The Gulf and the Search for Strategic Stability

The Gulf and the Search for Strategic Stability

Saudi Arabia, the Military Balance in the Gulf, and Trends in the Arab-Israeli Military Balance

Anthony H. Cordesman

Westview Press • Boulder, Colorado

Mansell Publishing Limited • London, England

This book is included in Westview's Special Studies on the Middle East.

Published in 1984 in the United States of America by Westview Press, Inc., 5500 Central Avenue, Boulder, Colorado 80301. Frederick A. Praeger, President and Publisher.

Published in 1984 in Great Britain by Mansell Publishing Limited, 6 All Saints Street, London N1 9RL, England

Library of Congress Cataloging in Publication Number: 83-10341
ISBN (U.S.): 0-86531-619-8

British Library Cataloguing in Publication Data available
ISBN (U.K.): 0-7201-1676-7

Printed and bound in the United States of America

5 4 3 2 1

Contents

Illustrations

Maps

Charts

Tables

Preface

Since the oil embargo of 1973–1974, the Gulf has become an area whose strategic importance to the United States rivals that of Western Europe or Japan. At the same time, it has become obvious that the Gulf is a politically explosive region that is threatened by the competition between the United States and the USSR and by its internal tensions. The fall of the shah and the Iran-Iraq War are only the most serious examples of the problems that may cause the West to lose its supplies of imported oil or to see control of these supplies fall into hostile hands.

The shah's fall has done more, however, than add another crisis to the region's long history of tension. It has deprived the United States of its principal military ally in Southwest Asia and destroyed the "two pillars" policy the United States has relied on since the British withdrew from the Gulf states. This has made Saudi Arabia the key to Western security in the region.

Saudi Arabia is now the only large pro-Western state in the Gulf. It and its smaller conservative neighbors are the only Gulf states that have supported the West in recent years. Yet even these allies are uncertain. All face growing external threats and pressures as well as internal security problems. These factors have recently been illustrated by riots and subversion in Bahrain, immigration problems in Qatar, the growing economic and demographic instability in the United Arab Emirates, the threat of a renewal of the Dhofar rebellion in Oman, and the Grand Mosque Uprising and Shi'ite riots in Saudi Arabia.

The challenge the West now faces is to establish strategic stability in spite of these changes. As the leader of the West, the United States must establish a strategic relationship with Saudi Arabia and the other conservative Gulf states that will protect them without threatening them and that will avoid the mistakes the United States made in Iran. The United States must simultaneously attempt to improve its relations with Jordan, strengthen its ties to Egypt and Pakistan, and reach some kind of modus vivendi or rapprochement with Iraq and Iran. Finally, the United States must checkmate the USSR, the expanding threat from Ethiopia and South Yemen, and the growth of other hostile radical movements that affect the Gulf.

This book analyzes these security problems through a net assessment of how the United States can improve its military relations with Saudi Arabia and its strategic ties to the conservative Gulf states. It reviews the overall trends in the military balance in the Gulf, discusses the options for increasing regional stability, and speculates on how the United States can best develop military forces to intervene in the area. Finally, it addresses the problem of how to best improve U.S. relations with the conservative Arab states in the Gulf while minimizing the problems caused by U.S. ties to Israel.

The assessment concentrates on security in the military sense, but it treats more than the military balance. It defines security to include such factors as the cultural and economic problems of development; political cohesion and ability to adapt to change; immigration and demographics; ethnic and religious stability; the organization of government, foreign policy, and regional affairs; and oil policy and the handling of oil revenues.

The assessment is divided into four main parts. The first introduces the overall problems in Gulf stability and summarizes the importance to the West of establishing improved strategic relations with the conservative Gulf states. The second traces the development of Saudi-U.S. military relations and the growth of Saudi military forces and analyzes the options for improving U.S. strategic ties with Saudi Arabia. The third discusses the overall patterns in Gulf security and options for expanding U.S. and Western military capabilities and collective security links with other Gulf nations. The fourth discusses the trends in the Arab-Israeli balance and how this will affect U.S. policy and options for a strategic partnership with Arab states.

One of the underlying principles in writing this assessment has been to provide a mix of quantitative analysis and historical data that can act as a useful reference in spite of the constant changes in the area. At least part of the problem with Western analyses of security trends in the Gulf is that they fail to bring together the wide range of quantitative data made available by various governments, the excellent work done by political and military historians on the region, and reporting on current military forces. This book attempts to tie these pieces together.

Such an assessment is a deliberately ambitious undertaking. It must often generalize or skip from area to area, and it must draw heavily on the work of others. Such sources are referenced wherever possible, but this work owes a debt to a wide range of experts on the Gulf, many of whom cannot be acknowledged because of their official status.

The assessment must also deal with a wide range of uncertainties—ranging from the spelling of Arabic names to the nature of key facts and events—that cannot be endlessly qualified throughout the text. The contemporary history of the region is extremely controversial, and it is further confused by the various "disinformation" campaigns of such states as the USSR, Israel, Egypt, Syria, and Libya. Many of the governments and nations discussed do not know their total population, their actual military capabilities and readiness, the strength of various internal political and ethnic movements, or the trends in their economy. At the same time, Gulf and Western governments classify much of the data on their military and internal security forces, while other information is hidden or invented for political or business purposes. The reader should be aware that many of the data presented are speculative or far less reliable than those available on Western industrialized states.

The reader should also be aware that the statistics used throughout this book must be regarded as uncertain general indicators and not precise measurements. A deliberate effort has been made to provide a range of sources when differences exist and to choose the best source for a given point or issue rather than to try to keep sources and numbers consistent. Nevertheless, even the best sources fluctuate in quality, and it often has been necessary to portray shifting time bases and use changes in definition to get results that seem likely to conform with reality. This is scarcely unusual in international statistics, but the reader should be warned to carefully check the footnotes and all the tables on any given point in order to understand the range of uncertainty involved.

For similar reasons, this assessment does not treat the details of the Gulf's complex politics when these do not have a direct bearing on Gulf security interests. This does not reflect a lack of fascination with the personalities involved, or with the intricacies of Gulf politics, but such relations are so volatile and the facts so uncertain that it seems desirable to avoid prolonged analysis. While it is possible to construct long discussions of such issues as the internal politics of a given tribal group, revolutionary state, or royal family, such discussions must often rest on the academic equivalent of bazaar gossip, and they do little to clarify the true nature of the security problems within the Gulf States. This book does, however, attempt to treat the relevant political issues. Where possible, it attempts to present the conflicting views of various experts and to make some judgments about which view is correct.

Finally, an attempt is made to predict future security trends in the area and make recommendations for action. This is done with the knowledge that many such predictions and recommendations tend to immediately be proved wrong by events, but in the hope that the detailed analyses that support such views will help the reader in organizing his or her own appraisals and speculations.

Anthony H. Cordesman

Acknowledgments

In addition to the many people in the Gulf, Europe, and the United States who contributed their help to this book, the author would like to thank Samuel Wells and the Wilson Center for the support he received during a year as a Wilson Fellow, Ruth Davis and Ronald Winkler of the Department of Energy for supporting the fellowship that made the book possible, his colleagues at the *Armed Forces Journal* for their support of research trips abroad, Susan McRory for many suggestions and improvements in her role as editor, Christopher Holshek and William Klun for research support, and Donna Watson for typing assistance. He also would like to thank Carole Foryst, Bridget Gail, Justin Galen, and Alexander Scott for their patience and editorial support.

A.H.C.

The Gulf and the Search for Strategic Stability

1
The Strategic Importance of the Gulf States

Since the fall of the shah of Iran in January 1979, the United States has struggled to find a new set of relationships in the Gulf and Middle East. It has sought to reestablish a reasonable degree of strategic stability, to protect its allies in the area, and to safeguard the West's supplies of imported oil. In practice, this search has proved to be dependent on four elements: U.S. ability to strengthen Saudi Arabia as a nation capable of defending itself against most regional threats and of guarding the other conservative Gulf states; U.S. ability to strengthen Egypt both militarily and economically; U.S. ability to find some solution to the Arab-Israeli conflict that will both meet Arab needs and offer Israel security; and U.S. ability to improve its power projection capabilities in the Gulf.

While the U.S. has other interests in the Near East, its primary objective is to secure access to the oil exports and reserves of the Gulf states. These states have 55% of the world's proved oil reserves. Regardless of fluctuations in the demand for imported oil, U.S. relations with the Gulf states have become pivotal to Western security. Oil also gives U.S. policy a clear set of priorities.

All of the Gulf states are important, but Saudi Arabia is the key to securing the West's energy supplies. Saudi Arabia alone has 25% of the world's proved oil reserves and roughly 30% of the sustained production capacity of the Organization of Petroleum Exporting Countries (OPEC). The fall of the shah has left Saudi Arabia the only major Gulf oil producer that is aligned with the West. Equally important, Saudi Arabia's geography, its influence within OPEC, and its wealth have made it the only regional power that can catalyze an effective collective security effort to protect all the conservative Gulf states and the West's primary source of oil imports.

The other conservative Gulf states are individually less important and cannot survive unless Saudi Arabia remains friendly and stable. They too, however, are of vital importance to the West. Collectively, they have roughly 50% of Saudi Arabia's oil production capacity and about 16% of world oil reserves. They are generally friendly to Western interests and have rarely been hostile to major U.S. policy initiatives, except in the case of Israel. In spite of their small size, several have large populations relative to that of Saudi Arabia. In hostile hands, each could greatly increase the political and military threat to the other conservative states and perhaps make effective defense of the southern Gulf impossible.

Finally, the West has a major strategic interest in preserving the independence of hostile or radical Gulf states like Iraq and Iran. While there is little real prospect of stable strategic relations with either state, Iran has another 8% of the world's oil reserves and Iraq has 6%. Friendly or not, it is vital to the West that both states retain their independence and ability to make their own oil export decisions. Their independence can be assured, however, only if the West and the other Gulf states can pose a strong counterbalance to Soviet pressure and influence.[1]

These strategic priorities are not easy "facts of life" for the U.S. to deal with. The U.S. must build ties to Gulf states that have different cultures and a different religion. While it has many areas of common interest with the southern Gulf states, there are also many areas of tension and conflict. The Gulf states are internally divided, and even the most friendly conservative Gulf states have different interests from the U.S. in pricing their oil and setting regional security policy. The U.S. must try to build a strategic partnership with the conservative Gulf states on the basis of a far more limited commonality of interest than it shares with its NATO allies.

This U.S. effort is further complicated by pressures from outside the region. Europe and Japan have an equal, if not greater, interest in securing the flow of Gulf oil, but they are unlikely to provide anything more than the most limited military support. They are also as likely to criticize U.S. action as support it. The U.S. must cope with both the domestic and international impact of the Arab-Israeli conflict and the fact that even the most friendly Gulf states are hostile to Israel. It cannot achieve its goals quickly or by reacting in a crisis. It can improve regional security only by slow and consistent action in a world in which fluctuations in global economic growth, the demand for oil imports, and the conflicts within the oil-exporting states can suddenly shift the situation from oil "glut" to oil crisis.

All these factors make it difficult for the U.S. to build a policy consensus around the need for a strategic partnership with the Gulf states, and even more difficult for the U.S. to deal with hostile or less friendly states like Iraq, Iran, and the Yemens. Nevertheless, the U.S. has little other option. It has assumed the de facto responsibility for the West's military security, and oil will link the West's strategic interests to those of the Gulf states for at least the next quarter century, regardless of shifts in the volume of the West's imports.

"Oil Power" and Western Security

These political and economic realities are so important that they deserve examination in detail. While the statistics involved in estimating "oil power" are controversial and complex, they are critical to understanding Western options in the Gulf and the pivotal role of Saudi Arabia. It is particularly important to understand just how deeply the West's dependence on the Gulf is embedded in its dependence on energy, and that the loss of Gulf oil can come only at the cost of massive global economic and political instability. Table 1.1 illustrates this point. It shows Saudi Arabia's ranking as a world oil producer and exporter in 1980. Saudi Arabia then ranked second in world oil production, first in world oil exports, and first in world oil reserves. This ranking has remained constant in spite of the shifts in the volume of exports caused by conditions ranging from war and revolution to global recession.

In 1980 Saudi Arabia was producing 2–3 million barrels per day (MMBD) more than its development plans required in order to meet the losses in Iranian and Iraqi oil exports resulting from the Iran-Iraq War. Although the world was already beginning a major recession, oil prices and the demand for oil exports were at near-panic levels because of the impact of the shah's fall and the war. Only Saudi Arabia's willingness to produce at its maximum capacity kept prices and supply in any kind of equilibrium. In 1981, a year of declining world economic activity but one in which the war prevented Iraq and Iran from being major exporters, Saudi Arabia produced 18% of total world oil production, 23% of all noncommunist oil production, 40% of all Organization of Arab Petroleum Exporting Countries (OAPEC) production, 60% of all Gulf production, and 67% of all production by pro-Western Near Eastern states.

In 1982, in the midst of a severe world recession and with Iranian production coming back on stream, Saudi production dropped to 12% of the world total, 16% of the noncommunist total, and 34% of the OPEC total. In the first half of 1983, which seems likely to be the worst point in the current world recession, Saudi Arabia produced 7% of the world total, 10% of the noncommunist total, and 23% of the OPEC total. It did so even though its oil production had sunk to monthly averages roughly one-third of its 1980 production level, the world recession had created a major "oil glut," and OPEC was involved in a serious price war.[2]

In spite of these reductions, Saudi Arabia played a critical role in allowing oil prices to drop to more economic levels and in creating the conditions for global economic recovery. Only the Saudi interest in sustaining high production levels kept the other members of OPEC from maintaining high prices by cutting production. Only Saudi Arabia's ability to produce large amounts of additional oil helped checkmate such efforts by radical member states like Libya and Iran.

TABLE 1.1 World Petroleum Supplies in 1980: the "Top Ten" Before the Iran-Iraq War

	Oil Production		Oil Exports		Oil Reserves		Gas Reserves	
Rank	Country	MMBD[a]	Country	MMBD[a]	Country	Billions of Barrels	Country	Billions of Cubic Feet
1	USSR	11.7	*Saudi Arabia*[b]	9.4	*Saudi Arabia*[b]	168.0	USSR	920,000
2	*Saudi Arabia*	9.9	USSR	3.0	Kuwait	67.9	Iran	485,000
3	U.S.	8.6	Iraq	2.3	USSR	63.0	U.S.	191,000
4	Iraq	2.6	Nigeria	1.9	Iran	57.5	Algeria	131,000
5	Venezuela	2.2	Venezuela	1.8	Mexico	44.0	*Saudi Arabia*	112,400
6	China	2.1	Libya	1.7	Iraq	30.0	Canada	87,300
7	Nigeria	2.1	Abu Dhabi	1.6	Abu Dhabi	29.0	Mexico	64,500
8	Mexico	1.9	Kuwait[b]	1.5	U.S.	26.4	Netherlands	62,000
9	Libya	1.8	Indonesia	1.2	Libya	23.0	Qatar	60,000
10	Kuwait	1.7	Iran	1.1	China	20.5	Norway	42,700

[a] Includes half of Neutral Zone.

[b] ARAMCO estimated daily average production of 9.82 MMBD, proven oil reserves of 167.85 billion barrels, NGL exports of 448,169 barrels daily, and gas reserves of 130,900 BCF in 1981.

Sources: Oil production and oil exports data are from ARAMCO; oil and gas reserves data are taken from *Oil and Gas Journal,* which uses a different estimative base from the CIA and ARAMCO.

It is impossible to predict which, if any, of these widely differing conditions will be typical of the future.[3] Predictions vary widely from rapid recovery to prolonged recession, and the U.S. can hardly base its strategic priorities on the assumption of continued global recession or even sustained reductions in the economic growth of the industrialized Western states. Its priorities must be based on the volume of oil exports necessary for global economic growth and political stability.[4] It seems likely, however, that the high Saudi production levels of 1978–1981 may be more typical of the average production levels of the 1980s and 1990s than the low production levels of early 1983. This conclusion is illustrated by the projections of the U.S. Department of Energy (DOE) and a wide range of other sources. The 1983 projections of DOE's Energy Information Administration (EIA) indicate that OPEC production will rise from 19.9 MMBD in 1982 to 25.8 MMBD in 1985 and 27.7 MMBD in 1990—roughly equal to OPEC production in 1980. This same report predicts that OPEC will experience a steep recovery in demand no later than early 1984 and that noncommunist importing nations will return to their 1980 level of imports by 1985. It also predicts that noncommunist oil-importing nations will then begin a slow but steady rise in oil imports through 1990, regardless of conservation and the development of alternative energy supplies.

These conclusions are generally supported by the independent projections of oil companies like Gulf, Standard Oil of California (SOCAL), CONOCO, and TENNECO and by the International Energy Agency (IEA). Although the world recession has brought total OPEC production to monthly levels as low as 14.4 MMBD, the lowest major independent projection of demand in 1985 is 21 MMBD (CONOCO), and the average projection of demand is 24.5 MMBD. The lowest demand projection for 1990 is 22 MMBD (SOCAL), and the average projection of demand is 27 MMBD—again roughly equal to the OPEC production levels in 1980.[5] Most important, all these projections are based on very limited levels of world economic growth compared to the average levels of the 1950s, 1960s, and 1970s. Whether or not they are correct in predicting the future, they provide a good picture of the level of oil production necessary to ensure a moderately healthy global economy.

Although such projections do not explicitly estimate Saudi exports, at least the DOE and IEA projections use input data that imply that Saudi production levels will increase to 7–8 MMBD by the mid-1980s, or to twice the production levels of the first few months of 1983. They also assume that oil prices (in 1982 dollars) will be about $28 per barrel in 1985 and $37 in 1990 versus $30 in 1983. This means that DOE and the IEA are assuming that Saudi oil production will return to its 1978 level by the mid-1980s, that real Saudi oil revenues will then begin to rise above their 1980 levels, and that sufficient Saudi production capacity will be available to the world market to keep the overall rise in oil prices to levels far lower than those demanded by the more radical members of OPEC.

This set of assumptions about the use of Saudi production capacity illustrates the fact that production and export levels are only one indicator of Saudi Arabia's strategic importance. Saudi Arabia's installed production capacity of 12.5 MMBD and sustained production capacity of 10 MMBD give it great influence in determining OPEC's price and production levels. No feasible combination of other OPEC states can raise prices beyond the level Saudi Arabia desires if it is willing to produce at near-maximum levels—something that Saudi Arabia has demonstrated in past confrontations with states as diverse as Libya, Nigeria, and Iran.

To put Saudi production capabilities in perspective, Saudi Arabia had 40% of the Gulf's total installed capacity before the start of the Iran-Iraq War and 64% of the capacity of friendly pro-Western Near Eastern states. These percentages almost certainly rose in 1980–1982 as a result of the damage the Iran-Iraq War did to Iranian and Iraqi oil facilities and the steady decline in maintenance and investment in Iran that has resulted from revolutionary turmoil.[6] Saudi Arabia's importance is further reinforced by the fact that it has the world's largest proved and probable oil reserves. Its probable reserves of 177.2 billion barrels are nearly 100 billion barrels larger than the next largest country, and at least 116.7 billion barrels of these reserves are proved.[7] Not only do they represent 25% of world reserves, they represent 65% of total Gulf reserves, well over 100% of the reserves of all Third World exporting nations outside the Gulf, and nearly one-third of the reserves of all Third World exporting nations including the Gulf. In spite of a massive worldwide oil exploration and development effort since 1973, Saudi reserves retained virtually the same statistical importance in 1983 that they had at the time of the 1973 oil embargo, and Saudi Arabia still controls the bulk of the free world petroleum reserves that are not committed to the domestic needs of nations holding such reserves.

Saudi Arabia is also important because its present economic development strategy ensures close ties to the West, high oil-production levels, and the "recycling" of the bulk of Saudi Arabia's petrodollars. Unlike many other exporting states, Saudi Arabia lacks domestic economic and political pressures that force it to try to maximize short-term revenue at the cost of long-term stability in oil income and profits.[8] This situation makes Saudi Arabia a natural economic and strategic partner of the West, although such a partnership depends as much on Saudi economic policy as on internal economic pressures.

The capital flows involved are immense. In mid-1981, a period that seems typical of the export levels implied in the previous demand projections, Saudi Arabia received almost $350 million per day in oil income. Even given the drop in production levels and prices that has occurred as the result of the present recession, Saudi oil and gas revenues seem unlikely to drop below $120 million per day, or $45 billion annually. The resulting surplus in oil revenues has given Saudi Arabia immense capital holdings. In mid-1983, Saudi Arabia had between $110 billion and $180 billion invested in the West, approximately one-third of which was invested in the U.S., and was earning between $15 and $20 billion annually from its investments.[9]

The value of Saudi Arabia's "recycling" of its oil income through purchases from the West is illustrated by the fact that between 1979 and 1982 U.S. exports to Saudi Arabia grew from $4.9 billion to $9.1 billion, Japanese exports grew from $3.8 to $6.8 billion, and German exports grew from $2.4 to $3.5 billion. All of the seven largest Western industrialized nations increased their exports to Saudi Arabia each year during 1979 to 1982 in spite of the world recession and drop in oil exports. In contrast, the U.S. imported $8–15 billion annually from Saudi Arabia during this period, Japan imported $12–21 billion, Germany imported $2.3–6.4 billion, and France imported $6–12 billion.

The control of such trade and capital resources is of considerable strategic importance. Fortunately, Saudi Arabia has pursued efforts to stabilize the dollar and Western currencies. Unlike many other OPEC states, Saudi Arabia has generally supported U.S. and Western monetary policy. At the same time, until the recession cut its oil flows in 1982, it spent roughly 4–6% of its national income on economic and military aid, most of it targeted toward assistance to states of major strategic importance to the U.S.[10] Major recipients included Egypt, North Yemen, Jordan, Lebanon, Turkey, the Afghan rebels, Pakistan, Sudan, Somalia, Oman, and other states where Saudi aid directly countered Soviet pressures or reduced threats to pro-Western regimes.

While Saudi Arabia has differed with the U.S. over many aspects of the Arab-Israeli conflict and the details of policy toward other Arab states, it has generally used its political and economic power, and its influence within Islam and the Arab world, in ways that have helped the West. Such efforts have included supporting President Sadat in breaking with the USSR, supporting the more moderate leaders of the Palestine Liberation Organization (PLO), helping to limit the conflict in Lebanon, funding the Afghan rebels, funding Pakistan's military purchases, and influencing Syria to limit the Soviet presence.

Equally important, Saudi Arabia is critical to the stability and survival of the conservative regimes in Bahrain, Kuwait, Oman, Qatar, and the United Arab Emirates (UAE)—states that earn up to $50 billion in annual oil income, that have roughly 8 MMBD of sustainable production capacity, and that control over 90 billion barrels of additional proved oil reserves.[11] Saudi Arabia's support of the creation of a Gulf Security Council, and of efforts to forge collective security arrangements with the other conservative Gulf states, provide the smaller conservative Gulf states with their only credible hope of preserving their internal security and creating a collective military deterrent that can secure them from their larger and more radical neighbors.

The Impact of Oil Production on Western Security

Table 1.2 helps put the importance of Gulf oil production into its broad strategic context. It also provides more detail on the fluctuations that can take place in Gulf oil production. The data on the period from 1973 to the shah's fall show a slow but consistent increase in Gulf exports. During this period, the West was able to count on marginal increases in energy supply at relatively limited increases in real cost.

This situation changed radically with the shah's fall. Revolutionary turmoil in Iran and the impact of the Iran-Iraq War cut the production of the two other large oil-producing states in the Gulf from a peak of 10.2 MMBD after the 1973 embargo to a little over 2 MMBD in mid-1981. Iranian production, which had been 5.2 MMBD before the start of the revolution, dropped to 3.2 MMBD in 1979, 1.7 MMBD in 1980, and 1.4 MMBD in 1981. It reached temporary lows of only 400 MBD, although production recovered to 2.2 MMBD in 1982 and 2.5 MMBD in mid-1983 and reached short-term peaks of 3.2 MMBD. Iraq, which produced an average of 3.5 MMBD in 1979, saw its production drop to 2.5 MMBD in 1980, 1.0 MMBD in 1981 and 1982, and 0.8 MMBD in the first half of 1983.[12]

The result was a sudden oil crisis, panic buying and increases in stocks, and a rise in oil prices and import costs that led to a global recession. This recession, in turn, created the "oil glut" shown in the data for 1982. Gulf production dropped by over 40% between 1980 and 1982 and continued to drop in 1983 as the recession worsened. The resulting major declines in total Saudi production provide a good benchmark for assessing Saudi Arabia's importance even in periods of minimal world demand.

It is interesting to note that although Saudi annual average production dropped from 9.6 MMBD in 1981 to 6.3 MMBD in 1982, Saudi Arabia still produced roughly the same amount of oil in 1982 as in the pre-embargo period of 1973. Even if one takes what is likely to approximate a record average monthly low in Saudi oil production—3.5 MMBD in March 1983— Saudi Arabia still produced 10% of the total oil production in the noncommunist world and 23% of all OPEC production. This production was also equivalent to about 5% of the world's total energy production from all sources of energy in quadrillions of Btus (quads).[13]

Under more normal conditions of economic growth and political stability, Saudi production levels are likely to be typical of those for 1978 and average between 6 and 8 MMBD. This means that Saudi oil, gas, and petrochemical product production is unlikely to drop below 5% of the world's total energy supply well into the 1990s. It also means that the Gulf as a whole must produce nearly 10% of the world's total energy supply for at least the next decade if the world is to sustain moderate economic recovery and growth.

Even these numbers understate Saudi Arabia's strategic importance during periods of major fluctuation in Gulf production or world demand.

TABLE 1.2 The Role of the Gulf in World Crude Oil Production (MMBD)

Country	1973	Peak Post-1973 Embargo	Pre-Fall of Shah, 1978	Pre-Iran-Iraq War in 1980	1981	1982
Saudi Arabia	7.4	10.0	8.1	9.6	9.6	6.3
Other Conservative Gulf States						
Bahrain	0.05	0.07	0.05	0.05	0.04	0.04
Kuwait	2.8	3.0	1.9	1.4	0.9	0.7
Neutral Zone	0.5	0.7	0.5	0.5	0.3	0.3
Oman	0.3	0.3	0.3	0.3	0.4	0.4
Qatar	0.6	0.6	0.5	0.5	0.4	0.3
UAE:	1.5	2.3	1.8	1.7	1.5	1.2
Abu Dhabi	(1.3)	(1.8)	(1.4)	(1.4)	(1.1)	(0.8)
Dubai	(0.2)	(0.4)	(0.4)	(0.3)	(0.4)	(0.4)
Sharjah	–	(0.06)	(0.02)	(0.01)	(0.001)	(0.001)
Subtotal	5.8	7.0	5.1	4.5	3.6	2.9
Total Conservative Gulf States	13.2	17.0	13.2	14.1	13.2	9.2
Other Gulf States						
Iran	5.9	6.7	5.2	1.7	1.4	2.2
Iraq	2.0	3.5	2.6	2.5	1.0	1.0
North Yemen	0	0	0	0	0	0
South Yemen	0	0	0	0	0	0
Subtotal	7.9	10.2	7.8	4.2	2.4	3.2
Total Gulf	21.1	27.2	21.0	18.3	15.6	12.4
Other Middle East/ African						
Algeria	1.1	1.2	1.2	1.0	0.8	0.7
Egypt	–	0.6	0.5	0.6	0.6	0.7
Libya	2.2	2.2	2.0	1.8	1.1	1.2
Subtotal	3.3	4.0	3.7	3.4	2.5	2.6
Total OAPEC	18.1	21.5	18.8	19.5	16.3	12.8
Total OPEC	31.0	31.1	29.8	26.9	22.7	18.8
Total Noncommunist World	–	48.6	46.4	45.2	41.6	38.7
Total World	–	62.6	61.3	59.5	55.8	53.1

Source: All data except for 1973 and 2nd Qtr. 1981 are taken from CIA ER IESR 81-004 (U), 28 April 1981 and exclude NGL. The 1973 data are taken from this source and Peter Mansfield, *The Middle East* (New York: Oxford University Press, 1980), p. 552. Some 1973 data include NGL. Totals may not always be consistent due to rounding. Data for 1981 and 1982 are taken from CIA DI EEI 83-013 (U), 24 June 1983.

Saudi Arabia has unique importance because its production capacity can make up for major variations in the production of the other exporting nations. This is reflected in the shifting role that Saudi oil has played in meeting the needs of individual Western states under the rapidly changing political and economic conditions of the late 1970s and early 1980s. While the world oil market has been extremely fungible, and importers have made major and rapid shifts in the sources of their oil imports over time, this fungibility has been heavily dependent on Saudi Arabia's willingness to provide a stable source of surplus production capacity and meet the needs of individual importing nations.

While U.S. imports from Saudi Arabia have been subject to particularly sharp fluctuations, the value of Saudi Arabia to the U.S. has not been altered as a result. The U.S. has bought from Saudi Arabia in periods of crisis or high demand and shifted to exporters that discount or have lower shipping costs in periods of recession and relative political stability. Saudi oil made up 17% of U.S. imports before the oil crisis began in 1973, and 21.1% in 1977, before the shah's fall. The percentage rose to 23.55% in early 1980 and to 25.7% in late 1980, when the Iran-Iraq War began. It dropped to 22.7% in March 1981 and to 15.2% in June 1982 and reached a record low of 9.4% in February 1983, when the political situation, the worldwide recession, and the availability of discounted oil with lower shipping costs shifted U.S. consumption away from secure supply to the lowest available marginal price.[14]

The other leading Western industrialized nations have been more consistently dependent on Saudi oil exports. Most have needed a stable source of oil that can be put on a long-term contract basis, and most are closer to the Gulf and have different marginal costs. This dependence is shown in Table 1.3. While the percentages in Table 1.3 fluctuate significantly over time, as individual importing nations have sought the best price and most secure oil supplies, Saudi Arabia has been consistently important to Europe and Japan. Saudi oil has provided about 30–50% of French imports since the start of the Iran-Iraq War, 9–48% of British imports, 12–35% of West German imports, and 36–47% of Japanese imports.[15]

During all these fluctuations, Saudi Arabia's large production and production capacity have ensured that the world oil market remains fungible enough to allow importing nations to shift exporters and compete against each other in seeking oil at the lowest marginal cost. If Saudi Arabia had been subject to the same sudden political and military pressures as Iran or Iraq, not only would the oil market never have approached the "glut" stage, but major Western nations would virtually have been forced into a massive competition to secure a source of oil from given exporters, and to do so at the expense of the Third World and of economic recovery in those Western nations least able to compete.

TABLE 1.3 Minimax of Monthly Shifts in Percentage of Western Oil Imports from the Gulf, 1980-1983 (range shown covers period from 1980 "high" to February 1983 "low")

	U.S.	Canada	Japan	United Kingdom	West Germany	France
Saudi Arabia	9-23	0-34	36-47	9-48	12-36	29-52
Other Conservative Gulf States						
Kuwait	0-0.5	0-3	0-4	0-11	0-0.2	–
Qatar	–	0	2-4	0	0-1	0-4
UAE	0.4-2	0-2	12-15	9-12	0-2	2-6
Minimax	0.4-2.5	0-5	14-23	9-23	1-3	2-8
Total Conservative Gulf States	9-26	0-39	50-69	18-68	12-39	37-58
Other Gulf States						
Iran	0-0.5	0-10	1-12	0-13	3-6	1-10
Iraq	0-2	0	0-4	?-9	0-3	0-3
Minimax	0-2.5	0-10	1-12	?-13	4-8	0-13
Total Gulf	9-28.5	10-39	60-70	54-77	20-46	38-69
Other Arab						
Algeria	1-4	6-13	1-2	0	5-6	5-6
Egypt	1-2	0	0	0-5	1-3	0-3
Libya	0-11	0-3	0-1	0-1	9-15	0-7
Minimax	2-18	6-13	1-3	0-5	15-24	5-16
Total OAPEC	17-43	13-47	61-73	21-81	38-56	52-70
Total OPEC	32-69	59-73	81-86	45-79	55-65	70-79
Total Imports (in MMBD)[a]	3.4-8.4	0.2-0.7	3.6-6.2	0.6-1.4	2.0-2.8	1.7-2.8
Total Oil Consumption (in MMBD)	14.7-18.8	1.3-1.9	3.6-5.8	1.2-1.8	1.7-2.7	1.2-2.5

[a]Peak buying in late 1979 leads to monthly peaks in imports that sometimes exceed peak consumption. Total import and total consumption data also sometimes treat product imports differently.

Source: CIA, GI IESR 81-011 (U), 24 November 1981, pp. 5-7; DOE/1A-0010/15, October-November 1981, p. 10; CIA GI IESR 82-009, 28 September 1982; CIA DI IESR 83-005 (U), 31 May 1983, pp. 4-7, 8-11, 13-16.

Totals may not add due to rounding. Range of subtotals is possible peaks and lows and mixes monthly and annual peaks and lows due to statistical inconsistencies in the CIA data base.

Trends in Western Oil Demand and Oil Vulnerability

The strategic importance of Saudi Arabia and the Gulf is also a function of the growth of competing energy supplies that can act as alternatives to imported oil. These alternatives fall into two major categories—oil stocks, or strategic reserves, and increases in domestic energy production.

The West has had considerable success in increasing domestic oil stocks and creating strategic reserves. Most Western countries now have sufficient oil reserves to cushion themselves against a short-term loss of oil or the worst effects of any repetition of the 1973 embargo. The United States has finally begun to make major progress in filling its 1-billion-barrel strategic petroleum reserve (SPR) and now has well over 300 million barrels of oil in the reserve. Most other Western industrialized nations are creating reserves equivalent to 90 days of imports.[16]

Such reserves do not, however, reduce the West's long-run dependence on Gulf oil; they simply act as temporary buffers that can reduce the impact of short-term crises or wars. Strategic reserves do not substitute for domestic sources of energy, they cannot cope with the destruction of critical oil facilities—whose repair often requires equipment with one-to-two-year lead times—and they cannot protect the West from a concerted effort by the major oil-producing states to use oil as a weapon. No Western nation, for example, plans to be able to cope with a major reduction in imported oil for more than six to nine months, and none can readily draw down on its reserves except in a major emergency. Western Europe will also soon add to its dependence on energy imports by importing massive amounts of Soviet gas.

The only long-term substitute for oil imports is to find alternative supplies of energy or methods of conservation that do not reduce economic activity. Unfortunately, no Western state has been able to approach the level of new energy production that it planned to reach in the mid-1970s in spite of a universal effort to find alternatives to importing oil. The present oil glut is the product of recession, not of Western success in reducing its dependence on the Gulf, and this recession has done as much to inhibit the growth of alternative energy supplies as to reduce oil imports.

The rise in oil prices from $3.39 per barrel in 1973 to $12.93 in 1978 led to substantial inflation, high interest rates, and excessive international borrowing even before the shah's fall. The seven leading Western industrial states (U.S., Japan, West Germany, France, United Kingdom, Italy, and Canada) averaged nearly 10% inflation in 1979, the ten largest Third World states had already encountered critical borrowing and/or growth problems, and most economies already exhibited significant structural distortion as the result of a shift to investment and plant with lower energy costs. The shah's fall, and the resulting rise in oil prices from $13.79 per barrel in the first quarter of 1979 to $34.85

in the first quarter of 1981, then served as major catalysts in reducing world economic growth. The rise in oil prices and panic buying nearly tripled the cost of oil imports in less than a year, and the seven leading Western industrial states saw their average consumer prices rise by 1.4–5.4% during the months leading to Khomeini's rise to power.

The U.S. went from a 4.4% increase in industrial production to a 3.6% decline in 1980, a poor 2.6% rise in 1981, and a catastrophic 8.1% decline in 1982. Japan's decline was slower, but it fell from 8.2% growth in 1979, to 6.8% in 1980, 3.1% in 1981, and 0.3% in 1982. West Germany went from 4.0% growth in 1979, to 1.8% in 1980, −0.2% in 1981, and −1.1% in 1982. France went from 3.3% growth in 1979 to 1.1% in 1980 and 0.2% in 1981; it achieved only 1.7% growth in 1982 at the cost of a massive borrowing and devaluation crisis in early 1983. The United Kingdom went from 2.5% growth in 1979 to a 6.5% decline in 1980 and a 4.6% decline in 1981. Britain eked out an 0.8% rise in 1982 only because of increases in its offshore oil production.[17] The trends in Western unemployment reached a crisis point, although government borrowing and welfare payments masked the loss of growth in gross national product (GNP). Even so, the annual shift in GNP in the seven leading Western industrial states dropped to 60% to −80% of the growth projected in the national budgets and energy projections each had made in early to mid-1979. The situation in the developing world's importing states was even worse, and the results ranged from political upheaval in Turkey to near-starvation in parts of Africa.[18]

The oil glut thus occurred only at the cost of major diversions of total economic effort away from normal market needs, reduced economic growth and increased inflation and unemployment, and/or exporting the oil-demand problem to less developed nations by outbidding them for imports at the margin. Further, the same recession that produced the glut exacerbated the long-standing shortfall between the West's goals of increasing its alternative energy supplies and its actual performance.

While it is difficult to develop comparable international figures on how far the West has fallen behind in its efforts to reduce its dependence on oil imports, Figure 1.1 does provide an example of such data for the U.S. It shows that the U.S. has fallen far short of its goals of the 1970s, and that U.S. government and other forecasts of future U.S. domestic energy supplies have had to be cut back virtually every year since the 1973 embargo. Equally important, the most recent annual report of the Department of Energy shows that U.S. efforts to increase nuclear power, synthetic fuel production, and coal use will almost certainly lag far more than the data in Figure 1.1 would indicate because of the same recessionary pressures that have reduced the demand for OPEC oil.[19]

Working level projections of the domestic energy supply efforts of other industrialized states are no more optimistic. European and Japanese efforts to increase synthetic fuels, nuclear energy, and the use of coal

CHART 1–1
CHANGING U.S. ENERGY SUPPLY PROJECTIONS FOR THE YEAR 1985[1]

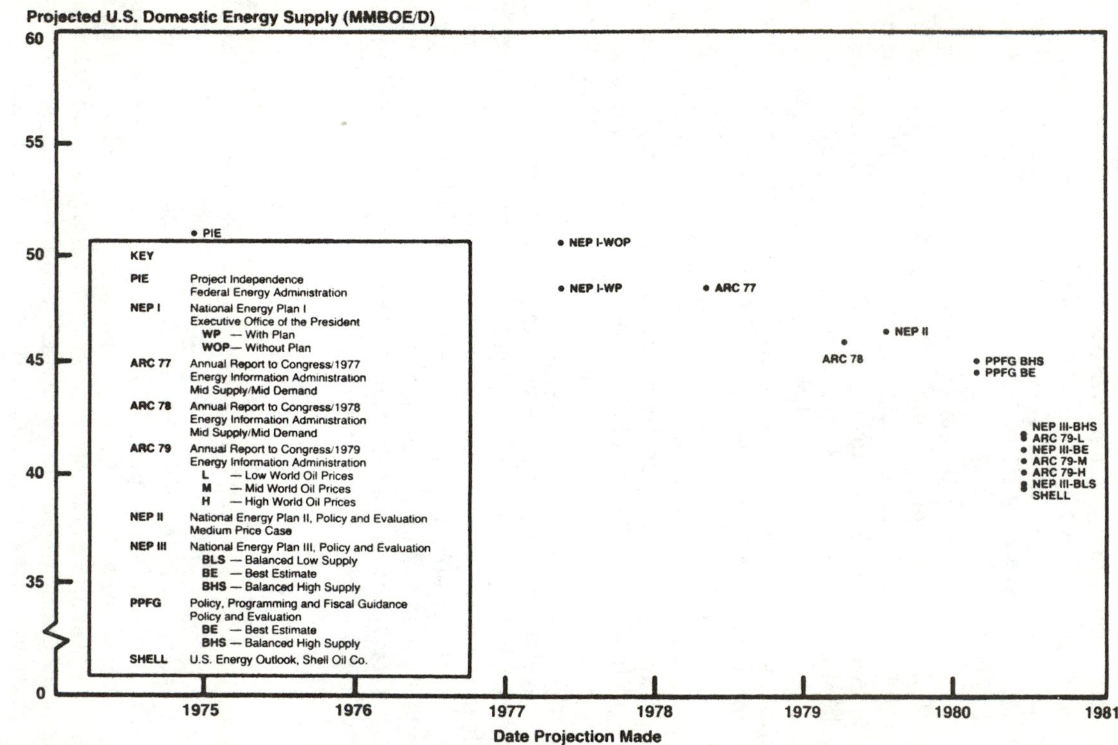

[1]This table is adapted from work by Anthony H. Cordesman and Richard Gilbert. While the trend is not relevant after 1980 due to increasing proximity to the year projected, the 1982 *Annual Energy Outlook* of the Energy Information Agency projected 7.3 quadrillion less Btu of domestic energy supply in 1990 than the *1981 Annual Report*. This was a decline of nearly 10% in one year. See DOE/EIA-0383(82), April 1983, pp. 87-88.

have also been cut back and delayed by unexpected problems, costs, and recession. According to DOE and IEA working data, the major Western industrial states will fall well below 50% of their 1975 projections of increases in these sources of energy through 1990, and they may fall well below 33%.[20]

If there is any reassuring side to the trends in the West's energy supplies, it lies in conservation. The ratio of total primary energy to gross domestic product (TPE/GDP) of the major industrialized states making up the Organisation for Economic Co-operation and Development (OECD) declined 13% between 1973 and 1980, while the total gross domestic product rose 19%. The ratio of oil consumption to GDP dropped 20% during this same period. Even this progress, however, has fallen short of most of the projections of conservation made in the mid-1970s, and it seems to be reaching a limit after which further improvements will come much more slowly.[21]

It is scarcely surprising, therefore, that the U.S. Department of Energy projects that noncommunist world demand for oil will resume its growth in the mid-1980s.[22] While experts may challenge the department's view of how rapidly the world will recover from the recession of the early 1980s, the department's estimates assume only 2% annual average world economic growth between 1980 and 1985 and 3.2% growth between 1985 and 1990. These estimates compare with growth averaging well over 5% annually during 1960–1973 and represent what is likely to be the minimal level necessary to preserve a reasonable level of political stability in Europe, Japan, and the developing world. Under these very moderate growth assumptions, oil consumption in the OECD nations—excluding Australia and New Zealand—is estimated to grow at an average annual rate of 1.5% between 1981 and 1985 in spite of the global recession of the early 1980s and to continue to grow at an average rate of 0.2% from 1985 to 1990 in spite of a return of real oil prices to their peak 1980 levels and Western increases in energy efficiency and fuel switching.[23]

Although the West's dependence on oil imports may diminish after the 1990s, DOE projects that between 1990 and 2000, a combination of declining oil reserves in most oil-producing states and continuing demand will sharply increase the importance of Saudi Arabia and Kuwait and increase oil prices by more than 50% above their level in 1980 dollars. It also projects that developing nations, many of which are strategically important to the West, will increase their oil consumption much more quickly. Oil consumption in the developing nations is projected to exceed that in Western Europe no later than 1984 and to increase by 20% between 1981 and 1990. At the same time, the OPEC nations are projected to increase their domestic oil consumption by more than 33% during the same period. These trends will sharply accelerate the critical problems the developing oil-importing nations already face in funding oil and petrochemical imports and will increase the pressure on the poorer OPEC states to raise prices.[24]

The Impact of Production Capacity

The demand projections discussed in the preceding section again highlight the strategic importance of Saudi Arabia's immense production capacity. Table 1.4 shows the details behind the summary estimates of production capacity provided in Table 1.1. Even these figures, however, understate the potential importance of Saudi production capacity. As has been touched upon earlier, Table 1.4 is based on CIA estimates that cannot reflect the ultimate result of the shah's fall and the Iran-Iraq War.

Iran's wartime production has swung from monthly average production levels of 0.6 to 3.2 MMBD; and Iraq's monthly production levels have reached lows of 0.6 MMBD and averaged 0.8 to 1.0 MMBD. Iran was producing well over 5 MMBD before the shah's fall, and Iraq was producing between 2.5 and 3.4 MMBD before the start of the Iran-Iraq War. It now seems unlikely that both nations combined can sustain average production levels of more than 5–6 MMBD once the war is over, although most prewar estimates indicated that their combined production would average 7–9 MMBD during most of the 1980s.[25] In fact, unless the Iran-Iraq War is truly settled, and Iran achieves enough political stability to prevent the continuing and irremediable decay of much of its present oil-production capacity, long-term Iranian and Iraqi oil-production capacity may drop to 50–70% of the 11 MMBD of installed capacity shown in the CIA's prewar/prerevolution estimates. This drop would further increase Saudi Arabia's strategic importance and raise the Saudi share of total installed oil-production capacity from 30% to 35% of OPEC capacity. It would also greatly increase the long-term leverage of a friendly Saudi regime in stabilizing oil prices.[26]

The scale of any such irremediable losses in Iranian and Iraqi production capacity is, however, impossible to estimate. The wartime damage to individual oil wells, processing plants, pipelines, pumps, loading facilities, and refineries can be repaired. What is less certain is whether ultimate recovery capability has been lost. Iran may have suffered serious damage to its oil fields and loading facilities because maintenance has been seriously reduced by the revolution and many of its technical personnel have fled the country. There is no way to estimate whether Iran can sustain long-term production above 3.5 MMBD without massive reinvestment on a scale that now seems politically unlikely. Iran has also lost most of its 610,000-BPD refinery at Abadan and is now considering either total reconstruction or writing off the facility and building a new one far to the east—a process that would require at least three to five years and would delay into the 1990s any resumption of its exports of oil products.

Iraq seems less likely to lose major production capacity, unless Iran succeeds in its invasion attempts. Iraq has, however, lost most of its oil-loading facilities in the Gulf. Even if Iraq can force or persuade

TABLE 1.4 Crude Oil Productive Capacity in the Gulf (in millions of barrels)

	Installed[a]	Maximum Sustainable[b]	Available[c]
Saudi Arabia[f]	12.5[h]	10.0	7.0
Other Conservative Gulf States			
Kuwait[f]	2.9	2.2	1.25
Neutral Zone[g]	0.68	0.6	0.6
Qatar	0.65	0.6	0.6
UAE:	2.57	2.42	1.25
Abu Dhabi	(2.15)	(2.04)	(0.87)
Dubai	(0.39)	(0.37)	(0.37)
Sharjah	(0.03)	(0.01)	(0.01)
Subtotal	6.9	5.8	3.7
Total Conservative Gulf States	19.4	15.8	10.7
Other Gulf States			
Iran	7.0	5.5[d,i]	3.2[e,i]
Iraq	4.0	3.5[i]	0.9[i]
Subtotal	11.0	9.0	4.1
Total Gulf	30.4	24.8	14.8
Total OPEC	41.4	34.7	23.7

[a] Installed capacity, also called nameplate or design capacity, includes all aspects of crude oil production, processing, transportation, and storage. Installed capacity is generally the highest capacity estimate.

[b] Maximum sustainable or operational capacity is the maximum production rate that can be sustained for several months; it considers the experience of operating the total system and is generally some 90-95 percent of installed capacity. This capacity concept does not necessarily reflect the maximum production rate sustainable without damage to the fields.

[c] Available or allowable capacity reflects production ceilings announced by individual members of OPEC. These ceilings usually represent a constraint only on annual average output, and thus production may exceed the ceilings in a given month. Iraqi total is determined by closing of Gulf ports and pipelines through Syria. It would otherwise be 3.5 MMBD.

[d] The precise loss in sustainable capacity remains uncertain.

[e] This figure represents the upper end of the range of available capacity, according to government statements.

[f] Excluding share of capacity in the Neutral Zone, shown separately.

[g] Capacity and production are shared about equally between Kuwait and Saudi Arabia.

[h] In Saudi Arabia, the concept of "facility," rather than "installed" capacity, is used. Facility capacity refers to the total installed capacity of gas-oil separating plants, main trunk pipelines, and oil-load terminals.

[i] Prior to the Iraq-Iran war. Iran and Iraq were both producing only 1.1 MMBD in August, 1981. Some estimates now put Iranian and Iraqi capacity at about 3 MMBD each.

Source: Adapted from CIA DI IESR 83-005(U), 31 May 1983, p. 2.

Iran to allow Iraq to rebuild its oil-loading facilities in the Gulf, it will take Iraq six months to a year to rig temporary replacements, and up to two years to deliver its prewar capacity of a little over 3.0 MMBD. Iraq also cut back significantly on oil development in 1982, and if the war drags on, its growing cutbacks in investment and maintenance may cut its near-term production capacity well below the levels shown in Table 1.4. While Iraq is expanding its pipeline system through Turkey from 700,000 BPD to 1.2–1.4 MMBD, and has considered constructing a new pipeline to Aqaba in Jordan or a new port near Yanbu in Saudi Arabia, these measures will only reduce its vulnerability in having to ship its oil through Gulf ports and terminals so close to Iran and/or through a hostile Syria. They would do nothing to expedite the recovery of Iraqi shipping capability.

Ironically, the result of these developments could be a situation in which an Iranian-Iraqi peace settlement could sustain the world oil glut in the near term because of both nations' desperate need for oil income, but worsen oil-supply problems in the longer term because of loss of capacity. In any case, the sheer scale of the uncertainties involved in estimating future Iranian and Iraqi production again highlights the importance of Saudi Arabia as a stable source of oil-production capacity.

Allocation and Downstream Capacity

Most oil-exporting nations are steadily improving their capability to allocate their crude oil or product exports. In 1972, the seven largest oil companies owned more than 50% of the noncommunist's world oil reserves, and produced 65% of its crude oil. In 1983, they owned less than 10% of world reserves and produced less than 20% of its crude oil. As a rough estimate, the exporting nations have cut the ability of the seven largest Western oil companies to allocate preferential access to Gulf oil from 60–70% before October 1973 to about 12% today and will cut it still further, to about 8%, by 1985.[27]

Many exporting states are also steadily converting their oil production from crude to product, a shift reflected in Table 1.5. Saudi Arabia and most of the other conservative Gulf states have, however, concentrated on developing refineries and petrochemical production facilities that make use of the low-cost gas feedstock they obtain from producing crude oil but cannot easily export. Saudi Arabia refined less than 7% of its crude oil exports during periods of peak demand in 1980 and 1981, and recent cutbacks in Saudi expansion plans mean that Saudi Arabia will not increase its refinery capacity to more than 850,000 BPD until the late 1980s at the earliest.[28] Saudi Arabia's present development plans also indicate that it will not fully staff the senior positions in ARAMCO with Saudi personnel before 1990, and that it will concentrate on selling low-priced crude oil well into the 1990s, rather than try to convert the bulk of its oil production into refined and processed petroleum products.[29] These decisions increase the flexibility of the West in pur-

TABLE 1.5 Refining Capacity in the Gulf Before and After the Start of the Iran-Iraq War (thousands of barrels per day)

	Refining Capacity		Average Daily Oil Production	
	1980	1981	1980	1981
Saudi Arabia[b]	585-662[f]	725	8,500	9,818
Other Conservative Gulf States				
Bahrain	250[e]	250	50	44
Kuwait[b]	634-645	623	1,500	1,180
Qatar	10-13	13	500	405
UAE[a]	14-15	128	1,600	1,482
Subtotal	908-923	1,014	3,650	3,111
Total Conservative Gulf States	1,493-1,583	1,739	12,150	12,929
Other Gulf States				
Iran[d]	995-1,121	530	1,700	1,184
Iraq[d]	319	169	2,500	951
Subtotal	1,314-1,440	699	4,200	2,135
Total Gulf Area	2,807-3,023	2,438	16,350	15,064
Related States				
Egypt	290-352	292	600	587
Libya	138-142	130	1,600	1,180
Other[c]	385	362	1,000	580
Subtotal	813-879	784	3,200	2,347
Total Region	3,620-3,904	3,222	19,550	17,411

[a] Abu Dhabi.
[b] Saudi Arabia and Kuwait include respective shares of Neutral Zone.
[c] Syria, Lebanon, Jordan, South Yemen, and Oman.
[d] Prewar.
[e] Bahrain's main refinery feedstock comes from Saudi Arabia.
[f] ARAMCO indicates Saudi capacity is divided as follows: 450,000 BPD at Ras Tanura, 20,000 BPD at Riyadh, 85,000 BPD at Jiddah, and 30,000 BPD at the Arabian Oil Company. 250,000 BPD for local use is under construction.

Source: Exxon, "Middle East Oil," Washington, D.C., 1980; and ARAMCO, *Facts and Figures, 1980,* p. 19, and *Facts and Figures, 1981,* p. 20. 1980 totals are Exxon figures.

chasing the types of crude oil it most desires and in refining the kinds of oil product it most desires. It will also reduce the West's future problems in allocating oil resources to meet market demand.[30]

The Impact of Gulf Oil Reserves

Saudi Arabia's importance is reinforced by the size and character of its oil reserves. Unlike most oil-exporting states, Saudi Arabia has not experienced depleting oil reserves and has not completed exploration and characterization of its readily recoverable reserves. This situation, combined with the fact that Saudi Arabia already has 121 trillion cubic feet of proved gas reserves and probably has far more natural gas than is left in the United States, means it has far less incentive than most OPEC states to conserve resources and limit oil production.

Table 1.6 shows the trend in Gulf oil reserves. There has been steady growth in Saudi reserves since 1950, and the importance of Saudi Arabia's oil reserves increased steadily between 1950 and 1980. According to these EXXON and DOE figures, Saudi reserves were 20% of total Gulf reserves in 1950, 45% of total Gulf reserves in 1965, and 60% of Gulf reserves in 1980. They were 25% of world reserves at the end of 1982, in spite of all the exploration during the previous decade. Moreover, the Saudi reserves shown in Table 1.5 are at least 10–15 billion barrels smaller than ARAMCO's latest estimate. This difference is equal to the total estimate of Saudi reserves in 1950, the total reserves of all the smaller Gulf states except Kuwait, or Britain's total oil reserves. While Saudi reserves are scarcely unlimited relative to the long-term demand for oil, the size and rate of growth of Saudi reserves are large enough to give Saudi Arabia great flexibility in sustaining long-term production levels of 7–10.5 MMBD. This flexibility will be even more important in the late 1980s and 1990s, when other nations have depleted more of their reserves; it means that Saudi Arabia's strategic value will steadily increase over time.[31]

The Importance of Gulf Capital Resources and Overseas Investments

At the same time, the events of the early 1980s have shown the West and Saudi Arabia that they have a strong common interest in preserving stable flows of oil and capital that is not shared by most of the other OPEC states. This commonality of interest is illustrated in Table 1.7, which provides a rough estimate of the capital accumulated by the Gulf states during 1980–1981. While the period shown in the table is one in which the combination of the shah's fall, the revolution in Iran, and the Iran-Iraq War combined to make the West and many Third World nations buy oil at panic prices, and must be described as "freak" conditions for the early 1980s, it may well be typical of the capital

TABLE 1.6 Estimates of Oil Reserves in the Gulf, 1950–1982 (billions of barrels)

	Cumulative Oil Produced (as of 1/1/80)	Estimated Probable Oil Reserves			
		1950	1965	1980	1982
Saudi Arabia	38.7	10.0	66.2	166.5[a]	165.3
Other Conservative Gulf States					
Bahrain	0.7	0.3	0.2	0.2	0.2
Kuwait	21.4	15.0	68.7	68.5	67.2
Oman	1.4	–	0.5	2.4	2.7
Qatar	3.0	1.0	3.0	3.8	3.4
UAE	6.3	–	10.0	29.4	32.4
Subtotal	32.8	16.3	82.4	104.3	105.9
Total Conservative Gulf States	71.5	26.3	148.6	270.8	271.2
Other Gulf States					
Iran	29.4	13.0	40.0	58.0	55.3
Iraq	14.6	8.7	25.0	31.0	41.0
Subtotal	44.0	21.7	65.0	89.0	96.3
Total Gulf Area	115.5	48.0	213.6	359.8	367.5
Related States					
Egypt	2.1	0.2	2.0	3.1	3.3
Libya	12.7	–	10.0	23.5	21.5
United States	124.3	25.3	31.4	26.5	29.8

[a]Saudi Arabia had proven reserves of 110 billion barrels and probable reserves of 180 billion barrels at the end of 1981. Only 15 of 47 Saudi oilfields have been produced, and recent exploration in the empty quarter and northern areas indicates that Saudi probable reserves could be as high as 250 billion barrels. See *Economist*, "Survey," 13–19 February 1982, pp. 19–20; *Middle East Economic Digest* (*MEED*), 22 January 1982, p. 42; *New York Times*, 10 February 1982.

Sources: Adapted from Exxon, *Middle East Oil*, 2d ed., pp. 5, 6, for 1950–1980; Department of Energy, *1982 Annual Energy Review*, DOE/EIA-0384(82) (Washington, D.C., April 1983), p. 45. Note that Exxon, ARAMCO, DOE, *Oil Gas Journal*, and CIA all use different definitions. Data are not comparable if based on different sources.

TABLE 1.7 Capital Resources of the Gulf States in 1980

	Nominal Current Value of Oil Production at Average OPEC Price of $35 Per Barrel ($ millions)		Capital Holdings in Investment in the West ($ billions)		Total Trade Surplus on Account (1980, in billions)	Trade with U.S. ($ billions)		
	Daily	Annual	Total	In U.S.		Exports	Imports	Balance
Saudi Arabia	350.0	127.8	110–150	40–60	50	5.8	13.3	-7.5
Other Conservative Gulf States								
Bahrain	1.6	0.6	54.9	—	—	—	—	—
Kuwait	52.5	19.2	—	—	14	0.9	0.5	+0.4
Oman	17.5	6.4	—	—	—	—	—	—
Qatar	10.8	4.0	—	—	3	0.1	0.3	-0.2
UAE	56.7	20.7	—	—	8	1.0	2.1	-1.1
Subtotal	139.1	50.9	—	—	25	2.0	2.9	-0.9
Total Conservative Gulf States	489.1	178.7	—	—	75	7.8	16.2	-8.4
Other Gulf States								
Iran	56.7	20.7	—	—	0	0.0	0.4	
Iraq	21.0	7.8	—	—	6	0.7	0.4	
North Yemen	0	0	—	—	—	—	—	
South Yemen	0	0	—	—	—	—	—	
Subtotal	77.7	28.5	—	—	6	0.7	0.8	-0.1
Total Gulf	566.8	207.2	—	—	81	8.5	17.0	-8.5
Total OPEC	738.5	296.6	—	—	107	17.8	54.8	-8.5

Source: CIA ER IESR 81-995, 26 May 1981; DOE IA Working Paper, 5 June 1981.

flows that will result from the previous projections of oil demand in the late 1980s. It also is an impressive demonstration of what a further oil crisis could do to disturb such projections.[32]

The changes in oil income and capital flows between 1979 and 1983 provide an important insight into the importance of a strategic partnership with Saudi Arabia. In 1979, the shah's fall caused the price of oil to rise from $16 per barrel in January to spot prices averaging over $35 per barrel in June. Posted prices rose from $14 before the shah's fall to $32 in 1980, and the average price of oil rose to levels that had not been expected before the end of the decade. As a result, the Saudi surplus on commercial international trade accounts rose to $6–7.5 billion for the U.S., about $15 billion for Japan, and $7 billion for France. The other industrialized states avoided massive trade deficits only because of Saudi recycling of its petrodollars. Saudi imports were worth about $2.5 billion to the Federal Republic of Germany (FRG), $4.5 billion to the UK, $6 billion to Italy, and $2 billion to Canada.

The other OPEC nations gained a similar increase in income. In 1981, the European Economic Community (EEC) imported $642 billion worth of goods from outside the Common Market, 34% of which was fuel products. Roughly 14% of total EEC exports went to OPEC versus 12% to the U.S. OPEC was the EEC's largest external customer, and 22% of EEC external exports went to OPEC nations. Even so, the EEC had a nearly $25 billion trade deficit with OPEC in 1981.[33] While Table 1.7 shows that all the oil-exporting states experienced a massive capital inflow, Saudi Arabia saw its oil income rise to roughly $350 million a day, or well over $100 billion a year. This income gave Saudi Arabia an annual surplus on account of nearly $50 billion in 1980 and a similar surplus in 1981. As a result, Saudi Arabia was able to increase its overseas investments to around $150 billion, of which $40–60 billion was invested in the U.S.[34]

The mix of capital flow and investment income could continue, however, only as long as Western economies could absorb the cost of oil. This became all too clear during 1982, when the same rises in oil prices that had given Saudi Arabia its new capital reserves helped lead to a worldwide recession. The West and Saudi Arabia learned an equally important lesson regarding the extent to which they shared a strong interest.

The conservative Gulf states suddenly found that the rise in their oil income had vanished with the West's economic growth, that they faced declining oil revenues, and that their investments in the West had taken on a radically increased importance. Saudi Arabia faced its first major budget and trade deficit since 1977-1978 and 1978-1979. The Saudi trade surplus dropped from $81 billion in 1981 to $38 billion in 1982, while imports rose from $35 to $40.5 billion. If Saudi Arabia had had to rely solely on the revenue from sales of crude oil, this deficit would have been $12–18 billion greater, which would have been critical in the 1982-1983 budget year, since actual income was only about $82 billion versus budgetary expectations of $102 billion.[35]

Even Saudi Arabia's investment income could not keep it from major cutbacks in 1983. Saudi oil production dropped to monthly averages of less than 4 MMBD, which forced Saudi Arabia to cut its 1983-1984 budget to $75.6 billion, or nearly $25 billion below its total budget obligations of the previous year. Saudi Arabia had to make major cuts in defense spending, new project starts, municipal facilities (27%), transport and communications (23%), and infrastructure spending (18%). Even so, the Saudi government had to base its budget on an estimated deficit of at least $10 billion. Further, this estimate was based on oil sales of approximately $51 billion, $1.5 billion from pilgrims, $4.1 billion from the sale of refinery products, and $2.9 billion in natural gas liquids (NGL). By mid-1983, Saudi Arabia faced the prospect that its oil sales might be as low as $35–40 billion and were unlikely to exceed $48 billion. As a result, outside experts predict deficits as high as $22–26 billion, and Saudi Arabia's $12.5–17.5 billion in overseas investment income became equal to 25–40% of its oil income.[36]

The global recession thus provided empirical proof to support the arguments of Saudis like Oil Minister Yamani, who had long argued that Saudi Arabia had to balance oil production and prices in ways that would sustain enough income to maximize real Saudi oil revenues and to protect the value of its overseas investments.[37] While Saudi Arabia had the income and investment reserves to maintain social services and enough public and private economic activity to meet the needs of its citizens, it became clear that the country's long-term economic health was as tightly linked to the West's economic health as that of the West was to the flow of oil from Saudi Arabia.

These arguments will be equally important once the West recovers from the present recession, and Saudi Arabia and the other conservative Gulf states resume their accumulation of surplus capital and their buildup of overseas investments. Saudi Arabia and its conservative neighbors can maximize their capital holdings and their revenue from oil sales and investments only if they set production and price levels that sustain Western economic growth. Saudi Arabia can maximize income only from maximizing sales. Unlike the other members of OPEC, it profits most from the sheer volume of oil it can sell, not from getting the highest possible price per barrel through restricting total OPEC production.[38] At the same time, the U.S. and the other Western states have realized that attractive as cuts in oil prices may seem, the West is dependent on relatively stable oil prices in structuring its international lending and the international monetary system. The increase in world borrowing, particularly by the developing states, has made it steadily more difficult for Western—or any other—financial institutions to cope with rapid shifts in income in the developing world and led to the somewhat startling event of U.S. Secretary of Treasury Donald Regan having to issue public warnings regarding the "risk" of further cuts in oil prices.[39]

The Impact of Gulf Oil Policy

This mix of forces also helps to explain Saudi oil policy and its value to the West. It is important to stress that the objectives of Saudi oil policy do not coincide with those of the West. Saudi pricing and production goals do not coincide with Western interests because Saudi Arabia seeks to maximize its revenues from the West. While this may mean showing enough moderation regarding oil prices to maximize revenue, it does not mean selling oil at prices one dime less than Western economies can afford. Further, the Saudi government has every incentive to use its oil power to make up for its other weaknesses. It does use its ability to manipulate oil production and prices to put political pressure on the West, and to show its displeasure with Western actions, particularly those of the U.S. toward Israel. It also has occasionally miscalculated the best way to maximize long-term revenues, or bowed to political pressures from within OPEC and the Arab world, and overpriced its oil or cut production in ways that harm the West.

Nevertheless, there has been enough common interest between Saudi Arabia and the West so that Saudi Arabia has generally taken the lead within OPEC in limiting oil price rises and in ensuring adequate production levels. This commonality of interest is reflected in Table 1.8, which provides a summary chronology of Saudi oil policy since the embargo of 1973–1974. It is also reflected in the events that created the global recession, and in a growing struggle between Saudi Arabia and the more radical members of OPEC.

The same pressures that forced the West into a recession created the oil glut of 1983, the shifts in Gulf production levels shown in Tables 1.1 to 1.3, and deep and potentially lasting divisions between the conservative Gulf states and the radical members of OPEC. While the reduction in Iranian and Iraqi oil exports kept up the production of other OPEC states in 1981, a combination of the worsening recession and Iran's ability to resume production began to radically change this situation in early 1982. Saudi production, which had averaged 9.6 MMBD in 1981, dropped to 6 to 7 MMBD by the early spring of 1982. Kuwait production dropped from 1 MMBD to 0.7 MMBD, and the remaining southern Gulf states also had to cut production. The other OPEC and exporting nations also experienced serious cuts in production and sales, which forced many exporters, including Iran, Nigeria, Libya, Indonesia, and Venezuela, to shift from charging a premium for their oil to discounting at prices that reached as low as $28.00 per barrel. Further, these cuts in demand occurred at a time when Iran badly wanted to recover the market share it had lost because of the revolution and war. Iran was producing only 1.1 MMBD but had the ability to produce at 2–3 MMBD, and it desperately needed additional revenue.

TABLE 1.8 Chronology of Major Saudi Oil Price and Production Policies, 1973–1981

1965, 1967	Saudi Arabia resists Iranian efforts to limit production to raise prices.
1973:	
June 1, July 4, and August 1	Saudi officials, including King Faisal, warn that oil production will be limited or frozen if progress is not made on an Arab-Israeli settlement.
October 6	October War begins.
October 12	Saudi Arabia warns the U.S. it cannot show moderation if U.S. provides arms aid to Israel.
October 12–13	U.S. airlift to Israel begins.
October 16	Posted prices rise from $3.01 to $5.11 per barrel. Six OPEC members meet in Kuwait and increase posted prices from $3.01 to $5.12 during October 1973 Arab-Israeli war.
	Ministers of OAPEC countries plus Iran meet in Kuwait. The majority support an immediate embargo. Saudi Arabia presses for more time for the U.S. and gets agreement on a 5% production cut per month.
October 17	President Nixon sends request to Congress for $2.2 billion in emergency aid to Israel.
October 18	UAE, Libya, and Qatar announce oil boycott against the U.S. Saudi Arabia resists and announces only a 10% cut in output.
October 20	Saudi Arabia joins boycott and cuts production from 8.3 to 6.5 MMBD, but allows ARAMCO to continue oil shipments to U.S. refineries in the Caribbean.
October 22	A cease-fire is declared, but fails to hold on the Sinai front as Israel drives to cut off Egyptian Third Army.
October 24	Second cease-fire, but final Israeli attacks halt only on the 28th.
October 26–28	Arab summit calls for hard line on embargo.
December 14	King Faisal tells Kissinger there can be no easing of embargo until progress is made on occupied territories.
December 23–24	The shah and most of OPEC press for a new posted price of $13.33. Saudi Arabia forces a compromise on $11.65.
December 24–25	OAPEC oil ministers agree to reduce their 25% production cut to 15%.
1974:	
February 14	Arab foreign ministers delay meeting on grounds insufficient progress has been made in peace talks, but Saudi Arabia, Egypt, Syria, and Algeria meet in a restricted summit and agree oil boycott should be dropped if U.S. makes constructive progress.
March 1	Kissinger presents disengagement proposals to Egypt and Syria.
March 13	Arab oil ministers meet. Saudi Arabia and Egypt agree to lift embargo. Syria and Libya oppose lifting and Algeria makes removal conditional.
May 28–31	Syria agrees to disengagement, and oil embargo ends.

TABLE 1.8 (continued)

June	OPEC economic experts press for an increase in the basic (national revenue) price per barrel from $4 to $7–11 to cut oil company profits. Saudi Arabia calls for a $2 cut in posted prices and forces a compromise that limits the price increase per barrel to 1.5%.
June 8	Saudi Arabia and U.S. establish Joint Commission on Economic Cooperation to ease impact of oil price rises and help recycle petrodollars.
September	Saudi Arabia again resists OPEC call for major price rises. Increase is limited to 3.5% per barrel.
1975:	
March and summer	At both the first OPEC summit in Algiers on 4–5 March and during the summer, Saudi Arabia resists price indexation and OPEC production limits.
October	OPEC meets in Vienna and increases price by 10%, a compromise between the 5% rise sought by the Saudis and the 15% favored by Iran.
1976:	
June	Saudi Arabia serves notice at OPEC ministerial meeting that it is in favor of a standstill in prices. Other ministers call for up to 20% rises.
September 24	Shah demands 35% price rise at OPEC meeting. African states call for 20%. Iraq calls for 26%. Saudis and Arab allies publicly push for 5% rise and privately for a maximum of 10%. Saudis threaten maximum production.
December 16	OPEC meets in Doha. Saudis and UAE agree only to a 5% price increase; the other states increase prices by 10%.
1977:	
January	Prince Fahd privately indicates Saudi Arabia will assist U.S. to create a strategic petroleum reserve equal to six months' consumption.
June	Reunification of OPEC prices. Saudis increase by 5%, others drop demands for additional planned July increases.
July 12–13	At OPEC conference, Saudi Arabia and Kuwait agree to raise prices 5% only if other states forego additional 5% price rise. Saudi Arabia agrees to limit production to 8.5 MMBD in exchange for price freeze to end of year.
1978:	
May 6–7	Saudi Arabia calls extraordinary an OPEC conference on long-term pricing and production strategy in Taif. Presses to avoid further price rises. Saudi production drops from 8.5 MMBD ceiling to slightly over 7 MMBD.
June 17–18	OPEC leaves prices constant. Saudi Arabia successfully resists effort to index dollar against other foreign currencies in face of oil glut and recession.
November–December	The shah's imminent fall causes a world price panic. Saudi Arabia increases production from 8.5 MMBD ceiling to over 10 MMBD.

TABLE 1.8 (continued)

December 16	Saudi Arabia resists call for immediate 15% further price rise. Gets OPEC agreement to four 5% quarterly price rises in 1979.
1979:	
January 23	Shah leaves Iran.
March 26–27	OPEC meeting coincides with signing of Arab-Israeli peace treaty. Members agree to disagree. Saudi Arabia holds to base price of $14.54 a barrel but limits production to 8.5 MMBD. North African producers raise to over $18 per barrel.
June	OPEC meeting sets general ceiling of $23.50 per barrel, plus $2 surcharge. Saudi Arabia raises to only $18. Raises production ceiling back to 9.5 MMBD.
December	OPEC in Caracas fails to reach unified price structure. Saudi Arabia increases to $24, retroactive to 1 November 1979.
1980:	
January	Saudis unilaterally raise price to $26, retroactive to 1 January 1980, to align prices closer to OPEC level in effort to restore common price front. Effort fails.
May	OPEC ministers meet at Taif in May: Saudi price increased from $26 to $28, retroactive to 1 April.
June	OPEC meeting in Algiers in June: OPEC prices increased from $32 to $37. Saudis stay at $28.
September–December	OPEC ministers meet in Vienna in September: Saudi Arabia increases to $30, retroactive to 1 August. Iraq-Iran War begins late September 1980. OPEC meets in Bali in December: Saudis increase to $32, retroactive to 1 November, but declare intention to keep production high to bring other OPEC prices down to Saudi level.
1981:	
June	OPEC ministers meet in Geneva and decide on price freeze. Surplus production is major problem, with spot prices falling sharply. Saudi Arabia continues high level of production to narrow price spread within OPEC.
September–November	Saudi Arabia initially resists pressure to cut back production to 6 MMBD or less. It cuts production to 9.2 MMBD in September and to 8.6 MMBD in November.
December	Saudi Arabia agrees at the OPEC meeting to raise its price to $34 per barrel and to cut production to 8.5 MMBD if other members of OPEC will cut their premiums on high-quality oil. This fails to stabilize average oil prices at a level low enough to maintain *demand.*
1982:	
February	Saudi Arabia allows liftings to "float" at market demand levels, but refuses to support OPEC efforts to cut production as prices drop below $34.
March	The spring ministerial meeting of OPEC reveals growing tensions within OPEC. Saudi Arabia accepts a temporary OPEC ceiling of 17.5 MMBD, but insists on a high ceiling on Saudi production of 7.5

TABLE 1.8 (continued)

	MMBD in March and 7 MMBD in May. This blocks OPEC efforts to freeze or raise prices above $34. Saudi production dips below 6.5 MMBD as spot market prices drop to $29.
July 9–10	Saudi Arabia rejects long-term production ceilings and efforts to raise prices at the OPEC oil ministers meeting, and calls for stable prices and increased production to allow world economic recovery. Iran calls for a cut in the Saudi quota to 5 MMBD.
December	Saudi Arabia and the conservative Gulf states split with Iran, Algeria, and Libya at the December OPEC ministerial meeting. Saudi Arabia again resists production quotas that would limit world oil availability and raise prices.
1983:	
January	Saudi Arabia consults with the U.S., IEA, Britain, France, FRG, and Japan on the problems that given oil production and price levels present to the world economy. It adjusts its plans to the prospect of a prolonged recession.
January 5	ARAMCO partners refuse to increase liftings.
January 16	Saudi Arabia, the GCC nations, and other OPEC moderates meet in Bahrain and agree to cut prices rather than accept major cuts in production.
January 23–24	A special meeting of OPEC oil ministers collapses because of irreconcilable differences between Iran and Saudi Arabia.
February 10	Saudi Arabia announces it will no longer maintain fixed oil prices, and plans to compete on the world market.

Source: This chronology is extracted from a wide range of articles in the *New York Times, Wall Street Journal, Middle East Economic Digest, Economist,* and *8 Days.*

When OPEC held its spring ministerial meeting in March 1982, Saudi Arabia became a natural target for the nations that lacked Saudi flexibility in altering price and production. Several members of OPEC, particularly Iran and Libya, put intense pressure on Saudi Arabia to cut production. Libya, for example, sought a Saudi production ceiling of 4.5 MMBD. Saudi Arabia refused, however, and the result was an awkward compromise in which OPEC agreed to set a production ceiling of 17.5 MMBD.

Although Saudi Arabia cut its production ceiling from 8.5 to 7.5 MMBD, this level was so high that it was impossible for the other members of OPEC to maintain price levels of $34.00 or more. The world economy continued to slip during the summer and fall of 1982, and OPEC oil continued to be discontented well below the official price of $34.00 per barrel. Saudi Arabia kept its price at the agreed OPEC level, but Iran, Libya, Venezuela, and several African nations had to continue to discount to maintain sales. While the demand for OPEC oil still averaged 18.8 MMBD in 1982, this demand dropped during the last two quarters of the year, and the resulting oil income was not high enough to fund the ambitious development plans and borrowing of key exporting states like Mexico and Nigeria or to allow Iran to produce at its desired level. Libya, Venezuela, and Algeria experienced a severe cash flow problem, and all of the heavily populated members of OPEC—which had overborrowed and overexpanded their development plans in anticipation of high revenues—ran into growing economic problems.

The cut in oil revenues affected not only Saudi Arabia but the other conservative Gulf states. Abu Dhabi's production dropped from more than 1 MMBD to 850,000 BPD in later 1982 and to 700,000 BPD in the first quarter of 1983. The United Arab Emirates as a whole dropped from 1.8 MMBD in the late 1970s to 1.2 MMBD in 1982 and then to roughly the UAE's quota level of 1.0 MMBD in early 1983. The UAE's oil revenues dropped by well over 25% in 1982 to levels around $7.5 billion and by another 25% in the first quarter of 1983. It had to make major cuts in its 1982-1983 budget, cut its 1983-1984 budget by 40%, cancel over $1 billion worth of construction plans, and make similar cuts in the rest of its development plans. Bahrain had to cut back on banking, trade activity, and investments. Oman maintained production but price cuts forced it to cut back on its budget and development plan. Kuwaiti production dropped to as low as 600–680,000 BPD, although Kuwait needs runs of over 850,000 BPD to feed its distribution and refinery system efficiently, and the country faced its first deficit on account in modern history. Qatar faced particularly serious problems because of production problems in gas and oil and saw its production drop from 500,000 BPD in 1979 to 328,000 BPD in 1982 and then to monthly average levels as low as 200,000 BPD in the first quarter of 1983. It faced a 41% drop in oil revenue and a $1.5 billion budget deficit.[40]

These cuts would have been far less drastic if the opposing interests of the OPEC states had not proceeded to turn what market forces would have made a limited downward adjustment in oil prices into a strategic confrontation. Saudi Arabia's strongest opponents in OPEC—Libya and Iran—produced almost twice their OPEC quota, although both constantly attacked Saudi Arabia for overproducing. These attacks were coupled to their overall radical political opposition to the conservative oil states and the West and to Libya's and Algeria's support of Iran in the Iran-Iraq War.

The result was an open battle at the OPEC ministerial meeting in December 1982. While the ministers did agree on an 18.5-MMBD ceiling, they could not agree on any production quotas by country, and OPEC had divided into a "moderate-conservative" bloc supporting relatively high production levels and de facto price flexibility and a "radical" bloc calling for major Saudi production cuts and high prices. Libya, which was undergoing a major economic crisis because of past overspending, called for a quota of up to 1.5 MMBD, as compared to its March quota of 750,000 BPD and actual sales of up to 1.5 MMBD.

Iran stated that it would produce at 3.02 MMBD or more, versus its March quota of 1.2 MMBD and a proposed compromise quota of 2.5 MMBD. It also tried to persuade the "moderate" exporters like Nigeria, Indonesia, and Venezuela to join it in pushing for major additional cuts in the Saudi production ceiling.[41] Saudi Arabia and the other members of the Gulf Cooperation Council (GCC) then joined together in surveying Western economic projections and views regarding oil prices, demand, and the impact on world debt payments of any sudden discounting of oil prices. The end result was that Saudi Arabia, Kuwait, Qatar, the UAE, and Oman concluded that they would have to act as a separate bloc in adjusting to a prolonged world recession. While the UAE and Kuwait wavered because of threats and pressure from Iran, the GCC states still theatened to meet as a bloc and to formally discount prices.[42]

These moves led to a special meeting of OPEC on 23 and 24 January 1983. The oil ministers met in Geneva at a time when Iran issued another ultimatum to Iraq, and Libya and Syria announced their unconditional support of Iran in the Iran-Iraq War. The issue became the extent to which Saudi Arabia would or would not cut production to hold prices and the other OPEC states would or would not continue to discount. Amid conflicting advice from the West—which wavered from calls for price cuts to requests to keep prices high so that the oil-exporting states could repay their debts—OPEC attempted to agree on a new quota system. However, the basic forces dividing OPEC, and Saudi Arabia and the other moderates from Iran and Libya, eventually blocked any agreement. The meeting broke up in the face of what Sheikh Yamani called "irreconcilable differences."[43]

This breakup was followed by a massive Iranian and Saudi lobbying effort within OPEC, and by meetings among Saudi Arabia, Kuwait, Qatar, and the UAE in late February 1983 to try to work out a common strategy for the conservative Gulf states. The eventual result was compromises between the conservative and radical members of OPEC over pricing, production, and quotas. In addition, another OPEC meeting was held in March 1983, and an awkward compromise was arrived at by which the members agreed to cut the posted price of oil from $34 to $29 per barrel (the first cut in OPEC's history), Iran agreed to keep to its production quota, and Saudi Arabia agreed to act as the "swing" producer that would help hold prices at $29. While the members agreed to keep to a 17.5 MMBD ceiling, the agreement left several major gaps. Iran did not agree to hold prices, and Saudi Arabia was left without any clear quota.[44]

Although Iran then did proceed to sell some oil at discount, particularly to Japan, rising world demand brought OPEC production up to 17 MMBD in the first half of 1983, and the OPEC states kept more or less to their quotas. The monitoring committee OPEC had set up to supervise the agreement met in June and again in early July and agreed that the new quota and price system was working well enough that it would not have to be an agenda item on the 18 July meeting of the OPEC oil ministers.[45] Nevertheless, as 1983 progressed, it became obvious that the new "unity" in OPEC was more apparent than real. It came at the cost of massive reductions in oil income and of papering over the differences between Iran and Saudi Arabia; it was sustained only because of a limited trend toward economic recovery in the West, and because Saudi Arabia was willing to defer any challenge to the new system until it saw the extent to which oil demand would rise in late 1983 and 1984. It also came at a time when Iranian payments to Syria continued to keep Iraq at minimal production levels, and Iraqi attacks on Iranian oil facilities, on top of a severe storm, had created a massive oil slick covering much of the Gulf.[46]

Regardless of what compromises may be worked out in the future, the tensions exposed during this period seem likely to make oil the continuing subject of a political struggle between Saudi Arabia and the other large producers, to exacerbate the growing political and economic conflict between Saudi Arabia and Iran, and to trigger a political battle for oil revenues and market shares that will continue regardless of any facade of unity within OPEC or the prices and quotas it formally agrees to. All the OPEC states now share a need for oil income that will tend to force them to produce at high levels, but they face an equally strong political temptation to try to maximize income and the value of their oil reserves at Saudi Arabia's expense. Saudi Arabia has also so far been the loser in the quota system, since Iran has been able to maintain its oil revenues while Saudi Arabia has not, and OPEC must still face the problem of what will happen when Iraq can again export at its prewar level.

Further, the present "oil glut" has given the Soviet Union a new incentive to put pressure on the Gulf. The recession and drop in oil prices forced the USSR to increase its oil exports to the noncommunist world by 40% in 1982 in a desperate effort to earn hard currency, and to cut its shipments to Eastern Europe by 10% in spite of continuing political unrest and cuts in the growth rates of its East European allies. Although the USSR also increased its arms sales, they represented only 17% of its exports as compared to 68% for energy, and even this export effort could not avoid a $4 billion deficit in Soviet hard currency earnings in 1982. Given the USSR's continuing export and hard currency problems, it has every incentive to join the hard-line OPEC states in putting pressure on Saudi Arabia.[47]

These pressures will tend to tighten the links between Saudi oil policy and the economic interests of the West and increase Saudi Arabia's strategic importance to the West as OPEC's "swing" producer regardless of how soon world oil demand recovers or of the outcome of the Iran-Iraq War. They also highlight the importance of creating a form of collective self-defense that can protect Saudi Arabia and the southern Gulf states from pressure by the more radical members of OPEC. Even an Iranian-Iraqi peace settlement that preserved both regimes could lead to joint Iranian-Iraqi pressure on the southern Gulf countries to cut production and raise oil prices. An Iranian victory could create conditions in which Iran and Libya could dominate OPEC in alliance with the African states.

Saudi Arabia's Political and Cultural Position

Saudi Arabia's political objectives differ from those of the West in many important ways. At the same time, Saudi Arabia's political and cultural position creates a core of common interest that reinforces its potential value in a strategic partnership. Saudi Arabia is the center of the conservative and moderate forces in Islam that offer the Arab world the option of modernization without radicalization. This position has led the Saudi government to take a pro-Western and anticommunist position and to systematically oppose Soviet efforts to expand its influence in the Arab world. It has led Saudi Arabia to consistently support a policy of political modernization in the Arab world and to serve as one of the key forces that has moderated the Palestinian movement.

Table 1.9 helps put this aspect of Saudi Arabia's strategic importance into perspective. It provides a chronology of Saudi diplomatic efforts that have been of assistance to the West, and it helps put the differences between U.S. and Saudi policy into perspective. It shows that Saudi Arabia has provided Oman with substantial aid in suppressing the radical and Soviet-backed Dhofar rebellion. It helped prevent a Nasserite and radical takeover in North Yemen. Its efforts to displace the USSR from South Yemen came close to success in 1978, helped push South Yemen into a peace with Oman in 1982, and are still the primary hope the West has of reducing Soviet influence in South Yemen. Though only partially successful, Saudi aid to North Yemen has been the main factor checking the growth of Soviet influence in that state.

The table also shows that Saudi Arabia has consistently encouraged Iraq and Syria to reduce their dependence on the USSR and that it is the only major pro-Western state with significant influence in both countries. It has used its oil wealth consistently in its own interest and that of the West to moderate Syrian actions in Lebanon and to try to work out a solution to the continuing civil war in Lebanon. Saudi diplomacy has been critical in reducing the risk of conflicts between Syria and Jordan and in reducing the tensions between Jordan and the Palestinians that grew out of the conflict of September 1970.

While Saudi Arabia opposed the Camp David accords on the grounds that they made no provision for Palestinian sovereignty on the West Bank and Gaza, or the creation of a peace settlement that would support Jordanian, Syrian, and Lebanese stability, it has long recognized the desirability of a peace settlement based on Israel's 1967 boundaries. For all its many differences with the U.S. over U.S. support of Israel and over the Arab-Israeli peace process, Saudi Arabia played a key role

TABLE 1.9 Saudi Diplomatic, Aid, and Military Initiatives in Support of Western Security Interests, 1970–1982

December 1969 to July 1972	King Faisal and his brother-in-law and chief of intelligence, Kamal Adham, are instrumental in persuading Sadat to break with USSR.
1970–1971	Saudi Arabia aids opposition to pro-Soviet National Liberation Front in South Yemen.
26 October 1974	Saudi Arabia agrees to pay $400 million per year to support an Arab League lease on Perim Island and secure the southern entrance to the Red Sea.
5 March 1975	Saudi Arabia aids in achieving the Iranian-Iraqi Algiers accord at the OPEC summit.
April 1975	Saudis agree to fund U.S. Hawk surface-to-air missile sales to Jordan.
September 1975	Saudi Arabia supports second disengagement agreement in Sinai. Previously provided $400 million in aid to Egypt.
August 1975	Saudi Arabia gives North Yemen $100 million in budgetary support and $400 million in economic aid to reduce dependence on USSR.
March 1976	Saudi Arabia starts efforts to link conservative Gulf states.
April–June 1976	Saudi Arabia agrees to fund Syrian intervention in Lebanon at Lebanon's request. Supports creation of joint peacekeeping force.
October 1976	Saudis apply heavy financial pressures on Syria and perform a key role in the resolution of the cease-fire in the Lebanese Civil War.
	Saudi-sponsored cease-fire in Lebanon. Saudi Arabia funds creation of Arab Deterrent Force.
1976–1977	Saudis offer aid to anti-Soviet regimes in Africa (e.g., Zaire) and to anti-Marxist Angolan forces under Savimbi. They also persuade Somalia to abandon the Soviet and espouse a pro-Western stance.
March 1976 to 26 June 1978	Saudi Arabia seeks to ease South Yemen away from USSR.
July to September 1977	Saudi aid to Somalia supports it in war with Ethiopia at time when U.S. and U.K. pledge military aid to Somalia.
Early 1977	First Saudi-funded U.S. arms transfers arrive in North Yemen.
April 1977	Saudi aid supports Muhammad Daoud of Afghanistan in 1978 in his effort to reduce dependence on USSR.
February 1978	Saudi Arabia presses the U.S. to also assist Somalia to thwart the Soviet/Cuban-backed Ethiopian forces operating in the Horn.
June 1978	Saudi Arabia finances airlift of 1,500 Moroccan troops to Zaire to suppress left-wing insurgents invading from Angola.
	Military aid is offered to Zaire, but requires U.S. approval to re-export such U.S.-made hardware.

TABLE 1.9 (continued)

8 March 1979	Saudi Arabia opposes embargo of U.S. and Egypt, and cutoff of aid and economic dealings with Egypt at Baghdad Conference on Camp David Agreement.
April 1979	Saudi Arabia goes along with the Arab economic and diplomatic boycott of Egypt, but privately assures Egypt of continued financial aid to purchase U.S. arms.
June 1980	King Khalid visits Germany, improving relations between the two powers, since Schmidt had come to Riyadh earlier to obtain a loan of about $1.7 billion to help finance the German balance-of-payments deficit.
October 1980	Riyadh breaks diplomatic relations with Libya after Qaddafi's vicious attacks on the U.S. for aiding Saudi Arabia in defence of the oilfields.
December 1980	Saudi mediation ends Syrian-Jordan border crisis after forces build up to 50,000 men and nearly 1,000 tanks.
1981	The Saudis provide critical aid to reduce Sudan's financial problems. In 1981 they supply the Sudan with over $300 million through the IMF.
May 1981	Though the Saudis publicly back Syria in the crisis with Israel, they send a high-level emissary to counsel restraint and effect a compromise with diplomatic and financial pressure.
August 1981	Fahd Peace Plan marks major advance in Arab willingness to recognize Israel and reach a peace based on Israel's 1967 boundaries.
November 1981	Saudi Arabia unsuccessfully seeks a consensus on the Fahd Plan at the Arab Foreign Ministers Meeting in Fez.
January 1982 to January 1983	Saudi Arabia works with the U.S. to bring a halt to the conflict in Lebanon, reach a peaceful outcome of Israel's invasion of Lebanon, and persuade Syria to evacuate Lebanon.
March 1981	Saudi Arabia agrees to fund Jordanian purchases of U.S. arms to give Jordan adequate self-defense capability and reduce pressure to seek arms *from* the USSR.
June 1982	Saudi Arabia outbids Iran, and provides the aid necessary to push South Yemen into accepting a Kuwaiti-mediated peace settlement with Oman in November.
July to September 1982	Saudi Arabia helps mediate the PLO evacuation from Beirut and southern Lebanon.
September 1982	Saudi Arabia takes the lead in catalyzing the Arab Summit to take a favorable stand on an Arab-Israeli peace settlement.
January 1983	Saudi Arabia continues to fund improved air defense links in the Southern Gulf, and provide strategic aid to Iraq, Pakistan, Jordan, Somalia, Sudan, and Afghanistan. Saudi aid to Syria remains a key counterweight to its military dependence on the USSR.

Sources: Taken from various editions of the *New York Times, Christian Science Monitor, Wall Street Journal, Middle East, 8 Days, Economist, Times* (London), and *Financial Times.*

in persuading Sadat to break with the USSR and in giving Egypt the financial and military support it needed to reach the initial Sinai accords. It helped persuade Syria to accept Egypt's second disengagement agreement with Israel in 1975 by trading Saudi aid to Syria and recognition of its right to head an Arab Deterrent Force in Lebanon for Syrian support of the Egyptian position and a cease-fire between Syria and the Lebanese Christians.

Although Saudi Arabia is still technically at war with Israel, this aspect of Saudi policy has been misunderstood because of Saudi Arabia's rejection of the Camp David accords.[48] Like Jordan, Saudi Arabia could not accept the vague language regarding the settlement of the issues of the West Bank and Palestinian rights. Unlike Egypt, which could afford to make such concessions because its primary interests lay in reducing its defense burden, expanding its economic ties with the West, and obtaining the return of the Sinai, Saudi Arabia could not turn a blind eye to this aspect of the Camp David accords. Even if Saudi Arabia had been willing to ignore the West Bank issue in spite of 30 years of commitment to the Palestinian cause, it could not sacrifice its legitimacy as the custodian of the Islamic holy places and weaken the basic underpinning of the Saudi regime. It would also have lost the support of many of its citizens, many of its foreign workers, and most of the smaller Gulf states.

This Saudi commitment to the Palestinian cause did not, however, preclude a willingness to recognize Israel. As early as 11 May 1977, Crown Prince Fahd talked of "complete, permanent peace" and a normalization of relations with Israel, stating that "all Arabs, including the Palestinians," were ready to negotiate a Middle East settlement with Israel if Israel recognized the full rights of the Palestinian people. Prince Fahd asked Carter to urge the Israelis to keep an open mind on a settlement that would be "just and lasting" and expressed "his strong hope that Israel would be reassured about the inclinations of his country toward the protection of their security."[49]

While upheaval in the Arab world following the Camp David accords led Saudi Arabia to step back from the peace issue, Prince Fahd reiterated these ideas once political tensions eased. In August 1981 he presented a formal eight-point peace plan that closely followed the UN resolutions supported by the United States.[50] The plan called for

- Israeli withdrawal from all territory occupied in the 1967 war
- recognition of the Palestinian refugees' right to return to their homeland, or to compensation if they do not wish to return
- establishment of an independent Palestinian state in the West Bank and Gaza Strip, with East Jerusalem, which has been annexed by Israel, as its capital
- a U.S. trusteeship of the occupied territories that would last only for a transitional period of a few months
- removal of all Israeli settlements from the occupied territories

- guarantees of freedom of worship in the Holy Land for all religions
- guarantees of the right of all states in the area to live in peace
- guarantees of such an agreement by the United Nations or "some of its members," presumably the United States and the Soviet Union

The first five points in the Saudi plan, and possibly the last three, were unacceptable to the Begin government in the precise form presented by Prince Fahd. Nevertheless, for all Saudi Arabia's hedging in public, advancing the Fahd plan constituted tacit recognition of Israel's right to exist.

Saudi Arabia consistently pursued such a peace strategy during the Lebanon crisis of 1981–1983. It made major diplomatic efforts to limit the conflict in Lebanon. It responded favorably to President Reagan's September 1982 peace proposal and backed the call for peace negotiations at the subsequent Arab summit meeting at Fez. It supported the agreement that the U.S. worked out between Israel and Lebanon in the spring of 1983 and the U.S. efforts to persuade Syria to accept some modus vivendi with Israel after the agreement failed to bring peace to Lebanon. Saudi Arabia has also disagreed with the U.S. position on many occasions, but it has never shown any serious desire to join the Arab confrontation states in direct military action against Israel.

The Impact of Saudi Strengths and Weaknesses

There is no doubt that Saudi Arabia is militarily weak and that its small population and developing economy create additional vulnerabilities. As will be discussed later, Saudi Arabia has internal problems, and it is vulnerable to pressure from Arab radical movements and the threat of terrorism and attacks on its government from any of the larger Arab states. This vulnerability has often led Saudi Arabia to avoid decisive political action or to support radical moves by states like Libya and Syria when it privately opposes them. Saudi Arabia is forced to take careful account of the desires of the Palestinian movement, events in the Yemens, and the views of Iran and Iraq.

Nevertheless, Saudi Arabia is by far the strongest and most influential conservative Gulf state, and it has broader prestige and influence because of its control over the key holy places of Islam. In spite of the growth of Muslim fundamentalism, the growth of a radical religious challenge in Iran, the uprising at the Grand Mosque in 1979, and attempts to use the flow of some 1.5–2 million pilgrims a year to subvert the Saudi regime, Saudi Arabia remains a powerful religious and cultural force in the Arab world.[51] Saudi Arabia is also able to combine its religious and cultural influence with the leverage it obtains from its oil wealth. Saudi Arabia has funded many major economic and military aid programs since the late 1960s, and most have served Western and U.S. interests.

Overt Saudi aid has been of major importance both to friendly states and to the world's financial institutions. Its more covert military and economic aid has been of equal importance in funding many of the initiatives listed in Table 1.8 and in countering Soviet and radical influence.[52]

Overt Saudi economic aid has been important since the early 1970s. It reached $11 billion in commitments during 1972–1975, only $3.2 billion of which was in loans. Saudi Arabia joined with France in initiating the Conference on International Economic Cooperation (CIEC) in 1977, a key step in maintaining a "North-South" dialogue, and it devoted 6% of its national income or well over $20 billion, to economic assistance during 1977–1981. Such aid averaged over $4 billion per annum and was equal to 41% of all aid from OPEC and 15% of all aid from the OECD. In 1981, before major cuts began in its oil revenues, Saudi Arabia spent $5.4 billion on aid, of which 40% was in grants and 60% was concessional development or cash loans. Saudi Arabia's contribution of 6% of its GNP compares with an average of 0.39% for the OECD nations and 0.27% for the U.S.[53] Such Saudi aid is of particular political importance because much of it is dispensed on a bilateral basis, combined with military or other unreported aid, and targeted toward the most vulnerable states in the Gulf, Arabia, Indian Ocean area, Red Sea area, the Middle East and Africa. Egypt, Somalia, North Yemen, Pakistan, Jordan, Zaire, Lebanon, and Sudan are examples of such states.[54]

Saudi Arabia has been one of the few OPEC nations to provide monetary aid to the West. It eased the shock of the rise in oil prices by granting outstanding loans to the International Monetary Fund (IMF) of $1.5 billion and by agreeing to extend special drawing rights (SDRs) of nearly $5 billion in 1981–1982, and it committed a further $4 billion in 1983. Saudi Arabia made $9.5 billion available to the IMF in May 1981 for recycling purposes. This brought recent Saudi commitments up to $12.8 billion, and while the cuts in Saudi oil income have delayed $4.3 billion of this funding, the Saudi commitment has still been substantial.[55] Saudi Arabia has also provided $3 billion to the World Bank, and the Saudi Arabian Monetary Agency (SAMA) supported long-term deutsche mark loans to the World Bank and bought 5.2 billion in deutsche mark promissory notes at below market rates in 1980 to ease West Germany's balance-of-payments problem. It helped rescue the International Development Authority (IDA) in 1982, and it provided massive loans to France. Saudi Arabia agreed to support over 50 billion yen in long-term notes for Japan and provided similar support to a number of other Western nations.

Not only has this aid given Saudi Arabia political strength that is of significant strategic importance, it also reflects further evidence of Saudi Arabia's understanding that its oil policy must be linked to the economic stability of the developing states. Further, Saudi Arabia has joined the U.S. in creating bodies like the Joint Commission on Economic Cooperation (JCEC), which the U.S. and Saudi Arabia established after the 1973–1974 embargo. Meetings between the Saudis and President Nixon's senior advisers and cabinet members led to an agreement that a permanent body would be established under the U.S. secretary of the treasury and the Saudi minister of finance, with working groups on industrialization, manpower, education, technology, and agriculture. This agreement resulted in the creation of the JCEC on 8 June 1974 and in a technical cooperation agreement that allowed the JCEC to begin operation on 13 February 1975.[56]

The commission has held seven ministerial sessions through mid-1983. It has completed 4 electric projects and agreed to 23, it sponsors the training of approximately 400 Saudis annually in the U.S., and it has approximately 250 Americans working in Saudi Arabia. Its projects are relatively small, but they are highly technical in character and have done much to increase U.S.-Saudi cooperation. They have included projects in areas as diverse as statistics and data processing, desalinization and water development, consumer protection, national park development, highway administration, solar energy research, and tax and customs administration.

The Prospects for Continued Saudi Cooperation with the West

The factors discussed in the preceding section reinforce the importance of keeping Saudi Arabia a friendly state and of creating a strategic partnership that will tie Saudi Arabia's government closely to the West. The risks the West faces go beyond access to a key source of imported oil. Any radical change in Saudi Arabia's government might well bring a regime to power that would be more interested in conflict with the West than in partnership. At the same time, the failure to give Saudi Arabia the ability to defend its territory could make even an otherwise friendly Saudi government far more vulnerable to political pressure from the more radical and price-oriented Gulf states. A political break between Saudi Arabia and the United States or a new crisis over the Arab-Israeli issue might put intense internal political pressure on the Saudi government to pursue a political rather than an economic strategy. Such an alienated Saudi Arabia might then use its oil capital against the West rather than to support it. As Tables 1.6 and 1.8 indicate, Saudi Arabia would have great leverage in such a hostile role. This leverage will also increase once the world economy recovers from its current recession, and it might be used to divide the U.S. from its allies.

A hostile Saudi Arabia would have considerable flexibility in cutting its oil sales and trade because its economic development plans do not "force" it to maintain high production levels to serve its development needs. Even before the substantial cutbacks begun in late 1982, Saudi Arabia's revised Third Five Year Plan optimized Saudi economic development on the basis of oil-production levels ranging from 6.5 to 8.7 MMBD, with less than the equivalent of 1 MMBD in gas production. Since that time, Saudi Arabia has learned that it can sustain most of its essential expenditures and development activity on production levels between 4 and 5 MMBD, and it made significant cuts in its development plans.

While a debate took place over the extent to which Saudi Arabia could cut its production during the peak period in Western demand in 1980, this debate ignored both economic and political factors. The recent cuts in the Saudi budget and five year plan have shown that Saudi Arabia can cut production below 3.5 MMBD and still sustain essential budget expenditures for a period of years. Saudi Arabia can reduce or delay its petroleum product development. Working-level data from several U.S. oil companies indicates that Saudi Arabia could slip its investment in "downstream" plants and associated industries to half the levels called for in the present development plan and still meet its need to create domestic jobs and increase domestic economic activity. In fact, if one allows for realistic slippage in the latest Saudi industrial development plans, Saudi oil production will not have to rise above 4 MMBD until 1990, and Saudi Arabia might then be able to further limit its oil production by shutting in the oil fields that do not produce gas, utilizing its other gas fields for petrochemical production rather than NGL, and concentrating on production of product rather than crude. Even using less conservative estimates, Saudi production could be kept to about 5–6 MMBD through the mid-1990s with limited impact on its Master Gas Development Plans.[57]

The key point, however, is not how low Saudi oil-production levels can go. It is rather that a friendly Saudi Arabia has the ability to increase its production levels to exert price restraint on the other members of OPEC in ways that serve both Saudi and Western interests. In unfriendly hands, or in a contingency in which Saudi oil-production capability was sharply reduced, the resulting cutbacks in Saudi oil production could have a devastating impact on Western trade balances, the stability of the dollar, and the stability of world investment flows.

One cannot ignore the example of Iran or the many other cases in the developing world in which political change has been more important than economic or strategic self-interest. The shah's fall led Iran to write off over $50 billion dollars worth of economic development projects and adopt a totally different economic strategy within a matter of months. Libya, Ethiopia, and Syria have also pursued anti-Western policies in conflict with their economic self-interest, and Iraq's attack on Iran provides a good example of a political action that imposed massive cost on the West without any deliberate intent. A strategic partnership must be founded on stable political and military relations, not simply on economic self-interest.

Saudi Arabia, the Gulf, and the West

Finally, Saudi Arabia's political links to the West are essential to developing broader regional security initiatives and catalyzing efforts toward collective self-defense. Even if one could ignore the other factors that give Saudi Arabia strategic importance, Saudi Arabia's territorial position and military forces would still dictate that no arrangement that excluded Saudi Arabia could bind together the other conservative Gulf nations and provide enough land and air forces to create an effective military deterrent. The geography of the Gulf leaves no other alternative, and while Saudi forces may be weak by Western standards, Saudi Arabia is the only conservative Gulf nation that has sufficient forces to create any kind of deterrent in being or to give the smaller Gulf nations the support they need in maintaining their internal security.

While the issues surrounding Saudi Arabia's role relative to the other Gulf states are a primary focus of this book, even the basic statistics in Table 1.10 show that the smaller conservative Gulf states lack the territory and population to act alone. Their geography makes them vulnerable to Iran, South Yemen, or Iraq. Their only hope of finding strength that approaches their wealth lies in collective action and in cooperation with Saudi Arabia. Such cooperation is of great strategic benefit to the West. The smaller conservative Gulf states have a combined population larger than the native population of Saudi Arabia, and they form a territorial bloc with Saudi Arabia that is far easier to defend than Saudi Arabia's Gulf and northern borders.

Fortunately, the conservative Gulf states have already taken some initiatives toward creating collective security arrangements and have eliminated many of the barriers that have divided them. Most reached acceptable border settlements in 1977, although most borders have still not been formally demarcated. Saudi Arabia and Kuwait have joined together to help Bahrain, the UAE, and Qatar recover from mismanagement of their economies and development, including overinvestment in showpiece projects like petrochemical plants and aluminum smelters. Most important, the creation of the Gulf Cooperation Council on 5 February 1981 may slowly lead to the kind of collective self-defense effort in which Saudi Arabia can be *prima inter pares* without reviving fears of the past conflicts among the southern Gulf states. Although most of the council's work in defense is still in the planning stage, it is seeking to create a local rapid deployment force, to further improve cooperation in internal security, to improve cooperation in air defense and weapons procurement, and to develop better-integrated weapons procurement and infrastructure.

Notes

1. These figures for percentage of world oil reserves are taken from the Energy Information Administration, *1982 Annual Energy Review,* DOE/EIA-

TABLE 1.10 Size and Importance of the Conservative Gulf States in the Pre-Iran-Iraq War Period[a]

	Area (thousand sq km)	Mid-1980 Population (thousands)	GNP (current $ millions)	National Budget ($ millions)	Mid-1980 Oil Production Capacity[g] (MMBD)	End-1980 Oil Reserves[h] (billions of barrels)	Annual Oil Revenues at Mid-1981 OPEC Prices[i] ($ billions)
Saudi Arabia	2,331[b]	10,112[c]	77,000[d]	74,000[e]	12.5	166.5	127.8
Other Conservative Gulf States							
Bahrain	0.6	392	1,700[d]	291[e]	–	–	0.6
Kuwait	16	1,418	23,500[d]	11,800[d]	2.9	68.5	19.6
Neutral Zone	–	–	–	–	0.7	–	6.4
Oman	212[b]	519	2,600[f]	2,200[d]	–	2.4	4.0
Qatar	10	225	5,000[d]	3,000[d]	0.7	3.8	6.4
UAE	83[b]	934	21,000[d]	8,600[d]	2.6	29.4	20.7
Abu Dhabi	–	–	–	–	–	–	(16.0)
Dubai	–	–	–	–	–	–	(4.6)
Sharjah	–	–	–	–	–	–	(0.1)
Subtotal	321.6	3,488	53,800	25,891	6.9	104.1	57.7
Total Conservative Gulf States	2,652.6	13,672	130,800	99,891	19.4	270.6	185.5
Other Gulf States							
Iran	1,647	39,097	81,700[d]	33,900[d]	7.0	58.0	20.7
Iraq	445	13,596	35,200[d]	20,000[j]	7.0	31.0	7.8
North Yemen	194[b]	5,305	3,800[d]	900[d]	–	–	0
South Yemen	287[b]	1,930	7,924[f]	423[d]	–	–	0
Subtotal	2,573	59,928	128,624	55,223	14.0	89.0	28.5
Total Gulf States	5,225.6	73,570	259,424	155,114	33.4	359.6	214.0

[a]*Source:* CIA, "NBI Factbook," July 1979; and CIA, "The World Fact Book, 1981," CIA GS-WF 81-001 (U). Numbers are often rough estimates based on previous years' figures.
[b]Some land disputed.
[c]Actual population is probably 4–6 million native Saudis and 1.5 million "guest" workers.
[d]1979.
[e]1977.
[f]1978.
[g]*Source:* CIA ER IESR 81-005 (U), 26 May 1981, p. 3, "installed" or "facility" capacity.
[h]*Source:* DOE IA-0010, 11 May 1981, pp. 5 and 7; Exxon, *Middle East Oil,* September 1980, p. 5, as of January 1981. Includes 1/2 Neutral Zone.
[i]*Source:* CIA ER IESR 81-004 (U), 28 April 1981, computed at average OPEC price of $35 per barrel, annually.
[j]Proposed FY1980–1981.

0384 (Washington, D.C.: Department of Energy, April 1983), p. 45. Estimates of probable and proved reserves used later differ in definition and are taken from the source referenced in the corresponding note.

2. These percentages vary slightly according to source. The figures quoted are derived from Central Intelligence Agency (CIA), *International Energy Statistical Review,* DI IESR 83-005, 31 May 1983, principally from p. 1. (All CIA documents quoted in this book are unclassified and are available from the National Technical Information Service, 5285 Port Royal Road, Springfield, Va., 22161.)

3. The problems in predicting oil production and demand are illustrated by the fact that an interagency task force of the U.S. government could not agree on how to project alternative demand levels for the 18 months following the March 1983 meeting of the OPEC oil ministers. The officials involved disagreed so sharply that the White House had to order them not to talk to the press. *Platt's Oilgram News,* 18 May 1983, p. 5.

4. It is important to note that a minor oil shock can have serious results even in a global recession. A study by Wharton Econometric Forecasting Associates indicated that the U.S. would lose 0.4–0.8% of its GNP if oil prices suddenly rose 10% even under the near-recession conditions the study predicted for most of 1984. See "Long Term Service Special Report," *Wharton Economic News Perspectives,* 20 June 1983, p. 6.

5. *Wall Street Journal,* 14 December 1982; *Economist,* 11 December 1982, p. 91; *Washington Post,* 21 December 1982. Views differ sharply over future world oil demand. While estimates have declined, this decline is generally based on a significant long-term decline in economic growth. Recent changes in estimates of free world demand are shown below:

	1985			1990		
	1979	1981	1982-83	1979	1981	1982-83
Texaco	64.3	52	47	71.7	54-55	49
EIA	–	–	51	52.6	50.4	53.1
SOCAL	63.5	49.3	48	67.8	51.3	51
BP	–	50-51	49	51-55	51	51
CONOCO	–	–	47	–	–	49
Shell	53	48	–	–	50-52	–
Gulf	–	–	48	–	–	51
Exxon	56	54	–	60	55	–
IEA	–	–	48-50	–	–	50-56

Non-OPEC production grew by 3.3% to 18.92 MMBD in 1981 and has grown 35.7% since 1975, but 12.8 MMBD of this 18.92 MMBD is produced by developed nations. The rest comes from Mexico (2.5 MMBD), Egypt (685 MBD), and a host of small producers (3.1 MMBD). It is unlikely that the mid-term growth of oil production in most non-OPEC developing nations can do more than meet local demand. See *Oil and Gas Journal,* January 1982; *New York Times,* 6 January 1982; *Wall Street Journal,* 27 January and 1 February 1982; and EIA, *1982 Annual Energy Outlook with Projections to 1990,* DOE/EIA-0383(82) (Washington, D.C.: Department of Energy, April 1983), pp. 12, 22–23.

6. The CIA has not revised its production capacity estimates since the beginning of the Iran-Iraq War. These estimates are based on 1983 data as presented in CIA DI IESR 83-005 (U), 31 May 1983, p. 2. See footnotes b and e.

7. ARAMCO figures as of mid-1982. These do not include probable gas reserves of 111,852 BCF and proven reserves of 70,810 BCF. The Department of Energy uses slightly different definitions. Its estimate of proved Saudi oil reserves is 165.3 billion barrels, and its estimate of gas reserves is 121,000 BCF. See EIA, *1982 Annual Energy Outlook,* p. 45.

8. The importance of Saudi flexibility in exporting oil is further illustrated by the fact that Saudi Arabia used only about 300,000 BPD of its crude oil for domestic consumption in 1981. Further, only 153,189,236 barrels were converted into product for export at Ras Tanura, although another 70,507,965 went to the refinery at Bahrain. The only other "dedicated" customer was Jordan, which received 25,951,842 barrels via the Tapline facilities at Qaisumah. This meant that in 1981 about 3.2 billion barrels, or over 90% of Saudi crude oil production, moved freely to world markets.

9. Estimates vary. William B. Quandt estimates Saudi overseas investments as being roughly $150 billion and as producing revenues of at least $15 billion a year. He notes that revenues from exports of NGL and from the pilgrims to Makkah add $2–3 billion of additional annual revenue. See William B. Quandt, *Saudi Arabia's Oil Policy: A Staff Paper* (Washington, D.C.: Brookings Institution, 1982), pp. 25–27. Data on OPEC exports and imports by country are taken from CIA, *International Energy Statistical Review,* DI IESR. The figures quoted come from the 31 May 1983 issue, pp. 11–12.

10. Saudi Information Office, September 1982. The Saudi estimate is "over 5%," but this does not track with recent Saudi data and CIA estimates of oil production and prices.

11. To put these figures into perspective, the 1981 period seems typical of the total world oil production and oil income most sources project for the middle to late 1980s. While it is unlikely that production by country will then be the same as in 1981, it is interesting to note that Saudi Arabia produced 16.6% of the world's oil in 1981. The upper Arab Gulf states produced 7.2%, the lower Arab Gulf states produced 4.6%. Iran produced 2.1%, and Arab Africa produced 5.8%. All communist countries produced 24.4%; the U.S. 14.5%, Venezuela 3.6%, Canada 2.5%, and the rest of Latin America 5.7%. Europe produced 4.1%, Indonesia 2.6%, and Australia and the rest of Asia 1.9%. In terms of comparative world oil reserves, Saudi Arabia had 25.9%, the upper Arab Gulf states 15.6%, the lower Arab Gulf states 5.6%, Iran 8.8%, and Arab Africa 5.5%. As for the rest of the world, the communist states had 13.3%, the U.S. 4.1%, Canada 1.0%, Venezuela 2.8%, the rest of Latin America 7.9%, Europe 3.6%, non-Arab Africa 3.0%, Indonesia 1.5%, and Australia and the other Far Eastern countries 1.6%. ARAMCO, *Facts and Figures* (Dammam: Al-Mutawa Press), 1980, pp. 24–27; 1981, pp. 24–26.

12. CIA GI IESR 81-011 (U), 24 November 1981, p. 3; CIA GI EEI 82-004 (U), 19 February 1982; CIA GI IESR 82-009 (U), 28 September 1982; CIA DI IESR 83-005 (U), 31 May 1983; CIA DI EEI 83-013 (U), 24 June 1983; *Wall Street Journal,* 4 November 1982.

13. The oil-production data are taken from CIA DI EEI 83-013, 24 June 1982, p. 8; CIA DI IESR 83-005 (U), 31 May 1983, p. 1. Estimates of quads are extrapolated from the data in EIA, *1982 Annual Energy Review,* pp. 2–20.

14. CIA GI ISER 82-009 (U), 28 September 1982; CIA DI IESR 83-003 (U), 31 May 1983.

15. Based primarily on CIA GI IESR-81-011 (U), 24 November 1981, pp. 5–7; CIA IESR 82-009 (U), 28 September 1982, pp. 6–9; CIA DI IESR 83-005 (U), 31 May 1983.

16. The U.S. strategic petroleum reserve held 312 MMB on 31 March 1983. Japanese strategic stockpiles were 78.7 MMB in early 1983. Total crude oil and product inventories in the first quarter of 1983 were 1.4 billion barrels for the U.S., 0.205 billion for France, 0.276 billion for Germany, 0.45 for Japan, and 0.131 for the UK. World inventory levels had risen from 4.3 billion barrels in 1976 to 5.1 billion in 1981 and remained over 5 billion in 1983. See U.S. Department of Energy, *Strategic Petroleum Reserve—Annual Report,* DOE/EP-0045/1 (Washington, D.C., 16 February 1983); CIA DI IESR 83-005 (U), 31 May 1983.

17. These statistics are taken from DOE and CIA weekly and biweekly bulletins and DOE monthly statistical summaries. The reader should be aware that these estimates often differ in detail from IEA, OECD, and oil company forecasts.

18. Unlike the industrialized states, the developing importing states also did not benefit from the recession in terms of lower costs. Their oil imports increased in 1982 even though their exports to the developing countries declined, and their current account deficit rose by about $16 billion, of which $4 billion was additional payments to meet international debts. Argentina, Mexico, Brazil, and Chile are typical of countries whose debt service payments exceeded the value of their total exports, and international lending to the non-oil-exporting developing states fell by 50% in spite of their increased need for borrowing. Their average growth rate has declined by nearly 50% since the shah's fall.

19. See EIA, *1982 Annual Energy Outlook,* for the latest projections to 1990. These projections make a grim contrast to the National Energy Plans issued under the Ford and Carter administrations, and it is interesting to note that the 1982 projections of Data Resources Incorporated (DRI) and Electric Power Research Institute (EPRI) for the year 2000 shown on pp. 99–105 of the EIA report are far more pessimistic than the DOE and EIA projections made in 1981. (EIA omitted projections for 2000 in its 1982 report for political reasons.) DRI, for example, projects 0.7 quads of synfuel production in 2000 versus 4.0 quads in DOE's 1981 *National Energy Plan* and 4.1 in the EIA's *1981 Annual Report.* It projects 6 quads less use of coal, and over 3 quads less nuclear power. The EPRI projections for nuclear power are even worse. They project that it will increase from only 2.7 quads in 1980 to 3.9 quads in 2000—5–6 quads less than the DOE and EIA projections. This mix of projections is more than 25 quads short of the Ford administration's projections of new domestic energy sources and 20 quads lower than the initial Carter administration projections. To put these figures in perspective, the total national domestic energy supply in 2000 is projected to be 81–100 quads.

20. For some of the trends involved see John R. Brodman and Richard E. Hamilton, *A Comparison of Energy Projections to 1985,* IEA monograph (Paris: OECD, January 1979); "Oil: The Once and Future Thing," *Economist,* 16 October 1982, pp. 91–92; and CIA IESR and EEI reports through July 1983.

21. Estimates of such figures vary in detail, but not significantly. The data used here come from the EIA, *1982 Annual Energy Outlook,* pp. ix, 3–26.

22. See ibid., pp. 7, 22–24.

23. Such projections could not anticipate the course of the recession in 1983, and they tend to exaggerate world demand. However, they are also far more optimistic about the U.S. need for oil imports than the Data Resources Incorporated and Electric Power Research Institute projections cited in note 20.

24. It is important to note that no major oil-importing developing nation could finance its oil imports without major international borrowing after 1979

and that International Monetary Fund and World Bank working data raise serious doubts about whether any developing importer can fund currently projected imports through 1985, much less 1990. The demand projections referred to here are taken from the EIA, *1982 Annual Energy Outlook,* pp. 3–24. Price estimates are based on the projections to 2000 shown on p. 11. The reader should also, however, carefully review pp. 95–223 for detailed assumptions, statistics, and alternative projections.

25. CIA ER-IESR 81-005 (U), 26 May 1981; CIA GI EEI 82-019 (U), 17 September 1982; CIA IESR 82-009, 28 September 1982; CIA DI IESR 83-005 (U), 31 May 1983.

26. These estimates are based on discussions with Japanese, British, and French experts familiar with current conditions in Iran and Iraq. Iran seems particularly vulnerable to long-term cuts in production capacity. It has failed to conduct proper facility maintenance for at least three years. Some critical oil field components began irremediable decay after no more than six months of improper maintenance, and many such items are special equipment with 1–2-year order lead times.

27. Working estimates based on de facto control of oil flows by company planners, country-to-country agreements affecting operator or company allocation, etc.

28. Half of this is committed in joint ventures to foreign partners. Reuters, 1 May 1983. A detailed table of all major Saudi oil refinery and petrochemical projects under way in 1983 is provided in Section V of "Survey: Saudi Arabia," *Financial Times,* 23 April 1983. An analysis by Louis Turner of the Royal Institute of International Affairs in London also indicates that Saudi Arabia will produce only 4.5 million tons annually of petrochemicals when all currently scheduled plants are complete. This will account for only 4% of world capacity. *New York Times,* 23 May 1983.

29. Sources vary. Exxon indicates that Saudi refining capacity reached 700,000 BPD in late 1980. Saudi plans called for 1.1 MMBD in domestic refining capacity and 1.8–2.3 MMBD in export-oriented capacity by 1985–1986. Pre-1983-1984 budget cut contracts existed for at least 835,000 BPD of new capacity. All these figures, however, include some gas facilities, and all predate the 1982 drop in oil revenues. For background see Quandt, *Saudi Arabia's Oil Policy,* pp. 27–28; Edmund O'Sullivan, "Saudi Budget Shifts from Infrastructure to Human Resources," *Middle East Economic Digest* (MEED), 30 April–6 May 1982; and "Survey: Saudi Arabia."

30. The "downstream" problem is extremely complex. The data now available on exporting-nation plans to convert crude production to domestically produced product indicate that it could be severe by the 1990s, particularly since no coordination existed within the exporting world to ensure that the overall increases in capacity now planned will respond to future market demand. Virtually all OPEC states miscalculated the near-term value of oil and gas products in the middle to late 1970s and overinvested in refineries, petrochemical plants, and industrial plants designed to use low-cost fuel. Few of these plants will be profitable under currently projected trends in world oil and gas prices, and they could exacerbate pressures to raise prices, sell on a cartel basis, or reduce total crude production within OPEC. Many of these plants are now being canceled, however, or are being rescaled to cut the required production level. There is no way to predict the seriousness of the "downstream" problem in such an environment. Saudi Arabia has already canceled plans to build a $1.5 billion petrochemical plant and is considering cancellation of up to $4.5

billion worth of refineries it once planned to build as part of the 1986–1990 development plan. ARAMCO had planned to increase its staff of 61,000 (33,000 Saudis) to about 80,000 by 1987, but it actually cut its staff by 1,000–2,000 in 1983. Although most of those cut were American, this is a major change; staffing rose by an annual average of 14% during 1977–1982. Saudi Arabia did announce plans to replace ARAMCO's U.S. president with a Saudi when the current president retires in 1984. It also announced, however, that it would continue to rely heavily on U.S. personnel well into the 1990s. Reuters, 1 May 1983; *Financial Times,* 25 April 1983; *Economist,* 8 January, 19 February, and 23 April 1983; *MEED,* 15 April 1983, pp. 52–54; *Wall Street Journal,* 30 December 1982; 19 May 1983.

31. It should be noted that this increase will be far less rapid than was indicated in most projections of depletion of world reserves made between 1973 and 1979. Many such projections, including those of the Department of Energy in 1980, indicated a massive shortfall in world oil supplies as early as 1985 or 1990. Current estimates indicate that depletion rates will be far slower and will not produce a major cut in export capability until some point well into the 1990s. It is, however, impossible to estimate the marginal cost of oil supplies much beyond 1990. The problem may be the cost of obtaining marginal oil rather than absolute depletion of reserves.

32. Any figures on Saudi or other OPEC state holdings are highly uncertain. This discussion of Saudi reserves draws heavily on work by Graham M. Benton and George H. Wittman in *Saudi Arabia and OPEC: An Operational Analysis,* Information Series No. 138 (Fairfax, Va.: National Institute for Public Policy, March 1983). Material is also drawn from various editions of the U.S. *Treasury Bulletin* and OPEC investment information background sheets furnished to the press by the Department of Commerce. Other sources include various issues of the *Financial Times,* particularly 4 October 1982 and 15 March and 25 April 1983; unpublished work by Dr. Odeh Aburdene of Occidental Oil; and Paul Barker, *Saudi Arabia: The Development Dilemma* (London: Economist Intelligence Unit, 1982).

33. See the *Economist,* special on EEC and OECD trade, 6 November 1981, pp. 56–58; ibid., 16 October 1982, p. 91; and the IEA and OECD energy forecasts issued for the fall 1982 meeting of the IEA.

34. While figures differ, Benton and Wittman give the following figures in various parts of *Saudi Arabia and OPEC:*

Total Cash Flow and Investment Income in Saudi Arabia (in billions of current dollars)

Year	Total Revenues	Total Spending	Foreign Assets	International Reserves	Investment Income
1975–76	31	25	–	–	–
1976–1977	41	39	–	–	–
1977–1978	39	42	–	–	–
1978–1979	39	45	–	–	–
1979	–	–	78	19.3	7.8
1979–1980	64	57	–	–	–
1980	–	–	125	23.4	12.5
1980–1981	105	71	–	–	–
1981	–	–	175	32.2	17.5
1981–1982	102	90	–	–	–
1982	–	–	175	31.4	17.5

35. Benton and Wittman, *Saudi Arabia and OPEC,* pp. 9–11; MEED, 15 April 1983, pp. 52–54.

36. *Washington Post,* 27 and 29 March and 2 June 1983; *Economist,* 23 April 1983; *MEED,* 15 April 1983; *New York Times,* 2 May 1983; *Financial Times,* 25 April 1983; *Wall Street Journal,* 23 March and 21 June 1983.

37. The Saudis have, however, tended to exaggerate the ease of making production cuts. For example, the Saudi minister of planning stated on 12 January 1983 that Saudi Arabia could easily adjust to a cash squeeze because its plans could be funded at production levels of 5.1 MMBD. This was propaganda and was based on budget and plan data that ignored Saudi Arabia's defense expenditures and high levels of aid to Iraq. In fact, Saudi Arabia had already been putting extreme pressure on the oil companies in ARAMCO to increase their liftings and imports to reduce Saudi Arabia's budget problems only a week before the minister spoke. *Wall Street Journal,* 4, 5, and 13 January 1983; *New York Times,* 5 January 1983.

38. The 2 March 1983 edition of the U.S. *Treasury Bulletin* showed that the total official investment position of the Gulf states (there are adjustment problems in the totals for Bahrain and Oman) in the U.S. increased from $69.5 billion to $77.9 billion between December 1981 and December 1982. These totals, however, exclude private investment equal to at least 25–50% of the totals tracked by the Treasury and do not yet reflect the major impact of the global recession on the Gulf. The flow of such investment capital to the U.S. was $6 billion in 1974, $9 billion in 1975, $11.5 billion in 1976, $7.7 billion in 1977, −$1.4 billion in 1978, $6 billion in 1979, $12 billion in 1980, $18 billion in 1981, and $8 billion in 1982. This trend disguises massive Iranian disinvestment in the U.S. following the shah's fall and the fact that Gulf holdings now belong largely to Saudi Arabia, Kuwait, Qatar, and the UAE. Occidental working data indicate that total Saudi investment in the West remained at well above $150 billion in mid-1983, that Kuwait had investment holdings of $65 billion and annual income of $6–6.5 billion, that the UAE had holdings of $30 billion, and that Qatar had holdings of $12 billion. Average Gulf return on investment now seems to be about 12–15%.

39. For typical reporting see the *Economist,* 11 and 25 June 1983; and *Wall Street Journal,* 29 June 1983. Odeh Aburdene provides a good analysis of the issues involved in "Falling Oil Prices and the World Economy," *American-Arab Affairs,* no. 4, (Spring 1983):46–53.

40. CIA DI IESR 83-005 (U), 31 May 1983; *Chicago Tribune,* 18 June 1983; *New York Times,* 5 February and 23 May 1983; *Los Angeles Times,* 4 April 1983; *Economist,* 5 February 1983; Reuters, 8 June 1983; *U.S. News and World Report,* 6 June 1983.

41. *Wall Street Journal,* 4 and 24 November and 7, 14 and 21 December 1982; 4 and 17 January 1983; *Washington Post,* 15 November and 21 December 1982; 17 January 1983; *Economist,* 11 December 1982, p. 99; *Chicago Tribune,* 21 December 1982.

42. *Wall Street Journal,* 4 and 17 January 1983; *Washington Post,* 17 January 1983.

43. *New York Times, Washington Post,* and *Wall Street Journal,* 23, 24, and 25 January 1983; *Economist,* 29 January 1982, pp. 57–60; 8 January 1983, p. 57.

44. For typical reporting see Reuters, 16 April 1983; *Wall Street Journal,* 22 and 28 February and 27 June 1983; *Washington Post,* 12, 13, 14, 15, and 16 March and 29 May 1983; *Christian Science Monitor,* 16 March 1983; *New York Times,* 22, 23 and 24 February and 12, 14, and 15 May 1983.

The shift in the quota system is summarized below (in MMBD):

	Old Quota March 1982[a]	Actual Production November 1982[a]	New Quota March 1983[a]
Saudi Arabia	7.15	5.8	5.0[a]
Iran	1.2	2.5	2.4
Venezuela	1.5	2.2	1.675
Nigeria	1.3	1.4	1.3
Iraq	1.2	0.9	1.2
Libya	0.75	1.7	1.1
UAE	1.0	1.2	1.1
Kuwait	0.8	0.9	1.05
Algeria	0.65	0.7	0.725
Qatar	0.3	0.4	0.3
Ecuador	0.2	0.15	0.2
Gabon	0.15	0.2	0.15
Total	17.5	19.4	17.5

[a]Saudi figure is a goal to be altered according to demand conditions, not a quota. Figures for for individual countries do not add to totals, but they do reflect available reporting.

Bahrain and Oman are not OPEC states and are not included in the quota system.

45. For typical reporting see Associated Press, 10 June 1983; Reuters, 9 June 1983; *New York Times,* 12 April and 9 June 1983; *Wall Street Journal,* 5 May 1983.

46. While it is possible to make only a rough estimate of the resulting loss in oil income in mid-1983, projections made in *U.S. News and World Report* on 6 June 1983 give a rough indication of the trend:

	Peak Income ($B)	1983 Income ($B)	Decline from Peak (%)
Saudi Arabia	115.5 (1981)	44.4	62
Iraq	26.0 (1980)	12.2	53
Iran	21.2 (1977)	21.2	0
UAE	18.0 (1980)	11.8	39
Kuwait	18.0 (1980)	10.0	44
Qatar	5.4 (1980)	3.2	41

For typical reporting see United Press International, 6 July 1983; and Reuters, 8 July 1983.

47. For an excellent summary of the trends involved see Jan Vanous and Daniel L. Bond, "Oil Prices Are Socking It to the Soviet Bloc," *Business Week,* 30 May 1983, pp. 101–103.

48. Saudi Arabia sometimes calls for an Arab "jihad" in opposing particular Israeli policies or actions. The term "jihad" literally means to struggle or endeavor in a holy cause. It does not mean "holy war." Saudi foreign policy and domestic political rhetoric has consistently used "jihad" in this manner in reference to differences with a number of states since the mid-1930s.

49. See "Saudi Arabia and the United States," Subcommittee on Europe and the Middle East, House Committee on Foreign Affairs, August 1981, p. 8; *Department of State Bulletin* 76, 27 June 1977, p. 637; *Christian Science Monitor,* 25 May 1977.

50. See *New York Times,* 12 August 1981; and *Baltimore Sun,* 10 August 1981.

51. For almost a decade, South Yemen and Libya have attempted to use the annual movement of pilgrims through Saudi Arabia as a method of intelligence gathering and subversion. Iraq supported parallel efforts of this kind until about 1975, and Kuwait has evidently allowed some minor radical parties to try to operate similar political efforts. Iran began similar practices during the 1980 pilgrimage and made significant efforts during the 1981 and 1982 pilgrimages to discredit Saudi handling of the pilgrimage with Shi'ite visitors. In 1982 roughly 100 Iranian Shi'ites under the Hojatolislam Mousaui Khoiniha had to be expelled. As a rough estimate, up to 300,000 members of Saudi Arabia's foreign-born work force have entered Saudi Arabia legally or illegally as pilgrims. Saudi Arabia's Minister of Planning Hisham Nazer has described the problem of controlling the pilgrims as the most serious internal security problem in dealing with foreign workers. The general security problems involved were illustrated in late 1979 by the uprising at the Mosque of the Prophet in Makkah (see Chapter 9).

52. "Overt" aid is defined in this case as the aid listed in Saudi reports to various international lending institutions. Other aid, or "covert" aid, is defined as aid that may be openly reported in various news sources but that is not reported to various international institutions and usually is politically sensitive or secret. The distinction is important because Saudi "covert" aid may have approached the "overt" aid in size.

53. These estimates are based on data provided by the Office of the Alternate Executive Director of the IMF, 6 July 1983. The data on OECD and U.S. aid are taken from the *Economist,* 11 June 1983, p. 74.

54. *Christian Science Monitor,* 26 April 1983.

55. *Wall Street Journal,* 29 June 1983.

56. The agreement was for five years and was renewed until 13 February 1985 in November 1979. The commission's objectives are to "help Saudi Arabia achieve its development goals by providing technical expertise in key areas; strengthen economic and political ties between the two nations; and encourage better understanding between the United States and Saudi peoples." For details see Saudi Arabian–United States Joint Commission on Economic Cooperation, *Annual Report 1982,* available from the U.S. Treasury, Washington, D.C., or Ministry of Finance and National Economy, Riyadh.

57. Benton and Wittman raise another issue in *Saudi Arabia and OPEC.* They analyze Saudi budget flows and conclude that Saudi Arabia must maintain very large production to make up for the fact that it actually obligates far more money than it budgets. This may well be an important factor shaping Saudi behavior under the current regime, but it has much less importance as the result of Saudi budget cuts in the 1983-1984 budget and current development plan, and it is still dependent on Saudi Arabia's pursuing its existing political and economic goals.

2
The Strategic Emergence of the Gulf

Vital as a strategic partnership among the West, Saudi Arabia, and the other conservative Gulf states may be, there is little point in harboring illusions about the ease of forging such a partnership. The conservative Gulf states combine strategic importance and vulnerability in an area that is comparatively near the USSR, but at the furthest global limit from U.S. military power. They are among the most tempting strategic targets in the world, with the possible exception of those African nations that provide the West with its supplies of strategic minerals, and the conservative Gulf states need Western military assistance as much as the West needs Gulf oil. Vulnerability alone, however, may not be sufficient motive to drive the Gulf states toward collective security or a partnership with the West.

U.S. ties to Israel divide Saudi Arabia and the Gulf states from the United States, the only nation that can underpin a Western military commitment to the Gulf. The history of Arab nationalism leads most Gulf states to fear any Western presence in the region, and where nationalism and radicalism are not a problem, a growing local resentment of "secularism" and "modernism" makes other groups hostile to further involvement with the West. The Soviet Union may be the closer threat on a map, and its long history of destroying cultures in its efforts to "liberate" them poses a grimmer threat to Gulf society than Western mores. It is the West, however, that now intrudes in the Gulf nations, and whose businessmen, military personnel, and societal customs seem more threatening on a day-to-day basis.[1]

Equally important, the United States is ill equipped to deal with the Gulf nations. Quite aside from its ties to Israel, the U.S. has a broad political and cultural ignorance of the Arab states. It has trained only a limited number of experts, and while few Americans have become xenophobic about the emergence of Arab oil power, many still regard the Gulf as an temporary sideshow in world affairs. The U.S. has long been oriented toward the threat of direct conflict with the Soviet Union in Europe or Asia. Its forces and military policy are not designed to

MAP 2—1
THE GULF

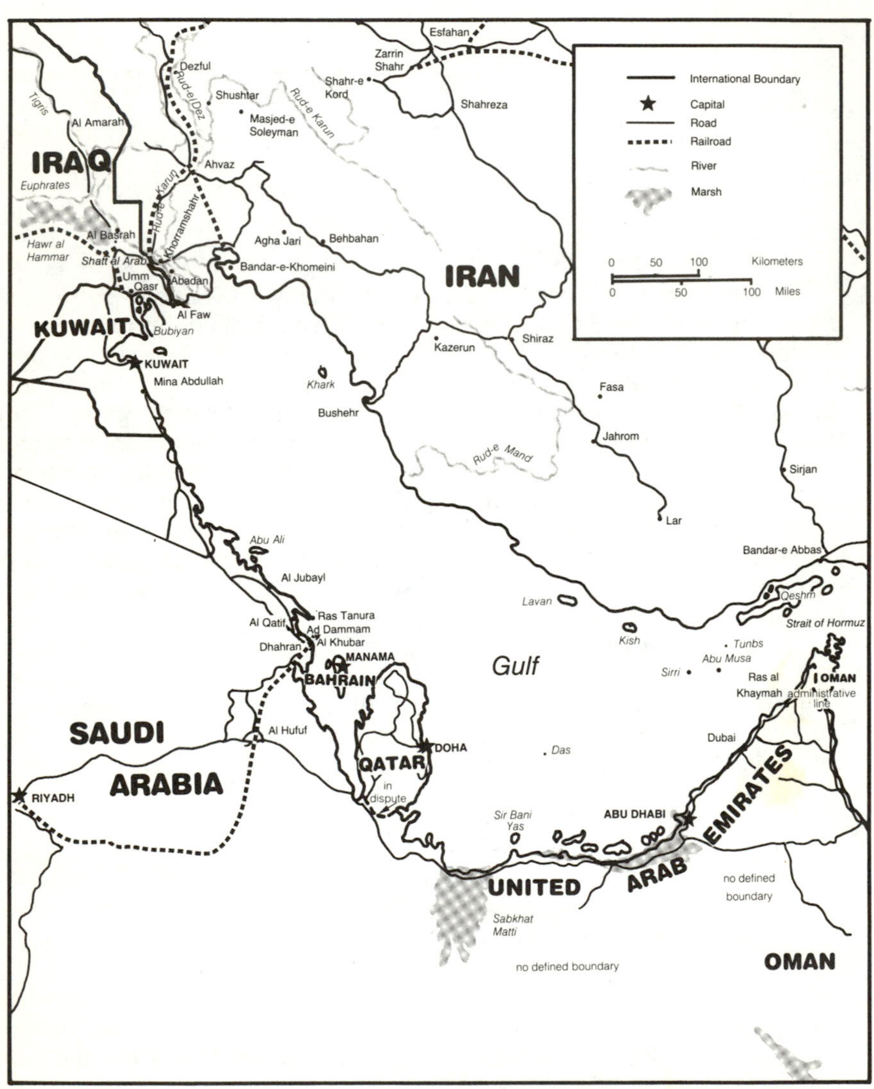

Adapted from CIA 504822 (546740) 7-81

deal with the complex regional and internal security threats in the Gulf or large-scale combat half a world away from current U.S. deployments.

It also is difficult for the U.S. to forge a domestic political consensus around military involvement in the Gulf or to make such a role convincing to its potential allies. Despite President Carter's declaration that the U.S. would defend its interests in the region, and President Reagan's even stronger promise to protect Saudi Arabia, U.S. military deployment capabilities remain uncertain and U.S. ability to act as a reliable source of arms and military assistance is questionable. The U.S. still lacks credibility in the eyes of the Arab states, Europe, and Japan, and there is a broad feeling that it has little current understanding of, or sympathy for, the complexities of Gulf and Arab nationalism.

At the same time, the history of the Gulf states divides each nation from the others and limits their capacity for collective action. These historical divisions are reinforced by the pressures of rapid change. The massive volume of arms transferred to the Gulf over the last decade symbolizes the transformation of the Gulf states from a relatively quiet colonial backwater into an area of continuing strategic crisis. This military buildup is, however, only one of the structural shifts that now threaten Gulf strategic stability. The massive political, economic, and cultural changes in the Gulf inevitably interact with this military buildup and with the changing competition between the superpowers.

The events of the last decade have also transformed a relatively low-level U.S. and Soviet struggle for influence in the Gulf area into an intense and potentially decisive one.[2] The risk of direct military confrontation between the superpowers has grown steadily, and the Gulf is so vital to the West that it is one of the few areas whose potential loss could trigger a third world war. This makes the military buildup of the Gulf states, and the various internal security threats to each Gulf nation, critical to all the powers concerned. On the one hand, they have raised increasing doubts about the ability of the Gulf states to absorb the arms transfers into the area, as well as to remain independent and secure without such arms transfers. On the other hand, they have linked these internal military and political developments in the Gulf closer and closer to the military interests and power projection capabilities of the U.S. and the USSR.

While the interaction between military developments in the Gulf and the region's changing military capabilities, and the military forces and arms sales of the superpowers are only one aspect of the strategic stability of the Gulf, they are a key aspect indeed. The other pressures transforming the Gulf—cultural change, economic development, a population explosion, labor migration, urbanization, the rebirth of Islam, and the creation of new political groups and social and economic classes—can dominate its future only if they are given the time and freedom to do so.

The Transition to Continuing Crisis

There is nothing new about military crises in the Gulf. The states in the region have been at war with one another for the last thousand years, and few Gulf states have had the opportunity to change rulers peacefully or without some form of military intervention.[3] Even the present confrontation between the superpowers has many historical precedents. The West has been strategically involved in the Gulf area for nearly four centuries, and for most of that time the West has been in a position of confrontation with Russia. The expansionary thrusts that gave Russia control over most of Central Asia were the cause of Britain's two Afghan wars, in 1838 and 1878, and led to the continuing struggle between Russia and Britain in Southwest Asia that came to be known as the "Great Game." While this struggle abated after the Anglo-Russian accord of 1880, it did not halt an Anglo-Russian contest for economic and political influence that started to involve oil the moment Britain made its first discovery in Iran in 1908.

The U.S. first came into formal diplomatic conflict with Russia shortly after the discovery of oil. It was Russia that successfully forced W. Morgan Shuster, President Taft's hand-picked financial adviser to Iran's first constitutional government, to leave the country. The struggle between the U.S. and USSR continued throughout the 1920s and 1930s, although Britain bore the brunt of the conflict with the new Soviet government until 1941. From 1942 onward, the Office of Strategic Services (OSS) and CIA engaged Soviet intelligence in a covert struggle for influence in the northern Gulf states. The U.S. created the Persian Gulf Command in 1943 to deal with the growing problems in Iran and the various threats to the area, which came to include the Soviet interest in the Gulf's oil long before the beginning of the Cold War. By the fall of 1944, tensions had reached the point where the USSR charged that the U.S. had persuaded Iran not to grant the Soviet Union the oil concessions it desired in the northern half of the country. This was a major reason why the USSR sponsored the Kurdish and Azerbaijani republics in Iran and massively boosted its aid to the communist and radical parties throughout the region.[4]

The U.S. became an equal partner with Britain in the West's effort to limit Soviet influence following the Tehran Conference, and the conflict between the U.S. and the USSR came to affect the postwar destiny of every Gulf state, particularly Iraq, Iran, Oman, and the Yemens. It meant overt or covert superpower participation in every internal and external crisis and helped drive the military buildup in most Gulf nations. No Gulf state was able to remain uninvolved in this competition between the superpowers, and the superpowers have only rarely been able to stand aside from the struggles within the Gulf. At the same time, the conflicts in the Gulf broadened to encompass nearby nations, such as Turkey, Libya, Afghanistan, Pakistan, Israel,

Egypt, Syria, Ethiopia, and Somalia, and eventually all the world's major industrialized powers.

The announcement of British withdrawal from the Gulf in the late 1960s gave a further impetus to this process. The withdrawal deprived the Gulf of a major stabilizing force, helped trigger an even broader regional struggle for power, and accelerated the regional competition between the U.S. and the USSR. The shah's fall in 1979 then removed the major regional military "pillar" that U.S. policy depended upon for stability, and the resulting power vacuum has forced both the U.S. and the USSR to greatly increase their power projection capabilities in the region.

British withdrawal from the Gulf and the shah's fall, however, are only the most conspicuous causes of the growing instability in the region. At least eleven major catalysts have helped accelerate regional conflicts and tensions. These catalysts have taken nearly two decades to become effective; they may take far longer to bring fully under control.

The Impact of the Arab-Israeli War of 1967

The initial catalyst was the Arab-Israeli War of 1967. Although Iran and Iraq had been involved in a low-level arms race since July 1958,[5] and each of the Gulf states had sought to modernize its military forces throughout the postwar period, it was Israel's massive defeat of the Arabs in June 1967 that triggered the present process of military modernization and expansion. The sheer scale of the Arab defeat, which peripherally involved several of the Gulf nations, left a legacy that no Arab nationalist or state could ignore. It virtually ensured an effort by every Arab state—including Saudi Arabia and Iraq—to build up its military forces and to try to compensate for the 1967 debacle.

This situation opened up further opportunities for the USSR to capitalize on Arab tensions with the West and to expand the influence it obtained through arms sales to the Arab states. At the same time, it gave a new impetus to Arab nationalism and to the struggle for control of Gulf oil assets. Egypt, Jordan, and Syria all lost territory, and Saudi Arabia lost two small islands it had leased to Egypt. The war created a whole new group of refugees and put the Arab population in the occupied territories under Israeli control. This created political issues that thrust the educated elites of the Arab world into a new level of conflict with Israel. The Palestinian Arabs—from whom the Gulf states obtained many of their managers, teachers, and military advisers—emerged as a far stronger and militant political force. This, in turn, precipitated civil war in Jordan and helped trigger Lebanon's civil war and collapse. This collapse began after the Israeli raids on the Palestinian bases in Lebanon, which began in January 1969, and it meant that the Gulf Arabs watched the spectacle of the destruction of an Arab state they knew intimately and where many had been educated. Most came to blame the wreckage of Lebanon on Israel and the United States, and the USSR took every opportunity to reinforce this belief.

The Impact of British Withdrawal from East of Suez

A second and more serious catalyst came from Britain's 17 January 1968 announcement that it intended to withdraw all its forces from "east of Suez" and to end its military and political presence in the Gulf. This announcement meant that the Gulf would lose the power that had dominated the region since the 1850s and that states that had never really had to rule themselves would suddenly become independent. It transformed the military rivalry among the major Gulf states from a relatively low-level contest to a Gulf-wide struggle for military and political dominance.[6]

Britain had laid the groundwork for a continuing crisis in southeast Arabia much earlier. Although it had withdrawn from a comparatively stable Kuwait earlier, in June 1961, its withdrawal from Aden and the Protectorates was a disaster. The British decision to withdraw from Aden was announced by the secretary of state for the colonies in May 1956. Given the impetus of the Suez fiasco, this announcement rapidly embroiled Aden and the surrounding Protectorates in an internal struggle for power and in Nasser's struggle for control over the Yemens. By October 1963, British efforts to create a stable local regime had foundered in a civil war that Britain could not control without returning Aden and the Protectorates to martial law. As a result, Britain announced in 1964 that it would grant the area independence by 1968. Although Britain made some attempts to create a viable South Yemen in the following three years, it had abandoned the area to the radical extremists in the National Liberation Front by November 1967. In the process Britain ignored the cries of both its former local allies in southwest Arabia and the objections of many Gulf rulers. It set a precedent for Western abandonment that still makes these Gulf governments leery of any Western security guarantees.

It is scarely surprising, therefore, that the British announcement that it would withdraw from all its remaining commitments in the Gulf precipitated a regionwide crisis. The announcement also left little time for the Gulf states to adjust to independence; the rulers of the Gulf received their first formal notification in January 1968. Iran reacted with an effort to seize control of several strategic islands in the Gulf near the Strait of Hormuz. Iraq and Kuwait became involved in territorial disputes as Iraq sought added security for its access to the Gulf. It was a first step in triggering the modern tension between Shi'ite and Sunni when Iran attempted to exploit its status as a Shi'ite state to win influence over Bahrain; it also helped to set free the twin forces of conservative Islam and radical nationalism through the southern Gulf area.

When British withdrawal finally came at the end of 1971, it left the smaller southern Gulf states deeply divided.[7] Although the former trucial emirates were linked together in the loose federation that became the United Arab Emirates, several members of the federation were involved in a serious internal power struggle, and Kuwait and Qatar refused an invitation to join. The smaller Gulf states remained the target of internal subversion and of external political pressure from Iran, Iraq, Saudi Arabia, the U.S., and the Soviet Union. The withdrawal also laid the groundwork for eventual Soviet control over South Yemen and deprived the West of most of its military bases in the area. The U.S. and UK retained inadequate contingency facilities in Bahrain and Oman, but their only sovereign base in Southwest Asia became the small atoll of Diego Garcia in the Chagos Archipelago. Diego Garcia had only token air and naval facilities and was some 1,000 miles from the tip of India, 2,200 miles from the Strait of Hormuz, and roughly the same distance from the western end of the Gulf as Dublin.

The "Two Pillars"

A third catalyst was the application to the Gulf of the "Nixon Doctrine." The failure of Britain and the U.S. to reach a viable accord over how to maintain Western military power in the Gulf led the Nixon administration to attempt to make Iran and Saudi Arabia the "two pillars" of U.S. security in the Gulf. However, Iran was seen as the only local military power that could hope to halt Soviet expansion in the northern Gulf and secure Western interests throughout the region without a Western military presence. Saudi Arabia was viewed as potentially capable of stabilizing the conservative states in the Arabian Peninsula, but was seen largely as a friendly source of oil.

As a result the Nixon administration reversed the past U.S. policy of limiting arms transfers to the region and gave the shah virtual carte blanche to buy U.S. weapons and expand his military forces. This decision was formalized in a meeting between President Nixon and the shah at Tehran airport in May 1971. The Nixon Doctrine did not, however, stabilize or unite the area.[8] As is described in more detail in the following chapters, Nixon's "blank check" to the shah fueled the latter's imperial ambitions and helped ensure the eventual collapse of his regime. Reports of the arrangement helped drive Iraq to sign a 15-year friendship treaty with the USSR on 9 April 1972. As the details became public, it also led Saudi Arabia to accelerate its military buildup. A side agreement also gave covert CIA aid to the shah in supporting the Kurdish revolt in Iraq. This CIA support helped give the shah the power necessary to force Iraq to concede the east side of the Shat al-Arab to Iran on 5 March 1975. It was Iraq's future president, Saddam Hussein, who was forced to settle Iraq's political differences with Iran on Iranian terms; this helped plant the seeds of the current Iran-Iraq conflict. It also inspired even stronger Iraqi efforts to build up the country's military forces.[9]

The October War of 1973

The October War of 1973 was a fourth catalyst; it reinforced the 1967 war's impact on the Gulf. It again expanded Arab nationalism and Palestinian consciousness throughout the Gulf, and it strengthened the links between the revolutionary elements in the Gulf and those in the other Arab states. It put pressure on each Gulf state to build up its military forces. It forced the conservative Gulf states to distance themselves from the U.S. and tended to separate the Arab Gulf states from Iran, which had tacitly supported Israel with oil and showed little interest in the Arab cause. It also gave the USSR new opportunities to exploit the internal tensions in the Gulf and Near East.

Most important, the war gave an incredible momentum to OPEC's efforts to raise oil prices. While Iran, Libya, and the other OPEC states would certainly have sought further price increases in any case, the October War gave the oil-exporting states the unity needed to launch an embargo. This tripled crude oil prices, provided a graphic demonstration of the West's weakness and dependence on the Gulf, and gave the Gulf states the wealth necessary to pursue the more destabilizing aspects of their military and economic competition.

The U.S. Defeat in Vietnam and Angola

The global decline of U.S. power was a fifth catalyst in the process. Two major events demonstrated to the Gulf nations the limits of U.S. power. The first was the U.S. defeat in Vietnam; the second was the failure of an ill-chosen U.S. adventure in Angola that was launched without a clear friend or enemy and with little regard for congressional willingness to sustain the effort. Of the two, it was the failure in Angola that proved more critical. The end result was defeat of the U.S.-backed faction in Angola, a massive victory of the Soviet-backed faction, and the sudden transformation of Cuba into a proxy force for projecting Soviet power. This defeat triggered new congressional constraints on U.S. military assistance that sent the Soviet Union a signal that it could operate throughout the developing word with little fear of active U.S. opposition. At the same time, the Soviet use of Cuban proxies—which originally stemmed from Soviet fear of U.S. military action—demonstrated that the Soviets had a power projection tool for which the U.S. had no clear counterpart.

The Soviet victory in Angola also allowed the USSR to exploit the growing conflict between black and white in Southern Africa and made radical political elements in states throughout the Indian Ocean area turn to the USSR for arms, aid, and political status. It helped ensure that Mozambique would grant the Soviet Navy better staging facilities to threaten the oil routes out of the Gulf and that the U.S.-Soviet struggle in the Gulf would be expanded to cover every Indian Ocean and West African state that the USSR might use as a threat to the West's oil and lines of communication or a potential military base.

The Conflict in Somalia and Ethiopia

The sixth catalyst was the crisis in the Horn of Africa. Only a year after its failure in Angola, the U.S. made another miscalculation that increased the threat to the Gulf.[10] At the urging of Saudi Arabia, the U.S. attempted to compensate for the overthrow of Haile Selassie in a Marxist coup, and the loss of Ethiopia as a friendly ally, by offering military assistance to the president of Somalia, Siad Barre. Barre then launched an attack to obtain Somali control over the Ethiopian provinces in the Ogaden, Nale, and Sidamo. Unfortunately, these U.S. overtures to Somalia backfired almost immediately when the Soviets offered a massive Soviet military aid plan and airlift to Ethiopia's new Marxist junta. By mid-1978, the Soviets had replaced the remnants of the U.S. presence in Ethiopia. The USSR built up a large Soviet, East German, and Cuban presence in Ethiopia. Combined with Soviet arms, this gave Ethiopia a military victory over Somalia and the ability to check the Eritrean rebels. Its strategic impact was to link the new Soviet initiatives in sub-Saharan Africa with the Soviet presence in South Yemen; to threaten the southern Red Sea, the Suez Canal, and Israel's access to the Indian Ocean and the Pacific; and to help force Israel's expulsion from Ethiopia.

Dhofar, South Yemen, and North Yemen

The seventh catalyst was South Yemen. As is described in Chapters 11 and 17, the series of radical governments that inherited Aden and its hinterland after the British withdrawal engaged in repeated attempts to radicalize the Gulf while reducing South Yemen's economy to a shambles. This made South Yemen increasingly dependent on Soviet arms, military training, economic aid, and technical assistance and transformed a "nationalist" Arab movement into a client state of the Soviet bloc. By late 1978, South Yemen's military forces, internal security services, and technical services were totally dependent on Soviet aid. While opinion differs over the exact extent of Soviet control over South Yemen since 1978 and Soviet ability to use it as a naval and air base, there is no doubt that Soviet control is now extensive. The Soviet-bloc presence in South Yemen steadily expanded, reaching 1,100 Soviet and East European and 1,000 Cuban military technicians by mid-1979. By 1980, the number of Soviet-bloc economic technicians had increased to 1,500; many of them were essential to the functioning of Yemen's airports, communications, seaport, and financial operations.[11]

In any case, South Yemen's support of the Dhofar rebels in Oman, its creation of large terrorist and revolutionary warfare training camps, and its invasion of North Yemen in 1979 have made it one of the most destabilizing influences in the Gulf and the Red Sea area. South Yemen's military pressure on North Yemen in 1979 forced the U.S. and Saudi Arabia into direct competition with the USSR in providing military assistance to North Yemen. This competition still threatens Saudi Arabia's principal supplier of foreign labor and is a source of continuing tension in the Gulf.[12]

The Fall of the Shah

The shah's fall from power in January 1979 gave these events a drastic new meaning. Until that time, Iran had seemed to give the United States military security in the region and made it easier for the U.S. to accept the previous intensification of the regional threats to its interests. Iran's high oil production and immediate recycling of its oil revenues also helped the West cope with the post-1974 increase in oil prices. In the months following the shah's departure, however, U.S.-Iranian relations degenerated into hostile chaos, the regular Iranian armed forces collapsed as a political force, and Iranian oil production declined precipitously. The average price of crude oil rose from $18.67 per barrel in current dollars in January 1979 ($10.64 in 1974 dollars) to $30.41 in current dollars in May 1980 (over $18.00 in 1974 dollars). Unlike in the 1973–1974 crisis, the West found itself without a military fulcrum in the Gulf area, with a new economic crisis it had little capacity to absorb, and with little immediate hope of reversing the situation. The U.S. suddenly found that it would have to be the military guarantor of the Gulf against the USSR and that its erstwhile "twin pillar" of security had become the region's greatest threat.

The Invasion of Afghanistan

In December 1979 the Iranian crisis was followed by the Soviet invasion of Afghanistan, the ninth major catalyst acting to create a continuing crisis in the region. It was the culmination of a takeover that began with a Soviet-backed Marxist coup in April 1978. The takeover was accomplished by Soviet, East German, and Cuban personnel, with the help of local forces. The Soviet invasion initially brought 80,000 Soviet troops and several hundred Soviet aircraft into the area; the number of troops has since risen to over 100,000. At the same time, the invasion led the Soviets to expand their land and air strength and their basing facilities and logistic capabilities in the North Caucasus, Transcaucasus, and Turkestan military districts. This buildup threatens Iran and Pakistan and has steadily increased Soviet capability to project power into the southern Gulf and Horn of Africa.

The Iran-Iraq War

The tenth catalyst was war between Iraq and Iran. In the fall of 1980 the aggressive efforts of Khomeini to include Iraq in his Shi'ite "revolution" and the ambitions of Saddam Hussein to make Iraq the dominant power in the region turned the long-standing tension between Iraq and Iran into an open war. Iraq launched an attack it hoped would overthrow Khomeini and end his efforts to cause Shi'ite unrest in Iraq, recover the east bank of the Shat al-Arab, which it had ceded to Iran in 1975, and possibly "liberate" Iran's oil-rich province of Khuzestan, 40% of whose population was Sunni Arab. This attack was accompanied by the covert efforts of several of the southern Gulf states to use the

Iraqi attack to reclaim the Tumb and Abu Musa islands, which the shah had seized after the British withdrawal from the Gulf.

Although the other Gulf states quickly backed away from Iraq when it became evident that Iraq would not win a quick victory and after they were threatened by Iranian air superiority, their tacit support of Iraq's attack broadened the Iran-Iraq conflict into an Arab-Iranian struggle with bitter Shi'ite versus Sunni overtones. It transformed Saudi Arabia's long-standing problems with the Shi'ites in its Eastern Province, and the conflicts over the status of Shi'ites in Bahrain and the other Gulf states with large Shi'ite populations, into a Gulf-wide religious problem. At the same time, it made Kuwait, which continued to help Iraq with supplies and transshipments, a target for Iranian threats and attacks.

The Israeli Invasion of Lebanon

The Israeli invasion of Lebanon in June 1982 became another catalyst in this process. As with the Iran-Iraq War and the Falklands conflict before it, the use of new weapons and technology during the fighting has greatly stimulated an already serious arms race. The main effect of the invasion, however, has been political. Although the Arab states stayed out of the fighting, showed considerable restraint in their dealings with the U.S. and the West, and took a generally moderate position, there is no doubt that the bloody Israeli siege of Beirut and the total of civilian dead caused considerable shock within the Gulf states. It seems likely that this might have triggered massive popular protests and forced several Gulf regimes to take reprisals against the U.S. if President Reagan had not succeeded in negotiating a cease-fire and the PLO's withdrawal and advanced his peace initiative.

Even so, the invasion has left a climate of tension and uncertainty. If the peace process eventually succeeds, it could free both the U.S. and the conservative Gulf states to develop the kind of regional deterrent that could do much to secure the Gulf against any threatening outcome of the Iran-Iraq War, the growing tensions in the Yemens, and the expanding Soviet presence in the Horn of Africa. It would also do much to stabilize the situation in Syria and to ensure the survival of a friendly regime in Jordan.

If the peace process fails or drags on too long, as now seems likely, it may act to discredit both the U.S. and the conservative Gulf regimes that have backed peace with Israel. It may force King Hussein to tilt toward the Soviet Union and force Syria into still closer dependence on the Soviets. It may lead to another major war between Israel and Syria and make Lebanon the partitioned "killing ground" for both states. It will make the entire Arab world more vulnerable to a possible Iranian victory in the Iran-Iraq War and to the rising pressures of Islamic fundamentalism and divisions between Sunni and Shi'ite. It also will act to alienate the Gulf's students, young technocrats, and military from the area's traditional regimes, even if they distance themselves from the U.S. It may also stimulate Gulf involvement in the almost inevitable next round between the Arabs and Israel.

The Problem of Strategic Stability

These catalysts have made the Gulf a strategic "jugular vein" of the industrialized democracies, as well as of much of the Third World. They have caused both superpowers to embark on a major buildup of their regional power projection capabilities and to become steadily more deeply involved in the military buildups of the various Gulf nations. They have allowed the Soviet Union to break out of its "containment" in Central Asia and to create a major presence in Afghanistan, Ethiopia, South Yemen, Syria, and several key states in Africa. At the same time, these catalysts have done more than transform the Gulf into an area of continuing military crisis. They have made it part of a broader "crescent" of crisis that sweeps from the Soviet Union in the north to the Cape of Good Hope in the south and from Morocco in the west to India in the east. They have tied Gulf security to the security of global oil movements to Japan, Europe, and the United States. To all intents and purposes, "Gulf waters" now extend from the Straits of Malacca to the South Atlantic.

No Gulf nation can afford to ignore the effects of these catalysts, any more than can any nation in the West. They mean that no conceivable combination of Gulf states can fully ensure Gulf strategic stability and that many Gulf nations are forced into tacit or overt dependence on outside security guarantees. The Gulf is ultimately just as vulnerable as the West to a Soviet thrust against Pakistan; to changes in the alignment of the nations that control access to the world's oil routes and the West's other strategic imports; to changes in Turkey and Jordan and their ability to secure the Gulf's "western flank"; to the military buildup in the southern USSR; to changes in the Horn of Africa and the Red Sea area; and to the risks inherent in another Arab-Israeli military conflict. Yet the West is equally unable to unilaterally secure the Gulf through any combination of its military forces. To achieve regional stability in spite of these catalysts, it must create strong, stable, and friendly Gulf states that can maintain their own internal security and eventually absorb most of the burden of their local defense. Western military capabilities are already strained throughout the world, and no probable set of U.S. or allied force improvements is likely to do more than keep pace with the buildup of Soviet-bloc capabilities in the Gulf area.

In short, in spite of all the problems involved, the Gulf states and industrialized democracies must find ways to structure a strategic partnership and to do so in spite of all its inevitable limits. The success of this effort will depend on whether Gulf states as diverse as Iraq and Saudi Arabia can deal successfully with Western states as diverse as

France and the United States and still preserve their independence and internal stability. It will depend on whether the West has learned enough from events in Iran and in the Arab world to provide the support the Gulf nations need without clutching them in an embrace that kills or that drives them toward the Soviet Union. At a minimum, this will require that both sides understand their relative military capabilities and the extent to which changes in Western and Gulf military capabilities can and cannot contribute to a mutual search for strategic stability. It also requires that their search for stronger strategic ties be conducted with a realistic understanding of the differing interests of the West, the Gulf nations, and the USSR.

Western Strategic Interests

The West's key strategic interest is obviously to secure the supply of oil imports from the Gulf region. Western dependence on Gulf oil may be a strategic cliché, but as was shown in Chapter 1, it continues to be a grim reality. At the same time, more is involved than simply providing short-term security for the West's present oil imports. The West must not only secure its present oil supplies but also secure them through at least the year 2000. In spite of all the hopes and claims after the 1973 oil crisis, the West is as far from true energy independence today as it was during the oil embargo.

As discussed in Chapter 1, virtually every new projection of the near-term increases in the West's other energy supplies reflects a new slippage in terms of past goals and objectives. Further, it has become increasingly clear that most of the recent decline in Western oil imports has been achieved only at the cost of reduced economic growth, increased inflation and unemployment, and a massive shift of real economic resources into domestic energy production. The oil glut has come at the cost of major reductions in the West's ability to combine real growth in industrial capacity with a steady rise in Western living standards.

Western strategic objectives also require that the West's oil imports be available at a reasonable cost and be provided with enough consistency to allow future economic growth and development. The problem is not simply one of maintaining a total volume of oil shipments, but also of ensuring that the West can count on the regular flow of the proper types of crude oil without having to buy on the spot market and without causing even minor panics in the world's capital and oil markets. In practice, this means that each of the Gulf oil-exporting nations must be a relatively stable source of oil. The West must seek a broad degree of stability within each major Gulf exporter.

Similarly, the problem of securing the capital flows and balances discussed in Chapter 1 is as important to the West as the problem of oil supplies. The total cost of Gulf oil to the U.S., Japan, and the leading industrial powers in Western Europe rose from $96 billion in 1978 to $185 billion in 1980, a figure that seems likely to be typical of Western expenditures during periods of high employment and economic growth.[13] The West cannot sustain expenditures on anything approaching this scale unless they are "recycled" through Gulf imports from the West. A viable balance of trade must be developed that ensures that the Gulf states do not simply accumulate capital in a form that stifles Western economic development or threatens the structure of the international monetary system.

Thus the West has a vital strategic interest in establishing stable economic relations with the Gulf states. It is not enough for the West to recycle dollars by massive arms sales or transfers of largely useless consumer goods or to market showpiece economic development projects that ultimately increase the internal security problems of the purchasing states. This approach to solving the West's oil and capital problems would be as suicidal for the industrialized democracies as for the Gulf states. It would virtually ensure the hostility of the Gulf exporters and the radicalization of precisely those Gulf states in which the West most wants to avoid such political change. It would also mean structuring Western economies to make unproductive investments in energy production, technology, and new plants.

Further, Western strategic interests go beyond finding a method of linking the West and the Gulf. The West must establish a stable pattern of three-way interdependence among the West, the Gulf oil-exporting states, and Third World oil-importing states. The oil-importing developing states had an oil-related debt of nearly $300 billion in early 1982, and most have since been forced into drastic cutbacks in development and debt rescheduling that may well continue throughout the 1980s.[14] The West cannot afford to watch the developing nations, upon which it depends for strategic materials and key export markets, collapse because of their oil problems. It cannot afford to see them become radicalized because of a continuing economic crisis. At the same time, Western ability to help such Third World oil importers has been steadily curtailed by the scale of the West's capital transfers to the oil states. Advancing Western loans and credits to such importing nations can only end in presenting both the West and the developing nations with an unpayable set of bills. This gives the West a vital strategic interest in having the Gulf oil exporters pick up much of the financial burden of helping Third World importers find a financial solution to funding their oil imports.

Finally, the West has a major strategic interest in helping friendly Gulf nations to improve their defense capabilities. There are obvious limits to such aid; it must be kept at limits that do not threaten the internal stability of the Gulf nations involved, exacerbate local tensions and conflicts, or become a conspicuous form of waste that threatens both the importing regime and popular support in the West. However, the West cannot afford to act as the day-to-day military guarantor of the individual Gulf states, and trying to meet any major threat in the region without local assistance would put an unacceptable strain on U.S. and European power projection capabilities. Further, any Western intervention in the Gulf area, except in the face of overt Soviet aggression or an attack by another Gulf state, virtually guarantees an eventual backlash against the West that will be as great as the short-term benefits of such an intervention.

In summary, the West's strategic interests force it to seek broad political, economic, and military ties to the Gulf that go far beyond simply finding solutions to the oil problem. They also force the West to look beyond solutions based on short-term expediency and the ready use of military force. The West must respond to the catalysts that have shaped the military crisis in the Gulf in a way that links the expansion of the military capabilities of the West and friendly Gulf nations to the creation of a broad economic and political partnership.

Western Strategic Vulnerabilities

The West must also be prepared to deal with a number of key vulnerabilities in its approach to the Gulf, one of the greatest of which is the West's division into sovereign nations with conflicting interests. Individual Western nations have very different degrees of dependence on oil imports, get their supplies from different Gulf nations, and must compete with each other to establish a stable pattern of petrodollar recycling. While the industrialized democracies have a common interest in a grand strategic sense, this in no way unites their interest in any specific instance.

Some competition is desirable. The pluralism and competition among the industrialized democracies in their economic relations with Gulf states have already helped to avoid any monolithic splits between the West and the Gulf and allowed the West to maintain relations with competing Gulf states. These factors minimize the risk that the West will be blamed collectively for the breakdown of individual Western relations with given Gulf states, that the entire West will be penalized for U.S. ties to Israel, and that the West's new ties with the Gulf will come to be regarded as a new form of economic or military "colonialism."

At the same time, the United States is the only Western nation that can provide significant direct military support to a Gulf state and that can protect the Gulf's economic lines of communication. This virtually ensures that the West as a whole is dependent on U.S. capabilities and willingness to act. It also ensures that the West as a whole will be at least partially identified with the action and policies of the United States and that the West's military ties with the Gulf will ultimately depend upon the success of U.S. military efforts. At the same time, the U.S. cannot prevent individual Western nations from exploiting short-term economic and military sale opportunities in the Gulf that can make effective U.S. policy and military action difficult or impossible.

The Problem of Israel

The most immediate source of division within the West, and between the West and the Gulf states, is Israel. The U.S. faces the problem that, on the one hand, it must seek to limit Israel's ambitions to permanently annex its occupied territories and Israeli military action against the Arab states and, on the other hand, it must support the defense of Israel and often take Israel's side in the political aspects of the Arab-Israeli conflict. The U.S. also must juggle its efforts to meet these competing objectives in a manner that will balance its support of Israel against its support of its Arab allies. It cannot hope to unite the Gulf around a stable political, military, and economic relationship with the West, or persuade it to react to the Soviet-bloc threat, if the U.S. is perceived as favoring Israel in a way that ends any hope of a peace settlement based on Israel's 1967 boundaries, that encourages further Israeli actions like the invasion of Lebanon, or that favors Israel's defense to the extent of denying the Arab allies of the U.S. the military assistance they need to create an effective defense.

Unfortunately, such a U.S. juggling act is virtually certain to displease both Israel and the Arab states much, if not most, of the time. Even if U.S. policy were "perfect"—and it obviously cannot be—the resulting balancing act would still lead it to take individual actions that favor one side at the expense of the other, and neither Israel nor any Arab state can be expected to freely accept such actions. The U.S. is also limited in its ability to maintain a balance by the strength of pro-Israel political action groups in the United States and by the broad ignorance about the Arab world in the Congress and much of the executive branch. As a result, U.S. policy has an almost inevitable "tilt" toward Israel, although the strengthening of U.S. ties to Egypt and Saudi Arabia and President Reagan's September 1982 peace initiative have helped restore a balance.

Even so, the U.S. will probably never be able to meet Arab expectations, or deal freely with the Gulf states, unless an Arab-Israeli peace can be reached on terms acceptable to all the parties involved, including the Palestinians. While the leaders of Egypt, Jordan, Oman, and Saudi Arabia are certainly sophisticated enough to understand the reasons for U.S. actions and the limits on U.S. ability to influence Israel, they cannot avoid continuing public confrontation with the U.S. over the Palestinian issue. Further, most Arab leaders friendly to the U.S. are deeply committed to the Palestinian cause on a personal level.[15] The U.S. and the West as a whole must thus walk a tightrope that allows the West to arm both friendly Arab states and Israel and to develop Gulf military capabilities in a way that minimizes the risk of any military confrontation between the Gulf states and Israel. This is necessary not only to protect Israel from the Gulf, but also to protect the Gulf from Israel. There is a greater risk that friendly Gulf states could be overthrown for not being sufficiently hostile to Israel than that they could ever present a serious military threat to Israel. Similarly, there is much more risk of an Israeli military overreaction against the Gulf states than of these states' playing more than a token role in any future Arab conflict with Israel.[16]

Differences over how to balance these conflicting objectives also tend to divide U.S. policy toward Israel from that of European countries and Japan. As a result, the U.S. has become Israel's only reliable military supplier and ally, while other Western states have tilted toward the Arabs. Thus U.S. flexibility in dealing with the Gulf has been weakened because the U.S. now stands virtually alone in meeting the West's moral commitment to Israel. Yet such policy divisions have not prevented European nations from supporting President Reagan's peace initiative; they have also served Western and Gulf interests. They have ensured that Europe and Japan represent a viable political alternative to the U.S. and the Soviet Union and that friendly individual Gulf states have been able to build up their military forces without becoming totally dependent on the U.S. or becoming enmeshed in U.S. domestic political debates over arms sales to Arab states.

"Revolutionary Movements"

The West must also find a method of living with the various Arab and non-Arab "revolutionary" and radical movements that affect the Gulf area. It cannot afford to rigidly divide the Gulf into conservative Western-backed states and radical states that have nowhere to go but the Soviet Union. The West must find some way of simultaneously supporting its conservative friends in the Gulf and reaching out to any Gulf regime or political movement that seeks either independence or diminished dependence on the Soviet bloc. This has been a critical problem in the past, particularly for the U.S., because of a Western unwillingness to distinguish between pro-Soviet and radical movements. The West must overcome this problem if it is to establish stable relations with Iran and Iraq, minimize their dependence on Soviet military support, and attempt to exploit any shifts in the government of South Yemen.

Global Military Stress

Finally, even if the West can create a viable strategic partnership with the Gulf nations, it will still face acute stress on its global military capabilities in the 1980s. There is little doubt that the overall military balance will continue to shift in favor of the Soviet bloc. This will leave the West little choice but to increase its military presence in the Gulf, but will increase the difficulty of defending the Gulf because of the growth of Soviet power and influence in surrounding areas. As a result, the West faces growing problems in simultaneously furnishing military guarantees to the Gulf against major Soviet aggression, providing security for the oil and cargo traffic to and from the Gulf, and blocking the expansion of Soviet power in the peripheral states near the Gulf and along the Red Sea.

Even with the help of strong local military forces, the scale of this military problem is so great that it will probably be impossible for the West to provide suitable military forces to support the Gulf states and at the same time increase its forces for other regions. The West thus will have to choose between the Gulf and its other commitments. This is particularly true of the United States, which may be able to assume the required role in the Gulf only by reducing its capabilities in Europe and Asia. This fact was formally recognized at the meeting of the NATO defense ministers in May 1982. The ministers agreed that member states had a commitment to defend the West's access to its oil supplies in the Gulf. This was not so much a pledge of collective action as a recognition of the need for a change in U.S. strategic commitments. The ministers knew that Britain planned to reduce its naval and air power projection facilities and that French power projection forces were declining. The agreement they signed was a tacit recognition that the U.S. had to draw on forces and reserves it had pledged to NATO if it was to commit significant forces to the Gulf and that this was as essential to Western defense as was the reinforcement of Europe.

The Strategic Interests and Vulnerabilities of the Gulf States

Although the strategic interests of the conservative Gulf states, and even Iraq, coincide with the West in several key areas, they differ in many others. The most important common bonds between the West and the Gulf states are long personal ties, oil, and economics. The Gulf states have almost as much need to export oil as the West has to import it. Oil revenues make up 70–95% of the GNP of the Gulf oil-exporting states. Although many Gulf states have built up substantial capital balances from their recent oil revenues, all but Saudi Arabia and Kuwait have effectively "mortgaged" their revenues through ambitious economic and military development plans, expensive social services, and the need to fund the transition to downstream petrochemical operations. The Gulf states must now export oil to survive. They have become dependent on trade with the West, on the stability of Western economies, and on the stability of the international monetary system. Their present wealth will be ephemeral if world trade ceases to be viable, and the stability of the dollar is now as important to the Gulf nations as to the U.S. Every Gulf nation has restructured its society to depend on Western goods and services, and as Iran is learning to its cost, major cuts in these imports would thrust the Gulf states backward in economic development to a point with which their societies could not cope.

Differences Between the Gulf States and the West

The Gulf states' dependence on Western markets for oil does not mean, however, that most Gulf states have an interest in producing the amounts of oil the West is likely to seek during periods of economic expansion, or in selling it at the price the West desires at any level of Western economic activity. Several Gulf states, particularly Saudi Arabia and Kuwait, cannot efficiently absorb the resulting income during periods of peak demand and have no alternative method of investing it at rates that will provide the same real return on investment as keeping the oil in the ground. Many—like Qatar and the UAE—cannot cope with the resulting rate of depletion of their oil reserves or have difficulty in coping with the shock to their societies of recycling petrodollars.

Some states—principally Iraq, Iran, and Oman—now have an urgent need to maximize revenues to support their military forces and economic buildup, even if this means a long-term loss of revenue or market share. Iraq and Iran face particularly brutal pressures because of the Iran-Iraq War, although both are now limited in what they can produce and export. All the exporting states, including Saudi Arabia, have an obvious interest in charging whatever oil price will maximize real revenues. Such prices are certain to be higher than the price that will optimize Western economic development during the West's slow transition to other energy sources.[17]

Likewise, the strategic interests of the Gulf nations do not include creating military ties to the West that are as close as some U.S. policymakers have desired. Quite aside from the problems such ties pose in terms of national sovereignty, because of the heritage of Western colonialism and interference in Gulf affairs, the Gulf nations have every reason to minimize the risk of becoming further involved in the broad sweep of U.S.-Soviet military competition—particularly given the trend toward a U.S. and Soviet buildup in the Gulf that could make the Gulf nations proxies for a U.S.-Soviet military conflict. Although the Gulf states need Western military support, and tacit U.S. guarantees that the U.S. would respond to overt Soviet aggression, they do not want the added complication of providing bases that would heighten their profile as targets for Soviet action or create more contingency risks than they resolve.

The Gulf nations also are broadly divided from the West in that they seek modernization, not Westernization. Although they have different political ideologies, the Gulf states face the common problem that their goal is not to adopt Western culture, but rather to transform and modernize their own societies at a pace their cultures can deal with. This problem affects the way in which the Gulf states build up their military forces. Gulf regimes are all too aware that past military buildups in the Third World, and military alliances with the West, have helped topple far more governments than they have protected. The Gulf states face the difficulty that their goal is not simply one of creating a viable defense or deterrent, but of doing so in a way that does not in the process destroy their political system. They naturally give political survival primacy over military effectiveness. It may be argued that the West should be equally concerned with matching the pace of Gulf military expansion to Gulf capacity for change, but historically it has failed to limit its actions accordingly.

The Problem of Survival

These differences between Western and Gulf strategic objectives are particularly important for the West to understand because the Gulf societies are far more vulnerable to the "oil problem"—and to the destabilizing impact of the strategic catalysts outlined earlier—than the West. Most Gulf states may find it difficult to survive even a successful strategic partnership with the West. Even the best such partnership will create a massive threat to their cultural identities and their right to create their own social order. The Gulf states risk losing two thousand years of cultural heritage in two generations and of ending up with a culture that is neither Western nor Middle Eastern—and probably not economically or socially viable.

The Threat to the Gulf's Cultural Identity

It should hardly be a surprise, therefore, that Gulf nations do not share the West's often patronizing attitude toward their inability or unwillingness to suddenly transform themselves into modern technical societies. Quite aside from a natural desire to control their own destinies, the Gulf states have already undergone a quarter century of massive social trauma. The combination of oil wealth and modern medical services has already more than doubled the population of every Gulf state and is leading to vast demographic shifts.

In 1970, for example, three of five Saudis lived in the desert, and one in a small town. In 1980 two of five lived in cities with populations of 100,000 or more, and the number in small towns had declined to a little over one in ten. The number living in the desert had dropped to about two in five, and most of these had become dependent on the services of an industrialized economy. The populations of the other conservative Gulf states have followed in the same path, and only Oman has taken minimally effective steps to reduce the pace of urbanization. The Gulf's oil wealth has transformed nomadic and peasant societies into new cultures oriented to a market economy, over half of whose people reside in cities or towns of over 10,000.[18]

The median age of the native population of the Gulf states is probably now less than 17, and something like two-thirds of the population of a once village-and-tribal-oriented society no longer live within 50 miles of their birthplaces. Education and modern communications have contributed to this process of cultural disintegration because they came long before the Gulf states could develop any concept of how they could be structured to preserve or productively change Gulf society. Again using Saudi Arabia as an example, in 1948 there were only 20,000 students at all levels, and 90% of the population was nomadic. In 1970 there were 590,000 students, and in 1980, 1.5 million. The number of schools tripled, from 2,047 to 6,641, during the 1970s. But these students will enter an adult population that is still 85% illiterate. The impact of these changes, and of the $53 billion annually that the Saudi government is now spending on education and youth services, is impossible to estimate.

Saudi Arabia's students will inevitably shape a very different society as they gradually come to dominate the country's economy and politics. Further, the Saudi population in service trades has risen from something like 3% in 1948, to 29% in 1970, and 46% in 1980. Only 4% of the Saudi population now works in Saudi Arabia's new basic industries, and according to Saudi figures, the Saudi share of the Saudi work force dropped from 92% in 1970 to 57% in 1980. These trends have continued into 1983, and other estimates indicate that over 1.5 million expatriate workers are active in the Saudi economy and that the number of native Saudis involved in agriculture is dropping by 10% every five years.[19]

The figures for the other conservative Gulf states follow the same pattern, but they reflect only part of the process of change. The economics of housing, food, water, and transportation have been revolutionized throughout the Gulf. Gulf legal and political processes have been destabilized by these changes, but no one now has a clear picture of what alternatives will best meet the needs of the societies involved. The average Gulf citizen has been thrust into a day-to-day dependence on Western consumer goods with even less preparation to judge the underlying meaning of such dependence than the average citizen in the West.

The Threat to Islam

The Gulf nations face a similar threat to their religion. It is tempting for Westerners to dismiss this or even to encourage it because of the Western separation of church and state and the fear of "Islamic fundamentalism." It is equally easy to dismiss the Arab and Persian cultural consciousness that goes with Islamic beliefs and to treat Gulf elites as backward and corrupt groups that must give place to Western political and cultural ideas. From a less ethnocentric viewpoint, however, it should be clear why even the "radical" Gulf states like Iraq have been deeply concerned with this process of change and with the ideological vacuum or extremism that often takes the place of traditional religious and cultural values. The problem is not simply one of the loss of religious ties or beliefs. It is the risk of creating a rootless and unstable society that can drift into borrowing the more extreme ideologies of the West or into a counterreaction in the form of an Islamic "fundamentalism" that is xenophobic in character, stifles the ability to adjust to social and technical change, and almost ensures eventual civil war. The risks to Islam of close contact with the West are infinitely smaller than such contact with a fundamentally hostile Soviet ideology, but they are still severe.

The Threats of Time and Opportunity

The threats of time and opportunity are linked to the fact that Gulf oil is a finite resource and that in general Gulf oil-production capacity is likely to diminish steadily over the next quarter century. The Gulf states are unlikely ever to have a similar opportunity to fund the transition to a level of development that liberates their people from dependence on subsistence agriculture. The West faces no similar risk. It has had nearly a century and a half to make the adjustments the Gulf must now make and has a far more secure prospect of long-term natural wealth.

The Threats of Corruption and Waste

The Gulf states are also vulnerable because of corruption, speculation, and waste. Corruption is perhaps the least serious problem of the three, although it gets the most attention in the West. It generally takes the form of minor transfers of state wealth through favoritism in contracts and land deals. While it is scarcely desirable, it often cushions the transfer of wealth to new elites, helps preserve the stability of Gulf regimes, and preserves traditional and ruling-party power structures. The term "corruption" is, in fact, much abused. The Gulf is not a Western market economy. It normally operates on the basis of favoritism, influence, and the use of economic transactions to preserve political power, reward loyalty, or buy off opposition. There is no question that a great deal of the economic decision making in the Gulf is made on such grounds and that ruling elites and their favored partners or power brokers regularly take a personal cut of the funds involved. In some cases, these practices are so blatant and divisive that they alienate the nation's rulers from the middle class, the military, and key technocrats. In many other cases, however, such activities are an accepted mechanism of Gulf politics. Unfortunately, there is no easy point at which to judge when favoritism in the use of state funds becomes corruption. The term should probably be applied only when no motive is apparent for the use of state funds other than personal profit and particularly when they are transferred out of the Gulf without any benefit to the state's citizens. This form of corruption is still serious, but it is far more limited than the use of economic power to maintain political power and internal security.

Speculation receives less attention in the West, but it is probably more dangerous to the Gulf states than corruption. Such speculation has involved the repeated collapse of the over-the-counter stock market in Bahrain, has produced billions of dollars worth of needless construction in Saudi Arabia and the UAE, has affected virtually every aspect of private and offshore banking in the Gulf, and has even affected the tourism, import, and service trades in "radical" states like Iraq. Such speculation is scarcely surprising—the same phenomenon marked the economic history of the West—but it still involves vast sums in spite of the growing efforts of Gulf states to control speculation since their first major "boom and bust" cycle in 1978.

The second collapse of the Kuwaiti parallel stock market in November 1982 involved paper losses of over $80 billion, and similar speculative activities had to be checked in Bahrain and the UAE.[20] There is no doubt that speculation, like the use of influence or corruption, produces large numbers of losers. It also tends to penalize those losers who are outside the power elite or who are traditional opponents of the regime. While Gulf rulers have increasingly realized the risks involved and have tried to both protect such losers and co-opt their opponents, both problems remain serious.

The involvement of Gulf ruling elites in corruption and speculation also presents an inevitable contradiction with the Gulf's emphasis on large-scale modern education: The Gulf's new class of technocrats and newly educated youth is far more critical of such actions than the preceding generation, and Gulf regimes will have to adapt accordingly if they are to remain in power.

It is waste, however, that is the most serious of the three problems. Unlike corruption and speculation, waste is often the product of precisely the same technocrats who criticize corruption on the part of Gulf rulers and speculation on the part of Gulf businessmen, and it is a problem common to both conservative and radical states. At a conservative estimate, more than half the major industrial and agricultural development projects that Iran built after 1965 would never have made a profit, produced a reasonable return on investment, or resulted in a productive transfer of technical and entrepreneurial skills. The shah's fall has led to the cancellation of many of the projects; but the result has been sheer waste, not restructuring them in a useful form.[21] Similarly, something like half the major construction in the southern Gulf between 1970 and 1980, or at least $30–50 billion worth of "economic development" projects, should probably have never been initiated in their current form, and much of the related infrastructure construction will never serve a meaningful economic purpose. The key danger is not simply one of mixing progress with corruption. It is rather the risk of wasting a limited national patrimony.

The Threat of Internal and Regional Division

These pressures have increased as the result of the current oil glut and the sudden dip in Gulf oil revenues. Each Gulf state is experiencing steadily growing internal tensions and divisions. The pressures of change are dividing Sunni and Shi'ite, "conservative" and "modernizer," old and emerging elites, and locally and Western educated. They are worsening every ethnic tension in the area. These tensions have been compounded by an explosive migration of foreign labor. More than half the work force in every southern Gulf state except Oman is now foreign, without citizenship and largely isolated from the society it serves. These tensions have also helped increase the divisions between the Gulf nations. The problems generated by change and sudden oil wealth have led to continual minor border crises, political conflicts, and efforts at subversion. In the case of Iran and Iraq, they have helped provoke the first really major war between Gulf states since the 1930s.

The Threat of Bureaucratization

The pressures of change have also forced each Gulf state to systematically expand the size and role of its government.[22] Primitive governmental structures have been steadily transformed into a growing bureaucratic apparatus that permeates education, economic planning, agricultural extension, town planning, import and export control, construction licensing, labor permit dispensing, and many other aspects of daily life in each Gulf state. Much of this expansion of government services has been beneficial, but it has occurred in states with little ability to manage the process efficiently, and it has been accompanied by a mix of self-interested outside advice and internal corruption that tends to separate each regime from its people. The negative effects of such bureaucratic alienation have been exacerbated by the nearly universal tendency in each Gulf state to try to maintain internal security by setting up competing and overlapping administrative centers of power and to overcentralize the information-gathering and major decision-making activities at the highest levels of government.

Most Gulf governments have also attempted to use bureaucracy to help maintain high employment for unskilled domestic workers and to absorb their newly educated youth into their economies. They have created large numbers of unnecessary jobs within their governments. Such "co-option" and disguised unemployment has helped to stabilize the Gulf states, but it has weakened the apparatus of government and increased its inefficiency and overinvolvement in Gulf life.

Bureaucratization has also tended to warp Gulf economic development because it has brought each Gulf economy increasingly under government control or influence and because most large contracts and economic transactions require government participation or approval. This spreads the impact of governmental inefficiency throughout the economy; it means many economic activities never learn to compete in the market place; and it alienates the losers in such struggles for influence from the regime. In many cases, bureaucratization has contributed to the spectacular waste and profiteering of new classes of businessmen, who develop ties to a young or changing government, and to the decline of the traditional Bazaari or merchant class, which has been a mainstay of the "popular" support for conservative regimes. Almost without exception, it has led to some degree of conflict between the new government elites and various ethnic, tribal, or clan leaders. Radical and conservative regimes alike have found themselves dealing with a growing new class of civil servants and government-oriented entrepreneurs, who inevitably come into conflict with the declining traditional elites.[23]

The Problem of Internal Security Forces

Almost unavoidably, all the Gulf states have also had to shift from a reliance on traditional checks and balances in controlling the competition for power and internal conflicts to a reliance on more modern internal security systems. The results have been most repressive in Iran, Iraq, and South Yemen and least damaging in the conservative Gulf states; but every Gulf state has been forced to sharply increase the size and power of its police, intelligence, and internal security forces.

The growth of such security forces has been particularly striking since the mid-1970s. Their scope has steadily broadened from monitoring the actions of traditional rivals to the regime, opposition political parties, and the various Gulf radical movements to a concern with the military forces, labor movements, foreign labor, and trends within the new economic and governmental elites. This growth, however, has generally been inefficient and has sometimes involved a crude borrowing of the worst of Western and Soviet security techniques. In the case of Iran, Iraq, and the Yemens, this has been combined with an equally brutal Gulf tradition of executing opponents and rivals for power. Many of the new security forces have proved corrupt and vulnerable to subversion. They may ultimately create more tension within the Gulf states than they control, and they have already become a steadily growing threat to the Gulf stability they are intended to protect.

The Threat of Militarization

The military buildup within the Gulf has introduced other internal threats to the Gulf states. Most Gulf military forces are dependent on foreign advisers and training, and this dependence has helped to politicize the Gulf military. The exposure of junior officers and noncommissioned officers to outside education, technology, politics, and living standards has transformed the traditional character of Gulf military forces. This has been particularly true since 1971, because the transfer of modern arms has meant vast increases in the number of Gulf military personnel who must receive technical training.

At the same time, the military buildup in the Gulf has led to a steady decline in the percentage of military officers, noncommissioned officers, and technicians who have traditional ties to Gulf regimes. Further, the traditional military elite has seen its status—or that of its families and ethnic group—decline in relative power, prestige, and wealth in many Gulf states. The "traditional" elements of the military have thus tended to be alienated from the regimes they serve. The fact that part of the Gulf military still comes from traditional groups is, therefore, misleading as an index of stability. These "traditional" groups are themselves increasingly unstable, and the internal tensions within them are creating new and unpredictable ties and conflicts between the "new" and "traditional" elements of the Gulf military.

This process of change has already helped to depose the shah of Iran and cause a long series of major political upheavals in Iraq and North Yemen. It seems certain to cause further changes in the future. The leadership of each Gulf military force is increasingly tied to its current government only to the extent that the government earns the military's loyalty and respect, provides financial incentives, and adjusts to the military's developing and uncertain political beliefs. The "traditional" Gulf army is disappearing; this is as true of "traditional" forces like the Saudi National Guard as it is of regular or expatriate armies.

The link between the expansion of Gulf military forces and increases in the number of foreign military advisers presents other problems. With notable exceptions, such foreign advisers have helped to exacerbate the cultural tension between the Gulf and the West. In fact, the very existence of Western and Soviet advisers in the Gulf is a symbol of foreign dominance or influence that many Gulf military personnel do not easily accept. The situation is worsened by the fact that many advisers have shown insufficient concern for Gulf culture and traditions and, consciously or unconsciously, have adopted an attitude of cultural and racial superiority to those they advise. Worse still, in most of the conservative Gulf states foreign military advisers have been hired from many different countries and regular military advisers have been mixed with nonmilitary advisers and businessmen. As will be seen in the following chapters, the result has sometimes been to tie Western military advice and arms sales to profiteering, personal excess, and internal rivalry for position and wealth. The resulting resentments affect not only the military, but also students, workers, officials, educators, the media, and businessmen. Many see military expansion as a form of repression, waste, and corruption or as serving Western interests rather than those of the Gulf. The resulting hostility to such poorly managed military buildups is now as common among the new middle class and students in Kuwait and the UAE as it was in Iran. Although this hostility varies in intensity in other Gulf states, it is always there.

These problems are compounded by the history of corruption in major foreign military sales. The military buildup in the Gulf has been accompanied by a continuing process of Western payoffs, short-term profiteering, and failure to live up to contractual requirements or meet specifications. The fact that many of the abuses are the result of overambitious plans for military expansion or the demands of venal Gulf officials, rather than deliberate corruption or inefficiency on the part of the Western arms sellers, is largely irrelevant. Every Gulf nation now has at least some reason to resent its foreign arms suppliers and military advisers.

These problems have been recognized, to varying degrees, by each Gulf state. Some, like Saudi Arabia and Oman, have made major efforts to control the resulting frictions and unrest and to ensure the loyalty of the military. None, however, has been fully successful, and this has led each Gulf state to expand the efforts of its internal security apparatus to include the military forces. This policy helps in some respects, but it hurts in others. Many of these internal security efforts have led to debilitating purges and upheavals in military forces that already face enormous stresses from conversion to modern technology. At the same time, such efforts have tended to punish almost as many of the innocent as the guilty and to introduce a new note of corruption in the process. They also have further weakened the ties between the military and the regime.

Such problems must not be exaggerated. Most Gulf military forces still remain collectively loyal to the regimes they serve and to the Gulf. The military are generally members of a privileged and often pampered class. Every Gulf ruling elite also understands the threat of military expansion and modernization, and each is acting to reduce this threat as much as it can. There is no inevitable relationship between an increase in Gulf military capabilities and the threat of a military takeover. Nevertheless, the risks are growing, and they are usually more immediate than the risk of foreign attack or internal subversion. Most important, the true nature of this risk has changed radically along with Gulf military forces. The current mixture of "new" and "traditional" elements in most Gulf military forces has, in effect, created a new class. If they do seize power, they are very unlikely to do so as a traditional junta or rival power group that otherwise maintains the status quo. With the possible exception of Iraq, no Gulf military force is now a fully known quantity. Each is staffed principally by the changing subelements within Gulf society, and these subelements have a very uncertain ideology and set of political alignments. Their political consciousness often consists of little more than a mixture of nationalism and the resentment of change, foreign advisers, corruption and waste, bureaucratization, and the other threats to the Gulf, not adherence to any given plan or ideology.

The Threat of Another Arab-Israeli Conflict

Finally, the Gulf states face the risk of another and even more serious Arab-Israeli conflict. Quite aside from any military threat that the Gulf may eventually pose to Israel, or that Israel now poses to the Gulf, every Gulf state and military force confronts the problem that since 1967, the Palestinian issue has become steadily more closely linked to the Arab political and cultural consciousness and has become a driving force in the attitudes of the region. This linkage is not simply the result of political pressures from the various Palestinian groups or the risk of Palestinian "terrorism" or "subversion" against Gulf states that fail to support the Palestinian cause. The Palestinian issue is a popular cause whose importance is steadily increasing. Virtually every citizen in the Gulf under the age of 25 (and this is probably something like 60% of the population) has grown up in a political atmosphere that has made the Palestinian issue a sine qua non of Arab consciousness. It permeates the Gulf media, education, and youth movements.

In spite of all the PLO's internal divisions and weaknesses, no Gulf state can afford to ignore the Palestinian movement, or to ignore the Palestinians in shaping its relations with the West. This does not mean that Gulf states have to reject the West as a whole, or the U.S. for its support of Israel. It does mean, however, that the Gulf rulers must balance their need for partnership with the West against the need to respond to each new crisis in the Arab-Israeli conflict. The uprising of popular feeling that followed Israel's invasion of Lebanon has shown that the Palestinian issue will not go away, be relegated to "benign neglect," or be subordinated to collective action with the West against a Soviet or Iranian threat. Even if no solution to the Palestinian problem proves possible, Gulf regimes must constantly seek one and must appear to support the Palestinian movement. If they do not, they may not survive. For similar reasons, if the U.S. is perceived as leaning too much toward Israel, Gulf regimes will have to back away from the U.S.

The Strategic Interests of the Soviet Union

The differences between Western and Gulf strategic concerns, and the various vulnerabilities of the West and Gulf states, furnish powerful mechanisms for asserting Soviet strategic interests. The Soviets can, and do, capitalize on these mechanisms and the opportunities they provide to expand the Soviet military presence in the region, to create or support friendly Gulf regimes, to threaten others, and to increase Soviet capability to control or threaten Western oil supplies.

Soviet Strategic Objectives

The Soviet strategic objectives in the Gulf are obvious. They are

- to neutralize or eliminate Western military power and political influence in the Gulf and Indian Ocean area
- to create alliances with friendly states throughout the Gulf
- to transform the Gulf states into Marxist or revolutionary states conforming to Soviet ideology
- to exploit the conflicts and tensions with the West and its allies in the region

- to expand Soviet influence on the surrounding states that affect Gulf security and to enlarge Soviet ability to threaten or control both the various oil shipment routes and other Western sources of oil and strategic minerals
- to build up Soviet military power and power projection capabilities in the region
- to use the Arab-Israeli dissension, wars in the Horn, Indo-Pakistani conflict, and every other opportunity to create a broad influence over the entire Middle East and Southwest Asia

Yet Soviet strategic interests involve more than achieving power over the region and control of the West's oil supplies. The Soviets must avoid war with the West, particularly over an area so vital that hostilities might escalate to nuclear conflict. The USSR must proceed slowly if it is to avoid polarizing the Gulf against it or its client states. It must constantly choose between short-term expediency in supporting "revolutionary" states that are not truly Marxist in character and steps that may create authentic communist regimes, actual clients, and true allies. It must choose between opportunities to play the "spoiler" role in achieving minor reductions in Western power and influence and a slower and more methodical effort to meet its long-term objectives.

The Soviet Union has had more than 50 years of experience in the Gulf and in achieving tactical victories that have proved to be strategically ephemeral. It has every incentive to avoid future "opportunism." Soviet actions in the Gulf have high political and strategic visibility in the West, and hostile action can threaten Soviet-bloc trade with the West and Soviet ability to capitalize on détente. Accordingly, while Soviet strategic goals may be obvious, the best way to attain those goals is not. The Soviet bloc also cannot ignore the facts that Eastern Europe increasingly depends on the region for oil and gas, that the USSR currently imports gas, and that the Soviet bloc must import an increasing amount of oil. The Soviet bloc must exploit the "revolutionary contradictions" of the Gulf with enough care to ensure that it will still have access to oil and gas and be able to maintain enough trade to help support its energy purchases.

This combination of experience and strategic interest makes it likely that the Soviet Union will generally move cautiously in responding to events like the revolution in Iran and act slowly and methodically in exploiting the areas where the Gulf is vulnerable. At the same time, the nature of Soviet strategic interests almost ensures that the Soviet struggle with the West and Gulf nations will result in a constant series of probes and tests. The USSR also seems likely to pursue a gradualist approach, rather than overt military threats or attacks, only as long as the West and the Gulf states can respond with a reasonable degree of military capability and political unity.

The Strategic Vulnerability of the Soviet Union

The problem involves more, however, than choosing among opportunities. The Soviet Union must simultaneously consider several major strategic vulnerabilities. The key vulnerability is the Soviet inability to provide a meaningful cultural and economic alternative to the West. The USSR cannot compete with the West as a source of ideology and intellectual concepts, technology, trade, and modernization. It lacks the economic capability and efficiency to meet Gulf needs. The Soviet mix of political objectives and ideology is also more alien to the Gulf than the West's mix of liberalism and capitalism. The illusions many Arab nationalists had about Marxism and the altruism behind the Soviet support of Gulf nationalism in the early postwar era were largely dissipated in the 1960s and 1970s. Even the left-wing elements within the conservative Gulf states and "radical" Gulf states like Iraq and Iran are now broadly aware of the risks of dealing with the Soviet Union and of its ultimate hostility to Islam and their national identities. The radical movements within most Gulf states find the USSR valuable only as a source of arms, money, and political support. They find Soviet ideology and "imperialism" to be just as passé as do many of the revolutionary movements in the rest of the world.

The USSR is only marginally more able than the West to create and sustain a major military presence in most Gulf states. Afghanistan may strain Soviet regional military capabilities for a generation, and the USSR faces a steadily greater threat of instability in Eastern Europe. Accordingly, a military occupation of Iran, or of any other Gulf state, would present major problems in terms of resources and logistics, quite aside from the probable hostile reaction of the other Gulf powers. In many ways, the Soviet Union is more vulnerable to problems of Gulf nationalism than the West. The emergence of strong national regimes in the Gulf may weaken Gulf military and political ties with the West, but the emergence of new "revolutionary" regimes in the Gulf states seems unlikely to reduce their trade with the West or their ties to Western economies. Even the current chaos in Iran has not really eliminated its economic dependence on the West. Revolutions may well end in replacing weak conservative regimes, which are vulnerable to Soviet threats and radical pressure, with strong new regimes whose foreign policy objectives are likely to be highly independent. Ironically, "revolutionary" states may be more independent and more able to resist Soviet pressure than traditional regimes. Iraq is a good case in point.

The Arab proverb that the "enemy of my friend is my enemy and the friend of my enemy is my enemy" does not therefore really serve Soviet interests, whether it refers to Israel or the current ruling elite in a Gulf state. The Soviets have the advantage that the vulnerabilities of the Gulf states allow the USSR to exploit their divisions, to play a "spoiler" role, and to obtain improved basing capability. They do not, however, offer much further opportunity to create Soviet client or communist states, or to integrate Gulf nations into the Soviet-bloc economic system. The Soviet Union's "friends" at any given moment may be its "enemies" in the long run.

Finally, one cannot totally dismiss the threat posed by the USSR's large Muslim and Central Asian ethnic minorities. Afghan rebels have been able to use such ethnic elements to operate within the USSR and the Soviets may yet face a serious internal threat as a result of the political and religious movements in the Gulf area. Events like the Iran-Iraq War and the Soviet intervention in Afghanistan risk doing more than expanding Soviet influence in the area. They risk a reaction by the ethnic groups whose superior birthrate is gradually displacing White Russians and Ukrainians as the dominant elements in Soviet society.

The Problem of Linking Western and Gulf Strategic Interests

The differences between the strategic interests and vulnerabilities of the Gulf and Western nations do not, therefore, preclude a partnership between them or necessarily offer the Soviet Union any long-term hope of achieving its strategic interests. Western and Gulf interests coincide far better than do Soviet and Gulf interests, almost regardless of the different political characters of the various Gulf nations. Iraq's Baath party, and even some elements of the Khomeini movement in Iran, have shown their consciousness of this fact. These differences do, however, require that the Gulf and Western states create a strategic partnership based on careful regard for the other's vulnerabilities. There must be no illusions that Gulf and Western interests are fully identical, that the solution to the Gulf's increasing security problems can consist simply of treaties, military guarantees, or Western military bases. The U.S., in particular, must be far more sensitive to the internal threats to the Gulf states than it was in the case of Iran.

Notes

1. For a detailed discussion of these issues as they relate to Saudi Arabia see William B. Quandt's study of Saudi and U.S. relations, *Saudi Arabia in the 1980s: Foreign Policy, Security and Oil* (Washington, D.C.: Brookings Institution, 1981); and William Ochsenwald, "Saudi Arabia and the Islamic Revival," *International Journal of Middle East Studies* 13, no. 3 (August 1981):271–286.

2. For a preliminary assessment of these threats, see Fredric S. Feer, Avigdor Haselkorn, R. D. McLaurin, and Abraham R. Wagner, *Middle East Net Assessment: Volume 1, Regional Threat Perceptions,* AAC-TR-9001/79 (Marina del Rey, Calif.: Analytical Assessments Corporation, January 1979). See also Abraham R. Wagner, Avigdor Haselkorn, and Lewis W. Snider, *The Energy Heartland—The Next Twenty Years: Military Aspects,* AAC-WN-7906 (Marina del Rey, Calif.: Analytical Assessments Corporation, December 1979); and Henry

S. Rowen, *Report on Persian Gulf Oil and Western Security,* PH80-11-LV7902-60A (Marina del Rey, Calif.: Pan Heuristics, November 1980).

3. From 1890 through 1974, no Trucial State changed rulers without family strife, a coup d'etat, or civil war.

4. See Barry Rubin, *Paved with Good Intentions* (New York: Oxford University Press, 1980), especially Chapters 1–4.

5. This can be loosely dated as beginning when General Abdul Karim al-Qassim led the coup that resulted in the death of King Faisal and Premier Nuri al-Said on 14 July 1958.

6. An interesting, if ethnocentric, description of British withdrawal is provided in J. B. Kelly, *Arabia, the Gulf and the West: A Critical View of the Arabs and Their Oil Policy* (New York: Basic Books, 1980). Kelly opposes the withdrawal; Fred Halliday provides a pro-Marxist defense in *Arabia Without Sultans* (London: Penguin Books, 1979). A more balanced military account is provided in Air Chief Marshal Sir David Lee's *Flight from the Middle East* (London: Her Majesty's Stationery Office, 1980).

7. In fairness to Britain, the U.S. could not agree internally on what course to recommend regarding a postwithdrawal British presence in the region and became bogged down in a long series of debates over a strategy of bases versus military presence and the use of sea power versus the use of air power. It also found little real parliamentary support for defense expenditures to help Britain maintain its presence or to replace the British presence with U.S. forces. The area was regarded as having limited strategic value and as being one where the U.S. should seek to avoid any superpower presence.

8. See Rubin, *Paved with Good Intentions;* and Francis Fukuyama, *The Soviet Union and Iraq Since 1968,* N-1524, AF (Santa Monica, Calif.: Rand Corporation, July 1980).

9. See George Lenczowski, *The Middle East in World Affairs* (Ithaca, N.Y.: Cornell University Press, 1980), pp. 220–221.

10. Not, incidentally, without strong Saudi urging. An interesting summary of these events is provided in Steven David, "Realignment in the Horn: The Soviet Advantage," *International Security,* no. 4 (Fall 1979):69–90.

11. See CIA ER 80-1031880, "Communist Aid Activities in Non-Communist, Less Developed Countries, 1954 to 1979," Washington D.C., October 1980; Francis Fukuyama, "A New Soviet Strategy," *Commentary,* October 1979, and *New Directions for Soviet Middle East Policy,* Rand P-6443 (Santa Monica, Calif.: Rand Corporation, 1980).

12. By late 1981, new conflicts had broken out in North Yemen. The main rebel faction had the backing of South Yemen and the USSR.

13. CIA GI IESR 81-011, 24 November 1981, p. 13. Such expenditures have since dropped sharply but continue to exceed $100 billion annually, even in the climate of a sustained world recession.

14. Estimates vary. For typical estimates see "A Survey of Saudi Arabia," *Economist,* 13 February 1982; *Economist, Banking on Recovery, A Survey of International Banking* (London, 26 March 1982); *New York Times,* 27 February 1983; *Economist,* 26 February 1983, pp. 46–47.

15. Both Israel and key Arab states have tended to have impossible expectations regarding U.S. support and freedom of action. Even sophisticated Arab analysts often regard the U.S. as a *deus ex machina* that could instantly solve the Palestinian problem if it were not the victim of a vast "Zionist conspiracy" or did not have sinister or covert motives for not acting. These Arab beliefs

are reinforced by a wide mix of anti-U.S. groups in Europe, which range from traditional anti-Semites to various Soviet fronts and extremist Marxist or right-wing political action groups.

In contrast, the attitudes of the Begin government toward the Arab world have taken on an increasingly extreme and racist character as the Israeli leaders in the Likud coalition who understood the Arab world, like Moshe Dayan and Ezer Weizman, have been replaced by relative extremists like Tamir Sharon. Israeli intelligence has also tended to become more extreme in seeing a Soviet hand behind every Arab action and in postulating steadily more sinister motives behind every Arab military purchase. Whatever the weaknesses of U.S. policy, and they are many, neither Israel nor the Arabs are generally impartial (or even intelligently selfish) judges of U.S. actions.

16. This was illustrated in November 1981, when Israel repeatedly overflew Tabuk, with up to 12 aircraft per flight, after the U.S. agreed to sell Saudi Arabia the AWACS. This was evidently the result of an effort to demonstrate Israel's military superiority over Saudi Arabia and to provoke a Saudi reaction that would discredit the Fahd peace plan. In the ensuing discussions between U.S. and Israeli defense officials before the AWACS sale, the Israelis again presented variations of an estimate of the Arab threat that Prime Minister Begin had originally presented to Secretary of State Alexander Haig in an effort to block the sale of the E-3A. While, as is discussed in Chapter 18, Israel has long painted pictures of the Arab threat that U.S. intelligence officials regard as exaggerated and unrealistic, the IDF studies presented in 1981 reached a level of overreaction that seriously disturbed senior U.S. foreign policy and intelligence officials.

17. See William B. Quandt's excellent discussion of this issue in *Saudi Arabia's Oil Policy: A Staff Paper* (Washington, D.C.: Brookings Institution, 1982), especially pp. 18–25.

18. These figures are taken from "A Survey of Saudi Arabia," *Economist,* 13 February 1982, pp. 5–33; and "Survey: Saudi Arabia," *Financial Times,* 25 April 1983. It is interesting to note that as Saudi economic development has expanded out of the Najd into the Hejaz and then into the Asir and the rest of the country, each phase has been accompanied by the systematic destruction of the former tribal, village, and class order of the developing region. Similar patterns are emerging in Oman, while the rest of the smaller Gulf states have already experienced a massive disintegration of their former social order. Ironically, the same trends in Iran and Iraq have tended to replace a traditional, locally oriented culture with often violent ethnic or religious "nationalism" or separatism. The more complex patterns of radicalism in South Yemen, and expatriate labor in North Yemen, are having equally shattering cultural effects.

19. Author's estimate based on various Saudi and other working papers. Approximately the same figures appear, however, in "Survey: Saudi Arabia," *Financial Times,* 25 April 1983; and *Middle East Review, 1983,* World Almanac publication 31009-8 (Essex, 1983), pp. 245–258.

20. Kuwait's "parallel" stock market, sometimes called the Souk Manakh or "camel park," collapsed for the second time in November 1982. The collapse occurred largely because the government set a 20 October 1982 deadline for registering checks deposited in the market and forced it to register deferred and partial payments on speculative investment. This investment consisted largely of postdated checks for stocks in nonexistent firms, and the speculation consisted essentially of trying to ride out the rise in share prices before the

entire market collapsed. The government had to set up a $1.7 billion fund to protect small investors of up to $6.8 million each, with immediate repayment of losses up to $340,000. At least four ministers and one member of the ruling Al-Sabah family were directly involved.

Bahrain was forced to check its offshore banking effort in late 1982 because it had become more a speculative lottery than a banking operation. Offshore banking had reached $68 billion in assets since 1975 and was growing at a rate of 44% annually. This growth was sharply reducing regional investment, and Saudi Arabia was both cutting back on investment and shifting funds to its own banks. The Central Bank of the UAE had been forced to act several months earlier. The number of banks in the UAE had risen to 50 independent banks and 347 branches for a nation with only 1 million citizens. Most of these banks had become badly overextended by speculating in high-risk loans without any security or even background investigation of the borrower. The UAE's moratorium on foreign banks, and regulations on the number of branches, affected some 83 branch banks, but this was only a first step in regularizing the UAE's banking operations.

While a great deal of emphasis is placed on "corruption" in the Gulf, such activities are almost penny ante compared to the kind of losses cited above, which totaled over $80 billion in paper transactions in 1982 alone. See David B. Ottaway, "Kuwait's $90 Billion Stock Market Collapses," *Washington Post,* 24 November 1982; *Economist,* 25 September 1982, p. 96; 30 October 1982, p. 82; "Bahrain Offshore Banking," *Economist,* 27 November 1982; and the survey of the UAE, "Central Bank Pulls in the Reins," *Christian Science Monitor,* 1 December 1982.

21. Author's estimate based on various World Bank and other working papers.

22. One Gulf nation estimates the average growth in the conservative Gulf states of the percentage of native labor dependent on government-funded projects or direct salary as having gone from no more than 10% for any state in 1960 to over 50% in all conservative Gulf states except Oman in 1975.

23. It has also created a new class of Western and Asian "profiteers" who provide the technical expertise and backing for such action. Few truly glaring examples of waste and corruption in the Gulf states have been achieved without the kind of equal partnership between the Gulf and the West that is least desirable for all concerned.

3
Saudi-U.S. Military Relations: The Formative Period

The West does not have many options in dealing with the complex mixture of strategic catalysts, capabilities, and vulnerabilities in the Gulf. The shah's fall has made Saudi Arabia the only major nation with which the West can forge a strategic partnership in the Gulf area. There is no practical near-term probability of reestablishing U.S. ties to Iran or of building up more than a fragile modus vivendi with Iraq. With the possible exception of Oman, no smaller conservative Gulf state can sustain a military relationship with the United States without at least the tacit support of Saudi Arabia. Even this option has severe limits. The West can have only a limited influence over the immense forces of social change in Saudi Arabia and the other Gulf states. No matter what the U.S. or the other Western states do, they cannot unilaterally stabilize the political situation in Saudi Arabia or any of its neighbors. The best the West can do is to strengthen its ties to Saudi Arabia and the other friendly Gulf states as much as possible and to take what steps it can to minimize the risks it cannot control.

U.S. military links to Saudi Arabia are only one of the areas in which the West must seek to improve its ties to Saudi Arabia and the Gulf, and stronger political and economic links will be equally important. Nevertheless, military relations are a crucial area for U.S. policy. They are the cornerstone to strengthening the other conservative Gulf states, which must ultimately build their collective security around Saudi Arabia. They are an area in which the U.S. can base its relations with Saudi Arabia on a unique ability to supply goods and services. They are an area in which the U.S. can provide "balance" in its relations with the Arab states and Israel; and they are a mechanism through which the U.S. can simultaneously minimize the need to commit U.S. forces to the Gulf and maximize their effectiveness if they must be committed.

Themes in Saudi-U.S. Military Relations

The history of Saudi-U.S. military relations extends back before World War II. The details of these relations are often obscure and controversial,

MAP 3—1
THE STRATEGIC POSITION OF SAUDI ARABIA

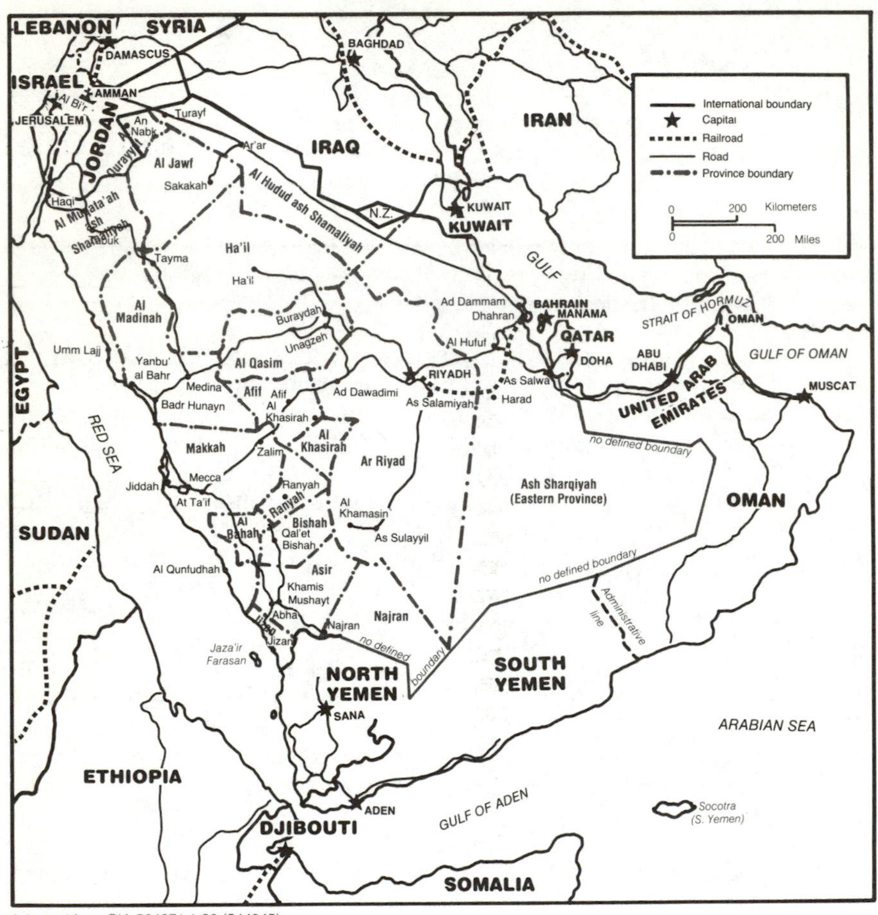

Adapted from CIA 504371 1-80 (544945)

but an understanding of their history is essential to any discussion of the current military situation in the Gulf. Without this background, it is difficult to understand Saudi attitudes and perspectives, the relations between Saudi Arabia and the other Gulf states, the forces that both unite and divide Saudi Arabia and the United States, and the challenges both nations must meet if more stable military relations are to be established in the 1980s. Without such historical background it is difficult to understand the strengths and weaknesses in Saudi forces, the relationships between Saudi Arabian external and internal security needs, and the limits to what the U.S. can hope to accomplish. Most of the problems in Saudi-U.S. military relations are the result of weaknesses in their respective political systems and are not the "fault" of either side. However, any meaningful improvements in their relations must take full account of the limitations that each nation has faced in dealing with the other.

One of these limitations is, in fact, the American lack of an "institutional memory." There is a fundamental difference between the experience of most Saudi and U.S. policymakers. Senior Saudi defense officials have often been in office for more than a decade. They have a detailed historical knowledge of Saudi-U.S. military relations, have met a long series of U.S. officials, have considerable personal decision-making authority, and are concerned with little else besides Saudi security. In contrast, most U.S. officials dealing with Saudi Arabia average less than three years in dealing with this area of responsibility, have had little historical background in Saudi-U.S. staff relations, and have had little staff continuity. Most generally have had authority over only a limited part of U.S. relations with Saudi Arabia, and they have usually focused on Saudi Arabia only as part of more general responsibilities for the Near East or the entire world. As a result, the perceptual differences between U.S. and Saudi officials have often been immense.

These differences have been compounded by the tendency of the Saudi Arabian government to keep Saudi Arabia a "closed society." The Saudi government has conducted its political and military relations without the public exposure of its decision-making process that is common in the West. As a result, little has been written about Saudi Arabia's military development. In addition, because of Saudi sensitivities, the U.S. and other Western governments have tried to avoid publicizing the details of their military relations with Saudi Arabia.

This situation compounds the problem the West faces in trying to understand Saudi Arabia, and it should be borne in mind in evaluating any attempt to write the history of Saudi-U.S. military relations. This history draws on interviews, official reporting, academic studies, defense research groups, and media sources that are so often in conflict that it seems pointless to iterate the various differences that exist on matters of detail. Nevertheless, some consistent themes do emerge that provide a useful overview of the patterns in Saudi-U.S. military relations and an introduction to their history.

• The U.S. has been the natural partner in Saudi Arabia's military development ever since World War II. Saudi Arabia more than any other regional power of comparable importance has needed foreign technical, training, operational, and maintenance support in every branch of its armed forces. It has had to change from a nontechnical, tribal-feudal state, with a small and largely illiterate population, to a state with a highly technical economy and modern military forces.[1] Its military requirements have evolved from a need for limited border defenses to a need for Saudi forces, and Western reinforcements, that can deter the massive, well-equipped armies and air forces of its neighbors. While Britain and France can still play an important role in providing Saudi Arabia with military support, their steady withdrawal from "east of Suez" has made the United States the only Western power that can provide Saudi Arabia with the full range of services it needs.

• Saudi Arabia has continued to maintain an extraordinary degree of dependence on the United States for the development of its modern armed forces. The first U.S. advisory mission arrived in Saudi Arabia in 1943, and since 1951 the United States has helped to shape each successive Saudi force plan and advised Saudi Arabia on both the development of its modern military infrastructure and its key purchases of military equipment.

• Similarly, Saudi Arabia's small native population of 4–5 million, and its far smaller pool of trained manpower, force it to sharply limit the growth of its armed forces and to seek quality rather than quantity.[2] In practice, this has meant a steadily increasing Saudi dependence on getting the most advanced "first line" military equipment, which has grown sharply since 1973. The other powers in the region have expanded their own forces and upgraded their military equipment at rates that have left Saudi Arabia no alternative than to buy the best military equipment available. This, in turn, has tended to reinforce Saudi ties to the U.S. While nations like France can provide equal or superior equipment in selected areas, the U.S. is again Saudi Arabia's natural partner. The U.S. has a unique ability to provide not only advanced aircraft like the F-15, but also the wide range of associated equipment and services necessary to operate such systems in a demanding and often hostile environment.

• The U.S. has been, and for all its present military weaknesses remains, the only Western power that can convincingly reinforce Saudi Arabia in an emergency. The U.S. has provided such reinforcements nine times since 1945, usually in the form of token deployments, and its "over-the-horizon" military presence has been invaluable to Saudi Arabia. While the Saudis often underplay the value of this over-the-horizon relationship, it remains one of critical strategic value to Saudi Arabia. To put its value in perspective, even a regional power as small as North Yemen is equal in population to Saudi Arabia. As a result, Saudi Arabia's vast wealth, its political skills, and its military forces cannot by themselves provide a convincing deterrent in a region where the other major states can draw on vastly larger manpower pools to expand their military forces.

• At the same time, the U.S. and Saudi Arabia have been deeply divided over the emergence of Israel and the importance of Arab nationalism. Although Saudi Arabia came to accept Israel's right to exist within its 1967 boundaries, it is still technically at war with Israel. Saudi acceptance of Israel's right to exist has come slowly and still involves major policy differences with the U.S. over control of Jerusalem and the rights of the Palestinians to a sovereign state on the West Bank and Gaza.[3]

• Saudi-U.S. military relations have been increasingly destabilized by the impact of Israeli and U.S. pro-Israeli politics on U.S. arms sales to Saudi Arabia. The first major Israeli effort to use U.S. Jewish groups to block U.S. arms sales to Saudi Arabia occurred in 1955. Since that time such pressures have steadily complicated Saudi-U.S. military relations and have led Saudi Arabia to turn to other nations for much of its army, National Guard, and navy equipment. As a result, Saudi-U.S. military ties are now largely the result of U.S. capability to supply Saudi Arabia's key military service—its air force.

• The U.S. and Saudi Arabia have also been divided by the Saudi commitment to various Islamic states and causes that the U.S. has not supported. There is no doubt that in many individual instances, Saudi Arabia has chosen to provide military, political, and economic support to Islamic movements or states that the U.S. has opposed. At the same time, there is equally little doubt that U.S. officials dealing with Saudi Arabia have sometimes miscalculated the importance of such actions to U.S. strategic interests. U.S. understanding of such Saudi actions has been undercut by the U.S. failure to realize that such Saudi action has the same ideological underpinnings as the U.S. struggle against communism. This perceptual difference has particularly affected Saudi-U.S. politico-military relations in regard to the PLO, but it has also created problems in Saudi-U.S. dealings with crises like the Ethiopian-Somali War, the overthrow of the imam in North Yemen, policy toward Nasser's Egypt, and a host of other cases.

• Since 1971, the history of Saudi-U.S. military relations has also been shaped by U.S. military relations with Iran. The "twin pillars" doctrine for the Gulf that the U.S. established in 1972 and that implemented the Nixon Doctrine announced in Guam in 1969 made Iran the key "pillar" in military terms. The U.S. virtually gave the shah of Iran a blank check to buy U.S. arms, while it sharply constrained Saudi arms purchases. The U.S. calculated that the shah would provide a military shield for the Gulf and that Saudi Arabia would need only limited military forces and internal security capabilities.

• The fall of the shah in late 1979 thus confronted Saudi Arabia with both the loss of an uncertain and somewhat unwelcome "shield" and the threat of aggressive radical Shi'ite movements throughout the Gulf. On the one hand, Saudi Arabia faced an immediate requirement to build up its armed forces to replace Iran; on the other hand, the complex politics in the Gulf made any U.S. force based on Saudi soil even more politically dangerous. Further, Saudi Arabia found itself in the position of having to support the other conservative Gulf states, which increased the need for effective Saudi military forces and forced Saudi Arabia into closer ties with nations with larger radical Arab political elements and/or ethnic divisions and conflicts. The resulting pressures again increased the limits on Saudi Arabia's ability to accept any permanent U.S. military presence.

• The Yemeni border war of 1979 and the Iran-Iraq War of 1980 allowed Saudi Arabia to temporarily accept a U.S. military presence on its soil in the form of the airborne warning and air control system (AWACS). It did not, however, change the fundamental Saudi need to avoid compromising its sovereignty in Arab eyes and establishing highly visible or formal military relations with the U.S. of the kind that would make Saudi Arabia a target for every Arab nationalist and radical movement.

• Unlike Iran, Saudi Arabia built its military forces slowly and laid the proper foundation for modernization in terms of training and infrastructure. It also established a modern command structure under King Faisal in 1964, which has since ensured tight continuity in Saudi Arabia's military development, with none of the constant purges, upheavals, and shifts in command that characterized the development of the Iranian military forces under the shah. Although the U.S. sold Saudi Arabia over $35 billion in military goods and services between 1950 and 1980, at least 90% of this went to training, military construction, and the other steps necessary to make Saudi Arabia ready to operate modern forces. This expenditure has now brought Saudi Arabia to the point where it is ready to operate the E-3A, the F-15, and other key equipment.

• The U.S. advisory effort supporting the Saudi Air Force encountered major problems long before the "AWACS crisis" of 1981. During the mid-1960s and the mid-1970s, Saudi Arabia accepted U.S. advice to buy second-line military equipment. In the mid-1960s, Saudi Arabia bought British fighters and U.S. surface-to-air missiles as part of a three-cornered deal between the U.S., Britain, and Saudi Arabia that gave Britain the funds to buy the F-4 Phantom and F-111. Because of delays in the delivery of U.S. Hawk missiles, Saudi Arabia was left facing a hostile Nasser with inadequate Lightning fighters and ineffective stocks of Thunderbird surface-to-air missiles. In the mid-1970s, Saudi Arabia accepted the F-5A and F-5E even though it sought more advanced fighters and felt threatened by U.S. sales to Iran of the F-14, F-4, and F-16. The present force structure of the Saudi Air Force has been heavily "mortgaged" by the impact of such U.S. sales and advice.

• Saudi Arabia is now seeking to create an air force with the capability to deter attacks on both its oil fields and those of the other southern Gulf nations. Again on U.S. advice, it has sought to create such a deterrent by mixing an advanced sensor, basing, and communications system with a limited number of F-15 fighters, E-3A AWACS, K-3 tankers airborne for refueling, and AIM-9L air-to-air missiles. These give it the capability to meet attacking fighters in head-on intercepts. Even with such equipment, Saudi Arabia will have only a minimally adequate deterrent, given the buildup of other Gulf air forces and the threat of such naval and air attacks as Iran successfully carried out against Iraq's oil facilities. Further, Saudi Arabia must plan to meet steadily increasing potential threats from the north, the Yemens, and across the Red Sea. Given its vast space and limited land forces, it can meet these threats only if it can mass its first-line fighters effectively anywhere in Saudi Arabia and use them in both the air defense and air attack roles.

• Saudi Arabia seems ready to operate such forces and to make major military progress during the 1980s. Few developing states have come so far so fast, and none has done so with the same manpower limitations. At the same time, Saudi defense institutions remain weak and will continue to require extensive foreign support throughout the 1980s. Saudi Arabia also has serious internal security problems, and these are compounded by the weaknesses in its defense structure and in the present process of U.S. military assistance to Saudi Arabia. The problem is not simply one of U.S. willingness to sell arms; it is one of meeting Saudi needs to improve its defense management, to improve its internal security apparatus, and to more carefully plan and manage its future military expansion.

In summary, the broad trends in Saudi-U.S. military relations have created a situation in which the U.S. still acts as Saudi Arabia's principal military ally and plays a major role in supporting the modernization of Saudi Arabia's most important military service, but in which the U.S. cannot base combat forces in Saudi Arabia in peacetime or even openly establish contingency capabilities. If the U.S. is to establish sound military relations with Saudi Arabia, it must do so in light of these facts and their consequences. The history of Saudi-U.S. military relations may be unfamiliar to most Americans, but it is all too familiar to Saudi officials, and it has created a heritage of problems that the U.S. must now seek to solve.

Saudi-U.S. Military Relations, 1930–1950

The Origins of Saudi Military Capabilities

Saudi military traditions have their origins in the rise of the Wahabi sect of Islam in the early 1700s and the partnership between the Saud family of the Najd and the Wahabi religious leaders. In 1803–1806, Saudi-led Wahabi forces took control of Makkah and Medina, and in 1808 they threatened Damascus. Although Muhammad Ali eventually seized control of most of the Arabian Peninsula, and at one point the Saud family was forced into exile in Kuwait, the rise of Arab nationalism and decline of the Ottoman Empire in the early 1900s led to a rebirth of the Saudi state.[4]

Under the leadership of Abd al-Aziz Ibn Saud, the Wahabi forces conquered most of northeast Arabia shortly before World War I. These Saudi forces were a combination of tribal warriors using light arms and machine guns, and religious warriors called Ikhwan; they remained the most effective military force in the Arab world following World War I and were consistently able to defeat the better-armed Arab forces of southern Arabia, Trans-Jordan, Iraq, and the Gulf. They conquered much of the Asir (southeast Arabia) in August 1920. They defeated the Rashid dynasty in November 1921 and the Shalan dynasty in July 1922, giving the Sauds control of most of the territory in Arabia north of the Hejaz and south of the British Trucial States.

Between 1922 and 1925, the Saudi forces defeated the far better-armed forces of the Hashemites in the Hejaz and conquered Makkah, Medina, and Jiddah. If it had not been for British protection, Saudi forces might well have conquered Trans-Jordan, southern Iraq, and the majority of the southern Gulf states. The British, however, checked the Ikhwan, using a combination of local forces, light armor, and air power. By that time, Abd al-Aziz had already turned to forging Arabia into a unified and peaceful country. This led to a revolt by the ultraconservative and militant forces in the Ihkwan, but Abd al-Aziz defeated the rebels at Sabillah and several subsequent battles in 1929 and captured their remaining chiefs in 1930 with British assistance. Abd al-Aziz formally proclaimed the existence of Saudi Arabia as a modern state on 22 September 1932.

Although King Abd al-Aziz established relatively close relations with Britain after the late 1920s, he continued to challenge the extension of the borders around the British-protected city-states and ports in the southern Gulf to cover the surrounding tribal areas. He did, however, sign treaties during 1933–1936 with Trans-Jordan, Iraq, and Egypt that established Saudi Arabia's borders with most of its modern neighbors.[5] The last major prewar Saudi conflict with its neighbors in the Arabian Peninsula was fought between Saudi Arabia and Yemen in 1934; it resulted in the defeat of the Yemeni forces.

Establishment of Saudi-U.S. Military Relations

The Great Depression created a crisis in Saudi finances that led King Abd al-Aziz to seek Western assistance in exploiting the nation's mineral wealth. This decision, coupled to aggressive U.S. competition with the British oil companies, led the king to grant an oil concession to a U.S. firm, Standard Oil of California, on 29 May 1933. SOCAL spudded its first well in Saudi Arabia on 30 April 1935 and struck oil on 4 March 1938. The export of Saudi crude oil began late that year, when oil was first barged to Bahrain for refining and export. Tanker shipments began from the small fishing port of Ras Tanura on 1 May 1939. During this period, the SOCAL operation was first renamed the California Arabia Standard Oil Company (CASOC), a part of CALTEX, which was formed when SOCAL had to obtain capital from TEXACO. CALTEX became the king's key economic tie with the West and provided the concession funds and loans necessary to allow the Saudi regime to weather the Depression.[6]

One critical effect of the ties that developed during this period was that King Abd al-Aziz rejected more favorable concession offers from both Japan and Nazi Germany during the late 1930s. Although both Axis powers made a major overt and intelligence effort to obtain Saudi concessions, the arrangement with CASOC was renegotiated on 13 May 1939.[7] While Saudi Arabia was not immune to pressures from Arab nationalists in Egypt, Iraq, and the Levant to establish ties to Nazi Germany, King Abd al-Aziz again rejected offers from the Axis powers in April 1941. He did so at a time when Britain's defeat seemed probable, and the German and Japanese threats to Allied shipping were forcing the West to suspend oil loadings in Saudi Arabia.[8] As a result, the Axis powers remained hostile to Saudi Arabia, and CALTEX had to halt all oil shipments in 1943. The war also sharply cut revenues from the hajj. Saudi income was reduced by about $10 million a year, pushing the Saudi government into near-bankruptcy and leading to an economic crisis that was avoided only by U.S. loans and by the eventual allocation of Lend-Lease assistance to Saudi Arabia in April 1943.[9] By 1947, the U.S. had provided Saudi Arabia with nearly $100 million in aid.

From that time on, the U.S. became the dominant Western force in Saudi Arabia, and the U.S. government became directly involved in Saudi Arabia's economic and military development. In early 1943, and long before the Nazi defeat in southeast Russia had eliminated the Axis threat to the Gulf, King Abd al-Aziz secretly granted the U.S. rights to build a military airfield in Dhahran. Although this agreement compromised Saudi neutrality, Dhahran eventually became the main U.S. base operating in the Egypt-Gulf area. This agreement also led to the further extension of U.S. economic and military assistance. A U.S. economic aid mission had already been sent to Saudi Arabia under K. S. Twitchell in 1942, and in December 1943 the U.S. sent its first formal military mission. Prince Faisal and Prince Khalid made the Saudi royal family's first visit to Washington in September 1943, and Saudi Arabian officials worked closely with the U.S. Middle East Command under Maj. Gen. Ralph Royce during 1944. At U.S. urging, Saudi Arabia preserved its formal neutrality to minimize the risk of any effort to limit U.S. operations in the area, but it declared war on the Axis on 1 March 1945. These Saudi Arabian services to the United States were kept a closely guarded secret during the war, but President Truman recognized them in 1946 when he awarded Prince Faisal the Legion of Merit.[10]

Saudi-U.S. Relations in the Postwar Era

Major oil shipments resumed in 1944, and CASOC was renamed the Arabian-American Oil Company (ARAMCO). Production, which reached

4–5 million barrels per year during 1939–1943, rose to 8 million barrels in 1944. It rose to 21 million barrels in 1945 and then to 60 million barrels in 1946, when oil revenues first exceeded $10 million. Saudi oil production expanded to 200 million barrels per year by 1949, bringing in roughly $50 million in revenue. It continued to rise at an annual average rate of 9% through 1970.[11] As a result of this new oil wealth, Saudi Arabia developed its first formal plans for economic and military modernization. These were, in fact, drafted largely by ARAMCO, U.S. officials, and Point Four advisory teams. They were announced on 17 July 1947, and they mark a minor milestone in Saudi Arabia's evolution as a modern state.

The arrival of Saudi Arabia's new oil wealth also, however, coincided with several major other trends in world events. The first was the growth of Arab nationalism, and particularly the growth of a largely anti-Western radicalism in many of the states that still preserved colonial or quasi-colonial relations. The second was the emergence of Israel. The third was the decline of Britain's power and ability to protect the Gulf. The fourth was a competition for influence in the Third World between an emerging global United States and a Britain that sought unsuccessfully to remain a global colonial power; and the fifth was the emergence of the Soviet Union as an aggressive and "neo-imperialist" power with strong ambitions in the Gulf and the Middle East.

The impact of these trends often conflicted, but they initially led to a reduction in Saudi-U.S. military relations. King Saud had received formal promises from President Roosevelt and President Truman that the U.S. would not support the creation of an independent state of Israel without Arab "consent."[12] As the Palestine crisis moved toward civil war, however, it became apparent that a separate Jewish state was likely to result from partition of the British mandate. Although Saudi Arabia continued to allow the U.S. to use the air base at Dhahran, King Abd al-Aziz sought British, rather than U.S., assistance in creating a modern army.

The king was in urgent need of such assistance. The U.S. team sent to Saudi Arabia in 1943 had confined its role largely to planning and discussions with the king's advisers and a few top officials. There were no Western advisers working to modernize Saudi forces, which remained a group of tribal levies of less than 40,000 men. Although King Abd al-Aziz had made effective use of radio, armored cars, and machine guns in his final battles against the Ikhwan and had employed artillery against Yemen in 1934, his army remained primitive.

Britain had sent Saudi Arabia four de Havilland biplanes with British pilots and maintenance crews in September 1930, and Mussolini had trained the first Saudi fighter pilots in 1934 as part of an effort to win local support for his Abyssinian campaign. In 1946, however, the Saudi Air Force still consisted of a few U.S.- and British-supported fighters in Dhahran.[13] Further, while Saudi Arabia had managed to parlay its discussions of oil concessions with the Axis into token arms aid from Italy in the late 1930s, and into the delivery of 4,000 rifles and the promise of an ammunition and small arms plant from Nazi Germany in August 1939, the country received few arms from either side during World War II.[14] By 1946, the king still relied largely on trucks equipped with machine guns as his principal mechanized force.

King Abd al-Aziz was thus ill prepared for a world in which Allied military power in the Near East melted away after the end of World War II and in which his Arab neighbors and Iran began to acquire a limited amount of modern armor and air power. His meeting with President Roosevelt after the Yalta Conference of February 1945 did not result in significant U.S. military equipment deliveries.[15] By the time the U.S. recognized Israel on 14 May 1948, he was in a position of almost total economic and technical dependence on the U.S. and lacked any modern military forces at a time when the first Arab-Israeli war was making such forces the key symbol of national power in the Arab world.[16]

The king responded by making limited changes in the Saudi Ministry of Defense in 1947[17] and by asking Britain to establish a military mission to create a lightly mechanized force of about 10,000 men along the lines of the Arab Legion the British had created in Jordan.[18] The king obtained this British support by playing on the growing Anglo-American rivalry in the region and threatening to turn to the U.S. The new British mission, however, proved ineffective, for several reasons. The first reason was that although Britain and Saudi Arabia initially held a common position regarding the rise of Israel, they did not hold a common position regarding British control of the southern Gulf states, Oman, Aden, and the South Arabian Protectorates, and Saudi Arabia opposed Britain's efforts to create some form of British-dominated Arab League. This led the Saudis to limit the British role to training in the area of Taif and Jiddah and to prevent British advisers from having access to the rest of the country.

The second reason was that neither the king nor his Saudi advisers had any real idea what military modernization meant. Although the king had given his twelfth son, Prince Mansour, the title of minister of defense in 1944,[19] neither this appointment nor the reorganization of the Ministry of Defense (MOD) in 1947 moved Saudi Arabia away from an almost total reliance on the unstructured and administratively chaotic royal cabinet. The king had no real conception of the scale of effort necessary to create armored and air power or of the kind of infrastructure involved. From 1945 until his death in 1953, King Abd al-Aziz spent about $400 million on economic development. This consisted of a few tarmac roads, a useful network of wells and water projects, and a costly showpiece railroad from Dhahran to Riyadh. Some further reorganization of the Ministry of Defense took place in 1951, when Prince Mishal (the eighteenth son) replaced his full brother

Mansour, and again in 1953, as part of a general reorganization in which Prince Fahd was made minister of education, Prince Sultan was made minister of agriculture, and Prince Talal was made minister of communications. But no serious progress was made in creating an effective defense organization until long after Abd al-Aziz's death.[20]

The third reason was that although the Saudi Army was recruited largely from the original Saudi power base in Najd, the Saud family did not entirely trust its loyalty. They were particularly concerned that the army's officers, NCOs, and technicians be recruited from families known to be loyal to the regime. The tribal base, however, was still largely feudal and could not provide the necessary trained or educated personnel.

The fourth reason was the king's inability to decide on the role of the new regular army relative to that of his tribal forces, composed of tribal family groups with direct ties to the Saudi royal family. It was these units that provided the Royal Guard and maintained internal security throughout Saudi Arabia. As a result, the army was kept away from the capital, and the Saudis rejected a number of key British proposals regarding improved logistic bases and mobility on the grounds that they might allow the army to seize the key ports in the south and the religious cities.

Although Saudi Arabia eventually sent two token battalions (400–600 men total) to assist the Arab forces during the first Arab-Israeli conflict in 1948–1950, it had virtually no capability to act as a modern military force.[21] Saudi Arabia's army had declined from the principal army in the Arab world in the 1930s to little more than an internal security force by the late 1940s. By 1950, Saudi Arabia still had no pool of trained manpower that could operate modern military equipment. The Saudi Army was unable to operate as a mobile infantry force even in Saudi Arabia because it lacked both combat and support vehicles. Saudi Arabia also lacked an organized air force and navy, and it had only token numbers of fixed-wing aircraft, which it operated largely for prestige purposes.

Saudi Arabia's Development of Modern Military Forces, 1950–1960

Fortunately for the U.S., the reduction in Saudi-U.S. military relations in the late 1940s did not lead to any lasting split between Saudi Arabia and the United States. The Saudi shift to Britain to provide an advisory mission for its army did not prevent an increase in Saudi-U.S. economic ties or military contacts. The U.S. continued to use the air base at Dhahran as one of its key air bases in the Middle East, the U.S. Navy visited the Saudi port of Dammam where it made its first visit to the Gulf in 1948, and ARAMCO continued to provide the Saudis with unofficial support in military and internal security planning.

The Resumption of Close Saudi-U.S. Military Relations

The slow end of the first Arab-Israeli conflict—which can be approximately dated to the Anglo-U.S.-French armistice guarantee of May 1950—reduced the pressures that then divided Saudi Arabia from the U.S. Coupled to the failure of the British advisory mission and Saudi Arabia's growing tension with Britain over Saudi claims to the Buraimi Oasis, parts of Oman, and disputed territory in the Trucial States, the political changes led King Abd al-Aziz to turn back to the U.S. as Saudi Arabia's principal source of military assistance.[22] The king asked the U.S. for a bilateral security treaty in 1949. Although the U.S. did not want a formal treaty, it quickly responded to the Saudi initiative. By doing so it sought to strengthen its position in competing with Britain for oil resources in the Gulf, to expand its use of Dhahran in response to the growth of the Soviet nuclear threat, and to obtain a forward base in the Gulf for U.S. strategic bombers.

In late 1950 the U.S. sent General O'Keefe on a mission to Saudi Arabia to survey Saudi defense needs and to start major negotiations to strengthen U.S. military ties to Saudi Arabia. As a result, the U.S. signed its first formal defense agreement with Saudi Arabia on 18 June 1951.[23] This agreement allowed the U.S. to continue to use Dhahran as a strategic air base and established a permanent U.S. military mission to Saudi Arabia.

The main part of the British mission was asked to leave, although a few Saudis continued on at Sandhurst, and Saudi Arabia did implement the mission's recommendation to buy Vampire fighters in 1952.[24] Saudi Arabia also diversified its dependence on the West by contracting with France to create two small munitions plants near al-Kharj and with West Germany for improved communications. It also obtained a small Egyptian military mission, which stayed in Saudi Arabia from 1951 until King Saud broke with Nasser in 1957.

It was the U.S. advisory effort, however, that replaced Britain as Saudi Arabia's chief source of support. This advisory effort benefited from the fact that a number of pressures were transforming Saudi society and giving it more of the unity, organization, and trained manpower it needed to operate more modern military forces. The increases in trained manpower were particularly important and resulted from a limited increase in formal education, the increases in the number of Saudis trained to operate modern industrial equipment that followed the start of large-scale oil production, and the shifts in Saudi society that resulted from migration to the cities and oil fields to take advantage of Saudi Arabia's new wealth. By the early 1950s, these changes had also begun to erode the Saudi government's past reliance on traditional village or regional ties in selecting its military personnel, to break down some of the past reluctance to recruit the comparatively well-educated Hejazis for the armed forces, to improve the overall organization of the Saudi government, and to create a bureaucratic climate that gave more recognition to technical training and skills and less to family origins. The king also reorganized the Ministry of Defense into the Ministry of Defense and Aviation in 1952 and slightly strengthened its staff and the quality of its reporting to the newly created Council of Ministers.[25]

As a result, the U.S. advisory team was able to make progress in several key areas. A military academy was established at Riyadh, and Saudi Arabia's two main training bases were reorganized and expanded. Saudi Arabia's force expansion plans, however, ran into serious problems. In 1952 the U.S. and Saudi Arabia set a goal of creating a force of five regimental combat teams, including modern infantry, engineer, signal, artillery, and technical elements. This force was supposed to be ready in 1956, but the lack of educated Saudi manpower, and initial Saudi insistence on relying on the less educated Najdis, delayed the achievement of this goal until 1962. Even then, it was made possible only by easing the restrictions on recruiting Hejazis and making them officers. The effort to create an air force was delayed even further and seems to have been allowed to lapse into training a few Saudi pilots in flying U.S. and British fighters.[26]

The Death of King Abd al-Aziz and Saudi-U.S Relations in the Early 1950s

Saudi-U.S military ties strengthened steadily during King Abd al-Aziz's final years, but these same years saw growing Arab nationalism and regional competition between the West and the USSR. As a result, King Abd al-Aziz's death on 9 November 1953 marked a watershed between the end of U.S. and British rivalry for influence over Saudi Arabia and the Gulf and its replacement by Western and Soviet competition to win influence over the forces of Arab nationalism and the increasingly more independent Gulf states.

Even before Abd al-Aziz's death, the U.S. and Saudi Arabia had been faced with the forces of change. From roughly 1950 onward, the kingdom's chaotic financing and failure to develop minimal social services led to increasing tension in the Eastern Province and some radicalization of the ARAMCO work force. The situation worsened steadily as overspending and waste gradually destroyed the nation's financial stability. By early 1950, military and police pay was four months in arrears, and even the security services began to be penetrated by Syrian and Iraqi nationalist groups. In March 1951 Saudi Arabia found it could not even finance $6 million for the French munitions plants it had purchased without pressuring the foreign banks in the kingdom. Out of its budget of roughly 500 million rials ($125 million), the country was spending 152 million rials on the king's court and on tribal subsidies. These expenditures were almost totally unplanned and uncontrolled. The kingdom was spending a similar amount on the armed forces, and some 90 million rials on debt service. A U.S. Point Four mission was sent to Saudi Arabia in 1951, and U.S. advice led to the formation of the

Saudi Arabian Monetary Agency in May 1952, but this only helped stabilize the nation's currency and did little to help its development.

By May 1953, these problems had begun to lead to serious unrest within the ARAMCO work force. The paternalistic character of ARAMCO had not extended to doing anything significant to modernize local conditions. The result was a formal petition protesting this situation, and when the workers' leaders were imprisoned in October, the workers attacked company and U.S. Air Force (USAF) vehicles in Dhahran. Most of ARAMCO's 19,000 workers then went out on strike, and a viable compromise between the company and the workers was not reached until November.[27]

These pressures led the king to give Crown Prince Saud and Prince Faisal increased powers in March 1953;[28] he made Saud commander-in-chief of the armed forces in August. However, Saud had no real authority until he was fully confirmed as the equivalent of prime minister on 10 October 1953. As a result, Saudi Arabia was weakly governed and experiencing serious internal problems when King Abd al-Aziz died in late 1953. Although the succession passed smoothly to Prince Saud on 9 November, it created new problems. Prince Saud was not a strong administrator and tended to be erratic and arbitrary in making major policy decisions. As a result, Prince Faisal was appointed Crown Prince, prime minister, and head of the Council of Ministers. This laid the groundwork for an almost inevitable rivalry between the two brothers and a split within the rest of the royal family.[29]

The royal family's pessimism about the new king proved justified. King Saud proved to be only slightly better able to administer a modern state than his father. Although his intentions were good, and he began with a competent Council of Ministers and made some useful administrative reforms in early 1954,[30] King Saud could not bring the kingdom's finances under control. He also failed to create any kind of civilian or military development plan. He did embark on a major building effort and created modern ministry buildings, schools, and a university. Each effort, however, was "layered" on the others, and although the kingdom's oil revenues rose from $56.7 million in 1950 to $234.8 million in 1954, King Saud continued to treat them as personal funds.[31]

These projects and the country's growing wealth led to an influx of experts, teachers, and commerical firms from the Levant and to increased contact between the newly educated Saudis and the currents of Arab nationalism. They also led to an effort by the Syrian National Socialist party to establish cells to overthrow the Saudi government—the first of a long series of outside attempts to "radicalize" Saudi Arabia. While the Syrian effort was not successful, and those involved were expelled from Saudi Arabia in the spring of 1955, the Saudis now had reason to fear any kind of relationship with the West that might give the impression of sacrificing Saudi Arabia's independence as an Arab state.

The situation deteriorated further because the long-standing restrictions Abd al-Aziz had placed on royal family participation in business died with him, and the corruption and profiteering in awarding and managing government contracts grew rapdily. The nation succeeded in spending even faster than its oil earnings could rise, and it failed to co-opt its merchant class, small educated elite, and newly trained army officers into the government. The king's personal household became increasingly corrupt, and serious irregularities began to take place in military pay and contracts.

These problems led to radical nationalist and Marxist penetration of the armed forces. Although King Saud tilted increasingly toward Nasser, whom he had visited in the spring of 1954, he began to lose the support of the army. The Saudi regime attempted to counter some of these pressures by agreeing to create a "unified command" with Egypt on 11 June 1954.

The king also capitalized on Saudi Arabia's new oil wealth to "expel" the U.S. Point Four economic aid mission in August on the grounds that the $6.4 million the U.S. was giving in technical aid was too small relative to what the U.S. was giving Israel.[32] This step had little practical effect since Saudi Arabia no longer needed the mission's money and generally ignored its advice. At the same time, however, King Saud allowed the U.S. to continue using the base at Dhahran, announced that he had refused Soviet offers of modern arms in August 1955, and purchased 18 tanks from the U.S. under the Dhahran Agreement of 1951. For all his rhetoric, King Saud maintained Saudi Arabia's reliance on the U.S. to help to modernize its military forces. By the end of 1955, this had led to U.S. plans to give Saudi Arabia a squadron of F-86 jet fighters, to equip one mechanized brigade with medium tanks, and to provide light tanks to improve the firepower of Saudi Arabia's remaining infantry brigades.

Neither expelling the Point Four mission nor provoking new border tensions with Britain did much, however, to win the support of the Saudi military. A minor mutiny took place in 1955, and an officer had to be executed. Communist-front literature was found circulating among police and army units in Al Hasa in early 1955,[33] and the army became steadily more politically insecure. King Saud then attempted to solve his internal political problems, and to strengthen his political hand with Britain, by bringing in a large cadre of additional pro-Nasser Egyptian military advisers. In January 1955 a 200-man Egyptian advisory team arrived in Saudi Arabia,[34] and Saudi Arabia began to send students, officers, and NCOs to Egypt for training. King Saud also provided Nasser with funds and propaganda support, joined him in rejecting the Baghdad Pact, cooperated in sponsoring a revolt against the British-backed regime in Oman, and turned the arbitration with Britain over Saudi Arabia's border claims into a significant confrontation.

A side result of these political shifts was that Nasser's "advisers" added a combination of "old Turkish" and "current Egyptian" bureaucracy to Saudi Arabia's existing administrative problem of referring all major decisions to the top. This heritage is still a cause of inefficiency in Saudi administration and defense management. King Saud's tilt toward Egypt did not, however, prevent another coup attempt by a group of army officers in Taif, or talk of other plots, including assassination attempts.[35] It also did nothing to prevent Britain from easily expelling Saudi Arabia's small forces from the Buraimi Oasis in October 1955.

The king's tilt also made Saudi military relations with the U.S. increasingly complex as Nasser's military buildup against Israel increased the political tension in the region, leading to serious fighting in the Gaza in August. This fighting forced Saudi Arabia to join with Syria and Egypt in signing a "defensive alliance" in October 1955. This, in turn, increased protests by U.S. pro-Israeli groups against U.S. plans to sell Saudi Arabia its first 18 U.S. tanks. The U.S. State Department responded by putting a temporary embargo on the sale, and Saudi Arabia was confronted with the prospect of being denied modern arms. If this embargo had continued, it could well have discredited the royal family in the eyes of the armed forces for relying too much on the U.S. Fortunately for Saudi Arabia and the U.S., President Eisenhower became convinced that Saudi-U.S. ties were vital to the U.S. and did not threaten Israel. Accordingly, although a new outbreak of fighting between Israel and Syria led to a U.S. embargo on arms sales to Israel and the Arab states on 17 February 1956, the U.S. lifted the embargo on tank sales to Saudi Arabia the next day.

The president's decision was particularly important, because King Saud found that placating Nasser simply made Saudi Arabia's internal security problems worse. Following Egyptian advice, Saudi Arabia welcomed a delegation from the People's Republic of China (PRC) and sent two princes to Moscow to discuss arms purchases in December 1955. During 1955, however, it became clear that some of the efforts to subvert the Saudi military had had at least tacit Egyptian backing. This discovery was followed by a three-day pro-Nasser strike by ARAMCO employees in early 1956, which Saud bin Jiluwi, the governor of the Eastern Province, put down by arresting 200 and publicly flogging 3 leaders to death.[36] This, if anything, made things worse. Nasser visited Saudi Arabia in September following his nationalization of the Suez Canal in July in order to persuade King Saud to embargo oil to the West. Nasser's appearance in Dammam proved so popular that it triggered the first mass political demonstration in Saudi Arabia's history.

King Saud responded by strengthening his bodyguard, building up a Royal Guard regiment of loyal tribal troops, and reviving an army of some 20,000–30,000 men, which was later called the National Guard. This army drew its manpower only from the tribes and was composed half of regular security troops (Firqa) and half of Bedouin irregulars (Liwa). The uniform of this force—the traditional Saudi robes—led to its being named the "White Army." Although it has since adopted regular uniforms, the guardsmen still wear the red-checked headdress of the traditional Bedouin warrior.[37]

King Saud continued to publicly back Nasser because the political pressures in the Arab world left Saudi Arabia little other choice. Like King Hussein, who had been forced to expel Glubb Pasha in March 1956, King Saud could not break with Nasser as long as the U.S., France, and the UK seemed united in support of Israel. As a result, Saudi Arabia refused to join in U.S. collective security initiatives like the Baghdad Pact and backed Nasser against the British, Israeli, and French invasion in October and November 1956. Saud even briefly embargoed oil shipments to the West.[38] Saudi Arabia did not, however, participate in the 1956 fighting between Israel and Egypt, although it did send token troops and military aid to Jordan. While Saudi Arabia signed a 10-year defense pact in Cairo on 18 January 1957, it limited its aid to providing a subsidy to Jordan and effectively distanced itself from the radical regime in Syria.

Saudi-U.S. Differences over the Need for Formal Collective Security Arrangements

While many of the problems in Saudi-U.S. military relations during this period can be traced back to problems within the Saudi government, it is important to note that the Saudi rejection of U.S. collective security initiatives was more than an effort to win support or tolerance from Nasser; it was partly a reaction to the Saudi fear that the Baghdad Pact would do far more to secure Britain's interests in the Middle East than to oppose Arab radicalism and Soviet influence. The Saudis were concerned that the pact was little more than an effort to maintain Britain as the dominant colonial power in the Gulf and that it would lead to a continued British presence in Aden and the South Arabian Protectorates. They were also afraid that it would mean the permanent loss of the key strategic and oil-exploration areas Saudi Arabia claimed on the borders of Qatar, the Trucial States, and Oman. Further, the Saudis feared that such arrangements would deprive the Arab nations that joined the Baghdad Pact of their legitimacy as independent Arab nations and make them the political targets of both moderate and radical Arab nationalists.[39]

Saudi refusal to support the Baghdad Pact thus reflected a difference between U.S. and Saudi policy that has been a continuing problem in Saudi-U.S. military relations. While the U.S. sought formal collective security arrangements, the Saudis preferred arrangements that relied on tacit guarantees of over-the-horizon protection from the U.S. that did not involve Saudi Arabia in superpower confrontations or arrangements that limited its regional diplomatic flexibility. Although the Saudis did not articulate their viewpoint in detail and took some time to rationalize their position, they reached conclusions that still govern Saudi policy. They concluded that Saudi Arabia's internal security was best served by (1) maintaining its own internal security without external aid; (2) avoiding any formal pacts or treaties with the West that make Saudi Arabia seem to be a U.S. client in an area where its powerful neighbors had to fight for their independence from Western colonialism and regarded any such ties as a fundamental violation of Arab nationalism; (3) building up Saudi military forces, predominantly with U.S. military support, so that it can deter any threat other than the largest possible outside attack by a neighbor or an outright Soviet attack; (4) avoiding any formal U.S. military presence or base in Saudi Arabia; and (5) relying on the U.S. to provide an ultimate security guarantee by deploying military power from outside Saudi Arabia in the event of a threat such as a Soviet invasion.

While the risks to Saudi security inherent in the wrong kind of ties to the West were as difficult for most Americans to understand in 1954–1956 as they are now, the wisdom of the Saudi position was supported by the events that followed. The complex British-Iraqi relations that led to the signature of the Baghdad Pact on 24 February 1955 resulted in the steady alienation of the Iraqi armed forces from the Hashemite dynasty and contributed to its overthrow in 1958. Similar problems occurred in Syria because of CIA efforts to overthrow a nationalist Syrian regime and in Egypt because of the CIA's sponsorship of Nasser in the hope he would be a strong anti-Soviet leader.[40] It became apparent during the mid-1950s that an Arab regime could survive only by paying as much attention to the internal impact of Arab nationalism as to any external threat.

Saudi Realignment with the U.S.

The radical and nationalist forces in the region in the mid-1950s might have forced Saudi Arabia into Nasser's camp and led to the eventual collapse of the Saudi regime if President Eisenhower had not persevered in trying to strengthen U.S. ties with Saudi Arabia and had not acted decisively following the Suez and Sinai invasions. As a result of decisions made in the White House, the U.S. continued to aid Saudi Arabia in its military modernization effort, although Saudi Arabia briefly restricted its renewal of the U.S. right to use Dhahran to a month-to-month basis after the 1951 Dhahran Agreement expired in June 1956.

This U.S. aid was essential to preserving U.S. ties to Saudi Arabia during a flow of events that included Nasser's nationalization of the Suez Canal, the French and British invasion of Egypt, and Israel's attack on Egypt and conquest of the Sinai. Equally important, President Eisenhower put sufficient pressure on France and Britain to force them to withdraw from Egypt on 22 December 1956. This action gave the U.S. new acceptability in the Arab world, which was reinforced by the announcement of the Eisenhower Doctrine on 1 January 1957 and by a speech by the president on 5 January that signaled that King Saud would be able to get arms from the U.S. without turning to the Soviet bloc.[41]

President Eisenhower and Secretary of State John Foster Dulles invited King Saud to visit Washington in February 1957. Although the king's visit was initially marred by anti-Saudi demonstrations in New York, the president helped make up for this by greeting King Saud at the airport—the first time he had so greeted any head of state. King Saud was also given firm assurances that the U.S. would provide Saudi Arabia with military support and would pressure Israel to withdraw from the Sinai in March. Eisenhower and Dulles also encouraged King Saud to begin a rapprochement with King Faisal of Iraq and later King Hussein of Jordan.[42]

The visit was so positive that King Saud stopped in Cairo on his way back from Washington and made a major effort to persuade President Nasser to break with the Soviets and to restore his ties with the U.S. The king's effort produced a hostile response from Nasser and eventually helped to lead Nasser to an open break with King Saud and to a series of Egyptian attacks on the legitimacy and Arab character of the Saudi government that did not diminish until 1967.

King Saud's and King Hussein's post-Suez tilt back toward the United States led Nasserite elements in Saudi Arabia and Jordan to back assassination and coup attempts against both leaders. The first attempt was made on King Hussein in April 1957, and King Saud responded by sending security officers and large amounts of funds. The coup attempt in Saudi Arabia was discovered later that month, when arms and ammunition were found stockpiled in Dhahran and Riyadh. The discovery led to mass arrests and deportations of pro-Nasser Palestinians and Egyptians and the arrests of some Saudis. The resulting interrogations traced some of the arms uncovered during the arrests to an assassination plot sponsored by the Egyptian military attaché in Jiddah, Colonel Ali Kashabah.[43] The Egyptians attempted to maintain their ties to Saudi Arabia in spite of these discoveries. President Shukri Kuwatli of Syria, Anwar Sadat, and Abdul Latif Bagouri, the Egyptian minister of labor, quickly flew to Riyadh in an effort to assure King Saud that Nasser had not been personally involved. However, this mission did not heal the breach. The Egyptian advisory team in Saudi Arabia was cut to the vanishing point, and the crisis brought Saud and Nasser to the edge of a public split. When Syria attacked Saudi Arabia as a "tool of America" in late June, Saudi Arabia temporarily withdrew its ambassador from Syria.

King Saud's Washington visit also resulted in a major renewal of Saudi military relations with the U.S. After talks in which the Saudis originally requested $300 million in arms deliveries, the U.S. and Saudi Arabia reached an agreement on 2 April 1957, in which Saudi Arabia granted the U.S. a five-year free extension of its lease on Dhahran. The U.S. responded by granting a $180 million increase in economic and military loans and aid. A grant of $25 million was provided in 1958 under the Foreign Assistance Act, and the U.S. agreed to provide about $50 million in military assistance over the five-year period of the lease.

The U.S. also agreed to help double the size of the regular Saudi Army, from 15,000 to 30,000 men, and to provide delivery of Saudi Arabia's first major supplies of modern arms. As a result, the U.S. provided 58 M-41 light tanks, 55 M-47 medium tanks, modern artillery, and 12 F-86 Sabre jets to Saudi Arabia during 1956–1958. The U.S. supported Saudi efforts to create a modern navy and air force as independent services, and the delivery of the first Sabre jets to Saudi Arabia in 1957 was accompanied by an expanded U.S. military training team and was a first step in forming the close relations between the Royal Saudi Air Force and the USAF that have now continued for roughly a quarter century.[44]

The U.S. aid effort did not, however, eliminate several major deficiencies in the Saudi forces. The Saudis showed a reasonable ability to operate the U.S. military equipment as it was delivered, but Saudi Arabia had to rely heavily on U.S. maintenance and logistical support. In addition, Saudi Arabia could deploy its regular forces only near its main cities, and it failed to develop anything approaching an effective modern command structure. It also had to continue to rely on the "White Army" for its internal security from the regular army.

The Saudi defense effort was further weakened by growing differences between King Saud and Crown Prince Faisal. King Saud used defense as one of his main power bases in strengthening his political position, and he appointed his sons to key positions: Fahd and Muhammid served as ministers of defense, Saud served as commander of the National Guard, and Bandar and Mansour served as commanders of the Royal Guard. This cut the key elements of the Saudi defense effort off from Prince Faisal's efforts at fiscal and administrative reform and gave them ineffective and relatively junior leadership.[45] King Saud also used defense funds as a source of royal patronage and political favor-giving. Senior positions and defense contracts were often awarded purely to consolidate King Saud's political position or strengthen his hand against Faisal.[46] As a result, few efforts were made to improve Saudi budgeting and administration; these were left almost solely to Saud's remaining foreign advisers. Major gaps remained in the effort to make Saudi Arabia's military forces effective.

The Creation of the United Arab Republic and the Fall of the Hashemite Dynasty in Iraq

At the same time, events outside Saudi Arabia steadily increased its need for modern military forces. A complex combination of internal political events in Syria, efforts by the CIA to trigger a coup d'etat by pro-Western elements in Syria, and efforts by Iraq and British intelligence to either create a friendly Syrian regime or absorb Syria into Iraq led to a major crisis in 1957.[47] Syria ejected the U.S. intelligence officers in Syria, turned to Egypt and the USSR for support, and became involved in major crises with Jordan and Turkey. By late 1957, Syria had become effectively isolated from all its neighbors except Egypt.

At the same time, Nasser reacted to the efforts by King Saud, King Faisal of Iraq, and King Hussein of Jordan to create a conservative "King's Alliance" by supporting an Arab "revolution" that called for the destruction of the conservative regimes in the Arab world and the creation of a single Arab nation. He capitalized on his political victory in gaining control of the Suez Canal, and Israel's withdrawal from the Sinai, to increase his influence over most of the major nationalist movements in the Arab world.

These pressures pushed Egypt and Syria closer and closer together. On 1 February 1958 Nasser and Syrian President Shukri Kuwatli signed an agreement that created the United Arab Republic (UAR). This agreement gave Nasser and radical Arab nationalism a massive new momentum that threatened every traditional Arab regime. The unification agreement also presented Saudi Arabia with an immediate security problem. The aging imam of Yemen saw the UAR as an opportunity to gain Arab support and military aid in his long-standing efforts to gain control of the various British protectorates in Saudi Arabia. His son—who had been educated in Egypt—saw it as an opportunity to unite Yemen with the rest of the Arab world. As a result, Yemen joined with the UAR on 8 March 1958 to create the United Arab States. This opened Yemen to a massive influx of advisers and political activists from Egypt and Syria and led to military ties between Yemen and the USSR. It also resulted in a major Egyptian and Yemeni effort to support anti-British movements in the protectorates that met with almost immediate success.[48]

These events took Saudi Arabia by surprise at a time when Crown Prince Faisal had long been out of the country receiving medical treatment for a nonmalignant stomach tumor. As a result, King Saud lacked effective advice, and this lack had a major impact on Saudi Arabia's future. With Faisal absent, King Saud attempted to bribe Syria's security chief, Colonel Abdul Hamid Serraj, to carry out a coup d'etat that would lead to Syria's secession from the UAR. In the process, Serraj was given three checks totaling 1.9 million Syrian pounds as a deposit on a total payment of 20 million. Serraj accepted the funds purely to embarrass King Saud, and he made a public announcement of the bribe attempt on 5 March 1958. This announcement had explosive implications for Arab politics, and its impact was reinforced when copies of the checks were widely circulated in the Arab press.[49] Further, Serraj identified one of King Saud's fathers-in-law, Abass Ibrahim, as the Saudi go-between in the plot. President Nasser followed with an open break with King Saud, and Cairo Radio began to call for the Saudi people to rise up and destroy the royal family.

The growing criticism of the king within the royal family and the upper echelons of Saudi society was reinforced by these events. King Saud's inability to manage, his lack of an organized budget, his overspending, and Saudi Arabia's increasing foreign debt[50] had reached the point of threatening the regime. As a result, the assassination plot led the king's brothers to demand that Prince Faisal be recalled as prime minister. Prince Abdullah acted as the principal spokesman for most of Abd al-Aziz's senior sons in demanding Crown Prince Faisal's recall, and King Saud had little choice. Faisal became head of government as prime minister on 24 March 1958, with full control over fiscal, domestic, and foreign affairs. He was able to reestablish relations with Nasser by late April, and Nasser even announced Faisal's appointment as a personal victory. It was at this point that Faisal also began to lay the groundwork for modernization of the armed forces.

Prince Faisal could not, however, eliminate the growing divisions between Saudi Arabia and Egypt, and he was rapidly confronted with a far worse crisis than the assassination fiasco. King Faisal of Iraq and his advisers made major efforts to reduce the strength of radical Arab nationalism during the course of 1957, but these efforts only exacerbated the internal problems created by Arab nationalism, anti-British sentiment, and the feeling of many Iraqi army officers that the Hashemites were an alien dynasty that had been forced on Iraq by the British. These problems came to a head when King Faisal announced a formal federation between Iraq and Jordan on 14 February 1958—largely in reaction to the creation of the UAR. The king's announcement catalyzed plans for a coup d'etat that elements of the Iraqi Army had been planning since the signing of the Baghdad Pact. On 14 July 1958, General Abdul Karim al-Qassim took advantage of movement orders from King Faisal to reinforce Jordan. He routed his troops through the capital, obtained ammunition from a fellow plotter, and led a bloody coup that resulted in the death of King Faisal, the Crown Prince, and Premier Nuri al-Said.[51]

This coup confronted a still weakened Saudi Arabia with the sudden creation of a radical Iraq and the transformation of the most powerful Arab state on the Gulf into a serious potential threat to Saudi interests. It also led to an Iraqi threat to invade Jordan that was a major factor in President Eisenhower's decision to send U.S. troops to Lebanon in July 1958. This decision was greeted with intense hostility throughout most of the Arab world, and although Egypt and Iraq showed little agreement over most issues in the months that followed, they both put significant pressure on Saudi Arabia to eliminate the U.S. military base at Dhahran.[52]

These problems were compounded by the ongoing conflict between King Saud and Crown Prince Faisal. Faisal's return in March 1958 had left King Saud in charge of the nation's defense establishment, the Royal Guard, and the Royal Household. Further, although Faisal was careful to make major increases in the pay of Saudi officers in the summer of 1959, his strict financial reforms alienated many tribal leaders and merchants. At the same time, Faisal's conservative, pro-Western policies alienated a number of Abd al-Aziz's sons who had been born in the mid-1920s to mid-1930s. These sons were called the "free princes"; they generally supported reform.

With the help of Gen. Said Abdullah Kurdi, the chief of Royal Intelligence, King Saud slowly built up a coalition with the free princes and with Prince Talal, their nominal leader. This gave King Saud the support of the more radical elements in the armed forces as well as in the "conservative" White Army and led to a renewed Saudi tilt toward Nasser and the more radical forces of Arab nationalism. In December 1960 King Saud capitalized on his new strength and Prince Faisal's illness to refuse to approve Faisal's new budget and to purge his supporters.[53] They were replaced with a mixture of Saud's sons and the free princes. He made his son Muhammid bin Saud the defense minister, Talal abd al-Aziz the finance minister, Badr the communications minister, Abdul Mushin abd al-Aziz the interior minister, and Fawwaz abd al-Aziz the chief of Diwan. Abdullah Taraki was made head of a new ministry for Petroleum and Mineral Resources, and Ibrahim Suwayl, a career diplomat, was made foreign minister.

The purge started a two-year period when Prince Faisal ceased to be foreign minister for virtually the only time in his adult life. More important, it removed Prince Faisal from his other sources of power and deprived the U.S. of its strongest support. It also gave power to a faction of the royal family that opposed any U.S. military presence in Saudi Arabia.[54]

The Dhahran Issue and the Break with the Free Princes

Oddly enough, however, it was the continued U.S. use of Dhahran that helped catalyze a break between King Saud and the free princes. Prince Talal—who had had to leave Saudi Arabia from 1955 to 1957 because of his Nasserite sympathies and association with the pro-Nasser officers involved in the coup attempt of 1955—pushed hard to end the U.S. presence in Dhahran.[55] As time went on, he also pushed hard for a "progressive" constitution and a council of government that would have sharply limited Saud's power and that of his sons. By August 1962, the resulting tensions had led to a split between Talal and King Saud, and Talal held a press conference in Beirut designed to force the king to support his views. He specifically mentioned the Dhahran issue as a key difference between them. King Saud responded by removing Talal from office, and he ousted the other leading free princes in September.

Given this background, it was fortunate that the Dhahran problem vanished over the next few years. Shifts in U.S. defense policy during the late 1950s and early 1960s eliminated the U.S. need to base a large portion of its strategic bomber force overseas. U.S. acquisition of intercontinental ballistic missiles (ICBMs) and submarine-launched ballistic missiles (SLBMs) reduced the need to base U.S. strategic forces in the forward area, and increases in Soviet bomber, medium range ballistic missile (MRBM), and intermediate range ballistic missile (IRBM) capabilities began to make such Strategic Air Command (SAC) bases increasingly vulnerable. As a result, the SAC force shifted increasingly to airborne refueling and to basing in the continental United States. After President Kennedy's election in 1960, his new secretary of defense, Robert S. McNamara, concluded that forward bases like Dhahran were not cost effective and rapidly phased out many of SAC's overseas facilities.

This change allowed the U.S. and Saudi Arabia to reach an agreement to end U.S. use of the base at Dhahran without seriously damaging Saudi-U.S. relations. Saudi Arabia gave the U.S. formal notice that it would not renew the basing agreement on 16 March 1961, and the U.S. "ceased" military operations at Dhahran on 16 April 1962.[56] This eliminated Saudi Arabia's vulnerability to charges that it remained a "colonial" nation and gave it improved leverage in dealing with the other Arab states.

The North Yemen Civil War and the Return of Prince Faisal

The U.S. withdrawal also, however, left Saudi Arabia without significant military forces of its own to protect its security, and in less than six months, Saudi Arabia was confronted by a major external threat from Egypt. The awkward union between the ultraconservative imam of Yemen and Nasser, the radical Arab nationalist, collapsed when the imam came to feel he was not getting adequate Egyptian support in his efforts to take over the South Arabian Protectorates and that the Egyptian presence in Yemen was becoming a threat to his regime. When Syria broke with Egypt in September 1961, the imam concluded that Nasser had begun to lose his influence in the Arab world and announced Yemen's withdrawal from the UAR.[57] By this time, however, a large part of Yemen's government officials and senior officers had become covert supporters of either Nasser or other Arab radical movements. When the old imam died in September 1962, the commander of the Royal Guard, Brigadier Abdullah Sallal, launched a military coup against the heir. Sallal's coup succeeded to the extent that it gained control over the capital, Sana, and the southern tribes. The new imam, however, managed to escape the coup and rallied the conservative northern tribes, which were the traditional power base of the imamate.

On the advice of Anwar Sadat, among others, Nasser then decided to intervene in support of the new "Republican" regime. He sent in troops and combat aircraft, and by October 1962, a major civil war had started on Saudi Arabia's southeastern border and Egyptian troops were pouring into Yemen in a strength far superior to Saudi Arabia's total regular armed forces. Saudi Arabia also found itself isolated from the United States because of internal problems in Saudi Arabia and because President Kennedy had immediately recognized the Sallal regime in an effort to reduce or eliminate the Soviet military advisory presence in Yemen.[58]

Saudi Arabia was poorly prepared to deal with these developments. The continuing power struggle between King Saud and his brother, Crown Prince Faisal,[59] and between their respective supporters in the government and royal family, had deprived the royal family of its strongest and most capable leader. This struggle might have undercut Saudi rule if King Saud's weaknesses and other events had not restored Faisal to power. While King Saud paid lip service to U.S. pressure for reform, he remained unable to administer Saudi Arabia as a state.

As had been the case in the late 1950s, Saudi expenditures and borrowing got out of control, which forced the king to make overtures to Faisal even before the Yemeni civil war. When a new crisis arose over Saudi policy toward the Syrian split with Egypt, King Saud recalled Prince Faisal for policy discussion, and Faisal returned to Saudi Arabia in mid-October. As a result, when King Saud's health collapsed on 17 November 1961, Faisal was given control of the budget and the practical administration of the kingdom's day-to-day affairs. King Saud's health recovered after medical treatment in the U.S., and he returned to Saudi Arabia. On 15 March 1962 King Saud again reorganized his government and personally assumed the premiership. However, this time King Saud kept Prince Faisal on as foreign minister. He also forced the remaining free princes out of the government. The events that followed are unclear, but Prince Faisal then left the country, apparently partly for medical treatment and partly to hold discussions in the West.[60]

The Yemeni civil war thus broke out at a time when Saudi Arabia had been without unified or effective leadership for two years and when major gaps and weaknesses had developed in the armed forces. It also began at a time when Prince Faisal and other members of the royal family had become concerned that King Saud's erratic talk of reform, coupled with the growing administrative chaos in the country, was creating a climate in which Saudi Arabia might follow in the path of Iraq. These concerns reached a turning point when the coup attempt in Yemen was followed by the defection to Egypt of several of Saudi Arabia's small staff of trained pilots, along with their aircraft.[61] The first such defection occurred when a Saudi cargo plane with three crew members was assigned to fly cargo to the Yemeni Royalists at the Saudi border town of Najran and instead flew to Cairo, where the crew immediately became Egyptian Air Force officers. The next day, two more pilots defected on a training flight.

It became apparent that all the Saudi armed forces, except the White Army, had strong dissident or pro-Nasserite elements. The air force, in particular, had to be grounded, and some two dozen officers were dismissed. Even worse, when King Hussein of Jordan responded by sending a squadron of Hunter fighters to Taif and King Saud proposed that they bomb Sana, the commander-in-chief of the Jordanian Air

Force and two of his pilots defected. The r
had to be recalled to Jordan.[62]

This chain of events led Saudi notables and
royal family to force King Saud to return Prince
Faisal returned to Saudi Arabia on 17 October 196
cabinet. He purged the last of the pro-Nasser elem
government. He made Prince Khalid deputy prime
Fahd minister of the interior, and Prince Sultan minister
31 October and signed a military alliance with Jordan on 4
By 6 November, Faisal had issued a 10-point reform program,
the freeing of slaves, and had begun to bring the nation's financ
full control.[63]

Faisal also began to counter the Egyptian military buildup in Ye
He instituted a subsidy to the Yemeni Royalists of 11 million rials
month, plus additional payments to the tribes, and deployed elements
of the White Army to positions at Jizan and Najran near the border with Yemen. He announced Saudi Arabia's support for Imam Badr and provided him with light arms, bases in Saudi territory, and funds to help pay troops and the services of a small number of Western mercenaries.[64] He also arranged with Britain to provide the Royalists with arms and other support from MI-6.[65] At the same time, Faisal made a concerted effort to persuade President Kennedy, who was then attempting to win back Nasser with about $200 million in annual aid, to end his support of the new regime in Sana. This shift in U.S. policy became inevitable when Egypt attempted to suppress Saudi support of the rebels by bombing the Saudi villages near the staging bases the Yemeni Royalists were using in the vicinity of Najran.[66]

The Egyptian air raids were repeated in January 1963 and were followed by the Egyptian use of poison gas inside Yemen. Faisal appealed to the U.S. for military assistance, and Saudi Arabia quietly agreed to allow the U.S. to use Dhahran. The U.S. then launched an operation called "Hard Surface." In March 1963 the U.S. sent a detachment of eight F-100s and a small number of paratroops to Dhahran and conspicuously deployed a destroyer in the region. It followed up by sending Ambassador Ellsworth Bunker to try to negotiate a cease-fire between the Saudis and Egypt.

Faisal's Military Reforms of 1963

Although Faisal supported the attempt to reach a settlement with Nasser, he also gave high priority to reforming and modernizing the Saudi armed forces. His reorganization of the Council of Ministers in October 1962 placed internal security and the Saudi armed forces under two of his senior brothers: Prince Fahd ibn Abd al-Aziz Al Saud (eighth son, born 1921) was put in charge of internal security as minister of the interior, and Prince Sultan ibn Abd al-Aziz Al Saud (thirteenth son, born 1924) was made a strong minister of defense.[67] Faisal continued

6 January 1963. He acted
recruits, and he mobilized
nificant, he raised defense
414 million in 1963. He
nder of the White Army
law Kamal Adham head
nce) and of the general
endent internal security
-6, the Service de la
ge (SDECE), and the
sons from an effective
ity.
into Saudi Arabia's
Prince Sultan were
while Prince Abdullah was
mmari mother. However, Faisal's changes
ship structure that remained for 17 years and gave
tion of Saudi military forces a stability unequaled in any other
developing country in the world.[70]

Faisal also resumed military relations with the UK and France. The French again took over operation of Saudi Arabia's small munitions plants, and a British military team was sent to train the White Army, which was renamed the National Guard in 1963. The British took charge of an effort to resettle the remaining nomads and to create strong tribal centers or towns that would be loyal to the royal family. A special effort was made to strengthen the ties between the Guard and the traditionally loyal Shammar tribe.[71] Prince Faisal also established the Saudi Navy as a full military service.

However, Faisal's ability to fully implement his defense reforms was limited by his continuing struggle with King Saud. Faisal had the power to provide a structure through which the Saudi forces could eventually be modernized, but his reforms were only first steps in a long effort to create a modern Ministry of Defense. They also did not include any serious attempts at dealing with the internal social and regional problems affecting the growth and stability of the armed forces, which caused severe difficulties in the late 1960s.

Equally important, the Saudi armed forces remained equipped and organized at a level that hardly prepared them to deal with the Egyptian presence that was building up in Yemen. The Egyptians rapidly increased their forces to 36,000 men, equipped with Soviet tanks and first-line combat aircraft. The regular Saudi Army still had only about 18,000 men in 1962; another 18,000 men served full- and part-time in the National Guard.[72] Although King Saud had spent roughly one-third of the defense budget on arms, the Saudi Army had no real capability for armored warfare, and only the National Guard was both loyal and combat effective.

Saudi Arabia's military bases consisted largely of small facilities located near major commercial centers, as well as the former U.S. airfield at Dhahran near the Gulf Coast. Saudi Arabia had only four operational military air bases and five small National Guard casernes.[73] It had no major naval facilities and no casernes near key border areas. Above all, it had no real air defense capability, since its 12 short-legged F-86 fighters and its obsolete Vampires had only a negligible combat air patrol (CAP) capability over even a limited part of the country, and many were no longer operational.

These deficiencies might not have mattered if the various Saudi efforts to negotiate a cease-fire with Egypt had been successful, but each series of negotiations failed. The Egyptian military presence in North Yemen grew from 36,000 men in March 1963, to 60,000 men in mid-1964, and to 70–80,000 men in the mid-1960s. Egyptian Il-28 bombers hit Jizan again in March and caused its population to flee the city. Egypt followed with air attacks on Abh Najran and Khamis Mushayt.[74] At the same time, the Yemeni civil war became the most intense and bloody war in modern Arab history, eventually killing more Arabs than any of the Arab-Israeli wars.[75]

The Egyptian military buildup and air raids also led President Kennedy to give Prince Faisal his full support. In spite of Operation Hard Surface, Kennedy had kept his options open. Both the president and his advisers deeply distrusted King Saud, had the feeling that Nasser would inevitably triumph, and distrusted the British and French personnel in charge of the operations in Yemen. It was only after the Egyptian buildup and bombings that Kennedy agreed to highly visible U.S. fighter flights over Riyadh and Jiddah and gave Nasser a strong warning against future raids.

The Departure of King Saud

Meanwhile, the struggle between Saud and Faisal reached its final stage, contributing to Saudi Arabia's problems with Egypt. King Saud had been in Switzerland and Austria for medical treatment from March to mid-September 1963, but he returned to the country determined to rule. He discovered, however, that Faisal had posted the tank and infantry units in his Royal Guard to the North Yemeni border area near Najran. Saud reacted by trying to block Faisal's budget, and he and his sons attempted to subvert the key tribes, including the Harb, Shammar, and Otaiba. He also reestablished contacts with Talal and the other free princes, and loose links to Nasser. When these efforts failed to weaken Faisal, King Saud deployed 800 men from the remaining portion of his Royal Guard to guard his palace at Nasariya.

By this time, however, Faisal had built an unbeatable coalition with the princes who favored stability and with several key princes with strong ties to the major Saudi tribes and regional cities. These included Prince Khalid (the present king, and fifth son, born 1912), Prince

Muhammed (the fourth son, born 1910), and Princes Fahd, Abdullah, and Sultan. Accordingly, Faisal made no efforts to compromise. He deployed National Guard units near Saud's palace and effectively checkmated the king. Although Faisal resisted Abdullah's urging to oust Saud by force, he denied Saud any power. The events from January to March 1964 remain somewhat obscure, but Faisal seems to have further isolated Saud by allowing Talal and the other free princes, who had been alienated by Nasser's propaganda and bombing attacks, to return to Saudi Arabia. Saud then came out of his palace and agreed to give Faisal power if Saud could continue to represent the royal family as head of state and act as a symbol of its unity. Faisal agreed to give him this status but excluded him from key negotiations with Nasser and Sadat. King Saud attempted to counter by dealing separately with Egypt at the Arab summit in the spring of 1964. He then demanded a restoration of his powers when he returned to Saudi Arabia on 13 March 1964. He also asked that at least two of his sons be placed on the Council of Ministers and threatened to have his Royal Guard fire its artillery against Faisal's villa.

This was the last straw. Faisal had Abdullah mobilize the National Guard. Although Saud had spent some $30–40 million attempting to bribe the tribes over the preceding six months, none rallied to his side, and the commander of the Royal Guard, Maj. Gen. Othman, swore allegiance to Faisal on 26 March 1964. Prince Faisal's supporters then arrested Saud's leading palace staff, including Saud's son Mansour, who was still titular chief of the Royal Guard and the last Saud supporter with any control over military force.[76] The leading princes, Council of Ministers, and *ulema* met on 28 March 1964, confirmed Faisal's powers, and cut King Saud's annual allowance in half, to roughly $40 million. Faisal then fully consolidated his control over the military and integrated the Royal Guard into the army, which placed it under the control of Prince Sultan. This still did not stop King Saud, who refused to abdicate and continued his informal contacts with Nasser. As a result, Faisal deposed Saud on 2 November 1964. Saud then went into exile in Cairo, where he made a long series of anti-Faisal statements and broadcasts.[77]

Saud's removal from power left the royal family and the country united around a strong leader for the first time since King Abd al-Aziz's death. It also coincided with a limited rapprochment between Saudi Arabia and Egypt. In spite of Saud's maneuvering and contacts with Nasser, Faisal had made considerable progress in reaching agreement with Nasser at the Arab summit meeting. This led Faisal to request U.S. withdrawal of Operation Hard Surface after an argument with the Kennedy administration over the terms of disengagement in North Yemen. Faisal's talks with Sadat and other Egyptians in March 1963 also helped bring the two countries closer together. In July 1964 Saudi Arabia reestablished relations with Egypt, and it made a major effort to use the September 1964 Arab summit to end the Yemeni civil war.

Notes

1. As late as 1974, 70% of all Saudi males over the age of 10 were estimated to be illiterate. In 1981 the CIA estimated overall literacy as 15–25%. See CIA GS-WF-81-001 (U), 1981, p. 173.

2. The population of Saudi Arabia remains a highly sensitive issue. The first Saudi census by the Central Statistics Department was conducted in 1962–1963 and estimated a native population of 3.3. million. It was suppressed. The Central Planning Organisation estimated 5.9 million Saudis and 790,000 foreigners in 1972, but it did not base this estimate on an actual count. The Second Five Year Plan was based on a guideline figure of 6.2 million, but following its publication, the government announced the ridiculously precise figure of 7,012,642. Later work by British experts estimated 4.2 million Saudis and 1.5 million foreigners as of 1974. These same experts estimated the total work forces as 1,799,900, of which 1,026,500 were Saudis and 773,400 were foreigners. Some 530,700 of the work force were estimated to be in agriculture and fishing, and some 277,100 in the civil service, police, and armed forces.

Estimates in 1981 were equally speculative. The Third Five Year Plan figures were highly political, and the CIA and IISS projections of a total population of 10,112,000, with a 5.6% current growth rate, seem to be little more than an acceptance of these heavily politicized Saudi estimates. These same sources indicate that the Saudi population is now 90% Arab and 10% Afro-Asian, that literacy is 15–25%, and that the labor force is one-third of the population and half expatriate. It is estimated that 44% of the labor force is in commerce, 28% in agriculture, 21% in construction, 4% in industry, and 3% in oil and mining. The *Economist*, which also seems to accept Saudi figures uncritically, indicates that the foreign labor force consists of 800,000 Yemenis, 400,000 Filipinos, 250,000 Palestinians, 250,000 Koreans, 200,000 Pakistanis, 150,000 Indians, 100,000 Thais, 200,000 Syrians and Lebanese, 45,000 Americans, and 40,000 Britons. These estimates of total population must be at least 2 million too high, and the figures for the Yemeni component of the foreign work force must be at least 50% too low. It is interesting to note that the somewhat less political projections in the Second Five Year Plan predicted a native work force of 1.5 million for 1980, with 1.47 million males and 48,000 females and an average growth rate of 3.4%. This would indicate a native population in 1981 at about 4.8 million. The plan projected the total foreign work force for 1980 as 813,000, growing at 21% annually. This would give Saudi Arabia a total population in 1981 of no more than 6.5 million. See David Holden and Richard Johns, *The House of Saud* (London: Sidgwick and Jackson, 1981), pp. 394–395; Saudi Arabia, *Saudi Arabia Five-Year Plan, 1975–1980* (Riyadh: Central Planning Organisation, 1975), p. 60; "A Survey of Saudi Arabia," *Economist*, 13 February 1982, p. 33; Adeed Dawisha, *Saudi Arabia's Search for Security*, Adelphi Paper no. 158 (London: International Institute for Strategic Studies, Winter 1979–1980); and CIA, *The World Factbook*, CIA GS WF 81-001 (Washington, D.C., 1981).

3. This issue has been complicated by Israeli occupation of the small islands of Sanafir and Tiran at the entrance of the Gulf of Aqaba. These islands were originally leased to Nasser, so that he could fortify them, during King Saud's efforts to work out a modus vivendi with Nasser. Nasser later seized the islands and claimed sovereignty, only to have Israel occupy them in June 1967. Originally, Israel planned to return them to Saudi Arabia to weaken the Egyptian threat

to its Red Sea lines of communication, but with the Camp David accords, it shifted its position to give them to Egypt as part of the return of the Sinai.

4. For an excellent discussion of many of these events, see Christine Moss Helms, *The Cohesion of Saudi Arabia* (Baltimore: Johns Hopkins University Press, 1981). Also see R. Bayly Winder, *Saudi Arabia in the Nineteenth Century* (London: Macmillan, 1965); the various books and articles of Sir John Glubb and Saint-John Philby; and Holden and Johns, *House of Saud.* Jose Arnold (*Golden Pots and Swords and Pans* [London: Gollancz, 1964]) and Robert Lacey (*The Kingdom* [London: Hutchinson & Co., 1981]) provide interesting popular background and gossip. John Sabin's *Armies in the Sand* (New York: Thames and Hudson, 1981) provides a good description of the earlier Saud conquest of Arabia in the 1800s.

5. King Abd al-Aziz Ibn Saud, often referred to in the West as "Ibn Saud," was born in 1880. He ruled as head of the Saud family from 1902 to his death in 1953.

6. The USSR attempted to split Saudi Arabia away from the West during this period and was one of the first countries to recognize Saudi Arabia. However, several major errors in Soviet trade policy and its conspicuous atheism led to irreconcilable differences. Although both nations formally have had diplomatic relations since 1927, no actual diplomatic relations have taken place since 1938.

7. See George Lenczowski, *The Middle East in World Affairs* (Ithaca, N.Y.: Cornell University Press, 1980), pp. 579–580; K. S. Twitchell, *Saudia Arabia* (Princeton, N.J.: Princeton University Press, 1947), p. 151; M. Childs "All the King's Oil," *Colliers*, 18 August 1945; Harvey O'Connor, *World Crisis in Oil* (London, 1962); Gabriel Kolko, *The Politics of War* (London, 1969), pp. 294–313; and Fred Halliday's pro-Marxist *Arabia Without Sultans* (London: Pelican Books, 1979), pp. 47–81.

8. Sources differ on the extent to which King Abd al-Aziz made overtures to Nazi Germany. The documentation written by his staff reflects their interest in German promises to give the Arab states full independence and remove the Jews from Palestine. The king, however, personally backed Britain. For summaries of the conflicting view of this era see Holden and Johns, *House of Saud*, pp. 123–127; and Lacey, *The Kingdom*, pp. 256–262.

9. Lenczowski, *Middle East in World Affairs*, pp. 584–586.

10. Ibid., p. 584; Holden and Johns, *House of Saud*, pp. 127–129; Lacey, *The Kingdom*, pp. 262–265.

11. ARAMCO, *Facts and Figures*, 1980 (Dammam: Al-Mutawa Press, 1981). The U.S. Navy was Saudi's principal customer at the end of the war.

12. Roosevelt pledged that "no decision would be taken with respect to the basic situation in that country without full consultation with both Arabs and Jews." *Department of State Bulletin*, 23 October 1945, p. 623. President Truman repeated this pledge on several occasions. See the *New York Times*, 18 May 1945; 16 October 1946. For a fuller summary discussion see Holden and Johns, *House of Saud*, pp. 133–138, 142–145.

13. Holden and Johns, *House of Saud*, p. 104.

14. Lacey, *The Kingdom*, p. 257.

15. Holden and Johns, *House of Saud*, p. 267.

16. Iraq called for a Saudi oil embargo only to have the king respond that without a $30 million payment, the kingdom would go bankrupt. Ibid., p. 289.

17. The ministry was titularly formed in 1940 but had nothing approaching a modern organization. The top questions in the Saudi defense establishment

have always been held by members of the royal family. Since its creation in 1940, the Ministry of Defense has had five ministers—three sons and two grandsons of Abd al-Aziz. The Ministry of the Interior, which has handled a number of key intelligence and internal security functions since its founding in 1954, has had six ministers—three sons and three grandsons of Abd al-Aziz. The commanders of the National Guard since 1958 have included two grandsons and one son of Abd al-Aziz. Princes have also filled the various deputy minister positions in the national security structure and headed the other intelligence branches. The key governors have similarly been members of the royal family, and some have earlier been military officers and defense officials.

18. Halliday, *Arabia Without Sultans*, pp. 53–55. J. C. Hurewitz, *Middle East Politics: The Military Dimension* (New York: Praeger Publishers, 1969), pp. 250–251.

19. He held this appointment until his death in 1951.

20. Holden and Johns, *House of Saud*, p. 160; Lacey, *The Kingdom*, p. 279.

21. Otto von Pikva, *Armies of the Middle East* (New York: Mayflower Books, 1979), p. 130.

22. Saudi Arabia notified the U.K. of its claims to roughly 50,000 square miles of the territory of Qatar, Abu Dhabi, and Musat on 14 October 1949. The most-publicized border dispute that resulted was the Buraimi Oasis dispute, largely because this was the major populated area in question. The real issue, however, was oil, and the oasis dispute symbolized a broad Saudi-U.S versus Anglo–Trucial State struggle for oil concession areas. See Chapters 11 and 14.

23. Richard F. Nyrop, *Area Handbook for Saudia Arabia*, Foreign Area Handbook Series (Washington, D.C.: American University, 1977), p. 335.

24. Holden and Johns, *House of Saud*, pp. 157–158; Halliday, *Arabia Without Sultans*, pp. 58–59.

25. Nyrop, *Saudia Arabia*, p. 311; Alvin J. Cottrell, Robert J. Hanks, and Frank T. Bray, "Military Affairs in the Persian Gulf," in Alvin J. Cottrell, ed., *The Persian Gulf States* (Baltimore: Johns Hopkins University Press, 1980), p. 140.

26. Hurewitz, *Middle East Politics*, p. 251.

27. Holden and Johns, *House of Saud*, pp. 158–170.

28. He had been declared Crown Prince as early as 1933.

29. King Saud was born in 1902 and was the son of King Abd al-Aziz's first wife, Wada bint Hazzam. Prince Faisal was born in 1906, and was the King's son by his second wife, Tarfa bint al-Shaikh. At the time he became king, Saud had 53 sons and daughters. He was to have over 165 grandsons, which added another echelon of rivalry to the struggle among the senior princes.

30. To put this in perspective, oil revenues were $2 million in 1939, $8–10 million in 1945, $56.7 million in 1950, about $90 million in 1951, $234.8 million in 1955, and over $250 million in 1956. The steady increases in Saudi oil production gave Saudi Arabia the revenues to make major new investments and expenditures. Saudi crude oil production reached 21 million barrels in 1944, 60 million in 1946, 90 million in 1947, 143 million in 1948, 174 million in 1949, 200 million in 1950, 278 million in 1951, 302 million in 1952, 308 million in 1953, 348 million in 1954, 352 million in 1955, and 361 million in 1956. ARAMCO; Lenczowski, *Middle East in World Affairs*, p. 589.

31. Holden and Johns, *House of Saud*, p. 180; Hurewitz, *Middle East Politics*, pp. 248–249.

32. Halliday, *Arabia Without Sultans*, p. 53.

33. Holden and Johns, *House of Saud*, p. 183.

34. Lacey, *The Kingdom*, p. 311.

35. Ibid., pp. 312–313.

36. Ibid., p. 314; Arnold, *Golden Pots*, p. 206.

37. The White Army was not renamed the National Guard (al-Haras al-Watani) until 1963, when Faisal brought a British military mission back to Saudi Arabia. Halliday, *Arabia Without Sultans*, p. 59.

38. The embargo was largely symbolic. The West was not sufficiently dependent on Saudi oil for the embargo to have a serious effect on the West. It did, however, cost King Saud about 40% of his national revenues at a time when he was deeply in debt. According to some reports, Nasser arranged to blow up Iraq's pipelines when it was slow to follow Egypt's lead, and this may have been a factor in King Saud's decision to impose the embargo. Lacey, *The Kingdom*, pp. 315–316.

39. Ironically, the U.S. itself never formally joined the Baghdad Pact and its successor, CENTO. The U.S. did, however, accept observer status and provided the bulk of the funds for the pact's economic activities, including microwave communications and the rail and road links between Iran and Turkey. It was the U.S. military assistance programs to Iran, Iraq, Turkey, and Pakistan that caused them to join the pact; the U.S. accepted full membership in the pact's economic, military, and countersubversive committees; and a U.S. general headed the pact's Combined Military Planning Staff.

40. For background on these events see Wilbur Crane Eveland, *Ropes of Sand: America's Failure in the Middle East* (New York: W. W. Norton, 1980), especially pp. 153–247.

41. Halliday, *Arabia Without Sultans*, pp. 53–54.

42. Lenczowski, *Middle East Politics*, pp. 287–289. King Saud met with key Iraqi officials while he was in Washington in early 1957. This led to a rapproachment by the Sauds and Hashemites against Nasser. Saudi Arabia provided troops to help put down a pro-Jordan coup in April 1957, and King Saud visited Baghdad in May 1957. Close talks with Iraq and Jordan followed.

43. Holden and Johns, *House of Saud*, pp. 194–196; Lacey, *The Kingdom*, pp. 317–318; Dawisha, *Saudi Arabia's Search for Security*, p. 2.

44. Nyrop, *Saudia Arabia,* p. 334. The U.S. virtually provided "turnkey" packages. There was essentially no defense planning effort by Saudi officials in developing these arms packages. For background see Lacey, *The Kingdom*, pp. 315–316; Holden and Johns, *House of Saud*, pp. 191–195; and Halliday, *Arabia Without Sultans*, pp. 53–55.

45. Some differences exist over the competence of King Saud's sons in these positions. Muhammed is sometimes regarded as a relatively strong figure, but he and Saud's other sons are not credited with being good administrators or with playing a major role in planning the Saudi modernization effort.

46. The first Saudi minister of defense was Mansour (1922–1951), King Abd al-Aziz's ninth son by Shahida Umm Mansour. When Mansour died in 1951, he was replaced by his younger full brother Mishal (the king's fifteenth son, born in 1926), who had been deputy minister. He was replaced in this role by his younger full brother Mit'ab (the king's sixteenth son, born in 1928). King Saud removed both brothers from power in 1957, during his struggles with Faisal. Although they returned to power when Faisal became king, they did not resume positions in defense.

47. See Eveland, *Ropes of Sand*; Holden and Johns, *House of Saud,* pp. 195–197; Lacey, *The Kingdom*, p. 317.

48. Richard F. Nyrop, *Area Handbook for the Yemens*, Foreign Area Handbook Series (Washington, D.C.: American University, 1977), pp. 37, 41–43; Peter Mansfield, *The Middle East* (New York: Oxford University Press, 1980), pp. 137–138; Lenczowski, *Middle East in World Affairs*, pp. 621–627.

49. Lenczowski, *Middle East in World Affairs*, pp. 594–595.

50. By this time Saudi Arabia had a debt of 1,800 million rials ($480 million), of which SAMA owned 700 million rials. International banks were refusing to lend, and the king was attempting to borrow from ARAMCO. The country could cover less than 14% of its paper currency with gold and foreign exchange, and the free exchange value of the rial had dropped from 3.75 per dollar to 6.25. The nation's oil revenues had leveled off at $340 million in 1956, inflation was seriously destabilizing the economy, hard currency was vanishing from the market, and the Saudis were rapidly moving their assets out of the country.

51. Richard F. Nyrop, *Area Handbook of Iraq*, Foreign Area Handbook Series (Washington, D.C.: American University, 1971), pp. 37–44; Lenczowski, *Middle East in World Affairs*, pp. 286–288; Mansfield, *Middle East*, pp. 330–332.

52. Faisal had had to make an earlier attempt to downplay the U.S. role in Dhahran in March 1957, in his effort to reduce the split with Nasser. Saudi Arabia announced there was no U.S. base in Dhahran and that Dhahran was not a depot for (U.S.) military weapons. Holden and Johns, *House of Saud*, p. 204; *Times* (London), 30 April 1958.

53. Faisal's budget was eventually implemented virtually intact. Defense and White Army expenditures then totaled 24 million rials, or 14% of the 1.729 million rial budget.

54. For a more detailed background on the various views of these events see Gary S. Saymore, "Royal Family Politics in Saudi Arabia," unpublished paper, Rand Corporation and Harvard University, 1981; Holden and Johns, *House of Saud*, pp. 208–211; Lacey, *The Kingdom*, pp. 321–327, 335–339.

55. He had quarreled violently with Prince Mishal, minister of defense, over these ties and served a period of "exile" as ambassador to France and Spain. Holden and Johns, *House of Saud*, pp. 209, 215; Lacey, *The Kingdom*, p. 341.

56. Nyrop, *Saudia Arabia*, p. 212.

57. This discussion is based on Nyrop, *The Yemens*; Lenczowski, *Middle East in World Affairs*; Mansfield, *Middle East*; von Pikva, *Armies of the Middle East*, pp. 21–22. See Chapters 12 and 16 for more details.

58. Lenczowski, *Middle East in World Affairs*, p. 630.

59. There are many differing accounts of these events. This discussion is based largely on ibid., pp. 594–597.

60. In August 1962 the "free princes" went into self-exile in Cairo and started "reform" broadcasts against the Saudi government. While most supported Nasser against Faisal over the Yemeni civil war, and Talal renounced his title and called for a republic, several of the "free princes" returned to Saudi Arabia and even to positions of influence in the government after King Saud's death.

61. Mansfield, *Middle East*, p. 115. Halliday (*Arabia Without Sultans*) states that nine pilots defected, but this total seems to include Jordanians.

62. Holden and Johns, *House of Saud*, pp. 226–227.

63. Saudi Arabia's finances were limited during this period by a world "oil glut" resulting largely from oil discoveries in the U.S. Saudi oil production, which had reached 0.95 MMBD in 1954, did not rise significantly above 1.0

MMBD until 1960, when it reached 1.2 MMBD. Even then, it rose comparatively slowly, to 1.4 MMBD in 1961, 1.5 MMBD in 1962, 1.6 MMBD in 1963, and 1.7 MMBD in 1964. During this period, oil prices often declined in real terms. Saudi marker prices were only $1.70 a barrel in 1970, and prices reached only $3.11 in October 1973. The rise in Saudi oil production after 1964 was more striking, and is shown below:

	Millions of Barrels per Day	Billions of Barrels per Year
1964	2.8	0.63
1965	2.0	0.74
1966	2.4	0.87
1967	2.6	0.95
1968	2.8	1.04
1969	3.0	1.09
1970	3.5	1.30
1971	4.5	1.64
1972	5.7	2.10
1973	7.3	2.68
1974	8.2	3.00
1975	6.8	2.49
1976	8.3	3.05
1977	9.0	3.29
1978	8.1	2.94
1979	9.3	3.38
1980	9.6	3.53
1981	9.6	3.51
1982	6.3	2.24

As these figures show, Saudi crude oil production reached its "mature" level in 1973–1974. Source: ARAMCO corporate data for 1964–1980; CIA DI EEI 83-013, 24 June 1983, p. 8, for 1981 and 1982.

64. Nyrop, *Saudia Arabia*, pp. 316–317; von Pikva, *Armies of the Middle East*, p. 21; Dawisha, *Saudi Arabia's Search for Security*, p. 3.

65. French intelligence also rapidly became involved, with the SDECE taking the lead. The British effort had high-level support from the conservative cabinet and continued through 1967. In 1965, without the Saudis' knowledge, MI-6 even air-dropped arms by flying out of Israel.

66. Nyrop, *Saudi Arabia*, p. 317; Lenczowski, *Middle East in World Affairs*, p. 317.

67. Nyrop, *Saudi Arabia*, pp. 317, 334; von Pikva, *Armies of the Middle East*, p. 21; Halliday, *Arabia Without Sultans*, pp. 58, 141.

68. Holden and Johns, *House of Saud*, pp. 231, 233.

69. Fahd and Sultan are two of seven sons of Abd al-Aziz's fourth wife, Hussa bint Ahmd al-Sudairi; they were born in 1921 and 1924 respectively. These brothers are sometimes called the Sudairi seven. Abdullah was the son of the fifth wife, al-Fahda bint Asi al-Shuraim; he was born in 1923.

70. Nyrop, *Saudi Arabia*, p. 317.

71. Hurewitz, *Middle East Politics*, p. 251; Halliday, *Arabia Without Sultans*, pp. 57–60.

72. Nyrop, *Saudi Arabia*, p. 320.

73. Ibid., p. 321.

74. Holden and Johns, *House of Saud*, p. 234; Lacey, *The Kingdom*, p. 347.

75. Judging from the above sources and several British books on the Yemeni civil war, at least 150,000 and possibly over 300,000 died during the war. According to Trevor N. Dupuy in *Elusive Victory: The Arab-Israeli Wars,*

1947–1974 (New York: Harper & Row, 1978), there were 15,000 Arab deaths in the 1948 war, 4,900 in the 1956 war, 4,296 in the 1967 war, and 8,528 in the 1973 war. This is a total of 32,724, or between one-fifth and one-tenth of the deaths in the Yemeni civil war.

76. There are countless versions of these events. This account is based on interviews; Holden and Johns, *House of Saud*, pp. 234–240; and Lacey, *The Kingdom*, pp. 322–353.

77. According to one fairly widespread rumor, Faisal allowed Saud to go into exile only because he had sworn an oath to his father never to harm his brother. In any case, one of the strengths of the Saudi royal family is that there has been little violence of any kind in the competition for political power among either its members or its allies.

4 Saudi Military Modernization, 1963–1970

King Faisal soon learned that achieving peace with Nasser could be as difficult as achieving peace with his brother. Instead of relaxing their military posture in Yemen, the Egyptians again built up their forces and attempted to defeat the Royalists. The Egyptian press and radio started a covert campaign against Faisal, and the Arab summit on 5–11 September 1964 produced only a cosmetic rapprochement between the two leaders. Although Yemen's Royalists and Republicans did agree to a cease-fire on 8 November 1964 and to a joint peace conference on 23 November, both sides started fighting even while the peace conference went on. By 10 November, the Egyptian bombing had started again, and peace seemed as far away as ever. By March 1965, it had become clear that Egypt might try to isolate the Royalist bases there. Even worse, from his position in exile King Saud had started to buy B-26, C-47, and DC-6 aircraft and to recruit mercenaries.

Saudi Arabia had no real military strength of its own to deal with such threats. Operation Hard Surface had ended in January 1964. Although a small British mission had been attached to the National Guard after Britain and Saudi Arabia resumed relations in 1963, and it was working with the Guard forces in the border area, the Guard was far too weak to face Egyptian troops. Guard members also lacked the education to absorb even simple systems like the Vigilant antitank guided missile. At the time the Royal Guards Brigade was transferred to the regular army in March 1964, the latter consisted of only four widely dispersed regimental teams, which had been trained to fight like Western light infantry forces by the U.S. The total Saudi armed forces did not exceed 45,000 men, with most split evenly between the army and National Guard. Further, many members of the former White Army were part-time levies rather than full-time soldiers. Saudi Arabia had no deployable armor, and its air force consisted of 12 largely inoperable fighters that could not be properly based and supported within range of Yemen. Thus the kingdom was in urgent need of both modern arms and military assistance.[1]

The Saudi Air Defense Package of 1964–1965

The resulting Saudi efforts to obtain modern air defenses led to the worst single failure in Saudi Arabia's military modernization efforts and perhaps the most damaging single U.S. mismanagement of a major military sale to any developing country.[2] The first step in this process was harmless. King Faisal bought additional light armor, modern artillery, 300 Vigilant antitank guided missiles, and other equipment to support air drops to the Royalists in Yemen. Saudi Arabia, however, also desperately needed modern aircraft, and it had no system or organization to buy such equipment or to train and maintain such aircraft. As a result, the Saudis turned to a young Saudi businessman, Adnan Khashoggi. Khashoggi had arranged several successful Saudi arms transfers to the North Yemeni Royalists, and he had become an informal intelligence agent for the Saudi government, reporting on Western arms and the U.S. and British military missions.[3] Khashoggi began by purchasing from Lockheed several C-130s for the Saudi Air Force to replace its C-126s at a commission of 2% of the sales price, plus $41,000 per aircraft—a total of about $400,000 per aircraft. This laid the groundwork for the commission scandals that not only affected Saudi Arabia's combat arms, but did so at a time when the nation faced a serious external threat.

These scandals might have been avoided if the U.S. had responded properly to Faisal's efforts to create a modern Saudi air force. At the time King Faisal requested Operation Hard Surface, he had also initiated talks with the U.S. on obtaining an advanced air defense system. The U.S. then provided its first comprehensive air defense study as part of an effort by Ellsworth Bunker to negotiate a peace between Faisal and Nasser. This was followed by several lesser studies of Saudi requirements by the U.S. Military Training Missions (USMTM), the U.S. Air Force, and the Office of the Secretary of Defense. The U.S. planning effort bogged down, however, because the USMTM did not give the effort sufficient priority. This failure was due to internal divisions within the Department of Defense over the nature of the system the Saudis required, Saudi-U.S. tensions over Yemen and Nasser, and competition between Northrop and Lockheed as to whose fighter the Department of Defense would recommend.

After Faisal became king, repeated Egyptian air raids on North Yemen again dramatized Saudi Arabia's vulnerability. Once the Saudi- and Egyptian-backed peace talks broke down in 1964, Faisal again sought U.S. assistance in developing a suitable system. By this time, however, the minister of defense and aviation, Prince Sultan, had sought advice from the British, and the French were actively competing for Saudi business. The result was an all-out brawl between the various competing agents and arms manufacturers. None of the Western nations involved placed proper limits on the efforts of their respective arms industries to obtain foreign contracts. The U.S. foreign military sales (FMS) effort was almost solely profit oriented and paid only limited attention to the impact of the resulting U.S. sales on the recipient country. The British and French were attempting to counter past U.S. dominance in Third World arms sales by any means possible.

The Saudis were also uniquely vulnerable. The long struggle for control of the Saudi government between Saud and Faisal during 1958 to 1964 had left the Saudi Defense and Finance ministries in a weak state of organization and without a modern procurement apparatus. The Saudis were almost totally unprepared to evaluate or manage Western proposals on their own. These Saudi shortcomings might not have mattered if Secretary McNamara had proceeded with the plan that his office had developed by early 1965. This plan was linked to a more general U.S. plan to expand Saudi forces that called for a U.S.-equipped air defense system and a training and support program to meet Saudi needs. Although Saudi Arabia was full of U.S., British, and French commission agents attempting to sell different aircraft and missile systems by the time the U.S. plan was completed, King Faisal and Prince Sultan seem to have been prepared to rely on U.S. advice.

If the plan had been adopted, it would have led Saudi Arabia to purchase a relatively modest air defense package based on Lockheed F-104 or Northrop F-5A fighters. Unfortunately for Saudi Arabia, the steady decline in British defense capabilities that had followed the Skybolt incident, and Britain's economic crisis, had reached the point at which Britain concluded it could no longer afford to develop its own advanced fighters and strategic forces. The British minister of defense, Denis Healey, was forced to make major cuts in British defense procurement, and the Labour government had to make major reductions in British defense R&D and in the British aircraft industry. As a part of this rationalization of the aircraft industry, Britain decided to cancel its own advanced fighter and buy the F-111 from the U.S. It lacked the money to do this, however, without a major export sale of its existing weaponry.

The result was that the U.S. and Britain reached a complex agreement that called for a three-cornered deal with Saudi Arabia whereby Britain would get the money to buy 50 F-111s at a cost of $725 million by selling 49 Lightning fighters, 25 Jet Provosts, air-to-air missiles, and Associated Electronics Industry (AEI) air defense radars to Saudi Arabia at a cost of $222 million. The U.S. was to get its money from the Saudis by selling 150 Hawk MIM-23A surface-to-air missiles. At the same time, Britain agreed to create a support firm called Airwork Services Limited to provide up to 1,000 people to train the Saudis in using their new fighters and radars and to maintain and support the new equipment. This program was initially estimated to cost an additional $61.6 million.[4]

It is unclear how much the Saudis knew about the real background to the resulting Anglo-American arms package when it was offered to them in November 1965. For political reasons, Secretary McNamara initially withheld at least some of the facts to prevent Lockheed and Northrop from protesting the nature of the sale,[5] and the British government avoided direct responsibility for the sale by giving the credit and commission to a British commercial agent and ex-RAF pilot named Geoffrey Edwards.[6] It seems doubtful, therefore, that the Saudi government knew either the full terms of the arms package it was buying or the hurried way it was arrived at.

In any case, the result was a political and military debacle. The early models of the Lightning F-52 fighter were an excellent short-range interceptor for a defense of Britain's limited airspace against strategic bombers.[7] Such intercepts depended on high-speed dashes from base to target and on using air-to-air missiles against large, slowly maneuvering targets at medium to high altitudes. They relied on using highly advanced air control and warning (AC&W) systems to avoid flying a prolonged fighter screen. They were, however, unsuited for Saudi Arabia; they lacked the range, combat air patrol capability, extended dogfight capability, and dual capability in the attack mission that the Saudis needed.

The U.S., in turn, never properly researched the Raytheon Hawk missile delivery schedule it promised the Saudis or the ability to "net" the Hawk properly with the British AEI warning radars. As a result, it quickly became apparent that the U.S. could not deliver the Hawk missiles on anything like the required schedule and that they would be far less effective than was originally specified in selling them to the Saudis.[8]

It also quickly became apparent that the British had sharply underestimated the training requirements involved, and this forced them to second British Royal Air Force (RAF) pilots to the Saudi Air Force to fly the fighters. Further, the British refused Prince Sultan's request to modify the agreement to have the RAF do the maintenance work and gave the job to Airwork Services. Airwork proved hopelessly unable to provide the full range of services required and the British government eventually had to bail the company out so it could provide even minimally adequate support.

The various delays in weapons deliveries then forced the Saudi government to buy an interim package of equipment from Britain (through Edwards) that came to be known as Operation Magic Carpet. For some £16 million, Britain agreed to provide 7 early model Lightnings and 6 Hunter light attack aircraft already in service with the RAF, plus 37 refurbished BAC Thunderbird I surface-to-air missiles, to be deployed at a new base at Khamis Mushayt near the Yemeni border. Airwork Services also recruited "ex"-RAF pilots to fly the aircraft, as well as set up the new base. This deal presented still further problems for the Saudis because the Thunderbird was not a successful design and never performed according to specification.[9]

Further, by routing the deal through a British commission agent, the U.S. and UK inadvertently involved in the sale Minister of Defense

Prince Sultan and his brother, Prince Abdul Rahman (seventeenth son, born 1911), as well as a leading Saudi financier named Gaith Pharaon, whose father was an advisor to King Faisal. At the same time, it excluded several other Saudi princes, Adnan Khashoggi, other British commission agents, and Americans like David Rockefeller and Kim Roosevelt. The resulting mix of publicity and lawsuits over sales commissions tarnished everyone involved. The Saudis got most of the blame in the Western press, although it was the parliamentary secretary to the British minister of aviation, John Stonehouse, who put the deal together, and virtually all of the commission problems involved were the fault of the U.S. and British governments.

The deal did have a few benefits for Saudi Arabia. The country gained a small fighter force flown by British pilots, and the Saudi pilots trained at the RAF base near Coltishall in Norfolk, England. Thus the Saudis were able to draw on an excellent cadre of "ex"-RAF pilots from 1965 to well into the 1970s. Further, although Airwork Services was never fully effective, it did provide the support and maintenance necessary to keep the Saudi jets combat ready. The British-piloted Lightnings were able to start flying patrols from the new base at Khamis Mushayt in July 1966, and they proved to be of critical value to Saudi Arabia when it fought a short border war with Yemen in 1969.[10]

The air defense package also gave Saudi Arabia experience with modern combat aircraft, radars, and surface-to-air missiles, but the package proved to be an almost total failure as an air defense system. Worse, it did nothing to teach the Saudis to improve their defense planning and procurement effort. Its only conceivable benefit in terms of defense management was that it led Saudi Arabia to place some tenuous initial controls on the size of the commission payments permitted for defense equipment. As a final irony, the F-111 escalated in cost, the British economy reached another crisis point, and the package collapsed in 1967, when the British were forced to cancel the F-111 deal with the U.S.

The Saudis were protected against the faults in their new air defense "system" by the conflict between the Arabs and Israel and by Israel's virtual destruction of the Egyptian Air Force in 1967, which forced Egypt to withdraw from North Yemen as the price of Saudi aid to Nasser in recovering from the June war.[11] These events made Faisal's diplomacy an "extension of air defense by other means," and its success came just in time. Egypt continued to fly long-range Tu-16 bomber attacks against Saudi territory from Egypt until early 1967, and the Saudis continued to lack more than the most minimal air defense capability.

The Groundwork for the Systematic Modernization of the Saudi Armed Forces

Fortunately for both the U.S. and Saudi Arabia, other aspects of Saudi-U.S. military relations during the mid-1960s proved more pro-

TABLE 4.1 Growth in U.S. Military Sales to Saudi Arabia Following the "Magic Carpet" Program of 1965[a] (in $ thousands)

Fiscal Year	Agreements	Deliveries
1950-64	87,026	75,426
1965	341,643	5,839
1966	8,652	12,200
1967	136,759	27,572
1968	13,696	36,856
1969	4,214	32,086
1970	80,910	31,937
1971	15,863	64,049
1972	371,004	159,646
1973	709,259	211,159
1974	2,031,250	329,971
1975	3,614,819	324,239
1976[b]	7,742,087	926,882
1977	1,888,155	1,502,104
1978	4,121,519	2,368,921
1979	6,468,701	2,471,531
1980	4,536,777	2,724,746
Total	32,172,334[c]	11,305,164

[a] Includes the value of Saudi Arabian Engineer Assistance Agreements projects requested by the Saudi Arabian minister of defense and aviation and approved by the U.S. government for management by the U.S. Army Corps of Engineers as follows: fiscal year (FY) 1965, $521,100; FY 1970, $65,820; FY 1973, $1,064,300; FY 1974, $1,389,400; FY 1975, $3,937,670; FY 1976, $3,744,995; FY 1977, $550,572; FY 1978, $1,522,100; and FY 1980, $2,393,444.

[b] Includes transitional quarter (FY 1977).

[c] These sales as of 1980 were 60% construction, 20% training, and 20% hardware.

Source: U.S. Department of Defense, Defense Security Assistance Agency, *Foreign Military Sales and Military Assistance Facts,* December 1980; and Congressional Research Service, *Saudi Arabia and the United States* (Washington, D.C.: Government Printing Office, December 1981), p. 48.

ductive than the air defense package. The joint Saudi-U.S. effort that King Faisal and Secretary McNamara launched to develop a comprehensive modernization program steadily broadened the military relationship. Although U.S. military sales agreements with Saudi Arabia had totaled only $87 million during the period from 1950 to 1964, as Table 4.1 shows, they rose to $341 million annually in 1965, and Saudi Arabia made major new purchases in each of the years that followed. Further, while the initial sale of C-130 aircraft to the Saudi Air Force in September 1965 involved many of the same commission problems as the air defense deal,[12] it gave Saudi Arabia its first effective airlift capability. More important, it initiated a Saudi shift toward the extensive use of air mobility. This shift was essential, given Saudi Arabia's large territory, limited manpower, and the range of potential political and military threats along its borders.

U.S. advisers also carried out an extensive study of the mobility requirements of the Saudi Army. Although this study was scarcely comprehensive, it recommended that Saudi Arabia slowly mechanize its army and that it progress by stages from truck-carried infantry to light mechanized forces and finally to modern armored units. The Saudi acceptance of these recommendations meant that Saudi Arabia did not follow many of the other Gulf nations in rushing into large purchases of tanks or armor that it could not crew or operate and started a process of slow force expansion that was essential to creating effective and well-trained Saudi units. The Saudi Arabian Mobility Program (SAMP) that resulted from these studies was formally approved in 1966. The initial survey of Saudi equipment by the U.S. contractor Commonwealth-Tumpane found the Saudis still had such oddities as two 1938 Humber halftracks. It also drew attention to Saudi Arabia's lack of basic military infrastructure and the need for extensive military construction, including roads, civil air facilities, and casernes. As a result, a major logistic base was set up in Taif, and work was started on bringing some order to Saudi Arabia's diverse equipment and logistics holdings.

The Role of the U.S. Army Corps of Engineers

The growing contacts between the U.S. and Saudi Arabia during this period also led to formalizing the long-standing arrangements between the U.S. Army Corps of Engineers and Saudi Arabia. An Engineering Assistance Agreement (EAA) was signed between the Saudi government and the Corps on 5 June 1965.[13] This arrangement put the Corps in charge of planning and supervising the construction of the major base facilities and installations that Saudi Arabia needed to support military forces that could compete with those being built up in Iran and Iraq.[14]

The agreement has led to the construction of three major military cantonments. The first cantonment, at Khamis Mushayt, was completed in 1971 at a cost of $81.4 million. The second, at Tabuk just south of the Jordan border, was completed in 1973 at a cost of $81 million. The third cantonment, called King Khalid Military City, is being built at Hafr (or Wadi) al-Batin, a barren stretch of desert south of the Iraqi border. It will house three brigades, an air force squadron, and an engineer's depot. The resulting city will have a population of over 70,000 including dependents. It is so large an undertaking that it will cost in excess of $7.8 billion and be completed only in the mid-1980s.[15] These projects involved an immense effort in a nation as underdeveloped as Saudi Arabia. Most Corps contractors had to bring in their entire labor force and provide them with housing, most of the construction machinery and material had to be imported, and it was necessary to build an

TABLE 4.2 U.S. Army Corps of Engineers Agreements with Saudi Arabia Affecting the Modernization of Saudi Forces (in $ millions)

FY 1950–1964		1,513.2
FY 1965	521.2	
FY 1966	–	
FY 1967	–	
FY 1968	–	
FY 1969	–	
FY 1970	65.8	
FY 1950–FY 1970		2,100.2
FY 1971	–	
FY 1972	–	
FY 1973	1,064.3	
FY 1974	1,389.4	
FY 1975	3,937.7	
FY 1976	3,745.0	
FY 1977	550.6	
FY 1978	701.6	
FY 1979	1,522.1	
FY 1980	2,393.4	
FY 1971–FY 1980		15,304.1

Source: Adapted from U.S. Department of Defense, DSAA, *Foreign Military Sales and Military Assistance Facts,* December 1977, 1978, and 1980. Covers projected value of Saudi Arabian Engineer Assistance Agreements: omits large amounts of military construction that the Corps of Engineers planned but did not manage or supervise.

entire new port on the Gulf at Ras Al Mish'ab with four general cargo berths, one bulk cement berth, onshore storage and related port facilities, and housing.

Other Corps projects under the EAA included the construction of the $298 million Ministry of Defense and Aviation headquarters complex and Royal Saudi Air Force headquarters in Riyadh, the $1.7 billion King Abd al-Aziz Military Academy near Riyadh, the Airborne and Physical Training School at Tabuk, and additions to the two existing cantonments. Many other projects are still in the planning or initial construction stage. These include the Army Engineer Center and School, the Signal Center and School, the Field Artillery Center and School, and the Infantry Center and School.

The growth of the EAA agreements through 1980 is shown in Table 4.2, but these figures are misleadingly low because, as time went on, the Corps came to play a major role in advising the Saudis on many

TABLE 4.3 U.S. Army Corps of Engineers Program in Saudi Arabia as of FY 1980 (in $ millions)

	Approved Department of Defense Funding[a]	Estimate of Total Cost
Status of program:		
Construction completed	1,546	1,488
Under construction	4,072	3,920
Out for contractor bids	1,499	1,495
Under design	4,668	11,514
In planning	949	3,880
Total program[b]	12,734	22,297
Components of program:		
Engineer assistance agreement[c]	8,510	14,140
Saudi Naval Expansion Program (SNEP)	2,455	4,688
Saudi Arabian National Guard (SANG)	369	2,010
Saudi Ordnance Corps Program (SOCP)	1,229	1,229
Ministry of Information	14	14
Other programs	1,387	1,445
Total program	13,964	23,526

[a] FMS cost. Congress approves projects, or "cases," totaling $25 million or more. Cost estimates may be lower than approved funding due to program changes.
[b] Excludes Saudi Ordnance Corps Program.
[c] Includes air force and army construction activities.
Source: U.S. Congress, House, Committee on Foreign Affairs, Subcommittee on Europe and the Middle East, Activities of the United States Army Corps of Engineers in Saudi Arabia, Hearing, 96th Cong., 1st session, 25 June 1979, p. 24; Congressional Research Service, *Saudi Arabia and the United States* (Washington, D.C.: Government Printing Office, December 1981), p. 49.

other projects that they did not actually construct or it planned projects without managing actual construction.[16] By 1981, the Corps had supervised over $5 billion worth of construction; it had $10 billion more under contract and issued $1.7 billion more in 1982 and $1.8 billion in 1983.

As Table 4.3 shows, the Corps also acquired new responsibilities under the Foreign Military Sales Act of 1968 and the Arms Export Control Act of 1976. These eventually included programs to modernize the Saudi Ordnance Corps, the Saudi National Guard, the Saudi Navy, and the Saudi Air Force. The logistics effort grew out of the Saudi Arabian Mobility Program, approved in 1966. A formal agreement was signed in 1967 that included both the Corps of Engineers and the U.S.

Army Material and Development Readiness Command in a continuing effort to supply end items and repair parts for wheeled and tracked vehicles and conventional armaments and to modernize the Royal Saudi Army's logistics system. As a part of this program, the U.S. also assumed responsibility for modernizing and providing limited maintenance for the army's fleet of nonarmored vehicles. This program was formally renamed the Saudi Ordnance Corps program in November 1972; it led to the sale of over 9,300 tactical and general-purpose vehicles by 1980.[17] It was renewed for two years in April 1979, bringing its total cost through 1982 to $2.47 billion.

The National Guard started to receive Corps assistance after the signing of a memorandum of understanding in 1973. This program was assigned to the U.S. Army Material Development and Readiness Command, but the Corps was responsible for designing and constructing all facilities. Corps support to the Guard included construction of a headquarters complex in Riyadh large enough to accommodate 3,500 people, which was completed in late 1980 at a cost of nearly $300 million. It has included training facilities, including classrooms, some 18 types of firing ranges, shops, and warehouses at Khashm al-An, near Riyadh.

Additional maintenance and training facilities are now under construction. Studies have been completed for a kingdomwide communications system, a fully integrated logistics and maintenance system, and a vehicle management program; initial procurement is under way. Another study is being completed that will produce a master plan to expand facilities at Khashm al-An. Planning is under way for two National Guard military cities, one near Al Qasim in north-central Saudi Arabia, and the other at Al Hasa near the east coast. The design of the city at Al Qasim is now completed.

Corps support of the modernization of the Saudi Navy began in 1972 when a memorandum of understanding was signed creating the Saudi Naval Expansion Program (SNEP). Corps activities came to include construction of deepwater port facilities at Jubail on the Gulf and Jiddah on the Red Sea and the naval headquarters complex at Riyadh. Both naval bases include facilities for ship berthing, dry docking and repair, fuel and ammunition storage, and base maintenance shops, as well as the necessary housing, mess, and recreation facilities for personnel. Jubail will also have naval training facilities.

An interim repair facility at Dammam on the Gulf has already been constructed by the Corps and is in operation. The Saudis now plan to maintain it as a permanent installation. Construction contracts for the naval headquarters in Riyadh and the various phases of the onshore and offshore construction at the two bases were initiated in 1975, 1976, and 1977. The Corps portion of this effort had an approved program cost of about $2.4 billion in 1982, out of a total program cost of $5 billion. The basic program was to be completed by 1984, but additional projects seemed likely to require Corps of Engineers participation through the latter 1980s.

While the Corps' projects in support of the Saudi Air Force began later, its activity in support of the F-5 and F-15 programs had reached a value of $700 million by 1982. Work included new facilities, shelters, taxiways, training buildings, and other services at Taif, Khamis Mushayt, Tabuk, and Dhahran. The Corps not only carried out design review on these projects, it performed full construction management as well.

Such Saudi arrangements with the Corps of Engineers did not prevent further waste and major abuses of the commission process in Saudi military construction. Abuses occasionally led to massive cost overruns and to the construction of a few projects that were so "gold plated" that they constituted literal examples of monumental waste.[18] However, these arrangements were infinitely preferable to the alternative of a wide range of competing and unintegrated efforts. Further, as with the Mobility Program, they meant that Saudi Arabia sought to expand its forces at a rate that it could reasonably hope to staff and operate. There is no doubt that such U.S. assistance was to Saudi Arabia's benefit. Unlike Iran, Iraq, and Syria—which bought massive amounts of combat equipment they had no practical hope of being able to integrate into effective combat units—Saudi Arabia followed the Jordanian model of focusing on quality rather then sheer quantity.

Most of Saudi Arabia's military excesses and mistakes after 1966 consisted largely of providing too many or too expensive facilities for its small armed forces, rather than funding a grandiose military expansion. Equally important, Saudi Arabia has avoided the shah of Iran's mistakes of trying to "force feed" the expansion of its military forces. The Saudi government did not ram new equipment down the throats of its officers, fire them for protesting its uselessness, or constantly override previous plans. This course showed considerable restraint, given the threats that developed in the region, but it was unquestionably a key factor in the relative success of Saudi military modernization after the mid-1960s and in the take-off period to follow in the 1980s.

The Saudi Security Position, 1965–1967

The growing military ties between the U.S. and Saudi Arabia were reinforced by King Faisal and Prince Sultan's growing contempt for the Labour government in Britain and their resentment of France's involvement in Algeria and its close military ties to Israel. In spite of repeated efforts to settle the war in North Yemen, King Faisal also found himself locked in a continuing confrontation with a steadily more bitter Nasser, and Egypt made repeated attempts to weaken or subvert not only Saudi Arabia but Aden and the South Arabian Federation. This increasingly polarized the Arab world into religious-conservative and radical-socialist factions and pushed Saudi Arabia further toward the U.S.

Nasser reacted strongly to these developments. A series of bombings took place in Riyadh and Dammam in late 1966. Clumsy assassination attempts were planned against King Faisal and Prince Fahd, and against Saud bin Jiluwi, the ruthlessly anti-Shi'ite governor of the Eastern Province.[19] These activities eventually proved to have been sponsored by pro-Egyptian Yemeni infiltrators who entered Saudi Arabia during the *hajj*. Most were captured in January 1967, and 17 were publicly beheaded in March as a warning to other "pilgrims" who used the *hajj* for subversive purposes.[20] Nasser's agents also made attempts to create radical labor groups in the Saudi oil fields, and Egyptian planes made a mass air drop of arms in the Hejaz. While all of this air drop was found untouched in the desert, and seems to have been targeted for an insurgent group that existed only in the imagination of Egyptian agents, the incident again demonstrated the vulnerability of Saudi air space to strikes from both Egypt and Yemen.[21]

Perhaps most unkind of all, Nasser began to manipulate ex-King Saud. The king, who had left Cairo for Athens, was persuaded to return to Cairo in December 1966. He proceeded to denounce Faisal as a U.S. agent who had seized power with the help of the CIA, and he turned up in Sana on 23 April 1967 to recognize the "legitimate" revolutionary government of Sallal. Sallal, in turn, greeted Saud as the "legal" king of Saudi Arabia.[22] There is no way to tell what might have happened if it had not been for the June 1967 war between the Arabs and Israel, but the "Six Day War" put a firm check to Nasser's actions. It left him financially and militarily bankrupt, and with greatly restricted political leverage.

Saudi Arabia did not play a serious role in the war, although it did declare a jihad and sent a brigade to support Jordan. The Saudi troops failed to arrive before the end of the fighting, although they were kept in Jordan to support King Hussein and demonstrate Saudi Arabia's commitment to the Arab cause. Saudi Arabia also joined the other Arab states in another brief oil embargo on 7 June 1967, after minor riots in Dhahran demolished the ARAMCO compound and the U.S. officers' club and consulate-general.

By July 1967, King Faisal had gained important leverage over Nasser. On 7 July, the king ended Saudi Arabia's participation in the oil embargo by declaring that he was responding to popular pressure, and he ignored the cries of Egypt, Iraq, and Syria. In August 1967, he dominated Nasser at the Arab Foreign Ministers' Meeting at Khartoum. The resulting agreement gave Egypt $280 million annually, Jordan $100 million, and Syria $14 million.[23] Saudi Arabia was to contribute $140 million annually, Kuwait $132 million, and Libya $74 million. These funds made Nasser dependent on Saudi Arabia's continued goodwill, and when Faisal met privately with Nasser on 31 August, Nasser agreed to end the Yemeni civil war on Faisal's terms and to put a stop to King Saud's attempts at return.[24]

The Transformation of Saudi Arabia's Security Position

While the third Arab-Israeli war of June 1967 put an end to the Egyptian military occupation in Yemen, it eliminated only one military threat to Saudi Arabia. In the years that followed, Saudi Arabia faced new threats on every border.

• Just to the southeast of Yemen, the British protectorates of Aden and South Arabia acquired their independence on 30 November 1967, under conditions that amounted to a British rout under the twin pressures of military insurrection and civil war. As a result, Saudi Arabia was suddenly confronted by an extreme radical Arab state that occupied an even longer portion of its border than North Yemen and that had strongly Soviet and Marxist leanings. Somewhat ironically, the British were forced to withdraw from South Yemen on 30 November 1967, only one week before the Egyptians finally left North Yemen on 7 December.[25]

• The collapse of Egyptian support of the Republicans in North Yemen was followed not by a Royalist victory, as was widely expected, but rather by divisions within the Royalist movement, which effectively destroyed it over the next six months. The result was an awkward Royalist-Republican coalition government that combined traditional religious and tribal leaders of North Yemen with a wide variety of Arab nationalists and left the Soviet Union still actively equipping and training a relatively modern North Yemeni Army and Air Force.

The Saudi government was slow to recognize the new regime and did so only after several overflights by MiG-17s flying out of Sana had again demonstrated the weaknesses of Saudi air defenses. It then found itself in the position of competing with the USSR and South Yemen in trying to win influence over a rapidly changing series of North Yemeni governments and facing the constant risk of a war between North and South Yemen.

• Directly to the east, the low-level tribal insurgency in Oman, which had ended in the late 1950s, was succeeded by a major radical effort to overthrow the sultan. This new rebellion was concentrated in the southern, or Dhofar, region of Oman. It was heavily backed by South Yemen, with some support from Iraq and Egypt. While the rebellion did not lead to a large-scale civil war until the 1970s, it was clear by the late 1960s that Saudi Arabia would soon confront the same kind of security problem in Oman that it had faced in North Yemen.

• These developments acquired added importance as the Arab defeat in the 1967 war created new pressures for Arab nationalism and radicalism. These pressures were reinforced by the riots that followed the fire at Jerusalem's Al-Asqa Mosque in August 1969. The Israeli occupation of the Golan Heights in Syria, Jerusalem and the West Bank in Jordan, and the entire Sinai in Egypt inevitably meant that the Arab world would arm for yet another war.

• At the same time, the Arab-Israeli War of June 1967 forced Saudi Arabia to temporarily reduce its ties to the U.S. and to deploy troops in support of Jordan and Syria. This scarcely threatened Israel, but the war had greatly heightened the sensitivity of the Israelis and U.S. pro-Israeli groups to any buildup of Arab military forces. As a result, Saudi Arabia found itself unable to count on military deliveries from the U.S.

• The 1967 war and Israel's seizure of the Muslim holy places in East Jerusalem also changed the Palestinian movement from a relatively powerless group of factions into a militant organization that acquired significant paramilitary forces and political power. The growth of PLO operations in Jordan created the threat that a radical regime might arise on Saudi Arabia's eastern border; the growth of the PLO also radicalized the large numbers of Palestinians in the Gulf.

• Another potential threat built up in the Horn of Africa. Fighting had started in 1965 between Ethiopia and Somalia, which was generally considered an Arab nation. While this fighting remained at a relatively low level, and an agreement to reduce tensions was reached in September 1967, it led Somalia to turn to the Soviet Union for equipment and advice. At the same time, a radical Muslim movement developed in Ethiopia called the Eritrean Liberation Front, which obtained strong support from Syria and other radical Arab movements. Coupled to political instability in Sudan, these conflicts meant that Saudi Arabia faced potential radical threats along most of its Red Sea coast.

• Most important of all, the further deterioration of the British economy led to a British declaration on 17 January 1968 that Britain would withdraw from the Gulf by the end of 1971 and would give the Trucial States full independence. This step suddenly deprived the Gulf of a key source of political and military stability. None of the various southern Gulf states had been prepared for such independence. Iran had extensive claims in the Gulf, including a claim to Bahrain. Iraq had made previous claims to Kuwait, and the prospect of British withdrawal encouraged all of the various Arab radical movements to try to follow the path of the successful radical movements in Aden.[26] Saudi Arabia was also confronted with the problem that its various border disputes with its conservative neighbors might have to be decided in the next few years.

In short, the events of 1967–1968 effectively transformed Saudi Arabia's national security position; it now faced major potential political and military threats on every border. Those events created the split between the radical Soviet-backed states and the conservative Western-supported states in the Gulf that still characterizes the Near East. They forced Saudi Arabia to become steadily more sensitive to Arab nationalist and Palestinian demands and to actively consider the situation in the Horn because of the potential threat to its Red Sea coast. Finally, they forced Saudi Arabia to diversify its sources of arms and military assistance, both to guard against the uncertainty of U.S. arms deliveries and because of political pressures to do so from the other Arab states.

Developments in the Saudi Armed Forces, 1967–1969

Saudi Arabia's initial response to these changes in its strategic situation was necessarily limited. The progress Saudi Arabia had made in modernizing its forces during 1962–1967 had only just begun to prepare it for large-scale military modernization.[27] Although its armed forces were the third largest in terms of numbers in the Gulf in 1967, this ranking depended heavily on the inclusion of the 25,000 part-time soldiers in the National Guard. While some elements of the Guard were probably the most effective troops in Saudi Arabia, and the Guard had a good cadre of British advisers, it still lacked the training and equipment for modern war. Saudi Arabia's regular army did not exceed 25,000 men and may have been as small as 18,000, its air force totaled 5,000 men, and its navy only 1,000.

The arms purchases that Saudi Arabia had made from the U.S. and UK in 1965 were still in the process of delivery or conversion. Saudi Arabia's pool of major combat equipment did not yet reflect major deliveries of the Lightning fighter and Hawk missile. The equipment of its five brigades consisted of a few aging M-24 and M-41 light tanks, a limited number of M-47 medium tanks, and Vigilant antitank guided missiles. The air force had about 20 combat aircraft: 4 Hunter light attack fighters, 4 Lightning fighters, and 8–13 aging F-86 fighters. It also had 4 C-130E transports, 6 C-47 transports, 2 Alouette III helicopters, and 40 trainers. Its navy had one U.S. patrol boat and some small craft.[28]

These manpower and equipment problems sharply constrained the expansion of Saudi forces during the late 1960s. Saudi Arabia did purchase French equipment to diversify its sources of arms and obtained AMX-13 light tanks, artillery, and light armored vehicles, including 220 Panhard AML-90 armored fighting vehicles (AFVs). The Saudi Air Force took delivery of its 40 remaining Lightning fighters and negotiated a further $54 million expansion of its air defense system with Britain.[29] It ordered 25 more BAC-167 Strikemaster light attack trainers to provide counterinsurgency and improved air attack capabilities in 1969–70 and purchased 20 AB-205 and AB-206 helicopters and 5 more C-130Es.

Saudi Arabia also obtained U.S. assistance in surveying its future naval modernization requirements and sought British, French, Pakistani, and U.S. advice in expanding its army and air force.[30] This advice was essential, because the limited defense reforms that King Faisal had begun in 1962, and which Prince Sultan had carried forward after Faisal's consolidation of power in 1964, had not given Saudi Arabia an effective training structure or organization of its armed forces to cope with the radical changes required. Saudi Arabia's highly personalized style of government had not evolved into anything approaching an effective defense staff or cadre of technocrats to handle weapons selections, logistic management, planning and programming, budgeting, or any of the other complex bureaucratic details of running a modern ministry of defense. The Saudi government continued to rely on the personal decisions of individual officials like the minister of defense in selecting sources of Western assistance and buying "packages" of arms, training, and support. There was essentially no coordinating structure linking the three regular armed services, no central budgeting in any programmatic sense, and little coordination between the chief of the General Staff, the various technical departments, and the regional commands. For a variety of historical, political, and internal security reasons, there also was no real coordination between the National Guard and regular armed forces at any level.[31]

The absence of coordination was demonstrated in December 1968, when Saudi Arabia backed an abortive attempt by the "Liberation Army" of South Yemeni exiles to invade South Yemen and seize power from the National Liberation Front (NLF). The force had the backing of Prince Sultan and Prince Khaled Sudairi, the governor of Najran. It did not, however, have the backing of Faisal's intelligence chief, Kamal Adham, or the aid of expertise from the National Guard. As a result, it was shattered by a few sorties from the British Provost fighters that South Yemen had inherited at independence.[32]

The Military Crisis of 1969

Even more important, although King Faisal had made significant reforms in Saudi society, the Saudi government had done little to truly modernize and develop the economy. It also had done little to overcome the historical differences between the Najd tribes, which were the Saudi family's original base of power, and the more cosmopolitan Hejazis, who lived in the urban areas like Jiddah, Makkah, and Medina. A disproportionate amount of the nation's oil wealth still went to the royal family and Najd leaders, and this had a critical impact on the armed forces. Although Saudi Arabia had to recruit a number of educated Hejazis beginning in the 1950s, it had been able to obtain most of its military manpower from tribes in the Najd until the mid-1960s. As oil wealth began to transform Saudi society, however, the number of Najdis living in traditional tribal areas declined precipitously. Further, because the government favored the Najdis in terms of development projects, employment in the oil fields, education, and other privileges, more and more Najdis began to move into urban areas or occupations, so that the better-educated Najdis had little reason to join the army.

At the same time, the more cosmopolitan Hejazis who joined the armed forces were often discriminated against, denied promotion for merit, and subordinated to "loyal" officers who were incompetent or corrupt. This discrimination limited the willingness of the Hejazis to join the armed forces and increasingly alienated those who did from the regime. Such problems were particularly important in the case of the air force, which had to draw on the Hejazis for many of its technicians, NCOs, and junior officers in order to get the skills it needed.

The air force was also the service with the most personnel who had been educated outside the country or whose contacts gave them exposure to outside influence from various Arab radical movements. It was the logical target of radical groups from the Yemens, Iraq, Syria, and the various Gulf liberation movements, and these groups capitalized on the ethnic and tribal divisions that built up within the service. As a result, the Saudi Air Force became infiltrated by small, disaffected nationalist groups by 1969, and considerable discontent developed regarding the pace of Saudi military modernization, the quality of much of Saudi Arabia's middle-echelon management, and corruption and nepotism within the armed forces. Several air force officers and NCOs became affiliated with a small radical terrorist group working within Saudi Arabia called the "Union of the Arab Peninsula," while other air force officers joined the army and navy officers and civilian elements to form "study groups" of the kind that had led to coups in other Arab states.

Although the full details are obscure, Saudi Arabia carried out large-scale arrests of suspected Yemeni exiles and among tribal groups in May 1969. It then arrested well over 130 members of the Saudi military between June and September. No coup as such seems to have been under way, and the timing and size of the arrests may well have been an overreaction to the military coup that overthrew King Idris of Libya on the first of September.[33] It is clear that the arrests went on long after there was any reason for them. Several hundred Shi'ites in Al Hasa were arrested, largely for being Shi'ites, and Saudi officers were arrested because they had suspect relatives or backgrounds. The chief of the General Intelligence Directorate, Omar Shams, seems to have arrested virtually every possible suspect and to have halted only after the direct intervention of the king, Prince Fahd, and Prince Sultan. Even then, some additional arrests took place in 1970, and many of those imprisoned were not freed until 1972–1975. Those arrested included the former head of Prince Sultan's office, the acting commandant of the Staff College, and the head of the College of Petroleum and Minerals. Even the pro-British commander of the air force, General Hashim S. Hashim, seems to have been suspect because he was a Hejazi.

These events clearly demonstrated the need to reform Saudi Arabia's treatment of its military personnel, but the royal family remained uncertain as to whether the armed forces could be trusted after such reforms and whether it could take the risk of further expanding Saudi forces. This uncertainty was resolved shortly thereafter, when the increasing tension between Saudi Arabia and the radical regime in South Yemen (People's Democratic Republic of Yemen—PDRY) led to a serious border skirmish during 26 November–16 December 1969. Again sources vary, but South Yemen seems to have reacted to continued

Saudi support of an exile group known as the "Hadraumi Legion" by launching a demonstrative infantry and armored attack against the Saudi frontier post at Al Wadiah, which was held by a few Bedouins in the Saudi Frontier Force. Not surprisingly, South Yemen quickly took the fort.

Saudi Arabia, however, now had Lightning F-53 fighters operational in the area. These Lightnings, led by Wing Commander Tony Winship, attacked the South Yemeni forces. They were followed by F-86s, some flown out of Khamis Mushayt. Although the PDRY's Provosts and Soviet-supplied MiG-17s retaliated, they could not encounter the Saudi fighters directly, and Saudi troops reoccupied the border area 10 days after the invasion started. Several Lightnings stayed on at Khamis Mushayt, and one later forced down a transport that was carrying the Iraqi chief of staff to Aden.[34]

Western observers who were resident in Saudi Arabia at the time feel that this victory had a tremendous impact on the Saudi armed forces and the royal family, one that was out of all proportion to the forces and events involved. First, it demonstrated that the Saudi forces could defeat an enemy. Second, it showed that when an outside threat appeared, the regular armed forces exhibited far more political unity than many members of the royal family had expected. Third, although the victory had been won by British-piloted fighters, it had become clear that the Saudis would soon be able to fight a similar battle. Fourth, it showed that the threat of invasion was real. And fifth, while Saudi Arabia continued to experience problems with its Lightnings, the victory did a great deal to erase the resentments that had resulted from the Anglo-American air defense package. More than any other factor, the "battle of Al Wadiah" persuaded the royal family to support the full modernization of the regular armed forces and gave the latter a vital boost in recovering from the arrests of 1969.

As a result, the Saudi government and royal family launched a serious effort to free the military from radical influences and to improve their living conditions, to reduce corruption and nepotism, and to base promotion on merit regardless of ethnic background. While this effort evolved slowly and had limited success until the end of the 1960s, it was one of the reasons behind the creation of the Saudi military cities, the "gold plating" of many Saudi military facilities, and the exceptional salary levels and privileges the Saudi military obtained in the early 1970s. The Saudi government also acted to reduce the divisions between Najdis and Hejazis beginning in the early 1970s, as Saudi Arabia steadily increased its oil wealth and began to implement its first five-year plan. Although the data involved are limited and unreliable, there seems to have been a major shift of development capital away from concentration on the Najd to a more balanced effort to develop the entire country and exploit the full potential of the Hejaz. This emphasis on nationwide development accelerated with the Second Five Year Plan, and the Third Saudi Five Year Plan seems particularly well balanced in this respect.

Accordingly, while the full integration of the Hejazi and other regional elements into the armed forces is still a problem, Saudi Arabia did respond effectively to the 1969 crisis in its armed forces. It solved many of the most critical problems in its treatment of the Hejazis and other non-Najdis within the armed forces by the mid-1970s. It is also important to note that Saudi Arabia's military intelligence operations did not follow the example of the SAVAK in Iran. Even the arrests in 1969–1970 were limited by Middle Eastern standards. There were no mass torturings or executions, and the primary emphasis was placed on co-opting the dissidents back into the armed forces rather than on the ruthless suppression of dissent. The internal security forces were reorganized to be significantly more efficient and less repressive. Further, all of those imprisoned in 1969–1970 were released by 1975, including many the Egyptian press had stated had been executed.

The long-term success of these Saudi reforms can also be judged by the fact that in the spring of 1977, Saudi military intelligence was able to thwart a heavily funded Libyan coup attempt that had infiltrated one of the Saudi Air Force units at Tabuk. Although the coup attempt initially led the Saudi government to cancel all attack exercises and restrict aircraft fuel to limit flight ranges, it turned out to involve only about 13 pilots in a rather awkward plot that was intended to seize control of the government by bombing key buildings in Jiddah and Riyadh. It also turned out to have been massively funded by Captain Muhammed Idris al-Shariff, then head of the Libyan Security and Military Intelligence Service. He was subsequently "turned" by the Saudis and made three "covert" attempts to oust Qadaffi before being arrested by him.[35]

There were no signs of any serious unrest among Hejazi officers and other ranks in the late 1970s, and by 1982, something like two-thirds of the air force and more than half of the regular army and navy was Hejazi or recruited from outside the traditional Saudi recruiting base in the Najd. While the Saudi armed forces found it difficult to recruit trained personnel in 1980–1981 because of the competition from the private sector, there were no signs of the acute internal conflicts within the armed forces that had surfaced in 1969, nor were there any indications that regional tensions within the armed forces remained a critical problem.[36]

As will be discussed later, however, this process of reform did not avoid other problems in the stability of the Saudi armed forces. It also did not eliminate the broader problems in Saudi internal security that resulted from regional, tribal, and religious discrimination. Leading Hejazi families continued to protest against economic discrimination, the Shi'ites in the Eastern Province continued to suffer from serious economic discrimination, and several major tribal groups, which traditionally had been hostile to the Saud family, seem to have been partly excluded from the nation's wealth.[37]

Saudi Defense Management

The Saudi government was less successful in reacting to the need to modernize the organization and management of the Ministry of Defense and Aviation (MODA) and the military services during the late 1960s and early 1970s. Although a long series of organizational changes and "reforms" were made after 1964, they still left the Saudi defense structure organized in a series of "vertical boxes," with every major element reporting to the minister of defense and aviation or to the top of a given service or subelement. There was little "horizontal" coordination between the elements of a given service. Even less coordination existed between services, or with other ministries, and Saudi Arabia attempted to make up for its lack of trained managers and technical personnel by buying outside support in individual "packages" that it lacked the ability to coordinate. The Ministry of Defense and Aviation did not modernize its budgeting and programming capability to keep pace with its increased defense expenditures and Saudi Arabia's civilian development projects. The MODA funded its projects so quickly that it constantly overspent the defense budget in any given year. It also dealt with manpower problems largely in political terms—by attempting to meet the human needs and the concerns of the personnel in a given service—while ignoring the need for overall management of training and career development.

The Saudi government partially reformed its promotion system to recognize merit and reduce regional, tribal, and family discrimination after 1969, but it did not develop a system for efficiently managing its overall personnel pool. Similar problems cropped up in the management and planning of logistics, supply, and service support. Further, although Saudi Arabia proved relatively efficient in getting competent outside support in individual areas, it did not develop efficient systems of management that could cut across individual areas, resulting in substantial waste and gaps in capability. Most important, the Saudi government did not significantly improve its procurement and weapons selection process. It continued to rely on a few top officials to make weapons selections on the basis of competing outside advice, although such advice was generally uninformed regarding Saudi Arabia's specific needs and tended to turn into a "liars' contest" among Western governments and manufacturers. It also made only faltering efforts to ensure that the equipment, munitions, infrastructure, and construction projects it purchased were fully compatible.

The F-5A Sale

This failure to improve Saudi Arabia's military procurement efforts had a critical impact on the next major step in Saudi Arabia's military modernization. The internal crisis within the armed forces resulted partly from the feeling of many air force officers that Saudi Arabia was not getting the modern aircraft it needed and had been sold ineffective fighters by Britain. This impression was reinforced by their knowledge of the Israeli efforts to obtain a tailored variant of the Mirage III that would improve its ability to sustain low-altitude air-to-air combat and provide an improved dual capability in the attack and fighter roles. Even the improved variants of the Lightning fighter that Saudi Arabia had purchased from Britain were unsuited in maneuver capability and avionics to deal with the "spiraling down" common in air-to-air combat between light fighters, particularly in air-to-air combat with the Soviet models operated by many of the potential threat nations in the Gulf. The Lightning also could not be adapted to effective performance in the attack role, since it lacked effective attack avionics. Although the BAC-167 attack-trainers that Saudi Arabia had bought from Britain were relatively effective in a light air-support role, they could not survive against hostile fighters, had little payload capability and accuracy, and had no prestige value.

Accordingly, the next step in Saudi Arabia's military modernization was almost inevitably the purchase of new fighters. This met the government's need to deal with the concerns of Saudi officers, to cope with the massive military buildup taking place in other Gulf nations, and to acquire the kind of first-rate fighters that would give Saudi Arabia the status it needed as a military power and would act as a deterrent to low-level attacks.

It was perhaps inevitable under these circumstances that the Saudis would not turn to Britain because of its problems with the Lightning and the unavailability of any British fighter with air-to-air performance characteristics superior to the then current models of the MiG-21. It is less clear why Saudi Arabia did not seriously consider France, but the Mirage had acquired a reputation for requiring extensive technical support and service capabilities. In addition, the most suitable French fighter would have been the Mirage V, which was an Israeli-designed variant of the Mirage III. The Israeli Air Force (IAF) had ordered 60 Mirage V aircraft in late 1966, with initial deliveries planned for late 1967. Since General de Gaulle put an embargo on the sale following the Arab-Israeli War of June 1967, they were available for purchase, but the politics were awkward. De Gaulle's temporary embargo turned into a formal embargo on arms sales to belligerents in the Arab-Israeli War in December 1969, after a series of border conflicts and raids developed between Israel and Lebanon, Jordan, and Egypt. This broader embargo, coupled with the fact that the Mirage V aircraft was a tailored redesign of the Mirage III that reflected most of the IAF's technical experience in air-to-air combat, may have inhibited French efforts to sell the aircraft, although it did not prevent the sale of 50 Mirages to Libya a year later.[38]

Perhaps equally important, Prince Sultan had been highly impressed by the effectiveness of U.S. fighters in Vietnam, and the U.S. was then heavily committed to selling an "export fighter," the Northrop Tiger, or F-5A. This meant that Northrop had the full support of the U.S. Department of Defense in trying to sell to Saudi Arabia. Although Prince Sultan had sought the F-4, the F-5A was an acceptable fighter for Saudi needs at a time when most potential threat fighters were short-ranged and lacked the ability to fly low-altitude attack sorties for any real distance. The Saudis also had little sensitivity at this time to the importance of advanced avionics in supporting air-to-air and air-to-surface combat, and they had as yet failed to develop any overall concept of air defense or air force modernization that made specific aircraft performance characteristics important. As a result, Saudi and U.S. interests coincided in the Saudi purchase of the F-5A, particularly because the U.S. could provide the combined training, support, and munitions aid that Saudi Arabia required.[39] Accordingly, unlike the sale of the Anglo-American air defense package in 1965, there was nothing inherently wrong with the Saudi purchase of the F-5A. Even so, the U.S. and Saudi handling of the sale proved as embarrassing as the handling of the earlier package.

Saudi efforts to reform the commission payment system following the Lightning-Hawk fiasco had had only limited success. Although the Saudi purchase of the Improved Hawk had given it an effective missile, and Saudi reliance on the Corps of Engineers had greatly reduced the abuse of commissions in construction projects, major problems still remained. Adnan Khashoggi, who had managed the sale of the C-130 to Saudi Arabia for Lockheed, had gradually become *the* agent U.S. arms manufacturers dealt with for sales to the Saudis. At the same time, his commissions had risen from 2% to over 7%, and he began to apply them to the sale of services and to cost-escalation changes as well. The chairman of Northrop Aviation, the manufacturer of the F-5A, became deeply involved in dealings with Khashoggi—at least partly because the Department of Defense, believing Khashoggi had the influence to ensure Saudi Arabia's purchase of the aircraft, had tacitly encouraged him to do so.[40]

It is unclear whether Khashoggi had such influence; if he did, he did not use it wisely. The payments to Khashoggi before the initial F-5A sale in June 1971 were not properly distributed to other Saudis, which made at least one member of the royal family furious. The resulting arguments over commissions led to an increasingly public scandal in Saudi Arabia as commission payments were made for follow-on sales and more arguments arose over their distribution. The eventual result was the exposure of both the Northrop payments and the distribution of commissions within Saudi Arabia in a series of brutal hearings before the U.S. Congress. These hearings discredited virtually everyone involved in the sale. While the Saudi royal family emerged in a considerably more favorable light did than the royal family of the Netherlands in a similar situation, the hearings scarcely enhanced its reputation, that of the U.S. government, or that of U.S. industry. The backlash from the F-5A sale is still remembered in Saudi Arabia and leads many Saudi officers and educated Saudis to question the integrity of U.S. military sales to Saudi Arabia.[41]

Notes

1. Richard F. Nyrop, *Area Handbook for Saudi Arabia*, Foreign Area Handbook Series (Washington, D.C.: American University, 1977), p. 345; George Lenczowski, *The Middle East in World Affairs* (Ithaca, N.Y.: Cornell University Press, 1980), p. 603; David Holden and Richard Johns, *The House of Saud* (London: Sidgwick and Jackson, 1981), pp. 241–245; Robert Lacey, *The Kingdom* (London: Hutchinson & Co., 1981), p. 376; J. C. Hurewitz, *Middle East Politics: The Military Dimension* (New York: Praeger Publishers, 1969), p. 251.

2. For a detailed account of many of the events described in this section, see Anthony Sampson, *The Arms Bazaar* (New York: Bantam, September 1978), pp. 174–181; John Stonehouse, *Death of an Idealist* (London: W. H. Allen, 1975); and Senate Foreign Relations Committee, *Arms Sales to Near East and South Asian Countries* (Washington, D.C.: Government Printing Office, 1967). Weapons numbers are taken from Nyrop, *Saudi Arabia*, pp. 334–335.

3. According to some sources, Khashoggi, who had picked up the maintenance contract once the U.S. left Dhahran, regularly entertained officials from the British and U.S. advisory teams and then forwarded detailed reports on any critical of the aid effort or the Saudis' comments to the Saudi government.

4. Sampson, *Arms Bazaar*, p. 178; Nyrop, *Saudi Arabia*, p. 334; Halliday, *Arabia Without Sultans*, pp. 59–61. Airwork Services later provided Oman with much of the air support services needed in the Dhofar rebellion.

5. Khashoggi was Lockheed's agent; Faisal's brother Muhammed was the agent for Northrop.

6. Edwards netted something like £7 million for the air defense package. According to Halliday, Edwards was also a close friend of Col. David Stirling, who helped organize the covert British military assistance to the royalists in Yemen and who attempted to overthrow Qadaffi. Edwards was later sued by Col. Richard Lawrence of Jersey, who claimed Edwards had defaulted on commissions from eight separate deals totaling $751 million and five more of unspecified value. See Halliday, *Arabia Without Sultans*, p. 77; *Sunday Telegraph*, 26 June 1966; *Observer*, 10 October 1971.

7. The versions of the Red Top and Firestreak air-to-air missiles then available lacked the sensors and maneuver or "G" capability for effective combat against other fighters, and the Lightnings had comparatively primitive air defense avionics.

8. The Hawk deal was initially costed at less than $60 million but was eventually worth $136 million to Raytheon. Even when the Hawks were finally delivered, they were placed in fixed sites that were far too compact and highly vulnerable to air attack. Until the shah's fall, the radar net and C^3 links servicing the Hawks had major gaps, even in key target areas like Ras Tanura, Dhahran, and Jiddah. Saudi operational doctrine also called for forward fighter defense with a "hand-off" to the Hawk units once enemy aircraft entered their range.

This "system" was poorly organized and integrated as late as 1981, except in the Dhahran area. The overall system also relied too heavily on prominent and highly vulnerable static radar sites with no real mobility and redundancy. For example, the key radar covering Ras Tanura, Dammam, Dhahran, Juaymah, and part of Jubail was on an "artificial hill" and a perfect target; it still gave only about 30 NM warning against low-flying fighters. The only backup was a voice and teleprinter link to the civilian air control radar in Bahrain.

9. In fact, the British Ministry of Defense used the Thunderbird as a case study of how *not* to develop a weapons system in several reviews of its R&D system and later in training staff personnel. See Halliday, *Arabia Without Sultans*, pp. 60–61.

10. Ibid., p. 60.

11. These events are discussed in more detail in Chapter 12. Nasser was forced not only to withdraw from Yemen but also to halt all efforts at subverting the Saudi government. King Saud was forced to leave for Athens, where he died in 1969. In a complex intrafamily negotiation, most of the "free princes" were allowed to return to Saudi Arabia and to some degree of power.

12. Sampson, *Arms Bazaar*, pp. 212–215; Lacey, *The Kingdom*, p. 468. Khashoggi eventually made more than $100 million from Lockheed, $54 million from Northrop, $45 million from a $600 million purchase of French armored cars, and even $4.5 million from a Belgian sale of small arms.

13. Nyrop, *Saudi Arabia*, pp. 334–335.

14. The bulk of the narrative in this section is based on U.S. Army Corps of Engineers data.

15. U.S. Army Corps of Engineers background paper, 1982.

16. The EAA agreements listed cover only directly supervised projects, which are only part of the total effort over which the Corps had direct and indirect control. For example, these include the preliminary planning of Jiddah Airport and the expressway from Jiddah to Makkah.

17. Congressional Research Service (CRS), *Saudi Arabia and the United States: The New Context in an Evolving "Special Relationship,"* a report prepared by the Foreign Affairs and National Defense Division, GPO 81-4940 (Washington, D.C.: Government Printing Office, August 1981), p. 49.

18. For example, the Officers Club in Riyadh cost $17.5 million, although the total number of officers in the area is relatively small, and the National Guard Academy cost over $110 million. In general, however, Corps-designed facilities were well designed and reflected considerable thought regarding the social transformations required to move from tribal or village society to modern military forces and allow for the steadily growing demands and expectations of Saudi officers, NCOs, technicians, and enlisted men.

19. He routinely referred to Shi'ites as "dogs," considered an unclean animal in Islam. He died of natural causes in 1967. The provinces were renamed in November 1963. Hasa became the Eastern Province; Mejd, the Central Province; Hejaz, the Western Province; Asir, the Southern Province; and the border area near Jordan and Iraq, the Northern Frontier Province.

20. Holden and Johns, *House of Saud*, p. 250.

21. Lenczowski, *Middle East in World Affairs*, p. 603; Nyrop, *Saudi Arabia*, p. 345.

22. Faisal at one point blamed U.S. jets for his overthrow and for "frightening" his Royal Guard. The regular Egyptian program directed over the "Voice of the Arabs" was called "The Enemies of God." It ended abruptly on 15 June 1967.

23. Adeed Dawisha, *Saudia Arabia's Search for Security*, Adelphi Paper no. 158 (London: IISS, 1980), p. 4.

24. Holden and Johns, *House of Saud*, pp. 252–254.

25. Richard F. Nyrop, *Area Handbook for the Yemens*, Foreign Area Handbook Series (Washington, D.C.: American University, 1977), pp. 52–54. The process of British withdrawal is described in detail in J. B. Kelly, *Arabia, the Gulf and the West: A Critical View of the Arabs and Their Oil Policy* (New York: Basic Books, 1980), and in Air Chief Marshal Sir David Lee, *Flight from the Middle East* (London: Her Majesty's Stationery Office, 1980).

26. The Iraqi threat in 1961 led to emergency British land and air deployments to Kuwait and serves as the only modern instance of a Western "rapid deployment force" entering the Gulf. The operation is described in detail in Lee, *Flight from the Middle East*. See Chapter 12 of this book for more details.

27. It is important to note that at this time the Saudi MODA was little more than a vertically structured staff for Prince Sultan. It relied almost solely on his decisions and personal review of U.S. and British advisory plans for structuring the Saudi modernization effort.

28. Alvin J. Cottrell, *The Persian Gulf States* (Baltimore: Johns Hopkins University Press, 1980), p. 142; and *The Military Balance, 1969–70* (London: IISS, 1970), p. 36; R. M. Burrell, *The Persian Gulf: The Implications of British Withdrawal*, Washington Paper no. 1, Vol. 1 (Washington, D.C.: Center for Strategic and International Studies, 1969), p. 82.

29. The new Lightnings had belly tanks and were converted to a limited attack role with rockets and iron bombs. They had no attack avionics, however, and retained the air combat maneuver (ACM) and other air combat defects of the earlier models.

30. Nyrop, *Saudi Arabia*, pp. 334–335; Halliday, *Arabia Without Sultans*, p. 61; *Times* (London), 8 July 1970.

31. From 1962 onward, Prince Abdullah and Prince Sultan kept their respective areas of responsibility tightly segregated, as did the princes allied with them. These included Prince Badr (Abd al-Aziz's twentieth son, born 1933), deputy commander of the National Guard in 1965, and Sultan's younger full brother Turki (twenty-third son, born 1934), who became deputy minister of defense in 1969. (Gary S. Saymore, "Royal Family Politics in Saudi Arabia," unpublished paper, Rand Corporation and Harvard University, 1981, pp. 12, 14.) The Egyptian press consistently reported during 1966–1967 that Interior Minister Fahd, supported by his full brothers Sultan (MOD) and Salman (governor of Riyadh), had sought to replace Prince Abdullah as commander of the National Guard with his son Muhammed but had these efforts blocked by King Faisal and Crown Prince Khalid. Like many reports of conflicts between the Sudairis and Abdullah, however, these reports had the clear intent of undermining Saudi stability and dividing the royal family. It is impossible therefore to interpret their validity. In general, it seems unlikely that this conflict took place. Although Sultan and Abdullah have been professional rivals, most Saudi sources indicate that their rivalry never went beyond the normal struggle for bureaucratic power and budget resources common among all senior Saudi officials. British and U.S. officials also indicate that they regard such reports as "disinformation." See Saymore, "Royal Family Politics"; *al-Ahram*, 3 March and 18 October 1967; *Middle East Record*, 1967.

32. Holden and Johns, *House of Saud*, p. 272.

33. Accounts of these events differ drastically. This description is based on interviews and references in ibid., pp. 277–282; John Keegan, *World Armies* (New York: Facts on File, 1979); Nyrop, *Saudi Arabia*, pp. 345–347.

34. Holden and Johns, *House of Saud*, pp. 281–282.

35. Keegan, *World Armies*, p. 620.

36. As will be discussed later, serious regional, tribal, and ethnic divisions still exist within Saudi society, although the improved distribution of the nation's oil wealth to all regions and elements of Saudi society is steadily reducing these tensions.

37. The Jabal Shammar area, which includes about 20% of Saudi Arabia's native population, is often cited as such an area. It was the center of the Rashid dynasty that once forced the Sauds into exile. It should be noted, however, that such senior Saudi princes as Abdullah are the sons of Abd al-Aziz's Rashid wives and that no signs of such discrimination were apparent in the economic activity going on in 1981.

38. Ironically, most are in storage. As was the case in Lebanon, France then lacked the kind of advisory and support capability to support Arab operation of so highly complex a fighter, and the Mirage as delivered by Dassault was one of the most difficult fighters to service in the field. As for the Israelis, a Swiss engineer named Alfred Frauenknecht stole the full technical plans for the Mirage V and gave them to the Israelis, who used them to manufacture the Kfir in Israel. See *From Mirage to Kfir*, War Data no. 2 (Jerusalem: Eshel-Dramit Ltd., 1979).

39. Which is not to argue that the F-5A was adequate as a basis for the large Saudi purchases the U.S. originally recommended. Like the Lightning, it lacked the payload, avionics, and growth capability to deal with the improved versions of the MiG-21 and Fitter. If the Saudis had not eventually shifted to purchases of the F-5A's successor, the much improved F-5E, or Tiger II, the F-5 sale might have been as unfortunate as the Anglo-American air defense sale.

40. See Sampson, *Arms Bazaar*, pp. 211–230, 305–323. It eventually turned out that Lockheed alone had provided Khashoggi with $106 million in commissions.

41. Based on interviews and discussions in Saudi Arabia.

5
Saudi Military Modernization from the British Withdrawal from "East of Suez" to the October War

At the beginning of the 1970s, Saudi Arabia still lacked many of the elements it needed for military modernization. The F-5A purchase was a stopgap in developing a modern air force. The reforms within the armed forces following the unrest in 1969–1970, and Saudi Arabia's arrangements with the Corps of Engineers, represented only limited progress in readying Saudi Arabia to absorb modern military equipment. Yet the country could not wait. The pressures that had begun to change Saudi Arabia's strategic situation gathered steady momentum throughout the early 1970s.

Changes in Saudi Arabia's Strategic Situation in the Early 1970s

The results of the British withdrawal from "east of Suez" were initially less threatening than might have been expected, particularly in the case of Saudi Arabia's two largest neighbors. Although Iraq did send a contingent of troops to occupy a Kuwaiti border post in March 1973 and laid repeated claims to two Kuwaiti islands near the Shat al-Arab in 1974 and 1976, it did not repeat its past claims to all of Kuwait, and there was no repetition of the kind of crisis that had led Saudi and other Arab League troops to be deployed to Kuwait during 1962–1964.[1]

In fact, Iraq became bogged down in a prolonged conflict with the Kurds that lasted until the mid-1970s and in a low-level border war with Iran over control of the Shat al-Arab. It also underwent a bloody series of internal purges and upheavals that upset its governmental structure and armed forces almost continuously, from General Hassan Al-Bakr's seizure of power on 17 July 1968 to Saddam Hussein's full consolidation of power in August 1979.[2] While these pressures did not until 1978 halt Iraqi ideological attacks on the conservative Gulf states or active Iraqi support of various covert radical groups, they did keep Iraq from being an active military threat.[3]

The shah of Iran similarly limited his ambitions, although he did lay occasional claim to the status of "guardian" or "protector" of the Gulf. He paid a state visit to Saudi Arabia in November 1968 to discuss the implications of British withdrawal and reached an amicable settlement with Saudi Arabia over the only territorial dispute between the two countries. Iran recognized Saudi sovereignty over the island of Al-Arabi in late 1968 in return for Saudi recognition of Iranian sovereignty over the island of Farsi. This agreement was partly aborted after the Iranian seizure of an ARAMCO oil rig, but it held throughout most of the shah's remaining tenure in power.

The shah also gave up Iran's claims to Bahrain in May 1970, although this may have been part of a complex bargain with Britain to allow him to seize several strategic islands and offshore oil fields in the Gulf. In any case, the shah confined his actions to a massive military buildup, to deploying an Iranian military presence on Qu'oin Islands in the Strait of Hormuz, and to seizing the Abu Musa and Tumb islands in the Gulf on 30 November 1971.[4]

While British withdrawal from the Gulf did not resolve Saudi Arabia's border claims against the southern Gulf States—which were not settled in the case of Qatar and Oman until 1977[5]—it did not lead to any major conflict between Saudi Arabia and the new states. Equally important, although Bahrain and Qatar refused to join the Gulf Federation that Britain had originally proposed, the rest of the former Trucial States joined the union of Arab emirates that formed around Abu Dhabi between December 1971 and February 1972. As a result, the smaller Gulf states founded a viable political framework, and all remained under conservative rule.

Finally, the struggle that developed in Jordan between the Palestinians and King Hussein was resolved between September 1970 and June 1971 by a series of battles that led to the total defeat of the Palestinians. Jordan also decisively checked Syria when it attempted to aid the Palestinians. This "Black September" secured Saudi Arabia's northwestern borders and reduced the ability of radical political groups to operate in western Saudi Arabia.[6]

Increasing Tensions in Oman and the Red Sea Area

These positive developments, however, did not provide a lasting increase in Saudi security or reduce the urgent need to expand and modernize Saudi forces. Just as the situation began to stabilize in the Gulf, tensions in Oman, the Yemens, and Somalia reached the crisis point. The first crisis was the result of the refusal of Oman's aging sultan, Said bin Taimur, to allow more than the most limited modernization and his failure to share the nation's new oil wealth. The consequence was a major new dissident movement in Oman that had strong radical leadership and a solid base in the disaffected tribes in the southern, or Dhofar, region of the country. This movement acquired steadily greater military capabilities during the late 1960s as a result of training and weapons assistance from the radical regime in South Yemen. The Omani movement built up strong ties with the Arab Nationalist Movements (ANM), and the new rebel force launched its first major military attack on the sultan's forces on 11 June 1970.[7]

This attack helped trigger a peaceful coup by the sultan's son, Qabus bin Said, on 24 July 1970. This coup established a far more progressive regime, but it came too late to avert a major civil war. Although the rebel forces were defeated in central Oman by 1972, the fighting dragged on in Dhofar because of the difficult terrain and the rebels' access to a sanctuary in South Yemen. Although the sultan won his initial victories with British assistance, the rebels were finally defeated only after the shah sent troops, Jordan sent 150 engineers, and Saudi Arabia provided massive financial aid to the sultan. Rebel elements remained active in South Yemen even after the final mop-up campaigns in 1976 and 1977, and their presence in camps in South Yemen continued to present a minor problem in late 1981.[8]

A second crisis arose as the continuing struggle between the various political elements in South Yemen and North Yemen led both nations into a strange pattern of border wars alternating with calls for unification, and to a continuously shifting set of internal and external political alliances in each country. In the case of South Yemen, Saudi Arabia made continuing efforts to try to split the more moderate elements within the South Yemeni government from the Soviet Union, only to see a Soviet-backed coup give a pro-Soviet faction total control in 1978. In the case of North Yemen, a three-cornered struggle for power among traditional tribal elements, more progressive moderates, and left-wing or radical extremists led to a constant shift in alliances with Saudi Arabia, South Yemen, the U.S., and the USSR. This conflict left Saudi Arabia uncertain at any given time as to whether North Yemen would join South Yemen in its hostility to Saudi Arabia and as to the probable impact of its continuing military buildup.

The third crisis involved Ethiopia. In October 1969 General Mohammed Siad Barre took control of Somalia and began to push Somali claims to the Ogaden region of Ethiopia. At the same time, low-level fighting between Ethiopian troops and the Eritrean Liberation Front (ELF) began to threaten the stability of Ethiopia. The government's massive mishandling of a famine was the third factor precipitating the Ethiopian army into action. Although Emperor Haile Selassie suppressed several coup attempts during the early 1970s, a "creeping coup" by the army eventually deposed him in September 1974.[9] The coup was followed by major ELF attacks on Ethiopia in 1975, a full-scale civil war in Eritrea, and a major war between Ethiopia and Somalia over control of the Ogaden that began in 1976. These events forced Saudi Arabia into more and more direct participation in the various Muslim and "Arab" movements in the Horn after 1970 and finally into providing major financial support to Somalia in its war with Ethiopia. The Somali offensive collapsed in 1977–1978, however, when the Soviet Military Transport Command moved nearly 200,000 Cuban troops into Ethiopia and launched a massive airlift, flying through Iran, Iraq, Afghanistan, and Libya.[10] As massive Soviet weapons deliveries built up, Saudi Arabia was confronted with a major Soviet-backed military power across the Red Sea.[11]

At the same time, Saudi Arabia faced a lesser crisis in Sudan. Since Col. Jaafar Muhammed al-Nimeiri came to power in May 1969, Sudan has been racked by constant coup attempts. They included an ultra-conservative Islamic tribal coup attempt in March 1970, a nearly successful communist-backed coup attempt in July 1971, Libyan-backed coup attempts in September 1975 and July 1976, and a host of lesser attempts. During this period, Nimeiri shifted from the left to a moderate position and formed an alliance with Egypt in 1976 with strong Saudi support. However, given Sudan's continued instability, Saudi Arabia had no assurance that it would not suddenly face another hostile radical regime across the Red Sea.[12]

The developing threats in the Red Sea area were compounded by a PLO attack on 11 June 1971 on the Israeli tanker *Coral Sea,* which was sailing near the Strait of Bab al-Mandeb at the southeastern entrance to the Red Sea. The attack had strong South Yemeni support, and it helped lead Israel to develop a long-range air strike capability. Israel further improved its long-range strike capabilities with fighter and tanker purchases after the October War of 1973. As a result, the Israeli threat to Saudi Arabia's cities, ports, and oil facilities increased significantly in the early 1970s.

The October War, Oil, and the Arms Race in the Gulf

These crises were joined by new problems after the Arab-Israeli conflict of 1973. While the October War did not involve Saudi Arabia in more than token military actions—the Saudi presence was limited to the deployment of a 1,500-man motorized infantry brigade and 10 tanks to Jordan—it still had an important impact on Saudi security.[13] The first effect was to further intensify the massive arms race throughout the Arab world and to add a new emphasis on obtaining the most advanced military technology available. Coupled to the impact of the war in Vietnam—which introduced precision-guided weapons, surface-to-air missiles, and sophisticated electronic warfare into the Third World—the October War essentially abolished the previous technological distinction between the forces of the great powers and the forces of countries in the Near East.[14]

This arms race is summarized in Tables 5.1 and 5.2, which reflect the virtual explosion in the growth of the military forces surrounding

TABLE 5.1 Numbers of Medium Tanks in the Gulf States, 1969-1982

	69-70	70-71	71-72	72-73	73-74	74-75	75-76	76-77	77-78	78-79	79-80	80-81	81-82	82-83
The Gulf States				0	0	0		0	0	0	0	0	0	0
Bahrain	n.a.	n.a.	n.a.	0	0	0	0	0	0	0	0	0	0	0
Iran	n.a.	n.a.	860	860	920	1,160	1,160	1,360	1,620	1,620	1,735	1,735	1,410	1,110
Iraq	535	645	860	860	990	1,390	1,200	1,200	1,350	1,700	1,700	2,600	2,600	2,300
Kuwait	n.a.	n.a.	n.a.	80	700	700	700	700	112	280	124	280	240	240
Oman	n.a.	n.a.	n.a.	0	0	0	0	0	0	0	0	0	18[a]	18
Qatar	n.a.	n.a.	n.a.	0	0	0	0	0	0	72	72	24	24	24
Saudi Arabia	"a few"	55	25	25	25	55	175	325	475	325	350	380	630	450
UAE	n.a.	n.a.	n.a.	0	0	0	0	0	0	0	0	0	75	118
YAR	n.a.	n.a.	n.a.	n.a.	30	30	30	30	30	220	232	864	714	714
YPDR	n.a.	n.a.	n.a.	n.a.	50	50	50	200	200	260	260	375	375	470
Subtotal	535	700	1,745	1,825	2,715	3,385	3,315	3,815	3,787	4,477	4,473	6,258	6,086	5,444
The Horn														
Ethiopia	n.a.	0	0	0	0	0	24	78	70	504	630	640	640	790
Somalia	n.a.	150[b]	150[b]	150[b]	150[b]	220[b]	250[b]	250[b]	300[b]	80[b]	80	140	190	140
Sudan	n.a.	50	120	130	130	130	130	130	130	130	130	130	197	190
Subtotal	n.a.	200	270	280	280	350	404	458	500	714	840	910	1,027	1,120
Arab/Israeli Confrontation States														
Israel	1,020	1,050	1,075	1,725	1,725	1,900	2,700	2,700	3,000	3,000	3,050	3,050	3,600	3,600
Egypt	825	1,225	1,450	1,970	1,850	2,000	1,920	1,920	1,850[b]	1,600[b]	1,600[b]	1,600	1,660	2,100
Jordan	329	310	290	344	420	490	490	490	520	500	500	609	516	569
Syria	450	850	750	1,140	1,140	1,600	2,300	2,300	2,400	2,500	2,600	2,920	3,300	3,990
Subtotal	2,624	3,435	3,565	5,179	5,135	5,990	7,410	7,410	7,770	7,600	7,750	8,179	9,076	10,259
Total	3,159	4,335	5,580	7,284	8,130	9,725	11,129	11,683	12,057	12,791	13,063	15,347	16,189	16,823

[a] 12 Chieftains on lease.
[b] Not all are operational.
Source: Adapted from *The Military Balance* (London: International Institute for Strategic Studies, various years).

TABLE 5.2 Numbers of Combat Aircraft in the Gulf States, 1969-1982

	1969-70	1970-71	1971-72	1972-73	1973-74	1974-75	1975-76	1976-77	1977-78	1978-79	1979-80	1980-81	1981-82	1982-83
The Gulf States														
Bahrain	n.a.	n.a.	n.a.	0	0	0	0	0	0	0	0	0	0	6
Iran	180	175	140	160	159	216	238	317	341	459	447	445[a]	100[b]	90[b]
Iraq	213	229	220	189	224	218	247	299	369	339	339	332	335	330[b]
Kuwait	n.a.	n.a.	n.a.	26	30	28	32	33	49	50	49	50	50	49
Oman	n.a.	n.a.	n.a.	15	12	12	47	44	50	46	49	52	50[c]	37
Qatar	n.a.	n.a.	n.a.	4	4	4	4	13	4	4	4	4	9	9
Saudi Arabia	43	75	75	71	70	90	95	97	137	171[c]	180[c]	177[c]	175	191[c,d]
UAE	n.a.	n.a.	n.a.	12	12	18	26	26	38	46	52	52	51	52
YAR	n.a.	n.a.	n.a.	n.a.	28	28	24[d]	28[d]	22	26	11	49	65	75[d]
YPDR	n.a.	n.a.	n.a.	n.a.	20	39[d]	27[d]	27[d]	33[d]	34[d]	109	111	111	114[d]
Subtotal	436	479	435	477	559	653	740	884	1,043	1,175	1,240	1,272	956	953
The Horn														
Ethiopia	n.a.	43	48	46	37	40	37	36	35	99	100	100+	100+	113[b]
Somalia	n.a.	18	20	21	21[a]	31[a]	52[a]	66[a]	55	25[a]	25[a]	33[a]	33[a]	55[a]
Sudan	n.a.	32	32	40	50	51	43	50	27	22	36	36	44	30
Subtotal	n.a.	93	100	107	108	122	132	152	117	146	161	169	177	198
Arab-Israeli Confrontation States														
Israel	275	330	374	432	488	466[b]	461	543	549	543	576	535	602	769[d]
Egypt	400	415	523	768[d]	620[d]	568[b,d]	500[d]	488	473	612[a]	563[a]	363	363[a]	429[a]
Jordan	11	38	33	50	52	50	42	66	78	76	73	58	84	94
Syria	145	210	210	210	326	300[b,d]	400[d]	440[d]	395[d]	392[d]	389[a]	395[a]	395[d]	450[b,d]
Subtotal	831	993	1,140	1,460	1,486	1,384[b]	1,403	1,537	1,495	1,623	1,601	1,351	1,424	1,742
Total	1,267	1,565	1,675	2,044	2,153	2,159	2,275	2,573	2,655	2,944	3,002	2,792	2,559	2,893

[a] Many aircraft believed nonoperational.
[b] Possibly inaccurate due to assessment difficulties.
[c] BAC-167s used in COIN/training role.
[d] Some aircraft in storage.
Source: The Military Balance (London: International Institute for Strategic Studies, various years).

Saudi Arabia. To put these numbers in perspective, it is interesting to note that the Germans had only 3,000 tanks on the entire eastern front in 1943[15] and that the International Institute for Strategic Studies (IISS) estimated that NATO had 2,539 combat aircraft and 10,531 medium tanks in Northern and Central Europe in 1982.[16] The more than fivefold increase in the number of medium tanks between 1969 and 1982 shown in Table 5.1, and the near-tripling of the number of combat aircraft shown in Table 5.2, made the Near East the largest arms-importing area in the world. It also gave the Near East total force levels of modern military equipment rivaling those held by NATO and the Warsaw Pact. Virtually all of Saudi Arabia's neighbors had acquired the capability to launch major air strikes against it by the mid-1970s, and most had acquired the ability to launch land attacks against Saudi Arabia, its allies, or its major lines of communication. Equally important, Saudi Arabia could not count on the stability of any given friendly regime. Events often eliminated or reduced potential threats, but Saudi military planners faced the grim reality that they could not plan on the friendship or even neutrality of any nearby state.

The second effect of the war was the transformation of the PLO and the Palestinian movement back into a major force in the Arab world and the Gulf. The Saudis strongly supported the PLO as an Arab cause, and such support was unavoidable if Saudi Arabia was to ensure the relative moderation of the Palestinian leadership and to avoid new efforts to radicalize the Gulf by pro-Palestinian student groups and the Palestinians working in critical jobs in most of the Gulf states. This necessity inevitably created still further tensions among Saudi Arabia, the U.S., and Israel.

The third effect was to trigger the massive increase in oil prices discussed in Chapter 1. OPEC's first major rise in oil prices, which resulted from the Tehran Agreement of February 1971, became "pin money." Posted prices rose from $3.11 per barrel on 16 October 1973 to $11.65 on 1 January 1974.[17] These increases in oil income transformed Saudi Arabia into an economic power, as described in Chapter 1, and led to a massive influx of new wealth. They forced Saudi Arabia into a faster pattern of modernization and into a race to transform Saudi society rapidly enough to cope with its new wealth before the wealth created tensions that tore the nation apart. Similar capital transfers affected the other oil-exporting states in the Gulf, many of which were far worse prepared to use their new oil wealth. More broadly, these changes made each oil-exporting state a major strategic target for both superpowers and for every radical movement in the Arab world.

The Iranian-Iraqi Arms Race and the "Two Pillars" Policy

Although virtually all the military developments shown in Tables 5.1 and 5.2 affected Saudi security, the Saudis became particularly concerned with the arms race between Iran and Iraq. A low-level arms race had started between the two states long before the British announced that they would withdraw from the Gulf, but once Britain left, the Iraqi-Iranian arms race became the dominant military development in the Gulf area. This arms race was fueled during 1969–1974 by occasional Iraqi and Iranian fighting over the control of the Shat al-Arab waterway, by attempts to sponsor assassination plots and hostile political groups in each other's country, by Iranian funding of the Kurdish rebels in Iraq, by tacit Iranian support of Israel, and by Iraqi conflicts with Kuwait in an effort to improve its naval position in the Gulf.[18]

The result from Saudi Arabia's point of view was to create two regional "superpowers" in the Gulf and to diminish its political and military influence. The broad patterns of this military development are shown in Table 5.3, along with the force ratios that resulted. It is also clear from the table that the Iraqi-Iranian arms race continued after the Algiers Accord of 1975. Moreover, the increases in Iranian and Iraqi force numbers were only part of the reason for Saudi concern. Unlike the other military forces that were potential threats to Saudi Arabia, Iraq and Iran had acquired enough trained manpower, aircraft, and armor to pose a major threat to Saudi oil facilities. They had also acquired the ability to project military forces into the other conservative states in the Gulf.

Iraq had a massive mobile logistic and combat support capability, including significant numbers of tank transporters, that gave it the power to move its armored forces comparatively long distances by road. Similarly, Iran's seaborne and air mobility increased steadily, and it had created the first major modern navy in the Gulf. Coupled to Iran's naval control of the strategic islands in the entrance to the Gulf and along its southern coast, this force gave Iran control over tanker and cargo vessel movements throughout the Gulf area.

Iraq was Saudi Arabia's most immediate concern. It remained politically hostile to the conservative Arab states in the Gulf until the late 1970s. Saudi Arabia had no major military bases nearer to Iraq than Tabuk and Dhahran, and while this was a major reason for building the new military city at Hafr al-Batin, it could not be completed before the mid-1980s. This combination of hostility and weakness led the Saudi government to seek closer cooperation with Iran, and the shah was glad to reciprocate. Although some periods of tension occurred between the two states—for example, when Saudi Arabia gave the United Arab Emirates token support in their protest against the shah's occupation of Abu Musa and the Tumb islands during the final days of Britain's departure from the Gulf—these periods of tension had little lasting effect. The normal pattern of Saudi-Iranian relations was one of presenting a common front against the radical regime in Iraq.[19]

Saudi Arabia and Iran cooperated in limiting Iraqi efforts to force Kuwait to cede the islands of Warbah and Bubiyan, facing Iraq's one

TABLE 5.3 Military Buildup of the Major Gulf Powers, 1969–1982

	Total Military Manpower (000s)				Combat Aircraft				Medium Tanks			
	Saudi Arabia	Iran	Iraq	Iran + Iraq % of Saudi Arabia	Saudi Arabia	Iran	Iraq	Iran + Iraq % of Saudi Arabia	Saudi Arabia	Iran	Iraq	Iran + Iraq % of Saudi Arabia
1969	62	221	78	482	43	180	213	914	?	n.a.	535	?
1970	60	161	95	426	75	175	229	538	55	n.a.	645	117[a]
1971	71	181	95	389	75	140	220	480	25	860	860	6,880
1972	51	191	102	575	71	160	189	497	25	860	860	6,880
1973	47	212	102	668	70	159	224	547	25	920	990	7,640
1974	69	238	113	509	90	216	218	482	55	1,160	1,390	4,636
1975	63	250	135	617	95	238	247	511	175	1,160	1,200	1,349
1976	72	300	158	636	97	317	299	635	325	1,360	1,200	788
1977	97	342	188	547	137	341	369	518	475	1,620	1,350	625
1978	94	413	272	666	171	459	339	466	325	1,620	1,700	1,022
1979[b]	65	475	222	980	178	447	339	441	350	1,735	1,700	987
1980[b]	67	240	242	719	136[c]	445	332	571	380	1,735	2,600	1,141
1981	82	195	252	545	139[c]	100	335	313	630	1,410	2,600	757
1982	84	235	342	687	128[c]	90	330	329	450	1,110	2,300	758
Average				603				517				2,399

[a] Iraq only.

[b] Figures for Iran may not be accurate; many men believed deserted and much equipment inoperable.

[c] Does not include 39 BAC-167 COIN aircraft used in a training role.

Sources: U.S. Arms Control and Disarmament Agency, *World Military Expenditures and Arms Transfers,* 1969–1978; *The Military Balance* (London: International Institute for Strategic Studies, 1969–1983).

military seaport of Umm Qasr, and in checking the influence of Iraqi-backed radical movements like the Popular Front for the Liberation of the Occupied Arab Gulf.[20] Saudi Arabia backed the shah in his efforts to force Iraq into a rapprochement on Iranian terms; this backing helped lead to the Algiers Accord of March 1975, which gave Iran joint control of the Shat al-Arab and stabilized Iraqi-Iranian relations until the shah's fall. Finally, the shah and Saudi Arabia cooperated in backing Sultan Qabus in his successful campaign against the Dhofar rebels.[21]

At the same time, Saudi Arabia was all too aware of the implications of the shah's steadily escalating claims to the status of protector of the Gulf; the shah was telling U.S. and other Western officials of how he would eventually have to save Saudi Arabia from the internal threats to its government.[22] The Saudis were also aware of the shah's concern with the future depletion of Iranian oil reserves, which was then predicted to begin in the mid-1980s, and of his efforts to increase his military influence over the other conservative Gulf states. As a result, Saudi officials viewed the deployment of Iranian troops to Oman with more than passing concern, and they became increasingly worried after 1973 that the shah had broader political-military ambitions in the Gulf and that the U.S. might support him in achieving his ambitions.

This Saudi concern was reinforced by the U.S. response to the British withdrawal from the Gulf. The U.S. involvement in Vietnam precluded any U.S. replacement of the British presence, even if this had been acceptable to the Gulf nations. Further, the "Nixon Doctrine," announced in Guam in 1969, called for a reliance on strong regional allies and the building up of regional powers to eliminate the requirement for the deployment of U.S. forces. The doctrine almost inevitably meant a U.S. alignment with Iran and support of the shah's efforts to make Iran a military power that could "secure" the region and check any expansion of Soviet influence. Although the U.S. publicly announced that it would rely on a "two-pillar" (or "twin-pillar") policy in the Gulf and build up both Iran and Saudi Arabia into centers of strategic stability, it actually pursued a "one-pillar" strategy. The U.S. relied on Iran for military security and treated Saudi Arabia largely as a source of oil. The two-pillar policy was also biased from the start by the recognition that any major U.S. attempt to build up Saudi Arabia military forces meant political confrontation with Israel and serious domestic political difficulties with U.S. pro-Israeli political action groups.[23]

This two-pillar policy was implemented at a time when the U.S. policy planning and intelligence effort was concentrated on the Vietnam War, and when major cutbacks were taking place in the U.S. political intelligence effort as the U.S. shifted to reliance on "technical means" of intelligence collection. The U.S. was thus deprived of the ability to improve its intelligence coverage of the Gulf just as vast increases were taking place in the strategic importance of the area. Further, for a variety of domestic political reasons, President Nixon's election in 1968 led to the dismissal or rotation of many of the senior U.S. career officials who had had long experience in the Gulf, had worked with the shah, or had been involved in the U.S. efforts to end the rebellion in Oman and to eliminate the Egyptian and Soviet presence in the Yemens. These changes meant that the U.S. implemented the two-pillar policy with only limited expertise in the area and a relatively poor institutional memory of the problems Iran faced in expanding its strategic role in the Gulf.

All these factors helped contribute to the fact that when President Nixon met with the shah in Tehran in March 1972, he gave the shah a "blank check" to buy any conventional arms in U.S. inventory and assured him of preferential treatment in terms of deliveries and the provision of military advisers.[24] He did so largely at the urging of Henry Kissinger, who had little background in the area, and who personally overruled the concerns expressed by the Department of Defense, the State Department desk officials for Iran, and the senior career State Department officials in Tehran.[25] This policy left Iran's limited financial resources as the only remaining restraint on the shah—a restraint that vanished with the rise in oil prices following the 1973 embargo.

Iran's new oil wealth gave the shah immense wealth and the ability to draw on Nixon's blank check. At the same time, the U.S. offered generous credit and financial terms, and made special arrangements to provide him with advisers and support personnel, in spite of congressional restrictions on the number of U.S. military personnel and officials that could be sent to Iran. After 1974, the U.S. acted as if the shah represented the only stable regime in the area and as if he had the wealth to buy virtually any arms he wanted. It assumed that he would simply recycle petrodollars because Iran's oil production had risen from 1.7 MMBD and an annual value of $482 million in 1964 to 5.9 MMBD in September 1973 and a value of $4.4 billion annually and then leaped to over $21 billion in 1974 for the same level of production.[26]

As a result, Saudi Arabia became steadily more concerned that the United States was providing it with an Iranian "shield" whose ultimate effect might be to make the shah a major threat to Saudi Arabia. The Saudis also found that when they quietly raised their concerns with U.S. officials, beginning in the early 1970s, the latter tended to echo the shah's claim that he would protect Saudi Arabia from internal threats and from Iraq—a response that scarcely allayed Saudi concerns. The Saudis were further disturbed when they found that most of the senior U.S. officials involved seemed generally unaware of the detailed political relationships among the states in the Gulf, of the risks inherent in creating such an Iranian shield, and of the details of many of the other political developments taking place in the region. Thus the Saudis had additional concerns over the possible consequences of the U.S. two-pillars policy, although Saudi intelligence was generally at least as ignorant of the internal problems building up in Iran as was the U.S., and Saudi

Arabia was in far worse position to appraise Iran's ability to absorb its weapons purchases than the U.S. military advisers working in Iran.[27]

Saudi Arabia could not respond to these trends by sharply accelerating the growth or modernization of its military forces. It certainly had the wealth to buy as much military equipment as Iraq or Iran, but it lacked the trained manpower and infrastructure to absorb it. The events of 1965, 1969, and 1971 had demonstrated all too clearly to Saudi leaders that there were severe limits to the increases that could take place in Saudi forces until Saudi Arabia laid the proper groundwork for full-scale military modernization. They made the Saudis realize that it would take at least a decade to bring this groundwork to the point at which Saudi Arabia could modernize its forces sufficiently to defend against the other two major powers in the Gulf.

Saudi Arabia could, however, react to Iran and Iraq's efforts by vastly increasing its investment in infrastructure and training. This policy did not offer immediate increases in military strength, but Saudi planners calculated that Saudi Arabia would have the time to transform its investment into larger military forces. The resulting policy decisions shaped the dynamics of Saudi Arabia's military buildup until the shah's fall, and they gave Saudi defense expenditures and imports a very different character from those of Iran and Iraq. This difference is illustrated in Table 5.4, which compares the total defense expenditures of the three major Gulf powers with their purchases of arms and equipment directly supporting combat equipment. The subtotal for 1978, the last year before the shah's fall, is particularly relevant. These figures show that while Iraq and Iran could concentrate on buying arms, Saudi Arabia was forced to devote an immense amount of its total defense expenditures to construction and infrastructure. Some estimates of such Saudi expenditures go as high 85–90% of the total. Even using the most generous definition of expenditures on items contributing directly to combat capability, Saudi Arabia spent at least 72% of its budget on construction and infrastructure through 1978.[28]

It is also important to note that the comparisons shown in Table 5.4 use U.S. Arms Control and Disarmament Agency (ACDA) and CIA data, which are biased by a systematic undervaluing of Soviet-bloc military equipment.[29] As a result, the figures for Iranian arms imports should actually be about 8% higher, and the figures for Iraqi imports about 30% higher, than those shown. Adjusting for these problems, Iraq was importing at least twice as many arms annually through 1978 as was Saudi Arabia.

The relevant flows of such U.S. assistance and arms transfers are shown in Table 5.5. No matter how Tables 5.4 and 5.5 are interpreted, the data show an incredible expenditure on defense following Britain's announcement of its withdrawal from the Gulf. These expenditures, however, bought Saudi Arabia and Iran very different things. At least 70% of Saudi purchases from the U.S. were for services, construction

TABLE 5.4 Defense Expenditures in the Gulf, 1969–1982 (current $ millions)

	Total Defense Expenditures					Arms Imports				
	Saudi Arabia	Iran	Iran as a % of Saudi Arabia	Iraq	Iraq as a % of Saudi Arabia	Saudi Arabia	Iran	Iran as a % of Saudi Arabia	Iraq	Iraq as a % of Saudi Arabia
1969	1,182	1,828	155	826	70	80	220	275	70	88
1970	1,481	2,045	138	822	56	30	160	533	50	166
1971	1,572	2,505	159	857	54	20	320	1,600	40	200
1972	2,115	3,093	146	977	43	110	525	477	140	127
1973	2,796	3,729	133	1,304	47	80	525	656	625	787
1974	3,182	6,303	198	1,686	53	340	1,000	294	625	184
1975	7,105	8,646	122	1,738	24	250	1,200	480	675	270
1976	9,288	9,521	103	1,837	20	470	2,100	447	1,000	213
1977	8,952	8,747	98	2,007	22	925	2,400	259	1,500	162
1978	10,284	10,598	103	2,136	21	1,000	2,100	270	1,500	150
1979	14,180	9,940	70	2,670	19	925	1,600	173	2,100	227
1980	20,700	4,200	20	2,700	13	1,400	220	16	1,600	114
Subtotal	82,837	71,155	86	19,560	24	5,630	12,370	220	9,925	176
1981	27,700	4,400	16	n.a.	n.a.	n.a.				
Total	110,537	75,555	68	19,560	18	5,630	12,370	220	9,925	176

Sources: U.S. Arms Control and Disarmament Agency, ***World Military Expenditures and Transfers,*** 1969–1978 and 1971–1980, Tables I and II; data for 1979, 1980, and 1981 from ***The Military Balance*** (London: International Institute for Strategic Studies, various years). Figures for 1982 not available.

TABLE 5.5 U.S. Arms Sales and Military Assistance to Saudi Arabia and Iran, FY 1967–FY 1976 (current $ millions)

	FY 1967–FY 1976: British Withdrawal to the Algiers Accord			FY 1970–FY 1979: Total Transfers from the Nixon Doctrine to the Fall of the Shah		
	Saudi Arabia	Iran	Total	Saudi Arabia	Iran	Total
Agreements and Planned						
Foreign military sales	8,555	12,504	21,059	30,012	14,014	44,026
Military assistance	0	70	70	0	a	a
International training	4	14	18	1	5	6
Total	8,559	12,588	21,147	30,013	14,019	44,032
Deliveries						
Foreign military sales	1,585	4,003	5,588	8,450	9,502	17,952
Military assistance	b	143	143	0	26	26
International training	4	17	21	2	5	7
Subtotal	1,589	4,163	5,752	8,452	9,533	17,985
Commercial exports	146	195	347	406[c]	636[c]	1,042[c]
Total	10,294	16,946	27,240	38,871	24,188	63,059
FMS Credits	129	365	494	12	0	12

[a] 341,000.
[b] $8,000.
[c] 1971–1976.

Source: U.S. Department of Defense, DSAA, *Foreign Military Sales and Military Assistance Facts,* various years. The data for a given year often do not track in these DSAA reports from year to year, and such totals must be regarded as approximate.

and infrastructure; these proportions were almost reversed in the case of Iran. Some 70% or more of the Iranian purchases shown in Table 5.5 were for equipment, munitions, and direct support to combat arms. The term "teeth-to-tail ratio" is somewhat misleading in assessing the figures in Table 5.5, since Saudi and Iranian purchases of arms, or "teeth," included both combat and service support, but it gives a rough idea of the impact of this difference. After the British announcement of its withdrawal from the Gulf, Iran spent over $12 billion on buying "teeth" from the U.S. during FY1967–1976; Saudi Arabia spent less than $3 billion. During FY1970–1979, Iran spent about $18 billion on "teeth," as compared to less than $10 billion for Saudi Arabia. Accordingly, during the critical period between Britain's withdrawal from the Gulf and the shah's fall, Iran outspent Saudi Arabia on "teeth" by far more than two to one. In contrast, Saudi Arabia spent almost five times as much on "tail." Further, a good deal of this "tail" includes civil expenditures like the creation of the Saudi Arabian television network and whole new seaports, roads, and major communications facilities whose main functions were civilian rather than military.

The Iranian emphasis on arms thus had the effect of making Iran, rather than Saudi Arabia, the key "pro-Western" military power in the Gulf. As time went on, however, this emphasis had other major effects on Saudi military development and Saudi-U.S. military relations. The disparity between the "teeth" each side obtained led to steadily increasing protests within the Saudi armed forces and government that the U.S. was favoring Iran. At the same time, U.S. observers, particularly in Congress, equated the Saudi military buildup with that of the shah on the basis of total dollars spent, although such comparisons were totally meaningless. This misunderstanding of the true nature of the arms buildup in the region has colored every congressional review of the U.S. arms sales to Saudi Arabia since 1974.

Saudi Air Force Modernization and the Evolution of the Peace Hawk Program

Given these conditions, Saudi Arabia was virtually forced to find some other means to compensate for its military weakness and the uncertainties in its strategic position. From 1971 onward, Saudi Arabia steadily increased its diplomatic efforts to support conservative and moderate regimes and political movements in the Arab world. These efforts were supported by the country's new oil wealth after 1973, which gave it the political and economic leverage to play a major role throughout the Gulf, the Near East, and Southwest Asia. As a result, Saudi Arabia began to substitute economic power for its lack of military power. It used its wealth to back King Hussein in Jordan, Sultan Qabus in Oman, President Sadat's break with the USSR, and President Nimeiri's shift to a moderate position in Sudan. It used economic aid as a major national security tool in its relations with the smaller Gulf states and, as will be described in Chapters 12 and 13, its new wealth gave it the flexibility to reach border settlements with most of its conservative neighbors, to achieve a modus vivendi with Iraq, and to play a more active role in the Yemens.

At the same time, Saudi Arabia took some important additional steps toward modernizing its military forces. The most important of these steps was to improve the organization of the Saudi Air Force and to finally obtain effective USAF and private contractor support in planning and managing the Saudi Air Force modernization effort. Somewhat ironically, it was Northrop that helped lead this effort, which contributed to overcoming the Saudi-U.S. tensions growing out of the October War and to persuading Saudi Arabia not to turn to the French for both fighters and air force support.[30]

In late 1971 Saudi Arabia followed its original F-5A purchase with the purchase of 20 F-5E Tigers, which were a greatly improved version of the F-5A. While this sale was not entirely free of the past problems with commissions, it gave Saudi Arabia the kind of fighter it needed. Equally important, the resulting deployment of the F-5A/B and F-5E to Saudi Arabia during 1972–1973 came with effective U.S. military and contractor support. The new F-5 purchase also gave the Royal Saudi Air Force (RSAF) much better access to training facilities in the U.S. and led to the stationing of a much larger cadre of USAF and U.S. contractor personnel in Saudi Arabia. As a result, not only was Saudi Arabia able to effectively take on a modern fighter, both countries acquired a better appreciation of the problems the Saudis faced, including the problems of operating fighters in the country's extremely demanding environment.

The outcome was a steady expansion of the role the USAF played in training the RSAF. The British mission established in the mid-1960s continued under a senior RAF officer, and in early 1973 a government-to-government agreement was signed that made the British Aircraft Corporation (BAC) the main British contractor for the air force. The British continued to operate the Saudi Air Academy at Riyadh, the technical studies institute at Dhahran (which had been set up to deal with the training problems exposed by the Anglo-American air defense system), the Saudi Air Force hospitals, and various other projects on Saudi Arabia's major air bases.[31] Further, BAC continued to service and carry out training on the Saudi Strikemaster and Lightning fighters; these tasks involved a total British staff of about 2,000.

However, the U.S. took over responsibility for ground crew training, basic pilot training, and all training for the Saudi Air Force personnel operating the F-5. The total size of the U.S. Military Training Mission expanded to 250, and the number of Technical Advisory Field Team (TAFT) and contract personnel expanded even further. In late 1975 the USAF also assumed responsibility for giving Saudi recruits the basic skills they needed to operate modern military equipment. A facility was set up at Lackland Air Force Base in Texas to train 400 Saudis a year in a course that included 4 weeks of basic training, 59 weeks of English, and one year of science and mathematics.[32] Further, as Northrop expanded its role as a major support contractor for the F-5A and F-5E, and in helping the Saudis in their conversion to the F-5s, its role changed from being one of many contractors competing for sales through commission agents to one of working closely with the Saudi Air Force and senior Saudi defense officials. Northrop proved considerably more effective in this role than its British predecessors, which gradually eliminated much of the resentment and lingering scandal that had surrounded the original F-5A sale.

These improvements in Saudi-U.S. military relations were complicated by Prince Sultan's efforts to buy the F-4, or Jaguar, and by a split within the U.S. Department of Defense over whether to sell the F-4 aircraft to Saudi Arabia. However, the U.S. and Saudi Arabia compromised on a Saudi purchase of more F-5Es and enough Improved Hawk surface-to-air missiles to provide a point defense of Saudi air bases, key cities, and oil facilities.

The political tensions that grew out of the October War faded quickly once the U.S. moved actively toward arranging a disengagement between the Arab and Israeli forces and Israeli withdrawal from part of the occupied territories. Saudi Arabia ordered the Improved Hawk,[33] and it used the first Saudi-U.S. talks after the disengagement agreement to establish a better-structured basis for Saudi-U.S. defense cooperation. Saudi Arabia gave this objective high priority in June 1974, when Prince Fahd led a mission to Washington as part of a broader effort to create a new overall relationship between the U.S. and Saudi Arabia.

The oil embargo had given the U.S. an equal incentive to establish stronger military ties, and the talks that followed not only set up the Joint Commission on Economic Cooperation, but a joint commission on Saudi defense and training requirements. This commission was initially headed by Prince Sultan and Assistant Secretary of Defense for International Security Affairs Robert Ellsworth. Once President Nixon had completed a reciprocal visit to Riyadh on 14–15 June 1974, the commission helped monitor a massive expansion of the U.S. military assistance effort to Saudi Arabia. U.S. foreign military sales agreements rose from $459 million in FY1973-1974 to $1,993 million in 1974-1975, and Saudi Arabia ranked second to Iran in buying U.S. arms. Although this U.S. assistance program was scarcely a tightly managed and well-planned effort, the U.S. mission in Saudi Arabia was reorganized and the planning and support effort in Washington received far more high-level attention than had previously been the case.[34]

This was particularly true of the plans the USAF prepared for the Saudi Air Force. The loosely structured plans the U.S. had previously furnished Saudi Arabia were replaced in 1974 and 1975 by a series of major Saudi-U.S. studies known as the "Peace Hawk" studies. These, and a number of supporting studies, examined the air threat to Saudi Arabia and Saudi air defense modernization requirements. These joint studies dealt solely with Saudi air power, and not with Saudi Arabia's overall defense planning, programming, and budgeting needs, but they had much more depth than previous joint studies and they did attempt to create a comprehensive plan for Saudi Air Force modernization.[35]

Saudi Arabia bought 30 more F-5Es and F-5Fs in 1974. These F-5Es and dual-seat F-5Fs were also heavily modified to provide a Maverick missile capability, a radar warning receiver, chaff, flares, and radar angle tracking. The Saudi Air Force was flying 20 F-5As and 14 F-5Es by the end of the year, which furthered the relationship between

Northrop and the RSAF. Saudi Arabia began to negotiate a formal agreement to make Northrop the main subcontractor for support of its air force modernization effort.[36] This agreement was signed in March 1976, and Northrop steadily increased the cadre of U.S. contractor personnel supporting the Saudi Air Force. This cadre reached 450 contract personnel by 1975; by that time its role had broadened to include responsibilities for construction. In the following years, Northrop's role in Peace Hawk expanded even further in a series of incremental planning efforts and programs. The staffing of its effort in Saudi Arabia rose to 900 by 1977, 1,100 in 1978, and 1,800 in 1980. Meanwhile, Lockheed got a contract in 1976 for a civil-military air traffic control system worth $611 million.

By late 1974, Saudi Arabia had a total of 126 F-5Es and F-5Fs on order.[37] Although this F-5E order proved overambitious and was cut back in 1978 when Saudi Arabia purchased the F-15, the Saudi Air Force was operating 65 F-5Es, 24 F-5Fs, and 16 F-5Bs in late 1980—a total of 105 F-5 aircraft. The success of the Saudi Peace Hawk program was demonstrated by the fact that the Saudi Air Force had reached proficiency levels superior to those of any other Gulf air force except Iran's.[38] By 1980, six follow-on Peace Hawk planning studies had been written for the Saudi government, and the total cost of the Peace Hawk program had reached $2.5 billion. Its importance to both Northrop and Saudi Arabia is shown in the growth of Northrop sales to Saudi Arabia analyzed in Table 5.6. Northrop's total sales to Saudi Arabia averaged over $1.2 billion annually during 1976–1980 and were 22–44% of its total sales. During this period, the Peace Hawk program also expanded to include building air bases "from taxi ways to snack bars," running English-language and basic technology courses for young Saudis in Texas, and a three-and-one-half-year "turnkey" program that combined on-the-scene support with training of Saudi replacements.[39] In August 1981, when Saudi Arabia extended the Peace Hawk program for the useful life of the F-5E,[40] it also requested an additional 4 F-5Es and 1 F-5F aircraft and 10 RF-5Es in early 1982. The RF-5Es will be Saudi Arabia's first aircraft dedicated to reconnaissance.[41]

The Congressional Arms Sale Debate of 1976

Without its previous modernization, Saudi Arabia would almost certainly have been left without an effective air force in the 1980s, and Saudi-U.S. military relations might have deteriorated to the breaking point. As it was, relations were severely strained by the congressional debates over U.S. arms sales to Saudi Arabia that occurred after 1974. Each major increment in the U.S. military sales program to Saudi Arabia led to a more serious debate in the U.S. Congress than had occurred over the previous sale. At the same time, new laws affecting the sale of U.S. military equipment led the U.S. to release more data than had previously been available to the Congress and the public. This

TABLE 5.6 Growth of the Northrop Peace Hawk Program, 1976-1980 ($ millions)

	1976	1977	1978	1979	1980
Total Northrop Net Sales to Saudi Arabia					
Aircraft	505.6	559.6	601.3	367.3	384.2
Services	183.5	288.1	366.5	453.6	470.2
Electronics/communications	143.9	160.8	188.8	235.4	312.9
Construction	110.5	298.4	294.0	62.7	19.3
Total	943.5	1,306.9	1,450.6	1,119.0	1,186.6
Net sales to Saudi Arabia as % of total Northrop sales	26	44	30	26	22
Peace Hawk Only					
Contract acquisitions	1,146	204	66	754	84
Net sales	208	485	546	365	320
Order backlog	980	699	219	608	372
Net sales to Saudi Arabia as % of total sales	16	30	30	23	19

Source: Northrop Corporation, *Annual Report,* 1980, pp. 31, 43–44.

information, in turn, helped trigger a more intense effort by various U.S. pro-Israeli groups to block U.S. sales.

This process first came to a head in late 1976, when the Senate Foreign Relations Committee, then chaired by Hubert Humphrey, held extensive hearings on U.S. arms sales to Iran and Saudi Arabia. None of the senators participating in these hearings seemed to be aware of the history of the Anglo-American air defense package, and the commission payments by Lockheed, Northrop, and Raytheon for the C-10, F-5, and Hawk sales had not yet become a matter of public record. The Department of Defense made this situation worse by restricting release to Congress of the threat and requirements studies it had conducted with Saudi Arabia and by not informing the Senate that it was the USAF and not the Saudis that determined Saudi purchase requirements.[42] It is clear from the text of the Senate hearings that Saudi Arabia was often blamed for making unrealistically large weapons requests when it was simply following U.S. advice and was submitting orders that its U.S. advisers had developed based on standard U.S. military planning factors. As a result, the Senate testimony constantly refers to possible covert Saudi motives, such as stocking arms for the

Arab forces threatening Israel. It is equally clear from the purchase requests published in the hearings that the U.S. was encouraging Saudi Arabia to buy more than it needed and that the U.S. advisory team in Saudi Arabia had not sufficiently improved its work that it was properly tailoring its advice to Saudi needs and operating conditions.[43]

These points are documented in Table 5.7, which provides a detailed overview of the general nature of U.S. arms sales and military assistance to Saudi Arabia in the mid-1970s. The Dragon and TOW purchases shown in the table are absurdly high, even after the cuts presented to the Senate, and they reflect a careless application of U.S. Army stock-level and lead-time planning requirements to Saudi Arabia. It is interesting to note that a later investigation by the Office of the Secretary of Defense forced major cuts in U.S. Army stock levels of Dragon and of TOW missile-to-launcher ratios that would have saved Saudi Arabia something like $20 million.

The purchase requests for Sidewinder (AIM-9) missiles were equally exaggerated. The Sidewinder was then in a process of considerable technical growth and modification and in any case required special handling in storage.[44] There was no reason for Saudi Arabia to buy such large numbers of existing types. Saudi Arabia, however, was advised to buy 2,000 missiles for an ultimate fighter strength of only about 100 user aircraft, of which it then had only 30 on hand—20 Sidewinder missiles per aircraft, based on projected Saudi operational aircraft needs in the early 1980s, and 67 missiles for each aircraft on hand. Such requirements might have made sense in the European theater, but they were far too high for Saudi Arabia, given its probable sortie rates and fighter loss-to-kill ratios. They also could not have been justified as part of a U.S. to effort to "prestock" for possible U.S. reinforcements, since the U.S. was then fully confident of Iranian stability. Even the eventual Saudi purchase of 850 Sidewinders that the Congress approved was too high, given storage problems and the "time window" for the availability of improved types.

The planning behind the Maverick and laser-guided bomb (LGB) requests was even worse. Even allowing for the fact that the U.S. and Saudi Arabia were discussing eventual Saudi purchases of up to 100 F-5Es, Saudi Arabia had an inventory of only 30 such aircraft when the hearings were held, and it was not scheduled to increase its inventory of missile- and LGB-using aircraft to more than 70 fighters until 1980. The original request would have provided Saudi Arabia with the USAF's ideal 90-day stock level—approximately three times the number of precision-guided missiles (PGMs) per aircraft that the USAF has ever been allowed to buy for its own aircraft. It would have given the Saudis 200 PGMs per user aircraft then in inventory and over 85 PGMs per user aircraft in inventory scheduled for 1980. Allowing for problems of storing and maintaining these weapons, predictable aircraft operational availability rates, and probable combat attrition, these purchases were

TABLE 5.7 Senate Foreign Relations Committee Examination of Saudi Arms Sales Requests, 1976

Nature of Sale	Value (in $ millions)	Number of Items: "Original" Request	Number of Items: Amount Presented to Senate
Prior to September 1:			
M60 tanks	118.0	–	150
Armored personnel carriers	124.0	–	1,000+
Vulcan antiaircraft cannon	41.0		
Maverick missiles	47.0	2,500[a]	1,000
Dragon antitank missiles	26.0	4,200	4,000
Al Batain cantonment	1,450.0	–	–
F-5 program expansion	1,500.0	–	–
Naval facilities	594.0	–	–
Ports	300.0	–	–
National Guard headquarters	158.0	–	–
RSAF uniforms	52.6	–	–
Ammunition	26.5	–	–
Pilot training	26.0	–	–
Ships–design	185.6	–	–
Trucks	25.3	–	–
Patrol gunboats–design	276.2	–	–
SA Army ordnance management assist.	223.3	–	–
Cement plant	235.0	–	–
Total	5,408.5		
Hardware	869.6		
Construction training	4,538.9		
Notifications dated September 1:			
Sidewinder missiles	25.0	2,000	850
Maverick missiles	30.0	1,500[a]	650
Naval training center equipment	130.0	–	–
Additional construction work at air force HQ	160.0	–	–
Family housing at Tabuk	88.0	–	–
Training Center equipment	130.0	–	–
Armored personnel carriers	10.0	–	77
F-5F aircraft	23.3		4
Vulcan antiaircraft guns	12.4		12
50 TOW (antitank) launchers and 1,000 missiles	7.9	1,800	1,000
Saudi National Guard training and modernization	215.0		
Total	831.6		
Hardware	238.6		
Construction, training	463.0		
1976 total to date, government-to-government[b]	6,110.1	–	–
1976 commercial sale of Hawk missiles	1,400.0		28 batteries
Total 1976	7,510.1		
1950–75 total	4,612.0	–	–
1950–76 total	12,122.1	–	–

[a]The original Saudi-U.S. field team request, referred to in the hearing as the Saudi request, was for 6,000 PGMs, including 1,000 Maverick optically guided air-to-surface missiles and 5,000 laser-guided bombs (LGBs). After review in the Office of the Secretary of Defense, this was cut to 2,500 Mavericks and 1,000 LGBs.

[b]U.S. planned military sales to Saudi Arabia for 1976, based on formal notifications sent to Congress. The figures are conservative because the administration was not required to report to Congress government-to-government sales smaller than $25 million prior to 30 June 1976 and smaller than $7 million following that date. In addition, there was no requirement for reporting commercial sales prior to June 30, and there is now a $25 million floor on reporting such transactions.

Source: U.S., Congress, Senate, Foreign Relations Committee, *U.S. Arms Sales Policy* (Washington, D.C.: Government Printing Office, 1977), pp. 54, 55, 58, 60, 70, 75, 78.

absurd. Even the sale of 1,650 Maverick AGM-65A missiles and 1,000 GMU-12 laser-guided bombs finally presented to Congress for approval were at least 30% higher than was logical to meet Saudi needs; they represented a waste of over $20 million.

The U.S. advisers making recommendations went "by the book"—or "buy the buck"—and did not respond to the Saudi Air Force's actual needs. The size of the "one year" purchase sent forth to the Department of Defense (DOD) also indicates that they were using a "package procurement" concept designed to maximize U.S. profits, and minimize production costs to the USAF, without proper regard for shelf life and maintenance, future changes in aircraft inventory, or changes in munitions types and modifications. The U.S. was overselling arms in large single purchases rather than recommending the kind of phased, tailored, and more flexible program that was obviously required.

Most of these problems in the U.S. advisory effort were too sophisticated for the Congress to detect. As a result, the Senate debate that actually took place over U.S. sales to Saudi Arabia showed little sensitivity to either Saudi needs or the role the U.S. was actually playing in Saudi Arabia.[45] This insensitivity would not have been of major importance if the 1976 debate had been only an isolated instance, or if the succeeding debates had been more sophisticated. However, most of the congressional debates and hearings that followed, such as the debate over the F-15 sale in 1978 and the sale of the AWACS package in 1981, were cast in the same mold. Although the Congress issued several excellent staff studies, the actual hearings involved only token discussion of the problems in Saudi-U.S. military relations, and the debates concentrated on rhetorical discussion of the destabilizing effect of selling arms to the Middle East, on the risk such sales to Saudi Arabia posed to Israel, on the danger that Saudi Arabia might become another Iran, and on the risk that Saudi Arabia would transfer its U.S. arms to another Arab power.

This situation became even worse when the details of Northrop's commission payments for the F-5A sale were finally exposed in 1977 as part of a long series of congressional hearings on corruption in international arms sales. These hearings also exposed the corruption of several European and Japanese leaders, and the stigma affected the Saudi royal family even though its senior members were not implicated.[46] Congressional debates over U.S. arms sales to Saudi Arabia came to include a constant series of broad references to the corruption of the Saudi government and royal family, although they conspicuously ignored the well-documented corruption of Western officials.

The result was steadily increasing tensions in Saudi-U.S. military relations between 1976 and 1980. The debates created growing Saudi doubts about Saudi Arabia's wisdom in relying on the U.S. for arms and military assistance. And they increasingly coupled Saudi-U.S. military relations with pressures from Israel and various U.S. pro-Israeli interest groups.

The Modernization of the Saudi Army

The modernization of the Saudi Army proceeded considerably more slowly than that of the Saudi Air Force during the early 1970s. At the same time, a number of factors led the Saudis to expand their relations with France. French involvement in Algeria ended, and French policy tilted away from Israel in the late 1960s and early 1970s. These developments made France a natural second supplier to the Saudi army. The French needed to recycle their expenditures on oil imports and to sell the AMX-30 tank and other military equipment to reduce the cost of production runs for their troops, and they were aggressively attempting to expand their export markets. In contrast, Britain was regarded as somewhat pro-Israel, still suffered from the taint of Airwork and the Lightning sale, was selling tanks to Iran, and lacked the kind of easily maintainable medium tank the Saudis needed. West Germany was precluded by its laws from selling the arms Saudi Arabia needed and was then concentrating its efforts to enter the Middle Eastern market on trying to sell the Leopard to Iran.

The Saudis were encouraged by their experience in helping Sadat obtain French arms after the expulsion of Soviet advisers from Egypt, and they began talks with the French. King Faisal visited Paris in May 1973, and Saudi Arabia ordered 200 AMX-30 tanks, additional armored cars, and other combat vehicles. Although President Pompidou had pledged not to sell arms to the parties in the Arab-Israeli conflict, France did not count Saudi Arabia as a confrontation state, and it pushed hard to become the principal supplier of the Saudi Army. By late December 1974, Prince Sultan and France's new president, Valery Giscard d'Estaing, announced a $900 million arms deal. It included the purchase of 38 Mirage V fighters for Egypt[47] and the purchase of 50 more AMX-30 tanks, 200 AML-60/90 armored cars, 500 AMX-10P infantry carriers, and AMX-30 SP antiaircraft guns for Saudi Arabia.[48] In addition, Saudi Arabia agreed to fund the development costs of the Shahine surface-to-air missile, a more sophisticated, long-range version of the Crotale, and gave France an oil allocation of 200,000 BPD.

At some point during this process, Saudi Arabia decided to organize its army into two major groups of combat units, the first group to be equipped with French equipment, the second group with U.S. equipment, including M-60A1 tanks.[49] These units were to be organized initially into one modern armored brigade—equipped with French armor—and four infantry brigades. They were then to be gradually converted to a strength of two armored brigades and four mechanized brigades,[50] plus two paratroop battalions, a tribally recruited Royal Guard battalion, and three independent artillery battalions. In addition, the army was to have 6 antiaircraft batteries and 10 surface-to-air missile batteries.

The table of organization and equipment (TOE) of these units was loosely based on U.S. and French models,[51] but it had several distinguishing features. First, it tended to be "tank heavy" and sought to provide maximum firepower and mobility with minimum manpower. Second, it was light on artillery, following French Army and pre–October War Israeli models, partly to reduce the need for logistic and combat support. Third, it emphasized air defense, reflecting the experiences of the Yemeni and Omani civil wars and the Arab wars with Israel. Finally, it equipped Saudi units with light armored fighting vehicles, rather than large numbers of armored personnel carriers (APCs), again in order to increase firepower relative to manpower and to improve maneuver capability.

This approach to planning the Saudi Army might have been successful if it had been implemented as part of a consistent plan, with strong central leadership and with proper regard to the training, logistic, and support problems in the Saudi Army. Unfortunately, the expansion of the Saudi Army lacked the kind of centralized joint planning and management that had characterized the Peace Hawk effort, and many key decisions were made in a relatively chaotic way. Although Saudi planning was supported by a series of French, U.S., and eventually British studies, the practical implementation of the Saudi Army modernization effort tended to hinge on individual major equipment purchases, and many of these purchases were made with little effort to examine their overall impact or how they could be integrated into an effective training and support system.[52]

The original Saudi decision to rely on two different countries and parallel lines of unit equipment created obvious difficulties. Even if the Saudis had stopped at buying U.S. and French equipment, they would have faced the problem of running two major training, logistic, and support organizations in their army, one tailored to supporting U.S. equipment, one to French.[53] The Saudis, however, turned to Britain as well. Saudi-British relations improved steadily during 1974 and 1975, and several major British sales teams were sent to Saudi Arabia. These teams were supported by intensive British diplomatic and political efforts to persuade the Saudis that Britain had to sell military equipment to Saudi Arabia to help recycle the balance-of-payments cost of its oil imports. As a result, the Saudis purchased Fox armored fighting vehicles, optically tracked versions of the Rapier surface-to-air missile, and some additional British armored cars.

These purchases met the needs of the Saudi Army in the sense that they were high-quality and relatively simple equipment, but they added yet a third line of logistic, service, and combat support requirements to the Saudi Army. This burden further complicated training, maintenance, and support problems and tended to divide Saudi combat units into battalion elements with different mixes of equipment and different training and support needs. These elements suffered from radically different rates of conversion as new items of equipment were delivered.

The Saudi purchases also created two additional problems. First, none of the equipment the Saudis had bought had a first-rate tank-killing capability. The antitank guided missiles they had purchased lacked range, punch, and rapid or accurate fire capability against Soviet-type armor. Even the AMX-30 tanks the Saudis purchased lacked advanced range finders and fire computers and were dependent on the "Obus G" HEAT round for antitank fire. This round was highly accurate but comparatively slow, had a high trajectory—in spite of claims to the contrary—and lacked penetrating power in comparison with other Western 105mm tank rounds.[54] The AMX-30 also traded simplicity for ease of operation and had a relatively poor and slow-moving transmission using a semisynchronized shift and only one reverse gear. Finally, the AMX-30 traded mobility for protection, which increased the need for Saudi skill in maneuver warfare at all levels of combat. Second, the Saudi Army did not buy enough artillery support to back its armor with suppressive fire and counter-battery support. Unlike other Arab armies, and Israel after the October War, the Saudis lacked the artillery strength to make up for their problems in maneuver skills with enough area fire to suppress infantry and antitank units. As a result, they remained highly vulnerable to such fire from an opponent.

These problems offset many of the advantages that the Saudi Army gained by its slow modernization and its concentration on first creating the necessary infrastructure and training. It also increased Saudi dependence on foreign support and intensified the Saudi Army's problem in operating its forces as coherent units—perhaps the most critical single problem for a unit without combat experience.

The Saudi Army also fell short of its force expansion goals. In 1978 the Saudi regular army still had only about 45,000 men, and its modern major combat units consisted of one under-strength armored brigade, one loosely organized mechanized "division," and three reinforced infantry battalions (sometimes listed as brigades). Its independent elements and support units remained weak. The Royal Guard battalion was roughly up to authorized strength, but its artillery, antiaircraft, and surface-to-air missile battalions were badly under strength.[55] Some units were little more than hollow shells, lacking trained personnel and technicians.

Saudi training was also disrupted by the deployment of units outside the country. Saudi Arabia kept a brigade stationed in Jordan from 1967 until 1977. The Saudi Army also had a brigade in Syria from 1973 to 1977, and at one time had 750 men in the peacekeeping force in Lebanon. These deployments seriously limited training and modernization, although the Jordanians did provide some advanced training support.

Saudi Basing Concepts and Military Modernization

The Saudis minimized some of the problems in their army by concentrating their French armor and equipment at Tabuk, their only major military base near Israel.[56] This policy helped to eliminate any risk that U.S. equipment and advisers would be involved in conflict with Israel and reduced the Saudi problem of getting U.S. consent to sell Saudi Arabia the other equipment it needed. However, the Saudi Army could not avoid making its bases dependent on using both U.S. and French equipment. These bases included King Khalid Military City at Hafr al-Batin, which guarded the Iraqi-Kuwaiti border; Assad Military City at al-Kharj, about 60 miles from Riyadh; and Khamis Mushayt, northwest of the border with North Yemen. A smaller base was later set up near Wuday'ah in the mountains of the Asir Province, about 60 miles north of the border with the Yemen Arab Republic.

The Saudis did, however, develop their bases into a more efficient structure during this period. New major air bases, and sectoral operating centers (SOCs) for the Saudi air defense system, were colocated near the main Saudi Army bases. Additional Saudi air bases were retained or established at Dhahran, Jiddah, Taif, Aghar, al-Kharj, Shaurara, Medina, and Yanbu. This basing structure effectively deployed Saudi Arabia's limited military strength against the most likely outside threats. It also helped isolate the Saudi armed forces from the political pressures of Saudi Arabia's main cities and made it far more difficult for any given commander or unit to launch a coup that could threaten the government.

These measures were reinforced by improvements in the deployment of the 35,000-man Saudi National Guard. Although much of its manpower remained paramilitary irregulars who were dispersed throughout the country to keep order, the Guard gradually moved into a major new cantonment at al-Qasim, in the center of Najd.[57] This step helped ensure that the Guard was located in a key region that would remain loyal to the Saud family, and it strengthened the Guard's recruiting base. Another such cantonment was set up at Al Hasa in the Eastern Province, which allowed the Guard to maintain security over the oil fields—where no heavily armed threat was likely—and gave the forces most loyal to the royal family control over the source of Saudi Arabia's wealth.

Finally, Saudi Arabia combined improved defense with improved internal security by placing its air defenses and Hawk batteries under the command of the army. The Improved Hawk facilities were sited at the key air bases at Dhahran, Khamis Mushayt, Hafr al-Batin, and Tabuk; at population centers like Jiddah and Riyadh; and at the approaches to key oil facilities. This siting policy had the secondary effect of ensuring that the Saudi Air Force could not be used in a coup attempt to attack an undefended major target. Further, by concentrating fighter and surface-to-air missile (SAM) operations into five SOCs, the Saudis added another central command echelon that would help block any coup attempt.

The Saudi Naval Modernization Effort, 1972–1975

The Saudis took a somewhat different approach in the case of the navy. Before 1971, Saudi Arabia had limited its naval expansion to purchases of small craft from Britain and the United States and had relied on the U.S. as its main source of foreign advisory support and help in expanding Saudi Arabia's naval bases. However, the British withdrawal from the Gulf created a need for expanded Saudi naval capabilities, and Saudi Arabia turned to the U.S. for help in expanding its navy because—as had been the case with the Saudi Air Force—the U.S. was then the only Western power organized to provide Saudi Arabia with the combination of equipment, support, and training services it needed.

As a result, Saudi Arabia sought U.S. assistance in converting its 1,000-man force—which had only one 100-ton ex–U.S. Coast Guard patrol boat, two 170-ton German-built Jaguar torpedo boats, six small patrol boats, eight SRN-6 British Hovercraft, two landing craft, and several small craft—into a navy that could provide some degree of "blue-water" capability and secure part of Saudi Arabia's long coastline.[58] This request resulted in the creation of a joint Saudi-U.S. study team, which built on the work done by the original U.S. Navy survey of Saudi naval requirements carried out in 1968. The recommendations of this study group led to a Saudi-U.S. agreement on naval modernization in February 1972. It also produced a plan (SNEP) that called for the Saudi Navy to expand to four 700-ton guided-missile patrol boats, nine 300-ton guided-missile patrol boats, four MSC-322 coastal minecraft, and eight other small craft. Further, the plan called for Saudi purchase of the Harpoon surface-to-surface missile, 76mm rapid-fire guns, MK-46 torpedoes, MK-92 fire-control systems, and AN/SPS surface search radars.[59]

Such plans meant revolutionary changes in the Saudi Navy at a time when the other services were being given priority and were already having difficulties because of Saudi Arabia's limited trained manpower resources. They also called for more equipment and a far higher caliber of advisers than the U.S. Navy could deliver. As a result, it became apparent that the Saudi-U.S. plan was overambitious, that the U.S. Navy was dumping low-quality personnel into its advisory effort, and that the Saudis lacked the management skills to implement the plan.

The U.S. and Saudi Arabia reached an agreement during 1972–1973 to modify the navy expansion plan and set less demanding goals. The U.S. Navy was to provide the Saudi Navy with improved training and support services during its expansion.[60] The formal signing of this agreement was delayed by the October War, but it eventually took place in April 1974. It called for the U.S. Navy to train key Saudi personnel and establish a naval academy in Saudi Arabia. The U.S. was also to design major Saudi naval bases at Al-Qatif/Jubail and Jiddah and a training center at Jubail; expand smaller naval facilities at Ras Tanura, Dammam, and Yanbu;[61] and provide architectural, engineering, and construction support in creating many of the remaining facilities the Saudi Navy would need. The agreement also called for a mix of regular

U.S. Navy and U.S. contract personnel support that effectively made the Saudi Navy dependent on the U.S. for its day-to-day operations.[62]

Neither country, however, proved able to implement even the revised agreement. Although the resulting modernization plan was originally appraised at $150 million, the cost had risen to over $2 billion by late 1977.[63] The Saudis lacked the trained manpower and managers necessary to effectively modernize the Saudi Navy even with additional U.S. support, but they demanded a much faster rate of expansion than the agreement originally called for. The Saudi Navy also proved to have particularly poor procurement management and logistic support, and the Saudi government gave the other services priority in getting high-quality recruits. At the same time, the U.S. Navy lacked the advisory experience of the other U.S. services, continued to provide low-quality or mediocre personnel, and continued to have serious problems in meeting its equipment delivery schedules. Significant reliability problems developed in much of the equipment that the U.S. Navy advised the Saudis to buy.

In short, the U.S. Navy did not prove as successful as the other services in helping the Saudis plan and manage their force expansion. This inadequacy led to the constant shifts in the Saudi Navy modernization plans shown in Table 5.8 and gradually exposed the fact that many European navies could sell patrol boats and other naval equipment that were better suited to Saudi needs. These difficulties, coupled with the friction on both sides inevitable in managing the Saudi naval modernization effort, helped contribute to a Saudi decision to seek additional naval equipment and support from the French in October 1980.[64] This decision was also, however, heavily political and arose out of internal tensions that led to the firing of the Saudi Navy's commanding officer in 1981.

Improving Saudi Military Training

Saudi Arabia did, however, make a number of broad advances in managing its military training effort during this period.[65] These included the efforts of the individual services described earlier and a significant expansion of the staffing and authority of the G-3 (Operations and Training) Section of the Saudi General Staff. The staff came to administer a school system including the army and air force academies and army schools for infantry and armor (at Tabuk), artillery (Khamis Mushayt), communications, physical training, ordnance, engineering, military police, administration, nursing, and music. It also included the Air Force Technical Institute at Dhahran for training warrant officers and the new facilities being built for the Saudi Navy.

The role of the Saudi G-3 expanded to include the coordination of foreign military training and the U.S., British, Jordanian, French, and Pakistani missions. The G-3 also seems to have exerted some degree of central control over the more than 1,600 Pakistani, Jordanian, Egyptian,

TABLE 5.8 Trends in Saudi Naval Modernization, 1969-1982

	1969	1970	1971	1972	1973	1974	1975
Manpower	1,000	1,000	1,000	1,000	1,000	1,500	1,500
Total vessels in service	1	7	13	31	43+	46+	46+
Corvettes	—	—	—	—	—	—	—
Patrol boats	1	7	3	21	31+	31+	31+
FAC(M)	—	—	—	—	—	—	—
FPBs/FPBGs	—	6	2	12	—	—	—
Over 100 tons	1	1	1	1	1	1	1
Over 50′	?	—	—	—	—	—	—
Under 50′	?	—	—	8	30+	30+	30+
Minesweepers	—	—	—	—	—	—	—
Coastal							
Torpedo craft	—	—	2	2	2	3	3
Ger. Jaguar type		—	?	?	2	3	3
Miscellaneous	—	—	8	8	10	12	12
Hovercraft			8	8	8	8	8
Reserve launches	—	—	—	—	2	2	2
Utility craft	—	—	—	—	—	2	2
Tug boats	—	—	—	—	—	—	—
Royal yachts	—	—	—	—	—	—	—
LCUs	—	—	—	—	—	—	—
Training craft	—	—	—	—	—	—	—
Coast Guard Craft	—	—	—	—	19	30	60
Hovercraft	—	—	—	—	8	8	8
Patrol boats	—	—	—	—	9	20	50
Rescue launches	—	—	—	—	2	2	2
On Order	2+ 2 45′ patrol boats; (?) mine-sweepers	20 20 small patrol boats	20 20 small patrol boats (under del.)	—	—	—	14 6 PFBs; 4 MCMs; 4 landing craft

1969: *Jane's* reports one patrol boat in service, while the IISS claims others, though of different types.
1970: IISS reports 7 craft, whereas *Jane's* submits only 2: the Ryadh-class patrol boat (ex-U.S. Coast Guard cutter delivered in 1960).
1971: Mainly IISS figures used. *Jane's* reports one Ryadh and two Jaguar-class boats. It is unclear whether the torpedo craft are Jaguar-types or not. Hovercraft are SRN-6 type.
1972: Ibid. Ten-year naval buildup program agreement signed with the U.S.: 4 MSCs; 6 large patrol craft; 4 LCTs; 3 training craft; 2 tugs (*Jane's*).
1973: *Jane's* figures used. IISS reports 10 patrol-type craft, 2 utility craft. Coast Guard figures not included in general total. Patrol craft are 20 45′ types, 10 Huntress types, and an unknown number of 20′ craft.
1974: Ibid., though IISS claims 24 patrol craft, 4 of the Jaguar type.
1975: Ibid. On-order figures from IISS.

TABLE 5.8 (continued)

	1976	1977	1978	1979	1980	1981	1982
Manpower	1,500	1,500	1,500	1,500	1,500	2,200	2,200
Total vessels in service	92+	93+	96+	141	145	100	94
Corvettes	—	—	—	—	3	3	4
Patrol boats	74+	75+	74+	114	115	63	63
FAC(M)	—	—	—	—	1	5	5
FPBs/FPBGs	—	1	—	—	—	4	4
Over 100 tons	1	1	1	1	1	1	1
Over 50′	—	—	—	20	20	53	53
Under 50′	73+	73+	73+	93	93	?	?
Minesweepers	—	—	4	4	4	4	4
Coastal			4	4	4	4	4
Torpedo craft	3	3	3	3	3	3	3
Ger. Jaguar type	3	3	3	3	3	3	3
Miscellaneous	15	15	15	20	20	20	20
Hovercraft	8	8	8	8	8	8	8
Reserve launches	2	2	2	2	2	2	2
Utility craft	2	2	2	2	2	2	2
Tug boats	2	2	2	2	2	2	2
Royal yachts	1	1	1	1	1	1	1
LCUs	—	—	—	4	4	4	4
Training craft	—	—	—	1	1	1	1
Coast Guard Craft	60	60	60	80	80	100	100
Hovercraft	8	8	8	8	8	8	8
Patrol boats	50	50	50	70	70	90	90
Rescue launches	2	2	2	2	2	2	2
On Order	14	14	18	21	14	11	10
	6 FPBGs; 4 MCMs; 4 landing craft	6 FPBGs; 4 MCMs; 4 landing craft; Harpoon	6 corvettes w/ Harpoon; 4 FPBGs; 4 gunbts; 4 landing craft	9 corvettes; 4 FAC (M) w/ Harpoon; 4 mineswprs; 4 LCMs	6 corvettes; 8 FAC (M) w/ Harpoon; Exocet; SSM	4 frigates; w/ Otomat; 1 corv.; 4 PAC (M) w/ Harpoon; 24 Dauphine	48 F-2000; 2 log ships; Otomat; 2 Atlantic ac; 24 Dauphine

1976: Ibid.
1977: Estimated from mainly *Jane's* figures. The FPBG is from IISS data; accuracy in question.
1978: Ibid.
1979: Mainly *Jane's* figures used here.
1980: Estimated mainly from *Jane's*. One fast attack craft (missile) out of four ordered was commissioned in 1980, three in 1979; three corvettes out of nine ordered were commissioned in 1980, and four more in 1981. IISS gives figure of 9 FAC(M) on order in 1980.
1981: Substantial cuts were made in smaller patrol craft in 1981.

Sources: The Military Balance (London: International Institute for Strategic Studies, 1969–1980; *Jane's Fighting Ships* (London, 1969–1976, 1979–1980). Manpower figures come from IISS data.

Bengali, Syrian, Iraqi, and Palestinian contract officers in the armed forces, most of whom were involved in training or logistics.[66]

Although the overall result of these changes was anything but efficient, even in 1981, they at least provided some degree of central coordination and helped reduce the competition between the regular services for Saudi Arabia's limited supplies of trained manpower. Unfortunately, they did almost nothing to standardize the effectiveness of Saudi training and exercise programs, which ranged from excellent for air force pilots to truly awful for naval enlisted personnel. They also left the Saudi Army training program with extreme variations in quality by specialty and region, a factor that sharply reduced its ability to act as an efficient coordinated force. These problems grew worse as modernization of the National Guard put new strains on Saudi Arabia's manpower base.

Modernizing the National Guard

Saudi Arabia also decided to further modernize the National Guard and to transform it into something closer to regular light infantry. King Faisal had proposed that the U.S. be contacted to provide such support following the problems with the armed forces during 1969–1970, and after some resistance by Prince Abdullah, Saudi Arabia requested U.S. assistance in developing a modernization program in September 1971. The resulting study led to the drafting of a detailed joint modernization plan and to U.S. agreement to equip and train the National Guard by 1973.[67] The October War again led to some delay in the implementation of a Saudi-U.S. agreement, but it was finally signed in April 1975.

The agreement was based on a plan that called for part of the National Guard to be reorganized into 20 light infantry battalions, of which 4 were to be equipped as light mechanized forces. These 4 battalions were scheduled to receive 150 Cadillac Gage V-150 Commando armored cars, 20mm cannon, 90 recoilless rifles, guns, TOW antitank guided missiles, Vulcan 20mm antiaircraft cannon, and an artillery battery with 105mm M-102 howitzers.[68] The goal behind this decision was to transform the National Guard into an organization that could deal with Saudi Arabia's modern internal security problems.

This was an ambitious step for a force then composed largely of tribal levies. This part of the Guard's most important role was to distribute part of Saudi Arabia's oil wealth among key tribal leaders. It was dispersed throughout Saudi Arabia, served only part time, and was paid only monthly. The rest of the Guard had some highly effective infantry units, but it was poorly armed and trained for modern warfare. Modernization meant turning a dedicated but largely illiterate cadre of infantry, with only a few trained officers and a limited number of British, Jordanian, and Pakistani advisers, into a force that could deal with well-armed and well-trained terrorists, dissident elements, and even insurgency by small elements of the Saudi armed forces. It required the National Guard to develop a capability to provide internal security for the Saudi oil fields against much more sophisticated threats and the development of a capability to work with modern intelligence techniques.

The modernization effort also presented significant problems because U.S. personnel were needed to handle training down to the squad level, which required large numbers of personnel. The April 1975 agreement to modernize the Guard had been reached on a government-to-government basis, and the various congressional restrictions on the use of U.S. military personnel overseas forced the U.S. to create a new private contractor capability to meet its training commitment.

The U.S. had originally proposed that Raytheon, which by then had had extensive experience with the Saudi Army, would be the primary contractor, at a cost of $330 million. However, it became clear in September 1975 that Khashoggi and King Faisal's eldest son, Abdullah al-Faisal, had received up to $75 million in a complicated deal that led the Department of Defense to certify that Raytheon was the only firm it could guarantee could do the work. When King Faisal and Prince Abdullah (who despised Khashoggi) found this out, they firmly rejected Raytheon.[69] Eventually the Vinnell Corporation of Anaheim, Calif., was selected under arrangements that involved the hiring of substantial number of U.S. ex-servicemen.

As might have been expected, initial progress was slow and faltering. The original Vinnell contract, signed in 1975 at an initial cost of $77 million, placed only 200 advisers in the country.[70] This number was inadequate to meet even the original Saudi requirements, and Saudi needs increased steadily as the Saudis came to understand the full implications of trying to modernize the Guard. As a result, the U.S. support effort expanded in 1976 to include a National Guard Academy and then to include the additional training necessary to make the Guard more equivalent in status to the army. The cost of Vinnell's part of the support program escalated to $215 million. Other "add-ons" came to include $12.4 million for 12 Vulcan AA guns, additional funds for the Commando armored cars,[71] and a National Guard Headquarters, which eventually had a price of $158 million.[72]

These changes increased the cost of the Guard, but they did not produce proportionate increases in its effectiveness. By the late 1970s, the National Guard had begun to consume about 8–10% of the greatly expanded Saudi defense budget, and although its equipment was further upgraded with TOW missiles, it remained a very lightly armed force for the now massive investment Saudi Arabia was making in it.[73] The Vinnell advisory team also expanded to 750 men, including at least 350 U.S. ex-servicemen. These personnel were supplemented by smaller support teams from the manufacturers of the Guard's equipment, which brought the U.S. support effort to nearly 1,000 men, and by a 75-man U.S. Army team headed by a brigadier general, which planned projects involving construction contracts of up to $1.2 billion each.[74]

Two of the four battalions to be mechanized completed their conversion by mid-1978, and a third was on the way, but the program's results remained uncertain throughout the 1970s. The personnel in the key units were still chosen on the basis of their traditional tribal loyalty to the Saud family, and they were often among the least educated and modernized Saudis in the armed forces.[75] While the NCOs and technicians often learned rapidly, they showed a strong cultural aversion to manual labor or routine service and maintenance functions. Similarly, the entire officer corps received training outside Saudi Arabia, at costs averaging $600 per man per month, but they did not meet the performance standards set by the armed forces. This was partly because the Guard recruited largely among the Najdi, on the basis of traditional ties rather than competence.

Since the Guard was not put to the test during the first 10 years of its modernization effort, these problems did not become fully apparent. Unlike the regular armed forces, the Guard—which had once been the most effective of all the Saudi forces—was difficult to evaluate on the basis of its equipment, training, and exercises. The seriousness of the Guard's weaknesses was demonstrated only in October 1979, when a group of ultraconservative tribal dissidents seized the Grand Mosque in Makkah and riots broke out in a Shi'ite city in the Eastern Province.[76] These events are discussed in more detail in Chapters 6 and 9, but it is important to note here that the Guard proved to be inadequately trained to deal with either the well-armed terrorists in the mosque or with riot control. Its officers did not perform well. The incident also revealed that the Guard had limited capability to deal with the growing problems of ensuring the internal security of the Saudi oil fields.[77]

The Guard also reacted to these incidents by seeking impractical increases in its equipment, including plans to buy 300–600 Leopard II tanks, 1,000 Marder APCs, and Gepard self-propelled antiaircraft weapons. The Guard was then the only force in over 30 Third World countries that could not maintain and service its own V-150 armored vehicles. It obviously lacked the trained manpower to operate such advanced systems,[78] and the equipment had little practical value against the kind of threats the Guard was organized to face.

These problems would have been serious if they had affected only Saudi Arabia's internal security capabilities. The National Guard tied up about one-third of Saudi Arabia's active military manpower during the 1970s in a force that provided a low military payoff per man employed. This deficiency would not have been so serious in a nation with a larger manpower base, but Saudi Arabia could not recruit more manpower, and the Guard's problems hurt all aspects of Saudi Arabia's military modernization.

The Saudi Armed Forces and Rivalry Within the Royal Family

Some of these modernization problems may have been affected by rivalries between Prince Abdullah and Prince Sultan and by other differences within the royal family that worsened after King Faisal's assassination on 25 March 1975.[79] Various sources provide radically different accounts of the extent and nature of such differences, but many agree on several points.

1. Conflicts over the Future Role of the National Guard. Sultan and Abdullah consistently disagreed on the role the National Guard should play and the armaments it should have. These topics were evidently a subject of serious debate during the reorganization of the Saudi government between March and October 1975,[80] during the finalization of the second Saudi Five Year Plan (1975–1980), which was distributed in June 1975, and during the Saudi debates that led to the original Vinnell contract.

This debate may have come to a head in July 1977, when Prince Fahd is reported to have proposed that the Guard's manpower be reduced, that all heavy weapons purchases be halted, and that the Guard be converted to a national police force, rather than a paramilitary organization. King Khalid, Prince Muhammid, and Prince Saud al-Faisal[81] are said to have resisted these efforts, and Khalid is said to have insisted that the National Guard and Royal Intelligence continue to report directly to the king. In contrast, some sources indicate that Crown Prince Fahd's power weakened in mid-1979 as a result of disputes over Saudi policy on the Camp David accords, that Abdullah began to chair the Saudi Council of Ministers, and that Abdullah used his influence to propose the German arms deal discussed earlier. They state that the deal was then allowed to die when Fahd returned to his position after Khalid's growing health problems and the uprising in Makkah and that the Saudi government signaled to Germany that it would not press its request for arms in the face of German public resistance.

2. Lack of Coordination Within Saudi Arabia's Internal Security System. Sultan and Abdullah did keep the Guard and regular armed services virtually isolated from each other until the Makkah uprising in November 1979. They made little attempt to create an effective communications interface, conduct joint planning, share intelligence, and carry out common training. Similar splits seem to have kept Royal Intelligence from fully sharing its information with the Guard or the military services, and the Ministry of the Interior (headed by Sultan's brother Prince Naif) failed to share data with the Guard. This isolation left Saudi Arabia's internal security structure in considerable disarray throughout the 1970s and meant that much of the Guard's attention focused on competing with the armed services rather than on its proper mission. The natural flow from police and intelligence to paramilitary security to regular military force did not exist.

3. Uncoordinated Resource Allocation. Effective national security coordination could not take place in allocating manpower resources and defense expenditures, in coordinating new intelligence and communications, and in reviewing the security needs or implications of the actions of other ministries. The lack of coordination contributed to a considerable waste of resources on duplicative or competing systems and to a lack of attention to passive security measures in key areas like the oil fields. It seems to have deprived Saudi Arabia of a coherent approach to guarding key facilities and to have left a mix of private contract personnel and poorly trained elements of different forces like the Coast Guard in charge of security tasks.

4. Divisions in the Foreign Advisory Effort. The competition between the two princes affected the foreign advisory effort. Coordination among Saudi Arabia's various advisory efforts was weak at best, but significant tension existed between the different sets of foreign advisers to the Guard and those of the Ministry of Defense and the Ministry of the Interior. At least until late 1979, the Guard seems to have received training from the Vinnell Corporation that was more appropriate to creating light mechanized forces for action in the field than to security work in Saudi Arabia's oil facilities and built-up areas.

Such training operations received only limited attention from the USMTM and other elements of the U.S. government. The tensions between the Guard and the regular armed forces also seem to have been a reason that Prince Abdullah sought equipment from the FRG—which was not a supplier to the regular armed forces and which did not present the problem of going to U.S. or French firms with ties to Prince Sultan. There are also indications that the Guard relied on advisers who had relatively hard-line positions on the Arab-Israeli conflict.

5. Problems in Decision Making. Although sources vary, the competition between Prince Sultan and Prince Abdullah was also used as an explanation for the tendency to refer directly to either prince all decisions that might involve the competition between them. The result, it is said, was often long delays in decision making or simply burying issues and decisions in a number of cases. This situation is said to have presented special problems even within the National Guard because Prince Badr, the deputy commander, was one of the former "free princes" who supported King Saud, and he did not have Prince Abdullah's full trust.[82]

6. Differences over Conscription. Saudi Arabia's two leading national security officials are also reported to have been involved in a continuing debate over whether to introduce conscription. Prince Sultan is reported to have backed an integrated national recruiting system that would eliminate tribal recruiting and tribally oriented units, that would be oriented toward feeding the most qualified manpower into the regular armed forces, and that would provide for some degree of broadly based conscription to supplement Saudi Arabia's long-service recruits and allow Saudi Arabia to significantly expand its forces.[83]

In contrast, Prince Abdullah is reported to have strongly backed retaining the tribal recruiting and unit system and to have resisted any kind of national recruiting and manpower allocation system. He is further reported to advocate reliance on relatively small professional military forces, and on close alliances within the Arab world, rather than on large military forces and ties to the West, to maintain Saudi Arabia's national security.

There is no evidence to firmly indicate the extent to which Prince Sultan and Prince Abdullah came into conflict before King Khalid's death in 1982 or to indicate how accurate the previous comments are in describing the development of the Guard, Saudi internal security, and Saudi defense policy during the late 1970s. Even Saudi officials differ sharply over the events involved and the importance of the splits within the royal family. Many, for example, feel that the differences between Prince Sultan and Prince Abdullah were exaggerated and that their differences were more typical of other policy disputes between senior members of the royal family. It is equally difficult to put any such dispute in perspective. One only has to imagine a Saudi analysis of the conflicts in the U.S. between "Princes" Schlesinger and Kissinger; "Princes" Brown, Vance, and Brzezinski; or "Princes" Clark, Haig, Allen, Weinberger, Meese, and Baker to show that it is impossible for the chief ministers of any modern society to avoid such disputes and for even inside observers to provide an objective picture of the differences among any nation's top officials.

There are indications, however, that the dispute between Prince Sultan and Prince Abdullah did go beyond a routine jockeying for power over the nation's security apparatus and normal differences over national security issues. Most reports of the power structure in the Saudi royal family that emerged between 1975 and 1982 indicate that the family was divided into two main factions based on the relationships shown in Chart 5.1. The first faction was reported to have been headed by the sons of King Abd al-Aziz whose matrilineal descent loosely or directly linked them to the Jiluwi family and Shammar tribe in northeast Arabia.[84] The chief members were King Khalid and Prince Abdullah, who was then commander of the National Guard and second deputy prime minister. The second faction was reportedly headed by the seven sons of King Abd al-Aziz's favorite wife, Hussa bint Ahmad al-Sudairi. These "Sudairi Seven" included King Fahd (then Crown Prince and deputy prime minister), Prince Sultan (the defense minister), Prince Naif (the interior minister and head of the police, Frontier Force, and Coast Guard), Prince Turki (former deputy minister of defense and former head of Military Intelligence), Prince Ahmad (Prince Naif's deputy), and Prince Salman (governor of Riyadh).

While accounts again differ, Abdullah's allies in the first faction were reported to represent a coalition of conservative or traditional princes who were sons of a number of King Abd al-Aziz's wives. In contrast, the Sudairi Seven were reported to represent a tightly knit prodevelopment, promodernization, pro-Western faction. The other princes re-

CHART 5—1
MAJOR RELATIONSHIPS IN THE HOUSE OF SAUD AFFECTING THE MANAGEMENT OF SAUDI NATIONAL SECURITY POLICY

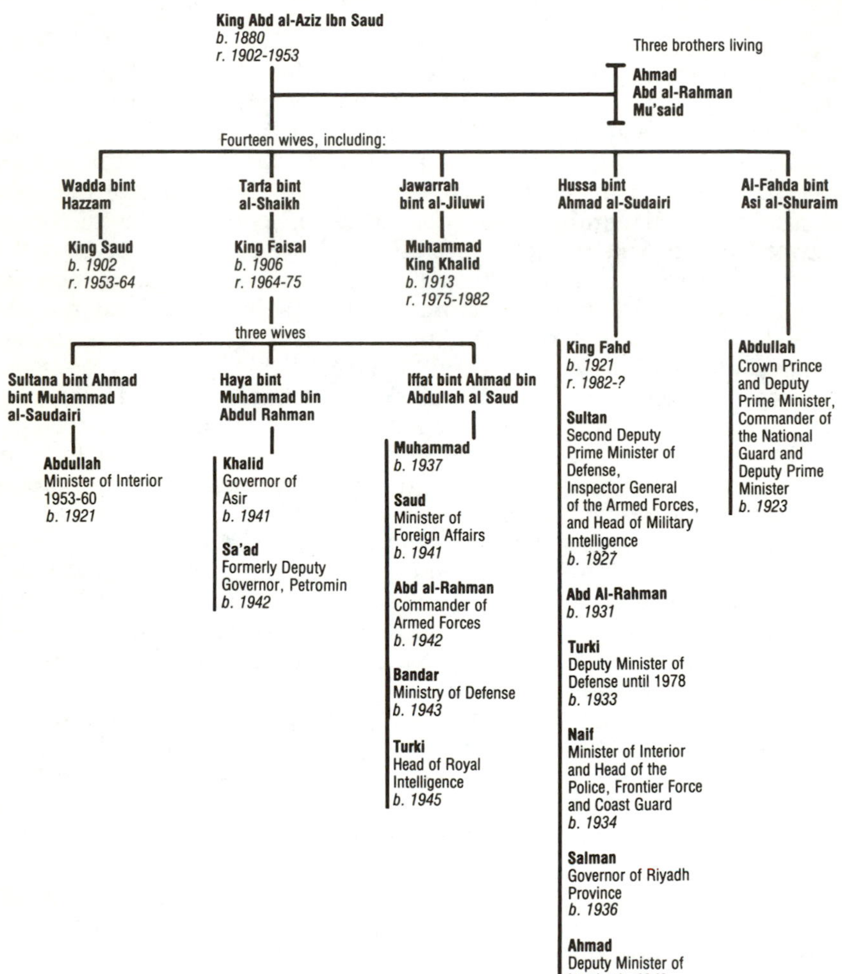

SOURCE: Adapted from Congressional Research Service, *Saudi Arabia and the United States, The New Context in an Evolving "Special Relationship,"* GPO 81-4940 (Washington, D.C.: Government Printing Office, August 1981), p. 18.

portedly aligned themselves with each faction according to their convictions, personal advantage, or family ties, although several sources indicate that King Faisal's sons represented a third faction. This third faction allegedly advocated creating a strong cadre of technocrats and administrators to govern, or administer, the country while the royal family gradually limited its functions to ruling the country by setting policy and making a limited number of major decisions.[85]

Some interviews indicate that the dispute between the factions led to a continuing struggle between Abdullah and Sultan as to who would follow Fahd in the succession to the throne, with the implication that if Sultan won, the Sudairi would become the main line of descent and orient Saudi Arabia even more strongly toward the West. According to these reports, this struggle came to a head in 1977, when Prince Fahd attempted to use the collapse of King Khalid's health and his probable need to relinquish the throne to obtain agreement that Abdullah would be bypassed for the succession in favor of Sultan.[86] According to other sources, there was no such struggle to eliminate Abdullah from the succession, but rather a debate over whether the Guard should be integrated into the army, placed under the command of Prince Salman, or placed under another prince once Abdullah stepped up to become Crown Prince.[87]

These latter reports now seem to be the more accurate, because Prince Abdullah's status as third in line seems to have been recognized long before King Khalid underwent open heart surgery in the U.S. in October 1978, and only limited signs of such a power struggle emerged after Khalid's death in June 1982. It is also interesting to note that one of Fahd's sons, Faisal, became a minister of state in July 1977, while one of Faisal's sons, Turki, was confirmed as minister of state and chief of Royal Intelligence in September; he had been deputy chief since 1978. These shifts argue that gradual realignments to prepare for the succession, rather than a major power struggle, took place.

In any case, these same factional disputes are reported to have led to major differences over Saudi policy toward cooperation with the other Gulf states and the West and toward the Camp David accords negotiated in September 1978 and signed by Egypt and Israel in March 1979. Prince Fahd is said to have wanted to take a more lenient attitude toward some kind of Arab compromise with Israel and toward dealing with Sadat than did King Khalid, Abdullah, and Saud. Similarly, Prince Sultan and Prince Naif reportedly supported stronger military ties to the West and collective security arrangements in the Gulf. According to some sources, Prince Fahd's faction was so strongly outvoted over the Camp David issue in late March 1979 that he had to take leave from his responsibilities, and Prince Turki was forced to resign as deputy defense minister and chief of Military Intelligence in May. Such sources feel that Abdullah clearly emerged as the third in succession and Sultan as fourth and that Abdullah and his supporters were preparing a major reorganization of government of the kind discussed in 1977–1978.[88]

Prince Abdullah did chair the Council of Ministers during this period and did take steps to buy German arms to make the Guard a major armored force. There are balancing reports, however, that Prince Fahd left for Spain in disgust because of his frustration over the failure of his efforts to deal with the Camp David crisis and because his weight had begun to pose a serious health problem. These reports have considerable credibility, because Prince Fahd returned to his normal duties by mid-May. It also has since become clear that Israel was conducting one of its periodic disinformation campaigns about the royal family in an effort to weaken Saudi-U.S. relations. Ironically, this Israeli campaign led to stories in the *Washington Post* on 15 April 1979 that the CIA had issued a report stating that the Saudi government had become extremely unstable. These reports later proved to have been a gross exaggeration of a CIA medical profile on King Khalid's health, but not until the *Post* article had caused serious problems between the U.S. and Saudi Arabia.[89]

It is also worth noting that Turki's resignation has been explained in many ways. Some reports state that it was the result of his position on the Camp David accords. Others indicate that it came as the result of personal reasons, a politically imprudent marriage, involvement in a business scandal, and/or a failure to deal with internal security problems.[90]

One thing is clear: Sadat's personal attacks on the royal family in May 1979 rapidly united it if it had ever been deeply divided. Abdullah and Khalid quickly compromised with the U.S. and increased Saudi Arabian oil production in June. Further, by the time King Khalid's health collapsed again in September, Prince Fahd had visibly returned to the mainstream of Saudi decision making. Virtually all reports agree that the uprising in Makkah and riots in the Eastern Province further united the royal family, and as is related in Chapter 10, the politics in the royal family have changed significantly since King Khalid's death.

Notes

1. George Lenczowski, *The Middle East in World Affairs* (Ithaca, N.Y.: Cornell University Press, 1980), p. 668; Peter Mansfield, *The Middle East* (New York: Oxford University Press, 1980), pp. 169–170. Some sources refer to a border settlement between Iraq and Kuwait in 1977 as stabilizing their borders, but this seems exaggerated in terms of past renunciations of such agreements in the Gulf.

2. Mansfield, *Middle East,* pp. 338–342; Lenczowski, *Middle East in World Affairs,* pp. 307–313.

3. Iraq did, however, greatly enlarge its embassy staffs in Bahrain and the UAE and provided radical groups in the southern Gulf with training, funds, and arms. This was symbolized by an incident in February 1972, when an Iraqi diplomat dropped his suitcase at Bahrain Airport and a Soviet-made AK-47 assault rifle fell out.

4. Lenczowski, *Middle East in World Affairs,* p. 657.

5. While most sources date the key Saudi border settlements to an agreement Prince Fahd initialed in 1974, negotiations with Abu Dhabi and Oman evidently continued through 1977. See J. B. Kelly, *Arabia, The Gulf and the West: A Critical View of the Arabs and Their Oil Policy* (New York: Basic Books, 1980), pp. 158–159, 210–212; David Holden and Richard Johns, *The House of Saud* (London: Sidgwick and Jackson, 1981), pp. 301–302.

6. These events also, however, triggered a process that has made Saudi Arabia's oil pipelines to the Mediterranean of little practical use. The Popular Front for the Liberation of Palestine (PFLP) first blew up the Tapline in 1969, when it was out of action for four months. An "accident" in Syria again cut the line in May 1970, and when Syria refused to allow it to be repaired, a crisis took place: Saudi Arabia blocked the entry of Syrian goods, and Syria blocked Saudi commercial overflights of Syria. The line was again repaired in 1972, but it has been blocked off and on by the Lebanese civil war since the mid-1970s and can reliably ship oil only to Jordan.

7. See Chapter 13 for more details.

8. Mansfield, *Middle East,* pp. 195–196; George Lenczowski, *The Middle East in World Affairs* (Ithaca, N.Y.: Cornell University Press, 1980), pp. 684–685; Kelly, *Arabia,* pp. 156–163; Otto von Pikva, *Armies of the Middle East* (New York: Mayflower Books, 1979), pp. 27–30; and Holden and Johns, *House of Saud,* p. 301. Qabus almost certainly had British support in his coup. British forces formally withdrew from the air bases in Masirah and Salalah in March 1977, but British officers and NCOs are still seconded to the sultan.

9. Although the Eritrean rebels later became identified as a Muslim rebel group, the rebellion started when Ethiopia annexed the area in 1962, because the residents of the former Italian colony were far more advanced and educated than the Ethiopians and resented Ethiopian commercial exploitation.

10. This was a matter of economics and demographics as well. Although both nations had per capita incomes of less than $70, Ethiopia has a territory of 472,000 square miles versus 246,000 for Somalia, a population of 30 million versus 3.2 million, and a GNP of $2 billion versus $250 million. The initial Ethiopian reverses occurred because the USSR had given Somalia the military equipment it needed to defeat Ethiopa at a time when half the Ethiopian army was engaged fighting the Eritrean rebels. The Somali edge over Ethiopia, however, was limited. It consisted of 52 aircraft (24 MiG-21s) to 37 for Ethiopia (9 F-5As); 250 tanks (T-34, T-54, T-55) to 62; and 300 APCs to 100. This "edge" was fairly easy to overcome when the USSR shifted from aid to Siad Barre to aid to the Dergue and Colonel Mengistu. Ironically, Saudi efforts to wean Somalia away from the Soviet bloc—which led Somalia to be the first non-Arab state to join the Arab League—were a key factor in the Soviet decision to back Ethiopia. It is interesting to note that the Soviet sea and air lift to Ethiopia that began on 24 November 1977 delivered roughly $3 billion worth of arms by mid-January, or about three times the total volume of U.S. military deliveries to Ethiopia during the previous quarter century. The Somalis were forced to announce their withdrawal on 9 March 1978. For a good discussion of these events see Steven David, "Realignment in the Horn: The Soviet Advantage," *International Security,* no. 4 (Fall 1979):69–90.

11. John Keegan, *World Armies* (New York: Facts on File, 1979), pp. 206–208, 210.

12. Ibid., pp. 652–655; Mansfield, *Middle East,* pp. 487–492. Still another major Libyan effort to threaten Sudan took place in late 1981 and coincided with Sadat's assassination.

13. That the timing of the October War came as a surprise to the Saudis is indicated by the fact that the commander of the Saudi Air Force and much of his senior staff spent the early hours of the war on 6 October 1973 arguing with the British Aircraft Corporation over the interpretation of a contract. The Saudi forces involved in the war arrived on the Golan only on 13 October and were deployed with the Arab Legion to the south of the main Israeli advance. Their action consisted of a minor encounter on 19 October, in which they claimed to have destroyed five Israeli tanks and crippled three for a loss of four armored cars, four 106-mm recoilless rifles, and nine men killed or wounded. The Israelis do not report such losses, but they did report the capture of several Panhard armored cars.

14. von Pikva, *Armies of the Middle East,* p. 36.

15. Strategy and Tactics, *The War in The East,* Staff Study No. 1 (New York: Simulations Publications Incorporated, 1977), p. 17. Germany attacked the USSR in June 1941 with about 3,680 tanks in inventory, about half of them light tanks.

16. *The Military Balance, 1982–83,* (London: IISS, 1983), pp. 132–133.

17. Saudi Arabia was then exporting between 7.3 and 8.2 MMBD. The value of Saudi oil exports in the 12 months preceding the October War was about $7.325 billion. In the following 12 months it was $33.815 billion.

18. Interestingly enough, many of the assassination plots on both sides were carried out by bribing officials of the other country's intelligence and internal security officials. The problem of *quis custodiet* became a life and death matter for the rulers of Iran and Iraq.

19. Adeed Dawisha, *Saudi Arabia's Search for Security,* Adelphi Paper no. 158 (London, IISS, 1980), p. 4.

20. Sources disagree over when Iraq halted this support. See Chapter 13.

21. Barry Rubin, *Paved with Good Intentions* (New York: Oxford University Press, 1980), pp. 140–141; Lenczowski, *Middle East in World Affairs,* pp. 219–222. See Chapters 12 and 13 for more details.

22. The shah regularly briefed visiting U.S. officials and congressmen on the inevitable need for Iran to "save" the Saudi royal family from a revolution or coup.

23. This concern was also affected after 1968 by President Nixon's need for Jewish votes and political action support in building the coalition that elected him.

24. The Kennedy and Johnson administrations pursued the opposing policy of trying to limit the shah's arms purchases through the end of 1968.

25. The author was assigned to the U.S. Embassy in Tehran during this period. The events involved are described in part in Rubin, *Paved with Good Intentions,* pp. 120, 124–130, 134, 136, 139–140, 148, 153, 161, 166, 174, 186, 186–192, 196–197.

26. Ibid., p. 130.

27. Saudi Arabia had virtually no intelligence on internal or external Shi'ite activities before the shah fell.

28. See Keegan, *World Armies,* p. 619; U.S. Congress, Senate Foreign Relations Committee (SFRC), *U.S. Arms Sales Policy,* September 1976 (Washington, D.C.: Government Printing Office, 1977), p. 56. White House background papers issued in September 1981 showed 60% on construction, 20% on training, and 20% on hardware.

29. All such U.S. data use a minimal estimate of cost for Soviet military goods and services, underestimate Soviet subsidies in the form of credit terms, etc., and fail to estimate goods and services that cannot be confirmed by intelligence collection although they are almost certainly provided.

30. Nyrop, *Saudi Arabia,* p. 335.

31. The current RSAF training facilities are highly effective and perhaps the best organized in the developing world. Visits to these facilities, and discussions with various foreign advisers in Saudi Arabia, indicate that they are able to produce pilots, technicians, and staff personnel of a higher quality than the equivalent facilities in any other Arab or Asian state. The other conservative Gulf states, Pakistan, and Iraq regularly send personnel to these Saudi schools.

32. Congressional Research Service (CRS), *Saudi Arabia and the United States: The New Context in an Evolving "Special Relationship,"* a report prepared by the Foreign Affairs and National Defense Division, GPO 81-4940 (Washington, D.C.: Government Printing Office, August 1981), pp. 51–52.

33. The order was placed in June 1974, for a tentative price of $270 million. The final contract, in 1977, was worth over $1 billion. Holden and Johns, *House of Saud,* p. 360.

34. Ibid., pp. 358–359.

35. SFRC, *U.S. Arms Sales Policy,* pp. 2, 10, 62.

36. Holden and Johns, *House of Saud,* pp. 360–361, 363, 365. The March 1966 contract was worth about $1.5 billion. Also see *Aviation Week,* 15 November 1982.

37. Unlike the F-5A, the F-5E had the performance characteristics necessary to equip it to deal with the later versions of the MiG-21 (although not the MiG 21-N) and Fitter. Its fair-weather combat performance is acceptable, although it lacks low-altitude, multi-aspect, and long-range intercept capability of the kind needed for the mid-1980s. Attack performance is acceptable, although its ability to deliver Maverick and laser-guided bombs under operational conditions, and particularly against defended targets, is limited.

38. *The Military Balance,* 1974–75 and 1980–81 (London: IISS, 1975 and 1981).

39. Louis Kraar, "Everyone at Northrop Is in Marketing," *Fortune,* 10 April 1978. Northrop *News,* December 1980; DOD background briefing, April 1981; Northrop *Annual Report,* 1980.

40. Visits to these facilities, and the new Peace Sun facilities in late 1981, indicated they were well organized, had exceptionally good Saudi and U.S. staffs, and were not "gold plated" in terms of staffing, construction, or facilities.

41. *Aviation Week,* 15 November 1982. The sale was part of a $350 million arms package. According to some reports, the new Saudi F-5Es will have ring-laser gyros.

42. SFRC, *U.S. Arms Sales Policy,* pp. 2–4, 10, 24.

43. Ibid., pp. 55, 58, 60, 78–79, 80, 82, 87.

44. See W. Shenk Meckenheim, "The AIM 9-L *Super Sidewinder,*" *International Defense Review* 3 (1976):151–155.

45. SFRC, *U.S. Arms Sales Policy,* pp. 2–4, 10, 24.

46. SFRC, *Multinational Corporations and U.S. Foreign Policy* (Washington, D.C.: Government Printing Office, 1976 and 1977), Part 12, pp. 149–151, 153–155, 171, 176, 199–238, 585, 594, 597, 625; Part 14, pp. 23–27, 52–53, 378, 380–383.

47. France sold the Mirage V on the basis that the sale was to Saudi Arabia, not Egypt. Holden and Johns, *House of Saud,* p. 362.

48. *The Military Balance,* 1974–75 and 1975–76 (London: IISS, 1975 and 1976).

49. U.S. FMS cases resulting from this plan included the sale of M-60A1 tanks, AVLB bridge launchers, TOW ATGMs, 155mm M-109 A1B howitzers, Redeye SHORAD missiles, Dragon man-portable ATGMs, 66mm LAW antitank rockets, and Vulcan 20mm AA guns.

50. *The Military Balance* (London: IISS, 1971–1975).

51. The first French-trained armored brigade was based at Tabuk, along with the French training mission. At the end of 1980, France had supplied about 400 AMX-30 tanks, 400 AMX-10P combat vehicles, and large numbers of APCs and artillery weapons.

52. Saudi weapons purchases were also affected by the commission problem. The French had no real restrictions on bribes and commissions and had paid a 25% commission on the sale of Panhard armored cars in 1968–1969. This compared to around 14% maximum for the UK and U.S. Khashoggi received a $45 million commission for the initial sale of 200 AMX-30 tanks, or 7.5% of their $600 million cost, and he was only one of several agents. The French did not place any real limits on such activities until 1977 at the earliest.

53. The only significant Saudi military equipment production facility is still the arsenal at al-Kharj. It assembles M-16s and M-1 rifles, M-60 .30- and M-2 .50-caliber machine guns and Heckler and Koch automatic rifles. It is now staffed with U.S. and West German advisers.

54. "Main Battle Tanks," *International Defense Review,* Special Series no. 1 (1976):16–17, 19, 21, 28, 35.

55. Alvin J. Cottrell, *The Persian Gulf States* (Baltimore: Johns Hopkins University Press, 1980), p. 143; Nyrop, *Saudi Arabia,* p. 320; *The Military Balance, 1978–79* (London: IISS, 1979), pp. 40–42.

56. Elements were later moved to Sharurah, far to the southeast, to deal with the threat created by the Yemeni border war of 1979.

57. Prince Abdullah, then commander of the Guard, maintains exceptionally close ties to the Shammar tribe in the Najd. The Shammar and other allied tribes are a major source of the Guard's recruits. See Dale Tahtinen, *National Security Challenge to Saudi Arabia* (Washington, D.C.: American Enterprise Institute, 1978), p. 17.

58. Nyrop, *Saudi Arabia,* pp. 334–335; *Jane's All The World's Navies* (London, various years).

59. Cottrell, *Persian Gulf States,* p. 144; *Jane's All the World's Navies.*

60. Nyrop, p. 335; *Jane's All the World's Navies.*

61. Small Saudi Coast Guard facilities exist at Sah Sharmah, Qisani, and Hagi, and stations exist at many locations on the Gulf and Red Sea coasts.

62. Nyrop, *Saudi Arabia,* p. 335.

63. Holden and Johns, *House of Saud,* p. 361.

64. *Baltimore Sun,* 16 October 1980; *Aviation Week,* 11 March 1980.

65. See Congressional Research Service (CRS), *Saudi Arabia and the United States: The New Context in an Evolving "Special Relationship,"* a report prepared by the Foreign Affairs and National Defense Division, GPO 81-4940 (Washington, D.C.: Government Printing Office, August 1981), for the source of much of this information.

66. Salameh, "Political Power and the Saudi State," *MERIP Reports,* no. 9 (October 1980):10. The vast majority of Saudi contract officers are Pakistani.

67. Tahtinen, *National Security Challenge,* p. 17; Nyrop, *Saudi Arabia,* pp. 320, 335. Cottrell, *Persian Gulf States,* p. 144; CRS, *Saudi Arabia and the United States,* pp. 45 and 50.

68. The V-150 series consists of a family of light, four-wheeled armored vehicles with good agility, a road speed of 89 kilometers per hour and a range of 960 kilometers. Its major variants are: (1) APC with a crew of 2 plus 10 infantry, armed with twin 7.62mm MG or one 7.62mm and one 12.7mm MG plus smoke dischargers; (2) mortar carrier with a crew of five and an 81mm mortar; (3) armed with a 20mm Oerlikon gun in a turret with powered traverse and elevation, a coaxial 7.62mm machine gun, a 7.62mm antiaircraft machine gun and smoke dischargers; (4) armed with a turret-mounted 90mm Mecar gun (2491.103), a 7.62mm coaxial MG, and a 7.62mm antiaircraft MG and smoke dischargers. Ammunition carried consists of 40 rounds of 90mm and 3,000 rounds of 7.62mm. Other models available include TOW missile carrier, command, and recovery vehicles. The decision to buy Cadillac equipment was delayed for several months because the Saudis confused Cadillac Gage with the Cadillac division of General Motors, which was then on the boycott list.

69. Holden and Johns, *House of Saud,* p. 364; *Washington Post,* 17 September 1975.

70. Nyrop, *Saudi Arabia,* pp. 323–332.

71. SFRC, *U.S. Arms Sales Policy,* p. 54.

72. Ibid., p. 75.

73. Keegan, *World Armies,* p. 612; Tahtinen, *National Security Challenge.*

74. *Los Angeles Times,* 23 January 1978, p. 1; Holden and Johns, *House of Saud,* p. 360.

75. *Los Angeles Times,* 23 January 1979; *Wall Street Journal,* 21 January 1980.

76. "Mecca Insurrection," *MERIP Reports,* October 1980.

77. Ibid.; Keegan, *World Armies,* p. 39.

78. *Financial Times,* 5 May 1981; Hayyan Ibn Bayya, "Open Letter to Saudi Arabia," *Nation,* 4 April 1981; *New York Times,* 20 March 1981; *Economist,* 28 February 1981.

79. Faisal was assassinated by a nephew, Faisal bin Musa'd bin Abd al-Aziz. He seems to have been a somewhat disturbed ultraconservative who blamed the king for the killing of his elder brother, Khalid, in 1966 as he led an assault on a television station that King Faisal had supported as part of his effort to modernize the kingdom. It is worth noting that the reorganization of the Saudi government after Faisal's assassination took roughly 24 hours, that a new Council of Ministers was selected four days later, and that Fahd was confirmed as crown prince and Abdullah as 2nd deputy prime minister and third in succession.

80. The following discussion is based in large part on interviews and on Holden and Johns, *House of Saud;* Lacey, *The Kingdom;* Gwynne Dyer, "Saudi Arabia," in Keegan, *World Armies,* p. 612; Gary S. Saymore in "Royal Family Politics in Saudi Arabia," unpublished paper, Rand Corporation and Harvard University, 1981; and the work of William S. Quandt. A deliberate effort has been made to exclude Lebanese, British, and Egyptian sources with obvious propaganda purposes and newsletters with connections to Israeli intelligence or Marxist sources.

81. Second son of King Faisal. He was generally regarded as an ally of King Khalid and was appointed minister of state for foreign affairs following King Faisal's death, and later foreign minister. While sources vary, he is reported to

have supported Fahd and Sultan in their efforts to modernize the kingdom but to have loosely aligned himself with Prince Abdullah in dealing with several disputes. Many sources indicate he represents a "third faction" of King Faisal's sons that includes Prince Turki, the chief of Royal Intelligence.

82. Badr is Abd al-Aziz's twentieth son, born in 1933. He is a Sudairi by a different wife from the mother of the Sudairi seven. He served as governor of Riyadh under King Saud, became deputy commander of the Guard in 1965, one year after Saud was deposed, and is the full brother of Abd al-Mujid, who was appointed governor of Tabuk in 1980. His son Faisal is deputy minister of posts and telegraphs.

83. Saudi officers serve 20–35 years, enlisted men 14–18 years. Most are recruited as youths, are trained in military schools, and are expected to serve for most of their useful working lives. The full implications of this system are unclear, since a modern military training and career system developed only in 1965–1969, and the volume of technically trained personnel that passes through Saudi military training schools has roughly doubled every four years since 1966.

84. Tribal and family affiliation descends through the mother in much of Saudi Arabia. None of this faction are full brothers.

85. Informal discussions with third-generation and collateral princes indicate that this policy does have broad support within the royal family and at least some support from Prince Abdullah, Prince Fahd, and Prince Sultan. Senior Saudi technocrats also indicate that the disagreement over this policy is one of timing and tactics, not strategy and objective.

86. Keegan, *World Armies,* p. 612.

87. Saymore, "Royal Family Politics"; *Financial Times,* 21, 28, and 30 June 1977; *Arabia and the Gulf,* 4 and 11 April 1977; 2 January 1978. Also see Keegan, *World Armies,* p. 612, which dates this to July–August 1977.

88. Saymore, "Royal Family Politics," indicates that one popular rumor was that Fahd's protégé Yamani would be replaced by Foreign Minister Saud, while Fahd would become foreign minister, and that the progressive minister of planning, Hisham Nazer, would become ambassador to the U.S. while Yamani replaced him. Other experts argue that Fahd's absence led to Saudi production cutbacks and changes in oil price policy that increase the impact of the shah's fall.

89. See Holden and Johns, *House of Saud,* pp. 506–507; Lacey, *The Kingdom,* pp. 453–454. The comment that these reports had Israeli origins is based on informal discussions with former and active NSC and State Department officials. Holden says the CIA station chief in Jiddah, George Cave, was blamed for such reports, but that the real source was James Schlesinger, who gave a background brief to the *Post.* Lacey blames "disgruntled State Department officials" who resented Saudi Arabia's lack of support for Camp David, etc.

90. Saymore ("Royal Family Politics") cites the *Middle East Contemporary Survey,* Vol. 3, 1979, and the *al-Nahar Arab Report and Memo,* 23 May 1979, for several of these stories. Holden and Johns raise the marriage story (*House of Saud,* p. 497).

6
Saudi Military Modernization, 1975–1980

In spite of the problems in its defense structure, Saudi Arabia seemed reasonably well positioned to deal with its national security problems at the start of the mid-1970s. Saudi Arabia had obtained the foreign support it needed to continue its military modernization, and its diplomatic and economic initiatives had helped lead to a rapprochement between Iran and Iraq. Iraq became steadily less hostile to the conservative Gulf states, and Saudi Arabia's efforts to wean South Yemen away from the Soviet bloc seemed to be having growing success. Egypt had developed into a strong military ally and conservative partner in the Arab world. The conservative and pro-Western forces supporting Sultan Qabus were headed toward an almost inevitable victory in the civil war in Oman. And, for all its risks, the "twin pillars" doctrine seemed to be succeeding in making Iran a military shield for the conservative Gulf states without making Iraq a threat. Although Saudi policy was unsuccessful in backing Somalia and the Eritrean rebels against Ethiopia, it was highly successful in supporting President Nimeiri in his efforts to move Sudan steadily into the conservative Arab camp. Further, Saudi Arabia was able to complete most of its border negotiations with its conservative Gulf neighbors and to prepare the groundwork for future cooperation in the Gulf.

The External Crises of 1975–1980

Once again, however, the regional security situation changed radically for the worse.

- Saudi Arabia faced a new crisis in its relations with the U.S. and Egypt over President Sadat's visit to Israel in November 1977 and the Camp David accords of September 1978. President Sadat could accept a settlement that focused on returning the Sinai to Egypt and that left the West Bank issue unresolved; Saudi Arabia could not. Like Jordan, Saudi Arabia could not survive association with an agreement that was fundamentally unacceptable to the Palestinians and to most Arab moderates, as well as to all Arab radicals and extremists. Although Saudi Arabia had used its economic power to help force Syria to accept the second Sinai accords, to limit its intervention in Lebanon, and to accept the Golan agreement, it was forced to break with Egypt over the Camp David accords. This step, in turn, divided Saudi Arabia from the United States and ensured stronger hostility of Israel and its U.S. supporters to U.S. strategic ties and arms sales to Saudi Arabia.

• The Arab-Israeli peace issue triggered new tensions in Jordan and Syria and helped turn the civil war in Lebanon into a grim struggle among Lebanese factions, the PLO, Syria, and Israel that divided the nation and presented the constant threat of new fighting between the Arabs and Israel.

• Saudi relations with Iraq improved steadily, particularly after a coup attempt against Saddam Hussein, backed by the Soviet Union and the Iraqi Communist party (ICP), misfired in late 1977. However, the potential threat to Saudi Arabia from Ethiopia grew steadily, and Libya poured money into radical and anti-Saudi movements in the Gulf. Thus Saudi Arabia and the other conservative Gulf states were confronted with steadily increasing risks of internal subversion and external terrorism.

• The complex efforts of Saudi Arabia and Iraq to wean South Yemen away from dependence on the Soviet bloc collapsed in June 1978. A bloody coup brought a strongly pro-Soviet Abd al-Fattah Ismail to power and effectively shifted South Yemen into the Soviet camp.[1]

• In early 1979 the rising tension between North and South Yemen led to a brief border war. While the war lasted only from February to March 1979 and was of limited intensity, it led to a complex U.S. and Saudi effort to provide North Yemen with military aid. Although this effort was initially successful, President Ali Abdullah Saleh of North Yemen reacted to the slow pace and limited size of U.S. arms deliveries, and to Saudi efforts to use the aid effort to maintain its influence over North Yemen, by seeking arms from the Soviet bloc. By late 1980, North Yemen was clearly playing both sides against the middle, but it seemed to be shifting toward a more pro-Soviet position. Nonetheless, the stability of North Yemen became more and more questionable during 1981, and by early 1982, the country had drifted into a state of low-level civil war.[2]

• Between June 1978 and January 1979, internal tensions in Iran exploded and drove the shah from power. His fall deprived Saudi Arabia of any "shield" from Iran, and in the months that followed, it became clear that the U.S. twin pillars policy had not only collapsed, but had turned into a disaster. Iran became a hostile and radical "Islamic" state dominated by an aggressive Islamic nationalism with ambitions to control the Shi'ite populations of the other Gulf states. As a result, Iran ceased to be a protector and became a major potential threat.

• To the northeast, Afghanistan went through several major convulsions. The king was overthrown by Mohammed Daoud Khan in July 1973. Khan, in turn, was deposed by a Marxist coup led by Nur Mohammad Taraki in April 1978. Takaki's efforts to turn Afghanistan into a Marxist state then brought the nation to near–civil war. This situation led to a Soviet invasion on 27 December 1979 that deposed Taraki and brought Babrak Karmal to power in a puppet government. Rather than bringing order to the country, however, the Soviet invasion triggered an all-out civil war, which forced the USSR to steadily expand its military presence and take full control of Afghanistan.

• The Afghan invasion led to a major expansion of the Soviet military presence and facilities in the southern USSR, bordering on Turkey and Iran, and to growing tension between the USSR and Pakistan. This situation was compounded by internal disarray in Pakistan and by the reelection of Indira Gandhi in India in January 1980, which was followed by a steady increase in tension between Pakistan and India.

• Within a year of the shah's fall, the settlement between Iraq and Iran of the Shat al-Arab dispute had collapsed. After several military incidents, Iraq invaded Iran on 22 September 1980, in what was intended to be a "lightning war." In fact, the attack misfired disastrously. Iraq's military performance proved to be inept at best. In the prolonged conflict that followed, oil facilities became a major military target for the first time in the Gulf's history and Iran demonstrated that limited air and sea attacks could rapidly destroy Iraq's oil-loading facilities in the Gulf.

This web of events confronted the U.S. and Saudi Arabia with a situation that was considerably worse than either nation had imagined as the "worst case" outcome of British withdrawal from Suez during their original planning in the early 1970s. It shifted the balance of power in favor of the USSR as the U.S. lost its Iranian bulwark and Soviet power built up in the southwestern USSR and in South Yemen, Ethiopia, and Afghanistan. For the first time, the U.S. was faced with the possible need for rapid deployment of U.S. forces half a world away, into an area where the USSR had major advantages in terms of distance and forces in being.

Coupled to the political backlash from Camp David, the loss of U.S. power and influence made it virtually impossible for most conservative Gulf states to allow the U.S. to base forces on their soil or even to be closely associated with it. With the exception of Oman, the conservative Gulf states were too dependent on expatriate Arab labor and technical expertise to alienate the Palestinian movement and its supporters and too vulnerable to combined pressures from Arab moderates and radicals to set themselves up as targets for the latter's hostility.

This left Saudi Arabia faced with several grim, and often contradictory, requirements. The first was the need to improve its military forces and its ability to deter external attacks much faster than it had planned in the early 1970s. The second was the need to redefine its military relations with the United States in a way that preserved its sovereignty, and independence from U.S. policy toward the Arab-Israeli conflict, but that created even tighter military relations with the U.S. in obtaining equipment and military assistance. The third was the need to resolve the extent to which Saudi Arabia would or would not depend on U.S. reinforcement and, if so, what kind. Finally, Saudi Arabia was faced with the need to seek immediate improvements in its collective security efforts in the Gulf, particularly with its conservative Gulf neighbors in the southern Gulf.

Saudi Force Planning and Defense Organization

The reversal in Saudi Arabia's security position following the external crises just discussed would have imposed a major strain on the planning capabilities of even the most sophisticated military power. In fact, this sequence of events would have precluded Saudi Arabia from systematic force planning even if it had been able to organize its Ministry of Defense to carry out such planning. Saudi Arabia, however, was far from ready to manage a major expansion of its forces on any basis. Although it had improved the operations of its Ministry of Defense and Aviation during the late 1960s and early 1970s, it still looked far more efficient on an organization chart than it was in reality.[3] Each element of the Saudi MODA still tended to operate autonomously in the middle and late 1970s and referred all important decisions to the top. Administrative procedures were poorly structured and even more weakly enforced. There was virtually no independent strategic planning. The Saudi defense procurement structure remained comparatively primitive, the ministry depended on outside advice for virtually every major purchase, and it lacked integration both into an overall plan and with its defense budget.

The MODA remained isolated from the other functions of the Saudi government, even in the areas in which no rivalry existed among the princes or with the National Guard. It began to acquire a trained permanent staff only when King Faisal established a career civil service in 1971. Although Saudi Arabia had started to base its economic development on formal five-year plans in 1970 and developed a cadre of well-trained economic planners who were backed by competent Western advisers, the MODA largely excluded itself from the planning process that created these plans, and it was eventually entirely omitted from the published version of the Third Five Year Plan.

The MODA also had little more than a theoretical budget. Regardless of what was approved by the Finance Ministry or Saudi Council of Ministers, the Saudi defense budget was perpetually being changed to meet the exigencies of the moment. The budget also was consistently overobligated and overspent. The MODA lacked even the limited controls the Finance Ministry and Ministry of Plans exerted over the civilian budget after 1975, and the defense budget was not subject to the "dialectic"

CHART 6—1
A WESTERN VIEW OF SAUDI DEFENSE ORGANIZATION IN 1975

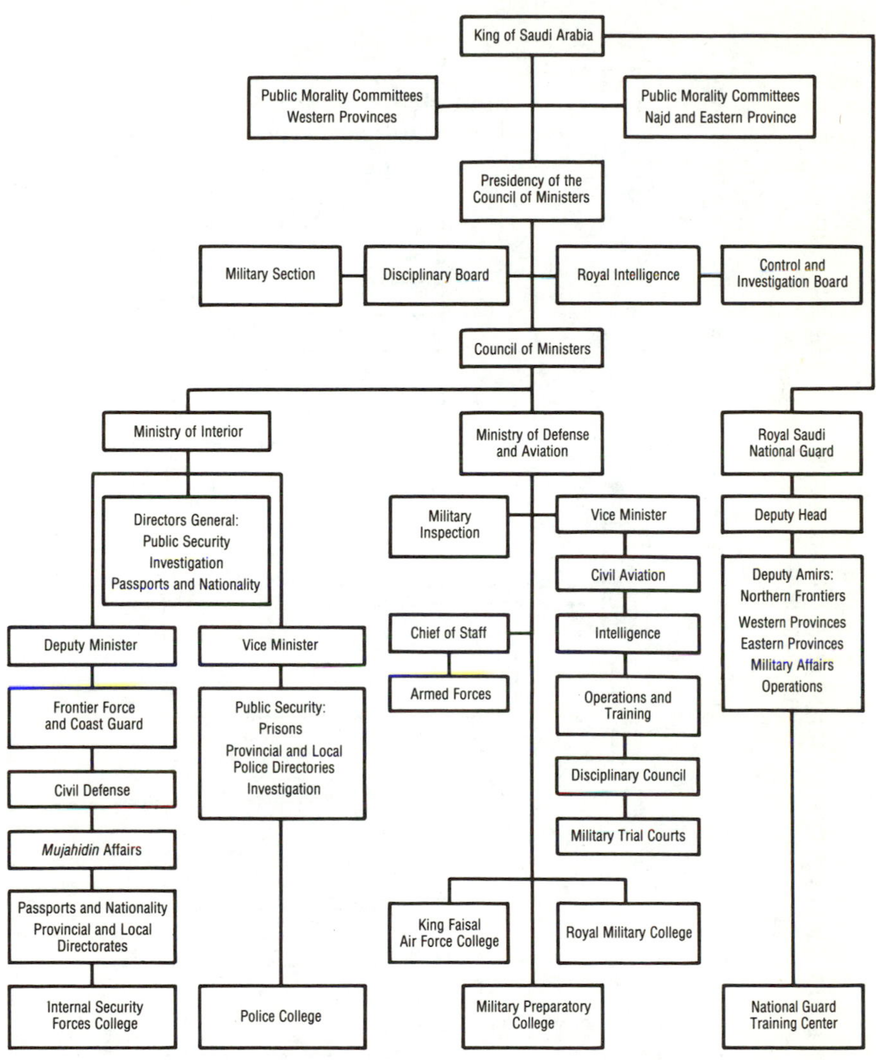

Adapted from Nyrop, *Area Handbook of Saudi Arabia.*

that resulted from the competition among civilian ministries for resources and authority.

These problems led to an effort to reorganize the MODA in October 1975, as part of a general reorganization of the Saudi government following King Faisal's death. The reorganization created six new min-

CHART 6—2
A SAUDI VIEW OF THE SAUDI ARABIAN REFORMS IN DEFENSE ORGANIZATION IN OCTOBER 1975

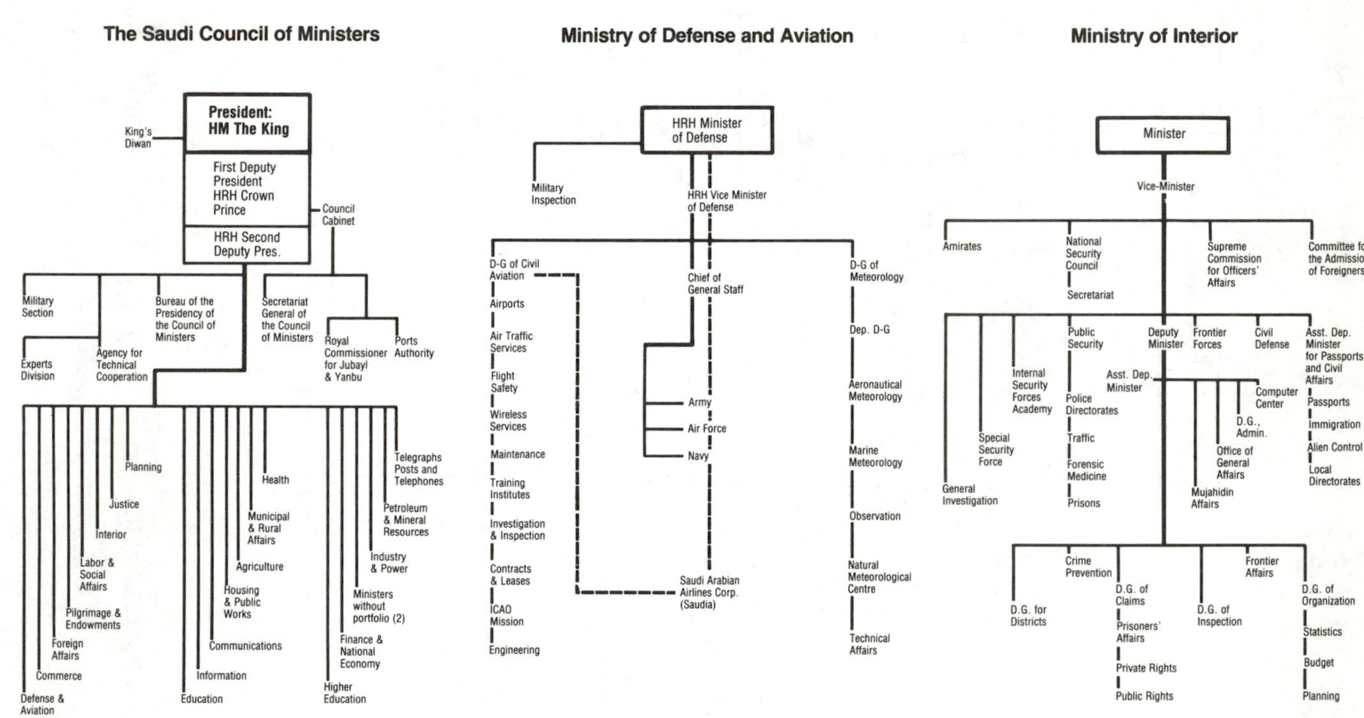

SOURCE: Fouad al-Farsi, *Saudi Arabia, A Case Study in Development.*

istries, including the Ministry of Plans,[4] and a small National Security Council was created within the Ministry of the Interior.[5] These changes gave Saudi Arabia the national security structure shown in Charts 6.1 and 6.2. Most authorities agree, however, that the October 1975 reorganization did little to substantively alter the defense structure of the Saudi government and that the changes that did occur were largely a reflection of the shifts that occurred in the responsibility of given ministers and princes after the assassination of King Faisal. As a result, the Saudi Ministry of Defense and Aviation had roughly the same structure under King Khalid that it had had under King Faisal.

The Limits of Saudi Force Expansion: Quality over Quantity

The problems within the MODA made Saudi Arabia almost totally dependent on outside assistance for the planning and execution of most of the technical and administrative details of its military modernization. This dependence was reinforced by several additional factors, including Saudi Arabia's severe manpower constraints, its problems with foreign labor, the growth in the number of its foreign advisers, and the costs imposed by creating modern military facilities in a country with such a limited infrastructure.

Constraints on Saudi Military Manpower

Saudi Arabia's manpower supply was so limited that it was forced to seek solutions to its growing military problems that substituted technology for manpower. As late as 1974, roughly 70% of Saudi adult males were still illiterate. Every increase in Saudi Arabia's oil wealth led to further increases in the civilian sector's demand for trained Saudi personnel who could use modern military technology.[6] Saudi student enrollments increased by nearly 100% between 1971 and 1976, but this still increased the proportion of students in the total population only from 7.4% to 11.7%. At the same time, Saudi Arabia's concentration of development in the areas most loyal to the regime meant that the manpower it most wanted to recruit for the armed forces had the best opportunities in the civilian sector.[7]

As a result, Saudi Arabia was forced to further speed up the regional integration of its armed forces and to increase the number of Hejazi and other non-Najdi personnel in the armed forces until they totaled well over half of the air force and roughly half of the army and navy. Although the Saudi government flirted with the idea of conscription as a method of obtaining more manpower and a better ethnic balance, this option was rejected during the 1970s because of the rivalry between Prince Sultan and Prince Abdullah and because of the risk that it would create more internal unrest than external security.

Foreign Workers and Security Issues

Other pressures compounded these manpower problems during 1975-1980 and limited the equipment Saudi Arabia could buy and absorb. The number of foreign workers in Saudi Arabia increased sharply along with its new oil wealth, doubling between 1974 and 1976. By the mid-1970s, Saudi Arabia depended upon roughly 1.3-1.5 million foreign workers, of whom nearly a million were Yemenis, 200,000 were other Arabs (Egyptians, Lebanese, Palestinians, Syrians, etc.), 260,000 Europeans and Asians, and 40,000 Americans. Although Saudi Arabia placed stringent controls on such workers and granted visas only for specific jobs except to the Yemenis and a few other Arabs, the large number of foreign workers presented a major potential threat to both Saudi Arabia's internal security and its national identity.[8] This threat was dramatized in March 1977, when Korean workers in Jubail—who were receiving 40% less than Westerners doing the same work—staged the first strike by foreign workers in Saudi Arabia's history.[9] It was reinforced when Turkish workers in Tabuk struck shortly thereafter.[10]

These strikes triggered immediate Saudi efforts to tighten controls over foreign workers, to segregate them from the Saudi population, to enforce the link between visas and specific jobs, and to force foreign firms to improve their control of their workers, but such efforts were only partially successful. Saudi Arabia's wealth was too great, and the demand for foreign labor was too high. A 1978 Saudi study found that 80% of the workers in Jiddah and 78% of those in Riyadh were foreign.[11]

The Ministry of Planning then attempted to limit the growth of foreign labor to the levels shown in Table 6.1 and to reduce dependence on foreign labor sharply beginning in the early to middle 1980s. However, the actual number of foreign workers still rose to 2 million by 1978-1980. These workers included roughly a million Yemenis; large numbers of Korean, Sudanese, and East Asian manual laborers; 150,000 Egyptians and Jordanians working in skilled and semiskilled jobs; 150,000 Indians and Pakistanis working as artisans and technicians; about 100,000 Americans and Europeans; and significant numbers of Palestinians, Taiwanese, Lebanese, and others.[12]

Severe competition existed between the civilian and military needs for Saudi manpower, particularly skilled manpower. The competition was intensified by a number of additional considerations. First, as late as 1975, something like 800,000 men in the Saudi work force of about 1.1 million were illiterate or semiliterate. Such unskilled manpower had increasingly limited value, even to the National Guard, as Saudi military equipment increased in sophistication and operating requirements. Second, although Saudi Arabia had a considerable "baby boom" and comparatively large numbers of educated students coming into the work force, the annual increment still totaled only about 0.2% of the work force per year. This increase fell far short of civilian demand, and most of the students not only expected more immediate economic rewards,

TABLE 6.1 Projected Civilian Employment, 1980-1985 (thousands)

	1979-80	1984-85	Net Change
Men			
Saudi	1,308.4	1,437.4	129.0
Non-Saudi	1,014.9	1,023.9	9.0
Subtotal	2,323.3	2,461.3	138.0
Women			
Saudi	103.0	120.0	17.0
Non-Saudi	44.9	44.9	–
Subtotal	147.9	164.9	17.0
Total			
Saudis	1,411.4	1,557.4	146.0
Non-Saudis	1,059.8	1,068.8	9.0
Total	2,471.2	2,626.2	155.0

Source: Saudi Arabia Ministry of Planning, Third Development Plan (Riyadh: Central Planning Organisation, 1975). It should be noted that the Second Five Year Plan projected a total of 1,470.0 Saudi men and a growth rate of 3.1% as early as 1980 and that non-Saudi men would increase from only 306,000 men in 1975 to 768,000 in 1980 (p. 60).

but they came from families and areas the Saudi government did not want to alienate through any form of conscription or pressure to serve in the armed forces. Third, every increase in Saudi manpower meant an increase in the number of foreign advisers and support personnel Saudi Arabia required to operate the armed forces.[13] The fact also remained that even if the Saudi Army doubled in size, it would not be able to compete in numbers with those of Iran and Iraq. It became all too clear that Saudi Arabia could not build either a credible defense or a credible deterrent simply by expanding its force structure and manpower.

Increased Numbers of Saudi Arabia's Foreign Advisers

The problems of foreign advisers was more than a passing consideration. Saudi Arabia already had approximately 35,000–40,000 foreign advisers and support personnel by the late 1970s, and it still had to rely heavily on training Saudi personnel abroad.[14] There were then special problems because of the risk that personnel trained overseas would become politicized. Although Saudi Arabia's internal training efforts were improving, most air force pilots scheduled for advanced combat training still had to be sent to the U.S. Many Saudi NCOs and warrant officers had to be sent to Lackland Air Force Base for technical training.[15] In the case of the navy, the youngest service, most advanced training was initially conducted in the U.S., particularly at San Diego, Calif. This foreign influence existed even within Saudi Arabia. Basic training for army and National Guard enlisted men was provided by Saudi NCOs and officers, but almost all subsequent specialized training came from one of the numerous contract training schemes provided by foreign armed forces or private companies, with foreign personnel as supervisors or instructors.

The other foreign military assistance efforts in Saudi Arabia also grew to disturbing proportions. The total number of U.S. citizens working on training, construction, and logistic support contracts with the Saudi armed forces reached a total of 30,000 by the late 1970s. The French training mission totaled at least several hundred military personnel by 1977, and 165 more arrived in January 1981 to assist the Saudi Navy. Another 2,000 British civilians supported the Saudi Air Force, and the number of Third World contract officers and NCOs exceeded 1,700 by late 1979.

By the late 1970s, the Saudis were still able to man their combat forces, but they had to use foreigners to provide training, maintenance, and logistical support to them. For example, the Bendix Corporation provided virtually all complex army logistical and maintenance services and was responsible for training of Saudi personnel to run such services in the field. The Raytheon Corporation had a contract for the maintenance of the army's Hawk and Improved Hawk SAMs and the training of their crews. The cost of the package deal to modernize the navy, which the Saudi government had signed directly with the U.S. government in 1974, had grown to over $2 billion. Even the small Saudi Coast Guard had to be trained by the Avco Corporation.

The RSAF became even more heavily dependent on outside support arrangements. As was discussed in Chapter 5, the initial four-year, $1.24 billion contract given the British Aircraft Corporation for servicing and maintaining the Saudi Air Force and operating the Air Academy and Technical Studies Institute was supplemented by the Peace Hawk program, which provided comprehensive support for the F-5. Other contracts were issued to Lockheed Georgia and Lockheed Aircraft Services to provide similar services for the air force's C-130 aircraft, to establish an air traffic control system, and to set up other major military communications functions. The air force also acquired a Pakistani Air Force advisory mission.

Foreign involvement in training and support became equally comprehensive in the "traditional" National Guard. The cost of the Saudi contract with the Vinnell Corporation of California escalated to $1 billion, and Saudi Arabia gave Vinnell responsibility for providing all training and all maintenance of modern weapons and military vehicles. About 75 U.S. Army officers were involved in this program by the late 1970s, but the Vinnell Corporation's civilian personnel (mostly ex–U.S.

Special Forces) came to number 308, and they bore most of the responsibility. Even then, the training effort, centered at Khashm al-An, was also supported by small British, Pakistani, and Jordanian military training missions, and the total number of advisory personnel was over 1,000.[16]

At the end of the 1970s, the Saudis were planning to increase their dependence on foreign support to at least 40,000–50,000 personnel by 1983, but they still could not establish a realistic schedule for phasing out many of their earliest foreign support efforts. The expanding technical demands of the Saudi armed forces utilized the full output of each new class from Saudi training schools without significantly reducing the need for foreign staff. Nearly one foreign worker per Saudi in uniform was required in the regular armed forces, and any further major increases posed obvious difficulties in recruiting trained personnel and in ensuring that significant friction did not develop between the Saudis and their foreign advisers.

The Rising Costs of Military Modernization

Table 6.2 shows the incredible costs of expansion and modernization, and the figures become even more striking when they are related to Saudi expenditures on support services from the U.S. In the period between fiscal 1950 and 1973, the United States sold Saudi Arabia about $213 million worth of weapons and ammunition, $65 million in support equipment, $59 million in munitions, and $1,975 million in support services, for a total of $2,312 million. The next year, primarily because of a naval modernization program and other efforts started before the 1974 survey, U.S. sales to Saudi Arabia began to escalate rapidly. As of 10 June 1981, the cumulative total for FY1950–1981 had reached $4.1 billion for weapons and ammunition and $25.5 billion for support services, for a grand total of $29.6 billion.[17]

By 1978, Saudi Arabia faced the problem that even its financial resources could not cope with the combined demands of the civilian sector, defense, and development. It faced a deficit in spite of truly incredible increases in its revenues. When the First Saudi Five Year Plan (1970–1975) was issued in mid-1970, petroleum income had just exceeded $1 billion annually for the first time, and oil revenues were not matching state expenditures. As a result, there was considerable doubt that Saudi Arabia could finance its $8 billion five-year plan, and defense faced considerable resource constraints. By July 1973, rises in oil prices and production had already given Saudi Arabia a budget surplus of 5.5 billion rials. With the impact of the oil embargo, this surplus increased to 23 billion rials in 1973–1974 and then to 65 billion rials ($18.4 billion) in 1974–1975. As a result, Saudi Arabia's gross domestic product increased from $4.9 billion in 1970, to $11.3 billion in 1973, and to $42.2 billion by mid-1975.[18]

When the Second Saudi Five Year Plan (1975–1980) was approved on 21 May 1975, it called for expenditures of roughly $141 billion. This

TABLE 6.2 Trends in the Expansion of Saudi Arabia's Armed Forces, 1966-1982

	Total Number of Men in Uniform (1,000s)[a]	Total Defense Expenditure (current $ millions)	Defense Expenditure as a % of GNP	Arms Imports (current $ millions)	Medium Tanks	Combat Aircraft
1966	45	150	6.3	25	0	12
1967	50	312	11.4	47	0	20
1968	60	203	6.4	79	0	57
1969	60	1,182	10.9	80	?	43
1970	65	1,481	11.9	30	55	75
1971	75	1,572	10.1	20	25	75
1972	75	2,115	11.8	110	25	71
1973	75	2,796	13.2	80	25	70
1974	80	3,182	10.7	340	55	90
1975	95	7,105	18.2	250	175	95
1976	95	9,288	21.5	470	325	97
1977	96	8,952	16.0	925	475	137
1978	93	10,284	16.1	1,000	325	171
1979	65	14,200	18.1	925	350	178
1980	67	20,700	14.4	1,400	380	136[c]
1981	82	24,400	21 [b]	n.a.	630	133[c]
1982	84	n.a.	n.a.	n.a.	450	128[c]

[a] 1966–1978: includes National Guard.
[b] Calculated from IISS figures.
[c] Excludes 39 BAC-167s used as trainers and some Lightnings in storage.
Sources: U.S. Arms Control and Disarmament Agency, *World Military Expenditures and Arms Transfers,* 1966-75 and 1971-80; *The Military Balance,* 1969-82 (London: IISS); Richard F. Nyrop, *Area Handbook for Saudi Arabia* (Washington, D.C.: American University, 1977).

was about 18 times the investment called for in the first plan, and 9 times actual allocations made under its various revisions. However, both the Second Five Year Plan and Saudi annual budgets after 1976 proved to be overambitious. The real price of oil did not rise as planned, and Saudi imports rose much faster. Even during 1970–1973, Saudi Arabia's imports had risen from about $1 billion to $2 billion annually. By 1975, they had reached $6.6 billion, by 1976 they were $11 billion, and by 1977 they were $15.7 billion. This growth was accompanied by increasing inflation, housing problems, difficulties with Saudi Arabia's sea and air ports, and delays and cost escalation in most development projects. Inflation also became a major problem during 1975–1977. The Saudi cost of living index used unrealistic categories; but the real rate of inflation reached 40–50% annually, and over 70% if rents were included.

Although the government attempted to cope with these problems through salary increases and subsidies, and it did raise civil service and military pay in 1976, the stage was set for a serious economic crisis with obvious internal security implications. This problem was compounded by the abuse of the commission system, which was applied on a percentage basis long after the amounts involved had escalated to almost incredible proportions, and by the role that various members of the royal family played in obtaining government contracts. Although the government first attempted to impose a ceiling on commissions of 3% in early 1977 and announced a ceiling of 5% in late December 1977, the actual rate of commissions paid continued to run up to 17% of the total sale. Only U.S. foreign military sales involved a serious attempt to stay within the 5% limit. Even these limits were often avoided, however, by paying higher margins on related civilian contracts.

As oil prices dropped in real value in 1978, Saudi Arabia abruptly learned that there were finite limits to its governmental and defense expenditures. During 1978–1979 Saudi government expenditures rose to over $42 billion annually and exceeded revenues by $4.3 billion. Further, the financial pressures discussed earlier drove defense and internal security expenditures to nearly $10 billion. The Saudi government was forced into a major economic crackdown. The government rescheduled spending, took measures to correct inflation, and set a 100 million rial limit on the size of the contracts that the MODA and National Guard could grant without approval from the Ministry of Finance. While both organizations violated this ceiling on numerous occasions, the combination of fiscal problems and inflation did lead to a more realistic understanding of the limits on defense expenditures and to growing caution over the allocation of defense contracts.

The F-15 Purchase and the Peace Sun Program

The combination of manpower and financial problems made it almost inevitable that Saudi Arabia would choose to concentrate on improving the quality of its equipment rather than trying to make major increases in its equipment numbers, and on upgrading its existing force structure rather than creating large numbers of new units. Although the price tag of individual purchases seemed high, the overall cost of the resulting force structure involved major savings in manpower and defense expenditures. It also helped deal with other problems. The facility and logistic limitations that had first forced Saudi Arabia to concentrate on improving its air force and military infrastructure in the 1960s still applied in the 1970s. If anything, they were proportionately more severe.

These factors led Saudi Arabia to give an even higher priority to upgrading its air force. The success of the Peace Hawk program, the high "teeth-to-manpower" ratio inherent in modern combat aircraft, and Saudi Arabia's vast distances made air power the military tool that could most easily be improved with the most effect. Saudi Arabia was encouraged in this choice by its close relations with the U.S. Air Force and by the fact that several of the younger Saudi princes had joined the RSAF and had acquired an intimate knowledge of the capabilities of advanced fighter aircraft like the F-14, F-15, and F-16 while training in the U.S.

As will be discussed later, the Saudi government also faced internal security problems within the RSAF that stemmed in part from charges that Saudi Arabia was not modernizing at the same rate as the other Gulf states, was taking second place to Iran, and was being denied modern U.S. aircraft because of U.S. relations with Israel. These pressures contributed to the Saudi decision to seek advanced fighter aircraft long before the shah's fall made this step absolutely critical.

The Decision to Procure the F-15

The Saudis had shown an interest in the F-4 as early as 1967, and Prince Sultan's desire for a first-line fighter was reinforced by the war of attrition of 1969–1970, the high technology of the air war in October 1973, the Vietnam War, and the shah's purchases up to 1973. The F-4, however, had sufficient offensive capability to raise major issues regarding its potential use against Israel. While the full details of the process that led the Saudis to select the F-15 are not yet available, it is clear that the Saudis made U.S. willingness to supply an advanced fighter a test of the strength of renewed Saudi-U.S. relations following the October War. Further, the joint Saudi-U.S. defense requirements and threat studies in the early 1970s indicated that Saudi Arabia would need a replacement for its Lightning fighters in the early 1980s and stressed the need to improve fighter coverage of Saudi Arabia's Gulf coast and its border with Yemen.[19]

These conclusions led to new Saudi-U.S. studies, and a U.S. study team recommended in 1974 that Saudi Arabia acquire advanced air defense aircraft to replace its aging British-made Lightning interceptors. In 1975 the U.S. Department of Defense invited a study team of Saudi experts to come to the U.S. to evaluate the F-14, F-15, F-16, and F-18. As President Carter stated in a press conference on 9 March 1978, this visit had led to a U.S. commitment to provide Saudi Arabia with advanced aircraft in the fall of 1975. After additional analysis, the RSAF determined in early 1977 that the F-15 was the preferred plane for its defense purposes. The proposed sale was approved by President Ford with the caveat that no action could take place in the 1976 election year. This approval was reaffirmed by President Carter in personal meetings with Crown Prince Fahd in May 1977 and with King Khalid in January 1978.

The F-15 was a natural Saudi choice and one that the U.S. Air Force unquestionably endorsed.[20] The F-14 would have been far too complicated, and it would have given the Saudis an air-to-air kill capability superior to that of any Israeli fighter. The F-16A then lacked the radar capability and growth potential to deal with "look-down shoot-down" situations. It also had high capability as an attack fighter, which meant the Congress would inevitably treat it as more of a threat to Israel.

In contrast, the F-15 was developed as an advanced air-superiority fighter. It was also an all-weather fighter with two engines, capable of speeds beyond Mach 2.5, and armed with a 20mm cannon and a computer-guided gunsight. The U.S. Air Force version was armed with four medium-range radar-guided AIM-7F Sparrow and short-range, heat-seeking AIM-9 Sidewinder air-to-air missiles. The F-15 had an advanced radar system that provided long-range detection and tracking as well as a modern electronic central computer and effective fire control. Equally important, it had excellent look-up/look-down radar and growth potential for shoot-down capability, which was seen as critical to defending Saudi oil facilities. The F-15 was designed for rapid plug-in and plug-out service, high reliability, and mission turnaround times of 12 minutes. It offered the potential to substitute high sortie rates for Saudi Arabia's limited aircraft numbers.[21]

Further, the F-15 could carry up to 12,000 pounds of external air-to-ground ordnance and could carry significant payloads without sacrificing its subsonic air-to-air capabilities. Although its combat range is still classified, unofficial sources estimate that the combat radius of the basic F-15 is at least 500 miles for an air-superiority mission and 300 miles even in low-altitude ground-attack missions. The F-15 thus combined excellent air-to-air capability with growth potential against low-altitude threats and eventual growth potential to multimission roles. At the same time, it was not designed for use as an attack fighter as was the F-16. While the F-15 could provide suitable "dual capability" in meeting Saudi attack mission requirements, in the Gulf and against Yemen, it lacked the advanced target-acquisition and munitions-delivery capability and attack avionics necessary to make it fully effective in the much more demanding combat environment that would exist in a war with Israel.

Finally, the F-15 did not offer an "edge" over Israeli fighters. Since the Israelis were already acquiring the F-15, President Carter could state in his 18 February 1978 press conference discussing the sale that the U.S. was "not introducing new weapons" in the Middle East (deliveries of 25 F-15s to Israel had already started and Israel was promised 15 more as a result of the F-15 sale to Saudi Arabia). By juggling payment schedules and selling Israel 75 attack-oriented F-16s, President Carter was able to claim that the sale would not prevent him from achieving his goal of reducing the amount of arms sales each year and that sale of the 60 F-15s to Saudi Arabia would not alter the strategic balance in the Middle East.

The Congressional Debate over the F-15 Sale

Much to the Saudi's displeasure, the Carter administration also assured Israel that the Saudi purchase of F-15s would be subject to the standard condition for all U.S. foreign military sales that transfer to any third party without prior U.S. approval would be prohibited. This condition could be enforced because of the special technology of the F-15s, which gave the supplier control through the continuing need for spare parts, for airfield and support equipment requirements, for special pilot and ground-crew training, for special computer programming and electronic warfare support, and for other special supports.[22] In fact, the *New York Times* pointed this out in an editorial supporting the proposed sale and commented that fear of transfer of F-15s to other states was "unwarranted" since it required a "formidable array of ground equipment and was not easy to fly. Even pilots who might master it could not handle its weapons systems without scores of hours in expensive ground simulators. And it would be virtually impossible to train pilots from other nations in Saudi Arabia without American and Israeli detection."[23] At the same time, the administration noted that delivery to Saudi Arabia of the F-15s would not commence until late 1981, and it argued that Israel would have the lead time to maintain its air combat superiority.

Such arguments did not, however, prevent another bitter round of debates when Saudi Arabia made a formal request to purchase 62 F-15 C/Ds, including 15 TF-15D trainers and 2 attrition reserves to be kept in the U.S. While part of the Israeli lobbying against the sale was unquestionably designed to seek increased U.S. aid and to work out a quid pro quo for U.S. sale of the F-15 and F-16 to Israel on favorable terms, both Israel and the groups supporting it in the U.S. mounted a major effort to block the sale.

These protest groups raised arguments that were still politically relevant when the Reagan Administration began its attempts to sell the AWACS package to Saudi Arabia in 1981, and they are worth summarizing because similar arguments are likely to be raised over future Saudi arms sales requests.[24]

- The F-15 was one of the most advanced air-superiority fighters in the world. It was capable of long-range attacks and interceptions and would enable Saudi Arabia to strike deep into Israel. It would provide the Saudis with 10 multirole fighter squadrons (7 squadrons of F-5s, 3 squadrons of F-15s), enhancing their combat capability dramatically. There would be a tenfold increase in the number of Saudi combat aircraft compared to 1967 and a threefold increase over 1973. The potential increase in weapons payload would be even greater: an increase of 2700 percent over 1967 and 500 percent over 1973. And the new aircraft would be superior in range, maneuverability, top speed, low-level penetration capability, avionics, weapons delivery equipment, electronic countermeasures, cannons, and missilery. Even if operated at 50% efficiency, the new equipment would represent a very significant augmentation of existing Saudi—and Arab—capabilities.
- The F-15 would be more difficult to maintain than the F-5. In fact, the USAF continued to rely heavily on McDonnell technicians to maintain its own F-15s. Thus there would be considerable involvement

of private U.S. personnel in Saudi combat support who would not be subject to control by the U.S. government.

• Saudi Arabia's arms purchases had already satisfied any foreseeable defensive needs. The Saudi armed forces were increasingly capable of sustaining offensive operations in the air, on land, and on the sea. Saudi Arabia was receiving 110 special upgraded F-5E fighters from the U.S. The Saudi F-5Es were equipped with Maverick television-guided air-to-ground missiles (which made F-5Es "potent" bombers) and Sidewinder AIM 9 air-to-air missiles. An exhaustive, year-long evaluation carried out by the U.S. Air Force and Navy had shown the F-5E to be a much more effective dogfighter than expected.

The Saudis had purchased 300 French AMX-30 and 250 American M-60A1 main battle tanks. Two thousand TOW and 4,000 Dragon antitank missiles had also been ordered from the U.S. For mobile air defense, the Saudis had bought the U.S. Improved Hawk, the British Rapier, and the French Shahine (Crotale) SAM missiles. For naval operations, the Saudis had ordered guided missile boats, patrol ships, attack craft, Hovercraft, and frigates.

• The Saudis were not merely buying an inventory of weapons but were engaged in a thorough and systematic program to develop a complete military capability from the ground up, including airfields, naval port facilities, radar and communications systems, supply depots and related logistical support, and maintenance and repair facilities. They had obtained support in training personnel to maintain, operate, repair, command, and administer the weapons and facilities. Where the Libyans, by contrast, were acquiring large amounts of equipment but lacked an infrastructure commensurate with their weapons inventory levels, Saudi Arabia was acquiring basing, operating, and maintenance facilities that exceeded the requirements of current inventories and laid the groundwork for considerable future growth.

• The effort to enhance Saudi capabilities would not end with acquisition of the F-15. The F-15 would require support from advanced ground or airborne radars. Its own radar could acquire targets at long ranges but could not scan wide, distant areas. It thus needed assistance to search for, acquire, and lock onto targets. Large support radar would be required to ensure accurate identification of distant targets as "friend or foe" (IFF). The sale of the F-15 would mean that an additional sale of advanced radar systems would be required in the future. Because of Saudi Arabia's large area and long borders, the likely candidates would be either the Grumman E-2C Hawkeye or the Boeing E-3A (AWACS). Such airborne radars would further enhance Saudi offensive capacity and further destabilize the Arab-Israeli military balance. The alternative to airborne radars would be ground systems requiring thousands of U.S. technicians.

• The presence of F-15s in Saudi Arabia would make direct Saudi involvement in any future Arab-Israeli war almost certain. If Saudi intentions were ambiguous or appeared to be leaning toward involvement in a war, the Israelis would have to take this fact into account. If the F-15s should be stationed at or transferred to bases in the northwest during an Arab attack against Israel, the threat might compel an Israeli Air Force faced with a multifront war to undertake immediate strikes against Saudi bases even if Saudi Arabia had not yet brought its forces into the war.

• The threat posed by F-15 aircraft in Saudi possession would constitute a much greater additional burden on Israeli defenses than any aircraft now with any Arab forces. Saudi F-15s would

- divert IAF squadrons from other theaters;
- complicate the identification problems of the IAF;
- pose a threat to the survivability of the Hawkeye airborne early warning and control system on which Israel now depends heavily and force the diversion of Israeli F-15s from other tasks to expand the combat air patrol dedicated to defending the Hawkeye; and
- significantly enhance the threat of Saudi strikes against Israeli military and civilian targets on the ground.

• The Saudis, for their part, would have to assume that Israeli attacks on the airfields in northwestern Saudi Arabia would be more likely than ever before. They might conclude that staying out of a war, which might otherwise be feasible, would be impossible because of the logic of the new situation. The transfer of advanced combat aircraft to Saudi Arabia might set in motion a cycle of defensive/preemptive calculations on both sides.

• Saudi troops had invaded Israel soon after statehood was declared in 1948. During the 1973 Yom Kippur War, Saudi units fought alongside the Syrian Army. Saudi Arabia was building a major field and support facility at Tabuk, only 125 miles from Israel's major southern port of Eilat and 140 miles from Sharm el-Sheikh at the Straits of Tiran, the gateway to Eilat. This base, constructed by the U.S. Army Corps of Engineers, was also the site of an airborne and paratroop training facility. During November 1977, a squadron of Saudi F-5E fighters participated in maneuvers at Tabuk. Other reports indicated that F-5Es would be permanently stationed at this air base. In addition, the civilian airfields at Gurayat and Turayf (250 and 300 miles respectively from the central Sinai) were being expanded for military use.[25] The Saudi F-15s would be able to operate in a war environment from all three airfields. These bases and the F-15 aircraft would present an added threat to Israel if, as Kuwait's *al Qabas* reported on 15 March 1977, Saudi Arabia planned to blockade Eilat in any future war with Israel. The Saudis might also use the F-15s in the southwest—from Khamis Mushayt, where F-5s are already deployed—to close the south end of the Red Sea to Israeli shipping.

• Saudi Arabia did not require the F-15s to protect its oil fields from Iraq and/or protect the Gulf shipping lanes. The F-5s and Improved Hawk force were totally capable of performing these defensive roles. It was unlikely that Iraq would ever bomb the Saudi oil fields. Control of intact oil fields might serve a political and economic purpose; control of ruined fields would not. Moreover, Iraq's own oil fields were far too vulnerable to a counterstrike. Most important, all Gulf oil producers use the Gulf and the Strait of Hormuz for tanker traffic. Each was the hostage of the other and each had a fundamental economic need to ensure continued freedom of passage.

• The F-15 could easily end up in the control of the radical elements and the Soviet Union, simultaneously endangering the regional position and technological security of the U.S.

• Saudi Arabia did not require F-15s because of the threat in Yemen or because of Soviet expansion in Ethiopia and northeast Africa. The Saudi monarchy had to avoid active roles in Gulf and African conflicts because of its limited manpower and the potential for internal instability. The Saudis have always used financial and political means to achieve their foreign policy goals. They had avoided military involvement against the Soviet-backed Marxist regime in South Yemen and also against the Soviet-aided rebels in Dhofar, Oman. Moreover, although the Soviet Union had maintained an active presence in South Yemen and northeast Africa for a decade, when Saudi Arabia was more vulnerable and less well defended than it is today, the Soviet Union did not menace the Saudi regime.

• Saudi Arabia was not ready to absorb the F-15. Following a study mission in Saudi Arabia, the General Accounting Office (GAO) issued a report to Congress by the comptroller general. The GAO report made the following observations:

- Delivery of the F-5s had successfully fulfilled DOD recommendations for Saudi defensive capability. On the basis of this fact and the maintenance and support problems now facing the Saudis, future sales of advanced aircraft would aggravate the problems of the Saudi Air Force.
- U.S. military advisers are active inside each Saudi armed service, not only at the headquarters level but also at military cities and bases. U.S. trainers and advisers were active in the Saudi National Guard, including "specialized U.S. teams to accompany deployed battalions," and U.S. advisory and training responsibilities in Saudi Arabia would continue to expand. This expansion would obligate the U.S. armed services to allocate a larger share of their own skilled people to assist the Saudis. Shortages might occur within the U.S. military.
- There were continuing problems in assimilating the F-5s, some of which had been delivered to Saudi Arabia six years previously.

- The "information we obtained indicated there is no imminent threat of Saudi Arabia's being overrun."
- "In Saudi Arabia there were no physical controls to prevent the unauthorized use of FMS equipment and services. Furthermore, it appears that physical control after the sale may not be practical to achieve." There should be tighter controls on sales of munitions and sounder evaluation of legitimate needs.

These arguments proved prophetic only in the case of the AWACS. They also had the weakness of simultaneously exaggerating and denigrating Saudi Air Force and Army capabilities, and they ignored or misstated virtually all of the major military and political shifts in the Gulf that increased the threat to Saudi Arabia. Yet for all their political rhetoric, they unquestionably reflected a far more serious Israeli concern with the F-15 sale than Israel had exhibited over any previous U.S. arms sales to Saudi Arabia. In fact, Israel proceeded to threaten the Saudis by conducting practice raids on the Saudi Air Force base at Tabuk.[26] This concern was also reflected in massive pressure on the Congress by Israel and U.S. pro-Israeli groups (which was a major factor behind the GAO study).There was just enough truth in the various arguments against the sale to have a powerful political effect.

The Saudis retaliated by dropping hints that Saudi Arabia would purchase the French Mirage 2000 or F-1 and by a variety of other steps. They finally agreed, however, to accept the F-15 in a configuration that eliminated the data link from the aircraft (deliveries of the F-15 to the USAF then also lacked the link), to not base the F-15 in the area near Israel,[27] to purchase the aircraft without the "FAST" kits necessary to extend its range and without the racks to use the F-15 in attack missions, and to buy the F-15 with only three, rather than five, hard points, which limited its future conversion capability to the attack mission. These limitations and assurances were stated to Congress in a letter sent by Secretary of Defense Harold Brown on 9 May 1978. The Congress narrowly approved the sale six days later.[28]

It is uncertain whether these concessions could have avoided a congressional refusal to approve the sale if the situation in the Gulf had not deteriorated so sharply during 1978, if a Soviet-backed coup had not taken place in Afghanistan two weeks earlier, and if a Soviet-backed Ethiopia had not just beaten Somalia and the Eritrean rebels. However, the Saudi compromises, and the administration's "packaging" of the Saudi sale with the sale of 15 F-15s and 75 F-16s to Israel and 50 F-5s to Egypt and with other increases in U.S. aid to Israel, eventually won the required margin of congressional support. As a result, Saudi Arabia acquired the basic combat tool it needed to cope with the changes in the surrounding area, although it did so under political constraints that virtually ensured another struggle to influence Congress in the near future.

U.S. Air Reinforcement of Saudi Arabia

The potential Saudi need for the F-15 was demonstrated only a few months later. The U.S. sent an F-15 squadron to Saudi Arabia in January 1979 as a preventive measure to deal with the crisis in Iran and the Yemeni border war. Ironically, this same U.S. "show of force" ended in demonstrating the need for increased Saudi forces in being and for the prestocking of equipment and munitions for any U.S. over-the-horizon reinforcement.

It took 42 aircraft to deploy 12 F-15s to Saudi Arabia.[29] Eighteen KC-135 tankers were required to refuel the fighters because the U.S. was denied the use of bases in Spain and limits were placed on its use of bases in Portugal. In addition, 6 backup F-15s had to be flown as far as Portugal to ensure that the U.S. could arrive with all 12 aircraft, an EC-135 had to be sent to control the deployment of the F-15s across the Atlantic, 2 C-141s and 2 C-5As were required to move the ground support equipment, and 1 Saudi C-130 had to be dedicated to provide airlift support in Saudi Arabia. An additional 293 U.S. personnel had to be deployed to Saudi Arabia to support the F-15s in country. As the U.S. Navy was quick to point out, deploying 12 unarmed F-15s cost the U.S. roughly the same amount as deploying an aircraft carrier.[30]

The need for advanced air defense technology in the Gulf was further demonstrated in March 1979, when the U.S. sent two E-3A AWACS to Saudi Arabia to provide air warning and control in the midst of the Yemeni border war. It was shown again in October 1980, when there was a risk that the Iran-Iraq war might expand to include Iranian air attacks on the Arab oil facilities in the southern Gulf. As a result, four AWACS had to be deployed to Saudi Arabia to cover the Gulf perimeter. This deployment forced the U.S. to airlift TPS-43E ground radar and support equipment to make up for the massive gaps in Saudi radar coverage left by the original Anglo-American air defense package of the 1960s. Unlike the British equipment originally sold to the Saudis, the TPS-43E was mobile, and it could detect aircraft flying at medium altitudes as far as 240 nautical miles (NM) and high-flying aircraft up to 350 NM. Creating minimal radar coverage of the Saudi oil fields on the Gulf required 396 U.S. personnel, including 300 to support the E-3A and 96 to support the TPS-43E, of whom 70 were operations and maintenance personnel.

Even then, the U.S. deployments left serious gaps in the overall radar coverage of the Gulf. The TPS-43E had not been designed for such a role and lacked suitable electronic countermeasure (ECM) resistance. It could at best provide 30–60 NM of very-low- to low-altitude range over the Gulf. The U.S. was forced to immediately fund an ECM upgrade program. The lesson was clear that Saudi Arabia would require much more sophisticated air defenses than the F-15 alone could provide.[31] It became apparent to both Saudi Arabia and the U.S. that Saudi Arabia needed to greatly improve its air control and warning capabilities, and

TABLE 6.3 Growth of the Royal Saudi Air Force, 1973–1982 (squadron/aircraft)

	1973	1974	1975	1976	1977	1978	1979	1980	1981	1982
Manpower	5,500	5,500	5,500	10,000	15,000	12,000	8,000	14,500	14,500	15,000
Combat Aircraft	120	149	195+	206	271	291	298+	293+	308+	
Interceptors	2/35	2/35	2/35	2/37	2/37	1/18	1/20	1/17	1/17	1/17[b]
Lightning										
F-52/53	35	35	35	37	37	16	18	15	15	15
T-55	–	–	–	–	–	2	2	2	2	2
Fighter-bombers	2/15	2/34	2/30	2/30	2/70	3/60	3/65	3/65	3/65	3/65
F86F	15	–	–	–	–	–	–	–	–	–
F5B	–	20	–	–	–	–	–	–	–	–
F5E	–	14	30	30	70	60	65	65	65	65
COIN										
FGA	2/20	2/27	2/30	2/30	2/30	2/35	2/39	–	–	–
BAC-167										
Strikemaster[a]										
OCU	–	–	–	–	–	3/58	3/54	3/54	3/57	2/40
F-5B						16	16	16	16	16
F-5F						24	24	24	24	24
Lightning/T-55						16/2	12/2	12/2	15/2	–
Transports	2/12	2/11	2/25	2/37	2/48	2/44	2/45	2/60[c]	2/72[c]	3/71
Heavy-medium	12	11	21	25	40	36	37	50	60	64
C-130	10	11	21	24	39	35	36	49	59	63
C-140 or Boeing 707	2	2	–	1	1	1	1	1	1	1
Light	–	–	2	4	4	4	4	4	4	9
Falcon			2	2	2	2	2	2	2	7
Jetstar			–	2	2	2	2	2	2	2
Tankers (KC-130)	–	–	4	4	4	4	4	6	8	6
Helicopters	2/30	2/37	2/52	2/53	2/53	2/64	2/52	2/46	2/46	2/46
Alouette III	1	6	6	12	12	22	2	2	2	2
AB-204	1	1	1	1	1	–	–	–	–	–
AB-205	8	10	25	24	24	24	24	12	12	12
AB-206	20	20	20	16	16	17	17	13	13	13
Bell 212	–	–	–	–	–	1	1	11	11	11
AS 61A	–	–	–	–	–	–	2	2	2	2
KV-107	–	–	–	–	–	–	6	6	6	6

TABLE 6.3 (continued)

	1973	1974	1975	1976	1977	1978	1979	1980	1981	1982
Trainers/Other	8	11	23+	25	33	12	23	51	51	58
T-33	1	1	–	–	–	–	–	–	–	–
T-55 (54/55)	–	3	3	5	7	–	–	–	–	–
Cessna 310K	1	1	–	–	–	–	–	–	–	–
Cessna 172G/H	6	6	–	–	–	–	11	12	12	12
T-41A	–	–	–	–	6	12	–	–	–	–
BAC-167 Strikemaster	–	–	–	–	–	–	–	–	39[d]	46[d]
F-58	–	–	20	20	20	–	–	–	–	–
Missiles										
AAMs	?	?	?	?	?	?	?	?	?	?
(Red Top, Firestreak, Sidewinder, Magic)										
ASMs	?	?	?	?	?	?	?	?	?	?
(Maverick)						x	x	x	x	x
SAMs	37	37	37	–	–	–	–	–	–	–
(Thunderbird Mk 1)										
On Order/Under Delivery										
F-5/F-4 (F-15)	140/30	126/–	100/–	100/–	20/–	–/(60)	–/(60)	–/(60)	–/(62)	15/16[d]
BAC-167/Mirage III	0/–	9/38	– /38	– /38	17/–					6/1
K-C 130/747		12/–	10/–	10/–		4/1	–/1	–/1	–/1	
C-130/CASA										40
C-212-200	4/–							–/20	–/20	
Alouette III/KV-107			x/–	x/–		–/6				
Sidewinder/Maverick					x/–			660/916	660/916	1179/916
E-3A AWACS	–	–	–	–	–	–	–	–	–	5

N.B. 20 F-Bs probably used in training role, 1975–1977, as were COIN aircraft in 1980; Mirages on order 1974–1976 believed to be for Egypt.
x = exact number unknown.
[a]BAC-167s used in a dual training/combat role.
[b]One interceptor squadron of F-15s forming.
[c]Plus an unknown number of CASA C-212s.
[d]BAC-167s used exclusively as trainers (not counted here as combat aircraft, though readily convertible to a combat role).
Source: The Military Balance, 1973–1983 (London: IISS).

CHART 6—3
THE BUILD-UP OF U.S. AIR SUPPORT FOR THE SAUDI AIR FORCE

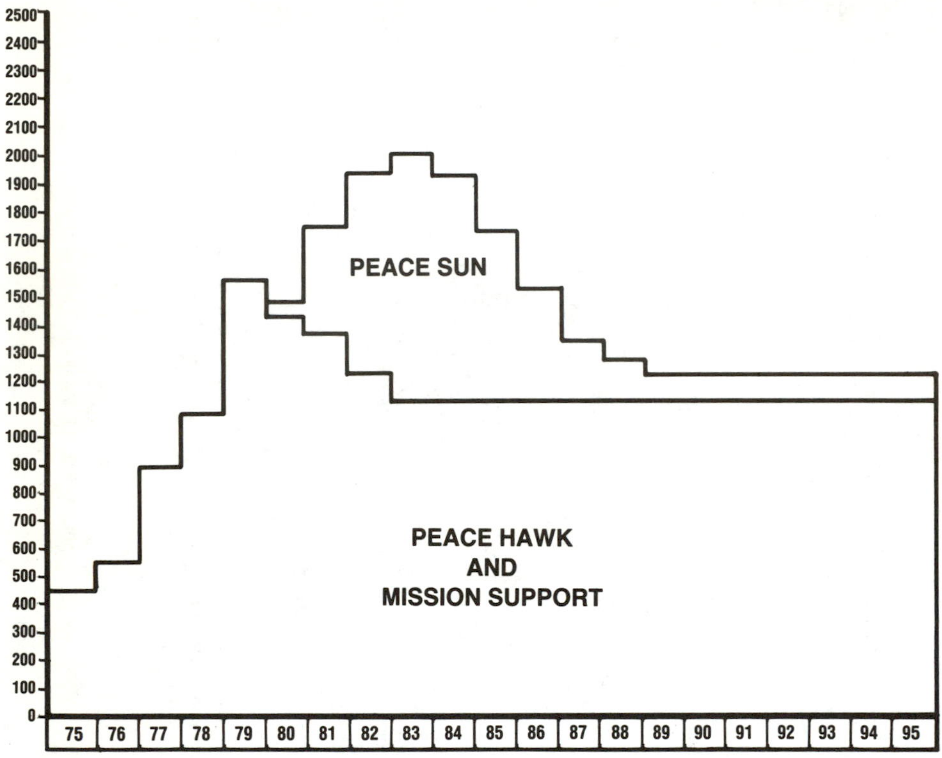

SOURCE: DoD Briefing, April, 1981.

to extend its fighter range and capabilities, if it was to meet the new threats developing in the Gulf.

The Overall Development of the RSAF

The overall development of the RSAF during the late 1970s is shown in Table 6.3. This table traces important, but relatively modest, changes in Saudi capabilities. The F-15 purchase was the only major combat aircraft purchase between the F-5E purchase and the end of the 1970s, but Saudi Arabia did expand its air mobility and transport capabilities significantly. It should also be remembered that because of the lead times involved, Saudi Arabia was still converting to the F-5E during this period. This process is reflected in the growth of the U.S. manpower required to support the Peace Hawk program shown in Chart 6.3, and it led to the gradual downgrading of the BAC-167 from COIN to trainer status. The chart also shows the timing of the Saudi conversion to the

F-15 and the buildup of the Peace Sun program to provide U.S. support for the F-15. It is interesting to note that the Peace Sun program could be implemented with relatively minor increases in manpower because of the solid training and support base established under Peace Hawk, the expansion of Saudi air base facilities, and the training of Saudi NCOs and technicians by the U.S.[32]

The Expansion of the Saudi Army

The expansion of the Saudi Army proceeded with deliberate speed. While the French advisory role grew steadily, the U.S. continued to work closely with the Saudis and agreed to expand its sale to Saudi Arabia of M-60 tanks and Improved Hawk surface-to-air missiles[33] and to provide the sights and fire-control systems necessary to upgrade the M-60Al to the M-60AlEl (A3). Saudi Arabia also purchased additional artillery weapons, air defense weapons, and heliborne missiles.[34] These changes did not provide Saudi Arabia with all the firepower and artillery support it needed to balance its combined arms, but they did mean that the Saudi Army would have a greatly improved short-range air defense capability and they laid the groundwork for creating air mobile units.

The growth of the army is shown in Table 6.4, and it seems worth stressing that this growth represented a relatively well-controlled force expansion given the pressures developing in the Gulf. The equipment mix of the Saudi Army continued to create serious problems in maintenance and support during this period, but most other Arab nations faced similar constraints. Saudi Arabia and Jordan were virtually the only major Arab countries that did not dilute army capabilities by overpurchasing equipment and spreading limited supplies of manpower over additional low-grade combat units.

The Saudi Army did, however, build up to two mechanized brigades by 1981, acquire two small paratroop battalions, and make major improvements in its basing and support facilities. For reasons discussed later, the Saudi Army construction schedule was speeded up in the late 1970s to help improve Saudi internal security, and two key army cantonments were completed at Khamis Mushayt and Tabuk by late 1979 at a cost of about $81 million each.[35] Saudi Arabia also made significant progress in completing King Khalid and Assad military cities, although the costs in 1981 dollars rose to $8 billion and $15 billion respectively,[36] and additional facilities were built at Sharurah near the Yemeni border.

As a result, Saudi Arabia was able to deploy a reasonably well-trained armored brigade and the key elements of four moderately well-trained mechanized brigades into new casernes by late 1980. These forces were split between Sharurah and Khamis Mushayt—which covered the potential threat from the Yemens—and Tabuk—which covered threats from Jordan, Israel, Iraq, and Iran.[37] Although the casernes at Hafr al-

TABLE 6.4 Growth of the Saudi Army, 1973–1982

	1973	1974	1975	1976	1977	1978	1979	1980	1981	1982
Total Manpower	39,500	62,000	56,000	60,000	80,000	80,000	55,000	51,000	65,000	60,000
Regular army	36,000	36,000	40,000	40,000	45,000	45,000	35,000	31,000	35,000	35,000
National Guard	3,500	26,000	16,000	20,000	35,000	35,000	20,000	20,000	30,000	25,000
Organization (unit size)	1 bn	1 bn	1 bd	1 bd	1 bd	2 bds	1 bd	1 bd	2 bds	2 bds
Armored	1 bn	1 bn	1 bd	1 bd	1 bd	2 bds	1 bd	1 bd	2 bds	2 bds
Mechanized (or reconnaissance)	1 bn	2 bns	—	—	1 div	—	—	1 bd	2 bds	2 bds
Infantry	4 bds	4 bds	4 bds	4 bds	2 bns	4 bds	4 bds	3 bds	2 bds	2 bds
Artillery	3 bns	3 bns	3 bns	3 bns	3 bns	3 bns	3 bns	3 bns	4 bds	4 bds
Paratroop	1 bn	1 bn	1 bn	1 bn	1 bn	2 bns	2 bns	2 bns	2 bds	1 bd
Antiaircraft	3 bns	3 bns	6 bns	6 bns	6 bns	6 bns	6 btys	18 btys	2 bds	18 btys
SAM	10 btys	10 btys	10 btys	10 btys	10 btys	10 btys	10 btys	10 btys	18 btys	18 btys
Royal Guard	1 bn	1 bn	1 bn	1 bn	1 bn	1 bn	1 bn	3 bns	3 bns	1 reg
Equipment										
AFVs	285+	315+	435+	585+	885+	575+	600+	630+	880	990
Medium tanks	25	55	175	325	475	325	350	380	530	450
Light tanks	60	60	60	60	210	—	—	—	—	—
Armored cars	200+	200+	200+	200+	200	250	250+	250+	350	540+
APCs	—	—	—	—	?	300+	350+	350+	1,250+	850+
Artillery	?	?	?	?	?	?	?	?	54+	?
SP	—	—	—	—	—	105,155mm	105,155mm	105,155mm	105,155mm	105/155/203mm
Field	?	?	105mm	105mm	105mm	105mm	105mm	105mm	105mm	105mm
RCL	—	—	75mm	75mm	75mm	75mm	75mm	75mm	75mm	75/90/105mm
Guided weapons	—	—	? SS-11; Harpoon	? SS-11; Harpoon	? SS-11; Dragon; Vigilant; Harpoon	? TOW	? TOW; Dragon	? TOW; Dragon	? TOW; Dragon	? TOW; Dragon; Hot
AA weapons	?	?	?	?	?	? M42; AMX-30	? M42; AMX-30	? M42; AMX-30	? M42; M163; AMX-30	? M163; AMX-305A
SAMs	10 btys Hawk	10 btys Hawk	10 btys Hawk	10 btys Hawk	10 btys Hawk; Rapier	10 btys Hawk	10 btys Hawk	10 btys Hawk; Crotale	18 btys Hawk; Crotale	18 btys Hawk; Crotale

TABLE 6.4 (continued)

	1973	1974	1975	1976	1977	1978	1979	1980	1981	1982
On Order										
AMX-30/M-60	30/–	150/–	250/ ?	100/250	x/200	–/175	–/150	370/100	170/150	–/150
Scorpion/Fox/Panhard	–	x/x/	250/–/–	100/–/–	–/50/–	–/50/–	–/50/–	–/50/x	–	–
AMX-13/AMX-10P	–	–	–	–/x	x/–	–/200	94 V-750	–/200	–	–
M-163 Vulcan/SPAA guns	–	–	–/x	–/x	–	x/–	x/86	x/86	–/40	–/60
V-150 Commando/AML	–	–	–	–	x/200	–	–	94/x	–	–
APCs	–	–	250	250	250	–	–	–	–	–
Guns/howitzers	–	–	x	x	x	–	–	–	–	–
Hawk/Improved Hawk	–	–/x	x/–	x/–	–/6 btys	–/6 btys	–/6 btys	–/6 btys	–/16	72
Rapier/Crotale	–	–	x/x	x/x	–	–	–	–/x	–	x/–
TOW/Dragon	–	–	–	–	x/x	x/x	–	–	–	–
Shahine/Redeye	–	–	–	–	x/x	x/x	x/x	x/x	6/x	x/–

x = exact number unknown.

1973: 1 reconnaissance battalion; M-47 medium, M-47 light tanks; AML-60, AML-90, some Staghound and Greyhound armored cars; Ferret scout cars.

1974: 2 reconnaissance battalions; 30 AMX-30 medium tanks; all other figures unchanged.

1975 150 AMX-30 medium tanks; all other figures unchanged.

1976: 300 AMX-30 medium tanks; all other figures unchanged.

1977: 400 AMX-30, 50 M60 medium tanks; Panhard M-3, Commando APCs; all other figures unchanged.

1978: 250 AMX-30, 75 M60 medium tanks; no light tanks mentioned; 200 AML-60, AML-90 armored cars; 50 Fox scout cars; 300 AMX-10P; M113, Panhard M-3 APCs; all other figures unchanged.

1979: 100 M60 medium tanks; 150 AMX-10P, 200 M113 APCs; all other figures unchanged.

1980: One armored brigade forming; 3 Royal Guard battalions comprise one regiment; 280 AMX-30 medium tanks; all other figures unchanged.

1981, 1982: 3 Royal Guard battalions comprise one regiment; 480 AMX-30, 150 M-60A1 medium tanks; M-60A3 conversion kits on order; all other figures unchanged.

Source: The Military Balance, 1973–1982 (London: IISS).

Batin were still unfinished, which left the Iraq-Syria-Kuwait border uncovered, this deployment of Saudi forces was a marked improvement over the past basing of Saudi units near Jiddah, Dammam, and Taif.[38]

The Saudi Army expanded its agreements with the U.S. Army Corps of Engineers to obtain aid in creating new combat and service engineering capabilities, and it started to create an Ordnance Corps in April 1979, at a total program cost of $984.3 million.[39] Finally the army began to acquire a modern telecommunications system, although this system had significant weaknesses because it was largely separate from the command and control (C^2) system of the air force, navy, and National Guard. This weakness seems to have contributed to the lack of coordination between the army and National Guard during the uprising at Makkah in 1979.[40]

Change in the National Guard

As Table 6.5 shows, the National Guard did not begin to expand beyond the levels discussed in Chapter 5 until 1981, and it remained a relatively lightly armed force. Prince Abdullah did, however, attempt to purchase 300 Leopard II tanks and other armor from Germany for the Guard. While the other senior members of the royal family took advantage of the reluctance of the German government to sell the weapons to let the sale die in early 1981, the debate over the Guard's expansion seems to have reflected the continuing indecision (discussed in Chapter 5) within the royal family over its role.[41]

The Growth of the Saudi Navy

The rationale behind the growth of the Saudi Navy has already been discussed, but several important changes occurred during the late 1970s. The new naval base at Jiddah and Jubail neared completion, and although progress in improving the quality of naval training and personnel lagged far behind Saudi and U.S. goals, significant progress was made toward creating the facilities necessary to give Saudi Arabia a "blue water" navy.

Saudi Arabia continued to be dissatisfied with the quality and responsiveness of the U.S. Navy advisory effort, however, and made an effort to diversify the sources of support for its naval expansion that culminated in the selection of France to supplement the U.S. as a major source of naval equipment and support. After stiff competition by the Italians, France was awarded a $35 billion contract in October 1980 to provide 4 2,000-ton frigates, 2 fleet oil tanker ships, 4 Otomat surface-to-surface missile craft, and 24 Dauphine naval attack surveillance helicopters with AS-15 missiles. France also agreed to second 165 regular officers and NCOs and to provide the required logistic and other services.[42] This contract followed an earlier Saudi purchase of Thomson

TABLE 6.5 The Saudi National Guard, 1973-1982

	1973	1974	1975	1976	1977	1978	1979	1980	1981	1982
Manpower[a]	35,000	26,000	16,000	20,000	35,000	20,000	35,000	20,000	30,000	38,000
Organization[b]										
Light infantry battalions	?	?	?	?	?	20	20	20	20	40
Mechanized battalions	0	0	0	0	0	0	2?	3?	4	4
Equipment										
Cadillac-Gage Commando variants	?	?	?	?	?	150	150	150	240	240
Vulcan AA guns	?	?	?	?	?	?	?	?	?	?
TOW anti-tank guided missiles	?	?	?	?	?	?	?	?	?	?
90 mm recoilless rifles	?	?	?	?	?	?	?	?	?	?

[a]Most are part time, and reporting varies sharply.
[b]Most formations are small, locally recruited detachments deployed in villages and towns or serving guard duty.

Source: The Military Balance (London: IISS, 1973-1982).

CSF TRS 3140 search/track-while-scan radars, and Otomat missiles, for shore-based defense and an agreement in principle in May 1980 that France would provide Saudi Arabia with the same kind of training and operational support the U.S. Navy provided for U.S. systems.[43]

This contract with the French did not sever Saudi dependence on the U.S. for support of the Saudi Navy. In May 1979 a business triumvirate called the HBH Company won a $671 million contract from the U.S. Navy to train Saudi Arabian naval forces to operate ships and maintain facilities as part of a three-year program, with the option to extend for two more years. HBH included Hughes Aircraft, Bendix, and Holmes and Narver, Inc., and the Saudi deal with the French did not affect this contract. The Corps of Engineers also continued to supervise work on the Saudi naval bases at Jubail and Jiddah and the naval headquarters complex at Riyadh.

The contract with the French did, however, introduce a major "dual source" of Saudi naval equipment and support and put major new demands on the Saudi Navy. The new French frigates were particularly high-performance ships, and they represented a massive step forward in technical sophistication for the Saudi Navy. The F-2000-class frigates were designed to be the most powerfully armed ship in the class in the world when they entered service in the mid-1980s. Although they were comparatively compact vessels—107 meters at the water line, 115 meters overall, and 12.5 meters at the waterline beam—they were equipped with a telescopic helicopter hangar, a Creusot-Loire 100mm gun turret, 8 Otomat surface-to-surface missile launchers, Crotale naval surface-to-air missiles, 2 Breda 40mm twin turrets, 4 antisubmarine warfare (ASW) torpedo launchers, and the AS.15 TT ship-to-ship missiles mounted on Dauphine 2 helicopters. They were also equipped with advanced search and tracking radar, an advanced electronic command center, fire-control radar, advanced electronic warfare equipment, towed and hull-mounted sonars, advanced optical trackers, and chaff launchers to defend against enemy ship-to-ship missiles. Even the all-diesel drive system was designed to be "state-of-the-art."[44]

The use of a heliborne antiship missile system was of particular interest. The Aerospatiale AS 365F Dauphine 2 helicopters were fitted with Thomason-CSF Agrion 15 maritime radar and AS.15 TT all-weather missiles with a range in excess of 15 km. The missile's initial targeting was handled by the Agrion 15 radar. After launch, the missile relied on automatic guidance for flight-to-target at low altitude above the sea surface. The Dauphine helicopter could carry four AS.15 TTs—two per side on a mid-fuselage stores platform, with growth potential to carry the Am.39 (Exocet), and the Agrion 15 radar antenna was to be nose-mounted in an under-fuselage swivel platform. Like the F-2000 frigates, the AS.15 represented an extremely sophisticated system for a force like the Saudi Navy, with very demanding training, maintenance, and support requirements. The AS.15 TT was capable of launch from various maritime patrol aircraft and from coastal missile batteries.

These purchases were particularly ambitious given that (1) the Saudi Navy was still operating only three fast patrol boats, one former U.S. Coast Guard cutter, four coastal minesweepers, and two utility craft in 1977; (2) the Saudi Navy had to absorb additional orders of six corvettes with Harpoon, four fast-missile patrol boats, four gunboats, and four additional landing craft; and (3) it still had only 1,500 men.[45] Although France agreed to provide logistic and training support for its share of the Saudi Navy's expansion, Saudi Arabia also committed itself to buying developmental equipment involving a substantial technical risk—a major departure from past Saudi practice, and one its weakest service seemed ill equipped to deal with. Such purchases almost certainly exceeded the navy's force expansion capacity; they constituted one of the few major "overbuys" that Saudi Arabia made during this period.

The "Explosion" of the Saudi Defense Budget

Most of the other changes in the Saudi forces adhered to the principles of creating the infrastructure and training base before the forces, working within Saudi Arabia's tight manpower limits, controlling the growth of the foreign advisory effort, and putting quality before quantity. However, such efforts still involved radical further increases in the Saudi defense budget. These increases were particularly severe because many of the expenditures on key construction projects came at the end of the projects, while most equipment purchases had to be paid for in advance. The resulting "explosion" in Saudi defense expenditures is shown in Table 6.6, and it is clear that the restraints imposed by Saudi Arabia's 1978 economic crisis quickly vanished under the twin impact of the shah's fall and the resulting rises in oil prices. The Saudi defense budget, which had already increased by about seven times during 1969–1974, increased another three times between 1975 and 1981 and then doubled again between 1978 and 1981. By 1981, Saudi Arabia had a defense budget roughly the size of the French or West German budgets.

This expansion put severe strains on the Ministry of Defense and Aviation from 1979 onward.[46] The MODA could not handle the burden of properly evaluating individual contracts and decisions or of integrating the activities of the different services and branches. The MODA's organization in 1980 is shown in Chart 6.4; it is virtually the same as it was in the mid-1970s. While Saudi Arabia's new oil wealth allowed the MODA to buy its way out of many defense management problems, even Saudi Arabia's wealth was not infinite. The country again had let its economic development plan and civilian expenditures get out of control. The Third Five Year Plan (1980–1985) called for expenditures of $220 billion, and this combination of civilian and military expenditure threatened to put Saudi Arabia into the deficit position it had faced in 1978.[47]

Moreover, the Ministry of Defense and Aviation continued to seriously overspend its annual budget, and MODA overspending more than

TABLE 6.6 The Econometrics of Saudi Defense Development

			Defense Expenditures as % of		Arms/Arms Imports		Manpower Effort		
	GNP ($ millions)	Defense Expenditures ($ millions)	GNP	Central Gov't Expenditures	Imports ($ millions)	As % of Total Imports	Total Population (millions)	Total Military Manpower (thousands)	Armed Forces per 1,000 People
1966	6,410	150?	6.3	–	25	–	4.8	45	9.4
1967	7,330	312?	11.4	–	47	–	5.0	50	10.0
1968	8,320	203?	6.4	–	79	–	5.1	60	11.8
1969	10,820	1,182	10.9	24.9	80	10.6	6.0	60	10.0
1970	12,448	1,481	11.9	27.2	30	4.2	6.2	65	10.5
1971	15,601	1,572	10.1	30.6	20	2.4	6.4	75	11.7
1972	17,973	2,115	11.8	34.1	110	9.6	6.5	75	11.5
1973	21,130	2,796	13.2	17.5	80	4.0	6.8	75	11.0
1974	29,738	3,182	10.7	19.3	340	11.8	7.0	80	11.4
1975	39,082	7,105	18.2	34.1	250	5.9	7.3	95	13.0
1976	49,312	9,426	19.1	35.5	470	5.4	7.7	95	12.3
1977	61,932	9,505	15.3	25.3	925	6.3	8.2	96	7.3
1978	67,734	10,751	15.9	29.0	1,000	4.3	8.8	93	10.6
1979	94,667	14,200	15.0	27.3	925	3.7	9.3	65	7.0
1980	116,636	20,700	17.7	26.7	1,400	4.4	9.3	67	7.2
1981	118,000	24,400	21	–	–	–	–	82	–
1982	–	–	–	–	–	–	–	84	–

Sources: The Military Balance (London: IISS, various years); ACDA, *World Military Expenditures and Arms Transfers,* various years. Figures are often inconsistent and may not track with other sources or with figures in text, which are taken from other sources when the latter seem more correct. The drop in Saudi total military manning in 1979 comes from changes in the way the IISS counts the National Guard. The inconsistencies in the defense expenditure and defense as percentage of GNP data for 1966–1969 reflect different sources, but the percentage of GNP data seems correct. See Chapter 10 for more recent reporting on 1980–1983.

CHART 6—4
THE ORGANIZATION OF THE SAUDI DEFENSE ESTABLISHMENT IN THE LATE 1970s

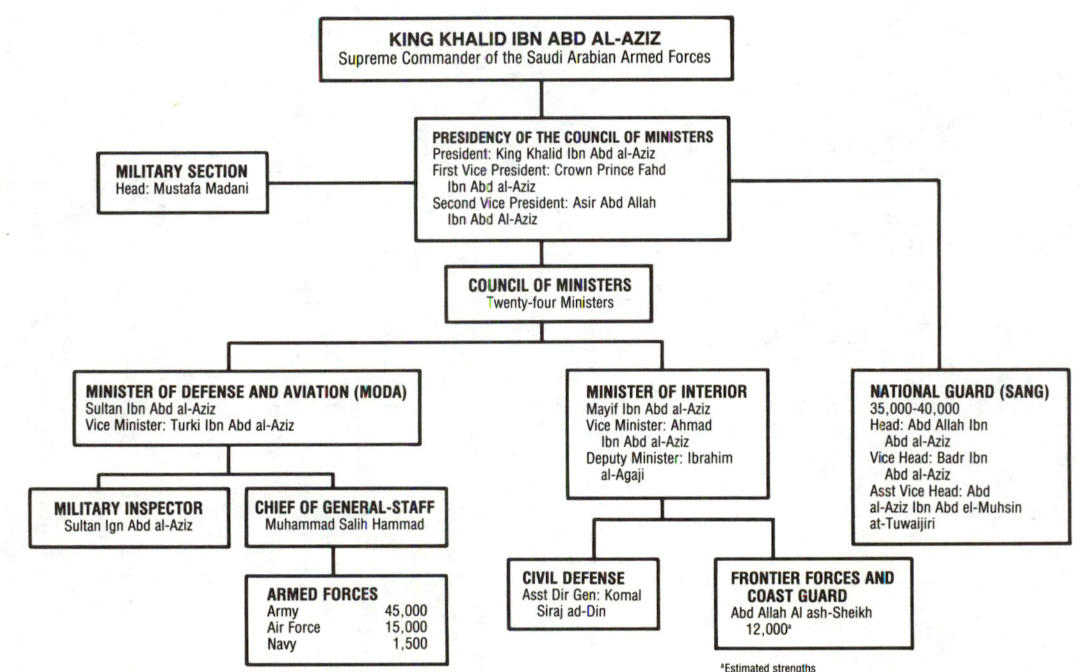

SOURCE: Arabian-American Oil Company; U.S. Congress, House, Committee on International Relations, *United States Arms Policies in the Persian Gulf and Red Sea areas: Past, Present, and Future*, Report, 95th Congress, 1st session, December, 1977; and *Middle East Economic Digest*, "Saudi Arabia and the United States," August, 1981, p. 46.

compensated for the failure of the other ministries to obligate their funds. The Ministry of Defense and Aviation simply could not improve its operations fast enough to cope with the problems it faced. It did increase its Saudi personnel, hire a number of outstanding young Saudi technocrats, and expand its use of foreign advisers.[48] It also attempted to adopt techniques like program budgeting, and it succeeded in improving its accounting and in adopting more modern business procedures. However, it failed to make such management systems fully effective, and most efforts to improve management had little operational impact because Saudi Arabia repeatedly had to suddenly accelerate its military modernization in reaction to shocks like the fall of the shah, the Yemeni border war, the invasion of Afghanistan, and the uprising in Makkah.

Further, senior Saudi officials continued to allocate resources on the spot, without regard to plans, administrative systems, and the other tools of management that Saudi Arabia was trying to introduce. Few of the foreign advisers helping the MODA and its components attempt to institute modern managements systems were willing to tell the Saudis they worked for that they should not exercise their former prerogative of making personal decisions and would have to follow the new system if it was to work.

The Saudis compounded these problems by continuing a style, or pattern, of administrative behavior that made most Saudis unwilling to keep fixed schedules, attend to administrative details, or conduct structured meetings and decision-making reviews. This behavior may have suited the informal character of Saudi society, but it left many decisions to meetings at which a host of different claimants and issues would struggle simultaneously for the attention of the prince or other decision maker and at which Saudi officials would rapidly shift from one issue to another and then take a decision without checking the data they had been provided. The end result often combined the worst of Saudi and Western administrative techniques. Lower-level officials in the MODA would not act on their own and normally referred all decisions upward or buried them in paperwork. In contrast, senior Saudi decision makers made quick decisions about critical issues on an unstructured basis and schedule.

At the same time, various groups of Western advisers developed proposals or plans to deal with individual issues. These plans normally had to be developed without proper coordination with previous plans, other defense activities, and the overall Saudi defense program. Yet many got Saudi approval and funding without further review and were then implemented on a piecemeal basis. While a constant series of adjustments and budget increases kept things working, these weaknesses crippled the MODA's efforts to improve its management and planning activities as much as did the need to respond to sudden changes in external threats.

It is interesting to note, however, that civilian development gradually became more of a burden than defense. Although Saudi military imports increased from under $100 million in 1970 to over $1 billion in 1978, they dropped as a percentage of Saudi Arabia's total imports, and this trend continued into 1982.[49] Saudi imports are largely the result of direct or indirect increases in government services; they indicate that it is Saudi Arabia's civilian development that may place the greatest burden on government in the mid-1980s.

Internal Security Issues

The rapid expansion of the armed forces, and the radical social and economic changes taking place in Saudi Arabia, also led to new internal security problems during this period. While these were far less serious than those that had arisen under King Saud, they were still important signs of the limits to Saudi Arabia's modernization.

New Tensions Within the Military

As has been discussed earlier, a minor coup attempt took place in the Saudi armed forces in May–June 1977, involving a dozen pilots at Tabuk Air Base. The reports available on this incident are sketchy at best, but the pilots evidently planned to bomb the palaces at Riyadh and Jiddah and to proclaim an Islamic republic. Although the plot had little support in the armed forces and was discovered well before anyone was ready to implement it, two of the pilots escaped in their aircraft to Baghdad. When the Saudis learned that the plot had massive funding by Libya, they forbade Saudi aircraft to carry munitions and more than 30 minutes' fuel for several months.[50]

More important, the investigations that followed showed that military pay had not kept pace with the increases in income in the civilian sector and that there was considerable dissatisfaction with living and training conditions. The Saudis solved some of these problems by the doubling of military salaries in 1976–1977, but the need to improve military living conditions involved longer lead times and could not be dealt with in this fashion.[51] By the late 1970s most of the construction projects for the armed forces lagged behind schedule, were inadequate to meet the growth in Saudi forces, or required further development.[52] The Saudi government responded by speeding military construction, improving military living standards and housing, and taking a number of other steps to improve training conditions and family housing facilities for enlisted military personnel. However, the coup attempt did serve as a further warning of the limits to Saudi Arabia's military expansion.

Regional Development Problems

The Saudis took several other important internal security decisions during this period. Perhaps the most important of these decisions was to improve the regional balance in Saudi Arabia's economic development. As has been discussed earlier, the first Saudi Five Year Plan (1970–1975) was formulated at a time when Saudi Arabia's oil wealth was still comparatively limited and the country's main needs were for basic infrastructure facilities such as telecommunications, roads, and airports. As a result, it did little to improve the distribution of the nation's wealth.

Saudi Arabia has five main regions: (1) the Najd, in the center, which includes Riyadh; (2) the Hejaz, in the mountainous west, which includes Makkah, Medina, and the Red Sea ports; (3) the Asir, in the relatively temperate mountains of the southwest; (4) the Northern Province, which combines several sparsely populated zones; and (5) the Eastern Province, along the oil-rich east coast bordering the Gulf. By the mid-1970s, Saudi Arabia's entire petroleum industry and most of its commercial activity, investment, and development projects were concentrated in the Eastern Province, along with a grossly disproportionate share of the country's wealth. The impact of these regional inequities became even sharper after 1973 as Saudi oil revenues steadily climbed. This led one Western journalist to warn that "social, political, and economic jealousies are growing acute among citizens to the north, south and west."[53]

By the time the Second Five Year Plan (1975–1980) was implemented, the rise in Saudi Arabia's oil wealth had created conspicuous problems in the regional and ethnic distribution of the nation's wealth. Although oil wealth helped the Hejaz, it did far less to improve conditions in the Asir, in the northwest, and in the southwest. The traditional system of appointing city and regional governors compounded these problems. Most governors had no real background or administrative staff to deal with the problems of urbanization, the new class of students and skilled workers, or planning on a regional basis. Many engaged directly in business or took commissions or shares for approving major projects and favors, and they paid little real attention to the regional inequities that were developing. The central Saudi ministries made things even worse by concentrating on major showpiece or centralized development projects, which overconcentrated Saudi development efforts in a few areas.

Further, a number of governors deliberately excluded elements of the population from the development process. For example, the Jiluwi governors of the Eastern Province had long adopted strict procedures to control both the Shi'ite and Sunni tribes in their regions and had left most economic development to ARAMCO. While Jiluwi rule softened in the late 1970s under Abd al-Mushin, his brother Saud and his father Abdullah were extremely strict in administering the province and controlling Shi'ite activities. The main Shi'ite cities of Qatif and Hofuf received little development other than that made possible by nationwide loan, grant, and subsidy programs. Shi'ites and certain Sunni tribes also faced serious discrimination in hiring and education. Other governors discriminated against traditional enemies of the Saud family or simply made no effort to include them in the development process. In at least some cases, this discrimination was compounded by family or personal feuds, which affected not only the areas that were the base of the Rashidi family's power, but many other families and areas throughout the country.

These divisions increased the resentment and tension within Saudi society as the "have nots" saw the wealth allocated to the "haves," and they contributed to the military unrest in early 1977. They also led to a growing, and regionally and ethnically oriented, resentment of real and rumored corruption in the government and royal family. Stories of $100 million commissions, multibillion-dollar profits from land speculation, and illegal profits resulting from advance knowledge of major future infrastructure and construction plans tainted the immediate families of several senior figures. This led James E. Akins, former U.S. ambassador to Saudi Arabia, to warn that "without dramatic internal reforms, the country faces serious problems, as the feelings about corruption are similar to developing feelings in Iran in 1976–1977."[54]

Fortunately, the Saudi royal family reacted to these pressures, and the Second Five Year Plan was revised during 1977–1979. Major efforts were made to broaden the regional distribution of the nation's oil wealth and to create new centers of development in the more depressed regions such as the industrial complexes at Yanbu and Jubail. Efforts were also made to improve conditions in the agricultural communities and smaller towns and for lower-income Saudis.[55] The government also seems to have significantly improved educational opportunities, expanded the distribution of public services and oil wealth into the less developed regions, and increased the ties between the government and royal family and the more underdeveloped areas. It did not, however, deal with the problems of inadequate administration by the governors or of regional, tribal, and family discrimination.

Changes in Saudi Internal Security

The Saudi government also continued to rely largely on the traditional structure of Saudi society to provide internal security rather than developing a massive internal security apparatus like SAVAK in Iran. The Ministry of Interior, Royal Intelligence, and the intelligence service of the Ministry of Defense did expand during the late 1970s, and they improved their cooperation with the other conservative Gulf states from 1978 onwards. They did not, however, become obtrusive or repressive.[56]

The Saudi government instead chose to tolerate wide-ranging criticism and dissent (as long as it did not take organized political form) and focused on co-opting potential sources of opposition into the government. It increasingly used development projects to deal with local unrest, and it increased popular access to the royal family and members of the government as a means of dealing with complaints on a case-by-case basis. It also seems to have improved the National Guard's ability to funnel money to tribal and village leaders, as well as to have increased the distribution of wealth to traditional tribal, regional, family, and religious leaders.[57]

But Saudi Arabia did leave several important gaps in its internal security system. First, it showed insufficient sensitivity to the impact of educating large numbers of Saudi students and military personnel overseas, particularly in areas where they would come into contact with Western or Arab radical and protest movements. Second, it did not create a particularly strong capability to provide surveillance over the more sophisticated radical and terrorist groups that were building up in the Gulf, and it relied too heavily on traditional sources of information and control within Saudi Arabia. Third, it failed to take sufficient account of Saudi demographics and urban migration and the fact that a whole new class of urban workers was being created that had steadily weakening ties to traditional Saudi leaders and roles. Fourth, Saudi Arabia's internal security arrangements and development plans underestimated the risk that traditional leaders and groups might react to modernization and the resulting social changes with growing hostility and might attack the development process rather than seek to benefit from it. Fifth, although many studies were carried out, only limited efforts were made to protect Saudi oil facilities from low-level or internal security threats. Finally, little effort was made to keep track of the Shi'ite groups in the Eastern Province, some Asiris, and some tribes and towns affiliated with the Rashid dynasty, which Saudi society had traditionally excluded on political, historical, and religious grounds.[58]

According to most Western sources, the Saudi government also continued to appoint the major regional military commanders and security officials on the basis of family ties or contacts rather than competence, to use governorship to balance political power within the royal family regardless of experience and competence, and to exempt many of the police and military organizations with internal security functions from the same demand for expertise and competence applied to the regular armed forces.

The National Guard

The rivalry and debates over how to modernize the National Guard continued to limit its ability to carry out internal security missions. The improvements in the Guard during 1976–1978 concentrated on increasing its capability in regular combat. While the Vinnell Corporation project to modernize the Guard described earlier was partially successful in giving the Guard four light mechanized battalions, many of the housing and facility projects for the Guard lagged significantly. Although the U.S. Army Corps of Engineers was given design responsibility for such facilities as the casernes at Qasim and at Hofuf in the Hasa Oasis near the oil fields, and the barracks at Khasham, construction was handled on an individual-bid basis and was often poorly managed.

Further, while the Guard acquired an ever-increasing number of well-trained junior officers and NCOs during the late 1970s, it continued to organize its nine regional commands by relying on tribal recruitment, with deployment away from the tribal area.[59] This gave the rest of the Guard—which consisted of 12,000–15,000 lightly armed part-time personnel and a 5,000–7,000-man militia—a relatively weak regional structure to deal with the problems of an increasingly sophisticated, urban, and mobile society.[60]

The lack of coordination between the regular armed forces and the National Guard continued, and only slightly better coordination took place between the armed forces and the small 6,500-man Security Force under Prince Naif in the Ministry of the Interior. A similar compartmentation existed in the case of the small Frontier Forces, Coast Guard, and Special Forces units.[61]

The Uprising at the Grand Mosque

The consequences of these problems in development and internal security were graphically demonstrated in November 1979, when a major uprising took place at the Grand Mosque in Makkah.[62] The full "truth" about this uprising is impossible to establish. Press and official accounts of the incident are such a mixture of rumor, propaganda, and feuding that the incident is reported to be everything from the act of a few religious extremists to a major nationwide political movement. Many details seem reliable, however, and track well with earlier Western reports on Saudi Arabia's internal security situation.

The Background to the Incident

As early as three months before the Makkah incident, Saudi authorities had questioned several junior army officers and even young princes suspected of disloyalty to the government, and a number of officers had been arrested in September 1979.[63] These officers were reported to be affiliated with a loose grouping called the "Movement," which included such radical groups as the Arabian Peninsula People's Union (APPU), headed by Nasir al-Said, which was little more than an umbrella organization of elements opposed to the Saudi royal family. These included groups within five Bedouin tribes, most notably the sizable Otaiba and Qahtani tribes. They also included small secret cells of disaffected officers and soldiers in both the Saudi Army and the National Guard, members of the Saudi intelligence service, university students, and immigrant workers.[64]

The Movement may also have been joined by elements from the Saut al-Taliah, or Voice of the Vanguard, a group of leftist Saudis outside the country that was founded in 1973, whose aim is to do away with traditionalism in the kingdom and which is financially supported largely by some of the approximately 13,000 Saudi students in the United States. It is doubtful that the Voice of the Vanguard played such a role, however, since the group is largely liberal and nationalist in character, rather than Islamic fundamentalist. It has attacked compulsory mosque attendance and has called for a democratic presidential system to replace the ruling royal family.[65]

In any case, small elements of the Movement emerged during 1978–1979, distributing subversive literature and creating minor disturbances in Dhahran, central Najd, Tabuk, and Medina. While such efforts initially aroused little concern, the National Guard and the army were placed on partial alert in the last week of September. Further, according to some reports, Saudi police in Makkah and Medina rounded up and detained 1,200 of the known participants in the unrest on 10 November. Since the yearly *hajj* (or pilgrimage) to Makkah was at its peak, the leaders of the Movement capitalized on the situation by staging a peaceful protest at the Grand Mosque; several hundred men, women, and children took part and soon became engaged in protracted clashes with local police.[66]

The Initial Stages of the Uprising

Ultimately, however, the ultraconservative tribesmen proved to be the only element of the Movement that posed any serious threat to Saudi security. On 16 November, four days before invading the Grand Mosque, small clandestine groups from some of the most puritanical Wahabi tribes scattered themselves throughout the Makkah-Medina region, including Yanbu and the area's lesser towns, to recruit new sympathizers.[67] The few foreign insurgents—from Egypt, Sudan, North Yemen, South Yemen, Iraq, and Kuwait—who were subsequently listed by the Saudi Ministry of the Interior as having been captured and executed seem to have joined the Movement at this stage.

Although such reports are disputed, the defection of small numbers of army and National Guard personnel may also have enabled the rebels to enter and raid local military armories. This could explain the appearance of several truckloads of weapons, some of them American-made, and of walkie-talkies. The bulk of the insurgents' weapons, however, were of Czech and Soviet origin and had been smuggled in from Lebanon, Iraq, and North Yemen. Such arms are still commonly available for private sale in the areas of North Yemen near the Saudi border. They were smuggled into the mosque in specially built coffins and a Toyota service vehicle.

Some reports indicate that a second rebel faction simultaneously raided Medina. These reports also indicate, however, that the Movement got no popular support and suffered hundreds of casualties at the hands of regular troops, who had been deployed there on alert since September. A third armed contingent is occasionally reported to have attacked Taif, just southeast of Makkah, in a poorly planned effort to capture King Khalid; but in any case the king had altered his travel plans and was elsewhere.[68]

Problems in the Saudi Reaction to the Uprising

The time the insurgents picked to strike at Makkah was ideal for a variety of reasons.[69] The influx of roughly a million and a half foreign pilgrims strained Saudi Arabia's police and internal security forces to the breaking point just to handle the crowds.[70] Although the uprising got no popular support, its members were able to move into the mosque without detection. Several senior members of the royal family were also outside the country. Crown Prince Fahd, who had just recovered from the strains imposed by the Camp David crisis and treatment for diabetes, was in Tunis for an Arab summit meeting. Prince Abdullah, who as head of the National Guard was responsible for protecting the royal family and the oil fields, was in Morocco. Further, according to several reports, the governor of Makkah, Prince Fawwaz Abd al-Aziz (twenty-fourth son, born 1934), was ineffective and paid little attention to his duties.[71]

As a result, King Khalid, who was ill with heart trouble at the time, ordered Prince Sultan and Prince Naif, the ministers of defense and interior, to rush from Riyadh to Makkah and direct the military operations. Since they were still uncertain about the extent and the source of the insurrection, the princes immediately contacted key foreign allies, ordered Makkah to be sealed off, and cut all communications within the kingdom. They dispatched troops to clear and patrol the streets in the main cities. The princes, however, faced several dilemmas in dealing with the actual uprising. The Great Mosque was a special responsibility of the Saud family and could not be damaged. Thus, if it was at all possible, they had to avoid using large-scale military force. It was still filled with pilgrims—some from important families—who could not be harmed. It was a privileged sanctuary under the laws of Islam, and in theory it could not be entered by Saudi state security forces.

King Khalid responded by calling upon the leading interpreters of Islamic law in the kingdom, the council of the *ulema*, for permission to use force against the insurgents. After some deliberation, the *ulema* sanctioned state intervention and the use of violence to protect the holy place. More than three hours passed, however, before any counterinsurgency personnel arrived at the mosque, although some 600 men from the Special Security Forces arrived by mid-afternoon. Fully 24 hours passed before a decision was taken in Riyadh as to the appropriate response. Further, Prince Sultan had to bring in troops, National Guardsmen, and police from Tabuk and Khamis Mushayt by C-130s to build up the strength he sought, and it took three more days to prepare Saudi Army troops to storm the mosque.[72]

The Great Mosque was an exceptionally difficult target for Saudi forces to clear. Because of the sanctity of the building and the pilgrims inside, heavy weapons could not be used in a frontal attack. Yet the structure was uniquely defensible against light arms. Its maze of pillared galleries, porticos, windows, small rooms, staircases, and grilled stonework provided ideal cover. The insurgents also held the advantage in terms of reconnaissance because they occupied the mosque's seven tall minarets and were able to use them for sniping shots.[73] According to some reports, the army tried a small heliborne assault but winched the troops down in daylight. This resulted in the slaughter of many of the men involved, and helicopters were driven off by machine-gun fire from the ground.

On the morning of the 21st, Saudi Army troops were finally committed to a frontal assault. Additional troops and armor were airlifted into Makkah. The mosque was surrounded by thousands of troops, a fleet of armored personnel carriers, armored cars, and other assault forces. Yet in spite of this buildup, the Saudi Army proved unable to advance. The Saudis lacked tear gas until this was provided through the U.S. Embassy. Because of rumors that the Otaiba and Qahtani tribes were implicated, officers from the mechanized battalions of the National Guard were brought in to command the tribal units. According to most reports, the Saudi forces were poorly coordinated. Saudi Army and National Guard officers argued over tactics and who was to blame for various mistakes, and the Saudi soldiers showed less dedication than their adversaries. Although some Saudi forces were now able to enter the mosque, fire from the insurgents kept them pinned down.[74] Casualties on both sides were heavy as the fighting continued.

Prince Abdullah returned from Morocco on the 22nd and joined in coordinating the seige, but the armed forces still advanced very slowly. The insurgents continued to control much of the mosque from behind barricades on the ground floor and from positions on the terraces and minarets. According to some reports, the Saudis then called in a small French antiterrorist squad with a planeload of special explosives and gas.[75] There is a broader consensus, however, that the head of Royal Intelligence, Prince Turki al-Faisal, had gradually emerged as a strong leader during the crisis, and he finally gained the authority to organize an effective attack.

In any case, the fighting on the 22nd and 23rd seems to have succeeded in dislodging the insurgents from the upper stories of the mosque and driven them to the ground floor. After another two days of fighting, the remaining insurgents retreated into the basement, a labyrinth of more than 200 rooms and passages. The final attack was launched on the night of 4 December, after nearly two weeks. In the early morning of 5 December, the insurgents' military leader and the last 170 insurgents were captured. The proclaimed Mahdi had been killed earlier. In two weeks of fighting 177 rebels had been killed and many more wounded. The government losses were 127 dead and 461 wounded.

Causes of the Uprising

While the Saudi government later insisted that this delay was inevitable if the insurgents were to be cleared without destroying the mosque and that the insurgents later proved to lack any broad base in the country, at least one Western commentator felt differently:

> Of the 500-odd men who joined the attack on the Grand Mosque, according to West European intelligence sources, 70 to 80 had been trained under Cuban and Soviet supervision at a camp at Lahej, 40 miles from Aden, which has also been used for instructing recruits of the Popular Front for the Liberation of Palestine. During the assault, in which Yemenis, Egyptians, Palestinians, and Kuwaitis took part, the South Yemeni army was mobilized along the Saudi border, together with its Soviet bloc advisers, apparently poised to intervene on the pretext of "defending the holy places," if the revolt showed signs of success. The rebels were equipped with a mixture of weapons—including old British rifles—to camouflage Soviet involvement, but large caches of modern Soviet-made arms were set up inside the South Yemeni border, ready for use if the moment presented itself. The whole exercise, which was supposed to include risings in Medina, Taif, and elsewhere, was supervised by a special Soviet command team.[76]

These charges seem distinctly exaggerated, and the Saudi position to be correct, but it is impossible to analyze the extent of foreign participation on the basis of the data available. What does seem clear is that the rest of the Movement does not seem to have been particularly strong or to have been able to provide even token popular support for the insurgents during the uprising. If anything, the mosque incident ultimately revealed that Saudi Arabia's main internal security problems lay in retaining Bedouin loyalty and the support of conservative religious groups, rather than from Arab radicals or the left.

Virtually all of the insurgents proved to be religious "ultraconservatives," although many of the Saudi rebels[77] came from the Otaiba and Qahtani tribes. These tribes are the traditional sources of loyal manpower to protect the royal family, of the members of the king's personal royal guard and of the 35,000-man National Guard, but their participation does not seem to have reflected any new tribal unrest. The Saudi insurgents came largely from tribal groups that still nursed grudges because of the suppression of the Ikhwan. The rebels' leader, Juhaiman ibn Muhammed ibn Saif al-Otaibi, was a former corporal in the National Guard.[78] His mother was foreign, but he had ties to some elements of the Otaiba tribes that had fought King Abd al-Aziz in the battle of Sabillah in 1929. Similarly, the head of one of the sniper groups, Affas bin Muhaya, was the son of an Otaiba chieftain who had been killed during Abd al-Aziz's suppression of the Ikhwan.[79]

The rebels' main motive, however, was clearly religious. Virtually all of the men involved in the uprising later proved to be religiously oriented youth, mainly theology students who were disoriented by or hostile to the social changes taking place in the kingdom. The few foreigners seemed to have similar backgrounds. The insurgents also identified themselves in their pamphlets as students of the *Shari'a* (Islamic law). They referred to their disgust at seeing their professors "bought by a corrupt regime with money and promises of promotion." One of their tracts claimed that the Grand Mufti himself was sympathetic to their cause and reproached them only for "concentrating their attacks on the Saudi regime when all Islamic regimes are corrupt." Their pamphlets also referred to several other fundamentalist groups, including the Muslim Brotherhood. The group does not, therefore, seem to have seized the Great Mosque with any of the goals of a modern insurrectionary movement but rather acted with the goal of restoring a purified, ultraconservative Islamic social order to Arabia.[80]

This conclusion seems further confirmed by the background of their leader. Juhaiman had left the National Guard after deciding that service to the state conflicted with service to God. In 1972 he became a student at the ultraconservative theological seminary at the Islamic University in Medina, which had been formed by members of the Muslim Brotherhood whom Nasser had expelled from Egypt. The university had been headed by Abd al-Aziz bin Baz, a fundamentalist whose literal acceptance of historical Muslim teachings had previously led him into a confrontation with the government because of his insistence that it was wrong to teach that the sun did not revolve around the earth. Although Juhaiman broke with Baz in 1974 and formed a faction of conservatives called the Salafiyya (Reformers), he absorbed a philosophy of literal observance of the Koran that brought him into direct opposition to every aspect of Saudi Arabia's modernization.

By 1978, Juhaiman had gathered around himself enough Saudi and foreign religious figures to be noticed by the security forces of the Ministry of the Interior. After his group began to circulate pamphlets printed in Kuwait that called for the overthrow of the royal family, he and 98 of his supporters were briefly arrested. Ironically, Baz was then called upon to interrogate them. He concluded that they were loyal but "misguided" Muslims. As a result, they were freed about two months later.[81] It was at this point they seem to have begun planning the uprising at the Grand Mosque. Considerable disagreement exists over their exact intentions, but Juhaiman seems to have concluded that proclaiming even a false Mahdi would catalyze the religious changes he sought and dramatize the need for a return to his concept of fundamentalism. Accordingly, Juhaiman's brother-in-law, Muhammed ibn Abd Allah al-Kahtani (al-Qahtani), who was a 27-year-old seminary student at the Islamic University, was proclaimed Mahdi.

Although the Saudi society forces had been aware of some of these developments, the uprising revealed far more religious tension than Saudi leaders had previously suspected.[82] It also dramatized the continuing importance of regional and tribal rivalries. In fact, the leader of the APPU, Nasir al-Said, attempted to capitalize on this tribal rivalry to explain the uprising in a way that supported his political position. He stated in an interview, "It is known that these tribes had feuds with the Saud family and rebelled against it in the past, after some of them had stood on the side of the Saud family, and staged revolutions led by (the chief of the Mutair tribe and . . . the chief of the Oteiba tribe), both of whom were killed by the Saudi tyrants in the ugliest manner."[83]

Saudi Reaction and Reform

The Saudi government took immediate steps to correct the military weaknesses revealed by the uprising and punished the rebels, but its primary reaction was political. In early January 1980 the chief of staff of the Saudi armed forces, the air force and land forces commanders, the chief of internal security, General Fayez Mohammed Aufi, and Prince Fawwaz were replaced in an extensive military and administrative shake-up. Sixty-three of the insurgents were publicly executed on 9 January 1980 in the central squares of eight different Saudi cities. The Saudi government simultaneously began to enforce many of the religious strictures that it had allowed to lapse regarding social conduct, the role of women, and the observation of religious law.[84]

The government modified the Third Five Year Plan to provide a slower rate of development, offered more financial incentives to the traditional elements of Saudi society, and strengthened the role of the religious and traditional tribal and family leaders in the councils and advisory bodies of the Saudi government. Sharp new restrictions were placed on study abroad, and schools were reorganized to emphasize the importance of Saudi traditions and religious customs. The government also made some efforts to correct its past failure to reform the various governorates, and its actions indicated a considerable strengthening of the unity of the royal family. Prince Fawwaz's replacement was Majid bin Abd al-Aziz (twenty-seventh son, born 1937). Although the governing of Makkah had traditionally been associated with the Sudairi, Majid was a supporter of Abdullah, who in turn gave up a supporting voice on the Council of Ministers when Majid resigned as minister of municipal and rural affairs.

Majid's appointment, however, was only one of several. In March 1980 Migrin bin Abd al-Aziz (forty-second son, born 1943), a former air force major and presumably an ally of Sultan, was appointed governor of Hail Province, and two of the full brothers of Prince Badr (deputy commander of the National Guard) were made governors. Abd al-Illah bin Abd al-Aziz (thirty-first son, born 1935) was appointed governor of Qasim, and Abd al-Mujid bin Abd al-Aziz (thirty-sixth son, born 1940) became governor of Tabuk. Like Badr, both are of Sudairi descent, although by a different mother than the Sudairi seven. At the same time, many subordinate positions in the various governorates were strengthened or replaced.[85]

The royal family initiated a massive effort to improve its contacts with tribal, religious, and regional leaders; to reduce corruption and conspicuous consumption; and to improve its reputation with the military and with younger Saudis. In March 1980 the government announced that King Khalid had authorized the formation of a nine-man commission (one prince, seven *ulema*, and one layman) to draw up two "charters": one for a national system of government based on statutes derived from Islamic law (*Shari'a*); and the second for a consultative council, or *shura*, to be composed of 50 to 70 members.[86] This council still does not exist, however, and it is unclear whether the royal family's substantive ruling powers will actually be transferred or whether these new institutions will ever really function.

Further Improvements in Internal Security

The Saudi government also sought internal security assistance from the U.S., Britain, France, Jordan, and Pakistan. After some study, it signed an agreement with France to train Saudi personnel in internal security methods on 2 November 1980. This agreement was supplemented by the establishment of a joint coordination bureau between the French and Saudi ministers of the interior. Saudi Arabia quietly made arrangements with Pakistan to airlift in Pakistani special forces in emergencies.[87] By early 1982, the Saudis had negotiated an arrangement with Pakistan that led a Pakistani armored division to begin to deploy to Tabuk to reinforce the under-strength Saudi armored units in the area and to provide an internal security hedge against any threat from the armed forces. The Saudis increased the number of British advisers to the National Guard, and they seem to have supported a complex deal through which British intelligence officers and members of the Special Air Services (SAS) began to assist North Yemen in dealing with South Yemeni–backed members of the National Liberation Front in late 1981.

A special counterterrorist unit was set up under the Ministry of the Interior, and the National Guard, Frontier Force, and Coast Guard security forces (at least 6,500 personnel) were further strengthened and given some improvements in equipment, training, and organization. These steps did not, however, lead to any integration of the National Guard and the various security services under Prince Sultan and Prince Naif. The general pattern was to strengthen all services, not to rationalize them or integrate their operations.

While the Saudis had often acted preventively rather than in response to existing dissent, there is no doubt that many senior Saudi officials emerged from the uprising with a different picture of the problems caused by development, of the internal security situation in Saudi Arabia, and of the need for caution in expanding the armed forces and National Guard. Both the royal family and Saudi technocrats had been given a shock of major proportions. They were forced to confront the limits to development as never before, as well as the need to preserve both the traditional order in Saudi society and their ties to all elements of that society.

The Shi'ite Riots

The Shi'ite riots that broke out shortly after the uprising in Makkah revealed a different kind of problem.[88] The Shi'ite population of the Eastern Province totals anywhere from 125,000 to 400,000,[89] and Shi'ites provide 40–60% of the work force for the oil fields.[90] They have long suffered from discrimination by the Sunni Wahabis, particularly in terms of education, job opportunities, and development. The Shi'ites also suffered uniquely harsh treatment by the Saudi government from the 1920s through the mid-1970s. Shortly after King Abd al-Aziz drove the Turks out of Al Hasa, he assigned its government to Abdullah bin Jiluwi, who instituted a ruthless set of security controls over the Shi'ite population and bloodily punished Shi'ite riots and disturbances. Even when his eldest son, Saud, replaced him as governor of the Eastern Province, the Shi'ites were systematically excluded from economic or political opportunity, and minor strike attempts led to executions. The capital of the province was moved from the Shi'a center of Hofuf to the historically insignificant port of Dammam, bypassing the Shi'ite-dominated city of Qatif, which had been the region's traditional trade center.

As a result, Dhahran, Dammam, and Al-Khobar became centers of development, while Qatif and Hofuf remained relatively primitive, although the situation eased somewhat when Saud's brother, Abd al-Mushin, replaced him as governor. Saudi construction statistics show that from 1976 to 1979, most of the Eastern Province's development activity was related to Jubail, localized ARAMCO projects, and the government's master gas-gathering system. Dhahran, Dammam, and Al-Khobar were the principal sites of the remaining activity. Qatif and Hofuf remained relatively neglected and were left unimproved except for the growth resulting from nationwide housing, small business, and agricultural loan programs. Further, the Bin Jiluwi governors became embroiled in personal land disputes and bureaucratic fights with the Plan Organization that further delayed development of the Shi'ite areas.

Even under Abd al-Mushin, the fact that the governorship remained in the hands of the Bin Jiluwi branch of the royal family helped ensure that few Shi'ites played any role in politics. They were excluded from any significant position in government, with the exception of a former minister of agriculture and Jameel Jishi, the director-general for the royal commission at Jubail.[91] This discrimination applied even at much lower levels. More than half the students at the University of Petroleum and Minerals in Dhahran have been Shi'ites, but few were permitted to run for student office.

The Shi'ites reacted by seeking upward mobility in the oil fields. They flocked to the training courses offered by ARAMCO and developed a work ethic not shared by other Saudis. At the same time, the Shi'ites began to react politically, leading to recurrent minor incidents with the police and National Guard, some of which became serious in the 1970s. The predominantly Shi'ite town of Qatif, to the north of Dhahran, was quarantined for a month in 1970 by government forces following protests against the monarchy. A similar confrontation in 1978 led to 50 arrests and a number of executions.

It was only after the Ayatollah Khomeini's triumphant return to Iran in early 1979, however, that the Saudi Shi'ite minority adopted a militant posture and did anything to challenge Saudi rule over the province. On 3–5 December 1979, two weeks after the Makkah Grand Mosque attack (and five weeks after the seizure of U.S. Embassy hostages in Tehran), thousands of Saudi Shi'ites—many bearing placards with Khomeini's picture—demonstrated in the oil region towns of Qatif and Khafji and near the major Ras Tanura refinery complex. They called for a more equitable distribution of wealth and for the royal family to support Iran's Islamic revolution.

In response, the government reportedly moved in 20,000 National Guard troops to quell the uprising; some reports indicate that at least five of the demonstrators were killed and hundreds arrested.[92] This violence seems to have been due to the Guard's lack of training and to a local commander who panicked and intervened with troops when this was not necessary. Nevertheless, it raised the specter that a significant part of the ARAMCO labor force might suddenly support the Khomeini movement.

In fact, Khomeini seems to have sought such a goal. On 7 January 1980, Tehran Radio and Radio Ahwaz beamed the first of several broadcasts across the Gulf demanding "death to the criminal and mercenary government of the Saudi family," whose members "are forcefully using all of the vast wealth of the land for their own gain."[93] The eastern Shi'ites demonstrated again for two days in early February, this time calling upon the authorities to release their fellow marchers jailed since the December incidents.[94]

The Saudi government reacted quickly and effectively to this threat. It again chose to rely on political and economic rather than military means as its primary method of dealing with an internal security crisis. Ahmad, Prince Naif's younger brother and his deputy in the Ministry of the Interior, immediately toured Qatif, heard complaints, admitted past injustices, and promised immediate progress in development. Prince Fahd ordered the release of all the political prisoners in Qatif.

Under the leadership of the minister of the interior, the government immediately began a massive new development plan. It initiated a $128 million electrification project in January 1980. Contractors suddenly worked after 10 at night repaving streets, and more than a million square meters of reasphalting was contracted in Qatif and other villages in the oasis. A site for a new hospital was selected, and new schools for boys and girls were completed. Millions of square meters of swamp were filled, with more reclamation planned. The government provided loans through the Real Estate Development Fund to town residents to build new homes. Contractors working on street lighting, sewage, communications, and improvement projects all seemed to have been instructed to make up for lost time.

This activity received a high profile in the official Saudi Press Agency. In one item the mayor of Qatif called attention to the award of 716 million rials in development projects and promised that more work was to be awarded to contractors within months.[95] The government did not make immediate political changes or replace the governor, but it did adopt a uniquely Saudi approach to the region's problems. It began to assemble both the Sunni and Shi'ite notables in the region and to conduct the equivalent of a "flying Majlis (open court)" with members of the royal family and officials of the various ministries flying from town to town and from project to project. As further proof of the government's concern for its Shi'ite citizens, the king traveled to Al Hasa and through Qatif and Hofuf during a 10-day visit to the Eastern Province in November 1980. During his stay, which began only five days after the "10th of Muharram," the king was constantly accompanied by town elders from Qatif.

These measures, plus the well-publicized turmoil and civil war in Iran, helped to deprive Khomeini of much of his support. As a result, the 10th of Muharram, a key Shi'ite holiday, passed uneventfully in 1980, 1981, and 1982. Although the Shi'ites were forbidden to carry out acts of self-torture, the Qatifis sat in the streets and listened tranquilly to the lamentations broadcast from the mosques, and both the Usuli and Khubari sects carried out the rest of their festival without incident. Further, in a unique religious compromise, those Shi'ites who were determined to perform the full ritual were flown to Bahrain, where Shi'a banners could be flown openly and self-torture was permitted.[96]

In this way much of the hostility building up within the native Shi'ite community was defused by the end of 1981, and Khomeini's increasingly bloody rule continued to convince most of Saudi Arabia's Shi'ites that there was little future in any political movement based on support of Iran. The Special Security Forces improved Saudi intelligence and internal security operations in the area, and the Saudis steadily improved their intelligence exchange groups with the other Arab Gulf states after 1979. They targeted these on Shi'ite and ultraconservative as well as radical groups.

Shi'ite disaffection, however, had not been eliminated. When major pro-Khomeini activities were detected in Bahrain in the fall of 1981, it became clear that they were part of a broader network in Saudi Arabia and the UAE. As a result, over 125 Shi'ites were arrested in Bahrain, Saudi Arabia, and the UAE in late December. Similarly, the Saudis had considerable problems in 1981 with Iranian pilgrims, who attempted organized protests and rallies in support of Khomeini in Makkah and Medina and who had to be suppressed with some violence.

Internal Security and the Saudi Bureaucracy

The series of internal security crises in 1979 and 1980 thus had a largely salutary effect. Like the military uprising in 1977, and the other postwar internal security crises in Saudi society, they focused the regime's attention on major political, social, economic, and ethnic problems without directly threatening its existence. Equally important, the Saudi regime reacted by seeking broad structural solutions to its internal problems rather than by relying on punitive internal security measures or trying to force through the process of development and military expansion regardless of popular feeling.

Such Saudi behavior contrasted sharply with the shah's actions in Iran, and the Saudi royal family did not have to learn from the shah's mistakes. The Saudi government had probably learned well the need for moderation, compromise, and co-option long before the shah fell. Accordingly, Saudi behavior is relevant to Iran only in providing such a striking contrast to the shah's actions during his final decade in power and to Khomeini's actions since.

Nevertheless, the events of 1979 and 1980 revealed problems in Saudi Arabia's internal security effort that have important implications for the future:

• First, problems in the Saudi internal security apparatus led to the failure of Saudi intelligence to properly track subversive activities, especially the recruitment of army and National Guard personnel, and trace the acquisition of substantial quantities of arms and vehicles.[97] The attack came as a surprise to the government, despite an eight-week-old partial alert of the kingdom's troops. The Saudi security system was evidently so oriented toward radical threats that it did not examine the sources of unrest in the traditional elements of Saudi society.[98]

• Second, the lack of a coordinated internal security structure and continuing conflict among the Guard, Royal Intelligence, and the Ministries of Defense and the Interior were compounded by an obvious lack of prior contingency training to deal with the insurgency, the long delays in arriving at a decision, and the poor coordination between army and the National Guard units when they did respond.[99]

• Third, the cost of "personalizing" the control of key posts in Saudi Arabia's internal security apparatus was clear. Quite aside from the problems caused by tensions within the royal family, the tendency of each service to report vertically to its head made effective management and reporting impossible. The absence of a merit promotion system in most of the intelligence and internal security forces, particularly at the top, seriously inhibited the upgrading of each branch's capabilities and its leadership.[100]

• Fourth, the lack of coordination in the response of the Saudi armed forces to the insurgency—and the tendency to wait for high-level decisions and to continuously pass the buck upward—revealed broader problems in modernizing Saudi Arabia's defense structure. Given the planned expansion of Saudi forces and the vast investment projects in the Third Five Year Plan, the Saudi government can deal with its military and economic problems only if the senior princes relinquish more of their direct control over the kingdom's military-industrial complex.

• Fifth, although neither the uprising at the mosque nor the riots in the Eastern Province revealed further instability in the Saudi armed forces, it is worth noting that military pay rates were again doubled in the spring of 1981 and that fringe benefits—including land grants—were also increased. While some of this raise was the result of the need to recruit and retain better manpower in the face of the increases in private-sector salaries, rather than the result of internal security problems, Saudi officials indicate that the government was concerned about the long-term stability of the armed forces. The Saudi government is to some extent the prisoner of its own policies in this regard. It cannot fully monitor the military without subjecting it to the controls of a police state, and if it attempted to do so, it might well create the disaffection it is trying to avoid. This problem makes the Saudi military something of an unknown quantity, although there is little sign of any radicalism within it.

• Sixth, the Grand Mosque incident revealed a broad lack of progress in integrating sufficient technical expertise into the defense and internal security staffs of the Saudi government. It is not clear, however, where such expertise will come from. The level of technical and financial expertise required to manage the Saudi government can come only from advanced Western education. But most of the Saudis who currently study abroad for graduate degrees opt for the rewards of the private sector. The remainder cannot possibly satisfy the government's civilian and military requirements for technocratic manpower, nor can Saudi Arabia's own institutes and universities.

Foreign experts will have to be imported in ever-greater numbers. The same is likely to be true of unskilled manpower. In future years, the labor force will have to absorb still more Yemenis, and Saudis will become a steadily smaller minority. These changes, however, will steadily increase both the problem of managing Saudi internal security and that of finding competent personnel to manage its internal security and intelligence systems.

In short, the problems in Saudi Arabia's internal security structure cannot be separated from the broader problems in the Saudi government. The base of popular support for the monarchy must broaden, new benefits must accrue to all Saudis, and minority elements must receive a larger share of political power and wealth. Further, as the economy becomes bigger and more sophisticated, and as bureaucratic power becomes more important, so does the need to transform the structure of the Saudi government into a modern bureaucracy and to find new sources of expertise.

Notes

1. The Saudi Ministry of the Interior has played a special role in strengthening Saudi-Iraqi relations. Interior Minister Nayif, one of Defense Minister Sultan's full brothers, negotiated an internal security agreement with Iraq in September 1979. Prince Nayif has also played a major role in strengthening Saudi security ties and foreign relations with the other Gulf states.

2. Prince Sultan, the minister of defense, is reported to have direct responsibility for Saudi-Yemeni relations, and the Saudi ambassador to Sana has recently been a lieutenant/general, Tirad al-Harithi. Saudi relations with both Yemens have long been regarded as a defense problem.

3. Foud al-Farsy, *Saudi Arabia: A Case Study in Development* (London: Stacey International, 1978), p. 93.

4. Ibid., p. 99; Richard F. Nyrop, *Area Handbook for Saudia Arabia*, Foreign Area Handbook Series (Washington, D.C.: American University, 1977), p. 318; Adeed Dawisha, *Saudi Arabia's Search for Security*, Adelphi Paper no. 158 (London: IISS, Winter 1979–1980), p. 13.

5. al-Farsy, *Saudia Arabia*, p. 116; David Holden and Richard Johns, *The House of Saud* (London: Sidgwick and Jackson, 1981), pp. 387–388.

6. See James Buchan, "Manpower," *Financial Times*, 5 May 1981, p. x; Dawisha, *Saudia Arabia's Search for Security*, pp. 13–15; "A Survey of Saudi Arabia," *Economist*, 13 February 1982, p. 33.

7. John Keegan, *World Armies* (New York: Facts on File, 1979), pp. 608, 616–618; *Al-Jazirah*, 11 May 1980.

8. Richard D. Erb, "The Arab Oil Producing States," *AEI Foreign Policy and Defense Review* (Washington) 2, nos. 3-4 (1980):14; Congressional Research Service (CRS), *Saudia Arabia and the United States: The New Context in an Evolving "Special Relationship,"* a report prepared by the Foreign Affairs and National Defense Division, GPO 81-4940 (Washington, D.C.: Government Printing Office, August 1981), p. 5. Such numbers are highly uncertain, and conflicting estimates are used deliberately in various portions of this text to illustrate the uncertainties involved.

9. *Financial Times*, 5 May 1981, p. x; Holden and Johns, *House of Saud*, p. 409.

10. They were airlifted home by Saudi Air Force C-130s.

11. *Financial Times*, 5 May 1981.

12. Keegan, *World Armies*, pp. 616–618. Other estimates differ strikingly in both directions. In its 13 February 1982 "Survey of Saudi Arabia" (p. 33), the *Economist* states:

> In the five years to 1980, according to the Saudi-tinted official figures, the local share of the workforce fell from 92% to 57%. Stepping into the breach have arrived some 800,000 Yemenis, some 400,000 Filipinos, some 250,000 Pakistanis, some 250,000 Koreans, some 200,000 Pakistanis, some 150,000 Indians and maybe 100,000 Thais to do the dogsbody jobs. About 200,000 Syrians and Lebanese and perhaps 45,000 Americans and 40,000 Britons do more exalted work.

These foreigners are unlikely ever to be dispensable. The number of Saudis in employment has actually declined over the past six years. . . . The number of Saudis employed in service trades has jumped from 29% to 42%. Most of them work in trade and local government, where thousands of well-paid, undemanding jobs are available. Only 4% of Saudis work in industry, the same proportion as five years ago and 15% fewer Saudis work in agriculture.

13. Prince Sultan evidently did not agree with this assessment, and some differences seem to have existed within the royal family over this issue. See Chapter 5.

14. Keegan, *World Armies*, pp. 616–618.

15. Basic training and most technical training were conducted in Dhahran, Riyadh, and Tabuk.

16. See Dawisha, *Saudi Arabia's Search for Security*, p. 16.

17. Staff report by the Senate Foreign Relations Committee (SFRC), *The Proposed AWACS/F-15 Enhancement Sale to Saudi Arabia* GPO 84-557-0 (Washington, D.C.: Government Printing Office, September 1981), p. 2.

18. This discussion is based on Saudi planning data and on figures quoted in Holden and Johns, *House of Saud*; the draft Third Five Year Plan; and *8 Days*, 16 August 1980.

19. Five Peace Hawk studies had been completed in 1978, and seven by 1980. Other studies were provided by Lockheed, BDM, and several additional U.S. firms.

20. It should be noted, however, that the F-15 sale was evidently the subject of considerable disagreement inside the Ford and Carter administrations. The *New York Times* reported on 8 July 1976, in an interview with then Deputy Secretary of Defense William Clements, that the Pentagon was advising Saudi Arabia that its air force was not ready to maintain and fly the F-15. According to Clements, the Pentagon's advice was that the Saudis should build their capability around the F-5 aircraft. Several governmental agencies also voiced reservations about or opposition to the sale. According to the 3 September 1977 *Washington Post*, the Arms Control and Disarmament Agency recommended that the sale of F-15s to Saudi Arabia *not* go through. ACDA and government officials confirmed the *Post*'s report. The *Post* also stated that the DOD's Office of Policy Analysis and Evaluation opposed the F-15 sale.

On the other hand, according to the 20 July 1977 *New York Times*, Saudi Arabia was later encouraged by the U.S. Air Force to buy the F-15 and to expand its air capacity beyond its original needs. Several sources told the *Times* that air force officials vigorously promoted the sale in order to amortize cost overruns on the F-15 program.

21. In the actual event, the F-15 proved to be very difficult to service without exceptionally large stocks of spares, and it still had engine and performance rating problems in late 1981.

22. The Saudi F-15s were not configured in the same way as the F-15s delivered to the USAF, and the distinctions involved were misunderstood even at the time of the AWACS debate in 1981, when many of those debating the AWACS referred to the Saudi version of the F-15 as if it had capabilities that did not exist on any USAF F-15.

Like most truly advanced fighters, the F-15 cannot be flown for maximum performance without on-board computer assistance, and it cannot be used against mass threats (such as a Saudi war with Israel) without digital links between its on-board computer and a sensor and control system like the AWACS. The Saudi F-15 lacks such digital data links, and the computer program on the Saudi F-15 is not designed for combat with other F-15, the A-4, or the F-16. These shortcomings reduce its effectiveness against U.S. or Israeli aircraft, although it is programmed for combat with the Iranian F-4 and F-14.

Further, as is the case with the F-15 in the Israeli inventory, the Saudi F-15 lacks the advanced program support (Mark IV Package PSP) or computer enhancement capability for its radar that may be fitted to the enhanced F-15 in the USAF inventory. As a result, the radar on the Saudi F-15 has no mapping or moving target indicator (MTI) capability, and it can see only land/water contrast and city-sized targets. It is not equipped for delivery of antitank missiles or similar PGMs. Further, the Saudi F-15 lacks advanced secure voice links and IFF capabilities. Source: DOD spokesman, 11 October 1981.

23. *New York Times*, 16 February 1978.

24. These arguments are excerpted or paraphrased in large part from "F-15s to Saudi—A Threat to Peace," American Israel Public Affairs Committee, Washington, D.C., January 1978.

25. To date, these bases have negligible military capability.

26. Henry Bradsher, "Israel Practiced Raids on Saudi Air Base," *Washington Star*, 27 March 1978. The IAF continued to overfly Tabuk regularly in demonstration flights through November 1981, when they finally provoked a Saudi military response and formal protest to the U.S.

27. This concession was made tacitly rather than formally, and it was fairly easy to make. With only 60 F-15C/Ds Saudi Arabia could deploy the F-15 only on three bases with a strength of 20 F-15C/Ds each. It had to concentrate its deployment to defend the key Saudi oil fields, cities, and ports. For geographic reasons this meant Dhahran, Taif, and Khamis Mushayt. The U.S. had also told Saudi Arabia that as a precondition for the sale, no U.S. military or contract personnel would move to Tabuk, the only Saudi base within practical operating range of Israel. This restriction effectively made it impossible to fly and fight the F-15 from Tabuk, even if the Saudis ignored the vulnerability inherent in relying on a single base well within the strike range of Israeli fighters.

28. The far more important constraints on aircraft data links, secure communications, and computer software were omitted from this letter. In retrospect, this omission seems to have occurred because Secretary Brown's staff underestimated their future importance.

29. *Armed Forces Journal*, March 1979, p. 12. Ironically, in the ensuing U.S. exercises with the F-15, the "bare bones" kit designed to provide F-15 basing mobility proved totally unable to meet the service requirements imposed by simulated F-15 combat sortie rates.

30. Ibid.

31. *Aerospace Daily*, 9 October 1980, p. 212; *Wall Street Journal*, 1 October 1980, p. 2; *New York Times*, 1 October 1980, p. 1.

32. By November 1981, virtually all of the Peace Sun facilities were on-line at Dhahran Air Base. Extensive use was made of Peace Hawk facilities, and there was no gold-plating of construction. Excellent simulator facilities were online for both the F-5E and F-15.

33. These were essential to provide the mobility, flexibility, and reduced vulnerability Saudi Arabia needed. The earlier Hawk program had provided

only one or two fixed sites per target, each of which was highly vulnerable to saturation attacks, surprise attacks, or antiradiation missiles.

34. Dak Tahtinen, *National Security Challenges to Saudi Arabia* (Washington, D.C.: American Enterprise Institute, 1979).

35. *Aviation Week*, 19 November 1981.

36. *Financial Times*, 5 May 1981.

37. Some Saudi Army forces were redeployed from Tabuk to Sharurah during the time of the Yemeni border war and remain there.

38. *Financial Times*, 5 May 1981.

39. U.S. Army Corps of Engineers, *Saudi Arabia Programs* (Washington, D.C., 1980), p. 10.

40. *Washington Post*, 27 April 1980; 31 January 1981; *Christian Science Monitor*, 12 March 1981.

41. By September 1981, the division within the Social Democratic party had forced the Schmidt government to formally notify the Saudis that it would not sell the equipment. By this time, however, there was no real Saudi request for the sale.

42. *Le Monde*, 10 January 1981. This contract may also have implicitly involved guarantees to France regarding future oil supplies.

43. *Aerospace Daily*, 8 October 1980, p. 212; *Baltimore Sun*, 16 October 1980, p. 1; *New York Times*, 4 May 1979.

44. *Aviation Week*, 3 November 1980, p. 33; November 29, 1982, pp. 84–86; *International Defense Review* 1 (1981):102, and 10 (1982):1393–1397. Saudi Arabia bought 20 armed and 4 unarmed Dauphine 2SX for delivery in mid-1985. Other equipment included Thomason-CSF vertical consoles for gun and missile control in the combat information center, the Thompson DR 4000 electronic support measures system, a new-generation jammer capable of jamming two targets simultaneously, Sea Tiger search radar, Castor II tracker radars, three CSEE optonic directors, and CSEE Dagaic chaff launchers.

45. *Baltimore Sun*, 16 October 1980, p. 1; *Aviation Week*, 20 October 1980, p. 23; 3 November 1980, p. 33. The Crotale was modified from a 50–3,000-meter altitude envelope to kill sea-skimming missiles down to 4 meters after the fighting in the Falklands.

46. Congressional Research Service (CRS), *Saudi Arabia and the United States: The New Context in an Evolving "Special Relationship,"* a report prepared by the Foreign Affairs and National Defense Division, GPO 81-4940 (Washington, D.C.: Government Printing Office, August 1981), p. 45.

47. Inflation caused a serious drop in real oil revenues, and as might have been expected, the initial peak in expenditures on the water projects following the 1973–1974 rises in oil prices all came due in the same year. The result was inflation well in excess of 50%, while many poorly planned development projects had to be "fixed" by throwing money at them.

48. The Saudis also purchased their own Pentagon, complete with mosque and shopping center, in late 1979, at a cost of $460 million. The new complex to house the MODA included office space, cafeteria, mosque, auditorium, underground command center, a 1,600-car parking garage, market facilities, gatehouses, mechanical and electrical equipment buildings, and all required roads, paving, utilities, landscaping, and sitework. Fred S. Hoffman, "U.S. Plans a Pentagon for Saudis," *Philadelphia Inquirer*, 9 September 1978, p. 34C.

49. For a recent and balanced summary of these problems see "A Survey of Saudi Arabia," *Economist*, 13 February 1982.

50. Keegan, *World Armies*, p. 620. Saudi accounts generally deny the importance of this incident. Jordanians and Pakistanis then present in Saudi Arabia confirm its existence.

51. Ibid., p. 617; Nyrop, *Saudi Arabia*, p. 324; Adeed Dawisha, *Saudi Arabia's Search for Security*, Adelphi Paper no. 158 (London: IISS, Winter 1979-1980), p. 17. The rise in March 1977 alone was 20–120%. The monthly salary of a private rose from $240 to $528, and a general's salary increased from $3,150 to $3,620.

52. For example, work at the key new military city of Hafr al-Batin began in 1978, rather than 1976, and fell three years behind schedule due to supply problems by 1980, forcing postponement of provisions to house a third brigade there. Since the complex was to house 70,000 personnel, including a key air and army base, and be the linchpin in defending Saudi Arabia's northeast borders, such problems caused considerable disruption throughout the Saudi Army.

53. Dawn H. Williams, "Trouble in Camelot—Arabian Style," *Christian Science Monitor*, 23 August 1979, p. 23.

54. Phillip Taubman, "U.S. Aides Say Corruption Is Threat to Saudi Stability," *New York Times*, 16 April 1980, p. A8; see also "Saudi Prince Is Said to Have Made a Fortune in Business," same page.

55. See English translations of the Second and Third Five Year Plans; *New York Times*, 26 October 1979, p. A2; 9 December 1979, p. D-1; 7 March 1980, pp. A-1, D-13; *Christian Science Monitor*, 23 August 1979, p. 534; *Economist*, 13 February 1982, pp. 20–29.

56. Prince Turki, who became head of Royal Intelligence in 1978, was an exceptionally sophisticated choice. Although he was then only 33 years old, he had served in Royal Intelligence for nearly a decade, and he became a strong influence in keeping Saudi intelligence professional and moderating the conduct and expansion of the internal security forces.

57. See the *Financial Times*, 5 May 1981; Dawisha, *Saudi Arabia's Search for Security*; and Lincoln P. Bloomfield, Jr., "Saudi Arabia Faces the 1980's" *Fletcher Forum*, Summer 1981, pp. 243–277. This, however, did nothing to deal with the problem of discrimination, since it simply moved money into the traditional ruling structure.

58. The National Guard's facilities in the Eastern Province were poorly developed until the start of the Iran-Iraq War because it was waiting for the completion of the new cantonment being built in the area. Only when the war started were two battalions sent into the area. Even in early 1982, its deployment and patrol activity were relatively poorly organized.

59. *Financial Times*, 5 May 1981.

60. Hayyan Ibn Bayar, "Open Letter to Saudi Arabia," *Nation*, 4 April 1981.

61. Keegan, *World Armies*, pp. 612–613; *Financial Times*, 5 May 1981; Tahtinen, *National Security Challenge*; Nyrop, *Saudi Arabia*, pp. 311, 320, 324; *Los Angeles Times*, 23 January 1978.

62. The spelling, "Makkah," rather than "Mecca," is used because Saudi Arabia made it official in 1978.

63. References include *Foreign Broadcast Information Service* (*FBIS*), NC 301154 and NC 301435, 30 November 1979; LD 131625, 10 December 1979; *Economist Foreign Report*, no. 1610, 28 November 1979, and no. 1613, 19 December 1979; *New York Times*, 26 November 1979; 18 November 1979 (2 articles); 30 November 1979, p. A-18, 5 February 1980, p. A-14; 25 February

1980, pp. A-1, A-10; *Christian Science Monitor*, 30 November 1979, p. 6; 11 January 1980, p. 4.

64. Helena Cobban, "A Growing Opposition in Saudi Arabia," *Christian Science Monitor*, 30 November 1979, p. 6; Youssef M. Ibrahim, "New Information Indicates Political Motivation Behind Mecca Mosque Takeover," *New York Times*, 25 February 1980, p. A-10; Bloomfield, "Saudi Arabia Faces the 1980's," pp. 249–251; *Washington Post*, 22 July 1980.

65. David Leigh, "Royal Family Target of Leftist Drive," *Washington Post*, 22 July 1980, p. A-8.

66. Bloomfield, "Saudi Arabia Faces the 1980's," p. 251.

67. For a discussion of Saudi religious pressures see William Ochsenwald, "Saudi Arabia and the Islamic Revival," *International Journal of Middle East Studies*, no. 13 (1981):271–286.

68. These reports of uprisings in Medina and Taif seem increasingly likely to be incorrect.

69. This account draws heavily on Jim Paul, "The Insurrection at Mecca," *MERIP Reports*, October 1980; Holden and Johns, *House of Saud*, pp. 515–532; Robert Lacey, *The Kingdom* (London: Hutchinson & Co., 1980), pp. 481–496; various issues of *Le Monde*.

70. Iranians used this vulnerability to stage pro-Khomeini riots during the pilgrimage in 1981 and 1982. To put the problem in perspective, there were only 107,632 pilgrims in 1950, 283,319 in 1960, 406,925 in 1970, and 918,777 in 1974. The Saudis have done a good job in coping with the influx but fully computerized even the entry records only in 1981. Holden and Johns (*House of Saud*, p. 482) note that rebels specifically attacked Fawwaz for a love of liquor and gambling.

71. William B. Quandt notes in *Saudi Arabia in the 1980s: Foreign Policy, Security and Oil* (Washington, D.C.: Brookings Institution, 1981) that Fawwaz was one of the free princes who had gone into Egypt in the early 1960s and later been reintegrated into the Saudi ruling elite. Other reports indicate that Makkah was much more tightly governed when Fahd and Sultan's younger brother, Ahmad, had acted as deputy governor, and the uprising revealed that broad weaknesses in its administration had developed after he became deputy minister of the interior in 1976.

72. Bloomfield, "Saudi Arabia Faces the 1980's," pp. 251–253.

73. Informal British, French, and U.S. Army studies of the military problems involved later concluded that Western armies would normally have faced similar difficulties. They required Special Forces, SAS, or commando-type units; special training; and long practical experience. The Saudis did have some Special Forces, but they lacked training for such missions.

74. Governor Fawwaz's driver was killed early in the fighting.

75. Major differences exist in the reports of French support. According to *Le Point*, King Khalid personally asked President Giscard D'Estaing to provide the assistance of a French antiterrorist squad. A five-man team, under the command of a Captain Barril, part of the Intervention Group of the National Gendarmerie (GIGN), flew to Saudi Arabia on 23 November. They drew up an assault plan, trained Saudi troops to carry it out, and largely directed the attack of 3 December that ended the two-week siege. One reason given for seeking French assistance was the friendship of Saudi Interior Minister Prince Naif with Count Alexandre de Marenches, head of the French intelligence service (SDECE). *Washington Post*, 28 January 1980, p. A-10.

The *Financial Times* (28 April 1980) reported that Saudi National Guard troops refused to obey U.S.-trained Saudi NCOs who had been brought in to replace regular tribal officers. The *Times* wrote that Prince Turki al-Faisal, head of Royal Intelligence, sought assistance from the U.S. and France, but that no "non-Muslims" were actually present for the siege. U.S.-supplied tear gas was used to drive the survivors out of the mosque's catacombs. Holden and Johns, (*House of Saud*, pp. 511–526) report that the Saudis received a flood of conflicting advice from the U.S., France, Pakistan, and others.

76. Robert Moss, "What Russia Wants," *New Republic*, January 1980, p. 25.

77. In fact, their beliefs departed sufficiently far from Wahabi teachings to deserve the adjective "radical" rather than "conservative."

78. Helena Cobban, "Saudis Reported Concerned About Security Despite Rebel Executions," *Christian Science Monitor*, 11 January 1980, p. 4.

79. Lacey, *The Kingdom*, p. 483.

80. See Quandt, *Saudi Arabia in the 1980s,* for a complete account of Juhayman's background.

81. Sheikh Abd al-Aziz bin Baz, chairman of the Board for Islamic Research of Riyadh, intervened on the principle that theology students should not be arrested. He later comdemned the sect as atheistic and a perversion of Islam. He then stated that although a mahdi would come, he would do so only with clear and decisive signs. Ironically, the rebels' action in profaning the mosque alienated most other ultraconservatives, who could not forgive the sacrilege.

82. Paul, "Insurrection at Mecca," *Washington Post*, 5 February 1980.

83. See Bloomfield, "Saudi Arabia Faces the 1980's," pp. 251–253; *FBIS*, LD 131625 London ADDUSTUR, "Special Interview with Nasser al-Saeed, Leader of the Arabian Peninsula People's Union," 10–16 December 1979.

84. This "laxness" should not be exaggerated, nor should any split between the government and the clergy. Three to four seats in the Saudi council are reserved for Wahabi descendants, and all Saudi schools, universities, and military training facilities include religious instruction. While the religious police, or "Organization for the Enforcing of Good and Preventing of Evil," have been denied the authority to make arrests and to inflict corporal punishment on those who drink, women who fail to dress properly, those who do not pray, and shops that do not close during prayer, these regulations were still enforced in most of the country even before the uprising. The "laxness" in Saudi mores tended to consist of secularism on the part of some Saudis and open Western violation of Saudi customs. Nothing approaching the split between church and state that exists in all other Arab nations exists in Saudi Arabia.

85. Gary S. Saymore, "Royal Family Politics in Saudi Arabia," unpublished paper, Rand Corporation and Harvard University, 1981.

86. "Saudi Arabia—Democracy Itch," *Economist*, 5 April 1980, p. 30.

87. CRS, *Saudi Arabia and the United States*, p. 52; *Times* (London), 4 November 1980.

88. The following description is taken in large part from Bryn Williams, "The Shiite Community," *Financial Times*, 5 May 1981.

89. Three conflicting samples: 125,000—Steven Rattner, *New York Times*, 28 November 1979; 200,000–300,000—Walter S. Mossberg, *Wall Street Journal*; and 10 percent of the total population (of perhaps 4 million)—*Washington Post*, 9 August 1979, p. A-16; 275,000—Holden and Johns, *House of Saud*, p. 528; 200,000—Lacey, *The Kingdom*, p. 488.

90. *Christian Science Monitor*, 20 February 1980, p. 12. ARAMCO sources argue 20–30% and for a much lower Shi'ite population, but they do not seem credible.

91. The governor in 1979–1980 was Abd al-Mushin ibn Jiluwi. Quandt notes that he was regarded as "a weak man who did little for his constituents."

92. "Saudis Are Said to Deploy Forces in Oil Region of East After Riots," *New York Times*, 4 December 1979. See also Fred Halliday, "The Shifting Sands Beneath the House of Saud," *Progressive* 44 (March 1980):39.

93. Walter Taylor, "Iran Calls for Overthrow of Saudi Rulers," *Washington Star*, 8 January 1980, p. A-7.

94. James Dorsey, "Saudi Minority Sect Is Restive," *Christian Science Monitor*, 20 February 1980, p. 12.

95. *Financial Times*, 5 May 1981.

96. Ibid.

97. The problem of arms transfers and seizures was detected in March 1979, but not its purpose.

98. These intelligence problems also affected the U.S. Within hours after the Holy Mosque was attacked, Saudi Arabia cut all communications with the outside world and maintained the blackout for at least 24 hours. The initial *New York Times* dispatch quoted "a senior American intelligence official" to the effect that his reports showed the insurgents to be Shi'ite Muslims from Iran. This, of course, turned out to be untrue, but for 24 hours it may well have been the United States's operative assumption on the affair. *New York Times*, 21 November 1979, pp. A-1, A-5.

99. *New York Times*, 25 February 1980, p. A-10.

100. These problems remain and are exacerbated by the Saudi handling of oil revenues. According to the *New York Times*, 26 October 1979, p. A-2, "The Royal Family receives yearly allotments of oil revenues determined by seniority and predominance in the hierarchy. Leading tribal figures get land and benefits. Senior officials who are not royalty are rewarded for services with land and cash, and so on." Since Saudi production above 6.7 MMBD has tended to be sold on the spot market by, or for, the princes, and officials often share in the Saudi firms that act as agents for contracts, considerable room exists for abuse.

7
Saudi-U.S. Relations at the Beginning of the 1980s

The late 1970s should logically have led to a steady tightening of Saudi-U.S. military relations. Saudi Arabia faced a mixture of external threats, limitations on its military expansion capability, and internal security problems that created a sharply growing need for U.S. military support. However, other factors intervened that still present serious problems in forging an effective strategic partnership between the U.S. and the Gulf states.

The Growth of U.S. Military Sales

As Table 7.1 shows, U.S. foreign military sales and assistance to Saudi Arabia did grow substantially. These sales also tended to create a closer U.S. military relationship with Saudi Arabia than they did with Iran because Saudi purchases were so heavily weighted toward services rather than weapons. Even in 1980, at least two-thirds of the Saudi agreements with the U.S. still involved training, construction, infrastructure, and support; only a third involved weapons and equipment. In contrast, U.S. sales to Iran involved virtually the reverse ratio of support to equipment, and U.S. sales to Israel had something like a six-to-one ratio in favor of equipment.

The U.S. sales shown in Table 7.1 also implied a massive and continuing U.S. commitment to Saudi Arabia. Saudi Arabia was agreeing to pay for U.S. services up to a decade in the future, and less than one-third of the Saudi-U.S. military sales agreements concluded during 1950–1980 had actually been delivered by mid-1981. If Saudi Arabia had not mortgaged its security to preserving its ties to the U.S., it certainly had come close.

Problems in Saudi-U.S. Military Relations

Nevertheless, the late 1970s saw a serious erosion in many aspects of Saudi-U.S. military relations. The brutal congressional debates over the F-5E and F-15 sales reinforced Saudi doubts regarding U.S. ability to be a reliable supplier of military equipment. The costs of maintaining a dual stream of equipment—U.S. and European—for the Saudi Army rose steadily. At the same time, the Saudis shifted to increasing reliance on French and Italian naval equipment, and the Saudi National Guard sought equipment from West Germany.

As is discussed in Chapter 10, the Saudi-U.S. effort in March 1979 to create a joint aid team to supply arms and assistance to North Yemen was not a success, although it did teach the Saudis some of the problems the Americans faced in providing assistance to Saudi Arabia.[1] Further, the split between U.S. and Saudi views regarding the Camp David accords created the divisions within the royal family discussed in Chapter 5, alienated many Saudis from the U.S., and sharply increased the problems the Saudi government faced in maintaining its relations with the U.S.[2]

Saudi Arabia also found itself in an awkward position in early 1979, when the United States sought to establish a military presence in Saudi Arabia in reaction to the shah's fall and the growing tension in the region. The U.S. was unaware of the depth of the debate within the Saudi government over the problems created by Sadat's rapprochement with Israel. Through communications failures on both sides, Secretary of Defense Harold Brown made a formal offer to establish a U.S. military presence in Saudi Arabia during his visit of 10 February 1979.[3] This offer seems to have resulted from a U.S. misinterpretation of Saudi comments on the U.S. deployment of the AWACS and F-15 to Saudi Arabia and of discussions between administration officials and some of the Saudi princes.[4]

Yet the same basic issues of Arab nationalism and Saudi sovereignty that had led to the closing of the U.S. air base in Dhahran in 1962 still applied. These pressures did not preclude Saudi Arabia's relying on the U.S. for most of its military support and accepting U.S. over-the-horizon reinforcements. Saudi Arabia could not, however, accept full U.S. bases or do anything that formally compromised its sovereignty in the eyes of the Arab world. Even if Camp David had not been an issue, the heritage of anticolonialism was too strong, as was the risk of alienating neighboring Gulf regimes, moderate Arab nationalists, and the Palestinians.[5] Permanent U.S. basing arrangements were particularly threatening to Saudi Arabia's delicate political dealings with Iraq and the other major Arab powers, and Saudi Arabia's security depended as much on these relations as on U.S. military guarantees. This dependence was demonstrated in October 1980, when Qadaffi's attacks on Saudi military relations with the U.S. grew so extreme that Saudi Arabia had to break diplomatic relations with Libya, and in a near-crisis over the same issue with Syria.[6]

Unfortunately, U.S. officials had little understanding of this situation, and under the pressure of the hostage crisis in Iran and the invasion

TABLE 7.1 Trends in Saudi-U.S. Military Relations, FY1960–FY1982

	Foreign Military Sales (FMS)		Foreign Military Construction	
Fiscal Year	Agreements ($ M)	Deliveries ($ M)	Agreements ($ M)	Deliveries ($ M)
1950–1965	214.0	20.5	n.a.	n.a.
1966	8.4	12.2	–	–
1967	49.3	48.9	–	–
1968	13.7	36.9	–	–
1969	4.2	32.0	–	–
1970	80.9	51.9	–	–
1966–1970	156.5	181.9	n.a.	n.a.
1971	15.2	64.0	–	–
1972	305.4	159.6	–	–
1971–1972	320.6	223.6	603.9[b]	257.8[c]
1973	140.7	64.1	1,027.0	146.9
1974	680.0	211.4	562.2	120.3
1975	1,084.8	190.7	4,679.7	138.9
1976[c]	1,996.1	461.4	5,453.7	465.5
1977	1,309.0	1,066.1	647.7	483.9
1978	2,706.6	1,129.2	667.4	1,239.5
1979	4,929.2	940.5	1,021.0	1,515.5
1980	3,023.3	1,152.5	1,551.8	1,458.5
1981	1,280.3	1,362.7	877.4	1,570.8
1982	5,574.0	1,785.5	1,845.7	1,946.9
1973–1982	22,723.9	8,363.6	18,333.6	9,086.6
1950–1982	23,397.2	8,789.6	18,937.5	9,344.4

[a] Includes MAP excess articles program. Saudi Arabia had no annual deliveries during 1970–1983. Total agreements after 1950 were worth $1,765,000; total deliveries were worth $1,765,000. The cost of the International Military Education and Training Program is also included in the figures for MAP. There have been no agreements with Saudi Arabia since FY1975. Agreements from FY1950–FY1972 had a value of $12,071,000. New agreements from FY1973 were worth $385,000. Deliveries had approximately equal value.

[b] Covers FY1950–FY1972.

[c] FY1976 includes transitional quarter (FY77).

TABLE 7.1 (continued)

Military Assistance Program (MAP)[a]		Commercial	Total Program		Saudi
Program ($ M)	Deliveries ($ M)	Sales ($ M)	Agreements ($ M)	Deliveries ($ M)	Military Trained in U.S.
31.7	–	n.a.	–	–	1,112
0.7	–	0.9	–	–	–
0.8	–	14.9	–	–	–
0.8	1.0	35.4	50.0	73.3	50
0.5	0.6	6.2	11.0	38.8	55
0.5	0.5	12.7	94.1	65.1	47
3.3	2.1	70.1	155.1	177.2	152
0.6	0.6	20.8	36.6	85.4	43
0.4	0.4	3.6	309.4	163.6	32
1.0	1.0	24.2	346.0	249.0	75
0.2	0.2	5.7	1,173.6	216.9	33
0.2	0.2	18.0	1,244.2	349.9	41
–	–	20.2	5,784.7	349.8	12
–	–	92.7	7,542.5	1,019.6	–
–	–	44.1	2,000.8	1,594.1	–
–	–	166.3	3,540.3	2,535.0	–
–	–	44.4	5,994.6	2,485.0	–
–	–	29.0	4,604.1	2,640.0	–
–	–	71.5	2,229.2	3,005.0	–
–	–	50.0	7,469.7	3,782.4	–
0.4	0.4	541.8	41,583.7	17,977.7	86
36.3	36.3	636.4	42,084.8	18,403.9	1,425

Source: The figures are taken from various editions of DSAA, *Foreign Military Sales, Foreign Military Construction Sales, and Military Assistance Facts.* The latest data are as as of September 1982. The reader should be aware that the final figures in arms sales can take up to ten years to obtain and that such figures are constantly being adjusted. The totals are DSAA figures and may not reflect the sum of reporting for individual years. Due to changes in reporting, foreign military sales and foreign military construction are totaled under Foreign Military Sales from FY1950 to FY1977. Construction costs include design services.

of Afghanistan, many found it difficult to accept the Saudi position. Tensions were further exacerbated by a long series of news reports about U.S. studies of how U.S. forces might intervene militarily in Saudi Arabia to save the royal family from some kind of coup, or seize the Saudi oil fields in the face of a radical takeover or another oil embargo.[7]

This was scarcely an ideal basis for a closer partnership. On the one hand, the U.S. felt Saudi Arabia was not cooperating with the U.S. to improve its own security and wanted something for nothing. The Saudis on the other hand, resented U.S. insensitivity in their political position and feared that any U.S. air or troop presence might actually be used against them.[8]

As the crisis in the Gulf mounted and was capped by the Iran-Iraq War, another issue arose to divide the two countries. The Saudis reacted to the growing air threat in the Gulf by seeking the FAST kits necessary to extend the range of the F-15, and other advanced air defense equipment. Given the promises the Carter administration had made to obtain congressional approval of the F-15 sale in 1978, and the fact that 1980 was an election year, the administration was forced to temporize. The result was to nearly provoke a major crisis between the U.S. and Saudi Arabia in July 1980. More than two-thirds of the Senate signed a letter to President Carter objecting to such sales. A confrontation was avoided only when the Saudis and the Carter administration reached a private agreement that the U.S. would accelerate delivery of the F-15 and would propose the sale of the additional equipment the Saudis sought once the November 1980 election was over. Even so, the Senate letter again raised the issue of U.S. unreliability as a supplier and laid the groundwork for yet another Saudi-Israeli struggle over congressional approval of U.S. arms sales to Saudi Arabia.[9]

Saudi-U.S. military relations were thus weakened at a time when both nations needed to strengthen these relations as much as possible. The Saudis could not make the transition to full-scale military modernization without massive U.S. aid. They had a steadily growing need to further improve the sophistication and quality of their forces as a substitute for larger force numbers, and they needed improved U.S. security guarantees of a kind that would provide protection against major threats without the destabilizing effects of a U.S. presence in the Gulf. The U.S., in turn, badly needed a strong ally in the Gulf and the kind of relations with Saudi Arabia that would lead it to pursue oil policies that would minimize the risk of further energy crises.

Other Aspects of Saudi-U.S. Relations

Unfortunately, the deterioration in Saudi-U.S. military relations was reflected in a broader division between the two countries. In fact, from a Saudi perspective, Saudi Arabia's strategic ties to the United States were sometimes more of a strategic liability than a strategic asset. This situation stemmed from the following issues and problems:[10]

• U.S. efforts to improve its military intervention capabilities in the Gulf after the fall of the shah were publicized in a way that increased the conviction of many Saudis that the U.S. was doing more to prepare to seize the oil fields in Saudi Arabia than to defend the Gulf and Saudi Arabia.

• Saudi reliance on uncertain supplies of U.S. weapons and aircraft created a growing feeling in the Saudi military and other elements of Saudi society that the Saudi regime was tied to an ally that provided neither objective advice nor the military equipment Saudi Arabia needed. These problems were reinforced by the lack of discipline members of the U.S. advisory team to Saudi Arabia showed in publicizing their criticisms of the Saudi government and the Saudi military effort.

• The shah's fall led to an obsessive discussion of every indicator of internal instability in Saudi Arabia by the U.S. national security community. This had the end result of publicizing every real or rumored problem in Saudi society throughout the Washington diplomatic community and began to persuade other nations that the Saudis were in trouble and vulnerable.

• Although the Saudi government conspicuously opposed the Camp David accords and the lack of U.S. support for self-determination in Palestine, Saudi Arabia continued to be identified as a supporter of the U.S. Every further incident on the West Bank and in Lebanon tended to increase Arab radical and moderate opposition to the Saudi government because of its continued ties to the United States.

• The U.S. was forced to pressure the Saudi government to produce oil at over 9.5 MMBD. By the late 1970s, however, a significant portion of the royal family, and many leading Saudi technocrats, had come to feel that the government was wasting its national patrimony by producing more oil than Saudi Arabia needed to sell and by underselling other exporting nations to keep world oil prices down. Many technocrats supported limiting production to 7–8 MMBD, and they were joined by conservatives who saw Saudi Arabia's high oil revenues as leading to uncontrollable change.

• Changes in U.S. law and tax structure helped to erode the former partnership between the U.S. private sector and Saudi Arabia in major construction and development projects. While major increases in South Korean and other foreign corporate activity in Saudi Arabia were inevitable, U.S. policy further reduced commercial links between the U.S. and Saudi Arabia that were critical to providing Saudi Arabia with a secure source of assistance in development and economic growth.

Problems in Saudi Perceptions of U.S. Military Power

Each of the problems discussed in the preceding section weakened Saudi-U.S. strategic ties. For example, the U.S. failure to support the shah and the failure of the U.S. attempt to rescue the hostages in Iran in April 1980 led many Saudis to conclude that in spite of U.S. rhetoric about using its rapid deployment capabilities in the Gulf to check the Soviet threat, the U.S. could not react effectively to any major threat to Saudi Arabia.[11] This feeling that the new U.S. Rapid Deployment Force (RDF) would continue to exist only on paper was compounded by a broad perception that the U.S. lacked the intelligence and special operations capabilities to deal with lesser threats. The Saudis and many other friendly Arab states in the Middle East and Gulf area came to feel that the CIA and U.S. military intelligence were hamstrung by the various legal and administrative constraints placed on U.S. covert action and that the new generation of CIA employees lacked the background, training, and support to be effective.

In fact, if the U.S. was preternaturally interested in every sign of Saudi instability, there was an almost equally obsessive Saudi interest in every indicator of growing U.S. military weakness. While the Carter administration was spending much of its time watching the Saudi royal family, the Saudi government was spending much of its time watching the Carter administration.

Saudi Sensitivity to the U.S. Debate over the RDF

The capabilities of the U.S. Rapid Deployment Force and the options for Saudi-U.S.cooperation are discussed in Chapter 18, but it is important to note here that the internal policy debate in the U.S. over the size and role of the RDF also hurt Saudi-U.S. relations during 1979 and 1980. A long series of press reports on the RDF provided detailed publicity on the U.S.'s inability to rapidly deploy forces that could deal with major conflict in the Gulf. Various special interest groups within the Department of Defense leaked such data in efforts to push some special force improvement or command interest, making the situation worse. During the critical period of May to July 1980, the Department of Defense publication *Current News*, which provides a daily summary of U.S. news reports on defense, contained an average of 2.5 detailed articles per day on weaknesses in U.S. readiness and military strength. It contained an average of nearly 1 article per day on problems in some aspect of U.S. military capability in the Gulf.[12]

These articles publicized a critical lack of U.S. airlift capability, shortfalls in skilled personnel, a 200,000-man shortage of adequate active and reserve manpower, and shortages in equipment numbers and types that would keep the U.S. from deploying effectively to a region filled with new tanks and first-line fighters. They included statements that it would take 5 days to airlift one marine brigade and 35 days to deploy an army division and that these troops could then be supported for less than 30 days of low-intensity operations. They reported problems in the manning and readiness of the 82nd Airborne and 101st Air Assault divisions, and the vulnerability and limitations on the equipment-carrying capability of the prepositioned equipment ships. They gave publicity to the limits on U.S. carrier forces and capabilities, USAF ability to deploy fighters into the Gulf area, and U.S. Navy (USN) mine warfare capabilities.[13]

Statements by senior U.S. officials reinforced this image of weakness. The Saudis were confronted with statements like that of Maj. Gen. David W. Twomey, commander of the 2nd Marine Division: "Even if the President put $1 billion on the table tomorrow, we wouldn't be able to do much with it. It takes years to design and develop the kind of equipment needed by an effective rapid deployment force."[14] Or that by General Voleny Warner, commander U.S. Readiness Command: "In no way could we go into the Middle East right now and defeat a Soviet force equivalent to what they have in Afghanistan."[15] By mid-1980, every defense ministry in the world knew that U.S. talk of major military intervention in the Gulf might be a bluff for much of the next decade. Some revolutionary literature in the Middle East even actively advocated deliberate action to force U.S. intervention on the grounds that it would be ineffective and would hasten the overthrow of the conservative states like Saudi Arabia by alienating much of the Arab world.

The publicity over the Rapid Deployment Force also reinforced the impression that the U.S. intended to use it not to protect the conservative Gulf states from a major Soviet or Soviet-backed threat, but rather to seize control of the Saudi oil fields. Even otherwise pro-American Saudi officers worried that the RDF, combined with the U.S. advisory team in Saudi Arabia, would allow the U.S. to seize the oil facilities in the northeast provinces and that the U.S. planned to do this in the event of another oil embargo.[16] While senior Saudi officials discounted this possibility—and knew that the U.S. was well aware that the long-range result of any such U.S. action would be to alienate the entire Arab and developing world—many middle-echelon officials took it more seriously. Even some senior Saudi officials were uneasy about the true purpose of the RDF, given the amount of ill-controlled talk about seizing the oil fields that went on in the Congress, the press, and the lower echelons of the Pentagon.[17]

This situation was not helped by public references by the RDF commander to a "preemptive strategy" under which the U.S. would deploy its forces as soon as possible to ensure that they would be in place before the Soviets could act. Both the Saudis and many European leaders felt that such a strategy would lead the U.S. to overreact and to try to beat the Soviets to the punch, creating a hair-trigger willingness to commit U.S. forces long before the need for such a commitment was clear. From the Saudi perspective, it meant that the U.S. might suddenly try to massively increase its presence in the Gulf, and demand Saudi support of that action, before the need for such action was clear. This course, the Saudis felt, could tie them to U.S. actions that would be so unpopular in the Arab world that they would isolate Saudi Arabia as a nation and greatly strengthen internal opposition to the royal family. The end result was that many Saudis became as worried over the possibility that the RDF would be used as over the possibility that it could not be used.

Saudi Doubts About the U.S. Military Assistance Effort

These same factors increased Saudi concerns regarding the U.S. military assistance effort that had built up in the mid-1970s. After the debate over the F-15 sale, the Saudi leadership increasingly came to wonder if the U.S. would provide Saudi Arabia with the equipment it needed to make effective use of the infrastructure the U.S. had sold Saudi Arabia and whether the U.S. might even be keeping Saudi Arabia deliberately weak rather than building up its strength.[18] Further, a number of senior Saudi military officers became concerned that in response to U.S. advice, Saudi Arabia had spent almost 70% of its defense procurement expenditures since 1968 on building up its military infrastructure, training base, and manpower skill levels to get ready to absorb modern weapons. They questioned whether U.S. advice had given or would give them the rate of improvement in military capability they needed and whether the U.S. had adequately considered the Saudi need to have large numbers of modern arms as a deterrent in a part of the world where few nations operated their equipment effectively and where equipment numbers and types had a major impact on local perceptions of military strength. Several stated that Saudi Arabia faced the prospect of having the world's most expensive military forces, in terms of dollars paid for firepower delivered, without being able to deal adequately with a single major regional threat.

Some senior Saudi officers also questioned the quality of U.S. military advice. Pro-American Saudis tended to feel that such problems were minor, resulting from U.S. ignorance of local capabilities and military conditions and the traditional conservatism and inflexibility of the U.S. military assistance effort; others felt that the U.S. was seeking to keep Saudi Arabia vulnerable and dependent. Still others felt that the U.S. advisers were patronizing the Saudis, or simply seeking to recycle petrodollars, and were far more ready to report to Washington on the problems in the Saudi armed forces than to work with the Saudis to solve them.

It is not surprising, therefore, that the Saudi government entered into negotiations with the French to fund development of the Mirage 2000 and 4000 as an alternative to the F-15 during this period.[19] Given the events of May 1977 and December 1979, the Saudi leadership had a strong incentive to do this for its own security. There were too many members of the Saudi military who questioned Saudi ties to the U.S. not to do so, and many Saudi technocrats—some of them quite senior—wanted Saudi Arabia to further decouple its military development from the U.S.

Interestingly enough, the Saudi government came under pressure to reach some arrangement to improve its forces from some of its neighbors that had previously opposed the buildup of Saudi forces. Bahrain, Kuwait, the United Arab Emirates, and Oman made it clear that they wanted Saudi Arabia to rapidly increase its military strength and to provide the southern Gulf states with air defense support. At the same time, the Yemeni crisis of 1979 went a long way toward convincing both Yemens that Saudi Arabia's military capability in no way matched its money and that Saudi Arabia could be vulnerable to military action even by powers as weak as South Yemen.

The U.S. "Threat" to Saudi Internal Security

The Saudis also felt threatened by an almost constant U.S. questioning after the shah's fall of Saudi Arabia's internal stability and of the cohesion of the Saudi royal family. Although it was not initially understood in Washington, the U.S. concern with the possibility that Saudi Arabia might become another Iran was watched with keen attention by every nation in the Gulf and Middle East, and each such nation became aware that the U.S. was acting as if the Saudi government were extremely vulnerable and could collapse at any moment.[20]

This awareness was reinforced by a lack of discretion on the part of a number of U.S. diplomats, military officers, CIA staff, and other U.S. officials. Several senior Saudis became firmly convinced that the U.S. mission in Saudi Arabia, and particularly the CIA, was responsible for a steady stream of reports indicating that Saudi Arabia was on the edge of collapse, that the royal family had split over Camp David, that Prince Fahd had lost power, and that King Khalid was about to abdicate.[21] They also worried that the U.S. was taking seriously the various British, Israeli, and Lebanese rumor mills and that U.S. intelligence ties with Israel were reinforcing a U.S. tendency to report instability in the Saudi government.[22]

The Saudis were infuriated early in the spring of 1980 by reports of a CIA background briefing that led *Newsweek* and the *Washington Star* to report that the Saudi royal family might be on the edge of internal conflict and unable to rule. They were particularly angry because the White House privately assured the Saudis of its confidence in Saudi stability almost simultaneously with the leak of the CIA report.[23] This situation came to a head in April, when the *Washington Post* quoted "U.S. intelligence reports" in an article discussing a possible split between Prince Fahd and King Khalid. The Saudis initially blamed George Cave, the CIA station chief in Jiddah, for the report. Prince Turki al-Faisal is reported to have summoned him for an angry interview and to have demanded that he leave the country. The situation was not improved when some press sources blamed Secretary of Energy James Schlesinger and then several senior State Department officials for the incident. While it developed some months later that the sources for these reports were largely Israeli, rather than American, the damage had already been done.[24]

The Saudis resented the fact that several former and active U.S. military advisers were publicizing both the weaknesses in the Saudi military establishment and their views that the Saudis were unable to properly absorb modern military equipment. They particularly resented testimony given to the House Foreign Affairs Subcommittee in May 1980 by Lt. Col. John Ruszkiewicz, the former U.S. Army attaché in North Yemen. Ruszkiewicz publicized the problems in the Saudi-U.S. military assistance effort to Yemen in great detail.[25]

Several senior members of the Saudi government complained during this period that the U.S. was speaking with two different voices. They claimed that at the official level, the U.S. was constantly reassuring the Saudis that it did not feel they were threatened, but it was impossible for them to visit a Washington party without being subjected to endless questions about whether Saudi Arabia would survive. Several stated that they would have left far more reassured if the U.S. had openly raised its concerns about their stability and at least allowed discussion that might help resolve them rather than unconsciously act as Saudi Arabia's most public and severe critic under conditions that alerted the Washington diplomatic corps.[26]

Some younger Saudi military officers and technocrats were more blunt. They felt that the U.S. was exacerbating problems that were difficult enough to solve without constant criticism and publicity from Saudi Arabia's closest ally. They found that many of their contemporaries in the Gulf were all too well aware of U.S. criticisms of everything from the Saudi Five Year Plan to Saudi ability to manage the Muslim shrines in Saudi Arabia. Since many had been educated in the U.S. and were well aware of U.S. economic and social problems, they felt the criticisms were both hypocritical and dangerous. The result was to alienate precisely the class of Saudis the U.S. was trying most to attract.[27]

The Saudi Reaction to Camp David

There is also no question that the Saudis felt increasingly threatened by the Egyptian-Israeli peace agreement at Camp David and by U.S. pressure to support the agreement. Camp David's impact on the royal family has already been discussed; the accords had several additional negative effects on Saudi-U.S. relations.[28]

- The Camp David accords made it possible for the Saudis to preserve their political and military ties with Egypt without being viewed as anti-Palestinian.[29] The resulting split with Egypt decoupled Saudi Arabia from the one Arab military power that could have been of major assistance in modernizing its forces and in providing military assistance.[30]
- The accords alienated the rest of the Arab world from the U.S. and increased the political costs of close Saudi ties to the U.S. The Saudis faced the problem that more than half the Arab world was under the age of 16, and all Arab schools and media constantly glamorized the Palestinians.

• The accords meant that Saudi Arabia might be forced in a future Arab-Israeli crisis to side with the Palestinians and Arabs against the United States, as well as making such a crisis more likely. In practical terms, this situation meant that the Saudis could be cut off from their principal military ally at almost any time.

• The accords led Saudi Arabia and Jordan to distance themselves from U.S. policy on the Middle East. Any impression that either country supported the Camp David accords meant being labeled in the Arab world as anti-Palestinian and entailed active opposition by Syria and Iraq. Given Saudi dependence on foreign labor, this was likely to lead to serious internal unrest and would be almost certain to alienate the large number of younger Saudis who support the Palestinian cause.[31]

• The resulting Israeli-Egyptian peace treaty traded what Saudi Arabia regarded as the comparatively unimportant issue of the Sinai for any active effort to deal with the problem of Palestinian sovereignty. As a result, the Saudis felt that the pressure for Saudi efforts to develop more moderate PLO positions regarding Israel had temporarily collapsed and that the pressure on Israel to compromise with the PLO had been removed.

• Camp David gave the impression that the U.S. had ceased to try to reach a meaningful peace settlement, was spending virtually all of its time trying to preserve Egyptian-Israeli ties, and was using the treaty for domestic political purposes.

One of the ironies of the situation was that, by the late 1970s, most of the Saudi leaders and technical staff wanted nothing more than a peace treaty between Israel and the Arab world. They had come to regard the ongoing struggle between Israel and the Arab states as one that was steadily radicalizing the Arab world and leading to ever-greater Soviet penetration into the area. In fact, many would have settled for a treaty that meant a very slow Israeli phase-out of military control of the West Bank, significant compromises on the western border of the occupied territories, and only token Arab sovereignty over a part of the old city of Jerusalem—such as the mosques—if Israel would accept a sovereign Palestinian state. The Saudis had no illusions that another war would end in an Arab victory or do anything other than accelerate virtually every regional trend that threatens their security. Camp David, however, created a situation that forced Saudi Arabia and Jordan to split with Egypt and that delayed any major Saudi peace initiatives until the "Fahd Plan" of 1981.

Tensions over Oil Policy

Saudi Arabia also increasingly resented U.S. pressure for Saudi oil production levels over 8 MMBD. Their view of the U.S. appetite for oil ran as follows:[32]

• Every barrel over 8 MMBD that Saudi Arabia produced was a waste of a limited national patrimony that should be saved for a future in which the Saudis will sell much smaller amounts of oil in the form of petrochemical products.

• The vast oil revenues that Saudi Arabia received were impossible to absorb. They were leading to instability and corruption, and they forced the Saudi economy to spend faster than the Saudis could control it. Their money could not be invested in Saudi Arabia, and foreign investment was far less remunerative than leaving the oil in the ground.

• The royal family was getting steadily greater internal criticism, some of it from very high levels in Saudi society, for producing more than the nation needed. This was another area in which a common ground existed among Saudi technocrats, the Saudi military, Saudi students, and more radical elements in Saudi society. It was one of the few areas in which all were willing to publicly criticize the royal family and the government.

• Saudi Arabia's high volume of oil sales tended to alienate Saudi Arabia from the other oil-producing states in the Arab world, many of which wished to maximize short-term revenues and felt the Saudis were depriving them of the price increase they would otherwise get.

• Such high levels of oil production helped identify the Saudis as a "client" of the U.S. They separated Saudi Arabia from the rest of the moderate Arab world and provided an issue that radical elements could exploit.

• The U.S. was not acting with any real urgency to reduce its oil imports; the end effect of high Saudi oil sales was U.S. inaction.

Most senior Saudi officials and oil experts regarded high production levels as essential to keeping world demand high and to preserving Saudi Arabia's share of world oil markets, but the fact remained that many Saudi technocrats, businessmen, and students increasingly opposed such high levels of oil production. While Saudi sales did a great deal to stave off a major recession in the industrialized world during 1980, many Saudis came to feel that they were threatening Saudi security.

The Declining Role of U.S. Business

Finally, these political and military problems coincided with a growing crisis in Saudi-U.S. business relations that continued into 1983.[33] U.S. business operations in Saudi Arabia play a powerful indirect role in ensuring Saudi security. They help forge strong economic links between Saudi Arabia and the United States that reinforce the national security ties between the two nations. They provide a source of the talent Saudi Arabia needs for stable internal development and the absorption of its oil revenues. They cushion the risk that foreign firms or labor will become a source of instability, and they provide a U.S. presence in Saudi Arabia that has done a great deal to develop popular pro-American sentiment.

During 1975–1980, however, U.S. construction firms slipped from first to twelfth place in the Middle East, where Saudi Arabia was 50% of the market. Between May 1978 and June 1979, about 220 major construction contracts, worth about $22 billion, were awarded in the Middle East. The U.S. won only 7 of these contracts, worth about $346 million. The market share of U.S. construction contractors in Saudi Arabia dropped from a 9% share in 1976 to a 6% share in 1978 and a 3% share in 1979–1980,[34] although the value of the contracts involved rose from $10 billion per year to $23 billion. The share of U.S. firms in U.S. Army Corps of Engineer contracts dropped from 35% in 1975 to 5% in 1978 and 2% in 1979.[35] During July 1976 to September 1979 U.S. firms fell so far behind competitors like South Korea that they got only $333 million of the $1.86 billion worth of contracts the Corps of Engineers managed for the Saudi Arabian government. In contrast, South Korean firms received $598 million worth of awards—and $287 million of the $333 million that went to U.S. firms involved a firm that had a Korean firm as a joint partner.

Part of this decline was an economic fact of life and resulted from normal competition in the marketplace. However, U.S. firms were also forced out of the Saudi market by Saudi resentment of U.S. foreign policy actions and by their own government. The U.S. provided no equivalent to the government financing of bid bonds and performance guarantees by nations like South Korea. A mix of badly drafted anti-boycott legislation, a lack of clear guidelines regarding the Federal Corrupt Practices Act, and regulatory problems like attempts to enforce the limits of the environmental protection acts on overseas operations made it extremely difficult for U.S. firms to compete on Saudi terms.[36] Further, U.S. tax laws added something approaching 25% to the cost of U.S. bids as a result of the 1978 Foreign Earned Income Act. The U.S. did remain Saudi Arabia's senior trading partner, but these pressures hurt the U.S. balance of payments and the U.S. economy. The end result was a growing separation between the U.S. and Saudi Arabia that did not aid either nation.[37]

Implications for the Saudi-U.S. Strategic Partnership

Some of the problems in Saudi-U.S. relations described in this chapter stemmed from an exaggerated Saudi reaction to U.S. policies and actions. They created growing pressures to limit Saudi Arabia's future strategic partnership with the U.S. and to force a test of U.S. willingness to provide Saudi Arabia with the advanced military equipment it was requesting. They also helped to shape the situation in 1981, when Saudi Arabia sought the advanced air defense equipment that the Carter administration had promised in 1980.

Notes

1. See Lt. Col. John H. Ruszkiewicz's statement before the Subcommittee on Europe and the Middle East of the House Committee on Foreign Affairs, 5 May 1980; *Washington Post*, 5 June 1980, p. 1; *New York Times*, 6 February 1980, p. 10; *Christian Science Monitor*, 29 November 1979, p. 1.

2. Few Americans understood that while Sadat could agree to the Camp David accords because they returned the Sinai to Egypt, Saudi Arabia and Jordan would have been alienated from much of their population and most other Arab states if they had accepted "autonomy" rather than self-determination and the annexation of Jerusalem. Saudi Arabia, whose legitimacy rested on its status as guardian of the Islamic holy places, was in no position to concede the control of the third holiest shrine. This led Prince Saud, the Saudi foreign minister, to term the agreement "an invitation to war rather than peace." *Le Monde* (Paris), 14 May 1979.

3. *Economist*, 13 October 1979; David Holden and Richard Johns, *The House of Saud* (London: Sidgwick and Jackson, 1981), p. 501.

4. See *Washington Star*, 3 March 1979, p. 3; *New York Times*, 23 February 1979, p. 7; 20 March 1979, p. 8; 16 May 1979, p. 7; *Los Angeles Times*, 23 April 1979, p. 14; *Washington Post*, 5 February 1979, p. 31; 7 May 1979, p. D-13; *Newsweek*, 26 March 1979, p. 37.

5. Roughly a month later, Saudi Arabia cut oil production at a time when it had a critical impact on prices and Western economies, and in May Prince Turki resigned as deputy minister of defense. While Sadat's attacks on the royal family, including Fahd, in June helped bring it together, this was not a particularly good period for U.S. basing initiatives.

6. *Washington Post*, 29 October 1980, p. 1.

7. The U.S. has never quite understood the political impact in the Arab world of publicly promising to save a friendly regime. The Arab media often portray this as the U.S. promising to protect a region from its citizens and as a symbol that a regime has lost its Arab character and legitimacy.

8. William B. Quandt notes in *Saudi Arabia in the 1980s: Foreign Policy, Security and Oil* (Washington, D.C.: Brookings Institution, 1981) that the Saudis had earlier been irritated by such articles as Robert W. Tucker's "Oil: The Issue of American Intervention," *Commentary*, January 1975, and "Further Reflections on Oil and Force," *Commentary*, March 1975; and Miles Ignotus's "Seizing Arab Oil: A Blueprint for Fast and Effective Action," *Harper's*, March 1975.

9. *Philadelphia Inquirer*, 17 December 1980, p. 13; *Washington Star*, 20 April 1980, p. 27; 20 June 1980, pp. 5, 7; 8 July 1980, p. 6; 10 July 1980, p. 1; *Wall Street Journal*, 14 November 1980, p. 1.

10. Many of the concerns expressed here and later in this chapter were stated formally by Prince Sultan in an interview in *U.S. News and World Report*, 12 March 1979, p. 25. Quandt discusses many others in *Saudi Arabia in the 1980s*.

11. This impression was reinforced by the faltering U.S. performance in dealing with the shah's fall and events in the Horn of Africa and Afghanistan.

12. Author's count. Excludes Early Bird and Special Editions.

13. See Jeffrey Record, *The Rapid Deployment Force* (Washington, D.C.: Institute for Foreign Policy Analysis, February 1981), for an authoritative discussion of these problems.

14. *Los Angeles Times*, 7 February 1980.

15. *Defense Week*, 30 July 1980.

16. One reason for such Saudi concerns was the kind of article the *New York Times* published on 5 July 1979. The article, which drew keen Saudi attention, analyzed possible U.S. military intervention in areas where U.S. vital interests were jeopardized. It listed a variety of circumstances that might be considered for U.S. intervention in Saudi Arabia, including an externally backed rebellion in Saudi Arabia; a PDRY invasion of Saudi Arabia with Soviet support; and a Saudi decision to reduce oil shipments to the United States for political reasons, such as dissatisfaction with U.S. policy over the Israeli-occupied territories.

17. Based on author's interviews in Saudi Arabia in May 1980.

18. Not quite ingenuously, a number of Europeans arms sellers pushed this theme in their discussions with Saudi defense officials.

19. *Strategy Week*, 22–28 September 1980. As is discussed elsewhere, this report is of doubtful authenticity.

20. Congressional Research Service (CRS), *Saudi Arabia and the United States: The New Context in an Evolving "Special Relationship,"* a report prepared by the Foreign Affairs and National Defense Division (Washington, D.C.: Government Printing Office, August 1981), p. 55; *Washington Post*, 12 April 1979.

21. The French kept a discreet silence about the fact that a four- or five-man French security team accompanied the Saudis into the underground rooms in the Grand Mosque. The Saudis appreciated the contrast. See Quandt, *Saudi Arabia in the 1980s.*

22. Prince Fahd formally protested the constant U.S. reports on Saudi instability and corruption in December 1980. *MEED* 24 (18 January 1980).

23. See also the *Baltimore Sun*, 23 January 1979, p. 4; and premature U.S. reports of King Khalid's death in the *Washington Post*, 21 February 1980, p. A-30. A high-level CIA official later had to formally apologize to Saudi Arabia. See Staff report, Senate Foreign Relations Committee (SFRC), *The Proposed AWACS/F-15 Enhancement Sale to Saudi Arabia*, GPO 84-557-0 (Washington, D.C.: Government Printing Office, September 1981), p. 47.

24. *Washington Post*, 15 April 1980; Holden and Johns, *House of Saud*, p. 506.

25. Particularly since this was Prince Sultan's personal responsibility and he had persuaded the royal family to rely on a joint partnership with the U.S.

26. Interviews with the author.

27. Ibid. Several made it a point to bring up Watergate, Abscam, and the General Services Administration (GSA) scandal.

28. Crown Prince Fahd expressed many of the following concerns in an interview in *Newsweek*, 26 March 1979, p. 37.

29. Saudi Arabia was initially willing to provide $525 million to Egypt for the cost of the F-5E program even after the break. The Saudis killed the deal only after Sadat openly attacked Saudi Arabia and its leaders on 1 May 1979. Even then, Saudi Arabia did not take economic reprisals by expelling Egyptian workers.

30. The Saudis generally supported the U.S. even after Sadat's surprise visit in November 1977. They became skeptical after the Camp David accords in September 1978 but broke with Egypt only when the peace treaty was signed in March 1979. Its indifference to the PLO and West Bank made Saudi support politically impossible. To the custodian of Islam it meant acceptance of Israeli

occupation of Jerusalem and the third holiest Muslim shrine. Nationally, it meant continued Israeli occupation of the Saudi islands of Tiran and Sanafir in the Strait of Tiran until April 1982. Politically, it meant supporting a position that ran counter to virtually all the Arab political movements in the Gulf. Even so, Prince Sultan stated in October 1979 that if Israel stopped its aggression and recognized Palestinian rights, "We would have no reason to remain hostile to Israel or refuse to deal with it." Riyadh Radio, 10 October 1979.

31. Saudi Arabia has only about 100,000 to 150,000 Palestinians in its work force, and few are in sensitive positions. These are offset by increasing numbers of largely anti-Palestinian Lebanese. However, virtually all its more than 1 million Egyptian, Jordanian, and Yemeni workers are pro-Palestinian, as are virtually all Saudi students.

32. Many of these Saudi arguments were raised by U.S. analysts in such documents as "The World Oil Market in the Years Ahead," CIA-NFAC, August 1979, and even by Deputy Secretary of Energy John Sawhill in hearings before the Senate Committee on Foreign Relations in late February 1980.

33. See deSaint-Phalle, Thibaut, "U.S. Productivity and Competitiveness in International Trade," Washington, D.C., Georgetown University Center for Strategic and International Studies, c. 1980.

34. American Businessmen's Group of Riyadh position paper, "American's Loss of Business in the Middle East, September 1980"; *MEED* special report, "Construction and Contracting," March 1981, p. 22; *MEED*, 24 September 1982, pp. 9–10. It had sunk to less than 2% by 1982.

35. U.S. Congress, General Accounting Office, *Report: Impact of Foreign Corrupt Practices Act on U.S. Business*, AFMD-81-34 (Washington, D.C.: General Accounting Office, March 4, 1981).

36. CRS, *Saudi Arabia and the United States.*

37. *Middle East*, December 1982, p. 16. The rank of major suppliers by country is shown below for 1976 and 1981.

	U.S.		UK		France		FRG		Italy		Japan	
	76	81	76	81	76	81	76	81	76	81	76	81
Bahrain	2	1	1	2	9	7	4	4	6	6	3	3
Egypt	1	1	5	6	4	2	2	3	3	4	7	5
Iran	1	8	4	3	5	5	2	1	7	4	3	2
Iraq	3	6	5	5	4	3	1	2	7	4	2	1
Jordan	2	2	3	3	6	4	1	1	5	6	4	5
Kuwait	2	2	4	4	5	7	3	3	6	5	1	1
Libya	5	6	6	3	3	5	2	2	1	1	4	4
Oman	3	3	1	2	9	9	4	5	10	10	2	1
Qatar	3	3	2	1	5	5	4	4	6	6	1	2
Saudi Arabia	1	1	4	4	8	6	3	3	5	5	2	2
Sudan	3	2	1	1	9	4	4	3	6	6	2	5
Syria	5	6	6	10	4	3	1	2	2	1	3	4
UAE	3	2	2	3	7	5	5	4	7	6	1	1

8
The Origins of the AWACS Sale

The Reagan administration inherited a distinctly mixed climate of Saudi-U.S relations when it took office in January 1981. Some advances had been made in military relations in the last months of the Carter administration, but the overall execution of U.S. policy toward the Gulf remained faltering and confused. The Reagan administration also took office with a mixed set of advantages and disadvantages from a Saudi perspective. On the one hand, the Saudis welcomed the new president's clear intention to reassert U.S. strength and military capability and the freedom the new administration had in maneuvering around the Camp David accords. On the other hand, they were concerned with the administration's lack of experience, the immediate conflicts that surfaced among its senior foreign policy officials, and President Reagan's strong and seemingly uncritical support of Israel and Prime Minister Begin.

For its part, the new administration showed an equal concern with what it felt to be a lack of proper Saudi understanding of the broader strategic changes taking place in the Gulf, with Saudi Arabia's "uncritical" support of the PLO, and with Saudi pressure on the U.S. to persuade Israel to grant some form of self-determination to the West Bank. From the Reagan administration's perspective, Saudi Arabia seemed to be far too concerned with what the U.S. regarded as a strategic sideshow at a time when the administration felt that Saudi Arabia should join the U.S. in forging a tacit "strategic consensus" among Israel, Egypt, and Saudi Arabia. A new U.S. administration once again had to learn that the Saudi concern with the Palestinian issue was not a *pro forma* gesture, but a major political commitment. It had to learn that Saudi policy was a response to the forces of Arab nationalism that shaped the Saudi regime's policy and gave it legitimacy and to the political forces in the Gulf area that made the active Saudi support of the Palestinian movement basic to both Saudi Arabia's internal security and Saudi influence over the other Gulf states.

This situation was complicated by the fact that Saudi Arabia and the United States had no way to predict the future political leadership of Israel. Prime Minister Begin's ability to form a new government remained in doubt until the first week of August 1981, which made it impossible to predict the progress that could be achieved in reaching an Arab-Israeli peace agreement and the extent to which even the loosest and most tacit strategic consensus could really be forged. The situation was further confused during the first six months of 1981 by Begin's increasingly aggressive stance toward Syria, Iraq, and the Palestinian movement. By the early spring, it had become apparent that Begin could ensure his reelection only by gaining the full support of Israel's growing majority of Oriental Jews and that as part of this effort he would have to take an exceptionally hard line toward the Arab world. Begin then proceeded to manipulate Israel's external tensions with the Arab world to create a series of crises, which he then used to gain political support in his effort to achieve reelection and to form a new coalition government.

As a result, Israel's domestic politics became linked increasingly to its military actions. These actions included increasing Israeli military support of the Christians in Lebanon, provoking a military crisis with Syria by shooting down two Syrian helicopters that were attacking Maronite forces in Lebanon, and provoking a crisis over Syria's retaliatory deployment of SA-6 surface-to-air missiles in Lebanon. They included Israel's destruction of the Osirak reactor that Iraq was building near Baghdad on the grounds that it would be used to produce nuclear weapons, and a series of major Israeli attacks on Palestinian forces in Lebanon that led to a broader political crisis when Israeli air attacks accidentally inflicted major civilian casualties.[1]

This series of Israeli politico-military adventures plunged both the U.S. and Saudi Arabia into a long series of efforts to contain each successive crisis that continued into 1983. While this had the beneficial effect of bringing the new administration into close contact with several Saudi leaders and of leading it to take a more critical approach toward the Begin administration, it also provided a poor basis for putting Saudi-U.S relations on a more stable plane or for developing a strategic partnership in the Gulf.

The Development of the "AWACS Package"

The U.S. did make important progress in putting its military relations with Saudi Arabia on a sounder footing as a result of several initiatives the Carter administration took during its last six months in office. As the Carter administration became aware of the reasons for Saudi Arabia's rejection of Secretary of Defense Harold Brown's offer of U.S. military bases during his trip to Saudi Arabia in February 1979,[2] and of the intensity of the problems in Saudi-U.S relations, it began to search for some method of meeting Saudi military concerns.

The chronology of events that transformed the Carter administration's 1978 pledges not to sell Saudi Arabia more advanced air defense equipment into the Reagan administration's "Saudi Air Defense Enhancement Package" of 1981 demonstrated both the strengths and weaknesses of Saudi-U.S military relations. It demonstrated the strengths by showing that both nations could evolve a viable military solution to the different political constraints they faced and could find a basis for putting their military relations on a more stable, long-term basis. It also showed that the U.S. could respond to the problems dividing it from Saudi Arabia and that the Saudis were flexible enough to cope with U.S. politics during an election year and a change in administration. At the same time, the process of Saudi-U.S planning that led to the "AWACS package" scarcely approached strategic elegance. Both nations were forced to continuously jockey for position, both to reach final agreement on what became the Saudi Air Defense Enhancement Package and to cope with external pressures and developments.

In brief, the Saudi Air Defense Enhancement Package grew out of the following developments:

May 1978: Still relying on the shah of Iran to provide Saudi Arabia with air security over most of the Gulf,[3] the Carter administration pledges limitations on future arms sales to Saudi Arabia to win Senate support of the F-15 sale by a vote of 52 to 44. A 9 May 1978 letter from Secretary Brown to Senator John Sparkman, then chairman of the Senate Foreign Relations Committee, stipulates the following:

> The F-15s we plan to sell to Saudi Arabia will have the same configurations as the interceptor model approved for the United States Air Force. The plane requested by Saudi Arabia will not be equipped with the special features that could give it additional range. Specifically the planes will not have conformal fuel tanks ("FAST packs"), i.e., auxiliary fuel tanks that conform to the body of the plane, and Saudi Arabia KC-130 tankers do not have equipment for air refueling of the F-15.
>
> Saudi Arabia has not requested that the plane be outfitted with multiple ejection racks (MER 200) which would allow the plane to carry a substantial bomb load. The United States will not furnish such MER's. . . . Saudi Arabia has not requested, nor do we intend to sell any other systems or armaments that could increase the range or enhance the ground attack capability of the F-15.

Secretary Brown reinforces these pledges in testimony before the House Foreign Affairs Committee on 9 May 1978, when he is asked whether the United States was planning to provide the Saudis with an aerial refueling capacity for the F-15s. In response, Secretary Brown states: "The F-15 does have a receptacle, but the Saudis don't have an aerial refueling capability with a probe, so they will not be able to refuel the F-15."

Assistant Secretary of State Bennett sends a separate letter to Congressman Lee Hamilton on 16 February 1978, making the following statements concerning the AIM-9L and AWACS:

> The Saudi Air Force is not scheduled to get the AIM-9L all-aspect *Sidewinder* missile which will be carried on the United States Air Force

> F-15's. . . . An F-15 sale will not lead to the sale of E-2C or E-3A (AWACS). The F-15 has an excellent radar. Were the Saudis to purchase an aircraft with less effective radar than the F-15, they would be more than likely to seek an airborne radar system.

August 1978: The film theater fire in Abadan kills 377. This is the sixth fire in 12 days, and the riots that follow show massive popular opposition to the shah.

September 1978: The first massive pro-Khomeini riot in Tehran on 7 September results in "Black Friday." The Iranian Army fires and wounds or kills 700–2,000. Defense Intelligence Agency (DIA) later predicts that the shah will continue to rule for the next 10 years. Jack Miklos and Henry Precht of the State Department and Robert Bowie of the CIA support this view in testimony to the Senate Foreign Relations Committee on 15 and 27 September. However, Iran is forced to cancel arms purchases, including 70 additional F-14s at a cost of $2 billion.

October–December 1978: Khomeini arrives in France after Iran asks Iraq to eject him. An active nationwide anti-shah campaign starts in Iraq.

2 November 1978: The U.S. forms a Special Coordinating Committee of the National Security Council (NSC) on the crisis in Iran.

5 November 1978: The shah sets up a martial law government in Iran under General Azhari. Ex-premier Hoveyda and ex-SAVAK head Nasiri are arrested on the 11th.

11 November 1978: President Carter protests the poor quality of U.S. intelligence on Iran.

25–27 December 1978: The shah appoints Shapur Bakhtiar, member of the opposition, as prime minister. Mass riots, troop fire, and tension increase.

16 January 1979: The shah flees Iran and goes into exile.

Late February 1979: President Carter agrees to send a token force of F-15s to Saudi Arabia, to deploy a carrier task force and to accelerate U.S. arms deliveries to the Yemen Arab Republic (YAR), in response to increased hostilities in Yemen and the collapse of imperial Iran.[4]

March 1979: Israel and Egypt conclude a separate peace treaty. Saudi Arabia and the other moderate Arab states break with Egypt and the U.S. over the treaty.

March 1979: Saudi Arabia fails to stabilize relations with Egypt following the Camp David accords. Prince Fahd leaves the country.[5]

April 1979: The Arab League expels Egypt, and member nations break off diplomatic and economic relations with Cairo. The Saudis provide verbal support of the general consensus but do not break economic relations, and they continue to finance Egyptian F-5 purchases.

Articles in the U.S. press about recent U.S. intelligence reports that question Saudi Arabia's political stability further strain relations. Defense Secretary Brown submits that the U.S. should be prepared to respond to a crisis in the Gulf even though the U.S. ability to do so is "questionable."[6]

Late April 1979: While visiting Washington, Prince Bandar ibn Sultan, son of the Saudi defense minister, is offered general reassurances regarding U.S. support of Saudi Arabia by Carter.[7]

March–April 1979: Two U.S. Air Force E-3A AWACS aircraft are deployed to Saudi Arabia in response to the conflict in Yemen and the possible threat to Saudi Arabia. Saudi officers gain a detailed knowledge of the E-3A and its ability to supplement ground-based radars.[8]

The Saudis cut oil production, increasing the impact of the oil crisis resulting from the shah's fall. Saudi Arabia takes an increasingly hard line toward Egypt.

May 1979: Saudi Foreign Minister Saud al-Faisal declares that "Saudi Arabia is keen on seeing its special relationship with the United States continue," while defending Saudi opposition to the Egyptian-Israeli peace treaty and stressing Arab unanimity and solidarity.[9]

June 1979: Sadat launches verbal and personal attacks on the Saudi royal family, including Prince Fahd. The Saudis unite in opposition to Sadat, but they do not fully break relations with Egypt.

Robert Strauss visits Saudi Arabia. Some reports indicate that he obtains an increase in oil production in return for a pledge of arms.

Late June 1979: During two high-level meetings between Secretary of Defense Brown and Secretary of State Cyrus Vance, a consensus emerges over the need to strengthen the U.S. military presence in the Indian Ocean and the Gulf. The Department of Defense is ordered to prepare a list of deployment possibilities to establish a permanent fleet in the region, as well as bases or contingency bases for land-based aircraft. King Khalid, however, warns against external military "intervention" and further states that the Gulf countries themselves must take responsibility for safeguarding the region, while reiterating that the Saudi-U.S. relationship is as friendly as ever.[10]

July 1979: Secretary Brown states that the U.S. intends to increase its security presence in the region and declares that "the United States would commit forces if we judged our vital interests were involved." State Department spokesman Tom Reston says that the United States clearly has vital interests in the Gulf. "An essential part of these interests is to preserve the independence, stability and sovereignty of the countries in it."[11]

13 July 1979: The Carter administration announces its recommendation to Congress for the sale of $1.2 billion in military equipment for continuation of the Saudi National Guard modernization program.[12]

30 August 1979: Saudi spokesmen continue to assert that oil production will not be employed as a political lever. President Carter declares that the U.S "would not let any Arab country blackmail the U.S. into any agreements," and that no Arab leader has "professed a desire for an independent Palestinian state" in any private session he had had with them.[13]

September 1979: The Saudis request a feasibility study to analyze the worth of an airborne surveillance system for the kingdom.[14]

1 October 1979: President Carter announces his order to form the Rapid Deployment Force.

4 November 1979: The U.S. Embassy in Tehran is seized and the long imprisonment of U.S. hostages begins.

12 November 1979: Saudi Second Deputy Prime Minister and National Guard Commander Prince Abdullah states during an interview that the kingdom's concern is to "prevent the Gulf region from becoming an arena for rivalry among the foreign powers."[15]

Late November 1979: The insurrection at the Grand Mosque in Makkah takes place, provoking questions regarding Saudi stability.

12 December 1979: Under Secretary of State for Security Affairs Lucy Benson states before the House Foreign Affairs Committee that the administration's decision to sell 660 AIM-9P Sidewinders, 916 AGM-G5A Mavericks, 3,435 GFBV-12 laser-guided bombs, 519 CBP-71 munitions, and 1,000 CBU-58 cluster bombs to Saudi Arabia has no direct link to Saudi oil production. Lt. Gen. Ernest Graves, director of the Defense Security Assistance Agency, states that such sales are justified in the light of the threat from Iraq and the PDRY.[16]

18 December 1979: The Defense Department announces that a joint State-Defense delegation will visit Saudi Arabia, as well as Oman, Somalia, and Kenya, for exploratory talks relating to creating contingency bases for U.S. deployments in the Indian Ocean area.[17]

27 December 1979: Soviet troops enter Afghanistan.

4 January 1980: Saudi Foreign Minister Saud confers with other Arab and Islamic representatives to seek a clear-cut, united stand calling for military and moral action in reaction to the Soviet invasion of Afghanistan, insisting that such strategic manifestations are the result of U.S. weakness and inconsistent, uncertain behavior.

Administration officials say that the United States has decided to maintain a permanent naval presence in the Indian Ocean.[18]

9 January 1980: The United States announces it will enhance its military presence in the region through regular facility usage in Oman, Kenya, and Somalia.[19]

12 January 1980: The U.S. informs Britain of its intention to expand its military facilities in Diego Garcia, the only permanent U.S. facility in the Indian Ocean.[20]

23 January 1980: President Carter delivers his State of the Union address and calls for a much greater U.S. involvement in the Gulf region: "Any attempt by any outside forces to gain control of the Persian Gulf will be regarded as an assault on the vital interests of the United States. It will be repelled by any means necessary, including military force."[21]

29 January 1980: President Carter states during a press interview: "I don't think it would be accurate for me to claim that at this time or in the future we expect to have enough military strength and enough military presence there to defend the region unilaterally."[22]

February 1980: National Security Adviser Brzezinski and Deputy Secretary of State Warren Christopher visit Riyadh to discuss U.S. security policy with Crown Prince Fahd. The following points are outlined by the Americans: (1) U.S. policy rests upon the president's determination to take concrete steps toward increasing security in the region, which Brzezinski termed the third central strategic zone of importance to the United States, after Europe and the Far East; (2) the United States will remain committed to achieving a peaceful accommodation between the Arabs and the Israelis, with particular recognition of the importance of making progress on the Palestinian issue; (3) the United States will undertake to establish a military presence in the region by acquiring regular access to military facilities and upgrading its military capabilities, and it is prepared to cooperate in military exercises in order to be ready for various contingencies; (4) the United States desires to cooperate militarily with Saudi Arabia and wants to discuss in detail what is required to make such cooperation possible; and (5) the United States is interested in maintaining a viable and united Iran in which the Soviet Union would not be tempted to intervene, and once Iran has released its U.S. hostages, the United States will be willing to assist that nation with its economic and military problems.

The Saudis respond by presenting a list of desired equipment, including the F-15 enhancement equipment and the AWACS. This list is then presented for review at the interagency level.[23]

March 1980: Crown Prince Fahd urges "friendly countries" to continue to supply Arab Gulf states with weapons for self-defense, emphasizing the principle of self-reliance.

23 April 1980: The U.S. tells Saudi Arabia that the request for the E-3A presents the U.S. with significant problems but promises it will conduct an unbiased feasibility study.[24]

24 April 1980: The U.S. rescue attempt in Iran ends in failure.

27 April 1980: Despite consistent support for the U.S. in its plight with Iran, the Saudi Foreign Ministry issues a statement that the rescue attempt "went beyond accepted limits of international conduct." Crown Prince Fahd stresses that it is Saudi policy to exclude direct foreign intervention in the region.[25]

May 1980: The Saudis issue their draft Third Five Year Plan (1980–1985), emphasizing a major expansion in military equipment and continued infrastructure growth, as well as political and social reform.

17 June 1980: The State Department announces that Saudi Arabia is seeking the purchase of F-15 enhancement equipment, including conformal fuel tanks and bomb racks.[26]

26 June 1980: Defense Secretary Brown meets with Saudi Defense Minister Sultan. This results in Brown's decision to consider the request for the E-3A, since the situation demands it (despite a May 1978 letter to Congress declaring that no such equipment would be sold to the Saudi Arabians).[27]

1 July 1980: The Carter administration orders that the air feasibility study promised to the Saudis in April 1980 begin on an informal basis.[28]

Mid-July 1980: Sixty-eight senators go on record in a letter to President Carter as being opposed to the sale of the F-15-related equipment to Saudi Arabia.[29]

8 September 1980: The air feasibility study is formally initiated.[30]

22 September 1980: Long-standing and intensifying border clashes between Iraq and Iran erupt into a major war.

28 September 1980: The chairman of the Joint Chiefs of Staff, General David Jones, visits Saudi Arabia. Urgent consideration is given to U.S. deployment of AWACS aircraft.[31]

29 September 1980: President Carter briefs key Senate members on the possibility of the formation of an international task force to protect Western interests in the Gulf.[32]

30 September 1980: The Defense Department confirms that four E-3A AWACS aircraft have been deployed to the kingdom for purely defensive purposes.

5 October 1980: The Defense Department further announces that ground radar and communications equipment is being shipped to Saudi Arabia, accompanied by about 100 support personnel. An interview in the *Washington Post* with Foreign Minister Saud reflects the Saudi decision to increase oil production to alleviate losses in Iranian oil exports resulting from the Khuzestan conflict.

22 October 1980: President Carter in an interview with RKO General Broadcasting states: "We will not agree to provide offensive capabilities for the planes that might be used against Israel and that obviously includes bomb racks."[33] Crown Prince Fahd and Defense Minister Sultan formally protest, and Prince Sultan threatens to cancel the F-15 purchase.

30 October 1980: Saudi Ambassador Alhegelan releases a statement that Carter's refusal to consider the request "had come as a surprise to Saudi Arabia."[34]

4 November 1980: President Carter is defeated in the presidential elections by President Reagan.

November 1980: The waning Carter administration agrees to sell the Saudis the E-3A and offers to complete the sale before President-elect Reagan takes office. Reagan and his staff decide that once in power they will review the matter separately.[35] Secretary of State Edmund Muskie and Secretary of Defense Harold Brown describe the climate of U.S. planning at this time as follows:

> Some time after the November election, the Carter administration, which had been considering the Saudi request, arrived at a tentative conclusion on how to handle the various elements of that request. . . . Among the various requests, we were favorably disposed toward an early and positive decision on sale to Saudi Arabia of conformal fuel tanks and of AIM-9L air-to-air missiles. (These latter are an updated version of the *Sidewinder* missiles already in the Saudi inventory, and had not been the subject of

an exchange between us and the Saudi in 1978.) We were also favorably disposed toward an eventual future sale of AWACS.

. . . Our conclusions were based on the changed situation in the Gulf since 1978, on U.S. military estimates of Saudi needs, on possible implications with respect to the military security of Israel, and on our judgment of U.S. security interests.

. . . A member of the Reagan Transition Team authorized to speak for the President-Elect was asked whether the new administration would care to make a joint representation with us to the Saudis on this matter. The answer given was that they did not wish to do so. Under those circumstances the Carter Administration concluded that it could make no firm decision, either affirmative or negative, on any of the items requested. We told the Saudis that we would convey our conclusions to the new administration when the new senior officials had been named and would, with the agreement of those officials, begin consultations with the leadership of the new Congress.

. . . Subsequent to the designation of a new Secretary of State and Secretary of Defense, further discussions were held by the two of us with those designees. The incoming administration then concluded that it wanted to review the situation itself, and take a decision in consultations with Congress after taking office on January 10.

. . . The Carter Administration thereupon informed the Saudis that we had indicated our views to the new administration, that they wanted to take an independent look at the problem, and that the Saudis would be hearing from the new administration thereafter.[36]

15 December 1980: The air feasibility study requested by the Saudis is completed.[37]

20 January 1981: The Reagan administration is inaugurated. The U.S. prisoners in Iran are freed. Crown Prince Fahd expresses his hope that the new administration will be better able to bring about positive changes in the Middle East situation.[38]

10 February 1981: In an interview with ABC, Saudi Information Minister Muhammid Abd al-Yamani cites the Camp David accords' inability to bring about a just and comprehensive peace in the region and calls for the rights of Palestinians to be taken into consideration and for the Palestinians to be allowed to participate in negotiations. He reiterates the Saudi decision to have no foreign bases on Saudi soil and the Saudi need for the requested U.S. air defense equipment.[39]

Late February 1981: Colonel Fahd Abdullah, the Saudi prince in charge of air operations, and Major General Charles L. Donnelly, Jr., the chief of the U.S. Military Training Mission in Saudi Arabia, discuss the broad implications of the combined impact of the Peace Hawk VII program and the Saudi Air Defense Enhancement Package. These discussions are followed by detailed discussions in the U.S. that resolve the problems inherent in preserving Saudi sovereignty and U.S. control over Saudi use of the AWACS, and they lead to informal understandings regarding Saudi willingness to provide a contingency capability to base U.S. over-the-horizon reinforcements.[40]

23 February 1981: State Department spokesman William Dyes states that the new administration has reversed U.S. priorities in the Middle East. The chief priority will be that of bolstering the deteriorating position of the West vis-à-vis the Soviet Union in the area, rather than pressing for a resolution of Egyptian-Israeli negotiations on Palestinian autonomy.

26 February 1981: The administration briefs the Senate Foreign Relations Committee on the basic outline of its decision to sell a new arms package to Saudi Arabia: AIM-9L missiles, conformal fuel tanks, and an airborne radar surveillance capability (AWACS).[41]

6 March 1981: The State Department announces that the Reagan administration will soon give notice to Congress of its intention to sell the missiles and the fuel tanks to Saudi Arabia.[42] The Saudis receive the air feasibility study requested in 1980.[43]

24 March 1981: Twenty U.S. senators declare their opposition to such a sale. Congressional opposition begins to mount.

4 April 1981: Secretary of State Alexander Haig begins his tour of Egypt, Israel, Jordan, and Saudi Arabia to persuade U.S. allies in the region to cooperate on the basis of opposition to the Soviets.

21 April 1981: The White House announces its decision to sell Saudi Arabia five E-3A AWACS aircraft in an Air Defense Enhancement Package that includes KC-135 tankers, AIM-9L air-to-air missiles, and F-15 conformal fuel tanks. It states that the sale is a continuation of the U.S. commitment to Saudi Arabia and that the sale is essential to protect U.S. interests in the region due to the deterioration of the security of the West in the region.[44]

This chronology documents a major shift in U.S. strategy toward the Gulf and a new approach toward U.S. military relations with Saudi Arabia. It is also clear that the Reagan administration's endorsement of the AWACS package had at least five major effects. First, it transformed the AWACS package into a tool for putting Saudi-U.S. military relations on a solid long-term basis. Second, it provided a potential keystone for Saudi force planning that could link Saudi Arabia's military forces to the West's and help the U.S. defend its oil supplies. Third, it endorsed a substitute for a U.S. base or military presence in Saudi Arabia that met Saudi political needs, but offered both nations many of the same military advantages. Fourth, it provided the groundwork for the first serious effort to directly defend the key oil fields in the southern Gulf and to give Saudi Arabia "360-degree" protection against the threats building up on its borders. And fifth, it inevitably made sale of the AWACS package *the* test of whether the U.S. would provide balanced military support to both Israel and Saudi Arabia.

The Peace Hawk VII Program

In order to understand the military logic behind this shift in U.S. policy, and the implications of the Reagan administration's decision, it is necessary to understand that both the U.S. and Saudi Arabia were responding to a series of studies by the U.S. Department of Defense and its contractors on how Saudi Arabia could best improve its air defense and protect its oil fields and urban centers.[45] Although these studies received little publicity during the congressional debate over the AWACS sale, they established a "logic of arms" that shaped many of the events in the previous chronology.

Even before the shah's fall, Saudi Arabia had asked the United States to consider how to upgrade the Saudi air defense system. As a result, the U.S. restructured its regular annual study of Saudi air defense requirements under the Peace Hawk program to examine how to carry out this task and then broadened it even further to deal with the military implications of the shah's fall. The USAF then produced a comprehensive four-volume survey of Saudi requirements for improved ground-based command, control, and communications (C^3) facilities that became known as "Peace Hawk VII." This study is classified, but it is clear that it made several important recommendations:[46]

- It recommended that Saudi Arabia establish a comprehensive C^3 system to integrate or net its ground-based sensor net, its ground-based air defenses, its fighter bases and fighters, and its various command systems into a system that was in many ways equivalent in sophistication to that of the NADGE system in NATO or the NORAD system in the U.S.
- It recommended that five sectoral operating centers be established in each of Saudi Arabia's five critical peripheral defense areas. These included the Eastern Province and the oil area around Dhahran, the western border area near Tabuk, the Iraqi border area near Hafr al-Batin, and the southern coastal area near Jiddah. These hardened command centers were to become highly sophisticated centers using digital secure communications and highly redundant radio nets with satellite backup.
- It recommended that a general operating center or central command center was to be established near Riyadh. This was to serve as the major command center for central control of both air war and the armed forces.

Although the Peace Hawk VII study did not address the need for airborne radar platforms, or U.S. capability to provide over-the-horizon reinforcements, it is clear that the study's analysis of the weaknesses in the Saudi radar system helped shape the initial Saudi requests for the AWACS.[47] Peace Hawk VII inevitably raised the issue of how Saudi Arabia could make the U.S.-recommended C^3 system work without an airborne sensor platform. As a result, the ensuing Saudi-U.S. discussions of the study had the same practical impact as if the U.S. had recommended that Saudi Arabia buy an AWACS. Further, the scale of the recommended system raised the issue of the size and nature of U.S. reinforcements to Saudi Arabia and led to discussions that resulted in the agreement that the Saudi system should be structured to allow U.S. reinforcement by roughly one wing of 70 U.S. fighters per base.

It is also important to note that the Peace Hawk VII study was written and discussed in a context in which previous U.S. plans had led Saudi Arabia to make massive purchases of air munitions and aircraft parts and support equipment. These "overbuys" had the virtue of providing any U.S. air reinforcements with prepositioned air munitions. Similar discussions had also led the Saudis to buy enough equipment for each Saudi F-15 base (which were to have only 20 Saudi F-15C/D aircraft each) to perform maintenance at peak loads for up to an entire fighter wing.

Thus, without ever reaching any explicit or written agreement, the U.S. and Saudi Arabia began to work out an over-the-horizon reinforcement arrangement that avoided the problem of establishing U.S. forces or contingency bases on Saudi soil. While Saudi Arabia and the U.S. deliberately kept the profile of these efforts as low as possible, during 1980–1981 Saudi Arabia committed itself to well over $5 billion in incremental expenditures to develop a U.S. reinforcement capability before the AWACS and the rest of the Saudi Air Defense Enhancement Package became a public issue.

Saudi-U.S. cooperation resulting from the Peace Hawk VII study also makes it moot whether the Saudis requested the AWACS first or the U.S. offered it first. The study created a logic behind the Saudi modernization effort that made an AWACS necessary. Further, the USAF knew it could not maintain an E-3A force in Saudi Arabia into the mid-1980s with the limited number of AWACS funded for U.S. forces. As programmed advances took place in NORAD, NATO, and U.S. forces in the Pacific, the U.S. would be forced to buy substantial additional numbers of E-3As. Accordingly, some arrangement had to be made under which Saudi Arabia would either lease or buy its AWACS, and the politics of the region ensured that Saudi Arabia would have to seek arrangements that meant eventual transition to Saudi command.

The Saudi Need for the AWACS Package

The momentum built up by the Peace Hawk VII study was greatly reinforced by the Iran-Iraq War. In December 1980 Iran retaliated against an Iraqi invasion by striking against Iraqi oil facilities, launching the first "oil war" between producing nations. More important, it demonstrated that a few sea and air strikes could destroy all of Iraq's oil-loading facilities in the Gulf and halt 3.2 MMBD of oil exports to the West. It provided tangible proof that the AWACS package was a response to legitimate requirements to enhance Saudi Arabia's air defense and protect the West's supplies of imported oil. It suddenly transformed the climate of U.S. and Saudi planning from considering theoretical scenarios to dealing with tangible realities.

This situation gave the USAF air feasibility study a special impetus. As described in the chronology earlier in this chapter, the U.S. agreed in April 1980 to provide this study, and it was formally initiated on 8 September. It was completed on 15 December 1980, after the Iran-Iraq War had begun, and was then held back for formal release to the Saudis until the new administration had completed its policy review. By the time the study was formally given to the Saudis on 6 March 1981, the Saudis had been fully aware of its contents for nearly four months, and both the Saudis and the USAF had already used it to plan a more comprehensive approach to Saudi air defense.

The Saudi "Strategic Axis"

The broad rationale behind the need to improve Saudi Arabia's air defense has been discussed in previous chapters, but in order to understand the results of the Peace Hawk VII and the air feasibility study, it is necessary to understand this rationale in more detail.[48] In strategic terms, Saudi Arabia must depend upon air power as its first line of defense. It is a nation of 873,000 square miles, or roughly the size of the U.S. east of the Mississippi, but it has a small population and very limited supplies of trained military manpower. Saudi Arabia can only defend its key economic facilities, cities, and ports by air. It faces potential threats on all its borders and must be able to rapidly change the deployment of its air power to mass it across long distances and from a relatively limited number of bases. In tactical terms, Saudi Arabia must be able to maintain a perimeter defense against the Yemens, Iraq, Jordan, Syria, and Israel, while concentrating its forces on defending the "strategic axis" that extends south from the Saudi oil facilities and cities on the Gulf (Jubail, Juaymah, Ras Tanura, and Dammam) through the capital at Riyadh and the holy city of Makkah to Taif, the key coastal port of Jiddah, the holy city of Medina, and the new petro-city and port at Yanbu.

The Oil Field or Core Area

The most vulnerable area in the strategic axis is Saudi Arabia's main oil facilities on the Gulf, or "core area." Its defense dominates both U.S. and Saudi planning, and it serves as an excellent case study of the air defense problems Saudi Arabia must deal with by the mid-1980s.

The total oil area covers 85,000 square miles, but Saudi oil facilities are concentrated largely in the 300-by-100-mile core area shown in Map 8.2. Although Saudi Arabia had some 47 oil fields, its core area ranges along a 250-mile axis that extends from the offshore field at Safaniya (the world's largest offshore field) to Ras Tanura and Berri on the coast to the southern tip of the Ghawar oil field (the world's largest onshore field). If various peripheral territories are included, the core area covers 10,000 square miles, or twice the area of the state of Connecticut.

MAP 8—1
MAJOR SAUDI MILITARY INSTALLATIONS

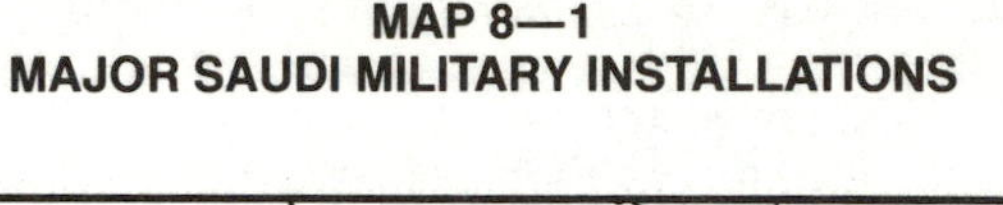

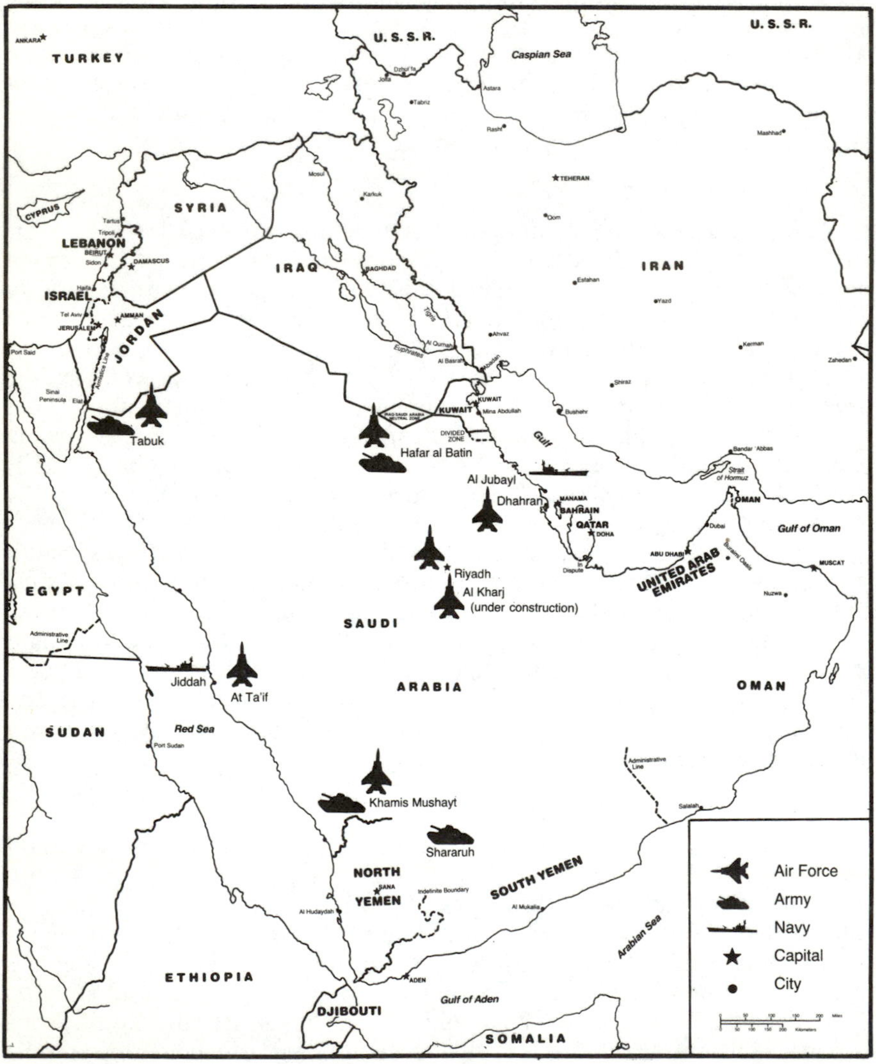

Adapted from a map prepared by the Congressional Research Service.

MAP 8—2
THE SAUDI CORE AREA

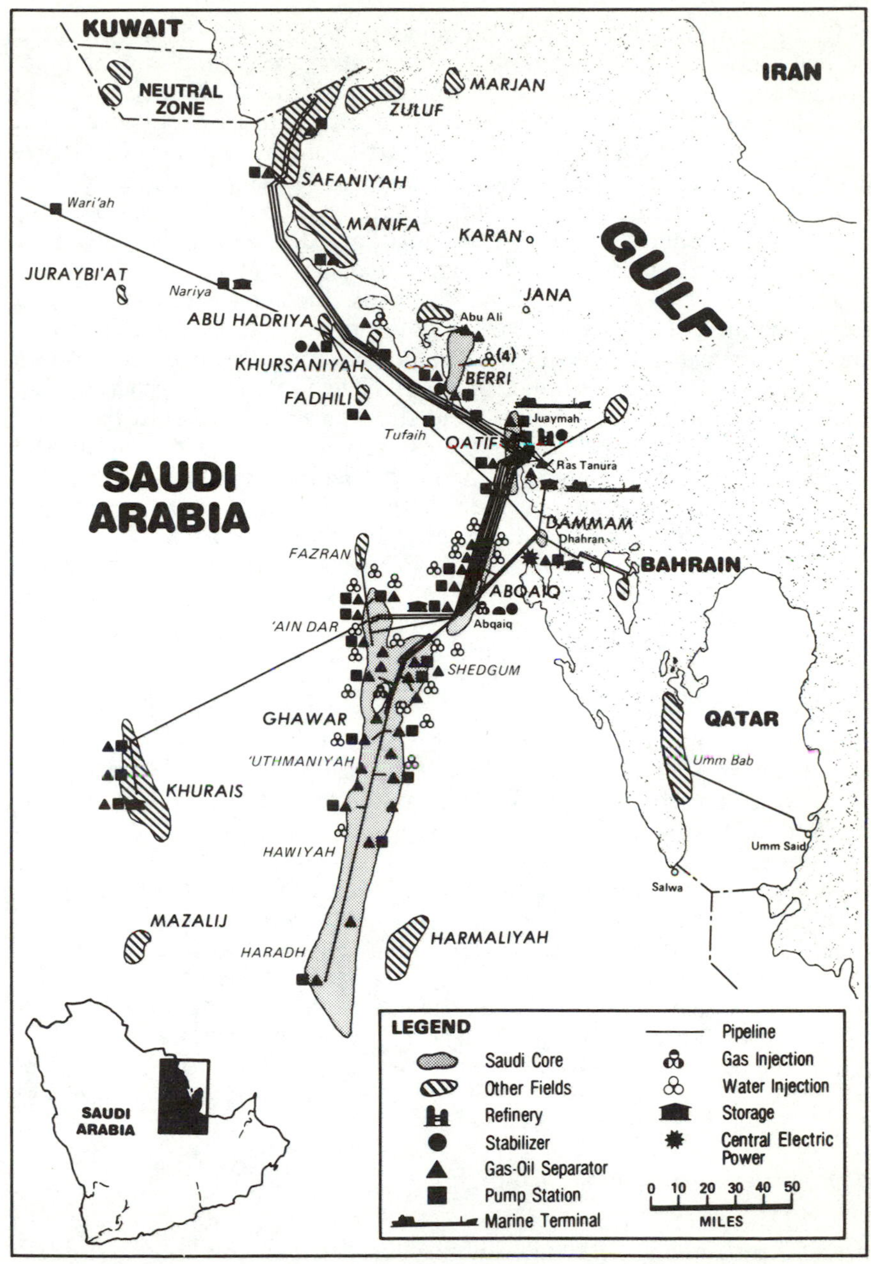

SOURCE: Adapted from Congressional Research Service, *Oil Fields as Military Objectives* (Washington, D.C., 21 August, 1975), p. 52. Does not show new fields at Dawl, Salsal, Juban, Nita, Jawb, Dhib, Faridah, Samin, Hamur, and Duhaynah, or the fields such as Shaybah, Ramlah Suhul, and the Kidans in the empty quarter. Virtually all Master Gas Distribution facilities, such as the new port at Ju'aymah, were built later.

Terrain Factors Affecting the Defense of the Core Area

Aside from the offshore portion, almost all of the core area is located on dry exposed plains with no natural cover or protection. During most of the year, key targets are easy to locate by air, and there are long periods during the day when such Saudi oil facilities produce enough image contrast for even first-generation air-to-surface missiles like Maverick to be effective. Many such facilities are also vulnerable to area bombing or to heliborne raids, and a number of key facilities are vulnerable even to light, shoulder-fired antitank rockets like the RPG-9 or to light antitank guided missiles like Milan or Dragon.[49]

Except for terrorist or commando raids, the terrain favors air and sea operations. The coastal area is covered by shallow sand flats and small hummocks that severely limit rapid movement by armored vehicles except along a limited number of roads. The shoreline is generally too shallow for amphibious landings, and the waterfront can shift back and forth by several miles in some places, depending upon the wind and the tide.[50] Salt flats are common and can become impassable with even limited rain. Coastal marshes often merge with the sea and create major trafficability problems. The dunes near the coast then transit into the Jafura sand desert. This desert becomes a mix of buttes, mesas, tablelands, and gullies at the Ghawar field, which is 150 miles long and 25 miles wide at maximum width. While the coastal area is relatively populated, there are no population centers in most of the oil fields except for small towns run by ARAMCO, and there is no local water. Temperatures can exceed 120° F in the summer. All of these factors limit the ability to rapidly seize the Saudi oil fields. In contrast, a successful occupation of all the key oil facilities within 40 miles of the Saudi coast, or a target raid on Abqaiq, Ras Tanura, or its sea islands, would provide control over most of Saudi Arabia's oil-loading and/or processing capabilities.

Weather conditions further complicate the problem of defending the core area. In the summer, prevailing northwest winds, called "*shamal*," create summer sandstorms. Line squalls are common, and visibility at the ocean surface can drop to zero. Thermal currents create a ducting phenomenon that can "blind" or obscure most radars. By taking advantage of these weather conditions, an airborne or seaborne attacker could hit Saudi oil facilities at a time when defenders on the ground would be virtually "blind" and have difficulty operating surface-based sensors and missile defenses.

The Distribution of Critical Targets

Critical targets for air or sea attack are scattered throughout the core area. The nature of these facilities is illustrated in Tables 8.1 and 8.2; each has different vulnerability characteristics.[51]

Most of the 646 onshore wells that Saudi Arabia was producing at the end of 1981 were free-flowing and required water injection to

TABLE 8.1 Key Oil Facilities in the Saudi Core Area at the End of 1976

Oilfield Facilities

	Abqaiq	Offshore	Onshore	Dammam	Ghawar	Qatif	Total
Producing wells	64	60	5	18	378	19	544
Shut-in wells	2	?	?	0	70	4	76
Producing well-platforms	0	15	0	0	0	0	15
GOSP stations[a]	4	1	1	1	24	3	34
Stabilizer plants	0	0	1	0	0	0	1
Gas injection plants	1	0	0	0	1	0	2
Water injection plants	6	7		0	16	0	29
Injection wells	54	15	5	0	151	0	225
Injection platforms	0	7	0	0	0	0	7
Supply wells	6	18		0	75	0	99
Pumping stations	2	3	0	0	9	2	16

Overall Oil Production Facilities

	In All Fields	At Junctions	At Terminals	Total
Producing wells	678	–	–	678
Shut-in wells	76	–	–	76
Producing well-platforms	15	–	–	15
GOSP stations[a]	34	1	1	36
Stabilizer plants	1	2	1	4
Gas injection plants	2	–	–	2
Water injection plants	29	–	–	29
Injection wells	225	–	–	225
Injection platforms	7	–	–	7
Supply wells	99	–	–	99
Pipeline miles[b]	–	–	–	972
Pumping stations	16	7	2	25
Tank farms	–	2	2	4
Refinery	–	–	1	1
Ship berths	–	–	21	21
Major power plants	–	2	1	3

Note: Many facilities are one-of-a-kind, and replacements would require special production. Some fields are being expanded. Figures above are thus minimums.

[a] GOSPs are gas-oil and desalting separators. Some stations have multiple units.

[b] It is not feasible to subdivide pipelines according to the categories above.

Sources: Data provided by ARAMCO and the Congressional Research Service.

maintain pressurization. While the individual wells are scattered targets, destruction of key high-output wells would have a considerable effect on Saudi oil production, as would destruction of key components of the water-injection system. Similarly, much of the Berri field is under water and feeds into 11 offshore platforms that regulate four to six wells each. In addition, eight more platforms maintain the water-well and

TABLE 8.2 Key Choke Points and Vulnerabilities in the Saudi Oil Distribution System, 1976

Pipeline Junctions	Number	Facilities
Alin Dar	4	Pumping stations, electric powered
Abqaiq	1	GOSP stations with 9 units on main line
	1	Stabilizer plant
	1	Pumping station (9 subordinate units)
	1	Tank farm
	1	Gas turbine–electric power plant
Qatif	1	Pumping station, electric powered
Dhahran	1	Pumping station, electric powered
(ARAMCO headquarters)	1	Tank farm
	1	Electric power plant
	1	Central power dispatch station
	1	Stabilizer plant
	1	Machine shop
Terminals	**Number**	**Notes**
Juaymah		
Onshore		
Storage tanks	9	Capacity 1,250,000 bbl each; 5 more under construction
Pumping station	1	8 electric booster pumps; 8 shipping pumps
Pipeline	2	Shore to anchoring platform 7 mi, 56 in diameter
	9	Metering platform to 3 single buoy moorings (SBM), 3 lines each, 42/48 in diameter
Offshore		
Central platform	1	Remote control for metering valves.
Metering platform	1	10 meters capacity 42,000 bbl/hr, direct crude oil in tankers at SMBs
Single buoy moorings	3	Located 8,000–11,000 ft from metering platform in water 95 ft deep. Each can handle 500,000 DWT tankers, 3,000,000 BPD total capacity
Ras Tanura		
Crude oil processing		
Refinery	1	Capacity 450,000 BPD
GOSP station	1	
Stabilizer plant	1	
Distribution		
Storage tanks	60	Crude and refined capacity about 28,000,000 bbl
Pipeline	5	From complex to loading piers, 6 mi, 20/42 in diameter
	4	From piers to sea island, 2 mi, 30/36 in diameter
	1	Juaymah to the Tamara shuttle, 15 mi, 20/22 in diameter
Pumping stations	1	
Loading points		
Onshore berths	10	North Pier 6 berths, 3,000,000 BPD capacity; South Pier, 4 berths, 1,000,000 BPD. Handles standard tankers
Offshore berths	8	Sea island, 1,400-ft platform 1 mi east on North Pier. 5 tankers up to 200,000 DWT; 3 more 400,000 + DWT
Miscellaneous		
Power Generating Plant	1	

Source: Congressional Research Service, ***Oil Fields as Military Objectives,*** No. S6-S520 (Washington, D.C.: Government Printing Office, 1975).

-injection system. These are connected by 25 miles of undersea pipeline ranging from 10 to 24 inches. Much of this piping is vulnerable to sabotage by ordinary scuba divers. Each of these platforms is an attractive target, and carefully planned strikes against a few of them could halt production from the entire Berri field.

An attack on Saudi Arabia's 12 offshore drilling and workover rigs could also affect Saudi production, but only in the very long run. So could an attack on the small island of Abu Ali, which is 20 miles off the Saudi coast, and where several main well and water-injection facilities are centralized, in addition to those for gas-oil separation.

The Saudi Oil and Gas Collection System

The Saudi oil and gas collection system is equally vulnerable to air attack. Crude petroleum from all the Saudi fields and a considerable amount of gas converge on Ras Tanura through well over 1,200 miles of pipe. Pipe diameters fluctuate between 12 and 48 inches, and many increase dramatically in size as lines pass gathering points. The overall security problems in protecting such facilities are less difficult, however, than the total pipeline mileage indicates. The length of the major pipelines in the kingdom exceeds 6,160 miles, and many redundant or backup links exist. Large pipes are difficult to destroy and small ones are easy to repair or replace. More than eight pipes share the same route from Abqaiq to the Qatif junction, five continue to the coast, and four pipes parallel the seaboard south of Khursaniyah. This redundancy makes them resistant to air attack and sabotage.

Still, there are many vulnerable choke points.[52] Saudi production depends on up to 12.5 MMBD of processed, nonpotable saline water. A single plant, the Quarayyah Seawater Plant, processes more than 4.2 MMBD of filtered and conditioned sea water. This is a highly vulnerable "one-of-a-kind" facility that could take up to two years to replace.

The Saudi power plants that service the fields are extremely large, and the loss of key plants could shut down large parts of the Saudi operations. Destruction of the 400-plus-MW facility at Ras Tanura might severely limit shipments from the port, and knocking out the 230-KV transmission line from Safaniya to Khurais could halt all southern field operations. The power available in the Eastern Province increased from 1,200 MW in 1976 to 2,928 MW in 1981, and four new 400-MW plants are being built at Ghazlan, but there will still be a limited number of high-payoff targets.[53] The evolving Saudi power system is also highly dependent on a single central computer facility located in Dammam. A successful attack on this facility might paralyze key aspects of Saudi production for months.

The Saudi oil pipeline system depends on 26 pumping stations, spotted anywhere from 5 to 50 miles apart. One new pumping station at Abqaiq alone processes 1.7 MMBD. One natural gas generator activates three pumping stations with three pumps each east of Abqaiq, and all nine pumps would be inoperative if the turbine failed. Other sensitive facilities are even more critical, and a loss of power to these facilities, or their sabotage, would virtually halt Saudi oil production. Thus, Abqaiq is Saudi Arabia's most critical single target area, although the coastal facilities are much more vulnerable.

Further, the three power plants that provide electrical current for 25 gas-oil separators (GOSPs), desalting facilities, pumps, and other purposes are controlled from a single dispatch center at Dhahran. If this center were destroyed, the ability to distribute power in the Eastern Province would be severely limited. A wide range of other computer centers controlling key oil facilities are equally vulnerable, and their destruction or seizure could have serious effects. Ain Dar is also the gathering place for all petroleum produced in northern Ghawar, plus Khurais on the west flank. Lines from Ain Dar and Haradh (in southern Ghawar) funnel into Abqaiq. Even more critical junctions lie farther east at Dhahran, Qatif, and Ras Tanura, and each of these centers has special vulnerabilities.

A new major target complex is being created at Shedgum at the north end of the Ghawar field, the center of the new transpeninsular gas and oil pipelines. This center has a new gas plant processing 1.5 BCFD, and a twin plant will be completed at Uthmaniyah by 1983. Each of the four gas modules at Shedgum is a target that processes 375 MFCD, and 237 kilometers of vulnerable high-pressure gas piping feeds the facility. The combination of gas, oil, and pipeline facilities—many, again, one-of-a-kind, with long replacement lead times—will eventually make Shedgum a target almost as attractive as Ras Tanura or Juaymah.

The new petro-city at Jubail, at the southern end of the Berri field, will also be a target after 1983. Jubail combines a new coastal population center with plants using gas fuel and feedstock. It will process over 270,000 barrels per day (BPD) in gas products, as will Janbu on the Red Sea. Jubail and Janbu will not be as attractive as the previous targets, but they will still require Saudi Arabia to extend its air defense perimeter.

Terminals and Port Facilities

The Saudi oil terminals shown in Map 8.3 are also vulnerable.[54] The main terminal facilities that serve all Saudi oil fields occupy a 50-mile arc along Tarut Bay between Ras Tanura and Al Khobar. They shipped 89% of total Saudi production in 1981, with 4.3% going to the Ras Tanura refinery and 84.2% going to the crude oil export terminals. Much of this crude was "sour" and had to be processed on-site or in facilities outside the United States. The Ras Tanura refinery and loading facility plays a critical role in ensuring the smooth flow of Saudi oil production. The refinery has a capacity of 450,000 BPD and processed 416,421 BPD of oil and 254,300 BPD of NGL in 1981. Equally critical are the stabilization plants on adjoining land, particularly those at

MAP 8—3
CRITICAL LOADING AND TERMINAL FACILITIES IN THE SAUDI CORE AREA

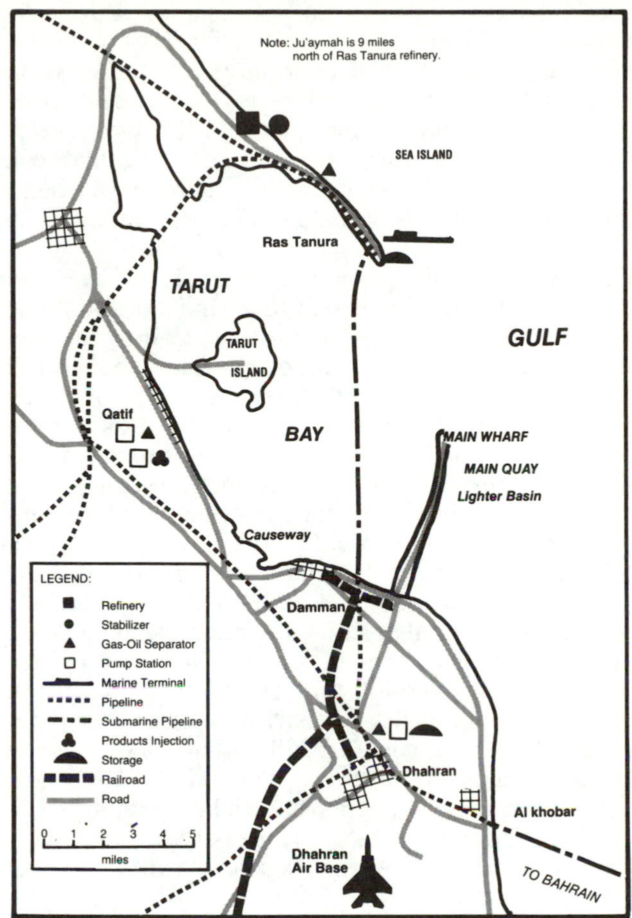

Adapted from map provided by Congressional Research Service.

Abqaiq, which remove poisonous and corrosive hydrogen sulfide from crude petroleum before it is piped aboard tankers. Crude oil and refined products awaiting shipment are stored in four great tank farms at Abqaiq, Dhahran, Ras Tanura, and the new port complex at Juaymah. The latter location includes 5 containers holding 1.5 million barrels each and 14 containers, each 72 feet high and 352 feet in diameter, that hold 1.25 million barrels each. Including pipelines and smaller storage facilities, the location stores up to 30 million barrels. The major storage facilities are extremely vulnerable to air or other attack.

Saudi port and loading facilities are attractive targets. Ras Tanura is the world's foremost oil port. It can berth 18 tankers. Its T-shaped northern loading pier can berth 6 tankers simultaneously, and its south pier can handle 4 more. An artificial "sea island," a mile farther out, can accommodate five supertankers up to 200,000 tons deadweight, as well as three more twice that size or larger. Because its new liquid propane gas (LPG) facilities have "layered" tanks and pipelines over the existing crude oil facilities and placed LPG tanks near new 1.5-MMBD oil storage tanks, there is an acute risk that conventional attacks—even by small craft—could cause a massive chain reaction. Ras Tanura's loading facility is probably the most attractive conventional target in the world.

ARAMCO also off-loads Arabian light crude oil at Juaymah, and Juaymah's capacity is steadily expanding. In addition to a new 10-kilometer offshore trestle and LPG twin-berth loading facility, Juaymah has single-point moorings (SPM) in deep water about 11 kilometers offshore. These can handle 500,000 deadweight ton (dwt) tankers with 95-foot drafts (currently the world's largest). The Ras Tanura terminal is limited to 65-foot drafts. Juaymah can simultaneously provide several grades of oil to six vessels. A pair of 56-inch pipes now connects the oil storage tanks on shore with a giant metering platform in 45 feet of water. This platform already can shunt oil to waiting ships at rates of over 140,000 barrels an hour. Juaymah started loading LPG in 1980 and shipped 92,313 BPD and 33.8 million barrels annually. Its two 30,000-barrel-per-hour loading facilities can handle 200,000-cubic-meter tankers. Like those at Ras Tanura, the key facilities at Juaymah are extremely dense, highly exposed, and could "chain react" under conventional attack. The throughput capacity at these two ports serviced 4,067 tankers in 1981 and loaded 3.2 billion barrels of crude oil product and natural gas liquids. Total capacity is 12 MMBD, and there is considerable redundancy of systems to handle Saudi production levels of 8.5–10 MMBD. Both terminals, the Sea Island, and the SPMs are extremely vulnerable to well-planned air or sea missile attacks.

Sabotage, Pressurization, and Blackmail

Sabotage, commando raids, and subversion can pose equally serious problems. Key facilities like the loading and refinery complex at Ras Tanura do have computer-card-entry security, special National Guard security forces, or support from units of the Coast Guard, other branches of the security forces, and the Ministry of the Interior. The work force, however, is mixed. It consists of 33,000 Saudis, 5,300 Americans, 6,000 Filipinos, 4,000 British, 2,000 people from Arab League countries, and 6,500 from the Indian subcontinent.

Unfortunately, however, even one or two men could introduce enough explosives to cripple a key facility, and there is poor badge and zone security and only minimal search activity. The facilities locate key targets within easy line of sight of small craft, helicopter fire, or the shore, and security guards have only light weapons, no physical barriers capable of stopping a heavy truck, and no protection against frogmen. They also have limited mobility and poorly protected and armed vehicles, and the 4,000-man National Guard force is of indifferent quality. One demolition charge, an RPG-9, Dragon, Milan, or heavier man-portable missile might be able to knock out a major part of such a facility from unguarded areas.

These Saudi defense problems are compounded by several other factors. Many of the facilities in the Saudi core area are pressurized systems. Unless Saudi Arabia can protect such systems with some confidence, it must respond to any major threat of attack by shutting in or depressurizing a wide range of facilities. Saudi Arabia also cannot produce more oil or gas than any given choke point allows, and most of these choke points depend on a few items of tightly grouped and specially fabricated equipment that were designed for maximum economy of scale and were located without any regard to vulnerability to military weapons. There is little or no redundancy or in-country repair capability for such equipment, and most such key items are not readily available on the world market. They must be specially fabricated to order, which can take up to two years.

Dependence on the Gulf and Alternatives to the Gulf Route

Saudi Arabia is dependent on the free movement of tankers to ship its oil. Virtually all of these tankers now move in and out of the Gulf through its narrow eastern opening at the Strait of Hormuz. Approximately 60 to 80 ships move through the strait each day.[55] About 30 to 50 of these ships are loaded outbound tankers. In 1981 an average of 11 tankers, carrying 8.9 MMBD of gas, oil, and petroleum products, came from Saudi Arabia. Another 0.2 MMBD, or 2.2% of total Saudi production, was shipped from the refinery at Bahrain.[56]

Saudi Arabia now has only two alternatives to the Gulf route.[57] The first is the "Tapline" pipeline, with 470,000 BPD capacity, that runs from Dhahran and Qaisumah through Jordan, Syria, and Lebanon to a port and 17,500-BPD refinery south of Sidon. This pipeline was built in 1950, and it requires exceptionally large amounts of manpower and service by modern standards. It is not economic in comparison with shipment through the Gulf by very large cargo carrier (VLCC), and it has been made even less economic through the lack of modernization and service that has resulted from the long series of disputes over transit fees. The pipeline's operation has been highly erratic. It intermittently shipped about 50,000–60,000 BPD from 1979 to 1982, a total of 20–29 million barrels, or 0.62–0.83% of Saudi crude production. Roughly 36,000 BPD has gone to support a refinery in Jordan, the rest to support the refinery in Sidon. There have been no exports to the

West. The link to Lebanon was cut during the fighting in 1981 and by the Israeli invasion in 1982. While the line could be quickly restored to 470,000 BPD, major investment would be needed to repair port facilities, improve efficiency, and to improve security against sabotage.

The second alternative is a pair of 1,170-kilometer pipelines from Shedgum in eastern Saudi Arabia to the new petro-city at Yanbu on the Red Sea. The "Petroline" has 1.85 MMBD capacity, and the 26–30 inch gas line has an initial capacity of 270,000 BPD of gas liquids. The oil line has a theoretical capacity of 2.35 MMBD. It moved 0.5 MMBD, or roughly 5.3% of Saudi production, in 1981. There is a slight possibility that another parallel line may be built to create a capacity of 3.6–4 MMBD. The capacity of the gas line can be raised to 405,000 BPD. Even then, however, Saudi Arabia would be heavily dependent on the free movement of tankers through the Gulf and on its ability to persuade tanker owners and captains that they can safely move through Gulf waters. The new pipelines will also make it dependent on convincing such owners and captains that they can safely move through the Red Sea.[58]

Each expansion in Saudi oil facilities tends to increase Saudi Arabia's air defense problems as well as reduce the vulnerability of a given sector. While the expansion of the new petro-cities at Jubail and Yanbu will reduce the concentration of Saudi oil facilities, and Yanbu may be able to ship up to 5 MMBD of oil, gas, and petroleum products[59] from the Red Sea coast by 1990, these facilities will require new air defense coverage and increase Saudi Arabia's defense problems. A review of the plans for Yanbu indicates that, unlike Jubail, it will have large numbers of one-of-a-kind oil storage and loading targets, so that a single air strike could paralyze a plant costing several hundred million dollars for up to two years. The new pipelines and pumping stations along the route to Yanbu will open up new opportunities for sabotage and long-range air strikes that bypass Saudi Arabia's radar system along the Gulf. Further, the new complex at Yanbu will force the small Saudi Air Force to defend two coastal areas more than 1,000 miles apart.

Long-Term Options to Reduce Saudi Vulnerability

Saudi Arabia is studying several long-term measures to reduce the vulnerability of its oil facilities. One of these options included the creation of a possible "Red Sea structure," or strategic petroleum reserve, with a capacity of up to 1.5 billion barrels (six months' capacity at Saudi Arabia's official production level of 8.5 MMBD) in the Hejaz mountains some 24 miles from Yanbu. The plans for such a reserve were developed by Riofines, a subsidiary of Rio Tinto Zinc, and were costed at about $2 billion. They included a series of parallel tunnels excavated in the rock.[60] Such a facility could reduce the impact of any attack on the oil facilities in the Eastern Province, as well as Saudi Arabia's vulnerability to political pressure or military threats. The recent "oil glut" has led Saudi Arabia to leave this plan in the study stage, and this is probably just as well. The reserve would almost certainly cost over $12 billion, rather than $2 billion, given U.S. estimates of the cost of similar types of strategic reserves. If started in 1984, it could store only 50 million barrels by 1988 at a rate of only 2.35 MMBD. Its use would still depend on uninhibited Saudi use of Yanbu and the Red Sea. This option seems increasingly unlikely given its cost and limited value.

Other long-term options to reduce Saudi vulnerability include a 50-million-barrel "operational reserve" near Yanbu, which would guard against minor sabotage or easily repairable attack damage, and a possible strategic pipeline from the junctions south of Ras Tanura through the UAE to an export terminal in Oman near Muscat or Masirah Island. Japan strongly urged in 1981 that such a pipeline be built in order to eliminate the vulnerability of its oil shipments to any cutoff of oil flows through the Gulf or Red Sea, and it formed a consortium called the Gulf Pipeline Development Council (GPDC). Such a line would have at least 2-MMBD capacity, run some 1,500 kilometers, and cost at least $2 billion. It would, of course, be valuable only if Saudi Arabia could continue to protect its capability to ship oil through the line. Petromin has also considered building a 250,000-BPD refinery and an improved deep-water port at Rabigh (between Yanbu and Jiddah). This port-refinery complex would draw on the Petroline for crude and would not significantly affect Saudi Arabia's vulnerability.

Finally, Iraq has studied the building of strategic pipelines to Aqaba in Jordan and/or to a new port northwest of Yanbu. Such lines would either bypass Kuwait or be tied into its facilities and would allow the shipment of 1–2 MMB. These plans remain in the conceptual stage, and Iraqi officials discussed them as "uncertain possibilities" in January 1983. They did indicate, however, that Iraq is seeking to create a secure export capability that could sustain its economy even if its lines through Syria and Turkey and its Gulf loading facilities were damaged. They also indicate that if strategic pipelines were not built, Iraq might seek to create a new port in Kuwait or on the Saudi Gulf coast to reduce its vulnerability to Iranian attack.

It seems likely that some combination of these steps will be taken regardless of the outcome of the Iran-Iraq War and the world recession. They are unlikely to be completed before 1990, however, and they would force the Saudi Air Force and Navy to cover a wider area.

Saudi Civilian and Urban Vulnerabilities

The problem of Saudi vulnerability extends beyond oil facilities. Saudi Arabia's modernization is making most Saudi cities acutely dependent on a limited number of water, desalinization, gas, and electric power facilities and on the use of a limited number of airports for food supplies. As is the case with the Saudi oil fields, past economies of

MAP 8—4
MAJOR OIL FIELDS AND FACILITIES IN THE GULF

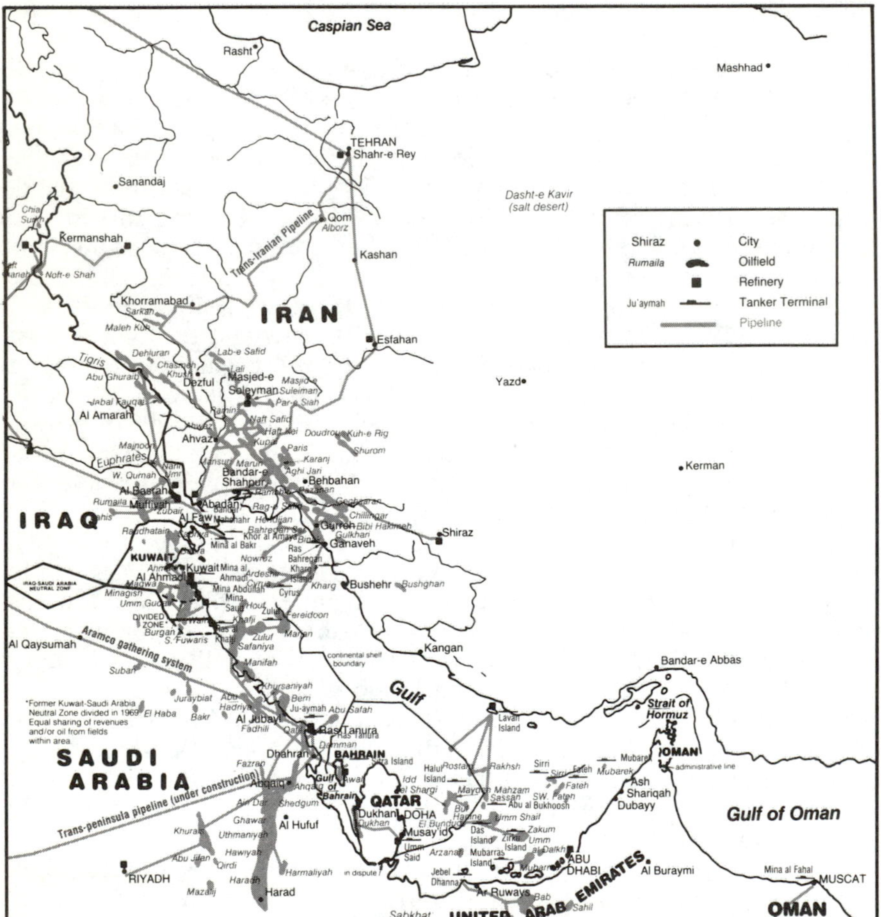

scale and technical manpower have led Saudi Arabia to buy extremely large one-of-a-kind facilities. An air attack on such facilities could deprive a given Saudi city in the core area of essential human services, and this vulnerability is growing steadily as more and more of the Saudi population becomes dependent on modern urban utilities. In fact, an attacker might well choose to put pressure on Saudi Arabia by attacks on its urban facilities rather than its oil facilities. While Saudi Arabia might well be able to ride out the temporary loss of oil facilities—although it is unclear that this would be equally true of the West—it could not ride out successful attacks on its population. It is also important to note that the key population centers serving the Saudi oil fields are concentrated in roughly the same coastal area as the Saudi core. These centers include Jubail, Dammam, Dhahran, Al Khobar, Ras Tanura, and Abqaiq.[61]

The Problem of Defending the Southern Gulf

Finally, Saudi Arabia's air defense problems extend beyond the defense of its own urban and oil facilities. If it is to maintain its influence as the leader of the conservative Gulf states and act as a major military force in the southern Gulf, it must be able to offer assistance to its neighbors. As a result, Saudi Arabia's air defense requirements must include coverage of urban facilities in each of the conservative Gulf states and the wider range of oil facilities located in a broad arc along the southern Gulf from Kuwait to Oman.

These facilities are shown in Map 8.4. Like the Saudi facilities, they have generally been designed as one-of-a-kind installations on the basis of purely economic criteria. As a result, they tend to use extremely large individual equipment items, without redundancy, to achieve economies of scale. Thus the destruction of a few key targets in the form of pumping stations, gas-oil separators, or other key equipment could lead to major cuts in production and in the loss of equipment that can take up to two years to replace fully.[62]

Notes

1. Press sources document this 1981 chronology of events:

10 February: The *New York Times* reports that Begin's political stability (and that of his coalition) had already been shaken by Dayan's resignation, the Lebanon crisis, a barely won vote of confidence, an ailing Israeli economy, and the recent resignation of Begin's finance minister. The date for the Israeli elections is finally set for 30 June by Parliament (*Washington Post*, 11 February 1981). Meanwhile, Begin's former foreign minister, Dayan, forms a new political party and Deputy Prime Minister Yadin announces he will retire from politics in June (*Washington Post*, 13 and 19 February 1981).

13 February: The *New York Times* reports that these political pressures on Begin continued to rise as Parliament decided to lift the immunity from prosecution of ministers and allowed Begin's minister of religion to be tried for corrupt practices.

3 March: Israeli planes heavily bomb Palestinian guerrilla camps in southern Lebanon after Begin fails to alter the election rules in his favor. Begin begins to pick up popular support for his "hard line" against the Arabs (*Washington Post*, 3 March 1981).

28 April: Israeli fighters shoot down two Syrian helicopters in support of Christian militia forces in Lebanon that are holding out against Syrian army attacks (*Washington Post*, 29 April 1981).

29 April: Syria deploys five SA-6 SAM batteries to the Bekaa Valley in Lebanon in retaliation (*Washington Post*, 30 April 1981). Tension reaches alarming levels almost immediately. Begin proclaims that Israel will attack the missile sites if the Syrians do not remove them (*Washington Post*, 2 May 1981), gaining him a massive increase in domestic political support (*Washington Star*, 11 May 1981).

12 May: Syrian missiles fire at Israeli aircraft over Lebanon. They miss, but again strengthen political support for Begin (*New York Times*, 13 May 1981).

15 May: A strong consensus builds up in Israel against Syria, causing both parties to decide on 18 May to avoid making the missile problem a debate issue (*Christian Science Monitor* and *Washington Post*, 19 May 1981). Nevertheless, the question of Syria and the missiles is heavily debated and becomes a divisive issue. This strengthens Begin's domestic position as Begin's tough stance steadily improves his popularity and poll performance (*Washington Star*, 25 May and 8 June 1981).

7 June: The Israeli surprise raid on the Osirak reactor further strengthens Begin's surging popularity (*New York Times* and *Washington Post*, 8 June 1981).

9 June: Begin justifies the Osirak raid in the light of the Holocaust—and repeatedly uses this as an explanation for Israeli activity against the Palestinians and the Syrians (*New York Times* and *Washington Post*, 10 June 1981). This argument is popular—but not unchallenged—in Israel. Peres, Begin's rival, charges on 10 June that his opponent planned the raid in time to boost his chances in the election (*Washington Post* and *Baltimore Sun*, 11 June 1981).

15 June: The results of a new poll show that Begin's popularity has soared dramatically (*Christian Science Monitor*, 15 June 1981; *New York Times*, 18 and 21 June 1981), especially among Sephardic Jews.

30 June: The election is too close to be decisive. Begin wins but is not able to consolidate his power. Israel is still politically divided and requires further stimulation to remain unified.

15 July: A series of rocket barrages is launched into Israel from Palestinian guerrilla positions, killing and wounding a small number of Israelis (*Washington Post*, 16 July 1981). The Israelis warn of stern action.

17 July: Israeli planes bomb Beirut, killing and wounding hundreds of people (*New York Times*, 18 July 1981; see also Geoffrey Godsell's article in the *Christian Science Monitor* on 27 July 1981). The air attacks continue steadily for over a week and a half (*Washington Star*, 20 July 1981), and shellings of Israeli towns intensify (17 July 1981).

29 July: The Syrians again come into the picture: A MiG-25 is shot down by Israeli aircraft over Lebanon (*Baltimore Sun*, 30 July 1981). Begin can now piece together his coalition, signaled by the appointment of war hero Ariel Sharon as defense minister (*Washington Post*, 5 August 1981; *New York Times*, 4 August 1981).

See also the chronology for the Beirut raid printed in the *New York Times*, 24 July 1981.

2. *Washington Star*, 27 February 1979, p. 1; Congressional Research Service (CRS), *Saudi Arabia and the United States: The New Context in an Evolving "Special Relationship,"* a report prepared by the Foreign Affairs and National Defense Division, GPO 81-4940 (Washington D.C.: Government Printing Office, August 1981), p. 54.

3. The first pro-Khomeini riots started in Qom on 18 January 1978 and resulted in police firing on the crowd. Riots in Tabriz on 18–19 February 1978 led to the killing and wounding of hundreds.

4. See CRS, *Saudi Arabia and the United States*, p. 54.

5. See Chapter 5.

6. CRS, *Saudi Arabia and the United States*, p. 55; *Washington Post*, 12 April 1979.

7. Ibid.

8. Senate Foreign Relations Committee (SFRC), *The Proposed AWACS/F-15 Enhancement Sale to Saudi Arabia*, GPO 84-577-0 (Washington, D.C.: Government Printing Office, September 1981), p. 3.

9. CRS, *Saudi Arabia and the United States*, p. 55; *Al Watan al-Arabi* (Paris), 18 May 1979.

10. CRS, *Saudi Arabia and the United States*, p. 55; *New York Times*, 28 June 1979; *As Siyassah* (Kuwait), 30 June 1979.

11. CRS, *Saudi Arabia and the United States*, p. 56. See also *New York Times*, 5 and 6 July 1979.

12. CRS, *Saudi Arabia and the United States*, p. 56; *New York Times*, 14 July 1979.

13. CRS, *Saudi Arabia and the United States*, p. 56; *Washington Post*, 27 August 1979.

14. SFRC, *Proposed Sale*, p. 3.

15. CRS, *Saudi Arabia and the United States*, p. 57; *Al Akhbav* (Jordan), 13 November 1979.

16. CRS, *Saudi Arabia and the United States*, p. 57. Also see *Washington Post*, 13 December 1979.

17. CRS, *Saudi Arabia and the United States*, pp. 57–58; *New York Times*, 19 December 1979.

18. CRS, *Saudi Arabia and the United States*, p. 58.

19. Ibid., p. 59.

20. Ibid.

21. State of the Union address, *Department of State Bulletin* 80 (February 1980): Supplement B.

22. CRS, *Saudi Arabia and the United States*, p. 59; *New York Times*, 30 January 1980.

23. CRS, *Saudi Arabia and the United States*, p. 59; SFRC, *Proposed Sale*, p. 4; *New York Times*, 6 February 1980; *Washington Star*, 18 August 1980.

24. SFRC, *Proposed Sale*, p. 4.

25. CRS, *Saudi Arabia and the United States*, p. 60.

26. Ibid., p. 61; *New York Times*, 18 June 1980.

27. CRS, *Saudi Arabia and the United States*, p. 61; *Washington Star*, 18 August 1980.

28. SFRC, *Proposed Sale*, p. 4.

29. CRS, *Saudi Arabia and the United States*, p. 61.

30. SFRC, *Proposed Sale*, p. 4.

31. CRS, *Saudi Arabia and the United States*, p. 61.

32. Ibid., p. 62.
33. Ibid., p. 63.
34. Ibid.
35. Ibid., pp. 62–63.
36. Letter to Senator Carl Levin on 1 April 1981 in response to the senator's request for information about Carter administration actions on the various F-15 enhancements and AWACS for Saudi Arabia. SFRC, *Proposed Sale*, p. 3.
37. Ibid., p. 4.
38. CRS, *Saudi Arabia and the United States*, p. 63.
39. Ibid.
40. *Washington Post*, 1 November 1981.
41. SFRC, *Proposed Sale*, pp. 5–6.
42. CRS, *Saudi Arabia and the United States*, p. 64.
43. SFRC, *Proposed Sale*, p. 4.
44. CRS, *Saudi Arabia and the United States*, p. 64; *New York Times*, 22 April 1981.
45. Other studies by Lockheed and BDM, and separate satellite communications and electronic warfare studies, contributed to this process.
46. The general character of the study surfaced in an article by Scott Armstrong on 1 November 1981, but many of the details later proved to be wrong. See "Saudi's AWACS Just a Beginning of New Strategy," *Washington Post*, 1 November 1981.
47. The Lockheed study evidently also played a major role in this regard.
48. Much of this discussion is adapted from CRS, *Oil Fields as Military Objectives, A Feasibility Study*, HD-9560 Gen. (Washington, D.C., 21 August 1975), especially pp. 42–47. It has, however, been updated with data obtained from ARAMCO, and during discussions in Saudi Arabia and the Gulf in late 1981.
49. Of the 47 Saudi fields, 14 are offshore, including Majun and Zuruf, less than three minutes' flying time from the coast of Iran or Iraq, 30 are onshore, and 3 extend both on land and under water. Fifteen are currently being produced. Ten fields were discovered in 1979–1980, only 4 of which are counted in the 47.
50. The CRS study of this issue cited earlier notes that

> the south central Persian Gulf, shallow and full of shoals, is generally a poor place for amphibious operations. The 6-fathom curve (36 feet) is 30 miles or more from the mainland in many places. Reefs, bars, oil drilling platforms, and piers often obstruct offshore approaches. Closer in, tidal flats, jetties, and fish traps are impediments. Opaque waters tend to obscure underwater obstructions. Beaches are marred by marshes. . . .
>
> As chance would have it, however, the best beach is just north of Ras Tanura. Channels, most of them marked, lead through reefs. Gradients in some places are steep. The core area south of Berri is a mix of dunes near enough a shoreline to permit dry-ramp LST landings. Prevailing winds produce choppy seas, but neither spring tides (about 5 feet) nor surf are particular problems for small craft. Once ashore, (attacking) forces would have instant access to the main coastal road.
>
> Over-the-beach logistic support might suffice for a short period, but port facilities would soon be imperative. Those at al-Khobar and Qatif, which currently serve fishing fleets and coasters, could handle U.S. lighters.

Ocean-going vessels depend on Dammam, the principal dry cargo port, whose precarious approach channel, 35 to 50 feet deep, is closely flanked by shallows. There is no clearcut harbor. Instead, a rubble and trestle causeway only slightly sheltered, extends almost 7 miles into Tarut Bay. Depths alongside the main wharf are 36 feet. Eighteen piers are in operation and throughput capacity exceeds 7 million short tons a year.

Extensive touring of the beach area also reveals irregular sand bars with 20–30 feet drops and fine sand or muck up to one mile from shore.

51. The information in these tables is dated, particularly in regard to LPG and other gas facilities. The total number of producing wells has been cut from 782 at the end of 1977 to 646 at the end of 1981. By 1983, ARAMCO will deliver 2 BCFD of sweet gas to Jubail, 375 MCFD of ethane to Jubail and Yanbu, and 600,000 BPD of NGL. Many of these facilities are colocated with Saudi crude oil facilities, particularly at Ras Tanura and Shedgum, and are under extreme pressure with poor or nonexistent attention to the chain reactions that could be caused by air or other attacks. Since 1976, ARAMCO has turned the Saudi fields into a massive time bomb.

52. Some details of this discussion have been altered to avoid precisely identifying key vulnerabilities. It is, however, representative of the problems involved.

53. Total power will reach 5,000 MW in 1982–1983.

54. All figures reported in this section are taken from ARAMCO reports, principally *ARAMCO 1980* (Dhahran: Al-Mutawa Press, 1981); ARAMCO, *Facts and Figures*, 1980 and 1981 (Dammam; Al-Mutawa Press, 1980 and 1981).

55. NBC Evening News, Marvin Kalb, 24 September 1980.

56. ARAMCO, *Facts and Figures, 1981*, p. 9. The refinery at Bahrain shipped a range of 69.6–77.5 million barrels, or 2.2–3.4% of total Saudi production, during 1977–1981.

57. Saudi Arabia does ship 69–73 MMBD to Bahrain annually for processing in its refinery, but this oil is exported through the Gulf.

58. See Roger Vielvoye, "Saudi Oil Development Thrusts West," *Oil and Gas Journal*, 7 July 1980, pp. 74–78; Grahn Benton, "Saudi Oil Safeguards Questioned," *8 Days*, 31 October 1981, pp. 36–38; and Francine Stock, "Pipe Dreams," *Middle East*, January 1982, pp. 62–63.

59. Includes products from gas.

60. *8 Days*, 30 October 1981, pp. 36–37.

61. Saudi seaports are too large to be major targets for tactical aircraft, and they are expanding quickly. They processed 53.325 million tons in 1980–1981, a 22.4% increase over 1975–1976. Jiddah processes 52%, Dammam 36%, and Jubail, Yanbu, and Jizan 12%.

62. See CRS, *Oil Fields as Military Objectives*; and regular CRS summary updates. Chapter 11 discusses the military problems involved in more detail.

9
The Saudi Air Defense Enhancement Package and the Lessons of the AWACS Debate

Given Saudi Arabia's defense requirements and vulnerabilities, it is clear why so much U.S. and Saudi attention focused on Saudi air defense after the shah's fall. Saudi Arabia's mix of vulnerabilities created the need for an exceptionally efficient and credible Saudi air defense system for the 1980s. To be effective as a deterrent or defense, this system had to be able to guard against sudden raids or saturation attacks on a 24-hour basis and to offer broad coverage over a wide area.

Further, while the Saudi core area in the northern oil fields occupies only 10,000 square miles, the total critical airspace to be defended in northern Saudi Arabia includes the Saudi cities in the area and is over 30,000 square miles. If the offshore fields and Neutral Zone are included, the area to be defended becomes 70,000 square miles, and the relevant airspace of friendly Gulf states is 5 to 10 times larger. Moreover, the Saudi defense problem is not simply one of detecting and intercepting hostile aircraft. Small craft or ships in the Gulf could be equally lethal against offshore and shoreline facilities, which means that ships have to be tracked and characterized.

Saudi Arabia faced major resource constraints in creating such a defense. It had to use limited numbers of fighter aircraft, sensors, and surface-to-air missiles to cover this large territory in a way that did not lock its forces into a "one-front" defense that could cover only the Gulf. It also had to deal with additional terrain problems. No mountains or high points exist near the Gulf coast. The terrain rises an average of only 5 feet for every mile from the high-water line until it reaches the Summan Plateau, which is too far inland to be useful in covering the Gulf. As a result, ground-based Saudi radars in the Gulf area could provide only about 30–50 NM of low-altitude coverage or 2–4 minutes of warning. These problems in sensor coverage are shown in Map 9.1.

MAP 9—1
COMPARATIVE SENSOR COVERAGE OF AIRBORNE AND GROUND BASED RADARS IN AN IRANIAN ATTACK SCENARIO

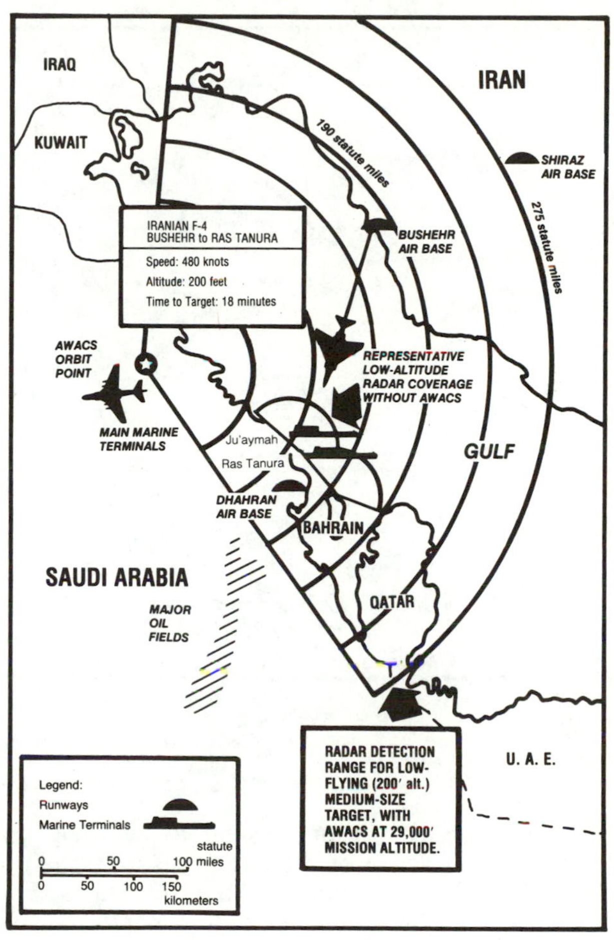

Map prepared by the Congressional Research Service.

Saudi Defense Needs

The Importance of the Saudi Basing System

Saudi Arabia's resource constraints meant that to cover the entire country its air defense system had to use only its five existing major air bases, their related sectoral radar and ground-based air defense centers, and the sixth base under construction near Hafr al-Batin.[1]

MAP 9—2
LOCATION OF MAJOR SAUDI MILITARY BASES, CENTER OF GOVERNMENT, AND CITIES AND POPULATION CENTERS

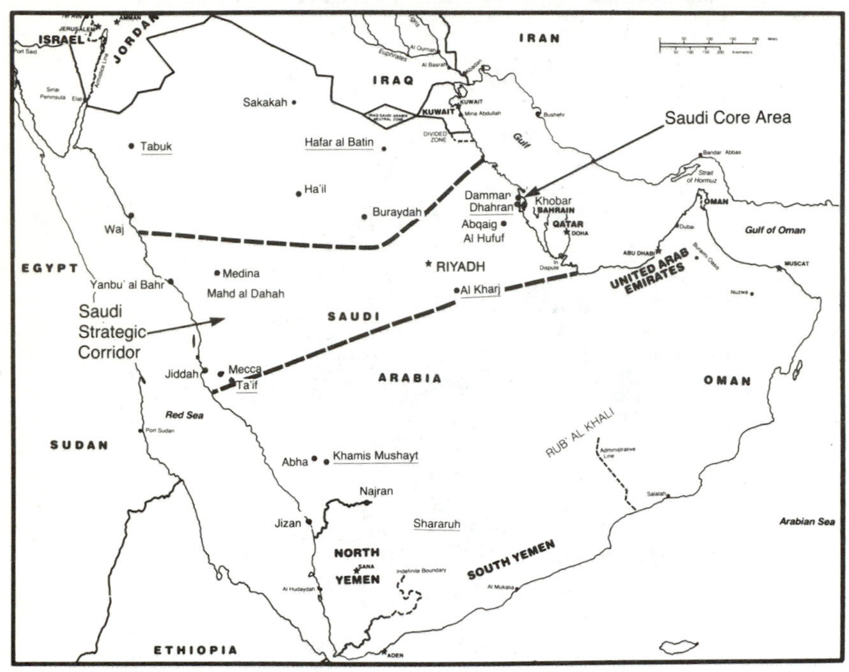

Saudi Air Bases are underlined.

SOURCE: Adapted from the *Financial Times*, 5 May, 1981; Department of the Army, *Middle East: The Strategic Hub*, DA 550-16, Washington, May, 1973, pp. 342-343; and CIA 504371 1-80 (544945).

The relation of the Saudi basing system to key defensive areas is shown in Map 9.2. Knowledge of the Saudi basing system is essential to understanding both the development of the Air Defense Enhancement Package and Saudi Arabia's current defense capabilities. The air base at Dhahran is especially critical. It must cover all the major oil facilities in the Gulf, the Saudi cities in the area, and those of the other conservative Gulf states. The other air bases also have to cover exceptionally wide areas. The base at Riyadh must cover the capital and its surrounding population centers, the base at Taif must cover the holy cities of Makkah and Medina plus Saudi Arabia's key port at Jiddah, and the base at Khamis Mushayt must cover the entire southeast corner of Saudi Arabia and the potential threat from South Yemen and the Horn of Africa.

Map 9.2 shows that Tabuk in northwest Saudi Arabia is currently the only main Saudi air base that is a threat to Israel.[2] However, the base at Tabuk also must cover the principal western land routes into

Saudi Arabia, and it is the only main operating base that Saudi Arabia can now use to assist a friendly state such as Jordan if a crisis like the 1980 border confrontation between Jordan and Syria should turn into war. This situation will change by the mid-1980s, however, when the new base at Hafr al-Batin will help Saudi Arabia defend against attacks by Iraq, "end-run" attacks from Iran, and attacks from Syria. Hafr al-Batin will also provide a limited backup capability to defend against attacks from Israel and Jordan.

The five Saudi bases now operational have Hawk surface-to-air missiles and 35mm antiaircraft (AA) guns; they will be sheltered with aircraft shelters and underground command facilities superior to those in NATO. The first such shelters were completed at Dhahran in late 1981. They allow four aircraft to be worked on in each shelter with a fifth on quick-reaction alert (QRA). They are twin-door shelters with shielded, camouflaged entrances and exits and four taxiways each, and they can house all air and service crews for 30 days without resupply. Dispersion is excellent, and the taxiways from each shelter are long enough to serve as runways. The Saudi munitions and fuel facilities are equally well sheltered, as are certain classified service facilities as well as the battle management or sector coordinating center (SCC). The base can fully shelter two squadrons in this manner. The base construction teams also have a rapid runway repair capability. The first F-15s arrived at Dhahran in December 1981, and the first Saudi F-15 squadron is now operational.

These features and facilities are so advanced that they sharply reduce Saudi Arabia's problems in relying on a single base per sector, and most civil air facilities will be relocated. Dhahran, for example will be purely military by the mid-1980s. This combination of civilian and military facilities will give Saudi Arabia 24 air bases with massive runway and taxiway facilities. It will then take the equivalent of a massive B-52 strike to use conventional hard bombs to inactivate a Saudi main military base. No Gulf air force could launch such an attack before 1990, and it is uncertain whether the USSR would be able to do so with conventional weapons.

The Problem of Vulnerability

Passive and active base defenses cannot, however, protect Saudi airfields against developmental air base suppression techniques, such as earth penetrators, cluster or modular glide bombs with minelets, or sensor weapons. They cannot protect such bases against updated versions of the hard-point munitions that Israel used against Arab targets in 1973, nor can they fully protect all the key facilities on these bases against conventional munitions delivered with the accuracy Israel demonstrated in its attack on the Iraqi Osirak reactor. As a result, U.S. and Saudi plans for an improved Saudi air defense system had to consider the fact that Saudi Arabia might still lose part of a forward air base like Dhahran and most of its fixed ground radars in a given area by

TABLE 9.1 Saudi Air Defense Radars in Early 1980: Planned and In Being

Type and Function	Status	Total	Number Integrated Into Air Defense System	Band
40TZ long-range radars (3-dimensional 300-NM range)	in being	5	5	S
Marconi S-654 radars (traffic management)	in being	3	1	L
TPS-43 mobile radars	deployed at Sana and Sharurah	3	2	S
Joint civil-military long-range radars	in procurement	12	12	L
Low-altitude radars	planned procurement	10	9	L/S
Modern long-range 3-dimensional radars	planned procurement	6	5	L/S

Figures do not include the long-range air traffic control radar in Bahrain, which is integrated into the Saudi system.

Source: Royal Saudi Air Force.

the middle or late 1980s. This situation imposed requirements almost as demanding as the sensor coverage problem discussed earlier.

The Saudis also faced the problem of radar numbers. Even if the air bases could survive, their effectiveness depended on land-based radars. Virtually all of these had to be sited in fixed and exposed positions dictated by the need to maximize low-altitude coverage. The main radar at Dhahran, for example, was permanently fixed on an artificial hill, and many other main radars were similarly fixed in position to allow rapid data transmission to each of the five sector operating centers[3] serving the local air base and army air defense control center (ADC).[4]

As Table 9.1 shows, Saudi Arabia had planned to expand its radar net even before the Air Defense Enhancement Package was sent forward and to shift to unattended radars of the type used by the U.S. and Canada. However, no expansion of its land-based radar system could eliminate the problems of vulnerability and the "blinding" of a large part of each base's defense zone by air or antiradiation missile (ARM) attacks on its radars, particularly since mobile radars could not provide the required data and communication links. Further, Saudi planners had to consider that if they lost the use of Dhahran, they would have to use remote sensors and the air bases at Taif and Khamis Mushayt to cover the Gulf, which would mean flying fighter missions of 600–800 miles. This is a longer operating radius than Israel flew in attacking the Osirak reactor—the longest-range offensive fighter air operation Israel has ever flown—and roughly equivalent to attempting to defend Chicago from Wichita or Dallas. Even when the base at Hafr al-Batin was completed, the Saudi Air Force would still have to fly 300-mile sorties to reach defensive positions near its closest major oil facilities, and Hafr al-Batin would not be permitted to support F-15 operations. Any such sorties would also be meaningless without local radar coverage, since the reinforcements would be too blind to be effective.

The Military Factors Behind the AWACS Package

Given these requirements, it is not surprising that the USAF and the Saudis produced an Air Defense Enhancement Package as sophisticated as the one shown in Table 9.2. While the military factors behind this package were complex, it represented the logical next step after the Peace Hawk and Peace Sun programs and it met Saudi Arabia's complex and demanding air defense system requirements. Above all, the Air Defense Enhancement Package dealt with the problems posed by the threat from Iran.[5] The collapse of the shah had suddenly added 432 fighters to the threat against Saudi Arabia, including 188 F-4D/Es, 166 F-5E/Fs, and 77 F-14As. While many Iranian fighters ceased to be fully operational once U.S. support was withdrawn or were lost in the Iran-Iraq War, the U.S. and Saudi Arabia had to plan for Iranian reequipment and for the possibility that Iraq might also come under hostile rule. The Carter administration had scarcely foreseen this possibility when it had pledged not to deploy additional advanced air defense weapons to Saudi Arabia in 1978.

As the staff report that the Senate Foreign Relations Committee commissioned to examine the Saudi need for the Air Defense Enhancement Package pointed out, the Iranian threat was the most difficult single problem in defending the Saudi core area. This was particularly true of the marine terminals at Ras Tanura and Juaymah. These not only transshipped 92% of Saudi crude oil exports, they were situated at a point on Saudi Arabia's coast that faced the Iranian air bases at Bushihr and Shiraz (see Map 9.1). Further, the key facilities at Abqaiq and in Saudi Arabia's multibillion-dollar natural gas development project, the Master Gas System, were only minutes further inland.

Saudi Air Defense Tasks

This coincidence of geography and politics represented an extremely taxing time and distance calculation for Saudi and U.S. military planners: An Iranian F-4, flying at 200 feet and 480 knots, could bomb the Sea Island at Ras Tanura or the offshore mooring stations at Juaymah only 16 minutes after taking off from Bushihr. If an enemy fighter loitered peacefully within Iranian airspace over the Gulf and then suddenly veered directly for Ras Tanura, the Saudi reaction time was reduced to

TABLE 9.2 The Saudi Air Defense Enhancement Package of 1981

Element	Number	System Cost	Delivery Schedule	Remarks
E-3A AWACS Aircraft[a,b]	5	$3.7 bn total	4 years	• Includes 3 years of spares and support equipment, plus logistic, maintenance, training, and technical support • Requires 170 aircrew and 360 maintenance personnel for 7 days of 24-hour flight
		$1.7 bn for aircraft		• Initial requirement for U.S. support manning was 480 contractor and 30 U.S. government personnel
Ground defense environment	22 major system elements of hardened command and control facilities, data processing and display equipment, new radars, and ground entry stations	$2.1 bn	6 years	• Result of 2-year USAF study • To be jointly operated by RSAF (10 systems) and Civil Aviation (12 systems) • First major modernization since 1960s
KC-707or KC-3 tankers[b,c]	6–8	$2.4 bn ($120 mn each)	40–44 months	• Includes 2 years of spares plus training, maintenance, and support • Purchase and with options to buy 2 • Requires 96 aircrew • Requires 320 initial contractor personnel support • Parts, engine, and airframe commonality with E-3A
Conformal fuel tanks or "fast kits" for F-15[d]	101 sets	$110 mn $900,000 per unit $200 mn	27 months	• Includes related spares, support equipment, training, and publications at cost of $110 million • No additional personnel required
AIM-9L air-to-air missiles	1,177	$200 mn total $98,000 per missile	30 months	• Includes 42 months of contractor training, maintenance, and logistic support • Supplements existing AIM-9F-3 and AIM-7-F • Will come out of USAF inventory as they are replaced by AIM-9M • No additional Saudi personnel required; 9 U.S. contractor personnel will be required for 3 years
Total		$8.5 bn		• 286 new full-time Saudi personnel • 130 additional U.S. government personnel • 809 new U.S. contract personnel

[a]The total price of the AWACS portion of the package was $5.8 billion. The price for 5 aircraft was $1.2 billion ($240 million each; included software modifications, engineering change orders, and an avionics integration lab). The price for spares was $536 million; support equipment was $44 million; contractor support and training was $1.3 billion; and miscellaneous program expenses were $664 million. Additionally, the price for upgrading the ground radar network was $2.0 billion.

[b]To be based at Riyadh and then al-Kharj

[c]The total price for the tanker was $2.4 billion. This included $962 million for 8 aircraft ($120 million each; included extensive engineering, design, and test work to make aircraft into a tanker), $316 million for spares, $34 million for support, $700 million for contractor support and training, and $387 million for miscellaneous program expenses.

[d]To be deployed at Dhahran, Taif, and Khamis Mushayt

8–9 minutes. The F-4, however, was a relatively slow-flying and limited-range attack fighter; the threats of the mid-1980s were likely to be faster, have much more lethal avionics and munitions, and have greater range and endurance.

In addressing this problem, both Saudi and U.S. Air Force planners had to take into account the fact that intercepting an enemy air attack involved more than the intercept itself. Saudi Arabia had to be able to perform several other tasks to provide an effective air defense for its cities and oil fields:

• *Detection.* The first task was to be able to recognize that a potentially hostile target was airborne. This task had to be accomplished using radar. Radar detection, however, is a function of target altitude and size. The higher the target, the greater the distance at which it can be "seen" by the radar; the larger the target, the better the chances become of receiving a discernible radar return. Radar also operates on a "line of sight" principle, and a low-flying fighter aircraft is screened by the curvature of the earth at ranges beyond 25–30 miles. Only by elevating the antenna or sensor system could Saudi Arabia extend the horizons of its radars significantly beyond this distance.

• *Identification.* The second task was identification. Once a radar operator "sees" a target on his scope, he must attempt to determine its identity or at least to categorize it as "potentially" or "probably" hostile. In wartime, one can assume that any target detected coming from a certain area is probably hostile. In peacetime, however, a specified sector of airspace is likely to be filled with numerous commercial, private, and military aircraft. By using identification of friend or foe and by cross-referencing filed flight plans and pilots' radioed position reports, a radar operator can eliminate most targets as nonhostile. The identity of a certain number of targets will remain unknown, however, and the determination of possible threats must rest on a more subjective reading of likely intent.

• *Decision.* The third task was to decide whether to intercept. A decision to order an intercept of an unidentified target can be pegged to an arbitrary rule: Any "unknown" aircraft that enters a certain zone will be intercepted. This is the approach used by the United States, which has established an Air Defense Intercept Zone, or ADIZ, which extends up to 300 miles beyond its east and west coasts. In the Saudi case, geography does not permit the luxury of such an extensive air defense zone that had to be kept within its borders or the limits of territorial waters in the Gulf and the Red Sea. The Gulf is just over 100 miles wide opposite Dhahran, and major air routes—connecting Baghdad, Bahrain, Abu Dhabi, Tehran, and other major cities to the northwest and southeast—lie just miles off the Saudi Gulf coast. If Saudi Arabia intercepted any unidentified aircraft flying as close as 100 miles from the oil fields, the RSAF would have to fly around the clock.

• *Scramble.* The fourth task was to have sufficient forces to scramble. Although Saudi F-5E and Lightnings then flew quick-reaction alert, and Saudi F-15s are beginning to take over this mission, such sorties take 3–5 minutes to launch. Fighter reaction time could be cut by several minutes by keeping the pilots in the fighter cockpit with the aircraft engines running, or using new quick-reaction laser gyros, but the cost of this approach in terms of jet fuel, engine wear, and pilot fatigue makes it impractical except when absolutely necessary.

• *Intercept.* The fifth task was to make intercepts successful. Once fighters are airborne, they must be able to engage the enemy, which means both closing on the target (Ras Tanura is about 30 miles from Dhahran) and maneuvering into a position from which short-range missiles can be fired. As a general rule, it takes much longer to get behind an enemy aircraft than to engage it head-on, and the effort to maneuver behind an attacker means that the defending fighter must expose itself to hostile fighters. While an RSAF F-15 could also launch radar-guided AIM-7 Sparrow missiles from beyond visual range, it must then track the enemy until the missile hits. This method would mean tying up the Saudi fighter while other hostile fighters could fly through or attack the Saudi aircraft.

Given these requirements, it was clear that the Saudi Air Defense Enhancement Package had to (1) improve the Saudi sensor and air control and warning systems, (2) improve Saudi head-on intercept capability, and (3) improve Saudi air endurance and deployment capability. Without a sensor like the AWACS, the RSAF would have had to rely on fixed, ground-based radars to detect enemy air attacks; even if such radars survived, they could not be adequate.

Radars cannot be sited on elevations higher than 1,000 feet in the Dhahran area because this is the maximum elevation on its flat coastal plain. As Map 9.3 shows, this requirement limited the radar horizon for small, low-flying (200 feet) targets to about 30 miles. Even an Iranian F-4, however, could fly directly toward Ras Tanura from Bushihr Air Base for 13 minutes at 200 feet before it could be detected by the ground-based radars in the Dhahran-Juaymah area. Once such a fighter was detected, it would still take the RSAF 12–15 minutes to intercept it east of Ras Tanura, and the fighters of the mid-1980s were likely to be much faster and to be able to penetrate at lower altitudes using conformal munitions.

This meant Iranian fighters could be over the target within 3 minutes of the time Saudi ground radars detected them. Even under optimal assumptions, a Saudi intercept based on warning from ground radars would occur 10 minutes too late, forcing the Saudis to defend the target with only surface-to-air missiles and antiaircraft guns. While the Ras Tanura–Juaymah–Dhahran area was defended by army air defense battalions made up of Hawk and Crotale missile batteries and 35mm Oerlikon guns, the Hawk batteries normally need about 10 minutes

MAP 9—3
IMPACT OF LIMITED WARNING FROM GROUND BASED RADARS ON SAUDI ABILITY TO DEFEND ITS KEY OIL FACILITIES

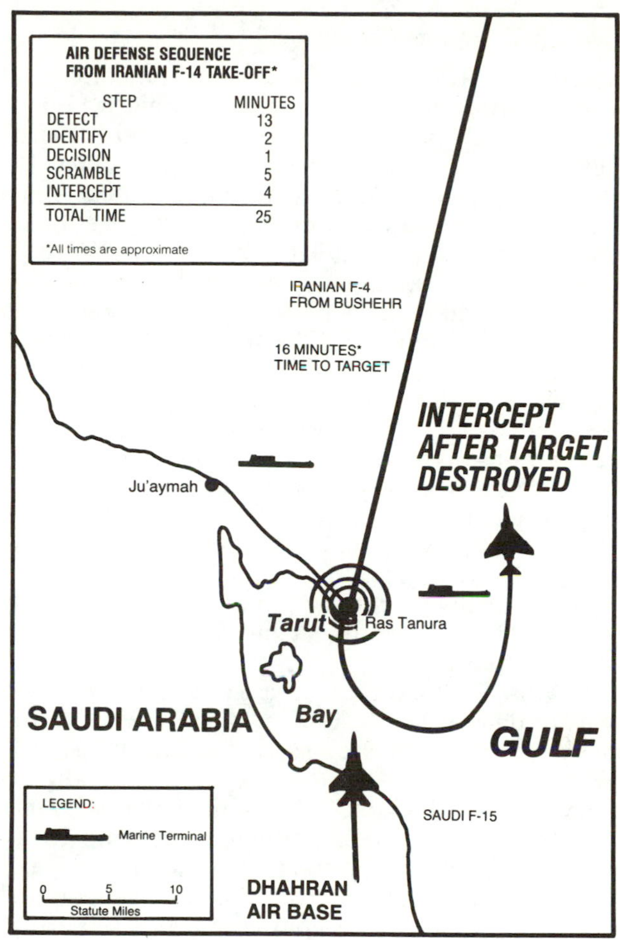

Map prepared by the Congressional Research Service.

warning to fire effectively, and the Crotale and Oerlikon weapons systems would probably be able to fire only as the attacker left the target. Even with extensive warning and more advanced systems like Patriot, the Saudis could not afford to rely on ground-based defenses. Moreover, the ground-based radars would have to work perfectly in detecting small, low-altitude targets to provide even 3 minutes of warning. Due to the temperature gradient between the air mass above the hot desert in Saudi Arabia's Eastern Province and the cooler air over the Gulf, ground-based radars experience serious performance degradations about 75% of the time. This phenomenon, known as "ducting," often impedes target detection until the enemy fighter is virtually on top of a ground-based radar.

Saudi Arabia's 360-Degree Threat

Saudi Arabia also had to plan for a multifront threat. The scale of this threat is illustrated by force trends summarized in Table 9.3.[6] According to the figures published in the Stockholm International Peace Research Institute (SIPRI) yearbooks and in the annual IISS *Military Balance,* the major potential threat nations and radical Arab states were building up their military equipment at close to twice the rate of Saudi Arabia. More details of the air threat that Saudi and U.S. planners had to consider are shown in the Department of Defense estimates in Table 9.4.[7] These numbers had to be evaluated in view of the fact that sudden political shifts in the countries on the periphery of Saudi Arabia were the rule rather than the exception. The recent life expectancy of the ruler of North Yemen, for example, had been slightly over four years, and the U.S. and Saudi Arabia were keenly conscious that they had received little warning of the shah's departure from power. Saudi-Egyptian relations had reversed themselves on six occasions since 1950, similar reversals have taken place in Saudi relations with Iraq, and virtually every other conservative Gulf state was deeply divided by foreign labor movements and internal religious and ethnic differences that could reverse currently friendly political alignments. In this sense, Saudi Arabia faced not only a "360-degree" threat but also an unavoidable inability to predict its direction.

The front with South Yemen is a good specific example of the problems involved. The South Yemeni Air Force had attacked Saudi installations in the Sharurah area as recently as 1973, had since been equipped with Soviet MiG-21s and Su-20/22s, and had more advanced aircraft on order.[8] Its fighters had the combat radius to strike at most targets in southwest Saudi Arabia, although Makkah, Riyadh, and the oil fields in the east were too distant for most Yemeni fighters. Saudi Arabia had an F-5E base at Khamis Mushayt, supported by ground-based TPS-43 radars, and had redeployed mechanized army units from Tabuk to Sharurah to defend against the land threat. However, the Saudi air defense system in this sector was as handicapped by the short warning time provided by ground-based radars as was the system in the Dhahran area. Ground-based radar coverage at Khamis Mushayt was especially limited due to the mountainous terrain, and Saudi officials had been impressed with the U.S. AWACS's superior capability to look over the mountains into South Yemen and provide advance warning of aerial activity during the fighting between North and South Yemen in 1979.

Further, both U.S. and Saudi planners had to consider other contingency threats to the Red Sea region. Ethiopia posed a growing threat

TABLE 9.3 Trends in the Military Buildup in the Gulf, 1969-1983

	Saudi Arabia	Iran	Iraq	Oman	UAE	North Yemen	South Yemen
Defense Expenditure (current billion $)							
1969	.343	.505	.280	n.a.	n.a.	n.a.	n.a.
1973	1.900	2.010	.467	.076	n.a.	n.a.	n.a.
1977	7.530	7.900	1.660	.457	.100	.079	.044
1983	21.952[a]	6.9-13.3[b]	7.722[b]	1.772[a]	2.915	.526[b]	.159[b]
Total Military Manpower							
1969	34,000	221,000	78,000	n.a.	n.a.	n.a.	n.a.
1973	42,500	211,500	101,800	9,600	11,150	20,900	9,500
1977	61,500	342,000	188,000	13,000	26,100	39,850	21,300
1983	51,500	2,000,000[e]	517,250[e]	23,500	49,000	21,550[e]	25,500[e]
Main Battle Tanks							
1969	"a few"	some	535	n.a.	n.a.	n.a.	n.a.
1973	25	920	990	–	–	30	30
1977	475	1,620	1,350	–	–	30	200
1983	450	940[c]	2,360[c]	18	118	714	450
Other Armored Fighting Vehicles							
1969	60+	some	40+	n.a.	n.a.	n.a.	n.a.
1973	260	2,000	1,300	some	96	70	–
1977	410	2,250	1,800	36	301	150	20
1983	1,490	900[c]	3,000[c]	36+	486	527+	300
Artillery							
1969	–	some	n.a.	n.a.	n.a.	n.a.	n.a.
1973	some	some	700	some	some	100	some
1977	some	874	790+	53	38	100	some
1983	74+	1,200[c]	800+	66+	70+	395	310+
Operational Combat Aircraft							
1969	43	180	213	n.a.	n.a.	n.a.	n.a.
1973	70	159	224	12	12	28	20
1977	137	341	369	50	38	22	33
1982	170[d]	70-90[c]	330[c]	37	43	75	113

[a] 1983 or 1983/84 figure.
[b] 1982 or 1982/83 figure.
[c] Very uncertain. IISS estimate as of July, 1983.
[d] 46 BAC-167 COIN aircraft used in training roles.
[e] Manning totals very uncertain. Data are from 1983/1984 *Military Balance.*

Source: The Military Balance (London: IISS, various years).

TABLE 9.4 Department of Defense Estimate of the Air Threat to Saudi Arabia in 1981

Country	Designation	Type	Number	Combat radius (NM)
Saudi Arabia	F5E	Fighter-bomber	65	650
	F 53	Interceptor	17	900
	F 53 and F	Interceptor	40	650
	F-15 (proposed)	Interceptor	60	500
Iraq	TU-22	Medium bomber	12	1500
	IL-28	Light bomber	10	600
	MiG-23B	Fighter-interceptor	80	700
	SU-7B	Fighter-bomber	40	300
	SU-20	Fighter-bomber	80	350
	MiG-21	Fighter-interceptor	115	400
	Mirage F1	Fighter-interceptor	34	350
Iran[a]	F-4 D/E	Fighter-bomber	188[b]	350
	F-3 E/F	Fighter	166[c]	120
	F-14A	Fighter-interceptor	77	580
	707	Tanker	13	–
	747	Tanker	9	–
Yemen	IL-28	Light bomber	8	600
	MiG-17F	Fighter-interceptor	37	300
	MiG-21	Fighter-interceptor	50	400
	SU-20/22	Fighter-bomber	12	350
Ethiopia	F-5	Fighter-bomber	7	120
	MiG-17	Fighter-bomber	37	300
	MiG-21	Fighter-interceptor	50	400
	MiG-23	Fighter-interceptor	12	700
Syria	MiG-17	Fighter-interceptor	85	300
	SU-7	Fighter-bomber	20	300
	SU-20	Fighter-bomber	30	350
	MiG-23	Fighter-interceptor	64	700
	MiG-25	Interceptor	25	500
	MiG-21	Interceptor	230	400

[a] Iran claims 3 TU-22 and IL-28 kills. Department of Defense does not confirm. Fifty of the Phantoms and 9 of the F-14s believed operational.
[b] IISS shows only 90 active.
[c] Number operational is unknown.
Source: Department of Defense Working Papers (U), 26 April 1981, updated to reflect IISS data as of September 1981.

to Saudi Arabia's oil shipments through the Red Sea, and Saudi Arabia could not plan its defenses for a decade into the future on the basis of a friendly Djibouti, Sudan, Egypt, or Jordan, nor could it plan on Israeli restraint. There had been over 30 military and paramilitary incidents in nations bordering Saudi Arabia in the previous 25 years, including repeated Egyptian bombings of Saudi Arabia during the civil war in North Yemen.[9]

Finally, Soviet ambitions in the area were scarcely any secret. Table 9.5 provides a tangible indication of the size and expansion of the Soviet presence in the area at the time Saudi and U.S. planners developed the air defense package.

The Reason for Selecting the AWACS E-3A

The factors discussed in the previous section virtually forced the selection of the E-3A. Work done by USAF Studies and Analysis in the "Air Feasibility Study" of July 1980 concluded that it would take a minimum of 48 large, fixed, and vulnerable radars to cover all of Saudi Arabia's borders without an airborne warning and control system. These radars would still leave major penetration gaps,[10] provide only 20–30 miles of low-altitude coverage, and give only token maritime surveillance capability. The USAF also found it would take 11–15 E-2C Hawkeyes and 34 ground radars to provide minimal coverage of the Gulf. Even this force could not provide 24-hour surveillance of Saudi Arabia's oil facilities for a 7-day period. Moreover, the E-2C could not effectively control Saudi fighters in the face of a large-scale attack over Saudi airspace, which is approximately 10–20 times the airspace of Israel, and it had electronic intelligence (ELINT) capabilities that would be useful in Saudi land and air offensives against Israel.[11]

In contrast, the USAF estimated that 5 E-3A and 18 ground radar installations could provide a single-front coverage of the oil facilities and cities in the Gulf, even under the assumption that one E-3A aircraft would be in a constant overhaul and refit status, another would be in regular maintenance, and three would be fully operational. Each E-3A could provide a minimum of 175 NM of low-altitude and maritime coverage and extend warning of an air attack on the Gulf front to a minimum of 7 minutes. As Map 9.4 shows, this warning would allow the E-3A to vector in an F-15 fighter to make at least one pass on an attacker before it hit a critical oil facility. It also would allow the Saudi Army to vector the acquisition radars of its Hawk batteries to enable them to engage effectively and would allow the F-5E to play a backup role. Further, as Map 9.5 shows, 5 AWACS could cover the entire front over the Gulf.

USAF planners estimated that even this small a number of E-3As would be survivable in defending the forward area over the Gulf front because there would be virtually none of the terrain masking at low altitudes that exists on Saudi Arabia's western border with Israel and

TABLE 9.5 Soviet-Bloc Military Presence in the Gulf and Middle East

	Arms Transfers ($ millions)		Soviet-Bloc Military Technicians		Military Trained in Soviet Bloc	
	1965–74[a]	1971–80[a]	1976[b]	1981[c]	1955–81	1969–81[c]
Gulf						
Bahrain	–	–	–	–	–	–
Iran	589	626	120	–	390	70?
Iraq	1,343	5,000	1,000	550	4,410	2,310
Kuwait	–	50	–	–	–	–
Oman	–	–	–	–	–	–
Qatar	–	–	–	–	–	–
Saudi Arabia	–	–	–	–	–	–
UAE	–	–	–	–	–	–
North Yemen	27	625	?	700	2,060	1,120
South Yemen	114	775	?	1,600[d]	1,115	665
Subtotal	2,073	7,076	1,120	2,850	7,975	4,165
Middle East						
Egypt	2,465	20	–	–	6,255	5
Israel	–	–	–	–	–	–
Jordan	–	–	–	–	–	–
Lebanon	4	–	–	–	–	–
Syria	1,758	5,400	2,500	3,300	5,515	2,670
Subtotal	4,227	5,420	2,500	3,300	11,770	2,675
Horn of Africa						
Ethiopia	–	1,900	–	13,900[e]	2,095	1,790
Somalia	134	150	1,100	–	2,600	205
Subtotal	134	2,050	1,100	13,900	4,695	1,995
Related Areas						
Afghanistan	309	450	350	2,000[f]	5,580	2,890
Libya	425	5,500	800	2,650	1,990	1,245
Subtotal	734	5,950	1,150	4,650	7,570	4,135
Total	7,168	20,496	5,870	24,660	32,011	12,970

[a]Source is ACDA, *World Military Expenditures and Arms Transfers,* various years.
[b]Source is CIA ER-78-10478U.
[c]U.S. State Department, "Soviet and East European Aid to the Third World, 1981," February 1983.
[d]1,100 Soviet and East European, 500 Cuban.
[e]1,900 Soviet and East European, 12,000 Cuban.
[f]Excludes 85,000 Soviet troops.

MAP 9—4
SAUDI F-15 INTERCEPT CAPABILITIES WITH THE E-3A AWACS AND AIM-9L

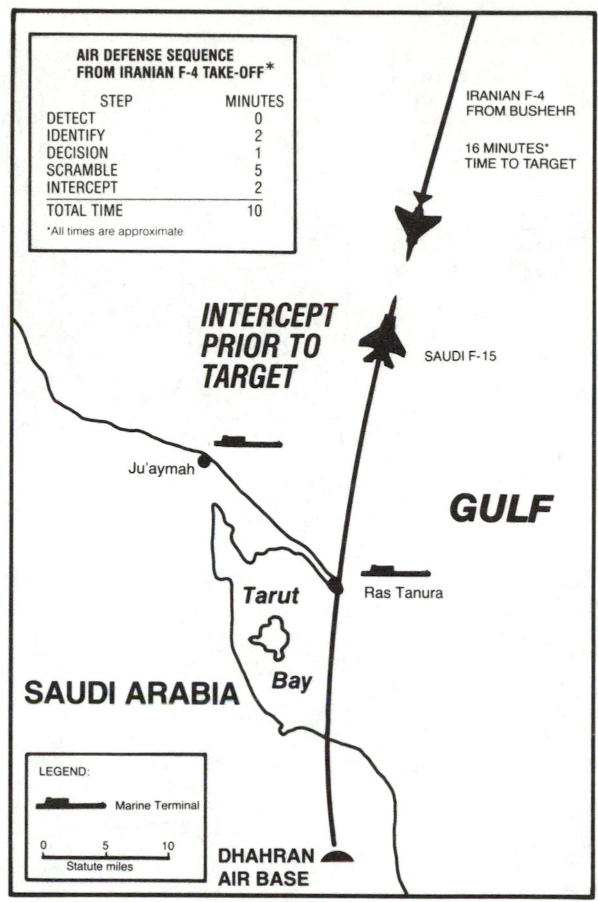

Map prepared by the Congressional Research Service.

Jordan, and the E-3As could operate far enough to the rear to withdraw if attacked. Moreover, the long flight times and limited air density of the Gulf would allow the E-3As to know they were under attack in time to react. Saudi fighters could then cover the AWACS; the E-3A could retreat or it could "pop down" below the coverage of most fighter radars. An individual E-3A could also fly for 11 hours on a single mission or 24 hours with refueling, allowing 2 hours for the refueling period. This long flight time would allow a crew of 17 men per aircraft (13 in the actual electronics role) to carry out the air control and warning mission more efficiently. The E-3A had more than three times the

MAP 9—5
LOW LEVEL WARNING RESPONSE TIME
(E-3A VS GROUND SITES)

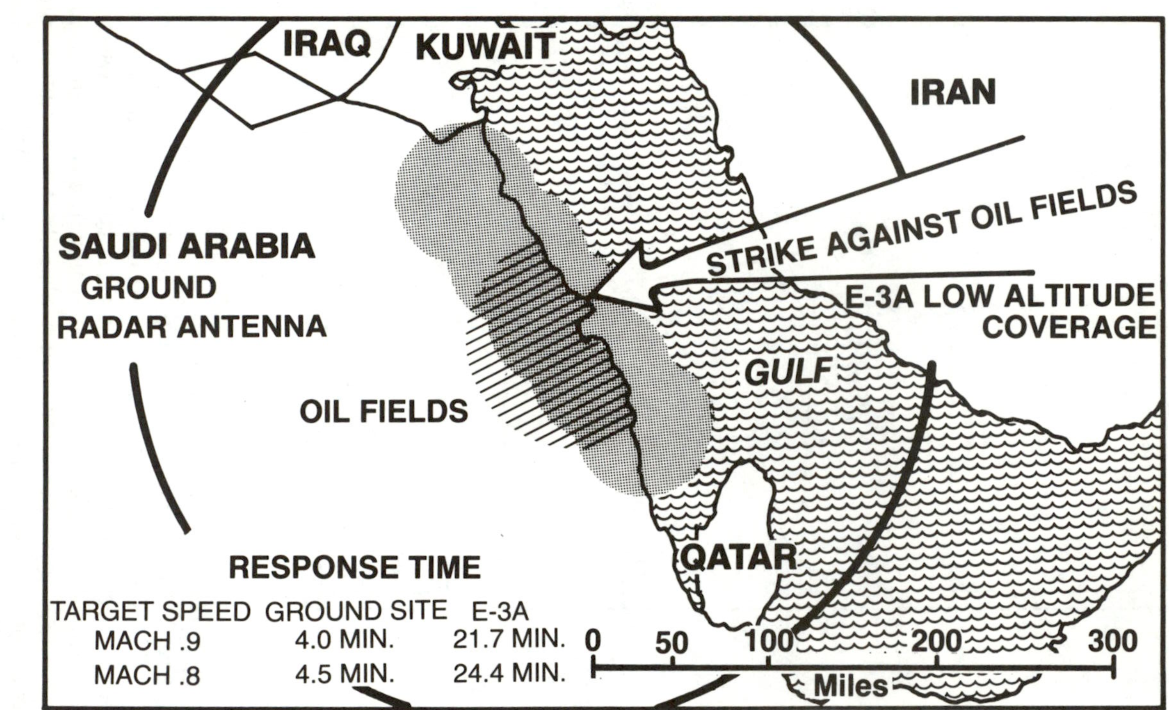

SOURCE: Boeing Corporation, August, 1981, and U.S. Air Force.

endurance of a force using the E-2C plus added ground radars, and it would require far fewer technicians.

Most important, the E-3A had the radar power to be highly jam-resistant, to track large, medium-altitude targets at 360-mile ranges, and to identify even small-cross-section fighters flying at altitudes above 200 feet at ranges of up to 175 miles ("cross-section" refers to the minimal radar profile of the aircraft, usually expressed in square meters). These features would allow the AWACS to fly about 50–100 miles inland from the Gulf and still provide a minimum of 5 minutes warning before the required moment of intercept. Each AWACS could independently track up to 300 targets and accept data on up to 200 more from another AWACS or ground radars. Under ideal circumstances an E-3A could engage and characterize up to 240 targets in terms of size, altitude, identity, speed, and direction. It could also direct 6–8 closely spaced intercepts and 3–6 simultaneous intercepts.[12]

Transferring the AWACS Technology

The USAF also concluded that the configuration of the AWACS sold to Saudi Arabia could omit the frequency-agile, secure voice and the jam-resistant joint tactical information distribution system (JTIDS) necessary to manage an air battle of the density that would be common in a NATO–Warsaw Pact or Arab-Israeli environment. Table 9.6 shows how the USAF tailored the E-3A to meet Saudi needs, concluding that such a configuration would be able to avoid creating a potential threat of technology loss to the U.S.—or a military threat to Israel—but still be able to handle most Gulf threats through the late 1980s.[13]

Equally important, the first E-3A configured to Saudi needs could be delivered in April 1985, and the other four at two-month intervals thereafter. The Saudis would thus be able to operate without U.S. crew support as early as 1986, although Saudi operation of the E-3A would still be dependent on at least 200 U.S. contractor personnel, 20–30 USAF personnel, and U.S. equipment replacements and overhauls during its entire operational life.[14] Saudi operation of the E-3A was absolutely critical. Any other long-term arrangement for deployment of the AWACS or basing of U.S. combat forces in Saudi Arabia would have been anathema in terms of Saudi sovereignty, internal political stability, ability to lead the other conservative Gulf states, and provocation of hostile reactions from the more radical Arab states.

The U.S. could sell the AWACS to Saudi Arabia with little fear that it would be hijacked or operated in ways hostile to U.S. interests. The E-3A aircraft could not be flown for more than a month without the full cooperation of the U.S. support personnel in Saudi Arabia, and all depot-level maintenance would have to be done in the U.S. Because of sensitive radar design and operating requirements, the key equipment on the AWACS could not be operated without U.S. support for more than a few days. The E-3A's mean time for service between major

TABLE 9.6 Saudi, U.S., and NATO AWACS

Feature	Current U.S. Score	Future Saudi	Future U.S.	NATO Standard
Block (production run)	1	10	20–25[a]	15
12 consoles/additional radios	No	No	Retrofit	No
Battle management positions	3	3	6	6
Simultaneous intercept capability[b]	3–6	3–6	6–12	6–12
Closely spaced intercept capability[b]	6–8	6–8	12–16	2–16
ESM/ESD (electronic support measures)	No	No	?	?
Radar[c]	AN/APY-1	AN/APY-2	AN/APY-2	AN/APY-2
Frequency agile	No	No	No	No
Maritime surveillance	Retrofit	Yes	Yes	Yes
Large computer (64K)[d]	No	Yes	Yes	Yes
Tactics package	T-5	Gulf-	?	?
Increased track capacity[e]	100	300	300	300
Mode IV IFF (AN/AOX-103)	Yes	Commer-cial	Yes	Yes
Secure Voice	U.S.	Commer-cial[f]	U.S.	U.S.
Have Quick (frequency agile jam-resistant voice)	Yes	No	?	No
Seek Talk (successor to Have Quick)	No	No	?	?
JTIDS (secure, ECCM, multi-user data net)	Retrofit	No	Yes	Yes
Tadil A (digital data relay)	Yes	Yes	Yes	Yes
Tadil C (interceptor control)[g]	Yes	Yes	Yes	Yes
ECCM enhancement	Retrofit?	No	R&D	No
Ground station oriented or tied	Optional	Yes	Optional	Optional
Delivery date	Current	1985	1985 start	1982

[a]20–25 adds additional C^3 or display facilities. 30–35 is an undefined R&D growth version.

[b]Average controller can handle one simultaneous intercept. Exceptional controller can handle two. Three is theoretical maximum.

[c]APY-2 adds maritime mode.

[d]Increases "K" (computing capacity over initial on-board computer) four times.

[e]Can handle 200 additional externally inputted tracks.

[f]Commercial system would not have frequency agile or spread spectrum. It is merely secure, not jam-resistant.

[g]Usable only with F-106 and U.S. carrier aircraft.

Source: Material provided by Boeing.

failures is 27.4 hours, and the time between system failures is 78 hours. As Table 9.6 shows, the variant of AWACS sold to Saudi Arabia could meet all Saudi requirements and still be left vulnerable to sophisticated U.S. communications jamming and to jamming by Israel.[15] It also did not need the sophisticated ECM gear or any of the ELINT capability of the four Grumman E-2C Hawkeyes now in Israel.[16]

As Table 9.7 shows, the sale of the E-3A also presented little risk of technical compromise because of its age and the special character of its technology. The AWACS was first flown in 1971. Only 10 of the more than 1,000 AWACS technical manuals were classified, none was classified higher than "secret," and all had already had broad release in NATO. The basic radar design of the E-3A was not sensitive—only the equipment used to produce it. This design could not be compromised by reverse engineering through acquisition of the aircraft. The production equipment involved vast amounts of software that would not leave U.S. hands and that represented an investment in special manufacturing capabilities of well over $1 billion.

In fact, since the E-3A would not be delivered to Saudi Arabia until 1985, it seemed likely that the Soviets would long since have deployed their new AWACS variant of the Il-76 Candid and have similar airborne radar capabilities operational in Europe. The rest of the electronics in the E-3A dated back to the late 1960s and would also be well within Soviet technical capabilities at the time the aircraft was transferred to Saudi Arabia. The E-3A's basic ECM defense and its key characteristics—operating frequencies, pulse repetition rates, pulse widths, side lobe characteristics, effective radiated power, antenna gain, transmitter power, scan rates, and receiver dynamic range—had already been acquired by Soviet ELINT systems.

The AIM-9L Air-to-Air Missile

The sale of 1,177 AIM-9L missiles[17] contributed to the Air Defense Enhancement Package by giving Saudi Arabia an all-aspect air-to-air missile with the shoot-down capability that it could use in "head-on" intercepts against low-flying attackers, without having to sacrifice the time and probability of intercept necessary to maneuver into a long, stern chase or "dogfight" position. Such a capability was essential given the limited warning time the AWACS could provide and the need for each Saudi F-15 to be able to engage more than one threat fighter per encounter. Although the Saudis already had 2,000 second-generation AIM-9J air-to-air missiles, 600 fourth-generation AIM-9-P-3s, and large stocks of "product-improved" AIM-7F radar-guided Sparrows, these missiles lacked the multi-aspect capability to enable the F-15 to avoid time-consuming and complex fighter maneuvers in meeting an attacking aircraft and lacked the energy of maneuver to be lethal at very low altitudes.[18] While the sale of the AIM-9L did create some risk of technology transfer, no other missile in the U.S. inventory had the requisite capabilities, and the U.S. gained compensating advantages.[19]

TABLE 9.7 Technology Transfer Risks of Selling the E-3A to Saudi Arabia

NORAD aircraft originally. Design set in 1970–1973, and unlike Nimrod and E-2C, E-3A was not designed or optimized to fight in electronic environment.

All hardware on the E-3A except the radar will be off-the-shelf in 1985 when deliveries start, including its navigation systems.

Its UHF radios are obsolescent and are now going out of production.

The E-3A's radar data correlator is the most important "state of the art" computer element. However, the logic jamming program will not be transferred and is easy to alter. The MECL 2 computer chip now so obsolete it is no longer made, and the USAF has had to stockpile it. By 1985 it will have been out of production for 10 years.

The E-3A's IBM CC-2 computer with quad memory is inferior to commercial CDC computers and will be inferior to small business computers by 1985.

The E-3A's ECM resistance is virtually all a function of the radar design and computer program and could not be compromised.

The key to E-3A's success is its computer program and software. There will be almost no risk of transfer. U.S. interceptor, tactics, and message formats will not be provided to Saudis. Most of the software will be kept in U.S. The software actually on the E-3A has little value. It consists of

- *Initialization:* value degenerates in hours
- *Tactics:* valuable, but to Saudi Arabia only, not U.S.
  Unsuited to war with Israel
- *Tadil A:* An old digital data relay. It is not sensitive, and a Soviet ship in Mediterranean seems to have entered (B and C are not relevant)
- *Guard Channels:* Can extract exact threshold of side-lobe jamming detection after months of analysis or prolonged flight, but 10ths of NM gain—matter of few DB. Minimum value to enhanced logic jamming

The Saudis would get only the USAF Mode 1, 2, and 3 IFF. The Soviets have Mode 3 for commercial flights to U.S. (1 and 3 for ATC, 2 for GCI). They would not get the USAF Mode 4—Secure IFF. The Saudi IFF will be compatible but not include the U.S. Crypto Chip. This is a U.S.-only technology.

The E-3A would have no ESM, ECCM, or ELINT equipment.

The Saudi E-3A will not get frequency agile secure voice and will be vulnerable to jamming if deployed near or forward of interceptors. The Saudis must tie their E-3As to ground links and will be vulnerable to Israeli early warning and electronic warfare systems and attack.

Security handling will include Form No. 1513 safeguards, plus special security provisions.

Source: U.S. Air Force.

The Reason for Providing Tankers

The sale of six KC-707 tankers, with the option to buy two more, provided Saudi Arabia with the ability to refuel its AWACS, F-15s, and F-5Es. This fueling capability would enable Saudi Arabia to mass its fighters and extend their combat air-patrol capability, as well as to accept reinforcements from U.S. carriers or air bases outside Saudi Arabia. The KC-707 also had airframe, engine, and parts commonality with the Boeing E-3A and could support wing-tip, probe, and drouge-type refueling.

Saudi Arabia's existing KC-130 tankers lacked both the required capacity and mission flexibility. They could not handle the F-15's and F-5E's combined need for beach pods, had no "hard points" to allow new mission features to be added, and could not provide the combination of the probe and drouge-type refueling needed for U.S. carrier aircraft and the boom refueling needed for USAF fighters. Without such tankers, a threat nation could fly peripheral missions that could force the Saudi E-3A and fighters to scramble until it exhausted Saudi combat air-patrol endurance; it could then attack. Saudi Arabia then would lack the capability to deter attacks on the air base at Dhahran and would not be able to fuel its forces to deal with two-front threats, such as attacks from both Iran and South Yemen. Saudi Arabia also would not be able to refuel over-the-horizon reinforcements from the U.S.

The Reason for Providing Conformal Fuel Tanks

The sale of 101 sets of conformal fuel tanks or "FAST" kits (two tanks per aircraft) for Saudi Arabia's F-15 fighters solved another problem. It gave individual Saudi fighters the endurance and range to maintain combat air patrol with a comparatively limited number of fighters and the ability to mass in the Gulf area for short periods even if Saudi Arabia should lose most of the facilities on its air base at Dhahran. The FAST kits gave the Saudi F-15 about 1,500 gallons more fuel per set. They extended the F-15's radius by 79% in the air-superiority mode and 93% in the interdiction mode and increased endurance by 65% in the CAP mode.[20] They also allowed the F-15 to retain its capability to carry four AIM-7F radar-guided missiles.

This increase in range was essential if Saudi Arabia was to use the F-15 in anything other than a relatively short-range point defense mode. Without the FAST tanks, the F-15 remained a relatively short-legged and low-endurance fighter. It was for this reason that the U.S. Air Force studies in 1978, which had led the U.S. to encourage Saudi Arabia to buy the F-15 rather than the F-14 or F-18, had recommended that Saudi Arabia be given these tanks. The kits also had the advantage that they could be provided in a form that would not allow Saudi F-15s to carry offensive attack munitions without U.S. technical support, since Saudi Arabia could not modify them unilaterally in ways that would allow a loaded F-15 to sustain its speed and maneuverability.

The Need for Hawk Data Links

Although the precise interface among the Saudi version of the E3-A, its air defense guns, and its Shahine and Improved Hawk missiles had not been decided upon when the USAF study was completed and was still under study in 1983, it was planned that Saudi Arabia would acquire data terminals at each major air defense site with digital processing capability and commercial encryption gear similar to the U.S. TADIL C. The radar problems discussed earlier made it essential that Saudi Arabia's limited fighter strength be able to "net" its fighters and Hawk surface-to-air missiles through the six ground-based sector coordinating centers and army air defense control centers (ADCs), so that the data collected by AWACS could be interpreted and transformed to provide the Hawk units with the search data they needed to back up the fighter screen. This combination of air and ground defenses allowed Saudi Arabia to greatly strengthen its point defense and to protect its Hawk against much of the ECM gear likely to be common in the Gulf in the mid-1980s. Similar terminals were planned for selected Saudi, short-range air defense (SHORAD) systems like the Shahine, but most Saudi short-range air defense systems were too limited in range, C^3 flexibility, and electronics sophistication to benefit greatly from AWACS data.

Improved C^3 and Air Defense Ground Environment Capabilities

As the Saudi Air Defense Enhancement Package progressed through the Pentagon, the U.S. also added features to improve the Saudi C^3 system and make optimal use of the improvements planned in Saudi Arabia's sector operating centers and General Operating Center (GOC) near Riyadh. These efforts drew on the Peace Hawk VII study and other studies begun after the sale of the F-15 to Saudi Arabia in 1978. Such an upgrading was vital. Many elements of the existing Saudi C^3 system dated back to the abortive Anglo-U.S. air defense system of the 1960s, and major improvements were required to make effective use of the AWACS. The improvements included new hardened command and control facilities, new data-processing and display equipment, and improvements to the ground radar surveillance network through replacement of existing radars and the addition of new radar sites to extend coverage. Special ground entry stations also had to be provided to allow optimal communications with the AWACS.

The final U.S. plans called for improvements to the Saudi command, control, communications, and intelligence (C^3I) system that would cost over $1.5 billion and take six years to complete. The resulting system was to be jointly operated by the Saudi Air Force (10 systems) and Ministry for Aviation (12 systems). It was also to be designed for defense of the Gulf against attacks by Yemen and attacks from across the Red Sea. Like the AWACS, it was to be heavily dependent on continued U.S. technical support throughout the 1980s, again reducing the risk that the AWACS package could be used unilaterally against Israel.

Links to Ships and Helicopters

Finally, the new air defense system had the advantage that it could be modified to interface with the ships in the Saudi Navy. It could link their radars and surface-to-air missiles to Saudi Arabia's other air defenses and conduct joint sea-air operations against any seaborne attacking force. The E-3A had 35–108 NM of range in the maritime surveillance mode against metal ships of 40 feet or more length operating in a normal sea. Given the probable proficiency of the Saudi Navy in the 1980s, some such battle-management system was essential if Saudi Arabia was to use its new vessels with any effectiveness.

Although it was not explicitly stated in the studies involved, Saudi Arabia had the option of using the AWACS to monitor transponders on Saudi Army vehicles and helicopters and potentially those of the National Guard. This capability would allow the Saudi Army and Air Force to locate such units precisely and to improve the effectiveness of air force air support to the land forces defending the Saudi oil fields and other critical facilities. It also offered a significant potential improvement in the ability to coordinate Saudi defenses against guerrilla or larger-scale terrorist attacks. Such combinations of ground, helicopter, and fighter operations are exceedingly difficult to coordinate even for Western armies, and the AWACS provided a potential battle-management and communications center for the kind of small-scale but delicate operation that would be involved in actions against guerrillas and terrorists.

The Advantages of the Air Defense Enhancement Package to the U.S.

Each of the 10 major elements of the Saudi Air Defense Enhancement Package thus contributed to a system that would upgrade Saudi air defense capabilities so that they could employ the necessary air defense tactics and form the cornerstone of the deterrent Saudi Arabia had sought since the early 1960s. The U.S. had a great deal more to gain from the sale, however, than simply strengthening Saudi ability to protect the oil fields. In the course of the negotiations, it acquired an over-the-horizon reinforcement capability far more important than the one Secretary Brown had sought in early 1979, and one far better suited to the region.

- The Air Defense Enhancement Package gave Saudi Arabia a credible local deterrent and defense capability against the most probable regional threats that could affect its security or the West's supplies of oil.
- The package gave Saudi Arabia the military power and status it needed to act as a counterweight to Iran and Iraq. It meant that the other smaller Gulf states could turn to Saudi Arabia for a credible strengthening of their air defense. It was an ideal form of "linkage"

MAP 9—6
THE OIL AXIS: KEY TARGETS IN SAUDI ARABIA, BAHRAIN, AND QATAR

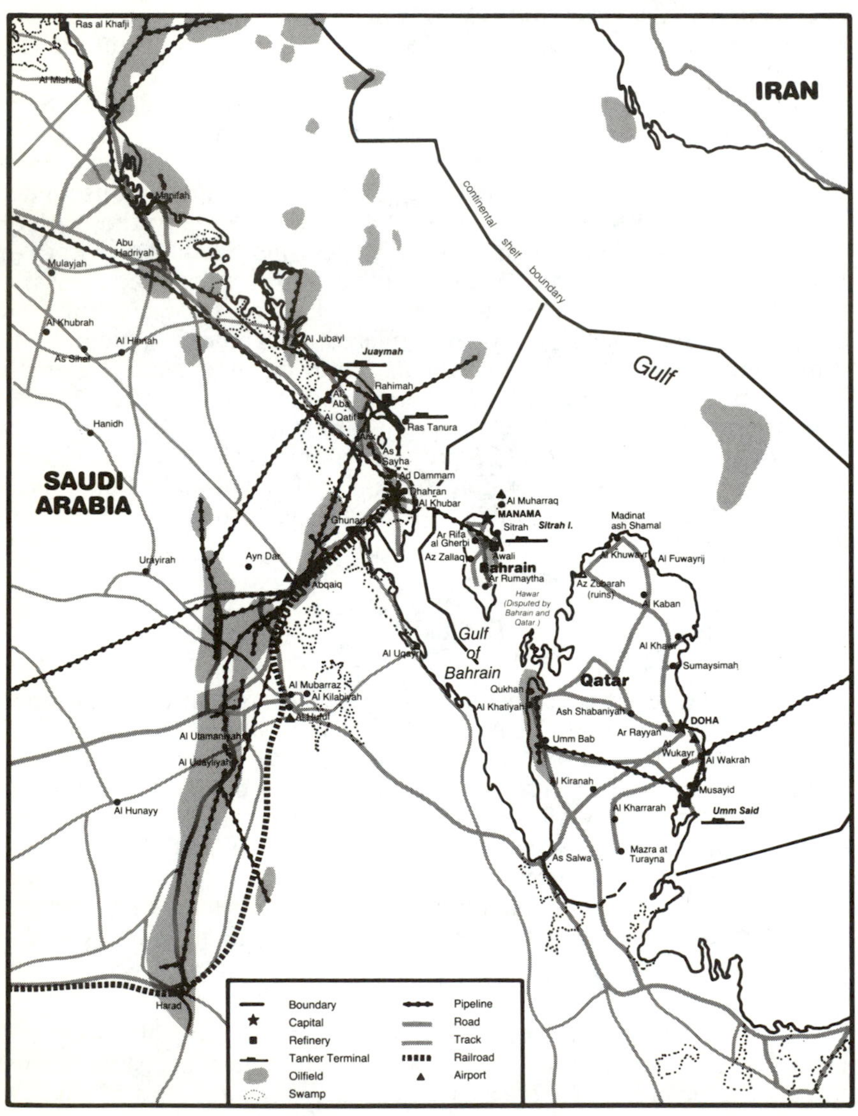

Adapted from maps furnished by the Department of Energy.

between Saudi Arabia and the smaller conservative Gulf states, which had something like 50% of Saudi Arabia's oil production capacity. It gave them the defensive coverage they need without threatening them and was an ideal means of uniting them behind the Gulf Cooperation Council and its nascent National Security Council.

• The package was a partial solution to the long-standing problem of convincing Saudi Arabia, particularly the Saudi military, that the country's military expenditures would be effective and would not jeopardize Saudi sovereignty and that the Saudi government had not miscalculated in maintaining its ties to the U.S. No single factor has been more important in destabilizing Third World military forces than the perception that their governments have failed to provide a credible basis for national defense and for maintaining national strength and independence.

• The package avoided formal military ties between the West and the conservative Gulf states, which half a century of Arab nationalism, the Arab-Israeli conflict, and the political history of Saudi Arabia had made untenable. It provided the U.S. with a means of strengthening Saudi Arabia while simultaneously preserving Saudi Arabian sovereignty and stability.

• The resulting Saudi-U.S. agreement, which is summarized in Table 9.8, gave the U.S. continued direct access to the information gathered by the AWACS while retaining control over transfers to third nations. Direct digital down links were to be available to the U.S.; these included data not only from the AWACS, but from the full range of sensors that make up the Saudi air defense system, many of which were not otherwise available.[21]

• The Saudis also agreed that the USAF and USN would be able to train and exercise jointly with the Saudi Air Force in a unique operating environment where such experience was essential to the effective projection of U.S. power. No substitute effort in the U.S., or elsewhere in the Near East, could provide such training and operational experience and give U.S. forces the "edge" necessary to maximize their effectiveness in the Gulf.

• The resulting improvement in Saudi capabilities greatly reduced the risk of having to send U.S. forces to deal with local or low-level threats. It also decreased the destabilizing effects of any such U.S. deployment without a threat great enough to unite the conservative Gulf states and moderate Arab opinion in support of such U.S. intervention.

• At the same time, the Air Defense Enhancement Package gave the U.S. the ability to deploy up to two wings, or roughly 140 USAF fighters, to support Saudi Arabia and the conservative Gulf states in an emergency. In fact, each main Saudi air base had the basic support equipment for 70 U.S. F-15 fighters in addition to supplies for its own F-15s. The package meant that Saudi Arabia would have all the necessary basing, service facilities, refueling capability, parts, and key munitions in place

TABLE 9.8 AWACS Letter of Offer and Acceptance (LOA) Terms and Conditions

	Standard LOA	Saudi Additions
Use of AWACS	Defensive use only	• No flights outside borders (without U.S. government prior consent)
Security of technology	Protect classified equipment with procedures similar to U.S. procedures	• U.S. government approval of security plan • U.S. government semi-annual inspections • High-technology security facilities • Only U.S. and Saudi people have access to equipment and documentation • New information security agreement • Computer software (machine language) remains U.S. government property
Third-country transfer	No transfer of equipment without U.S. government approval	• Third-country modifications to equipment forbidden • Third-country personnel forbidden to perform maintenance
Information sharing	None	• AWACS data exchanged between U.S. and Saudi Arabia at all times • No AWACS data to other countries without prior and mutual consent of U.S. government and Saudi Arabian government

Source: Adapted from material provided by U.S. Air Force.

to accept over-the-horizon reinforcement from USAF F-15 fighters. No conceivable improvement in U.S. airlift or USAF rapid deployment and "bare basing" capability[22] could come close to giving the U.S. this rapid and effective reinforcement capability.

• The package allowed the U.S. Navy to use its airpower effectively in the Gulf. U.S. carriers were too vulnerable to deploy into the Gulf, even during the Iraq-Iran War of 1980. The TF-70 Task Force sent to the region had to stay in the Gulf of Oman in 1980 because of the threat posed by Iranian forces, but carrier-based fighters lacked the range and AC&W capability to defend the central and western Gulf. The Saudi Air Defense Enhancement Package provided both the airborne refueling and AC&W capability to overcome this problem.

• None of the key elements of the system would be operable without U.S. support throughout their useful life.

• Something like two-thirds of the Saudi expenditure on the air defense system was to be on fixed ground facilities, bases, and defenses that will help protect Gulf oil facilities, oil shipments, and the Red Sea, but could not pose any meaningful threat to Israel.

• The facilities that would become part of the Saudi system would also help to strengthen U.S. ability to deploy forces from the eastern Mediterranean and project them as far east as Pakistan in those contingencies that threatened both U.S. and Saudi interests. No conceivable buildup of U.S. strategic mobility, or of U.S. staging bases in Egypt, Turkey, Oman, Somalia, or Kenya, could act as a substitute for such facilities in Saudi Arabia. The closest other U.S. facility in the region was at Diego Garcia, which is as far from the western Gulf as is Dublin, Ireland.

• The system's maritime mode provided a potential method of solving many of the problems in Saudi Arabia's naval defense and the modernization of its naval forces and in improving the coordination of its diverse U.S. and French vessels and equipment.

• The package solved the critical problem of financing the defense of the Gulf by having Saudi Arabia assume the full cost of the system. The Air Defense Enhancement Package was projected to cost $8.5 billion in current dollars, with only three years of spares and support. Even this cost estimate depended on exceptionally efficient U.S. assistance in managing the construction and training effort. Allowing for a 10-year life-cycle, systems growth, and normal cost growth, the true cost was projected to be at least $15 billion. The package also built on past and future U.S. military assistance expenditures, which then totaled $33–38 billion, some $20–25 billion of which was still to be delivered, and it meant the dollars were to be spent in the U.S. rather than in France or Britain. At least 50% of this expenditure was to be on construction, and some 80% of it will contribute directly to the defense of Gulf oil exports. The U.S. lacked the financial resources and the forces to create any credible alternative.

• The package was inherently defensive in character and did not threaten other regional powers. At the same time, the Saudi ground stations, SAM defenses, E-3A, and other elements of the package could be upgraded in the future in direct proportion to any growth in the threat.

In short, the Saudi Air Defense Enhancement Package offered Saudi Arabia the ability to provide a highly capable "one-front" fighter screen over the oil facilities in the Gulf and to protect against long-range attacks from Iran, Iraq, and the USSR in the north, with excellent capability on any other front and some "two-front" capability. It did this at minimum cost relative to alternative technologies, probably by a factor of two or three. It avoided the issues of sovereignty that prevented Saudi Arabia from accepting U.S. forces or bases in peacetime, yet it allowed Saudi Arabia to make far better use of over-the-horizon U.S. reinforcements if these should prove necessary. And it simultaneously gave Saudi Arabia the capability to deal with relatively unsophisticated attacks from South Yemen on a "two-front" basis. Perhaps most important, the package was a potential solution to more than two decades of problems in creating an effective military relationship between Saudi Arabia and the U.S. It linked both countries firmly in a synergistic way while minimizing any increase in the military threat to Israel.

The Vulnerabilities of the New Air Defense System

The Air Defense Enhancement Package did, however, create a number of significant risks for Saudi Arabia. While the system was certainly "state-of-the-art" for the region, it still had the following military vulnerabilities:

Surprise attack. The Saudis could not plan on keeping an AWACS on station at all times in peacetime, in the Dhahran area or any other area. The five AWACS would normally be on the ground at the al-Kharj main operating base, except for routine training, maintenance checkout, or proficiency flights or when practicing intercept procedures with fighter units or ground-based radar facilities.

In the event of a crisis, with clear indicators of imminent hostilities, the RSAF could maintain a single AWACS radar orbit over the oil fields (or elsewhere in the kingdom) for only seven days without U.S. AWACS reinforcements. Maintaining 24-hour AWACS radar coverage in peacetime, or for longer than seven days during a time of political tension, required many more AWACS. Thus if Iran or any other country attacked Saudi Arabia without political or strategic warning, it could probably avoid confronting an AWACS on station in the forward area.

Attack after prolonged strategic warning. An attacker could bluff Saudi Arabia into mounting a continuous AWACS orbit, either by verbal threats or provocative aerial maneuvers, and then wait for a week or more until the capabilities of the AWACS fleet had been degraded due to normal maintenance and logistics factors. Once the RSAF was forced to abandon continuous orbits for random orbits, Iran could attack when all five AWACS were at the al-Kharj base. An air attack would then encounter only ground-based radars.

Helicopter attack. The system was vulnerable to missile-equipped helicopters. The E-3A cannot detect slow-flying helicopters, although it can sometimes detect their blade motion.

Deceptive flight plans. Commercial air service is maintained between Saudi cities and many potential threat nations. Without sophisticated electronic support measures (ESM) equipment (which the U.S. does not plan to sell to Saudi Arabia) a Saudi E-3A could not tell from a radar presentation alone whether a target originating from a location like Tehran that purported to be a civilian aircraft and that complied with a duly filed flight plan to Dhahran or Bahrain was in fact a tight group of threat fighters imitating the speed and route of the civil aircraft.

Reduced warning attack. As previously mentioned, attackers could cut Saudi reaction time, even with the AWACS, by exercising or loitering peacefully in nearby airspace before veering off for an attack.

Multifront attack. A coordinated, large-scale attack on two or more fronts could prevent the Saudi AWACS from being effective in covering two fronts or force Saudi Arabia to choose one front over the other.

Further, the attacker could expand the area the E-3A would have to cover by attacking Saudi Arabia and its allies at both ends of the Gulf, by attacking from two countries simultaneously, or by extending a Red Sea attack to cover the north and south ends. As a result, Saudi Arabia is dependent on reinforcements by USAF E-3As to deal with large-scale attacks.

Missile attack. The Air Defense Enhancement Package was not designed to deal with the "smart" conventional missile attacks that may become possible in the late 1980s. A Phoenix-like, "smart," long-range antiaircraft missile might well then be able to track and kill the AWACS before it could retreat. Even today, conventional cruise missiles could penetrate the AWACS system with only a limited risk of detection, and in the future they will have improved guidance that should allow them to "kill" or incapacitate various oil facilities. Line-of-sight attacks by small, ship-mounted missiles would be effective against tankers and sea-based oil facilities, and the E-3A could not detect small ships, wooden ships, or ships operating in a high sea. The E-3A also provides no defense against high-speed missiles homing on terrorist or saboteur-installed designators.

Saturation attack. The Saudi E-3A and Saudi F-15 "net" could normally handle only 6–9 simultaneous intercepts at low altitudes. This could be increased only to 10–15 simultaneous intercepts even under the best circumstances. The AWACS-linked Saudi Air Force of the mid-1980s will also lack the fighter numbers necessary to provide full or continuing coverage of the targets in the Gulf area. The 62 Saudi F-5Es lack the data links, radar power, and heads-up display (HUD) necessary to fly "head-on" or effective multi-aspect intercepts, and its F-5E could not be economically upgraded. Even if the Saudi force expands to over 200 fighters or replaces its F-5Es with advanced fighters like the F-18A or F-16C, it would still be possible for an attacker the size of Iran or Iraq to outmass the Saudi air defense system. Accordingly, the system would be vulnerable to saturation unless USAF fighters were deployed on the scene.

Counter-AWACS attack. The system was not designed to deal with an opponent that also had an AWACS. Because of the extremely demanding time-on-target capabilities imposed by Saudi Arabia's small number of fighters, an enemy could use its AWACS to vector its fighters to end-run or avoid the Saudi defenders. Similarly, an enemy AWACS could spot any "stand-down" in the Saudi E-3A net or any gap that resulted from refueling.

Communications Problems and Interoperability

The vulnerabilities of the new air defense system were compounded by the risk that the U.S. might have underestimated Saudi Arabia's electronic warfare requirements. The Saudi configuration of the E-3A lacked the JTIDS, secure digital data links, the Have Quick and Seek

Talk frequency agile voice links, and the three extra data-display consoles in the USAF versions of the E-3A. Thus the Saudi E-3A was vulnerable to the level of ECM-capability electronic warfare that neighboring powers could acquire in the late 1980s.

The lack of JTIDS and Have Quick reduced the capability of the AWACS package to handle high-density attacks because of the need to rely on slow communications without automated support. The efficiency of the Saudi system in coordinating with U.S. air reinforcements was thus limited because:

- The Saudi E-3A would not have the JTIDS used by U.S. forces;
- The Saudi AWACS would not have the Have Quick anti-voice-jamming improvement common in U.S. forces;
- The Saudis would be sold sanitized, U.S.-government-controlled "commercial" secure data links in lieu of the U.S.-"military"-encrypted digital and voice communications gear for the E-3A, and they would be sold only a controlled "commercial" secure voice system for radio communications with the RSAF F-15s;
- The Saudi IFF for Modes 1, 2, and 3 would be the same as on the U.S. E-3A. However, the Saudis would be sold only U.S.-government-controlled and -sanitized "commercial" cryptographic equipment rather than U.S. military secure Mode 4 IFF cryptographic equipment;
- The Saudis would not be provided the computer software needed for TADIL C data links with interceptors or U.S. Navy F-14 fighters; and
- The Saudi F-15 would lack the advanced air-intercept program support package to be provided on U.S. F-15 C/Ds, and would lack the ability to fight enemy fighters on equal terms.

Even with these limitations, however, the new system offered the U.S. and Saudi air forces a substantial degree of interoperability. For example, the RSAF AWACS will be able to transmit or receive digital data using TADIL A high-frequency links with U.S. AWACS, navy ships, or air force ground-based tactical reporting and control posts (provided the formatted data is not passed through the noncompatible Saudi and U.S. cryptography equipment). The Saudi E-3As will be able to communicate by voice with U.S. E-3As and fighters using UHF radio (again provided that neither side passes transmissions through noncompatible secure voice equipment). The RSAF AWACS will also be able to interrogate U.S. AWACS and fighter IFF transponders using Mode 3 (but not the secure Mode 4).

Further, the communications equipment on the Saudi E-3As will be designed to have "form, fit, and function" interchangeability with the USAF E-3A, which means that Saudi interoperability with U.S. forces can be significantly upgraded with modifications that can be quickly and easily performed in the field. The RSAF secure voice and IFF equipment can be removed and replaced with U.S. "black boxes" in about four hours, giving both air forces fully compatible secure voice data and IFF capabilities. Alternately, the U.S. AWACS could replace its gear with Saudi "black boxes." U.S. Air Force mission tapes and TADIL C software can quickly be programmed into the RSAF AWACS computers. Only the installation of JTIDS and Have Quick require depot-level installation in the U.S.

The AWACS Debate

The technical arguments about the AWACS, however, had little impact on the long and bloody debate within the Congress that followed the sale. This debate was virtually a pure political struggle between the Reagan administration and supporters of Israel, and it came within four votes of killing the sale for several reasons: First, in order to pass its domestic program, the Reagan administration deferred any lobbying on the sale until late August 1981. Second, the lobbying effort was initially headed by President Reagan's national security adviser, Richard Allen, and the NSC staff. The staff, however, was new and had no practical experience in lobbying the Congress. Allen was also severely undercut by several members of his staff who opposed the sale and who privately briefed the Congress. Third, the administration underestimated the need to persuade the Congress with carefully reasoned arguments, as distinguished from using the new president's popularity. Fourth, the administration relied on polls predicting that Prime Minister Begin would be defeated in the elections Israel was to hold in the spring of 1981. When he was reelected, it then miscalculated that it could persuade his government to accept the sale through a combination of persuasion, increased aid, promises of strategic ties, and veiled threats. Fifth, the administration underestimated the skill and leadership quality of its opposition in the Senate and House and of the various pro-Israeli lobbying groups in the U.S.

Sixth, the administration allowed Prime Minister Begin and senior Israeli officials to lobby the Congress without opposition and to "lock up" votes before it began its own lobbying effort. Seventh, the administration overestimated the negative impact of the Israeli Osirak and Beirut raids on the Congress and congressional responsiveness to Saudi support of the U.S. during the Lebanon crisis of 1981. Finally, and perhaps most important, the administration miscalculated the effect of the shah's fall on the Congress, most of whose members interpreted it as a signal that no Arab ally could be stable or be trusted with sophisticated equipment rather than as a sign that the U.S. needed to strengthen its other major ally in the Gulf.

The Chronology of the AWACS Debate

Once again, a chronology of events is instructive, in explaining how the Reagan administration overcame these handicaps and in providing a detailed picture of the interactions that shape Saudi-U.S. military relations:

26 February 1981: The administration briefs the Senate Foreign Relations Committee on the basic outline of its decision to sell a new Saudi arms package: AIM-9L missiles, conformal fuel tanks, and an airborne radar surveillance capability.[23]

6 March 1981: The State Department announces that the Reagan administration will soon give notice to Congress of its intention to sell the missiles and the fuel tanks to Saudi Arabia.[24]

24 March 1981: Twenty U.S. senators declare their opposition to such a sale.[25]

1 April 1981: Senator John Tower of the Senate Armed Services Committee argues that the F-15 enhancement equipment to be sold to Saudi Arabia is beneficial even to Israel's long-term interest.[26]

2 April 1981: Opposition continues to rise, highlighted by a colloquy of 27 senators wary of the sale.[27]

20 April 1981: Former Carter officials (Secretary of Defense) Brown and (Secretary of State) Muskie release a letter stating that they are "favorably inclined" toward the sale of AWACS and F-15 equipment.[28]

27 April 1981: The White House announces its decision to sell Saudi Arabia five AWACS systems in a package including KC-135 tanker planes along with the F-15 equipment. It defends the sale as a continuation of the U.S. commitment to Saudi Arabia in a series of military programs, stating that it is essential for the protection of U.S. interests in the Gulf due to the deterioration of the security of the West in the region.[29]

May–June 1981: Representatives Long and Lent release a resolution with 225 signers opposing the sale. The Senate sends a letter opposing the sale with 54 signatures to the president.[30]

25 June 1981: Senate Foreign Relations Committee Chairman Charles Percy recommends that the proposal for the sale be delayed.[31]

28 June 1981: Secretary of State Haig announces a delay in the formal proposal of the sale.[32]

10 July 1981: Secretary Haig sends a letter sharply warning Begin regarding his overt opposition to the AWACS sale and implicitly linking the resumption of F-16 deliveries to Israel and Begin's anti-AWACS posture.[33]

29 July 1981: Haig announces again that formal submission to Congress of the sale will be delayed until September.[34]

5 August 1981: President Reagan launches his campaign to win support for the AWACS sale by sending a letter to the Republican and Democratic leaders of both houses. Secretary Haig visits Riyadh to confirm security-related positions; during the visit the Saudis sever diplomatic relations with Afghanistan.[35]

Early August 1981: Crown Prince Fahd indicates Saudi Arabia's interest in a peace in the Middle East that includes Israel.[36]

24 August 1981: President Reagan formally proposes to Congress the sale of the AWACS package to Saudi Arabia. Opposition remains strong.[37]

September 1981: Prime Minister Begin arrives in Washington and expresses open opposition to the sale. During the course of his stay, Begin meets with a number of U.S. pro-Israel lobby leaders and U.S. legislators, as well as with the president, to discuss strategic issues. Begin returns to Israel and steps up his opposition. Reagan responds by implicitly warning Begin not to meddle with U.S. foreign policy decision-making. Israeli-U.S. relations are further strained. Begin asserts, however, that he has not interfered in the internal U.S. decision-making process and that there is no link between the sale and Israeli-U.S. ties.[38]

11 September 1981: The U.S. Congress is again in session: The House is opposed to the sale, the Senate remains split. The lobbying, particularly by President Reagan, heats up, highlighted by personal meetings with various senators. Reagan manages to sway several senators in his favor, though he is still far short of the votes to approve the sale.[39]

Late September–Early October 1981: Reagan manages to rally more votes, but still has far from enough. He obtains aid from other political figures, such as Henry Kissinger and former Presidents Nixon and Ford. The Congress debates the notion of a joint command of the planes with Saudi Arabia, which flatly refuses such a proposal even though President Reagan sends an envoy to Riyadh to explore the Saudi reaction to the suggestion. Secretary Haig then informs the Congress there can be no further concessions on the package.[40]

1 October 1981: Secretary of Defense Caspar Weinberger testifies before the Senate Foreign Relations Committee, defending the administration's decision to sell the package.[41] President Reagan brings his case before the public in a televised speech, during which he defends the sale and vows that the U.S. will not allow Saudi Arabia to become another Iran and will protect Saudi internal security.[42]

5 October 1981: A nationwide poll by Cambridge Reports, Inc. (conducted 16–19 September) indicates that a strong majority of Americans favor the sale and do not feel the AWACS is a threat to Israel; they do feel congressional disapproval will greatly impair the president's prestige and ability to conduct foreign policy. A senior Saudi official indicates that his country does not plan retaliatory action if the sale does not go through, but that such a failure would be a great letdown by a "hitherto trusted friend."[43]

6 October 1981: Egyptian President Anwar Sadat is assassinated in Cairo, with telling effect on the AWACS debate: 9 more senators decide to vote in the president's favor, arguing that the uncertain situation requires greater support of the president. The opposition, however, argues that the assassination only demonstrates the instability of the region, and opponents focus more and more upon direct comparison between the Saudi kingdom and imperial Iran. Both the Israelis and the Saudi Arabians attempt to use the assassination to support their views.[44] The House Foreign Affairs Committee and the Senate Foreign Relations Committee decide to delay their votes on the issue.[45]

7 October 1981: President Reagan meets with 43 Republican senators in the White House.[46]

9–11 October 1981: Former Presidents Carter, Ford, and Nixon attend the funeral of Anwar Sadat along with former Secretary of State Kissinger and Secretary Haig. All publicly express support of the AWACS sale.

15 October 1981: The Senate Foreign Relations Committee submits a resolution opposing the sale.[47]

13 October 1981: The U.S. secretaries of state and defense affirm the U.S. intention to temporarily dispatch AWACS planes for Egyptian defense. The next day, two aircraft begin their trek to Egypt.[48]

14 October 1981: The House votes against the sale, 301 to 111.[49]

15 October 1981: The Senate Foreign Relations Committee recommends (9–8) opposition to the sale, overshadowing the Armed Services Committee's endorsement,[50] although the opposition drops from an initial vote of 14 to 3 against.

23 October 1981: During the summit meeting in Cancun on world economic development, President Reagan meets with Prince Fahd, though claims are made that there was no discussion of the AWACS sale. An influential Democratic senator, Dale Bumpers, announces his opposition to the sale.[51]

25 October 1981: President Reagan intensely lobbies the proposed sale throughout the Senate. Senator Howard Baker expresses his confidence in the president's ability to swing the necessary votes.[52]

27 October 1981: President Reagan picks up a substantial number of votes after personal lobbying efforts to persuade key senators.[53]

28 October 1981: The Senate votes on the resolution: 52 vote in favor of the sale, largely as a result of President Reagan's brilliant last-minute lobbying. The president sends the Senate a letter stating that Saudi Arabia has agreed not to transfer AWACS data to third parties. The fierce personal campaign included such lobbying as a helicopter trip to Richmond with Senator Warner, during which the president persuaded another senator to see his point of view.

As this chronology shows, President Reagan proved able to use his personal prestige to win Senate acceptance of the sale by a thin margin. While this vote was more a personal triumph for President Reagan than a reflection of congressional understanding of the role that Saudi Arabia could play in stabilizing the Gulf, the Senate's approval still laid the essential groundwork for sustained Saudi-U.S. military and strategic cooperation in the 1980s.

The Lessons of the AWACS Debate

The AWACS debate left some lasting scars. By the time the president's victory occurred, the sale had something of a "no win" impact for the U.S., Saudi Arabia, and Israel alike. The struggle between Reagan and Begin seriously hurt U.S. relations with Israel. At the same time, the debate led to so many public criticisms in the U.S. of the Saudi government and to so much public denigration of the E-3A that it deprived Saudi Arabia of much of the political and deterrent value of the sale. Further, the debate gave the impression that the new administration lacked the ability to lead consistently and to manage foreign relations.

These negative effects were softened by the fact that most of the resentment that built up during the debate was temporary and channeled toward Prime Minister Begin. Senior officials of the Saudi government had also expected what happened. Unlike the situation in 1978, they had no illusions about the cost of winning the sale or the president's powers to prevent an excruciating public debate over Saudi instability and military competence. Finally, the president's triumph reduced the negative impression caused by the administration's initial mishandling of the sale.

Still, the debate left several messages for the future. First, no U.S. administration can hope to make such arms sales without a long lobbying effort and a skillfull campaign to inform the Congress of the sale's technical merits. The Congress and the media must be approached as far in advance as possible, and the debate must be elevated to one over facts rather than emotion in time to allow serious discussion. Second, both the U.S. and Saudi Arabia need to improve their efforts to communicate the nature and mutual benefit of their military relationship. As was the case in 1978, much of the debate stemmed from a broad ignorance of the history and nature of that relationship. A continuing effort, not simply an episodic treatment focused on a major arms sale, is required. Third, the U.S. cannot hope to persuade Israel to accept close U.S. ties to an Arab state, or to buy Israel off, under current political circumstances. The U.S. can hope to minimize Israeli concerns, but it must expect a political battle over every major arms sale to Saudi Arabia and act accordingly. Last, some improved method is needed in dealing with arms sales that will allow tacit communication among the U.S., friendly Arab states, and Israel. While agreement between Israel and the Arab states is impossible, many of the problems that occurred in the AWACS debate were the result of technical "surprises" that Israel lacked the time to understand properly and to which it then overreacted. Quite similar problems have occurred when Arab allies have reacted to U.S. transfers of technology to Israel. One solution might be to publicly announce long-term U.S. military aid plans to Israel and the Arab states alike. Such announcements would allow a quiet debate at the senior political level and minimize the risk of explosive public debates over aid and sales to a single side.

The need to learn these lessons is scarcely academic. As will be discussed in the next chapter, the Reagan administration has already repeated many of the mistakes of the Carter administration and the AWACS debate. The inability to create even a modest modus vivendi among the U.S., Saudi Arabia, and Israel again threatens U.S. efforts to forge a strategic partnership with Saudi Arabia, and Saudi Arabia will have enough self-inflicted problems in modernizing its forces. The U.S. must take every step possible to minimize the impact of any further problems imposed by the Arab-Israeli conflict on U.S. politics and diplomacy.

Notes

1. At the time the USAF air feasibility study was completed, the RSAF F-5B fighter-bombers, as well as 36 Lightning fighter aircraft, were to be phased out in part as F-15s were delivered. The main combat squadrons were deployed throughout the country. No. 2 Squadron flying Lightning F-53 fighters was stationed at Dhahran Air Force Base (AFB) on the Gulf. A similarly equipped No. 6 Squadron was stationed at Khamis Mushayt on the Yemeni border. Dhahran also housed the other combat utility (OCU) squadron of F-5E fighter bombers, No. 7 Squadron, as well as an operational F-5E squadron, No. 15. Taif and Tabuk AFBs—the former on the mountains just behind the Red Sea, the latter 200 kilometers from Eilat in Israel—based four squadrons of F-5Es between them, but Tabuk had the only main operating base. In the past, one of these squadrons had taken part in an inter-Arab exercise in Syria; another was attached to Mafraq AFB in Jordan. Riyadh AFB housed the King Faisal Air Academy, two light attack squadrons flying BAC-167 Strikemasters, and a transport squadron. Two more transport squadrons were scattered throughout Saudi Arabia's air force bases.

2. Under its 1978 agreement with the U.S., Saudi Arabia may not deploy F-15s to Tabuk or Hafr al-Batin, although the latter is more than 300 NM from Israel. F-15 support is available only at the bases at Dhahran, Taif, and Khamis Mushayt. No support equipment or U.S. F-15 technicians may be deployed at either base. This requirement effectively precludes Saudi Arabia from sustained F-15 operations against Israel. Redeployment of support equipment would take several months, and loss of U.S. technicians would effectively deprive Saudi Arabia of the use of its F-15s within three months at most. Cutting off U.S. spare parts would have the same effect much sooner. Saudi Arabia is now dealing with this problem by concentrating all its later-model Lightnings at Tabuk as the F-15s are delivered.

3. Only the SOCs and Tayma (Tabuk), Riyadh (also the GOC), Dhahran, and Taif (alternate GOC) were fully operational. Only Dhahran had an advanced sector coordinating center.

4. ADCs exist at Tabuk, Dhahran, Hafr al-Batin, Riyadh (army GOC), Taif, and Khamis Mushayt.

5. This discussion is excerpted in part from SFRC, *The Proposed AWACS/F-15 Enhancement Sale to Saudi Arabia,* GPO 84-557-0 (Washington, D.C.: Government Printing Office, September 1981), especially pp. 16–19.

6. Taken from *The Military Balance, 1981–82.* (London: IISS, 1982). Iraq probably had about 2,900 medium tanks and 370 combat aircraft before the

spring 1982 offensive, and the North Yemeni Air Force has increased to about 80–90 aircraft.

7. Trends are estimated from the annual IISS *Military Balance* (1969–1981), SIPRI yearbooks through 1980, and SIPRI computer printouts on arms transfers.

8. See George Lenczowski, *The Middle East in World Affairs* (Ithaca, N.Y.: Cornell University Press, 1980), for a history of many of these incidents.

9. This forced the U.S. to deploy F-100 fighters in Saudi Arabia's defense. See ibid., p. 589; and Richard F. Nyrop, *Area Handbook for Saudi Arabia,* Foreign Area Handbook Series (Washington, D.C.: American University, 1977), p. 334.

10. As Table 9.1 shows, Saudi Arabia had five such radars in 1981, plus some smaller mobile TPS-43 radars.

11. The E-2C navy airborne early warning and control (AEW&C) aircraft has been in service since the 1950s. Although originally designed only for maritime operations, the E-2 series has since been equipped with a highly capable pulse-doppler radar for detecting low-flying targets over land. The E-2C has been purchased by Israel, Egypt, and Japan and is being considered by Australia and France. Compared to the AWACS, the Hawkeye has a slower cruise speed and significantly less range and endurance. This means that it takes an E-2C longer to arrive at its orbit point, and it can remain on station for a shorter amount of time before having to return to its home base for fuel. For example, almost twice as many E-2Cs as AWACS are required to maintain a continuous orbit 200 NM from a home base (a distance that approximates the radius of current AWACS radar orbit points from Riyadh). For orbits more than 500 NM from the home field, approximately three times as many E-2Cs as AWACS are needed. This problem could be minimized if E-2Cs were based near their orbit points—at Dhahran, for instance, for oil field defense. The Saudi air defense requirement, though, calls for one home base for the AWACS fleet, rather than dispersed basing around the kingdom. Maintaining the AWACS fleet at one base simplifies the associated logistics, maintenance, and training requirements and minimizes the risk of surprise or preemptive attack.

Since the E-2C cannot cruise at as high an altitude as the AWACS, its radar horizon is slightly less than that of the AWACS. As a general rule of thumb, the AWACS detects low-flying (200-foot) targets about 20 NM sooner than would an E-2C. In addition, the E-2C's detection range for high-altitude targets is less than that of the AWACS. The E-2C's overland height-finding capability is also less effective than that of the AWACS, and its main radar beam is more vulnerable to jamming.

The E-2C does, however, have some capabilities superior to those of the AWACS. For example, the Hawkeye can use its passive defense system (PDS)—an electronics system not currently installed on AWACS—to detect and track radar emitters of a wide range of air, land, or sea platforms, including such systems as tank fire-control systems, artillery-spotting radars, and the missile-control radars on fighter aircraft. The E-2C's PDS could therefore be employed to monitor armor or artillery units even if they were not moving along the ground. Unlike the AWACS, the E-2C can use its main radar in modes that permit it to track very slow-moving objects, including helicopters and standard army vehicles (tanks, self-propelled guns, trucks, etc.).

On balance, the E-2C could be said to have radar, computer, and automation capabilities generally comparable to those of the AWACS; however, the range and endurance limitations of the basic airframe make it more suited to "point defense" scenarios (such as defending an aircraft carrier or a small state like Israel) than for area defense of large landmasses. See SFRC, *Proposed AWACS/F-15 Enhancement Sale,* p. 26–27, for more details.

12. *Congressional Record,* 7 April 1981, p. H-1379. Such estimates had the merit of being based on practical tests. At an exercise at Nellis AFB, two E-3A Sentinels coordinated 134 friendly aircraft against 274 "enemy" planes.

13. Ibid. This may be a comparatively high-risk decision by the mid-1980s. It is unclear that Saudi forces could handle a high-density threat without JTIDS of the kind that might well develop in the Gulf by the mid-1980s, and this lack will severely degrade USAF and USN ability to operate with AWACS in providing over-the-horizon capability.

14. This discussion is summarized from the transcripts of unclassified DOD briefings issued to the press on 24 April 1981.

15. Some U.S. industry sources believe that Israel already has the capability to jam the AWACS radar. Since the AWACS radar is not frequency agile, Israel could use its MN-53 electronic warfare system, developed originally by the Elbit Company for the Israeli Navy, to intercept and identify the RSAF AWACS radar frequency. At this point, even a low-power jammer set on the AWACS radar frequency could "penetrate" the AWACS's main radar beam, effectively blocking 100 degrees of the AWACS scan. Assuming that the AWACS orbits 180 miles from Israeli airspace, Israel could establish a continuous screen of radar jamming by deploying low-power noise jammers every 3 miles along whatever sector it wished to cover. Such equipment is produced by AEL, Israel, Ltd.

The Israeli E-2C would be available to assist Israeli interceptors to compensate for support provided to Saudi fighters by AWACS. Any adjustments in flight patterns made by Saudi aircraft to avoid Israeli defenders could be quickly observed and countered by the Israeli E-2C. Using its ESM equipment, the Israeli E-2C could detect the Saudi AWACS and vector scrambled Israeli F-15s to an intercept. Even if the attacking Israeli fighters did not shoot down the AWACS, they could force it to turn and run, thus removing it as a factor in the air engagement. NATO AWACS are instructed to stay behind the forward edge of the battle area (FEBA) during war.

16. The loss of JTIDS and the Have Quick and Seek Talk secure communications equipment would make the Saudi version of AWACS vulnerable to the generation of jamming equipment that Israel had begun to manufacture in the late 1970s. While it is doubtful that such jamming would be effective for power reasons in the wide patrol area covered by the AWACS in the Gulf, it would probably be effective in the much smaller territory involved in an Arab-Israeli conflict. There the approximate location of AWACS can be easily predicted, reliance must be placed on reliable links to SAM systems, and many Arab aircraft will have relatively poor on-board communications capabilities. For a description of such Israeli capabilities see the special series on Israeli avionics in *Aviation Week,* 10, 17, and 24 April 1978.

17. The AIM-9L is the third generation in the Sidewinder family of short-range, air-to-air infrared (heat-seeking) missiles. It incorporates an "all aspect" guidance and control system that allows head-on attack. The major improvements of the AIM-9L over the AIM-9P-3, currently possessed by the Saudis, included an improved seeker, providing all-aspect and better look-down/shoot-down capabilities; increased maneuverability; and improved warhead lethality. The seeker and fuse technology allows this version of the Sidewinder missile to be fired at enemy aircraft from any angle, rather than only from the rear.

Approximately 4,000 AIM-9Ls were in USAF and USN inventories. The AIM-9Ls proposed for sale were to come from U.S. inventories on a one-for-one basis as the more advanced AIM-9M series is procured. The estimated unit cost was $98,000, but that does not include spares, support, training, etc. Other purchasers include Israel, United Kingdom, Germany, Norway, Italy, Japan, Australia, Greece, and Sweden.

18. See "The AIM-9L Super Sidewinder," *Combat Aircraft,* special issue of *International Defense Review,* 1976, p. 151.

19. The AIM-9L did present a danger of technology compromise because of its advanced seeker and fuse technology. While the Soviets were aware of the basic cooling technology involved, they did not yet have the manufacturing capability to produce a comparable all-aspect missile. The similar French Super Matra had, however, been sold to Iraq. AIM-9L technology had thus far been limited to NATO countries, Japan, Australia, New Zealand, and Israel. It was being coproduced with several NATO countries, but all fuses as well as all guidance and control systems were produced in the United States (seekers were being coproduced only with West Germany). The physical security of the AIM-9 was difficult to control because 1,177 missiles would eventually be stored in several locations. However, the missiles sold to Saudi Arabia were to have very stringent security procedures developed specifically for the AIM-9L.

Raytheon Corporation no longer produces AIM-9Ls, having converted its assembly line to the production of the more advanced AIM-9M. Since the U.S. was retiring its AIM-9L missiles in favor of the AIM-9M anyway, the Saudi AIM-9L sale effectively subsidized U.S. upgrading of a significant portion of its short-range air-to-air missile inventory. The AIM-9M has a more advanced optic seeker, capable of distinguishing the target from flare decoys, and a cleaner-burning propellant, which makes it more difficult for an enemy to detect the missile in flight.

20. McDonnell-Douglas Company, "FAST Pack Conformal Fuel Tanks—The Eagle Enhancers," April 1980. The kits weighed about 2,000 lbs empty and could carry 9,750 lbs of fuel. They were supplied to Israel and Japan, but not the USAF SFRC, *Proposed AWACS/F-15 Enhancement Sale,* p. 63.

21. Testimony during the AWACS debate showed that the U.S. had had such down links to U.S. Navy ships in the Gulf from the first day the AWACS was deployed in the Gulf. Although some confusion arose in the press over the status of these agreements after Secretary of Defense Weinberger's visit to Saudi Arabia in January 1982, they were implemented in full.

22. "Bare basing" refers to the ability of U.S. C-5A or C-141 air transports to fly in enough equipment to support minimal fighter operations from a foreign base. The weaknesses in this capability were confirmed by U.S. experience in the "Bright Star" exercises of January 1982. See "Bright Star," *Current News,* (Department of Defense), Special Edition, nos. 812 and 813 (3 February 1982).

23. SFRC, *Proposed AWACS/F-15 Enhancement Sale,* pp. 5–6.

24. Ibid., p. 64.

25. Ibid.; *Washington Star,* 25 March 1981.

26. *Washington Post,* 2 April 1981.

27. *Near East Report* 25, no. 15 (10 April 1981).

28. *Washington Post,* 21 April 1981.

29. SFRC, *Proposed AWACS/F-15 Enhancement Sale,* p. 64. See also *New York Times,* 22 April 1981.

30. *Washington Star,* 24 June 1981; *New York Times* and *Wall Street Journal,* 25 June 1981.

31. *Washington Star,* 26 June 1981.

32. *Baltimore Sun,* 29 June 1981.

33. *Washington Star,* 7 July 1981.

34. *Washington Post,* 30 July 1981.

35. *Washington Star* and *Baltimore Sun,* 4 August 1981; *Wall Street Journal* and *Washington Post,* 6 August 1981.

36. *Christian Science Monitor,* 11 August 1981; *Baltimore Sun,* 10 August 1981; *New York Times,* 12 August 1981.

37. *Washington Post,* 25 August 1981; *Aviation Week,* 31 August 1981.

38. *Washington Post,* 30 August and 7, 14, and 21 September 1981; *New York Times,* 21 September and 6 October 1981; *Christian Science Monitor,* 8 and 9 September 1981; *Baltimore Sun,* 3 October 1981.

39. *Washington Post,* 12 and 14 September and 9 October 1981; *Wall Street Journal,* 15 September 1981; *New York Times,* 11 and 18 September and 7 October 1981; *Aviation Week,* 28 September 1981.

40. *Washington Post,* 30 September and 6 October 1981; *New York Times,* 4 October 1981; *Baltimore Sun,* 6 October 1981.

41. *Washington Post* and *New York Times,* 2 October 1981.

42. *Los Angeles Times,* 3 October 1981.

43. Cambridge Reports release, 5 October 1981; *Baltimore Sun,* 6 October 1981.

44. *Washington Post,* 7 and 9 October 1981; *New York Times,* 7 October 1981.

45. *Washington Post,* 8 and 9 October 1981.

46. *New York Times* and *Washington Post,* 10–14 October 1981.

47. Ibid., 16 and 17 October 1981.

48. *Baltimore Sun,* 14 October 1981; *Washington Post,* 15 October 1981.

49. *Washington Post, New York Times,* and *Baltimore Sun,* 15 October 1981.

50. *Baltimore Sun* and *Wall Street Journal,* 16 October 1981.

51. *Washington Post,* 24 October 1981.

52. *Washington Post* and *Baltimore Sun,* 26 October 1977.

53. *Baltimore Sun, New York Times,* and *Washington Post,* 28 October 1981.

10
Trends in Saudi Military Modernization and Saudi-U.S. Military Relations

It is difficult to look beyond the AWACS debate and make any precise predictions of the growth of Saudi military capabilities, of the trend in Saudi-U.S. relations, or of Saudi Arabia's role in the region. As is discussed in the following chapters, the future may well be shaped by factors beyond Saudi and U.S. control. These factors include the aftermath of Israel's invasion of Lebanon; the long-term outcome of the Iran-Iraq War; the success of the conservative and radical states in the Gulf area in forging collective military strength; the rate of world economic recovery and recovery of the demand for Saudi oil; the future rate of arms transfers into the area; and political developments that take place in the Yemens and the Red Sea area. Some of these trends will act to divide the U.S. and Saudi Arabia in spite of the AWACS sale. Others may forge an even tighter military relationship or even diminish Israeli opposition to U.S. strategic ties to Saudi Arabia. There are, however, several things that can be said about the forces shaping Saudi Arabia's military future and Saudi-U.S. military relations. These forces will strongly influence Saudi Arabia's ability to act as the fulcrum of a Western strategic partnership with the Gulf states.

The Transition to Full-Scale Military Modernization

During the 1980s, Saudi Arabia will realize many of the fruits of its immense investment in construction, training, and infrastructure. As Table 10.1 shows, the early 1980s mark a transition period during which many of Saudi Arabia's efforts to expand its facilities and manpower base are beginning to be translated into major equipment deliveries and a growing force structure.

While Saudi Arabia can be expected to show continued restraint in its military expansion—particularly in view of the world recession of the early 1980s and the resulting decline in oil revenues—it is gradually

TABLE 10.1 Trends in the Modernization of Saudi Arabian Armed Forces, 1974-1982

	1973-74	1974-75	1975-76	1976-77
Total population	8.4	8.67	8.9	5-6
Defence expenditures (DE) (billions)	1.9	1.8	6.77	
GNP (billions)	6.8	24.8	37.2	
DE % of GNP	28.0	7.3	18.2	
Total military manpower	42,500	43,000	47,000	51,500
Army				
Manpower	36,000	36,000	40,000	40,000
Equipment				
Medium tanks	25	55	175	325
Major types	M47	AMX-30	AMX-30	AMX-30
Other AFVs	260	260	260	260
Major types	AML-90	AML-90	AML-90	AML-90
Field/light artillery	some	some	105mm	105mm
SP guns	—	—	—	—
AA weapons	some	some	some	some
ATWs	Vigilant	Vigilant	Harpon	Harpon
Missiles	Hawk	Hawk	Hawk	Hawk
Navy				
Manpower	1,000	1,500	1,500	1,500
Total craft	22 2 torpedo 10 patrol 2 utility 8 Hover-craft	32 24 patrol 8 Hovercraft	4 4 patrol	3 3 patrol
Air Force				
Manpower	5,500	5,500	5,500	10,000
Total combat aircraft	70	90	95	97
Fighters	35	35	35	37
Major types	Lightning	Lightning	Lightning	Lightning
Fighter bombers	35	55	60	60
Major types	BAC-167	F-5	F-5	F-5
Transports	12	11	25	31
Major types	C-130	C-130	C-130	C-130
Helicopters	30	37	52	53
Major types	AB-206	AB-206	AB-205	AB-205
Other (numbers/types)	1 trainer 7 light ac 37 SAMS	4 trainers 7 light ac 37 SAMS	3 trainers 37 SAMS	25 trainers
Paramilitary forces				
Manpower	3,500	26,000	22,500	26,500
Craft			50 patrol 8 Hovercraft	50 patrol 8 Hovercraft

[a]GDP

[b]39 BAC-167 COIN aircraft used in dual role in 1979 reduced to trainer status in 1980

TABLE 10.1 (continued)

1977–78	1978–79	1979–80	1980–81	1981–82	1982–83
6–7	7.73	7.98	8.22	10.4	8.1
7.53	9.63	14.2	20.7	24.4	–
55.4	64.2	96.6[a]	(1)	119	–
13.6	15	17.8	–	20.5	–
61,500	58,500	44,500	47,000	51,700	52,200
45,000	45,000	35,000	31,000	35,000	35,000
475	325	350	380	630	450
AMX-30	AMX-30	AMX-30	AMX-30	AMX-30	AMX-30
410	550	600	600	1,600	1,390
AML-90	AMX-10P	M-113	M-113	M-113	M-113
105mm	105mm	105mm	105mm	105mm	105mm
–	some	155mm	155mm	105mm	105mm
some	M42	M42	M42	AMX-30	35mm
Dragon	TOW	TOW	TOW	TOW	TOW
Hawk	Hawk	Hawk	Hawk	Hawk	Imp. Hawk
1,500	1,500	1,500	1,500	2,200	2,200
5	10	134	86	77	76
5 patrol	4 patrol	124 patrol	76 patrol	5 PGM	4 PGC
	4 mine-	8 Hover-	4 mine-	3 PCM	5 PGG
	sweepers	craft	sweepers	4 MSC	3 FAC
	2 utility	2 LCU	6 landing	53 LPC	54 PC
			craft	12 landing	4 mine
				craft	6 LC
15,000	12,000	8,000	14,500	14,500	15,000
137	171	178[b]	136[b]	139	128
37	36	34	34	34	15
Lightning	Lightning	Lightning	Lightning	Lightning	Lightning
100	135	144	105	105	113
F5E	F-5E	F-5E	F-5E	F-5E	F-15
46	44	47	70	69	71
C-130	C-130	C-130	C-130	C-130	C-130
53	66	54	40	41	38
AB-205	AB-205	AB-205	AB-205	AB-205	AD-205/6
35 trainers	12 trainers	23 trainers	12 trainers	51 trainers	58 trainers
41,500	41,500	26,500	26,500	36,500	31,500
50 patrol	50 patrol		150 APCs	240 AFVs	240 AFVs
8 Hovercraft	8 Hovercraft		70 patrol	90 patrol	9 patrol
			8 Hovercraft	8 Hovercraft	8 Hovercraft

Source: The Military Balance (London: IISS, various years).

becoming a significant modern military power. During the mid-1980s, the emphasis in Saudi defense expenditures will shift to acquiring weapons and advanced military technology, and the character of U.S. and other Western military assistance must change accordingly. The challenge for both Saudi Arabia and the West will be to make the Saudi absorption of its new equipment purchases militarily effective and to avoid making Saudi Arabia another center of the "Arab disease"—buying military equipment without being able to operate it effectively.

Saudi Dependence on Foreign Manpower

One key aspect of this challenge will be to give Saudi Arabia the kind of foreign help it needs. Saudi Arabia's new arms will keep it dependent on foreign technical assistance and support well into the 1990s. Saudi Arabia's reliance on volunteers to man its forces in a country with a native population of 4–5 million (slightly larger than that of North Yemen) will continue to force it to concentrate most of its military personnel in combat arms.

As a result, Saudi Arabia will need more than its current 5,300 U.S. technicians and the 425 U.S. military personnel who provide maintenance support for its U.S. weapons systems, military advice, and training.[1] As Chart 10.1 shows, the Air Defense Enhancement Package will add significantly to that total, and it is only part of the story. Saudi requirements for highly trained U.S. military and technical and personnel may double in the next decade, although the overall total of Americans should drop as construction activity phases down. Saudi Arabia will need more British and French advisers as well. Saudi Arabia will also need *better* advisers and support personnel. The U.S. military training mission has improved steadily in recent years. Both the Department of Defense and the Commander-in-Chief, Europe (USCINCEUR) now give Saudi Arabia more attention. The personnel at the mission's headquarters in Dhahran and those supporting the joint Saudi-U.S. section at Riyadh have been upgraded, and the head of the mission now exerts more direct authority over the activities of the Middle East district of the U.S. Army Corps of Engineers, the Saudi National Guard modernization program, and the Saudi Naval Expansion Program.

The U.S. aid effort is, however, still of mixed quality. The Saudi Air Force generally gets excellent national support, and the temporary deployment of USAF air defense equipment provides additional "hands on" support. The USAF effort has teams at the Saudi Air Force headquarters, at Riyadh Air Base (C-130 support), King Abd al-Aziz Air Force Base at Dhahran (F-15 and F-5 support), and the King Faisal Air Academy, and at each Saudi air base. Senior Saudi Air Force officers have also been pleased with the impact of the Elf-1 unit that is operating four E-3As, KC-135 tanker aircraft, and TPS-43 gap-filler radars during the period before the U.S. delivers the Air Defense Enhancement Package to Saudi Arabia. The approximately 500-man unit is based at Dhahran

CHART 10—1
U.S. CONTRACTOR MANNING IN SUPPORT OF THE SAUDI AIR FORCE BUILD-UP: 1973-1983

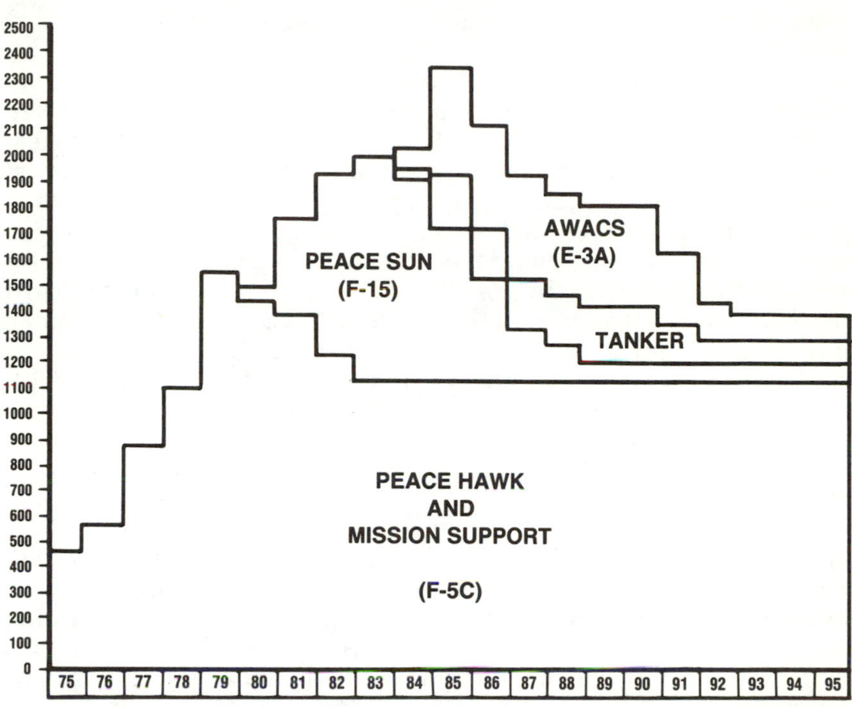

SOURCE: DoD Briefing, April, 1981.

Air Force Base and has already provided Saudi Arabia with key training in operating an air defense system and using the AWACS. In addition, increasing use is being made of special task teams assigned for specific missions on a temporary duty basis.

The Saudi Air Force is equally pleased with its civilian contractor teams from Northrop, Lockheed, Boeing, and McDonnell Douglas, and it is making use of independent consulting firms like Braddock, Dunn, and McDonald (BDM). In 1983, BDM had at least $7.4 million worth of contracts with the Saudi Air Force, including a $3.9 million contract for operating Saudi Arabia's logistics-oriented reporting, analysis, and management information system (RAMIS) and a $3.5 million aeronautical engineering support contract. Saudi Arabia also seems happy with the British personnel supporting the remaining Lightning fighters, BAC-167, and various training missions.

Saudi and U.S. officials do, however, feel that more support is needed in managing major acquisitions, in planning and managing major projects, and in providing independent studies and analyses to examine force improvement options. The Saudis seem particularly concerned with the depth and independence of analysis provided by the U.S., while U.S. personnel complain that it is difficult to raise problems, to conduct frank discussions of issues, or to ensure that projects are kept from escalating in cost once begun.

The army training effort draws less praise, both from the Saudis and from former U.S. and French personnel. There seems to be a general consensus that the army is not only modernizing far more slowly than the air force, but that it has weaker teams and poorer contractor support. Ironically, the Saudis tend to criticize the failure of their advisers to be frank, to raise issues, and to warn about problems in cost growth, project expansion, and Saudi management. U.S. and French personnel, however, criticize the Saudi Army for being unwilling to listen to negative or controversial advice, for failing to plan and execute realistic training efforts, for accepting the advice of whichever foreign adviser is most positive (Pakistani and Egyptian advisers receive the most criticism in this regard), for delaying or not taking decisions, for failing to properly administer, for allowing parallel or conflicting management and project efforts to go on, and for not meeting its training and maintenance goals or setting proper standards.

It also seems fairly clear that the advisory effort supporting Saudi Arabia's ground-based air defenses has been far less tightly and efficiently managed than the support for the Saudi Air Force. Contractor advice seems to have been weak, and the U.S. Army advisory effort often seems to have simply accepted problems and failed to try to solve them. The competition over Saudi Arabia's future ground-based air defense system that has grown out of the sale of the Air Defense Enhancement Package may help correct this situation, but it remains a critical problem.

The U.S. has improved the quality of the personnel assigned to the Saudi Naval Expansion Program. This program is headquartered at Dhahran, but has training teams at the Saudi Navy bases at Jiddah and Jubail and at the main training base at Dammam. While the U.S. team is still criticized both by the Saudis and by its own personnel for not providing Saudi Arabia with more objective advice and for not bringing up key issues, it has corrected many of its severe personnel selection problems. The program initially had far too many personnel who lacked the proper experience, were on their last tours, or were alcoholics. This was particularly embarrassing during the period before the Saudis turned to the French for additional naval support, although the Saudis now criticize the French for a failure to provide timely support and meet their training and technical support agreements at least as much as they criticize the Americans.

The U.S. Army Corps of Engineers effort presents different problems. Both U.S. and Saudi personnel seem to recognize that the Corps lacks the power to ensure proper control of the development of major construction projects and that many are allowed to grow without proper control of costs, new features, or modifications. The end result, even in the air force, can be changes to shelter designs that omit communications links, or "gold-plating" facilities that either should not be built or should be constructed for a limited life and later replacement. Unfortunately, neither the Corps nor any Saudi has responsibility or authority to tightly manage construction efforts, and contractor and other foreign advice is oriented almost solely toward expanding construction efforts and getting the largest profit possible.

The U.S. has tightened up the quality of the regular uniformed personnel assigned to the National Guard and has improved the analytic and contracting support provided to the mission in both Saudi Arabia and the United States. Nevertheless, the National Guard remains a critical problem. The Guard's modernization continues to lag and much of the input of its foreign advisers is ignored. These problems have grown to the point where it has been necessary to impose strict security limits on any discussion of these problems by current or former advisers. Prince Abdullah has made it clear that the U.S. role in advising the Guard must be kept more limited than in advising the regular services, and the 1,800 men in the Vinnell Corporation have a more independent role than that of other contract advisers. Thus the part the U.S. government can play in ensuring that the Guard gets the advice and support it needs is weakened. It is also unclear that the contract teams advising the National Guard have sufficient technical support personnel. This seems to have delayed the Guard's effort to learn how to maintain its Cadillac Gage armored vehicles, and Saudi Arabia has evidently been slower in converting to self-maintenance of this equipment than any of the other 30-odd developing nations that have bought it.[2]

Further, Saudi Arabia will continue to need foreign construction workers to help build its military infrastructure. If such personnel are included in the total of advisers and contractors, the Saudi regular armed forces of about 58,000 men and the National Guard of 35,000 men will need a total of something like 20,000–40,000 U.S., British, French, Pakistani, Jordanian, Egyptian, Korean, and North Yemeni personnel for construction services, technical support, supply, training and modernization through at least 1990.

There is, therefore, little prospect that Saudi Arabia can make major reductions in the number of its foreign advisers and support personnel before the late 1980s, and a near-certainty that it will need new advisers and more advanced technical support with each passing year. This situation has the advantage of creating a partnership between Saudi Arabia and the West, and a human infrastructure that can aid the effectiveness of any over-the-horizon reinforcements from the U.S. It ensures that Saudi Arabia will act defensively and avoid any attacks or adventures outside its own territory. It has the disadvantages that both nations must depend heavily on civilians outside the military in both peace and war and that such personnel are difficult to recruit, retain, and manage. In general, the advantages now offset the disadvantages, and the problem of upgrading the advisory and contract effort seems manageable.

Saudi Arabia's future need for the deployment of foreign military combat units is more uncertain. Saudi Arabia does allow the U.S. Elf-1 to operate on Saudi territory pending the transfer of the new air defense system it is buying from the U.S. It also takes advantage of warning and intelligence data from U.S. vessels in the Gulf and regularly exercises with U.S. naval and air forces.

What is less clear is Saudi Arabia's dependence on foreign security and land force units. Rumors that it has obtained the support of Thai and South Korean security forces cannot be confirmed. There is, however, considerable evidence that Saudi Arabia has sought contingency support from Jordan and Pakistan and that some Pakistani forces are in the country. U.S. officials indicate that Pakistani training "brigades" are deployed at Saudi army bases like Tabuk, which have the combat strength of reinforced battalions. While it is doubtful that Pakistan has a true "tank brigade in Tabuk only 20 km from Eilat," as Lt. General Rafael Eytan—then Israeli Chief of Staff—charged on 21 February 1983, there are probably around 7,000 Pakistani now in Saudi Arabia and some reports go as high as 20,000. These forces provide the cadres necessary to allow Pakistan to rapidly deploy substantial combat forces in an emergency if Saudi Arabia or another conservative Gulf state were attacked by a major regional power. Like the French advisory effort at Tabuk, they are also a deterrent against Israeli attacks.

Saudi and U.S. efforts to help Jordan build up its contingency capabilities to intervene in the Gulf were leaked to the press in October 1983. These reports indicated that Jordan was developing a two-brigade force of 8,500 men. The Jordanian forces were to receive training assistance from the U.S., to airlift from 8 C-130 transports, and to be armed with TOW antitank weapons, Stinger surface-to-air missiles, DIVAD antiaircraft guns, tank-mounted bridging equipment, and modern C^3I equipment. The U.S. was to sell Jordan three additional C-130s, to give it a total of eight, but this would only provide lift for 50 troops per aircraft. The U.S. was to provide large-scale lift in an emergency. The initial cost of the program, which included the land force equipment, was $220–230 million. This was to come from U.S. foreign military sales loans, and Saudi Arabia was to provide Jordan with the money. Further sales of up to $470 million of FMS equipment were to include F-16 fighters and other major equipment necessary to allow Jordan to resist a major air or armored threat.

It seems likely, therefore, that Saudi Arabia is making contingency arrangements that could provide substantial "over-the-horizon" reinforcements from Pakistan and Jordan as well as from the U.S. Such forces could be of great potential value to Saudi Arabia, the other conservative Gulf states, and the West in the face of any major threat from Iran, Iraq, Syria, or South Yemen. They have the great advantage of being Muslim and, in the case of Jordanians, of speaking Arabic, unlike U.S. ground troops who lack language skills and would open Saudi Arabia to countless cultural and political problems. They also would ease the problems the U.S. would face in trying to deploy both large-scale land and air forces or in committing U.S. ground troops to any complex contingency where the case for U.S. intervention was unclear.[3]

As for the effects of Saudi Arabia's dependence on foreign personnel, they must be kept in perspective. There are now something like 2 million foreign workers in Saudi Arabia, and as many as 100,000 Americans will be involved in civilian and economic modernization programs under the current five-year plan. Saudi Arabia also differs radically from Iran in that the living standards of Western workers in Saudi Arabia are not excessively high in comparison with those of most Saudis they work with, and Saudi Arabia does not have large numbers of recently educated students who feel displaced and discriminated against by the hiring of Western workers. As a result, the military portion of Saudi Arabia's foreign labor pool is not excessive or destabilizing, and much of the foreign manpower supporting Saudi forces will leave in the late 1980s as Saudi Arabia completes its massive military equipment construction program.

The Saudi Air Force

The Saudi military buildup seems likely to be most successful in the case of the air force. The air force is almost certain to continue to get priority over the other services because it is the only service that can cover Saudi Arabia's 2.3 million square kilometers of territory and its 4.5 million kilometers of border. The air force is also virtually certain to expand beyond the levels called for in the Saudi Air Defense Enhancement Package. As Table 10.2 shows, the recent expansion of the Saudi Air Force has brought it to the point at which it should be able both to absorb the Air Defense Enhancement Package effectively and to expand its air attack and transport capabilities. In fact, its transition to the F-5E and F-15 has been smooth enough to indicate that the Saudis can effectively operate a modern air force of nearly 200 combat aircraft by the mid-1980s.[4]

Saudi Arabia has already solved its most serious near-term problems in fighter modernization. The first of its 62 F-15C/D fighters arrived in the country on 13 January 1982. Saudi conversion to the aircraft has been unusually rapid, and the first squadron of F-15C/Ds was operational in Dhahran by early 1983. A second squadron was due to complete formation at Taif by the end of 1983, and a third was due to begin formation at Khamis Mushayt in July 1983. The delivery of

TABLE 10.2 The Saudi Air Force, 1983-1984

Manpower	14,000-16,000
Total combat aircraft	170
Organization and strength	3 air defense/attack sqns with 65 F-5Es[a] Other combat units with 24 F-5Fs and 16 F-5Bs[a] 1 interceptor sqn with 15 Lightning F-53s, 2 T-55s[b] 3 interceptor sqns with 60 F-15C/Ds (2 forming)[c] Trainers: 46 BAC-167s[d] and 12 Cessna 172 G/H/Ls 2 transport sqns with 39 C-130Es and 25 C-130Hs[e]; 5 B-747s 6 KC-130Hs; 2 Jetstars 2 helicopter sqns with 14 AB-205s; 12 AB-206Bs; 25 AB-212s Other aircraft include 1 B-707; 2 Falcon 20 transports; 2 Alouette IIIs, 14 AB-206, 1 Bell 212, 1 AB-204B, and 10 KV-107 helicopters 2 air defense batteries, 1 with Improved Hawk and 1 with 6 Shahine/Crotale surface-to-air missiles 5 Marconi 40t2 air defense radars 6 TPS-43 3D S-Band gap-filler radars
Major munitions	AAM: Red top, Firestreak, Sidewinder, R-530, R0-559 Magic, 1,000 Sparrows (some still on order) ASM: 2,400 IR-guided Maverick, laser-guided bombs
Major orders	10 RF-5Es; 5 F-5Es; 1 F-5F; 5 E-3As; 6 KC-707s; 40 CASA C-212-200 tpts; 1,177 Sidewinder AIM-9L and 1,000 AIM-7F Sparrow AAM; 916 TV-guided Maverick ASMs; Honeywell H-421 ring-laser gyro for F-5E refit; ALQ-135 ECM; 101 ship sets of conformal fuel tanks for F-15s; 762 Mark 12, Mode 4 Teledyne IFF units; 9 TPS-43 radars.

[a]38 of the F-5B/E/Fs operate from Dhahran. They have an air defense and training role, although the IISS lists most as attack aircraft. Two other F-5 squadrons (Sqn 3 and Sqn 10) with 35 F-5Es and 9 F-5Fs are deployed at Taif, one primarily in an air defense role. Khamis Mushayt has a single F-5 sqn with 18 F-5Es and 9 F-5Fs.

[b]Reports of current F-53 strength vary from 10 to 25 fighters. The main Lightning unit is based at Tabuk, but a limited number of Lightnings are based at, or rotated through, Dhahran. Although the fighter has British support, it now has an extremely high mean time between failures, and average operational strength may be as low as 12 aircraft.

[c]The Saudi F-15C/Ds were first delivered to Dhahran in January 1982. The 13th Saudi Air Force sqn at Dhahran is rapidly building up to 30 operational F-15C/Ds. It already flies advanced training and aggressor sqn exercises. A second Saudi F-15C/D squadron, 5th Sqn, is forming at Taif. A third squadron with 20 F-15C/D fighters is forming at Taif and will have 30 fighters. However, 20 of 5th Sqn's fighters will eventually deploy to Khamis Mushayt. The Saudi F-15C/Ds are equivalent to USAF fighters except for planned growth in secure communications and data links. They have 17% more internal and centerline tank fuel than the original F-15A/Bs and improvements to their Hughes APG-63 radar, computer, and data displays.

[d]The ground attack role has been retained for the BAC-167, but its primary role is as a trainer. Only about 20 are normally active, and they have little contingency value. There are 25 former RAF instructor pilots using the BAC-167s for flight training.

[e]These figures are taken from the IISS and may exaggerate the number of C-130s in Saudi Arabia. Other sources indicate that a total of 43 have been delivered.

Sources: The Military Balance, 1983-84 (London: IISS, 1983); *Washington Post,* 24 February 1982; *Wall Street Journal,* 3 March 1982; *Aviation Week,* 23 May 1983, pp. 61-64.

the 101 ship sets of F-15 conformal fuel tanks began in June 1983. As has been discussed earlier, these tanks add 9,750 lbs of fuel and are extending Saudi combat air patrol mission times to a maximum of 3 hours per sortie.

The rest of the $2.85 billion Peace Sun program is also on schedule. Training and the deployment of technical advisers and support personnel has proceeded smoothly. (Estimates vary, but the McDonnell Douglas staff evidently will build up to 1,220 personnel, with 150 in administration, 80 instructors, 880 maintenance technicians, and 44 supply personnel, before phasing down as Saudis replace U.S. contract personnel.) All major construction for both the Peace Sun and expanded Peace Hawk program was completed by the summer of 1983, and preliminary planning for depot-level maintenance facilities had begun. The McDonnell Douglas portion of the Peace Sun program began extensive training of Saudi maintenance and ground personnel by late 1982, and the F-15s at Dhahran were meeting their goal of a 70% operational availability rate by May 1983. The Saudi air base expansion program seemed on schedule, and the first sheltered facilities for the F-15s were operational at Dhahran.

This progress is supported by equal advances in the Peace Hawk program. Peace Hawk will complete its eighth increment by the mid-1980s, has reached a cost of about $3.8 billion, and has delivered 114 variants of the F-5 to Saudi Arabia. This investment has allowed Northrop to begin making major reductions in U.S. personnel as they are replaced by Saudis, and several Saudi units are now maintained almost solely by Saudi personnel.

The Saudi Air Force is also seeking to extend the useful life of Saudi Arabia's F-5Es and improve their air defense mission capabilities by retrofitting them with Honeywell H-421 ring-laser gyros. This would allow the F-5E to align its gyros and take off within 30 seconds versus about 3 minutes for a fighter using an ordinary gyro. The mission effect would be the equivalent of allowing an F-5E to reach 17,000 feet at 10 NM at Mach 0.9 before a fighter using a conventional gyroscope could take off. While this would scarcely bring the F-5E up to the sensor capability of first-line Western fighters, it would allow them to meet most currently foreseeable regional threats until the late 1980s.

Further, the Saudi Air Force is considering a letter of offer for 15 additional F-5s, including 10 RF-5Es. This would cost $320 million, but it would give the Saudis an aircraft with selectable mission pallets that allow the choice of four advanced sensor packages, including an advanced night reconnaissance mission capability. Although Saudi Arabia already has 20 conversion kits, or "noses," to allow its F-5s to fly recce missions, these lack the stand-off range, oblique area coverage, and night mission capability of the RF-5E. Providing such mission capabilities would significantly improve Saudi ability to use its attack aircraft against potential threat air forces with limited air-to-air combat capability, like the air forces of South Yemen or forward-deployed Iranian forces, and improve its ability to locate and strike at small insurgent or tribal forces.[5]

Even if Saudi Arabia obtains the ring-laser gyroscope and RF-5Es, however, it will need to modify its F-15s to fly attack missions and to obtain additional aircraft beginning in the mid-1980s. The attack mission capability is needed to help make up for Saudi Arabia's limited ground strength, and it is a growing sore point in Saudi-U.S. relations. In 1981 the U.S. and Saudi Arabia completed a joint study recommending such dual capability as part of a more general study of Saudi attack mission requirements, but the U.S. has been unable to implement its recommendations because of problems in obtaining congressional approval of the sale of the necessary bomb racks.[6] While the F-15 C/D lacks the avionics to fly advanced attack missions, it can deliver a considerable amount of ordnance with great accuracy against an enemy lacking good air cover and ground-based air defenses, and it can eventually be used to deliver "smart" or terminally homing area munitions. This means it can play a critical role against a threat like South Yemen, against any landing on the Saudi coast, or even against the kind of comparatively limited armored forces the northern Gulf states are likely to be able to deploy in any invasion before the late 1980s, although the latter mission would be heavily dependent on at least local air superiority or the lack of enemy fighters with "look-down/shoot-down" capability.

Saudi Arabia will also need at least 30–40 more F-15C/Ds as it phases out its Lightnings. Although it has a paper strength of about 25–27 fighters, it probably has fewer than 10 operational Lightnings at any given time, and even its newer fighters are beginning to show structural wear. While the Saudi Air Force extended its support contract with Britain in mid-1981 to cover the period through 1985, the Lightning imposes special maintenance and support costs that make it far more expensive to operate than the F-15 because of the need to fund special British support and training facilities for less than one operational squadron of aircraft. The new contract with British Aerospace (Warton Division) will cost $595 million and bring the total cost of the Saudi-UK program to $2.31 billion. The contract includes a wide range of other services—including basic air crew training, logistic procurement, and construction—but the Lightning portion is extremely costly for the capability provided.[7]

The Lightning lacks the avionics, range, and air combat maneuver performance to be integrated into Saudi Arabia's new air defense system or to compete with the newer Soviet-made fighters, including most modern marks of the MiG-21. Even if Saudi Arabia is willing to avoid basing F-15s at Tabuk, it would need approximately 100 F-15C/Ds to cover its other major air bases, provide an operational reserve, and compensate for maintenance losses. Assuming that Saudi Arabia's F-5Es are available in the backup role, this is the minimum force Saudi

Arabia would need to provide normal peacetime coverage of the Gulf, Red Sea, and border with South Yemen *plus* to be able to deploy enough F-15s in a crisis to ensure effective deterrence along the Gulf or guarantee rapid local air superiority against South Yemen.

Any requirement beyond this point tends to be speculative, and much will depend on the rate of rearmament in Iran and elsewhere in the region. The F-5E will remain adequate only as long as potential threat nations do not deploy fighters with superior "head on" kill capability, look-down/shoot-down capability, and superior radar range. While the F-5E will still be able to engage such fighters, it will lack the superior performance or edge to allow Saudi Arabia to use its air force to make up for its lack of ground forces or to avoid massive losses. This creates a potential requirement for up to 150 new fighters in the late 1980s, although with luck, Saudi Arabia will not need to complete phasing out its F-5Es until well into the 1990s.

Saudi Arabia will face similar uncertainties in translating its purchase of the E-3A and the rest of the Air Defense Enhancement Package into a fully effective system. The five E-3As will provide a considerable air defense sensor and command and control capability even without full integration into a land-based sensor, air defense weapon, and command and control system. They can cover Saudi oil facilities on the Gulf, key facilities in Bahrain and Qatar, and most facilities in the UAE provided that they have sufficient warning to deploy and sufficient recovery time so that their endurance is not pushed beyond its limit.

They are not, however, a panacea. The unusual temperature conditions in the Gulf radically alter the range at which radar can function, and Saudi Arabia will need the new technology developed by Ferranti even to predict the loss of radar range at given altitudes caused by the reflection of radar waves by heat, or "ducting." The purchase of five aircraft means that Saudi Arabia will be able to average only one E-3A mission a day under normal operating conditions, or about 3 hours of coverage with a maximum range of 180–200 miles. This coverage is sufficient for deterrence, but as has been pointed out earlier, it is hardly sufficient to cover the entire coast or even the Saudi core area and can scarcely prevent individual aircraft from flying in undetected or deal with a surprise attack.

At least one defecting Iranian F-4 crew has already flown over Ras Tanura undetected, and an Iranian B-707 flew undetected across Saudi Arabia to Cairo. While the failure of the E-3A to detect those aircraft is partly explainable by the presence of other aircraft in the area, the problems of relying on any sensor are illustrated by the fact that the Iranian F-4 also flew undetected over one of the five U.S. Navy radar picket ships in the area.[8] These penetrations also occurred at a time when the E-3As flown by the Elf-1 Task Force flew only as far west as the "Fahd Line," or a line drawn from Abadan to the Iraqi-Iranian border. Saudi Arabia will have to fly further west if it is to cover the new base at Hafr al-Batin that will become operational in 1984, and this will create still more "gaps" in its E-3A coverage.

Accordingly, Saudi Arabia and the U.S. now face the problem of developing a mix of land-based sensors, command and control systems, and air defense weaponry that can complete the air defense package, and this will not come easily. The U.S. and Saudi Arabia experienced some problems even with the E-3A and KC-707 part of the package, or Peace Sentinel program. When in December 1981 Saudi Arabia signed the U.S. letter of offer for the sale of five E-3As[9] and six KC-707 tankers with an option to buy two more, neither country had really completed plans for basing the aircraft, defining the engines and IFF systems the aircraft were to use, or for the training of Saudi personnel.

The U.S. Department of Defense had done even less planning of the ground-based, or Peace Shield, phase of the enhancement package. It had not really costed the plan it presented to the Saudis and Congress, had not developed detailed construction schedules, and had heavily "gold-plated" its proposals rather than sought cost-effective systems integration. As originally planned, Peace Shield was to be issued as a sole-source $3.5 billion contract. It rapidly became apparent, however, that a better basis was needed both to define the project and to select a prime contractor. Accordingly, while the basic contract for Peace Shield was left at $3.8 billion, the U.S. and Saudi Arabia agreed that a competitive contract would be issued for a one-year-projection definition phase. This phase was to have at least two competing contractors. The Saudi and U.S. governments were then to select both the best plan and the winning firm as the prime contractor for the rest of the project.

The competition for this phase of Peace Shield was originally supposed to begin shortly after Saudi Arabia signed the letter of offer for Peace Sentinel. The U.S. rapidly found, however, that it could not even issue the request for proposal (RFP) seeking contractor bids without further definition of the Peace Shield program and major improvements to the communications aspect of the Peace Shield system. This need caused the RFP to be slipped to early 1983, although progress did not halt improvements in the ground-based portion of the Saudi air defense system. Saudi Arabia obtained additional TPS-43 gap-filler radars during this period as part of another program and purchased 762 commercial versions of the Mark 12, Mode 4 IFF system. It also agreed on the selection of 17 unattended GE FPS-117 "Seek Igloo" radars, of the kind developed for the Dewline (North American air defense warning) system, as the key sensor in the Peace Shield radar network, in spite of serious uncertainties regarding "Seek Igloo" performance and reliability.[10]

If the U.S. had gone ahead with the RFP before the cuts in Saudi oil revenues, it would still have run into major problems and probably caused new friction in Saudi-U.S. military relations. First, the U.S. was proposing a $3.8 billion program for a system it had never built for its own use and could not properly define. Second, an ongoing $1.5

billion effort to integrate Saudi Arabia's Improved Hawks into its air defense system was experiencing major problems because of weak project definition and management by the contractors involved and the Department of Defense. Third, the U.S. officials involved knew that the Saudis had not had time to evaluate the system definition in the contract proposal. Fourth, several of the potential competitors for the contract were not really ready to bid. And fifth, the U.S. officials involved had not taken proper account of the fact that several senior members of the Saudi royal family, including Crown Prince Abdullah, were deeply concerned with the U.S.'s past failure to help Saudi Arabia obtain proper planning and contract support.

However, the cut in Saudi oil revenues continued to delay the start of the contract effort and forced the U.S. and Saudi Arabia to take a more modest approach. Saudi Arabia had to put much tighter cost constraints on the effort, and by August 1983, the cost of the initial phase of Peace Shield had been cut to $1.2 billion. Further, the timing of the project became more realistic. The project definition phase was not to be completed until January 1985 (which allowed proper time for planning and evaluation), and construction was to be phased in over the period between January 1985 and 1989.

These delays allowed three major consortia, led by Boeing, Litton, and Hughes, to fully prepare to compete for the award, which was scheduled for late 1983. They also allowed a great deal more staff work to take place between Saudi and U.S. Air Force officers, which helped build confidence within the Saudi government. A great deal of unnecessary communications equipment had been eliminated, along with overautomation and overcentralization. At the same time, the elements of the revised Peace Shield system seemed to meet both Saudi needs and the original intent of the Saudi Air Defense Enhancement Package.

Saudi Arabia was to obtain the communications and automation it needed, a nationwide network of TPS-43 radars and 17 FPS-177 unattended radars, a major hardened headquarters at the Saudi Air Force headquarters in Riyadh, and five decentralized sector centers at Taif, Tabuk, Khamis Mushayt, and al-Kharj. Six of the TPS-43 radars were to be directly linked into the automated C^3 system, and 5–10 automated ground entry stations were to be set up to accept data from the E-3As at strategic points throughout the country. Though scarcely cheap, the revised plan for Peace Shield seemed well designed to meet Saudi needs.

This history is not reassuring, however, for what it says about U.S. ability to manage its military relations with Saudi Arabia or the other Gulf states. There is no question that the Saudi Air Force, U.S. Air Force, and U.S. contractors have moved closer together and that the Saudis are steadily increasing their planning and management role in air force projects, but most of the improvements in the Peace Shield program came more by chance than by U.S. effort. Further, there are still some aspects of the project that indicate that the U.S. is not playing a proper role. The new plan called for $600 million of the $1.2 billion program to be spent in ways that would support Saudi Arabia's industrialization effort and provide a high amount of technology transfer. The proposals presented to the Saudis have probably promised far more benefits to Saudi Arabia than the U.S. can deliver. So have proposals to re-engine the E-3As and KC-707s with GE CFM-56 engines and to set up service and other offset facilities in Saudi Arabia. While the Saudi desire for technology transfer is both natural and a potentially excellent idea, the U.S. has not exerted the kind of control necessary to ensure that such transfers would be successful or to lay the groundwork for stronger Saudi-U.S. cooperation.[11]

The technology transfer issue is also important because the U.S. will need to help the Saudi Air Force to upgrade its C^3I and AC&W capabilities as the other major powers in the Gulf acquire their own advanced sensor C^3I and AC&W systems during the late 1980s. The U.S. must be prepared to help Saudi Arabia to steadily improve its air defense system to preserve an "edge" over a South Yemen possibly equipped with the Candid 2 version of an AWACS, or an Iran possibly equipped with electronic countermeasure aircraft and high-performance attack fighters like the MiG-27 and Su-24. This will mean upgrading the Saudi E-3As in the late 1980s and possibly buying additional "mini-AWACS" and electronic warfare and intelligence aircraft.

The U.S. will have to find some solution to helping Saudi Arabia strengthen its air defense in the north and west, which is essential to cover potential threats from Iran, Iraq, and Syria and—from the Saudi viewpoint—to check Israel. The U.S. cannot deal with this problem indefinitely through its current policy of restricting deployment of the F-15 to Tabuk and Hafr al-Batin and supporting Saudi protests against Israeli overflights. The need to guard against the uncertainties created by the Iran-Iraq War may already be forcing the U.S. to take a new approach to the problem.

Finally, the U.S. must decide how to treat Saudi Arabia's ties to Jordan, which are as much an issue in terms of air power as they are in terms of Jordanian contingency capabilities in the Gulf. Both Saudi Arabia and Iraq have helped fund Jordan's air defenses in the past. Saudi Arabia paid for the 14 Improved Hawk launchers Jordan bought in 1978. In 1979 it bought two TPS-42 radars for Jordan, which will be delivered in 1982 and which will provide 240 NM of medium- to high-altitude coverage. It bought five more mobile TPS-63 gap-filler radars in early 1981, to be delivered in 1982. At the same time, Iraq is paying $225 million to give Jordan 20 SA-8 missile launchers and 16 ZSU-23-4 AA guns, and has tentatively agreed to fund a limited purchase of Roland.

Jordan now, however, faces a critical need for air modernization and Saudi Arabia has tentatively agreed to help fund four squadrons of F-20As or F-16s, mobile Improved Hawk missiles, and Stinger man-

TABLE 10.3 The Saudi Army, 1983–1984

Total combat manpower	35,000
Major combat formations	2 armored brigades (1 forming) 2 mechanized brigades 2 infantry brigades (1 to be mechanized) 1 airborne brigade (2 paratroop battalions, 1 special forces company) 1 Royal Guard regiment (3 battalions) 5 artillery battalions 18 antiaircraft artillery battalions 16 SAM batteries with Improved Hawk (Air Force assigned) and 2 with Shahine (12 launchers, 48 missiles)
Medium tanks	300 AMX-30s, 150 M-60A1s
Armored personnel and fighting vehicles	200 AML-60/90 armored cars, Ferret, 100 Fox scout cars, 20 OTO Melara VCC-1 with TOW, 350 AMX-10Ps, 800 M-113 APCs, Panhard M-3 armored cars
Artillery	54 Model 56 105mm pack howitzers; M-101 105mm, 18 M-198 towed 155mm and GCT 155mm SP howitzers; 81mm and M-30 107mm mortars
Antitank weapons	TOW, Dragon, HOT, and Vigilant ATGM; 75mm, 90mm, 106mm RCLs
Air defense weapons	Improved Hawk, M-163 Vulcan 20mm, AMX-30SA, 30mm, 86 35mm, M-42 40mm SP AA guns; Redeye, Shahine/Crotale SAM
On order	150 M-60A-3 conversion kits, 60 AMX-10P MICVs, Shahine launchers, 180 VCC-1 TOW AFV, 200 FH-70 155mm howitzers, 100 M-60A3 tanks, 400 JPz SK-105 SP antitank guns, and TOW

Sources: IISS and SIPRI printouts; *Financial Times,* 25 April 1983.

portable SHORADs to improve Jordan's air defenses against Israel and Syria and Jordan's ability to protect Saudi Arabia. Further, Saudi Arabia is seeking to create secure cable and voice links to Jordan's now largely obsolescent air defense center and to improve its capabilities.[12] These plans depend on U.S. foreign military sales, however, and the U.S. will have to work out some kind of modus vivendi that will protect Saudi and Jordanian and Israeli interests if these plans are to go forward.

The Saudi Army

The importance of putting Saudi-U.S. military relations on a sound basis is further illustrated by the limitations that will continue to exist in the Saudi Army, whose current structure is shown in Table 10.3. Its modernization and expansion will be significantly slower than that of the Saudi Air Force, although the army should be a reasonably effective defensive force by the late 1980s. Even then, however, the Saudi Army will lack a proper balance of modern equipment. It also will not be large enough to concentrate significant forces on a given front for a week to 10 days, and it will lack the massive armored forces of its stronger neighbors.

Training has been a particular problem. Many of the army's training plans have not been executed, and maneuver training has been poor. The army's mix of U.S., French, and British equipment still presents major conversion problems, and the army has been much slower in providing the trained manpower necessary to absorb such equipment than the air force. Much of the equipment also has required modification or changes to its original technical and logistic support plan before it could be operated in large numbers, and some key items still present major serviceability problems. These problems have been compounded by the wide dispersal of the army throughout the kingdom, the erratic quality of contractor support, and an overambitious effort to create a modern logistic system that has lacked proper Saudi and U.S. advisory management.

As has been discussed earlier, the Saudi Army's mix of many different types of armor has prolonged and exacerbated these problems, and its 300 AMX-30s lack the armor, firepower, and operational availability to be kept in service much past the 1980s. The AMX-30 has exceptionally light armor and is not competitive with any of the newer Soviet- and other Western-made tanks now being deployed in the region (e.g., T-62/72/80; M-60; Khalid; Merkava; Chieftain; Challenger). While the adoption of newer anti-armor round technology has made up for the lack of penetrating power in the Obus G rounds that France originally sold the Saudi Army, the AMX-30's fire control and range-finding capability is totally inadequate to help Saudi tank crews make up for their lack of experience, and the AMX-30 lacks the power, cooling, and filtration for desert combat.

This need to replace Saudi armor, however, presents severe problems, and it has already created a new source of tension between Saudi Arabia and the United States. The U.S. has had a natural interest in testing its new M-1 tank and M-2 fighting vehicle in the Gulf and began preliminary discussions of a test and evaluation effort in Saudi Arabia in 1982. By early 1983, not only had these discussions produced a test plan, but Saudi tank and maintenance crews had begun training on the M-1 tank at Fort Knox, Ky., and the Saudi Army was actively interested in procuring the M-1 and in standardizing on U.S. equipment.

The Saudi-U.S. discussions focused on a preliminary purchase of 200 M-1 tanks that would occur only after the U.S. completed the upgunning of the M-1 from a 105mm to a 120mm gun and after the Saudi Army had evaluated the M-1 and M-2. These 200 M-1s would have been delivered after 1985, with the tentative goal of replacing all the Saudi AMX-30s with another block of 200 M-1s by 1990. Saudi Arabia would then have the option of building up to a force of 800–1,200 M-1 medium tanks. This would have allowed it to replace its M-60s and expand its force structure by some point in the mid-1990s.

These discussions took place in late 1982 and in early 1983, at a time when shifts in the politics of the Arab-Israeli conflict and the impact of President Reagan's 1982 peace initiative made such a sale seem possible without serious Israeli and congressional opposition. They also offered both sides a mix of additional advantages. The net effect was to lower the unit cost of the M-1 and M-2 to both the U.S. and Saudi Arabia, to standardize on a mix of armor that would be used by both Saudi forces and U.S. reinforcements, and to provide a large pool of armor in the region that U.S. forces could use without the major problems inherent in trying to deploy such equipment from over the horizon.

The discussions leaked to the press, however, and were published in the February 1983 issue of the *International Defense Review.* They then got major press play in the *New York Times* on 4 March 1983, in an article by Richard Halloran, and in a form that stressed a goal of 1,200 tanks rather than an initial purchase of 200. The senior Pentagon official who had provided the data on a background basis had failed to consider Saudi, Israeli, or congressional sensitivities. As a result, the story came out in a form that turned preliminary talks into a plan and that almost seemed designed to create massive U.S. domestic political opposition. Worse, the leak was accompanied by discussion of Saudi Arabia's problems with reduced oil revenues and of costs per tank of $2 million. This immediately led to discussions in Saudi Arabia about the possible waste of Saudi funds on a highly controversial tank that was still having teething problems in U.S. forces.

This embarrassment was compounded because the U.S. then had to deny the story. On 15 March, the Associated Press carried both a report on the sale and a categorical denial by Henry Catto, the assistant secretary of defense (public affairs). When Halloran repeated the story with more details on 4 April, the Pentagon issued another denial, this time on a nonattributable basis. By then, however, a web of rumors surrounded the discussions, including reports that 800–1,000 of the tanks would be prepositioned solely for the use of U.S. rapid deployment forces. By 26 March, the BBC was picking up major propaganda attacks on the sale from groups like the Soviet-backed Radio Peace and Progress, which attacked both the Saudi royal family and U.S. "imperialism."[13] Ironically, the Congress was notified of an actual tank purchase on 2 August 1983. The purchase, however, was of 100 M-60A3 tanks and not 1,200 M-1s. While the M-60A3 did have modern laser range finders and thermal night sights, it was the first U.S. sale affecting Saudi armor since 29 July 1980, the date the U.S. agreed to sell Saudi Arabia 150 M-60A3 conversion kits to modernize its 1960-vintage M-60A1s. Such a sale had no real impact on the regional balance in the Gulf, much less the Arab-Israeli conflict.

This mishandling of U.S. and Saudi affairs came during a period when the U.S. was actively trying to persuade Saudi Arabia to put pressure on King Hussein of Jordan to support President Reagan's peace initiative and on Syria and Lebanon to reach an agreement on Israel's withdrawal from Lebanon. The U.S. was also seeking Saudi support in persuading the other Gulf states to standardize on U.S. air defense systems. Needless to say, it did little to enhance the prospects for peace or to improve Saudi-U.S. military cooperation.

Saudi Arabia was forced to respond by looking for other sources of arms and it renewed its contacts with West Germany. In late May, Saudi Arabia announced that Prince Sultan would visit Germany for health reasons. In fact, he met with West German Chancellor Helmut Kohl at the latter's home in Ludwigshafen to discuss possible arms purchases. This was announced officially in Bonn on 13 June, and the announcement was followed by reports that Saudi Arabia might buy up to 800 Leopard II tanks, 800 Marder armored fighting vehicles, and 200 Gepard air defense vehicles. At the same time, Saudi Army experts visited France to examine France's new AMX-32 and AMX-40 tanks, although Saudi Arabia's experience with French tanks and advisers had led the Saudis to be far more interested in the West German equipment.[14]

It is impossible to predict the net result of these events, and Saudi Arabia still lacks any clear source of the army equipment it needs. The Saudi Army may well be forced to buy equipment that is not standardized with U.S. equipment and to rely on West German army and contract support that has no meaningful postwar experience in aiding a developing nation.

These problems in the Saudi armor procurement effort are compounded by the Saudi Army's need for improved air defense, artillery, and helicopter strength. As has been discussed earlier, the U.S. contractor effort to improve the integration of Saudi Army Improved Hawk, Shahine (Improved Crotale), antiaircraft gun, and land-based radar and C^3 systems has not been particularly successful. While U.S. and Saudi officers feel that much of the blame must go to the Saudis as well as the U.S., it both exacerbates the other problems in U.S. relations with the Saudi Army and is of considerable military importance. The effectiveness of the Saudi Army depends heavily on the quality of its air cover and the ability of the Saudi Air Force to link its operations with those of the army and to provide air cover and air support. Thus it is essential that the army both improve its own air defense and develop fully successful C^3 links to the air force.

Saudi Arabia's problems with its artillery are largely a matter of numbers and the need for better mobile fire-control and ammunition supply equipment and may be solved by orders for the FH-70 155mm howitzer. The helicopter, however, raises different issues. The Saudi Army is now deployed nearly 600 miles from the Eastern Province, and even when part of its strength deploys to its new base at King Khalid City near Hafr al-Batin in 1984, the Saudi Army will still be heavily dispersed throughout the kingdom. Attack and troop lift helicopters offer a potential solution to this problem and both provide rapid concentration of force and allow Saudi Arabia to make up for its lack of experience in large-scale maneuver. It is far from clear, however, where Saudi Arabia can get the attack and troop lift helicopters it needs or the kind of advisory and technical support required. While the Saudi Army is actively examining the option of developing a helicopter force, this option raises yet another problem for the future.

Finally, the Saudi Army will continue to face serious demographic and training problems. Although the Saudi Army has made major progress and should steadily improve in manpower quality and experience during the 1980s, there is no apparent solution to its lack of available manpower as long as substantial amounts of manpower go to the National Guard and the Saudi civilian sector offers far greater economic attraction. The army's strength of seven brigades would normally call for 70,000 men rather than Saudi Arabia's present active strength of about 34,000–36,000. Even under the most favorable projections of the Saudi birthrate and the success of Saudi training programs, there is little prospect that the Saudi Army can usefully expand to much more than 45,000 men before 1990. This situation helps explain why Saudi Arabia is so dependent on foreign support and is interested in aid from nations like Jordan and Pakistan; even the most successful Saudi Army modernization effort must remain dependent on foreign support and cannot match the efforts of the heavily populated northern Gulf states like Iran and Iraq. This is particularly true when Saudi Arabia must disperse its forces to cover the threat from the Yemens and station a significant portion at Tabuk. While the Saudi Army cannot check any major Israeli attack, it also cannot afford the political and military consequences of leaving a major base undefended, of not covering the Red Sea area, and of not having forces to cover its troubled western border.

Trends in the Saudi Navy

The Saudi Navy will have still less capability to absorb its modern equipment, and it will have to depend even more on air support. As was discussed in Chapter 6, the navy force structure (shown in Table 10.4) is almost certainly over ambitious, and it will expand strikingly by 1986.

The Saudi Navy is now completing two major, fully modern naval bases at Jiddah and Jubail. These bases will have up to five years of stocks on hand, with initial deliveries of two years' worth of inventory. The Jubail base is now the second largest naval base in the Gulf and stretches nearly 8 miles along the coast. It already has its own desalinization facility and is designed to be expandable up to 100% above its present capacity.

The Saudi Navy is procuring an automated logistic system similar to that in the other services, with extensive modern command and control facilities. It will have this system operational, complete with

TABLE 10.4 The Saudi Navy, 1983–1984

Major combat manpower	2,200–2,500
Major combat forces	4 PCG-1 corvettes with 2x4 Harpoon SSM 1 large patrol craft (ex-U.S. coastguard cutter) 9 PGG-1 FAC(M) with 2 twin Harpoon SSM 3 Jaguar FAC(T) 4 MSC-322 coastal minesweepers 4 ex-U.S. LCU; 8 ex-U.S. LCM-6 53 coastal patrol craft
Bases	Jiddah, Al Qatif/Jubail, Ras Tanura, Dammam, Yanbu, Ras al Mish'ab
Recent major orders	4 F-2000 ASW frigates ? Crotale SAM (naval) ? Otomat SSM at cost of $3.4 billion 24 Dauphin 2 helicopters with 200 AS-15TT ASM 2 Durance-class oilers ($ 218 million), to be delivered in 1984
Total major equipment on order	4 frigates with Otomat SSM, Crotale SAM 1 PCG-1 corvette with 8 Harpoons 4 PCG-1 FAC(M) with 2 twin Harpoon SSMs 2 logistic support ships/light replenishment tankers 2 Atlantic II maritime reconnaissance aircraft 24 AS-365N Dauphine 2 helicopters (4 SARs, 20 with AS-15TT ASMs)

Sources: IISS and SIPRI printouts.

hardened control centers at Riyadh, Jubail, and Jiddah, by the end of 1984. It will also acquire automated data links to the E-3A, with the ability to obtain AWACS data when the aircraft is in the ocean surveillance mode, and to Saudi land-based command centers. Other typical facilities include a meteorology laboratory, a Harpoon missile and Mark 46 torpedo maintenance facility, an advanced technical training school, and a Royal Naval Academy.

The Saudi Navy will take delivery by the end of 1986 on all of the 15 ships it now has on order, which will give it a 34-ship force, plus 24 missile-equipped helicopters. It plans to expand its manpower from 2,500 to 4,500 and to expand its status from Gulf and Red Sea fleets to operations in the Indian Ocean and possibly even the eastern Mediterranean. The major deliveries under the U.S. phase of this effort are nearing completion; they will give the Saudi Navy nine patrol gunboat, missile (PGG) craft and four patrol chaser, missile (PCG) craft. The navy has also procured four coastal minesweepers, two large harbor tugs, two utility land craft, and eight LCM-6 mechanized landing craft.

The first two PGGs, built by Peterson Builders, became operational at Jubail in February 1983, and four more left the U.S. for Saudi Arabia with Saudi Navy crews in late April 1983. These PGGs have computerized fire-control systems with twin Harpoon surface-to-surface missiles. They have both gas turbine and diesel engines and can go from 16 to 30 knots. They displace 495 tons and are 190 feet long. Each is also armed with Oto Melera 76mm guns, Mark 67 20mm cannon, Mark 19 40mm grenade launchers, Mark 2 81mm mortars, and the Vulcan/Phalanx close-in defense system. They have Speery Mark 92 fire-control systems and full communications, radar, navigation, and IFF equipment.[15]

The PCG will displace 903 tons and have roughly the same weapons as the PGGS, plus the Mark 309 antisubmarine warfare system, Mark 32 torpedo tubes, and Mark 46 torpedos. The U.S. has already delivered 162 Harpoon missiles, 28 Mark 46 torpedos, and ammunition for the 76mm guns and other weapons. The U.S. Navy Expansion Program team in Saudi Arabia had 23 military and 4 civilian government employees in mid-1983.[16]

The basic details of the systems the Saudi Navy ordered from France in 1980 have already been discussed. This program is now called Sawari (Mast) I. It has reached a minimum value of 14 billion French francs, or $1.9 billion, and may have escalated in cost to over $3 billion. It will deliver 4 missile-equipped 2,000-ton frigates and 24 missile-equipped helicopters, 2 fuel supply vessels, Otomat missiles for the frigates, AS-15 missiles for the helicopters, and additional training services. Saudi crews are already training in France to operate the vessels.

The end result of all these U.S. and French sales will be a two-fleet Saudi Navy with ocean surveillance, coastal defense, antiair, antisurface, and antisubmarine capabilities and some of the most modern equipment in the world. It will also be a navy that would normally require at least 10,000 men, and probably close to 20,000. The Saudi Navy is unlikely to meet its goal of 4,000 men by 1990, however, and even with automation and foreign support, it will not be able to operate much of its equipment and bases effectively before the early 1990s.

Saudi Arabia is, however, already examining options that would expand it still further. Prince Sultan met with France's President François Mitterrand and Defense Minister Charles Henru in May 1983, and only Saudi Arabia's reduced oil revenues seem to have prevented agreement on a new program called Sawari II. Saudi Arabia has been much happier with the support it has obtained from the French Navy than that from the French Army. It had already signed a follow-on contract to Sawari I in February 1982 to provide additional training support, naval facilities, and land-based coastal defense, and the new Sawari II program would have cost an additional $1.6–2.12 billion. It would have included at least two more 2,000-ton frigates and possibly 4,000-ton frigates as well. Further, it may have included two AMD-Breguet Atlantic Nouvelle Generation (ANG) maritime patrol aircraft as the first step in the procurement of a much larger force. Other equipment may have included lift and troop-carrying helicopters, surveillance and intelligence equipment, and special warfare equipment.[17]

This program indicates that the Saudi Navy may be in for serious indigestion problems during most of the 1980s. It should be able to use many of its major combat ships effectively and to pose a reasonably effective conservative counterbalance to regional powers like Iran, Iraq, South Yemen, and Ethiopia—all of which have severe problems of their own. At the same time, it cannot absorb what it already has on delivery, and new orders will simply increase the overload.

Thus the role of adviser to the Saudi Navy may be even more difficult than in the past. It is unclear, however, that the French Navy is ready for this challenge. It will soon have to make the transition to the role of training and supporting a major naval force that uses equipment that is not standard in the French Navy and in a region where the French Navy can no longer play any serious military role. As for the U.S. Navy, its advisory role will continue. On 1 March 1983 the Saudi Navy added $31 million more worth of technical services contracts to its previous total of $49 million. The U.S. advisory mission will, however, shift to a distinctly secondary role unless the U.S. displaces France in selling Saudi Arabia the 4,000-ton frigates the Saudi Navy desires. The U.S. has tentatively proposed sale of the FFG-7 class of frigates, but it seems more likely that the U.S. Navy will be limited to projects like building weapons stations and the Naval Academy, integrating French and U.S. equipment, providing training and range support, and providing landing and logistic ships.[18]

This may be just as well for the U.S. Both the Saudi Navy and its principal adviser are in for a troubled decade. While the Saudis do not face the kind of unplanned expansion that characterized the Iranian Navy under the shah, far too many promises have been made that cannot be kept. This seems particularly true of the "turn key" defense industrial complex France has promised to set up in Saudi Arabia as part of the Sawari I program. Like similar U.S. promises, much of this effort seems unnecessary or far too costly.[19] The pause in Saudi naval expansion caused by reductions in Saudi oil revenues is not likely to do more than ease the situation. The U.S. Navy has already gotten into trouble once over the navy expansion program. Both the U.S. and the West as a whole may benefit from the fact that France seems likely to have to help the Saudis through what are certain to be troubled waters.

Trends in the Saudi National Guard

Although its future may depend upon the complex politics within the Saudi royal family following King Khalid's death, the Saudi National Guard seems likely to remain a lightly armed internal security force whose main mission is to ensure the loyalty of Saudi Arabia's traditional tribes. While its current purchases do not seem overambitious, and the Guard is now better trained and deployed, it cannot absorb large numbers of heavy arms. Even if it is given them for political reasons, the National Guard will continue to have little value as a regular combat force. In fact, the greatest single uncertainty in the Saudi military modernization process is whether the National Guard can deal with terrorism and paramilitary threats and what role the army, air force, and navy should play in aiding it in this mission.

Prince Abdullah has talked about expanding the Guard to 30,000 men, about adding a second mechanized brigade, and about building up to three mechanized brigades by 1989. While these would be motorized infantry units by Western standards, they would have modern infantry support and antitank weapons.

The Guard has begun to hold significant training exercises for its 6,500-man Imam bin Mohammed al-Saud Mechanized Brigade, and it has established a limited oil field security force in the Eastern Province. The mechanized brigade held a 10-day exercise in the desert about 250 miles west of Riyadh in early 1983. While it did not maintain its armored equipment, relied heavily on foreign support, and exhibited a habitual problem with translating tribal into military discipline, the brigade did carry out three days and two nights of reasonably effective maneuvers. Units moved from as far away as the Eastern Province, and there were no signs of unrest. If anything, the Guard personnel in the mechanized forces seemed to have become more conservative and traditional regardless of their Western training—or perhaps in reaction to it.

Nevertheless, the bulk of the Guard is still a traditional tribal force. It is dominated by the 11,000 men in its *firqa* (full-time tribal) and *liwa* (part-time irregular) units. Many of its "troops" are actually retired military, descendants of the troops that fought with King Abd al-Aziz, or the sons or relatives of tribal leaders. The Guard's manpower also serves to the age of 60–65, much of it is directly recruited and paid by tribal or regional chiefs, and many positions have a quasi-hereditary status. It is heavily recruited from the Otaiba and Mutair tribes (of the areas between Makkah and Riyadh and the northeast). It has only gradually recruited new and educated personnel who are loyal to a service rather than a given leader or subleader.[20]

As was described in the previous chapters, the National Guard is more a means through which the royal family allocates funds to tribal and Bedouin leaders than a modern combat or internal security force. The Guard helps key princes maintain close relations with the tribes in each region; it has not evolved into a force that can deal with urban disorders, oil field security problems, border security problems, and ethnic or other internal divisions. The Guard is politically vital, but it has not found a clear military mission. Further, as Table 10.5 shows, the Guard's current force structure and equipment also fail to provide air mobility and the specialized units necessary to deal with urban warfare and terrorist activities.

Such specialized forces might come from the army and air force, but there seem to be no clear plans for this. As a result, the lack of a clear

TABLE 10.5 Saudi Paramilitary Forces, 1983–1984

National Guard	
Total manpower	25,000–31,500 plus 10,000 foreign contract military personnel
Major formations	Brigade headquarters 4 all-arms battalions 16 "regular" infantry battalions (full time) 24 irregular infantry battalions (part time) 1 ceremonial cavalry squadron Support units
Major equipment[a]	240 V-150 Commando APCs; M-102 105mm how; 81mm mortar; 106mm RCL; TOW ATGW; 20mm Vulcan; 90mm AA guns
Major orders	489 Commando AFVs (now in process of delivery); V-150 SP 20mm AA; SP TOW ATGW; 90mm gun armed AFVs
Other formations	Counterterrorist unit (Ministry of Interior): French-trained heliborne force 8,500 Frontier Force and Coast Guard with some helicopters, 169 coastal and 300 small patrol boats, and 12 SRN-6 Hovercraft (MM-40 Exocet SSM and 2 SRN-6 on order) General Civil Defence Administration units

[a]Some reports still show large purchases of German weapons, but these are inaccurate. See the *Economist*, 8 May 1982, and *Washington Times*, 28 May 1982, for a correct report. The report on German sales in the *Middle East*, December 1982, pp. 31–33, is almost entirely in error.

Sources: IISS and SIPRI printouts.

thrust behind the Guard's modernization means that Saudi Arabia may not be doing an adequate job of preparing to deal with the kind of low-level military threats that it may find more dangerous on a day-to-day basis than the major military threats on its borders. French and Pakistani aid can help in the interim, as can the small security units being built up under the Ministry of the Interior, but better Saudi planning and Western advice are needed in this area.

Trends in Saudi Internal Security

It is impossible to ignore the shah's fall in discussing future trends in Saudi Arabia. Saudi Arabia bears little resemblance to Iran's combination of a one-man autocracy, popular poverty, and a yawning gulf between the ruler and his people and their religious leaders. However, the question still arises whether Saudi Arabia is stable enough to support the strategic partnership that will grow out of expanding Saudi-U.S. military relations. There is no simple answer to this question. As the previous chapters have shown, Saudi Arabia does suffer from problems in maintaining its internal stability. It is undergoing a rate of social transformation and modernization that has no parallel in history, and regardless of the level of its oil revenues, it will face incredible difficulties during the 1980s in trying to modernize without westernizing. This task will force the Saudis to redefine many social norms, religious customs, and patterns of cultural behavior. At the same time, Saudi Arabia must cope with both its massive influx of foreign workers and long-standing internal divisions.

The Problem of Foreign Workers

There is no doubt that the problem of Saudi Arabia's foreign workers will grow with time. Although the Saudi Third Five Year Plan indicates that there are only 1.1 million foreign workers out of a labor force of 2.5 million and that there will be only negligible future increases in the number of foreign workers, these figures seem to have been issued largely for political purposes.[21] Saudi Arabia almost certainly had well over 1.5 million foreign workers at the end of 1982. This economic dependence on foreign workers raises much more serious issues than the country's need for foreign military advisers and support.

About 0.6–1.0 million of these workers are Yemeni, many of whom are de facto permanent residents, although Saudi arabia has attempted since 1979 to limit the economic role of its Yemeni workers and their ability to stay in the country. Another 400,000 are other Arabs, including 300,000 Egyptians, 100,000 Palestinians and Jordanians, 40,000 Syrians, 15,000 Lebanese, and 50,000 Sudanese. Some 50,000 Muslims from other Arab states are resident. The numbers of Palestinians and Egyptians are dropping as Saudi Arabia imposes special visa and residence restrictions. They are being replaced by Jordanians and other foreigners: There are now 100,000 Koreans, 50,000 Thais, 200,000 Filipinos, 300,000 Pakistanis, 75,000 Indians, 50,000 Somalis, 40,000 Turks, 20,000 Afghans, 15,000 Bangladeshis, 15,000 Indonesians and Malays, and 7,000 Chinese in the country.[22] "Western" residents include 40,000 Americans, 15,000 French, 13,000 Italians, 10,000 Germans, 10,000 Greeks, 5,000 Japanese, and 13,000 of other nationalities.

These foreign workers will continue not only to dominate the operations of the Saudi economy in the 1980s but also to provide most essential technical skills. Even using Saudi educational statistics and the somewhat optimistic estimates of the revised Saudi Third Five Year Plan, less than half of Saudi Arabia's projected labor force of 1.5 million in 1985 will be fully literate and experienced enough to use Western machinery and technology.[23]

Yet although at least 25% of Saudi Arabia's foreign workers are either illegally present in the country or work at illegal or improperly registered occupations, Saudi Arabia seems likely to be able to exert reasonably tight controls on its foreign labor. Even most Yemenis eventually return home. Unless events in North Yemen deteriorate so far that it is taken over by the South Yemeni–backed National Liberation Front, and "home" for all of Saudi Arabia's Yemeni workers becomes a Marxist and pro-Soviet state, it should be possible for Saudi Arabia to deal with the problems for at least the short term. Saudi Arabia also maintains more rigorous controls over its other foreign workers. It has established steadily more effective controls over its foreign construction workers since 1977 (when a small group of Koreans launched the first major strike by foreign workers in Saudi Arabia's history), and the Saudi government has forced major construction projects to provide proper housing and tight labor controls.[24] Only the "illegals" who enter during the annual pilgrimage still seem to be a major problem.

The Shi'ite Issue

Saudi Arabia still faces problems with the Shi'ite population in its Eastern Province. As was discussed in Chapter 6, the Shi'ites now total around 275,000 and make up 30–60% of the population in the oil region, with 150,000 in the Qatif north of Daharam and 100,000 in the al-Hasa about 100 miles south of Daharam.[25] They have long been subject to repression and discrimination. Unless the Saudi government is careful to bring an end to this discrimination, and to build on the progress it has made since 1980, it will face a growing threat that the Shi'ites may turn to Khomeini or become politically alienated. Khomeini has already attempted to exploit the situation. Shortly after his rise to power, he sent "messengers" to try to link the Saudi Shi'ites to his "Islamic revolution," and these Iranian efforts have continued throughout the Iran-Iraq War.[26]

The last two pilgrimages, for example, have seen Iranian riots in Makkah and Medina. In October 1982 Saudi Arabia expelled 69 Iranians from Medina after they launched a pro-Khomeini riot. A "Hojatolislam Khoeininha" was also arrested for pro-Khomeini and anti-Saudi propaganda, and Saudi Arabia faced both protest marches and threats of massive sit-down strikes. Similar rallies and protests had been staged since 1979, but they first became openly violent in 1981, and only prompt action by the Saudi police avoided large-scale violence in 1982.[27]

The Shi'ites are important for other reasons. The modern element of the Saudi Shi'ite population has the strongest "work ethic" of any segment of Saudi society and makes up a large portion of the skilled workers in the oil fields. The Shi'ites also have a rising political consciousness. They have carried out strikes or protested Saudi labor policies and discrimination several times since the early 1960s. They have long joined the protests against Saudi restrictions on the celebration of Shi'ite holidays. It was such restrictions on the observance of the death of a Shi'ite martyr on the 10th of Muharram that culminated in major riots less than nine days after the seizure of the mosque in Makkah.[28]

Even though the Shi'ites have faced considerable educational discrimination, they now make up more than 50% of the student population of the University of Petroleum and Minerals in Dammam. They have failed to emerge as a force in student politics only because they were barred from student office, and they are now emerging as a new political force in spite of this discrimination. Long before the riots in the Eastern Province, Shi'ite students at the university launched a successful boycott of student elections because the elections had denied the Shi'ites the right to campaign for student government.

Fortunately, the Saudi government now seems committed to reforms in its treatment of the Shi'ites. It has continued to give the Shi'ites far more attention. It has instituted major changes in its revised Third Five Year Plan that will expand the development of Shi'ite cities and towns, and it has eased the discrimination in the university and educational system and started to bring more Shi'ites into senior government positions. In spite of anti-Saudi reports in various Lebanese papers, the National Guard has been kept carefully controlled, and the other security and Special Forces elements in the area have been reorganized to minimize the risk of further friction. The primary means of dealing with religious unrest has been a temporary local curfew, and few political prisoners have been taken. Senior Saudi officials have continued to regularly tour Shi'ite areas and talk to Shi'ite leaders. The issue of self-flagellation—which the Wahabi view with extreme religious distaste as a corruption of Islam—has been resolved by allowing those Shi'ites who wish to perform the ceremony to fly to areas where it is permitted.[29] The government did not overreact to the Khomeini-inspired coup attempt in Bahrain in late 1981, and it is struggling to minimize the growing tension between Sunni and Shi'ite that characterizes the rest of the Near East.[30]

This Saudi reaction to the Shi'ite crisis is particularly important because it indicates that Saudi Arabia will rely on cooperation and flexibility in the future rather than on rigid development plans or repression. In fact, this Saudi ability to react to the forces unleashed by social and economic change is the best guarantee of Saudi Arabia's future internal stability and also gives the country a unique ability to assist its conservative neighbors in the Gulf. The other Gulf states lack the combination of size, political institutions, and wealth to allow them to deal with such crises without assistance. While Saudi Arabia cannot prevent all violent internal reactions to the forces of change, it is the only Gulf state that offers any long-term prospect of being strong and cohesive enough to cope with them.

The problem, however, is not a simple one. During 1981, close ties developed among the Shi'ite-led governments of Syria, Iran, Libya, and South Yemen. The Bahrain plot did disclose that some Saudi Shi'ites were receiving military training in Iran, and it later became apparent that a new, radical younger element in North Yemen's Shi'ite tribes also had links to the Khomeini movement and to South Yemen as well. It is possible to trace increasing arms flows from Libya, Syria, and Iran to other Shi'ite radical groups in Lebanon, Iraq, and Bahrain, and it seems almost certain that such flows will go to Saudi Shi'ites and some of the North Yemenis in Saudi Arabia. It also seems likely that the various Shi'ites in Saudi Arabia will be heavily influenced by the outcome of Iran's war with Iraq, and if Iran continues to be victorious, they may become more amenable to the influence of the Khomeini movement.[31]

Tribal and Regional Rivalries

Saudi Arabia will also continue to be divided by the tribal and regional rivalries discussed in Chapter 6. Only since the early 1970s have the more urbanized and better-educated native Saudis from the Hejaz been brought fully into the armed forces or given equal treatment as technocrats. There are still merchant families in the south who resent past discrimination against the Hejazis and tacitly oppose the royal family. Similar rivalries still exist in the north, some of which date back to the suppression of the Ikhwan and the complex tribal struggles between the Saud and Rashid families before King Abd al-Aziz's triumph in the early 1900s.[32]

These rivalries should diminish steadily in the 1980s, however, under the pressures of population growth, labor mobility, and urbanization. UN statistics indicate that something like 60% of Saudi Arabia's population is under 18 and that more than 50% now live comparatively far from their tribal homes. As a rough estimate, about 50% of Saudi Arabia's population is now urban, and traditional tribal life now involves less than 300,000 Najdis and fewer than 600,000 Saudis from all parts of the country. Allowing for agricultural changes in areas like the Asir, the traditional tribal basis or structure of Saudi society should further wane, losing something like 7–10% of the population per year through the mid-1980s.[33]

The end result should be a steady decline in the traditional frictions within Saudi society, although they may be replaced with a broader set of tensions between religious and political conservatives, who wish to preserve traditional family, social, and religious customs, and modernists, who feel that the only alternative to radical leftist or ultraconservative reactions is to integrate Saudi Arabia's changing population into an industrialized society.

The Stability of the Saudi Military

There is no way to guarantee that Saudi Arabia will be free of problems with its military, although any Middle Eastern country that pays its privates $12,000 a year has obviously done much to reduce the likelihood of such problems.[34] Saudi Arabia has, however, been careful to limit the combat units in the capital to the specially recruited 1,000-man Royal Guard, and it does not suffer from the most serious problems in Iranian military modernization: the shah's constant purges and changes in military command structure in order to speed "modernization" and to secure his personal power over the armed forces. Saudi Arabia has managed to steadily "professionalize" the training and career structure of its armed forces and to give them continuity at the top. The same Saudi princes have led the armed forces since the early 1970s, and approximately 60 other cadet princes occupy key slots in the armed forces. At the same time, most of the senior positions in the armed forces are now occupied by career officers who have earned their positions.

Saudi military intelligence has continued to conduct its counterintelligence operations in a low key, and with fewer abuses than its Iranian counterparts under the shah or the ayatollah. As was discussed in Chapter 6, Saudi intelligence was unprepared for the incident at the Grand Mosque in Makkah in 1979 and for the riots that followed in the Eastern Province. However, many Western observers feel that the Saudis have since continued to restructure their various military and counterintelligence branches and that they are making significant progress in improving those aspects of the army and National Guard that deal with internal security. Most important, the Saudis have again done so without overreacting and without repression. Saudi Arabia has no parallel to the SAVAK in its armed forces. The Saudi government has continued to rely on its traditional dealings with the tribal, regional, and leading-family groups of Saudi Arabia for internal security. The field forces of the National Guard are not full time, do not exercise SAVAK-like functions, and are used largely to maintain contact with Saudi Arabia's traditional elites.

But the Saudi armed forces, National Guard, Royal Intelligence, and Ministry of the Interior have not solved the problems discussed in Chapters 5 and 6. The Saudi military is unlikely to be entirely stable during the 1980s, and Saudi Arabia's rapid transition to a modern state will be no easier for its armed forces than for any other element of Saudi society. Nations like Libya and South Yemen will continue to conduct active efforts to subvert the Saudi armed forces, students, and technocrats and various regional groups, as well as the country's Shi'ites. This Libyan and South Yemeni effort is so large that it is almost certain to find weak spots in the Saudi armed forces and internal security structure.

There seems to be little immediate prospect, however, of a serious military coup attempt, or of any massive anti-American reaction within the armed forces—particularly as long as Saudi Arabia can count on its present military and economic relations with the West. The only factors that seem likely to change this situation are (1) an unsuccessful Saudi-Israeli conflict; (2) an unsuccessful war or other conflict between Saudi Arabia and its neighbors; (3) a massive mismanagement of the "cash squeeze" caused by the current world recession; (4) a crisis in U.S. arms sales that would lead Saudi officers, technocrats, and students to believe that the U.S. was favoring Israel at the expense of Saudi Arabia's defense; (5) the broad conviction that the Saudi armed forces could not count on reasonable or "balanced" treatment from the U.S.; or (6) the conviction that the Saudi government was not putting enough pressure on the U.S. over some vital issue.

It should also be remembered that the Iranian armed forces had little to do with the shah's fall, except to the extent that his ambitions eventually led him to obligate so much of Iran's income to defense that he had to make massive cutbacks in economic development. This is scarcely likely to be the case in Saudi Arabia, which faces no foreseeable risk of encountering Iran's 1979 economic problems, large numbers of unemployed urban poor, or massive retrenchment in its economic development.[35]

The Risk of an Anti-Western Backlash

Many Saudis, including senior Saudi officers, technocrats, and even members of the royal family, do, however, question a number of aspects of Saudi Arabia's military relations with the West. This is particularly true of the military construction that the U.S. has persuaded Saudi Arabia to buy since 1974 and of its internal political impact in Saudi Arabia. The lack of "teeth" Saudi Arabia has obtained in proportion to its vast expenditures on "tail" has become a political issue within Saudi Arabia, especially with students and younger military officers.

Ironically, therefore, Saudi Arabia's problems tend to be the reverse of those of Iran. Unless the air defense enhancement effort proceeds smoothly, there could be a substantial backlash—a popular feeling that Saudi Arabia's military buildup has proceeded so slowly that its forces lack internal and external credibility and do not match the country's economic and political power.[36] This feeling may soon be accompanied by charges that the U.S. is encouraging waste if Saudi oil revenue remains low and the Saudis become increasingly cost conscious. There also is no doubt that the AWACS debate has dramatized the U.S.'s uncertain willingness to provide Saudi Arabia with modern military equipment, while Israel's invasion of Lebanon has again made the government's ties to the U.S. a liability. These events have produced growing internal unrest over the U.S. advisory presence in Saudi Arabia and have cast doubt on Saudi Arabia's ability to deter an attack on its territory and back up its collective security initiatives in the Gulf.

In short, if Saudi Arabia is to ensure the stability and loyalty of its armed forces, counter the concerns of its students and young professionals, and deal effectively with its potential allies and enemies in the Gulf, it must have a military credibility it can get only by translating its immense investment in military infrastructure and U.S. equipment and services into effective military forces. The Saudi government must be able to demonstrate internally and externally that the U.S. is a credible and reliable security partner.

The Impact of the Economy

As was discussed in Chapter 1, there is little prospect of an economic crisis in Saudi Arabia, although it now seems doubtful that its oil revenues will recover before the mid-1980s or will then grow at anything like the rate of the previous decade.[37] A lower growth rate, however, may help Saudi Arabia's development and stability. It should cool down its inflation rate, which had started to rise again in 1980–1981, and help put Saudi industrialization plans in a more realistic perspective.[38] Certainly, the Saudis seem to have created overambitious plans for petrochemical development. They have already spent something like $8.6 billion on investment in petrochemical and fertilizer plants since 1975, and they had expected to spend at least $11 billion more before 1985. Saudi estimates of demand and probable price were optimistic even when they were issued, and the slowdown in such development projects would almost certainly help Saudi Arabia to adjust to more realistic goals.[39]

As for the rest of the "cash squeeze" that Saudi Arabia will experience until the world's economy recovers, there is little prospect that the country will have to cut back on the increases it has made in the living standards of its average citizens. Saudi Arabia now has at least $150 billion and probably closer to $175 billion, invested abroad.[40] Even if Saudi oil revenues continue to remain low in the early and middle 1980s, it still will cost Saudi Arabia only about $0.60 per barrel to lift its oil and only $4 and $6 to deliver it at the tanker, including the capital cost of future exploration and development. Accordingly, although Saudi Arabia's Third Five Year Plan is now costed at over $235 billion, the country has immense leeway in cutting back on this plan without affecting Saudi living standards.[41]

The rise in Saudi living standards has been already impressive. To put it in perspective, in the 20 years from 1951 to 1970, Saudi oil revenues rose from $57 million per year to $1.2 billion. By 1974, they had risen to $4.3 billion a year, a rise of 257% over the 1970 figure. By the end of 1981, they were approaching $100 billion annually. By the time the Second Five Year Plan had been completed in 1980, at a cost of $160 billion, some 50% of the expenditures under the plan had been spent on basic infrastructure like roads, utilities, schools, water projects, and hospitals that changed the life of virtually every Saudi. In spite of inflation, the average real wage of all Saudis rose 70% between 1975 and 1979, and social services increased this income by a further 29%. In addition, the government provided 100,000 free houses and interest-free loans for 200,000 more, and many Saudis acquired extensive capital wealth as a result of government loans and grants and the general expansion of the economy.[42]

While this allocation may not be optimal from the viewpoint of economic development, it is also important to note that some 39% of the growth in Saudi Arabia's gross domestic product (GDP) under its

$235 billion Third Five Year Plan will be in the service sector, which again contributes directly to living standards. This figure compares with 30% for the oil sector, 8% for construction, 5% for manufacturing, 5% for utilities, and 4% for agriculture and mining.[43] According to Saudi Arabian Monetary Agency estimates, this growth has involved $3 billion in private, non-oil-related capital investment in manufacturing and $4.5 billion in government soft loans since 1976.[44] As a result, the number of Saudi factories, or small entrepreneurial manufacturing enterprises, rose from 350 in 1976 to about 900 in 1979. In spite of the recent cuts in oil revenues, another $4.5 billion in soft loans should raise this total to nearly 2,500 by late 1985.[45]

Accordingly, there are strong signs that Saudi Arabia can cope with the socioeconomic problems of adjusting to the shifts in its oil wealth and still maintain high living standards. Still, as was discussed in Chapters 1 and 2, the future will not be easy. By the middle to late 1980s, Saudi Arabia will have to decide what it is really going to do about its foreign workers, particularly about the problem of absorbing its semipermanent Yemeni work force.[46] It will have to decide how much of a service industry it can afford to create and what long-term role Saudi workers and entrepreneurs will play in the new economy. It will have to learn how to use its newly educated population, and it will have to adjust to broadening popular participation in its government.

The Impact of the Defense Budget

Saudi Arabia's flexibility also extends to its defense budget. Many individual projects can be delayed or cut back to avoid any choice between "guns" and "butter" or to minimize any budget deficit or use of Saudi investment reserves. Saudi Arabia has completed its basic military infrastructure, and the timing of the improvements needed in its land, air, and naval forces allows them to be postponed by up to several years without significantly affecting Saudi security. There have already been some cutbacks in construction, the air defense effort, and naval procurements. The Ministry of Defense and Aviation has, for example, cut $350 million off the cost of the al-Kharj Air Base and postponed some E-3A and KC-707 expenditures. This indicates that reduced oil revenues may well end in encouraging the same kind of healthy look at defense spending that has already produced cutbacks in petrochemical development and civilian construction.

As for the actual size of the Saudi defense budget, this is very much a moving target. According to the plans Saudi Arabia announced in April 1983, Saudi defense and internal security expenditures would be 82.5 billion rials in 1981-1982 (out of a total budget of 298 billion rials), 92.89 billion rials in 1982-1983 (out of a total budget of 313 billion rials, or $90.7 billion), and 75.7 billion in 1983-1984 (out of a total budget of 260 billion rials). These figures imply a 19% cut in defense spending in 1983-1984, which is slightly higher than the 17% overall cut planned in the total budget. The actual cut may be higher, however, as only 57.7 billion rials ($16.7 billion) of the 75.7 billion rials ($21.9 billion) would go to the MODA and regular forces. The remainder would go to the internal security forces, and the split between the MODA and other expenditures implies that the government may be deliberately compensating for the effects of reduced economic activity by using the Guard to increase transfers to the tribal and other traditional leaders or that Abdullah's status as Crown Prince may be giving the Guard a higher funding priority.[47]

The Saudi Finance Ministry has since reported that the 1983-1984 budget will be regularly reexamined beginning in August 1983 and that total spending will be adjusted according to the size of the Saudi deficit and the trends in the oil market. Given the fact that the oil revenue projections in the mid-July and fall 1983 OPEC meetings were considerably lower than Saudi Arabia's expectations in formulating its budget, it seems likely that further defense cuts are in store. Saudi officials have, in fact, indicated that they are reviewing major contracts and payments on a monthly basis and that obligations are lower than the schedule called for in the 1983-1984 budget. If true, this is a striking reversal, since obligations usually run substantially above the defense budget projections.[48]

Saudi Arabia has great flexibility in adjusting its defense expenditures. Virtually one-third of its total defense and internal security expenditures goes to construction or construction-related services, and almost all can be postponed or scaled back, given progress to date in creating Saudi bases and facilities. Roughly another third goes to procurement that does not affect the living conditions of the Saudi military or affect Saudi businessmen heavily. While such procurement cannot always be postponed, Saudi Arabia's rate of new obligation has been so high a percentage of total expenditure that simply delaying major new project expenditures can produce massive savings. Because of Saudi investment reserves and the country's ability to alter its defense trade terms to barter oil for goods and services or schedule payment in the out-years when higher demand for oil is likely, defense spending should be both controllable within the limits made possible by Saudi oil revenue and relatively unimportant in shaping Saudi internal security.[49]

The Royal Family as a Force for Stability

The Saudi royal family has so far dealt with these conflicting pressures by simultaneously supporting the enforcement of traditional Saudi customs, cutting back on Saudi Arabia's massive modernization efforts, and continuing to fund all social benefits and a rise in personal income for most individual Saudis. The government has divided the country into areas where advanced development is encouraged and areas where the more traditional tribes are sheltered from foreign intrusion and modernization. The Saudi government consists of a broad mixture of conservative and modern ministries, which gives the government considerable flexibility in dealing with the forces of change, as does the size of the royal family.

The Saudi royal family now consists of as many as 20,000 people, including collateral branches and related families like the Jiluwis. There are some 2,000–3,000 princes at its core including those with the first- and second-generation ties to Abd al-Aziz, his brothers, and the collateral descendants of Abdul Rahman, Abd al-Aziz's father.[50] Coupled to a tradition of the open court, or Majlis, where any element in Saudi society can talk directly to one of the princes, the size of the royal family means that it can represent virtually every faction in Saudi society and keep in touch with most potentially alienated elements.

The royal family thus provides a broader and more representative structure for integrating Saudi society in the face of major social change than that of other Gulf states, including the radical Gulf regimes. However, it still leaves many serious problems in governing Saudi society. As was discussed in Chapter 6, the struggles between "conservative" and "modernist" were a major reason for the rising at the Mosque of the Prophet in November 1979. While the force that seized the mosque was small,[51] the uprising did reveal tensions in Saudi society that had been serious enough to lead the Saudi government to place new restrictions on the modernization of Saudi social customs and the role of women and to continue to revise its modernization plans to reduce internal tension.[52]

Further, it is impossible to dismiss the succession issue. It is true that King Khalid's death in June 1982 resulted in a succession that was even smoother and more rapid than the one following the assassination of King Faisal. Within 24 hours of Khalid's fatal heart attack, Prince Fahd had become king, Prince Abdullah had become Crown Prince and deputy prime minister, and Prince Sultan had become second deputy prime minister and third in line to the throne. Even though Khalid died in the midst of a major Israeli attack on Lebanon, there were no delays and few signs of any of the tensions or frictions among the princes discussed in Chapter 5.[53]

This does not mean, however, that the organization of Saudi Arabia's national security apparatus (shown in Chart 10.2) is likely to remain unchanged. Some "succession" must eventually be found to command of the National Guard, control of the MODA, and control of Saudi intelligence and internal security. King Khalid's death has created pressures that will ultimately lead to new ministers' replacing the senior princes and to a new hierarchy's taking power within each organization.

Some friction, in fact, is already emerging. Rumors of a coup attempt by the National Guard in January 1983 eventually seemed to trace back to anti-Saudi groups operating in London and Lebanon. At the same time, a flood of more substantive rumors began that indicated that there was tension between King Fahd and Crown Prince Abdullah, between

CHART 10—2
SAUDI ARABIA'S DEFENSE ORGANIZATION IN 1983

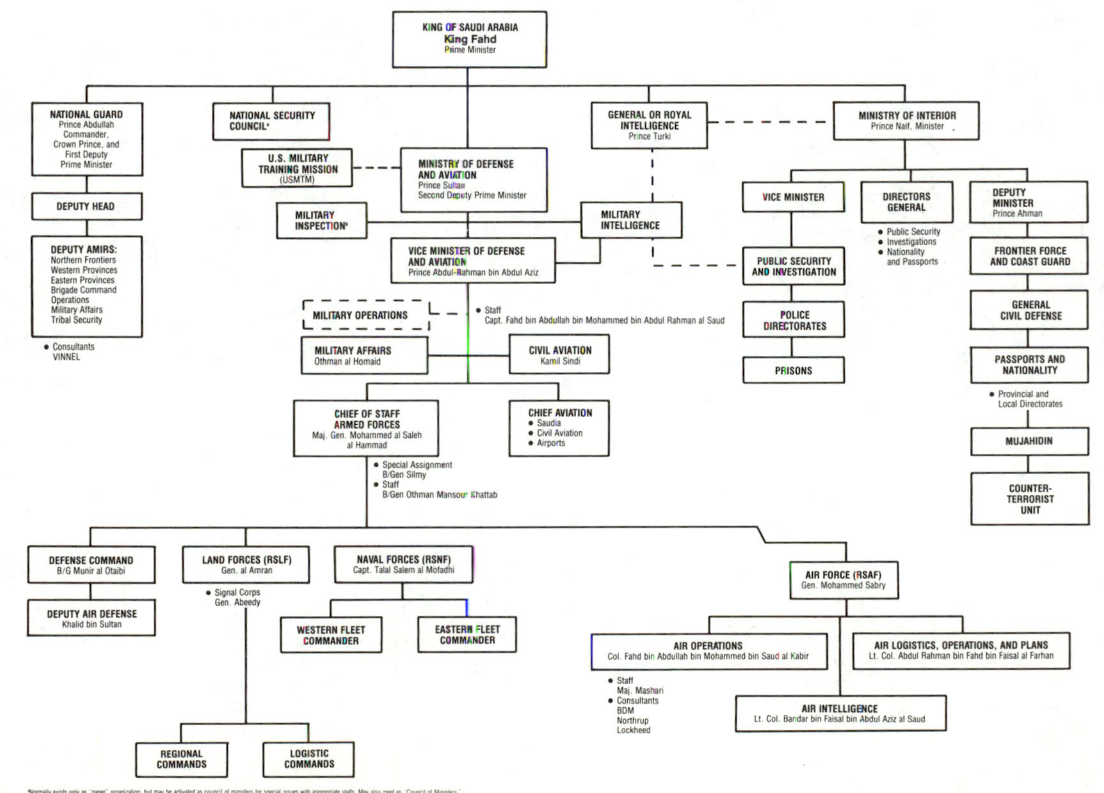

[a]Normally exists only as "paper" organization, but may be activated as council of ministers for special issues with appropriate staffs. May also meet as "Council of Ministers."
[b]Disciplinary Council and Military Trial Courts may report to Minister or Vice Minister.

Adapted from tables provided by the Embassy of Saudi Arabia; from Clarence Robinson, "Saudi Arabia," *Aviation Week*, 23 May 1983, pp. 54 and 76, and from Holden and Johns, *The House of Saud*, pp. 267, 512-13, and 523-24.

the traditionalist elements in Saudi society and the modernists, and between the advocates of drawing on Saudi Arabia's investments to maintain development spending and the fiscal conservatives who wanted to avoid any budget deficits and use of Saudi Arabia's investment reserves. These rumors accelerated still further when Abd al-Aziz al-Quraishi resigned as head of the Saudi Arabian Monetary Agency on 13 April 1984, just as the 1983-1984 budget was announced, and when the Saudi minister of information, Muhammid Abdur Yamani, was dismissed, evidently for allowing rumors of dissension within the royal family to surface in a 25 April 1983 *Financial Times* special section on Saudi Arabia. They gathered still greater force as rumors arose that Oil Minster Ahmed Zaki Yamani (no relation to Mohammid Yamani) and Finance Minister Mohammed Abalkheil would soon be forced to resign and take the status of advisers to the king.

By May, rumors were circulating that King Fahd and Prince Sultan had attempted to displace Prince Abdullah's supporters in the National Guard and among the tribal leaders. At the same time, rumors emerged that Abdullah had threatened a National Guard–backed coup, and still other rumors emerged that the king had left the Council of Ministers in anger or was ignoring Abdullah and failing to consult him on decisions. These rumors extended to cover the other senior members of the royal family, although many differed by province, a natural result of the fact that 7 of the 14 provincial governors, or emirs, are brothers or half brothers of the king, five are Sudairis, and two belong to the Ilawi tribes in the northern provinces.

Such rumors also came to include the military. One rumor noted that Prince Abdullah and the National Guard had been given exceptional public attention and that Abdullah was publicly involved in decisions affecting the Ministry of Defense and Aviation. These points were interpreted to mean that Abdullah was increasing his power. Another set of rumors focused on the fact that the king had named Prince Abd al-Rahman deputy minister of defense and that this gave the Sudairis new authority, because it meant that Sultan and Abd al-Rahman controlled defense, and Prince Naif and his deputy, Prince Ahman, controlled the Interior Ministry. By June 1983, the royal family was forced to take the unique step of officially announcing that the rumors were untrue, something Prince Abdullah proceeded to confirm in interviews.

No one can confidently sort out this mixture of rumors and denials or predict what new rumors will surface over the next few years. There are also a host of other factors that affect the situation; for example, King Fahd does not like to make decisions publicly or attend long conferences or meetings, particularly public meetings like the Majlis at which protocol dictates that he cannot smoke. This has tended to isolate the king, while Abdullah's elevation to the status of Crown Prince has inevitably given him a new role. Further, his ties to Syria have given him an additional role both in trying to deal with the Arab-Israeli dispute and in seeking Syrian help in bringing an end to the Iran-Iraq War, while Prince Sultan has dealt with the West. These roles have led to reports that Abdullah is anti-American or anti-West while Sultan is pro-American.

It seems likely, however, that there is some fire underneath this smoke. First, the cut in oil revenues is forcing Saudi Arabia to make choices it has never had to make before, and the National Guard's ability to help provide internal stability must take priority over new defense projects. Second, King Fahd does not like to coordinate decisions with Prince Abdullah, and there is some friction between them. Third, a coalition has built up between the supporters of sustained modernization, symbolized by King Fahd and Prince Sultan, and the supporters of cutbacks and tradition, symbolized by Prince Abdullah. Fourth, Prince Abdullah is supported by a number of technocrats and members of Saudi Arabia's senior business families who would also like to see a more modest development effort, and possibly by some of the key nephews of the senior princes like Foreign Minister Prince Saud al-Faisal, who would like Saudi Arabia to shift more toward the Third World and away from involvement in the kind of politics that involve superpower confrontations. Finally, there is continuing jockeying for power simply because the national security organization lends itself to divisions along family lines.

Such divisions may actually help Saudi stability by allowing the royal family to represent the forces of change and adapt to new conditions, but they also mean that sooner or later the U.S. may have to deal with both *King* Abdullah and a much more demanding coalition of younger princes, technocrats, and Saudi power figures than it deals with today.[54]

Further, while Prince Abdullah and Prince Sultan seem to have ended any competition that may have existed over the succession, the problem still arises as to what succession will follow the death of King Fahd, Prince Abdullah, and Prince Sultan. This problem does not seem likely to surface in the early or middle 1980s. In late 1983 Fahd will be 62, Abdullah 60, and Sultan 59. One of the three seems likely to survive for the next decade, and for all the various reports of conflicts among them, they are politically sophisticated men who fully understand the need to balance the political pressures on the kingdom. They will probably deal with most issues and acts of government in much the same way.

The succession problem seems more likely to surface after these senior princes depart from power, and some experts predict that it will do so after the death of Prince Abdullah. The sheer size of the royal family ensures that future members cannot have the power and privileges that its members enjoyed in the past. It is also unclear how the Saudi family can make a transition to a more stable form of rule as long as the succession passes from brother to brother, rather than from father to son. There are, after all, 36 sons of Abd al-Aziz, and 8 surviving sons were born after 1939. They, in turn, already have had more than 170 sons, and the number is growing. These numbers make it difficult, if not impossible, to create a stable power structure unless a more orderly succession can be established.

Another key question is whether the royal family can gradually cease to "rule" and let the new generation of Saudi officers and technocrats take responsibility for governing or whether it must continue to govern as well. When Westerners compare Saudi Arabia to Iran, they often raise the issue that the shah was the source of many of the pressures that tore Iran apart. However, the royal family now governs the Saudi state to the extent that it is the prime source of most of the pressures that hold Saudi Arabia together. The Saudi princes now so dominate Saudi Arabi's administrative apparatus and politics that there is a good chance that any coup that deposed the royal family would lead to civil war between such Saudi factions as the modernists and traditionalists. The answer, at least until the mid-1990s, may be that the royal family will continue to govern, but will do so more and more indirectly. For example, the junior and cadet princes of the royal family now provide a layer of competent officers who can act as partners of the emerging generation of Saudi military professionals and technocrats.

A wide range of junior princes either are pursuing military careers or have used military careers as a way station.[55] These include Ibn Saud's forty-second son, Migrin; Faisal's son Abdul Rahman, commander of the first Saudi armored brigade; Faisal's son Bandar, an air force officer; Faisal's son Turki, director of Royal Intelligence; the younger son of Crown Prince Fahd, who is a major in the army; two of Sultan's sons—Khalid and Bandar—who are officers; two of Abdullah's sons—Mit'ab and Turk—who are officers in the National Guard; Prince Salman's son Ahmad, an army officer; and two of Prince Nasir's sons—Turki and Muhammed—one an officer in the air force, the other an officer in the army. Several of Abd al-Aziz's brothers also have sons in the armed forces, including Abdullah's son Fahd, a naval officer. Fourth-generation princes are also beginning to be active. One of Prince Muhammed's great-grandsons, Bandar, is an army officer. Prince Fahd bin Abdullah, the chief of Air Force Operations, is an example of a member of a collateral branch of the family who has emerged as a key figure in the MODA. There is, in fact, no precise count of how many junior or cadet princes are in the armed forces. The role and identity of members of the collateral branches is not well understood in the West, and even tracking the grandchildren of Abd al-Aziz is difficult, particularly since they are now reported to total over 167 males and 165 females.

Although such a dual command structure does provoke resentments and presents the problem that a prince whose formal rank is that of a major or colonel may be the de facto superior of a general, it should be remembered that the Saudis have lived with this situation for centuries.

Further, the personal relations between prince and career professional seem surprisingly sound in practice. These relations are more flexible and easier than those among the members of the senior ranks in many other Arab armies, and they are strengthened by the fact that many of the younger princes understand that the royal family must steadily limit its role in the direct command of the armed forces if Saudi career professionals are to remain loyal. These younger princes seem certain to become increasingly important as Prince Abdullah and Prince Sultan broaden their responsibilities to cover the government of the entire country and transfer the command of the armed forces and National Guard. Most of the younger princes are also far more used to concepts of Western administration and the delegation of authority than their fathers. They are typical of a new royal elite that clearly sees the need to strengthen the role of Saudi Arabia's technocrats, professionals, and the middle class.

Ironically, the royal family may be readier to share its power and to give an increasing role to the civilian government than the nation is ready to accept such changes. There are strong indications that the family's reluctance to supplement the Majlis with a consultative assembly has been as much the result of pressures from religious and tribal figures as of any unwillingness on the part of the royal family. It also seems likely that much of the Western debate over the "conservatism" of Prince Abdullah stems from the fact that he has been the principal spokesman within the royal family for the conservative forces in Saudi Arabia. As such, he has expressed a caution regarding the pace of modernization that all of the princes share. It is important to remember that Saudi Arabia is a nation, not simply a family. The Saudi royal family survives because of its ability to represent all the major factions in Saudi Arabia, not because of its ability to suppress them. Still, it faces a major challenge. It must find a new approach to monarchy at the same time that Saudi society must develop new patterns of politics and mores. This is scarcely impossible. Many of the world's nations have had to go through similar transitions during the last decade. However, few have done this so quietly and without incident.

At a minimum, the Saudi government will need a better and more modern method to staff senior ministerial positions. The Saudi system of keeping senior appointees in office unless they make catastrophic mistakes does provide continuity, and it can develop great expertise when these appointees are competent; but it provides for little change or adaptability. Few senior appointments changed between King Khalid's accession to the throne and his death six years later. Many ministers have been in office even longer—Yamani has now served as oil minister for nearly two decades—and major changes seem virtually inevitable in the next year or so. In several cases, the Saudi government has obviously retained incompetent officials long after they should have been replaced, and new junior appointments have had to be made to bypass such senior officials.[56]

In summary, Saudi Arabia needs to define a suitable future role for the royal family, to create a broader forum for popular representation like a consultative assembly, to modernize the government's organizaiton, and to "professionalize" the government to the extent that major appointments are changed more often. It needs to crack down on extravagance, waste, and corruption and to pay very close attention to preserving the royal family's legitimacy in terms of custom and Islamic law. It must find ways to make its military and bureaucratic structure more adaptable to current needs and pressures. The royal family does not seem threatened, but it must react to the new Saudi Arabia it has done so much to create. Its greatest vulnerability is that it has unleashed forces it may fail to lead.

Implications for a Saudi-U.S. Strategic Partnership

The trends discussed in the previous section argue strongly that the problem of forging a Saudi-U.S. military partnership will require as much attention in the future as in the past. If Saudi Arabia is to become a more modern state, establish a stable balance between royal and career professionals, create effective military forces, and join the U.S. in an informal strategic partnership in the Gulf, it will need increasing U.S. aid in improving its planning, budgeting, and management systems and in developing tools it can use to improve the collective security efforts of bodies like the Gulf Cooperation Council.

Improving the Quality of Western Military Assistance

Although Saudi Arabia is acquiring a large number of young technocrats with all the required academic credentials, these technocrats lack the practical experience to develop the needed management systems. Saudi Arabia will also need outside help in breaking down the present vertical organization of the Saudi military organization and bureaucracy.

Similarly, the U.S. must improve the quality of its planning and advice. It cannot simply recycle petrodollars and make any kind of strategic partnership work or leave the quality of its planning and advice to the Saudis at its past level of sophistication. If the U.S. is to translate its new military relationship with Saudi Arabia into an effective partnership, it must give Saudi Arabia plans and advice that have the same level of sophistication and safeguards that would be demanded in the U.S. The U.S. must recognize the risks inherent in the failure of any U.S.-proposed system to meet Saudi needs adequately.

Saudi air defenses, for example, will have extraordinarily sophisticated technology. Even with the cutbacks described earlier, they will involve a life-cycle investment of well over $15 billion between 1984 and 1994. Yet the U.S. failed to systematically cost the key elements, create meaningful project plans for the major pieces—much less for the entire system—address the issue of systems integration, and independently validate its recommendations before advancing the Air Defense Enhancement Package, although it involved Saudi expenditures of several billion dollars per major element. No real "cost-to-defeat" or threat-growth analysis was performed as part of the Peace Hawk VII or "Air Feasibility Study" efforts. No real project plan was developed before the Congress approved the sale. The costing was perfunctory at best, and the sensitivity analysis in both studies failed to look at major cost-benefit trade-offs or to offer the Saudis a reasonable selection of options.

Peace Sentinel and Peace Shield have since begun to overcome these problems, but this state of affairs cannot be allowed to continue. The U.S. cannot keep on selling before it plans, and it must increasingly eliminate gold-plating and consider the costs to Saudi Arabia. More well-educated military and civilian technocrats enter the Saudi Ministry of Defense every year, and their impressions of the wisdom of maintaining close military relations with the U.S. will be determined by the quality and integrity of U.S. military advice. This advice is now well intentioned and conceptually sound, but it falls far short of what it should be.

It is also apparent that Saudi Arabia can never develop all the relevant analytic and planning capabilities that are common in the U.S.—Saudi Arabia simply cannot afford to devote the skilled manpower resources to developing such skills for one-time systems designs, even if it could do so on a timely basis. Accordingly, the U.S. cannot credibly transfer responsibility to the Saudis for managing the details of the U.S. advisory effort or reviewing its advice. The U.S. must assume responsibility for making its advice cost effective and making it work.

For the same reasons, France, Britain, and Italy need to improve their advice and planning support to Saudi Arabia even more. All three nations have shown a greater tendency to "oversell" their technology than has the U.S., with even less concern for the details of whether the Saudis can properly operate it and the kinds of follow-on support the Saudis will require. The problem with this approach is that Europe's dependence on Saudi oil is unlikely to go away and that, once again, the new generation of Saudi officers and technocrats is not going to "forget and forgive" problems in any nation's advice and equipment transfers.

The U.S. cannot afford to worsen its present reputation for exploiting Saudi defense purchases. It also cannot afford the kind of action that a Boeing vice-president suggested shortly after the AWACS sale to Saudi Arabia—that the U.S. Air Force "would load it on the Saudis" in pricing the E-3A.[57] It cannot afford to promise Saudi Arabia offsets, technology transfer, and industrialization in return for its defense dollars and then see these promises turn into "buzz words" that are little more than pious frauds. The U.S. must be extremely careful to give Saudi Arabia fair value for money if it is to preserve close relations. The recent cuts in Saudi oil revenues have already made Saudi Arabia much more cost conscious, and this consciousness is likely to continue once Saudi revenues have recovered.

Accordingly, the character of U.S. military relations with Saudi Arabia must change strikingly over the next few years. The Saudi force structure is maturing to a much more sophisticated level, which will require the U.S. to increase the sophistication and quality of its planning and advisory effort. Extreme care must be exercised if many of the Saudi purchases are to be made militarily effective. As Robert Osgood once said of NATO, Saudi-U.S. military relations are becoming an "entangling alliance." The U.S. is not only getting advantages from the Saudi purchase of new air systems and improved reinforcement capabilities, it is also acquiring new responsibilities and increasing obligations to Saudi Arabia.

The Need for Long-Term Planning

The U.S. must also stop using major arms sales as "bandaids" for the more fundamental problems in Saudi-U.S. relations. Both the U.S. and Saudi Arabia now tend to deal with every new security problem in the Gulf, or crises in Saudi-U.S. relations, by negotiating a major new arms package. Far too often, this leads to hurried planning and poorly structured programs, to dramatic increases in arms technology that trigger new U.S. political debates, and to overpurchases and waste. The solution is a far more methodical planning process that meets both nations' long-term needs.

As part of this long-term planning effort, the U.S. must again seek to include the French and British and possibly West German governments. The problem of whose arms will be sold to Saudi Arabia may inevitably limit the extent of such cooperation, as may the various political differences between the U.S. and its allies over the Middle East and the Gulf. Nevertheless, France is now the joint supplier of Saudi Arabia's navy and army, and Britain seems likely to remain an important supplier to its air force. No matter how the U.S. strives to develop a tacit or overt strategic consensus between Israel and Saudi Arabia over the next decade, it cannot plan to supplant its allies in their present advisory role. This means that the U.S. may have to try to create a long-range planning forum that will include its European allies. Such a forum could both help put Saudi forces on a solid footing and improve the cooperability of French, British, U.S., and Saudi forces. Such planning should include an effort to minimize Saudi Arabia's burden of trying to support equipment from several major suppliers and some effort at rationalization and standardization. It should also consider how to shape the Saudi Army and Navy to solve their respective equipment replacement and expansion problems and to reduce the costs of foreign support and construction. U.S., British, and French competition in supplying Saudi Arabia has its healthy side, but it must be accompanied by as much cooperation as possible.

Priorities for Improved Planning

Further, the U.S. must consider how it can best help Saudi Arabia in several critical areas of its planning during the 1980s:

• The first such area is internal security and the problem of adapting Saudi intelligence and security forces to deal with the steadily more sophisticated threat from nations like Libya and South Yemen. U.S. assistance can be particularly important in this area, although major help can come from France or Britain. The U.S. can help Saudi Arabia improve its coordination, crisis management in dealing with complex politico-military crises such as the uprising at the Grand Mosque, and its training of Saudi special forces to deal with such problems. It can help Saudi Arabia improve the interface between its army and National Guard and find the best way of organizing both services to deal with internal security problems. The West cannot hope to resolve the political and historical differences between the two services. It can, however, offer technical and military options that will give both services a meaningful role and help them cooperate. These options could include developing complementary equipment mixes and force concepts for each service and improved C^3 systems that will allow them to net without necessarily eliminating their independence.

• Second, the U.S. needs to help Saudi Arabia develop the kind of air mobility and defense systems necessary to guard its key civilian and oil facilities against limited guerrilla or terrorist attacks or sabotage. Some such steps are under way, but they remain faltering and poorly organized. Further, the large area to be covered, and the wide range of potential threats involved, mean that the National Guard and army cannot hope to deal with the problem solely through area defense. More attention is needed to passive defense, less vulnerable facility design, and systems redundancy. The Saudis must become able to rapidly deploy by air and helicopter units that are specially trained and equipped to deal with the kinds of crisis that may arise and that can surpass any terrorist or guerrilla forces in firepower and speed of reaction. The AWACS can help by locating such forces when they are equipped with transponders and in providing a mobile command center and basis for coordinating helicopters and firepower. It might even be possible to add special terminals and software for such purposes.

• Third, the U.S. must help Saudi Arabia solve some of the problems in the organization of its defense effort and the management of its defense budget. The problems in the present Saudi system described in Chapters 6 and 7 are now widely recognized by many Saudi technocrats, and the Saudi government seems ready for such aid. It is essential to build public and military confidence that Saudi Arabia's defense effort is effective and honestly managed and also to reduce the tension that has built up over the feeling that the U.S. and other Western nations are profiteering from Saudi Arabia's defense expenditures.

• Fourth, the U.S. must help Saudi Arabia organize the rest of its disparate and uncoordinated military electronics and C^3 systems. The AWACS is a paradigm in that it focuses on solving critical problems in Saudi military effectiveness without massive deployments of new weapons and on Saudi Arabia's battle-management problems. Similar aid is required for the Saudi Army, for Saudi ground-air cooperation, and for linking the armed forces and the Saudi political leadership. Such systems also have the added benefit of improving the ability of U.S. and Saudi forces to cooperate in a larger-scale conflict or crisis or in assistance to one of the other conservative Gulf countries.

• Fifth, the U.S. must help Saudi Arabia deal with its mobility and firepower problems. As is discussed in Chapters 17 and 20, Saudi Arabia needs to learn from recent wars in the region and develop the kind of forces that can help make up for its lack of experience in armored maneuver and its lack of large armored forces. For example, a properly structured helicopter force would act as a powerful deterrent to any land or amphibious action by Iran and Iraq and would give Saudi Arabia the ability to react quickly to any terrorist or insurgent threat in the southern Gulf. Recent wars have shown that helicopters can check superior armored forces and can match tactical airpower as a solution to Saudi Arabia's unique combination of manpower and time and space problems. It will, however, take massive initial U.S. help to make such a program effective. Helicopter forces require extensive training, support, and adaptation to local tactical conditions to deliver their potential.

• Sixth, the U.S. must organize to systematically aid Saudi Arabia in working with the other conservative Gulf states and in developing effective contingency arrangements for U.S. over-the-horizon reinforcements. The following chapters outline recommendations to this end; implementing these recommendations will require the U.S. to provide both formal and informal assistance to Saudi planners.

U.S. Diplomacy and the Problem of Israel

Finally, the U.S. still faces the need to improve its diplomacy. The Reagan administration has taken some useful initiatives in this area. During the AWACS debate, on 26 October 1981, it reasserted the U.S. pledge to defend Saudi Arabia in a formal statement to the Joint Economic Committee.[58] It also sent Secretary of State Caspar Weinberger to Saudi Arabia in January 1982 with detailed proposals to strengthen Saudi-U.S. defense cooperation, to create a joint committee for military projects under the chairmanship of Prince Sultan and Secretary Weinberger, and to set up a joint effort to assist the Gulf countries in strengthening their defense.[59]

At the same time, the Reagan administration has shown that it has not learned many of the lessons of the AWACS debate, and it has repeated some of the mistakes of the Carter administration made in 1979 and 1980. One of these mistakes was the inability to accept an informal strategic partnership. Like its predecessor, the Reagan administration could not appreciate the fact that Arab states like Saudi Arabia, Jordan, and Egypt must operate in the Arab as well as the Western world and cannot afford the risk of full and open alignment with the U.S. Rather than accept the success of its informal ties with Saudi Arabia, the administration sought to put its military arrangements on a formal basis and gave this effort inordinately high publicity before making sure of Saudi agreement. Further, it combined these efforts to strengthen defense cooperation with an equally public effort to put formal limits on the use of the E-3As it was selling to Saudi Arabia that would have compromised Saudi sovereignty in the eyes of the Arab world, but that added nothing to the real-world technical constraints described earlier.

These U.S. attempts culminated in a trip by Secretary of Defense Caspar Weinberger to Saudi Arabia in early 1982. Although Weinberger's visit was a success in every practical sense, and the U.S. and Saudi Arabia worked out a series of informal agreements that laid the groundwork for close strategic cooperation, Weinberger than proceeded to announce the relationship before the press. Although a silent Prince Sultan stood with him at the conference, Saudi Arabia immediately backed away from Weinberger's announcement and then went on to deny any embarrassing details of Saudi-U.S. military relations that appeared in the press.[60]

At one level, the episode reflected a conflict between cultures that may be unavoidable. U.S. security policy operates openly and formally and in an atmosphere of constant media exposure. Saudi security policy, like that of most other nations in the world, is kept secret and as informal as possible. The U.S. always seeks formal and structured relations and rarely acts quietly behind the scenes. Saudi Arabia seeks to avoid any open action that would unnecessarily arouse the hostility of any state or political movement or force it to choose publicly between ties to the West and to the Arab world. Its combination of strength and weakness forces it to keep as low a public profile as possible.

At another level, however, this episode reflected the continuing problem the U.S. has in dealing with Israel. Quite aside from incidents like the M-1 tank fiasco discussed earlier, the Reagan administration has been unable to smooth over the almost inevitable frictions resulting from U.S. support of Israel. Even before Israel's invasion of Lebanon led to a new round of fighting in the Middle East, Israel's annexation of the Golan Heights led Prince Fahd to cancel a planned 19 January 1982 visit to Washington. This was the second time in three years that Prince Fahd had canceled a visit to Washington, and it was not a propitious beginning to the year in which he became King.[61] Although Prince Fahd had met with President Reagan in Cancun in October 1981 and twice with Secretary Haig before this cancellation, the Saudi government used all three meetings to express its opposition to the administration's public call for a "strategic consensus" that linked Saudi Arabia and Israel.

The complex events since Israel's invasion of Lebanon in June 1982 have not eased this situation. Only President Reagan's fall 1982 peace initiative prevented a serious crisis in U.S.-Saudi relations.[62] The continuing crisis in Lebanon that has grown out of Israel's invasion has involved the U.S. in a complex juggling act with Israel, Saudi Arabia, and other Arab states that constantly threatens to link the U.S. to Israel in ways that could seriously damage U.S.-Saudi relations.

The Reagan administration had to tell the Saudi government in early 1983 that it could not support any major new Saudi military modernization efforts because of its concern with pro-Israel lobbying in the Congress and the 1984 elections. It then had to repeatedly seek Saudi help to prevent the Lebanese crisis from causing the permanent division of Lebanon and a new Israeli-Syrian war.[63] In spite of the progress made in the interim, the 1984 election promised to raise many of the same problems in diplomacy and U.S. efforts to balance relations with Israel and Saudi Arabia that had occurred in 1980.

This situation requires more professional and more subtle diplomacy. It also requires a more careful balance in U.S. relations with Israel, Saudi Arabia, and the Arab world. As is discussed in the last chapter of this book, the most serious problem in achieving strategic stability in the Gulf does not lie in U.S.-Saudi military relations, in achieving unity among the conservative Gulf states, in coping with the risks posed by the Iran-Iraq War, or in checking Soviet ambitions—it lies in ensuring that there is enough movement toward a just and lasting peace between Israel and its Arab neighbors so that years of patient effort in the Gulf are not destroyed by the political and military consequences of the Arab-Israeli conflict.

Notes

1. Estimates vary. The figures shown here are taken from the *New York Times,* 9 March 1983. They do not include approximately 500 personnel manning and supporting the USAF E-3As, radars, and other temporary air defense equipment in Saudi Arabia that will be phased out as the Saudi Air Defense Enhancement Package is delivered.

2. Very little written literature is available on this aspect of Saudi affairs, and much of it is contradictory. The preceding comments are based on interviews by the author and Clarence Robinson; "Military Mission Increasing Advisory Role," *Aviation Week,* 23 May 1983, pp. 55–57; "Business Briefs," UPI, 12 April 1983; "Saudi Arabia," *Financial Times,* Special Survey, 5 May 1981, p. xv; *New York Times,* 9 March 1983.

3. Few data are available on the Pakistani armored "division" or "brigade" that may be deployed to Tabuk in support of the Saudi 12th Armored Brigade. Roughly 800 Pakistanis have already arrived in a support role, and there have been reports that this force will build up to over 12,000 men. While Saudi sources deny that they have provided Pakistan with some $1.2 billion as a *quid pro quo* for this aid, they are funding part of Pakistan's current FMS purchases from the U.S., including the F-16, and have discussed using Pakistani forces to set up a "mini RDF" to assist in securing the Gulf. The reports involved are complicated by constant Pakistani efforts to exaggerate Pakistan's role and

influence in the Gulf and Arab world and by Israeli efforts to exaggerate the Arab threat for political or aid purposes. See "Setting the Limits of Power," *Middle East,* January 1982, pp. 13–16; Shirin Tahir-Khali and William I. Staudenmaier, "The Saudi-Pakistani Military Relationship," *Orbis,* Spring 1982, pp. 155–171; British Broadcasting Corporation (BBC), *World Summary,* 19 January and 23 February 1983; and "Zia's New Role in the Gulf," *Middle East,* April 1983, pp. 33–34. For reporting on Jordan see *Washington Post,* 15 and 22 October 1983, *Los Angeles Times,* 15 October 1983, and *New York Times,* 22 October 1983.

4. These comments are based on extensive visits to Saudi air facilities. For an independent version see Clarence Robinson's special report on Saudi Arabia, *Aviation Week,* 23 May 1983.

5. Ibid.; *Wall Street Journal,* 3 March 1982; *Boston Globe* 9 February 1982, p. 11.

6. *New York Times,* 14 January 1982, p. 4.

7. *Armed Forces Journal,* October 1982, p. 17.

8. See Clarence Robinson, "Persian Gulf Air Defense Poses Difficult Challenge," *Aviation Week,* 23 May 1983, p. 81; and *Financial Times,* 25 April 1983, p. xv.

9. The E-3A designation is confusing. The Saudis will receive the equivalent of an E-3C in terms of CC-Z computer capability and full maritime capability (ability to "blank" land signals so that ships near shore or at dock can be detected). Saudi Arabia will not get the secure communications and data links on the USAF E-3B. U.S. and NATO E-3As in the blocks 1–20 will be refitted with CC-Z computers to E-3B status, but only block 25 onward will get full maritime capability on the E-3C. The Saudi E-3A is, therefore, an E-3C in every respect except secure communications and data links capability and the extra console position demanded by NATO.

10. Westinghouse sold 5 TPS-43 radars, plus narrow band communications using digital target extraction, for $60 million as part of a program called "Peace Pulse." It was providing nine more improved TPS-43 radars as part of a $1.5 billion Litton program to provide a defense acquisition radar system and proposed to provide 8 TPS-63 two-dimensional gap-filler radars. The GE FPS-117 radar is an automated, computer-aided system based on the GE 592 three-dimensional radar that is highly jam resistant and provides automatic unattended data transmission to an air defense center. It requires very low power and has a highly redundant and jam-resistant communications capability. It has an exceptionally low mean time between failures, and the system can easily be expanded to cover other Gulf states. Saudi Arabia bought 364 systems from Teledyne for the air force, 329 for the army, and 69 for the navy at a cost of $149 million. These were fully adequate to meet Saudi needs. *Aviation Week,* 18 April 1983, p. 80; 23 May 1983, pp. 42–45, 85–87; *Aerospace Daily,* 24 March 1983, p. 142; *Defense and Foreign Affairs,* 14 February and 11 March 1983.

11. For a more positive view of the technology transfer aspects of the Peace Shield program see Clarence Robinson, "Saudis Employing Offsets to Expand Industrial Base," *Aviation Week,* 23 May 1983, pp. 85–87.

12. Based on the author's interviews in Jordan in January and September 1982.

13. *International Defense Review,* February 1983; *New York Times,* 4 and 9 March and 4 April 1983; Associated Press, 15 March 1983; BBC international

affairs summary, SU/7295/A4/1, 30 March 1983; *Philadelphia Inquirer,* 16 March 1983; *Christian Science Monitor,* 5 April 1983; *Defense and Foreign Affairs,* 8 and 11 April 1983; *Washington Post,* 29 April 1983.

14. BBC ME/7336/A/1, 18 May 1983; *New York Times,* 14 June 1983; Associated Press, 14 June 1983; *Defense and Foreign Affairs,* 1 July 1983.

15. *Defense and Foreign Affairs,* 21 February 1983; Reuters, 7 February 1983.

16. For a full description of the U.S. effort see Clarence Robinson, "Saudi Naval Force Grows Toward 34 Vessel Fleet," *Aviation Week,* 23 May 1983, pp. 75–78.

17. *Aviation Week,* 23 May 1983; *Financial Times,* 12 May 1983; Xinhua News Agency, 12 May 1983; *Defense and Foreign Affairs,* 6 April 1983; *France,* MEED Special Report, April 1982, pp. 53–61.

18. Reuters, 1 March 1983.

19. *Wall Street Journal,* 1 February 1982, p. 16; *Omani Daily Observer,* 6 February 1982, pp. 1–3; *Washington Post,* 1 February 1982.

20. For recent reporting see Michael Field, "Social and Military Institution," *Financial Times,* Section III, 25 April 1983, p. xv; *New York Times,* 14 June 1983; Reuters, 14 March 1983.

21. These estimates are based on the revised Third Five Year Plan issued in 1980. The Saudis had a South Korean firm attempt to analyze the foreign labor pool in 1979, but it had no real data to work from. The Saudis keep their published figures low to minimize internal protests and the foreign view of their vulnerability. They similarly have claimed a native population of 7 million, when the true figure is unlikely to be much above 5.5 million. Estimates of 3–4 million native Saudis seem too low and to ignore the almost incredible reduction in the infant death rate since 1950. The range of estimates involved has already been discussed in Chapters 1, 2, and 6.

22. These figures are extrapolated from John A. Shaw and David E. Long, *Saudi Arabian Modernization: The Impact of Change on Stability,* Washington Paper 83 (New York: Praeger Publishers, 1982), pp. 45–48; John Keegan, *World Armies* (New York: Facts on File, 1979); press sources like the *Financial Times* analysis of 5 May 1981; Richard D. Erb et al., "The Arab Oil Producing States of the Gulf," *Foreign Policy and Defense Review* (AEI) 2, nos. 3 and 4 (1980). At least 25% of the foreign labor force is in the country illegally or working at unregistered or improperly registered occupations. These figures are more recent than the CIA data quoted earlier, and special credit should be given to John A. Shaw for his work in improving such data.

23. *Revised Third Five Year Plan,* November 1980.

24. *Financial Times,* 5 May 1981.

25. The American Enterprise Institute estimates 50%. See Erb et al., "Arab Oil Producing States of the Gulf," no. 3, p. 15. The *Washington Post* (2 January 1982) estimates only 150,000.

26. See Peter A. Iseman, "Iran's War of Words Against Saudi Arabia," *Nation,* 19 April 1980, pp. 463–466.

27. *New York Times* and *Baltimore Sun,* 9 October 1982.

28. A good recent account of the problems involved is Bryn Williams, "The Shi'ite Community," special section on Saudi Arabia, *Financial Times,* 5 May 1981, p. xviii.

29. The author spent two weeks in the province in November, much of it talking to students, and found most to be far more interested in jobs and the Palestinian issue than in Khomeini.

30. See David C. Ottaway, "Allegations of Iranian Plots," *Washington Post,* 2 January 1982. Later 13–25 Saudi Shi'ites were beheaded for their role in the plot.

31. See ibid.; *Washington Post,* 3 January 1982; 4 March 1982, p. 22; *New York Times,* 28 January 1982; *Christian Science Monitor,* 21 December 1981.

32. See Jones Buchan, "Take Counsel Among Yourselves," *Middle East,* September 1980, pp. 34–36; *Washington Post,* 3 January 1982; *New York Times,* 18 October 1981; 21 February 1982.

33. Based on U.S. *Demographic Yearbook,* 1978, and *Statistical Yearbook,* 1977. As was noted earlier, the *Economist* estimates that in 1970 one Saudi in five lived in a town of over 15,000, but that in 1980 more than two in five lived in towns of over 100,000 ("A Survey of Saudi Arabia," 13 February 1982, p. 33).

34. *Economist,* 13 February 1982, p. 17.

35. See Abul Kasim Mansur, "The Crisis in Iran," *Armed Forces Journal,* January 1979, pp. 26–33; and Barry Rubin, *Paved with Good Intentions* (New York: Oxford University Press, 1980), pp. 158–252.

36. For example, Assad Military City near al-Kharj, one of half a dozen military cities being built in Saudi Arabia, has been reported in the press to have a total planned cost of $15 billion, although its real cost may actually be about half that total. The National Guard Academy at Khashm al-An has been reported to have cost $133 million. The Saudi Ministry of Defense complex is reported to cost over $400 million. Many such facilities have been planned and managed by the U.S. Army Corps of Engineers. Press reports of these costs are producing a steadily more hostile reaction among educated Saudis. Even the costs of such projects reported by the Corps seem ambitious, in spite of Saudi Arabia's almost total dependence on imported goods and labor. Several younger Saudis have quoted Corps figures on such construction projects as examples of the kind of "waste" the U.S. is encouraging Saudi Arabia to invest in. See Keegan, *World Armies,* pp. 610–611, 617–619.

37. See UPI, "OPEC," 3 April 1982; *New York Times,* 8, 10, 20, and 22 February 1982; *Wall Street Journal,* 29 October 1982; 30 December 1982.

38. Saudi sources report rises as high as 40% in 1981. The IMF shows inflation as less than 5% annually in 1970–1972, 15% in 1973, 20% in 1974, 33% in 1975, 32% in 1976, 12% in 1977, and less than 5% in 1978–1981, but such figures are totally unrealistic. See the *New York Times,* 21 January 1982.

39. For an excellent recent treatment of Saudi Arabia's economy and modernization effort see Shaw and Long, *Saudi Arabian Modernization.* For other recent discussions of the issues involved see *8 Days,* 2 May 1982, pp. 2–4; *Middle East,* January 1982, pp. 62–64; *Wall Street Journal,* 5 February 1982; 16 March 1982; *New York Times,* 21 January 1982; *Economist,* 6 February 1982, pp. 76–78; and "Survey of Saudi Arabia."

40. See Chapter 1. Additional data can be found in the *Economist,* 13 February 1982, p. 25; *Wall Street Journal,* 29 October 1982.

41. The above costs for the Third Five Year Plan are taken from new reports that use 1979 dollar equivalents based on the text of the revised Five Year Plan, which was costed at $235.1 billion, with a spending ceiling of $249.7 billion. Cost estimates in current dollars exceed $300 billion, or 1 trillion rials. See Shaw and Long, *Saudi Arabian Modernization,* pp. 26–60.

42. See ibid., pp. 19–26; *Economist,* 6 February 1982; and "Survey of Saudi Arabia."

43. See *The Third Five Year Plan* (Riyadh, 1980). Shaw and Long quote somewhat different figures. (*Saudi Arabian Modernization,* p. 29).

44. "SAMA: Are Changes on the Way?" *8 Days,* 2 May 1981.

45. *Economist,* 21 February 1982; *Wall Street Journal,* 29 October 1982; *Financial Times,* 25 April 1983.

46. Shaw and Long estimate this Yemeni work force at 600,000, with a range of 400,000–800,000, (*Saudi Arabian Modernization,* p. 44). Other estimates go well over 1 million.

47. *MEED,* 15 April 1983, p. 54; *Defense and Foreign Affairs,* Special Edition, 12, no. 77 (28 April 1983): 1; *New York Times,* 14 June 1983.

48. Ibid.; *Washington Post,* 2 June 1983; *Aviation Week,* 23 May 1983, p. 52; *Financial Times,* 25 April and 9 May 1983; BBC, ME/7308/1, 15 April 1983; *Economist,* 19 February and 23 April 1983.

49. For a much more pessimistic analysis see Graham M. Benton and George H. Wittman, *Saudi Arabia and OPEC: An Operational Analysis,* Information Series no. 138 (Fairfax, Va.: National Institute for Public Policy, March 1983).

50. Shaw and Long, *Saudi Arabian Modernization,* pp. 59–65; David Holden and Richard Johns, *The House of Saud* (London: Sidgwick and Jackson, 1981), pp. 460–462; Gary S. Saymore, "Royal Family Politics in Saudi Arabia," unpublished paper, Rand Corporation and Harvard University 1981. Other estimates routinely refer to 4,000 princes and 4,000 princesses (e.g., *Economist, New York Times, Washington Post*) but it is doubtful that such estimates are accurate.

51. In a 3 January 1982 *Washington Post* article, based on interviews in Saudi Arabia, the number of insurgents is given as 300, but this figure now seems significantly low.

52. See John M. Goshko's article in the *Washington Post,* 20 December 1982.

53. For a good summary of the succession, see *MEED,* 18 June 1982, pp. 28–31.

54. The above analysis is based largely on those rumors repeated in the major newspapers and interviews. It deliberately excludes the more extreme rumors in terms of possible conflicts, coup attempts, and attacks on personal behavior. For typical reporting see Reuters, 14 March 1983; *Defense and Foreign Affairs,* 10 February 1983; *Economist,* 10 February 1983, Survey, p. 8; *MEED,* 15 April 1983, pp. 60–61; *Defense and Foreign Affairs,* May 1983, p. 53, and Volume 19, No. 19, Number 35, Third Series, p. 6; *Wall Street Journal,* 2 June 1983; and Joseph Kraft, "Letter from Saudi Arabia," *New Yorker,* 4 July 1983, pp. 41–59.

55. See Saymore, "Royal Family Politics"; Shaw and Long, *Saudi Arabian Modernization,* pp. 63–64; and Holden and Johns, *House of Saud,* pp. 462–463.

56. Rumors of such shake-ups began in July 1982. For example, see the *Economist,* 17 July 1982, p. 17.

57. James Grafton, as quoted in the *Chicago Tribune,* 11 December 1981, p. 1. The E-3A was priced at $68 million in "fly away" condition at end 1981, but at $128 million including R&D. By adding in an R&D "slice" not charged to the USAF, the U.S. could effectively double the cost of the aircraft.

58. *New York Times,* 27 October 1981.

59. Ibid.; 5, 8, 9, 13, and 26 February 1982; *Washington Post,* 10 February 1982.

60. See ibid., plus the *Baltimore Sun* and *Washington Post,* 2 and 3 March 1982; and *8 Days,* 20 February 1982, p. 27.

61. *Washington Post,* 24 December 1981, p. 7. Prince Fahd was originally scheduled to meet President Carter on 1 March 1979. Haig met with Fahd in Riyadh in the spring of 1981 and again in Malaga, Spain, in September 1981.

62. King Fahd issued a highly publicized "warning" to President Reagan to bring Israel under control during its siege of Beirut in August 1982. See the *New York Times,* 6 August 1982, p. 3.

63. For typical reporting on these trends see Reuters, 10 April 1983; BBC, 19 and 29 April 1983; *New York Times,* 13 May 1983; *Washington Post,* 13 May and 5 June 1983; *Chicago Tribune,* 22 June 1983.

11
Strategic Stability and the Other Gulf States: The Historical Background

Saudi-U.S. relations are the key to increasing the strategic stability of the Gulf, but the West must do more than establish a sound military partnership with Saudi Arabia.[1] The West must encourage collective security among the conservative Gulf states, improve its relations with Iraq, and minimize the risk of Iran's becoming a Soviet client state. It must help Oman deter the threat posed by South Yemen and find methods of coping with North Yemen's efforts to play East off against West.

As the leader of the West, the U.S. cannot hope to achieve these goals by relying solely on its own diplomacy or military forces. U.S. influence is sharply constrained by the complex politics of the region and the limits on U.S. power projection capabilities. The U.S. must act in cooperation with key regional allies or not at all. It has little more hope of working through formal alliances with the rest of the Gulf states than it does with Saudi Arabia. Their recent history, political dynamics, and security problems preclude any such option. As a result, the U.S. must rely on efforts to build collective security within the Gulf through organizations like the Gulf Cooperation Council and through informal relationships with the smaller conservative Gulf states.

Iraq poses a more difficult problem. Its recent politics, and the uncertainties growing out of the Iran-Iraq War, make close diplomatic ties impossible. While U.S.-Iraqi relations can be improved, any strategic relationship between the U.S. and Iraq will have to be indirect and be based largely on the ability of Saudi Arabia and the other conservative Gulf states to improve their security relationships with both Iraq and the United States. Nations like France may be able to achieve closer ties with Iraq, but even those ties seem likely to remain limited and uncertain.

Western relations with Iran will be even more difficult to stabilize or improve. In the short run, there may be nothing the U.S. can do, other than avoid a relationship with Iraq, that would preclude later improvements in U.S.-Iranian relations. The U.S. can help the other Gulf states build up an air shield over the southern oil fields to guard against an Iranian threat and can strengthen its over-the-horizon capabilities. These measures will limit the risk that events in Iran can pose to the other Gulf states or to Western interests. The other Western states can strengthen their commercial ties and keep the door open if internal political changes move Iran closer to the West, but it is unlikely that any Western nation can do more.

As for the Yemens, the West again has few options. If there is any hope of South Yemen's being freed of its current dependence on USSR, it lies in the diplomacy and actions of the Arab states in the Gulf. Similarly, the U.S. and its allies have little choice other than to back Saudi Arabia in its complex struggle with South Yemen over the future of North Yemen. The U.S. lacks the political skill and military resources to play its own game in North Yemen, a fact that has been demonstrated all too clearly over the last 15 years. While Britain does help North Yemen in internal security and counterinsurgency, its influence is weak, and no other Western nation has significant influence.

In order to understand the West's opportunities and constraints, however, it is necessary to understand the recent history of the Gulf states, the interactions that shape their present security, the broad dynamics of the military buildup in the Gulf, and the extent to which the security situation in each Gulf nation permits the development of improved collective security and better relations with the West.

The Larger Gulf States: Iran, Iraq, and Saudi Arabia

Much of the recent history of security interactions among the largest Gulf states has been outlined in the previous chapters, and the tensions among them are familiar from the turmoil reported in the daily press. Nevertheless, there are several trends in each country that are important to understanding the options for expanding Western security ties in the area.

Iran

The key trends in Iran are its internal revolution, its violent shift away from strategic ties with the U.S., its growing alienation from its Arab neighbors, and its effort to obtain political control over the Shi'ite minorities and majorities in nearby states like Iraq, Syria, Bahrain, and Lebanon. Although the shah's fall represents a radical change in Iran's recent pattern of interaction with other Gulf states, it is not inconsistent with Iran's history. Tensions between Iran and its neighbors are more the rule than the exception.

These tensions have grown out of many factors. Historically, Iran has always had to struggle to preserve its separate cultural, linguistic, and religious identity. When Iran has been weak, this struggle has been to maintain control over the Iranian plateau. When it has been strong, the struggle has been one to control the river valleys of Iraq, the Gulf, and even India. Since the Fourth Caliphate, Iran has split from the rest of Islam, sometimes isolating itself in new forms of mysticism, at other times attempting to proselytize all of Islam and to assert dominance over the world's Shi'ites. For at least the last two thousand years, there has never been a decade during which some sort of conflict was not taking place on Iran's borders.

Even in modern times, Iran's brief periods of close relations with the U.S., during 1953–1978, and with its Gulf neighbors, during 1971–1978, are something of a historical anomaly. Russian and British pressures destroyed the Iranian constitutional and republican movements in the early 1900s and led to conflicts with the West that lasted until the mid-1950s. British naval strength opposed Iran's ambitions in the Gulf in modern times, and Iran's current conflict with Iraq dates back to Reza Shah's efforts to block Britain's sudden creation of Iraq as a Hashemite state.

Further, Iran's current hostility toward its neighbors and its efforts to expand its power in the Gulf are to some extent the natural legacy of the actions of the shah of Iran. Between the late 1960s and 1979, the shah used Iran's oil wealth to transform Iran into the dominant military power in the Gulf and to make it the "protector" of the conservative Gulf states. His efforts brought Iran into an almost inevitable conflict with Iraq, particularly after the revolution that overthrew the Hashemite dynasty in 1958. This conflict was only tentatively resolved by the Algiers Accord of 1975.

The shah's ambitions also led to a series of crises with the other Gulf states. Iran came into conflict with Bahrain when the shah made an attempt to annex it shortly after Britain's announcement that it intended to withdraw from the area and with the United Arab Emirates when Iran acquired Abu Musa Island by *force majeure* during the final stages of Britain's withdrawal from the Gulf. Both crises were resolved without military conflict, but the shah's actions left a legacy of Arab resentment and reinforced the historical tensions produced by similar Iranian efforts during the Qajar dynasty.

Conflicts between Iran and its neighbors are not, however, inevitable. The shah moderated his policy and sought a rapprochement with the other Gulf states in the mid-1970s when it became clear that Iran's security depended on the stability and independence of the other conservative Gulf nations. Between 1974 and 1979, the shah succeeded in establishing acceptable relations with all the Gulf states. With the help of the U.S. and Saudi Arabia, he pushed Iraq into a favorable settlement of Iran's claims to the Shat al-Arab and then brought a halt to the constant low-level political conflict between the two states. While the resulting settlement may not have been exactly what Iraq desired, it served Iraqi and Iranian needs well enough to reflect a reasonable basis for a modus vivendi.

From the mid-1970s until his fall, the shah systematically mended his fences with the conservative Gulf states. He supported Kuwait during its periods of tension with Iraq, recognized Bahrain's independence, provided aid to the new United Arab Emirates and particularly to Dubai, gave military support to Oman in suppressing the Dhofar rebellion, helped North Yemen replace its Soviet arms, and furnished arms to Somalia. Although the shah scarcely quelled the other Gulf states' fears regarding his military buildup and ultimate ambitions, his actions presented little tangible threat to the other Gulf nations.[2] In fact, the shah's military buildup relieved the Arab Gulf states of immediate concern for their external security and of the need to develop close ties or seek collective security.

The shah's efforts might well have stabilized Iran's relations with its neighbors if his departure from Iran in January 1979 had not marked such a radical change in Iran's politics. However, the sudden rise of Khomeini confronted the other Gulf states with a revolutionary Iran ruled by a radical Shi'ite theocrat. The southern Gulf lost a somewhat grandiose but largely unthreatening protector and saw him replaced by a leader who threatened the security of every other Gulf state.

Even before the shah's departure, several Gulf intelligence and internal security organizations had detected "messengers" from Khomeini who actively attempted to proselytize the Shi'ite citizens of Iraq, Kuwait, Bahrain, the UAE, and Saudi Arabia. By the spring of 1979, Iranian efforts had begun to go beyond political propaganda. Iran began to transfer small arms and supported paramilitary training efforts in Iran and the other Gulf states. After mid-1979, these actions led to a covert war between the Iraqi security forces and Khomeini's "messengers" that caused several deaths a week.[3]

This covert conflict was unquestionably a major factor in causing the Iran-Iraq War, along with Iraq's resentment of the Shat al-Arab accords and Saddam Hussein's desire to make Iraq the Gulf's dominant military power.[4] The fear of Iran's radicalism, and of its efforts to control the Shi'ite population in the other Gulf nations, helped cause the other Gulf states to back Iraq in its attack. It led Bahrain, the UAE, and Oman to initially support Iraq's plan to attack the Iranian-held Tumb and Abu Musa islands, and it led the conservative Arab states to provide financial aid to Iraq once its offensive bogged down in failure.

No one can now predict the result of these trends. Theoretically, Iran has a long-term interest in preserving the stability of the other Gulf states and in minimizing any risk of creating threatening or anti-Islamic regimes. Iran has an equal interest in avoiding any instability that might exacerbate the competition between the U.S. and USSR in the Gulf area. In fact, Iran has everything to gain from pursuing a more moderate version of the shah's strategic policies of the mid-1970s. Yet the Khomeini regime and its most probable successors seem likely to be so radical or nationalistic that such rational security considerations will have only a limited impact on Iran's relations with its neighbors. The Iran-Iraq War is already causing lasting hostility between Iran and Iraq, and between Sunni and Shi'ite, hostility that will continue regardless of how the fighting is resolved.

The southern Gulf states cannot predict whether Iran will remain oriented toward Shi'ite radicalism, tilt more toward the left, fall under Marxist or Soviet influence, move back toward the more "moderate" position of a Bani Sadr, or even fall under some kind of military rule. They can be sure, however, that Iran will continue to be a significant military power with a large navy and control over many of the Gulf's strategic islands. As a result, they and the West are virtually forced to plan for the contingency that Iran will emerge from the present war as a hostile and disruptive force throughout the Gulf area.

Iraq

Since 1978, the changes in Iraq's national security position have been almost the reverse of those in Iran. While Iran has moved away from the other Gulf states, Iraq has moved toward them. As was described in Chapters 5 and 6, Iraq moved closer to Saudi Arabia and strengthened its relations with the other conservative Gulf powers. These moves were reflected in steadily growing Saudi-Iraqi cooperation, reductions in the tension between Iraq and Kuwait, and a virtual end to Iraqi support of the various radical or liberation movements aimed at overthrowing Oman, the UAE, and other Gulf regimes.

These developments had their origin in the mid-1970s as the result of two factors. First, Iraq's new oil wealth gave it the income it needed to fund its own weapons purchases and economic development for the first time. Iraq changed from a "have not" nation, whose oil wealth was still partially under foreign control, to a "have got" nation with true financial independence. This change led to a major decline in Iraq's economic relations with the USSR. The Soviet Union dropped from being Iraq's largest trading partner in 1973 to a 10% share of Iraq's trade in 1975. Second, the Baath became involved in conflict with the USSR over Soviet support of Kurdish nationalism and the Iraqi Communist party (ICP) and over Soviet efforts to keep the Baath from suppressing the Kurds and ICP by force.

These factors contributed significantly to Iraq's 1975 settlement with the shah. Although Iraq reached a brief rapprochement with the USSR, and both nations opposed Syria's initial move into Lebanon, Iraq kept its distance from the USSR. The Baath concentrated on consolidating its power, on internal development, and on building closer ties to Jordan and other Gulf states.[5] This trend accelerated toward the end of the 1970s because the ICP made a Soviet-backed coup attempt to overthrow the Baath, because of Soviet aid to Abd al-Fattah Ismail in the overthrow of South Yemen's pro-Iraqi President Salim Rubai Ali in June 1978, and because of the Soviet invasion of Afghanistan on 27 December 1979. By early 1979, Iraq was actively promoting new collective security arrangements in the Gulf and seeking intelligence ties with the other Gulf states and cooperation against Khomeini's messengers.

Iraq also increasingly turned to the West for arms. In May 1979 Iraq purchased $250 million worth of arms from France and Spain, and while its army remained dependent on Soviet equipment, Iraq sought advanced antitank weapons and aircraft from France, small arms from Spain, and ships from France and Italy. Iraq also turned to France and Jordan for military advice and technical assistance when its attack on Iran misfired in late 1980. The Iran-Iraq War made Iraq steadily more dependent on its conservative neighbors and the West. Iraq's defeats, the closure of its Gulf ports, its dependence on the Gulf states and Jordan for economic and logistic support, virtually forced the Baath to act moderately in dealing with other Arab states.

The key question is what regime will emerge from the Iran-Iraq War. It seems doubtful that Iraq will remain dominated by a small, closely knit political elite whose leaders come from the village of Takrit, but no one can predict what regime will take its place. While a military or more broadly based Baath government seem the most likely alternatives, Iraq may come under a Shi'ite regime, and it will have to deal with strong Kurdish and lesser Turkish ethnic movements and with the ICP.

This uncertainty limits the extent to which the other Arab states can afford to maintain close relations with Iraq's current regime. On the one hand, none of the conservative Gulf states want to see Iraq defeated or Iran emerge as the strong man of the Gulf. On the other hand, Iraq's Arab neighbors have good reason to be uncertain about its future. They cannot count on the survival of Iraq's current regime or future friendship or on Iraq's not turning toward Iran or the USSR.

Saudi Arabia

Saudi Arabia's military development has been described in depth in previous chapters; its diplomatic history has not. It is important to stress the extent to which the 1970s marked an end to Saudi Arabia's long-standing border conflicts with many of the conservative Gulf states. These shifts have made Saudi Arabia the one major Gulf power the smaller Gulf states have little reason to fear. Saudi Arabia now has more oil wealth (and related developmental problems) than it can easily deal with and little incentive to pursue its past territorial claims. It has become the conservative protector of the traditional Gulf regimes and Sunni Islam. Saudi diplomacy is undoubtedly the most sophisticated and best managed in the Gulf area, and Saudi Arabia has demonstrated in recent years that it will support collective economic and political security in the Gulf without using its economic strength to dominate its smaller neighbors.

This transformation is the result of several underlying pressures that seem likely to make Saudi Arabia a relatively stable future partner for its Gulf neighbors. First, Saudi Arabia's small population precludes it from becoming a military power that can do more than deter limited outside aggression. Second, Saudi oil wealth is now so large in per capita terms, and its oil reserves so large, that it has little incentive to seek control over the wealth of other Gulf states. Third, Saudi Arabia's severe internal problems in coping with social change preclude it from attempting to acquire direct influence over other Gulf states, which would force it to absorb those states' social problems. Fourth, the legitimacy of the Saudi royal family and government increasingly have become tied to the legitimacy and stability of the Gulf's other traditional rulers. Fifth, any hostile Saudi action against one of its Gulf neighbors would probably unite the others against it. Saudi Arabia cannot afford any such reaction, given the potential threat posed against it by the Shi'ite radicalism of Iran or the underlying political hostility of even a friendly Iraq. Finally, no process of direct Saudi interference in Gulf affairs could offer the Saudis as many benefits as collective efforts at economic development and security. In this sense, Saudi Arabia's combination of vast oil wealth and cultural and military vulnerability act both to unite it with its neighbors and to help stabilize the Gulf.

The shifts in Saudi policy do, however, reflect a considerable change in Saudi attitudes. Several Gulf states have good reason to remember the Ikhwan's attempts to conquer the Gulf area in the 1920s and the long series of border disputes that followed. Although Saudi Arabia's transformation from an aggressive religious movement to a stable kingdom began as early as King Abd al-Aziz's defeat of the Ikhwan rebels at the Battle of Sabillah in March 1929, Saudi Arabia pressed its neighbors for territorial concessions from the early 1930s until the late 1960s. It made major efforts to secure territory from Oman and the Trucial States as late as the mid-1970s. Although Saudi Arabia settled its borders with Kuwait and Iraq with the creation of the Neutral Zone in 1922, it occasionally made additional claims until the late 1960s. It ended these efforts only in 1973 when Iraq tried to seize the islands of Warbah and Bubiyan from Kuwait, and Saudi Arabia formally backed Kuwait's territorial claims to help counter Iraqi pressure. These events made support of Kuwait's territorial integrity a vital aspect of Saudi policy.

Although the Saudis improved their relations with Qatar's ruling Al-Thani family after 1939, they continued to claim part of Qatar as part of a long-standing border conflict with Abu Dhabi. When oil production began in Qatar in 1949, Saudi Arabia engaged in a low-level border dispute over the Khaur al-Udaid inlet in the far south of the Qatar peninsula that did not result in a modus vivendi until 1965. The agreement was, however, a peaceful one, facilitated by the fact that the Al-Thani family was linked to Saudi Arabia by blood and a common adherence to the Wahabi faith.[6]

The other southern Gulf states were not always so lucky. The Saudis were unable to profit from the kind of informal deals with the British that gave Iran control of Tumbs and Abu Musa islands, but they forced Abu Dhabi into major border concessions through paramilitary action in 1976. The Saudis used political and military pressure to force minor concessions from Oman in 1976–1977, although some of these Omani concessions seem to have occurred because Abu Dhabi mistakenly ceded Omani territory. In any case, there is a history of low-level tension between Oman and Saudi Arabia that has continued in spite of Saudi aid to Oman during the Dhofar rebellion and that is an additional factor behind Oman's continuing effort to seek a British and U.S. military presence to guarantee its security.[7]

To the south, Saudi Arabia has been at swords' points with the radical leaders of South Yemen for most of that country's short history. This hostility was reinforced by the same Soviet-backed coup in Yemen in 1978 that helped to alienate Iraq from the USSR. Saudi Arabia has had difficult relations with North Yemen since the early 1960s. The Saudis have long imported over 30% of their labor force from North Yemen, and they have attempted to exert tacit control over North Yemen's internal and external affairs. Saudi Arabia has made major payments to North Yemeni officials and tribal leaders—a policy it continues to a lesser extent in Oman—as well as provided aid to the central government. This policy has led to a constant Saudi rivalry with South Yemen over control of North Yemen, which was a major cause of the conflict between North and South Yemen in 1979. It was the source of new tensions between the Yemens in 1981 and has involved increasing competition between the U.S. and USSR to back the various Saudi and Yemeni efforts.[8]

The past rivalries between Saudi Arabia and its neighbors must, however, be kept in careful perspective. Such jockeying for power has been the rule in the region for centuries, and most of the border claims Saudi Arabia pursued between 1930 and 1977 had at least as much justification as the claims of the opposing Gulf states. The "validity" of the area's borders after the 1850s was determined largely by British arms, and the "legality" of the Gulf's modern borders often depends on decisions British officials made unilaterally during the 1920s and 1930s. These decisions were often poorly documented, arbitrarily made, and enforced only by *force majeure.* Similarly, Saudi Arabia now has little alternative to seeking influence over the southern Gulf states, Oman, and the Yemens. This too is a political and foreign policy process that has gone on in the Gulf for centuries, and the internal tensions in the Yemens are so great that Saudi Arabia must continue to seek such influence in its own defense.

The end result is to create a situation in which each of the smaller Gulf states now seeks Saudi help in maintaining its security, while seeking help from outside the Gulf in preserving that security from the

Saudis. At the same time, the smaller conservative Gulf states fear equally the reverse situation. They are as frightened of the possibility of the overthrow of the regime in Saudi Arabia as Saudi Arabia is frightened of changes in their leadership. This fear limits their willingness to become too dependent on Saudi Arabia for collective security.

Several Gulf states, including Kuwait and Bahrain, have also been subject to Saudi pressure to halt steps toward internal modernization that these states have felt are essential safety valves in dealing with the changes that oil wealth is causing in the area. The smaller Gulf states sometimes feel they are pressured by Saudi Arabia's conservatism as well as by Iraq's radicalism and Iran's Shi'ite extremism. It is true, however, that the younger Saudi leaders recognize the risk of moving too slowly and that Saudi efforts to block political reform in the southern Gulf have faded sharply in recent years.

The Smaller Conservative Gulf States

The conflicting pressures discussed in the preceding section are acquiring growing strategic importance to the West, but they can be understood only in the context of the history of the smaller Gulf states. Each of these states has a history of interactions with its neighbors that constrains the extent to which it can work with them and the West. At the same time, several states, most notably Oman, have a recent history of civil war that has broad implications for future military contingency planning in the Gulf and for the design of any efforts to link the conservative Gulf states.

Kuwait

Kuwait's strategic interactions with the other Gulf states are similar to those of Saudi Arabia in that they are partly dictated by a mixture of immense oil wealth and military weakness. Kuwait's military weakness, however, is of a fundamentally different character from that of Saudi Arabia.[9]

Kuwait is a small nation of 17,600 square kilometers, including the Neutral Zone, with about 1.5 million people.[10] It is sandwiched between Iran, Iraq, and Saudi Arabia and has 459 kilometers of land boundaries and 499 kilometers of coastline. It has a strong Shi'ite minority, and its economy and government are dominated by Palestinians, Indians, Pakistanis, and other foreigners. It cannot govern, or even live, except through the efforts of foreign workers. Expatriates make up more than 58% of the population, over 65% of the workers employed, and a substantially higher proportion of the skilled or competent workers who actually work. Its total population is 41% "other Arab," 7% South Asian, 4% Iranian, and 6% other.[11]

This mixture of wealth, small size and population, and dependence on a largely Palestinian foreign labor force means that Kuwait must try to be all things to all its neighbors.[12] Kuwait is compelled, as is Saudi Arabia, to provide extensive amounts of economic aid to secure the influence and security it cannot obtain through military force. It also is forced to support radical and conservative causes alike, to avoid overt commitments to any superpower or other Gulf power, to back the Palestinians in any major issue, and to be tolerant of political movements that operate in Kuwait but that do not directly threaten Kuwaiti security.

The resulting Kuwaiti diplomatic juggling act has often been brilliant, and Kuwait's political structure has contributed to its success. Kuwait is still ruled by an oligarchy of roughly 15 families, one of the most sophisticated political structures in the Gulf. Under the leadership of the ruling Al-Sabah family, it has taken advantage of Kuwait's oil wealth to build up political and economic ties throughout the Gulf and Arab worlds. Even when Kuwait has given its neighbors more rhetoric than money, it has generally been able to do so in a way that has aroused a minimum of outside hostility and has exhibited a superb capability to bend with the wind.

This skill has not, however, protected Kuwait from periodic tension with Iraq, Iran, and Saudi Arabia. Iraq made several attempts to annex Kuwait in the 1930s and might well have succeeded in 1939 but for the timely death of Iraq's King Ghazi Ibn Faisal and the discovery of oil in Kuwait. While Iraq's claims lay in abeyance until Britain gave Kuwait independence in June 1961, Iraq renewed them less than a week after the British departed. It took the overthrow and death of Iraq's dictator, General al-Qassim, a quiet Kuwaiti payment of $85 million to his successors, and an expression of Kuwaiti intent to end military relations with Britain to secure Iraq's formal recognition of Kuwait's independence and borders of 5 October 1963.

During the early 1970s, Kuwait was caught up in Iraq and Iran's dispute over the Shat al-Arab. Iraq's need to find some way to load large tankers without being vulnerable to Iranian military action, and its reliance on a waterway that was subject to silting and placed its ports within Iranian artillery range, led Iraq to seek a less vulnerable location. As can be seen from Map 11.1, however, Iraq could not achieve such security within its own territory or territorial waters. While Iran could solve many of its oil shipment problems by shifting its major crude oil-loading facilities to Kharg Island, some 175 miles to the east of the Shat, Iraq did not have such an option. Iraq's Gulf coastline was only 38 miles wide, and the only part of its coast that was not dominated by the Iranian shore was dominated by the Kuwaiti islands of Warbah and Bubiyan.[13]

As a result, Iraq reacted to the shah's seizure of Abu Musa and the Tumbs by building up its port and naval facilities at Umm Qasr and by demanding access to Kuwaiti waters and territory to build an offshore oil-loading facility with pipelines crossing Bubiyan. Kuwait refused

MAP 11—1
AREAS OF CONTENTION IN THE KUWAIT IRAQ BORDER DISPUTE OF 1971

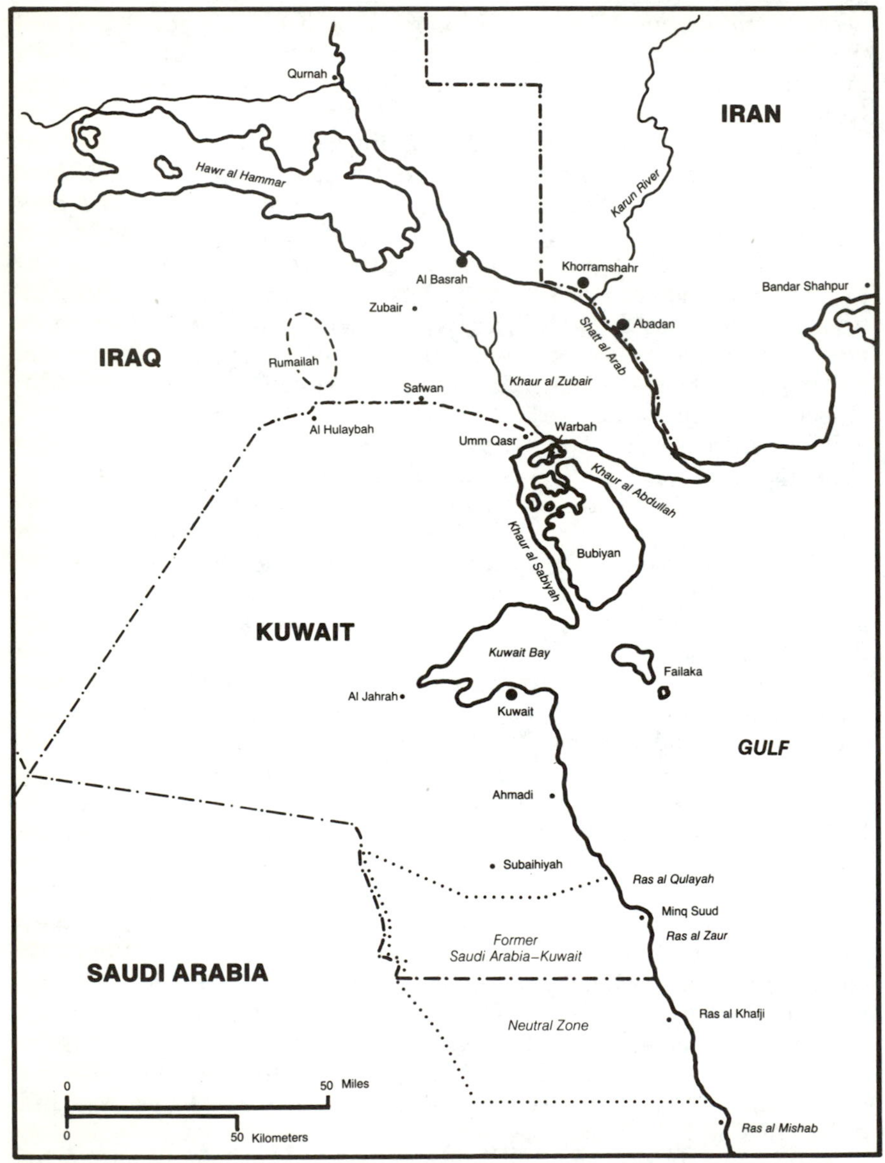

SOURCE: J. B. Kelly, *Arabia, the Gulf, and the West,* Basic Books, 1980, and Department of the Army, *Middle East: The Strategic Hub,* DA 550-16, Washington, May, 1973, pp. 182-183.

because of its fear that Iraq would permanently seize the islands, and Iraq sent troops into northern Kuwait on 20 March 1973. Only a combination of Saudi and Iranian pressure, and a Kuwaiti payment of several hundred million dollars, led to an partial Iraqi withdrawal. The resulting agreement left Kuwait limited to civil authority over the two islands, and Kuwait obtained the right to conduct occasional military patrols only after considerable further tension.[14]

Kuwait, therefore, can never be entirely sure that some upheaval in Iraq—or even a Kuwaiti civil war or conflict with its foreign workers—will not be followed by a renewal of Iraq's claims. This is one reason Kuwait has given Iraq so much support in the Iraq-Iran War, although Iraqi threats and Kuwait's fear that Iran might subvert the Shi'ite minority in Kuwait were also important incentives.

Kuwait's relations with Saudi Arabia have been far less tense. Although King Abd al-Aziz briefly blockaded Kuwait in the early 1920s in an attempt to annex it, Saudi Arabia has recognized Kuwait's borders and those of the Neutral Zone since the 1930s. Saudi Arabia was so concerned over the risk that Kuwait might be taken over by "radical" or "reform" elements in the early 1970s, however, that it strongly pressured Kuwait's ruling Al-Sabah family to adhere to Muslim strictures and to limit the country's political modernization. Further, after a debate over seabed oil reserves and oil pricing policy in 1976, Saudi Arabia occupied the islands of Umm al-Maradem and Gharo in the disputed area and solved the dispute by force.[15]

Although Saudi-Kuwaiti relations are now friendly, and there is a limited degree of kinship between the Saudi royal family and the Al-Sabah family, there also is continuing political and cultural tension between the two states. This tension is compounded by the fact that Kuwait, as the first of the oil-rich states, has played the role of "sophisticate" to a "primitive" Saudi Arabia. Many Saudis still resent what they regard as patronizing Kuwaiti attitudes.

Such tensions have made it difficult for Saudi Arabia and Kuwait, the strongest and wealthiest conservative Gulf states, to cooperate fully in improving Gulf economic cooperation and collective security. Quite aside from the fact that Kuwait has had to limit its links to the Saudis to avoid irritating Iraq and Iran, there is a natural rivalry between the Kuwaiti and Saudi elites that is tinged with Saudi resentment of past Kuwaiti attitudes and Kuwaiti resentment of the Saudis as the Gulf's *nouveaux riches*. The result has often been quite Saudi-Kuwaiti rivalry in forums like OPEC and the Arab League and unnecessary competition in trying to influence the other Gulf states.

Recent trends have eased some aspects of Kuwait's regional juggling act while making others more difficult. The slow rapprochement between Iraq and Saudi Arabia reduced the risk of conflicting Saudi and Iraqi pressures on Kuwait. Saudi Arabia's shift to a policy of seeking collective security within the Gulf has improved Kuwaiti-Saudi cooperation and eased Kuwait's security problems. Iraq's break with the Soviet-backed regime in South Yemen in 1978 led to the end of Iraqi pressure on Kuwait to allow various Gulf liberation movements to continue to operate on its soil.

Unfortunately for Kuwait, these positive trends have been more than counterbalanced by the rise of Khomeini. Kuwait has been forced to try to simultaneously placate its Shi'ite elements, support Iraq in the Iran-Iraq War, and avoid being dragged into the conflict.[16] Kuwait is even more strategically vulnerable to Iran than Iraq, since Iraq has some ability to ship its oil through pipelines to the West and has widely dispersed population centers. In contrast, Kuwait depends heavily on the willingness of the Iranian Navy and Air Force to allow Kuwait to ship its oil. Over 90% of Kuwait's population is located in Kuwait City, which has no practical air defenses and is less than 15 minutes' flying time from the nearest Iranian air base. As Kuwait learned early in the Iran-Iraq War, when Iran "mistakenly" bombed border posts in Kuwait, Kuwait's security is as dependent on Iranian tolerance as it is on the support of Iraq and Saudi Arabia, and Iran has since reinforced this lesson with further air attacks and a massive propaganda campaign.

Kuwait also became steadily more dependent on the goodwill of the Palestinian movement during the 1970s and came under increasing pressure to show this support. This is one of the reasons that the Al-Sabah family revived the popular assembly it had suppressed in August 1976 and then helped rig the elections of "Islamic conservatives," who were actually a front for the traditional leading families. Kuwait's conservative oligarchy then tried to use these elections to unite its native population and to present a stronger front against both the Palestinians and Iranians, although the end result was an assembly that showed sufficient independence to force its virtual suspension.

This mixture of pressures also explains why Kuwait has established and maintained relations with the USSR. Such relations have given Kuwait the status of the USSR's only "conservative" friend in the region and helped ensure that the Soviet Union will discourage radical movements and any internal unrest among Kuwait's Palestinians. Such ties, however, provide only limited protection. As will be discussed in Chapter 15, Kuwait has growing internal security problems and external problems with Iran and Iraq.

Bahrain

Like Kuwait, Bahrain is a small nation that is vulnerable to pressure from any of the three major powers in the Gulf.[17] It is the smallest state in the Gulf, and its territory consists of several small islands. Only the island of Bahrain has any size. Even it has only 161 kilometers of coastline and 596 square kilometers of landmass. This landmass compares with 10,360 square kilometers for Qatar and 16,058 for Kuwait. Bahrain's total population is slightly less than 40,000.[18]

Bahrain's history is similar to that of Kuwait in that the general decline of the Gulf as a trade route and pearl fishing area after the mid-1880s led to a slow decline in Bahrain's importance as a Gulf power and in its ability to maintain influence over the Gulf coast immediately to the south. While the establishment of treaty relations with Britain in 1861 freed Bahrain of the risk of Turkish domination, the rise of the Al-Thani family in Qatar deprived Bahrain of its former control over most of Qatar's territory and of several small islands between Qatar and Bahrain. As a result, Bahrain's political importance between the late 1880s and the discovery of oil stemmed almost solely from the British presence on the island. Only British military strength kept Bahrain from falling under Qatari, Saudi, or Iranian control.

Fortunately, many of these tensions are "old history" by Gulf standards. Bahrain's ruling Al-Khalifa family has accepted its borders since the 1930s, and has intermarried with the Saud and Al-Thani families. Bahrain differs sharply from Kuwait, however, in that its oil production has dropped to about 50,000 BPD and that it faces relatively near-term depletion of its reserves. This prospect represents a major change for a Gulf state in which oil was first discovered in 1932 and first exported in 1934 and whose small size allowed it to create educational and social services in the 1950s and 1960s that produced a well-educated and reasonably broad native elite. As a result, Bahrain has recently faced the risk of a second period of decline.

Bahrain's alternative has been to transform itself into a Gulf-wide financial and commercial center to offset the loss of its status as a significant oil producer. It has been fairly successful in this regard, but at the cost of committing its economic future to becoming a "service" state for Saudi Arabia. For example, more than 120 banks operated in Bahrain in 1982. Because of the tolerance of the Saudi Arabian Monetary Agency, they could also operate in Saudi Arabia in a way that gave them a significant advantage over outside banks, which has guaranteed Bahrain a reasonable amount of commercial success. Without this advantage, Bahrain probably would not have been successful in becoming a Gulf financial center. In recent years, Saudi Arabia has also provided Bahrain with more than 70% of the crude oil necessary to support its large refinery and with support for its major aluminum smelter.

This dependence on Saudi Arabia will increase steadily during the 1980s. Under both Saudi and Bahraini economic plans, Bahrain is to become more and more of a service center for the Saudi economy. Development will also mean the end of Bahrain's island status, since a 25-kilometer causeway will be completed between the Saudi mainland and Bahrain in the mid-1980s.

Demographics will also reinforce Bahrain's dependence on Saudi Arabia. Although Bahrain's oil revenue and other income is still increasing in real terms, the fact that Bahrain was one of the first Gulf states to sell oil and had a small and heavily concentrated population led to rapid reductions in infant mortality in the 1930s and 1940s that have culminated in a 4% annual birthrate and in a population that is now largely under 15 years of age.[19] Since 1971, Bahrain has had a reasonably effective system of mass education. There is no way that the ruling Al-Khalifa family can hope to employ this population and stabilize Bahrain internally unless Saudi Arabia provides the necessary jobs. In fact, Bahrain's civil service is now so overloaded with "make work" jobs for Bahrain's youth, and its economy so limited in internal opportunities for real growth, that Bahrain must count on nearly a one-to-one correlation between the expansion of its labor force and the expansion of economic ties with Saudi Arabia.

Bahrain will also need Saudi support to cope with the problems it faces in dealing with Iraq and Iran and the pressures for radical change. Bahrain is ruled by a small conservative oligarchy under an Al-Khalifa emir. This oligarchy rules the country through its control of more than 50% of the senior posts in government and through its dominance of a council, or Diwan, which is far more conservative than that of Kuwait. There are growing demands for reform by the Sunni portion of Bahrain's population, which is the element with the best education and the most exposure to Arab nationalism and radicalism. While Iraq's support of radical Sunni elements in Bahrain ended in 1978, it has been replaced by South Yemeni support of a number of dissident elements, and South Yemen and Libya have actively tried to subvert the Al-Khalifa family and traditional Sunni oligarchy. A new and hostile regime in Iraq could make this situation more threatening.

The combination of this problem with that of Bahrain's Shi'ite population is an explosive one. Bahrain's native population has up to 10% more Shi'ites than Sunni, and an additional 8% of its total population is Iranian.[20] There have been several street riots in the country since 1950 involving various combinations of Sunni and Shi'ite political elements, but the Shi'ites have dominated the opposition. Bahrain's flirtation with a true popular assembly ended because of such pressures, and there is a constant risk that the Al-Khalifa oligarchy could be isolated on two sides: from the "left" by a movement composed of the Sunnis who have been excluded from Bahrain's oil wealth and from the "right" by its increasingly radicalized Shi'ite majority.

This situation is the outgrowth of both discrimination against the native Shi'ite population and Shi'ite immigration from Iran. Only about 63% of Bahrain's population is native born, and it includes large numbers descended from recent Persian immigrants. These "immigrants," combined with those who retain Iranian nationality, compose much of Bahrain's merchant class and skilled labor. They have aligned themselves with the original Shi'ite residents of the islands, who were conquered by the Al-Khalifa family and who perform most of the low-income jobs in Bahrain. Together, the three Shi'ite elements constitute about 65% of the total population, and most are now linked to Iran by at least some family ties. The Shi'ite clergy in Bahrain also includes a mixture of native and Persian-descended religious figures. The younger and more radical elements of Bahrain's Shi'ite clergy have ties to both the Khomeini movement in Iran and to radical elements of the Shi'ite clergy in Iraq.[21]

The Khomeini movement has presented a special problem. Iran has never entirely abandoned its historical claims to Bahrain. Although the shah legally agreed to give up such claims in 1973, Iran's religious claims are stronger than its legal ones. Khomeini's influence has transcended national boundaries, and the religious leader of the Shi'ites has traditionally been separate from—and superior to—the secular ruler. He has traditionally been the spokesman of the oppressed and their leader in protest and revolt.

Khomeini potentially fills this role and has sought to claim it in every nation with a significant Shi'ite population. His concept of an "Islamic" state includes Iranian control over all Shi'ite populations, and his "messengers" arrived in Bahrain at virtually the same time they started operations in Iraq. As was the case in Iraq, the appearance of these "messengers" was followed by small Iranian arms shipments, and some Bahraini Shi'ites have undergone paramilitary training in Iran. While the evidence is scanty, the pro-Khomeini elements in Bahrain seem to be more aligned with the left-wing elements of the Khomeini movement than the Iraqi Shi'ites who trained in Iran, which has allowed them to broaden their influence in the island.

The risks this situation creates were demonstrated all too clearly early in the Iran-Iraq War. Bahrain's ruling oligarchy miscalculated Iraq's chance of an early victory. Bahrain backed Iraq politically and seems to have offered staging facilities for the Iraqi Air Force and for an invasion of Abu Musa.[22] These steps triggered a series of pro-Khomeini protests and street riots by Shi'ite elements that rapidly taught the oligarchy the limits of its power. Bahrain has since had to juggle its tacit support for Iraq against "neutral" aid to Iran and to turn even further toward the Saudis for protection. As will be described later, however, this policy has not shielded Bahrain from Iranian coup attempts and a rise in internal subversion.

Qatar

Qatar is another of the Gulf's small oil-producing states, but its interactions with its neighbor states are more secure than those of Bahrain and Kuwait. Its territory is about 10,360 square kilometers, and it has a 56-kilometer border with Saudi Arabia. Qatar still produces about 400,000 barrels of oil per day, and it has oil and gas reserves that afford it considerable economic independence.

As has been discussed earlier, Qatar reached a de facto border settlement with Saudi Arabia in the early 1970s. It has not been subjected to repeated challenges to its sovereignty by the other major Gulf powers. Its sea frontiers were demarcated in 1916 as part of Britain's World

War I effort to stabilize its presence in the Gulf and to secure it against Turkey. This demarcation has since helped to protect Qatar from confrontations over its border and oil rights in the Gulf. The Al-Thani of Qatar are also more closely aligned by marriage with the Saudi family than are the other ruling families in the Gulf, and they follow the Wahabi rite. This alliance has kept Qatar more conservative than the other Gulf states.

The slower rate of change in Qatar has helped to shield it from outside threats and interactions, although the rate has accelerated sharply since 1977. Oil wealth came to Qatar nearly 20 years later than to Bahrain and Kuwait. Qatar did not receive major oil revenues until the early 1950s, and the ruling sheikh of the Al-Thani family, Sheikh Ahmad, personally controlled all major funds until this policy began to cause major popular dissent. As a result, Qatar's modernization did not really begin until 1963, when a general strike forced the Al-Thani to disburse Qatar's oil funds more equitably. Even then, the Al-Thani family continued to control most of Qatar's oil wealth under a system referred to as the "rule of the Four Quarters:" This meant a quarter for the ruling sheikh, a quarter for the other sheikhs, a quarter for the other lower-ranking members of the Al-Thani family and oligarchy, and a quarter for the rest of the population.[23] Nothing like Kuwait's welfare system was set up during the 1960s, although the fact that the Al-Thani family numbered between 450 and 750 out of a native population of only 50,000 and was widely intermarried with the rest of Qatar's social and economic elite broadened the impact of Qatar's wealth.

It was only after Britain's withdrawal from the Gulf, and the surge in oil wealth that followed OPEC's raising of oil prices, that major economic and political changes began to occur in Qatar and its relations with the other Arab states. These changes came to a head in 1971, when the Al-Thani family split over whether to join a federation of former Trucial States following British withdrawal from the Gulf. According to various reports, in the resulting internal power struggle Abu Dhabi backed the ruling sheikh and Saudi Arabia backed his younger cousin. At first, Britain and Abu Dhabi prevailed, and Qatar aligned itself with the new federation, the United Arab Emirates. Qatar adopted a provisional constitution in April 1970, which allowed it to meet the UAE's requirement that each member have its own constitution.

As British power faded, however, Saudi influence expanded. In September 1971 Qatar broke with the UAE and formally declared its independence. In February 1972 Sheikh Ahmad was overthrown by his Saudi-backed cousin, Sheikh Khalifa bin Hamad, who then revised the original constitution to reflect Qatar's independence and give it the status of a conservative Islamic government with no popular representative body. The resulting Provisional Constitution of April 1972 is still the formal basis for Qatar's system of government and closely parallels the Saudi system of government.

Although the events involved are uncertain, the change in government also seems to have led to a complex set of negotiations among Saudi Arabia, Qatar, and Abu Dhabi (see Map 11.2). These negotiations eventually forced Abu Dhabi to give up its claims to the territory that connected Qatar and its western borders for a cash payment in 1974, although the arrangement acquired a more formal status only in 1977. These negotiations also, however, gave Abu Dhabi control over most of the disputed oil resources. They largely ended both nations' disputes with Saudi Arabia and eliminated the last major dispute over Qatar's southern border. The resulting territorial settlement also cut Qatar off from direct geographic contact with the UAE and probably eased the internal security problems created by Qatar's shift toward modernization after 1972.

Sheikh Khalifa's takeover in 1972 was rapidly followed by a worldwide spiral in oil prices that raised Qatar's oil wealth from several hundred million dollars a year to about $1.8 million in 1975 and $3.6 million in 1979. This new wealth gave the sheikh the means to adopt a policy of co-option and of sharing Qatar's new oil wealth with its population. This policy, however, inevitably increased the size of Qatar's government, its modern economic institutions, and its social and welfare facilities. Such reforms were less developed in Qatar than in Kuwait and Bahrain, but they led to massive changes in Qatar's society and in the four quarters system that spread Qatar's oil wealth much more broadly among its population.

These changes also had the effect of causing a massive labor migration into Qatar. Although Qatar had a 4.4% annual birthrate, 75% of its population was foreign by mid-1981.[24] Depending upon the estimate, foreign workers numbered between 100,000 and 150,000; the native work force was only 10,000 to 15,000.[25] Foreign technicians came to virtually run the country through such bodies as the civil service, the Qatar General Petroleum Company, the Qatar Investment Board, and the Qatar Monetary Agency. Even Qatar's Arab complexion has begun to disappear. Its total population is now 34% South Asian, 20% other Arab, 16% Iranian, and 5% other.[26] But Qatar also has a large European, predominantly British, technical elite. The role of the rest of its labor force is widely mixed. Pakistanis and Indians dominate the less-skilled jobs. Baluchis and Iranians perform mid-level technical and commercial tasks. Other unskilled workers come from Oman and North Yemen. A skilled elite of about 5,000–7,000 Palestinians, Egyptians, and Jordanians is employed in various professional posts. Accordingly, although about 70–90% of Qatar's labor force is foreign, its composition is so varied that it does not constitute a bloc that naturally aligns itself with any other Gulf nation.

Further, the Qatari security forces help prevent such alignments and ensure that labor contracts are enforced to prevent workers from engaging in political activity. Qatar relies on Baluchis for its internal security

MAP 11—2
AREAS OF CONTENTION IN THE QATAR, ABU DHABI, SAUDI BORDER DISPUTES

A. CLAIMS DURING 1913-1955

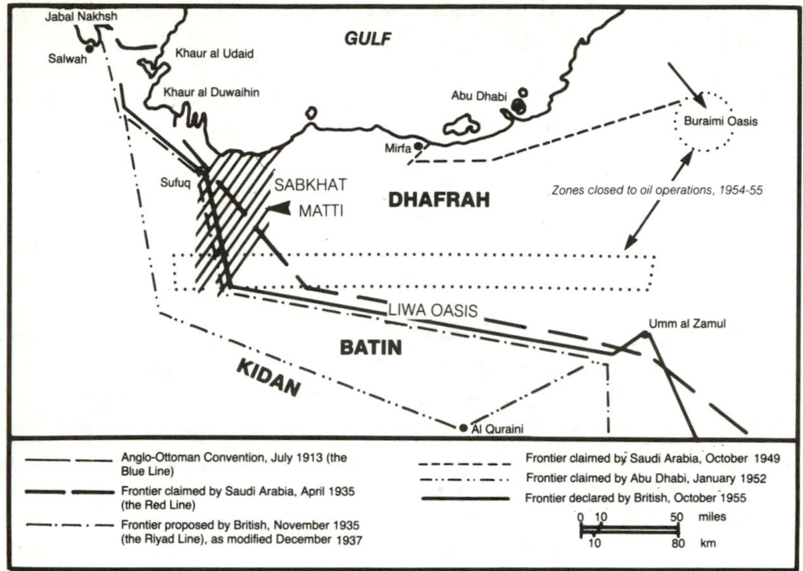

B. PROCESS OF SETTLEMENT: 1955-1977

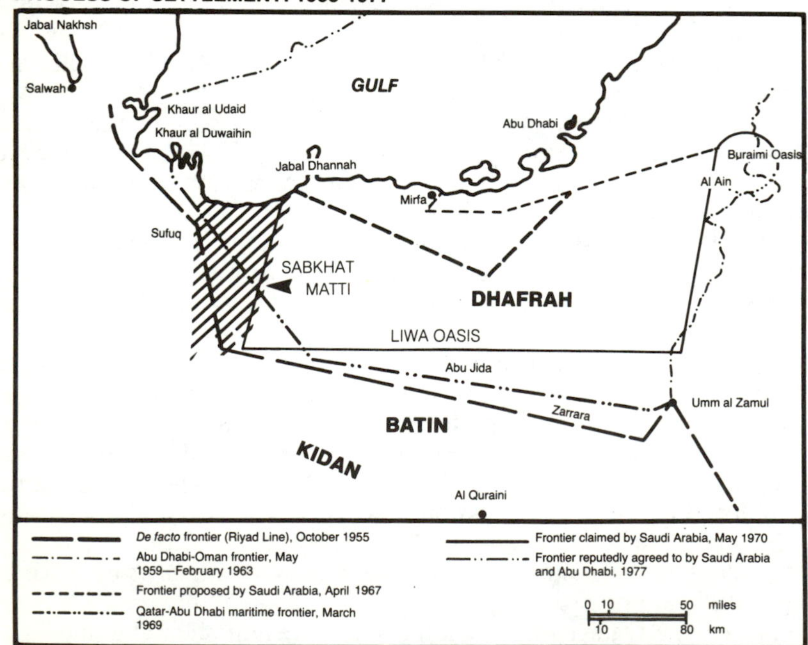

Adapted from J. B. Kelly, *Arabia, the Gulf, and the West,* Basic Books, 1980; and Will D. Swearingen, "Sources of Conflict Over Oil in the Persian/Arabian Gulf," *Middle East Journal,* Volume 35, No. 3, Summer, 1981. Research by Kelly is altered slightly to use the outline mapping in DA Pamphlet 550-16, Department of the Army, Washington, May 1973, pp. 181-182.

forces and on Omani and Yemeni mercenaries for its defense forces. These forces report to separate, and sometimes contending, elements of the Al-Thani family, and they maintain surveillance over the native Qataris as well as foreign laborers. They can also operate with considerable ruthlessness, although their conduct has moderated since the mid-1970s, and Qatar now tends to rely more on deportation than on brute force. Much of the Qatari civil service, which employs something like a third of all native Qataris, also has a direct or indirect role in controlling foreign labor, and the Qataris are assisted in this task by the internal security forces of Saudi Arabia.[27]

With the exception of its labor problem, Qatar remains relatively secure. It aligns itself closely with Saudi Arabia and does not face an immediate threat from Iraq or Iran. South Yemen has recently provided limited support to the small radical and revolutionary movements in the Qatari labor force, and the growing political consciousness among the younger Qataris is leading some to look toward the more radical Arab states for political ideas and support. These threats from Qatar's neighbors are minor, however, and this situation seems unlikely to change as long as Saudi Arabia remains stable.

The United Arab Emirates

The United Arab Emirates is a loose federation of the smaller Trucial States.[28] It is roughly 83,000 square kilometers in area and has 1,094 kilometers of land boundaries. The UAE is centered on the largest and wealthiest state, Abu Dhabi, and consists of seven states whose previous history has been one of constant internecine conflict. The UAE's eastern territory is composed of a bewildering mix of tribal and historical enclaves, shown in Map 11.3. Although the two largest states, Dubai and Abu Dhabi, have more orthodox borders, they are still divided by a "neutral zone" along the southern border of Dubai.

It is difficult to put the size and influence of the different members of the UAE in perspective, but a fairly accurate census was held in 1975. This census recorded a total population of 655,937. Abu Dhabi had a population of 235,662, with 128,000 in Abu Dhabi City and 50,000 in Al Ain City. Dubai had a population of 206,861. Sharjah had a population of 88,188, Ras al-Khaimah had 57,282, Umm al-Qaiwain had 16,879, Ajman had 21,566, and Fujairah had 26,498.[29] The native population has since grown at a rate of about 4% annually. This growth and the immigration of outside labor raised the total population to 934,000 in January 1981. Such growth, however, does not seem to have altered the relative importance of the member states.[30]

In terms of economics, Abu Dhabi has a maximum sustainable oil-production capacity of 2,035 MBD, Dubai has 370 MBD, and Sharjah has only 10 MBD. Abu Dhabi has at least 50 years of reserves at production rates of over 1.2 MMBD. Dubai has proven reserves of 1.4 billion barrels and can produce at 340–360 MBD for several decades.

MAP 11—3
MAJOR ENCLAVE AREAS IN THE EASTERN UAE

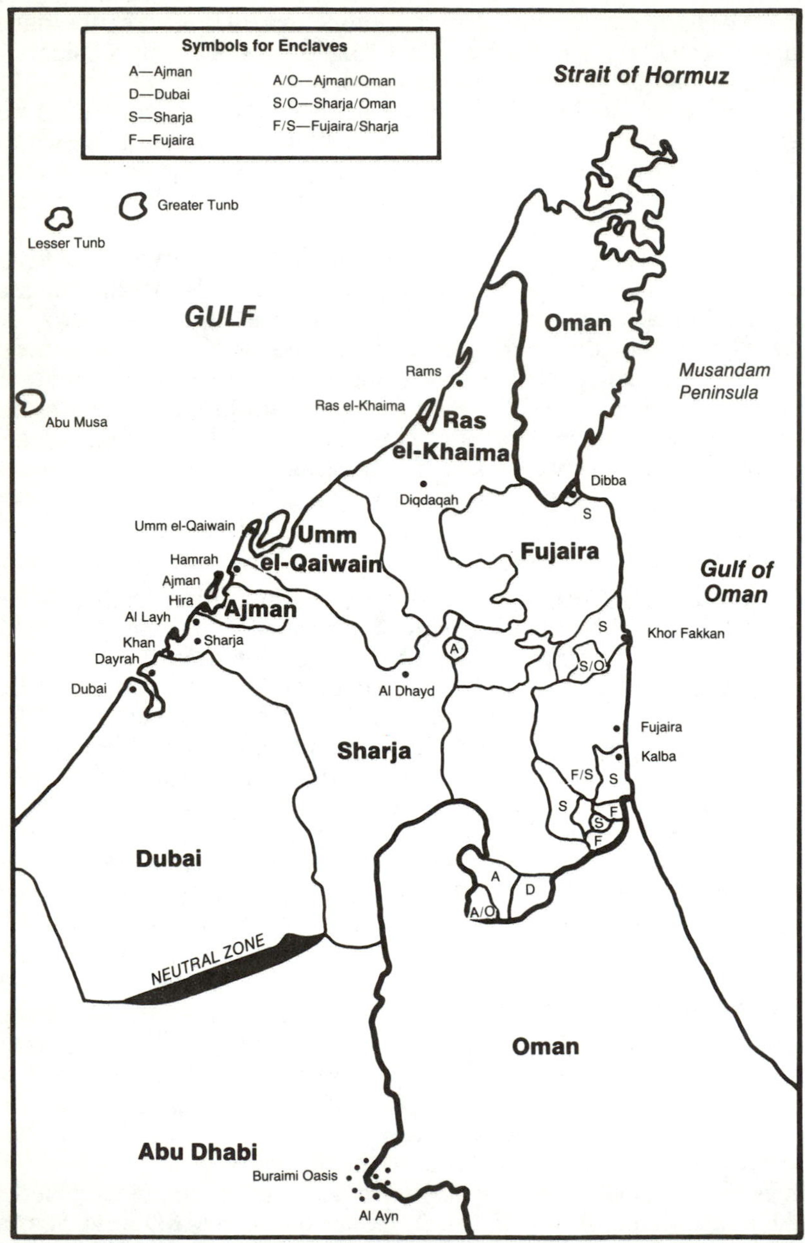

SOURCE: Adapted from Lenczowski, *The Middle East in World Affairs,* 4th Edition, Cornell, 1980, p. 677; maps furnished by the UAE information service; and Department of the Army, *Middle East: The Strategic Hub,* DA Pamphlet 550-16, Washington, 1973, pp. 182-183.

While Sharjah has significant gas resources, its proven oil reserves are only 11 million barrels, and production has declined from 38 MBD in 1975 to 9 MBD in 1981.[31] Abu Dhabi and Dubai also have major gas reserves.

The only major industrial areas in the UAE are at Ruwais in Abu Dhabi and Jebel Ali in Dubai. These consist largely of petrochemical facilities and cement plants. Sharjah has some light industry, and Ras al-Khaimah has two large cement plants (1 million tons per year each). The agricultural importance of each state is loosely indicated by its area under cultivation. In 1977 Ras al-Khaimah had 7,400 hectares (ha), Abu Dhabi 2,870 ha, Sharjah 2,400 ha, Fujairah 1,357 ha, and Dubai 479 ha. Ajman and Umm al-Qaiwain had negligible cultivated areas.[32]

All of the states that now make up the UAE initially came under British influence in the 1820s when Britain sought control of the Gulf to protect India and established an agent in Sharjah. Britain took formal control of these states in 1892. Fear of Russian, French, and Turkish efforts to expand influence in the Gulf area led Britain to make a series of "exclusive agreements" with the "Trucial States" that obligated them to cede their territory to no foreign nation but Britain.

British control did not, however, bring a halt to the constant fighting between them or to their internal struggles for family and tribal influence. The emirate of Fujairah, for example, emerged after one such controversy in the early 1900s; it acquired formal treaty status only in 1952. Many of the current enclaves in the eastern UAE represent disputed areas where the present borders and rulership arrangements had to be agreed on as part of the negotiations of the Union's foundation.

Even in the mid-1960s, the various emirs often supported rival factions in the ruling families of other states and conspired against each other within the limits imposed by the British agents. The emirates also remained comparatively isolated and backward. Oil wealth came late to the area. It was not discovered in Abu Dhabi until 1959, in Dubai until 1966, and in Sharjah until 1972. Before that time, the general economic decline in the southern Gulf following the end of the pearl trade had left the emirates a strategic backwater. Only Sharjah had a British base. This base had originally been established in 1932 as a commercial refueling facility; it was expanded to an RAF base in 1940. Although the base was comparatively small, it made Sharjah the key state in the UAE until the discovery of oil and British withdrawal from the Gulf.[33]

Another factor that delayed the development of the area was that Saudi Arabia still had significant claims to the border areas surrounding Abu Dhabi. As was described earlier, these claims included the narrow slice of territory between Abu Dhabi and Qatar. They also included potential oil resource areas in the south and a critical water and potential oil resource area on Abu Dhabi's eastern border with Oman known as the Buraimi Oasis. Such claims made any effort to formally structure the borders of the emirates highly controversial. Further, Britain simplified its task in ruling each emirate by encouraging the various emirs to compete and by promoting family and tribal rivalries over territory. These "divide and rule" tactics did nothing to create a solid basis for regional self-rule.[34]

Once oil was discovered in Abu Dhabi, however, both modernization and confrontation with Saudi Arabia became almost inevitable. The Saudi dispute over control of the Buraimi Oasis dated back to the 1800s. It was a continuing source of contention and minor military skirmishes between Abu Dhabi and Saudi Arabia after 1934, as was the dispute over whether Abu Dhabi had a "land bridge" with Qatar. These border disputes worsened in the early 1950s, when it became probable that oil fields existed in both the disputed southeastern part of Abu Dhabi and near the Buraimi Oasis. The resulting tension led to several small military encounters between Saudi and Abu Dhabi forces in the early 1950s and to a suspension of oil exploration while Saudi Arabia and Britain attempted to arbitrate the issue.

The failure of this arbitration led to more incidents in the late 1950s. Finally, in 1966, the British issued a formal warning to Saudi Arabia that it would defend Abu Dhabi. This warning was severely undercut in January 1968, however, when Britain announced its intention to withdraw from the Gulf. The announcement encouraged Saudi Arabia to again press its claims, as did the gradual discovery that Abu Dhabi had large reserves of oil. As the time for British withdrawal drew closer, the Saudis pressed their claims further and further, leading to more incidents, more drilling controversies, and the sequence of claims and counterclaims shown in Map 11.2.[35] British departure from the Gulf left Saudi Arabia with the upper hand. As a result, Saudi Arabia obtained major concessions from Abu Dhabi between 1972 and 1977. In August 1974 Abu Dhabi gave up part of its western territory and its rights to the Zarara oil field in the south for Saudi recognition of the UAE and Abu Dhabi's rights to most of the disputed fields in the southwest and the Buraimi Oasis.[36] In June 1977 Saudi Arabia forced Abu Dhabi to move its border 20 miles further west on the Gulf coast, although it paid Abu Dhabi's ruler, Sheikh Zayid, some $33 million in personal compensation. The result was the borders shown in Map 11.3.[37]

Although the long border controversy ended in Saudi Arabia's favor, Abu Dhabi did not really suffer from the settlement. In fact, Abu Dhabi gradually aligned itself closely with the Saudis after King Faisal's death in 1975, which created some friction between Abu Dhabi and two other emirates. Dubai chose to align itself more closely with the shah, partly in an effort to counter Abu Dhabi's oil wealth and Saudi power.[38]

The announcement of British withdrawal from the Gulf also led to another territorial dispute. The shah demanded control over several of the strategic islands in the Gulf. These islands included the Greater and Lesser Tumbs and Abu Musa. While none of these islands "controlled" the main tanker passages, Iranian occupation of the Tumbs and Abu Musa meant that Iran could extend its waters to the edge of the southern Gulf and gained offshore areas with significant offshore oil potential. In October 1970 Iran formally renewed the claims to the Tumbs and Abu Musa that it had last made in the 1930s and indicated that it would not recognize the UAE until it obtained control over all the islands. Britain, which saw the shah as the principal future source of stability in the Gulf, was not prepared to make an issue of the matter and made an arrangement with Iran that allowed it to occupy the islands immediately after British departure.[39]

This arrangement was reached with some degree of amicability in the case of Abu Musa. Sheikh Khalid of Sharjah agreed to Iran's military occupation of the island in exchange for a nine-year annual payment of $3.5 million, which was to be increased if oil production in the surrounding area exceeded $7 million in annual value. This was a relatively minor concession on Khalid's part. The sheikh desperately needed money, since oil had not yet been discovered in Sharjah, and Abu Musa was little more than unpopulated rocks. The agreement further benefited Sharjah when oil was discovered near Abu Musa in 1972. Sharjah had a 35% share in the field, Iran had 50%, and Umm al-Qaiwain had 15%. A combination of unit operation and rapid Iranian exploitation of the field gave Sharjah oil wealth far more quickly than would have been possible if it had had to negotiate directly with the oil companies.

In the case of the Tumbs, however, the shah made unequivocal claims for total sovereignty. These claims were resisted by the ruler of Ras al-Khaimah, Saqr bin Muhammed al-Qasimi, partly because of his desire to become a major leader of the UAE.[40] He based this ambition on the fact that Ras al-Khaimah then had most of the UAE's water and much of its arable land, and these were the traditional sources of power. This assessment ignored the new realities created by oil wealth, and Ras al-Khaimah's dependence on grants by Abu Dhabi and Dubai, but Sheikh Saqr continued to resist British and Iranian pressure to turn the islands over to the shah. The shah responded by using the controversy to demonstrate his new power in the Gulf. On 30 November 1971 he occupied the Tumbs, even though Britain still had a formal legal obligation to protect the rights of Ras al-Khaimah until 2 December. The evidence is uncertain, but the presence of a British carrier in the immediate area during the Iranian occupation, and a number of other British actions, indicated British complicity in the shah's invasion.

This incident not only helped to divide the UAE in its relations with Iran; it also had several wider effects. Britain and Iraq were already in a state of political confrontation, and the indications of British complicity triggered an explosive Iraqi response. They helped lead to the Iraqi pressure on Kuwait described earlier, the breaking of Iraqi diplomatic relations with Britain and Iran, the expulsion of Iranian workers from Iraq, and the nationalization of the remaining holdings of the British Iraqi National Petroleum Company. Libya seized on the incidents as an excuse to nationalize assets of the British Petroleum Company, and Libya and Iraq both greatly increased their support of various radical movements in the Gulf in an effort to overthrow the British "puppet states."

Such Iraqi reactions may seem extreme, but it should be remembered that Britain had helped give the shah much greater control over Iraq's lifeline through the Gulf. Moreover, the British effort to link the UAE's security to Iran threatened Iraq's lifeline from both sides of the Gulf and was a major challenge to the Baath's emphasis on an Arab national consciousness. One ironic consequence of this Iraqi reaction was that an unsuccessful Iraqi-backed coup in Sharjah may have resulted in the death of the same sheikh who had made concessions to the shah over Abu Musa.

This division and controversy between the newly formed UAE and each of the Gulf's three major powers was followed by problems in the UAE's interactions with Oman. By the early 1970s, the UAE had three reasonably large oil-exporting states: Abu Dhabi, Dubai, and Sharjah.[41] Their oil wealth led to a rivalry in their foreign affairs with the other Gulf states that was based on Abu Dhabi's attempts to exploit its status as the wealthiest oil state, on Dubai's efforts to take advantage of its higher-level development, and on Sharjah's efforts to capitalize on its former status as the British headquarters in the Gulf. It also led the three "oil-rich" members of the UAE to compete for influence over the four oil-poor members: Ajman, Umm al-Qaiwain, Ras al-Khaimah, and Fujairah.[42]

Abu Dhabi had a natural advantage in this competition in terms of wealth, willingness to support a strong federation, and willingness to agree to share its oil wealth. It also, however, faced the problem of securing its eastern border and the area around the Buraimi Oasis. It could accomplish this only by ending its long historical rivalry with the rulers of Oman and by buying the loyalty of key tribes.[43] As a result, Abu Dhabi provided Oman with several hundred million dollars in direct assistance between 1966 and 1974 and gave Oman's sultans millions more to help secure the loyalty of the various tribal groups in Oman's Musandam region and in its northwest territory.

At the same time, Ras al-Khaimah was making recurrent efforts to claim territory and offshore rights from Oman. In November 1977 these efforts finally led to an armed confrontation between Ras al-Khaimah and Oman that ended like a comic opera when the large number of Omanis in Sheikh Saqr's forces refused to fight Oman's forces. However, the president of the UAE, Sheikh Zayid of Abu Dhabi, backed Oman in the dispute, which both exposed the UAE's vulnerability to pressure from Oman and led to continued tension between Sheikh Saqr and other members of the UAE. The UAE has quietly provided aid to Oman as a means of securing its borders ever since.

Fortunately, the UAE's interactions with its conservative neighbors stabilized considerably between 1974 and 1979. The various border conflicts ended in producing the boundaries shown in Map 11.4, and the Dhofar rebellion in Oman and the constant turmoil in the Yemens provided the UAE's rulers with a warning of what might happen if any member of the UAE carried its disputes to the point of conflict. The shift in the nature of the Gulf's oil wealth after 1974 also removed much of the incentive to compete for most of the border areas, which proved to have only limited potential resources. Finally, the flood of oil wealth into the UAE led even the smaller members to concentrate on building up its ports, cities, and central infrastructure and made control over tribal areas and land rights less important.

The shifting interactions among the major Gulf powers also benefited the UAE. Between 1972 and 1978, Iraq's support of various radical movements in the Gulf led Saudi Arabia and Iran to cooperate in supporting the growth and stability of the UAE. After the settlement of its border claims in the mid-1970s, Saudi Arabia steadily became a source of aid rather than a threat.

While most cooperation between the UAE and Iran ended with the shah's fall, the members of the UAE initially had only limited vulnerability to Khomeini's influence on their Shi'ite minorities. Shi'ites are only about 6.5% of the UAE's population,[44] and Iran gave these Shi'ites comparatively little attention until mid-1981. Iraq's shift to a position of supporting the other Arab states in the Gulf after 1977, and its break with South Yemen, also helped to compensate for the change in Iran's position.

The shah's fall, however, has presented increasing problems. Abu Dhabi was careless in publicizing its initial support of Iraq in the Iran-Iraq War, and Sharjah remains dependent on Iranian cooperation for its oil wealth. Dubai also has long had close ties to Iran and has a significant Shi'ite minority, although the initial efforts of the Khomeini "messengers" in the UAE have been tentative and concentrated more on Iranian migrant laborers. Abu Dhabi has recently started to make quiet payments to Iran in an effort to buy security, and a low-level Iraqi-Iranian-Saudi struggle for influence is already under way.

The internal tensions within the UAE, and the incredible rate of labor migration from the outside, have also become a growing threat to its stability. As is discussed in more detail in Chapter 15, there has been a continuing struggle between Abu Dhabi and Dubai for power within the UAE, and other demographic shifts seriously threaten its stability. The combined demographic impact of the importation of foreign labor and cuts in infant mortality has been incredible. The Trucial States had a total population of less than 180,000 in 1965. The UAE alone had a population of 655,000 in 1975 and nearly a million

MAP 11—4
DIVISIONS OF TERRITORIAL LIMITS IN THE GULF FOLLOWING THE IRANIAN SEIZURE OF THE TUMBS AND ABU MUSA

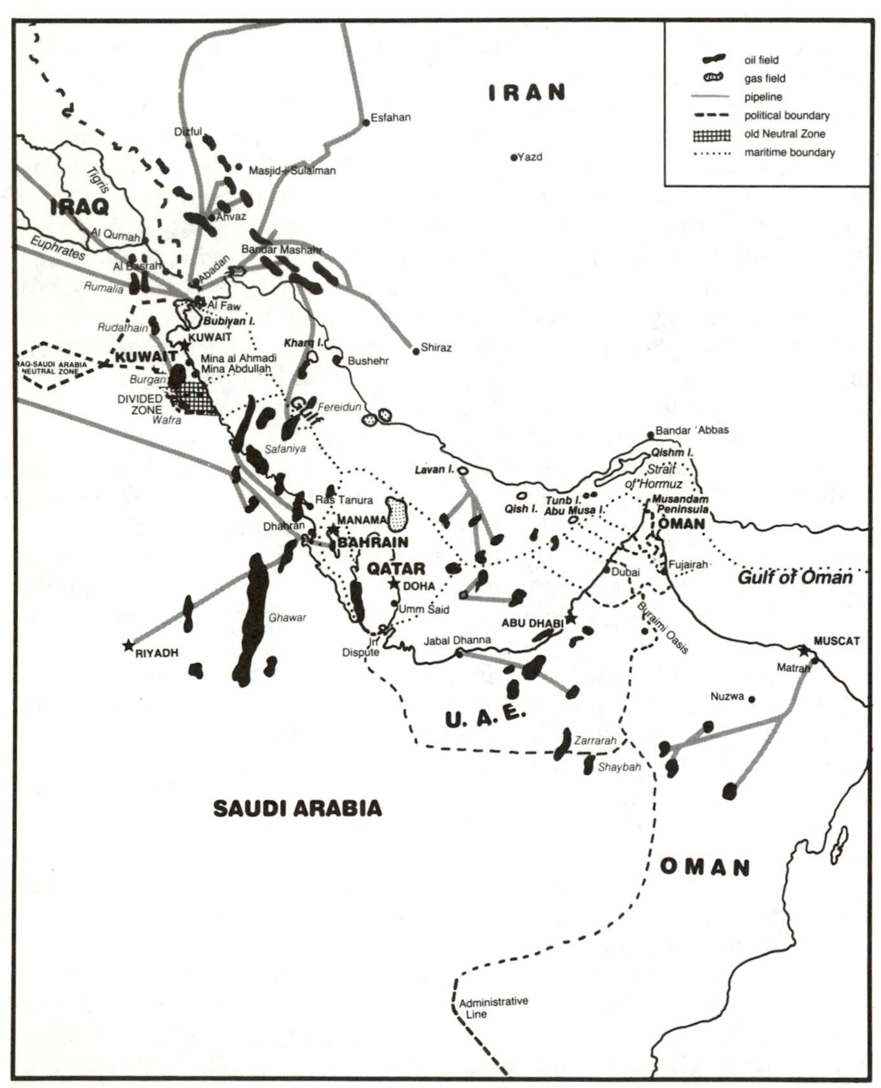

Adapted from Lenczowski, *The Middle East in World Affairs*, 4th Edition, Cornell, 1980, p. 659, and Will D. Swearingen, "Sources of Conflict over Oil in the Persian/Arabian Gulf," *Middle East Journal*, Volume 35, No. 3, Summer, 1981, pp. 315-330.

in 1981. Approximately 81% of the UAE's current population is now foreign, including large numbers of unregistered or illegal workers; this population has limited privileges and no hope of citizenship. In 1981 the total population was 19% native, 23% other Arab, 50% South Asian, and 8% Western and East Asian.[45]

The UAE's native population has not only increased radically, it has shifted so that at least 70% of it is now "urban," market-oriented, and living in areas or an environment outside traditional family or tribal locations.[46] Literacy has risen from less than 5% in 1960 to over 25% today. In 1981 there were already 96,000 telephones in the country, and six radio and nine television stations. These changes are inevitably altering the political consciousness of the emirates.

Interactions Among the Major Gulf Powers and the Smaller Conservative Gulf States

While it is dangerous to overgeneralize about the interactions among the major Gulf powers and the smaller conservative Gulf states, a number of patterns emerge:

- Iran and Iraq have been almost continuous rivals, as much because of differing national and political interests as because of different political ideologies. The smaller Gulf states have had to position themselves to avoid being the target of this rivalry and have tended to seek the support of whatever state was least likely to intervene in their affairs at any given time.
- Saudi Arabia has continuously had to adjust its policies to seek the support of either Iran or Iraq and to minimize the risk of hostile action by either power. Although Saudi Arabia is the dominant power in the southern Gulf, it has lacked the military and political strength to ignore its larger northern neighbors. In some ways, however, Iraq has been Saudi Arabia's natural ally because it is smaller and wealthier in per capita income and has been governed by a Sunni elite.
- All the larger Gulf powers have a long heritage of border claims against their smaller neighbors. These claims have been largely settled in Saudi Arabia's case, and Saudi Arabia now has a strong incentive to avoid border conflicts and to cooperate with its smaller neighbors. Iraq still has tentative claims to part of Kuwait, but the Iran-Iraq War has demonstrated that acquiring the Kuwaiti islands facing Iraqi Gulf ports and access channels has little value in the face of Iranian air power. In contrast, while the shah settled most of his claims against the smaller Gulf states, it is far from clear that Iran's new government will leave in peace any southern Gulf state with a significant Shi'ite minority.[47]
- The smaller Gulf states have a long heritage of mutual conflict and conflict with their large neighbors. Such conflicts have, however, lost

much of their importance since the mid-1970s. While some tensions remain within the UAE, most of the southern Gulf states are now well positioned to increase their cooperation and to seek collective security.

- All of the Gulf states have internal divisions that interact with their external tensions and relations. The divisions of the most immediate concern are those between Sunni and Shi'ite, but the southern Gulf states also face serious class divisions and major problems in dealing with immigrant labor.
- The conservative Gulf states have an obvious strategic interest in ties to the West. At the same time, they also have to fear the reactions of Iraq and Iran and the impact of being tied to Israel's principal ally. Further, sufficient time has elapsed since British withdrawal so that it is extremely difficult for them to accept any formal Western base on their territory.

The full implications of these patterns become clear, however, only when they are analyzed in terms of the events that have shaped the interactions between Oman and the Yemens, the current military balance in the region, and the relevant capabilities of the two superpowers.

Notes

1. This chapter draws on many sources, including interviews during four trips to the Gulf. The primary statistical source is the CIA *World Factbook*, 1981, NFAC GS WF-81-001 (U), April 1981. This is supplemented by a number of other references, including the World of Information, *Middle East Review*, 1981 and 1983 (London, 1980 and 1983). Extensive use has been made of the U.S. Army Area Handbooks for the Gulf States, Iran, Iraq, and the Yemens; Alvin J. Cottrell, *The Persian Gulf States* (Baltimore: Johns Hopkins University Press, 1980); W. B. Fisher's classic, *The Middle East* (London: Butler and Tanner, Ltd.), especially the 1963 edition; Fred Halliday's Marxist analysis in *Arabia Without Sultans* (London: Pelican, 1979); Donald Hawley, *The Trucial States* (London: George Allen & Unwin, 1970); Derek Hopwood, ed., *The Arabian Peninsula: Society and Politics* (London: George Allen & Unwin, 1972); John Keegan, *World Armies* (New York: Facts on File, 1979); J. B. Kelly, *Arabia, the Gulf, and the West: A Critical View of the Arabs and Their Oil Policy* (New York: Basic Books, 1980); George Lenczowski, *The Middle East in World Affairs*, 4th ed. (Ithaca, N.Y.: Cornell University Press, 1980); Peter Mansfield, *The Middle East, A Political and Economic Survey* (New York: Oxford University Press, 1980); Otto von Pikva, *Armies of the Middle East* (New York: Mayflower, 1979); Muhammad Sadik and William P. Snavely, *Bahrain, Qatar, and the UAE* (Lexington, Mass.: Lexington Books, 1972).
2. These steps involved at least some elements of rivalry with Saudi Arabia. Iran's ties to Oman, and the December 1977 agreement between Iran and Oman to jointly patrol the Strait of Hormuz (the key channels are in Omani waters), were seen as a potential challenge by the Saudis. Similarly, the Iranian support to Dubai was a counterweight to the Saudi support for Abu Dhabi, and the shah's limited support of North Yemen in creating a new base south of Mokha included support to then President al-Hamdi at a time when he was at odds

with Saudi Arabia. Iranian-Saudi rivalry also arose over Bahrain, where Saudi Arabia built an air base, but the shah tried to expand his military and political influence. The only area where the shah's actions did not involve at least some hint of rivalry between the two powers was in Somalia. There the shah's arms transfers, coupled to massive Saudi aid payments of $400 million during the expulsion of Somalia's Soviet advisers and $200 million during its invasion of Ethiopia, were the key to avoiding U.S. unwillingness to transfer arms.

3. Based on interviews in Iraq and with Iranian exiles.

4. It should be remembered that no conceivable Iraqi gains in the Shat al-Arab or along its border can secure Iraq's access to the Gulf, protect its narrow coast on the Gulf, or achieve any other major strategic objective. The control of the Shat is important in terms of prestige but is militarily meaningless. What Iraq can hope to accomplish is to seal the border, cause unrest among Iran's minorities, and isolate Iran's Shi'ite proselytizing while appealing to the Sunnis in Iran.

5. This is a marked contrast to the period before 1976. It was Iraq that blocked Oman's original attempts to link the eight Gulf states into a regional security pact during the conference Oman sponsored in 1976 on the grounds that the pact was U.S.-sponsored and that the Omani proposal did not include Iraq.

6. See Kelly, *Arabia, the Gulf and the West*, pp. 57–58, 187–188.

7. These themes consistently emerged in talks with various Omani and UAE officials in 1980 and 1981.

8. U.S. Congress, House Committee on Foreign Affairs, *U.S. Security Interests in the Persian Gulf*, 97th Congress, 1st Session, March 16, 1981.

9. In addition to the sources listed earlier, use has been made of Ralph Shaw, *Kuwait* (London: Macmillan, 1976), and various official Kuwaiti publications.

10. CIA, *World Factbook*, 1981, pp. 110–111.

11. Ibid.

12. For example, when Kuwait replaced some key Palestinians in sensitive positions in 1976 with Egyptians, it increased its payments to the PLO.

13. Ironically, the Iran-Iraq War has now led Iraq to discuss building a 3.5–5.0-MMBD pipeline to a new port near the Saudi port of Janbu and led Iran to discuss building a pipeline and refinery complex somewhere near the Strait of Hormuz to replace the one at Abadan.

14. Another result was that Iraq finally built its offloading facilities near al-Fao and at Khor al-Amaja following the riverine line of the Shat al-Arab rather than to the west near Kuwait. This location was only about 60 miles by sea from the Iranian naval port at Bandar Shahpur, and the design of the facilities was highly cost effective in that it relied on a few very large components and only two surface facilities. These features made them more vulnerable than most Gulf port facilities. As a result, Iranian commando and naval forces were able to destroy the Iraqi facilities easily in 1981.

15. This occurred in June 1977. Kuwait officially denies that the occupation took place. Keegan, *World Armies*, p. 417.

16. Opinions in Kuwait and the Gulf differ sharply over the strength of Shi'ite factions in Kuwait, and there are conflicting opinions as to whether these factions are becoming more or less pro-Khomeini. The CIA estimates 17% of Kuwaitis are Shi'ite. See 630814 12-81 (U), 1981.

17. Some data are taken from Bahrain, Cabinet Affairs, Directorate of Statistics, *Bahrain, A Statistical Abstract* (Doha, September 1979).

18. CIA, *World Factbook*, 1981, p. 12.

19. Ibid., p. 13.

20. Ibid.

21. These estimates are taken from ibid. Other estimates of the Shi'ite population tend to be slightly lower. The rest of Bahrain's population is 13% Asian, 10% other Arab, and 6% other.

22. Based on interviews in the Gulf. Some experts feel only the UAE and Oman were involved.

23. Kelly, *Arabia, the Gulf and the West.*

24. CIA, *World Factbook*, 1981, p. 164.

25. Ibid. Some estimates of the Qatari work force go as high as 40,000.

26. Ibid.

27. Based largely on interviews in the Gulf.

28. Much of the discussion in this section is from Lenczowski, *Middle East in World Affairs*; Mansfield, *Middle East*; Ali Mohammed Khalifa, *The United Arab Emirates: Unity in Fragmentation* (Boulder, Colo.: Westview Press, 1979); and Keegan, *World Armies*. Additional statistics are taken from UAE Ministry of Information and Culture, *United Arab Emirates: A Record of Achievement, 1979–1981* (Abu Dhabi, 1981).

29. World of Information, *Middle East Review 1981*, p. 344.

30. CIA, *World Factbook*, 1981, p. 204.

31. World of Information, *Middle East Review 1981*, p. 348; CIA, GI IESR 81-011 (U), 24 November 1981, pp. 1, 3.

32. World of Information, *Middle East Review 1981*, p. 350.

33. Mansfield, *Middle East*, p. 183.

34. See Hawkey, *Trucial States*, and Halliday, *Arabia Without Sultans*, for the pros and cons of this process.

35. See Kelly, *Arabia, the Gulf and the West*, pp. 84–88, 210–212.

36. According to some sources, Abu Dhabi inadvertently also ceded territory claimed by Oman to Saudi Arabia. This led to Saudi-Omani talks in 1977 and further adjustments of the border.

37. See Kelly, *Arabia, the Gulf and the West*, pp. 56, 66–78, 84–87, 210–211; and Lenczowski, *Middle East in World Affairs*, p. 680.

38. One example of this rivalry occurred in February 1978, when President Sheikh Zayid of Abu Dhabi suddenly named his 18-year-old son, Colonel Sultan Bin Zaid, as commander in chief of the UAE's armed forces without consulting Sheikh Rashid of Dubai or his son, who was the UAE's defense minister. This appointment led Dubai to withdraw temporarily its forces from the joint UAE command and put them on one-hour alert. Prince Sultan of Saudi Arabia responded by immediately congratulating the new commander in chief on his appointment, and the shah responded by immediately inviting the minister of defense to Tehran. Zaid resigned in early 1982 without a public explanation.

39. See Lenczowski, *Middle East in World Affairs*, p. 730; Mansfield, *Middle East*, p. 190; Kelly, *Arabia, the Gulf and the West*, pp. 87–89, 93–97.

40. The sheikh joined the UAE later than the other members, and he has laid informal claims to Sharjah on the grounds that it is legitimately a part of a larger Qawasim state. He did not fully support the UAE before the shah's fall and at one point unilaterally invited Soviet military technicians to Ras al-Khaimah.

41. By 1976, Abu Dhabi was exporting 1,600,000 BPD, Dubai 350,000 BPD, and Sharjah 50,000 BPD.

42. Ras al-Khaimah exports some oil.

43. Kelly, *Arabia, the Gulf and the West*, pp. 84–88, 210–212.

44. CIA 630814 12-81 (U), 1981. The Christian and Hindu population is almost as large, at 4%.

45. CIA, *World Factbook*, 1981, p. 205.

46. World of Information, *Middle East Review 1981*, pp. 348–352.

47. The end of open rivalry over borders is as much the result of political agreement as of formal demarcation of borders. The following major boundary problems remain:

Offshore Boundaries: Roughly two-thirds of the offshore borders in the Gulf are not formally demarcated. Those boundaries that are demarcated include Saudi Arabia–Bahrain (1958), Saudi Arabia–Iran (1968), Abu Dhabi–Qatar (1969), Abu Dhabi–Dubai (1969), Iran–Qatar (1970), Iran–Bahrain (1972), and Iran–Oman (1975). For a good summary discussion see Will D. Swearingen, "Sources of Conflict over Oil in the Persian/Arabian Gulf," *Middle East Journal* 35, no. 3 (Summer 1981).

Saudi Arabia–Qatar–Abu Dhabi: Opinions differ over the status of the agreement between Saudi Arabia and Abu Dhabi regarding the Khaur al-Udaid inlet southeast of the Qatar Peninsula and the adjacent coastal area. The 1974 negotiations between Abu Dhabi and Saudi Arabia definitely granted Saudi Arabia access to the inlet via a territorial corridor between Qatar and Abu Dhabi. This was part of the Buraimi Oasis settlement. The negotiations did not, however, produce a definitive border settlement.

Musandam Dispute Between Oman and the UAE: Oman has sporadically made claims to part of Ras al-Khaimah, as well as to offshore drilling rights near the junction of the border and coast that are claimed by Ras al-Khaimah. Another dispute centers on the proper disposition of territory held by the Shihuh and Habus tribes in the area northeast of Musandam. The village of Dibba, the focus of the dispute, is now divided into three parts administered by Sharjah, Fujairah, and Oman.

The Saudi-Iraqi Border: The 2,500-square-mile Neutral Zone seems to provide a fairly stable separation of the two states, but it is not a formally demarcated border.

The Internal Borders of the UAE: The seven emirates that compose the UAE have extremely complex internal boundaries. Only Abu Dhabi and Umm al-Qaiwain are territorially integral units. Even Ajman, the smallest emirate with only 150 square miles, is divided into three separate territorial units within the UAE's boundaries. Abu Dhabi and Dubai, Dubai and Sharjah, and Fujairah and Sharjah have dormant border disputes, and only Abu Dhabi and Dubai have reached a firm agreement on offshore oil rights.

12
Oman and the Yemens: The Lessons of War

The remaining three states in the Arabian Peninsula—Oman, North Yemen, and South Yemen—all have a recent history of war.[1] This history of conflict is important not only because of its impact on the future strategic stability of the Gulf but because of its implications for the kind of wars that the Gulf states and the West must guard against in the future.

Oman

Oman has been involved in two civil wars since the mid-1950s. These wars involved Egypt, Saudi Arabia, Iran, Iraq, and South Yemen, and their heritage still affects relations between Oman and the other Gulf states. Unlike the situation of the Gulf states discussed earlier, the threats to Oman's security and stability have not been theoretical or limited to minor border conflicts. Oman has been involved in over two decades of open warfare. The first of these two civil wars, a Saudi Arabian–backed rebellion by Oman's western tribes, is now fading into history. It has little current impact on Oman's relations with Saudi Arabia or its willingness to join the other southern Gulf states in collective security arrangements. The second civil war involved a much more serious South Yemeni–backed attempt to seize control of the entire country, and a long and grim guerrilla war in Oman's southern province of Dhofar. The heritage of this war has left Oman facing the constant prospect of military conflict with South Yemen.

The Origins of the Omani Civil Wars

The origins of these civil wars lie in earlier conflicts in the eighteenth century. In the early 1700s, a series of civil wars broke out in Oman that threw the country into chaos and led to a brief Persian occupation during 1737–1744. These wars ended with the emergence of the present ruling family, the Saids, but left the country divided among hostile tribal factions that proceeded to renew their struggle for influence and power whenever a weak member of the Said family gave them the opportunity.

Such internal conflicts were muted from about 1750 to 1856 by Oman's emergence as a major Arab naval power. Oman's traders sailed as far east as Indonesia, and its forces pushed Portugal out of most of its northeast African possessions. By the early 1800s, Oman controlled Zanzibar and a substantial portion of the East African slave trade. As a result, Oman's sultans were content to concentrate on their overseas possessions and made less and less effort to control Oman's primitive and tribally divided interior.

The division of the country was reinforced by the indifference of the Said sultans to the initial Wahabi raids on Oman's western tribes and by a split between the roles of sultan and imam. After 1806, the imam became the de facto leader of the western tribal areas, as well as the custodian of the Ibadi sect of Islam. The Said sultans and their followers showed little interest in tribal affairs, which brought them little revenue and power. They became increasingly cosmopolitan, further preventing them from playing a strong role as leaders of the Ibadi sect.

This situation was altered after 1856 by a division of the kingdom between the two sons of Sultan Sayyid Said. This split effectively deprived Oman of its African possessions, which passed to the son based in Zanzibar. At the same time, Oman suffered from the ending of the slave trade and conversion of the Indies trade to steam after 1862; it increasingly came under British influence. A treaty of friendship was signed between Oman and Britain in 1839, and it was the governor general of India who formalized the division of Oman between the two sons in 1861. As a result, Oman lost most of its strategic importance. It became little more than another British protectorate, although Oman never formally sacrificed its independence as the Trucial states did.[2] Oman had signed a friendship pact with Britain as early as 1646, but it did not sign a formal treaty fully establishing its relations with Britain until 20 December 1951, when the growing tension over the Buraimi Oasis led both states to establish a relationship that would help protect Oman's border from Abu Dhabi and Saudi Arabia. Nevertheless, Oman remained a strategic backwater from 1861 to the 1930s. It was of little interest to its neighbors or the outside world. British efforts to limit tribal war and maintain control of the Gulf both isolated Oman and kept it relatively secure from its neighbors.

The conservatism of the Ibadi sect, and a constant series of upheavals and civil wars in Oman that followed the split of 1861, also contributed to Oman's isolation. The main port of Muscat was sacked by one of the western imams as late as 1895, and it avoided similar sacks in 1877 and 1915 only because of British intervention. An end to these upheavals did not come until 1920, and it was the result of compromises between the Said family and the Ibadi imam that ensured Oman would stay a conservative and isolated state. This peace occurred because the assassination of an imam closely allied to the tribal factions hostile to the sultan allowed the British to reach a compromise that made a pro-sultan candidate, Muhammad ibn Abdullah al-Khalili, the new imam.[3]

This compromise gave al-Khalili a substantial degree of autonomous control over much of Oman's western interior and the sultan control over the coast and the agricultural area of Dhofar. The compromise was reinforced in 1932 when an unpopular Said sultan, Taimur ibn Faisal, abdicated in favor of his son, Said. Said was highly conservative, and his adherence to Ibadi customs made him considerably more acceptable to the inland religious and tribal leaders. A long war between the Harithi and Ghafri tribes, which had begun in the 1700s, also ended during this period. The resulting Harithi-dominated coalition reduced this source of internal squabbles and conflicts and created a relatively stable ruling structure in Oman, although one with little interest in modernizing the country or developing contacts with the outside world.

The West's concentration on oil exploration in Iran and the western Gulf also helped to keep Oman comparatively isolated until the late 1930s. When Oman did finally grant oil exploration concessions in 1937, it did so only in time to see all exploration activity suspended until the end of World War II.

The Civil War for Western Oman

When oil exploration activity was renewed in 1947–1948 Oman became involved in a long conflict with Saudi Arabia. Exploration activity in Oman was initiated at the western border of the country near the Buraimi Oasis,[4] which had been a contested area in eastern Arabia for centuries. The exploration activity began after only token consultation with the imam and the area's tribal rulers and without any sharing of the money paid for exploration rights. It involved a part of Oman that had been the scene of a long series of bloody clashes between the Wahabi and Ibadi sects, that was religiously one of the most conservative parts of Oman, and that was a traditional source of separatist movements. It also inevitably involved Oman in the conflict between Abu Dhabi and Saudi Arabia over the Buraimi Oasis.

Although the tension between the western tribes and Sultan Said grew steadily between 1952 and 1954, the sultan consistently refused to share his oil wealth with their leaders and did not try to win their political support. The Saudis took advantage of these failings to encourage the separatist elements within the western tribes, and they occupied part of the Omani side of the Buraimi Oasis in 1950 and 1952. From 1952 to 1954, the Saudis supported the growing opposition to Said's actions and actively encouraged several of the leaders of the western tribes to break with the sultan when his long-standing ally, Imam Salim Bin-Rashid al-Kharusi, died in 1954.

The key leaders involved in the resulting rebellion were Suleiman bin Himyar of the Beni Riyam tribe, which controlled the Jebel Akhdar

Mountains in the northwest, and Sheikh Salih bin Isa of the tribes in the southwest. These leaders not only sought a share in Oman's oil wealth, they were the traditional autonomous rulers of part of Oman where the sultan had no troops and that he never visited. As a result, they were happy to accept substantial funds from the Saudis and to work with them to elect a new imam, Ghalib ibn Ali, who could be counted on to support the rebel cause. The rebels were able to obtain the backing of a coalition of Saudis seeking control over the Buraimi Oasis area, Egyptians seeking any opportunity to oppose British imperialism, and ARAMCO officials seeking to displace the British from concession rights in the area.

From 1952 to 1955, Britain sought to deal with the Omani–Abu Dhabi border issue through international arbitration and through counterbribes to the western tribes. However, Britain failed to outbid its competitors, and the arbitration process collapsed during 1955. The British reacted in two ways. First, they sent in the Trucial Oman Scouts from the emirates and forced the Saudis to leave the Abu Dhabi side of the Buraimi Oasis. Second, they gave Sultan Said the backing he needed to send his British-trained Muscat and Oman Field Force (MOFF) to occupy the key towns and villages in the Jebel Akhdar.

Since the imam's forces had no real military organization, the sultan's forces were able to occupy Western Oman relatively quickly in December 1955. The Beni Riyam rebels withdrew into the mountains, however, and the Saudis provided the imam and his brother with arms, training facilities, and military advisers. As a result, the rebels were able to build up a substantially improved military capability by 1957. They also obtained the support of Saudi Arabia and Egypt in seeking recognition from the Arab League and the United Nations as an independent state. In May 1957 the rebels reentered Oman in strength. While they were defeated in the southwest, they lured the MOFF into a major ambush in the Jebel Akhdar. This victory allowed the imam to return to western Oman and to occupy several key towns in the northwest, shown in Map 12.1. The rebels then gradually expanded their control of the roads and paths in the area by a constant series of ambushes of the remaining forces of the MOFF. The Saudis provided U.S. arms and mines, and the poorly organized MOFF proved unable to operate effectively in minesweeping or offroad operations.

The British then agreed to reorganize the sultan's forces into a new force called the Sultan's Armed Forces (SAF) and provided regular British troops from the various guard regiments, the Special Air Services, and other units. They also helped the sultan recruit Baluchi troops, who eventually provided about 80% of the manpower for the new SAF.[5] RAF Shackelton bombers and Sea Venom attack fighters were deployed to give air support as well as improved armored cars and light armored vehicles. A considerable force was built up by late 1957. Between November 1957 and January 1958, the British and SAF were able to

MAP 12—1
KEY LOCATIONS IN THE REBELLION IN WESTERN OMAN: 1955-1959

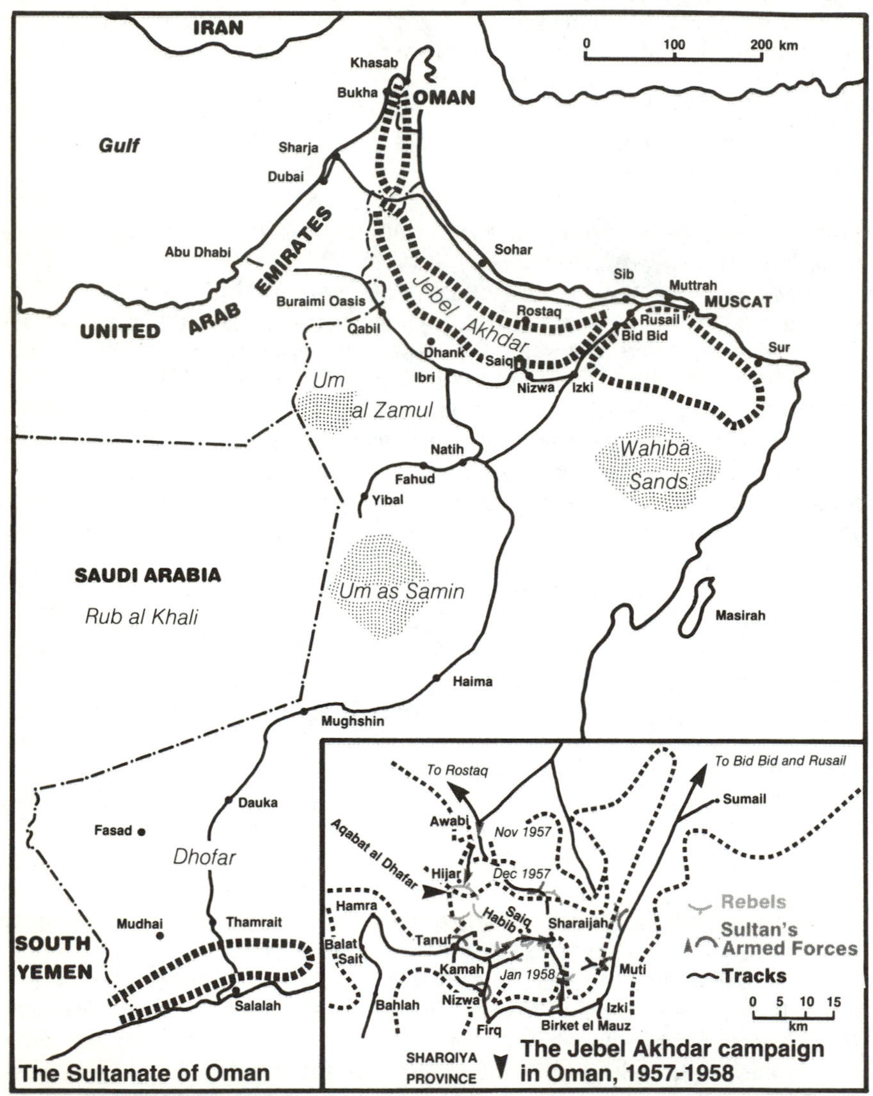

Adapted from Otto von Pivka, *Armies of the Middle East*, Mayflower, 1979, p. 57, and U.S. Department of the Army, *Middle East: The Strategic Hub*, DA Pamphlet 550-16, Washington, May 1973, pp. 181-183 and 342-343.

systematically seize control of each of the key villages in the northwest. By January 1959, there were essentially no rebel forces operating in western Oman.

While British support of the sultan would probably have proved decisive in any case, the rebels' defeat was speeded by two additional factors. First, the rebels were never able to reassert themselves militarily in the southwest after 1955, and Sultan Said eventually compromised with Sheikh Salih bin Isa to the point of sharing his oil revenues, which split the southern and the western tribes. Second, the Saudi defeat on the Abu Dhabi side of the Buraimi Oasis led the Saudis to shift their attention to Abu Dhabi's southern border and to press their border claims in an area where the disputed oil fields were geographically related to the Saudi fields.

The imam's defeat did not prevent the Saudis from backing him and other defeated western leaders in an appeal to the U.S. during 1959 and 1963. However, the Saudis gradually phased out their support of the rebel leaders when these leaders established relations with radical elements in South Yemen and as Saudi Arabia became steadily more hostile to Nasser's Egypt. As a result, the rebels had no real Saudi support after 1961, and the eventual UN report on the rebels' claims issued in 1965 had no real political audience.[6]

The Dhofar Rebellion

Unfortunately for Oman, Sultan Said's victory failed to provide any real stability in Oman's internal affairs or interactions with its neighbors. Just as Sultan Said was putting down the rebellion in the west, new problems arose in Dhofar. Said's control over the far southern part of Oman was even more tenuous than his control over the west, and during the late 1950s the tribes in the southern province of Dhofar experienced a severe economic crisis when the monsoon rains failed to provide enough water for even minimal agriculture. The sultan provided no aid of any kind, which created a wave of popular resentment and opposition. Since the Dhofaris were loosely aligned with the Yemeni tribes to the south, they became involved with radical Arab movements based in Aden that were attempting to undercut British influence and the rule of the traditional sheikhs. The Saudis also provided support to various Dhofari factions in an attempt to expand the western rebellion and provided paramilitary training to the more "conservative" factions of the Dhofar rebels.

During the early 1960s there was a steady buildup of rebel elements in Dhofar. These linked themselves to the other groups in Oman that resented Sultan Said's unwillingness to share his limited oil and customs income and to provide minimal government services, medical facilities, and schools. The Dhofar rebels gradually established a network of paramilitary and revolutionary cells with close relations to the "radical" or Arab nationalist elements in the merchant classes of Oman's coastal cities, many of whose sons had been politically sensitized during their education in Lebanon and Kuwait. The Dhofar Liberation Front (DLF), which was linked to most of the other Arab radical parties in the area, was formed in 1969. By early 1965, the DLF felt it had the power to launch a popular rebellion. Accordingly, during 9–12 June 1965, it launched a series of attacks and uprisings against the sultan throughout much of the Dhofar province. It was able to get Egyptian, South Yemeni, and limited Saudi recognition of its claims to sovereignty in the area.

The DLF simultaneously attempted to seize the north and take advantage of the widespread hostility to Sultan Said. While the June uprising was not particularly successful outside Dhofar, it did give the rebels control over many of the tribes and villages in the south. This control allowed the rebels to expand their operations during the next year, and a DLF-sponsored coup and assassination attempt came close to killing the sultan in April 1966. The rebels, however, were constrained by the lack of a secure base of operations. By mid-1965, the Saudis had become worried enough about the DLF's radical political alignment to cease providing a sanctuary in Saudi Arabia, and as long as the British remained in Aden, the rebels had no secure base in the south. Nasser's catastrophic defeat in the June War of 1967 also meant that Egypt had to cease support of any movement not backed by the Saudis. Thus the rebels lost much of their outside political support, and these shifts would probably have ended the rebellion if other events in the Gulf had not intervened.

The loss of India, Pakistan, and Britain's Far Eastern empire deprived Aden of most of its strategic value, and the continuing economic crisis in Britain led it to cut back on the rest of its military commitments in the Gulf. The cuts included plans to withdraw from South Yemen, which were accelerated by a complex civil war that led Britain to leave in 1967. The British departure allowed the radicals in Aden to suppress the traditional leaders in the inland areas, especially in the Hadramaut tribal areas just south of Dhofar. Iraq then reacted to Britain's announcement that it would withdraw from the Gulf by 1971 by expanding its backing of Gulf nationalist and radical movements. Further, the emergence of strong Marxist-Leninist elements in the NLF and South Yemen led the PRC to provide the NLF with military support and funds and to become actively involved in training the Dhofar rebels.

The NLF was then reorganized under the title of the Popular Front for the Liberation of the Occupied Arab Gulf (PFLOAG) at a conference held in Hamrin in central Dhofar. As a result of this conference, Iraq made major increases in its financial and propaganda support of the rebels, China started large-scale training of rebel military leaders in the PRC, and cadres of Chinese and South Yemeni military advisers were sent into southern Dhofar. This reorganization also resulted in a systematic and murderous purge of the less Marxist members of the NLF and gave South Yemen steadily greater influence over the PFLOAG.

The sultan proved extremely slow in reacting to these changes in the threat, and his continued failure to share properly his oil and customs revenues made it steadily more difficult for his British advisers to rally much of the country to his support. Oil had finally been discovered in Oman in 1963, and production had started in 1967. The issue of sharing the nation's oil revenues then changed from a debate over the limited amount of money paid for exploration rights to a debate over a relatively massive influx of wealth.[7] The sultan also increased resentment by hoarding most of his arms to prevent a coup and blocked efforts to win back the moderate elements of the DLF by offering the rebels only surrender or death.

The sultan then reacted to the growing opposition among his own supporters by imprisoning and exiling other members of the Said family and many representatives of the other leading tribal and merchant families. As a result, the sultan found himself isolated from his natural allies and began increasingly to distrust the British because of their pressure to "modernize" the country. He refused to properly fund the expansion of the SAF because of his fears that the troops might turn against him.

The rebels were thus allowed to seize control of the town of Rakhyut in Dhofar, to gain control over most of the mountain areas in the south and many of Dhofar's coastal villages, and to virtually isolate the RAF base at Salalah in southern Oman (see Map 12.2). By June 1970, the rebels were operating as far north as Izki in central Oman. On 11 June they launched an attack on the SAF garrison in the area that was intended to spark a general uprising by radical elements in the SAF. This attack misfired only because of the efforts of British intelligence and small units of the SAS. The British were faced with the prospect that Oman would fall into radical hands if Sultan Said continued in power. As a result, they removed the sultan's long-time British military adviser, which allowed Sultan Said's son Qabus to get the backing of key officials and officers and to force his father into permanent exile at the Dorchester Hotel in London. The commander of the sultan's guard, Buraik ibn Hamud, was the man who placed Sultan Said under arrest, and the coup had the support of most members of the Said family and most of Oman's traditional elite.

Qabus became sultan on 23 July 1970.[8] He had considerable qualifications. He had graduated from Sandhurst in 1964, served with the 1 Cameron Battalion, and studied government in London. Although his father had held him under virtual house arrest in the years before the coup, he had also made a world tour and had a broad understanding of the modern world.

The British acted immediately to help Qabus improve his forces. They had little choice. Oman's collapse, or partial collapse, might well have triggered major upheavals in the other Trucial States just at the point when the British were trying to forge the UAE and arrange for

MAP 12—2
KEY LOCATIONS IN THE DHOFAR REBELLION OF 1965-1976

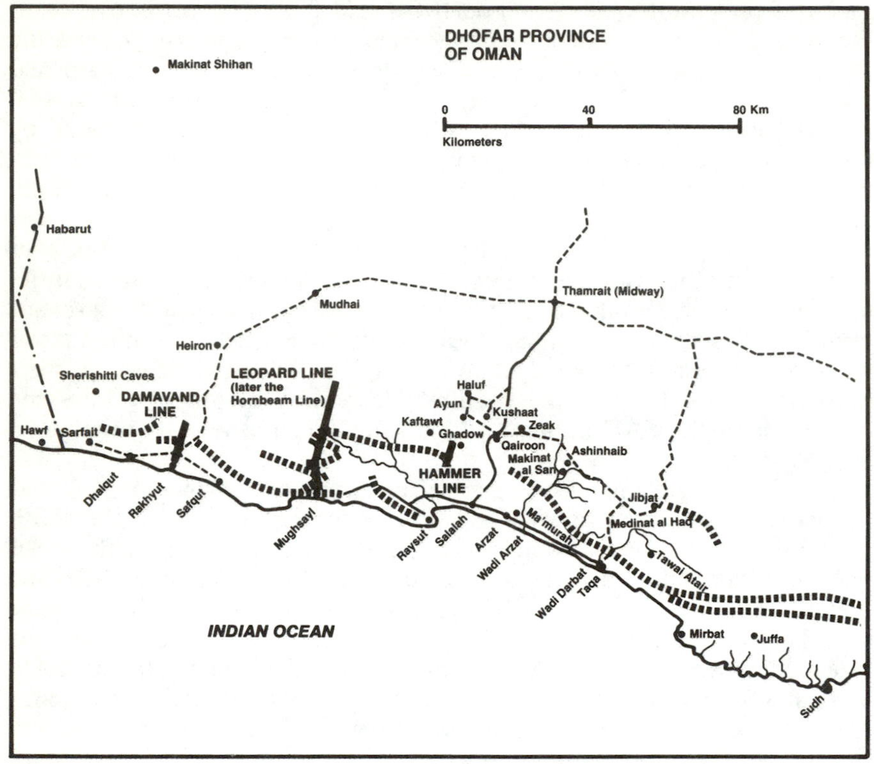

Adapted from Otto von Pivka, *Armies of the Middle East*, Mayflower, 1979, p. 70; and Defense Mapping Agency, special insert to Department of State Publication 7835, Revised March, 1971.

a stable withdrawal from the Gulf. If also would have meant radical control of the Strait of Hormuz and the entrance to the Gulf. As a result, British officers and NCOs were provided for the SAF, special SAS units were sent to Oman, and British and Pakistani pilots were recruited on a contract basis to provide air cover. At the same time, the British expanded their intelligence support and made a systematic effort to suppress the PFLOAG operations in the other Trucial States.

These military measures were backed by significant reforms. Qabus immediately began to share Oman's oil wealth, first with the tribal leaders and ruling elites in the coastal cities and then with the people of Oman. He initiated a broad program of funding medical, educational, water, and transport projects. This "pacification" program was combined with an offer of sweeping pardons to the Dhofar rebels and other opponents of the former sultan. The offer had a powerful effect because the extreme Marxism of the PFLOAG's South Yemeni–backed leaders, and their brutal treatment of the Dhofaris, alienated many of the NLF's leaders and ordinary Dhofar tribesmen.

Within a year, the sultan had put the PFLOAG on the defensive. In November 1971 the sultan's forces launced an offensive that pushed the PFLOAG forces south of Tawai Atar. Although the rebels returned to northern and central Dhofar when the monsoons halted air operations, the sultan's forces and the British began interdiction operations by establishing the Hammer Line, the first of a series of defensive lines of strong points and wire barriers designed to interdict rebel movement. The Saudis also began to provide financial aid to Sultan Qabus for the first time during 1971, while the shah of Iran started to provide both funds and military equipment. Jordan provided training aid and combat engineers. Further, from 12 September 1970 on, many traditional Dhofari leaders and tribesmen backed the sultan against the PFLOAG. Anti-PFLOAG members of the NLF attempted to arrest the PFLOAG leaders on that date, and although their attempt failed, large numbers of Dhofaris joined the sultan's tribal forces, or *firqats*.[9]

As a result, the PFLOAG became steadily more dependent on South Yemen for sanctuary, training, and military equipment, a situation that created new problems for the rebels. The collapse of South Yemen's economy between 1967 and 1970 made it totally dependent on Soviet aid, which gradually led the Chinese to withdraw from South Yemen and to end their support of the PFLOAG. While the Soviets could easily replace the PRC as a source of military equipment, they proved incapable of providing effective training and support for revolutionary and guerrilla warfare. This problem weakened the rebels militarily and eventually led to a number of important defections as the old leaders of the NLF became alienated from a PFLOAG increasingly dominated by the Soviets and South Yemenis.

The sultan's forces steadily expanded their operations, and in early 1972 they occupied Sarfait near the South Yemeni border. The PFLOAG attempted a disastrous counteroffensive further up the coast at Mirbat on 19 July. The plans for the offensive were betrayed to the sultan by hostile elements in the PFLOAG—which deeply resented a further South Yemeni–backed purge of the organization in November 1971—and the sultan's forces inflicted a defeat on the rebels that substantially reduced their future ability to engage the SAF in conventional military operations.

By the fall of 1972, the war had entered a phase in which the sultan was able to start permanent interdiction operations in southern Dhofar, and he used his British support to create a new defensive barrier, called the Leopard Line, to cut off the south from the rest of Dhofar. He was also able to recruit many ex-rebels into the SAF and to establish a Home Guard in many of the villages and tribal areas in the north and central Dhofar. These steps provided only minimal regional security, but they were enough to make the peaceful aspects of the sultan's pacification program effective in many areas. The rebels were thus placed at a severe disadvantage, since they could not compete with the economic benefits the sultan provided, and their attempts at collectivization, "land reform," and forced education in Marxism won little popular support.

The British and the sultan, however, lacked the manpower and mobility to secure all the coastal villages and simultaneously conduct hunt-and-kill operations in the mountain areas. This shortcoming might have led to a stalemate, or even a reversal, as the Soviets expanded their aid efforts in the south and the rebels acquired the experience to exploit the sultan's lack of manpower and mobility. At this point, however, the shah of Iran chose to use Oman as a demonstration of his new role as "protector of the Gulf" and as a major testing ground for his new army.[10] The shah began a troop buildup in December 1973 that eventually reached over 3,500 men, giving Sultan Qabus the additional manpower he needed, plus additional air support, artillery, and heliborne mobility. Of equal importance, the shah was willing to accept relatively high casualties to the Iranian forces. The sultan could not accept such casualties without risking the breakup of the SAF, and although some 1,000 British "troops" were in the country, this combination of serving and contract personnel could not incur high casualties without causing severe domestic political problems in Britain.

This additional margin of support allowed the sultan's forces to seek out the rebels and sustain intense combat. It also allowed them to permanently open the north-south road in Dhofar, which ran from Salalah through the Qara Mountains to Thamarit, in December 1973. The sultan's forces then had the strength to stay in the secured territories when the monsoon began in January 1974. They used this presence to steadily reinforce the Leopard Line and to block the north-south routes about 50 miles from the Yemeni border. During this period the reinforced line became known as the Hornbeam Line.

By mid-1974, the PFLOAG had so suffered that it was little more than two armed bands of about 1,800 men. In contrast, the SAF had expanded from a force that totaled only 2,500 men in 1970 to one that totaled 12,500. The resulting loss of military and political influence led to a meeting in Aden in August 1973, at which the PFLOAG split between those who advocated continued conflict and those who advocated political action. The advocates of continued conflict formed the Popular Front for the Liberation of Oman (PFLO). They also obtained Cuban and Cuban-trained Libyan advisers through the USSR in an effort to rebuild their military capabilities.

These events had virtually no military effect, however, and the sultan was able to use his increasing oil wealth and Saudi aid to win the loyalty of much of the population of southern Dhofar and to supplement the shah's forces with additional units from Jordan. Jordanian and British engineers, backed by Iranian ground forces, then began to move out from the villages and coastal towns in central Dhofar and to establish a network of tracks through the mountain areas. These tracks gave the sultan's forces superior mobility in the mountain areas for the first time and forced the PFLO rebels to concentrate their forces in Rakhyut, the only major town still under rebel control, and in a series of caves and narrow wadis near the South Yemeni border known as the Sherishitti Caves.

This new rebel deployment was not successful. Iranian forces were able to seize control of Rakhyut in January 1975, and the sultan's forces reduced the rebel presence in the Sherishitti Caves and forced the rebels to virtually withdraw from the area. The sultan's forces then conducted sweeps of the remaining rebel pockets in the mountain areas while the Iranians constructed a final barrier called the Damavand Line near Rakhyut, which cut off the major routes through the mountains. These operations destroyed most of the remaining rebel forces in Dhofar between February and August 1975 and allowed the sultan to establish a final defensive barrier near the South Yemeni border, known as the Sarfait Line. By late October 1975, the rebels had again been forced to shelter in the Sherishitti Caves area, and they could mount only a token occupation of two small towns, Mughsayl and Dhalqut.

The sultan's forces and allies were then strong enough to interdict the coast and any major PFLO movements across the border with South Yemen, and the sultan's forces could move faster than all but the smallest rebel units. Further, his monopoly of air power and artillery superiority allowed him to strike with superior firepower virtually anywhere in the area. Former members of the NLF helped the sultan to establish intelligence links with the remaining rebel forces in the Sherishitti area, which gave the sultan's forces the information they needed to defeat most of the remaining rebels. Finally, the sultan's British-operated air force attacked rebel headquarters at Hauf in South Yemen with Iranian support on 17 October 1975, and it was made clear that further air attacks on South Yemen would follow.[11] The combination of air attacks and continued defeats on the ground proved to be the last straw. The rebels withdrew from the last two coastal villages without a fight, and only a few small elements returned to South Yemen. On 11 December 1975 Sultan Qabus announced that the war was over.[12]

Other events helped to reinforce the PFLO's defeat. By October 1976, the Saudis had become so concerned with the Soviet buildup in South Yemen that they offered to replace Soviet aid to South Yemen in return for a halt in Yemeni efforts to radicalize the Gulf. The Iraqis supported this effort, and the Saudis had some success in obtaining agreement to such an arrangement by the more moderate Marxist elements in the leadership of the PDRY. From October 1976 until a pro-Soviet coup and the execution of South Yemen's moderate leader, Rubai Ali, in June 1978, Oman was able to enjoy reasonably stable relations with its southern neighbor.

Oman's Interactions with Its Neighbors After 1976

Unfortunately, the peace settlement with South Yemen did not bring an end to the problems caused by Oman's civil wars. The aftermath of the conflict created several new problems, and Qabus found that his problems with his neighbors were far from solved. First, Britain informed Qabus in July 1976 that it was permanently withdrawing its remaining SAS and regular army units and that it would withdraw from the RAF bases at Salalah and on Masirah by March 1977. While British-contracted and -seconded officers and NCOs remained, and Oman was sold 12 Jaguar fighters with Harpoon missiles and a cadre of ex-RAF pilots and technicians to operate them, the withdrawal deprived Qabus of an outside protector that could help guarantee Oman's security against his Saudi and Iranian allies. Second, Saudi Arabia cashed in on its support of Qabus by obtaining his agreement to settle Oman's eastern boundary disputes. This border agreement was not punitive because of Saudi Arabia's desire to avoid future conflicts and its need to reach a compromise with both Oman and Abu Dhabi, but it did involve some tension between the two states.[13]

Third, although the shah withdrew most of his forces in January 1977, he made it clear that he regarded himself as being just as much a "protector" of Oman as the Saudis.[14] In December 1977 he capitalized on his support of the sultan in the fighting to obtain Oman's agreement to jointly patrol the Strait of Hormuz, which gave the shah de facto control over the main tanker channels through the Gulf. The shah's fall two years later ended Iran's immediate ambitions to control the Gulf and Western Indian Ocean, but it left Qabus with another problem. Oman's total population is less than 2% Shi'ite, and its Shi'ites do not present a threat. Qabus has, however, only gradually extended his modernization programs into Oman's mountainous northern enclave, the Ruus al-Jibal, and is only now building up his basing and defense capabilities. As a result, the shah's fall has left Qabus facing a major threat from Iranian naval and air bases just across the Strait of Hormuz, and there is a slight possibility that the Shi'ite ferment in the Gulf might affect Oman.

Fourth, the Soviet-backed coup in South Yemen that deposed Rubai Ali in June 1978 ended Saudi and Iraqi ability to limit Soviet influence in South Yemen and led to a renewal of South Yemeni support of the Dhofar rebels. The PFLO was also reorganized into a broader movement called the National Democratic Front for the Liberation of the Occupied Arab Gulf (NDFLOAG) and started efforts to subvert the Arabs in the Shihu tribes in the Ruus al-Jibal. These efforts had had negligible success, however, and South Yemen began serious peace negotiations in mid-1982, although it continued to pose a radical threat on Oman's southern border.[15] Fifth, although price rises and new oil and gas discoveries increased Oman's oil revenues—and Oman also has copper, chrome, and gas reserves—Oman continued to need economic aid and some source of military aid and protection from outside the Gulf area to ensure its independence. This need was a key reason Sultan Qabus was later willing to provide the U.S with contingency bases in Oman, in spite of substantial Iraqi and Iranian opposition. Although Qabus moderated such Iraqi opposition by supporting Iraq in its conflict with Iran, he still faced opposition from his Arab neighbors and the constant threat that Oman might become a cat's-paw in any struggle for control of the Strait of Hormuz.[16]

Nevertheless, Oman did a good job of weathering the changes in its external relations between 1976 and 1982. Although its economy seriously overheated in 1978, it had recovered by 1980, and its economic development has provided steadily increasing benefits to all regions of the country. The development of Dhofar and the Ruus al-Jibal was particularly striking after 1979 and helped to reduce the operations of the few remaining rebels in Dhofar to the level of petty bandit raids.

Further, the sultan and several of his Omani ministers played a leading role in creating and strengthening the Gulf Cooperation Council. While Oman miscalculated and backed Iraq too visibly early in the Iran-Iraq War, it quickly distanced itself from Iraq when Iran threatened military action. After a brief "face off" between four Iranian destroyers and three Omani gunboats in the Strait of Hormuz in late 1980, Oman worked out a modus vivendi with Iran. Iran ceased to send ships into Omani waters, and Oman ignored overflights by Iran's maritime patrol and reconnaissance aircraft.

Equally important, the sultan steadily increased the role of native-born Omani officials and military officers after 1976. He made several ex-rebels into ministers and gave an increasing number of Western-educated Omanis high positions. Finally, on 21 October 1981, the sultan established a 45-man Consultative Council led by his former minister for social affairs and labor, Khalfan bin Nassir al-Wahaibi. The council had 17 members from the government, 11 from the private sector, and 17 from the regions. It met for the first time in November 1981. None of the members was under 30, and all had been chosen by the sultan. However, this was a major step forward in giving Oman's government a popular character. Along with Oman's growing ties to the U.S., such changes significantly reduced the sultan's dependence on Britain without costing the sultan the loss of key British advisers and technocrats.

South Yemen

The Yemens are unique, even in the Gulf. South Yemen has been the scene of bloody political conflicts for roughly a quarter century, and North Yemen has experienced a civil war that produced more casualties than any other war in modern Arab history. The recent history of both states has been one of internal turmoil that has increasingly decoupled them from the rest of the Arab world. While this decoupling is most severe in the case of South Yemen, both Yemens now seem to be becoming a major long-term threat to the interests of the conservative Gulf states and the West.

The Origins of South Yemen as a Radical Marxist State

If Oman's recent history of interaction with its neighbors is grim, South Yemen's has been painted in blood. South Yemen's emergence as a state has involved it in constant conflict with Oman, Saudi Arabia, and North Yemen, and South Yemen has established a level of hostility with its neighbors that seems likely to be one of the most consistent aspects of Gulf politics. At the same time, this history has made it increasingly dependent on the USSR.

The origins of these developments stem from the initial British occupation of southeast Arabia. Britain seized the port of Aden in 1839, when its population was approximately 500, in a routine effort to suppress piracy and to control all the key ports that other powers might use to threaten India. Over the next century, Aden steadily expanded into one of the most cosmopolitan and advanced cities in the Gulf area, and its modernization was accelerated by a steady influx of Indians, Pakistanis, and other foreigners. The opening of the Suez Canal in 1869 made Aden the most important port in the Gulf and Red Sea area, and its economy was further expanded by making it a duty-free port and by the establishment of extensive British naval and dockyard facilities. Aden also acquired a large refinery in 1954, when Britain chose it as a "stable" location to replace the Anglo-Iranian Oil Company refineries that had been nationalized in Iran.

These developments also made Aden the Gulf's politically most developed city. It was the first city in the Gulf area to acquire a major labor movement, and the broad process of education in Aden made it a natural center for the Arab nationalist movements that arose in the 1920s. Because of its connections with India it was one of the first Arab areas to come under extensive communist and Marxist influence, which led to the creation of a number of small, extreme-left Marxist study groups.

In contrast, Britain had virtually no interest in the inland mini-states that surrounded Aden (see Map 12.3), which remained under the rule of tribal sheikhs and sultans. Britain applied the same divide-and-rule techniques to keep these leaders loyal that it used in its other colonial possessions, and it confined its role largely to controlling tribal warfare and ensuring that the imam of Yemen did not succeed in threatening British control of the area's western tribes. Even in the mid-1950s, Britain had not established firm administrative arrangements with all of the protectorates, and much of South Yemen remained in virtually the same condition as in the 1830s.

This situation provided an explosive recipe for change when Britain announced in 1954 that it would gradually transform the various tribal

MAP 12—3
THE PROTECTORATES OF SOUTH ARABIA IN 1962

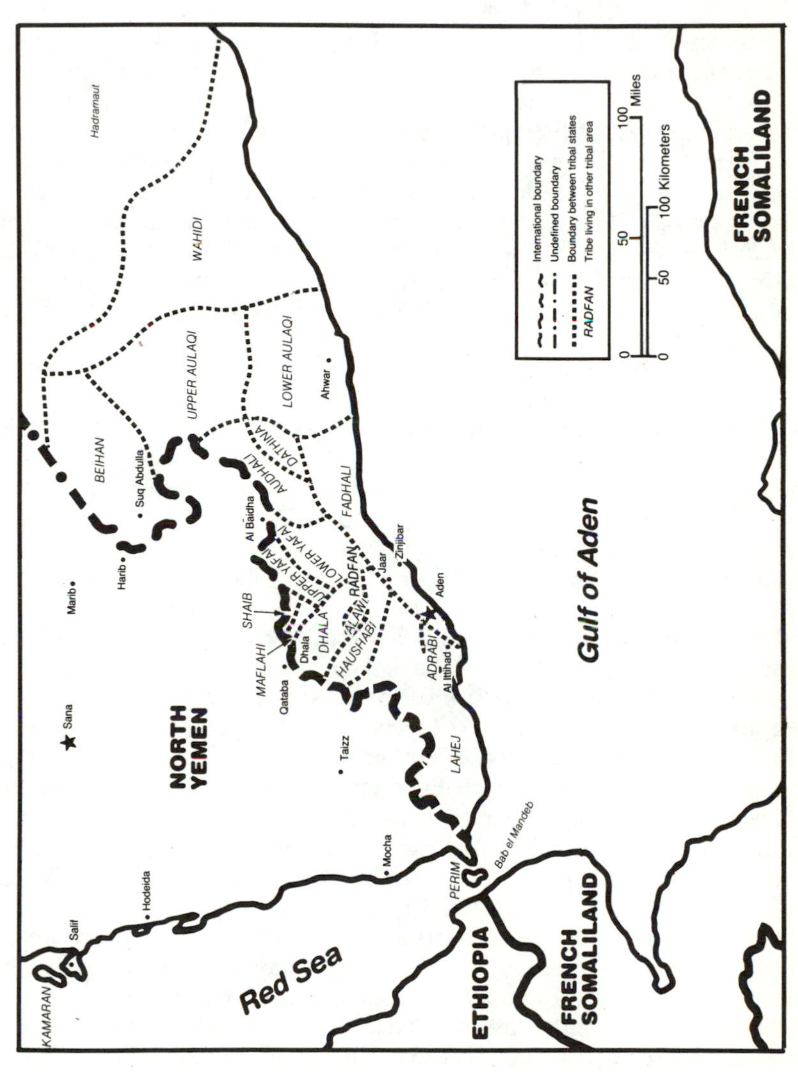

D A Pamphlet 550-182, *Area Handbook for the Yemens*, Washington, 1977, p. 44.

protectorates in South Yemen into the South Arabian Federation. North Yemen reacted by attempting to block the federation and actively reasserted its claims to the area. The Saudis reacted by supporting various anti-British groups and seeking control over the area, and the various Marxists and Arab nationalists in Aden immediately began a struggle for power over Aden and the various traditional protectorates.

The Suez crisis of 1956 and the Iraqi revolution of 1958 added new fuel to these fires. The Egyptians and Iraqis alike denounced all moderate or pro-British elements in Aden, and the traditional rulers of the protectorates as British puppets. The political climate in Britain also forced it to accelerate its efforts to give the area independence, and the protectorates were made into a federation in 1959, leaving Aden as a Crown colony. This arrangement might have had some success, but in 1962 the civil war in North Yemen brought Egyptian military forces into the area and made North Yemen a source of direct military and political support for the anti-British radical groups in Aden. These events led rapidly to the formation of organized revolutionary groups like the People's Socialist party.

When Britain included Aden in the federation in 1963, it virtually ensured that some kind of civil war would break out between the growing radical elements in Aden and the surrounding conservative protectorates. After October 1963, South Yemen became the scene of steadily increasing radical efforts to drive Britain out of the area and to seize control of the entire country. These radicals gradually formed into three major groups: the Front for the Liberation of South Yemen (FLOSY), which was loosely aligned with North Yemen and Egypt; the NLF, which was far more nationalist and left wing; and the SAL, which was comparatively moderate. Each group fought the others as well as the British, creating a mixture of terrorism and low-level civil war that led Britain to announce on 22 February 1966 that it would withdraw from South Yemen by 31 December 1968.

Aden's radical parties had no intention, however, of allowing Britain to withdraw in a way that gave the other parties a continuing role in ruling the state which left the traditional rulers of the protectorates and the merchant elite in Aden in power. As a result, an open war broke out between the NLF and the FLOSY in June 1967. The NLF gained the upper hand and defeated the FLOSY, which had been weakened by the defeat of Egypt in the "Six-Day War" and the chaos in North Yemen. The NLF gradually obtained control of the protectorates by subverting the South Arabian Federal Army, which speeded British withdrawal to 29 November 1967. The NLF deliberately attempted to embarrass the British by declaring the creation of the People's Republic of South Yemen two days earlier.

The ruling regime that emerged after independence was strongly Marxist. It was divided, however, into a faction led by the new president, Qahatan al-Shaabi, who supported a relatively moderate course of action and efforts to maintain good relations with Aden's neighbors, and a much harder-line Marxist faction backed by Salim Rubai Ali, Ali Nasr Muhammed, Muhammad Ali Haythan, and Abd al-Fattah Ismail. In March 1968 the NLF split over these policy differences, and al-Shaabi emerged as the initial victor.[17] He then concentrated on eliminating the remaining opposition to the NLF. On 20 March 1968, al-Shaabi announced that a coup attempt had failed, and he then used this as a reason to systematically purge his opponents. He started a series of mass imprisonments and executions that characterize South Yemen's politics to this day. His purges also divided the NLF. They ended with al-Shaabi dependent for his support on the army, the less-Marxist left, and various tribal elements. In contrast, Ali, Ismail, the more radical members of the NLF acquired control of the party apparatus and the new People's Militia set up to oversee the army.

If al-Shaabi had been able to keep control of the NLF party apparatus, South Yemen might eventually have established smoother relations with its neighbors and avoided its heritage of tension with Oman, North Yemen, and Saudi Arabia. However, the closing of the Suez Canal during the Arab-Israeli War of 1967 effectively deprived South Yemen of the economic reason for its existence. The closure of the British military base in Aden had previously thrown some 14,000 men out of work, and the civil wars just before independence had driven out many of Aden's remaining industries and clients. As a result, al-Shaabi was forced to turn to the communist nations for aid and, when this appeal proved unsuccessful, to the West. Ismail used his position within the NLF to capitalize on Yemen's growing economic problems and al-Shaabi's turn to the West to gather support from his fellow Marxists. When al-Shaabi broke with one of his key tribal associates, Ali and Ismail used the opportunity to force him from power.[18]

Conflict with Saudi Arabia and North Yemen, 1969–1976

The Revolutionary Council, which came to power on 22 June 1969, took a more radical approach to South Yemen's internal development and its relations with neighboring states. It launched a new set of purges aimed at eliminating all remaining moderate and traditional leaders and used the People's Security Court that al-Shaabi had established in May 1968 to carry out numerous death sentences.[19] By the end of 1969, South Yemen had about 350,000 citizens in exile.[20] While these exiles were composed of a bewildering mixture of tribal, conservative, FLOSY, and NLF factions, their common hostility to the government in Aden ensured that South Yemen faced a constant risk of hostile action from North Yemen and Saudi Arabia. Rubai Ali and Ismail also alienated South Yemen's neighbors more directly by making major increases in the support that South Yemen provided to the PFLOAG and the Dhofar rebels and by attempting to subvert the tribes in North Yemen and Saudi Arabia that had ties to those in South Yemen.

Since this shift in South Yemeni policy occurred at a time when the long civil war in North Yemen was finally winding down into an awkward coalition of the moderate Republicans and the Royalists, it was fairly easy for South Yemen's leaders to establish ties to the more radical factions in the Republican movements, who had been largely excluded from power in the coalition government. The situation was complicated, however, by the fact that the NLF was allied with some radical factions in North Yemen while the PFLOAG was aligned with others, and the Baathists, Nasserites, and communists had their own separate factions in both Yemens. While Rubai Ali and Ismail had a considerable capability to harass the new Iriani regime in North Yemen, the political divisions in the opposition to Iriani limited their success, and Rubai Ali and Ismail proved vulnerable to counterpressure when North Yemen began to support the less-Marxist elements in South Yemen.[21]

The South Yemeni efforts to back radical elements in North Yemen also steadily increased Saudi concern over the political changes taking place in South Yemen. So did Rubai Ali and Ismail's reliance on Egyptian and East German advice in drafting a new constitution, which was ratified in November 1970. A series of economic "reforms" followed that nationalized virtually every major foreign-owned firm except the BP refinery and attempted to convert South Yemen's primitive peasant agriculture to a Marxist model. This series of actions, which became known as the "Corrective Revolution," further isolated South Yemen from its neighbors and cut most of its remaining economic ties to the West. At the same time, it created a perpetual South Yemeni dependence on outside aid.[22]

Saudi Arabia and North Yemen retaliated by attempting to subvert South Yemen's border tribes and by backing various groups of South Yemeni exiles who wanted to overthrow Rubai Ali's regime. Some significant military border clashes resulted between Saudi Arabia and South Yemen near Sadiah in December 1969 and March 1970. The Saudis initially suffered minor reversals.[23] By mid-1970, however, they had built up their troop strength in the area. The buildup, combined with major Saudi payments to some of the South Yemeni tribes, forced South Yemen to reduce the fighting along its Saudi border to minor encounters between Saudi- and Yemeni-backed tribal factions. Further, Saudi Arabia built up an "Army of Deliverance" out of Yemeni exiles, which unsuccessfully attempted to seize the Hadramaut from South Yemen in 1971.[24]

Similar clashes occurred along the border with North Yemen between 1960 and 1972, but these were initially less intense because North Yemen was unable to win significant support from the Shaafi tribesmen who dominated both sides of the border area, and South Yemen chose to concentrate on other revolutionary activities in support of the PFLOAG in Oman, the PLO, and other radical Arab groups. South Yemen had become involved in a loose alliance with Iraq, Libya, and Algeria in encouraging such movements, and it began to establish training centers for the PLO and other groups interested in revolutionary warfare. South Yemen was originally supported by the PRC in these efforts, but Cuban influence became increasingly important after 1972.

Neither South nor North Yemen stopped seeking control over the other's border areas, and a low-level conflict developed by early 1972. As a result North Yemen closed its side of the border and banned all South Yemeni exports in March, and both countries started to engage in a series of firefights in the border area of fairly serious proportions. By August, it seemed increasingly likely that these incidents could lead to all-out war, which became still more likely in September, when North Yemen seized the Kamaran Islands in the Red Sea from South Yemen. Saudi Arabia, Iraq, Egypt, Algeria, and Libya joined in an effort to bring the two countries together under Arab League auspices, which led to peace talks in Cairo in October 1972 and further talks in Tripoli in November.[25]

Accounts differ sharply as to the reasons for what happened next, but on 28 November 1972 the leaders of both countries announced they would move in phased steps toward unification. Unification suited the ideology and formal policy declarations of the ruling political parties of both countries, but the real motives behind the announcement seem to have been more practical. President Rubai Ali of South Yemen faced a major economic crisis, the near-certain defeat of the Dhofar rebels, and increasing rivalry from Abd al-Fattah Ismail and other members of his Revolutionary Council. Unification offered him the prospect of Arab aid, an end to South Yemen's isolation, and increased security from his pro-Soviet rivals.[26] President Abdul Rahman Iriani of North Yemen probably had a more serious philosophical commitment to unification, but he also had equally strong pragmatic motives. Unification offered him increased independence from the various factions surrounding him, particularly from the Zaidi tribal leaders, who represented the dominant ruling elite in the country. It also offered him the prospect of reduced dependence on Saudi Arabia and the ability to increase the rate of modernization and centralization within North Yemen. From 1972 to 1974, therefore, both leaders made reasonably serious attempts to move toward unity, although accounts differ as to their respective intentions.

Saudi Arabia gave these efforts some public support but privately firmly opposed them. The unification of the Yemens threatened to create a strong Marxist state on its borders with a larger population and armed forces equal or superior to its own, to deprive it of a secure source of imported labor, and to create a constant source of political agitation located near key cities like Jiddah and Medina. Accounts differ as to how much support Saudi Arabia gave to the Zaidi leaders in North Yemen, who opposed the unification efforts, and how much encouragement Saudi Arabia gave to the various factions of South Yemeni exiles operating in North Yemen, who launched minor border attacks during 1973. Some sources indicate that the problems with the unification effort in both Yemens were largely internal, and some indicate that the Iraqi Baath party opposed unification on ideological grounds. There is substantial evidence, however, that the Saudis made a massive effort to reduce North Yemeni support for the unification program.

As early as December 1972, the North Yemeni government divided over the unification issue. President Iriani pushed ahead with the effort, however, and the two nations established a Unification Council on 13 February 1973. Iriani also made repeated attempts to suppress Zaidi tribal opposition and to forge a coalition supporting unification between the remaining Zaidi leaders and those of the Shaafi tribes. He ultimately failed in these efforts, however, and the Zaidi leaders gained more power. The North Yemeni military also was increasingly subverted by Iriani's opposition, and several key officers became convinced that the unification effort would simply threaten their independence and the nation's security. This led to a coup d'etat in June 1974, which deposed Iriani and put a temporary end to active North Yemeni support for the unification effort.[27]

The Struggle Between Ismail and Rubai Ali

The situation in South Yemen was as complex as that in North Yemen. Elections held in March 1972 effectively divided control of the country between the state apparatus of power, run by Rubai Ali, and the party apparatus, run by Ismail.[28] As South Yemen's economic situation worsened, Rubai Ali increasingly found himself in a position in which he could survive only with outside Arab economic aid and in which Saudi Arabia was the only Arab nation willing to provide the scale of assistance he required. It was clear, however, that such Saudi assistance would continue only if South Yemen ended its support of the Dhofar rebels and broke with the USSR.

The Saudis did not make things easy for Rubai Ali. They were slow in providing the financial aid they promised, and they used their growing financial power to take a number of steps that isolated South Yemen from the rest of the Arab world. Rubai Ali thus tended to lose strength between 1973 and 1975, and when South Yemen's state security apparatus was organized into a Ministry of State Security in 1974, and new Homeland Defense Laws were passed, Ismail seems to have been able to purge some of Rubai Ali's key supporters.[29]

Ismail also benefited from the fact that he had long had the status of an orthodox Marxist-Leninist with close ties to the USSR. Rubai Ali was aligned with the PRC and was a more theoretical and gradualist Marxist in the Arab nationalist mode.[30] As long as Saudi Arabia refused to provide major aid, South Yemen's only real source of military and economic assistance was the USSR. This situation invariably favored

Ismail, and it allowed him to strengthen his ties to Yemen's Soviet, East German, and Cuban advisers and to obtain their aid for his People's Militia. Although South Yemen signed friendship agreements with the PRC in November 1974 and with the USSR in December 1975, this sequence of events was misleading. The PRC was to all intents and purposes on its way out, and the USSR was on its way in.

The Saudis came to recognize this fact in 1975, and the defeat of the Dhofar rebels enabled Rubai Ali to meet the Saudi demand that a cease-fire take place between South Yemen and Oman. In 1976 Saudi Arabia offered Rubai Ali $100 million as the first of a series of loans that would have freed South Yemen from dependence on the USSR, and South Yemen signed the cease-fire with Oman discussed earlier. Iraq joined Saudi Arabia in backing Rubai Ali because of its reaction to a coup attempt within the Iraqi military and Baath party that had had strong communist and Soviet support.[31]

Ismail did not ignore these efforts, however, and he countered by including two smaller extreme leftist parties in the National Front and by taking advantage of developments in North Yemen. Although the new leader of North Yemen, Colonel Ibrahim al-Hamdi, initially seems to have had Saudi and Zaidi support in ousting Iriani, he soon proved he was even more committed to reducing Saudi influence and suppressing the power of the traditional Zaidi tribal leaders than was his predecessor. He also later proved to have had long-standing ties to the Nasserite movement and extensive clandestine contacts with South Yemen.[32]

As a result, Ismail entered into talks with al-Hamdi that were superficially intended to lead to a mutual defense pact between the two countries, but which in reality led to an alliance between Ismail and al-Hamdi to control their respective countries.[33] Al-Hamdi evidently felt that he had the strength to bring this off because he had removed many conservative officers and Zaidi leaders from office. They proved, however, to have more strength than he estimated and organized a countercoup. Al-Hamdi was assassinated on 10 October 1977, just as he was about to leave for Aden to formalize the mutual defense pact. He was replaced by a pro-Saudi and conservative Zaidi leader, Colonel Ahmid Ghashmi.[34]

A complex duel developed between Rubai Ali and Ismail between 1977 and 1978. On the one hand, Saudi Arabia, Iraq, and North Yemen under Ghashmi attempted to support Rubai Ali and create a situation in which South Yemen would split with the USSR and become a relatively moderate Arab state. This effort acquired growing urgency as the USSR built up South Yemen as the staging point for its airlift to Ethiopia and as senior Soviet officials provided growing aid to Ismail.[35] As a result, the Saudis and Iraqis encouraged the leaders of both Yemens to renew their unification efforts under circumstances that would have created a loose, conservative federation designed to secure their respective positions.[36]

Rubai Ali seems to have relied on his control over the formal apparatus of the state, on a victory that strengthened his titular control over the National Front in late 1975, and on his ties to various tribal and administrative leaders. In contrast, Ismail steadily improved his control over the party apparatus in South Yemen and used his links with the Soviets and Cuba and management of South Yemen's support of Ethiopia to gain increasing control over key state functions and the army.

In October 1977 Ali Nasr Muhammed was replaced as minister of defense by an all-out supporter of Ismail, Lt. Col. Ali Antar. Soviet-bloc advisers at many levels helped Ismail broaden his influence over the administrative structure of the state, and Ismail also seems to have had considerable success in working with al-Hamdi's supporters. These supporters were composed largely of North Yemeni groups that opposed the traditional Zaidi elite and Ghashmi's attempts to strengthen his relations with Rubai Ali. Ismail's strength built up steadily. In late 1977, the USSR evidently added a substantial number of security "advisers" who supported Ismail under the cover of staffing the "air bridge" to Ethiopia that it was staging through Aden. In late 1977 Ismail seems to have provoked new fighting with Saudi Arabia in the Wadiah area, and he used this fighting to distance South Yemen from Saudi Arabia. In February 1978 the USSR also made an offer to Ali Nasr Muhammed, who was then prime minister, to double the size and strength of South Yemeni forces, which evidently brought him into the pro-Ismail, pro-Soviet camp. His support gave the Ismail faction the strength to purge 150 of the top pro–Rubai Ali officers in the army, and a key supporter of Ismail, Minister of State Security Muhammed Said Yafai, publicly attacked Rubai Ali for admitting subversive elements into the army and then launched a series of further purges.

The South Yemeni defense minister, Antar, then went to Moscow. As a result, a delegation led by Admiral Gorshkov came to Aden, and a secret 15-year military and economic cooperation agreement was signed in June 1978. This agreement virtually turned South Yemen into a Soviet satellite. It provided for a Soviet naval base in the Bay of Turbah, fighter base facilities at Khoramskar, intelligence facilities on Socotra, and a Soviet logistic installation at Al Mukalla. In return, South Yemen got immediate delivery of missile patrol boats, about 30 MiG fighters, and a radar defense system.[37]

Events finally came to a head on 24 June 1978. Rubai Ali attempted to plan a last-minute countercoup against Ismail with Ghashmi, but a courier from Rubai Ali to Ghashmi unknowingly delivered a booby-trapped briefcase. The resulting explosion killed both the courier and Ghashmi. Ismail then launched his own coup against Rubai Ali with full Soviet, East German, and Cuban support, and he was able to execute Rubai Ali along with many of his followers two days later.[38] In retrospect, it seems likely that the Saudis, Iraqis, and Rubai Ali failed to fully understand the power that Ismail and his colleague Nasr

Muhammed had obtained and seriously miscalculated Soviet willingness to give them open military and political support in a crisis.

The 1979 Border War with North Yemen and Ismail's Ouster

Ismail's rise to power made South Yemen a virtual client state of the USSR. He, Antar, and Ali Nasr Muhammed ended the effort to achieve union with North Yemen on moderate terms and eliminated any remaining element in the NLF with ties to the Baathist movement, the PRC, and any other faction that was not felt to be solidly pro-Soviet.[39] South Yemen further increased its dependence on Soviet advisers, allowed the USSR to expand its naval facilities in the area, and initiated negotiations that led to the signing of a 20-year friendship treaty with the USSR on 25 October 1979.[40]

As he consolidated power, however, Ismail became steadily more extreme, and he made two major mistakes that eventually resulted in his ouster. The first was his support of yet another set of Marxist reforms of South Yemen's already crippled economy. The reforms not only made South Yemen even more dependent on increasing amounts of Soviet economic aid, they also made it virtually impossible for the country to expand its trade with its neighbors in the Gulf and to get sufficient foreign loans and credits. Ismail increasingly became an embarrassment to both his own party and the USSR by unnecessarily cutting South Yemen off from outside economic aid and support.[41]

Ismail's second mistake was to back the efforts of the NLF-supported front in North Yemen in a poorly timed effort to seize control of the country. While his initiative almost unquestionably had broad support from his colleagues in the South Yemeni government, Ismail seems to have sharply overestimated the capability of the rebel forces he supported to establish a secure foothold in the southern part of North Yemen.[42] When the rebels failed to do more than seize control of a few areas along the border, Ismail then tried to "reinforce failure" by providing air cover and a limited amount of armored support. However, the Saudis reacted by seeking U.S. aid for the North Yemeni forces. Since the U.S. was looking for an opportunity to reassert its power in the Gulf—the rebel attacks on North Yemen came shortly after the fall of the shah—it responded to the Saudi request with comparative haste. The USSR and Ismail's colleagues were suddenly presented with the prospect of a major North Yemeni military buildup, a sharp increase in Saudi influence in North Yemen, and U.S. replacement of the USSR as North Yemen's principal military supplier.

At the same time, Iraq and Syria supported Saudi Arabia in its efforts to pressure South Yemen into ceasing its active support of the rebels. Iraq was still smarting from Rubai Ali's execution and its loss of influence over South Yemen, and it was seeking to improve its relations with Saudi Arabia. As a result, South Yemen faced the threat of total isolation from other Arab states. Since the USSR was then having serious problems in its relations with Syria and Iraq, this threat could not have come at a worse time, and it put further pressure on Ismail to agree to a cease-fire under Arab League auspices. Ismail gave in and agreed to a cease-fire and withdrawal in March 1980.[43]

By this time, Ismail's extremism had become a major embarrassment to his colleagues and the Soviet Union. He also had alienated his defense minister, Ali Antar, who had consolidated his control of the armed forces and used his power to obtain Soviet backing in ousting Ismail. As a result, Ismail's resignation due to "ill health" was announced on 21 April 1980.[44] Ali Antar did not have the power to take control of the country, however, and Ali Nasr Muhammed became the PDRY's new leader. He proved to be a superb manipulator. During the next year he systematically replaced or eliminated most of Ali Antar's supporters in carefully planned stages. He consolidated his control over both the party and the internal security apparatus, and by early 1981 he was able to remove Ali Antar from the Defense Ministry, which Ali Antar had controlled since 1977. He also removed the foreign minister, Saleh Mutea, who had become a lesser rival.[45]

Opinions differ on the extent to which Ali Nasr then moved toward a more moderate position. At first, he seemed as committed to reliance on the Soviet Union as his predecessor. The overall distribution of Soviet-bloc advisers in the Gulf, shown in Table 12.1, reflects a major growth in the Soviet role in South Yemen during Ali Nasr's initial year in power. Depending on the source, the Soviet presence had risen to 1,500–2,500 technicians and military and other advisers by early 1983. Roughly 800–1,500 Cubans held jobs ranging from working in hospitals to training the Popular Militia, and roughly 325 East German advisers dominated the state security apparatus.[46]

Soviet aid helped South Yemen sustain imports six times its exports in the early 1980s, and Soviet-bloc advisers dominated South Yemen's economic development and infrastructure. A typical Soviet aid project—a small fish-canning plant—had 15 Soviet staff out of a total staff of 65. Soviet oil exploration teams ran South Yemen's oil effort. The USSR helped South Yemen build strategic roads to its border areas, ran its ports, modernized the main air base near Aden, and helped build a new major operating base in the eastern Hadramaut near Oman. According to some reports, the PDRY also reached a security agreement with both the USSR and Ethiopia in June 1980 that gave the Soviet Navy responsibility for helping both countries patrol local waters. This agreement may have put the base on Socotra under joint PDRY-Soviet command and given the USSR the right to build submarine pens.[47]

Soviet development aid did not, however, prove particularly successful. The Soviet light industrial projects were inefficient, and Soviet promises of new power and desalinization plants did not materialize. The USSR provided loans rather than grants and tied these to the purchase of inefficient Soviet-bloc plants and machinery. As a result, Ali Nasr inherited an economy in desperate straits. South Yemen reached the point of importing 75% of its cereals, and it cultivated only 0.2%, or 76,000 hectares, of its 330,000 square kilometers of territory. The land reforms of 1968 and 1970 had produced a process of collectivization, state-controlled mechanization, and water development that had severely limited the PDRY's agricultural growth. Although the government invested roughly 25% of its capital in agriculture (it will invest 22% of the $274 million in its 1981–1985 development plan), it had little more to show by way of results in 1981 than most states that followed the Soviet model.[48] Every farm over 16 hectares had come under state control, and the state farms and collectives failed to provide suitable pay incentives, pricing, fertilizer, and machinery. Further, although deep groundwater was found in the Hadramaut, it was not developed, and the PDRY's water development became strangled by a large party and government bureaucracy.

As a result, Ali Nasr tilted back toward trade with the West. South Yemen's trade with the OECD countries rose by about 50% annually after 1979, from a base of $370 million, and Japan, Britain, Australia, and France became South Yemen's largest trading partners. The PRC and USSR dropped in rank to sixth and seventh. Western firms took over such projects as the construction of hotels, new power plants, a civilian airport, and office buildings and feasibility studies. Even some hard-liners in the Yemeni socialist party were struck by the fact the Soviet oil-exploration effort in the Sanaw area had to be paid for as development aid and produced nothing other than border clashes with Oman, whereas an Italian concession found oil near Al Mukalla for nothing.[49]

South Yemen also tilted slightly toward the West at the diplomatic and military levels, although the signals were conflicting. Ali Nasr started yet another series of unification talks with North Yemen, although he simultaneously revitalized South Yemen's backing of the efforts of the rebels in the National Democratic Front (NDF) to seize power in North Yemen. He conducted a complex cycle of "carrot and stick" tactics in which South Yemen and the USSR tried to block North Yemen from accepting arms and aid from the U.S. and Saudi Arabia by threatening its internal security on the one hand and by offering unification and Soviet arms on the other. These tactics initially proved effective, for several reasons. The National Democratic Front, or National Front, had a core of about 700 Marxist-Leninists, most of whom had direct links to South Yemen. The PDRY was able to use this cadre, its own forces, and tribes in the border area to put pressure on North Yemen at will. Yet it could call new unity talks with equal speed. In fact, the PDRY was able to simultaneously negotiate for unification and support the NDF in raids on North Yemen.[50]

South Yemen was able to do this through the end of 1981 because North Yemen was suffering serious internal difficulties and experiencing

TABLE 12.1 CIA and Israeli Estimates of Soviet-Bloc Military Presence in the Gulf and Middle East

	Soviet-Bloc Arms Transfers ($ millions)			Soviet-Bloc Military Technicians in Country	
	1965–74[b]	1974–78[b]	1976–80[b]	1976[c]	1981[d]
Gulf					
Bahrain	–	–	–	–	–
Iran	589	310	625	120	–
Iraq	1,343	3,600	5,000	1,000	1,065
Kuwait	–	50	50	–	5
Oman	–	–	–	–	–
Qatar	–	–	–	–	–
Saudi Arabia	–	–	–	–	–
UAE	–	–	–	–	–
North Yemen	27	50	625	?	130
South Yemen	114	370	775	?	2,100[e]
Subtotal	2,073	4,380	7,075	1,120	3,300
Middle East					
Egypt	2,465	430	20	–	–
Israel	–	–	–	–	–
Jordan	–	–	–	–	–
Lebanon	4	–	–	–	–
Syria	1,758	2,700	5,400	2,500	2,480
Subtotal	4,227	3,130	5,420	2,500	2,480
Horn of Africa					
Ethiopia	–	1,300	1,900	–	14,250[g]
Somalia	134	300	150	1,100	–
Subtotal	134	1,600	2,050	1,100	14,250
Related Areas					
Afghanistan	309	330	450	350	4,000[h]
Libya	425	3,400	5,500	800	1,820[i]
Subtotal	734	3,730	5,950	1,150	5,820
Total	7,168	12,840	20,495	5,870	25,850

[a] IDF, "National Security Issues," August 1982, p. 21. Israeli estimates track closely with Egyptian estimates issued by Defense Minister Lt. Gen. Ghazala, *Aviation Week*, 14 December 1981.

[b] ACDA, *World Military Expenditures and Arms Transfers*, various years.

[c] CIA ER-77-10296, 1977.

[d] CIA ER-80-1031U, 1980, includes USSR, Eastern Europe, and Cuba; Department of Defense, *Annual Report*, FY1983, Annex A, p. 84.

[e] 1,100 Soviet and East European, 1,000 Cuban.

[f] 1,000 tanks, 600 artillery pieces, 150 APCs in emergency stores.

TABLE 12.1 (continued)

Military Trained in Soviet Bloc		Total Soviet, East European, and Cuban Military Presence in 1982[a]	
1955-76[d]	1976-79[d]	Soviet and East European	Cuba
—	—	—	—
325	?	?	?
3,600	1,150	1,200	0-200
—	—	—	—
—	—	—	—
—	—	—	—
—	—	—	—
—	—	—	—
1,100	260	150	—
800	325	550	1,000
5,825	1,735	1,900	1,000
6,250	—	—	—
—	—	—	—
—	—	—	—
—	—	—	—
4,150	1,305	2,580[f]	—
10,400	1,305	2,580	—
—	1,790	1,400	6,500
2,500	80	—	—
2,500	1,870	1,400	6,500
3,975	35	85,000	—
1,125	370	1,750[j]	200
5,100	405	86,750	200
23,825	5,315	92,630	7,700

[g]11,250 Soviet and East European, 13,000 Cuban.

[h]Excludes 50-85,000 Soviet troops.

[i] No estimate of Cubans.

[j] 1,500 tanks, 1,000 artillery pieces, 500 APCs, and 100 combat aircraft in emergency stores.

Note: The estimates shown in this table are illustrative. The author's estimates are used in the text. CIA, Israeli, and Egyptian estimates show many inconsistencies over time, and no reliable source exists.

growing dissatisfaction with the scale of U.S. and Saudi aid. President Ghashmi's successor in North Yemen, Major Abdullah Saleh, was seeking both to reduce his dependence on the Saudis and to secure his position. Ali Nasr was able to exploit this weakness, while the USSR won back much of its influence by offering both North and South Yemen arms.[51]

Ali Nasr was slower to change South Yemen's other alignments. He initially backed Libya in its efforts to transform the Steadfastness Front—which Algeria, Ethiopia, Libya, the PDRY, and Syria had established in 1977 to resist any compromise on an Arab-Israeli peace—into a body that could counter conservative and moderate bodies like the Gulf Cooperation Council.[52] Ali Nasr's actions were motivated partly by the promise of some $400 million in Libyan aid, but they also reflected a personal commitment to radical politics.[53] During 1982, however, South Yemen's economic problems became even more severe, and the PDRY experienced disastrous floods that caused a major agricultural crisis. Libya also began to experience a cash squeeze because of the cut in its oil revenues, and the USSR refused to provide a major increase in grant aid. Either these events forced Ali Nasr to become more moderate or he took advantage of them to shift the PDRY toward the rest of the Arab World.

Ali Nasr responded by expanding his contacts with both the West and Oman and reduced the PDRY's military support of the NDF. The PDRY restored full diplomatic relations with Britain, France, Denmark, West Germany, Italy, Belgium, and Switzerland. It ignored North Yemen's rejection of the unification effort and quietly restored relations with most of the conservative Gulf states. It then negotiated the equivalent of a peace treaty with Oman. This agreement was reached with the mediation of Kuwait and the UAE. It was signed in Kuwait on 27 October 1982 and was formally announced on 15 November 1982. It provided for the exchange of ambassadors, noninterference in internal affairs, negotiations on border disputes, and negotiations on the future status of facilities for foreign powers. Ironically, the Omani foreign minister who signed the agreement, Youssef al-Alawi, had once been a leader of the Dhofar rebels. Although the foreign minister of both nations immediately declared it would not affect their respective ties with the USSR and U.S., the PDRY did put an immediate halt to any overt activity by the PFLO, and its radio attacks on Oman from stations based in the PDRY halted on 6 November after nine years of daily broadcasts.[54]

Thus the agreement left South Yemen in a state of comparative peace with its neighbors for the first time in its national existence. It was far from clear, however, that it was more than a temporary expedient. The agreement with Oman was "a close run thing." It occurred as the result of Saudi promises of major amounts of aid during a visit by Prince Naif, the interior minister, on 6 June 1982. The timing of Prince Naif's visit was particularly striking because Aden had announced on 3 June that it was pulling out of the talks scheduled with Oman in Kuwait and because an Iranian representative visited Aden on 4 June as part of the regular meetings Iran was holding with members of the Steadfastness Front. While it is impossible to do more than speculate, this timing implied that Saudi Arabia achieved peace by outbidding the competition, an interpretation that is confirmed by the timing of transfers of funds and aid from Abu Dhabi and Kuwait.[55]

North Yemen

Many of the recent developments in North Yemen have already been discussed in tracing South Yemen's relations with its neighbors in the Gulf. However, North Yemen's complex interactions with Saudi Arabia, South Yemen, and its other neighbors have particular importance because they provide a case study of the revolutionary change, civil war, and outside military interference that could envelop each of the Gulf countries under traditional rule.

North Yemen is also important because of its comparatively large population. Although it is only 194,000 square kilometers in size, or about 10% of the total territory of the Arabian Peninsula, it has almost one-third of its total population. It now has at least 5.3 million people, including about 1.5 million Yemenis working abroad. These figures compare with 4–6 million native Saudis, and a population of 1.9 million in South Yemen.[56] Although the population growth rate in both Yemens is only 2.1–2.4%, this figure is misleading. Improved hygiene practices and medical services have gradually reduced the infant death rate in North Yemen from something like two out of three to one in five, while the amount of arable land the number of economic opportunities have declined. As a result, a "population explosion" has developed that has made North Yemen Saudi Arabia's leading source of foreign labor. It also has increasingly forced North Yemen to rely on emigration to other Gulf nations as a safety valve and on cash transfers from expatriate workers for its national income. This need for emigration has been accelerated by the impact of the various civil and tribal wars in the area, by the disruption of farming in North Yemen's fertile highlands, and by a steady conversion of regular agriculture to the growing of *qat*, a mild narcotic of the region.

While North Yemen's recent history of internal conflict and tension with its neighbors has its tragi-comic aspects, the fact remains that North Yemen represents a major potential threat to the stability of Saudi Arabia and the UAE and that a successful Marxist takeover in North Yemen, an expansion of the kind of Soviet influence that now dominates South Yemen, or union between North and South Yemen under a leader like Ismail would radically shift the balance of power in the area.

The Origins of the Yemeni Civil War and North Yemen's Conflicts with South Yemen and Saudi Arabia

Although the monsoon rains gave North Yemen something like 50% of the Arabian Peninsula's fertile land, and its highlands normally receive 16 to 32 inches of rain a year, it has virtually no major economic resources. Unlike most Gulf states, it has had no major economic links to the West, few trade links to the Arab world, and virtually no strategic importance in terms of trade routes.[57] Thus North Yemen remained isolated from the rest of the world until the mid-1950s. It was cheaper to leave the area alone than to take up the burden of governing it.

North Yemen's isolation was encouraged by the fact that it was ruled by an imam of the Shi'ite sect and by a quasi-religious Shi'ite oligarchy that gave power to a limited number of members of its Zaidi tribes, called Sayyids, who claimed descent from the Prophet. This system created an elite of about 300,000 that dominated the country until the late 1950s. Its rule depended upon recognition of its legitimacy within the Zaidi tribe and on its political control of the largely Sunni Shaafi tribes in southern and eastern Yemen, who represented 60–70% of the population. Since the Shaafis dominated trade throughout North Yemen, and most of its limited manufacturing, they tended to be better educated and more cosmopolitan, which led the Zaidi imam to try to reduce any foreign contacts that would increase the chances of a Shaafi rebellion or weaken Sayyid control over the Zaidi tribes.

Imam Yahya pursued this policy from 1918, when he expelled a small Turkish garrison and seized control of the country, to his assassination in 1948.[58] While he had ambitions to restore the control the Zaidi had once exerted over the protectorates and southeast Arabia before the appearance of the British and the rise of the Wahabi in Saudi Arabia, the British easily checked his ambitions in the Aden protectorates. When he challenged the Saudis in the Asir highlands in the 1920s and early 1930s, the resulting war with Ibn Saud's forces led to the crushing defeat of Yahya's forces. The subsequent peace agreement at Taiz in March 1934 left the imam's territory more or less intact, but together with Yahya's lack of any real interest in the outside world, it established a pattern of Saudi dominance over North Yemen that forced North Yemen's isolation.[59]

The British remained indifferent as long as North Yemen did not bother the Aden protectorates, and there were no other pressures on North Yemen to end its isolation. The West's indifference was reinforced by the Depression and World War II, and North Yemen remained one of the most backward countries in the world.

Between the mid-1930s and late 1940s, however, some Zaidi and Shaafi officers, merchants, and civil servants received Western and Levantine educations. The rise of this small educated elite laid the groundwork for an almost inevitable conflict between the imam and the forces for modernization. The imam contributed to these pressures by keeping most of the country's limited revenues from the coffee trade in his personal coffers and by ruling by terror. Like Sultan Said in Oman, the imam made so few concessions to the pressures for modernization and to the need to buy the loyalty of the traditional tribal leaders that he almost ensured a revolt.[60] In 1946 and 1947, Yahya weakened significantly from age, and in February 1948 his closest adviser, Abdullah al-Wazir, led a coup in which he was assassinated.[61] This coup misfired, however, when the imam's 56-year-old son, Crown Prince Ahmad, escaped and rallied the Zaidi tribes. Ahmad succeeded in restoring control of the country, executed al-Wazir and his supporters, and reorganized the state around an even more rigorous form of personal rule.

Ahmad does seem to have been slightly more interested in modernization than his father. Unfortunately, he proved equally unwilling to share his wealth and even more willing to rule by terror. He often flew into murderous rages. On several occasions this led him to execute leading tribal, court, and government officials on the spot, and he often imprisoned others without cause. Such actions inevitably led to further conflicts between the imam and the reform elements.[62]

Ahmad also had his father's ambitions to restore Zaidi control over the protectorates. Between 1948 and 1951, he began to seek control over the tribes in the various protectorates and funded separatist movements in Aden. This policy brought him into conflict with Britain, which had begun to try to modernize the protectorates and to ready them for self-rule. The British presence in the protectorates surrounding Aden rose from 2 agents shortly before World War II to some 3,000 administrators by the early 1950s, and Ahmad responded by provoking tribal conflicts and raids. The British attempted to mediate in 1951, but although Ahmad signed a treaty with Britain, he had no real intention of adhering to it. He stepped up arms shipments and payments, sponsored increasingly bloody clashes between rival tribal elements, and attempted to get several South Yemeni sheikhs and sultan's to break with the British. He also attempted to capitalize on the rise of the Arab nationalism and the Third World. In July and October 1954 Ahmad protested British actions to the UN. In December he went further and attempted to seize a key strong point in South Yemen called Fort Mukeiras. Ahmad, however, had no more military luck than his father. The RAF and the British-led Aden Protectorate Force responded immediately and decisively defeated the imam's forces.[63]

By 1955, the British and most of the traditional leaders in the Aden protectorates had become hostile to the imam, and Ahmad's mixture of ultraconservatism and failure to obtain control over the protectorates made him seem weak to many of the army and government officials around him. As a result, his brother, Saifal Islam Abd Allah, and various Army leaders tried a coup. The attempt failed when Ahmad escaped to his personal fortress, which held all of the army's fuel and ammunition. His son al-Badr also escaped to rally the northern tribes, which led to a brief civil war during March and April 1955. Al-Badr succeeded in defeating the rebels. He then proceeded to systematically exterminate the Abd Allah faction.[64]

Given Ahmad's failing health and the desire of the Zaidi tribal leaders for a stronger government, al-Badr emerged from this victory as the effective head of government. He also initially gained Ahmad's trust and strong support. These changes did more than give North Yemen a younger leader. Al-Badr had been educated in Egypt at a time when Nasser was coming to power, and he had come under considerable Arab nationalist and Marxist influence.[65] His resentment of Britain and the West over the creation of the South Arabian Federation was reinforced by the tensions that were driving Britain and Egypt toward the Suez crisis. Further, al-Badr recognized that some kind of reform was necessary to ensure the regime's survival and that he needed military assistance to cope with the buildup of the protectorates' military forces.[66]

As a result, al-Badr took several important steps. He opened up the old imam's personal coffers and began the first major government expenditures on modernization in North Yemen's history. He reorganized the country's administration into the districts shown in Map 12.4. He granted oil concessions to a U.S. company to counter British influence, and he sought a source of aid that would make him independent of both British and Saudi policy. He thus turned to Egypt and the USSR, beginning a pattern of balancing alignment with the USSR against alignment with Saudi Arabia that North Yemen's leaders have tended to follow ever since.[67]

North Yemen's new ties to the USSR gave it enough military aid for Ahmad and al-Badr to attempt to capitalize on the British reversal in Suez and on the general unrest in Aden caused by the closing of the Suez Canal. As a result, they prepared for another attack on the protectorates. By early 1957, the imam had acquired about 30 medium tanks, 30 combat aircraft, and extensive stocks of Soviet small arms. He then transferred his older light weapons to tribes in the protectorates, taking one hostage for every 10 rifles. While he avoided direct military confrontation with the British, the tribal forces started a series of raids that led to some 50 military incidents in the first year and to a continuing low-level border war.[68]

Ahmad could not, however, achieve any serious military success without outside support in training, maintaining, and operating his forces, and this realization seems to have helped al-Badr to persuade him to turn to Nasser as well as the USSR as a source of military assistance and arms. Ahmad and al-Badr established steadily closer relations in Egypt. When Egypt announced its federation with Syria in February 1958, North Yemen effusively supported it and then applied to join them in an alliance that became known as the United Arab States (UAS). This application was granted on 8 March 1958.

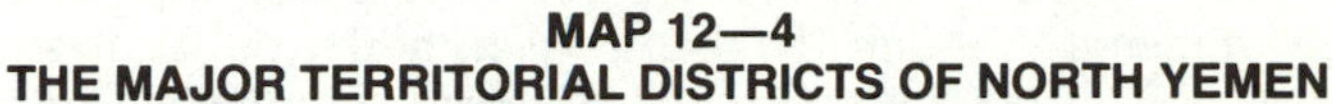

MAP 12—4
THE MAJOR TERRITORIAL DISTRICTS OF NORTH YEMEN

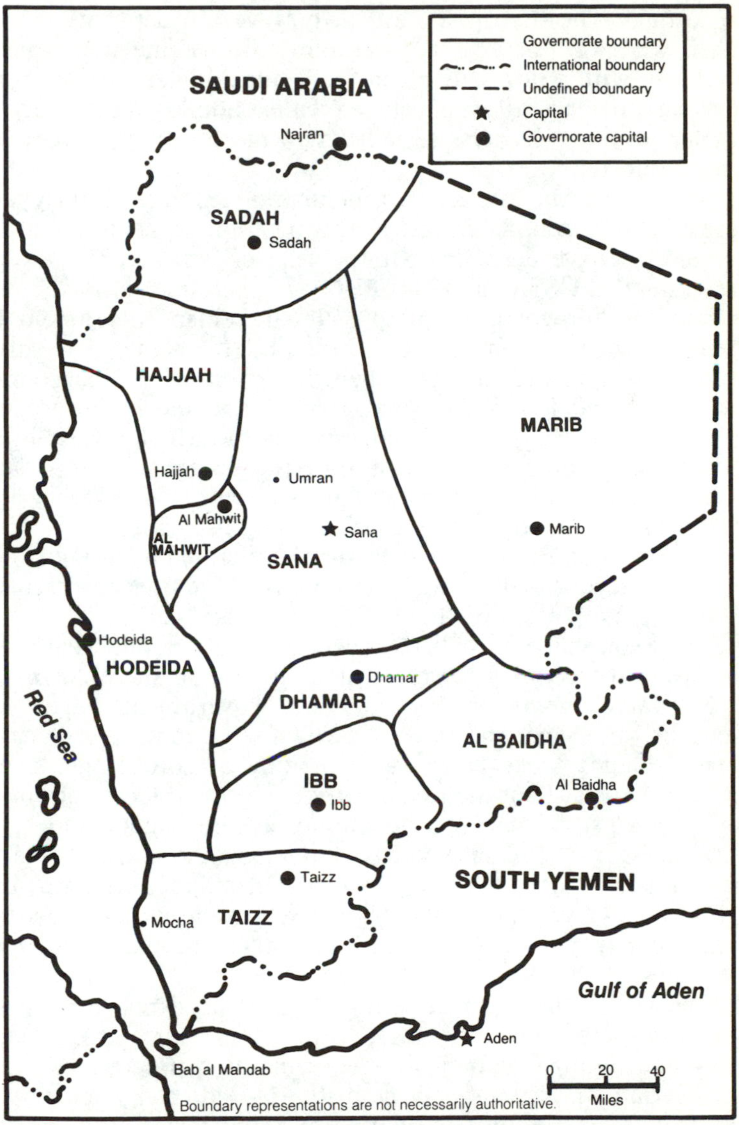

DA Pamphlet 550-182, *Area Handbook for the Yemens,* Washington, 1977, p. 162, and DA Pamphlet 550-16, *Middle East: The Strategic Hub,* Washington, May, 1973, pp. 404-405.

This "Act of Union" gave Ahmad the backing of the pro-Nasserite radical movements in Aden. It also gave him the political strength to persuade several of the key sultans in the protectorates to support him, which created the first real risk that some of the protectorates might fall to Ahmad. The British succeeded, however, in deposing the sultan of Lahej, who was the key to the imam's immediate ambitions, and replaced him with a pro-British cousin. While Ahmad did have a major influence in blocking British efforts to create a South Arabian Federation based on traditional leaders, he failed to win any permanent influence over the protectorates.[69]

By late 1958, Ahmad had largely abandoned his military efforts. However, he then found himself in the position of being an ultraconservative religious leader with complex ties to Egypt, radical movements in the Gulf, the USSR, and the PRC. At the time, al-Badr's ties to Egypt and the "progressives" in the North Yemen government began to create growing tension between him and his father. The division between them worsened in 1959, when the failure of the monsoon rains caused widespread famine in North Yemen and the imam accepted a U.S. offer of aid. He accompanied this tilt toward the West by quiet contacts with Saudi Arabia, which split the government into factions supporting father and son, various Pan-Arab and radical factions, and tribal factions centered on the Zaidi and Shaafi tribes. This division between Ahmad and al-Badr was further accelerated as al-Badr brought more Yemenis educated outside the country into the government, as well as some supporters of the FLOSY and the NLF.

The situation came to a head when Ahmad's failing health forced him to leave the country for medical treatment in the U.S. in March 1960. Several elements in the army and government started minor uprisings in Taiz, Sana, and Hodeida, which seem to have been designed to force al-Badr to take power and institute a more progressive government.[70] While al-Badr did execute several of the leaders and imprison others, Ahmad still regarded his conduct as too lenient and came to feel that al-Badr might have tacitly supported the coup. Ahmad also became violently angry with Nasser when he stopped in Cairo in July on his way back from Egypt and Nasser refused to give him troops for internal security purposes and another attack on the Aden and the protectorates.

The result was that Ahmad split with al-Badr, expelled most of his Egyptian advisers—including those running the air force and police schools—and eliminated many of the remaining progressive elements in the government. He canceled the bribes al-Badr had given to the key Hashid tribe after the uprisings and suppressed them by force. He also expelled the former commander of the military forces in Lahej, who had defected to North Yemen at the height of Ahmad's efforts to seize control over part of the federation. These moves meant that the pro-Egyptian factions in North Yemen could no longer support such groups in South Yemen. They deprived the FLOSY of much of its military support from Nasser and were one of the factors that ultimately contributed to the NLF's victory over the FLOSY. These measures further divided an already unstable country. Minor uprisings and unrest followed throughout the rest of 1960, and in November there was another series of purges, which Ahmad rather erratically followed with an amnesty. This helped lead to an assassination attempt on Ahmad in March 1961, in which four of Ahmad's body guards were killed and he was severely wounded. He was forced to turn back to al-Badr, but he also attempted to reassert his control over the country through a new series of executions and imprisonments.

It became apparent in March 1961 that Nasser had at least tacitly supported the assassination attempt and was still actively encouraging Ahmad's overthrow, which led Ahmad to begin an active campaign against Nasser. When Syria broke with Egypt in September 1961, Ahmad concluded that Nasser would be critically weakened. He ended North Yemen's membership in the UAS by the unusual expedient of reading an insulting poem over Sana radio—which proved to be Ahmad's "last hurrah." In October his health became so poor that he was forced to formally name al-Badr as his successor.[71] By then, however, Nasser was no longer willing to rely on al-Badr or to support the imamate. He called a conference of the tribal and progressive leaders who were hostile to the imam in December and strongly encouraged them to overthrow the new imam. This step created a reasonably strong coalition, but it excluded the Zaidi tribes and many moderates. As a result, Nasser's efforts divided the country and the army, with many officers supporting the Nasserite movement and most of the troops supporting conservative Zaidi tribal leaders to whom they owed primary allegiance.

The situation steadily deteriorated, and when Imam Ahmad finally died on 18 September 1962, a new group of officers called the "Free Yemeni" movement attempted a coup. On 26 September, Colonel Abdullah al-Sallal, the commander of the Royal Guard, surrounded and shelled al-Badr's palace with a force of six tanks. He then announced al-Badr's death, and a new "Republican" government. The circumstances behind this coup were unique even for North Yemen. Ahmad had kept al-Sallal chained to a wall for several years, and al-Badr had pardoned him in an effort to gain the support of the Nasserite faction.[72] Once again, however, a coup by the North Yemeni Army misfired because its key target escaped. In fact, not only did al-Badr escape but so did most of his family. Since al-Badr was now imam, and he had broken with Nasser, the conservative Zaidi-dominated tribes rallied around him. Saudi Arabia and Jordan pledged him military support. The groundwork was laid for civil war.

The USSR naturally supported al-Sallal as the conflict developed, but the West was divided. The U.S. initially saw al-Sallal's coup as an opportunity to wean North Yemen from the Soviet bloc, and it promptly supported UN recognition of his regime in December 1962. In contrast, the British strongly opposed al-Sallal because of his ties to Nasser, his regime's support of the FLOSY in South Yemen, and his links with the PFLOAG in Oman. The French joined Britain in opposing any Nasserite-backed government. The U.S. was thus placed in a somewhat ambiguous position, but still both sides received major foreign support.[73]

The Yemeni Civil War

The eight years of civil war that followed made North Yemen a "killing ground," the site of a continuing competition between King Faisal of Saudi Arabia and President Nasser of Egypt, and the scene of a similar competition between the USSR and the U.S., Britain, and France. It also resulted in one of the bloodiest wars in modern Arab history. While North Yemen's isolation from the West meant that the civil war got comparatively little attention in the U.S. press, the Yemeni civil war produced well over 60,000 casualties and at least 20,000–30,000 combat deaths—more fatalities than the total of Arab deaths in the first five Arab-Israeli wars and the Dhofar and western tribal civil wars in Aden.

The conflict involved major forces from the outset. It was marked as well by the use of poison gas, the routine execution of prisoners of war, and the systematic torture and murder of civilians. Yet most of this bloodshed took place in support of political labels that were little more than illusory. The "Royalists" who rallied around al-Badr were predominantly conservative, but much of al-Badr's immediate entourage still had ties to Arab radical movements and had supported him in his tilt toward the USSR. Although al-Sallal's Revolutionary Council was dependent from the start on Egyptian support for its survival, the "Republicans" were composed of a wide mixture of opponents to al-Badr and traditional Zaidi rule. Many were "conservative" by any normal standard.

It is clear that the Egyptians seriously miscalculated both al-Sallal's popular support and his ability to eventually develop an army. Thus Egypt committed military forces to Yemen on the basis of a false picture of the extent of the commitment that would be required. Anwar Sadat, who was one of the key Egyptian officials who visited North Yemen after al-Sallal's takeover and who shared responsibility for Nasser's miscalculation, later referred to North Yemen as "Egypt's Vietnam."

The course of the civil war favored the Royalists during the first few months, as a combination of the Zaidi tribes, Saudi and Jordanian support, and a limited number of British, Belgian, and French mercenaries gave the Royalists control over the north and allowed them to move toward Sana. Nasser quickly sent in Egyptian troops and combat aircraft, however, and he increased his strength to 36,000 men by April 1963. The Egyptians then began a combination of armored, artillery, and air attacks on the Royalist forces and air and gas attacks on Royalist-

MAP 12—5
MAJOR COMBAT AREAS IN THE NORTH YEMENI CIVIL WAR

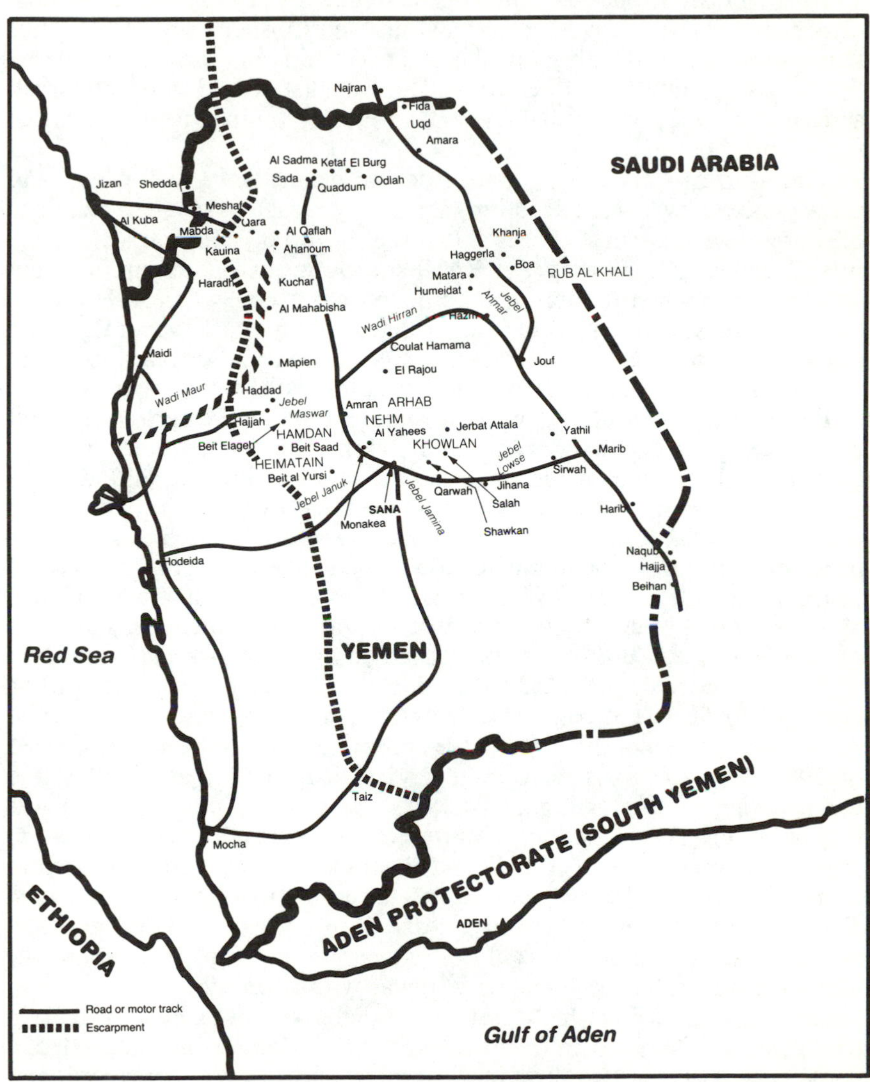

Adapted from Otto von Pivka, *Armies of the Middle East*, Mayflower, 1979, p. 69; U.S. Department of the Army, *Middle East: The Strategic Hub*, DA Pamphlet 550-16, Washington, May 1973; and CIA 501283 7-73.

held villages. This campaign might have proved decisive, but the Egyptian troops lacked experience in mountain or guerrilla warfare, and Nasser's first offensive had failed by July with very high casualties on both sides.[74] Nasser then increased his forces to 40,000 men, but a pattern of conflict developed that foreshadowed the U.S. experience in Vietnam and the Soviet experience in Afghanistan. Nasser's troops lost most minor encounters with the guerrillas but won most major battles. Thus the Republicans had little control over hostile territory, and they suffered from constant attrition. In contrast, the Royalists could win only small actions, and they were unable to oust the Egyptians from control of their strong points.

This kind of warfare gave both sides an incentive to seek peace, and these pressures were catalyzed into action when each side suffered serious military reversals. In October 1964 the Egyptian commanders badly miscalculated and allowed the Royalists to ambush a major Egyptian armored force when it attempted an offensive in the northeast. However, the Royalists suffered a similar major defeat in an attack on an Egyptian strong point during the summer. As a result, Saudi Arabia and Egypt were ready to push their respective clients toward the conference table.[75]

Peace talks began in Sudan in November 1964, and a serious attempt was made to reach a cease-fire. Unfortunately, the complex mix of factions on both sides made any peace agreement difficult, and al-Sallal and al-Badr came into irreconcilable conflict over the future of the imamate. The Revolutionary Council faction refused to accept any peace based on continuing the imamate, and al-Badr's faction refused to accept peace on any other terms. While another peace effort was made in April 1965 by Ahmad, the premier of the Revolutionary Council, this attempt quickly collapsed. Both sides then tried to arm for a decisive military victory.[76] Nasser increased the Egyptian troop strength to some 60,000, and the Royalists got bazookas, light artillery, and heavy mortars.[77]

Another set of bloody major battles followed in the spring and summer of 1965. The Royalists were largely victorious, and these battles tied down a significant portion of Nasser's forces at a time when he was preparing for confrontation with Israel. As a result, Nasser flew to Jiddah in August 1965 in an effort to trade Egypt's withdrawal from Yemen for Faisal's support of Egypt in its confrontation with Israel. The two leaders then agreed on a cease-fire that was intended to result in a Royalist-Republican coalition government, a plebiscite on the imamate, and total Egyptian withdrawal within one year.

As a sign of good faith, Nasser sent al-Sallal on an extended vacation to Egypt in October and ensured that the Republicans attended a conference with the Royalists in November and made a serious attempt to implement the Jiddah accords. The Royalists and Republicans proved as unable to agree in 1965, however, as they had in 1964. The Royalists and the Saudis also may have felt that they had the strength to force Egypt to withdraw militarily, and King Faisal had no real desire to increase Nasser's power and freedom of action. King Faisal quietly concluded a major arms deal with the UK and the U.S., and he began to negotiate with the shah to create a conference of conservative Islamic leaders that would have deliberately excluded Nasser from a major role.[78]

Once Faisal's actions became known to Nasser, he halted the Egyptian withdrawal—which had reduced Egyptian strength from a peak of 70,000 in mid-1965 to 20,000 men—and built his forces back to about 40,000. He also withdrew his forces to a "triangle" of relatively secure pro-Republican tribal areas between Taiz, Sana, and Hodeida. Nasser was encouraged in these actions by Britain's February 1966 announcement that it would withdraw from southern Arabia by 1968. Nasser seems to have estimated that Egypt could ensure a FLOSY victory and dominate South Yemen and that he could engage the Royalists in a two-front war. As Egypt's confrontation with Saudi Arabia accelerated, Nasser also started to carry out demonstrative air strikes against the Royalist sanctuaries in Najran and Jizan in the Asir region of Saudi Arabia. Nasser launched the first such air strikes against Saudi Arabia in October 1966, and he organized his forces for yet another spring and summer offensive against the Royalists in 1967.[79] At the same time, he persuaded the Soviets to expand their military aid to the Republicans and to send in a greatly expanded team of military advisers. Finally, the Egyptians and Soviets provided al-Sallal with large funds to buy the loyalty of Royalist tribes and leaders.

This Egyptian effort came to a brutal end a few months later. Israel's shattering defeat of Egypt in June 1967, and Nasser's desperate need for funds to buy arms and sustain Egypt's economic subsidies, forced him to reconcile with Faisal. As a result, Nasser met with Faisal in Khartoum from 29 August to 1 September 1967. The Khartoum Conference produced an agreement that Egypt would withdraw immediately from North Yemen and that Saudi Arabia would halt its aid to the Royalists. In practice, however, the agreement was one-sided, with Egypt agreeing to withdraw from North Yemen, and it meant the end of the Egyptian support to both the Revolutionary Council and FLOSY.[80]

If this agreement had come earlier, al-Badr would unquestionably have won the civil war by late 1967. However, the war had dragged on so long that the Revolutionary Council forces had finally begun to acquire a considerable military capability. These forces were also able to obtain Algerian, Syrian, and Soviet support in continuing the conflict and quickly acted to broaden their internal support. The more moderate members of the Revolutionary Council ousted al-Sallal on 4 November, and welcomed back many of the other moderates whom he and Nasser had exiled or imprisoned. They obtained the support of some 300,000 FLOSY and other South Yemeni exiles who had fled South Yemen after the National Liberation Front won the battle for control of the country in November 1967. The Republicans also initiated a new series of contacts with moderates on the Royalist side, many of whom had no great love for al-Badr, Saudi Arabia, the imamate, or traditional Zaidi rule.[81]

The Royalists responded by launching an all-out attack on the Republican positions in December 1967. They besieged Sana, cut many key roads, captured Amran, and seemed postured to take control of the country. They moved far too slowly in attacking Sana, however, and operations were slowed by their observance of Ramadan, which gave the Revolutionary Council time to mass the new firepower it had been provided by the USSR and to obtain some 600 troops from South Yemen. As a result the Royalist forces were unable to take Sana by frontal assault, and while they besieged the capital, they became divided over who would govern once they won.

Al-Badr either overestimated the importance of the traditional Zaidi leaders or had become so dependent on them that he did not take the proper steps to secure the loyalty of the moderates and the key officers running his army.[82] By February, the Republicans were able to take advantage of the growing divisions within the Royalist ranks. They launched a complex campaign that mixed military action, assassination, and bribery. By May, the Republicans had managed not only to break out of the Royalist encirclement but also to isolate al-Badr politically so that he had to give up the imamate and designate a relative, Muhammad ibn Husayn, as his successor.[83]

The reorganization of the Republicans, under a military government headed by Lt. Gen. Hassan al-Amri, gave the Revolutionary Council more effective military leadership. It also allowed them to steadily co-opt the moderates in the Royalist forces. While this alienated the more extreme leftists, it gave the Republicans a still broader political base. In contrast, in August 1968 the Royalist forces split completely over who would govern a country they were rapidly losing, and the Republicans defeated the last Royalist offensive in September.

On 18 September Gen. al-Amri established a joint Revolutionary Council, which included a wide range of moderate factions, with seven Shaafi and nine Zaidi members. On 10 October he persuaded the commander of the Royalist forces, Gen. Qisim Munassar, to defect. From this point on, the reorganized Revolutionary Council systematically defeated the Royalist forces in a series of minor actions and simultaneously co-opted the Zaidi tribes in the liberated areas. Further, once the defeat of the Royalists became certain, the Saudis reduced their support. King Faisal ended all support to the Royalists in March 1969, and the Republicans were so strong by February 1970 that al-Amri was able to step down, and the leadership of the Revolutionary Council was returned to civilian control under Mohsin al-Aini.

The Republican victory became official in March 1970, when al-Aini went to the Islamic Foreign Ministers Conference in Jiddah. His visit led to talks between the Republicans and Royalists that resulted in a further reorganization of the Revolutionary Council in May. A coalition government was then formed with minority Royalist representation. The Royalists got 2 places on the Council, 4 ministerial portfolios, and 12 seats in the National Assembly. In return, it was agreed that the members of the imam's family would remain in exile. In July the Republican government received recognition from Saudi Arabia, the UK, France, and Iran.[84] This Saudi recognition included the formation of a Yemeni-Saudi Coordinating Committee, chaired by the Saudi defense minister, Prince Sultan bin Abd al-Aziz, which channeled Saudi economic and military funds to the new government. It still acts as a primary mechanism for exerting Saudi influence over North Yemen.

Peace came, however, only after the civil war had shattered North Yemen for a generation. Its end result was the devastation of the country, a regime so divided that it could not effectively govern, economic dependence on Saudi aid and military dependence on the USSR, and the loss of a decade in any serious efforts to modernize the nation's economy. While the sheer magnitude of the North Yemeni civil war tended to discourage further civil warfare, its heritage virtually assured that the awkward coalition of Royalists and Republicans would dissolve in another series of struggles for power.

The Border War with South Yemen and Its Aftermath

During the initial period after the civil war, President Abdul Rahman Iriani was able to keep these pressures from turning into open conflict and to juggle North Yemen's factions so that they did not come into open conflict. These factions were split into five main groups: the tribal chiefs, the conservative Muslim clergy, the moderate Republicans, the "progressives," and extreme leftist factions with ties to South Yemen. The latter represented a confusing mixture of former Nasserites, communists, Baathists, supporters of FLOSY, supporters of South Yemen's NLF, and other diverse political elements. The tribal faction was equally divided between major and minor tribes and between Zaidi and Shaafi; and the clergy were divided into Shi'ite and Sunni and into regular clergy and the Sayyidi who claimed descent from the Prophet. The end result was conflict over every action of the central government, and each faction sought outside support.[85]

Iriani was able to survive the first coup attempt by an Iraqi-backed Baathist group, and he generally turned a blind eye to Saudi efforts to buy the loyalty of the northern tribes. However, he proved unable to win a consensus on how to deal with North Yemen's growing economic problems, transform the Presidential Council, which had replaced the Revolutionary Council, into an effective government, and build up North Yemen's declining military strength. This military decline became critical when South Yemen began to use its military buildup to threaten North Yemen. The USSR virtually cut off aid to North Yemen while making an eightfold increase in military deliveries to Aden.

This mix of pressures resulted in the June 1974 coup led by Col. Ibrahim al-Hamdi discussed earlier.[86] Al-Hamdi tilted the government away from the religious and traditional tribal leaders and aligned with Saudi Arabia while increasing ties to Iraq. He reorganized the Presidential Council into the Military Command Council (MCC), which established a balance of Zaidi and Shaafi interests and also maintained close ties to the key Hashid and Baikal tribal confederations.

These measures at first allowed him to establish a relatively strong and reform-oriented rule. However, al-Hamdi's reforms brought him into steadily greater conflict with the tribal and religious leaders, and indirectly with Saudi Arabia.[87] Although al-Hamdi was a Zaidi and seems to have had Saudi money in ousting Iriani, he evidently had covert political ties to the more radical factions and felt that the threat of Saudi control was as great as the threat from South Yemen and that the government would have to reduce tribal influence if any efforts at reform were to be successful. As a result, he expelled the traditional tribal leaders from the MCC in 1975, and in 1976 he dissolved the tribally dominated People's Assembly. He then took other measures that increasingly isolated him from Zaidi support, particularly from that of the Hashid and Baikal tribes. He did, however, maintain his ties to Saudi Arabia during this period, and he closed the Soviet naval facilities at Hodeida. Further, he reacted to the reduction in Soviet arms by making a Saudi-backed purchase of U.S. weapons and support.

Al-Hamdi might have been able to retain power if he had moderated his suppression of the tribal confederacies, but he did just the opposite. As a result, he became involved in a new civil war with the Hashid and Baikal tribes by early 1977. Further, al-Hamdi became involved in the complex struggle between Ismail and Rubai Ali. Al-Hamdi covertly backed Ismail in these political struggles and got the backing of the National Front in South Yemen in checking the tribes in North Yemen and in countering an increasingly concerned and hostile Saudi Arabia.

These shifts helped trigger his assassination on 10 October 1977, two days before he was scheduled to visit Aden, sign a mutual defense pact that had Ismail's backing, and lay the groundwork for unifying the two countries. His overthrow was made possible when he and his brother, the commander of one of the three brigades that were the source of his power, were shot. The two men were killed along with two French women in a rest house outside Sana, under conditions designed to make it look as if they were consorting with prostitutes. Al-Hamdi's brother-in-law, who was the commander of the armored brigade commanding the capital, was arrested at the same time. The commander of the remaining brigade in the area, the paratroop brigade, Major Abdullah Abdul Alim, was part of the coup attempt.[88]

The exact extent to which the coup was backed by Saudi Arabia is uncertain, but the leader of the coup, Lt. Col. Ahmid Ghashmi, was the chief of staff and the member of the MCC responsible for managing Saudi aid funds. This aid evidently amounted to over $1 million a month at the time of the coup, which enabled him to buy control of the army.

Ghashmi immediately reestablished the autonomous tribal areas in the north, which were the traditional centers of Saudi influence and which al-Hamdi had abolished. He restored power to such Saudi-backed elements as the Zaidi tribal faction, conservative business leaders, and the clergy. He also recalled the People's Assembly and restructured the cabinet so that it included a Zaidi-dominated coalition with two exiles from Aden who strongly opposed Ismail.[89]

Part of the army and government responded by opposing Ghashmi as being a Saudi front, which started a new low-level civil war in which South Yemen became involved as the result of the power struggle between Ismail and Rubai Ali. Ismail supported the creation of a National Democratic and Liberation Front, composed of all the radical factions that had backed al-Hamdi, in February 1978. The NDF included various minor radical parties, the more extreme Baathists and ex-Nasserites, the communist-oriented Democratic Party of Popular Unity, and the Revolutionary Democratic party, which Ismail had long backed and supported through the NDF.[90]

Ismail also supported an attempted revolt by one of Ghashmi's partners in the coup, Maj. Abdullah Abdul Alim. His forces included his paratroop unit, part of the "Giants" brigade formerly commanded by al-Hamdi's brother, and tribal groups centered in the southern part of the country around Taiz. Ghashmi's forces were put under the command of the new chief of staff, Lt. Col. Ali Abdullah Saleh, and they quickly crushed the rebellion. They bombed key villages using North Yemen's MiG-17s and made effective use of their monopoly of armor. Alim escaped, however, and joined the NDF, giving the rebel faction new support in the tribal areas in the Taiz, Sana, and Damar districts, and the rebels were joined by elements of the military units that had been loyal to al-Hamdi. The rebels, the Shaafi tribes, and other Ismail-backed factions also united into a common coalition under the NDF.[91]

This combination of political and military forces led to the major border fighting in June 1978 that was discussed earlier. It triggered the final confrontation between Rubai Ali and Ismail that resulted in Ghashmi's assassination and Rubai Ali's execution. These events, in turn transformed the struggle between the radicals and conservatives in North Yemen into a split between Saudi- and South Yemeni–backed forces.

Ghashmi's replacement was the Lt. Col. Abdullah Saleh who had suppressed the rebels.[92] He reacted by taking new repressive measures against the radicals and by strengthening the role of the tribes in the government, including the Hashid and Baikal tribal confederacies. He also called on the Saudis for further military aid to provide increased compensation for North Yemen's loss of arms supplies from the USSR and to meet the growing South Yemeni threat. This step split his faction from many of the nationalists who had backed Ghashmi but who opposed strengthening the tribes and thereby Saudi influence.[93]

The split led to yet another attempted coup. An assassination attempt was made on Saleh on 12 October 1978, and four army units attempted to seize power while Saleh was in Saudi Arabia on 15 October. The coup attempt seems to have involved elements of the NDF, Baathists with ties to Libya, and elements of the "June 13th movement." This movement claimed to support al-Hamdi's policies and called for the punishment of al-Hamdi's assassins, the end of exclusive relations with Saudi Arabia, and unification with South Yemen. The call for punishment of al-Hamdi's assassins had special relevance because Saleh was sometimes reported to have led them.[94] The rebels proved unable to obtain the support of North Yemen's armored forces, which caused the coup to collapse. On 27 October there occurred the bloodiest purges since the civil war. Nine army officers, the minister of labor and social affairs, and numerous other nationalists and radicals were arrested. Something approaching 100 executions followed over the next two months, and thousands were imprisoned.[95]

These purges weakened Saleh's political support, and Ismail seems to have calculated that the NDF could overthrow Saleh or at least seize control of North Yemen's southern provinces. Although the initial NDF attack faltered, Ismail provided air cover to counter the North Yemeni Air Force, and South Yemeni armor and artillery gave the NDF enough assistance to move up to 25 miles across the border and seize the towns of Qataba, Bayda, and Harib.

The result was the February 1979 border war discussed earlier, a bloody but highly localized conflict. Up to 7,000 deaths have been reported, but the actual figure was probably much lower and most casualties seem to have been civilians or tribal irregulars. Ismail also quickly learned that he had miscalculated the strength of the NDF forces. While the support of South Yemen's forces allowed the rebels to occupy the territory near North Yemen's border with South Yemen, they lacked significant popular support. Saleh was able to move large numbers of his forces—including many Hashid tribesmen—down to suppress the NDF. As a result, the rebellion was halted in March 1979, although South Yemeni forces continued to threaten North Yemen.

Saleh used this South Yemeni "invasion" to convince Saudi Arabia and the U.S. that he faced a major direct threat from a Soviet-backed South Yemen. Saudi Arabia and the United States would normally have treated these claims with considerable reservation, particularly given Saleh's history of shifting alliances. However, a number of factors led both countries to overreact in supporting him. The USSR had just demonstrated how rapidly it could build up the military forces of Ethiopia. It had made massive increases in South Yemen's military forces in the year following Rubai Ali's death. Saudi intelligence depended on reports coming from various Zaidi factions, and these factions provided exaggerated reports of intense fighting along the border. The U.S. had no real political intelligence of its own about what was happening.

And the U.S. was urgently looking for a way to reassert its power in the Gulf that would reduce the image of U.S. weakness left by the shah's fall.[96]

As a result, the U.S. agreed to speed the military aid to North Yemen it had first promised in 1976 and to expedite delivery of a new arms package that Saudi Arabia agreed to fund. The resulting aid package was a joint Saudi-U.S. effort, however, and failed to give Saleh the direct access to U.S. aid and advice he had sought. It thus failed to meet his true political goal, which was to obtain security from both the South Yemeni threat and independence from further Saudi control. Saleh did initially welcome the Saudi-U.S. arms deal, and the U.S. deployment of a small task force in the Gulf of Aden, including the aircraft carrier *Constellation*. However, he soon came to the conclusion that the deal failed to offer him the scale of arms deliveries he sought, as well as direct ties to the U.S. The new arms package provided only limited numbers of major weapons: 12 Northrop F-5 Fighters, 64 M-60 tanks, 50 M-113 APCs, and a small number of artillery weapons.[97] While the deal also included Vulcan antiaircraft guns and modern antitank guided weapons, it fell far short of giving North Yemen military independence and of matching the levels of aid the USSR was providing South Yemen. Saleh and many other key army officers felt that North Yemen was being made permanently dependent on Saudi Arabia.

As a result, Saleh took advantage of the terms of the peace agreement with South Yemen to tilt back toward the Soviet bloc. The border war had ended in a cease-fire on 4 March 1979, which came as a result of both the buildup of North Yemeni forces, and the intervention of Kuwait, Iraq, Syria, and the other Arab League states. The cease-fire was followed later in March by a meeting in Kuwait at which both sides agreed that they would pursue further unity talks under Kuwaiti auspices and at which South Yemen was given assurances it would receive aid from Kuwait and the UAE.[98]

This peace agreement theoretically had Saudi blessing, but only to the extent that it offered a way to wean South Yemen from the Soviet bloc. Saleh, however, saw it as a means of reducing the threat from both South Yemen and Saudi Arabia. In June 1979 he agreed to hold popular elections prior to "unification" that would include candidates from the South Yemeni–backed National Front. More important, he reorganized his government to reduce Saudi influence and brought in members who formerly had been supporters of al-Hamdi.[99]

Saleh could then go to the USSR for arms. In August he concluded a military and economic aid pact with the USSR without consulting either the U.S. or Saudi Arabia. The pact provided for some $600 million worth of Soviet arms only months after Saudi Arabia and the U.S. had agreed to provide $390 million worth of arms to counter Soviet and South Yemeni influence.[100] It led to an increase in the Soviet advisory team from 200 to 500–600 men and to the training of some 1,000

North Yemenis in the Soviet Union.[101] It also provided for the rapid transfer of MI-8 attack helicopters, some 70 fighters including at least 36 late-model MiG-21s and 24 Sukhoi attack fighters, and enough T-54 and T-55 tanks to raise North Yemen's active strength to over 700 tanks. The Soviet agreement to deliver advanced fighters had a particularly favorable impact on Saleh because the Saudis and the U.S. were then telling the Yemenis they would need Taiwanese contract officers to fly even 15 F-5Es.[102]

Saleh then proceeded to describe his new arms deal to the Saudis as being much smaller than it was and defended it as part of his effort to neutralize Soviet backing of the threat from South Yemen. He used this same excuse to continue the unification talks. Several of the committees formed in March reported in November 1979, leading to public statements in December that agreement had been reached on plans to unify the armed forces of the Yemens.[103] In January 1980 an additional agreement was reached on plans to unify transport and communications. Saleh announced plans for unification elections in February but did not announce an election date.[104]

Relations with the Saudis deteriorated further because many of the U.S. arms promised to North Yemen were kept in Saudi Arabia, and the Saudis kept tight controls on the ammunition and spare parts for the rest.[105] However, North Yemen remained dependent on the Saudis for economic aid, the security of its northern tribes, and the imposition of any controls over smuggling from Saudi Arabia. These controls were critical because such smuggling avoided North Yemen's high customs duties and threatened to virtually destroy its economy. As a result, the Saudi discovery of the true scale of the Soviet arms deliveries to North Yemen in early 1980 provoked a considerable crisis.[106] Saudi Arabia responded by trying "carrot and stick" tactics. The Saudis threatened to cut off some $700 million in promised aid and all funds to pay for the U.S. military equipment still held in Saudi Arabia.[107] This threat forced Saleh to agree to halt further Soviet arms purchases and to pull back from his unification efforts.

The new agreement broke down by July. Saleh refused both to expel his Soviet advisers and to ratify a new border agreement desired by the Saudis.[108] It seems likely that Saleh was influenced by Ismail's forced retirement from the leadership of South Yemen in April and his replacement by the more "moderate" Ali Nasr Muhammed, by promising developments in oil exploration in North Yemen, by increases in the amount of Soviet arms to a value well in excess of $1 billion, and by a series of incidents indicating that the Saudis had been actively subverting the northern tribes.[109] In any case, Saleh continued to seek arms from the USSR and to pursue unification talks with South Yemen. He also was still able to obtain Saudi economic aid. The Saudis could afford to cut off weapons shipments, but they could not risk severing economic aid.[110]

At this point, however, the game began to get even more complex. The U.S., which had increased its FMS agreements from $1.3 million in FY1978 to $172.1 million in FY1979, cut them back to $1.5 million in FY1980 and $17.75 million in FY1981.[111] It halted the licensing of most commercial arms agreements and did not provide aid. The only continuing U.S. program was in military education and training, which cost $684,000 in FY1978, $561,000 in FY1979, $506,000 in FY1980, and $934,000 in FY1981. This aid totaled less than the program provided to Tunisia during the same period.[112]

The Saudis increased economic aid to nearly $400 million a year plus additional development aid,[113] but they made no effort to halt the smuggling that threatened to destroy the North Yemeni economy. North Yemeni imports rose to nearly $2 billion annually in 1981 and 1982 plus up to another $1 billion in smuggled goods, while exports totaled only about $30 million. Inflation rose to 30% in 1981 and over 40% in 1982, and reserves fell by roughly 50% to about $800 million in 1981. North Yemen reached a $350 million trade deficit in 1982.[114] Saudi Arabia also increased its payments to the northern Zaidi tribes, provided them with large numbers of additional automatic weapons and possibly even SA-7 missile launchers, and increased its support to two conservative Islamic movements hostile to Saleh, the Yemeni Muslim Brotherhood, and the Democratic Cooperative Movement (the Shura of Tawawun).[115] Finally, Saudi Arabia refused to support North Yemeni membership in the Gulf Cooperation Council and to pay its arms debts to the Soviet Union.[116]

By early 1981, Saleh had lost a great deal of his control over the northern tribes and much of the customs revenue he depended on for an independent source of income. Worse, his efforts to introduce conscription had reduced his income from expatriate workers, an increasing number of whom found ways to transfer income and goods without paying customs duties. The Saudi pressure led Saleh to arrest the leading pro-Saudi official in his government, Foreign Minister Abdallah Asnaq, in March for informing the Saudis of the full details of his relations with Moscow. It also led him to try to isolate the Saudi Embassy from contact with Yemeni officials and to accelerate his efforts to remove pro-Saudi Zaidi tribesmen and officials from power.[117]

These steps did not succeed in neutralizing South Yemen. While Ali Nasr Muhammed made the first major visit by a South Yemeni leader to Kuwait, Saudi Arabia, and the UAE since 1977 and pursued a moderate public course toward North Yemen, he also actively increased South Yemen's support to the National Front. By early 1981, the Front had been reorganized as the National Democratic Front around a core of about 100–800 strongly pro–South Yemeni and Marxist leaders led by its secretary, Sultan Omar. The NDF was able to command a force of about 600 defectors from the North Yemeni Army and 5,000 North Yemeni and 6,000 South Yemeni irregulars.[118]

During early 1981, Saleh's delays on unification led Ali Nasr to take further action. It became apparent that Saleh would not hold the unification referendum that had been the quid pro quo for North Yemen's cease-fire—its third—with the NDF in 1980. The NDF forces—who were largely Sunni Shaafi tribesmen—then started putting gradual military pressure on North Yemen in the area from Ibb and Dhamar to the border. They also were able to conduct scattered raids in the area bounded by Hodeida, Sana, Jibleh, Taiz, and the coast. Only the fact that some 300,000 anti-NDF South Yemeni exiles lived in the area around Taiz gave the southern part of the country some degree of security. By mid-1981, Saleh was in serious trouble. Various opposition movements were able to operate in Sana at night, and Ali Nasr pressed hard for progress on the unity talks. Then, in October 1981, the NDF forced the North Yemeni Army into a new border conflict that involved heavy fighting.

While Saleh was able to use his tanks and fighters to check the NDF in any given battle, it became clear that his success was largely dependent on the extent to which he could obtain Soviet support or to which Ali Nasr limited his support of the NDF forces. Further, Ali Nasr's consolidation of power in South Yemen made Saleh Mousleh, a relative hard-liner, minister of defense.[119] Saleh responded by appealing to Moscow. He flew to the USSR on 26 October 1981 and was greated at the airport by Brezhnev and a number of senior Soviet military officials.[120] While the details of his talks are unclear, Saleh seems to have reached some agreement with the USSR that North Yemen's "positive neutrality and nonalignment" would tilt toward the Soviet Union, and the Soviets responded by promises to intervene with South Yemen and to provide more arms. The resulting communiqué referred to "striving to broaden and perfect" military relations.[121]

Although the exact sequence of the resulting Soviet arms transfers is not currently available, U.S. intelligence sources reported in April 1982 that the volume of Soviet arms transfers following Saleh's August 1979 pact with the USSR had increased to between $1 and $2 billion, that 650 tanks and 400 armored fighting vehicles had already been delivered, that fighter deliveries totaled three squadrons of MiG-21s and one Su-24 squadron, and that North Yemen had been given large helicopter forces. Equally significant, the number of Yemenis training in the USSR had been increased to 1,500, in comparison to roughly 25 per year in the U.S.[122]

In any case, Saleh's growing ties with Moscow seem to have given him the confidence to resist pressure from the PDRY and NDF. Ironically, this latest break in the "on-again, off-again" talks between North and South Yemen came after Saleh made his first official visit to Aden for the PDRY's fourteenth independence celebration at the end of November 1981.[123] The visit resulted in a fourth cease-fire with the NDF, which Saleh and Sultan Omar signed with Ali Nasr present as a witness. Ali

Nasr's quid pro quo for the cease-fire seems to have been Saleh's agreement to make a draft constitution public and to hold the unification referendum that he had dodged in 1981. The 136-article document called for a United Yemeni Republic with Sana as its capital and a socialist state with Islam as its official religion. It also called for a referendum in both nations during 1982 to approve the constitution.

Although Saleh continued to support the unification talks for the rest of 1981, he seems to have felt he had a sufficient balance of Soviet guarantees and Saudi aid to strengthen his position. Just when the PDRY first publicized the constitution and agreement to a unification referendum, Saleh created a whole new series of political obstacles. As a result, Kuwait announced a formal end to the unification talks because of irreconcilable ideological differences on 27 January 1982.[124] Saleh had miscalculated, however, and by March 1982, North Yemen was engaged in another round of fighting with the NDF. It is difficult to be sure of what would have happened if South Yemen's economy had not run into critical difficulties, or if Saudi Arabia and the other conservative Gulf states had not "outbid" Iran for influence in the PDRY. North Yemen could not suppress the NDF, and it ran into serious economic problems. The reductions in Gulf oil revenues limited any prospect that it could get the funding it needed for its $6.5 billion five-year (1982–1986) plan, and its efforts to woo Western capital had only token success.[125]

North Yemen's problems in expanding its service sector, light industry, and tourism continued into 1983, as did its difficulties with smuggling and inflation. It also continued to have critical problems with its agricultural sector. Agriculture employed 70% of the work force but produced only 28% of the GDP. Although North Yemen's new five-year plan called for 4.8% annual growth, the country averaged less than 1% annual growth in agricultural output between 1978 and 1983. The new plan also reflected a continued emphasis on overambitious projects; it called for $971 million for 56 projects with 58% foreign financing. It ignored the failure of past water projects, mechanization with the wrong kind of tractors (over 5,000 of the wrong type were imported), misuse of fertilizer, overambitious fishery projects, and efforts to bring government control to farming activity.[126] Although the government had some significant successes in building light roads and smaller water projects and in the Wadi Zbid project, it did not prove competent to cope with the broad pressure on the economy. Competition from Saudi Arabia and other Gulf economies led to the abandonment of 7.4% of North Yemen's cultivated land between 1975 and 1981, cereal production dropped by 14%, and cotton production dropped by 63%. Fewer than 66 of 90 local water supply systems were completed, and only 28 of 60 extension centers were completed. In contrast, *qat* production rose to 46,000 hectares, or 7% of North Yemen's cultivated land.[127]

Thus the economic situation scarcely promised Saleh much security and gradually added a new threat to the long list of threats to North

Yemen's independence and stability. While the traditional leaders of the Zaidi tribes are pro-Saudi, largely because of heavy subsidies, these tribes are largely Shi'ite. Many of the younger tribesmen, particularly those who have worked in Saudi Arabia, have become increasingly anti-Saudi and independent since 1976. Some of the emerging young Zaidi elite has made contact with the Khomeini movement in Iran, which may well have contributed to North Yemen's expulsion of the chief Iranian envoy in North Yemen on 31 December 1981 (the formal reason was his verbal attacks on Iraq).[128] While such Zaidi unrest was still limited in early 1983, it reflected the almost inevitable process of change in Zaidi politics. It also seems likely to accelerate because of the government's failure to develop the economy and agricultural sector, resentment of the tax system enforced by the tribal leaders, the almost universal carrying of automatic weapons by the tribesmen, and the growing wealth and education of many expatriate workers.

Notes

1. In addition to the sources listed in note 1 of Chapter 11, this chapter draws on Phillip Durby, *British Defense Policy East of Suez, 1947–1968* (London, 1973); Sir Ranulph Fiennes, *Where Soldiers Fear to Tread* (London: Hodder & Stoughton, 1975); Jane Smiley Hart, "Basic Chronology for a History of the Yemens," *Middle East Journal* 17 (Winter-Spring 1963):144–153; Donald Hawley, *Oman and Its Renaissance*, (London: Stacey International, 1980); J. C. Hurewitz, *Middle East Politics: The Military Dimension* (New York: Praeger Publishers, 1980); Air Chief Marshal Sir David Lee, *Flight from the Middle East* (London: Her Majesty's Stationery Office, 1980); Richard F. Nyrop, *Area Handbook for the Yemens* (Washington, D.C.: Department of the Army, 1977); Edgar O'Ballance, *The War in the Yemens* (Hamden, Conn.: Archon Books, 1971); Oman, *Oman in Ten Years* (Muscat: Ministry of Information, 1980); Christine Osborne, *The Gulf States and Oman* (London: Croom Helm, 1977); John E. Peterson, *Oman in the Twentieth Century: Political Foundations of an Emerging State* (London: Croom Helm, 1978), and *Yemen: The Search for a Modern State* (Baltimore: Johns Hopkins University Press, 1982); D. L. Price, *Oman: Insurgency and Development*, Conflict Studies no. 53 (London, 1975); Robert W. Stookey, *Yemen: The Politics of the Yemen Arab Republic* (Boulder, Colo.: Westview Press, 1978), and *South Yemen: A Marxist Republic in Arabia* (Boulder, Colo.: Westview Press, 1982); John Townsend, *Oman: The Making of a Modern State* (London: Croom Helm, 1977); Manfred W. Wenner, *Modern Yemen, 1918–1966* (Baltimore: Johns Hopkins University Press, 1967).

The "standard" references on the Middle East have been footnoted where appropriate. The above sources, and other materials used, conflict in many details. Extensive use has also been made of *Merip, 8 Days, MEED*, the *Economist* (including its research publications), and the *Financial Times*.

2. See George Lenczowski, *The Middle East in World Affairs*, 4th ed. (Ithaca, N.Y.: Cornell University Press, 1980), p. 680; and Peter Mansfield, *The Middle East* (New York: Oxford University Press, 1980), pp. 192–195.

3. J. B. Kelly, *Arabia, the Gulf and the West: A Critical View of the Arabs and Their Oil Policy* (New York: Basic Books, 1980).

4. Ibid. It should be noted that while Kelly and various British sources tend to imply the oasis was difinitely not part of Saudi Arabia, no clear title of any kind seems to emerge at any point in recorded history.

5. The Gwadur enclave of Baluchistan was part of Oman until Sultan Said sold it to Pakistan in 1958. The Baluchi are not foreigners by Omani standards.

6. Lenczowski, *Middle East in World Affairs*, p. 682; Otto von Pikva, *Armies of the Middle East* (New York: Mayflower Books, 1979), pp. 19–20; Lee, *Flight from the Middle East.*

7. The scale of this wealth should, however, not be exaggerated. Oil was not produced in Oman until 1 August 1967. The total value of Oman's exports was about £1 million in 1960. Oil raised them to £13 million in 1967 and to £73 million in 1970. MEED, *Oman: Practical Guide* (London, 1981), p. 18.

8. For all practical purposes, the "coup" was planned and implemented by British "advisers" who were members of British intelligence. Fred Halliday's account, while biased, seems fairly accurate. *Arabia Without Sultans* (London: Pelican, 1975), pp. 332–333.

9. Ibid., pp. 336–338.

10. At the height of Iran's intervention, Iran had a full brigade operating in Oman, a squadron of eight F-5s at the air base at Thamarit, and a joint radar base nearby, plus independent artillery units and heavy lift helicopters. By December 1974, 3,500 men were deployed, and self-contained logistic units followed.

11. John Keegan, *World Armies* (New York: Facts on File, 1979), p. 525. Iranian destroyers are also reported to have shelled South Yemen.

12. About 40 guerrillas remained active in Dhofar, and about 200 remained in camps in Yemen. The war cost about 500 lives on the sultan's side and 1,000 on the rebels'.

13. Another version of events indicates that Sheikh Zayid of Abu Dhabi inadvertently signed away Omani territory when he made his border settlement with Saudi Arabia in 1975 and that Saudi Arabia returned the territory to Oman in 1977. Keegan, *World Armies*, p. 526.

14. About 1,000 Iranian troops remained until the shah's fall in 1979, when they were replaced by 200 Egyptians. The shah continued to fly Iranian RF-4 recce sorties over Oman until his fall.

15. In 1980 and 1981 the rebels in South Yemen were almost totally quiet and seemed to be seriously disorganized. The only tension in the area was with South Yemeni troops protecting Soviet oil crews, who repeatedly moved into Yemeni territory. See the *Middle East*, December 1982, pp. 18–20; *Washington Times*, 22 October 1982; *Washington Report on Middle East Affairs*, 10 January 1983, p. 4.

16. In November 1981 reports circulated that Saudi Arabia had offered Oman $1.5 billion to replace U.S. aid if it would cancel its contingency base arrangements with the U.S. It supposedly did this at a meeting of the Gulf Cooperation Council, and with the full backing the council's other members. These reports seem totally false.

17. This account of events is based largely on Nyrop, *Area Handbook for the Yemens*, pp. 96–99. Keegan, *World Armies*, pp. 809–810; Halliday, *Arabia Without Sultans*; "Hitched to a Red Star: The People's Democratic Republic of Yemen," *MERIP Reports*, 1974.

18. See Nyrop, *Area Handbook for the Yemens*, pp. 96–97; Lenczowski, *Middle East in World Affairs*, p. 648.

19. See Mansfield, *Middle East*, p. 158.

20. In the months that followed the coup, about 300,000 more political refugees left the country. In addition, the army was ruthlessly purged of officers, NCOs, and men from the Awaliq tribes of the Fourth and Fifth Governorates, many of whom were tortured to death. They were replaced by officers and NCOs from the Dathina area (Third Governorate), which was President Rubai Ali's home territory. Ali then steadily increased the number of regular military personnel from his own area, especially from the Hadramaut in Eastern Yemen near Oman. In contrast, the party secretary, Abd al-Fattah Ismail, ruthlessly purged the old General Security Units and formed a Popular Militia based on the party as his personal power base. The third leader of South Yemen, Prime Minister and Defense Minister Ali Nasr Muhammed, seems to have backed Ali more than Ismail at this time.

21. See Lenczowski, *Middle East in World Affairs*, pp. 634, 649–651; Mansfield, *Middle East*, p. 159.

22. See Nyrop, *Area Handbook for the Yemens*, pp. 97–99, 111–120; Mansfield, *Middle East*, pp. 160–161.

23. See Nyrop, *Area Handbook for the Yemens*, pp. 147–148; and Lenczowski, *Middle East in World Affairs*, p. 650.

24. Keegan, *World Armies*, p. 811.

25. See Nyrop, *Area Handbook for the Yemens*, pp. 99–100, 212–213; Lenczowski, *Middle East in World Affairs*, pp. 634, 650–651; and Mansfield, *Middle East*, pp. 143, 159.

26. See Mansfield, *Middle East*, p. 159; Nyrop, *Area Handbook for the Yemens*, pp. 100, 213–214; and Lenczowski, *Middle East in World Affairs*, pp. 633–634, 650.

27. See Nyrop, *Area Handbook for the Yemens*, pp. 213–214; Lenczowski, *Middle East in World Affairs*, p. 635; and Mansfield, *Middle East*, p. 142.

28. See Nyrop, *Area Handbook for the Yemens*, p. 99.

29. See Mansfield, *Middle East*, p. 158. Prime Minister and Defense Minister Ali Nasr Muhammed seems to have been largely neutral in this struggle.

30. See ibid., p. 154.

31. See Frances Fukuyama, *The Soviet Union and Iraq Since 1968*, RAND, N-1524, AF, 1980, and "A New Soviet Strategy," *Commentary*, October 1979.

32. Lenczowski, *Middle East in World Affairs*, pp. 635–637. Accounts differ sharply over the precise details of these events.

33. See Mansfield, *Middle East*, pp. 142–143.

34. See Lenczowski, *Middle East in World Affairs*, p. 637. While some reports claimed the Saudis instigated al-Hamdi's overthrow, it was largely the result of local opposition.

35. Soviet Navy commander-in-chief, Admiral Sergei Gorshkov, visited South Yemen in late 1976; the Soviet first deputy defense minister visited in February 1977.

36. See Mansfield, *Middle East*, pp. 157–158; Lenczowski, *Middle East in World Affairs*, pp.651–652.

37. This analysis is based largely on interviews, but see Keegan, *World Armies*, pp. 812–813; *Manchester Guardian Weekly*, 10 September 1978; and *Financial Times*, 29 June 1978.

38. See Mansfield, *Middle East*, p. 155; Keegan, *World Armies*, p. 812. The fighting in Aden was extensive, and much of the armed forces remained loyal to Rubai Ali. According to some reports, Ethiopian and Cuban troops were

flown in to quell pro-Ali forces, and widespread fighting in the countryside lasted until November. Elements of the armed forces up to a brigade in size defected to North Yemen.

39. See Mansfield, *Middle East*, p. 158; Lenczowski, *Middle East in World Affairs*, p. 652; Fulvio Grimaldi, "Whose War in the Yemens?" and *Middle East*, April 1979, pp. 56–57.

40. *New York Times*, 26 October 1979.

41. David Shirrelf, "Five Year Plan Goes Back to the Drawing Board," *MEED*, 30 May 1980.

42. In retrospect, it is important to note that pro-Rubai Ali forces fought pro-Ismail troops in the First, Fourth, and Sixth Governorates and much of the eastern Hadramaut. The purges and executions necessary to suppress these forces scarcely made South Yemen ready to launch an invasion.

43. *Washington Post*, 20 and 27 March 1979.

44. See Nyrop, *Area Handbook for the Yemens*, pp. 97–101; *Neue Zurcher Zeitung*, 22 April 1980; World of Information, *Middle East Review, 1981* (London, 1980), p. 301; and Andrea Maleta, "Unity on Every Lip," *Middle East*, October 1980, pp. 25–27.

45. Michel Szwed Cousins, "The Wooing of the Two Yemens," *8 Days*, 30 May 1981, pp. 18–19.

46. *Washington Post*, 14 July 1982; Israeli Embassy, *National Security Issues*, August 1982; DIA estimate issued as background for Department of Defense press release.

47. *Washington Post*, 14 July 1982; *Middle East*, August 1982, pp. 20–21.

48. Chris Kutschera, "Snags in Boosting Aden's Production," *Middle East*, October 1982, pp. 70–72.

49. Chris Kutschera, "South Yemen: A Slow Move Towards the West," *Middle East*, August 1982, pp. 20–21.

50. *Economist*, 16 January 1982, pp. 44–45; "North Yemen: Is It War?" *Arabia: The Islamic World Review*, January 1982, p. 24; *8 Days*, 2 May 1981, pp. 4–8, 54; 20 May 1981, pp. 18–19; 30 January 1982, pp. 6–7; 20 February 1982, pp. 17–19; *MEED*, 7 May 1982.

51. Lt. Col. John J. Ruszkiewicz, "A Case Study in the Yemen Arab Republic," *Armed Forces Journal*, September 1980, pp. 62–72.

52. *Christian Science Monitor*, 20 August 1982, p. 1; *New York Times*, 28 January 1982.

53. *New York Times*, 28 January 1982; *Washington Post*, 14 July 1982.

54. *Middle East*, July 1982, p. 12; August 1982, pp. 20–21; December 1982, pp. 18–20; *Economist*, 20 November 1982, p. 53; *Washington Report on Middle East Affairs*, 10 January 1983, p. 4.

55. *MEED*, 9 April and 6 and 14 June 1982; *Economist*, 20 November 1982, p. 52.

56. See Mansfield, *Middle East*, pp. 46–47; and CIA, *World Factbook*, 1981, NFAC GS WF-81-001 (U), pp. 217–218.

57. Although Yemen's coffee crop has been a luxury export, and its jewelry has been important in Bedouin economics as far west as North Africa, its total volume of trade has long been small. Ironically, most "Yemeni jewelry" is now generally made in small factories outside the area, and imported European gold jewelry in replacing silver jewelry among the now largely settled Bedouin. In 1979 North Yemen exported only minor amounts of *qat*, cotton, coffee, hides, and vegetables.

58. Nyrop, *Area Handbook for the Yemens*, pp. 25–28.

59. See Lenczowski, *Middle East in World Affairs*, pp. 615; and Mansfield, *Middle East*, pp. 135–136.

60. See Nyrop, *Area Handbook for the Yemens*, pp. 35–37; and Mansfield, *Middle East*, pp. 137–138.

61. Mansfield, *Middle East*, p. 136; Lenczowski, *Middle East in World Affairs*, p. 616; Nyrop, *Area Handbook for the Yemens*, p. 36.

62. Nyrop, *Area Handbook for the Yemens*, pp. 36–37; Mansfield, *Middle East*, pp. 137–138.

63. Mansfield, *Middle East*, p. 137; Nyrop, *Area Handbook for the Yemens*, pp. 36–37; Lenczowski, *Middle East in World Affairs*, pp. 617–618.

64. Nyrop, *Area Handbook for the Yemens*, pp. 37–38; Lenczowski, *Middle East in World Affairs*, pp. 619–620.

65. Nyrop, *Area Handbook for the Yemens*, p. 37; Lenczowski, *Middle East in World Affairs*, p. 620.

66. Nyrop, *Area Handbook for the Yemens*, pp. 619–620.

67. Lenczowski, *Middle East in World Affairs*, pp. 622–623; Mansfield, *Middle East*, p. 137.

68. Nyrop, *Area Handbook for the Yemens*, p. 38.

69. Ibid., pp. 38–41; Halliday, *Arabia Without Sultans*, p. 98; Wenner, *Modern Yemen*.

70. Nyrop, *Area Handbook for the Yemens*, pp. 41–42.

71. Ibid., p. 42; Halliday, *Arabia Without Sultans*, pp. 97–99.

72. This account of events is based largely on Nyrop, *Area Handbook for the Yemens*; Mansfield, *Middle East*; Halliday, *Arabia Without Sultans*; Wenner, *Modern Yemen*; and articles by Eric Rouleau in *Le Monde*, December 1962.

73. Nyrop, *Area Handbook for the Yemens*, p. 43; Mansfield, *Middle East*, p. 138; Lenczowski, *Middle East in World Affairs*, pp. 623–624; William R. Brown, "The Yemeni Dilemma," *Middle East Journal*, Autumn 1963.

74. Lenczowski, *Middle East in World Affairs*, pp. 628–631; von Pikva, *Armies of the Middle East*, pp. 20–22.

75. von Pikva, *Armies of the Middle East*, p. 21; Halliday, *Arabia Without Sultans*, pp. 110–112. Egypt lost 15,195 men killed between October 1962 and June 1964. These were Egypt's best-trained troops, and their loss seriously weakened Egypt in the 1967 conflict with Israel.

76. Mansfield, *Middle East*, p. 139.

77. von Pikva, *Armies of the Middle East*, p. 21.

78. Nyrop, *Area Handbook for the Yemens*, p. 50; Mansfield, *Middle East*, p. 140; and Halliday, *Arabia Without Sultans*, pp. 110–114.

79. von Pikva, *Armies of the Middle East*, pp. 21–22.

80. Nyrop, *Area Handbook for the Yemens*, p. 95; Halliday, *Arabia Without Sultans*, pp. 117–119.

81. See Mansfield, *Middle East*, p. 141; Nyrop, *Area Handbook for the Yemens*, p. 210; Halliday, *Arabia Without Sultans*, pp. 118–122.

82. Ibid.

83. See von Pikva, *Armies of the Middle East*, p. 22; and Mansfield, *Middle East*, pp. 140–141. Halliday provides a strident defense of the leftist factions that broke with Amri (*Arabia Without Sultans*, pp. 121–124).

84. Nyrop, *Area Handbook for the Yemens*, p. 210; Halliday, *Arabia Without Sultans*, pp. 126, 131; *Economist*, 23 May 1970.

85. See Mansfield, *Middle East*, pp. 142–143; Lenczowski, *Middle East in World Affairs*, pp. 633–635; and Nyrop, *Area Handbook for the Yemens*, pp. 212–213; Halliday, *Arabia Without Sultans*, pp. 132–135, 146–147.

86. See Lenczowski, *Middle East in World Affairs*, pp. 635–636; Mansfield, *Middle East*, p. 143; and Nyrop, *Area Handbook for the Yemens*, p. 142.

87. See Mansfield, *Middle East*, p. 142; and Lenczowski, *Middle East in World Affairs*, pp. 635–636.

88. See Nyrop, *Area Handbook for the Yemens*, p. 216; Lenczowski, *Middle East in World Affairs*, pp. 635–637; and Keegan, *World Armies*, pp. 803–804.

89. See Lenczowski, *Middle East in World Affairs*, pp. 637, 651–652; and Mansfield, *Middle East*, p. 142.

90. *MERIP Report*, no. 81, pp. 21–23; various working papers by Jean Geuyras of *Le Monde*. Sources differ in their use of National Democratic Front (NDF) and National Liberation Front (NLF).

91. Working papers by Jean Geuyras; Lenczowski, *Middle East in World Affairs*, p. 637.

92. Keegan, *World Armies*, pp. 804–805.

93. Based on working papers by Jean Geuyras.

94. "North Yemen Faces Embryonic Civil War," *MERIP Report*, no. 81, pp. 21–22; Keegan, *World Armies*, p. 804. Libya is reported to have provided $2 million worth of arms to the rebels.

95. "North Yemen Faces Civil War"; Grimaldi, "Whose War in the Yemens?" pp. 56–58.

96. See Grimaldi "Whose War in the Yemens?"; David R. Griffiths, "Congress Probes Yemeni Arms Policy," *Aviation Week*, 26 May 1980; Ruszkiewicz, "A Case History in the Yemen Arab Republic"; Col. Alfred B. Prados, "Bilateral Military Aid in the Middle East: The Yemen Program," unpublished papers, National Defense University, May 1978.

97. *New York Times*, 7 May 1980; *Wall Street Journal*, 12 March 1980.

98. World of Information, *Middle East Review, 1981*, p. 385.

99. Ibid.

100. *Economist*, 16 January 1982.

101. Ibid., estimates 600. The DIA estimated 475 Soviet, no Cuban, and 5 East German advisers of all types in mid-1981. Department of Defense, *FY1982 Annual Report*, Annex A, p. 84.

102. *Economist*, 16 January 1982; World of Information, *Middle East Review, 1981*, p. 385; *Washington Star*, 17 January 1980; *Baltimore Sun*, 19 March 1980; *Washington Post*, 28 May 1979.

103. World of Information, *Middle East Review, 1981*, p. 385.

104. Ibid.

105. Ibid.

106. *New York Times*, 7 May 1980; Amos Perlmutter, "The Yemen Strategy," *New Republic*, 5 July 1980.

107. World of Information, *Middle East Review, 1981*, p. 385; *Baltimore Sun*, 17 January and 19 March 1980; *Washington Post*, 20 February 1980.

108. World of Information, *Middle East Review, 1981*, p. 387.

109. *Washington Post*, 21 April 1982.

110. *Economist*, 16 January 1982.

111. OSD/DSAA computer printout as of 30 September 1981.

112. Ibid.

113. *Economist*, 16 February 1982; *Christian Science Monitor*, 14 January 1983.

114. *Economist*, 16 February 1982; Tony Hall, "North Yemen Seeks Its Niche in Modern Arabia, *8 Days*, 2 May 1981, pp. 4–54; *Christian Science Monitor*, 14 January 1982.

115. "N. Yemen: Is It War?" *Arabia: The Islamic World Review*, January 1982, p. 24.

116. *Christian Science Monitor*, 29 October 1981.

117. "N. Yemen: Is It War?" p. 24; *Economist*, 16 February 1982; "The Changing Face of Arabia," *Middle East*, January 1982, pp. 14–15.

118. "N. Yemen: Is It War?" p. 24; *Economist*, 16 February 1982; *Washington Post*, 21 February 1982; Michel Szwed Cousins, "Yemens Step Up Unity Talks," *8 Days*, 30 January 1982, pp. 6–7.

119. "N. Yemen: Is It War?" p. 24; *Economist*, 16 February 1982; "Changing Face of Arabia," pp. 14–15.

120. *Christian Science Monitor*, 28 October 1982.

121. Ibid., 29 October 1981.

122. *Washington Post*, 21 April 1982.

123. Hall, "North Yemen Seeks Its Niche," pp. 4–8, 54; "N. Yemen: Is It War?" p. 24; *Economist*, 16 February 1982; "Changing Face of Arabia," pp. 14–15.

124. *New York Times*, 28 January 1982; Szwed Cousins, "Yemens Step Up Unity Talks," pp. 6–7.

125. "Yemen Woos British Investment," *Middle East*, December 1982, p. 63.

126. *Christian Science Monitor*, 14 January 1983.

127. *MEED*, 11 June 1982, p. 70; Susannah Tarbush, "Arabia's Fertile Fringe," *Middle East*, September 1982, pp. 60–61.

128. *Washington Post*, 1 January 1982.

13
Dynamics of the Military Balance

Just as the recent interactions among the Gulf states shape their ability to cooperate, the military dynamics in the Gulf shape their power and stability. There are exceptions to this rule: Saudi Arabia and Kuwait have oil wealth that gives them political and economic power far greater than the size of their military forces would indicate. In broad terms, however, power in the Gulf is determined largely by military power, and stability is largely the result of the local military balance and the ability to use military force to maintain internal control.

The Military Balance in the Gulf in the Early 1980s

It is not surprising, given the Gulf's wealth and recent history, that it has experienced the fastest rate of military buildup of any region in the world. All of the factors that have driven Saudi Arabia's military expansion have also driven that of the other Gulf states, as has the constant history of tension throughout the region. Only a few of the smallest Gulf states were able to avoid participating in the Gulf arms race in the years between the announcement of British withdrawal and the shah's fall. Since 1980, every Gulf state has been forced to devote a steadily increasing proportion of its oil wealth to competing with the other Gulf states and/or neighboring states outside the Gulf.

This growth has been so explosive that it has compounded the normally serious problems in Gulf statistics. It has also been accompanied by many reports of arms transactions that have not been completed, false reports of force strength, and "guesstimates" as to manpower and defense expenditures. This makes it impossible to standardize on one source or time base and makes uncertain any analysis that compares a wide range of nations. Even so, some dynamics do seem to emerge consistently from most of the data available, and others seem to be correctly described in broad terms in given sources even if they are not correct in detail.

Force Strengths and Force Ratios

Table 13.1 summarizes the military balance in the Gulf in 1983–1984, using data taken from the IISS. It shows that Iraq and Iran dominate the Gulf as the largest military powers. They are followed by Saudi Arabia, and the other Gulf states have only limited forces and military capability. The disparity between the larger and smaller Gulf powers is, in fact, greater than the table indicates. Iran, Iraq and Saudi Arabia are the only Gulf states with the combination of manpower and wealth to buy and operate the most modern military equipment. The other conservative Gulf states lack the manpower skills to operate such equipment effectively, and the two Yemens lack both skilled manpower and money.

At the same time, Table 13.1 shows that if the smaller conservative Gulf states can develop effective collective security arrangements they can create a formidable force by regional standards. Such a force would be limited to operating in the territory bordering the southern Gulf, would be dependent on Saudi Arabia as a senior partner, and would still have serious qualitative problems. However, it should be capable of checking the potential regional threats to the conservative Gulf states. The military forces of potential threat nations have qualitative problems of their own. This collective security option is illustrated in more depth in Table 13.2, which shows how the present forces of Saudi Arabia and the other conservative Gulf states compare with those of the potential threat nations in the Gulf. The resulting comparisons indicate that Iraq or Iran, or the Yemens acting in combination with another state, could pose a serious threat to any combination of the conservative Gulf states. However, the force ratios are not so unfavorable that the conservative states could not create a considerable deterrent capability even under worst-case conditions.

Geographic Factors Affecting the Gulf Balance

There are additional factors that favor the conservative Gulf states in any confrontation involving indigenous military forces and that tend to make air power the critical form of military power in the Gulf.

- The geography of the region limits the ability of Iran and Iraq to deploy their land strength effectively against most of the southern Gulf powers and provides a similar protection of Saudi Arabia and Oman from the two Yemens.
- Geography and the region's roads force Iraq and Iran to move through Kuwait if they are to conduct extended land force operations in the southern Gulf, and Iran would first have to move through Iraq. Both Iraq and Iran would have to move through Saudi Arabia to conduct extensive land force operations against any of the smaller Gulf states except Kuwait. Iraq's western land routes to Saudi Arabia—which bypass Kuwait through An Najaf and Rafha—are improving but will be unable

TABLE 13.1 IISS Estimates of the Military Balance in the Gulf, 1983–1984

	Iran	Iraq	Saudi Arabia	Kuwait	Bahrain
Total population (millions)	41.5	14.3	8.0	1.5	0.4
GNP ($ billions)	121.7	31.8	152.0	20.2	4.5
Defense Expenditure	6.9–13.3	7.7	22.0	1.6	0.3
Total active manpower	2,000,000	517,250	51,500	12,400	2,700
Army					
Manpower	1,000,000+	475,000+	35,000	10,000	2,300
Major combat units[a] (divisions/brigade equivalents)					
Armored	3/2	6/2	0/2	0/1	1 sqn
Mechanized	2/2	4/–	0/2	0/2	–
Infantry	-/-	-/24	0/2	–	1 bn
Paratroop	1/-	-/3	0/1	–	1 bty
AFVs					
Medium tanks	940	2,360	450	200	0
Other AFVs	900	3,000	1,490	485	142
Artillery	1,200+	800+	74+	20+	15
Reserves	500,000+	250,000+	–	–	–
Navy					
Manpower	20,000	4,250	2,500	500	300
Total craft					
Destroyer/Frigates	9	1	4	–	–
Patrol craft (missile)	12	10	9	–	2
Other craft	15	18	8	47	–
Landing vessels	17	3	12	6	2
Air Force					
Manpower	35,000	38,000	14,000	1,900	100
Combat aircraft	80–100[c]	290	216[b]	49	6
Attack/FGA	72–92	133	159	30	6
Recce	3	–	–	–	–
Air defense	5	157	57	19	–
Transports	–	58	72	7	–
Helicopters	76?	397?	66	31	12
Paramilitary	2,650,000	250,000+	34,500	18,000	2,680
AFVs	–	100+	240	–	–
Patrol craft	–	–	181	–	18
Aircraft	–	–	–	–	9

[a] Includes Saudi Arabia, Kuwait, Bahrain, Qatar, UAE, and Oman.

[b] Presently under expansion; Saudi Arabia forming 3 squadrons of 60 F-15s in 1983–1984. Totals include 46 BAC-167s in training role with COIN/FGA capability.

[c] Iranian aircraft figures are for operational combat aircraft: 30 of 90 F-4s believed serviceable, as well as 5 of 77 F-14s; up to 50 F-5s operational. Does not include reports of up to 100 Chinese F-6 and North Korean MiG-19/21 fighters.

TABLE 13.1 (continued)

Qatar	UAE	Oman	Conservative Gulf States[a]	North Yemen	South Yemen
0.3	1.1	1.0	12.3	7.2	2.0
6.8	28.7	6.5	233.0	2.6	1.1
0.2	2.9	1.8	28.8	0.5	0.2
6,000	49,000	23,500	145,100	21,550	25,500
5,000	46,000	19,950	118,250	20,000	22,000
1 bn	0/1	0/1	0/5	0/5	0/1
1 rgt	0/1	0/1	0/7	0/1	0/2
5 bns	0/2	0/2	0/7	0/9	0/9
–	0/2	0/1	0/4	0/2	0/1
24	136	27	837	714	450
201	486	36+	2,840	527+	300
14	70+	66+	259+	395	310+
–	–	–	–	–	–
700	1,500	2,000	7,500	550	1,000
–	–	–	4	–	1
2	6	3	22	2	6
44	9	9	117	10	12
–	–	6	26	–	7
300	1,500	2,000	20,100	1,000	2,500
11	43	37	362	75	113
11	13	37	256	50	77
–	–	–	–	–	–
–	30	–	103	25	36
4	24	32	139	11	45
9	31	28	177	33	3+
?	?	3,300+	58,480+	25,000	30,000
–	–	–	–	–	–
–	41	12	–	–	–
5	–	15	–	–	–

Source: Adapted from *The Military Balance, 1983-84* (London: IISS, 1983). The IISS figures differ in many details from the data estimated by the author and used elsewhere in the text.

TABLE 13.2 The Ratio of the Conservative Gulf States' Military Forces to Those of Potential Threat Nations, 1983–1984

	Defense Expenditures[a]	Total Military Manpower[b]	Main Battle Tanks	Other Armored Fighting Vehicles	High-Performance Combat Aircraft[c]
Saudi Arabia:					
Iran	5:1	1:5	1:2	2:1	1.4:1
Iraq	8:1	1:7	1:5	1:3	1:3
South Yemen	197:1	2:1	1:1	4:1	1:1
Iraq and South Yemen	8:1	1:7	1:6	1:3	1:3.5
North and South Yemen	54:1	1:1	1:3	1:1	1:1.4
Iraq and the Yemens	7:1	1:8	1:8	1:3	1:4
Conservative Gulf States (Saudi Arabia, Bahrain, Kuwait, Oman, Qatar, UAE):					
Iran	6:1	1:2	1:1.3	3:1	3:1
Iraq	9:1	1:3	1:3	1:1.4	1:1.2
South Yemen	235:1	5:1	2:1	7:1	2.5:1
Iraq and South Yemen	9:1	1:3	1:3	1.5:1	1:1.6
North and South Yemen	65:1	2:1	1:1.4	3:1	1.5:1
Iraq and the Yemens	8:1	1:3	1:4	1:2	1:2

[a]The ratios including Iraq and North and South Yemen are probably high against that particular country in defense expenditures, since the 1980 figures are used respectively.
[b]Not including Saudi National Guard.
[c]Iranian combat aircraft figures include only estimated operational planes. Saudi figures do *not* include 36 DAC-167 trainers or the squadron of F-15s forming in 1983.
Source: Adapted from *The Military Balance, 1982–83* (London: IISS, 1983).

to support major armor operations through the late 1980s. Their use would also force Iraq to enter Saudi Arabia far from any major military objective.

• Although the land routes connecting the nations along the southern edge of the Gulf are good and will be greatly improved over the next ten years, they are limited in number, and wide expanses of the area present serious problems to off-road movement because of desert terrain, sand, shallow wadis, and the like. These problems further limit the ability of Iran or Iraq to operate large-scale land forces against key objectives in Saudi Arabia or any other southern Gulf state.

• In contrast, the Gulf's geography gives every Gulf power great flexibility in deploying air and naval power against another. No violations of third-country territorial waters and airspace are required for most attacks, and most Gulf countries have highly vulnerable oil or other critical facilities near the Gulf coast. As a result, air power has unique importance in the Gulf area, and even limited heliborne or naval and amphibious forces can have considerable impact.

• Oman, North Yemen, and South Yemen face special geographic and terrain barriers from mountains, deserts, and poor land lines of communication. North Yemen can move against southeastern Saudi Arabia only along two land routes that cross extremely rough and easily defensible terrain. South Yemen has no major lines of communication with Saudi Arabia and is far from any critical strategic objective in Saudi Arabia. South Yemen's land routes to Oman are similarly limited and are guarded by the extensive defensive barriers put up during the Dhofar rebellion.

• No Gulf country, including Iran and Iraq, is organized to sustain prolonged military land force operations far from its borders. Even the two largest Gulf powers cannot project most of their combat units for long distances into hostile territory because of maintenance problems, inadequate combat and service support, lack of logistic equipment, and inadequate C^3I.

• Iran and Iraq have "armor heavy" land armies. They lack amphibious and major airborne capability. Iran's once-massive helicopter, air transport, and amphibious capabilities have degenerated strikingly under the pressures of revolution and the Iran-Iraq War, and Iraq is just beginning to develop such capabilities.

• The Yemens and Ethiopia do not, however, face similar problems in using air or naval power. While the Yemens are out of tactical fighter range of most Saudi oil facilities, they are within range of Jiddah and the holy cities, and North Yemen was successfully used as an Egyptian base for air strikes on Saudi border cities. Egypt also flew strikes against Saudi Arabia directly from Egypt during the Yemeni civil war, and fighters based in northwestern Ethiopia can provide excellent coverage of the Saudi targets on the Red Sea coast.

The geography of the Gulf thus favors the less populous, but wealthy, conservative Gulf states by limiting the ability of their potential opponents to use their land force superiority against key strategic targets. It gives air power, and sea and air mobility, a special strategic importance in the region. While all the Gulf states can develop such capabilities, the conservative Gulf powers can afford to buy the best available equipment and Western support. They can develop the relatively limited numbers of trained manpower required to operate an air force, which gives the conservative states an advantage in using air power and collective security to help "equalize" the balance.

Qualitative Problems and Issues

At the same time, the various military forces of the Gulf nations suffer from a wide range of qualitative problems that sharply limit the ability of the conservative Gulf states to act in unison or use their individual air forces effectively. These qualitative problems favor Iraq and Iran, at least in the short run:

• The conservative Gulf states have not designed their forces to cooperate with each other, and they now have little interoperability. While some improvements have recently taken place, they remain limited and most are still in the planning stage. In contrast, Iraq and Iran have already built up modern air forces, and Iran at least has considerable naval capabilities.

• With the exception of Iraqi, Iranian, and some Omani units, no Gulf force has ever engaged in modern combat. This lack of experience severely reduces their fighting capability, regardless of their organization, equipment, and training.

• All conservative Gulf forces rely heavily on foreign advisers and technicians, and many rely on contract officers and mercenaries. Forces dependent on foreign support have rarely performed well in combat, although Oman is a significant exception. Further, the quality of the contract personnel in some Gulf nations is relatively low.

• Many Gulf forces have major imbalances in their equipment that will prevent or limit effective large-scale interservice or combined arms operations (see Table 13.1). For example, tanks are being purchased without suitable AFV/APC and artillery support or transporters. High-performance fighters have been purchased without high-performance munitions and missiles. Small numbers of widely diverse types of aircraft and armor are maintained in service regardless of the maintenance and training problems involved, and these problems are especially severe in the conservative Gulf states.

• The ratios of total manpower to total major combat equipment are often impossibly low. For example, the air forces listed in Table 13.1 exhibit radically different numbers of manpower per combat aircraft. In most of the smaller Gulf states these manpower ratios are far too low to adequately support air operations—even allowing for support from foreign contract personnel. Similar problems emerge in most Gulf navies.

• Many Gulf forces suffer from an obvious effort to gain prestige by buying the most modern equipment, regardless of its suitability, and from a tendency to buy in small lots from too many suppliers or countries. This is again particularly true of the smaller conservative Gulf states.

• In virtually every case, Gulf forces are now being radically restructured and modernized, often at conversion rates that have proved impractical even for highly sophisticated Western military forces with long experience in the use of modern weapons. Many Gulf nations, for example, are attempting new types of fighter aircraft over much shorter periods than would be attempted by the RAF, Luftwaffe, or French Air Force.

The most serious problem the conservative Gulf states face, however, is political rather than technical. Their recent history has just begun to encourage collective security efforts, but most can overcome the previous problems only through collective security efforts and a mix of standardization and interoperability. The efforts of the Gulf Cooperation Council, and the Saudi and Omani efforts to develop cooperative defense relations with Qatar and Bahrain, are important steps toward this end. However, these efforts are still nascent, have been disrupted by Iranian pressure on Kuwait and the UAE, and lack the Western technical advice necessary to give them cohesion.

Other Factors Shaping the Gulf Military Balance

The problems discussed in the preceding sections are compounded by other factors. Most Gulf military forces also suffer from the following problems: (1) a lack of suitably educated personnel; (2) a rigid separation in terms of status of officers and enlisted men that prevents adequate leadership and cooperation; (3) an unwillingness on the part of officers and NCOs to become involved in training and maintenance that is regarded as "manual labor"; (4) a similar lack of willingness to become involved in complex maintenance and logistic procedures; (5) chronic overcentralization of decision making and management; (6) a resulting lack of interservice cooperation and coordination; (7) a failure to operate management and administrative systems effectively; (8) nepotism or "politicization" of the promotion process; (9) overreliance on foreign assistance and advice; and (10) unwillingness to report factually on politically threatening or career-threatening readiness and force improvement problems.

These difficulties are endemic in the social structure of most Arab states, but they are compounded in the conservative Gulf states by "imported" problems. These include the tendency of foreign advisers to emphasize military sales rather than meet actual host-country requirements; a tendency to apply Western military models to a different culture and set of area military requirements; a lack of personal commitment by foreign advisers to the force being advised or supported; an emphasis on short-term profits over long-term relations; and an unwillingness or inability to call attention to politically embarrassing issues or weaknesses in the force being advised.

The demanding climatic conditions in the Gulf make the situation even worse. The failure to effectively administer Gulf forces leads to a uniquely rapid deterioration of military equipment and munitions. Even properly stored or maintained equipment has only one-half to one-third the operational life it would have in Europe, and slight departures from proper handling can have major effects. For example, minor errors in storage procedures can greatly reduce air-to-air, air-to-surface, and antitank missile performance. Such errors have destroyed major amounts of military inventory, even in more experienced nations like Turkey and Vietnam.

Modernizing for Status Rather Than Military Capability

The rulers of several conservative Gulf states have only recently understood that they must make a serious attempt to transform their military forces into an effective defense or deterrent that could increase the cost of an attack to the attacker and buy time for their allies or the West to come to their support. Kuwait and several members of the United Arab Emirates have engaged in a complex internal competition for military "status," in which status has been determined by which royal family or ruling elite can buy the most prestigious arms and create the illusion of having large military forces most quickly.

This competition is reflected in Table 13.3, which compares summary measures of the military buildup in the Gulf during 1969–1981. Most of the states shown in the table are only now acquiring a modern technical base, and most have failed to follow Saudi Arabia's example in creating a suitable military infrastructure; hence Table 13.3 documents a process of waste and poorly controlled growth.

The Importance of the Human Element

Tables 13.1 and 13.2 disguise some critical aspects of the dynamics of the military buildup in the Gulf. The impressive force numbers on these tables do not reflect the vast diversity of incompatible equipment types, munitions, and military infrastructures that have been built up in most Gulf states. They do not show the rapid turnover of new equipment types or reflect the rate of turnover among senior military officers and foreign military advisers. They also do not reflect the political problems in the military forces of the radical Gulf states, which in many ways counterbalance the weaknesses of the conservative Gulf countries. These include massive purges in Iraq and Iran, involving the execution and imprisonment of thousands of officers and NCOs, and proportionate political upheavals in North and South Yemen.

These factors make the Gulf very different from Europe. Western military analysts measure the relative capabilities of NATO and Warsaw Pact military forces largely in terms of unit numbers and type, total manning, equipment numbers, and the quality and size of support forces. There are good reasons for using such criteria in assessing European forces. NATO and Warsaw Pact forces have tended to evolve in similar ways, to develop common training and performance standards, and to equip and structure their support and logistics to allow them to match the capabilities of their potential allies and enemies.

The situation is radically different in the case of military forces, like those in the Gulf states, that are undergoing rapid modernization. There is no movement toward common levels of military effectiveness. Unit structure is in constant turmoil. Equipment conversions often exceed 20% of major equipment a year. Training is erratic, and units evolve in very different ways even in the same country. There is no common

TABLE 13.3 Key Trends in the Military Force Buildup in the Gulf, 1969-1983

	Northern Gulf		Conservative Gulf		
	Iran	Iraq	Saudi Arabia	Bahrain	Kuwait
Defense expenditure[b] (current $ millions)					
1969	505	280	343	–	202
1973	2,010	467	1,900	34	360
1977	7,900	1,660	7,530	70	1,115
1982/83	6,900-13,300	7,700	21,952	253	1,561
Arms imports (current $ millions)					
1969	220	70	80	–	30
1973	525	625	80	–	0
1977	2,400	1,500	925	–	310
1980	220	1,600	1,400	20	50
Total military manpower					
1969	221,000	78,000	34,000	–	10,000
1973	211,500	101,000	42,500	3,000	14,000
1977	342,000	188,000	61,500	2,000	10,000
1983/84	2,000,000	517,250+	51,500	2,700	12,400
Main battle tanks					
1969	some	535	"a few"	–	–
1973	920	990	25	–	100
1977	1,620	1,350	475	–	112
1983/84	940[c]	2,360	450	–	200
Other AFVs					
1969	some	40+	60+	–	–
1973	2,000	1,300	260	16	250
1977	2,250	1,800	410	16	240
1983/84	900[c]	3,000[c]	1,490	142	485
Artillery					
1969	some	n.a.	–	–	–
1973	some	700	some	6	30
1977	874	790	54+	6	30
1983/84	1,200[c]	800[c]	74+	15	20+
High-performance combat aircraft					
1969	180	213	43	–	–
1973	159	224	70	–	30
1977	341	369	137	–	49
1983/84	80-100[c]	290-330[c]	216[d]	6	49

[a] Figures often inaccurate due to a lack of data.
[b] Figures are either for 1982 or 1983.
[c] Much equipment, especially aircraft, is low in serviceability. Large war losses affect totals, especially in armor and operational aircraft.

TABLE 13.3 (continued)

Conservative Gulf				Southern Gulf	
Qatar	Oman	UAE	Conservative States[a]	North Yemen	South Yemen
–	–	–	545	–	–
187	76	n.a.	2,557	–	–
n.a.	457	100	9,272	79	44
166	1,772	2,915	28,619	526	159
–	0	n.a.	110	0	10
–	10	10	100	5	40
40	50	140	1,465	30	120
90	100	160	1,820	490	240
–	n.a.	n.a.	44,000	n.a.	n.a.
3,000	9,600	11,150	83,250	20,900	9,500
n.a.	13,000	26,100	112,600	39,850	21,300
6,000	19,950	46,000	118,250	32,100	26,000
–	–	–	some	–	–
–	–	–	125	30	50
–	–	–	587	30	200
24	27	136	837	450	714
–	–	–	60+	–	–
48	some	96	670+	70	–
48	36	301	1,051	150	20
201	36+	486	2,840	527+	300+
–	–	–	–	–	–
4	some	some	40+	100	some
4	53	38	131+	100	some
14	66+	70+	259+	395	310+
–	–	–	43+	–	–
4	12	12	128	28	20
4	50	38	278	22	33
11	37	43	362	75	113

[d]BAC-167 aircraft used in training roles are counted, as are squadrons of F-15s forming in 1983.

Sources: The Military Balance (London: IISS, 1969–1984); defense expenditure and import figures from ACDA, *World Military Expenditures and Arms Transfers, 1971–1980,* Table I!I.

structure or standard of readiness, and every country tends to improvise to meet its particular needs. As a result, even those units that can fight effectively in set-piece defensive actions may collapse without warning in the face of the unfamiliar.

For precisely these reasons, several key officers or units in a given Gulf military force can make an incredible difference. An exceptional Iranian brigade commander may, for example, be able to easily halt two Iraqi divisions, whereas another might put up virtually no resistance. Similar human factors affect air, helicopter, naval, and commando performance in the Gulf. A good squadron commander might be able to incapacitate an enemy airbase in minutes; a conventional commander might be totally ineffective or abort his attack in the face of limited fighter or missile defenses. A good ship commander might be able to do incredible damage to tanker or offshore facilities in an hour; other officers might fail to exploit the obvious vulnerabilities.

It is true that huge differences among commanders and units often average out in large-scale combat. The outstanding officers on any given side tend to be counterbalanced by much larger numbers of ordinary or incompetent leaders. The weight of numbers shown in Table 13.1 may well be decisive in an all-out war between a large Gulf power like Iraq or Iran and a smaller Gulf power. Many military operations in the Gulf, however, seem likely to be limited actions designed to achieve a limited objective or probe the weaknesses of a neighboring nation. In small operations, differences in manpower quality will give a great advantage to the side that is capable of choosing the right unit or leader for a carefully planned application of force. This applies not only to commando operations but also to limited uses of armor. Ariel Sharon, for example, was able to support his crossing of the Suez Canal for more than six hours with only three to six tanks and limited Israeli infantry forces against two brigade-sized Egyptian forces. The outcome of Gulf conflicts will often depend on the conduct of a few officers whom the West and other Gulf states have never previously heard of, or on the professionalism of a few key units, and not on mass arms quality or weapons numbers.

Defense versus Internal Stability

The difficulty of analyzing the military effectiveness of the Gulf states is compounded by the problems they have in maintaining internal stability. No Gulf or neighboring state is totally stable, and most have either unstable and repressive radical regimes (Iraq, Iran, North Yemen, and South Yemen) or conservative quasi-feudal regimes whose ability to cope with their current pace of modernization is uncertain (Kuwait, Qatar, Bahrain, Saudi Arabia, Oman, and the UAE). In such a situation any military officer might seek to be the next head of state, and a major political crisis, economic crisis, or struggle for power could trigger a military coup. Every Gulf state is thus forced to be as worried about the potential internal threat from its military forces as about the threats posed by foreign military powers. Further, no Gulf state has been able to expand its army without drawing extensively on new social classes, or foreigners and other groups outside the ruling elite, for its officers and NCOs. No Gulf power now has a "traditional" army or air force. In every case, the bulk of the officers and NCOs are either foreigners or "new men" who lack the previous mix of family, economic, and political ties to the ruling regime.

The Gulf states have found four main solutions to this problem. First, they co-opt the military into the ruling elite; Saudi Arabia has perhaps been the most successful state in this regard. Second, they rely on a mixture of citizens and mercenaries, who, it is hoped, will not threaten to become rulers; the UAE has been the most successful practitioner of this strategy. Third, they systematically purge and murder any officers who hint at opposition; Iran, Iraq, and South Yemen have mastered this skill. Fourth, they create a paramilitary security force to watch the military; almost all the Gulf states have chosen this option, but Saudi Arabia, Iran, and Iraq seem to be the most successful, although the three nations use radically different approaches. No assessment of the military balance in the Gulf can be adequate, therefore, without considering internal security and the interaction between the military and the internal security forces. The most important military balance in most Gulf nations is often the one that prevents their own military forces from seizing power.

The Dynamics of the Gulf Military Buildup

The dynamics of the military buildup in the Gulf tend to be more important than the current military balance. Table 13.3 has already dramatized the extent to which Gulf forces are in a state of "perpetual becoming." Although many cultural and historical factors shape the capability of each Gulf force, each is the product of its relative level of arms imports, defense effort, manpower, and rates of absorption of modern military equipment. These trends, or "dynamics," are thus important indicators of what Gulf forces may become over the next 10 years and of how the U.S. might best cooperate with friendly Gulf states. The challenge is not to structure deterrence on the basis of this year's forces, but rather to provide a long-term capability to counter the trends in potentially hostile forces.

This challenge cannot be confined to the Gulf or Saudi Arabia. The military dynamics in neighboring states are creating significant potential threats from outside the Gulf region and new relationships between the increases in Gulf forces and those of neighboring states. The Iraqi military buildup, for example, cannot be divorced from that of Turkey and Syria or from the trends in the Arab-Israeli conflict. Although Jordan is not a Gulf state, it is a vital Western buffer for Saudi security, and any shift in its relative military position affects that of Saudi Arabia.

Similarly, no Gulf state can afford to ignore events in the USSR and in Afghanistan. The trends in the Northern Tier states also do much to determine the balance between Western and Soviet influence, while trends in the India-Pakistan conflict help determine the stability of the Indian Ocean area and the Gulf trade routes and labor supplies. Trends in Ethiopia, Somalia, and Sudan help to determine the security of the Red Sea and Saudi Arabia's air defenses, while trends in the military buildup of Egypt, Syria, and Libya have a powerful effect on which nation and political trends dominate Arab nationalism.

The Race in Arms Imports

The annual volume of arms transfers provides another measure of military dynamics. Although the unclassified data the U.S. government makes available on such arms transfers lag years behind current transfers and show remarkably little consistency over time, they still provide a useful picture of the shifts taking place throughout the region. Unlike most industrialized states, the Gulf nations and their neighbors must import virtually all their military equipment. The data on arms transfers are thus roughly equivalent to a measure of each Gulf state's total investment in military modernization and in new major combat equipment and munitions. These data are shown in Table 13.4[1] but it is important to note that they include only major military equipment transfers and exclude imports like services and construction. They also have the defect that although they are the best available measure of the extent to which given nations are acquiring new "teeth" and armaments, they are taken from ACDA reports based on CIA sources, which underprice Soviet arms deliveries.

Several key trends emerge from the data in Table 13.4:

• The first is how much greater the long-term expansion of Iranian and Iraqi forces has been relative to that of the other Gulf nations. As was discussed in Chapter 7, many of the defense expenditure data commonly used in comparing Gulf forces are misleading in that they equate the trend in total Saudi or conservative Gulf state defense expenditures with a buildup in weapons or "teeth," or they treat expenditures by the conservative states as if they were comparable to the expenditures of Iraq and Iran. As Table 13.4 shows, however, the other Gulf states lagged far behind Iran and Iraq in terms of weapons imports until the shah's fall.

• Second, both Iraq and Iran imported well over $1 billion (in constant dollars) worth of arms per year from 1976 onward. Until the shah's fall, however, Iran had a clear lead, spending over twice as much on arms as Saudi Arabia and about half again as much as Iraq. Since Iran could then buy modern Western equipment that was unavailable to Iraq, Iran was able to get far more for its arms expenditures.

Reliable unclassified data are not available on what has happened since the shah's fall. The Iranian government did cut back on arms

TABLE 13.4 Arms Imports in the Gulf, 1969–1980 (constant 1977 $ millions)

	1969	1970	1971	1972	1973	1974	1975	1976	1977	1978	1979	1980
Gulf												
Bahrain	—	—	—	—	—	—	—	—	—	—	20	18
Iran	428	272	547	862	815	1,419	1,555	2,465	2,907	2.063	1,600	199?
Iraq	136	85	68	229	971	887	875	1,232	1,744	1,738	2,100	1,450
Kuwait	58	—	8	8	—	—	64	98	360	325	60	45
Oman	—	17	17	8	15	14	51	12	58	293	10	90
Qatar	—	—	—	—	—	—	12	—	46	21	20	81
Saudi Arabia	155	51	34	164	124	482	323	542	1,017	1,194	925	1,269
UAE	—	—	—	16	15	70	38	123	151	43	150	145
South Yemen	19	8	8	32	62	56	51	49	139	152	250	217
North Yemen	—	—	—	16	7	14	25	24	34	97	450	444
Total	796	431	682	1,335	2,009	2,942	2,994	4,545	6,456	5,926	5,585	3,958
Arab-Israeli Confrontation States												
Egypt	214	1,104	598	903	1,320	326	453	184	290	412	625	453
Jordan	136	85	85	49	62	99	90	172	139	184	100	475
Lebanon	38	8	8	32	31	14	12	12	—	21	20	36
Syria	97	101	188	459	2,020	1,171	492	770	755	977	2,000	2,175
Subtotal	485	1,298	879	1,443	3,433	1,610	1,047	1,138	1,184	1,594	2,747	3,139
Israel	311	391	444	492	357	1,348	939	1,202	1,279	1,004	525	747
Libya	38	101	171	262	279	468	712	1,232	1,395	2,172	2,300	1,903
Total	834	1,790	1,494	2,197	4,069	3,426	2,698	3,572	3,858	4,770	5,570	5,789
Northern Tier/Indian Ocean												
Afghanistan	77	51	34	32	124	113	51	61	127	97	200	9
India	272	169	410	344	295	269	220	604	843	315	525	657
Pakistan	155	101	85	180	202	141	129	234	255	184	190	253
Turkey	467	425	444	246	77	212	285	394	162	238	170	226
Total	971	746	973	802	698	735	685	1,293	1,387	834	1,085	1,145
Horn of Africa												
Ethiopia	19	17	17	16	15	14	38	61	511	1,194	210	435
Sudan	38	67	8	32	15	42	—	61	220	130	100	90
Somalia	19	17	—	32	62	127	90	123	93	260	130	172
Total	77	101	25	80	92	203	128	245	824	1,584	440	697

Source: ACDA, *World Military Expenditures and Arms Transfers,* 1970–79, and 1971–80. These data are highly uncertain, and past years are often revised in each new edition of this document. The 1969 and 1970 import figures have been converted into 1979 dollars by the author. Data may not track with other estimates cited in the text from different sources and dates. Totals may not agree due to rounding.

imports in 1979, and this process was accelerated in 1980 by the hostage crisis. While Iran led Iraq in arms imports by 1.4 : 1 in 1978, Iraq led Iran by 2 : 1 in 1979. It is also clear that Iran had serious problems in obtaining Western munitions and spares during the first years of the Iran-Iraq War and that the balance of supply continued to tilt in Iraq's favor through mid-1981. Iran, however, learned to buy arms from other sources and got emergency aid from Israel. At the same time, the USSR refused to resupply Iraq. These events have left the current trend in imports unclear. U.S. experts estimate that Iran obtained arms worth between $250 and $350 million from Belgium, France, Greece, Israel, Libya, and Portugal during 1980–1981, worth well over $600 million from North Korea, and worth about $250 million from the USSR. They are unwilling to hazard a similar guess regarding the value of Iraq's purchases, although France alone may have sold Iraq over $600 million worth of arms in 1980. Both sides have failed to obtain massive arms transfers from either the U.S. or the USSR or even the spares necessary to fully maintain their surviving equipment.

• Third, the figures for the Arab-Israeli confrontation states reflect several important events. One is the Soviet break with Egypt, which resulted in major cuts in Soviet arms shipments to Egypt, a loss of at least one-third of Egypt's Soviet-supplied equipment, and Egypt's being forced to undertake a slow process of conversion to Western equipment and eventually to make major force cuts. These changes have reduced Egypt's ability to play a military role in the Red Sea area. At the same time, as Table 13.4 shows, Syria has generally outpaced Iraq in arms imports and the hostility between the two regimes acts as a potential check to Iraqi action in the Gulf. In spite of the peak deliveries to Jordan in 1980, Jordan has fallen far behind Syria and most Gulf nations in its rate of military modernization. It has moved from a position of superiority to Syria in the early 1970s to one where it is now modernizing at less than 15% of the rate of Syria. This trend has weakened Saudi Arabia's western buffer state, and it reflects a sharp downward shift in Jordan's long-term military influence in the region. At the same time, the almost incredible growth in Libya's arms imports reflects its growing importance as a "wild card" in the region and as a potential source of arms and military assistance to radical Gulf states and political movements.

• Fourth, the trend in arms imports has favored South Yemen over North Yemen in most of the years covered in Table 13.4. This imbalance, however, led to a major increase in North Yemeni imports in 1979–1981 that greatly strengthened North Yemeni forces. Since this has been matched by a buildup in Soviet deliveries to South Yemen, the arms race between the two Yemens has triggered a major increase in the potential threat to southeastern Saudi Arabia.

• Fifth, Table 13.4 helps to put the military trends in the Northern Tier and Indian Ocean area into perspective. While military powers like Turkey, India, and Pakistan imported far more arms than the Gulf states at the start of the 1970s, their arms imports are now at "token" levels in comparison to those of the Gulf and Arab-Israeli confrontation states. It is interesting to note that Kuwait imported more arms in 1978 than any Northern Tier nation, although Kuwait's military forces have since received more modest imports and have little more than token capability.

• Finally, Ethiopia has built up much faster than the other nations in the Horn, particularly Sudan and Somalia. The long-run importance of this shift is difficult to estimate, but it is clear that if it continues, Ethiopia will become the dominant power in the Horn and a major power in the Red Sea area and will pose a growing threat to Saudi Arabia and Western interests. It is also important to note that U.S. access to basing points in Somalia, and French facilities in Djibouti, will not parallel the immense military infrastructure and facilities that the USSR is building up in Ethiopia and South Yemen, many of which will be completed in the mid-1980s.

If these trends in arms imports continue, they will lead to significant shifts in the military balance in the Gulf and Southwest Asia.

The "wild card" in this process is the Iran-Iraq War. Neither Iran nor Iraq has yet turned to the U.S. or the USSR for major arms deliveries or created any kind of "client" relationship. As is discussed in depth in Chapter 17, however, this situation can continue for only a year or two more. Regardless of the final outcome of the war, Iran and Iraq must find a new major source of arms or risk the other's military dominance. Iran also faces the dilemma that its immense investment in U.S. equipment leaves it with only two choices in buying its arms: to find some modus vivendi with the U.S. or to align itself with the USSR. Iran either must have access to extensive supplies of U.S. equipment or be able to get the kind of large-scale rapid deliveries of totally new equipment that only the USSR can provide. Iraq faces somewhat similar problems in terms of choosing between France and the USSR, but its equipment is already more diversified. While it is not possible to rule out a scenario in which Iraq and Iran fight each other into paralysis, or in which a peace settlement or the political instability in both nations halts a massive postwar military buildup, such scenarios seem unlikely. As a result, the forces of the conservative Gulf states will almost certainly have to be built up to compensate for both the near-term shift in favor of Iran and the risk of an Iranian or Iraqi shift to dependence on the USSR for arms imports.

At the same time, as Table 13.4 shows, Saudi Arabia faces significant changes in the capability of the forces facing its western and southern borders. The balance in the Horn and Red Sea area is shifting steadily in favor of the more radical and anti-Western states. The military balance is also shifting away from Jordan and Egypt in favor of the more radical states like Syria and Libya. While such shifts may have more political than military importance to the Gulf states, they do have the effect of increasing the military isolation of the conservative Gulf forces and their need for deterrent capabilities.

The Balance of Defense Effort

Trends in defense expenditure are another major factor shaping the military dynamics of the Gulf, although the full implications of these trends can be only understood in terms of how such expenditures relate to each nation's defense effort. Table 13.5 provides an estimate of the comparative defense efforts of the individual Gulf states in 1980, the latest year for which truly comparable data are available. While the table has been dated by the same trends that have affected the post-1979 balance in arms imports, it reveals a number of further factors that shape the military dynamics in the Gulf.

Two sets of statistics in Table 13.5 are of particular importance. The first is military expenditure per soldier. This measure normally provides a good rough indicator of manpower and equipment quality. In the case of most conservative Gulf states, however, it reflects the immense cost of converting to modern military forces. Saudi Arabia, for example, has the highest total military expenditures per man, but these are not disproportionate to those of the other conservative Gulf states, particularly when their lack of matching effort in infrastructure and training in the smaller Gulf states is considered.

The figures for military expenditures per soldier for the other Gulf states are more complex. Recent data are not available on Iran and Iraq, but before the shah's fall Iran was spending almost twice as much per soldier as Iraq. Iraq's past expenditure levels seem far too low to build a modern army in the Gulf region, and they almost certainly reflect inadequate salary, training, and infrastructure expenditures. This inadequacy may help explain the relatively poor performance of Iraqi forces during the first two years of the Iran-Iraq War. At the same time, Iranian expenditures per soldier fell substantially below those of Iraq between 1978 and 1979, while Iraq's rose steadily, in spite of the expansion of Iraq's forces. If this trend had continued long enough before the Iran-Iraq War it might have tilted the balance in favor of Iraq. The war broke out, however, before Iraq could obtain any significant advantage from its superior defense effort.

The data on spending per soldier in the Yemens are so low that they indicate that the threat either nation can pose to Saudi Arabia is much lower than the force ratios in Table 13.2 or the arms imports figures in Table 13.4 would indicate. In contrast, the data for Oman reflect the high rate of expenditure necessary to build an effective force.

The other important statistic in Table 13.5 is the figure for arms imports per soldier. These show equipment transfers, or "modernization" expenditures, per man. They make a particularly interesting contrast with the data on defense expenditure per soldier. Again, however, some

TABLE 13.5 Comparative Measures of Defense Expenditure Efforts in the Gulf, 1980 (1979 dollars)

	Gross National Product (millions)	Military Expenditures (MILEX) (millions)	MILEX/ GNP (%)	Central Government Expendi-tures (CGE) (millions)	MILEX/ CGE (%)	GNP per Capita	MILEX per Capita	MILEX per Soldier	Arms Imports (millions)	Arms Imports per Soldier	Arms Imports/ Total Imports (%)
Saudi Arabia[a]	105,744	15,176	14.4	56,764	26.7	11,370	1,631	226,507	1,269	18,940	4.4
Other Conservative Gulf States											
Bahrain	2,628	50	1.9	754	6.6	8,762	166	25,000	18	9,000	0.5
Kuwait	28,077	1,192	4.2	8,442	14.1	20,055	851	119,500	45	4,500	0.6
Oman	4,339	1,069	24.6	2,430	44.0	4,821	1,188	76,357	90	6,429	6.2
Qatar	6,024	503	8.4	2,498	20.1	30,120	2,515	100,600	81	16,200	6.3
UAE	23,604	1,503	6.4	3,636	41.4	23,604	1,503	50,133	145	4,833	1.8
Subtotal (Average)	64,672	4,317	(9.1)	17,760	(25.2)	(17,472)	(1,245)	(74,378)	379	(8,192)	(3.1)
Total Conservative Gulf States (Average)	170,416	19,493	(11.8)	74,524	(26.0)	(14,421)	(1,438)	(150,413)	1,648	(13,566)	(3.7)
Other Gulf States											
Iran[c]	65,875	n.a.	n.a.	n.a.	n.a.	1,697	n.a.	n.a.	199	710	16.0
Iraq	35,484	n.a.	n.a.	n.a.	n.a.	2,708	n.a.	n.a.	1,450	6,590	12.3
North Yemen[b]	3,533	295	8.3	983	30.0	679	56	9,833	444	14,800	n.a.
South Yemen[b]	897	114	12.8	250	45.7	472	60	5,700	217	10,850	n.a.
Subtotal (Average)	105,789	410+	(10.6)	1,233+	(37.9)	(1,389)	(58)	(7,766)	2,310	(8,238)	(14.2)
Total Gulf States (Average)	276,205	19,903+	(11.2)	75,757+	(32.0)	(7,905)	(748)	(79,090)	3,958	(10,902)	(8.9)

[a] Includes Saudi National Guard.
[b] Discrepancy in data.
[c] Figures for Iran for 1978.

Source: ACDA, *World Military Expenditures and Arms Transfers,* 1971–80.

historical perspective is necessary to understand the major structural differences between the Saudi and Iranian military modernization efforts. Iran spent nearly 60% as much as Saudi Arabia in terms of arms imports per man for a vastly larger force structure, but only 28% as much in terms of total defense expenditures. It is interesting to note Iraq's overall defense spending per man was only 1.5 times as much as its spending on arms imports per man, while the figure for Iran was over 4. This statistic again reveals Iraq's overemphasis on equipment before the Iran-Iraq War and the lack of a balanced military modernization effort.

The imports per soldier figures also reveal a high level of imports relative to total expenditure per man in uniform for North and South Yemen. The Yemens were spending far too little relative to their arms imports to hope for an effective force. The data on other countries are generally predictable, with the exception of those for Bahrain. Bahrain "opted out" of the Gulf arms race until the shah's fall and spent almost nothing on arms per man.

The figures on military expenditures as a percentage of GNP may seem high by Western standards, but they are not unusual for such developing states. It was only under the shah that military spending posed a strain on a Gulf nation before the start of the Iran-Iraq War. Iranian defense spending reached 14.2% of GNP under the shah, and this was far too high given Iran's mix of population, civil economic needs, and development activities. This strain is also reflected in the past figure for Iran's arms imports as a percentage of total imports, and was at least a minor indicator of the pressures that helped overthrow the shah.

The Dynamics of Defense Expenditures

Tables 13.6 and 13.7 show the trends in overall defense expenditures in the region in both current and constant dollars. In some ways, such measures are more important to the economist than to the analyst of strategic stability in the Gulf, since they tell less about military capability than the previous data on arms imports or military expenditure per man. They are important, however, in documenting the sheer scale of the arms race in the Near East in the 1970s and the extent to which the arms race in the Gulf has outpaced the arms race in the Arab-Israeli conflict, the Horn, and in the Northern Tier and Indian Ocean area. Further, these figures do provide some additional insights into the military dynamics of the region. Table 13.7, for example, traces a consistently low level of defense expenditure on the part of the Yemens and reflects the qualitative limits to their forces in much the same way as the snapshot of the defense effort provided in Table 13.5.

The data on Iraq and Iran reflect an even sharper Iranian superiority over Iraq before the shah's fall than did most of the previous measures. This superiority was also the result of a much greater Iranian effort in all aspects of military expenditure, including bases, training, support

TABLE 13.6 **Defense Expenditures in the Gulf, 1969–1981 (current $ millions)**

	1969	1970	1971	1972	1973	1974	1975	1976	1977	1978	1979	1980	1981[a]
Gulf													
Bahrain	–	–	–	–	4	7	14	28	39	49	57	55	135
Iran	1,828	2,045	2,644	3,266	3,927	6,654	9,128	10,038	9,242	11,342	7,700[b]	4,200[b]	4,400[b]
Iraq	826	822	762	816	1,168	1,510	1,555	1,684	1,891	2,148	2,671	3,790[b]	4,500[b]
Kuwait	202	203	185	210	234	568	731	1,086	1,043	1,076	1,181	1,315	1,300
Oman	–	127	46	77	121	342	698	785	686	768	779	1,179	1,690
Qatar	–	–	–	52	114	104	124	167	230	264	458	555	893
Saudi Arabia	1,182	1,481	573	792	1,187	2,670	6,519	9,426	9,505	10,751	13,851	16,740	24,400
UAE	–	–	–	16	13	20	32	81	505	791	1,151	1,658	1,700
South Yemen	32	31	39	37	46	53	46	61	65	96	104	114	150[b]
North Yemen	14	27	36	37	41	59	85	105	130	155	373	325	135[b]
Total	4,084	4,736	4,285	5,303	6,855	11,987	18,932	23,461	23,336	27,440	28,325	29,931	39,303
Arab-Israeli													
Egypt	435	645	811	1,031	1,073	1,524	1,929	1,472	1,834	2,044	1,984	1,362	2,100
Jordan	100	78	155	184	182	186	192	337	283	310	382	399	425
Lebanon	46	48	44	48	54	85	86	93	98	–	–	–	232
Syria	227	282	235	290	508	497	1,014	1,055	1,077	1,273	1,577	2,205	2,390[b]
Subtotal	808	1,053	1,245	1,553	1,817	2,292	3,221	2,957	3,292	3,627	3,943	3,966	5,147
Israel	1,196	1,663	1,492	1,352	2,878	2,799	3,502	3,761	3,786	3,409	4,814	5,051	6,060
Libya	183	302	140	134	193	388	243	364	479	729	500	523	630
Total	2,187	3,018	2,877	3,039	4,888	5,479	6,966	7,082	7,557	7,765	9,257	9,540	11,837
Northern Tier/Indian Ocean													
Afghanistan	29	26	25	31	36	36	49	72	61	69	64[b]	80[b]	97
India	1,395	1,564	2,181	2,210	2,002	2,343	3,105	3,167	3,313	3,812	4,155	4,521	5,260
Pakistan	388	446	530	588	658	650	793	863	833	976	1,054	1,265	1,890
Turkey	750	875	1,224	1,285	1,361	1,507	2,712	3,293	3,535	3,555	3,155	3,546	2,620
Total	2,562	2,911	3,960	4,114	4,057	4,536	6,659	7,395	7,742	8,412	8,428	9,412	9,867
Horn of Africa													
Ethiopia	39	40	43	50	42	46	101	139	178	159	334	427	387
Sudan	70	91	175	164	155	136	131	133	188	227	227	260	333
Somalia	11	14	19	20	21	27	27	28	33	81	84	93	–
Total	120	145	237	234	218	209	259	300	399	467	645	780	720

[a] Adapted from *The Military Balance,* 1981–82 and 1982–83 (London: IISS, 1982 and 1983).
[b] Figures highly uncertain; often estimated by author.
Sources: Adapted from ACDA, *World Military Expenditures and Arms Transfers,* 1969–78, and 1971–80.

TABLE 13.7 **Defense Expenditures in the Gulf, 1969–1981 (constant [1979] $ millions)**

	1969	1970	1971	1972	1973	1974	1975	1976	1977	1978	1979	1980	1981 [a]
Gulf													
Bahrain	–	–	–	–	7	10	19	35	45	54	57	50	122
Iran	3,528	3,763	4,524	5,365	6,103	9,447	11,828	12,377	10,747	12,320	n.a.	n.a.	3,960[b]
Iraq	1,594	1,512	1,303	1,340	1,816	2,144	2,015	2,076	2,199	2,334	2,671	n.a.	4,050
Kuwait	389	374	317	345	364	807	948	1,340	1,213	1,168	1,181	1,192	1,170
Oman	–	234	79	127	189	485	905	968	798	834	779	1,069	1,521
Qatar	–	–	–	85	177	147	160	205	267	286	458	503	804
Saudi Arabia	2,281	2,725	981	1,301	1,845	3,792	8,448	11,623	11,053	11,678	13,831	15,176	21,960
UAE	–	–	–	27	21	29	42	100	587	859	1,151	1,503	1,530
South Yemen	62	57	39	37	46	53	46	61	65	96	104	114	135[b]
North Yemen	27	50	61	61	63	84	110	129	151	168	373	295	122[b]
Total	7,882	8,714	7,304	8,688	10,631	16,998	24,521	28,914	27,125	29,797	20,605	19,902	35,374
Arab-Israeli Confrontation States													
Egypt	840	1,187	1,387	1,694	1,669	2,164	2,500	1,815	2,133	2,221	1,984	1,235	1,890
Jordan	193	144	266	302	283	264	248	416	329	337	382	361	383
Lebanon	89	88	76	79	85	122	112	115	114	n.a.	n.a.	n.a.	209
Syria	438	519	402	477	790	706	1,314	1,300	1,252	1,382	1,577	1,999	2,151
Subtotal	1,559	1,938	2,131	2,552	2,827	3,256	4,174	3,646	3,828	3,940	3,942	3,595	4,632
Israel	2,308	3,060	2,553	2,221	4,473	3,974	4,539	4,638	4,402	3,703	4,814	4,579	5,454
Libya	353	556	239	220	300	551	315	449	557	792	500	474	567
Total	4,221	5,553	4,923	4,993	7,600	7,781	9,028	8,733	8,787	8,435	9,256	8,648	10,653
Northern Tier/Indian Ocean													
Afghanistan	56	48	43	51	56	51	64	89	71	75	n.a.	n.a.	87
India	2,692	2,877	3,731	3,630	3,111	3,327	4,024	3,905	3,853	4,141	4,155	4,099	4,734
Pakistan	748	821	906	966	1,023	922	1,028	1,064	968	1,061	1,054	1,146	1,701
Turkey	1,448	1,610	2,093	2,111	2,116	2,140	3,515	4,061	4,111	3,862	3,155	3,215	2,358
Total	4,945	5,356	6,773	6,758	6,306	6,440	8,631	9,119	9,003	9,139	8,364	8,460	8,880
Horn of Africa													
Ethiopia	75	74	74	83	65	65	130	172	207	173	334	387	348
Sudan	135	167	300	270	242	193	170	164	218	247	227	236	300
Somalia	21	26	33	34	33	39	35	35	38	88	84	84	–
Total	232	267	407	387	340	297	335	371	463	508	645	707	648

[a] 1981 dollars are converted at 0.9.

[b] Figures uncertain; many are author's estimates.

Sources: The Military Balance (London: IISS, various years); ACDA, *World Military Expenditures and Arms Transfers,* 1969–78 and 1971–80. 1969 expenditures are converted at 1.93; 1970 expenditures are converted at 1.84. 1971–1980 conversions are by ACDA.

facilities, and military communications. Accordingly, the data in Tables 13.6 and 13.7 indicate that the simple force measures shown in Tables 13.1 and 13.2 understate the strength Iran built up before the shah's fall. They provide a further explanation of why Iran has been able to check Iraqi attacks in spite of the disarray of the Iranian military and the lack of a steady source of resupply. Iran's expenditures under the shah had built up a "bank" of added superiority on which Iran is now drawing.

The data for Kuwait again reflect an almost incredible level of spending for a nation with token military forces, particularly when they are compared to the defense expenditure data for the UAE, which is often used as an example of Gulf overspending on military forces.

The data in Tables 13.6 and 13.7 also reveal some insights into the dynamics of defense expenditure in neighboring states. They again show Syria's emergence as the dominant Arab military power among the Arab-Israeli confrontation states and the relative drop in the defense efforts of Jordan and Egypt. This drop is, in fact, much greater in the case of Egypt than is initially apparent because Egypt has had to fund an extraordinarily large force structure and manpower base.

The expenditure data indicate that India's superiority to Pakistan is increasing at a faster rate than is reflected in the arms transfer data in Table 13.4. India has outspent Pakistan by 3–4:1 in total defense expenditures over the last decade versus about 2 : 1 in arms imports. Since India has a comparatively efficient force structure and can manufacture a substantial amount of its own military equipment, the long-term trend will make India far superior to Pakistan. The data also indicate, incidentally, that it is unlikely that any credible amount of U.S. or Saudi military aid could substantially alter the balance in Pakistan's favor.

The data on the Horn indicate a much higher level of effort by Sudan than do the arms transfer data. This is consistent with its force structure, because Sudan has a large amount of manpower but little modern equipment and military capability. The trends in arms import data shown in Table 13.4 are unquestionably valid in indicating that Ethiopia is becoming the dominant military power in the Horn.

Finally, the data in Tables 13.6 and 13.7 provide a useful counterbalance to the critics of military spending by the conservative Gulf states. While the tables reflect a regionwide tragedy in terms of overall waste and unproductive expenditure, the high defense expenditures of the conservative Gulf states are the result of pressures in the region that make them almost inevitable. The conservative Gulf states, which are largely attempting to defend the status quo and their own national wealth, cannot stand aside from the defense efforts of their radical neighbors. While some, like Kuwait, unquestionably went too far in the period before the Iran-Iraq War, the others would have virtually been forced into the levels of expenditure shown in these tables. These pressures become even clearer when the "snapshot" of defense effort shown in Table 13.5 is analyzed by individual trend.

Other Aspects of the Dynamics of Defense Effort

The trend in defense expenditures as a percentage of GNP is shown in Table 13.8, and the trend in defense expenditures as a percentage of central government expenditures is shown in Table 13.9. Unfortunately, the data in Table 13.8 are uncertain, and they predate the full impact of the shah's fall, the Iran-Iraq War, and the resulting rises in oil prices. Table 13.8 does, however, dramatize the strain that the Dhofar rebellion imposed on the Omani economy, the growing strain military expenditures put on the Iranian economy, and the considerable pressure defense spending put on the economies of Iraq and South Yemen. Similar strains did not occur in the cases of Saudi Arabia and Kuwait because of their comparatively small populations and their ability to fund military expansion without reducing either the growth of consumer benefits or economic development.

The data for defense expenditures as a percentage of total central government expenditures (CGE), shown in Table 13.9, convey roughly the same message. However, the strain the shah's ambitious military expansion plans imposed on Iran's economy is shown even more clearly than by the figures for GNP. Iran had a comparatively large market economy outside the governmental sector, but it depended directly or indirectly on governmental economic development expenditures for the bulk of the jobs in its construction sector. It was also Iran's central government expenditures that created most new agricultural jobs and absorbed the nation's growing population into the Iranian economy. Seen from this perspective, Table 13.9 shows that the shah spent so much on defense in the mid-1970s that he helped generate the pressures that forced his massive development cutbacks in 1978. The resulting unemployment of many workers and youth who had migrated into the cities or sought rural employment helped create the social and economic basis for the popular movement that overthrew him.

In contrast, Iraq avoided many of these strains because its economic development plans were less ambitious, its urban migration was more limited, and its urban development was better balanced. Ironically, the shah's fall also greatly eased Iraq's problem in maintaining a high level of CGE on defense until it launched its invasion of Iran. The rise in oil prices caused by the Iranian oil production cutbacks that followed the shah's departure gave Iraq the resources to fund high levels of both military expansion and economic development.

The Saudi figures for defense spending as a percentage of CGE are slightly disturbing, given the limitations on Saudi Arabia's market economy outside the range of government expenditure. However, many of the Saudi expenditures shown in 1969–1978 went to finance infrastructure development with broad benefits to the civilian economy.

TABLE 13.8 Gulf Defense Expenditures as a Percentage of GNP, 1969–1981

	1969	1970	1971	1972	1973	1974	1975	1976	1977	1978	1979	1980	1981
Gulf													
Bahrain	—	—	—	—	1.3	1.0	2.0	2.7	2.8	3.0	2.8	1.9	n.a.
Iran	8.3	7.8	8.4	8.5	8.3	11.8	14.3	13.5	11.6	14.6	n.a.	3.7	n.a.
Iraq	13.8	12.9	12.3	11.5	13.6	15.7	11.8	11.0	10.7	9.9	8.0	7.6	n.a.
Kuwait	3.1	2.9	4.8	5.6	5.8	5.0	5.4	7.0	6.3	6.0	4.4	4.2	4.2
Oman	n.a.	15.2	15.9	25.0	37.5	28.3	40.9	39.9	31.6	34.2	26.0	24.6	43.2
Qatar	—	—	—	11.3	19.0	5.2	5.7	6.8	9.2	8.9	9.7	8.4	13.6
Saudi Arabia	10.9	11.9	10.1	11.1	13.2	10.9	17.4	19.1	15.3	15.9	18.1	14.4	20.5
UAE	—	—	—	1.4	0.6	0.3	0.4	0.7	3.4	5.5	6.1	6.4	n.a.
South Yemen	8.7	8.2	9.4	10.5	11.7	13.5	11.0	10.9	9.3	12.4	12.1	12.8	n.a.
North Yemen	2.7	4.3	4.6	4.2	3.7	4.8	5.4	5.0	5.0	4.9	11.2	8.3	n.a.
Arab-Israeli Confrontation States													
Egypt	9.6	12.8	12.9	15.1	14.7	18.5	19.6	12.1	12.9	12.2	10.5	6.0	n.a.
Jordan	17.8	14.9	17.3	18.1	17.6	16.2	14.1	17.2	13.3	12.2	14.2	12.0	n.a.
Lebanon	2.9	2.7	2.5	2.4	2.4	3.2	5.1	11.0	17.6	n.a.	n.a.	n.a.	5.5
Syria	10.1	11.7	8.3	8.3	14.6	10.3	15.6	14.4	14.1	14.3	15.7	18.1	19.9
Israel	20.3	25.1	22.7	17.6	34.1	28.6	31.9	32.7	30.0	24.3	30.7	29.1	28.7
Libya	1.9	2.8	2.9	2.6	3.0	3.3	2.2	2.5	2.7	4.3	2.2	1.7	12.8
Northern Tier/Indian Ocean													
Afghanistan	2.1	1.7	1.6	2.0	1.9	1.6	1.9	2.5	2.0	2.0	n.a.	n.a.	3.0
India	3.0	3.0	3.5	3.5	2.9	3.0	3.4	3.2	2.9	2.9	3.1	2.8	3.3
Pakistan	5.9	5.8	6.4	6.7	6.6	5.7	6.1	6.0	5.2	5.3	5.0	5.0	6.9
Turkey	4.3	4.2	4.4	4.1	3.9	3.7	4.4	6.0	5.9	5.4	4.4	4.5	5.1
Horn of Africa													
Ethiopia	2.6	2.3	2.4	2.5	1.9	1.9	3.8	4.9	5.7	4.8	8.7	9.7	n.a.
Sudan	2.6	3.4	4.9	4.5	4.4	3.2	2.6	2.3	2.8	3.0	2.9	3.0	2.7
Somalia	5.1	5.9	3.4	3.2	3.2	4.6	3.2	3.2	3.2	6.7	6.3	6.3	n.a.

Sources: Adapted from ACDA, *World Military Expenditures and Army Transfers,* 1969–78, and 1970–79, Table I. The Reader should note that these data are taken from a document issued in March 1983; they differ from other ACDA statistics used in this book. Data for 1981 taken from *The Military Balance, 1981–82* (London: IISS, 1982).

TABLE 13.9 Gulf Defense Expenditures as a Percentage of Central Government Expenditures, 1969–1980

	1969	1970	1971	1972	1973	1974	1975	1976	1977	1978	1979	1980
Gulf												
Bahrain	—	—	—	—	4.3	3.6	4.6	5.4	5.8	6.7	8.7	6.6
Iran	28.4	25.8	26.4	27.7	30.2	29.1	32.1	32.2	24.8	27.4	—	—
Iraq	38.2	37.6	30.9	32.4	30.7	32.8	20.2	23.9	24.1	14.4	13.4	—
Kuwait	8.4	7.7	15.3	14.2	12.8	14.8	18.9	19.7	14.7	15.3	13.3	14.1
Oman	—	60.2	35.0	37.6	45.8	31.4	47.9	45.5	44.3	47.3	41.4	44.0
Qatar	—	—	—	9.5	14.2	11.3	7.6	8.9	10.5	14.7	20.9	20.1
Saudi Arabia	24.9	27.2	30.6	34.1	17.5	34.7	34.1	35.5	25.3	29.0	27.3	26.7
UAE	—	—	—	43.0	13.2	10.8	10.5	12.5	31.1	40.3	50.7	41.4
South Yemen	53.2	46.0	44.4	45.2	45.8	47.8	46.9	43.6	42.2	50.5	47.2	45.7
North Yemen	30.2	33.3	31.0	30.5	30.0	33.8	37.0	34.2	33.9	27.1	38.2	30.0
Arab-Israeli Confrontation States												
Egypt	27.3	32.4	32.1	33.8	32.1	33.7	31.6	25.8	25.1	23.1	25.2	16.4
Jordan	46.9	47.0	41.6	39.6	35.1	31.3	23.8	35.9	25.1	27.3	23.7	23.4
Lebanon	18.6	17.4	17.3	16.4	15.7	20.4	15.7	15.8	16.4	—	—	—
Syria	36.7	37.6	16.9	17.2	16.7	18.1	31.1	29.9	28.5	27.4	26.5	28.4
Israel	42.0	47.6	42.1	39.8	54.8	43.3	43.3	41.0	34.8	34.0	38.6	34.2
Libya	6.9	9.9	8.8	6.1	6.7	8.9	5.1	6.2	7.3	10.0	6.2	4.5
Northern Tier/Indian Ocean												
Afghanistan	20.0	19.9	20.6	19.0	19.8	18.5	17.9	18.5	17.0	17.3	n.a.	n.a.
India	19.4	18.8	21.6	20.0	20.3	21.0	19.6	18.5	16.7	15.1	17.5	16.0
Pakistan	29.0	31.9	43.6	40.9	33.4	28.3	26.5	26.1	23.8	24.5	21.6	23.2
Turkey	19.0	20.4	19.0	21.1	19.9	19.9	26.1	26.0	21.4	20.0	16.5	19.1
Horn of Africa												
Ethiopia	23.7	21.1	21.2	18.4	13.7	13.9	20.2	24.7	29.2	23.0	42.7	42.6
Sudan	15.3	19.6	20.4	19.3	18.4	16.2	11.0	10.7	12.2	14.7	11.4	12.2
Somalia	22.5	25.3	19.3	16.4	12.8	11.5	10.9	10.2	12.6	21.2	17.0	18.4

Sources: ACDA, *World Military Expenditures and Arms Transfers,* 1969–78 and 1971–80, Table I. The data are only slightly less uncertain and subject to change than the data in Table 10.8.

Further, the rise in oil prices following the shah's fall initially reduced the pressure defense put on the total Saudi budget. This situation has since been altered by the world recession of the early 1980s, but it is too soon to predict a trend.

Oman and South Yemen exhibit levels of central government expenditure on defense that are far too high for orderly economic development. The tragedy for Oman is that the Dhofar rebellion effectively cost Oman most of its limited oil wealth for a decade and imposed an awkward and limited economic development program oriented toward achieving internal security rather than balanced growth. This situation has changed significantly since 1978, but Table 13.9 shows that Oman had to spend an incredible amount of national income on the war for a nation with comparatively limited oil reserves and that its victory over the Dhofar rebels may have been achieved only at the cost of future economic growth and political stability.

The CGE figures for South Yemen reflect the impact of the brutal national history outlined in Chapter 12. Expenditure levels have remained far too high for a developing nation that perpetually skates on the edge of economic collapse, and it is clear from Table 13.9 that they have helped drive North Yemen to a similar level of stress. Tables 13.8 and 13.9 show that the cultural and political causes of internal instability in both Yemens have been structurally reinforced for more than a decade by an arms race that neither country can afford.

Table 13.8 shows as well that the nations involved in the Arab-Israeli dispute have also suffered severely from the need to maintain exceptionally high defense expenditure levels. It is obvious that Syria and Israel have been under severe economic stress in funding their forces for nearly a decade, while both Jordan and Egypt have chosen to reduce their comparative defense effort. It is also apparent that Libya's exaggerated arms purchases impose little real strain on its overall economy.

The data in Table 13.9 are particularly interesting for the Arab-Israeli confrontation states because they confirm the structural shift in Egyptian and Jordanian governmental spending away from defense over half a decade. Such figures are somewhat confusing because they do not always count military and economic aid receipts accurately or report expenditures within the right year (this is particularly true of loans and new loan obligations). Nevertheless, these trends for Jordan and Egypt are supported by the previous data on arms imports and total defense expenditures, and they indicate a major reduction in both nations' efforts to challenge Israel that could not be quickly reversed. At the same time, the GNP and CGE data on Syria and Israel reflect the same trends as in Table 13.8 and show the extent to which both powers have severely strained their national budgets to support their respective defense efforts.

The data on the trends in the Northern Tier countries have largely been overtaken by events. They are overoptimistic in that they do not reflect the major post-1978 upsurge in Indian and Pakistani defense expenditures that have reversed the downward trend between 1974 and 1979. They reflect a situation in Afghanistan that has been totally changed by the Soviet invasion of that country. Similarly, the data on the Horn only hint at the resurgence of the arms race in that area, which Somalia triggered in 1978 and which has been followed by major new defense efforts in both Somalia and Ethiopia from 1979 onward. Preliminary data for 1980 indicate that the percentage of CGE that Somalia and Ethiopia now spend on defense is so large that it consumes most of the resources that could go to economic development.

Comparative Manpower

Assessing manpower trends or dynamics in the Gulf is complicated by the fact that the nations in the Gulf and neighboring regions have such disparate manpower resources. Differences are a matter not only of total population but also of different educational and skill levels and varying dependence on foreign workers. Further, Gulf manpower statistics are uncertain and are often political in nature or the product of erratic estimates made without the use of modern statistical methods or census inputs.

These problems are illustrated in Table 13.10, which shows typical IISS and UN manpower data for the Gulf countries. The data in the table present roughly the same problems regardless of the choice of source:

- Nations like Saudi Arabia with limited populations exaggerate their estimates of total population and fail to provide supporting data. The numbers of legal and illegal foreigners (at least 70% of the population in the case of Qatar) suffer from even more erratic counts.
- The data on age-group distribution of males—which should be reasonably accurate, given the current emphasis on educating young military-age males in most Gulf countries, reflect severe undercounting, even when such data are available. There seems to be a failure to count a substantial number of privately educated males, males who are not in school, males still outside the school system, and males outside urban areas. Given the case-study data available on shifts in infant mortality, even in relatively backward areas in most Gulf countries, the percentage of youthful males must be much higher than available Gulf country or U.S. data indicate.
- Table 13.10 does not show data on numbers of teachers, students, and graduates, but such statistics are equally lacking or confusing. Some of these data are shown in Table 13.11, but some nations seem to report the capacity of their schools rather than actual output and a few countries seem to include the output of schools in the planning stages or under construction. The data in Table 13.11 on North and South Yemen seem particularly exaggerated in this regard. There is no doubt, however, that the table is accurate in showing that many Gulf countries, particularly

TABLE 13.10 Comparative Measures of Defense Manpower in the Gulf, 1981–1982

	Total Population[a] (thousands)	Armed Forces[a] (thousands)	Armed Forces per 1,000 People[a]	Male Population (thousands)				Annual Growth Rate (%)
				Total	Age 15–19	Age 20–24	Age 25–29	
Saudi Arabia	8,100	52.2	6.4	–	–	–	–	3.1
Other Conservative Gulf States								
Bahrain	400	2.6	6.5	116.3	11.6	9.6	9.1	10.5
Kuwait	1,400	12.4	8.9	581.2	48.0	51.6	52.8	6.1
Oman	948	18.0	19.0	–	–	–	–	3.1
Qatar	240	6.0	25.0	–	–	–	–	5.4
UAE	1,040	48.5	46.6	110.8	–	–	–	7.7
Subtotal	4,028	87.5		–	–	–	–	6.6
(Average)			(21.7)					
Total Conservative Gulf States	12,128	139.7		–	–	–	–	6.0
(Average)			(11.5)					
Other Gulf States								
Iran	39,100	235.0	6.0	17,337.2	1,821.9	1,335.6	1,009.2	2.2
Iraq	13,600	342.3	25.2	6,182.9	488.3	602.4	422.8	3.5
North Yemen	7,200	32.1	4.5	–	–	–	–	2.3
South Yemen	1,995	26.0	13.0	889.2	76.8	62.2	54.2	3.1
Subtotal	61,895	635.4		–	–	–	–	2.8
(Average)			(10.3)					
Total Gulf States	74,023	775.1		–	–	–	–	4.8
(Average)			(10.5)					

[a] Data are uncertain. Figures in the *CIA Factbook* for 1981 and 1983 are quite different. The figures are taken from the IISS deliberately to allow a contrast with the CIA data used elsewhere.

Sources: For the first three columns, *The Military Balance, 1982–83* (London: IISS, 1983). Male population figures are from United Nations, *Demographic Yearbook,* 1980. (Note: Data vary because different years are indexed for each country; average index year: 1976.) Annual growth rate figures are from United Nations, *Statistical Yearbook,* 1979–80.

TABLE 13.11 Educational Enrollment of Males in the Gulf States

	Overall Literacy (%)	Primary	Secondary Total	Technical	University	Total
Iran	37	2,800,000	1,400,000	121,000	96,000	4,417,000
Iraq	20–40	1,200,000	350,000	18,000	56,000	1,624,000
Saudi Arabia	15–25	440,000	157,000	4,500	21,000	622,500
Kuwait	60	61,000	59,000	1,700	3,500	125,200
Bahrain	40	25,000	10,000	1,470	340	36,810
Oman	10	40,000	1,200	84	–	41,284
Qatar	25	13,000	5,000	370	330	18,700
UAE	25	55,000	13,000	620	–	68,620
North Yemen	15	227,000	27,000	566	2,200	256,766
South Yemen	10[a]	139,000	33,000	550	780	173,330

[a]25% in Aden.

Sources: United Nations Yearbook, 1979. See tables under "Education." Figures are rounded. Note that data have since ceased to be reported by the UN. Literacy figures taken from CIA, *World Factbook, 1981,* GS-WF 81-001 (U).

Iran, Iraq, and the conservative Gulf states, have made massive progress in educating their male populations and that large numbers of literate males, with sufficient technical background to operate modern military equipment, are now entering the labor force in most Gulf countries. At the same time, the statistical data involved seem so uncertain as to make detailed comparisons among countries pointless.

• The data in Table 13.11 generally imply that most Gulf states instituted large-scale education in the mid-1970s, although this effort is really just beginning to be successful in most states. This point is particularly important because it indicates that the military manpower base in most Gulf countries will not have the educational background to operate modern equipment until the middle to late 1980s.

• Recent reports on Qatar and the UAE indicate that educational progress is more uncertain in these countries than in the other conservative Gulf states. Recent reports on Iran—which are admittedly hearsay—indicate that the educational system is experiencing widespread collapse, which could eventually tilt the balance in favor of Iraq if Iran does not win the current war. Finally, the limited data available on both Yemens indicate a failure to develop effective education systems: South Yemen's system is regressing in capability and that of North Yemen is failing to advance.

These trends in manpower and education must be kept in mind in appraising the military balance in the Gulf. Like the long-term trends in defense expenditures, they inevitably shape the extent to which the forces and force ratios shown in Tables 13.1 and 13.2 can, in fact, be translated into military capability.

Foreign Manpower and Ethnic Minorities

Foreign manpower and ethnic minority demographics in the Gulf states are summarized in Table 13.12. While the data in this table are drawn from many sources, and virtually all such sources conflict, it does provide an overview of the extent to which each Gulf nation is divided against itself and to which its society and economy are dependent on expatriate labor. These statistics have several broad implications for the dynamics of Gulf security and defense:

• Ethnic movements, particularly that of the Kurds, are strong enough in both Iran and Iraq to constantly threaten internal security. There have been five major Kurdish revolts in Iraq since the late 1940s, and low-level violence still continues from various Kurdish independence movements. The Kurds in Iran were relatively quiet from 1948 to 1978, but they have been an increasing source of friction since the shah's fall and the outbreak of the Iran-Iraq War. Kurdish nationalist activity now virtually forces both Iraq and Iran to maintain a large troop presence in Kurdish areas.

• Iran is also divided by Turkish minorities in the northwest, Baluchis in the southeast, and Sunni Arabs in Khuzestan—Iran's major oil province and the area Iraq invaded at the start of the Iran-Iraq War. Although the Sunni minority in Iran showed a surprising lack of support for the Iraqi-backed liberation efforts, it and the other minorities in Iran have long been forcibly suppressed and have shown considerable resistance to the Khomeini regime.

• Iraq is predominantly Shi'ite, but it is ruled by a minority Sunni elite that is currently dominated by a relatively small cadre of senior Baathist officials from the town of Takrit. Long-standing discrimination against the Shi'ites has led to a number of riots and to limited purges of Shi'ite officials. Khomeini's efforts to exploit this situation, and to obtain influence or control over the Shi'ite majority in Iraq, were a major reason for the current Iran-Iraq War.

• Shi'ite minorities exist in most of the other Gulf states. Recent events have indicated that the Shi'ite population in the southern Gulf countries is probably larger than has previously been estimated, particularly in the Eastern Province of Saudi Arabia and in Bahrain and Kuwait. The Shi'ites are a majority of the native population in Bahrain, and large native and expatriate Shi'ite populations exist in Qatar and the UAE.

• The Foreign population in many of the southern Gulf states is so large that they have been forced into steadily more rigorous efforts to control labor permits and illegal immigration since the mid-1970s, and most states face serious long-term problems in dealing with a large male population of foreign workers that exceeds the native male population. Qatar unquestionably has the most severe problem in this regard, but all the conservative Gulf states face the problem. Only Saudi Arabia and Oman can close their societies enough to monitor their current

TABLE 13.12 Foreign Labor and Ethnic Minority Demographics in the Gulf States

Iran	• CIA estimates population as 42,490,000 in July 1983, rising at 3.1% annually • Roughly 88–93% of the population Shi'ite, including non-Persian Shi'ite minorities. 5% is Sunni, 2% other. • "Foreign" population uncertain (200,000 Iraqi Kurds, 1977) • Population 47% urban in 1976 and rising rapidly • Ethnic minorities concentrated in the north and northwest peripheries. Out of total population 3% are Kurds, 18% are Turkic, 3% are Sunni Arab, 13% are other Iranian, and 1% are Christian, Jews, etc. • A great number of small, ethnically diverse tribes, the largest being the Baluch, comprising 3% of the population. Frequent tribal uprisings sometimes met with brutal eradication. Most tribes have become sedentary • 45.5% of the population under 15 in 1975 • About 33% of the12-million-man labor force is agrarian • A sharp shortage of skilled labor occurred in 1977 • Actively employed as percentage of total population fell from 32.6% (1956) to 28% (1975) • Trends in growth, urbanization, and modernization moderated in the 1970s, but effects of revolution in 1979 remain uncertain • Literacy is 50% • Total population was 14,509,000 in July 1983
Iraq	• Foreign population uncertain, but not large • Population 62% urban in 1975, and rising very rapidly; concentrated in the center and river valley plains • Growth rate 3.2% in 1973–1975 and 3.3% in 1983, ignoring effects of war • Population is 71% Arab, 18% Kurds, 0.7% Assyrian, 2.4% Turkoman, and 8% other • 55% are Shi'ite, 40% Sunni, 5% Christian and other • 48% under 15 (1976) • Majority of Bedouin tribes sedentary and integrated • Shi'ites a majority, but Sunni minority dominates government • About 30% of the 3.1-million-man labor force in the agricultural sector, 27% in industry, 21% in government, 22% other • Agricultural population declining rapidly as people flock to cities • CIA estimates literacy at 30%; government claims as high as 90%
Saudi Arabia	• Total population between 6.4 and 10.4 million, rising at 3.4% per year 4.3–8.7 million natives (2.1–4.2 million males) 1.7–2.1 million foreign workers • Foreign workers uncertain in number. One recent estimate is 600,000 Yemenis, 300,000 Egyptians, 100,000 Palestinians and Jordanians, 200,000 Filipinos, 300,000 Pakistanis, 100,000 Koreans, 50,000 Sudanese, 75,000 Indians, 50,000 Thais, 40,000 Turks, 40,000 Syrians, 15,000 Lebanese, 50,000 Somalis, 40,000 Americans, 5,000 Japanese, 61,000 Europeans, 10,000 other Arabs • Native work force 1.1 to 1.8 million: 37% agricultural, 5% regular armed forces, 3% National Guard, 3% government, 48% commerce and services, and 3% other private sector • Population about 2/5 urban (rising steadily), 1/4 nomadic (falling) • Population concentrated in Eastern Province and areas around Makkah, Riyadh, and Jidah

TABLE 13.12 (continued)

	• Total growth rate 3%, 1970–1975; 3.4% in mid-1983 • Shi'ites up to 1/2 Eastern Province population, 6% total population • 45% of population under 15 in 1974 • 35% of oil work force Bedouin tribesmen in 1975 • Foreign population has experienced highest growth rates in country • Native population 90% Arab, 10% Afro-Asian • Literacy 15–25%
Kuwait	• Total population 1,652,000 in July 1983 • 78% of total population Arab, 9% South Asian, 4% Iranian, 9% other • 61% of population foreign • 70% of 360,000-man (1978) labor force foreign • Foreign labor roughly distributed as follows: 18% non-Arab (8% Iranian, 6% Indian, 3% Pakistani, 1% other), 40% Jordanian/Palestinian, 12% Egyptian, 9% Iraqi, 8% Syrian, 13% other Arabs • Literacy about 60% • Population mostly urban and in capital/Hawali area • Overall growth rate was 10% in 1976 due mainly to immigration; native Kuwaiti growth rate was 6.2% in 1983 • 50% of Kuwaiti citizenry under 15 • 2.5% of labor force agricultural • 11% of population shanty-dwelling Bedouins • Loyalty to tribal customs remains high • Arab population mostly Sunni, but 17% Shi'ite
Bahrain	• Total population 393,000 in July 1983 • Foreign population is 21% (1965), 17+% (1971), 37% (1983); 10% other Arab, 13% Indian and Pakistani, 8% Iranian, 3% British, 4% Yemeni, 3% Jordanian • Population about 80% urban (rising), concentrated in northeast • Growth rate 5.6% (1971–1975), 4.0% (1981), 4.0% (1983) • 27% of nationals under 15 (1971) • 59% of 140,000-man labor force foreign • 7% of labor force agrarian • Literacy about 40% • Labor, even skilled, in good supply, due to excellent domestic education system • Tribal groups do not play a role, no nomadic Bedouin population • Shi'ism approaches 65%, including Iranians; 35% Sunni
Oman	• Total population 978,000 in July 1983; growth rate 3.1% • Foreign population (including small groups of Iranians) small (4% of the total is Indian and Baluchi), but occupies more advanced economic sectors • Indigenous manpower poorly educated and unskilled until recently; 50% of 300,000-man cash-economy work force is foreign • Population quasi-urban, concentrated in cities and towns on the coastal plains, especially in Batinah area • Literacy has risen steadily to 50% • Large influx/outflux of population • During 1970s, population trebled, mainly due to immigration • Dependence on foreigners for skilled labor high • 75% of native work force agrarian • Sizable number of Baluchi and foreign non-Arabs in cities • 1/6 of population believed to be Bedouin • Schism exists between the Ibadi and Sunni, who occupy mainly the southeast and northwest provinces, respectively • Northern enclave has some Shi'ites, but Shi'ites only about 1% of total • Population 267,000 in July 1983; growth rate 3.4%

TABLE 13.12 (continued)

Qatar	• Population 267,000 in July 1983; growth rate 3.4% • 80% of population foreign; of this, 25% other Arab, 34% South Asian, 16% Iranian, 5% other • Lebanese, Egyptians, and other northern Arabs fill professional positions • Westerners have some senior management posts • 90% of 100,000-man labor force foreign (1980) • Approximately 10% of population nomadic • Pronounced Wahabi affiliation, but 8% of population Shi'ite • Literacy 25%
UAE	• Total population 1,374,000 (July 1983), rising at 10.7% annually • 81% of population foreign (rising): 23% other Arab, 50% South Asian, and 8% other expatriate • Population largely urban, living mainly in Abu Dhabi and Dubai • Growth rate 10.7% (overall), 4% indigenous (1980) • Literacy 25% • 71% of population is male (mostly 20–40-year-old foreigners) (1977) • 80–87% of work force of 541,000+ foreign (56% in services): Iranians and Pakistanis—manual labor Indians—clerks, traders Arabs—professional types Europeans—managers • Intradynastic tribal rivalry common, tribal status still relevant • Arab population mainly Sunni, but 6% of total is Shi'ite; Shi'ism is concentrated (50%) among Iranians and in Dubai
North Yemen	• Population 5,744,000 July 1983 (CIA estimate); growth rate 2.7% • Split between Zaidi (Shi'ite) in north, Shaafi (Sunni) in south • Formerly ruled by religious oligarchy of Sayyids in Zaidi tribes • Major tribal confederations in North still feud with each other and central government • 90% of native population settled tribesmen in small towns and villages • Population is 90% Arab, 10% Afro-Arab • Significant indigenous population of South Yemeni refugees • 20% of population (mostly males) works outside the country • Literacy is 15%
South Yemen	• Total population 2,086,000 in July 1983 (CIA estimate) • Population overwhelmingly Yemeni • Some other Arabs, Indians, and Somalis • Population 33% urban, 57% rural, and 10% nomadic • Urbanization continues as urban fertility rates are higher • Population concentrated mainly in Aden and central areas • Intrastate migration forcibly curtailed, with adverse economic effects • Emigration significant, much of it illegal • Annual growth rate 2.7–3% • Population not supported by agriculture • About 50% of population under 17 (1975) • Tribal groups and affiliations dissolved by force

Sources: Alvin J. Cottrell, *The Persian Gulf States* (Baltimore: Johns Hopkins University Press, 1981), based on the respective statistical abstracts of the Gulf countries in the 1970s; John Keegan, *World Armies* (New York: Facts on File, 1979); Richard F. Nyrop, *Area Handbook for the Yemens* and *Area Handbook for the Persian Gulf States,* Foreign Area Handbook Series (Washington, D.C.: American University, 1976 and 1977); Richard D. Erb et al., "The Arab Oil Producing States of the Gulf," *Foreign Policy and Defense Review* (AEI) 2, nos. 3 and 4 (1980); CIA, *World Factbook,* 1983, CR-83-11300 (U) (Washington, D.C., May 1983).

foreign labor population with any great success, and even Saudi Arabia is unable to control the immigration of its large Yemeni minority and the increasing numbers of Ethiopians and other illegals who stay on after the annual *hajj*.

• The portion of this work force that comes from Pakistan, India, Southeast Asia, Africa, and other non-Arab states probably poses less of a long-term problem. In most cases, the non-Arabs are more than willing to return home after they earn the wealth that brought them to the Gulf in the first place. Only the Pakistanis seem likely to try to stay on in the Gulf countries, and many have already been assimilated into Gulf society.

• The Arab foreign workers in the Gulf present a different problem since most have steadily less incentive to return home. This is particularly true of the Yemenis, but it is also true of the Egyptians, Jordanians, Lebanese, and Palestinians. The latter two groups represent a quasi-permanent minority whose importance is far greater than their size would indicate. Their education and training have given them important positions in Gulf countries, and their pro-Palestinian politics are an important factor behind Gulf support of the PLO.

• These problems are compounded by the stratification of the native Sunni populations in all of the southern Gulf countries. To a greater or lesser degree, the various classes of Bedouin and town-dwelling Arabs, whose status once ranged from a quasi-nobility to virtual untouchables, still influence Gulf society. Such class problems affect the modernization of every Gulf state. The development plans of most conservative Gulf state show a clear bias toward favoring higher-status tribal groups and urban clans, a bias characteristic of the military and civil service as well. Data are lacking on the details of such discrimination, but it often seems to have a more powerful effect than conventional nepotism on the ability to run a military establishment on the basis of merit.

In short, there are many hidden currents in the demographics of the Gulf states that strongly influence their internal security and military professionalism. The West is just discovering these currents, but most of the Gulf states are equally unable to estimate their strength and nature with any accuracy. The lack of meaningful census data, widespread corruption in the issuing of labor permits (or tolerance of workers without papers), and the lack of understanding of the dynamics of the changes taking place lead most Gulf countries to ignore these problems or to deal with them on the basis of a mixture of past history and current propaganda.

Total Military Manpower

The dynamics of Gulf military manpower are shown in Table 13.13. Like most Gulf statistics, they present significant uncertainties. Some Gulf states report authorized or required manning levels rather than

TABLE 13.13 Military Manpower Trends in the Gulf, 1969-1984 (thousands)

	1969	1970	1971	1972	1973	1974	1975	1976	1977	1978	1979	1980	1981	1982	1983	1984
Gulf																
Bahrain	—	—	2	3	3	4	5	5	2	2	2	3	3	3	3	3
Iran	225	245	255	265	285	310	385	420	350	350	410[a]	280[a]	195[a]	235[a]	400[a]	2,000[a]
Iraq	90	95	105	105	105	110	155	190	140	140	220[a]	220[a]	252[a]	342[a]	350[a]	517[a]
Kuwait	10	10	14	14	14	15	25	25	10	10	10	10	12	12	13	13
Oman	4	4	4	4	8	10	12	18	12	12	14	14	14	18	18	24[a]
Qatar	—	—	—	2	3	3	5	5	5	5	5	5	10	6	6	6
Saudi Arabia	60	65	75	75	75	80	95	95	95[b]	94[b]	65[b]	67[b]	83[b]	84[b]	80[b]	77[b]
UAE	—	—	—	10	11	19	21	27	25	25	30	30	43	49	44	49
South Yemen	9	9	10	13	12	14	19	21	20	20	20	20	24	26	26	26[a]
North Yemen	14	13	13	20	31	35	42	42	40	40	30	30	32	32	32	22[a]
Total	412	441	478	511	547	600	764	848	699	699	806	678	668	807	972	2,737
Arab-Israeli Confrontation States																
Egypt	230	225	315	390	390	410	400	400	350	350	350	340	367	452	449	447
Jordan	60	70	65	70	70	70	60	65	70	70	70	70	68	73	74	73
Lebanon	19	19	20	20	20	25	20	0	9	n.a.	9[a]	23[a]	24	24	26	35[a]
Syria	75	75	110	115	115	130	230	230	225	225	225	250	223	223	276	223[a]
Subtotal	384	389	510	595	595	635	710	695	654	645	654	683	682	772	825	778
Israel	100	105	130	130	130	160	190	190	165	165	165	165	172	174	238	172
Libya	25	18	19	20	20	25	25	25	30	50	51	53	55	65	68	73[a]
Total	509	512	659	745	745	820	925	910	849	860	870	901	909	1,011	1,131	1,023
Northern Tier/Indian Ocean																
Afghanistan	89	91	91	91	91	130	130	142	143	110	90[a]	40[a]	43[a]	46[a]	40[a]	40[a]
India	1,510	1,550	1,560	1,590	1,620	1,620	1,670	1,440	1,270	1,300	1,286	1,286	1,104	1,104	1,110	1,120
Pakistan	390	390	404	350	466	500	502	604	588	518	544	549	451	479	485	485
Turkey	545	540	610	610	545	535	453	460	540	566	566	567	569	569	569	569
Total	2,534	2,571	2,665	2,641	2,722	2,785	2,755	2,646	2,541	2,494	2,486	2,442	2,167	2,198	2,204	2,214
Horn of Africa																
Ethiopia	45	45	45	50	50	45	50	65	225	233	234	240	230	251	255	259
Sudan	25	25	35	35	35	35	50	50	50	71	71	68	71	58	58	58
Somali	18	20	20	25	25	30	30	31	53	54	54	54	63	63	65	68
Total	88	90	100	110	110	110	130	146	328	358	359	362	364	372	378	385

[a] IISS Figures exceptionally uncertain. Iran should total more than 1.5 million from 1980 on. Iraq should exceed 800,000.

[b] Including National Guard (IISS figures).

Sources: ACDA, *World Military Expenditures and Arms Transfers, 1969-78,* Table I; data for 1981 and 1982 taken from *The Military Balance,* 1981-82 and 1982-83 (London: IISS, 1982); 1983 and 1984 estimates include adjustments by the author. Input data to estimates normally lag up to one year behind year shown.

the actual number of men in uniform. Most Gulf states do not report accurately on the use of foreign military personnel or advisers, and many vary their count of paramilitary manpower from year to year in ways that make such figures highly uncertain. It is also difficult to interpret the manpower totals in Table 13.13 because of the very different systems of recruiting and conscription used in each Gulf country.

Iran's current military manpower is impossible to estimate because of the impact of the revolution. Some estimates indicate that the 1979 and 1980 totals are only 50–66% of those shown; others indicate that the 1980–1981 totals should be well over 400,000. Iraq's manpower reporting has always been politicized and erratic, but the sudden buildup after 1978 has considerable credibility. Iraq unquestionably further expanded its forces in reaction to the shah's fall and the threat perceived from the Khomeini regime. Its true 1980 and 1981 totals are probably well over 300,000.

Saudi Arabia's manpower reporting is erratic because of changes in the way it counts the National Guard and a tendency to exaggerate army and National Guard manpower. It is also difficult to compare the Saudi figures to those of Iran or Iraq because Saudi Arabia has to provide about twice as much logistical manpower (and expenditure) per tank or aircraft deployed as nations like Iraq and Iran with more adequate manpower.

The figures for Kuwait present different problems. The manpower trends for Kuwait in Table 13.13 make a sharp contrast to the data in the previous tables. Kuwait's growth in total manpower is so slow relative to its arms purchases and defense expenditures that it confirms the fact that Kuwait is wasting vast amounts of money on forces too small to be effective. Similarly, the manpower data on the other small conservative Gulf states dramatize their inherent weakness as individual powers.

It should be remembered in this context that military forces are particularly subject to economies and diseconomies of scale. A small total national military manpower base is incredibly inefficient because the required cadre of essential support services cannot be reduced below a given level and still allow the nation to maintain an effective force. Bahrain, Kuwait, Qatar, and the UAE all face critical diseconomies of scale. These problems are compounded in the case of the UAE by its tendency to maintain separate "national" force elements.

Oman's manpower trends are interesting. Oman shows limited increases in military manpower for a comparatively populous Gulf state, particularly since it was the only conservative Gulf state involved in war during most of the period shown in Table 13.13. The Omani figures serve as a warning that manpower totals and trends may not be a valid measure of military capability.

The figures for North and South Yemen mirror the defense expenditure and arms import data in showing a strong military buildup by South

Yemen. These figures are somewhat misleading in the case of North Yemen, however, because the North Yemeni army has many part-time elements, is subject to constant attrition from desertion, and has not reached the overall level of education common in other Gulf forces. The quality of the North Yemeni manpower shown in Table 13.13 has also declined relative to that of other Gulf forces during the last decade, both because of a failure to improve the nation's educational base and because of the loss of personnel trained during the Yemeni civil war of the 1960s. In contrast, South Yemen has enforced draconian recruiting and conscription procedures and combined them with superior progress in education and postrecruitment training.

The data for the countries neighboring the Gulf tend to be more accurate than that on the Gulf states, and they generally more than reinforce the previously discussed trends. Israel and Syria show a sharp growth in military manpower that matches their overall increase in defense expenditures and effort. The growth of Syrian manpower is particularly striking—rising from 115,000 at the time of the October War to about 223,000 in 1983. However, this growth has been more than offset by the improvements in the Israeli reserve system, and in Israel's total pool of military manpower, which are not reflected in Table 13.13.

The manpower data for the Northern Tier states show some relaxation in India's military buildup, but this seems to reflect a shift to emphasizing quality over quantity rather than any drop in fighting capability. The data for the Horn again reflect Ethiopia's massive military buildup, although Somalia has also increased its forces. The totals in Table 13.13 do not include the large number of Somali rebels who are now effectively part of the Somali forces.

Qualitative Trends in Manpower

Trends in total manpower, however, tell only part of the manpower story. There are a number of other factors that shape manpower quality and the capabilities of each Gulf force. The problems caused by the small total military manpower base in virtually all of the conservative Gulf states are compounded by the conflicting demands for skilled native labor and technical personnel of the military and civilian economies. While it is impossible to make precise estimates, the number of civilian jobs exceeds the number of available trained or educated native workers by at least two to one, and by more than five to one in many of the key skills relating to military service. This forces the conservative Gulf forces to hire large numbers of civilians and expatriates and to offer exceptionally favorable terms to the native military.

The demand for skilled manpower also creates major retention problems in most Gulf forces. With the exception of Saudi Arabia, Oman, and the UAE, most Gulf countries offer better opportunities in the civilian sector. Although many states theoretically forbid resignation before 14–35 years of service, resignations are common. In Iraq and North Yemen there is a particularly high flow out of the military into the civilian sector, and in both North and South Yemen there is large-scale desertion as the troops leave the country to take up jobs in Saudi Arabia, Oman, and the other conservative Gulf states. Further, in most Gulf countries—particularly Iraq, Iran, the UAE, and the Yemens—officers and NCOs periodically leave the military because of political instability or purges within the force structure.

This combination of pressures makes it almost impossible to estimate the manpower quality of a given Gulf army. It is certain that many key slots in most Gulf countries are now filled by officers who lack the proper training or by expatriates. It is equally certain that manpower retention problems are compounded by political factors, influence peddling, and a nepotism that leads to the promotion of the incompetent and the alienation or resignation of career military. All these problems have been compounded in nations like Iraq and Iran by the reluctance to assign foreign-trained officers to sensitive positions until they have proved their loyalty and by the tendency in the Gulf states to divert officers and NCOs with specialist training into generalist positions because they have superior ability and education.

Further, the military has often been the career path in the Gulf countries for those students with the least family influence or connections. This increases the leadership problem since such personnel have the weakest ties to the regime, and the Gulf states must balance the appointment of such officers to key positions with tight internal security procedures or ensure that expatriates or loyalists are kept in key positions regardless of competence.

Similar factors apply to the recruiting and retention of NCOs and technicians, with the added problem that most Gulf educational systems do not do a good job of producing technically trained military personnel to perform jobs that are regarded as manual labor. The social bias against "hands on" jobs leads to a considerable competition to avoid such appointments after attending technical schools and to leave them as soon as possible. This problem is compounded in several Gulf armies by overrigid discipline in the enlisted ranks, traditionally sharp divisions between officer and nonofficer, and a tendency of officers to avoid the kind of close work with their NCOs and technicians that is regarded as manual labor or demeaning. Such attitudes are fundamentally incompatible with modern and well-equipped military forces. They exacerbate recruiting and retention problems and have often led to forced retention or to long-term tours of duty that alienate many of the NCOS and technicians involved. At the same time, they reinforce the tendency to use foreign contract civilians, or expatriate military, in support functions, and they weaken the cohesion and effectiveness of many conservative Gulf states' forces.

Use of Expatriate Military Manpower

A rough estimate of Gulf dependence on expatriate military and advisers is shown in Table 13.14. The data now available, however, are so contradictory and confusing that it is often impossible to do more than flag the problem in a given country. Further, it is impossible to estimate the trends involved, since many conservative Gulf countries do not report such data, falsify it to improve their image of strength, or report only episodically and then only some of the expatriates in uniform or serving in civilian roles. It also is difficult to interpret the meaning of the available data. While British officers and NCOs have succeeded in supporting Oman's forces and have previously "stiffened" the fighting capabilities of many of the Trucial States, other expatriate-led forces have often been ineffective. Further, the reliance some of the conservative Gulf states place on expatriate support is so high that—regardless of the accuracy of the particular data shown—it is clear that their forces suffer severely from overdependence on foreign support and that such forces could hope to fight only if that support continued.

The importance of the problems that can result are illustrated in the case of Iran. Iran lacked the ability to operate its helicopters and much of its aircraft once it expelled its U.S. advisers, and its army suffered critical shortages early in the Iran-Iraq War because it depended on foreign support to operate its computerized supply and inventory system. Iran initially could not bring much of its weaponry to bear against Iraq or make use of many of the munitions and parts it had in inventory. Iran has since suffered severe equipment attrition in addition to that it lost in the fighting because it lacked the ability to replace expatriate maintenance and repair services.

Paramilitary and Reserve Manpower

The importance of paramilitary and reserve manpower is illustrated in Table 13.15. It is now almost impossible to determine the true state of affairs in Iran and Iraq, but the remaining data seem approximately correct. At least some of this manpower, however, is counted as "active" in the reporting provided in Table 13.13. The bulk of these paramilitary and reserve forces are useful largely for internal security purposes.

Trends in Defense Expenditure per Man in Uniform

The importance of data on defense expenditure per man in uniform has already been briefly analyzed in the "snapshot" of defense efforts shown in Table 13.5. Such data generally are a good measure of the extent to which given nations are managing their manpower and defense expenditures in ways that provide an effective ratio of expenditure per man. These trends are shown (in constant dollars) in Table 13.16. The details are uncertain, but the trends are broadly correct.

To put these data in perspective, it takes a minimum of about $10,000 per year for each active man in uniform to maintain minimum effec-

TABLE 13.14 Method of Military Recruiting and Dependence on Foreign Military Manpower in the Gulf

Country	Method of Recruiting	Dependence on Foreign Military and Civilians
Iran[a]	2-year universal conscription (shah) No conscription in 1979 Universal conscription after 1980	Formerly 30–40,000 U.S. military and civilian technicians (1977) Now some Israeli, North Korean, and Soviet support
Iraq[a]	2-year universal conscription	Heavy economic, military, and diplomatic support from USSR. Over 1,000 Soviet-bloc military technicians. 8,000 Soviet, 2,200 Cuban, and 160 East German military and economic technicians in country Growing Western influence, particularly French, plus some Egyptian advisers
Saudi Arabia	Voluntary, plus tribal levies in National Guard, males 18–35, and youths trained from 14	Up to 40,000 U.S., British, French, Pakistani, Jordanian, Egyptian, and other foreign military and civilian personnel
Kuwait	Titular 2-year Kuwaiti male conscription since 1978, but in reality voluntary plus expatriates (18 months)	U.S.-trained Hawk operators and A-4 pilots, 20+ Soviet advisers for SA-6/7s. 30 other Soviet-bloc. 125 British officers for aircraft, armor. Also French contingent for Mirage training, as well as Egyptian advisory team for infantry tactics, Jordanian and Syrian officers aiding in conscription, and Pakistani naval advisers. Many officers trained in Jordan, Pakistan
Bahrain	Voluntary	U.S. naval school, use of port facilities. Saudi airbase at Awali-Zalag roads
Oman	Voluntary	450 British officers, including ¼ of acting army officer corps, 1/3 of army are Baluchi Specialists training in Britain, Egypt, Jordan, Saudi Arabia, and UAE
Qatar	Recruited from Bedouin tribes	Expatriates from Britain, other Arab countries, and Pakistan
UAE	Recruited from outside, particularly from Oman	Jordanian officers, ex-Pakistani pilots, British contract officers. Mostly Omani forces
North Yemen	3-year selective conscription	Up to 400 Soviet-bloc, some Saudi advisers, and a U.S. advisory effort. British advisers on internal security
South Yemen	2-year conscription	Training missions from Soviet Union (400–800), East Germany, and other Warsaw Pact (300), Cuba (300), and North Korea. 2,100 Soviet, 800 Cuban, and 325 East German technicians. Soviets train regular forces, Germans police, and Cubans paramilitary. Soviet, Cuban pilots and troops. Some Ethiopian, and Libyan liaison team

[a]Pre-war. Iran and Iraq have since conducted mass mobilization.

Sources: The Military Balance (London: IISS, various years); John Keegan, *World Armies* (New York: Facts on File, 1979).

TABLE 13.15 Comparative Reserve and Paramilitary Manpower in the Gulf, 1982–83

	Number, Type	Equipment	Comments
Iran	Bassej volunteers, mostly youths, small arms, ancillary to main Field Forces; Gendarmerie (5,000); *Pasadaran* (150,000 plus), Hezbollahi (Home Guard) (2,500,000). *Mostazafin* (Guards); Border Tribal Militia.	Cessna 185/310 light aircraft; 32 AB-205/206 hel.; 40 patrol boats[a]	Up to 500,000 ex-conscripts and actives may have been mobilized in various capacities.[b]
Iraq	4,800 security troops; 450,000 People's Army	100 T-34 tanks	Army includes 75,000 to 250,000 mobilized reserves. People's Army under under party control; perhaps 10,000 foreign Arab volunteers
Saudi Arabia	25,000 National Guard; 8,500 Frontier Force and Coast Guard; counter-terrorist unit; General Civil Defense Administration units	240 V-150 Commandos; M163 Vulcans; 106mm RCL; TOW 90mm AA guns; 169 coastal and 300 small patrol boats; 12 SRN-6 Hovercraft	Guard organized into 16 regular and 24 irreg. inf. bns.; 15,000-man militia acts as reserve. 10,000–20,000 foreign contract military personnel.
Kuwait	18,000 police	Some helicopters(?)	No reserve, but may be forming from ex-conscripts
Bahrain	2,500 police; 180 Coast Guard	2 Scout; 3-BO-105; 2 Bell 412; 2 Hughes 500 D hel.; 1 Hovercraft; 2 landing craft; 17 small patrol	
Qatar	Police	3 Lynx M-28; 2 Gazelle hel.	No reserves; armed tribes
Oman	3,300 Firqats; Police Marine and Air Wings	1 Learjet; 2 Turbo-porters; 2 Merlin IVA; 2 Buffalo aircraft; 5 AB-205; 3 AB-206 hel.; 12 patrol boats	Firqats are Tribal Home Guard from Dhofar, mainly former rebels
UAE	Coast Guard	41 coastal patrol boats. 6 on order.	No reserves[c]
North Yemen	20,000 tribal levies 5,000 Ministry of National Security Force	Unknown	Tribes may still field up to 200,000 armed men largely outside government control.
South Yemen	Popular Militia; Public Security Force 30,000[d]	Well equipped in relation to regular units	Mostly urban males, Cuban-trained

[a] Losses make figures uncertain.
[b] Creation of Revolutionary Guard in February 1979 integrated many former militia elements and guerrilla groups.
[c] The Union Defence Force and the armed forces of the UAE were formally merged in May 1976.
[d] Presently undergoing expansion.

Sources: The Military Balance (London: IISS, 1973–1984); John Keegan, *World Armies* (New York: Facts on File, 1979).

TABLE 13.16 Defense Expenditures Relative to Military Manpower, 1969–1981 (1979 dollars per man on active duty)

	1969	1970	1971	1972	1973	1974	1975	1976	1977	1978	1979	1980	1981
Gulf													
Bahrain	–	–	–	–	2,333	2,500	3,800	7,000	22,500	27,000	28,500	25,000	40,667
Iran	15,680	15,359	17,741	20,245	27,414	30,474	30,722	29,469	30,706	35,200	–	–	20,308
Iraq	17,711	15,916	12,410	12,762	17,295	19,491	13,000	10,926	15,707	16,671	12,140	–	16,071
Kuwait	38,900	37,400	22,643	24,643	26,000	53,800	37,920	53,600	121,300	116,800	118,100	119,100	97,500
Oman	–	93,500	19,750	31,750	23,625	48,500	75,417	53,778	66,500	69,500	55,643	76,357	108,642
Qatar	–	–	–	42,500	59,000	49,000	32,000	41,000	53,400	57,200	91,600	100,600	80,400
Saudi Arabia	38,017	41,923	13,080	17,347	24,600	47,400	88,926	122,347	116,347	124,234	212,786	226,507	264,578
UAE	–	–	–	2,700	1,909	1,526	2,000	3,704	23,480	34,360	38,367	50,133	35,587
South Yemen	6,888	6,333	3,900	2,846	3,833	3,786	2,427	2,905	3,250	4,800	5,200	5,700	5,625
North Yemen	1,928	3,846	4,692	3,050	2,032	2,400	2,619	3,071	3,775	4,200	9,833	9,833	3,813
Average	19,131	19,760	15,280	1,700	19,435	28,330	32,096	34,097	38,805	42,628	25,565	27,137	52,771
Arab-Israeli Confrontation States													
Egypt	3,652	5,275	4,403	4,344	4,279	5,278	6,250	4,538	6,094	6,347	5,669	3,633	5,150
Jordan	3,217	2,057	4,092	4,314	4,043	3,771	4,133	6,400	4,700	4,814	5,468	5,157	5,632
Lebanon	4,684	4,632	3,800	3,950	4,250	4,880	5,600	–	12,667	–	–	–	8,708
Syria	5,840	6,920	3,655	4,148	6,870	5,430	5,713	5,652	5,564	6,142	7,009	7,996	9,646
Subaverage	4,060	4,625	3,739	4,289	4,751	5,127	5,879	5,246	5,853	3,008	6,028	5,264	6,792
Israel	23,080	29,142	19,639	17,085	34,408	24,838	23,889	24,411	26,679	22,442	29,176	27,751	31,709
Libya	14,120	30,889	12,579	11,000	15,000	22,040	12,600	17,960	18,567	15,840	9,804	8,943	70,309
Average	8,293	10,245	7,470	6,702	10,201	9,499	9,760	9,596	10,350	7,483	10,639	9,598	11,719
Northern Tier/Indian Ocean													
Afghanistan	629	527	473	560	615	392	492	627	497	681	–	–	2,023
India	1,783	1,856	2,391	2,283	1,920	2,054	2,410	2,712	3,034	3,185	3,231	3,187	4,288
Pakistan	1,918	2,105	2,243	2,760	2,195	1,844	2,048	1,762	1,646	2,048	1,937	2,095	3,772
Turkey	2,657	2,981	3,431	3,460	3,883	4,000	7,759	8,828	7,613	6,823	5,800	5,670	4,144
Average	1,951	2,083	2,541	2,559	2,317	2,312	3,133	3,446	3,543	3,664	3,364	3,464	4,098
Horn of Africa													
Ethiopia	1,667	1,644	1,644	1,667	1,300	1,444	2,600	2,646	920	742	1,427	1,613	1,513
Sudan	5,400	6,680	8,571	7,714	6,914	5,514	3,400	3,280	4,360	3,479	3,197	3,470	4,225
Somalia	1,167	1,300	1,650	1,360	1,320	1,300	1,167	1,129	717	1,630	1,556	1,556	–
Average	2,636	2,967	4,070	3,518	3,091	2,700	2,576	2,541	1,107	1,419	1,797	1,953	2,153

Sources: Adapted from ACDA, *World Military Expenditures and Arms Transfers,* 1969–78 and 1971–80. Figures for 1981 adapted from IISS figures: Some 1981 figures might be inaccurate because of turmoil that year; some figures are author's estimates.

tiveness even for those few Gulf forces that can really draw on conscript manpower. This figure rises to at least $20,000–$30,000 per man per year in the case of the conservative Gulf states, because they must rely largely on high pay and other incentives. It should probably be about $30,000–40,000 in the smaller Gulf states, allowing for the diseconomies of scale. Figures below $15,000 per man per year indicate seriously inadequate manpower or equipment quality (or both) for a major part of the force structure. Figures below $3,000 per man imply massive qualitative deficiencies for a major part of the force structure.

The data for the Gulf area show that most of the conservative Gulf states are now spending the required amounts. They also reveal the extraordinary cost impact on Saudi Arabia of completing its investment in military infrastructure—with expenditures running well over $100,000 per man per year. At the same time, several conservative Gulf states—particularly the UAE—show erratic trends in defense expenditure per man in uniform that match their rather patchy and episodic records of arms imports. Kuwait's totals also again reflect excessive levels of expenditure that cannot be explained by the kind of infrastructure effort that justifies Saudi Arabia's high totals.

The long-term trends in expenditures per man are particularly striking for the Gulf's two largest armed forces. Table 13.14 shows that Iranian expenditures per man have been adequate for a partly conscript force, but the decline in 1979 points up what has since been a steady underfunding of Iranian expenditure per man and a corresponding decline in Iran's ability to operate modern forces. The data on Iraq reflect a marginal funding of the total force structure, particularly in 1979 and 1980, when the manpower data reported by Iraq indicate a gross underfunding of the army's expansion in the period leading up to the war. Even allowing for conscription, Iraq did not spend enough per man over the last decade to create an effective military force structure.

The expenditure trends for the Yemens are as low as those shown for 1978 in the "snapshot" in Table 13.5. They are somewhat misleading in the case of South Yemen, however, because the real totals would be about twice those shown in Table 13.16 if Soviet-bloc military assistance was costed at the same prices as Western assistance. The figures for North Yemen are probably broadly correct, however, and they reveal a chronic underfunding of North Yemeni forces that correlates with the previous data on the decline of its forces. While the totals for North Yemen have been increased since 1979 by U.S. and Soviet-bloc aid, North Yemen's low levels of expenditure per man over the last decade do much to explain its comparatively poor performance in its 1979 border war with South Yemen and its problems with manpower attrition.

The data for the Arab-Israeli confrontation states reflect different conditions from those of the Gulf states. Nevertheless, the Arab states are clearly grossly underspending, and Table 13.16 provides a good picture of their tendency to maintain inflated military force totals they cannot afford to train or equip. The totals for Egypt and Jordan, for example, show a critical underfunding of their respective force structures. The figures for Jordan also do much to explain the convulsions of the Jordanian forces and pay "strikes" of the middle and late 1970s.

The data for Lebanon are largely meaningless, as is the Lebanese Army, as the real military forces in Lebanon are still Israeli, "Christian," PLO, and Syrian. Syria was shifting toward more realistic expenditure levels per man before Israel's invasion of Lebanon, but only Israel reflects the expenditure levels necessary to make modern forces effective. The contrast between trends for the Arab states and Israel in Table 13.16 are particularly striking because Israel operates lines of communication and does not need the support structure required to operate most Arab armies. Israel also has a much better base of educated manpower and has received substantial grants in aid from the U.S. since the October War that are not counted in the table and that only recently have been provided to Egypt.

The Arab-Israeli data are also interesting because they show that Syria has consistently underinvested in its forces since 1973, which may help explain its poor performance against Israel in June and July 1982. The Arab states have tended to be their own worst enemy in this regard, since they have so diluted their resources that they have reached the point of diminishing returns. Both Egypt and Jordan, for example, would have to cut their current military manpower in half, or double their defense budgets, to make their forces properly effective. Further, given their financial history, it would take at least half a decade for the results of such a policy to materialize. This analysis confirms the previous indications that the balance has shifted in favor of the more radical Arab confrontation states.

The date for the Northern Tier and Horn states in Table 13.16 are more difficult to interpret because most such countries have much lower military pay rates than the Gulf confrontation states, and they use military conscription and appointments to reduce unemployment and serve internal political needs. Nevertheless, the totals are so low that they confirm that the average quality of the forces of such states is falling behind those of the Gulf and the industrialized states in capability. It should be noted, however, that India, Pakistan, and Turkey depend upon a relatively limited number of key land forces and elite navy and air force combat units. Still, the average expenditures per man in Table 13.16 do indicate that something like 70–80% of the total armed forces in every Northern Tier and Horn country must be underequipped and undertrained for use in anything more than minimal light infantry functions. This is true even when one allows for such "pay" programs as that of Ethiopia, in which most conscripts receive no pay other than subsistence.

Trends in Major Military Equipment

Given this background, it becomes easier to make realistic judgments about the equipment totals shown in Tables 13.1 and 13.2 and about the impact of trends in the buildup of military equipment. Quite aside from any underlying ethnic or cultural differences among the military forces shown in these two tables, it should be clear that there are substantial differences in manpower, expenditures, arms import patterns, and other factors that shape the degree to which each Gulf nation can operate the equipment it buys. It should be equally clear that most Gulf and neighboring nations have bought more equipment than they can operate effectively. Equipment totals are still, however, a useful measure of military strength, particularly when they are put into some kind of qualitative perspective. It is also possible to measure how rapidly forces are changing by comparing changes in the numbers of key equipment, and rates of equipment transfer indicate the extent to which each country is buying more equipment than it can absorb. As a rule of thumb, even Western and Soviet-bloc armies and forces cannot increase their total holdings of key weaponry like tanks or aircraft by more than 10–15% per year without sharply diluting their manpower quality or putting their manpower base on a wartime footing. These equipment conversion and absorption problems increase in direct proportion to the weakness in the military infrastructure of less developed nations and their inability to fund suitable training and support. The Gulf nations and their neighbors obviously face far more serious constraints in absorbing new equipment and expanding their forces than the West and the Soviet bloc.

The Trends in Medium Tanks

Tables 13.17 and 13.18 and Chart 13.1 show these equipment trends for medium tanks and armor. Table 13.17 shows the total number of medium tanks in the active force structure for each year reported. The number of medium tanks is a good overall measure of equipment trends and army modernization rates in the Near East because the success of Israeli armor in 1956 and 1967 has made the tank the primary weapon throughout the region. Chart 13.1 supplements these figures with a rough estimate of future trends and a qualitative estimate of tank modernization trends. Finally, Table 13.18 gives an illustrative estimate of the armor on order in early 1982. Such estimates, and the estimates of aircraft purchases that follow in Table 13.20, are extremely uncertain and attempt to map a constantly changing landscape. They do, however, serve to illustrate the rate of future force expansion in the region.

To put these data in perspective, a modern division in an industrialized state has about 300–350 tanks, and there are about 6,000–7,000 medium tanks in all the NATO forces in the Central Region. Seen from this perspective, Table 13.17 shows that the Gulf has the equivalent of about

TABLE 13.17 Numbers of Medium Tanks, 1969–1984

	1969	1970	1971	1972	1973	1974	1975	1976	1977	1978	1979	1980	1981	1982	1983	1984
Gulf																
Bahrain	n.a.	n.a.	n.a.	0	0	0	0	0	0	0	0	0	0	0	0	0
Iran	n.a.	n.a.	860	860	920	1,160	1,160	1,360	1,620	1,620	1,735[a]	1,735[a]	1,410[a]	1,110[a]	900[b]	940[b]
Iraq	535	645	860	860	920	1,390	1,200	1,200	1,350	1,700	1,700	2,600	2,600[b]	2,300[b]	1,500[b]	2,360[b]
Kuwait	n.a.	n.a.	n.a.	80	100	100	100	100	112	280	124	240	240	240	200[c]	200[c]
Oman	n.a.	n.a.	n.a.	0	0	0	0	0	0	0	0	0	12	18	27	27
Qatar	n.a.	n.a.	n.a.	0	0	0	0	0	0	12	12	24	24	24	24	24
Saudi Arabia	a few	55	25	25	25	55	175	325	475	325	350	380	630	450	450	450
UAE	n.a.	n.a.	n.a.	0	0	0	0	0	0	0	0	0	75	118	136	136
South Yemen	n.a.	n.a.	n.a.	n.a.	50	50	50	200	200	260	260	375	375[b]	470	520[c]	520[c]
North Yemen	n.a.	n.a.	n.a.	n.a.	30	30	30	30	30	220[a]	232[a]	664[a]	714[a]	714	750[b,c]	714[b]
Total	535+	700	1,745	1,825	2,045	2,785	2,715	3,215	3,787	4,417	4,413	6,018	6,080	5,444	4,507	5,371
Arab-Israeli Confrontation States																
Egypt	845	1,255	1,500	1,960	1,910	2,000	1,945[c]	1,945[c]	1,850[c]	1,600[c]	1,600[c]	1,600[c]	1,660[c]	2,100[c]	2,100[c]	1,910[c]
Jordan	329	310	290	344	420	240	240	490	420	500	500	609	516+	569	670[c]	670[b,c]
Lebanon	n.a.	40	40	40	60	60	60	60	nil	nil	nil	nil	nil	nil	36	54
Syria	450	880	780	1,170	1,170	1,600	2,100	2,300	2,500	2,500	2,600	2,920	3,700	3,990	4,100[c]	4,200[c]
Subtotal	1,624	2,485	2,610	3,514	3,560	3,900	4,345	4,795	4,770	4,600	4,700	5,129	5,876	6,659	7,106	6,834
Israel	1,020	1,050	1,075	1,700	1,700	1,900	2,700	2,700	3,000	3,000	3,050	3,050	3,500	3,600	3,750[c]	3,750[c]
Libya	n.a.	6	121	221[a]	221[a]	271[a]	345[a]	715[a]	1,200[a]	2,000[a]	2,000[a]	2,400[a]	2,700[a]	2,700	3,000	3,000[c]
Total	2,644	3,241	3,806	5,435	5,481	6,071	7,390	8,210	8,970	9,600	9,750	10,579	12,076	12,959	13,856	13,584
Northern Tier/Indian Ocean																
Afghanistan	n.a.	n.a.	—	—	200	450	350	700	700	700	800[b]	1,200[b]	1,200[b]	850[b]	800[c]	650[b]
India	980	1,150	1,200	1,200	1,700	1,690	1,680	1,880	1,780	1,700	1,850	2,120	2,120	2,128	2,260	2,200
Pakistan	—	400	575	450	850	950	950	1,000	1,000	1,000	1,000	1,000	1,285	1,285	1,390	1,321
Turkey	—	—	—	—	1,400	1,800	1,500	2,500	2,800	2,800	3,500	3,000	3,500	3,650	3,650	3,577
Total	980	1,550	1,775	1,650	4,150	4,890	4,480	6,080	6,280	6,200	7,150	7,320	8,105	7,913	8,100	7,748
Horn of Africa																
Ethiopia	n.a.	0	70	30	50	50	12	78	70	504	630	640	790	790	850[c]	890[c]
Sudan	n.a.	50	120	130	130	130	130	130	130	130	130	130	197	190	215[c]	205[c]
Somalia	n.a.	150[a]	150[a]	150[a]	150[a]	220[a]	250[a]	250[a]	300[a]	80[a]	80[a]	140+	390[d]	190	220[c]	140[b]
Total	n.a.	200	340	310	330	400	392	458	500	714	840	910	1,377	1,170	1,285	1,235

[a]Serviceability is low
[b]Figures uncertain
[c]Some tanks in storage
[d]Includes 200 Centurions paid for by Kuwait. *International Defense Review* 1 (1982):11.

Source: The Military Balance (London: IISS, 1969–1984). Estimates for 1983 and 1984 include inputs by the author and do not necessarily agree with figures shown elsewhere from other sources. Data inputs to estimates often lag up to one year behind year shown.

TABLE 13.18 Armor on Order in the Gulf, 1983–1984

Country	Number	Item
Bahrain		None
Egypt	52	M-109 A2 155mm SP howitzers from U.S.
	100	M-106 A2, M-125A2 SP mortar carriers from U.S.
	100	Kuerassier light tanks from Austria (known also as SK-105 Jagdpanzer Ks)
	189	M-60A3 from U.S.
	600	BMR-600 APCs
	750	M-113A2 APCs
	200	TOW launchers from U.S.
Iran	150	T-55/62/72 medium tanks from Libya, North Korea, and Syria
Iraq	?	T-62 medium tanks
	?	AMX-30 medium tanks
	85	155 GCT 155mm SP guns from France
	100	T-55s from Poland (delivered through Saudi Arabia)
	150	T-72s from USSR (war interrupted delivery)
	100	EE-9 Cascavels and EE-3 Jararaca armored cars
	80	EE-11 Urutu APCs
	?	SP-73 152mm SP howitzers
	?	Soviet-made artillery weapons and AFVs from Egypt
Israel	?	M-107 SP guns from U.S.
	125	M-60A3s from U.S. (100 under delivery)
	800	M-113 APCs from U.S.
	200	M-109 A1B 155mm SP howitzers from U.S.
Jordan	?	Chieftains from Iraq (gift of captured tanks)
	36	M-60A1s from Iraq (gift of captured tanks—delivered)
	248	Khalid MBTs from Britain (some in delivery)
	40	M-60A3s from U.S.
	78	M-113 APCs from U.S.
Kuwait	?	Scorpion light tanks from Britain
	188	M-113A2 APCs from U.S. (under delivery)
	56	M-901 Improved TOW vehicles from U.S.
	?	French tank transporters
	160	Night-vision sets for Chieftain tanks
Lebanon	?	M-48 MBTs from Jordan
	228	M-113A2 APCs
Libya	300	T-72s from USSR
	100	Lion or Leopard 1 tanks from Italy
	100	Urutu APCs
	?	Fiat 6616 armored cars from Italy
	188	Palmaria 155mm SP howitzers from Italy
	?	EE-9 Cascavel armored vehicles (Enqsea)
Oman	15	Chieftain MK 7 medium tanks
	?	Palmaria 155mm SP howitzers
	?	Scorpion light tanks
	?	Stormer APCs
Saudi Arabia	100	M-60A3 medium tanks
	150	M-60A3 conversion kits
	?	Ensaga armored cars
	180	VCC-1 TOW AFVs from U.S. and Italy
	60	AMX-10P APCs from France
	400	JPz SP-105mm anti-tank guns
	72	FH-70 155mm SP howitzers
Sudan	80	M-113 APCs from U.S.
	?	M-163 Vulcan 20mm SP AA guns from U.S.
Syria	?	BMP-1 IFVs from USSR
	?	BIR-60 APCs from USSR
	?	M-1974 122mm SP from USSR
	?	M-1973 152mm SP from USSR
UAE	20	Scorpion light tanks
	100	AMX-32, Challenger or Valiant medium tanks
	36	OF-40 medium tanks
	66	Ensaga Urutu APCs with TOW
	?	Cascavel armored cars
	?	OF-40 medium tanks
North Yemen		None
South Yemen		None

Sources: The Military Balance (London: IISS, 1983–1984); SIPRI computer printout, April 1981; *Defense and Foreign Affairs,* 18 April 1983.

CHART 13—1
SHIFTS IN TANK STRENGTH AND QUALITY IN THE MAJOR POWERS IN THE NEAR EAST: 1973-1983

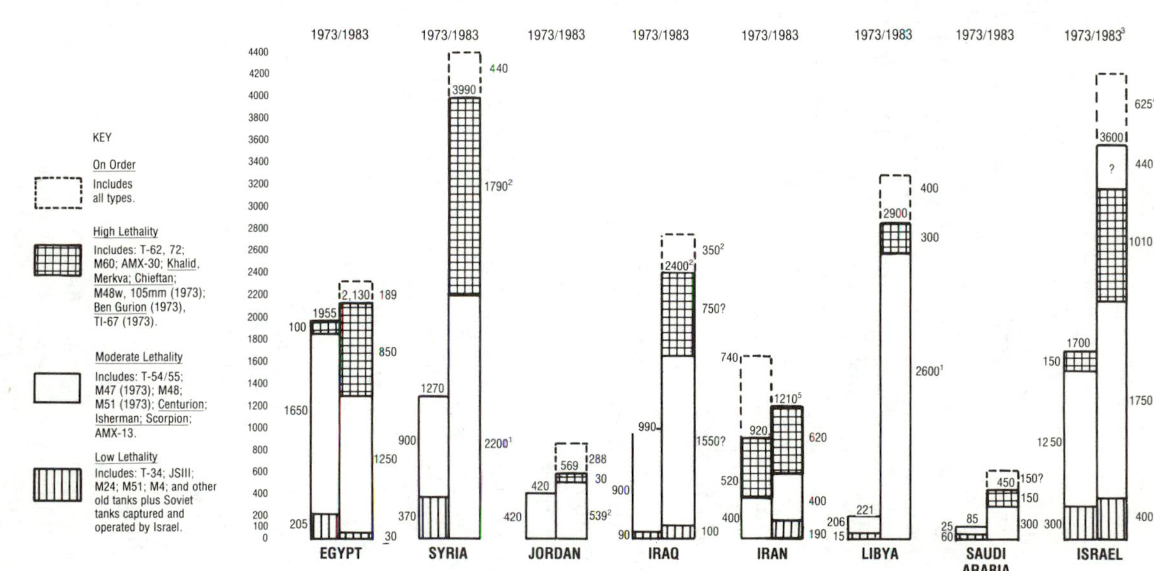

[1]Data given as including T-62 and T-72 types, though numbers unknown.
[2]The T-72s in Syria and Iraq are believed to utilize composite armor. Syria has approximately 400 T-72s in delivery. Iraq's current strength is highly uncertain.
[3]The Israelis are famous for modifying captured or older tanks—so much that models considered mediocre in other countries are very lethal in Israel. The Israelis often up-gun older or captured vehicles and add on fire control improvements and new engines.
[4]Israel had 3600 tanks in its active force structure in 1983, but only 3160 could be identified by type. It had 625 tanks on order with 125 M-60s in delivery and 500 Merkva to be built in Israel. Israel also, however, planned to retire and sell up to 900 Chieftains.
[5]Strength unknown, but may be closer to 600. Low lethality tanks include Soviet-made types. Some are T-62s.

SOURCES: *The Military Balance*, I.I.S.S., London and experimental SIPRI computer runs. Exact counts and categorization vary from other tables as is explained in footnotes.

20 modern NATO divisions' worth of military equipment and a total tank inventory roughly equivalent to that of the NATO Central Region. At the same time, it shows that many Gulf nations have an annual rate of expansion far greater than even the world's best military forces could absorb.

Iraq suffers particularly from too rapid expansion, which does much to explain its comparatively poor performance in tank maneuver warfare in the Iran-Iraq War. The Iranian totals are also disturbing in that they level out only in 1978 and only at the point at which the shah was already in trouble. In previous years, Iran had built its armor up far more quickly than its numbers of trained manpower justified, and it has compounded its problems by buying many different types. These factors help to explain Iran's poor performance in launching armored counteroffensives in the Iran-Iraq War and its problems in moving its armored units. It is not surprising, in view of the data in Tables 13.17 and Chart 13.1, that many Western experts felt that both nations bought nearly twice as many tanks as they could operate and severely diluted the effectiveness of their armored forces in the process.

The data for the other Gulf countries reveal a number of fluctuations stemming from reporting problems, but they again confirm such trends as the methodical nature of Saudi Arabia's military buildup during the 1970s and Kuwait's emphasis on showpiece purchases of equipment. The totals for the two Yemens also show the impact of the arms race that began in 1979, and the fact that the USSR is now delivering much larger numbers of tanks than either nation can hope to operate effectively in the near future.

The data on the Arab-Israeli confrontation states in Table 13.17 reveal the expected massive military buildup by Syria and Israel and the decline in Egyptian capabilities. Chart 13.1 shows that Egypt is converting to U.S. tanks at a comparatively slow rate and that the decline in Egypt's capabilities is likely to be even sharper than the previous tables in this chapter have indicated. It also shows that Syria is acquiring the same T-72s as Iraq and that Jordan is acquiring a larger number of tanks than its defense expenditure and manpower data have indicated. These acquisitions have been made possible by Saudi and Iraqi aid, which has enabled Jordan to buy the order of modern British tanks that Iran forfeited. This change will tilt the regional balance slightly back in favor of Jordan.[2]

The figures for Syria in Table 13.17 are also interesting in that they again reveal that Syria expanded its force structure far faster between 1973 and 1982 than its pool of trained manpower permitted, particularly as many of its best units were tied down in Lebanon. In contrast, Israel leveled out its tank strength at a point of near-saturation and had the time to complete most of its major expansions and conversions. While the delivery of more advanced tanks to Jordan and Syria may eventually force Israel into conversion to new types of armor and anti-armor weaponry, it seems unlikely that such conversion will pose anything like the problems for Israel that its Arabs opponents will face in converting to tanks with advanced sights, fire-control computers, faster rates of maneuver, longer-range fire, night operations, and combined arms operations. As a result, the trend in armor through the mid-1980s should favor Israel much more than is apparent from the force numbers.

The data for the Northern Tier countries reveal the impact of the various coups in Afghanistan in increasing the Afghan forces, although Afghanistan now has little more than a paper army. The figures for India confirm the trade-off between quality and quantity discussed in the previous section; the Indian Army has the trained manpower to make much of its new armor effective. In contrast, as shown in Table 13.17, Pakistan has been forced to "level off" its military expansion since 1975. Turkey has increased the quality of its tank strength more than its trained manpower permits. Like India, however, Turkey is feeding its tanks into a long-established and previously underequipped force structure. Turkey may, therefore, be able to solve its conversion problems more rapidly than most of the other Near Eastern states.

The tank data on the Horn reveal Ethiopia's overexpansion of its forces, although this has been largely offset by dependence on Cuban "advisers" and "volunteers." The figures for Sudan illustrate the static trend in its force structure, and its relative decline in regional importance, while the figures for Somalia reflect that country's defeat in the Ogaden and its slow recovery since. These trends again confirm the shift in favor of Ethiopia and the emergence of a strong Soviet-backed force on the southern edge of the Red Sea.

The Trend in Combat Aircraft

Tables 13.19 and 13.20 and Chart 13.2 show similar data on trends for combat aircraft. It should be noted, however, that expanding and modernizing air forces is even more difficult than improving modern armored forces. It can take up to three years for even a highly trained squadron to convert to a significantly more advanced type of fighter. The success of such a conversion is also highly dependent on related major improvements in C^3I capabilities, as well as on massive changes in training methods and facilities. As a result, many Third World nations never properly convert to the combat aircraft they buy. They buy new types before they have absorbed their most recent purchase, and their pilots and technical personnel are placed in a constant state of turmoil. Training and training facilities, air doctrine, AC&W systems, air support and air defense exercises, and all the other elements of effective air power never have time to come together in the form of effective units, and the end result can be little more than a very expensive military practical joke.

Most Gulf nations are no exception to this rule, although Saudi Arabia's modernization has been well planned and Iran avoided some

TABLE 13.19 Numbers of Combat Aircraft in the Gulf, 1969–1984

	1969	1970	1971	1972	1973	1974	1975	1976	1977	1978	1979	1980	1981	1982	1983	1984
Gulf																
Bahrain	n.a.	n.a.	0	0	0	0	0	0	0	0	0	0	0	6	6?	6?
Iran	180	175	140	160	159	216	238	317	347	459	447	445[a]	200[b]	90[b]	70?[a,b]	80-100[a,b]
Iraq	213	229	220	189	224	218	247	299	369	339	339	332	335[a]	335[a]	280?[b]	290-330
Kuwait	n.a.	n.a.	n.a.	26	30	28	32	33	49	50	49	50	50	49	47	49
Oman	n.a.	n.a.	n.a.	15	12	12	47	44	50	46	49	52	38	37	40	37
Qatar	n.a.	n.a.	n.a.	4	4	4	4	13	4	4	4	4	9	9	14	11
Saudi Arabia	43	75	75	71	70	90	95	97	137	171[c]	180[c]	177[c]	178[c]	174[c]	187[c]	216[c]
UAE	n.a.	n.a.	n.a.	12	12	18	26	26	38	46	52	52	51	52	58	43[d]
South Yemen	n.a.	n.a.	n.a.	n.a.	20	39[d]	27[d]	27[d]	33[d]	34[d]	109	111	118	114	114[d]	113[d]
North Yemen	n.a.	n.a.	n.a.	n.a.	28	28	24[d]	28[d]	22	26	11	49	65	75	75[d]	75[d]
Total	436	479	435	477	559	653	740	884	1,049	1,175	1,240	1,272	1,044	947	891	920-980
Arab-Israeli Confrontation States																
Egypt	400	415	523	768[d]	620[d]	568[b,d]	500[a,d]	488[a]	365[a]	612[a]	563[a]	360	290	429	430[a,d]	498[a,d]
Jordan	11	38	33	50	52	50	42	66	78	76	73	58	84	94	114[d]	103
Lebanon	n.a.	24	21	18	18	18	24	27	21	21	16	7	0	8	8	8
Syria	145	210	210	210[d]	326[d]	300[b,d]	400[d]	440[d]	395[d]	392[d]	389[d]	395	448	450[d]	475	467
Subtotal	556	687	787	1,046	1,016	936	966	1,021	859	1,101	1,041	820	822	981	1,027	1,076
Israel	275	330	374	432	488[d]	466[b,d]	461[d]	543[d]	549[d]	543	576	535	602[d]	634	711[d]	683[d]
Libya	n.a.	7	7	22	44	70[d]	92[d]	129[d]	162[d]	178[d]	201[d]	287[d]	408	555	605	533
Total	831	1,024	1,168	1,500	1,548	1,472	1,519	1,693	1,570	1,822	1,818	1,642	1,832	2,170	2,343	2,292
Northern Tier/Indian Ocean																
Afghanistan	n.a.	n.a.	100	120	112	150	160	152	184	144	169[b]	160[b]	120[b]	117[b]	110[d]	150[b,d]
India	625	625	625	650	842	731	725	950	670[c]	661[c]	620[c]	630[c]	614	635	680[d]	727[d]
Pakistan	250	270	285	200	248	283	278	217	247	257	256	256	220	219	250[d]	259[d]
Turkey	500	310	360[d]	288[d]	288	290	292	370	319	339	303	290	325	402	430[d]	340
Total	1,375	1,205	1,370	1,258	1,490	1,454	1,455	1,689	1,420	1,401	1,348	1,336	1,279	1,373	1,470	1,476
Horn of Africa																
Ethiopia	n.a.	43	48	46	37	40	37	36	35	99	100	100+	115+	113[b]	115[a,d]	107[b]
Sudan	n.a.	32	32	40	50	51	43[d]	50	27[d]	22	36	36	44	30	36	31
Somalia	n.a.	18	20	21	21[a]	31[a]	52[a]	66[a]	55[a]	25[a]	25[a]	33[a]	35[a]	35[a]	35[a,d]	64[a,d]
Total	n.a.	93	100	107	108	122	132	152	117	146	161	169	194	178	186	202

[a]Spares are short and not all equipment is serviceable.
[b]War losses make this difficult to ascertain.
[c]Some now in a training role.
[d]Some are (or are believed to be) in storage.

Source: The Military Balance (London: IISS, 1969–1984). Figures for 1983 and 1984 include estimates by the author and do not necessarily agree with figures shown elsewhere from other sources. Data inputs to estimates often lag up to one year behind year shown.

TABLE 13.20 Combat Aircraft on Order in 1983–1984

Bahrain	6 F-5E/Fs ?
	60 Aim 9P air-to-air missiles
Egypt	20 Mirage 2000 from France
	16 Mirage SE:2 from France
	35 Alpha jets from France
	100 Chinese F-7 fighters
	24 Cobra helicopters with TOW
	36 Gazelle helicopters with HOT
	70 F-16A/2s from U.S. (Egypt requested 160; U.S. offered up to 120 along with 250 M-60A-3s)
Iran	? North Korean MiG-19/21 fighters
	100 Chinese F-6 fighters
Iraq	150 Alpha jets from France (under negotiation)
	150 MiG-23/25/27s from USSR
	42 Mirage F-1C/-1Bs from France (32 delivered in 1981)
	5 Super Etendard fighters with Exocet
	? Mirage 2000/4000 fighters
	? Mi-24 attack helicopters
	? CH-6 from PRC
	? CH-7 from PRC
Israel	11 F-15s from U.S. (total of 51 now ordered)
	72 F-16As from U.S.
	60 Kfir TC-2 trainers
Jordan	13 Mirage F-1s from France
	20 F-5E/Fs from U.S.
	24 AH-1Q Cobra helicopters with TOW ATGM
	? F-FG (F-20) from U.S.
	? F-16 from U.S., Mirage 4000 from France, or P-115 from UK
Kuwait	12 Mirage F-1 C/D fighters with Matra S-550 AAMs from France
	6 Super Puma helicopters with Exocet missiles from France
Lebanon	6 Gazelle helicopters
Libya	50 MiG-25s from USSR
	140 MiG-23s from USSR
	40 Mirage F-1s from France
	12 G222 attack trainers from Italy
Oman	12 Jaguar FGA attack fighters
	6 Bell 214 ST helicopters
Qatar	14 Mirage F-1 attack fighters (some delivered)
	6 Alphajet attack trainers
Saudi Arabia	31 F-15 Eagles from U.S.
	15 TF-15s from U.S.
	5 E-3A AWACs from U.S.
	10 RF-5E recce fighters
	4 F-5E attrition reserves
Sudan	6 F-5E U.S. fighters
Syria	40 MiG-27a from USSR (some delivered)
	? MiG-23 fighters from USSR
	2 TU-126 Recce aircraft
	18 AB-212 missile-equipped helicopters
	12 Super Frelon helicopters
UAE	18–40 Mirage 2000 fighters from France
	6 Alpha jets: FGA/trainer from France
	24 Hawk trainers from UK
	4 AS-332F Super Puma
North Yemen	None
South Yemen	None

Sources: The Military Balance (London: IISS, 1983–1984); SIPRI computer printout, April 1981; *Defense and Foreign Affairs,* 18 April 1983.

CHART 13—2
SHIFTS IN COMBAT AIRCRAFT STRENGTH AND QUALITY: 1973-1983

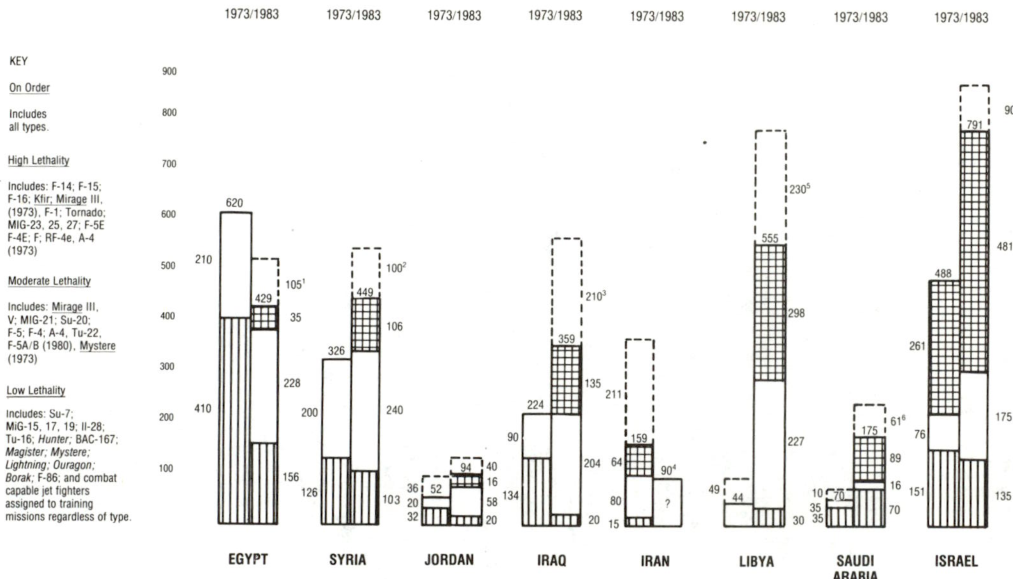

[1]Figures for Egypt in 1973 grossly exaggerate true operational strength which is closer to 270 aircraft. Orders include 70 F-16 A/B, 20 *Mirage* 2000, 16 *Mirage* S-E-2, and 15 Alphajet attack aircraft, but not 30 Alphajet trainers.
[2]Rapid changes in inventory are adding approximately 100 high lethality fighters to totals shown. Many low lethality types cannot be made operational.
[3]Iraqi figures inaccurate due to war losses and do not include recent Chinese sales, if any.
[4]Many aircraft inoperable. Only 90 considered operational; about 100 F-5s may still be in inventory; 9 out of 77 F-14s possibly serviceable; most *Phantoms* no longer operational. Some North Korean-made fighters being delivered.
[5]Does not include 2 Tu-22, 12 *Magister*, and 119 SF-2600WL trainers because they lack combat capability.
[6]Includes 39 BAC-167s used as trainers.
[7]In 1983, Israel had a full time active fighter strength of about 634 combat aircraft with up to 270 more aircraft in storage and 77-162 aircraft in training and reserve roles. It would like to phase out over 400 fighters by 1990, and maintain a force of around 600 high lethality fighters including the Lavi. It is trying to sell many of its A-4s, and is examining a re-engined "super" F-4.

Adapted from *The Military Balance*, I.I.S.S., London and experimental SIPRI computer runs. The exact count and categorization differs from the other tables in this section and is explained in the footnotes.

of these problems under the shah by purchasing massive amounts of U.S. training and technical and maintenance support. Iran also relied on training in the U.S. to create a fairly competent pool of pilots and squadron commanders. The shah's purchases were so massive that they enabled Iran to maintain air superiority in the Iran-Iraq War through the end of 1981, although only about one-third of Iran's fighters were operational and Israel could provide Iran with only limited spares. Even though the Iranian Air Force steadily dropped in capability once Iran split with the U.S., and Iran could operate its F-14s only as radar warning platforms and with infrared (IR) missiles, it still proved a match for Iraq until it finally lost the ability to keep its planes flying. In fact, the Iraqi Air Force was a model of how not to organize effectively during the period before the war began. Table 13.19 shows it bought far too much too quickly. Equally important, Iraq was not able to match Iran in buying the foreign support it needed to make its military buildup effective, even though it did not approach Iran in aircraft quality. As a result, Iraq's real level never approached the level indicated by its aircraft numbers.

The smaller conservative Gulf states have generally done no better than Iraq. Oman alone has matched Iran and Saudi Arabia in buying effective foreign support for its small air force, which was effective during the Dhofar rebellion only because it relied on foreign pilots and technicians. It is unclear how soon Oman can "Omanize" its air force, but it can rely on former RAF pilots as it increases its Jaguar force from 8 to 20 fighters.

The UAE and Kuwait bought air power largely as a status symbol, and their almost total reliance on foreign support did little to make their forces effective. The 30 Mirage Vs the UAE has acquired have only token readiness, and the 30 A-4KUs and 20 Mirage F-1s in Kuwait are strictly "showpiece" buys. Bahrain did not buy combat aircraft during the period shown, and Qatar has limited itself to token purchases of Mirage F-1 fighters designed to coordinate with Saudi Arabia.

The data for the two Yemens reveal the same rapid buildup after 1978 that is reflected in tanks and the other measures of defense dynamics, although the speed of this buildup indicates that neither country has yet had time to develop an effective air force. The sheer scale of the purchases in Table 13.19 does indicate, however, that the South Yemeni Air Force could become a significant threat to Saudi Arabia by the mid-1980s and that North Yemen is reversing its long period of decline. More recent data also indicate that South Yemen may well be building up to a force of over 150 combat aircraft and North Yemen to well over 100. These forces could pose a significant threat to Saudi Arabia in the mid-1980s.

The data for the Arab-Israeli confrontation states in Table 13.19 and Chart 13.2 indicate that Israel reached something of a plateau in first-line air strength around 1976 and then began to concentrate on aircraft quality. They also show that Syria has sought to convert to more advanced combat aircraft types while trying to expand the size of its air force. This focus on obtaining new types has been forced on Syria by its constant defeats by Israel in air-to-air combat, but the effort to simultaneously build up its numbers reveals a lack of effective organization and planning.

Table 13.19 and Chart 13.2 show Egypt's decline in air strength and its commitment to a long period of conversion to U.S. types that will reduce its overall effectiveness even further through the mid-1980s. The data on the Jordanian Air Force demonstrate that Jordan is not keeping up in air strength and aircraft quality. This failure is critical because Jordan may be unable to provide effective air cover or support for its land forces. The numbers in Chart 13.2 indicate that at best Jordan will have to remain in a defensive role and rely on F-5Es, which are no match for most Israeli fighters.

The data on the Northern Tier countries are interesting largely because they reflect a period of comparatively static air force strength for India, Pakistan, and Turkey. All are now making major new arms purchases, but it will be years before any of these nations have the ability to project air power beyond their own boundaries. The data for the Horn show the growth of Ethiopian capabilities relative to those of Somalia and the Sudan, and the emergence of a significant potential Ethiopian air threat to Saudi Arabia.

Overall Trends and Options to Improve Regional Stability

The mix of military dynamics, capabilities, and vulnerabilities described in this chapter does not lend itself to any simple "bottom line." As might be expected, the military situation in the Gulf is as complex as the political trends described in Chapters 11 and 12, and the extent to which the West must treat each Gulf country as a potential partner or threat, or even as an unstable risk, depends on the specific conditions in that country. Nevertheless, the analysis does convey some broad messages:

• If the war gives it enough time, the balance in the Gulf will shift in favor of Iraq. While Iran will remain a major military power by Gulf standards, it will need a massive new outside source of arms to keep from becoming a second-rank power relative to its main potential opponent.

• The geography of the Gulf now limits the military power that Iran and Iraq can bring to bear on the conservative Gulf states and gives air power a special importance. Air power is an area in which the conservative Gulf states are now individually weak—only Saudi Arabia has real capability—but in which they are well positioned to improve their cooperation in the future.

• The large size of Iranian and Iraqi forces is somewhat misleading. Both countries have severe imbalances in the defense effort that supports their current force structure. As a result, the dynamics of the Gulf military balance may favor the conservative Gulf states more than the current military force strengths would indicate, although that both Iran and Iraq have hundreds of thousands of experienced troops is an important factor.

• The conservative Gulf states are now paying far more for their military expansion than the other Gulf states, but the small manpower base in most conservative Gulf countries makes these individual defense efforts extremely inefficient. Kuwait in particular is spending massive amounts without producing even the image of strength. Such weakness creates a strong incentive for cooperation if the political heritage described in Chapter 11 can be overcome by the efforts like the Gulf Cooperation Council. There is an equal incentive for rationalization of military facilities, for standardization, and for integration. At the same time, any Western over-the-horizon reinforcements should at least provide the option of helping the conservative Gulf nations compensate for the internal weaknesses and imbalances in their defense efforts.

• If the conservative Gulf states are to counter the superior forces of their northern neighbors, both their armed forces and any over-the-horizon reinforcements must take account of the special conditions inherent in trying to defend the southern Gulf. These include the need to be able to defend key oil facilities and to provide area defense of both airspace and surrounding waters. Given the size of the military forces of the smaller Gulf nations, and the special problems of air and sea defense in the Gulf, these needs can be met only by creating some kind of collective security arrangements centered on sensor and battle-management systems like the Saudi AWACS.

• The problem of Gulf defense goes far beyond the risk of a Soviet attack, or one by Iraq or Iran. The dynamics of the military buildup in the Gulf, and the vulnerability of Gulf lines of communication, are increasingly creating a "360°" threat to the West's oil supplies. North and South Yemen are rapidly expanding in force strength, although neither country now seems able to provide enough finances to make its entire force structure effective. The air and naval threat from South Yemen seems particularly dangerous, and may grow to serious proportions by the late 1980s.

• The military balance in the Horn or southern Red Sea area is steadily shifting in favor of Ethiopia, which is creating a significant potential air threat to Saudi Arabia. The dynamics of this shift are so strong that it would take either renewed political convulsions in Ethiopia, or an almost incredible military miscalculation, to prevent it from eventually dominating the southern coast of the Red Sea area. This further increases the threat to the Bab al-Mandeb, to traffic through the Suez Canal, and to Saudi Arabia's new oil export facilities at Janbu.

• The Arab-Israeli balance is tilting away from the conservative Arab states such as Egypt and Jordan. Syria is emerging as a major military power in terms of force numbers, and although its fighting with Israel during Israel's invasion of Lebanon did little to demonstrate that it could make these numbers effective, Syria has greater strength relative to its Arab neighbors than in 1973. Libya also represents a massive pool of equipment support for radical causes even if it bears little resemblance to an effective military force. While Syria now suffers from acute imbalances and overexpansion, the long-term trends indicate that it will become the dominant regional Arab military power in the mid-1980s.

In contrast, Jordan will need major arms transfers to recover its former level of relative military capability. Jordan will otherwise steadily lose its importance as a military shield to Saudi Arabia throughout the 1980s. Egyptian military power is also likely to decline for most of the early 1980s and with it any Egyptian capability to balance the various threats to the Gulf. Jordanian and Egyptian military weakness reduces the ability of Egypt and Jordan to protect Saudi Arabia and increases the threat to road and pipeline routes to the Gulf.

• As might be expected, most of the Northern Tier states seem unlikely to have an immediate impact on the military balance in the Gulf. Turkey might, however, be able to significantly counterbalance any Soviet or Iraqi attack on the Gulf. The current trends indicate that India is now unquestionably the superior military power in the Indian Ocean area and that it will become increasingly superior over time. Pakistan may recover some of its former capability if it gets large deliveries of new U.S. equipment, but it will take time for it even to begin to build up momentum. It has been qualitatively and quantitatively stagnant for more than half a decade. The full importance of these trends becomes clearer, however, once they are considered in terms of the current military and internal security shifts in each Gulf state.

Notes

1. Wide disagreement exists over how to count such numbers. Constant dollars are used in Table 13.4 because they both show the trend in real terms and avoid portraying amounts in current dollars that may be misinterpreted as actual prices. For discussion of the issues involved see ACDA, *World Military Expenditures, 1977–1980,* pp. 27–30 and 37–38; SIPRI, *Yearbook,* 1978 (New York, Crane, Russak and Co., 1978), pp. 280–293; and Edward T. Fei, "Understanding Arms Data Problems," in Stephanie Neuman and Robert E. Harkavy, *Arms Transfers in the Modern World* (New York: Praeger Publishers, 1980), pp. 37–48.

2. Recent reports indicate that neither the export T-72 nor the Shir I will have advanced armor capable of defeating modern kinetic antitank weapons.

14
Oil, Lines of Communication, and Strategic Vulnerability

The special strategic objectives and vulnerabilities created by the Gulf's oil industry, and its dependence on long lines of communication to ship its oil and receive its imports, create another set of factors that shape the strategic stability of the region. Military capability and deterrence in the Gulf are uniquely linked to the ability to protect or threaten key oil facilities and the potential choke points limiting the movement of oil exports and critical imports.[1]

Gulf Oil as a Military Objective

The problem of defending key Saudi oil facilities and the Saudi core area has already been discussed in Chapter 8. These facilities are the most critical to the West, but all the Gulf's oil facilities are of strategic importance. The damage done to Iraqi and Iranian oil facilities in the Iran-Iraq War has already demonstrated that the "oil weapon" can be used with great lethality against Gulf countries and with a devastating effect on oil prices and Western economies. It has shown that even the most powerful Gulf states cannot protect their facilities without enhanced air defenses and that even a limited short-term loss of Gulf oil exports can have a major destabilizing impact on Western economies and world oil prices.

There is no reason why similar attacks could not have a major impact even if they were targeted against the smaller Gulf producers. An attack on Bahrain or Qatar might, for example, be used to force its alignment with another Gulf state, to help overthrow a conservative Gulf regime, or to demonstrate willingness to attack a larger Gulf state. Such attacks could be used to threaten the West or to force general compliance with an oil boycott. Given the panic that might follow in terms of a disruption of movements, rises in tanker insurance, oil prices, or shifts in the political alignment of other Gulf states, such attacks might have consequences almost as disastrous as attacks on the Gulf's largest oil producers.

Even a small attack can have major effects. A combination of a tanker collision with a well and Iraqi attacks on three offshore wells in Iran's Nowruz fields started an oil spill in February and March 1983 and the release of anywhere from 1,200–10,000 BPD into the Gulf. By July 1983, the resulting oil slick, or "black ghoul," had reached as much as 1.5 million barrels and had forced facilities like the desalinization plant at Al Khobar to shut down and threatened the shorelines of Kuwait, Bahrain, Qatar, and Saudi Arabia.

Iraq found that the threat of blocking efforts to cap the wells had given it new leverage over Iran and the southern Gulf states, and it promptly obtained more Exocet air-to-surface missiles and an agreement to obtain the loan of five super Etendard fighters from France to extend its attack range. Iran sought Japanese assistance in examining how it could best attack offshore wells, and the southern Gulf countries commissioned similar studies of their attack and defense options. The Gulf had clearly discovered that oil wars could be tailored to almost any size the attacker desired.

There also is no doubt regarding the inherent vulnerability of most Gulf states. Table 14.1 shows the distribution of key oil facilities in the Gulf, and their impact on trade in 1981—a year that may be slightly more representative of the future than the figures for 1982 and 1983. These facilities differ in capacity and importance, each is a relatively vulnerable military objective and most can be attacked by air and sea from virtually any Gulf country. This vulnerability is shown in Map 14.1, which shows the overall distribution of major oil facilities in the Gulf area.

The Gulf oil producers do, however, differ in geographic vulnerability. Iraqi production is based predominantly at the fields at Kirkuk, which are near Iraq's border with Iran but 400–500 miles from the Gulf. Iraq's main refinery facilities are near the Iranian border and have also been a target in the war, while its loading facilities in the Gulf are limited to areas near its short 30-NM stretch of Gulf coastline. Iraq's output can be shipped via pipeline through the Mediterranean, as well as through the Gulf, which has allowed Iraqi production to continue at a diminished rate in spite of the loss of its oil-loading facilities in the Gulf during the Iran-Iraq War.

Iran, which now seems limited to a maximum production of about 3.5 MMBD, has its oil fields scattered along a 300-mile corridor near the Zagros Mountain range.[2] The land routes in and out of the region are poor, but they proved to be well within the range of Iraqi armor and artillery early in the Iran-Iraq War. Iran's main oil-extraction and -production facilities are now concentrated in vulnerable core areas like the crude oil-loading facilities at Kharg Island, and although the island is barely within the effective range of current Iraqi fighters, it will be fully within the range of Super Etendards and Mirage 2000s that will be deployed by the mid-1980s. Iran's main refinery facilities were located

TABLE 14.1 Illustrative Data on Gulf Oil Fields and Production

	Bahrain[a]	Iran	Iraq	Kuwait	Oman	Qatar	Saudi Arabia	UAE
General Geography								
Size of oil-producing area (miles)	20 x 10	300 x 100	500 x 100	100 x 50	175 x 25	120 x 35	300 x 100	100 x 25
Distance from U.S. (miles)	7,000	6,650	6,280	6,700	7,450	7,100	6,950	7,200
Oil Extraction								
Total major oil fields	1	11	4	13	3	3	14	8
Offshore	0	2	0	2	0	2	7	5
Onshore	1	9	4	11	3	1	7	3
Percentage offshore	0	18	0	15	0	66	50	63
Active wells	211	330	160	1,040	160	70	775	275
Oil Production								
Refineries								
Number	–	5	7	5	0	1	3	1
Capacity (BPD)	–	911	169	712	0	10	586	15
Pipeline mileage[b]	unknown	3,720	3,690	740	unknown	120	2,800	400
Loading facilities	1	7	2	7	4	7	11	14
Ports	1	5	2	4	1	2	4	6
Single buoy moorings or other offshore	–	2	0	3	3	5	7	8
Oil Exports[c]								
Total production	0.05	1.7	0.7	1.6	0.3	0.5	10.2	1.2
Exports to:[d]								
U.S.	0.001	0.4	0.1	0.03	n.a.	0.04	1.4	0.3
Western Europe[e]	negl.	0.9	1.7	0.9	n.a.	0.2	3.6	0.7
Japan	0.03	0.5	0.3	0.6	n.a.	0.1	1.9	0.5
Oil production as % of total imports								
U.S.	negl.	21.5	8.9	20.2	3.8	6.3	129.1	15.6
Western Europe	1	22.0	9.0	20.8	3.9	6.5	132.5	15.5
Japan	1	30.3	12.5	28.5	5.4	8.9	182.1	21.4

Figures rounded to show order of magnitude rather than precise accounting.

[a]Data on Bahrain taken from Special Subcommittee on Investigations of the Committee on International Relations, *Oil Fields as Military Objectives* (Washington, D.C.: Government Printing Office, 1975), p. 32.

[b]Approximate pipeline mileage for major crude carriers.

[c]Data taken from NFAC, *International Energy Statistical Review,* ER IESR 81-005, 26 May 1981.

[d]Data as of 1979.

[e]Includes Great Britain, West Germany, France, and Italy.

Source: Adapted from John M. Collins, *Petroleum Imports from the Persian Gulf: Use of U.S. Armed Forces to Ensure Supplies,* Issue Brief no. IB79046, Congressional Research Service, 1982, p. A-1.

MAP 14—1
DISTRIBUTION OF OIL FIELDS AND FACILITIES IN THE GULF

Adapted from maps furnished by the CIA.

at Abadan, near the Iraqi border, which led to their destruction during the Iraqi land offensive against Iran.[3] They may now be rebuilt on the Iranian coast in the eastern Gulf near Bandar Abbas or the Gulf of Oman.

Unlike Iraq and Iran, where oil fields and ancillary installations are scattered, highly redundant, and often separated by sizable distances, Kuwait has five refineries and five loading facilities on the Gulf, and all its oil facilities are concentrated into an area of only 500 square miles. Kuwait is so close to Iraq, Iran, and Saudi Arabia that it is unclear that its oil facilities can be militarily defended, and they certainly cannot be defended without an advanced AWACS-type air and maritime warning system.[4] Kuwait has only 740 miles of pipeline, versus 3,720 miles for Iran and 3,690 miles for Iraq, but it has roughly the same number of refinery complexes, and its seven loading facilities equal Iran's loading capacity and far outstrip that of Iraq. Thus it has a number of very attractive key targets, and the Iranian Air Force exploited this in 1981 by launching air attacks designed to make Kuwait reduce its support to Iraq in the Iran-Iraq War.

The oil facilities in the littoral states of Bahrain, Qatar, and the UAE are positioned along a 600-mile arc. The total production of these states was 1.8 MMBD in 1981.[5] Establishing a defensive perimeter around the combined fields would, at a minimum, encompass an area of 6,900 square miles and again require an advanced air defense using an AWACS. Many of the wells in all three countries are located offshore, which further complicates defensive operations.[6] The oil produced from Qatar's wells is loaded at Qatar's maritime terminal at Umm Said, and its product exports are refined at a nearby refinery, which makes this a key potential target. Bahrain is connected by pipeline to Saudi facilities, and although it has a small oil field at Awali, this is now largely a processing center for refining Saudi crude. Its refinery terminal at Sitra Island and its other oil facilities are vulnerable to air attacks from all Gulf states. Further, the oil facilities in both Qatar and Bahrain are vulnerable to sea attacks by even light missiles like the SS-12 mounted on small craft. The facilities of the UAE, which are concentrated in Abu Dhabi, are equally vulnerable to naval and air attack, although some are beyond the effective range of current Iraqi fighters.[7] Oman's small facilities, which are concentrated at the loading facility at Mina al-Fahal near Muscat, are comparatively isolated from most Gulf countries but lie well within the range of Iranian F-4s and fighters based in South Yemen.

The Early Lessons of the Iran-Iraq War

The Iran-Iraq War provides a tangible illustration of the vulnerability of these Gulf oil fields and their potential importance in a future conflict.[8] Iraq initially seems to have hoped to seize the Iranian oil facilities in Abadan more or less intact and perhaps also the key pipelines moving domestic product north to Iran's cities. As is described in detail in Chapter 16, Iraq launched a major ground attack on the Iranian oil province of Khuzestan in late 1980, accompanied by massive air raids on Iran's air bases. When these attacks failed, Iraq attempted to deliberately disrupt Iranian domestic oil flows and oil exports. In addition to shelling the Abadan refinery and the major storage facilities nearby, Iraqi fighters attacked Iran's other refineries and its main crude export facility at Kharg Island. Iraq launched only limited attacks against any of the Iranian crude oil-production and oil field processing facilities, largely because it lacked the air power to do more.[9]

Iraq's artillery attacks on the refinery at Abadan were successful, virtually destroying the 610,000-BPD refinery. Iraq also achieved limited success in its air strikes on the 80,000-BPD refinery at Tabriz and the 200,000-BPD refinery at Isfahan, although both were back in operation in early 1981. Its air attacks on the 225,000-BPD refinery at Tehran and the 40,000-BPD refinery at Shiraz largely misfired. The Iraqi Army also failed to cut the main north-south pipelines in Iran, and the Iraqi Air force failed to hit key facilities at Kharg Island.

The facilities at Kharg were theoretically an attractive target because they handled about 90% of all crude exported from Iran, which is fed from the mainland to Kharg through six 43-kilometer underwater pipelines ranging in diameter from 30 to 52 inches. In addition, one of Iran's major offshore fields (Fereidoon) fed into Kharg Island via a 20-inch, 100-kilometer underwater pipeline from the southwest, and oil was produced from another field (Darius-Kharg) at Kharg Island. Although the pipelines were buried or under water, and the facilities were highly redundant, Kharg had two vulnerable points. The first was the Sea Island loading facility on the west side of Kharg, which was fed by underwater pipelines and was capable of handling four VLCCs simultaneously. Two large metering and control systems channeled the crude flow to the north and south platforms, and all crude oil-loading operations would have stopped if these systems had been disabled. Replacement or repair would have taken at least several months. The second was a set of storage tanks ranging in capacity from 250,000 barrels to 1 million barrels each. While these had firewalls designed to contain spills and reduce fire damage, the individual tanks were highly vulnerable to explosives. Further, Iraqi raids could have struck at the valve or control systems in the storage tank area and created large spills and major fires.

Such attacks, however, required a degree of planning and coordination that proved beyond the capacity of the Iraqi Air Force. It also lacked effective targeting intelligence, especially at the start of the war, and Iraq's Soviet-built fighters generally had a shorter effective range than Iran's U.S.-built fighters. As a result, many key Iranian facilities, such as Kharg Island, were at the outer limit of the practical range of Iraqi fighters. This quickly became apparent when repeated Iraqi attacks destroyed only a few tanks, and Iraq then proved unable to strike at smaller targets like the Sea Island facilities with any accuracy.

Further, Iraq rapidly learned it was no match for Iranian fighters in air-to-air combat and that Iran was more than able to retaliate in kind. During the early weeks of the war, Iranian planes repeatedly attacked a variety of Iraqi petroleum installations, including export terminals, production and processing facilities, and major and minor refineries.

The raids were conducted against installations deep in Iraq as well as against facilities near the Iranian border.[10] Despite the large number of raids, the damage was initially limited. This situation changed radically, however, in November 1980, when Iran's air attacks were supplemented by an Iranian naval and commando attack on Iraq's two crude export terminals in the Gulf, with a combined export capacity of 3.2 MMBD. The damage at the first terminal, Mina al-Bakr, included destruction of its control facilities and major fire and blast damage to both of its main platforms and to its pipes, valves, metering equipment, and loading arms. The second facility, at Khor al-Amaja, suffered even more massive damage, including extensive fire damage to the platforms and destruction of controls, pipes, valves, loading arms, and metering and electrical equipment. In addition, the walkway connecting the two principal platforms, which carries the main crude oil line, was severed. Iran followed this success by inflicting additional damage with further naval and air attacks.

Although this series of Iranian attacks involved comparatively small forces, it demonstrated just how vulnerable Gulf nations could be. Iraq was left with just a small export terminal at al-Fao that could handle only the smallest tankers and sustain loadings of only about 100,000 BPD. Iraq also found that it could do little to repair the damage while the war continued, other than ordering long-lead-time equipment. Even then, a considerable debate arose among Iraq's consultants regarding just how long even temporary repairs would take once the war was over. One group estimated that a temporary single-point mooring buoy system could be installed in about a month if the equipment was available. Another estimated that over a year would be required if equipment and controls had to be fabricated as well as installed. Further, these Iraqi and Western experts agreed that only enough buoys could be installed to restore about one-third to one-half of prewar loading capacity because of the draft limitations imposed on tankers.

In any case, the loss of its loading facilities in the Gulf forced Iraq to shift its oil exports to oil pipelines that loaded at ports in the Mediterranean. However, these lines had a maximum theoretical capacity of 1.9 MMBD, and even this estimate of capacity assumed that *all* pipelines to the Mediterranean could be operated at full capacity. In fact, there had been substantial degradation in the capacity of the Iraq-Syria pipeline system during the years, when it was either not operating or was operating only at reduced levels because of Iraqi-Syrian disputes over fees, the Lebanese civil war, and various other political issues. The 400,000-BPD Tripoli/Baniyas spur of the Iraq-Syria pipeline had not been used since 1976 and could not be brought on line immediately, and the Lebanon spur—with a capacity of 500,000 BPD—could not be brought on line at all because of the Lebanese civil war. The lines through Turkey, which terminated at Dortyol and Yumurtalis, had the drawback of passing through Kurdish areas in both Iraq and Turkey.

Iran retaliated against Iraq's use of these pipelines by directing its air attacks against oil installations in northern Iraq in an attempt to prevent Baghdad from maintaining a high level of crude exports. When Iraq restored a significant flow of crude to its Mediterranean Sea terminals in late November 1980, the Iranians increased air strikes against Iraq's petroleum installations. Damage to the Iraqi oil-processing facilities at Kirkuk forced Baghdad to suspend major shipments from the field. Iran also launched attacks on Iraq's refineries that forced Iraq to shut down its largest refinery at al-Basrah for several months and to close several other key facilities, including gas-oil separators and tank farms, for varying periods of time. Both sides gradually tapered down their air attacks in 1981 and 1982 as it became apparent that they were mutually destructive and as the attrition of the Iranian Air Force from combat and inadequate maintenance forced Iran to conserve aircraft.

The Impact of the Iran-Iraq War on Oil Shipments

Following the mutual attacks on oil facilities, the war illustrated another aspect of oil vulnerability. Various Kurdish and Lebanese groups sabotaged the pipelines carrying Iraqi oil through Turkey, Syria, and Lebanon on five occasions between September 1980 and April 1982. While such attacks caused only temporary cuts in shipments out of Turkey, they proved critical in halting shipments out of Lebanon, where it proved impossible to secure pipeline facilities against repeated attacks or to repair them without the consent of the various warring factions in the area.

Iraqi ability to ship oil through the Hadithah-Baniyas pipeline through Syria also became increasingly tenuous as Iraq's relations with Syria went from bad to worse. The long heritage of rivalry between the Baath parties of the two nations was compounded by Syria's resentment of Iraqi support for the more conservative Arab states, by its feeling that Iraq had failed to properly back it in the Arab-Israeli conflict, by its fear of the consequences of an Iraqi victory over Iran and Iraq's military dominance of the region, by its fear of the developing alliance between Jordan and Iraq, and by the fact that Syria's secular government was headed by members of a Shi'ite sect. All these factors made Syria increasingly reluctant to let Iraqi oil flow through Syria, making Iraq's pipelines through Turkey more vulnerable since they passed within 30 kilometers of the Syrian border. On at least one occasion, the "Kurdish" saboteurs cutting the Iraqi line in Turkey may have been Iranians operating out of Syria.[11]

This Syrian hostility toward Iraq steadily accelerated during 1981 and early 1982. In mid-April 1982 Syria refused to ship any further Iraqi oil and seized roughly 1.5 million barrels' worth of Iraq oil waiting in tanks in the Syrian port of Baniyas.[12] While this deprived Syria of about $127 million in annual oil transit fees, it also cut Iraq's oil shipments by about 300,000–400,000 BPD (out of total exports of

900,000–1,000,000 BPD) and eliminated its ability to increase its oil shipments through the Tripoli spur of its eastern pipeline.[13] Syria then announced that it had reached an agreement with Iran to trade 8.7 million tons of crude oil annually for 10 years in return for Syrian exports of food. There are some indications that the first Iranian oil shipment arrived in Baniyas about nine days before Syria suspended Iraqi oil shipments, and that Syria stockpiled Iraqi oil in order to seize the maximum possible amount.[14] Iraq responded by announcing that it was examining plans to build new pipelines through Jordan to Aqaba or through Saudi Arabia to a new port on the Red Sea. Iran announced that it would build a parallel line through the same Kurdish areas in Turkey that had given so much trouble to Iraq and that it was studying pipelines to a port on the Gulf of Oman. Ironically, Iran found itself involved in renewed fighting with its Kurds less than a week later.[15] Both nations had become involved in a pipeline war that was almost as serious as the attacks they had launched against each other's oil facilities early in the fighting.

Luckily for the West, this struggle over oil exports occurred in the midst of a world recession and at a time when oil prices were already so high that substantial surplus capacity existed. The results of the war were also fortunate for the West in several ways: Neither side had really planned its attacks well enough to take advantage of its opponent's vulnerability, both sides were limited in their air attack capabilities, and the fighting had its worst effect on refinery facilities that were most important in serving Third World nations or domestic markets in Iran and Iraq.[16] As a result, the West was able to substitute other sources of oil, although only at the cost of still further price rises and a deepening economic recession.

This same situation applies in 1983, even though Iraq resumed occasional air attacks on Gulf oil shipping and on Kharg Island after Iranian forces had pushed Iraq out of Khuzestan and began to threaten Iraq. Although Iran's air force declined in operability so that it could no longer use its aircraft to defend its airspace, and Iran could not make most of its Western-made surface-to-air missiles operational, it was able to obtain large numbers of ZSU-23-4s and other AA guns, as well as Improved SA-7s and other light surface-to-air missiles, from Syria, Libya, and North Korea. These weapons allowed Iran to build up very strong short-range air defenses over Kharg and other key targets. Iraq's MiG-21s, MiG-23s, and Mirage F-1s lacked the combination of range, endurance, payload, and delivery accuracy to deal with this situation. Further, the ECM gear and other air defense suppression equipment sold to Iraq required more skill and training than the Iraqi Air Force had yet acquired. As a result, Iran was able to export an average of 2.5 MMBD, and peaks of 3.2 MMBD, in spite of a steady increase in the number of Iraqi attacks—more than enough to keep prices low and oil supplies high in the climate of a worldwide recession.

The Future Vulnerability of Oil Facilities in the Gulf

There is no reason to assume, however, that such military attacks will remain so ineffective or that the West will always be so "fortunate" in terms of oil supply and demand. The Iraqi attacks on Iran's offshore wells discussed earlier have shown that limited strikes can be highly effective and are already leading to improved attack planning throughout the Gulf. Iraq's order of 5 Super Etendard with Exocet and the orders of new attack aircraft shown in Chart 13.2, coupled with other orders of more advanced air munitions, will allow most Gulf states to launch far more lethal air attacks on Gulf oil facilities with each passing year. So will the equally large purchases of assault and attack helicopters now on order, as well as the missile-carrying patrol boats either now on order or in the final negotiating stage.

Oil industry experts also indicate that the military forces of the larger Gulf states and peripheral powers have devoted a significant amount of time to examining the vulnerability of their neighbors' oil facilities since the start of the Iran-Iraq War, to studying how to improve the lethality of attacks against them, and to formulating strategic options for using such attacks to influence their potential enemies in the Gulf or to put leverage on the West. While the scale and effectiveness of such planning are open to question, there is little doubt that the problem of oil field vulnerability and defense will become steadily more critical throughout the 1980s and that the Iran-Iraq War has set an exceedingly dangerous precedent.

It is also important to note that there is another class of threats to the Gulf and the West's oil supplies. As was noted earlier, Kurdish terrorists succeeded in blowing up a key pumping station on the 700,000-BPD pipeline from Iraq to Ceyhan in Turkey early in the Iraq-Iran War and in shutting this last remaining Iraqi export route for several weeks. Kurdish, Lebanese, and other saboteurs have since cut Iraq's pipelines on five other occasions. The pipeline is only one of many Gulf oil facilities that is vulnerable to terrorist or covert action, to air attacks, or to small sea and heliborne raids, as well as to major air attacks. The key targets for such raids include the following:[17]

- *Manifold Stations:* These regulate the types and amounts of crude that flow into pipelines. They consist primarily of a surge tank and pipelines. Damage to such facilities would significantly diminish the ability to export crude oil, but repairs can generally be made relatively quickly.
- *Gas-Oil Separating Plants:* These plants separate associated natural gas from oil at the fields. They are generally extremely large in the Gulf, and many are "one-of-a-kind" facilities that involve equipment with long replacement lead times. Even minor acts of sabotage against such facilities could have serious effects, since up to two years might

be required to replace one of the larger GOSPs, although smaller or "makeshift" separating facilities could be set up in a few months for temporary operation at most fields. Temporary repairs could present a problem, however. Such plants use multistage separators to avoid the loss of the more valuable crude component, such as butanes and pentanes, that would occur if the separation process took place all at once at atmospheric pressure. A considerable loss of oil would be likely if simple flow tanks—designed to handle crude containing little associated gas and to produce at low pressure—were used to separate oil from large quantities of high-pressure gas through foaming or misting. In some cases this problem would be further complicated by their need for desalting capability.

• *Booster Stations:* These are large pumping stations that maintain the flow of oil along pipelines in the Gulf. Many are redundant, or sited to reduce vulnerability, but many are heavily concentrated and use one-of-a-kind equipment. These are good targets for aircraft and sabotage. Each such pumping station usually houses several large gas capacity combustion turbines. Sufficient power would usually still be on line to maintain crude flows, even if one or two turbines were seriously damaged. But larger-scale damage would have a major effect on production and exports. It might take two years or more to replace the turbines and 18 months to replace other rotating equipment because of long manufacturing lead times. Manufacturers generally do not stock equipment, although smaller pumps might be used to temporarily achieve up to 1 MMBD of pumping capacity.

• *Electric Power System:* The electric generating facilities that support petroleum production and exports are essential to maintaining petroleum output. Backup units are now increasingly redundant, and some are "netted" with other power systems. Power plants still, however, make attractive targets. Key vulnerable points include turbines, boilers, and transformers. Electricity is also essential to maintaining electrolytic anticorrosion devices, and pipelines could become vulnerable to corrosion in a short period without this protection. In a few fields, power is also critical to water injection and gas injection and could affect the pressure point and long-term recovery. Well-planned attacks on both a few key plants and key points in the associated distribution system could have considerable effect.

• *Onshore Pipelines:* Because of the long distances involved, onshore crude oil pipelines cannot be completely protected. However, even if most pipelines were severely damaged—and carefully placed explosives would be required—repairs could be accomplished relatively quickly. Spare pipe is almost always available, and repeated attacks are required against pipelines to keep them closed.

• *Underwater Pipelines:* Submarine crude pipelines in the Gulf are usually installed as buried lines. Underwater currents generally wash this cover away, however, and the exposed pipelines are then sandbagged.

Although anchorage is forbidden in the sea lanes near pipelines because of the risk that ships could drag anchors and sever the pipelines, they remain vulnerable to surface dragging as well as to frogman-type operations. Most can be reached using ordinary scuba equipment at some point along their length, and many can be attacked covertly without any serious risk that the attacker can be firmly identified.

• *Oil Wells:* A few high-yield wells are sensitive targets. If most individual oil wells are damaged, however, they can be easily isolated from the pipeline collection network, and their loss will have little impact on total oil deliverability. Large stocks of spare parts are available for repair of damage to most surface production equipment. It can, however, take weeks to months to repair a well, and special expertise is required to stop a fire. If a substantial number of wellheads were destroyed, there could be a significant impact on reservoir pressures and a risk of lower ultimate recovery. Blowing up an oil well can be accomplished either by using explosives or by loosening wellhead fittings and igniting the leaking fluid.

Oil well fires in some Gulf states pose another problem because tubing is rarely installed inside the wellbore. If the wellhead is destroyed, or if it leaks, it is difficult to shut in the well. In many cases, it may be necessary to drill a relief well—a process that may take a month or more—to put out a well fire. Moreover, access to control valves and bottom flanges would be limited, which further complicates fire protection.

• *Natural Gas Liquids Plants:* NGL facilities separate out the heavier components of associated natural gas production so that dry gas can be shipped. Gas cannot be delivered without such facilities, but their loss would have little effect on oil output because gas can be flared at the fields. During the 1980s, however, many Gulf states will become dependent on gas exports or gas to support their "downstream" operations and economic development. Such plants can be damaged by conventional sabotage, by contaminating the dehydration facilities, or by tampering with the carbon dioxide removal system, as well as by sabotage of the compressors.

• *Gas Storage Facilities:* Gas storage facilities are equivalent to depots with several tons of high explosives. They can be set off by most light antitank weapons. Many are colocated with crude oil-loading facilities, and a well-planned land, air, and/or sea attack could have a greatly increased impact by creating large-scale secondary effects.

• *Gas Treatment Plants:* These plants remove hydrogen sulfide from associated gas, a "sweetening" process that is essential to maintaining large-scale deliveries through gas pipelines. The cryogenic equipment at such plants is particularly difficult to replace because of long manufacturing lead times.

• *Offshore Oil Facilities:* These facilities are uniquely vulnerable to missile attacks or heliborne and amphibious raids. Such raids require careful planning and targeting, but they could generally quickly destroy long-lead-time components on a given facility. Most offshore wells have spill and fire protection, but this can be bypassed with careful planning and expert assistance. Further, even ineffective conventional bombing or other military raids might well force large-scale evacuation of such facilities in the Gulf, many of which are dependent on foreign technicians.

As Iraq's February 1983 attacks on Iran's offshore wells demonstrated, it is also possible to use attacks on offshore wells for a variety of political purposes. The wells are particularly vulnerable because it is difficult to provide warning of air or sea attacks, given the distances involved and normal traffic in the region, and because the wells make high-contrast targets that allow the use of air-to-surface missiles like Exocet or Harpoon or any medium to large surface-to-surface missile with terminal homing. While the kill probability of any given missile will be limited, it is far higher than trying to attack a complex and defendable target with miles of surface area like Kharg Island.

Oil company sources confirm that the vulnerability of such wells is often increased by inadequate maintenance or the failure to install, or properly install, safety devices, a problem that is compounded by the fact that there has been sufficient fraud in the Gulf area that it is difficult for many countries to identify wells that lack adequate safeguards. Once successful, such attacks also offer the advantage that the wells cannot be capped without exposing the ships used in the capping effort to further attack. Unlike with land wells, repair crews can approach only in an easily detectable form, and one that forces the repair crew to work from a stationary target that is easily identified and attacked using aircraft or ship radars and terminally guided missiles.

Such attacks also tend to be useful in putting pressure on the southern Gulf states because they need Gulf water for desalinization and water-injection purposes. In contrast, Iran is much less dependent on unpolluted Gulf waters, and Iraq has no economic interest in restricting such oil spills. Like undersea pipelines and offshore pumping facilities, offshore wells provide a uniquely tempting method of conducting limited or anonymous oil strikes, and a defense is virtually impossible without the kind of radar warning that can be provided only by an AWACS with both air defense and maritime surveillance capability or complex new systems like tethered radar sensor balloons.

• *Refineries:* Refineries involve a number of critical long-lead-time, or one-of-a-kind, components whose loss can often halt operations or reduce capacity for months or even several years. They do, however, allow for better area defense than many of the smaller facilities listed above, and they are very difficult air targets because they require either mass raids or extremely well-trained pilots using precision-guided munitions. The relatively small vulnerable area of critical components protected crude oil refineries against long-term damage in the Iran-Iraq War and has had a similar effect in past wars. The vulnerable area also cannot be identified with the radars on current ships and aircraft, and radar missiles with terminal homing cannot "lock on" the parts of a complex that are vulnerable. Current electro-optical missiles also lack the discrimination and data links to permit effective attacks. Military proficiency in the Gulf air forces can, however, be expected to improve in time, and heliborne assaults could be highly effective in destroying key components like "crackers."

• *Tank Farms:* It is generally easy to destroy individual tanks, but in most crude oil tank farms the tanks are spaced far enough apart so that conventional bombs from limited numbers of air attacks have surprisingly low lethality. Artillery fire can be more precise, but smoke from the initial tank fires often so obscures the target as to protect the farm from further fire, depending on the angle of attack and the wind direction—and whether targets are preplotted or not. Sabotage is obviously a major problem, although tank farm perimeter defense can be effective when the farm is sufficiently isolated from nearby towns and facilities and is large enough to merit such defense.

This matrix of vulnerabilities can be dealt with by area denial of enemy ships, aircraft, and assault forces; by establishing defensive perimeters against terrorists; by effective internal security measures; and by the threat of reprisals in kind. However, economies of scale and the relatively wide dispersion of key vulnerability points usually preclude such measures as the deployment of rapid repair kits and prestocking long-lead-time equipment. While "passive" defense measures can be effective in critical cases, the Gulf states can generally protect their fields only by direct defense of their territory airspace and territorial waters.

Waterways, Ports, and Airports

The military dynamics of the Gulf are also shaped by the fact that the Gulf states are dependent on a relatively few road nets, major ports, and international airports for key imports. Like their cities and oil facilities, such lines of communication (LOCs) are essential to the functioning of most Gulf states. All the Gulf states are food importers to a greater or lesser degree, and most import a large part of their consumer goods and durables. Most are also dependent on the relatively free flow of both tankers and freighters to move oil out of the country and bulk imports in.

Waterways

The key waterways affecting the Gulf include the Suez Canal, the Red Sea, the Indian Ocean, the Cape route, and the Gulf itself. Iran also has an important seasonal waterway through the Caspian Sea, which can be used for relatively high volumes of shipment through the

USSR. All these waterways are vulnerable along their entire length. Modern small craft can carry armor-piercing, surface-to-surface missiles fully capable of sinking most tankers or bulk carriers. Aircraft can locate large ships on their radars, and most patrol aircraft and attack fighters can now carry air-to-surface weapons that are lethal against such vulnerable naval targets as tankers and container ships. Even the smaller Gulf navies are capable of effective hit-and-run raids against shipping. As a result, Gulf shipping is vulnerable to even small-scale terrorist raids, particularly since few private firms would risk a ship or even pay wartime insurance premiums to complete a voyage to a Gulf country. It also is impossible for a single Gulf navy to patrol the Gulf or Red Sea effectively because of the long distances involved, the vulnerability to air or sea attack from neighboring countries, the high density of traffic, and the many points of attack along the major shipping routes.

These same problems preclude the adequate defense of shipping lanes by most Gulf air forces, although the maritime reconnaissance mode of the E-3A, E-2C, and Nimrods and the sensors of Iran's P-3C Orion maritime patrol aircraft could provide the required analysis and C^2 capability and greatly improve the effectiveness of ships and fighter aircraft alike.

The Iran-Iraq War has so far disguised the vulnerability of Gulf sea lanes for a number of reasons. Iran has been able to halt Iraq's oil shipments through the Gulf without such attacks, and is unlikely to launch attacks that might keep tankers out of the Gulf as long as it can maintain its own oil exports and has no reason to try to put military pressure on the entire region. Iraq has (to date) been incredibly clumsy in launching such attacks, and has confined itself to wild damage claims that both tanker companies and insurers have learned to ignore. While Iraq has recently begun to hit a few ships near Iraq's coastline, it still lacks proficiency. French advisers to Iraq point out with contempt that Iraq launched two helicopter-borne Exocets to hit one 6,000-ton tanker and that most of Iraq's few fighter attacks on tankers and Iranian offshore wells have failed when they would have been certain successes if conducted by a Western air force.

This state of affairs is, however, unlikely to characterize the future. The presence of loose naval mines in the Gulf floating down from waters near the Shat al-Arab is already a subject of concern. France's loan of five Super Etendard fighters will give Iraq an aircraft specially configured for antiship attacks and that can detect and characterize very or ultra large tankers at the limit of the Exocet's 50–70-kilometer range. Exocet is also typical of modern ship-to-ship and air-to-ship missiles in that its sea-skimming flight profile makes it hard to detect and that its warhead-to-total-weight ratio (165kg : 654 kg) gives a high kill probability against a tanker for very limited total payload weight.

Other such systems are already in service in the Gulf, including the Italian-made Otomat, which is in service in Saudi Arabia and Libya, which has a maximum range of 180 kilometers, 209 kg : 780 kg warhead-to-total-weight ratio, and an active radar-seeker homer. The U.S.-made Harpoon, which is in service in Saudi Arabia and Israel and has a 160-kilometer range in the air-launched mode (55 kilometers sea-launched), a 230 kg : 531–668 kg warhead-to-total-weight ratio, an advanced radar seeker, and advanced missile to launch electronics interface. And the Soviet-made Styx, which is in service in Iraq and South Yemen, has a 40-kilometer range, a 500 kg : 16,000 kg warhead-to-total-weight ratio, and a mix of radio, IR, and active radar guidance.

It also seems likely that most tanker captains would turn back if attacked even by light air-to-surface missiles like Maverick or AS 12, and it is interesting to note that the Hawk and other long range surface-to-air missiles can be used against both tankers and offshore wells. An Israeli Hawk did, in fact, set a land well on fire during the 1973 fighting when the Hawk crew mistakenly identified the oil well as an enemy helicopter. The Hawk can be used against such targets at ranges up to 40 kilometers, while Soviet missiles have even greater range. The SA-6 can deliver an 80-kg warhead 30–60 kilometers, the SA-3 can deliver a 130+ kg warhead up to 30 kilometers, and the SA-2 can deliver a 130 kg warhead up to 50 kilometers.

By the late 1980s, the situation will have moved far beyond even today's advanced systems like the Exocet or Harpoon and far beyond expedients like the use of surface-to-air missiles. Newer missiles with "smart" warheads will provide an over-the-horizon capability that can home in on specific classes or tonnages of tankers from land-based fire points at ranges of over 200 kilometers, while shorter-range missiles should have the sensors to attack tankers in port or land-based oil targets. Successfully sinking a tanker at a mooring could effectively block a loading facility for months.

The sea routes to the Gulf also present the problem that they move through three key choke points: the Strait of Hormuz, the Suez Canal, and Bab al-Mandeb.

The Strait of Hormuz. Before the Iran-Iraq War, about one-third of the world's daily oil production, and one-fifth of Gulf imports, passed through the Strait of Hormuz. The main shipping channel through the strait, which utilizes the shortest route around the Musandam Peninsula of northern Oman, is 30–35 kilometers long and 8–13 kilometers wide. Under the shah, the strait was dominated by Iran. While Oman nominally controlled the Qu'oin Islands in the middle of the strait and the key passages to the south, Iran had naval and air supremacy from bases just to the north. It also held Abu Musa and the Tumb Islands in the southeastern Gulf, which it had seized in late 1971. The shah's December 1977 agreement with Oman to share security responsibility over the entire strait even gave him authority to patrol the key tanker routes in Omani waters. He also moved Iran's naval headquarters from Khorramshahr to Bandar Abbas at the northern bend of the Strait of Hormuz and developed a new port at Chah Bahar on the Iranian coast of the Gulf of Oman, giving Iran a "blue water" port for its expanding navy.[18] The disintegration of Iranian forces since the shah's fall has ended Iran's naval domination of the strait. Iran has not entered the key tanker passages between the Omani-held Qu'oin Islands and the Musandam Peninsula since an abortive attempt to challenge British and Omani vessels in late 1980, although it has renewed threats to do so in mid-1983 if Iraq should successfully attack Iranian oil facilities.

The channels are also too large to be highly vulnerable to any terrorist attack. The inbound and outbound channels are separated by a prohibited area about 2 kilometers wide. Depths in the channel generally range from 75 meters to more than 200 meters. The outbound main channel is wide enough and deep enough to enable shipments to continue even if two supertankers were sunk in it. Outbound tankers can also avoid any danger in the channel by passing through the broad, shallower part of the strait north and east of the Qu'oin Islands, where depths range from 45 to 80 meters. This depth is more than adequate to permit passage of the largest supertankers. The currents in the area are also erratic and uncharted, and the straits would be difficult for any regional power to mine.[19]

The Gulf states now have few current alternatives to use of the Strait. The pipeline routes that bypass the Gulf are limited and politically vulnerable. As Map 14.2 shows, there are now only three pipelines with Mediterranean outlets, with a maximum theoretical capacity of 2.5 MMBD, and only the Iraq-Turkey pipeline discussed earlier is operating at near its full capacity of 600,000 BPD. Current efforts to improve compression and pumping rates can at most raise sustained capacity to around 1.2 MMBD.[20] The other two lines—the Iraq-Syria route[21] and the Saudi Tapline—are subject to constant military or political interruption and have very uncertain strategic value. The Iraq-Syria line carried about 250,000–300,000 BPD until Syria suspended shipments from Iraq. The 1,213-kilometer Saudi Tapline has a 470,000-BPD capacity, but Saudi Arabia has run into constant problems with Lebanon over arrangements to finance the line and protect its operation. The Tapline has recently been used only to supply a 36,000-BPD refinery in Jordan and occasionally to supply a 17,500-BPD refinery in Lebanon near Sidon. The Lebanese link was sabotaged in 1981 and was cut again during Israel's June 1982 invasion of Lebanon. The only other line that can now bypass the strait is the new 1,215-kilometer Saudi Petroline from the Ghawar oil fields in the Gulf to Janbu on the Red Sea, which now carries 1.85 MMBD.[22]

The recent surge in Gulf imports of consumer and industrial goods from the West can also be affected by interdiction in the strait. Most of the raw materials and building equipment and much of the food for the Gulf nations must be imported. Gulf countries imported about $80 billion worth of goods in 1980 and similar amounts in 1981. No

MAP 14—2
CURRENT AND PROPOSED STRATEGIC PIPELINES

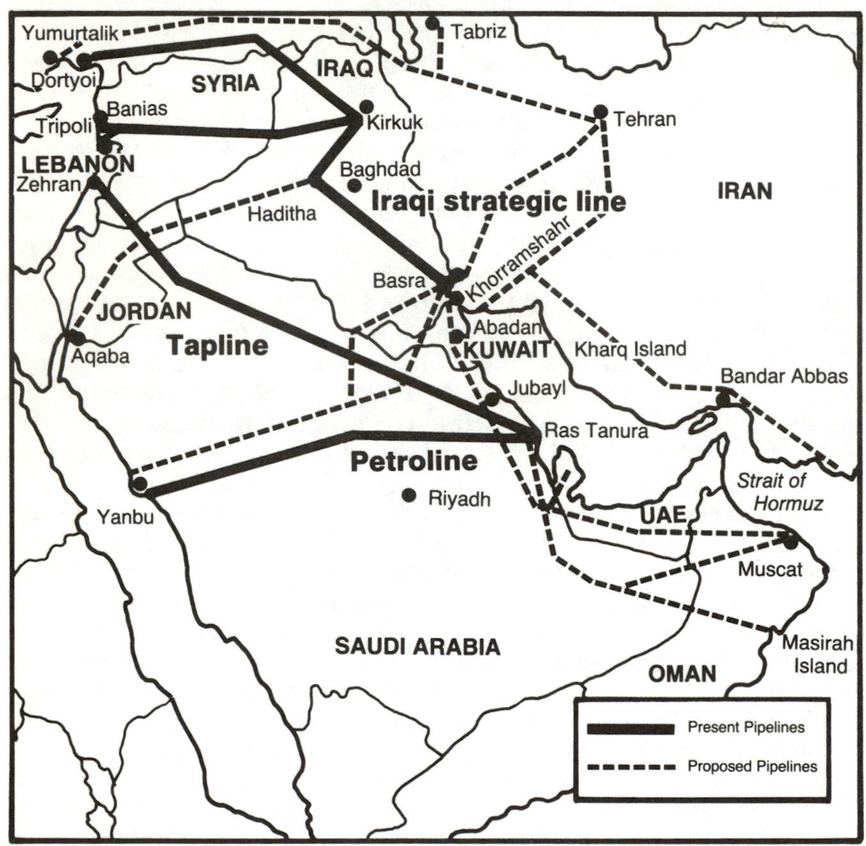

SOURCE: CIA 504295 1-80 (544807) U and France-Stock, "Pipe Dreams," *The Middle East,* January, 1982, p. 61.

dependable alternative overland transportation system now exists that is capable of handling such a large volume of goods. The imports that do arrive overland must go through Turkey, the USSR, Syria, or Jordan, countries that have often been at political odds with many of the Gulf states.

While air and road shipping could certainly supply essential food and consumer goods, they are not economic substitutes for cargo vessels in carrying bulks or heavy material. A halt to shipping could, therefore, put pressure on the Gulf states, although Saudi Arabia has access to deliveries via the Red Sea. It can reduce its dependence on imports through the strait in any emergency and can do so without depending on the limited road or port capacities of its Western neighbors. Oman's major ports are also located outside the Gulf, although these have little value in transshipment to other Gulf states.

The Suez Canal. The Suez Canal was expanded in December 1980, following a five-year, $1.5 billion expansion project that added three new bypasses and increased the draft limit from 12 to 16 meters. The canal can now handle fully laden tankers of up to 150,000 deadweight tons (dwt) and ships without cargo of up to 380,000 dwt. The canal previously could accommodate fully laden 60,000-dwt ships and 150,000-dwt ships in ballast. More than one-third of world tanker tonnage can now go through the canal with cargo, and more than 90% can make the transit in ballast. The new bypasses have made nearly half of the 160-kilometer waterway into a two-way channel, greatly increasing capacity.

The importance of the Suez Canal is reflected in the immense saving it can make in fuel, distance, and time of transit. The distance from Florida to the Gulf is 43,400 kilometers by the Cape route and 38,500 by Suez; the distance from Rotterdam is 42,000 kilometers by the Cape and 23,900 by Suez. Ships making two-way transits of the canal can cut 4,900 kilometers from the U.S. round trip and 9,000 kilometers off the run to Rotterdam. Ships up to 380,000 dwt can save the same distance on each round trip by making the return voyage in ballast through the canal. The value of this saving depends heavily on the size of the ship. Ships larger than 250,000 dwt can still use the Cape route at less cost than smaller tankers traveling through the canal. A new 300,000-dwt tanker, for example, is roughly 50% more efficient per unit of cargo than a 150,000-dwt ship. For unladen ships on trips from Europe, however, the canal offers a clear cost advantage.

The Suez Canal is also important because of the new Saudi crude oil and gas pipelines being built from the Saudi core area near the Gulf to the new Saudi industrial city and port at Janbu. The 1,170-kilometer gas pipeline already carries 270,000 BPD of ethane and NGL, and the Petroline opened late in 1981, with a capacity of 1.85 MMBD. The Petroline is scheduled to expand to 4-MMBD capacity in the mid-1980s; it will significantly reduce Saudi Arabia's dependence on Gulf shipping routes.

Map 14.2 shows that several more "strategic" pipelines may be built if the conservative Gulf producers give oil output and transport vulnerability the high priority they are now discussing. As was noted earlier, Iraq is expanding its existing pipeline through Turkey and is considering several additional lines, including a 1–2-MMBD pipeline through Jordan to Aqaba and a pipeline to a new airport near Janbu with up to 5 MMBD of capacity. The line to Aqaba has already reached the point where pipe is being procured. It could be completed fairly quickly by joining existing Iraqi lines to the Saudi pipeline through Jordan and adding links south through Amman to Aqaba. Iran is considering lines to Turkey and the Gulf of Oman. Saudi Arabia and the other conservative Gulf states are examining pipelines to Oman and to Jordan on the Gulf of Aqaba, northwest of Janbu. Recent studies indicate that such strategic pipelines could be completed by the late 1980s. These may all be coupled to some variant of the strategic petroleum reserve Saudi Arabia is now studying.[23]

It is also worth noting that the routes to Janbu and ports near Aqaba can not only be protected by Egypt, but cut the distance to Rotterdam to only 14,000 kilometers—one-third the distance of a round-trip voyage around the Cape of Good Hope. Loading at Janbu also cuts the trip to the United States by 45%, to 24,000 kilometers. Equally important, such tankers do not have to expose themselves to any attack in the Gulf in a time of crisis or passage through the Strait of Hormuz.

Bab al-Mandeb. Such ports would also be important because they bypass the strait at the southeastern end of the Red Sea. The Strait of Bab al-Mandeb funnels down from 200 kilometers to a narrow mouth of 40 kilometers and is dominated by the South Yemeni–held island of Perim.[24] The Arabic name of the strait means the "gate of lamentation" and was evidently first applied because of the hot, humid climate and bleak topography of the region. The name, however, might just as well apply to the strait's current strategic position. The island of Perim is about 8 square kilometers in area—just large enough for an air strip and limited fortification. The northern channel near Yemen is about 3.2 kilometers wide, and the southern channel, which is much deeper, is about 16 kilometers wide. Thus theoretically most of the passage lies in international waters, but South Yemen has claimed a territorial limit of 12 miles (19.3 kilometer) from Perim, and Djibouti, on the southern side of the strait, has not made formal claims. As a result, the size of the international channel, and control of the waters in the strait, remains uncertain.

Terrorist attacks from the many small coves in the coastal area also present a potential threat to Red Sea traffic. The reality of this threat was demonstrated in 1971, when South Yemen gave PLO agents the use of a small, missile-equipped patrol boat to attack the Israeli tanker *Coral Sea,* and the situation has worsened steadily ever since.

Explosives, anti-armor rockets, and light guided missiles have been distributed to many of the rebel forces in the area. The USSR has gained steadily greater access to naval and air facilities in Ethiopia and South Yemen. It has established major anchorage near the island of Socotra in the mouth of the Gulf of Aden, and it seems to be expanding military facilities on the South Yemeni–held Kamaran Islands about 320 kilometers north of the strait. The military facilities in the Ethiopian ports of Asawa and Assab are also being steadily expanded, along with the military air bases in both countries. French naval and air forces seem likely to remain in Djibouti, which has a pro-Western government, and the U.S. is improving its staging points in Egypt, Somalia, Diego Garcia, and Oman. There is no doubt, however, that the Bab al-Mandeb poses a growing threat to Western and Gulf use of the Suez Canal. In fact, only the French presence in Djibouti now gives the West a good chance to secure passage through the Bab al-Mandeb. While the U.S. does have contingency access to Berbera in Somalia, the USSR already has a strong presence in Aden and the port of Assab in Ethiopia. The strait is within range of Saudi, Israeli, and Egyptian fighters with airborne refueling, but a nearby naval presence would be required to keep them open on a sustained basis. A sophisticated airborne sensor capability would also be needed to handle the problem of "slash and run" raids by small craft or fighters.

Land Routes

There is vast variation in the climate and terrain in the Gulf states, but most have two things in common: first, extraordinarily demanding climatic conditions with sharp seasonal variations and, second, terrain that severely inhibits off-road movement. The larger Gulf states also have long land distances between settled or industrialized areas. These conditions give the land routes in the Gulf states special strategic importance, since they are the logical routes for most land forces, particularly given the inability of most Gulf armies to cope with the repair burden of trying to move armor through anything but the most favorable terrain.

The road and rail nets of the northern Gulf states are critical economic supply lines for their economies and large populations, as was demonstrated early in the Iran-Iraq War.[25] Iraq, which lost access to all of its ports on the Shat al-Arab, was able to meet its basic import requirements only because it could quickly develop land transshipment routes through Jordan, Kuwait and Saudi Arabia, and because its Arab neighbors were largely sympathetic and cooperated in Iraqi resupply efforts. Iraq got nearly 80% of its imports through the Gulf before the war. These imports totaled roughly 8.2 million tons, of which food imports accounted for about 3.5 million tons. They entered Iraq through three Gulf ports. Al-Basrah, on the Shat al-Arab waterway, handled imports of nearly 5 million tons. The remaining seaborne imports came through the Gulf ports of Umm Qasr and Az Aubayr. The remaining imports came overland through Jordan, Turkey, Kuwait, and Syria. Iraq was able to compensate for the closing of the Shat al-Arab that resulted from ship sinkings and gunfire because it had readily accessible, high-capacity port facilities and could use all of the surplus capacity of the overland routes through Jordan, Kuwait, Turkey, and Saudi Arabia to handle cargoes diverted from its Gulf ports. Iraq imported about 1 million tons of goods over these routes in 1979, and the total for 1980 was vastly increased. Although Iraq's heavy use of Aqaba strained logistical resources in Jordan, led to some congestion, and increased waiting times for vessels, this transshipment route served Iraq well. About 65 vessels were reported in the port in mid-November 1981, compared with a normal 16 to 17 before the war. Iraq and Jordan also moved quickly to improve the efficiency of operations at Aqaba and to minimize transshipping interruptions. These measures allowed Iraq to avoid seeking help from a hostile Syria and to keep to a minimum the strain it put on a friendly but highly vulnerable Kuwait.

In contrast, Iran found itself in a more difficult position. The Iran-Iraq War denied Iran the use of three of its five major Gulf ports. The closed ports of Bandar Shahpur (Khomeini), Khorramshahr, and Abadan normally handled 40–50% of Iran's total imports. The remaining transportation links—the ports of Bandar Abbas and Bushihr and overland links via the Soviet Union and Turkey—handled some inbound cargoes but quickly became congested and could not significantly expand capacity to compensate for Iran's lost ports. Bandar Abbas and Bushihr had normally handled about 20% (1.5–3 million tons) of total imports before the war, transit routes through the Soviet Union had accounted for 15% of total trade, and routes through Turkey had handled only a small percentage of imports.

The difficulties in making use of the remaining routes derived from a combination of long-existing problems, increased shipments, the war, and other factors outside Iran's control. Heavy congestion occurred at Bandar Abbas because of diversions from other ports, and operations slowed because of insufficient handling equipment, spare parts shortages, lack of experienced staff, and shortages of fuel. Azadi, a new port 23 kilometers west of Bandar Abbas, was hampered by unfinished facilities and poor clearances resulting in 20-day waiting periods, although some cargoes are being received. Bushihr did not have such problems, but its contribution to Iran's import needs was limited because of its small size. Iran also faced problems because of a backup of rail cars moving through the USSR, which often led to temporary bans on Soviet acceptance of new transit shipments. The Soviet inland waterways to the Caspian freeze from November to March, and the winter also disrupts road traffic through Turkey and the USSR. In contrast, the Iraqi routes through Jordan and Kuwait experience occasional heavy rains, which temporarily flood key roads but do not seriously affect their normal capacity.

The Iran-Iraq War is thus a case study in the problems inherent in movement into the Gulf, but it is difficult to generalize the extent to which potential interdiction or control of land routes could put economic pressure on any given Gulf state. Both Iran and Iraq were able to cope with the situation and have now more or less adjusted to the problems caused by the war. The southern Gulf states face more serious problems because of their lack of alternative borders with Western countries or the USSR and their limited road capacity; but they are improving their land routes to Europe, they have small populations and limited amounts of critical imports, and they can make greater use of sea and air routes.[26] Accordingly, land routes seem more critical to the southern Gulf states as potential routes of invasion.

It is also uncertain what the future importance of the Shat al-Arab will be. It seems unlikely that Iran will ever rebuild its port at Khorramshahr or its refinery at Abadan, at least to anything like their past level of importance. Iran can site replacement facilities in the eastern Gulf or Gulf of Oman, or connecting with pipelines through Turkey, at almost the same cost. Short of a total victory over Iraq, Iran will have every incentive to expand its Gulf ports. It also will take at least a year to clear the Shat al-Arab, which is a rapidly silting river that requires constant dredging. In the past, the normal channel depth was maintained at about 8 to 10 meters, although this has fluctuated. At times its depth has been as low as 7 meters. Since this silt will accumulate with each month the war lasts, Iran will have less and less incentive to clear the Shat.

In contrast, Iraq will be under considerable pressure to reopen it. Al-Basrah needs to be reopened if Iraqi economic activity is to return to normal. Iraq's supply routes through Jordan, Kuwait, and Saudi Arabia are much more expensive to use, and they lack the capacity to carry normal civilian imports and military goods and are politically insecure. It is possible, therefore, that the Iran-Iraq War will ultimately deprive the Shat al-Arab of much of its strategic value to Iran while leaving Iraq vulnerable to Iranian intransigence in maintaining the waterway and to Iranian attacks on Iraqi port facilities to which Iraq would have difficulty in replying in kind. It may even end in forcing Iraq to resite its oil- and cargo-shipping facilities through Saudi Arabia, Turkey, and Jordan in spite of the cost.

Seaports and Airports

The southern Gulf states are considerably more vulnerable than Iran and Iraq to attacks on key port facilities, cities, and communications facilities. Their lack of arable land, their oil wealth, and their recent urbanization have concentrated their population in a comparatively few cities. It has also made the smaller Gulf oil states dependent on seaports and airports for much of their food supply, and there is little stocking of food reserves. While such states could cross-supply each other by land, interdiction of their seaports would be capable of seriously straining their economy and food supplies and simultaneously interdicting oil shipments. Most southern Gulf states are also heavily dependent on air traffic for perishable food supplies and time-sensitive equipment shipments. This dependence could be important in a future conflict because most Gulf international airports are highly vulnerable targets for even a few fighter sorties, while Gulf ports are usually large and redundant and could not be effectively attacked by air or most Gulf ships.

Cities and Communications

The concentration of the population of the Gulf states into a relatively few urban centers has a further important consequence. In the case of Saudi Arabia and the other conservative Gulf states, any serious conflict in the Gulf may ultimately lead to urban warfare. Space is rarely strategically important in the Gulf area. Strange as it may seem in an area that has so many of the world's bleak deserts and mountains, it is the cities that are the means to political and military power. Most Gulf cities are now so built up that they have become not only key strategic targets, but also excellent defensive positions. If two Gulf states do reach the point of large-scale warfare, a decisive conflict may take the form of house-to-house fighting. This kind of battle makes armored maneuver and the effective use of tactical airpower almost impossible. Iraq has learned this the hard way in the Iran-Iraq War, but urban warfare has previously proved critical in the struggle for Aden and in the decisive battles for the control of North Yemen discussed in Chapter 12.

Any fighting related to internal security or civil war may also be urban. The control of the capital city or key cities in most Gulf countries is the key to power for any given faction, especially control of the communications facilities, government buildings, and utilities that are the traditional power centers in any coup attempt. It is easy to lose sight of the strategic importance of Gulf cities in counting tanks and aircraft, or discussing oil field defense or shipping lanes. In practical terms, however, the urban warfare capability of any Gulf army may be as critical as any other aspect of its military strength.

The Military Implications of Oil and LOC Vulnerabilities

There is no way to predict how this complex set of vulnerabilities will affect future conflicts or crises in the Gulf. It is clear that both the Gulf states and the West are acutely vulnerable to attacks on Gulf oil facilities, and on the lines of communication through the Gulf, but there are so many possible methods of attack and so many forms that conflict can take that a highly redundant mix of new defense and shipping capabilities will be required to provide any serious protection. Still, the security of the southern Gulf states is heavily dependent on finding some collective method of securing their oil fields, cities, and ports against naval and air attacks and the threat of terrorist attacks. This is not simply a matter of protecting against the damage such attacks could inflict and the long lead times necessary to repair certain facilities. It is also a matter of the willingness of the Gulf states to resist political pressures or military threats by a major power like Iran or indirect Soviet pressure. The fragile nature of the oil facilities and lines of communication in the Gulf makes the smaller Gulf states uniquely vulnerable to "blackmail" unless they are confident that they have a credible air and maritime defense and can count on other states for aid against terrorist operations.

The Iran-Iraq War has demonstrated the need for an improved strategic pipeline system. The Gulf states are already building redundant airport and seaport facilities and are building improved road networks that will reduce their vulnerability to supply interdiction. What they must now also build are the kind of pipeline and oil facilities that would reduce their vulnerability to local attacks and to the cutoff of any given maritime route. Future oil and gas facility construction in the Gulf also needs to be designed to reduce the vulnerability to air and sea attack, to reduce the risk of chain-reaction effects, and to allow some degree of standardization and stockpiling of key components to allow more rapid repair.

Finally, the discussion of new oil ports in Jordan, Saudi Arabia, and Oman should eventually be translated into action. The growing vulnerability of the middle and southeastern Red Sea makes dependence on any port southeast of Janbu relatively risky. In contrast, shipments from Oman or the Red Sea coast northwest of Janbu seem likely to be relatively easy to secure as long as Jordan and Egypt remain friendly to the West. Pipelines through Oman can be protected from the contingency bases Saudi Arabia and Oman could make available to the U.S. in an emergency, and they are not vulnerable to interdiction of the Strait of Hormuz or the Bab al-Mandeb. Although such actions are costly, they seem far more cost effective than trying to buy equivalent military protection, and unless such steps are taken, the Iran-Iraq War seems likely to be only the first of the oil wars in the Gulf.

Notes

1. The data in this section are taken from a number of sources, including various governmental and oil company working papers. Many data, however, are built around studies that were last fully updated during 1975–1977.

2. Estimate based on CIA GI IESR 82-002 (U), 22 February 1982, p. 3. Installed capacity before the revolution and the Iran-Iraq War was 7.0 MMBD. Maximum sustainable capacity was 5.5 MMBD. Peak actual production was 6.68 MMBD in November 1976.

3. Special Subcommittee on Investigations of the Committee on International Relations, *Oilfields As Military Objectives: A Feasibility Study* (Washington, D.C.: Government Printing Office, August 1975) (hereafter *Oilfields*), p. 26. Iran is now considering plans to relocate the refinery complex on its eastern Gulf coast.

4. At Mina al Ahmadi, Mina Abdullah (two refineries), Mina Saud, and Ras al-Khafji in the Neutral Zone.

5. *International Energy Statistical Review,* ER IESR 81-005, 26 May 1981, pp. 1 and 9.

6. *Oilfields,* pp. 25 and 30.

7. Abu Dhabi produces about 80% of the UAE's oil, is now producing extensive amounts of LPG, and has more than 50 years of production from proven reserves at 1 MMBD, as well as several undeveloped fields. Its loading facilities are dispersed, with key links at Ruwais, Jebel Dhanna, Das Island, Zinku Island, and Mubarras Island. It is exceptionally vulnerable to attacks on its offshore loading facilities. Dubai has about 20% of the UAE's oil, and its production and reserves are slowly declining. The key target in Dubai is its offshore loading facilities at Fateh. Sharjah's declining offshore field now produces only abouat 9,000–10,000 BPD, and is dependent on the offshore loading facility at Mubarak.

8. The description of events in this section is based on press sources as corrected by interviews in the Gulf, with U.S. experts, and with personnel from foreign oil companies.

9. Iran has refineries at Abadan, Masjed-e-Soleyman, Kermanshah, Tabriz, Tehran, Isfahan, Shiraz, and Lavan Island. Unlike Iraq, whose only loading facilities in the Gulf are at colocated offshore terminals at Khor al-Amaja and Mina al-Bakr, Iran has terminals at Bandar Mashahr, Ras Bahregan, Kharg, Cyrus, Lavan, Abu al Bukhoosh, and Sirri.

10. The key targets in Iraq, aside from pipelines, are the refinery and collection facilities at al-Basrah and Muftiyah near the Gulf, at Khanaqin near the border with Iran, at Karkuk in the Kurkuk oil fields, at Ad Dawrah near Baghdad, at As Samawah on the pipeline to the east of al-Basrah and Muftiyah, at Qayyarah, northwest of Kirkuk, the key pipeline and pumping junction near Bavil, and at the pipeline junction near Syria at Al Hadithah. The largest refineries are at al-Basrah (70 MBD), Karkuk (30 MBD), and Ad Dawrah (80 MBD).

11. *Washington Post,* 7 January 1982; Francine Stock, "Pipe Dreams," *Middle East,* January 1982, pp. 62–64.

12. *New York Times,* 15 April 1982.

13. *Los Angeles Times, New York Times,* and *Wall Street Journal,* 12 April 1982.

14. *New York Times,* 19 April 1982.

15. *Chicago Tribune,* 17 April 1982.

16. Iran continued sporadic air attacks on Iraqi and Kuwaiti oil facilities through late 1981.

17. Much of this analysis is taken from working papers of the Congressional Research Service and of oil companies operating in the Gulf.

18. George Lenczowski, *The Middle East in World Affairs,* 4th ed. (Ithaca, N.Y.: Cornell University Press, 1980), p. 730.

19. Based on discussions with Omani officers in the area in February 1982.

20. Design capacity is 700,000 BPD, but current actual capacity is lower.

21. Kirkuk to Baniyas in Syria and Tripoli in Lebanon. The system has 1.2–1.4 MMBD design capacity, but the Tripoli link has been closed since 1975, and current capacity is much lower. The Lebanon section has 400,000 BPD design capacity, but current rated capacity is only about 200,000 BPD.

22. The Tapline was built in 1950 and is now relatively labor intensive and costly to operate. It is cheaper to ship oil through the Gulf by VLCC. Unlike the other ARAMCO property sold to Saudi Arabia in 1980, the Tapline is still owned by the ARAMCO partners.

23. See Chapter 8 for details.

24. Egypt held the island on a lease paid by Saudi Arabia from 1974 to 1978, and it has reasonably good military facilities. Lenczowski, *Middle East in World Affairs,* p. 732.

25. This analysis is drawn from a combination of news sources, including *8 Days, Middle East, Economic Digest,* and several private commercial newsletters. It has been informally reviewed by Gulf and U.S. experts.

26. Ironically, overbuilding of Gulf international airports gives them well over 10 times their presently utilized cargo capacity.

15
The Military and Internal Security Situation in the Smaller Conservative Gulf Countries

Although it is the broad trends in the Gulf's military forces and vulnerabilities that shape its balance of power, the strategic stability of the region is equally dependent on the individual ability of each Gulf regime to survive and deter aggression while maintaining internal order. The previous chapters have described the historical evolution of the interactions and tensions that form the attitudes of each Gulf nation and the broad pressures that shape their military capabilities. Each, however, faces different military and internal security problems. These problems must be reduced or eliminated if the conservative Gulf states are to remain stable and develop effective strategic relations with the West.

The military and internal security situation in Saudi Arabia has already been described in detail. The other conservative Gulf states all border on the southern edge of the Gulf. They include—from west to east—Kuwait, Bahrain, Qatar, the United Arab Emirates, and Oman. Chapter 1 showed that these states collectively average half the petroleum production of Saudi Arabia. Chapter 13 showed that they have the military resources to potentially constitute a powerful military bloc, and one of immense strategic importance. Yet, as Chapter 11 and 12 described, the southern Gulf states are now a bloc only in the sense that each is led by a traditional family regime and has a conservative political system. Each pursues a separate, uncoordinated path to building up its armed forces and to internal security.

This situation must change if strategic stability is to be established in the Gulf. The conservative and moderate Gulf states must develop effective collective security arrangements in spite of their history of conflict and rivalry. They must offset the problems inherent in trying to create modern military forces out of small and disparate national elements by developing interdependent forces. Ideally, they must be linked with Saudi Arabia into a defense structure that can (1) preserve their sovereignty and independence, (2) provide effective regional air and naval defense of all their respective oil facilities, (3) deter aggression by Iraq and Iran, (4) defend against amphibious or armored raids, (5) maintain internal security without external intervention, and (6) develop the capability to support over-the-horizon reinforcement by the U.S. to deal with "worst-case" contingencies. The following analysis indicates that such progress is possible, but that achieving it will be difficult indeed.[1]

Kuwait: Deterrence and Instability

Kuwait is in some ways both the strongest and the weakest of the smaller conservative Gulf states. It is the strongest in the sense that it was the first Gulf state to have an oil income that vastly exceeded its immediate needs and that it has completed the transition to full independence as a modern state in a manner that has given it a well-developed private sector, a strong educational base, and a relatively effective government. As a result, Kuwait has emerged with the most sophisticated economy and ruling elite of any Gulf state, and it has been able to use its immense wealth to buy off potential threats and establish close political relations with virtually all the powerful movements in the Arab world. It is the weakest conservative Gulf state in the sense that it is strategically exposed to pressure from Iraq, Iran, and Saudi Arabia. Kuwait is within artillery range of Iran and has a long common border with Iraq and Saudi Arabia. It is particularly vulnerable to Iraqi pressure because Iraq can deploy its armor against Kuwait with only minimal warning, and Iraq has the strength to quickly seize military control of Kuwait.

Iraq also has a strong incentive to exert political and military influence over Kuwait. Kuwait has been the source of up to $8 billion in war "loans," and the land routes that run through Kuwait to the Mediterranean have become Iraq's main supply routes since the start of the Iran-Iraq War. Kuwait has served as a "neutral" port and staging point for shipments from Jordan, and it is the only route free of Iraq's problems with Syria and the Kurds. Iraq desperately needs Kuwait's support to sustain its war effort, and it has quietly threatened the Al-Sabah family with personal reprisals if they should give way to Iranian pressure.

These pressures will not end with the war, regardless of its outcome. The 130-kilometer border between Kuwait and Iraq has never been demarcated. As was described in Chapter 11, Kuwait possesses two islands in the Gulf, Bubiyan and Warbah, which face the Iraqi port of Umm Qasr and Iraq's 0.58 kilometers of seacoast. Bubiyan is about 1.6 kilometers from Kuwait and 8 kilometers from Iraq. Warbah is about 3.2 kilometers from Kuwait and 1 kilometer from Iraq. Both are generally recognized as Kuwaiti. Umm Qasr, however, is Iraq's only port that is not on the Shat al-Arab and that will not be within easy artillery range of Iranian military installations once the Iran-Iraq War is over. The islands are also critical to the future security of Iraqi oil-loading facilities in the Gulf. For these reasons Iraq occupied the island of Bubiyan in 1973, as well as the area surrounding the Kuwaiti border post at Samita, and caused the closing of the Kuwaiti-Iraqi border from 1972 to July 1977. Relations have steadily improved since 1975, and Iraq formally abandoned its claim to all of Kuwait as early as 1965. The island of Bubiyan is now under Kuwaiti control, and a $52 million bridge now connects the uninhabitable island with a spot on the mainland. It has been referred to as "connecting nothing with nothing." The "island" is basically a salt marsh whose maximum elevation is 1.5 meters.

The Iran-Iraq war has also created growing problems in Kuwait's relations with Iran. Iran has made major efforts to influence Kuwait's Shi'ite population since Khomeini's rise to power, has repeatedly threatened Kuwait for its support of Iraq in the Iran-Iraq War, and has launched several air raids against Kuwait to deter further expansion of that support.[2] These Iranian raids forced Kuwait to build air raid shelters and provided a practical demonstration of Kuwait's extreme vulnerability to Iranian air or naval raids. This Iranian pressure has been more successful since Iran's victories in early 1982. Kuwait put its armed forces on a state of maximum alert on 26 July 1982 during one offensive and has greatly increased its efforts to end the war since the spring of 1982.

Iran's military success also has combined with growing internal problems in Kuwait. That country's Shi'ites are not great supporters of Khomeini, but they generally oppose Saddam Hussein's control of Shi'ite movements in Iraq. They have long been subject to discrimination, and many deeply resented the government's manipulation of the constituencies in Kuwait's February 1981 allocations that reduced Shi'ite representation from 10 seats to 4.[3] Iran exploited such tensions and its military threats to weaken Kuwait's willingness to give Iraq additional aid and Kuwait's support for collective security initiatives in the Gulf Cooperation Council. Kuwait played down its support of Iraq in 1982 and joined with the UAE in limiting the progress made in expanding military cooperation at the council's third summit meeting in Bahrain in November 1982.[4]

These forces have also brought Kuwait under increased pressure from Saudi Arabia. While the two states have no meaningful strategic differences, they are still arguing over who has sovereignty over the islands of Umm al-Maradem and Qarwa, which are 17 and 40 kilometers off the coast of the Neutral Zone and which Saudi Arabia occupied in June 1977. The Saudis have also backed stronger support of Iraq and more immediate action on GCC defense initiatives and have pressed Kuwait to take a highly conservative approach to development. Although such Saudi initiatives did not threaten Kuwait's external security, they did contribute to the suspension of Kuwait's parliament between 29 August 1976 and February 1981, and they have contributed to the government's reluctance to accept constitutional reforms that would expand the powers of the Kuwaiti Assembly. They also have contributed to such social acts as the decision to suppress any open celebration of Christmas in 1982.

All these pressures demonstrate that Kuwait is a natural target of any conflict or tension among the Gulf's major powers, and Kuwait is particularly vulnerable because it is a nation of only 16,058 square kilometers and 1.65 million people.[5] Expatriates total almost 970,000 and make up over 61% of the total population. Roughly 624,000 are expatriate Arabs. Roughly 10% of the nonnative Arabs are Iraqi, 8% are Syrian, 12% are Egyptian, and as many as 39% may be Palestinian. A large number of these "Palestinians" are in fact permanent residents who cannot own property or shares in Kuwaiti companies but who virtually dominated the upper echelons of the Kuwaiti civil service until some began to be replaced with Egyptians and other Arabs in 1976. These Palestinians virtually all pay taxes to the PLO and are mostly at least parlor socialists. They have also backed the various "alphabet soup" radical movements that have operated in Kuwait such as the NFLB, ANM, PFLP, PFLO, PFLAOG, SLF, FNR, and FNLSA.[6]

In addition, something like between 144,000 and 170,000 Indians and Pakistanis, originally brought in as construction laborers, have become de facto permanent residents. Another 4–6% of the population is Iranian, and 9% is classified as "other." These expatriates not only make up 70% of the work force, their large numbers are creating a serious political and cultural problem in Kuwaiti society.[7] There are still over 125 expatriate males per female, and the Iranians, Omanis, and Yemenis occupy low-status, dead-end jobs and have over 500 males to 1 female. Virtually all real work in the country is done by non-Kuwaitis, although many senior positions are filled by Kuwaiti citizens who "front" for work that is really done by foreigners.[8]

The Capability of Kuwait's Armed Forces

The Kuwaiti armed forces are now little more than a hollow shell.[9] While Kuwait has increased its arms imports from around $2.5 million in 1973 to over $400 million annually, and its defense budget to about $1.3 billion annually, it still is buying a "deterrent" whose day-to-day management and operations depend on foreign support personnel and advisers. In fact, it is sometimes unclear whether Kuwait is attempting to develop serious military capabilities. Kuwait instead seems to rely largely on its oil wealth to achieve national security by providing foreign aid and assistance to various Arab causes and Soviet-bloc states in ways that minimize the immediate threat of hostile Iraqi action or Palestinian and Marxist opposition to the government.[10] Similarly, Kuwait is the only conservative Gulf state with ties to the USSR, and it uses these ties to ensure that no Soviet-backed movements are targeted against it.[11]

The recent history of Kuwait's military buildup is shown in Table 15.1. Although Kuwait established a seven-year Defense Development Plan in 1976, following further Iraqi penetrations across Kuwait's border and the disbanding of Kuwait's National Assembly, its recent defense efforts have had limited success. Kuwait still procures far more equipment than its small infrastructure and manpower base can absorb. Kuwait has made large purchases of impressive hardware, but it has paid little attention to logistic management and efficient equipment mixes. Although Kuwait's arms purchases have recently become somewhat more sensible and moderate, and its armed forces seem to be becoming slightly more effective, Kuwait will have little real combat power for most of the 1980s. Its rapid military modernization and buildup have been substantially less competently managed than that of most neighboring states.

Kuwait's army had 10,000 men, one tank "brigade," two mechanized infantry "brigades," and a surface-to-surface missile battalion at the end of 1983. By Western standards, such a force would require a minimum of 20,000 men and probably 40,000. Only the armored units, however, can be described as "combat effective" against the forces of Iraq or Iran. Kuwait's diverse mix of 160 Chieftains, 70 Vickers, and 10 Centurion tanks presents serious training and maintenance problems, which will be further complicated by the arrival of the Scorpion light tanks now on order and by Kuwait's tentative plans to buy new advanced main battle tanks. Kuwait's light armored forces are now equipped with 175 U.S. M-113 APCs, 100 Saladin armored cars, 80 Ferret scout cars, and 130 Saracen APCs. About 188 U.S. M-113s are under delivery, some with TOW antitank guided weapons, as are additional Soviet weapons. Kuwait has also recently ordered 56 M-901 Improved TOW vehicles, 4,840 Improved TOW missiles, 16 more M-113 A2 APCs,[12] French tank transporters and modern night sights for its chieftains. Its artillery includes 80 French AMX F-3 155mm SP guns, a few old British 25-pounders, 81mm mortars, and Soviet FROG-7 surface-to-surface missiles. Antitank weapons holdings are impressive, but the army's effectiveness is reduced by its wide mix of SS-11, HOT, TOW, and Vigilant antitank guided weapons (ATGWs). The air defense force has 50 Improved Hawk missiles (6 launchers), grouped into four mobile batteries. About 60 additional Improved Hawks are on order. However, the Kuwaiti ground-based air defense "system" now has only token effectiveness.

Although the Kuwaiti Army is moving into a new $100 million base about 20 miles from Kuwait City and is acquiring French tank transporters, its ability to use most of its equipment effectively is limited by poor training, particularly at the exercise level. Many of Kuwait's officers have trained at Sandhurst, and major efforts have been made to recruit competent NCOs and technical personnel, but only its officer cadre shows any real signs of reaching the required professional standards. The conscription system introduced in April 1978 has been a corrupt failure, and most Kuwaitis with influence escape the system. While token Kuwaiti armored units served on the Suez front in 1973, the army has not conducted realistic large-scale training exercises or taken any other serious steps to make up for the inevitable weaknesses resulting from a lack of combat experience and rapid modernization. A small National Guard exists, but it seems limited to minor internal security functions.

The Kuwaiti Air Force (KAF) is the closest force Kuwait has to a real deterrent. It is well based and has an emergency dispersal agreement with Bahrain. The 1,900-strong air force, advised by U.S., French, British, and other expatriates, consists of an interceptor squadron of 19 Mirage F-1Cs and F-1B trainers, located at its original base at Kuwait City. Kuwait ordered 12 more Mirage F-1s in December 1982, along with Matra Super-530 air-to-air missiles, at a cost of 2.7 billion French francs (then about $550 million). Although it is proving extraordinarily difficult to maintain, and its radar is unreliable and lacks the quality of computer support and the "look-down/shoot-down" capability critical for air combat in Kuwait's small airspace, the Mirage F-1 is still an acceptable fighter for the air combat role. This unit is loosely "integrated" with the Improved Hawk force, the Soviet missiles, and evidently some Crotales to provide low-altitude defense. Kuwait has an adequate medium- to high-altitude AC&W system, including long-range radar, gap-filler radars, and an operation and communications center, and France's Thomson-CSF and the U.S. Hughes Corporation are competing to provide a more advanced system with longer range, better low-altitude coverage, and better netting of fighter and land-based air defense weapons. Such a system would also allow better links to the other Gulf states, but it could not be operational before the mid-1980s and could not effectively cover Kuwait's limited airspace or provide long-range warning without information from an AWACS.

Kuwait's air attack force includes two fighter-bomber squadrons of 30 A-4KU Skyhawks located on one of two new sheltered bases built with Yugoslavian aid. Kuwait's air forces could also be dispersed to other Gulf bases. Air weaponry includes a stock of Red Top, Sky Streak, 300 AIM-9H Sidewinders, and R-550 Magic air-to-air missiles. Kuwait has a variety of air-to-surface missiles and laser-guided bombs, including the R-530. Kuwait also has a comparatively large helicopter force. A squadron of 9 Pumas performs troop transport and assault and logistical support, a squadron of 12 Gazelles provides reconnaissance and liaison, and a second Gazelle squadron, armed with HOT missiles, acts as an assault helicopter antitank force. Kuwait also ordered 6 Super Puma helicopters with Exocet missiles from France in June 1983 and will train its helicopter pilots at the IUT (University Technological Institute) in France, which has trained Iraqi and Syrian pilots. Its combat forces

TABLE 15.1 The Military Buildup in Kuwait, 1972–1982

	1972–73	1973–74	1974–75	1975–76	1976–77	1977–78	1978–79	1979–80	1980–81	1981–82	1982–83
Total population (millions)	0.9	0.957	1.1	1.21	1.04	1.09	1.2	1.16	1.32	1.46	1.40
Defense expenditures (DE) ($ billions)	n.a.	n.a.	.162	.230	2.06	.336	n.a.	.979	1.1	1.3	n.a.
GNP ($ billions)	3.565	4.7	11.0	n.a.	12.6	11.9	n.a.	23.5	n.a.	30.7	n.a.
DE as % of GNP[a]	n.a.	n.a.	1.5	n.a.	16.3	2.8	n.a.	4.2	n.a.	4.2	n.a.
Total military manpower	9,200	10,200	10,200	10,200	9,700	10,000	11,100	12,000	12,400	12,400	12,400
Army											
Manpower	7,000	8,000	8,000	8,000	8,500	8,500	9,000	10,500	10,000	10,000	10,000
Equipment											
Medium tanks	80	100	100	100	100	112	280	124	280	240	240
Major types	Centurion	Centurion	Centurion	Centurion	Centurion	Centurion	Chieftain	Centurion	Chieftain	Chieftain	Chieftain
Other AFVs	some	250	250	250	240	240	250	250	250	410	477
Major types	Saladin	Saladin	Saladin	Saladin	Saladin	Saladin	Saladin	Saladin	Saracen	Saracen	Saracen
Artillery	—	30	30	30	30	30	30	30	90	90	90
SP guns	—	—	—	—	20	20	20	20	80	80	80
ATWs	—	—	Vigilant	Vigilant	Vigilant	Vigilant,TOW	Vigilant,TOW	Vigilant,TOW	Vigilant,TOW	HOT,TOW	HOT,TOW
Other	—	—	—	SS-11	SS-11	SS-11	SS-11	SS-11	FROG-7	FROG-7 SAM	FROG-7 SAM
Navy											
Manpower[b]	200	200	200	200	200	500	200	500	500	500	500
Total craft	10	10	20	29	31	31	31	36	46	60	60
Numbers/Types	8 patrol 2 landing craft	8 patrol 2 landing craft	18 patrol 2 landing craft	27 patrol 2 landing craft	28 patrol 3 landing craft	28 patrol 3 landing craft	28 patrol 3 landing craft	33 patrol 3 landing craft	43 patrol 3 landing craft	57 patrol 3 landing craft	57 patrol 3 landing craft

TABLE 15.1 (continued)

	1972–73	1973–74	1974–75	1975–76	1976–77	1977–78	1978–79	1979–80	1980–81	1981–82	1982–83
Air Force											
Manpower[b]	2,000	2,000	2,000	2,000	1,000	1,000	1,900	1,000	1,900	1,900	1,900
Total combat aircraft	26	30	28	32	33	49	50	49	50	50	49
Fighters	14	12	12	14	12	24	20	20	20	20	19
Major types	Lightning	Lightning	Lightning	Lightning	Lightning	Mirage	Mirage	Mirage	Mirage	Mirage	Mirage
Fighter-Bombers	12	18	16	18	27	25	30	29	30	30	30
Major types	Hunter	BAC-167	BAC-767	BAC-767	BAC-167	BAC-167	A-4KU	A-4KU	A-4KU	A-4KU	A-4KU
Transports	6	5	6	5	5	7	5	4	5	4	3
Major types	light	med. light	Caribou	Caribou	Caribou	Hercules	DC-9	DC-9	DC-9	DC-9	DC-9
Helicopters	4	5	7	7	38	48	44	42	34	34	32
Major types	AB-205	AB-205	AB-204B	AB-205	Gazelle	Gazelle	Gazelle	Gazelle	Gazelle	Gazelle	Gazelle
Other		4	8	6	6	6	8	6	8	8	9
Numbers/Type		4 trainers	8 trainers	6 trainers	6 trainers	6 trainers 50 Imp. Hawk SAM	8 trainers 50 Imp. Hawk SAM	6 trainers 50 Imp. Hawk SAM	8 trainers 50 Imp. Hawk SAM	8 trainers 50 Imp. Hawk SAM	9 trainers 50 Imp. Hawk SAM
Paramilitary	1,500 (army)	1,500 (army)	—	—	—	9,500 Guard	15,000 Police	—	15,000 Police	18,000 Police	18,000 Police

[a]Calculated.
[b]Does not include expatriates.
Source: The Military Balance (London: IISS, various years).

are reinforced by nine Strikemaster ground-attack/trainers, which can act as COIN aircraft. Its small transport force has little tactical value.

This air force is large enough to provide some air defense and to inflict at least limited damage upon an opponent's oil fields and combat forces in the initial stages of a limited conflict. Kuwait is also examining the purchase of more advanced fighters, although it has evidently been quietly told that it cannot get congressional approval of a purchase from the U.S. and has decided to reject the Mirage 2000 because of budget problems and the aircraft's maintenance burden and inadequate avionics. However, the Kuwaiti Air Force is dependent on expatriate pilots and technical personnel, and although it is sheltered and has improved active air defenses, it is vulnerable to a large, preemptive strike by Iraq or Iran. It lacks modern air defense and air attack training as an organized force, and although individual pilot proficiency is sometimes good, the KAF would be no match for Iraqi or Iranian forces without outside help. Overall organization, readiness, and command proficiency are still weak, although the force is steadily improving.

The 500-man Kuwait Navy is little more than a token force. It has 57 light patrol craft (only 15 of which are armed) and three 88-foot landing craft. It is now organized as a coast guard and internal security force and has long been assigned to the Ministry of the Interior. It does have a new $30 million naval base, and it plans to expand its combat capability with 8 Lürssen TNC-45 light patrol craft and heavier patrol craft with Exocet MM-38/40 surface-to-surface missiles and to buy 12 support ships from Britain's Cheverton Workboats, including four 30-meter landing craft, two firefighting harbor tugs, and six 8.2-meter launches. However, it will be at least five years before the Kuwaiti Navy could have even the most minimal military effectiveness.

These military forces are now under the direct command of a competent young member of the Al-Sabah family, Sheikh Salim al-Sabah, who is the ruler's cousin and who also commands the security forces of the Ministry of the Interior, which are nominally under the command of Kuwait's minister of the interior, Sheikh Nawwaf al-Ahmad, and Maj. Gen. Yusuf Badr al-Kharafi. Other Al-Sabahs occupy most of the senior command positions in both the armed forces and the security services. This situation, and the extremely high rates of pay, make it likely that the armed forces will stay loyal to the ruling family. They could put down any internal threat and could make a token defense in response to an Iraqi invasion. They had no effectiveness against the Iranian air attacks in 1981, however, and the Kuwaiti warning system now cannot distinguish effectively between sorties directed against Kuwait and Iraq. Kuwait's forces might be able to deal with a limited Iranian amphibious or helicopter raid if Iran did not provide heavy air cover.

The officer corps has received close attention from the ruling Sheikh and Crown Prince, and natives are recruited from traditional family and tribal supporters of the Al-Sabah family. The officer corps has excellent pay and privileges. Much of it is trained at Sandhurst, and it is backed by a diverse range of advisers from the U.S., France, Britain, Pakistan, Jordan, and the USSR.[13] Advanced training is provided in several foreign countries, including Jordan, Pakistan, Britain, and the U.S. Nonetheless, there was one serious outbreak of unrest by cadets in Kuwait's Infantry College in 1979. There are also serious structural problems in Kuwait's military manpower. Kuwaiti society is extremely stratified and has one of the most complex "pecking orders" in the Gulf. Key promotions and selections are made on the basis of loyalty and family background, which has weakened Kuwait's military management and leadership. The 18-month conscription period is far more theoretical than real. Kuwait recruits most of its "other Ranks" and career forces from the portion of the native labor force that cannot compete in the regular economy. Given the opportunities open to Kuwaiti citizens in the civilian economy, this ensures that enlisted and other ranks are relatively low in quality. It has also meant that the army's other ranks consist predominantly of former Iraqi Shi'ite Bedouins, although they include Saudi Bedouins and some Asians as well.

Even if these problems did not exist, the Kuwaiti military would still face the problem of geography. Not only does the country's small size and position make it strategically vulnerable to its three large neighbors, its topographical features create additional tactical problems. There is little that even the best Kuwaiti forces could do against concentrated air and ground attacks. Aside from the rough terrain on Kuwait's western border, and low ridges in the north, there is no substantial cover behind which its army units can maneuver, except the urban areas they must defend. The air force also cannot operate with effective warning without support from an AWACS, and it could be kept pinned in its shelters unless it is supported by a neighboring force.

Regardless of whether it organizes more effectively in the future, all Kuwait can hope for is to build a deterrent based on an immediate ability to inflict casualties on an Iranian or Iraqi attacker and to create a defense based on reinforcement by friendly Gulf states. Kuwait's geographical situation, though helpful in maintaining internal security (the population is highly centralized, for the countryside is mostly harsh desert), provides almost insuperable difficulties in defending alone against external threats.

Internal Security

The ruling Al-Sabah family has generally done a good job of juggling the competing external and internal pressures that affect Kuwait's security. It restructured Kuwait's constitution to favor its ruling families in 1980 and successfully reintroduced a popular assembly in February 1981. Although the vast majority of the 500 candidates were left-wing, they were so divided that most of the 50 seats went to Bedouins or conservatives. This process was aided by the fact that only 43,000 Kuwaiti males, or 3% of the population, were eligible to vote. The government has since tolerated considerable dissent. There have been significant debates on constitutional issues, the rights of women, aid to Syria, prohibition of alcohol, and a number of other issues that generally cannot be openly discussed in Gulf politics. The government has also shown a willingness to expand the assembly's powers, although scarcely to the extent that various members of the assembly have demanded.[14]

There are, however, many problems in Kuwait's internal affairs. The government does face opposition from the native middle and professorial class and has long had political problems with its elections. In 1967 the government was able to rig an election by suddenly naturalizing 100,000–200,000 Saudi and Iraqi Bedouins and by drawing upon traditional family and tribal powers. It was also able to rig the 1981 elections to produce the same results. The former nomads are joining the rest of Kuwait's citizens in forming a well-educated and politically active group, however, and it is clear that the government will have to move with the times even in dealing with the Sunni majority.

Kuwait's economy is also a problem. Its heavy subsidies, low, government-set interest rates, and lack of development planning have tended either to drive capital out of the country or to channel the nation's wealth into chaotic speculation. In 1982 this tendency led to a major domestic crisis that aroused new concern over the government's management of the domestic economy and the integrity of the Al-Sabah family. As was described in Chapter 2, Kuwait allowed a massive over-the-counter stock market to develop called the Souk Manakh, or camel market. This market speculated in the rise in share value of paper corporations using postdated checks. Profits of 500% were produced in early 1982, but the balloon burst in September. When trading was finally suspended, postdated checks worth some $90 billion were on call, and although many of the checks represented self-canceling debts between the various investors, real losses approached $28 billion. In fact, eight major dealers with close or direct ties to the Al-Sabahs or Kuwait's leading families had issued checks worth $63 billion.[15]

To the government's credit, it dealt with the crash reasonably well. It protected "small" investors with holdings of less than $6 million and dealt quite firmly with the larger investors. Still, this was the second crash of its kind, and the government had had clear warning of what was going to happen as early as 1981. As a result, the crash reinforced growing objections to "corruption," waste, and mismanagement within the Sunni community—and radicals, conservatives, and students all seem more likely to press for added powers for the popular assembly and more checks on the Al-Sabah family and Kuwait's merchant elite.

Kuwait's expatriates are a time bomb. Aside from the Palestinian problem discussed earlier, Kuwait has problems with its Shi'ites. Native

Shi'ites probably make up about 17% of the population—roughly 100,000. In 1981, Kuwait had 40,000 Iranian, 45,000 Iraqi, and 12,000 Saudi residents, many of whom are also Shi'ite.[16] The rise of Khomeini reinforced a growing political consciousness among these elements, which the Al-Sabah family had formerly had some success in manipulating by buying blocks of votes from the lower-income Shi'ites. The government initially reacted to these pressures by attempting to suppress Shi'ite political movements and by expelling as many as 20,000 Shi'ite expatriates.[17] This, however, was a potentially explosive solution to the problem. Some of the expelled Shi'ites showed up in Iranian training camps, and Iran stepped up its threats. At the same time, Kuwait's native Shi'ites tended to move to the left and demanded a fairer share of the nation's wealth, the right to construct mosques (Kuwait had torn down many old Shi'ite mosques as "urban renewal" but had generally built only new Sunni mosques), the right to shares in Kuwait's legitimate stock market, and political rights. From 1981 onward, the government increasingly had to meet these demands and offer its own Shi'ites increasing equality and economic rights.[18]

The Al-Sabah family faces the same difficulty with its student population as the other conservative Gulf countries, but in Kuwait there are stronger left-wing and radical elements in the universities and secondary schools, reinforced by strong radical Palestinian movements. The Kuwaiti birthrate is variously estimated at from 4.3 to 6.3% annually.[19] While Kuwait's low death rate of 5 per 1,000 limits the rate of demographic shift to a younger population more than its most Arab countries, its rate of natural increase is still nearly 4%. Coupled to Kuwait's relatively long history of modern education, this means that something like two-thirds of the native population has been educated at a level that has raised the political consciousness of Kuwait's youth. A majority now back some form of left-wing or radical movement, and a limited resumption of representative government may not be enough. There are also growing pressures among Kuwait's middle class to limit the Al-Sabah family to a constitutional role and to place much tighter limits on its wealth and use of state income.

The Kuwaiti internal security services and police are reasonably well trained and organized. They have received growing support from Saudi Arabia, Bahrain, and the UAE since 1976, as part of a broad effort among the conservative Gulf states to improve cooperation in reporting on the activities of various radical groups, on labor problems, and on various religious factions. Kuwait's security services are fairly effective, and they have expert expatriate advice. While some disaffected elements exist—and have ties to Iran and radical Palestinian groups—they do not seem to pose a current threat. Kuwaiti cooperation with other Gulf services was also strengthened by an agreement among the members of the Gulf Cooperation Council to create a coordinated internal security system that was reached at Taif in August 1980. This agreement has helped Kuwait deal with its expatriates and radical groups, and Kuwait, Bahrain, Qatar, the UAE, and Saudi Arabia have cooperated in making joint arrests of various radicals since September 1981.[20]

The problems in Kuwait's internal security efforts are becoming more serious, however, as Kuwait proves unable to prevent foreign influence from increasing over every technical and bureaucratic function of the state, as Kuwait continues to expel illegal foreign workers, as the various grievances of the expatriate population rise, and as Kuwaiti students become more politicized. Kuwait also faces the prospect of growing problems with a relatively radicalized labor leadership and even more serious opposition from its Shi'ites.

Given these tensions, the survival of the Al-Sabah regime is likely to rest more on its continued ability to use the nation's oil wealth to buy off foreign and domestic opposition than on the armed forces and internal security forces. So far, the Al-Sabah family has done a good job of making such adjustments, and Kuwait has over $80 billion invested in its Kuwait Fund for Future Generations, which is intended to provide income for the nation after 2001, and which now earns $8–9 billion in interest annually. In spite of a 25% cut in its total oil revenues to $20.8 billion in 1981 and a 40% decline to around $10 billion annually in 1982 and 1983, Kuwait has little reason for concern. It is budgeting about $10.5 billion for 1983, and it earns $8–10 billion annually from its investments. Kuwait now has proved oil reserves of 72 billion barrels, or 10% of the world's known reserves. This is enough for 140 years even at Kuwait's maximum target rate of 1.3 million barrels per day.[21]

Some talk arose in early 1982 that Kuwait would go bankrupt in four years if oil prices stayed low and Kuwait continued to export at only 650,00 BPD, but this scarcely seems likely. Kuwait's projected $1–2 billion deficit in oil revenues on its 1982 budget of $12.3 billion could easily have been avoided without cutting into defense or social services, and the country had amassed a budget surplus of over $6 billion in 1981.[22] Kuwait had $50–70 billion in public investments on 31 December 1982, and it earned an estimated $868 million on private investment and $1.4 billion on finance house investment in 1982. Its revenues from investments reached $8.7 billion in 1981 and $8–9 billion in 1982. Oil revenues exceeded $7 billion in spite of the world recession and began to move upward in mid-1983. If anything, Kuwait experienced more trouble from having to spend over $5 billion to rescue its citizens from their near-lunatic speculation than from cuts in its oil income.[23]

Kuwait can also continue to use its "aid weapon." It provided roughly $11 billion in aid during 1970–1978 and continues to provide massive aid to the PLO and United Nations Relief and Works Agency (UNRWA) to win Palestinian support. It is still aiding Iraq, although it is now making quiet overtures to Iran. It openly aided Syria until it broke with Syria early in 1982 over the latter's support of Iran in the Iran-Iraq War, and it still provides covert payments to buy off Syrian threats to the regime.[24] It also can exploit its neutral stance. It has opposed the U.S. military presence in the Gulf and has taken a strong pro-Palestinian line on the Arab-Israeli peace issue. At the same time, Kuwait has tilted just enough toward the USSR to minimize hostile pressures from Soviet-backed movements or the more radical Arab movements. The Al-Sabah family has also continued to buy Soviet arms and has made tentative offers of oil sales to the USSR.

What is less clear is whether Kuwait can emerge from its present depression in oil revenues without broadening its economic base. Its heavy subsidies are not a valid substitute for its lack of real economic growth and inability to develop a manufacturing sector or even a petroleum sector that will keep more of its wealth in the country, distribute it more broadly, and create real jobs for its growing educated class. National income is not enough. The nonoil sector of Kuwait's economy has shrunk since 1979, and Kuwait's total GDP shrank by 8% between 1980 and 1981, largely because of the outflow of capital. Showpiece $1 billion investments in petrochemical plants will not suffice. Kuwait needs much sounder and more balanced economic development.[25]

At the same time, it seems likely that the Al-Sabah regime will either be forced to take a steadily more generous attitude toward the naturalization of expatriates, hasten the pace of political reform, and offer its Shi'ites more wealth and power or fail to survive through the mid-1980s. In fact, several senior British and Israeli experts feel that the Al-Sabah family may already be in more serious trouble than is generally reported. These experts feel that the Kuwaiti armed forces now have some radical cadres and that Palestinians and quasi-Marxist elements are achieving so much influence over the routine operations of government that they will come to dominate Kuwaiti decision making in spite of the Al-Sabah family's efforts to bring in Egyptians and other more trustworthy expatriates and to create more loyal cadres of native Kuwaitis. A few also feel that Arab radicalism has had more influence over Kuwait than even the Saudis realize and that the bureaucracy, or "real government," tends to tilt toward the radical Arab world while the "official government" continues to be conservative in its financial and diplomatic dealings with the southern Gulf states.

These British and Israeli views seem somewhat pessimistic, but even if the Iran-Iraq War does not spill over into Kuwait or create a new internal crisis, Kuwait cannot be sure that it can buy off its northern neighbors.[26] An Iraqi defeat in the Iran-Iraq War might rapidly force Kuwait to align itself significantly closer to Iran, Syria, and the USSR. If the war continues, however, it will give Iraq and Iran a growing incentive to compete in bringing directly under their influence and to obtain authority over Kuwait's islands and facilities. Kuwait's future is likely to be extremely tense unless it can rapidly develop collective security arrangements with its southern neighbors.[27]

MAP 15—1
THE STRATEGIC POSITION OF BAHRAIN

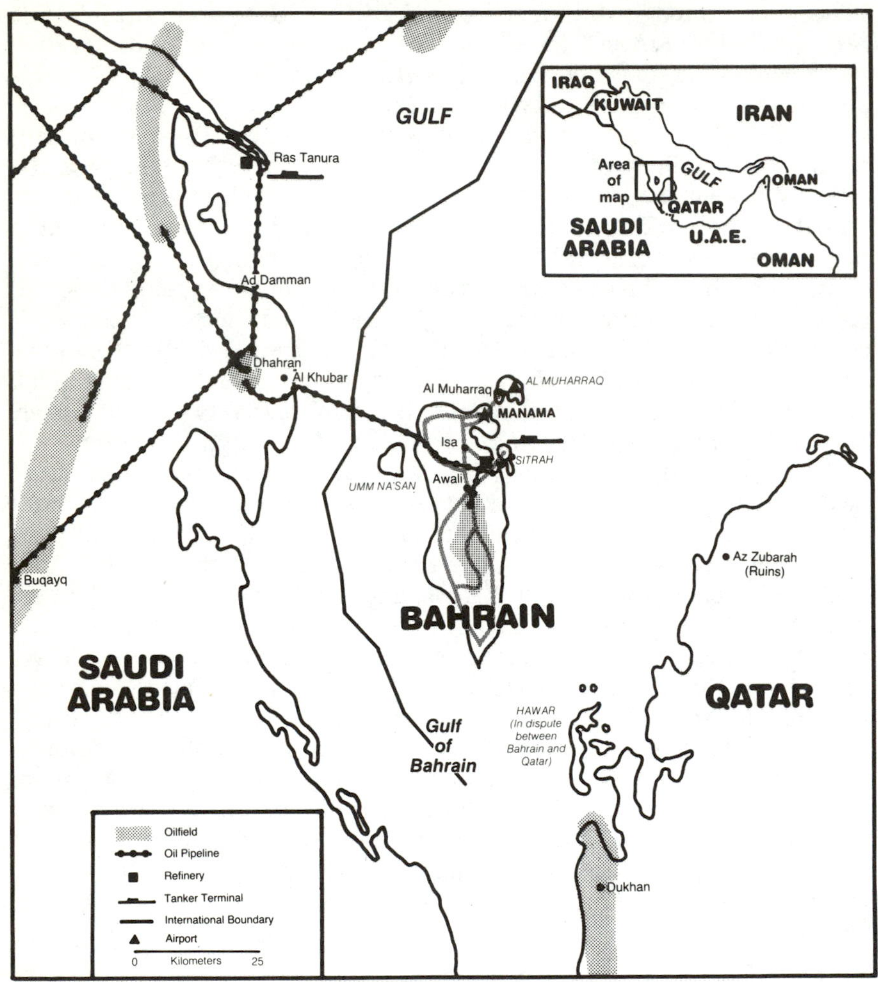

Adapted from CIA 626961 4-80

Bahrain: The Image of Stability

Bahrain and Qatar are the only two Gulf states that did not join the arms race that dominated the actions of other Gulf nations during the 1970s. In Bahrain's case, this was a result of both its size and its geography. Bahrain consists of one main island, only 596 square kilometers in area, and 32 smaller islands. These territorial limits leave

Bahrain unable to manage its own defense, and its location on the coast of Saudi Arabia makes it heavily dependent on Saudi Arabia for its security. The limits on Bahrain's military strength are reinforced by the nature of its population and economy. Bahrain has a population of only 393,000; about 37% is expatriate, and 65% is Shi'ite. As a result, Bahrain can create no more than token armed forces. Bahrain's oil economy is fading. The country now produces about 42,000 BPD, increasingly from the Abu Saafah offshore field, which it shares with Saudi Arabia.[28] This field has a limited life, although recent seismic studies offer some hope of sustaining production. Bahrain's only other economic resources are its limited nonassociated gas production resources, a drydock with a 500,000-ton ship capacity, a 165,000-ton aluminum smelter, and improving downstream production facilities. None of these facilities can sustain Bahrain's oil wealth, and the drydock and smelter may prove to be economic white elephants.

Bahrain has thus been forced into the economic dependence on Saudi Arabia described in Chapter 11, although the relationship has so far benefited both countries. Bahrain has a reasonably well-educated population with more advanced technical skills than that of most other Gulf states. While Saudi Arabia has supplied Bahrain with nearly $1 billion annually in direct and indirect aid, and $50 million annually in balance-of-payments aid, Bahrain has been able to provide skills Saudi Arabia needs and to maintain its economy by acting as an "open" banking, trade, industrial, transport, and service center for Saudi Arabia and the rest of the Gulf area.

Bahrain's economy has otherwise done quite well. Its GDP has risen from 414 million Bahraini dinars (BD) in 1975 to 964 million in 1979. Industrial output has risen at an average of 9% per year since 1973, and light industry has increased in annual output by 10–15%. Bahrain has dealt with the near-term impact of the reduction in Gulf oil income by raising automobile tariffs (10–20%), the cost of alcohol (70–100%), and the price of gasoline. Its 1983 budget will be 643 million BD in obligations and 630 million BD in actual spending. This is more than adequate to meet Bahrain's social and defense needs.

The aluminum market has also started to improve, and Bahrain evidently has the funding to proceed with its 2.3 billion BD four-year plan (1982–1985). This plan will improve Bahrain's telecommunications, airport, aluminum smelter, and refinery. Bahrain will build about 2,000 houses annually and start a wide range of new cooperative light industry projects with other nations on the Gulf. Bahrain has also drawn some protection from its tenuous status as the informal "home port" for the five ships in the small U.S. Middle East Task Force deployed in the Gulf. Following British withdrawal in the late 1960s, Bahrain formally offered the U.S. naval and air facilities in return for military training and a payment of $4 million per year. While the October War created tensions that led to a formal cancellation of this agreement in June

1977, the U.S. Navy still makes frequent visits. It played a major role in establishing Bahrain's small naval training school and still stations 65 personnel on the island.[29] This protection has become increasingly uncertain, however, in the face of the growing threat from Iran, and Bahrain can no longer count on economic cooperation with Iran to preserve its security.

Bahrain's Military Forces

Bahrain's military buildup is traced in Table 15.2. It shows only token growth, tailored almost entirely to internal security requirements. Total defense expenditures were very small by Gulf standards through 1980. Outlays in 1981 were only about $135 million and took up only about 6% of the budget, although they rose to $224 million in 1982 and $253 million in 1983 in response to the growing threat from Iran. The Bahraini defense forces now total only a little over 2,700 and are directly under the command of the minister of defense, Crown Prince Sheikh Hamad Bin Isa Al-Khalifa.

Bahrain's 2,300-man army is organized into an infantry battalion, an armored car squadron, an artillery battery, and small administrative and support units. At the end of 1983, the army had 8 Saladin armored cars and 8 Ferret scout vehicles, 20 Panhards (AML-90), 110 M-3 APCs, 8 light guns, 6 81mm mortars, 6 120mm Mobat recoilless rifles, and 6 RBS-70 surface-to-air missiles. Bahrain's 300-man navy is a token coast guard placed under the Ministry of the Interior; it consists of two Lürssen 45-meter TNC-45 fast patrol boats with Exocet missiles and two other 38-meter Lürssens with guns. Bahrain has a small 100-man air force with 12 AB-212 helicopters. It is, however, transitioning to 4 F-5IIs and 2 F-5F trainers, and Saudi Arabia established a dispersal base at the old RAF airstrip on the Awali-Zalaq road during 1978–1979, with facilities for 25 fighters. Bahrain is also taking delivery on MBB Bo 105 and Hughes 500D helicopters, some of which may be equipped with TOW. Bahrain has voice and teleprinter links to Saudi Arabia's traffic control radars and is equipping its international airport, which has a 13,000-foot runway, as a military dispersal and support base.

The above orders reflect a broader process of modernization. France reached an agreement in May 1980 to sell Bahrain sophisticated radar and electronics equipment, training services, missile-launching patrol boats, and antisubmarine corvettes. The agreement was signed in Riyadh, and the Saudis agreed to provide much of the $700 million funding. Further, the U.S. agreed to sell Bahrain 6 F-5E/F fighters and 60 AIM-9-P3 air-to-air missiles for $114 million on 19 April 1982. This was part of a package designed to give Bahrain the ability to take part in the air defense system sold to Saudi Arabia. It may eventually include Hawk surface-to-air missiles and suitable C^3I links to create a common air defense system throughout the southern Gulf if the efforts of the Gulf Cooperation Council are successful.[30] The U.S. has discussed

TABLE 15.2 The Military Buildup in Bahrain, 1972–1982

	1972–73	1973–74	1974–75	1975–76	1976–77	1977–78	1978–79	1979–80	1980–81	1981–82	1982–83
Total population (millions)	0.216	0.233	0.240	0.250	0.260	0.270	0.345	0.355	0.373	0.400	0.400
Defense expenditures ($ millions)	n.a.	n.a.	n.a.	n.a.	n.a.	n.a.	43	98	n.a.	135	n.a.
GNP ($ billions)	n.a.	n.a.	n.a.	n.a.	1.6	1.7	n.a.	1.7[a]	2.27	n.a.	n.a.
DE as % of GNP	n.a.	n.a.	n.a.	n.a.	n.a.	n.a.	n.a.	5.8	n.a.	n.a.	n.a.
Total military manpower	1,100	1,100	1,100	1,100	1,600	2,300	2,300	2,300	2,300	2,500	2,550
Army											
Manpower	1,100	1,100	1,100	1,100	1,600	2,300	2,300	2,300	2,300	2,300	2,300
Equipment											
AFVs	0	16	16	16	16	16	16	16	109	126	146
Major types	Saladin, Ferret	Saladin, Ferret	Saladin, Ferret	Saladin, Ferret	Saladin, Ferret	Saladin, Ferret	Saladin, Ferret	Saladin, Ferret	Panhard	Panhard	M-113, AML-90
Artillery	0	0	0	0	0	0	0	0	0	8	8
Numbers/Types	ATk guns	6 ATk guns 6 81mm mortars	6 ATk guns 6 81mm mortars	6 120mm RCLs 6 81 mm mortars	6 120mm RCLs 6 81 mm mortars	6 120mm RCLs 6 81 mm mortars	6 120mm RCLs 6 81 mm mortars	6 120mm RCLs 6 81 mm mortars	6 RCLs 6 81mm mortars	8 105mm 6 RCLs 81 mm mortars	8 105mm 6 RCLs 6 81 mm mortars
Navy											
Manpower	n.a.	n.a.	n.a.	n.a.	n.a.	n.a.	n.a.	200	200	200	150
Total craft	some patrol boats	some patrol launches (police)	some patrol launches (police)	2 2 patrol launches (police)	5 5 patrol launches (police)	9 9 patrol launches (police)	9 9 patrol launches (police)	11 9 patrol launches 2 landing craft	22 18 patrol 3 landing craft 1 Hover-craft	18 15 patrol 2 landing craft 1 Hover-craft	2 FAC(M) 2 FAC (G) 18 patrol 2 landing craft 1 Hover-craft
Air Force											
Manpower	—	n.a.	n.a.	n.a.	n.a.	n.a.	n.a.	n.a.	n.a.	n.a.	
Aircraft	—	some	2	2	2	2	2	2	7	17	
Numbers/Types		police helicptrs	2 Scout helicptrs (police)	2 Scout helicptrs (police)	2 Scout helicptrs (police)	2 Scout helicptrs (police)	2 Scout helicptrs (police)	2 Scout helicptrs (police)	7 heli-cptrs	10 AB-212 other helicptrs	6 F-5E/Fs
Paramilitary	—	—	—	—	—	—	—	—	2,500 police	2,500 police	2,680 Coastgrd, police

[a]GDP

Source: The Military Balance (London: IISS, various years).

possible follow-on deals that would enable Bahrain to make the transition to F-20A or F-16 aircraft and train Bahraini pilots and 100 ground crew personnel in the U.S. while providing U.S. technicians in the interim.[31] These arrangements now seem highly uncertain, however, because U.S. officials have had to tell Bahrain that the U.S. Congress will not approve the sale of an advanced fighter. This may force Bahrain to turn to France for Mirage aircraft and could even kill the Hawk purchase.

Bahrain has also established some paramilitary forces of police and coast guard, which have obtained most of their equipment from the other services. The 2,000-man police force has strong Baluchi and North Yemeni elements and acts as both a police and paramilitary force. It is under the command of a member of the royal family and is part of the Ministry of the Interior. Its equipment includes helicopters and modern riot-control equipment.

Many of the senior officers in both the Special Branch and Security Force are still British, Jordanian, or Pakistani. This force is effective and often ruthless, although it relies on detention and expulsion and avoids the torture and murder common in the Yemens and northern Gulf. It has worked closely with the intelligence forces of the Saudi Ministry of the Interior since 1976 and with the other southern Gulf states since August 1980, and it is felt to be reasonably effective, particularly in intelligence gathering. Pay and housing are considered equal to or better than in equivalent civilian jobs, and there are usually more volunteers than necessary.

Internal Security

Bahrain is, therefore, taking what steps it can to improve its defense and internal security. Until recently, Bahrain's stability was aided by a steady increase in oil revenues and its success in becoming the banker of the Gulf. The rise in oil prices increased Bahrain's oil revenues from \$115 million in 1973 to about \$750 million in 1981, and 1982 revenues approached \$600 million in spite of the drop in oil production. Banking quadrupled Bahrain's nonoil revenues between 1973 and 1982. It was also responsible for giving Bahrain high foreign reserves in spite of a continuing long-term trade deficit and provided the resources to maintain a high standard of living and reduce the incentive to challenge the Al-Khalifa regime.[32] In late 1982 Bahrain did, however, have to cut back sharply on its banking activity, which had become involved in the same kind of speculative pressure that had gripped Kuwait.[33] Bahrain was forced to halt a considerable amount of its offshore banking activity, which led to substantial losses by private investors. Although Bahrain emerged with its banking system intact, it seemed unlikely to be able to maintain its past levels of activity until the world economy recovered and oil demand and revenues rose.

Bahrain's agricultural sector has virtually collapsed in the face of competition for manpower and from imports. In spite of massive Saudi aid, Bahrain has not been particularly successful in its industrialization efforts, nor is it likely to unless Saudi Arabia can make its new industrial complex in Jubail a major success.[34]

Bahrain also lacks political unity. Although it held elections in December 1972, it was forced to dissolve its 42-member National Assembly on 26 August 1975. The stated reason was "left-wing elements," but the reality was that the 22 elected members would have been both left-wing and Shi'ite and that the government also acted in response to Saudi pressure to end a reform that Saudi Arabia found politically unsettling.[35] Bahrain has since proved unable to suppress the Popular Front of Bahrain (an offspring of the PFLOAG) or the National Liberation Front of Bahrain (the front name of the Communist party, founded in 1955). Leftist elements have also built up in the expatriate population. There are about 2,000 Palestinians in Banrain, and while they are usually in skilled jobs and are not generally aligned with radical elements in the Palestinian movement, they have played an increasing political role.

These problems have been reinforced by tensions between Bahrain's wealthier Sunnis and a Shi'ite majority that makes up about 60% of the population.[36] As a result of Saudi prodding, the ruling Al-Khalifa family has prohibited labor unions, kept the National Assembly suspended, and limited Bahrain's popular institutions to the traditional Majlis. Rapid native population growth of roughly 4.0% annually has created a student body—Shi'ite-dominated—that now makes up a majority of the total population. This student body now faces limited overall job prospects, continuing employment discrimination against Shi'ites, and serious barriers to upward mobility for even Sunni students outside the traditional ruling elite.

Further, Bahrain became a major labor importer in the mid-1970s, and 42% of its population is now expatriate. This has created growing tension between the native Shi'ite workers and the non-Shi'ite foreign workers, who now make up half the work force. The native Shi'ites have increasingly formed a bloc with expatriate Iranian workers, who now make up about 10% of Bahrain's population. This bloc's natural resentments have been reinforced by erratic management of inflation, housing, and urban services and the neglect of the traditional agricultural and fishing sector.

The Shi'ite Issue

The tensions described in the preceding section were reduced in the period before the rise of Khomeini by the fear of the older and more conservative Shi'ite leaders that they could lose control to younger radicals. Shortly after his rise to power, however, Khomeini declared that Bahrain was part of Iran, and his "messengers" had an almost immediate impact on Bahrain's Shi'ites. About 1,500 Shi'ites demonstrated in August 1979, and the authorities expelled a pro-Khomeini sheikh and several Shi'ite clergy in October. Further Shi'ite protests, which included violent attacks on the U.S., occurred during the Iranian hostage crisis. The ruling Al-Khalifa family then reinforced Khomeini's influence when it badly miscalculated Iraq's strength in the early days of the Iran-Iraq War. Although reports of the Al-Khalifa family's actions are conflicting, it seems to have felt that it could deal with its Shi'ite problem by giving Iraq political support and by allowing Iraqi fighters to disperse in Bahrain. As it became clear that Iraq's initial victory claims were exaggerated, the family tilted back toward a more neutral position. It did so too late to prevent further Shi'ite protests in support of Khomeini in April 1980. The British-led security forces then detained some 50 Shi'ite leaders and began a process of crackdowns and arrests that still continues. This action left a legacy that accelerated Sunni-Shi'ite tensions.

Khomeini neither forgot nor forgave this support for Iraq. This became all too clear in mid-December 1981, when Bahrain arrested 73 people, including 58 Bahraini nationals, 13 Saudis, 1 Kuwaiti, and 1 Omani, and eventually deported up to 300 others. All were Shi'ite members of a group called the Islamic Front for the Liberation of Bahrain, and they had planned a coup attempt for Bahrain's national day on 16 December. They had trained in Iran and had slowly infiltrated in men, arms, and $120,000 in cash by air and in small boats. The groups had obtained Bahraini police uniforms and planned to assassinate key members of the Al-Khalifa family and government officials. They planned to then proclaim an Islamic republic when their leader arrived from Iran.[37]

The plot was discovered by an immigration officer in Dubai, who noticed suspicious transit movements through the country, and Bahraini internal security officials then found that the Iranian chargé d'affaires in Manama was bringing in equipment like walkie-talkies in his diplomatic pouch from London, as well as "bankrolling" the group. Another 13 members were found to be operating in Saudi Arabia and others in the UAE. Although the arrests failed to arouse any public protests, the group was found to have considerable support in the Diraz and Awali districts of Bahrain and to have 150–200 guerrillas training in Iran. It also had ties to Hadi al-Modarasi, a mullah who lived in Bahrain while the shah was in power and who now heads the Gulf Affairs Section of the Iranian Revolutionary Guards. These discoveries led Bahrain to be very cautious in trying the rebels and in dealing with other Shi'ites. It carefully avoided triggering public protests when in 1982 it tried the rebels and expelled 200–300 additional Shi'ite dissidents, rather than trying them.[38] It was very careful to keep further arrests in 1983 as quiet as possible and to avoid public tension with Iran over new evidence of subversion.

Bahrain also took steps to improve the economic opportunities open to its Shi'ites, particularly students. It expanded the number of Shi'ites in government positions, and here it was able to build on reforms it had begun much earlier. Five of 17 cabinet members were Shi'ite even in 1975, and over half the ministers and most heads of government departments were nonroyal in 1982. The government could thus hire new Shi'ites without appearing weak. It also increased the number of Shi'ites in teaching positions.[39]

These reforms do not, however, seem likely to prevent a steady rise in Shi'ite pressure on the government, a growing popular shift to left-wing and radical movements, and new attempts at subversion. Accordingly, much will depend on whether Saudi Arabia and the other Gulf states can improve their capacity to help Bahrain in an emergency. Airlifted or heliborne Saudi reinforcements would probably be decisive if they could arrive in time, and this course should be increasingly feasible over the next few years. The Saudi dispersal base near the Awali-Zalaq road could be used as a 25-kilometer staging center, and a land causeway will be built between Bahrain and Saudi Arabia in the mid-1980s.[40] When it is completed in 1986–1987, it will allow Saudi Army forces to rapidly move in strength into Bahrain, particularly against the Shi'ite elements in the city. It seems unlikely that any uprising that did not have the full support of the Bahraini armed forces could have the strength to seize control of the airfield or future causeway and thus block Saudi movement.

It still seems possible, however, that Bahrain could suddenly become a radical and anti-Western state at any point in the mid-1980s. Much will depend on the unity of the Al-Khalifa oligarchy, the course of the Iran-Iraq War and Iranian revolution, Saudi Arabia's willingness to allow sufficient social reform, and Bahrain's treatment of its Shi'ites and poor and foreign workers in the future. A failure in any of these areas might well serve as a political catalyst that could ultimately bring down the Al-Khalifa regime.

The long-term prognosis for the Al-Khalifa family is, therefore, uncertain. In some ways, it has suffered from Saudi pressure to remain conservative. While Saudi aid has provided Bahrain with vital major direct and indirect economic support, Saudi policies have helped to divide the regime from the population. The Bahraini Army and internal security forces should be able to deal with any normal radical elements in the short term, but they may be unable to deal with the more serious Sunni-Shi'ite tensions building up in Bahraini society.

Qatar: Moving in the Direction of Kuwait

Qatar is another small Gulf country, with about 10,360 square kilometers of territory. It has only 56 kilometers of land boundaries, although the peninsula has 563 kilometers of coastline. Like Kuwait and Bahrain, Qatar has little cultivable soil, and herding, trade, and the sea are its only sources of income other than oil—which accounts for about 90% of Qatar's income.

Qatar's main security problem is its large expatriate population. Its total population was reported to be 167,000 in July 1979, 225,000 in January 1981, and 260,000 in early 1983.[41] Virtually all sources agree that almost 80% of Qatar's legally resident population is now expatriate and that significant additional numbers of illegals are present in the country. Its legal population is estimated to be about 20% Qatari, 25% other Arab, 16% Iranian, 34% South Asian, and 5% other. An additional 5% or more of its population consists of illegal workers. As in Kuwait, most of the real work in Qatar is done by expatriates. About 90% of its 100,000-man work force is foreign, with a ruling and business elite of native Qataris. Native literacy is only about 25%.

Its present government seems relatively secure. Qatar is ruled by Sheikh Khalifa bin Hamad al-Thani, a Council of Ministers (9 of whose 13 members are also Al-Thanis), and a 20-man Advisory Council appointed by the sheikh. Khalifa deposed his ultraconservative cousin, Ahmad bin Ali al-Thani, in a bloodless coup in February 1972, and the Al-Thani regime has since been relatively stable.

Qatar's oil wealth is more recent than that of Kuwait, and unlike Kuwait, Qatar does not yet face organized labor unions, major political pressure from its growing population of educated young professionals, or significant pressures from Palestinian immigrants. A number of clandestine groups are active, but they are still small.[42]

Like Kuwait, Qatar has done a good job of passing its oil wealth down to its native population. Until recently, however, it did a wretched job of developing its economy. Its initial NGL plants were a technical disaster, and one entire plant burned to the ground because of improper safety standards in April 1977. Qatar funded a number of major showpiece projects that were not profitable and that increased the need for foreign labor. Inflation reached the crisis point in 1976–1978, and Qatar's oil development and production were poorly managed, and occasionally its oil fields produced beyond their maximum economic recovery point[43]—which reduces ultimate oil recovery. Qatar has sharply improved its economic management since 1978, however, and in the early 1980s it dropped its oil-production targets to the 400,000-BPD levels indicated by its reserves of 4,700 million barrels. This was at least 35 years of reserves at the target rate. It also cut back on its petrochemical development plans in 1982. These are still overambitious, but they are much better structured, and Qatar now has sounder plans to exploit its extensive gas reserves of 300 million cubic feet. Qatar has also greatly improved its fertilizer and steel operations, and these are now profitable if one ignores the write-off of early capital and operating costs.

If Qatar's development plans continue to be successful, it should have the income to continue to provide excellent economic opportunities to native Qatari and expatriate alike. Saudi Arabia has also provided Qatar with extensive economic support by integrating projects like its 378,000-ton iron and steel complex into the Saudi economic development program centered around Jubail and by "bailing out" the otherwise uneconomic Qatari projects started during 1974–1977.[44]

Qatar has recently had some trouble in maintaining oil production, which has dropped from annual averages of 400,000–500,000 BPD in 1979–1981 to 202,000 BPD in 1982 and monthly averages as low as 170,000 BPD in 1983. Oil reserves may drop to around $3.2 billion in 1983 versus $5.4 billion in 1980, and Qatar has had to slash its 1983-1984 budget to $1.07 billion versus a 1982–1983 budget of $2.6 billion (this budget covered an 18-month period). This has forced Qatar to cut back on its defense budget, which was projected as being as high as $896 million in 1981–83. Only 15.7%, or $165.9 million, of the 1983-1984 budget is allocated to defense, Qatar should, however, have more than enough money to maintain civilian and development spending until its oil revenues recover.

Qatar's Military Forces

Although Qatar's forces increased to 6,000 men in 1982, Qatar is similar to Bahrain in that it has not really joined the Gulf arms race.[45] Qatar's military development is shown in Table 15.3, and the limited growth of its forces reflects the decision to focus on internal security capabilities plus a limited ability to protect against small border incursions.

In late 1983, Qatar has fairly well-organized military forces that still reflect a sound heritage of British organization and training. They are composed mainly of a 5,000-man army, organized into one tank battalion, one Royal Guard infantry regiment, five regular infantry battalions, and one artillery battalion. The army's equipment and infrastructure is a mixture of British and French types. The army has 24 AMX-30 tanks, 10 Ferret scout cars, 30 AMX-10Ps, 25 Saracen and 136 VAB APCs, 6 155mm howitzers, 8 25-pounder guns, and a handful of aging guns, howitzers, and mortars. The army is composed of 18 nationalities and has a large number of Omani, Dhofari, Yemeni, Baluchi, and Iranian expatriates. It also has a number of British officers, and some Jordanian and Pakistani expatriates, although most officers are now Qataris. It is acquiring a number of well-trained native officers and NCOs, new $100 million casernes, and modern training, communications, and supply facilities. Morale seems to be good by Gulf standards.

Hawk and Rapier missiles are now under delivery as part of an effort to increase the army's air-defense capabilities, and they are now planned to be relatively tightly integrated with Saudi forces. Five Tigercat surface-to-air launchers are also installed at Doha, but these are largely ineffective. Saudi Arabia has bought and supplied a network of Thomson-CSF surveillance radars, and it plans to provide Qatar with Shahines (improved Crotale) surface-to-air missiles.

The Qatari Air Force is 300 strong and is based on a facility at Doha that is being converted from a single-runway airport to a modern air

TABLE 15.3 The Military Buildup in Qatar, 1972–1983

	1972–73	1973–74	1974–75	1975–76	1976–77	1977–78	1978–79	1979–80	1980–81	1981–82	1982–83
Total population (millions)	0.15	0.089	0.09	0.09	0.09	0.2	0.205	0.21	0.22	0.23	0.24
Defense expenditures ($ millions)	n.a.	n.a.	n.a.	n.a.	n.a.	n.a.	61	n.a.	59.5	893	n.a.
GNP ($ millions)	280	n.a.	n.a.	425	n.a.	1,000	n.a.	5,000	n.a.	6,580	n.a.
DE as % of GNP	n.a.	n.a.	n.a.	n.a.	n.a.	n.a.	n.a.	n.a.	n.a.	13.6	n.a.
Total military manpower	1,800	2,200	2,200	2,200	2,200	4,200	4,000	4,700	4,700	9,700	6,000
Army											
Manpower	1,600	1,600	1,600	1,600	1,600	3,500	3,500	4,000	4,000	9,000	5,000
Equipment											
Medium tanks	—	—	—	—	—	—	12	12	24	24	24
Major types							AMX-13	AMX-13	AMX-13	AMX-30	AMX-30
Other AFVs	39	48	48	30	48	48	72	80	68	65	201
Major types	Saladin	Saladin	Saladin	Saladin	Saladin	Saladin	Saladin	Saladin	AMX-10P	AMX-10	VAB
Field Guns	—	4	4	4	4	4	4	4	10	14	14
Other											
Numbers/Types	— —	81mm mortar	81mm mortar	81mm mortar	81mm mortar	81mm mortar	81mm mortar	81mm mortar	81mm mortar	81mm mortar	81mm mortar
Navy											
Manpower	—	n.a.	n.a.	n.a.	n.a.	400	200	400	400	400	7,000
Total craft		4	4	4	4	11	37	35	35	37	46
Numbers/Types		4 patrol	4 patrol	4 patrol	4 patrrol	11 patrol	37 patrol	35 patrol	35 patrol	37 patrol	2 FAC(M) 44 patrol
Air Force											
Manpower	n.a.	n.a.	n.a.	n.a.	n.a.	300	300	300	300	300	300
Total combat aircraft	4	4	4	4	13	4	4	4	4	9	9
Numbers/Types	4 Hunter	4 Hunter Tigercat	4 Hunter 2 helicptrs Tigercat SAMs	4 Hunter 1 trnspt 6 helicptrs Tigercat SAMs	13 Hunter 1 trnspt 2 helicptrs Tigercat SAMs	4 Hunter 1 trnspt 8 helicptrs Tigercat SAMs	4 Hunter 1 trnspt 11 helicptrs 1 trainer Tigercat SAMs	4 Hunter 1 trnspt 11 helicptrs 1 trainer Tigercat SAMs	4 Hunter 1 trnspt 11 helicptrs Tigercat SAMs	3 Hunter 3 Alpha-Jet 11 helicptrs Tigercat SAMs	2 Hunter 3 Alpha-Jet 4 trnspt 9 helicptrs SAMs
Paramilitary	—	—	—	—	—	—	—	—	—	—	Police 3 Lynx M-28 2 Gazelle helicptrs

Source: The Military Balance (London: IISS, various years).

base. It possesses 6 Alpha jets, 2 Hunter FGA-6s and 1 T-79 trainer, and several British helicopters. The Hunter pilots are mainly seconded from Britain. The other aircraft have a combination of native and expatriate fighters, although Qatar is now training additional native pilots. Fourteen Mirage F-1 fighters and Puma helicopters are on order, and Qatar is examining French and U.S. proposals to acquire more advanced fighters. It is at best a minimal "trip wire" without adequate strength or C^3I capabilities, although Bahrain would evidently have placed a $650 million order with France for more F-1s and Alpha jets, plus radars, air defense equipment, and naval equipment, in April 1983 if it had not faced budget problems. Like Bahrain, Qatar has been told by U.S. officials that it cannot expect near-term approval of any purchase of advanced U.S. fighters because of problems in obtaining congressional approval of such a sale.

Doha is also the base of the army's 700-man naval branch. It is being equipped with three La Combattante IIIM fast attack craft with MM-40 Exocets. It also has 6 British Vosper large patrol craft with 40mm guns, two 75-foot patrol craft with 20mm guns, 27 much smaller patrol craft with machine guns, and 2 Interceptor fast assault and search-and-rescue craft. Serviceability is generally high.

Qatar's military manpower is composed of a mixture of foreign officers, NCOs, and technicians and native troops. The native manpower was traditionally recruited from nonurban tribes and Bedouin tribes that migrate between Qatar and Saudi Arabia, but it has been drawn largely from settled villages in recent years. Qatar is likely to have increasing recruiting problems if it tries to expand to 10,000–15,000 men in the mid-1980s. Native Qatari recruits still tend to lack technical skills, although the tribal intake has shown surprising adaptability in operating modern military equipment.

Both the native and expatriate leadership of the armed forces seems loyal to the regime. The officer corps also has a number of members of the royal family. The commander and minister of defense is Major General Sheikh Hamad bin Khalifa al-Thani, the son of the ruling sheikh and a Sandhurst graduate. The deputy commander, who exercises operational control, is a member of the closely allied Attiyah family.

Internal Security

Qatar also has a competent police and security force under the Ministry of the Interior, but these forces are not large or unusually oppressive. The police include a substantial number of Yemenis. Both forces are commanded by a member of the royal family trained at the British police college at Hendon, and the government relies largely on routine security police surveillance to deal with its limited number of native radicals and foreign workers.

There are approximately 800 sheikhs in the ruling family out of a native population of 60,000, and the Al-Thani family has intermarried extensively with other Qatari families in the century it has been in power. The Al-Thani family must, however, now begin to cope with a society that has had a 90% increase in the number of its students over the past 10 years, and which had 43,000 students in school out of a total population of 240,000 in 1981. The family also has done a poor job of co-opting the rest of the small native work force and in sharing its wealth. Qatar remains a nation divided between rich and poor.

Qatar's labor policies ensure that its 40,000 Iranian workers are clearly identified by the security services and that it is the Pakistanis and other Asians who receive the least desirable jobs. Although Qatar has Egyptians, Jordanians, and Palestinians in key positions, it relies on 15,000 Western expatriates for most of its skilled labor. This provides an ethnic basis for separating out the most dissatisfied expatriates.

The security forces did prove corruptible in crackdowns on expatriate workers in 1979 and 1980, but they have still proved competent enough to deal with the overall problem. Qatar is also protected by the fact that it contributes heavily to the PLO and has strongly supported "nonalignment" with the superpowers. Its narrow 56-kilometer land border is protected by Saudi Arabia, and Qatar and Saudi Arabia have increasingly shared intelligence and security services since 1976.

Although Qatar is subject to the same political uncertainties as the other Gulf nations that are dependent upon a small and traditionalist royal family, there does not appear to be any major short-term internal threat to its security, other than a long-standing rivalry over the succession. The current ruler succeeded in having his son, Sheikh Hamad bin Khalifa al-Thani, named Crown Prince in May 1977, but his younger brother, Sheikh Suhaim, the minister of foreign affairs, has continued to make informal claims to the throne. He has also fought with the ruler's younger son, Abd al-Aziz, the minister of finance and oil, over the position of prime minister.

Qatar is involved in several comparatively petty border disputes with Bahrain and Saudi Arabia. Bahrain has a claim to the Hawar Islands, which are less than a kilometer off the northwest coast of Qatar. While the largest of these islands is only 5 square kilometers in area, they do affect offshore drilling rights. The islands are generally considered to belong to Bahrain, and Qatar has largely avoided the issue, but it resented Bahrain's naming one of its patrol boats *Hawar* and stationing it near the islands just before a Gulf foreign ministers' conference in February 1982.

There is also a minor dispute between Bahrain and Qatar over Bahrain's claim to the Zubarah strip on the northwest coast of Qatar. This also affects the demarcation of offshore oil and gas zones, although the issue seems comparatively minor and may well be resolved by a compromise giving Bahrain sovereignty over the Hawar Islands and Qatar sovereignty over the Zubarah strip.

The dispute with Saudi Arabia, which affects the UAE as well, concerns the coast along the Khaur al-Udaid inlet at the southeast base of the Qatar Peninsula. This dispute seems to have been resolved in 1974–1977 by a complex trade that gave Saudi Arabia a corridor to the coast, the UAE sovereignty over the Buraimi Oasis, and Qatar a cash payment plus the larger part of the offshore gas rights in al-Salwa Bay (west of Qatar).

In any case, Qatar now has close relations with Saudi Arabia. The de facto settlement of the Qatari-Saudi border dispute has strengthened the ties between the Saudi and Qatari governments and ruling families. The Saudi Army has, in fact, intervened indirectly on one occasion to back the Al-Thani family. In 1972 it backed the coup that brought the current ruler to power, financially, politically, and with a show of armed force at the border. Saudi Arabia engaged in joint defense planning with Qatar long before the formation of the Gulf Cooperation Council and encouraged Qatar to order Mirage F-1s to provide an air unit that could cooperate directly with the Saudi Air Force. Qatar has since worked closely with Saudi Arabia in planning its land-based air defenses, and Qatar's Hawk units will be linked with the Saudi C³I system that will be part of the Air Defense Enhancement Package. Qatar's border with Saudi Arabia also allows direct Saudi military reinforcement in the event of any internal security crisis.

Qatar has also done a better job than most of the conservative Gulf states in controlling the influx of Palestinian and other radical elements, although it has many Iranians, Iraqis, and Egyptians in its civil service, and there are large numbers of Lebanese. If the Iran-Iraq War does not spill over into the southern Gulf, Qatar should be able to control its limited expatriate Shi'ite population and to build up reasonably effective joint air and sea defenses with the Saudis by the middle to late 1980s.

In the long run, however, the Al-Thani family and the other Qatari native elites must find a way to absorb most of Qatar's Arab expatriates as full citizens. Their influence, coupled to modern education, is politicizing the younger native-born population, and pressures for modernization and a broader sharing of the nation's wealth should mount steadily over the next five years.[46] It seems doubtful that the present system of government can survive these pressures without significant reform. Radical groups like the Islamic Revolution Organization in the Arabian Peninsula and the Human Rights Defense Committee now have virtually no serious influence in Qatar, however, and there may be sufficient time to broaden the government to avoid violent change by the military or by revolutionary pressures.

The United Arab Emirates: The Most Unstable?

The classic description of the Holy Roman Empire is that it was "not holy, not Roman, and not an empire." As Chapter 11 showed, the origins of the UAE have given it a somewhat similar character. Although it has only 82,880 square kilometers of territory, it has rarely been united since its founding in 1971, and it has often acted more like an alliance of squabbling mini-states. It has not really been Arab: About 80% of the total population of the UAE is expatriate, and only 42% of the total is Arab.[47] It is, in fact, more than 50% South Asian, with another 8% East Asian, Western, and "other." And it has not been composed of seven equal emirates. It has rather been the scene of a power struggle between Abu Dhabi and Dubai, with Ras al-Khaimah and Sharjah causing problems in the "wings."

Collectively, the UAE has been the worst governed and most divided of the conservative Gulf states, and it has done one of the worst jobs of equitably distributing its oil wealth. It has also seen the steady buildup of internal opposition. While substantial improvements have taken place since 1978, when Saudi Arabia and Kuwait helped to halt the UAE's steady internal decline, the UAE is still the southern Gulf "state" that now seems most vulnerable to being taken over by an anti-Western radical regime.

The UAE's Military Force

The recent history of the UAE's military buildup is shown in Table 15.4.[48] Its expansion has been more moderate and realistic than that of Kuwait, but the UAE has maintained the highest per capita defense expenditure in the world with only limited results. Its forces have also reflected the deep political divisions within the UAE discussed in Chapter 11. Since the UAE achieved independence in 1971, its military forces have been dominated by the UAE's president, the sheikh of Abu Dhabi, Zayid Sultan al Nuhayan. He has controlled virtually all of the UAE's oil income and 90% of its central budget expenditures. Sheikh Zayid began building up a modern military force in Abu Dhabi when Britain first announced its intention to leave the Gulf, and he has steadily increased the UAE's annual arms imports from about $10 million in 1973 to well over $100 million annually in 1980. By the mid-1970s, the Abu Dhabi Defense Force (ADDF) was five times the size of the Federal Union Defense Force (UDF). This led Dubai and Ras al-Khaimah to create their own forces. While all these forces were "unified" in May 1976, each emirate has continued to expand its forces as de facto national forces, although they have been called regional commands.

The UAE's total armed forces expanded from about 10,000 in 1973 to nearly 50,000 by the end of 1983. The 46,000-man army now consists of one Royal Guard "Brigade," nine mechanized infantry battalions, five armored car battalions, an artillery brigade of three battalions, and one air defense brigade of three battalions. The major equipment in the armored units consists of 100 AMX-30 and 18 OF-40 Lion (Leopard) medium tanks, 60 Scorpions, 90 AML-90 armored cars, Saladin, VBC-40, and 6 Shorland armored cars. It is interesting to note that Dubai's armored forces have standardized on the OF-40, are buying 66 Engesa Urutu APCs with TOW, and may buy Rapier surface-to-air missiles, while Abu Dhabi is examining the Challenger, Valiant, and AMX-32 tank, and plans to buy different APCs and AFVs. Seventy Saladins and 60 Ferrets are in storage. The nine infantry battalions are equipped with 30 AMX VICs and 300 Panhard M-3 APCs and have a dozen Saracens in storage. The three artillery battalions have 81mm mortars, 84mm recoilless launchers, over 20 British 25-pounders, 50 105mm guns, and 20 French AMX self-propelled 155mm SP howitzers. The air defense battalions are armed with Rapiers, Crotales, RBS-70 SAMs, and some light AA weapons. Other weapons include 120mm recoilless rifles, Vigilant antitank guided weapons, and a mix of late-model SAMs. Eighteen more OF-40 tanks, 20 Scorpion light tanks, 54 TOW launchers, and 7 Improved Hawk batteries with 42 launchers and 343 missiles are on order.

The army is just converting to its medium tanks and beginning to acquire a minimal capability for modern armored warfare. The army also improved its organization and efficiency in the late 1970s and early 1980s through the efforts of its chief of staff, Maj. Gen. Khalidid (a Jordanian veteran with training at Sandhurst and Fort Leavenworth). It also has made some efforts to rationalize and centralize its major equipment procurement. Training is improving, although the overall quality of training is still poor to mediocre.

Equipment is adequate; but all elements of the UAE's land forces have major problems in troop proficiency, maintenance, and unit operations. About 75% of the army consists of the forces of Abu Dhabi (Western Region), while another 20% belong to Dubai (Central Military Region), and 5% belong to Ras al-Khaimah (Eastern Region). These national differences make logistics a nightmare. There are far too many equipment types. For example, the mix of light AFVs is amazing, while the ATGWs are operated by poorly trained troops. Similar problems occur in the air defense missile units, reflecting the low technical knowledge and general educational level of the rank and file throughout the armed forces.

Omanis and Baluchis, sometimes of indifferent quality, provide up to two-thirds of the army's manpower and the bulk of the NCOs and junior officers. Although competently trained native officers have entered the armed forces in significant numbers, many of the senior and technical staff positions are still filled by Jordanian, Pakistani, and British military on contract. Since Oman gives its officers and NCOs strong incentives to eventually return home, the loyalty of such expatriates is uncertain. Attempts to balance this situation by recruiting from North Yemen did not succeed in solving the problem, although the UAE has been successful in persuading many Jordanian officers to become naturalized citizens.

Attempts to introduce conscription since 1976 have been unrealistic and cosmetic, designed more to expand Abu Dhabi's power and find a means of bringing "loyal" citizens into the armed forces than to meet military needs. Manning levels, turnovers, training and operations, maintenance, and virtually all aspects of readiness are poor, and the

TABLE 15.4 The Military Buildup in the United Arab Emirates, 1972–1983

	1972–73	1973–74	1974–75	1975–76	1976–77[a]	1977–78	1978–79	1979–80	1980–81	1981–82	1982–83
Total population (thousands)	131.8	163.8	170.6	220	n.a.	690	875	905	920	950	1,040
Defense expenditures ($ millions)	24.2	n.a.	n.a.	n.a.	n.a.	100.6	661	750	1,200	n.a.	n.a.
GNP ($ millions)	n.a.	n.a.	n.a.	n.a.	8,500	7,700	12,000	21,000	29,680	n.a.	n.a.
DE as % of GNP[b]	n.a.	n.a.	n.a.	n.a.	n.a.	1.3	5.5	n.a.	4.0	n.a.	n.a.
Total military manpower	9,850	11,150	12,000	15,550	21,400	26,100	25,900	25,150	25,150	42,500	48,500
Army											
Manpower	8,850	10,150	11,000	13,000	18,800	23,500	23,500	23,500	23,500	40,000	46,000
Equipment											
AFVs	81	96	102	74	116	301	188	178	201	561	604+
Numbers/Types	Saladin	Saladin	75 Saladin 21 Ferret	47 Saladin 15 Ferret	47 Saladin 36 Ferret 27 Scorp.	125 Saladin 60 Ferret 80 Scorp.	80 Saladin 60 Ferret 30 Scorp.	70 Saladin 60 Ferret 30 Scorp.	150 AML-90 45 Scorp.	75 AMX-30[b] 25 Ferret 60 Scorp.	100 AMX-30 18 OF-40 300 Pnhds 60 Scorp.[c]
Field guns	some	some	16	16	25 pdr., 105mm	22	22	22	22	40	50+
SP guns	—	—	—	—	16	16	16	6–10	6–10	20	20
Other	—	81mm mor.	81mm mor.	81mm mor.	81mm mor.	81mm mor.	81mm mor.	81mm mor.	81mm mor.	81mm mor.	81mm mor.
Numbers/Types				Vigilant	Vigilant Rapier	Vigilant Rapier	Vigilant Rapier	Vigilant Rapier	Vigilant Rapier	Vigilant Rapier Harpoon	Vigilant Rapier Crotale

TABLE 15.4 (continued)

	1972–73	1973–74	1974–75	1975–76	1976–77[a]	1977–78	1978–79	1979–80	1980–81	1981–82	1982–83
Navy											
Manpower	n.a.	150	150	200	800	800	600	900	900	1,000	1,000
Total craft	16	15	15	12	24	29	15	9	15	11	15
Numbers/Types	12 patrol 4 dinghy	9 patrol 4 dinghy 2 dhows	9 patrol 4 dinghy 2 dhows	9 patrol 3 dinghy	20 patrol 4 dinghy	29 patrol	15 patrol	9 patrol	15 patrol	11 patrol	6 FAC(M) 9 patrol
Air Force											
Manpower	n.a.	350	1,200	1,200	1,800	1,800	1,800	750	750	2,000	1,500
Total combat aircraft	12	12	18	26	26	38	46	52	52	51	52
Fighters	—	—	10	14	14	24	32	32	32	30	30
Major types			Mirage	Mirage V	Mirage V	Mirage V	Mirage	Mirage	Mirage	Mirage	Mirage
FGA/COIN	12	12	8	12	12	14	14	20	20	21	22
Major types	Hunter	Hunter	Hunter	Hunter	Hunter	Hunter	Hunter	MB-326	MB-326	Hunter	Hunter
Transports	6	6	9	9	11	11	14	17	17	16	21
Major types	n.a.	n.a.	n.a.	n.a.	C-130	Islander	Islander	Islander	Islander	Islander	Islander
Helicopters	4	10	16	21	25	38	37	34	29	42	44
Major types	n.a.	AB-206	AB-206	AB-206	AB-206	AB-205	Alouette	Puma	Puma	Gazelle	Gazelle
Other	—	—	5	4							
Numbers/Types			4 MB-326 1 Cessna 182	3 MB-326 1 Cessna 182	8 MB-326			AAMs ASMs	AAMs ASMs	AAMs ASMs	3 PC-7s AA/SMs
Paramilitary	—	—	—	—	—	—	—	—	—	Coast Guard pt. boats	Coast Guard pt. boats

[a]The Union Defence Force and the armed forces of the United Arab Emirates (Abu Dhabi, Ras Al Khaimah, and Sharjah) were formally merged in May 1976.
[b]Calculated.
[c]Twenty-five more OF-40 Leopard tanks and 20 more Scorpion light tanks are on order.
Source: The Military Balance (London: IISS, various years).

handling of funds within the army has involved continuing abuses and corruption. Extensive tribal and provincial divisions within the comparatively small and strained force structure have also reduced effectiveness and efficiency.

The UAE Air Force (UAEAF) has been dominated by Abu Dhabi. Although it is gradually becoming a "native" force at the officer level, it is still staffed largely by contract expatriate personnel, largely Pakistani and British. It has shown marked growth in aircraft strength, and its manpower has risen, but its 1,500-man strength is not sufficient to operate its existing 43 combat aircraft and 7 combat helicopters, much less the 6 additional British Alpha Jet fighters now being delivered. Reliance on expatriates and civilian contractors does, however, allow the UAEAF to keep many of its aircraft operational, and it does have some good native, Pakistani, Jordanian, and British pilots.

The air force is now organized into an interceptor-strike wing, with two squadrons of 25 Mirage V strike interceptors with three additional reconnaissance and two combat-training variants. These units are based in Abu Dhabi. An additional ground-attack squadron is based in Sharjah with 12 rebuilt Hunter FGA-76s (2 are trainers) is converting to the 6 Alphajets. A COIN squadron of 10 Italian MB-326K light attack aircraft and one SF-260OWD is based in Dubai. Its remaining aircraft are dispersed mainly between Abu Dhabi and Dubai. Transport capabilities are fair, and expansion is planned. The UAE also has a force of 44 helicopters with a mix of French and U.S. types, 7 of them (Alouette IIIs) attack helicopters. More helicopters are on order, and the UAE has managed to keep this force operational and has developed reasonable proficiency standards. It evidently agreed to buy 18–40 Mirage 2000 fighters from France in March 1983, and the purchase of 24 Hawk fighter trainers and of Skyguard 35mm air defense systems from Britain was confirmed in April 1983.

The UAEAF, however, is not effective as an integrated air force. Its training has little practical value in combat, it has an unfortunate record of past mismanagement of its procurements and support services, and it is now crippled by its lack of an effective air defense and AC&W system. While some medium- and high-altitude radar warning coverage exists over the entire coast, the UAE has no long-range warning capability and erratic short-range coverages, and it lacks the C^3I, electronic warfare, and IFF capability to use its forces effectively or to cooperate with other Gulf states. If funded, its purchase of the Mirage 2000s will give it fighters with marginally adequate radars and computers to provide the long-range warning and the look-down/shoot-down capability it will need to defend its coast and offshore oil facilities. The Mirage 2000s are, however, dependent on rather poor avionics for the demands of the middle to late 1980s. The UAE is procuring a more advanced AC&W and C^3I system from the UK, but this will not be capable of optimal integration with the system the U.S. is providing to Saudi

Arabia and could not significantly improve its capability until the mid-1980s at the earliest. In the interim, the U.S. and Saudi E-3As would have to provide immediate C³I capabilities if the UAEAF was to have more than the most minimal capability.

The 1,500-man navy has had British organization and leadership, but it is only beginning to shift from the status of a coast guard to that of a real navy. It consists of 3 lightly armed British Keith Nelson–type coastal patrol craft, 6 larger British Vosper patrol craft, and 6 Lurssen TNC-45 fast attack patrol boats with two twin Exocet missile launchers, based primarily at Abu Dhabi. More patrol craft are on order. A separate contingent of 45 small machine-gun craft also exists under the command of the Marine Police. Serviceability and operational proficiency have reached acceptable levels. There is a small chance that the navy could deal effectively with minor attacks by Iraqi or Iranian forces, especially against craft armed with light missiles. It will progress to the stage of being able to fight a limited "blue water" conflict only after the mid-1980s. British experts also believe that some elements in the navy may have ties to radical groups.

Saudi and Kuwaiti sources regard the UAE federal police and security forces as relatively clumsy and occasionally oppressive, as incompetent except for their expatriate elements, and as being for sale to local business elements and radicals alike. This situation is changing, however, as increasing cadres of younger native personnel with modern education enter the forces and cooperation with the forces of the other conservative Gulf states improves. The elements of the national police and security forces that have had British and Jordanian training are also regarded as competent, especially the Special Branch.

Internal Security

If the shah's fall had not provided a salutary lesson to the UAE's squabbling rulers, it seems likely that the ruler of at least one member state would have been overthrown and that the UAE's ruling structure might have crumbled.[49] A major breach developed between Dubai and Abu Dhabi in February 1978, when the UAE's President, Sheikh Zayid of Abu Dhabi, suddenly appointed his 18-year-old son as commander-in-chief without consulting Sheikh Rashid of Dubai or the latter's son, the UAE's defense minister. This breach paralyzed the country at a time when it was experiencing a considerable economic crisis as a result of the mismanagement of its development program, growing problems with expatriate labor, and popular unrest because of the inability of the UAE's archaic legal system to establish land rights and ownership. These problems were compounded by the abortive unilateral attempt of Sheikh Saqr of Ras al-Khaimah to seize Omani territory and offshore areas in November 1977 and by the emirates' different reactions to the shah's seizure of the Tumbs and Abu Musa.

This situation seriously discredited the UAE's traditional rulers with its technocrats, younger officers, and educators, many of whom already had little sympathy with the rivalry among the rulers of Abu Dhabi, Dubai, and Ras al-Khaimah. Worse, it began to discredit the sheikhs with the traditional ruling elites, major business families, and senior officers in the military. These attitudes showed up clearly in the history of the UAE's National Assembly, which continued to meet even though the Supreme Council could not meet as long as the key sheikhs would not talk to each other. Although the National Assembly was a purely advisory body, appointed by the UAE's rulers (eight members each for Dubai and Abu Dhabi, six each for Sharjah and Ras al-Khaimah, and four each for Ajman, Umm al-Qaiwain, and Fujairah), its conservative members still seized the initiative. They sponsored an amnesty on illegal immigration, and in three meetings between January and March 1979, they drafted a joint memorandum calling for full federal unification and something approaching true parliamentary democracy.

Saudi Arabia and Kuwait did their best to bring Dubai and Abu Dhabi together and helped offset the UAE's economic problems by integrating its development projects into their own development plans. It still seems likely, however, that the divisions between the ruling sheikhs would have unified almost all of the various political elements in the UAE against them if the shah's fall had not frightened Sheikh Zayid and Sheikh Rashid into reaching an agreement in early 1979. The resulting compromise expanded the role of Sheikh Rashid from that of vice-president to that of prime minister in June 1979 and gave him joint control over the government and expanded administrative authority over the civil ministries.

Sheikh Rashid then formed a cabinet in August 1979, which unified the UAE's conservatives while expelling the members who had backed moves toward parliamentary rule. He again cracked down on expatriate labor, reinforced some of the traditional Muslim social restrictions, and started a campaign of arrests, firings, and deportations designed to control the UAE's growing student unrest, radical movements, and disaffection among its native Shi'ites. The new government did, however, improve the allocation of resources directly to the poorer areas and classes of the UAE, and it acted to ease the legal problems of determining landownership. Given the small size of the organized opposition groups, and the willingness of the technocrats to give the "new" regime a chance, the sheikhs at least had a breathing spell, if little serious popular support. Nevertheless, one of the results of Britain's insistence that every member of the UAE should have a constitution and that there should be some form of popular assembly has been to give the UAE's native population a growing political consciousness, and the sheikhs increasingly rule by superior force rather than loyalty.

As is the case in Kuwait, even the so-called conservatives or Islamic purists have little real reason to maintain traditional loyalties to any of the ruling families. This is particularly true of the Al-Qasmi family in Sharjah and Ras al-Khaimah, who tend to treat Abu Dhabi and

Dubai as nouveaux riches, but who are strongly disliked by the UAE's emerging middle class and technocrats. Sheikh Saqr of Ras al-Khaimah is probably the least popular ruler in the southern Gulf. His gross mismanagement of Ras al-Khaimah's economy has left it without adequate electric power to run its air conditioners and threatened to make it a ghost town of uncompleted projects even before the drop in the UAE's oil revenues in 1982.[50] The government of Abu Dhabi has been considerably better run and maintains its own National Consultative Council.

It may be possible to deal with these pressures by more internal security crackdowns of the kind conducted in 1981 and 1982. It seems more likely, however, that the UAE's traditional rulers can survive only by bending with the wind, by giving the Federal National Council more power, and by sacrificing their own power for national unity.[51] While the political pressures that have built up within the UAE are not revolutionary, and the various Marxist and radical groups in the area are weak, it seems unlikely that the native population and the UAE's merchant elite, educators, and technocrats will long tolerate either a delay in reform or any further major divisions among the key ruling families—particularly if the ruling families cannot find a successor to the one successful traditional leader in the UAE. Sheikh Zayid Sultan al-Nuhayan of Abu Dhabi has won considerable respect for his support of unification, his willingness to use Abu Dhabi's oil wealth to meet the nation's overall economic needs, and his tolerance of limited amounts of reform. While Sheikh Zayid is not old, he is reported to be ill and his sons and close relatives do not have his popularity or seem to share his competence. In fact, several of his sons are widely regarded as unfit to rule.

Territorial and Economic Divisions

Regardless of the pace of reform, the UAE will need time to make a peaceful transition to the point at which it can survive without a strong traditional figure. It is unclear who this figure will be. Neither Sheikh Rashid nor his family seems capable of assuming the role, and none of the lesser sheikhs could now hope to claim such a position. Stable leadership in Abu Dhabi and Dubai is also important because of the continued feuding between the emirates.

All of the states except Abu Dhabi and Umm al-Qaiwain have noncontiguous enclaves, and although about two-thirds of the resulting border controversies have been resolved, nearly a dozen remain. One such dispute between Fujairah and Sharjah led to tribal battles that killed 20–35 people in May 1972. Sharjah and Fujairah established a commission on disputes in 1980, but frictions continue. Border conflicts between Dubai and Sharjah threatened to lead to fighting in August 1976. Other "settled" disputes involved long-standing conflicts over oil. For example, Sharjah successfully seized an oil area from Umm al-

Qaiwain in 1971, and Umm al-Qaiwain now has only a third share in the field after Sharjah and Iran.

These feuds have been further compounded by sharp internal competition over roads, ports (Sharjah has deliberately designed its port at Khor Fakkan to try to divert trade from Dubai), and industrial facilities. Both Abu Dhabi and Sharjah are still actively competing with Dubai. Abu Dhabi has already acquired status as the capital, and it will be the first state to benefit from the new highway links to Europe. It is planning to use this fact to take commercial markets away from Dubai. Similarly, Sharjah is hoping that its new port at Khor Fakkan on the Gulf of Oman will lead ships to avoid transit through the straits and use it instead of Dubai. At a more traditional level, there is still substantial gun-running and backing of opposition movements of rival members of the ruling family among the various emirates.[52]

The Impact of Economic Problems

The reduction in oil revenues in 1982 brought an end to the economic boom in the UAE that seemed likely to continue through the mid-1980s. Overall GDP growth slowed from 34% annually in 1979 and 1980 to 8% in 1981, and nonoil growth seems likely to drop to about 1.7% in 1982. Oil production slipped from 1.7 MMBD in 1980 to about 1 MMBD in 1982 and 1983, with Abu Dhabi producing 700,000 BPD, Dubai producing 325,000 BPD, and Sharjah only 7 BPD. The UAE's oil revenues, which reached $19.3 billion in 1980, may drop as low as $11.8 billion in 1983. This does not mean that the UAE is likely to face a cash "squeeze." The shah's fall and the resulting rise in oil prices gave the UAE a sudden $6 billion increase in oil revenues in 1980 (for a total of $18.5 billion), at a time when the UAE had had to retrench to cope with a major overheating of its economy in 1977 and 1978 and had learned to place some limits on its spending. While the UAE did overspend some of its new income, it also built up substantial cash and investment reserves. Its surplus on account reached $11 billion in 1981, and its balance-of-payments surplus exceeded $5.6 billion. It earned nearly $17 billion in oil revenues in 1982, in spite of declining demand. These earnings give the UAE a substantial economic cushion for the future.[53]

Nevertheless, the UAE had serious problems even before the cut in oil income. It regularized the federal budget only in March 1980, when Sheikh Rashid and Sheikh Zayid agreed to put half their oil revenues into the national treasury. A central bank was not created until December 1980, and the UAE did not have any economic development plan until the Council of Ministers approved the First Five Year Plan (1981–1986) in early 1981. Even then, most states continued to operate as individual units. Ras al-Khaimah refused to participate in the plan, and a continuing effort had to be made to bail out Sharjah after disastrous mismanagement of its economy in 1980 and early 1981.

Accordingly, it is significant that the UAE had to scale down its Five Year Plan in 1982 and to reduce its 1982-1983 national budget to $6.1 billion from a 1981-1982 level of $7.1 billion. Its 1983-1984 budget will be 40% lower than its 1982-1983 budget, and the UAE had a $1.2 billion deficit in 1982-1983. It is delaying on or not paying debts to foreign customers, forcing foreign banks to reduce their presence, cutting its Central Bank assets, and tightening defense spending. The result is that total government expenditures are unlikely to rise significantly until world oil demand rises sharply.[54] This spending drop seems likely to accelerate pressures to modernize the management of the UAE's economy, to stop building economic white elephants, and to limit the private spending of its traditional rulers. It also may mean that many expatriates will become increasingly discontented and the lower-income groups will become more vulnerable to radical pressure.

The Problem of Iran

The UAE seems likely to experience increasing problems with Iran. Although only 6% of the UAE's population is Shi'ite, it is heavily concentrated (Dubai has up to 100,000 Shi'ites and a strike has shown that its port cannot function without Iranian workers), and past discrimination and ties to Iran led to early contacts with the Khomeini movement. While the UAE continued to recognize Iran, and Dubai and Umm al-Qaiwain privately established good relations, Abu Dhabi strongly opposed both Khomeini's rise to power and any radical Shi'ite influence over the UAE.[55] Thus the UAE aligned itself with Iraq at the start of the Iran-Iraq War. There were numerous news reports that Abu Dhabi was prepared to serve as a base for Iraqi fighters and ships and that several members of the UAE would back an Iraqi invasion of the Tumb and Abu Musa islands in return for the promise that the islands would be returned to Iraqi sovereignty.

Although the UAE became far less supportive of Iraq once it became clear that the latter had not won a quick victory, its support laid the same groundwork for conflict with Iran as that of Bahrain and the other Gulf states that had put too much faith in Saddam Hussein's early victory claims. Further, the UAE continued to aid Iraq—providing over $1.4 billion in aid by November 1982—and initially gave strong backing to Saudi and Omani efforts to unite the Gulf states into strong collective security initiatives through the Gulf Cooperation Council. By late 1982, the UAE position had created an increasingly dangerous situation. Dubai and the other emirates with Shi'ite minorities had to covertly pay "aid" to Iran. While Abu Dhabi kept up its payments to Iran, it had to reduce its support of collective security initiatives at the third summit meeting of the Gulf Cooperation Council in October 1982. Interestingly enough, Abu Dhabi also carried out a vulnerability study that indicated even before the oil slick crisis of mid-1983 that it would face an immediate crisis if Iran should attack its power and desalinization plants.

In short, the UAE now finds itself as threatened by the Iran-Iraq conflict as do the small southern Gulf states.[56]

Oman: Growing Competence

Oman's recent military and political history was described in Chapter 12. Oman now has a population of around 591,000 to 978,000.[57] It is developing rapidly, and it is strategically one of the most important Gulf states. It has about 212,400 square kilometers of territory, 1,384 kilometers of land boundaries, and 2,092 kilometers of coastline. Its control over the Musandam Peninsula and the main shipping channels at the Strait of Hormuz makes it critical to ensuring the free passage of Gulf oil. Oman also has a number of strategically significant air and naval facilities, principally at Salalah, Thumrait, and Masirah, which make it a key potential staging point for any U.S. over-the-horizon reinforcement of the Gulf.

The Omani Armed Forces

Within the limits imposed by their equipment and organization, Oman's 23,550-man military forces are among the best in the Gulf.[58] Their expansion is shown in Table 15.5. They have continued to have good British military advice (and de facto leadership) and have had extensive operational experience in dealing with the rebellion in southern Dhofar. They are under the command of Gen. Sir Timothy Creasy, formerly commander of UK land forces, and they still have over 200 British military advisers, a small cadre of Pakistani advisers, and several thousand Baluchi troops. About 3,700 of the 23,550 man force are foreign. Oman's forces are, however, steadily reducing the number of British and Baluchi officers, and the transition to Omani command is relatively smooth. The number of Omani officers has grown to over 500. Oman has also been able to sharply reduce its dependence on Baluchi other ranks in recent years.

Oman's military forces have been well financed. Defense expenditures are 35–45% of the Omani national budget and 25% of the GNP, and defense expenditures have grown at a rate of roughly 11% per year, and totaled $1.71 billion in 1982 and $1.78 billion in 1983. Saudi Arabia, the UAE, and several other Gulf states continue to provide financial aid. Although there have been reports of corruption among Sultan Qabus's British and other expatriate advisers, these seem to be largely Marxist propaganda. The overall British military assistance effort has been sound, honest, and well tailored to Omani needs.

The Omani army reached 19,950 men by the end of 1983, but it is still basically a light infantry force. It is composed of an armored regiment of three armored car and two tank squadrons, an independent armored car squadron, eight infantry battalions, a paratroop squadron, and one Royal Guard "brigade." Five battalions in northern and central

MAP 15—2
OMAN

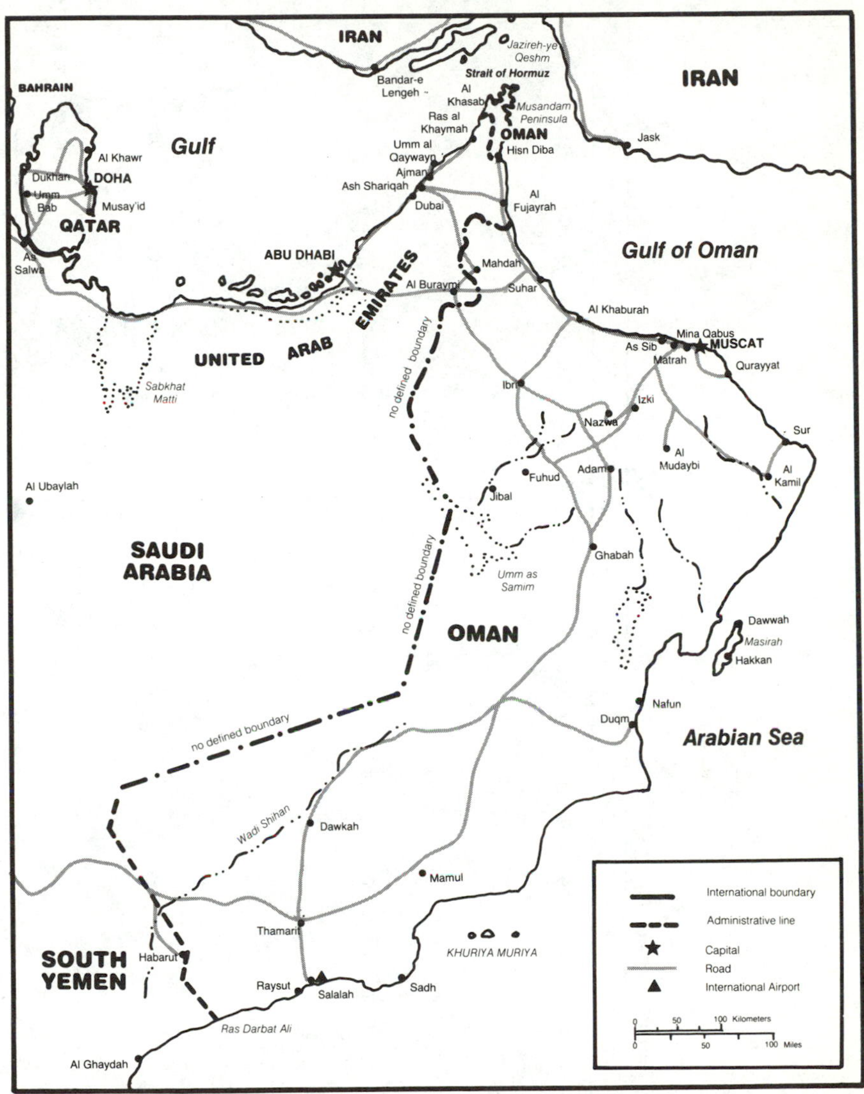

Oman are largely Omani, and the three in the south are largely Baluchi. There is also provision for operational flexibility, with two brigade headquarters. The army has an impressive array of special combat support units for so small an army. These include two light artillery regiments with 105mm guns, one medium artillery regiment with Soviet-

TABLE 15.5 The Military Buildup in Oman, 1970–1983

	1972–73	1973–74	1974–75	1975–76	1976–77	1977–78	1978–79	1979–80	1980–81	1981–82	1982–83
Total population (thousands)	750,000	71,000	740,000	760,000	790,000	806,000	837,000	870,000	930,000	930,000	948,000
Defense expenditures ($ millions)	n.a.	77.5	169	359	768	457	767	688	879	1,690	n.a.
GNP ($ millions)	n.a.	n.a.	n.a.	n.a.	n.a.	2,500	2,600	n.a.	n.a.	3,910	n.a.
DE as % of GNP	n.a.	n.a.	n.a.	n.a.	n.a.	17.9	29.5	n.a.	n.a.	43.2	n.a.
Total military manpower	6,000	9,600	9,700	14,100	14,150	13,000	19,200	19,200	14,200	14,500	18,000
Army											
Manpower	5,500	9,000	n.a.	12,900	13,200	11,800	16,200	16,200	11,500	11,500	15,000
Equipment											
Medium tanks	—	—	—	—	—	—	—	—	—	18[a]	18
Major types										Chieftain, M60A1	Chieftain, M60A1
Other AFVs	—	—	—	68	78	36	36	36	36+	36+	36+
Major types	Saladin	Saladin	Saladin	Saladin	Saladin, etc.	Saladin	Saladin	Saladin	Saladin Scorpion	Saladin V-150	Saladin V-150
Artillery	9	n.a.	n.a.	n.a.	n.a.	53	36	36	47	85	85
Field	9	75mm,5.5′	75mm,5.5′	75mm,5.5′	how.,guns mort.	105mm, etc.	105mm, etc.	105mm, etc.	105mm, etc.	105mm, etc.	105mm, etc.
SP guns	—	—	—	—	—	—	—	—	—	12	12
ATWs	—	—	—	TOW	10 TOW	10 TOW	TOW	TOW	TOW	TOW	TOW
AA weapons	—	—	—	—	—	—	—	—	4 ZU 23-2	4 ZU 23-2	4 ZU 23-2
Missiles	—	—	—	—	—	—	28 Rapier	28 Rapier	28 Rapier	—	—

TABLE 15.5 (continued)

	1972–73	1973–74	1974–75	1975–76	1976–77	1977–78	1978–79	1979–80	1980–81	1981–82	1982–83
Navy											
Manpower	200	200	200	200	400	450	900	900	900	1,000	1,000
Total craft	1+	5	7	6	9	12	18	18	19	15	15
Patrol	1	2	4	4	6	7	14	13	13	9	9
Minesweepers	—	—	—	2	—	—	—	—	—	—	—
Landing craft	—	—	—	—	3	4	3	3	5	5	5
Other	Armd dhows	3 Armd dhows	3 Armd dhows	—	—	1 trg.	1 trg.	2-log, trg.	1 log, 5 pt	1 log	1 log.
Air Force											
Manpower	300	400	500	1,000	550	750	2,100	2,100	1,800	2,000	2,000
Total combat aircraft	15	12	12	47	44	36	32	35	38	38	37
Fighters	6	—	—	—	—	—	—	—	—	—	—
Major types	T-52 trs.										
Fighter-bombers	9	12	12	47	44	36	32	35	38	38	37
Major types	BAC-167	BAC-167	BAC-167	Hunter, BAC-167	Hunter, BAC-167	Hunter, Jaguar	Hunter, Jaguar	Hunter, Jaguar	Hunter, BAC	Hunter, Jaguar	Hunter, Jaguar
Transports	11	16	18	31	30	28	16	30	29	29	32
Major types	Skyvan	Skyvan	Skyvan	Skyvan	Skyvan	Skyvan	Skyvan	Skyvan	Skyvan	Skyvan	Skyvan
Helicopters	12	12[b]	14[b]	22	22	29	27	26	24	27	26
Major types	AB-205	AB-205	AB-205	AB-205	AB-205	AB-205	AB-205	AB-205	AB-205	AB-205	AB-205
Other										28 Rapier	28 Rapier
Paramilitary	—	2,000	2,000	2,000	2,000	3,000	3,300	3,300	3,300	3,300	3,300
Home Guard (Firqats)	—	1,000	1,000	1,000	2,000	3,000	4 aircrft	5 aircrft	5 aircrft	7 aircrft	7 aircrft
Gendarmerie		900	1,000	1,000			6 Hlcptrs	6 Hlcptrs	6 Hlcptrs	8 Hlcptrs 5 patrol boats	8 Hlcptrs 11 patrol boats

[a]12 Chieftains on lease from Britain.

[b]3 on loan (Iran).

[c]Gendarmerie not listed after 1975–76. Paramilitary forces include Firgats, Police Marine Wing, and "Air Wing" in 1982–83 edition of *The Military Balance*.

Source: The Military Balance (London: IISS, various years).

built D-22 130mm guns supplied by Egypt, a signals regiment, one special force unit, and an engineer and a paratroop squadron. Units are ethnically segregated, personal amenities are good, and morale is high. There is a 3,500-to-5,000-man home guard or *firqat* force in Dhofar, which now has two regular companies and a third forming. Two of the eight Omani infantry battalions regularly rotate from the Northern Command to the Southern Brigade in Dhofar, and there is local rotation of the 50-to-150-man *firqat* units. All Iranian troops have left.

Oman is also forming a locally recruited, company-strength Musandam Security Force, a Coastal Security Force for the east coast, and a Western Border Security Force. There is an air defense regiment in the making, as well as the first women's army corps in any Arab state in the Gulf. A gendarmerie exists, nominally as a battalion, although it is locally employed and has never been consolidated.

The armored regiment's equipment consists of 6 M-60A1s and 12 Chieftain tanks in two main battle tank squadrons, and three armored recce squadrons with 36 Saladin armored cars, which are now being replaced with Scorpion light tanks. The army has a total of 36 light 105mm guns and 12 130mm medium guns, 12 155mm self-propelled howitzers, and 81mm, 4.2 inch and 720mm mortars. Oman is now gradually retiring its 25 World War II–vintage British 25-pounders. It is improving its antitank capability by acquiring U.S. TOW ATGWs and will replace its older Soviet ZU-23-2 twin 23mm AA SP guns with U.S. antiaircraft weapons. It has 15 Chieftain tanks and Palmaria 155mm self-propelled howitzers on order, and is now taking delivery on 200 Steyr cross-country vehicles, 30,000 Steyr AUG 5.56mm assault rifles, and Pilkington night-vision devices.

While the Sultan of Oman Land Forces (SOLF) possess little offensive capability against the armored forces of South Yemen, it has enough antitank armament to be adequate in a defensive role, and it is steadily improving its offensive, maneuver, and firepower capabilities. The British have concentrated on training the SOLF in military roles in which it can become effective relatively quickly and have given it considerable competence in dealing with guerrilla and light infantry forces. British officers and NCOs also assist Omani forces in most actions against the small remnants of the Dhofar rebels, and some elements of the SAS are still in the country.

It is less clear that Oman's army can adapt to heavy weapons and armor. It still lacks the educated and technical manpower to operate large numbers of sophisticated systems. However, the service school near Muscat is now turning out reasonably proficient Omani NCOs and officers, and they are steadily replacing expatriates in leadership positions. This process of Omanization is reflected in Table 15.6, which shows the now dominant role of Omanis in the army. The first 60 Omani officer cadets will complete training in early 1982, and 14 Omani officers are now studying in overseas staff colleges.

TABLE 15.6 Manning of the Omani Army and Air Force, 1982

Army

	Total Strength		
	Officers	Other Ranks	Total
Omani	389	8,816	9,205
Baluchi	68	3,794	3,862
Firqat	75	3,616	3,691
Total	532	16,226	16,758

	Foreign Advisers			
	Officers		Other Ranks	
	Seconded	Contract	Seconded	Contract
British	32	130	67	111
Jordanian	5	1	16	3
Egyptian (transport)	4	–	4	–
Pakistani (logistics)	3	16	1	1,041
Indian (medical)	29	25	5	98
Sri Lankan	–	1	–	35
Other	–	3	–	4

Air Force

	Officers	NCOs/Airmen
Omani	150	1,500
British	200	100
Others	–	300
Total	350	1,900

Source: Government of Oman.

The sultan has ambitious plans to equip the army with additional armor, artillery, long-range antitank weapons, and helicopters, although Oman's effort to obtain increased military assistance from the U.S. is leading it to reevaluate its army modernization plans. It originally planned to buy 37–49 Chieftain medium tanks and 4 armored recovery vehicles, all up-engined with Condor 12V800 engines. It also planned to buy additional British Scorpion light tanks and Stormer APCs. These plans are now being reconsidered in the light of possible conversion to U.S. equipment, and its seems likely that Oman will add only 12–15 more Chieftains with the regular L-60 engine to the 12 it has already obtained from British war reserves.[59] This number seems adequate for a defensive force whose only immediate threat is South Yemen. The terrain and logistic factors in the border area severely limit the amount of armor that South Yemen can deploy, and Oman has a definite edge in the quality of its other forces. While the army may not modernize at the rate Sultan Qabus desires, it should steadily improve in quality during the 1980s.

The Sultan of Oman's 2,250-man Air Force (SOAF) was first formed in 1959 and flew its first combat aircraft in 1964 and its first jet fighters and helicopters in 1969. It now operates roughly 100 aircraft and is building up to a strength of 3,000 men. With extensive aid from Britain, the SOAF has evolved into a small, efficient air force, developed around the ground attack mission. As Table 15.6 shows, it has a good cadre of British officers and pilots, many of whom have been replaced by Omanis. Roughly one-third of Oman's fighters have Omani pilots and 30 are in training; the training of Omani helicopter pilots has proceeded more slowly.

The SOAF is organized into two fighter/ground attack squadrons. One is a squadron of 12 Hunter FGA-6s and 4 Hunter reconnaissance/training planes at Thumrait, and one is a squadron of 7 dual-purpose Jaguar S(O) Mk 1s, plus 2 Jaguar trainers. The Jaguars have laser range-finders and 30mm cannon and carry a normal payload of 8 British-made 600-1b cluster bombs. Laser-guided bombs are on order. The Jaguars are based in Thumrait. As a result of somewhat controversial purchases in 1981, Oman will acquire 12 more Jaguars, which will be based at Masirah. This purchase led to charges that the sultan's British advisers were buying sophisticated aircraft that Oman did not need as a favor to Britain, and for commissions. These charges seem false. The Jaguar is well suited to attack missions in the area and is a good aircraft for a transition to more sophisticated types in the middle and late 1980s.

There is also a COIN/training squadron with 12 BAC-167 Strike-masters and a 23-aircraft helicopter squadron, which performs transport and light support duties. They are equipped with AB-205s, Bell 214s, and Augusta Bell 214s. The SOAF has fixed-wing aircraft that can also be used in ground support roles even in Oman's rough terrain, and it makes extensive use of its Skyvans. The transport wing consists of three squadrons of largely antiquated light planes, but Oman has a Saudi Air Force C-130 on loan, has bought three C-130s, and is buying one more C-130 and two DHC-5D transports.

A new air defense wing, with two squadrons of 28 Rapier surface-to-air missiles and 28 Blindfire radars, is being integrated with the Jaguars in the air defense role. Oman is acquiring 250 AIM-9 air-to-air missiles and will provide a limited protective air umbrella by the mid-1980s. One Rapier squadron is deployed at Thumrait and another at Salalah, and they can be rapidly redeployed to Seeb or Masirah. They are now day-only defense systems, but the Blindfire radars will provide the Rapier with all-weather capability. Air defense radars are located at Seeb and Thumrait; an additional one became operational in Masirah in 1982. Oman has a troposcatter communications system to link its forces in spite of its mountain barriers, and is buying Racal Jaguar frequency-hopping radios and ECM gear for all its services.

The air force is now deployed at civilian military bases at Seeb and Salalah and at military bases at Masirah and Thumrait. Thumrait is the main strike base, Salalah is the main transport and army support base, Seeb is a logistic and transport base, and Masirah is being built up as a training and second-strike base. The air base at Thumrait is sheltered and hardened, and the other bases will be sheltered by the mid-1980s. There are 15 other light air strips in Oman. The air strips in the Musandam Peninsula are best suited for helicopters and light transports, but a military base is being built up at Khasab.

A further expansion and upgrading of the air force is planned, and Oman has been trying to persuade Saudi Arabia to pay for an order of Tornado multirole fighters, but Oman lacks the trained indigenous personnel for rapid expansion. An air force technical school has been established, but it will not provide the required cadres until after the mid-1980s. While the Omani Air Force still depends on contract pilots, and sometimes seems more an extension of the RAF than truly Omani, it is well balanced and should eventually change to fully Omani command.

The SOAF would now face serious problems if it had to deal with a large-scale Iranian air or naval attack, and it has no real maritime surveillance or reconnaissance capability, although at least two U.S. P-3 Orion maritime patrol aircraft are kept on station at Saab or Masirah and the purchase of such aircraft is now under study in the navy. The air force does, however, have a considerable capability to deal with internal security threats and probably could deal with any air attacks from South Yemen. This situation may change over the next few years because Yemeni air strength is expanding much faster than that of Oman, and South Yemen is building new military bases near the border. Oman's Jaguar fighters are not superior to the MiG-23-B-1 or MiG-21N in air-to-air combat capability, and Yemen could easily use pilots who were Soviet-bloc "volunteers." Oman could, however, equip its Jaguars with AIM-9Ls, which would probably give them air superiority over South Yemen in any limited conflict.

The Sultan of Oman's Navy was formed in 1975. It is a light patrol force that can barely cover Oman's long coastline against terrorist infiltration or arms smuggling and that has limited ability to deal with more serious threats. It now has about 2,000 men and consists of 2 former Dutch Wildervank minesweepers, a converted royal yacht with a 40mm gun, 2 Brooke Marine MM-38 37-meter patrol boats with two MM-38 Exocet missile launchers, a Province fast attack craft with two triple launcher MM-40 Exocet missile units, four Brooks Marine craft with Otto Melara 76mm guns, four Vosper-Thorneycroft inshore patrol boats with 20mm guns, 5 LCUs, and a light logistic support ship (LSL),

MAP 15—3
THE STRAIT OF HORMUZ

Adapted from CIA 625450 7-79

based at Khor Muscat. The LSL can carry tanks and 200 troops. The navy also has two more 56-meter Province patrol craft with Exocet and 76mm Otto Melara guns, four 25-meter patrol craft, 3 Skima-12 Hovercraft, and a landing craft medium (LCM) on order. These orders will give Oman at least a limited capability to defend the Strait of Hormuz against Iranian forces.

The Omani Navy is well trained and organized by Gulf standards. It performed well during 1977, when Ras al-Khaimah attempted to install an oil rig in Omani waters.[60] It also showed reasonable proficiency in expanding its patrols during late 1980, when tension in the Gulf heightened after Iranian threats to close the Gulf at Hormuz. The Omani Navy also confronted the Iranian Navy in September 1980, when three Iranian frigates based at Bandar Abbas entered Omani waters above the Qu'oin Islands. Omani patrol boats based at Goat Island, just north of the Musandam Peninsula, faced down the frigates at a range of 3 NM, and the Iranians left. Iran has threatened the strait only once since this time, when an Iranian Navy vessel deliberately violated Oman's traffic scheme in the strait in early 1982, but Iranian P-2Cs regularly fly over the area, and Iranian ships still sometimes enter Omani waters.

The Omani Navy needs to expand, and it can justify its current orders for additional ships, but it faces problems. Most Omani ships have Omani captains, but the oldest Omani officer was 30 years old in 1982. Most of Oman's petty officers were in their 20s; the average age in other navies was 35 to 40. While extensive training is under way, it is unclear how quickly the navy can grow from a late 1981 strength of 1,500 men, with 60 Omani officers, to a goal of 3,000. Further, Oman's current ships are too small to operate in the monsoon, and Oman's main base at Khor Muscat cannot be used when the *shamal* winds blow from the south. Its base at Goat Island is still being expanded, and main bases at Masirah and in the south are still in the planning stage.

Unlike most Gulf navies, the Omani Navy has a clear mission. It faces a serious threat from the Iranian Navy, and it has had to check infiltration by the Dhofar rebels and South Yemen along a 2,092-kilometer coast. It must police the passage of 50–60 ships a day through the Strait of Hormuz (1,462–1,585 ships per month in 1980 and 1,422–1,919 in 1981). Roughly 25% of the world's tanker traffic will pass through the strait when the world's economy recovers, and the navy patrols the tankers waiting in the Gulf of Oman. This task has led it to take on a far more serious character than the other conservative Gulf states' navies, and it may well be able to make its expanded forces effective.

Internal Security

The internal security situation in Oman is complex and difficult to evaluate. The Dhofar rebels had been suppressed long before the Oman–South Yemen peace agreement of November 1982. Their last significant military act was to shoot down a few SOAF aircraft with SA-7 missiles in 1975, and there have been only two minor incidents since 1979. The regular armed forces and tribal internal security forces do an excellent job of controlling both the urban and tribal areas. They have good British contract advisers, and they now seem to have more trouble in dealing with PDRY and PFLO deserters and refugees from South Yemen than with the Dhofar rebels. Even the PFLO "radio" was a front operated by Radio Aden before its broadcasts stopped following the peace agreement. The rebel forces outside Oman would now be little more than a token threat even if South Yemen broke the peace agreement. They consist of a small camp in South Yemen near Dhofar with fewer than 500 men. The camp's training facilities shut down in 1977 because of a lack of recruits, and the regional chairman of the PFLO now works as a used car salesman.

Omani forces did find South Yemeni forces and oil survey teams 7–10 kilometers within Omani boundaries near Shahar in March 1981 and exchanged fire with their PDRY escorts before they withdrew. These incidents were repeated in April and November 1981, although none were serious. In fact, Oman has had more serious internal security problems with its *firqat*, or Home Guard forces, which have tended to feud and occasionally have abused their authority. The regular Omani police and internal security forces are not overrepressive, however, and do not seem to have any covert elements hostile to the sultan. They also are relatively well equipped, especially in the case of the Police Marine Wing, which has absorbed much of its equipment from the regular services.

The internal economic situation is somewhat different. Oman had little industrial development before 1976 because of its long series of civil wars. Peace then led to a spurt of poorly managed economic development plans in 1977–1978 and even more poorly managed overspending and overborrowing using short-term credits. These problems have since been brought under control, however, and economic growth is now proceeding fairly smoothly. Oman issued a new five-year development plan in 1980, which is still one of the best in the Gulf, and Oman's recent economic development activities have been sound, although some cutbacks had to be made in 1982 and 1983 because of the fall in oil revenues.[61] Most of Oman's population does, however, still work at near-subsistence occupations in agriculture and fishing, in low-paying service jobs in urban areas, or outside Oman. Its educated middle class is growing rapidly and is creating a significant force of entrepreneurs, merchants, and civil servants, which has a considerable capability to assist the government and to survive in a modern economy.

Sultan Qabus has also done a good job of balancing tribal elements and regional economic development since 1979, and he has deliberately structured his immigration policy so that most expatriate labor is non-Arab Asian. Only a few hundred Palestinians are allowed to live in the country and Shi'ite elements are small. Thus, although according to CIA estimates about 50% of Oman's 300,000-man work force is expatriate, expatriate workers do not represent as much of a threat as in many other Gulf states, and the internal security forces keep reasonably good control of work permits and immigration, although they have sometimes proved subject to bribery.

There has been some Omani resentment of the better-paid foreign elements in the country, which reached its peak around 1978 because of corruption or profiteering by a few foreign advisers and officials. The foreign advisers around the sultan have been given the title of the "Muscat Mafia" by various opposition groups and are a potential source of conflict between him and the people. The role of the sultan's British advisers has been a particular issue. Various British and Lebanese journalists have reported that the younger and better-educated Omanis feel the sultan's British advisers profited personally from helping British firms get military contracts the nation did not need. One must be leery of such reports. Many of these same sources have attacked every pro-Western element in the Gulf.[62] Defense is now consuming much less of the nation's wealth, however, and Oman's purchases of electronic equipment, aircraft, tanks, and ships seem fully justified in view of the rise of the Iranian threat.

The sultan also has not been insensitive to the need to gradually eliminate Oman's dependence on Britain. Oman's ministries are increasingly being run by Omani ministers, including many former senior rebel leaders. Oman's rising middle class and technocrats have also replaced the armed forces as the major modern element in Omani society, and the sultan's 45-member Consultative Council now has 11 members from the private sector and 17 from the regions.[63]

The sultan does face another potential internal security problem. Oman had 900 boys in 3 schools in 1970. It had 110,000 boys and girls in 373 schools in 1981. About 15,000 of these were in preparatory schools and 1,500 in secondary classes; Qabus University will open in 1986. This expansion of the nation's education system will inevitably create large numbers of students who have new career and political demands. Recent oil and gas discoveries indicate that Oman will not deplete its reserves, and it may be able to increase oil production from 315,000 BPD to over 370,000 BPD by the mid-1980s. In fact, Oman reached 335,000 BPD in 1982, and raised production to 360,000 BPD in early 1983. This increase is important because oil accounts for 60% of Oman's gross domestic product and 90% of its government revenues. The increase in production, recent gas discoveries, and the ability to smelt high-grade copper located near the gas wells indicate that Oman may still be able to expand its economy in the 1980s to the extent called for in its 1980–1984 Five Year Plan, provided that world oil demand recovers.[64] It remains unclear, however, that Oman is fully prepared to cope with its new class of students or to offer them adequate economic opportunities. At the same time, migration is taking place from Oman's agricultural sector into its cities. Oman has done a better job of dealing with this growth than most Gulf states, but such shifts are accelerating the decline of tribal and traditional ties.[65]

External Threats

The main threats to Oman seem likely to be external. Oman will face a steadily more serious threat from Iran if Iran continues to be the victor in the Iran-Iraq War. It seems likely that the Khomeini movement will eventually attempt to reassert the control the shah once exercised over the Strait of Hormuz, and it is at least possible that Iran may eventually revive its ancient claim to the Musandam Peninsula.

Oman will also continue to face a threat from South Yemen, in spite of the November 1982 peace agreement. Oman now has one "brigade," the South Oman Brigade, to cover the border with South Yemen. The brigade has four regular infantry battalions, one regiment of guns, a *firqat* battalion, and a desert regiment on the border near Sarfait. One battalion is near the border in the north, one is on the border near the coast, and two are up the coast.

The PDRY forces deployed against the border with Oman consist of three brigades, two regular and one militia. One regular brigade is about 15 kilometers from Sarfait, one is about 185 kilometers from Harbrout, and the militia brigade is based at Al Ghaydah. There are about 1,500 more PDRY militia in scattered positions near the border. The other nine PDRY brigades are currently deployed near the border with North Yemen. These PDRY brigades are not much of a current threat. They are generally only at 30–40% of authorized strength, and the best is manned at only 1,000 men out of an authorized total of 1,500. The PDRY's attempt to introduce conscription in 1980 did raise their strength from only 300 to 500 men, but is also led to so many desertions that Oman had to close its border to stop the influx of deserters. The PDRY does, however, have two squadrons of T-34/55/62 tanks near the Omani border and an extra squadron in the area. There were 60 tanks near the border and 160 tanks in PDRY forces in the north in late 1982. South Yemen is also building a military air base at Al Ghaydah, about 85 kilometers from the border. This will give the PDRY its first major capability to overfly Oman; the closest PDRY military air base is now at Al Mukalla (Ash Shihr), about 450 kilometers from Sarfait. South Yemen is also expanding its air facilities at Thamud on the edge of the Empty Quarter and at Hadiboh on Socotra.

Omani and British intelligence officers now feel, however, that the PDRY's strategy is to concentrate on taking control of North Yemen, and to turn on Oman only when it has reasonable control over Sana. Although they are somewhat worried that the PDRY's armor could attack a limited objective like Oman's key air base in the southern desert at Thumrait, which is only five hours' drive from the border, they feel that it would take virtually the entire PDRY army and air force to mount a direct military logistic threat to Oman. They feel that South Yemeni forces would face serious terrain problems even in attacking Thumrait and that they now lack anything approaching the professionalism of the Omani forces. Their main concern has been the improving ties among Iran, South Yemen, Syria, and Libya—all of which have vehemently attacked the sultan for his support of the U.S. They estimate that there were 5,000 Soviets in the PDRY in 1982, 25% in military functions, and 16,000 other Soviet-bloc personnel, including Cubans. They estimate that every PDRY brigade has at least four full-time Soviet advisers and that many also have Cuban and East German advisers. As a result, Oman will face both steadily improving PDRY forces and the threat of renewed radical support of the Dhofar rebels or some successor.

These factors help explain the sultan's efforts to improve his relations with Saudi Arabia and the other conservative Gulf states and to strengthen his ties to the U.S. Although Oman's loose alliance with the U.S. has led the other conservative Gulf states to protest such ties, the sultan has structured them in ways that minimize any U.S. presence on the mainland and the visibility of the limited U.S. construction and support personnel on Masirah.

The sultan has strongly backed the Gulf Cooperation Council, and Oman has led the movement toward collective security and improved internal security cooperation since the council had its first major meeting in March 1981.[66] This position has helped him improve Oman's ties to most of the conservative Gulf states. Oman cooperated with the RDF in 1981, 1982, and 1983, when no other Gulf state except Saudi Arabia would even conduct joint training exercises, but it limited these exercises and ensured that they had a low public profile.[67] Oman also has ensured that U.S. contingency facility projects in Oman in no way limit Omani sovereignty over such facilities and that they will serve Oman's immediate needs.

The U.S. is improving facilities at Masirah, Al Khasab, Thumrait, and Seeb. The facilities at Masirah include petroleum, oil, and lubricants (POL) and ammunition storage, billeting and mess, runway improvements, new power and desalinization facilities, a new water distribution system, aircraft parking and maintenance facilities, and warehousing. The U.S. will also preposition extensive stocks of supplies for air operations by the end of 1983. These improvements to Masirah will give Oman a modern air base to cover its seacoast that is outside the effective range of most Iranian and Yemeni fighters, and the tacit guarantee of over-the-horizon reinforcement from the U.S., without having sacrificed any aspect of Omani sovereignty. The improvements at Al Khasab will give Oman a base in the Musandam Peninsula near the strait and its northern naval base at Goat Island with a 4,800-foot paved strip and aircraft parking aprons. The work at Thumrait and Seeb will improve POL distribution and storage, ammunition storage, parking aprons, warehousing, power generation, and maintenance facilities. At the same time, the U.S. is quietly helping Oman improve secure communications and AC&W, is setting up secure links between Omani headquarters and the U.S. forces in the Indian Ocean, and is cooperating with the United Kingdom in helping Oman improve its maritime surveillance capability.[68]

The U.S. completed virtually all of the negotiations necessary to make such arrangements effective during 1983. Many contracts have already been let and all are scheduled to be complete by August 1985. They will cost the U.S. between $250 and $280 million and involve only six permanent and a few hundred rotational U.S. personnel. The cumulative result should be to provide a fully effective deterrent to Iran and South Yemen that Oman could not otherwise afford. This deterrent may well constrain South Yemen even if it does succeed in taking over North Yemen, and it may already have contributed to South Yemen's willingness to sign a peace agreement.

Prospects for Cooperation Among the Conservative Gulf States

Given this background, the prospects for cooperation among the conservative Gulf states seem mixed. Only Bahrain and Qatar have a recent history of significant military cooperation with Saudi Arabia, and they have the smallest military forces of all the Gulf states. Kuwait faces significant political problems with Iraq and Iran if it expands its military cooperation in ways that might limit their influence, and Kuwait's combination of poorly structured military forces and an exposed strategic position presents significant problems for Saudi reinforcement. The UAE has a poor history of internal cooperation and an only slightly better military base to build upon. It has also shown an increasing fear of irritating Iran. Oman has relatively effective forces, but it has some problems in cooperating with the UAE because of its minor conflicts with Ras al-Khaimah over offshore drilling rights and the Shihu and Habus tribal areas.

Options for Strengthening Military Cooperation

There are technical as well as political barriers to improved cooperation. The previous discussion of each country's military equipment orders shows that there is little movement toward standardization or interoperability. Further, any attempt to rationalize and standardize the military buildup of the conservative Gulf states will complicate the problems created by their different equipment mixes, manpower problems, and internal divisions. At least in the short term, they will have serious difficulties in using what they already have on order, much less converting to the additional types necessary to standardize or achieve interoperability. Their armies have different force mixes, training patterns, and equipment, which will make it difficult for them to cooperate under most combat conditions and will prevent their deployment as effective forces in any area away from their main bases. While such problems would be far less severe in providing internal security support to a neighboring country, they make it extremely difficult for one Gulf army to cross-reinforce another against any significant external military threat.

The conservative Gulf navies lack the sensors, communication systems, electronic warfare (EW) capability, and on-board weapons to cooperate effectively in anything other than light patrol activities. The Gulf navies should ideally be able to act jointly in securing a given nation's coast against guerrilla incursions and gun-running, and to secure critical offshore oil facilities, but the Gulf Cooperation Council began to study this issue only in late 1981. In fact, aside from Oman and Saudi Arabia, most Gulf navies seem to lack any strategic or tactical rationale even in purely national terms. The thrust behind their modernization is more a matter of buying the largest and most capable ships a given country's former Coast Guard can credibly absorb than a result of serious study of the military or internal security missions such forces will have to perform. Further, the manpower and training problems in the conservative Gulf states' navies are more severe than those in most Gulf armies and seem likely to remain so through the end of the 1980s.

At the same time, the difficulties in improving land force and naval cooperation should not be exaggerated. The problems in the Gulf armies and navies can be corrected over a period of years by cooperative training, standardization or interoperability in key munitions and equipment, improved and standardized communications, and organization along more compatible lines. Short-term problems can be minimized by creating specialized internal security and counterinsurgency units and airmobile forces that can deal with the kind of limited threats that now seem to be the most probable contingencies Gulf forces will face. It should be possible to standardize relatively rapidly in such key areas as oil field defense.

The near-term problems in improving air force cooperation should also be less severe than those for naval and land forces. It is true that the forces of each state now differ so sharply in training, relative air combat capability, communications and IFF systems, and basing that they would find it difficult to cooperate effectively. It is possible to provide joint training for the conservative Gulf states' air forces far more quickly than for land and naval forces, however, and the incompatibilities and inadequacies in current and planned C^3I systems can be overcome. Most can be eliminated with comparative ease over the next few years. While it may be a decade before the individual air forces can fully cross-service each other, they can already cross-disperse, arm, and fuel each other's aircraft. Saudi Arabia and Oman will also be able to cross-shelter friendly fighters by the mid-1980s.

The real issue, therefore, is the will to cooperate and to provide at least the common air battle management capability and the joint training necessary to allow the Gulf air forces to fight as a common unit. The smaller Gulf air forces are even more dependent on an AWACS-type sensor and effective C^3I links than is Saudi Arabia's. All of the Saudi problems discussed in Chapters 7 and 9 are increased when a nation has only one real air base or exceedingly limited numbers of modern air defense fighters, if any. No smaller conservative Gulf nation can hope to provide a credible radar coverage of its oil facilities or other critical targets without some form of AWACS. All will require an AWACS to provide C^3I links to their fighters, land-based command centers and air defenses, and links to their neighbors to make up for their limited numbers of fighters. Without such links, Iran, Soviet long-range aviation, or even the Yemeni and Iraqi forces of the late 1980s may be able to attack the smaller conservative states at will.

The smaller conservative Gulf states' air forces also need air training facilities that no single state can afford. While the widespread use of advanced simulators of the type the U.S. has already provided to Saudi Arabia could help to increase proficiency levels, the smaller Gulf states will need the kind of large-scale facilities that will allow them to fly regularly against the equivalent of an "aggressor squadron," and they must conduct air combat training under conditions that allow telemetry and computerized analysis to diagnose the mistakes of individual pilots to reduce the risk of training losses. They need greatly improved and tactically realistic attack training facilities, which again use modern automation to substitute for the lack of training experience and proficieny. Fortunately, the core of such facilities already exists at or near Dhahran Air Force Base in Saudi Arabia, although Saudi low-altitude air combat and attack mission training facilities and doctrine are still inadequate. As was discussed in Chapter 9, the Gulf air forces could build on such facilities to create a much more effective force by the mid-1980s.

The same is true of land-based air defenses. Saudi Arabia, Qatar, and Kuwait—and possibly Bahrain and the UAE—are procuring or considering the procurement of Improved Hawk surface-to-air missiles. There will also be a rough "standardization" on shorter-range systems with similar characteristics, like the Rapier, the RBS-70, Crotale, and Shahine surface-to-air missiles. If all the conservative Gulf nations buy Improved Hawks and compatible C^3I links for their AA guns and missiles, and then standardize on the improved Rapier or Shahine, they could use readily available data links and IFF systems to develop a credible collective deterrent against local threats without sacrificing their sovereignty and could simultaneously increase the credibility of over-the-horizon reinforcement from the U.S. without making any formal arrangements or agreements with the U.S.

Most conservative Gulf states will have to acquire new fighter aircraft during the middle to late 1980s or are already planning to do so. Virtually all of these aircraft will be from U.S. or European manufacturers, and most will have advanced enough avionics and munitions-carrying capabilities, or sufficient upgrade capacity, to allow them to operate far more effectively in cooperation with the Saudi Air Force and AWACS than existing combat aircraft. In most cases, it should also be possible to tailor such aircraft orders to select the avionics, on-board computers and software, IFF and EW systems, air armament, and refueling and outboard tank compatibility on Gulf aircraft to sharply improve their ability to operate as a unified air screen.

The smaller Gulf navies' boats and ships are not equipped with effective air defenses and compatible communications and sensors, but the maritime mode on the AWACS could remove many of these limitations and help in conducting joint fleet operations. So could the purchase of a "Gulf Force" of maritime patrol aircraft like the P-2C, the Nimrod, or Atlantique; or of a "mini-AWACS" with maritime patrol capabilities like those under development by Ferranti and Lockheed. Common training, standardization of on-board communications, and common planning could further increase the effectiveness of these navies in defending key oil facilities and in performing internal security missions by the mid-1980s. It should also be possible to change current naval modernization plans to further standardize on weaponry, sensors, and communications while taking advantage of the maritime reconnaissance and tracking capabilities of the AWACS.

The problem of cooperation is also reduced by the relatively limited military effectiveness of potential local threats. Many of the weaknesses in the forces of the smaller Gulf states will be important only if these forces can be decoupled from those of their neighbors and from the possibility of reinforcement from the U.S. As is discussed in Chapters 13, 14, and 17, Iran, Iraq, the Yemens, and Ethiopia have serious military weaknesses of their own. It will take time for Iran and Iraq to rebuild their forces after the massive losses they are now taking and for their economies to recover from the damage each country has done to the other. Thus both Iran and Iraq might well be unwilling to risk attacks on any conservative Gulf state if they felt such a state would receive timely support from its neighbors.

Passive Defense and Improved Internal Security

The Gulf states can do much over the next five years to reduce their vulnerability by cooperating on passive defense measures. These could include (1) improving the netting and redundancy of pipelines and port facilities to reduce the impact of the destruction of one key facility; (2) standardizing new oil field equipment to allow prestocking of key parts and training and planning for joint repair efforts; (3) standardizing new petrochemical plants in the same manner; (4) creating strategic pipelines to the coast of Oman, the Red Sea, and through Turkey and Jordan; (5) netting gas systems and water treatment plants; (6) netting electric power to allow wheeling if a key plant is lost; (7) instituting joint vulnerability studies and follow-on efforts to harden and disperse key equipment; and (8) developing compatible security measures.

Internal security can also be enhanced by passive defense. For example, the Gulf states are already beginning to computer-code visa stamps and identity cards. This system could be used to allow Gulf-wide detection of a security problem and create a central Gulf-wide identity card system to control expatriate labor. It might even be cost effective to create central equipment depots to preposition ships with critical equipment and to create a joint capability to rapidly rig single-point moorings to provide emergency tanker loading facilities.

Such options offer the conservative Gulf states an incentive for improving their efforts at collective security. They are, in fact, the only means through which any of the smaller conservative Gulf states—with the possible exception of Oman—can hope to make their military forces effective and develop strong enough internal security capabilities to overcome the pressures that threaten to tear them apart. No other course of action can compensate the conservative Gulf states for the loss of Iran as a strategic shield and its transformation into a long-term potential threat.

The Will to Cooperate

More generally, cooperation is the only way the southern Gulf states can cope with the forces of change, the dynamics of the military buildup, and the threats in the region. The various forces that now shape the trends in the military balance in the Gulf cannot be dealt with in the piecemeal way that the conservative Gulf states formerly attempted. Most cannot cope with the expenditure levels required, and none can cope with the mix of manpower problems inevitable in trying to create and maintain a modern military force structure that can deal with the kind of threat that Iran and Iraq will pose in the future.

The incentives and options for cooperation do exist. The issue is one of will, particularly one of whether the Gulf's conservative leaders can understand and react to the forces at work. While most of the Gulf's princes and sheikhs have had to become superb politicians to survive within their traditional framework, they have been conditioned to compete within the rules of a previous era. Most are only beginning to understand the broad forces outlined in Chapter 13 and the problems inherent in the kind of military forces they are trying to create.

Yet the rulers of the conservative Gulf states have shown since 1979 that they do understand the threat posed by the shah's overthrow, the prolonged low-level civil war in Iran, the Iran-Iraq War, and the Soviet invasion of Afghanistan. They have shown that they understand that the Iran-Iraq War has set the precedent of using air and sea power against critical oil and economic facilities and that regardless of how friendly Iraq may be in the short run, its instability and emergence as the dominant military power in the Gulf require some kind of military counterbalance. Admittedly, the rhetoric of Gulf cooperation has often been far stronger than the reality. Even so, the chronology of cooperation shown in Table 15.7 shows not only a steady increase in cooperation in the face of external threats, but an ability to overcome past jealousies and rivalries. It also shows that the formation of the Gulf Cooperation Council has led to growing military cooperation in spite of pressure from nations like Iran, and this history has been supported by cooperation in a number of economic projects. Important symbols of joint economic cooperation include the following:

- The Gulf Aluminium Rolling Mill Company (GARMCO). Six Arab Gulf states—including Iraq, but with the noticeable absence of the UAE—signed a joint venture agreement on 10 February 1981.
- Proposals for a fourth oil refinery to be built at Yanbu using funds from several Gulf countries.
- The Saudi-Kuwait and Saudi-Bahrain Cement companies. The latter now has an installed capacity of 1,500 tons a day, following tests on the first kiln in 1981.
- The Aluminium Bahrain (ALBA) plant, in which the Saudi Arabian Basic Industries Corporation (SABIC) took a 20% stake rather than develop its own capacity in Jubail and which is considering further capacity expansion.
- The Sitra methanol-ammonia project in Bahrain, which has as shareholders the Bahrain National Oil Company (BANOCO), Kuwait's Petrochemical Industries Corporation (PIC), and SABIC.
- The Arab Iron and Steel Company (AISC), which is also to be sited in Bahrain and which will feed iron pellets to the various steel plants around the Gulf.
- The agreement reached between Bahrain and the Saudi state oil agency, Petromin. Under the arrangement, Petromin will sell 100,000 BPD of crude direct to the Bahrain Petroleum Company, which by nationalizing its refinery has forfeited secure supplies of ARAMCO crude stemming from the 60% share in the refinery held by SOCAL and Texaco.
- The Gulf International Bank (GIB), with transnational ownership.
- The Iran-Iraq War Insurance Risks Syndicate, the Arab Reinsurance Group (ARIG), and the numerous banks that have set up overseas banking units (OBUs) in Bahrain to serve the Saudi market.
- The planned university for all the GCC states in Bahrain. The institution will have a bias toward vocational training in specialized areas for which there would not be sufficient demand to establish such training in a single country.
- Ras al-Khaimah is the focus of regional interlinking in the health field, with a pharmaceutical factory endorsed by the health ministers as a pan-Gulf industry.
- Various specialized schools in television technology that were established along the Gulf to avoid duplication and the Gulf News Agency (GNA), Gulf Air, and the Arab Air Carriers Organization (AACO).
- The United Arab Shipping Company (UASC) (jointly owned by Iraq, Saudi Arabia, Kuwait, Qatar, Bahrain, and the UAE), which has announced plans to buy six further container ships.

The Gulf Cooperation Council

The key to whether the conservative Gulf states can create a fully effective strategic partnership is the Gulf Cooperation Council, and it

TABLE 15.7 Chronology of Movements Toward Cooperation by the Conservative Gulf States

1973–1974	Gulf foreign ministers hold discussions on creating a single political and economic plan for the Arab Gulf states.
March 1973	Gulf Air is established, to be owned jointly by Bahrain, Oman, Qatar, and the UAE.
April 1974	The shah of Iran seeks a collective security agreement excluding all the superpowers and Iraq. Saudi Arabia rejects the shah's call for a Gulf military cooperation agreement, but Defense Minister Sultan calls for security arrangements within the "Arab nation."
March 1975	The Algiers Accord between Iran and Iraq is signed.
April 1975	Free trade agreement is signed between Bahrain and Saudi Arabia.
May 1975	Kuwait signs separate bilateral agreements with Bahrain, Qatar, and the UAE to unify import policies relating to foodstuffs.
May 1975	Saudi Arabia joins Kuwait, the UAE, and Qatar in contributing $1 billion to the Arab Industries Organization, designed to manufacture armaments within the Arab world. While the effort proves abortive because of tensions with Egypt over Camp David, it represents a major first step in military cooperation.
June 1975	As part of complex negotiations within the Gulf to persuade all Gulf nations to exclude superpower forces, Saudi Arabia conducts joint military maneuvers with the Bahrain Defense Force, steadily strengthening Bahraini-Saudi military ties.
Mid-July 1975	At a meeting of the Gulf foreign ministers in Jiddah, all ministers agree to exclude superpower forces and to deny the superpowers bases.
August–September 1975	Internal crisis in Bahrain leads Sheikh Issa bin Sulman al Khalifa to suspend National Assembly. Saudis provide extensive tacit security support. Bahrain notifies the U.S. it must withdraw from its naval facility by mid-1977.
March 1976	King Khalid of Saudi Arabia visits Kuwait, Bahrain, UAE, Qatar, and Oman seeking a conservative Gulf defense cooperation effort. Little progress is made because of Oman's dependence on the shah's forces in Dhofar and resulting pressures from Iran on the other Gulf states.
May 1976	The United Arab Shipping Company (UASC) is established; shareholders are Bahrain, Iraq, Kuwait, Qatar, Saudi Arabia, and the UAE.
June 1976	Formation of Saudi-Kuwait Cement Company is agreed on, under the aegis of the Saudi-Kuwait Joint Industrial Committee.
October 1976	The Gulf Ports Union is formed with the participation of all seven Arab Gulf states.
October 1976	Saudi Interior Minister, Prince Naif, tours the conservative Gulf states and quietly establishes joint internal security and intelligence "council" and cooperative agreement. This agreement steadily strengthens over the next few years.
November 1976	Following the Algiers accord, Iran and Iraq jointly argue at the Gulf foreign ministers' meeting for a collective security agreement involving all Gulf states. The conservative Gulf states again decline.
November 1976	The six conservative Gulf states plus Iraq form the Gulf Organization for Industrial Consultancy (GOIC). Its purposes include cooperation and coordination among the member countries, especially in chemical and petrochemical, basic metal, and other industrial projects.
November 1976	The Gulf International Bank is established with the same shareholders as UASC.
February 1977	The Gulf Organization for Industrial Consulting is set up in Doha, with the sponsorship of all seven member states.

TABLE 15.7 (continued)

August 1977	Agreement on the Saudi-Bahrain Cement Company is reached.
October 1977	The first general conference of Arab Gulf trade ministers proposes the creation of a common market among the Gulf states.
March 1978	The Gulf News Agency (GNA) begins transmission under overall authority of all seven states.
26 June 1978	President Rubai Ali is executed in South Yemen. The execution of Rubai
Mid-1978	Ali in South Yemen, the Soviet airlift to Ethiopia, and Iraq's purge of its communist party lead to high level talks between Iran, Iraq, and Saudi Arabia that cause Saudi Arabia to support a cooperative security agreement involving all the Gulf states.
Mid-Late, 1978	The Saudi-initiated cooperative internal security and intelligence links between the conservative Gulf states are greatly strengthened. Iraq began to feed the conservation Gulf states security and intelligence data for the first time.
16 January 1979	The shah leaves Iran.
1979	Following the shah's fall, Oman proposes a $100 million plan for joint efforts to secure entry through the Straits of Hormuz. Iraq calls for the creation of an Arab Gulf Security Force. The Saudis oppose both funding the Omani effort and a joint military force with Iraq.
May 1979	Important meeting of planning ministers in Doha agrees to treat the Arabian Peninsula as a single economic unit.
July 1979	First significant cooperative military maneuvers by the conservative Gulf states are conducted at Khamis Mushayt in Saudi Arabia.
Autumn 1979	Gulfert (a forum on Gulf fertilizer industries joined by Saudi Arabia, Qatar, Iraq, Iran, and Kuwait) agrees to meet commitments of thè Shahpur Chemical Company, shut down by the revolution.
27 December 1979	Soviet troops enter Afghanistan.
1980	A second meeting of planning ministers in Doha; the establishment of the Gulf Federation of Chambers of Commerce and Industry; a number of bilateral security pacts signed to improve the flow of sensitive intelligence information among the various interior ministries; the groundswell for joint industrial ventures leads to the signature on 10 February 1981 of the agreement to set up the Gulf Aluminium Rolling Mill Company (GARMCO), dubbed by Saudi Industry Minister Dr. Ghazi al-Gosaibi as the first pan-Gulf industrial scheme.
Late 1980	Saudi Interior Minister Naif visits Kuwait and Pakistan and holds talks with the other conservative Gulf States regarding a "collective security plan" based on five principles: (1) collective efforts at internal security, (2) cooperation in response to the request of any state threatened by local or imported sabotage and in halting activities by international terrorists, (3) strengthening police cooperation and joint communications systems, (4) denial of entry or refugee status to all hostile elements, and (5) other measures to ensure collective security.
Late 1980	A joint Saudi-Jordanian security committee is established. Saudi-Jordanian Iranian cooperation in air defense is strengthened.
22 September 1980	Iraqi troops, after a continuous escalation of hostilities, pour into Khuzestan, Iran.
4 February 1981	The foreign ministers of the conservative Gulf states meet and agree to form the Gulf Cooperation Council. They also agree to a Kuwaiti version of the Saudi security cooperation plan. The main focus is on internal security, but a Gulf "national security council" is formed. Oman agrees

TABLE 15.7 (continued)

	to defer discussion of joint defense of the strait, and Iraq states that it cannot join such an arrangement while the Iran-Iraq War is still in progress.
March 1981	Establishment of Gulf "National Security Council."
26 May 1981	The first formal Gulf Cooperation Council Meeting at the summit level. The conservative Gulf states again discuss methods of increasing internal security. Saudi Arabia offers links to its new computerized internal security system, which is to come on line in late 1981. Oman and the other conservative states split over Omani efforts to greatly increase the military cooperation and aid aspects of the council's activities. Oman is the "odd man out" because of its acceptance of Camp David and willingness to act as a staging base for the U.S.
July 1981	Dr. Abdullah Hamad al-Muajil of Saudi Arabia, formerly professor at the University of Petroleum and Minerals in Dhahran, is appointed secretary general of the GOIC for a four-year term, and it becomes fully operational. Projects include a 15-year metal smelter strategy for the Gulf, an aluminum rolling plant in Bahrain, a float glass plant in Iraq, and a tire plant in Kuwait. All proceed except the glass plant, which is suspended because of the war.
August 1981	Army chiefs of member states meet in Riyadh.
November 1981	Gulf Cooperation Council meeting leads to studies to strengthen joint defense planning, exercises, and air defense and maritime cooperation, but Oman's call for more ambitious efforts is again rejected. The council encounters continuing problems because of Oman's special status, and its agreement to grant the U.S. staging bases. The industrial development activities of the council also run into problems because the Gulf Organization for Industrial Consulting (GOIC) includes Iraq, and joint cooperation between the conservative states and Iraq does not prove easy.
December 1981	Saudi Arabia signs bilateral security pact with Bahrain and offers similar pacts to other GCC members.
Late January 1982	GCC defense ministers meet in Riyadh and discuss coordination of defense strategies. They review (1) a report by the GCC's secretary general on regional defense needs; (2) the recommendations of the Army chiefs, reporting on studies growing out of their August 1981 meeting; (3) a report on the Iranian threat; (4) a report on air defense cooperation, and (5) a report on arms procurement policies and armament plants. They agree in principle to establish a joint military strike force and a collective air defense system, including a joint command. Agreement is reached to draft a two-year implementation plan and a similar study of arms procurements and establishing an arms industry.
Late January 1982	GCC finance ministers agree to coordinate financial policies and establish joint investment fund.
1 February 1982	GCC oil ministers meet in Riyadh on "oil glut" in first of continuing joint discussions of oil price and production policies.
Early February 1982	Secretary of Defense Weinberger asks Prince Sultan to help undertake a coordinated security assistance program to the Gulf Cooperation Council states.
6–7 February 1982	GCC interior ministers meet on internal security in Kuwait and warn Iran against subversive actions. Iran state radio calls for overthrow of Saudi regime.
March 1982	GCC chiefs of staff spend two days discussing Iranian threat, defense cooperation, and possible contingency assistance from Egypt and Pakistan.

TABLE 15.7 (continued)

November 1982	GCC nations hold their third summit meeting in Bahrain. While little progress is made in defense cooperation, they agree on enhanced cooperation in development and oil planning, freer movement of trade and citizens, and the establishment of a $2.1 billion joint investment cooperation with each state paying equal shares of $350 million each.
March 1982–March 1983	GCC nations steadily expand their cooperation in oil pricing and oil development planning. GCC analysis is increasingly separate from that of OPEC.
1 March 1983	"Mini-Common Market" agreement goes into effect. Key points are (1) no duty on agricultural, manufactured, or petroleum and mineral products originating in the GCC states, plus agreed-upon tariffs to protect the GCC industries; (2) free access for GCC-flag ships to ports in any member state, and exemption of passengers and goods from fees and taxes; (3) freedom of GCC nationals to operate in any GCC state and to start business with or without local partners; (4) coordinated petroleum policies; and (5) a $2.1 billion investment corporation, headquartered in Kuwait, to handle regional and international investments.
March 1983	Prince Sultan announces that GCC plans for a joint military industry are the subject of "intense study and cooperation." The GCC study group examines a plan based loosely on the Arab Organization for Industry, suspended in 1979 because of the breach with Egypt over its support of Camp David. Joint membership, including a more industrialized Arab state like Iraq, Egypt, or Jordan, is under study.
11 May 1983	GCC finance and national economy ministers meet in Riyadh. Discussions take place on next steps in expanding the mini-common market agreement.
12 May 1983	The GCC assistant secretary general for political affairs leads a delegation to the PDRY to discuss cooperation between the GCC states and South Yemen.
22 May 1983	Meeting of GCC defense ministers. A spokesman announces plans to establish a joint command.
	"Moderating Group" of the GCC is established to coordinate efforts to eliminate sources of tension and conflict in the region. A key priority is said to be resolution of the Iran-Iraq conflict.
30 May 1983	Agreement on a joint military industry is announced at a meeting of GCC defense ministers in Doha.
June 1983	GCC announces that it is setting up a rapid deployment force of earmarked battalion-sized contingents from Saudi Arabia, the UAE, Kuwait, and Oman. Units will include armored mechanized, paratroop, and special forces elements. Plans are announced for exercises in the UAE in October 1983.

Sources: adapted from *8 Days,* 14 March 1981; *New Times,* 11 November 1981; *Khaleej Times,* 31 January 1982; *Oman Daily Observer,* 4 and 6 February 1982; *Middle East,* September 1981, pp. 35–36., and October 1981, pp. 25–26; *New York Times, Wall Street Journal,* 5 November 1981; 30 March 1982; *MEED,* 11 June 1982, pp. 30–31; *Baltimore Sun,* 16 November 1982, *Christian Science Monitor,* 26 October 1982; 30 March 1983; *Washington Times,* 9 and 12 November 1982; *Washington Post,* 10, 12, and 25 November 1982; *Economist,* 19 February 1983; BBC ME/7348/A/1, 1 June 1983; ME/7339/1, 21 May 1983; ME/W1237/A1/1, 24 May 1983; Reuters, 11, 26, and 30 May and 12 June 1983.

is important to stress that the council is a new and still developing institution. It was formed in February 1981, largely as the result of the shah's fall and the Iran-Iraq War, and includes the UAE, Bahrain, Saudi Arabia, Oman, Qatar, and Kuwait. Its headquarters have been established in Riyadh. It has a Supreme Council, a Ministerial Council, and a Secretariat General. The Supreme Council consists of heads of state, with a rotating presidency. Its charter calls for it to meet annually, or in emergency session at the request of any member. Each member state has one vote, and it must pass its resolutions unanimously. It also has a Commission for the Settlement of Disputes between member states. The Ministerial Council is made up of the foreign ministers of each state. It has a rotating presidency and is supposed to meet every three months. Two-thirds of the members must attend for its meetings to be valid, and it has a sufficiently broad charter to address virtually any issue. It appoints the assistant secretaries general of the GCC. Again, each member has one vote and decisions must be unanimous. The Secretariat has a secretary general appointed for three years by the Supreme Council. It is staffed to conduct plans and studies for cooperation in a wide range of areas. Assistant secretaries general and staffs now deal with virtually every area of Gulf activity.

When the Gulf Cooperation Council had its first formal meeting in May 1981, it agreed to establish a National Security Council. Although the members were divided over how close their cooperation should be, agreement was reached to cooperate on future defense plans, to seek improved cooperation in air and maritime defense, and to establish a secretariat that could study ways to improve cooperation in internal security and defense planning and to perform some of the functions of the international staffs of NATO. These defense efforts acquired increased momentum after the abortive coup in Bahrain in December 1981. On 1 December 1982 plans were formulated to set up a strong Defense Council and to improve the standardization and integration of internal security systems and the tracking of terrorist or radical movements between Gulf countries. Progress was also made on studies of joint air and maritime surveillance, a unified high command, cooperative training, and equipment standardization.

As 1982 progressed, however, a number of factors weakened the unity of the various member nations. Oman became concerned that its fragile economy was not ready for a major reduction in trade barriers or free movement of traders and technicians from the other GCC states. Kuwait and the UAE remained concerned with the political risks posed by Oman's ties to the U.S. and the threat of increased radical or Soviet-backed activity if they supported too strong an effort toward collective self-defense. Kuwait and the UAE also came under intense pressure from Iran, which steadily increased its threats to all the southern Gulf states after its victories over Iraq in the spring of 1982, but which put particular pressure on Kuwait and on the other members of the UAE to check Abu Dhabi's moves toward defense cooperation. This pressure helped prevent Kuwait from joining the other GCC states in signing bilateral security agreements with Saudi Arabia following the coup attempt in Bahrain. It also led both Kuwait and the UAE to advocate mediation in the Iran-Iraq War and to reduce their support for Iraq. Further, the member states proved unable to agree on exactly what form of defense cooperation would be most acceptable, and some old problems, such as the UAE's fear of Oman's influence over the UAE's large numbers of Omani troops, became an issue.

This situation became further complicated as the various members of the GCC tried to adapt their budgets, development plans, and oil-pricing and -production policies to the drop in their oil revenues. The members of the GCC began to compete for a share of the declining world market, which tended to divide the smaller states from Saudi Arabia because several felt their markets could be sustained only if Saudi Arabia made further cuts in production. Iran put the same pressure on the smaller conservative states to support Iranian oil policy that it used to pressure them against increased cooperation and support of Iraq in the Iran-Iraq War. As Iran and Saudi Arabia became involved in a growing conflict over oil quotas, Iran's military struggle with Iraq became joined to a political and oil struggle with Saudi Arabia.

As a result, the council's third summit meeting in Bahrain in mid-November 1982 produced limited progress. While the various states remained united, they deferred agreement on creating a Defense Council and integrated command. The council limited action on the war to describing Iran's attacks on Iraq as "dangerous," deferred any action on common oil and development policy for study, and deferred action on a freer "common market" until March 1983. As Table 15.7 has shown, the meeting's major results were to establish a $2.1 billion joint investment fund, with each member contributing $350 million, and to agree to reduce tariffs, ease capital flows, and improve labor mobility on 31 March 1983.

During early 1983, however, it became clear that Iran did not pose a massive threat of internal subversion within the conservative Gulf states and that it did not pose an immediate threat of defeating Iraq. Equally important, the pressures caused by cuts in oil revenues created still another force pushing the conservative Gulf states together. This force, patient Saudi and Omani diplomacy, and the efforts of the GCC staff helped bring the states together and reach agreement on the announcement of a Gulf rapid deployment force and plans to create a joint command and joint arms industry (see Table 15.7). By late 1983, the GCC states were able to hold the first joint military exercise in their history and to conduct a quiet contingency planning effort to discuss military measures if Iran should broaden its attacks in an attempt to halt oil traffic in the rest of the Gulf. Just as important, they allowed renewed progress in political and economic cooperation and gave the GCC a rising formal status in Gulf affairs.[69]

While there is still a risk that the council may prove to be nothing more than a political shell, there are strong forces that will push it toward success. The Gulf rulers are generally served by a "new class" of military and civilian technocrats who combine regional expertise with Western education, and who generally have far less interest in the rivalries described in Chapters 11 and 12. This class often remains comparatively junior in terms of influence and position in many Gulf states, but it is fully able to understand the pressures and trends in the region in a broader and more modern sense than are the Gulf 's traditional rulers.

All the Gulf elites also are clearly sensitive to the lessons of Iran, the Afghan invasion, the Iran-Iraq War, the Soviet buildup in South Yemen, and the long history of failures to radically transform Arab and Third World states. As a result, the Gulf's new class should be able to give the Gulf Cooperation Council and its National Security Council real meaning. It can be expected to counterbalance the traditional influences on the Gulf rulers and help them to take a broader view of their own national interests. It is hoped that this new class will also have a powerful impact in pushing the Gulf rulers toward a viable approach to political modernization and to dealing with expatriate labor and ethnic minorities.

Prospects for Cooperation with the U.S. and the West

Regional cooperation, however, is only part of the story. The issue then arises as to what cooperation can be developed between the conservative Gulf states and the West. The answer is clear in at least one sense. There is no practical prospect of any formal ties or regional security treaties. Not even the most friendly Gulf states will be willing to do anything that will jeopardize their sovereignty, link them formally to the U.S. before an Arab-Israeli peace settlement, or make them a major target for the Soviet Union. None is going to be willing to risk shattering the hard-won progress in regional cooperation by forcing the weaker conservative Gulf states to face the kind of Iranian, Iraqi, or Arab challenge that would result from formal ties between the GCC states and the U.S. or any other Western state. This is particularly true in view of the dismal historical record of the Baghdad Pact and the Central Treaty Organization (CENTO).

It is also unclear that the West is any more ready for such ties than the Gulf. NATO specifically rejected expansion of its role to cover the Gulf at its spring 1983 ministerial meeting. Britain and France lack the resources to maintain any permanent bases or presence or do more than they are already doing in the region. Germany and Japan have no power projection capability, and they have more immediate defense needs on their borders. The U.S., for all its plans and rhetoric, has found that formal commitments are currently unacceptable to the Congress and that it cannot even sell the key equipment needed for air and sea defense to the smaller Gulf states because of political resistance from Congress and the supporters of Israel.

This, however, is neither a sign of weakness nor a barrier to strategic partnership—particularly to the kind of partnership that can form a lasting deterrent in the region with a minimum risk of provoking direct superpower competition or political backlash. Informal relations can be made strong and effective—probably much more so than those that could be set forth in a formal treaty. While the U.S. and the conservative Gulf states may never define exact arrangements for cooperation in regional defense or in over-the-horizon reinforcements, Table 15.8 shows that many of the key elements of informal cooperation are coming into existence. These elements may lack coordination and efficiency, and some plans may never materialize, but the core elements needed for cooperation are there.

Every further step in military cooperation among the conservative Gulf states will have two effects: first, to reduce the need for U.S. or other Western intervention and, second, to make it easier and more effective. Gulf cooperation in C^3I, in cross-basing, in planning, in creating a joint command structure, in creating an effective air defense system, and in training and support will inevitably increase the risk any attacker will face that a successful attack on the southern Gulf states will simply bring U.S. forces into the region. These same steps will increase the ease with which the U.S. can support a friendly Gulf state against a major military coup, terrorism, or insurgency and will allow the U.S. to increasingly substitute technical aid, training support, or equipment transfers for the deployment of forces.

In this sense, the work on the U.S. Rapid Deployment Force during 1979–1983 has laid the groundwork for a unique kind of strategic partnership: one that does not require treaties, forces in being, or even open admission of its existence where this is embarrassing to a Gulf or Western state. There is, however, much that can be done even within this context to make such a partnership more effective, and without any peacetime U.S. basing, prestocking of supplies, or prior contingency planning and exercises. Such options could include the development of cross-basing capabilities throughout the Gulf that allow the immediate deployment of U.S. air reinforcements. This would involve stocking the required munitions, major spares, and service equipment to support reinforcing U.S. units; providing full AC&W and IFF compatibility; providing expanded air base facilities and shelters to allow reinforcement by outside aircraft; and developing standard shelters that could accommodate both U.S. and other Gulf fighters. It also would mean deploying all the ground equipment and infrastructure to support U.S. military airlift and possibly stocking compatible munitions and spares for US-CENTCOM (RDF) forces.

Such arrangements could be made on an informal basis, without any formal agreement with the U.S., an added U.S. presence, or joint training

TABLE 15.8 Developments and Key Facilities in the Gulf Affecting the Informal Collective Security Capabilities of the West and the Southern Gulf States

Saudi Arabia

Central C^3I system costing up to $4.6 billion to be constructed by 1990, with options for links to other GCC countries.

Air Force General Operating Center (GOC)—an underground command operations center to coordinate massive air operations, which is already under construction in Riyadh. It will cost $500 million, excluding the C^3 system, which was part of the AWACS package.

Construction of five sector command centers and five sector operation centers costing $1.3 billion that will conduct air operations in five regions, each tied to major bases, local radar sites, surface-to-air missiles, smaller bases, two operations centers, and two sector operation centers where data is collected and processed.

Over-capacity Saudi air bases that can each handle more than a wing (70 F-15 fighters). This includes reinforced runways, parking ramps, shelters, spare parts, munitions storage, oversized storage facilities for U.S. use in each corner of the country at a cost of $1 billion plus.

Saudi Army C^3 system designed by Litton Data. These command systems will tie army units, bases, and Hawk missile units to a master C^3 network with its central command in Riyadh, at a cost of $1.6 billion.

Land forces facility construction—the King Khalid Military City at Hafr al-Batin in the northeast will be a major army command center and potential sixth sector command and operations center in the C^3 system ($6.3 billion).

M-1 tank and M-2 fighting vehicle test will examine performance of key U.S. Army equipment in Gulf conditions.

Saudi Navy C^3 systems will link ships and communications stations at Jiddah, Jubail, and Riyadh to the military headquarters in Riyadh at a cost of more than $1 billion.

Naval facility construction—the Corps of Engineers is supervising construction of two new naval facilities, one on the Red Sea near Jiddah, the other on the Gulf at Jubail, built to U.S. Navy requirements ($5.2 billion).

Satellite and hookups for C^3I dedicated to military use at an estimated cost of $200 million to $300 million.

Civil aviation ground radar. In addition to the 10 sets of long-range radars and ground entry stations sold under AWACS, there are 12 more sets being purchased commercially by the Civil Aviation Administration and tied into military as well as civilian network ($700 million plus).

Mobile ground radar. Six previously purchased mobile ground radars will be tied into C^3 system purchases as part of AWACS package ($39 million).

Five E-3A AWACS planes purchased.

Electronic warfare and intelligence equipment. Some will be ground based and some will be mounted on C-130 aircraft and linked to the C^3I system purchased as part of AWACS package ($39 million).

Surface-to-air missiles—16 improved Hawk missile batteries plus more missiles will be added and tied into C^3 network ($1.4 billion).

F-15 aircraft. The 60 Saudi F-15s purchased in 1978, plus 2 spares stored in United States, will cost $4.5 billion, including follow-up contracts.

F-15 conformal fuel tanks—101 ship sets to extend range.

F-15 bomb racks or comparable equipment in the future.

Oil storage—a network of hardened oil-storage facilities, including some refined fuel for U.S. RDF, at Yanbu and elsewhere as a back-up if Gulf oil facilities are attacked. The cost will be more than $2 billion (excluding value of oil).

Prepositioned equipment and munitions sufficient to sustain U.S. forces during intensive combat for 90 days or more. This makes available not only the AWACS but also other military equipment just purchased, including 1,177 AIM-9L Sidewinder missiles, 6 Boeing 707 aerial refueling aircraft (plus option for 2 more) that can refuel the U.S. carrier-based F-14s, as well as Saudi aircraft. The cost is more than $1 billion (excluding the AWACS package).

Mini-Rapid Deployment Force—a special project to protect the oil fields from saboteurs, including R&D on nonfriction ballistics and special remote-controlled sensors (costs unknown).

TABLE 15.8 (continued)

United Arab Emirates

Purchase of 18–40 Mirage 2000 fighters from France and 6 Alphajet attack fighters.

Air defense study in August 1980, recommended purchase of advanced C^3I and surface-to-air missile system.

Seven batteries of Improved Hawk surface-to-air missiles are currently being purchased, with data links planned to the Saudi C^3 system. ($800 million.)

British C^3I Air Defense Project, including ground radar, electronic warfare equipment, brigade-level command posts, an integrated air defense operations center, and equipping one or more C-130 aircraft with electronic intelligence (ELINT), signal intelligence (SIGINT), and communications intelligence (COMINT) gear (up to $1 billion).

C-130s for the electronic intelligence (cost unknown).

Twenty-four Hawk attack trainers from Britain.

Purchase of Skyguard 35mm air defense guns and radar system from UK.

Oman

New British frequency agile communications and ECM system.

Overall defense study in October 1977 by Defense and State departments at U.S. expense.

U.S. facility study in early 1980 to identify needed improvements for use by U.S. forces.

Purchase of 24 Blindfire radars and 28 Rapier surface-to-air missiles from UK.

Purchase of 19 Jaguar attack fighters with sidewinder air-to-air missiles.

Purchase of AM-39 Exocet air-to-surface missiles from France.

Possible purchase of advanced Tornado fighters.

Upgrading of facilities at Khasab and Masirah for USCENTCOM forces.

Basing of U.S. P-3C maritime patrol aircraft.

Expansion of naval, air, radar and C^3I facilities at Goat Island and Musandam Peninsula.

Kuwait

Purchase of 12 Mirage F-1 C/D fighters from France with Matra R-550 AAMs. Will give total of 31 Mirage F-1 C/D.

Purchase of AM-39 Exocet for fighters.

Purchase of 6 Super Puma helicopters with Exocet.

Crotale short-range surface-to-air missiles from France.

Surface-to-air missiles, including 27 Improved Hawk launchers, 164 missiles, and other associated systems ($1 billion plus).

Planned purchase of Thomson-CSF or Hughes C^3I and AC&W system.

Bahrain

Purchase of 6 F-5E/F fighters and 60 AIM-9P missiles in 1982 with AC&W links to Saudi forces. Advanced fighter purchase under study.

Teleprinter and voice links to Saudi Arabian C^3I system—already operational, with new $700 million improved AC&W and sea surveillance system under study.

U.S. Army study recommending purchase of Improved Hawk missiles.

Improved Hawk surface-to-air missiles—to be paid for by Saudi Arabia and integrated into the Saudi air defense network (over $200 million).

Improved air bases at international airport and main military base.

Qatar

Purchase of 14 Mirage F-1 and 8 Alpha jet fighters from France. Planned procurement of an advanced air defense fighter.

Improved Hawk surface-to-air missiles.

Five Tigercat surface-to-air missile fire units from the UK to be replaced by more extensive Crotale or Shahine defenses.

Gulf-Wide

C^3I coordination of 100–150 fighter planes. When completed, the Saudi C^3I–E-3A system will be able to coordinate between 100 and 150 fighter planes purchased by the other regional states; estimated costs, including contractor training, maintenance, and support—$5–10 billion.

Source: Adapted in part from the *Washington Post,* 1 November 1981, IISS, *Military Balance, 1983-1984,* and *International Defense Review,* Volume 16, No. 10, 1983, pp. 1405–1419.

and contingency planning. They would send the same deterrent message as deliberate cooperation without having any of the political visibility and liabilities. It is also important to note that the U.S. could support such arrangements by developing special programs for the Saudi E-3As to improve interoperability among the forces of the conservative Gulf states and with those of the U.S. These programs could be tailored to Gulf conditions to avoid increasing the threat to Israel. While the precise benefits of such an option are speculative, it is well within the state of the art.

Notes

1. The major written sources used in this chapter have already been listed in note 1 to Chapters 11 and 12. Unless otherwise stated, statistics are usually taken from World of Information, *The Middle East Review*, 1981, 1982, and 1983 (London, 1980, 1981, and 1982), or CIA, *World Factbook*, 1981 and 1983.

2. The first raid, early in the war, was a token raid on border facilities that Iran claimed was an accident. Iran then attacked a Kuwaiti ship. It bombed refineries in Kuwait on 1 October 1981, and this time made it clear that it was a deliberate effort to show its displeasure for Kuwait's tacit support of Iraq. For a good summary of recent developments see the *Christian Science Monitor*, 22 March 1983.

3. *MEED*, 27 February 1981, p. 21; 11 June, 1982, p. 30.

4. *Washington Post*, 12 and 25 November 1982; *Economist*, 24 July 1982, p. 33; *Christian Science Monitor*, 26 October 1982.

5. The area, including the Neutral Zone, is 17,818 square kilometers. The distance between the extreme points of state boundaries, from south to north, is about 100 kilometers; that from west to east along parallel 29°N, about 170 kilometers. The total length of frontiers is 490 kilometers, of which 250 kilometers form the frontier with Saudi Arabia in the south and west. The frontier with Iraq is 240 kilometers in length, and there are 195 kilometers of coastline. The total area is just under 18,000 square kilometers. The earth slopes gently from east to west. The land surface is generally flat with the exception of a few rocky hills ranging in height from 180 to 300 meters above sea level. Shallow depressions are found in the desert. There are several islands, of which the largest is Bubiyan, located in the northeast corner. To the north of Bubiyan is Warbah Island. At the entrance to the Bay of Kuwait is Failaka Island, and there are two smaller islands, Masken and Oha, nearby. There are three small islands, Kobbar, Qarwa, and Umm al-Maradem, near the southern coastline. In the Bay of Kuwait are Korein Island and another small island, Umm Al Namir. Saudi Arabia occupied Qarwa and Umm al-Maradem in June 1977.

6. Total naturalizations averaged only 6,700–8,900 during 1973–1977, and few Palestinians were accepted. These various radical groups were, however, small, often short-lived, and more prone to talk than act.

7. The growth of the expatriate population has also been exceptional. There were only 73,500 in 1957; by 1965 the total had risen to 247,000. In 1970 expatriates already made up 47% of a total population of 738,662, and there were 147,000 Palestinians. At the end of 1973, the population was 907,000, with 500,000 expatriates; in 1975, the population was 972,500, with 532,000 expatriates; and in 1979 the population was 1.4 million, with 800,000 expatriates.

In spite of various immigration crackdowns, Kuwait still projects that by 2000 its population will be well over 2 million and that more than half will be expatriate. See Avi Plascov, *Security in the Persian Gulf: Modernization, Political Development and Stability* (Aldershot: Gower, 1982), pp. 72–74; and CIA, *World Factbook*, various years.

8. For an excellent analysis see Shaiman Y. Alessa, *The Manpower Problem in Kuwait* (London: Keegan Paul, 1981).

9. The main statistical sources utilized in this section are interviews in the Gulf in 1982; CIA, *World Factbook*, 1981 and 1983; World of Information, *Middle East Review*, 1981, 1982, and 1983. For the army: John Keegan, *World Armies* (New York: Facts on File, 1979), pp. 416–420; *The Military Balance, 1982–83* (London: IISS, 1983). For the air force: Mark Hewish, Bill Sweetman, Barry C. Wheeler, and Bill Gunston, *Air Forces of the World* (New York: Simon and Schuster, 1979), pp. 166–167; *Military Balance, 1982–83*; and Keegan, *World Armies*. For the navy: mainly *Military Balance, 1982–83* and Keegan, *World Armies*. See also Otto von Pikva, *Armies of the Middle East* (New York: Mayflower Books, 1979), p. 118; Alvin J. Cottrell, *The Persian Gulf States* (Baltimore: Johns Hopkins University Press, 1981), pp. 165–167; Y.S.F. Al-Sabah, *The Oil Economy of Kuwait* (Boston: Keegan Paul, 1980); and Europa, *The Middle East and North Africa, 1982–83* (London: Europa, 1981).

10. See Kuwait, *The Annual Statistical Abstract* (Kuwait City, 1981), Edition 17, sections 290–294, for a description of Kuwait's aid effort. During 1962–1980, Kuwait balanced its aid effort so that a typical program, the Kuwait Fund for Arab Economic Development, gave 11.9% to Jordan, 5% to Bahrain, 10.3% to Tunisia, 2.3% to Algeria, 13.4% to Sudan, 7.6% to Syria, 2.8% to Somalia, 1.6% to Iraq, 2.5% to Lebanon, 14.9% to Egypt, 9.1% to Morocco, 6.5% to Mauritania, 5.9% to North Yemen, 3.6% to South Yemen, 2.2% to Oman, and 0.4% to Djibouti. The timing of virtually all the projects funded shows that they were security oriented. Kuwait also offers loans to Soviet-bloc states, which amount to aid for the same reason. These include a $50 million loan to Hungary in March 1980, an $85 million loan to Romania in April 1981, a $150 million loan to Hungary in March 1981, and a $117 million loan to Yugoslavia in March 1981.

11. It also uses them to put counterpressure on the U.S. and Saudi Arabia and to reduce pressure from Iraq and Iran. Even very conservative members of the Al-Sabah family have pushed Saudi Arabia and the other Gulf states to "balance" their relations with the USSR to reduce the risk of problems with the PLO and the Yemens, avoid a superpower confrontation in the Gulf, and prod the U.S. into achieving an Arab-Israeli peace settlement. This is a significant policy difference between Kuwait's leaders and those of the other Gulf states.

12. *International Defense Review* 3 (1982):345; *Financial Times*, 23 February and 22 April 1983; *Defense and Foreign Affairs*, 29 April and 6 June 1983.

13. About 20 Soviet military experts, headed by a general officer, arrived in April 1978 to provide SA-6, SA-7, and FROG training. The total Soviet delegation in Kuwait is slightly over 100, which is suspiciously large given the fact that the USSR provides about 0.02% of Kuwait's imports. *Christian Science Monitor*, 11 March 1982.

14. The 50-member assembly is elected by literate males over 21 with "first class" citizenship (limited to people present in Kuwait before 1920). It is now the only popularly elected assembly in the southern Gulf. It rejected votes for women in January 1982 by 27 to 7. *New York Times*, 20 January 1982; *Los*

Angeles Times, 12 December 1982; *Washington Post*, 25 May 1983; *Financial Times*, 23 February 1983.

15. *Wall Street Journal*, 2 December 1982; *Washington Post*, 24 November 1982; *Economist*, 25 September 1982, p. 96; 30 October 1982; 4 December 1982, p. 86; 19 February 1983, pp. 19–25; *Washington Times*, 10 December 1982.

16. CIA 630814 (U) 12-81, 1981.

17. *Washington Post*, 25 November 1982.

18. *Economist*, 24 July 1982; *Washington Post*, 25 November 1982; *MEED*, 11 June 1982, pp. 30–33.

19. This is an area of considerable controversy. A mid-1981 census indicates the Kuwait rate may be nearer 5% while the non-Kuwait rate may be well above 5.9%. For a different view see Torbe B. Larsen, "Running to Stand Still," *Middle East*, July 1979, pp. 57–60.

20. World of Information, *Middle East Review, 1981*, p. 213. See Richard F. Nyrop et al., *Area Handbook for the Persian Gulf States*, DAPAM 550-18 (Washington, D.C., 1977), pp. 183–204, for historical background on the internal security services.

21. *Economist*, 19 February 1983, pp. 19–25; *Wall Street Journal*, 10 March 1982; *New York Times*, 15 February 1983.

22. *Wall Street Journal*, 26 April and 26 October 1982; *New York Times*, 22 February 1982.

23. *New York Times*, 5 April 1982; 15 February 1983; *Christian Science Monitor*, 22 March 1982; *Washington Post*, 19 March 1982; 16 March 1983; *Washington Times*, 10 December 1982; *Wall Street Journal*, 2 December 1982; *Economist*, 19 February 1983, pp. 19–25; 5 February 1983, pp. 38–39; *Financial Times*, 23 February 1983.

24. World of Information, *Middle East Review, 1981*, p. 213; *Christian Science Monitor*, 3 December 1982.

25. Kuwait may be able to make a petrochemical industry work in the long run. It paid $2.5 billion in December 1981 to acquire Santa Fe International and its subsidiary, C. F. Brauk, which gave it considerable expertise in oil exploration and process plan construction. Nevertheless, the economic projections behind its $1 billion new petrochemical plan and $3.5 billion investment in refinery expansion seem dubious. Further, even if they work, the internal job-creation effect on the Kuwaiti native population may well be only 5–10% of what the government estimates because of Kuwait's overreliance on foreign firms and expatriates.

26. "A War That's Good for Business," *Economist*, 27 March 1982, p. 35.

27. This course will, however, force Kuwait to take the political risk of allying itself to Saudi Arabia, and Kuwait is afraid of both the Iranian and Iraqi reaction and Saudi pressures on Kuwait to slow its political and social modernization.

28. Bahrain's onshore Jebel al-Dukhan field produced most of Bahrain's 66,000 BPD in 1974.

29. *U.S. News and World Report*, 24 November 1982, pp. 30–31; *Time*, 25 October 1982, pp. 47–50; *Economist*, 11 December 1982, pp. 62–64.

30. *Washington Post*, 20 April 1982; Associated Press, 19 April 1982; World of Information, *Middle East Review, 1981*, p. 125.

31. *Washington Post*, 23 September 1982; *Aviation Week*, 27 September 1982, p. 19; *Washington Times*, 18 July 1983, p. 7.

32. Sources include Nyrop, *Area Handbook for the Persian Gulf States*, pp. 231–234; Keegan, *World Armies*, pp. 42–44; and *Military Balance, 1982–83*, as well as von Pikva, *Armies of the Middle East*, p. 86; Cottrell, *Persian Gulf States*, pp. 167–168; Europa, *The Middle East and North Africa, 1982–83*; MEED specials on Bahrain in 1981 and 1982; Shahram Chubin (ed.), *Security in the Persian Gulf: Domestic Political Factors* (London: IISS, pp. 5–8, 39–43, 64–65; Plascov, *Modernization, Political Development, and Stability*, pp. 27–30, 60–65, 71, 74, 151–155; "Focus on Bahrain," *The Middle East*, February 1983, pp. 57–60.

33. *Economist*, 27 November 1982, p. 96.

34. "Bahrain," Special Report, *8 Days*, 30 January 1982, pp. 21–28; various issues of the *Economist*.

35. See Emil Nakleh, "Democracy in the Gulf," *Middle East*, August 1980, pp. 32–35; "What Are the Internal Threats," *8 Days*, 23 May 1981; *Washington Post*, 25 November 1982; Chubin, *Domestic Political Factors*, pp. 5–8; and Plascov, *Modernization, Political Development, and Stability*, pp. 151–154.

36. CIA 630814 (U) 12-81 and CR 83-11300 (U) 5-83; *Washington Post*, 25 November 1982; *8 Days*, 30 January 1982, pp. 22–24; Plascov, *Modernization, Political Development, and Stability*, pp. 28, 132–133, 141, 151, 169.

37. Estimates vary. *8 Days* reported arrests of 60 people—45 Bahrainis, 13 Saudis, one Omani, and one Kuwaiti. It reported that 12 additional Bahrainis were given three months to return and face trial. *8 Days*, 30 January 1982, p. 23. Also see *Time*, 25 October 1982, p. 49.

38. He is also reported to have acted as a "stringer" for the KGB while living in Bahrain. *Time*, 25 October 1982, p. 49.

39. *Economist*, 13 March 1982, pp. 59–60; *New York Times*, 18 and 19 December 1982; *Wall Street Journal*, 10 February 1982; *Washington Post*, 31 March and 25 November 1982; Plascov, *Modernization, Political Development, and Stability*, p. 141.

40. *Jordan Times*, 20 January 1982; *Wall Street Journal*, 7 September 1982. The four-lane causeway will have five bridges, cost $564 million in 1982 dollars (or nearly $1 billion in current dollars), be 15.6 miles long, be built by Ballast-Nedam of the Netherlands, and have a capacity of 3,000 vehicles per hour. Also see *New York Times*, 6 March 1983.

41. CIA, *World Factbook*, 1981, p. 165 and 1983, p. 183; *Military Balance, 1982–83*.

42. Qatar promulgated a constitution on 2 April 1970 in the belief that it would join the UAE. It withdrew from the UAE in September 1971, and its amended constitution does little more than recognize an absolute monarchy, Wahabism, and the *shura*.

43. The *MEED* is a good source on Qatar's development; a good summary is presented in "Focus on Qatar," *Middle East*, October 1982, pp. 37–41.

44. For recent discussions see Michael Petrie-Ritchie, "Qatar Celebrates 10 Years of Cautious Progress," *MEED*, 19 February 1982, pp. 26–27; Richard D. Erb, "The Arab Oil-Producing States of the Gulf," *Foreign Policy and Defense Review* (AEI) 2, nos. 3 and 4 (1980); Emil Nakleh, "Democracy in the Gulf"; *Financial Times*, Survey, 22 February 1983; *Defense and Foreign Affairs*, June 1983, p. 1; World of Information, *Middle East Review*, 1981 and 1983.

45. Principal sources used in this section include the following: For the army; Keegan, *World Armies*, pp. 585–586; *Military Balance, 1982–83*; for the air force, the same sources plus Hewish et al., *Air Forces of the World*, p. 167; for

the navy, the same sources as for the army. See also von Pikva's *Armies of the Middle East*, p. 128; Cottrell, *Persian Gulf States*, pp. 161–165; MEED specials on Qatar of August 1981 and August 1982; MEED, 8 April 1983, pp. 30–31; Europa, *The Middle East and North Africa, 1981–82*; Ragaei El Mallakh, *Qatar: Development of an Oil Economy* (London: Croom Helm, 1979); Rosmarie Said Zahlan, *The Creation of Qatar* (London: Croom Helm, 1979); Plascov, *Modernization, Political Development, and Stability*, pp. 62–75, 102, 138–148; and Chubin, *Domestic Political Factors*, pp. 4–5, 41–43, 70–76.

46. A 3,000-student university opens north of Doha in 1983.

47. CIA, *World Factbook*, 1981, pp. 205–206, and 1983, pp. 229–230.

48. Sources include the following: For the army: Nyrop, *Area Handbook for the Persian Gulf States*, pp. 323–337; *Military Balance, 1981–82*, p. 49; Keegan, *World Armies*, pp. 747–752; for the air force, the same sources and (mainly) Hewish et al., *Air Forces of the World*, pp. 165–166; for the navy, the same sources as for the army. See also Muhammad Morsy Abdullah, *The United Arab Emirates, A Modern History* (New York: Barnes & Noble, 1978); Ali Mohammed Khalifa, *The United Arab Emirates: Unity in Fragmentation* (Boulder, Colo.: Westview Press, 1979); MEED Special, "UAE, Tenth Anniversary," November 1981; Mana Saeed Al-Otaiba, *Petroleum and the Economy of the United Arab Emirates* (London: Croom Helm, 1977); John Daniels, *Abu Dhabi: A Portrait* (London: Longman, 1974); Plascov, *Modernization, Political Development, and Stability*, pp. 101, 105, 108, 145; and Chubin, *Domestic Political Factors*, pp. 19–37.

49. For background on these developments see *8 Days*, 23 May 1981, pp. 6–13; *Middle East*, July 1979, p. 12; August 1979, p. 17; June 1980, pp. 29–33.

50. *Economist*, 30 January 1982, p. 44; Plascov, *Modernization, Political Development, and Stability*, pp. 142–145; Chubin, *Domestic Political Factors*, pp. 19–37.

51. This often highly vocal body now has eight members each from Abu Dhabi and Dubai, six members each from Sharjah and Ras al-Khaimah, and four each from Fujairah, Umm al-Qaiwain and Ajman. See United Arab Emirates, *A Record of Achievement, 1979–1981* (Abu Dhabi, 1981), p. 18.

52. World of Information, *Middle East Review, 1981*, pp. 341–384; UAE, *A Record of Achievement*, pp. 14–94; *8 Days*, 23 May 1981, pp. 6–13; 16 January 1982, pp. 37–38; *Middle East*, June 1979, p. 18; August 1979, p. 17; June 1980, pp. 29–33; January 1982, pp. 58–59; *Economist*, 30 January 1982, p. 44; John Duke Anthony, "The UAE in Transition," in Chubin, *Domestic Political Factors*, pp. 19–33.

53. *Washington Post*, 2 December 1982; 16 March 1983; "United Arab Emirates," *Christian Science Monitor*, special report, 1 December 1982; *The UAE: A Practical Guide* (London: MEED, 1982), pp. 1–6, 89–121; *Economist*, 5 February 1983; 19 February 1983, p. 4; *U.S. News and World Report*, 6 June 1983, p. 47.

54. Ibid.; *Financial Times*, 16 May 1983; Reuters, 9 May 1983; *Washington Post*, 21 June 1983; *Defense and Foreign Affairs*, 9 May 1983, p. 2.

55. CIA 630814 (U), 12-81; *Economist*, 20 November 1982.

56. *Economist*, 20 November 1982, p. 53; *Christian Science Monitor*, 26 October and 12 November 1982; 1 December 1982; *Washington Times*, 22 October 1982; *Washington Post*, 12 and 25 November 1982; *MEED*, 11 June 1982, pp. 30–31.

57. CIA, *World Factbook*, 1983, p. 171.

58. The main source is briefings in Oman. Other sources include the following: For the army, Nyrop, *Area Handbook for the Persian Gulf States*, pp. 385–407; Keegan, *World Armies*, pp. 524–527; *Military Balance, 1982–83*; for the air force: Hewish et al., *Air Forces of the World*, pp. 164–165; *Military Balance, 1982–83*; Nyrop, *Area Handbook for the Persian Gulf States*; for the navy: mainly Nyrop, *Area Handbook for the Persian Gulf States*, and *Military Balance, 1982–83*. See also von Pikva, *Armies of the Middle East*, pp. 27–29, 125–127; Cottrell, *Persian Gulf States*, pp. 159–161; John Akehurst, *We Won a War: The Campaign in Oman, 1965–1975* (London: Michael Russel, 1982); F. A. Clements, *Oman, The Reborn Land* (New York: Longman, 1980); Michael Carver, *War Since 1945* (London: Weidenfeld and Nicolson, 1980); MEED special, "Oman," November 1982; MEED, *Oman: A Practical Guide* (London, 1982); J. E. Peterson, *Oman in the Twentieth Century: Political Foundations of an Emerging State* (London: Croom Helm, 1978); Chubin, *Domestic Political Factors*, pp. 4, 19, 39–43, 70–76; Plascov, *Modernization, Political Development, and Stability*, pp. 7–8, 71, 74, 102, 119, 141–142; and "Oman—Special Survey Section," *Financial Times*, 21 December 1982.

59. *International Defense Review* 1 (1982):11.

60. This incident occurred in November 1977. Sheikh Zayid was forced to back down by a combination of Omani naval action, army maneuvers that strayed 3 miles into Ras al-Khaimah territory, and unrest among the many Omani personnel in Ras al-Khaimah forces.

61. *Wall Street Journal*, 29 October 1982; *Washington Times*, 22 October 1982.

62. The key sources of such charges are Marxist; they backed the Dhofar rebels and the PDRY position throughout the fighting.

63. *Oman: A Special Report*, MEED, November 1980; *Third Five Year Plan*; and Oman, *Oman*, 1979, 1980, and 1981 (Muscat: Ministry of Information and Youth Affairs).

64. Ibid.

65. Omani government statistics.

66. See *8 Days*, 14 and 21 March 1981; Reuters, 14 March 1981; *Christian Science Monitor*, 26 October and 12 November 1982; *Wall Street Journal*, 29 October and 12 November 1982; *Washington Post*, 12 November 1982.

67. *Economist*, 11 December 1982, pp. 62–64; *U.S. News and World Report*, 29 November 1982, pp. 30–31; *Washington Times*, 25 October and 19 November 1982; *Baltimore Sun*, 21 July 1982; *Wall Street Journal*, 19 July 1982; *Time*, 25 October 1982; pp. 47–50; *Washington Post*, 23 July 1983.

68. U.S. Army Corps of Engineers, *Middle East Division's Oman Project*, Fact Sheet, 22 September 1982.

69. *Washington Post*, 10, 12, and 25 November 1982; *Christian Science Monitor*, 12 November 1982; 30 March 1983; *Wall Street Journal*, 29 October and 21 November 1982; *MEED*, 11 June 1982; 20 November 1982, pp. 18–20; *Middle East*, December 1982; *Washington Times*, 9 and 12 November 1982; *Economist*, 19 February 1983, "Survey," pp. 25–26; Gulf Cooperation Council, *Cooperation Council for the Arab States of the Gulf, Information Handbook* (Riyadh: Bahr Al-Olum Press, 1982); Reuters, 11, 26, and 30 May and 12 June 1983; BBC ME/7339/1, 21 May 1983; ME/W1237/A1/1, 24 May 1983; and ME/7348/A/1, 1 June 1983.

16
The Military and Internal Security Situation in the Northern Gulf Countries

The West has few opportunities for cooperation with the more "radical" Gulf states, and many reasons to fear them as a threat to its regional allies and oil suppliers. Only Iraq and North Yemen now offer any serious potential for even the most loosely structured and tacit partnership in stabilizing the Gulf. Iran, South Yemen, and several of the "radical" nations surrounding the Gulf must be considered largely in terms of the threats they pose to the region.[1]

The Iran-Iraq War: The Broad Implications for the Gulf[2]

The most threatening single development among the "radical" Gulf states is currently the Iran-Iraq War. It threatens to create new, unstable military and political alignments throughout the northern Gulf and perhaps throughout the entire Middle East. It is also exceptionally difficult to predict the outcome of the fighting, the political and military future of Iran or Iraq, their future alignments with their neighbors and the superpowers, or the extent to which they will pose a direct threat to the southern Gulf states.

The war has so disrupted the "normal" pattern of economic activity in the Gulf that it is difficult to predict postwar changes. It has virtually destroyed economic growth in Iran and Iraq. The war has already cut Iraq's average daily oil production from over 3 million BPD to well below 1 million. The fighting cost Iraq at least $1–2 billion a month in 1981 and $2.5–4 billion per month in 1982, and it has forced an oil-rich Iraq into a massive deficit in structuring its 1983 budget. This same fighting virtually consumed Iran's national reserves in 1980 and 1981, forced it into becoming OPEC's "cut-rate" oil merchant, and led it to try to sell its crown jewels. Iran began to recover in 1982, but it still faces devastating economic losses. Informed estimates of the damage to the oil facilities and civilian economies of the two countries all go above $100 billion, and a few go as high as $400 billion.[3]

Yet the present war has many of the signs of a preliminary bout. Many experts on both nations feel that any cease-fire or peace will be no more than the prelude to rearmament or revenge and that hatreds have been built up throughout the Near East that will explode periodically into future conflicts even if one side does achieve "victory." If Iraq should fall to Iran, many Gulf officials and Western intelligence officers feel that the forces of nationalism, and the more modern and secular character of Iraq, will eventually lead any initially pro-Iranian or pro-Khomeini successor regimes there to renew its hostility to Iran.

The depth of the hostility between the present political regimes in Iran and Iraq has been clear since the first days of Khomeini's rise to power. Although Khomeini spent much of his long exile in Iraq, it was Iraq that expelled him at the shah's request, and one of his sons died there under mysterious circumstances. It is also clear that Khomeini deeply resented Iraq's secular character and felt that it should fully adhere to Shi'ite law and custom. Khomeini first began to call for an Islamic revolution in Iraq within months of his rise to power. The war started largely because of his efforts to overthrow Iraq's Sunni and secular rule, and his government has since been unwavering in calling for the total destruction of Sunni and Baathist control of Iraq as the price for peace.

Iraq just as clearly is unwilling to tolerate the threat posed by Khomeini. It launched the war because of its fears of the influence that Khomeini could have on Iraq's population. Out of Iraq's total population of 13.6 million, only 40% is Sunni and only 70% is Arab. Roughly 55% of Iraq's population is Shi'ite, and while Shi'ites have shared in the nation's oil wealth and acquired a growing role in the middle levels of the Baath leadership, many still have little reason to be loyal to the regime and good reason to be loyal to the Shi'ite cause.[4] Iraq has tried to deal with this situation by creating a nationalist fervor and by telling its soldiers that Iran has shot its prisoners and even that Khomeini has declared that the key Shi'ite martyr, Ali, is buried not in Iraq but in Qom. These steps, however, have scarcely eliminated the ideological and cultural threat posed by Iran.[5]

The struggle between the two nations has also had an impact that has gone far beyond Iran and Iraq. The war has led to a growing alliance among the Shi'ites of Iran, the Alawites who rule Syria (some 13% of the population), the Shi'ites of Lebanon (who now may be approaching a majority of the native Muslims), and those Druzes in the Golan who now are siding with the Alawites in Syria. For Jordan, the risk is increasingly one of facing a broad "front," rather than simply separate threats from Syria and Israel. For Lebanon, the Iran-Iraq War is contributing to a new civil war between the Christians and wealthier Sunnis on the one hand and the Druze and Shi'ite factions on the other.

The Shi'ite factions now represent a majority of Lebanon's Muslim population, but they are themselves divided between ties to Syria and local factions.[6]

The war has threatened the southern Gulf since its beginning. Iran has bombed Kuwait three times, and Kuwait lost millions of dollars' worth of oil and storage facilities in the 1 October 1981 Iranian raid on Umm al-Aysh. The war helped lead to the Shi'ite coup attempt in Bahrain in December 1981. It has caused similar arrests or political tension in the United Arab Emirates, Saudi Arabia, and North Yemen. An oil slick caused by storms and Iraqi attacks on Iranian wells in February and March 1983 continued to pour 2,500–5,000 barrels of oil per day into the Gulf well into the summer. In the fall of 1983, Iraq purchased 5 French Super Etendard fighters with Exocet missiles in a new effort to threaten Iran's oil facilities. Iran replied by threatening both to close the Gulf and set the entire Gulf "on fire." While such statements died down at the end of 1983, the military threat remained.

The smaller southern Gulf nations face a growing risk of Iranian subversion if Iran continues to be the victor in the war. Kuwait is already having serious problems with its native Shi'ites and its Iranian expatriates. Bahrain's native population is at least 57% native Shi'ite and 8% expatriate Iranian. The UAE has some strong Shi'ite elements, many with ties to Iran. Saudi Arabia has at least 130,000 Shi'ites in the Eastern Province, where its oil facilities are located, and while few have proved pro-Khomeini, the threat of subversion remains. Similarly, North Yemen's dominant northern tribes are members of a Shi'ite sect, and Iranian efforts at subversion led to the Iranian ambassador's expulsion in December 1981.[7]

The Khomeini regime's view of Saudi Arabia has shifted from antipathy to gut hatred. During 1982, the tone of Iranian broadcasts changed so that Iran's attacks on Saddam Hussein seemed almost mild in comparison to its attacks on the leading members of the Saudi royal family. Iran made a major effort to disrupt the pilgrimage of Makkah, Jiddah, and Medina in September 1982 and, during 1983, it steadily increased its efforts to subvert Saudi Shi'ites and establish pro-Khomeini cells among the Shi'ite North Yemeni workers in Saudi Arabia. Iran turned its oil policy into economic warfare with Saudi Arabia and into an OPEC-wide struggle for markets, revenues, and influence. This struggle split OPEC in January 1983 and seems unlikely to diminish even when world economic activity and oil demand recover.[8]

As has been discussed earlier, these tensions have sometimes weakened the Gulf Cooperation Council's efforts to strengthen collective defense. Iran and Saudi Arabia have become locked in a conflict to influence Kuwait and the UAE. This conflict has affected not only the GCC's defense efforts but also its economic and oil policy. It may also be only a taste of things to come. In the future, Iraq may be as serious a threat as Iran. Iraq too will have to compete for a share of the oil market, major conflicts may arise over repayment of its war "loans" from the southern Gulf states, and Iraq will have an enhanced interest in acquiring the Kuwaiti islands near its small seacoast on the Gulf. It is also possible that Iraq may put pressure on the GCC states for war recovery aid and political support.[9]

For much of the Arab world, the main lesson of the Iran-Iraq War is already that Iraq's miscalculation in starting a war it could not finish will threaten their security and unity for a decade. The "pan-Arab" euphoria that followed Iraq's initial victories has turned into the grim knowledge that nothing can be worse than fundamental mistakes in grand strategy. Those Arab states that now support Iraq do so in the effort to contain Khomeini and in the fear of what a radical Shi'ite-dominated Iranian-Iraqi-Syrian axis would do to the Arab world. The southern Gulf states and the West can, however, learn other lessons from the battles that already have been fought. While some lessons are tragically familiar, each new war serves as a further warning of how important these battles will be to Western and Gulf security. At the same time, new lessons that are emerging out of the confusion must be considered in structuring Gulf and Western strategy to deal with the uncertain threat from the north.

The Iraqi Attack: Lessons in Grand Strategy, Assessment, and Tactics

Iraq's precise goals in launching its 22 September 1980 attack will never be known. Only Saddam Hussein and his closest advisers could have defined them at the start of the war, and it seems likely that they have by now convinced themselves that their initial goals were as modest as Iraq's military failures have since forced them to claim. It is clear, however, that Iraq's goals had to involve some mix of the following objectives:

- First, to secure the Baath regime against Khomeini's declared intention to overthrow it and against his efforts at subversion. According to some Arab sources close to Saddam Hussein, he felt that he would inevitably lose a struggle if he allowed Khomeini to undermine his regime religiously, but that he could defeat Khomeini if he turned the conflict into a national one. As one put it, "Hussein felt he would lose a conflict with the Shi'ites, but not between the Arabs and the Persians."
- Second, to secure Iraq's borders from a long series of military incidents and to claim the 200–300 square kilometers of territory near Qasr-e-Shirin and Behran covering the main Iranian approach to Baghdad, which the shah had promised to turn over to Iraq as part of the 1975 accord on the Shat al-Arab.

MAP 16—1
INITIAL IRAQI ATTACK ON IRAN

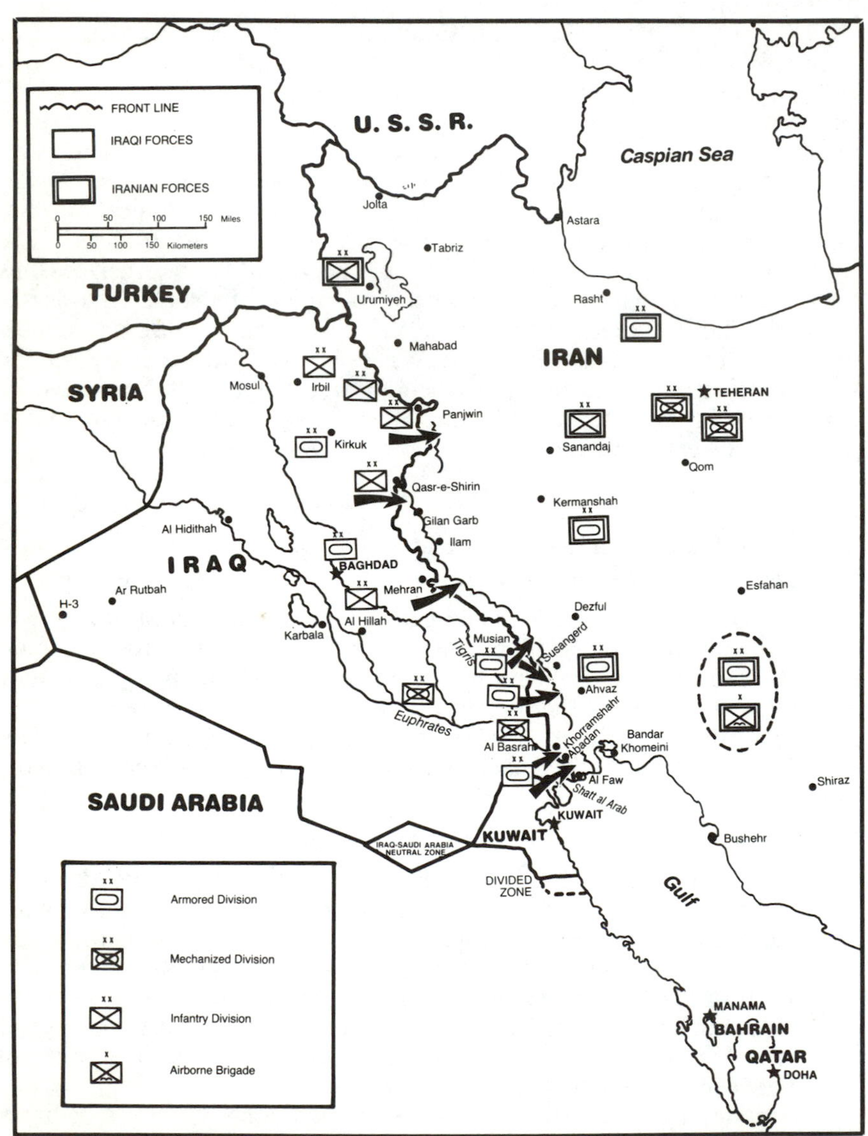

SOURCE: *Armed Forces Journal International*, April, 1982, p. 46.
Adapted from work by Col. W. O. Staudenmaier, U.S. Army Strategic Studies Institute.

MAP 16—2
THE SHATT al ARAB AREA

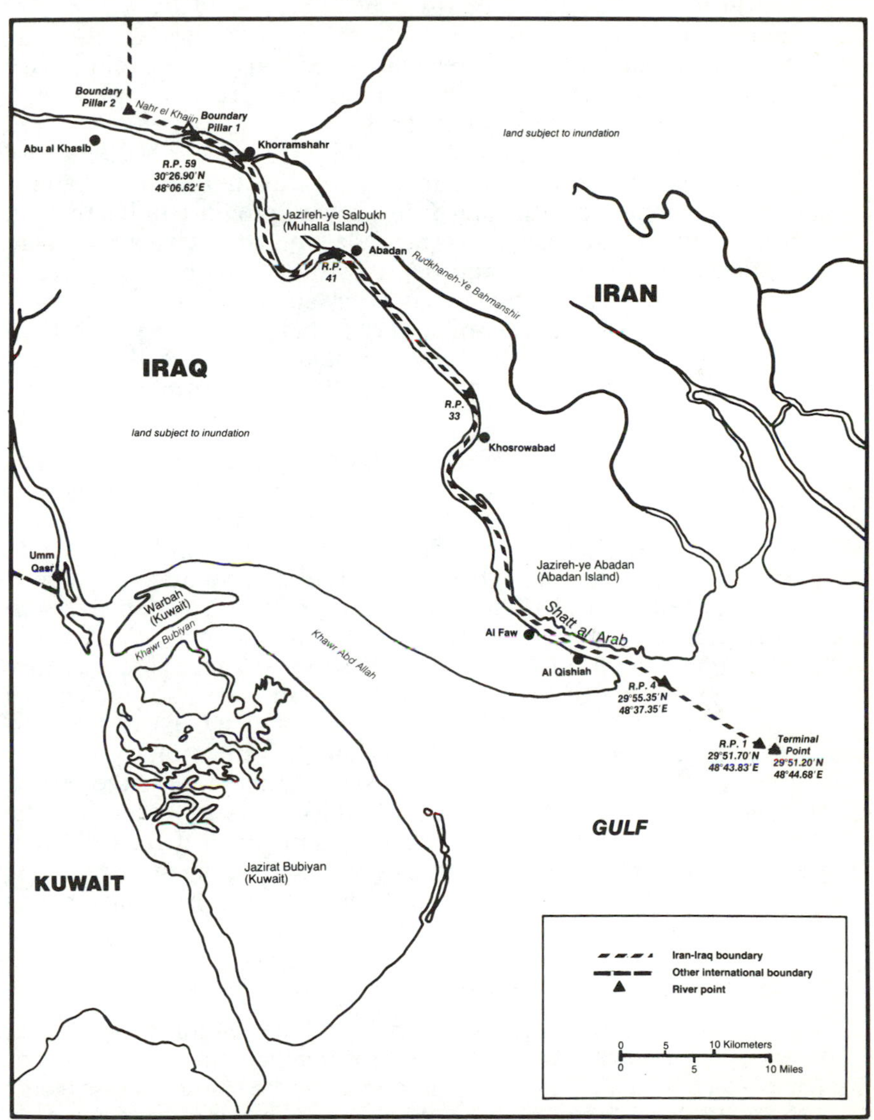

SOURCE: CIA 503692 4-78 (543694).

- Third, to redress the Algiers Accord and to give Iraq total control over the waters of the Shat, to demonstrate that Iraq and not Iran was the dominant power in the Gulf, and to enhance Iraq's status at the 1982 meeting of the nonaligned Nations.
- Fourth, to destroy Iranian military power while Iran was still weakened by the purges of its armed forces and by the virtual cutoff of U.S. supplies and support during the hostage crisis, while it was still converting from regular armed forces to Revolutionary Guards (Pasadran), and while most of the Iranian logistic and maintenance system was in chaos.
- Fifth, to create conditions that would overthrow Khomeini and lead to his replacement by a more orthodox and secular regime.
- Sixth, to conquer or "liberate" Iran's key oil province of Khuzestan, place it under Iraqi or Sunni Arab rule, and simultaneously secure Iraq's access to the Gulf and deprive Iran of the economic assets needed to recover as a major Gulf power.
- And seventh, to become so powerful that no conservative Gulf nation would risk Iraqi hostility and that the hostile Baath party in Syria would be forced to recognize Iraq's power and influence.

While the Iraqis have claimed in recent months that their goals included only the first three objectives, they were much less modest at the start of the war, and their statements then indicated that they had all seven objectives clearly in mind. There are strong indications that Iraq was planning to announce that a free Iranian government had been set up in Khuzestan when it "liberated" the province. Saddam Hussein also came perilously close to formally declaring that Iraq would annex Khuzestan in a speech on 4 November 1980 stating that Iraq's victory had "imposed its own claims."[10] This interpretation of Iraq's objectives is born out by the nature of the Iraqi attack and by the efforts Iraq made to catalyze a revolt in Khuzestan and to gain military support from Oman and the other conservative states. Accordingly, the weight of evidence argues strongly that Iraq's ambitions greatly exceeded the capability of its grand strategy to achieve them. Even if they did not, however, Iraq made critical mistakes in grand strategy in starting a war that it did not know how to finish and that left Iraq as vulnerable as its enemy.

Iraq's Mistakes in Grand Strategy

Iraq had considerable provocation in launching its attack. Khomeini had done far more than talk about overthrowing Saddam Hussein, whom he once referred to as a "dwarf pharaoh." He had sent "messengers" to subvert Iraq's Shi'ite population, and he had sponsored assassination attempts on Iraqi officials. He and Bani Sadr had publicly appealed for an "Islamic Revolution" in Iraq, had launched attacks on Iraqi border posts, and had shelled Iraqi towns near the border in early September

1980. While Iraq must bear a good part of the blame for the long-standing rivalry between the two nations, and for some of the incidents just before the war, even Iran's current supporters do not deny that it was behind most of the roughly 240 military incidents that occurred between the two countries in the year before Iraq invaded.[11] Khomeini seemed determined both to export his revolution and to avenge his expulsion from Iraq.

The Iraqis also had ample reason to believe Iran was weak and divided. A coup attempt had been made on Khomeini in August, and Iranian high command and officer corps had been purged, and most of Iran's minorities were becoming increasingly hostile to Khomeini.[12] Just as Britain and the conservative monarchies of Europe hopelessly misread the French Revolution, Iraq mistook an intensely nationalist upheaval for divisions it could exploit to rapidly defeat Iran's disorganized military forces, to conquer its oil-rich province of Khuzestan, and then to leave Iran militarily and economically shattered. Iraq ignored the countless times in history that an outside invasion has united a revolution into a lethal military force.

Like many of their predecessors, the Iraqis created a situation that redirected an internal civil war against the outside threat. They also acted to radicalize the Iranian revolution and to make its extremism seem justified. Khomeini was able to point to a legitimate "foreign devil," he and the radical clergy around him were eventually able to make "moderates" like Bani Sadr into traitors, and Khomeini used the war to mobilize the bulk of the native Persian population against Iraq and rival ethnic factions in Iran. It is unlikely, for example, that Khomeini could have been so effective in suppressing Massoud Rajavi's Mujahedin e-Khalq guerrillas—which at the start of the war had over 20,000 armed men—without the lever furnished by the Iraqi invasion. It is equally unlikely that anything else could have done as much to unite Iran on religious grounds. Iran may be only 63% Persian—with 3% Kurds, 18% Turkic, 3% Arab, 13% tribal, and 1% other—but it is 93% Shi'ite.[13] Iraq launched its invasion in an atmosphere in which it drastically miscounted the first set of figures and totally ignored the second.

The Problems of "Arabestan." Iraq also made a fundamental miscalculation in treating Khuzestan as if it were an Arab extension of Iraq. This portion of Iran, which Iraq calls Arabestan, is located on a river plain that is a continuation of the Tigris-Euphrates. It is geographically isolated by the Zagros Mountains to the east, which are 620 miles long and 120 miles wide and which have heights of up to 5,500 feet. It is about 9,800 square miles in area, and it contains many of Iran's oil and pipeline facilities, its major port, and its largest refinery. It also has about 3.5 million people. Only between 33% and 40% of this population can now be called Arab. Further, many of these "Arabs"—real or titular—now hardly speak Arabic and are Shi'ites loyal to the Iranian clergy.

The Iraqis did not simply set out to conquer this part of Iran. They let their ideology persuade them that the population would side with the "Arabs" and against the "Shi'ites," although their rationale for this belief seems to be almost totally one of ideological preconviction. While the Bani Kab tribe, which had settled the area before Reza Shah consolidated power, may have come from what later became Iraq, its last independent leader—Sheikh Khazaal—had been overthrown by one of Reza Shah's generals in 1925. In the following 55 years, Iran had systematically "Persianized" Khuzestan through every means from forcible resettlement to the suppression of Arabic in the schools. Rebellions from 1929 to 1945 led to forced changes in the character of the region.[14] By the time pro-Arab groups like the People's Liberation Front of Al-Ahwaz arose in the mid-1950s, they had lost much of their popular base. When the Arab oil workers in the area rioted against the Khomeini government in early 1979 and early 1980, they acted in protest against their pay and promotion prospects. They showed few signs of being pro-Iraq.

The Iraqis also seem to have failed to properly analyze the nature of their economic objective. They seem to have given Abadan, whose main function was to refine oil for export, and the port of Khorramshahr far more strategic importance than they really had. There is no question that such objectives were important, but they were not critical or crippling to Iran. The revolution had already greatly reduced Iran's needs for imports through its Gulf ports, and the vast majority of Iran's oil pipelines, oil fields, and oil-loading facilities are east of Ahwaz. In fact, Iran's main oil-loading terminals are far to the east at Kharg Island. To control "Arabestan," and to economically cripple Iran, Iraq had to advance at least as far east as the key pipeline junctions east of Ahwaz and Bandar Mashahr (Khomeini). Ideally, Iraq had to advance to the Zagros, or the towns and river barriers along a line drawn from Lali through Gazin and Bandar Deylam.

Iraq never seems to have understood either the amount of territory it had to conquer or to have firmly decided whether it wanted control of the province or the border area near the river. Yet unless it achieved control over most of the province, it stood little prospect of being able to terminate the conflict on strategically advantageous terms unless the Khomeini regime collapsed of its own accord under the tensions of revolutionary turmoil. This possibility was far too uncertain to justify an Iraqi attack.

Failure to Understand Vulnerabilities. Further, Iraq seems to have failed to fully analyze its own vulnerabilities. Quite aside from the risks inherent in sending a largely Shi'ite army, with Sunni officers who were not always popular, to fight a Shi'ite revolution, Iraq ignored its own geography and logistics and the vulnerability of its oil industry. Iraq has a coastline of only 93 miles. Its three ports—al-Basrah, Umm Qasr, and al-Fao—can all be interdicted by any conflict in which Iraq cannot

MAP 16—3
KEY OIL VULNERABILITIES

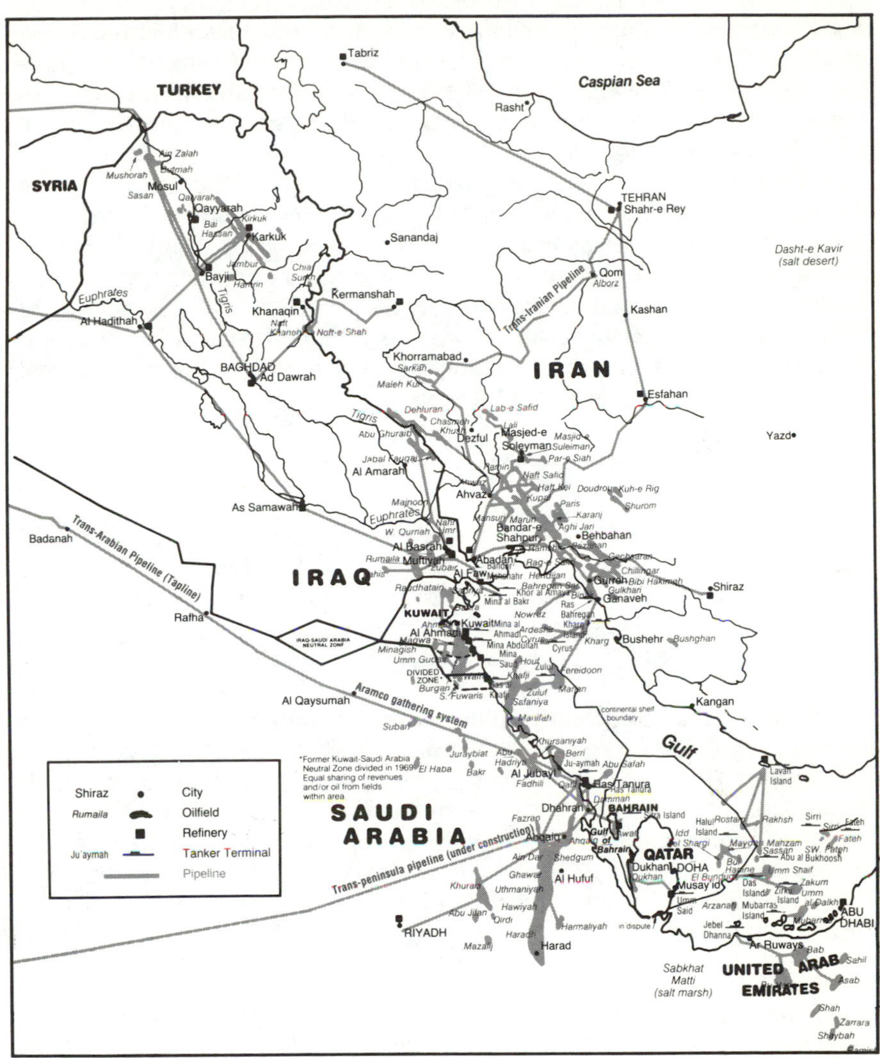

shield this narrow coast. Al-Basrah, its main port, is well within artillery range of Iran. The Shat al-Arab is also extremely difficult to secure. It is 136 miles long, and al-Basrah is 47 miles up this passage from the Gulf. The river is only 1/4 to 3/4 mile wide and silts up quickly unless it is dredged, which makes Iraq's lines of communication vulnerable to any war that closes the Shat.[15] Equally important, Iraq's only major oil-loading facilities on the Gulf were at Khor al-Amaja and Mina al-Bakr, and these were closer to the Iranian shore than to Iraq. They also were highly vulnerable to Iran's navy, which most experts still felt clearly outclassed Iraq's naval forces at the time Iraq launched its attack. Iraq's only alternative economic lifelines were limited-capacity oil pipelines through Turkey and Syria. The first was vulnerable to the Kurdish rebels, the second to Syrian political hostility and the vicissitudes of the Lebanese civil war.

In fairness, however, it should be said that one of the key lessons of the war was that Iraq made most of its mistakes in grand strategy for reasons that could just as easily have been made by any other state. It would be difficult to name a single Western nation that started any significant military conflict in this century with a realistic picture of what it wanted to achieve and how it would terminate the conflict it was engaging in. If Iraq marched somewhat carelessly off into a political void, it followed in a long tradition.

The True Definition of "An Intelligence Failure": The Problem of Assessment

The Iraqi failures in grand strategy involved important failures in intelligence, but they also involved far more. While they provide a case study in some of the fundamental limits to intelligence on the politics and military capabilities of the Gulf States, they have broader implications for any effort to assess the forces shaping the Gulf.

Intelligence Warning Versus Warnings About Intelligence. It is obvious in retrospect that Iraq badly underestimated not only the capabilities of Iran's regular military force, but also those of its new Pasadran, or Revolutionary Guards. In this sense, the war involved massive "intelligence failures," which ranged from the inability to predict the capabilities of individual units to an inability to understand the basic forces driving an enemy state. These failures involve some lessons that are almost as familiar from recent military history as the inability to formulate and implement grand strategy:

- No clear methodology exists for estimating the combat effectiveness, adaptability, or will of enemy forces that have not been tried in combat. It is remarkably easy to issue estimates of such capabilities, but it is virtually impossible to support them with indicators or defendable reasons why these indicators should be valid. To the extent that the outcome of a policy or war depends on such intelligence judgments, it involves a high degree of risk.
- These risks increase greatly when such estimates must be made about the forces of developing nations, forces in political transition, and forces acquiring new tactics and technologies.

- They increase even further when reliable human intelligence (HUMINT) is not available in great detail, and when equally detailed intelligence is lacking on recent training, exercise, and combat performance. Order of battle intelligence, technical intelligence, and data on manning and stock levels are important, but they are valuable largely in interpreting HUMINT and readiness intelligence. They are dangerously misleading without such intelligence.
- And they increase to the point of disaster when intelligence on the capability of military forces cannot be related to how they will be commanded in war and the probable political behavior of the high command.

While these lessons are a warning to the West and the conservative Gulf states to improve their HUMINT and intelligence analysis, such efforts can only minimize future failures. The real lesson of these intelligence failures, and one that goes beyond the issue of Gulf security, is that uncertainty must be planned for and that all nations may suddenly blunder into war half-blind. The issue is not one of how intelligence can correct this situation, it is rather to realize just how specious any "intelligence" that claims special vision must inevitably be.

Lessons Regarding Introspection and Assessment. Iraq's problems also stemmed from a lack of self-assessment. It lacked the capability to honestly assess the training, readiness, and weaknesses of its own forces. The extent of this failure becomes clearer when one compares the total military forces and resources on both sides when the war began. These forces are shown in Table 16.1. Seen from an Iraqi perspective, they seem relatively well matched. The ratios favor Iraq in some respects and Iran in others, but Iraq obviously managed to build up a suprisingly large military force structure, given the differences in population and GNP. Further, although such numbers disguise a general technical superiority in the equipment on the Iranian side, they make no allowance for Iranian losses of manpower and combat-ready equipment as a result of the revolution. Up to a point, it was reasonable for Iraq to assume that Iran could not commit most of its forces to battle or take advantage of most of its technological superiority.

The Assessment of Air Power. There are, however, several aspects of the Iranian force structure that Iraq should have found deeply worrying and that none of the Iraqi statements at the time or since indicate that Iraq properly considered. The first is that Iran's air force was primarily offensive. This shows up in the numbers in Table 16.1, but it becomes even clearer when the aircraft types involved are considered. Iran's attack aircraft included 188 F-4D/Es and 166 F-5E/Fs. Iraq's attack aircraft included 12 Tu-22s, 10 obsolete Il-28s, 80 export-version MiG-23BMs, 40 Su-7Bs, 60 export-version Su-20s, and 15 Hunters.[16] All of the Iranian attack aircraft were advanced types with high-quality avionics, as well as the ability to carry advanced attack munitions. None of the Iraqi aircraft had more than mediocre avionics, and most could not

TABLE 16.1 Iraqi and Iranian Forces and Resources at the Beginning of the Iran-Iraq War

	Iran	Iraq
General		
Total population (millions)	38.3	13.1
GNP ($ billions)	76.1	21.4
Defense expenditures ($ billions)	4.2	2.7
Arms imports, 1974–1978 ($ billions)	8.3	5.7
Total military manpower	240,000	242,200
Conscript manpower	180,000	177,200
Additional paramilitary manpower	75,000	79,800
Army		
Armored divisions	3	4
Mechanized infantry divisions	3	4
Mountain divisions	0	4
Independent brigades	4	3
Active army manpower	150,000	200,000
Reserve manpower	400,000	250,000
Medium tanks	1,735	2,750
Other AFVs and APCs	1,075	2,500
Self-propelled artillery	564	?
Towed artillery	1,000+	800
Air Force		
Air Force Manpower	70,000	28,000
Total combat aircraft	445	332
Bombers and attack	354	217
Air defense	77	115
Recce	14	0
Helicopters (Army and Air Force)	746	277
Navy		
Naval manpower	20,000	4,250
Missile destroyers	3	0
Missile frigates	4	0
Corvettes	4	0
Missile patrol boats	9	12
Large patrol boats	7	5
Maritime patrol aircraft	6	0

Sources: Adapted from *The Military Balance, 1980–81* (London: IISS, 1981), p. 42; ACDA, *World Military Expenditures and Arms Transfers, 1969–78.*

carry advanced munitions. This means that an Iraqi victory was highly dependent on the extent to which the revolution made Iran's fighters inoperable and on the extent to which Iraq could destroy them or their bases.

Western estimates made at the time of the Iraqi attack indicated that only 18–50% of Iran's attack aircraft were operational.[17] To this day, it is unclear what the truth was, but these figures still seem reasonable. Discussions in the Gulf also indicate that Iraq relied as much on estimates in the Western press as on its intelligence sources. Iraq should have realized that Iran had enough air strength left to strike at Iraq's oil facilities and key economic targets, many of which have only 100–200 miles of strategic depth. It should have realized that in any prolonged war, it would face an enemy that could strike at its economic survival and reply to Iraqi victories on the ground with air power.

Iraq compounded these mistakes by grossly overestimating the capabilities of its own air force. Unlike Israel, Iraq seems to have let ideology and rhetoric delude it into assuming that its air force and ground-based air defenses had high effectiveness. Iraq did so even though

- its most effective attack squadrons and all its bomber squadrons had been kept under Hussein's thumb to prevent them from threatening the regime and had had only third-rate range training;
- its fighter pilots had received limited training in the USSR and no modern air-to-air training in Iraq—in fact, they were virtually untrained for combat except in one-on-one encounters at altitudes above 5,000 feet;
- the October War had clearly demonstrated just how difficult it is to attack a sheltered or protected air base, and Iraq's pilots had shown relatively poor combat accuracy in strikes against the Kurds and in range performance before the war;
- it had almost no low-altitude radar coverage and serious netting and reliability problems in medium-altitude coverage;
- the October War had provided lessons regarding the acute performance limitations on the SA-2 and SA-3 missiles, and Iraq had only about 25 SA-6 launchers, which were manned by half-trained crews, and which were not netted into anything approaching a capable air defense system;
- it had conducted only *pro forma* close air exercises with the army, and in real world terms, it was able to sustain less than 50% on-line operational readiness in even its best squadrons;
- and it had no real reconnaissance and target analysis capabilities, and no command and control structure suited to either carrying out close air support missions or conducting an integrated air defense.

In short, Iraq forgot an "iron law" of air power that the two previous

Arab-Israeli wars should have made clear to every senior Iraqi official and officer: You are only as good as your sustained performance in realistic exercises and combat training, and you are never likely to be better than your methods and equipment have proved in previous combat.[18]

The key lesson that emerges from these Iraqi mistakes is exactly the one that emerges from most modern wars: Air forces are defeated or weakened at least as much by their internal illusions as by the enemy. The minute readiness data cease to be realistic, training is cut back or separated from realistic combat conditions, effectiveness is exaggerated, equipment performance and lethality are overstated, gaps in training and doctrine are ignored, and an air force becomes a bureaucracy rather than a ruthlessly self-critical fighting machine. It places itself in a position in which it must try to carry out in war the preparation it should have carried out in peacetime.

The Assessment of Sea Power. The second critical weakness, and perhaps an excusable one for a land power, is that Iraq ignored Iran's naval superiority. This time, it did so in the face of accurate reporting that while the Iranian Navy had serious problems, it was still able to send its larger ships to sea, to fly its six P-3Fs armed with Harpoon, and to threaten not only Iraq's facilities in the eastern Gulf but tanker movements in the entire Gulf region.[19] Iraq also ignored the Iranian Navy even though it had clear knowledge that its own navy was largely ineffective. Iraq's leaders knew that most of their 12 Osa-I and Osa-II with Styx missiles had poor readiness and operational training. Iraq had approached two Western European navies in 1978 and 1979 and asked for help in training and improving their readiness. Iraqi officers then had stated quite openly that Soviet training had proved inadequate and that the missiles on their ships were not proving effective even in an EW-free environment.

The Iraqis should have known that much of the Iranian Navy was based outside the effective range of the Iraqi Air Force and that the Iranian Air Force could provide it with considerable air cover. They should have realized that even if Oman and the UAE did allow them to use their bases for a heliborne assault on the Tumbs and Abu Musa, this was quite different from acquiring the sustained air power capabilities necessary to strike at the Iranian Navy in areas outside the normal range of Iraqi air bases. They should have known that the Iraqi Air Force had no training for striking against naval targets. Further, even if they ignored all these factors, they should have realized that no Iraqi invasion was likely to occupy Abadan Island in less than a week and that there was a good prospect that by that time, Iranian artillery might have effectively interdicted Iraq's ports.

In this case, assessment is less complex and controversial than for air power. The Iraqis launched a war in which they had terrible vulnerabilities to sea power, and with a total disregard of their own lack of effectiveness. It is a basic principle of strategy that the military balance and the outcome of war must be viewed in terms of an accurate assessment of the ability to fight the enemy's entire force.

The Assessment of Land Power. Iraq's problems in assessing its land power are more complex. Conversations with a number of senior officers from Arab countries who talked to Iraqi senior officers before and after the war started to indicate that Iraq seriously miscalculated the technical superiority of Iranian army equipment and the importance of the immense stockpiles of material that the shah had purchased. Iraq did, therefore, underestimate Iran's potential qualitative edge and the extent to which it could fight a long war without resupply if it was given the chance to do so. Iraq evidently also placed high reliance on the impact of the political turmoil in Iran in causing Iran's mobilization system to collapse and in disrupting Iran's ability to move material and men to the front and on reports that Iran's reliance on a computerized logistic system had left it unable to find many of its holdings of parts and ammunition. Iraq almost certainly underestimated the fighting power of individual Iranian units and Iran's ability to sustain a war.

This was probably a relatively minor miscalculation, however, compared to Iraq's overestimate of the capability of its own land forces. Senior Arab officers from several countries friendly to Iraq have all noted one of the consequences of the extreme politicization of the Iraqi armed forces is a heavy emphasis on morale, on nationalism and the impact of revolutionary fervor, on the impact of masses of manpower, and on highly demanding physical training. These officers note that Iraq's ideology caused it to ignore the weaknesses in its force structure and to underemphasize realistic training. A combination of ideology and constant political purges led Iraq to ignore most of the Western and Israeli commentary on Arab military weaknesses and failures and to create a highly centralized command structure that does not tolerate problems in reporting on readiness and in converting to new weapons and technology, as well as the host of minor problems affecting military capability.

Virtually every Western military expert would confirm these judgments, and several have added that Iraq's limited military experience led it to seriously overestimate its capabilities. One aspect of this overestimation was evidently caused by Iraq's experience in the October War. Iraq did prove successful in moving large formations to the front very quickly and without warning and in making effective use of its tank transporters. As a result Iraqi planners sharply overestimated the mobility that Iraq could achieve in advancing through Iran, while they conveniently forgot that Iraq had been halted dead the moment it encountered serious Israeli opposition.

Further, the long campaigns against the Kurds—which produced some 60,000 Iraqi casualties between 1968 and 1975—had led the Iraqi forces to adopt a special style of fighting. The Iraqi forces could not suppress the small Kurdish guerrilla units, so they adopted tactics based on massing against Kurdish villages, towns, and strongholds. These tactics involved massing against the objective, sealing it off, and then methodically using artillery fire and strafing to disorganize the defense. Armor and infantry would advance slowly and would be used in ways that essentially added to the bombardment. Tanks would be dug in whenever they proved vulnerable. If the strong point continued to resist, more artillery would be used and tanks would continue to be used as artillery. This method worked well in advancing against a half-trained and poorly equipped force that could not be effectively resupplied. Even so, however, the Kurds were defeated only when Iraq's 1975 accommodation with the shah led him to cut off support to the Kurds and to have the CIA halt all training and supply.[20]

In the years that followed, ideology and selective memory turned these "victories" over the Kurds into memories of high military effectiveness. The Iraqi Army and Air Force also seem to have enshrined many of the tactics and procedures involved in their training and planning without realizing the implications. They overlaid Soviet tactical concepts regarding mass and maneuver without ever conducting realistic field exercises. This was not the way to prepare for a very different kind of war with Iran, and it was not the way to develop a realistic understanding of the capability of Iraq's forces.

Assessment of Politicization. Finally, the problem of assessment was compounded by the fact that Iraq seems to have been as unable to understand the impact of its own revolution as it was unable to understand that of Iran's. The Iraqi Baathists surrounding Saddam Hussein had legitimate reason to be proud of the progress they had made in uniting the country after 1978. The suppression of a military coup backed by the Iraqi Communist party had been followed by progress in economic development and in sharing the nation's wealth, which merits considerable respect. Similarly, the Revolutionary Council had greatly relaxed Iraq's internal security effort and had taken a wide range of measures to win popular loyalty and ease the past tension among Kurd, Sunni, and Shi'ite. It is easy in the West to underestimate this progress, but it is apparent to any recent visitor to Iraq who can remember the country in the mid-1970s. Even some Arab opponents of the Baath and Saddam Hussein give Iraq considerable credit for this progress.

Nevertheless, the Iraqi high command had been extensively purged in 1978, the key offensive forces of the Iraqi Air Force were kept under Hussein's personal control, the capital was kept surrounded with politically loyal combat units that were under constant supervision by the security services. Iraq's T-72 tanks were kept in reserve elements specially chosen to secure the regime. The government treated honest reporting of military problems as failure or disloyalty, and it overcentralized every aspect of decision making. Iraq thus went to war against an opponent that it regarded as crippled by internal politics with crippling political weaknesses of its own.[21]

In fact, Iran was in the grip of revolutionary, ideological, and religious fervor. It was ready to endure high casualties to defend its revolution, and it was already socially and politically committed to a national state of war. In contrast, Iraq's political cohesion lay in the belief of its citizens that, regardless of politics, life was getting better. Iraq's unity depended on avoiding casualties, on maintaining the rise in living standards, and on avoiding any circumstances that could lead to friction among Kurd, Sunni, and Shi'ite—particularly because the Iraqi officer corps were largely Sunni and the troops were largely Shi'ite. These problems did not matter if Iraq won a quick, decisive victory, but they meant that Iraq was acutely restricted in the casualties it could accept and its need to preserve the unity of its armed forces if it did not.

Lessons for the West and the Southern Gulf States. Iraq's mistakes present some obvious lessons regarding the importance of politics to war and the need to assess relative politicization in the military forces of developing states. They are yet another point of evidence to support the thesis that most armed forces organize and train to win their last war and that this helps prepare them to lose the next. The key lesson, however, is that the success of military planning depends to an extraordinary degree on an honest net assessment of the comparative strengths and weaknesses of one's own forces, those of one's allies, and those of the threat. The corollary of this lesson is equally apparent, and it is one of the key lessons the U.S. learned from air combat in Vietnam and that Israel learned from the October War. The key to stripping away the illusions that bind one's own military effectiveness is to conduct constant training in as realistic a manner as possible. The key to readiness is not simply equipment strength, ammunition stocks, small parts inventories, or manning levels: It is also training and continuity.

The Problem of Strategy

It is important to iterate that the problems in the strategy of the Iran-Iraq War are not solely those of Iraq. Iran virtually provoked the war but had no defensive strategy. Iran provided yet another case study in the fact that revolutionary societies can suddenly embroil themselves in wars that they have made no attempt to be ready to fight.[22] It is also somewhat speculative to draw conclusions about the war's strategy since the evidence regarding Iraq's exact intentions is uncertain. Nevertheless, some aspects of Iraq's strategy seem clear.

The Strategy Behind the Timing of the Attack.[23] Iraq faced a relatively narrow time window in terms of weather if it was to strike in 1980. The rainy season in the area starts in November and can continue through April. Southern Khuzestan is crossed by a number of major water barriers and something like 640 minor ones. It is subject to flooding, which can be enhanced by opening key dikes or dams. The central and northern fronts are subject to rain, cold weather, and snow

MAP 16—4
KHUZESTAN PROVINCE

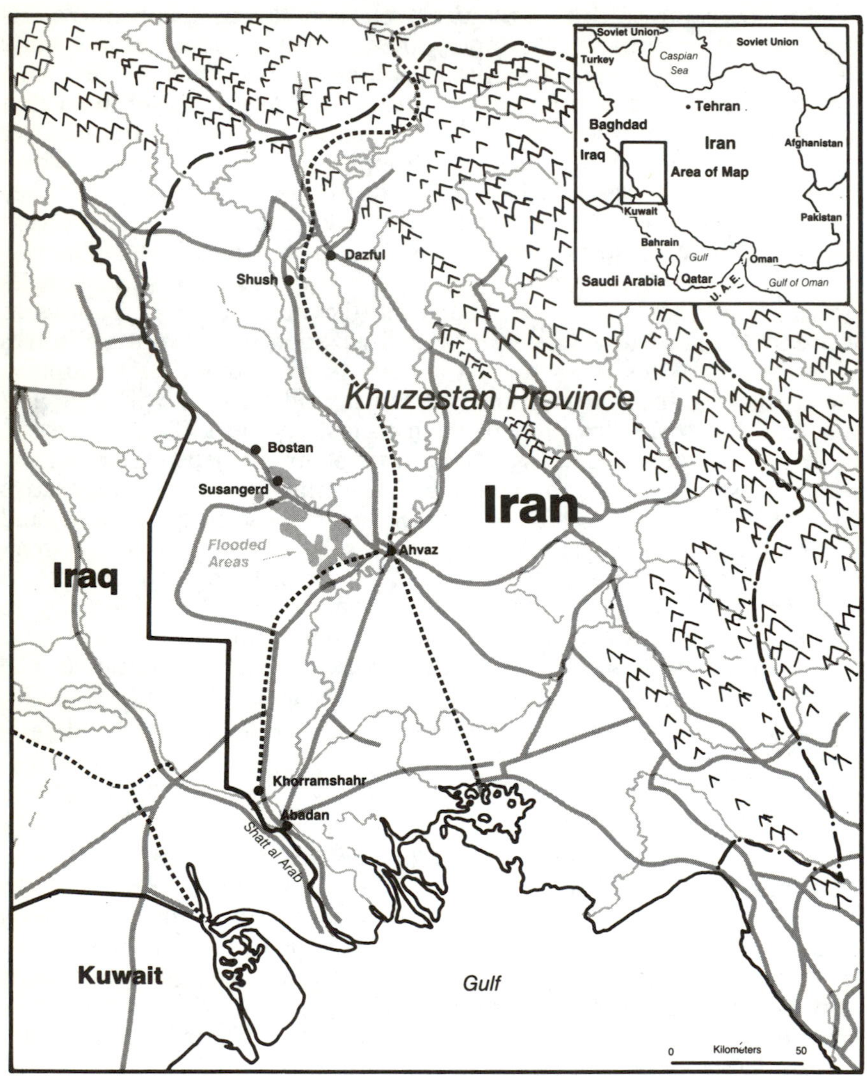

in some areas and are extremely hot and dry in others, depending on the time of year. Iraq had to strike while the terrain was relatively dry, but also relatively cool. Iraq could not predict whether the turmoil in Iran would be reduced. It faced an Iran in near-civil war, with its military purged, and cut off from U.S. parts and ammunition by the hostage crisis. The Carter administration had publicly hinted that it would resume shipments if the hostages were released, and the regular armed forces opposing Iraq were being steadily strengthened by Revolutionary Guards.

Further, Iraq had had only limited military resupply from the USSR after the coup attempt in 1978, and its conversion to Western equipment—if it could be accomplished at all—would not come before the mid-1980s. It got its first 4 Mirage F-1s, for example, only in February 1981, although it had first ordered 36 of the aircraft in 1977. It was not able to operate most of its French army equipment effectively and did not have the numbers of equipment it would require to replace its Soviet equipment on order, much less that in the process of delivery. Its navy could not make the transition to the ships it had on order before 1983 at the earliest. In short, its Soviet-equipped force structure was a wasting asset.

Iraq also faced several political problems. One was the need to rapidly assert its leadership of the Gulf. The second was its uncertainty regarding future U.S. and Soviet ties to Iran and its ability to attack a still isolated Iran when the rains ended in the spring. The third was the fact that it had a second hostile Shi'ite-dominated power on its western border and had no way to predict the impact Shi'ite or Kurdish unrest would have if it did not attack. Finally, it was hosting the Nonaligned Nations Conference in the fall of 1982, and a victory would give it immense influence.

Seen from this perspective, the timing of the Iran-Iraq War seems to have been well judged and an almost natural outcome of the forces and pressures involved. The only difficulty, and the key lesson involved, is that it took the West about a year after the war started to become aware of these pressures. While the West had relatively good intelligence warning of some of the military moves involved, it is impossible even with hindsight to say that it could have been warned of the degree to which such forces would suddenly threaten, and then reduce, its oil supplies.

The Strategy of the Land Attack. The nature of Iraq's strategic objectives—and its expectations regarding its ability to conquer Dezful, Ahwaz, Abadan, and Khorramshahr—is still a matter of conjecture. The rest of its land attack strategy, however, is fairly clear. Even in peacetime, Iraq faces three distinct military problems on its border with Iran. The first is that it must secure the northern part of the border to ensure security against both an Iranian invasion and problems with its Kurds. It can reduce its concentration of forces in the area only at the cost of a sharply increased risk of Kurdish insurgency. The second is that in the central part of the border, Baghdad is only 100 miles from Iran, and while there are fairly good rough terrain and mountain barriers on the Iranian side, it is a "straight shot" at Iraq's capital from the Iranian border garrison of Qasr-e-Shirin. It is almost impossible for Iraq to advance to Tehran and the key Persian cities in Iran, but it is comparatively easy for Iran to threaten Iraq's capital, and it is unlikely that a Sunni-led government could survive the capital's fall. The third is that any attack on Iran on the southern part of the border must reach Dezful and Ahwaz to have any chance of creating an Arabestan, securing Iran's oil industry, seizing Iran's key military bases in Khuzestan, and securing a military victory. Iraq must control Abadan Island and Khorramshahr to provide minimal security to the Shat al-Arab, and it must secure Bandar Khomeini to give that security even the slightest sustained credibility. The size of an Iraqi advance through the south quickly became limited by the roads and engineering equipment. It was not possible to move more than three to five divisions through the area without creating immense problems in creating new roads, crossing water barriers, and the like.

These factors forced Iraq to divide its forces to cover three fronts. The only issue was the extent to which it should try to take the offensive on all three fronts, and here certain terrain and strategic factors became critical. Any advance in the north meant moving through easily defensible mountains and into a void. Even a capture of Mehebad or Tabriz would present more problems to Iraq in occupying such cities than their loss would present to Iran. The most Iraq could hope for would be to link up to Kurdish or other elements hostile to Iran. A central front offensive meant fighting through defensible terrain to at least Kermanshah. Even Kermanshah, however, is a minor objective; it is important only if it allows Iraq to wheel its forces south against Dezful.

The general land force strategy of the Iraqi attack is shown in Map 16.1. Iraq began its deployment with five divisions in the north, two guarding the central area near Baghdad, and five in the south. These included three armored divisions and two mechanized divisions. Opposed to this, Iran had four of its nine under-strength divisions along a 1,300-kilometer frontier. One was an infantry division near Urumiyeh in the far north, the second was an infantry division at Sanandaj covering the threat from the Iranian Kurds and reinforced by the Pasadran. The third was an armored division at Kermanshah and a brigade at Qasr-e-Shirin. The fourth was an armored division in Ahwaz, which covered the south and shielded Iran's key air base at Dezful. A battalion group garrison was added to the town of Mehran just before the war began.[24]

Although the exact details are uncertain, Iraq's strategy in dealing with this situation was to hold defensively in the north, although an Iraqi infantry division finally attacked toward Panjwin in December in an effort to secure the oil fields at Kirkuk and link up with anti-Iranian Kurds. Depending on the source, one infantry division, and possibly an armored division as well, attacked across the central front at Qasr-e-Shirin with the goal of pinning down or destroying the Iranian armored division at Kermanshah. Another Iraqi infantry division advanced against Mehran, although some elements may initially have been held in reserve. On the southern front, which would decide the success of Iraq's strategy,

Iraq attacked with one armored division against Dezful and Susengard, one armored division against Ahwaz, one armored division against Abadan, and two mechanized divisions—plus special forces and other independent brigades—in reserve. This gave Iraq an initial advantage of something over 5–6 : 1 in the southern front. In theory, it should have been decisive. Iran was not prepared for the attack, and at least from 20 to 23 September, it was wide open to the Iraqi advance.

Iraq failed because of the grand strategic reasons discussed earlier, because of its failures in assessment, and because of tactical failures that will be discussed shortly. It also failed for strategic reasons that provide important lessons for a future war. First, Iraq compounded its inability to concentrate all its forces on the most critical front by diverting a substantial portion against Abadan before it defeated the Iranian regular division at Ahwaz and captured the Iranian main air base near Dezful. It sacrificed its most critical advantage, and the most critical moments of the war, because it failed to concentrate first on defeating the enemy's ability and/or will to fight—a basic violation of Clausewitz and virtually every writer on strategy since.

Second, Iraq was unprepared for urban warfare and warfare in built-up areas. The ability of random mixtures of Iranian regular troops, rapidly reinforcing militia and reserves, Revolutionary Guards, policemen, and naval commandos to use the combination of water barriers and the cover provided by buildings to halt largely unsupported and totally untrained and unprepared armor in an urban warfare environment came as a complete surprise. This became immediately apparent when the Iraqi army entered Khorramshahr. Its untrained troops waited for orders, called in artillery fire, and found that without far more independent decision-making authority than NCOs and junior officers had previously been given, they could not react in time to protect themselves.

An Iraqi special forces brigade then had to be called in and to fight its way through the city without even the advance preparation of being equipped with street maps. Like the Israelis who fought in Suez City in the final days of the October War, the Iraqis found that urban war deprives armor of its advantage, makes mass artillery fire largely ineffective against enemy forces, and gives even untrained infantry a great advantage in the defensive against partly trained attackers. At least 1,500 Iraqis died in a kind of fighting that Iraq's strategy had ignored, which led Iran to rename Khorramshahr "Khuninshar," the city of blood. This should be a warning to the planners shaping southern Gulf and USCENTCOM forces. These forces are at least as likely to die in some Gulf city as in the Zagros Mountains, and if they are to live, they should receive as much training to fight in a Gulf city as in the desert.[25]

The Air Strategy. Iraq's air strategy was quite simple. It launched as many planes as it could for the first three days of the war. While it attacked a total of 10 Iranian air bases, it concentrated on the 6 Iranian air fields nearest to Iraq and the Iranian early warning stations at Dehloran and Naft e-Shah. It also struck at ammunition dumps and key interdiction targets. For unknown reasons, however, Iraq attempted to deal with the problem of Iran's sheltered air bases by trying to crater runways. It either missed the large numbers of parked aircraft in the area or ignored them, and it did not hit at selected soft facilities. The results were militarily absurd. Iraq has since blamed its failures on Soviet munitions and charged that only one munition in six exploded, but this claim seems more rationale than reality. Iraq's Soviet fighters lacked the kind of avionics necessary to provide the accuracy needed for such attacks with conventional ordnance, and Iraq had obviously neither trained for such an attack nor made any attempt to analyze how it could best be carried out. It chose a strategy to deal with Iran's key advantage in air attack capability that was in direct contradiction to everything written about the probable lethality of such attacks in Vietnam, the Arab-Israeli conflict, and the India-Pakistan wars.

The end result was that during the first days of the war, much of the Iraqi Air Force had to flee to dispersal bases in Jordan and elsewhere in the Gulf. This step invited Iran to attack into Iraqi territory, and Iran quickly discovered that formations of two to four F-4s, flying at low altitudes, were virtually immune to both Iraqi fighters and its SAM defenses. By the second day of the war, Iran had hit Baghdad as well as Iraq's air bases, and after Iraq's artillery hit the refinery at Abadan on the third day, Iran began to strike at Iraq's virtually undefended oil facilities. Iraq not only failed to formulate a meaningful offensive air strategy, it failed to formulate a defensive strategy, as well, which virtually dictated Iran's strategy of exploiting a key Iraqi vulnerability.

There are lessons here, but most are painfully familiar. First, no strategy can be implemented without tactical capability, training, and the proper technology. Successful air attacks require long preparation against exactly the kind of target mix involved; no air force in history has proved flexible in suddenly adapting general training in peacetime to effective missions in the offensive role. In spite of all the nonsense about the flexibility of air power, air forces have been successful in implementing only those offensive strategies for which they received specific training and equipment. Second, air forces—and particularly those in developing countries—seem to have an infinite capacity for self-delusion about their effectiveness in offensive missions. Third, Western air training, avionics, munitions, and range payload capabilities are still far more effective than their Soviet counterparts, at least in the export version. This was true in Iran's case, even in the course of a revolution when some of the pilots had to be let out of jail to fly. And fourth, conventional bombing of area targets may have great shock value, but the true operational accuracy of such attacks is so poor—particularly when they have even minimal AA gun defenses—that it has little tactical effect. It took the U.S. Navy something like 66 1,000-pound bombs to crater one gravel road just once at the start of the interdiction campaigns against the resupply routes in Vietnam. Something like a third of the Pakistani attacks on Indian air bases in the last Pakistani-Indian war were directed at nearby service roads and totally missed the base, much less the runway.

The Naval Strategy. If Iraq had a naval strategy, it has not yet become apparent what it could have been. Iraq may or may not have hoped that the Iranian Navy was incapacitated, that Iraq's patrol boats could somehow protect its oil-loading facilities, or that its air power could destroy the Iranian Navy.

The Iran-Iraq War: The Shift from Iraqi Invasion to War of Attrition

The war's lessons regarding tactics, training, technology, and supply have equally important implications for Gulf security; in order to understand them, it is necessary to understand the flow of events that shaped the war after Iraq's initial miscalculations. The war has so far had six phases. The first was a series of incidents and provocations on both sides that helped cause the Iraqi invasion. The second was the Iraqi invasion and the brief period in which it scored its major victories. The third occurred in October and November 1980, when the Iranians succeeded in holding the Iraqi forces outside the key towns in Khuzestan and started a series of attacks on Iraqi oil facilities that eventually destroyed Iraq's ability to ship oil through the Gulf. The fourth was a period of virtual stalemate, from November 1980 to September 1981. The fifth was the round of fighting from September 1981 to May 1982, during which Iran drove Iraq from most of its key positions on Iranian soil. The sixth was a series of bloody Iranian offensives designed to destroy the Iraqi Army and/or occupy critical strategic areas in Iraq and overthrow the regime of Saddam Hussein. This phase continued into 1983.

The Initial Phase: Provocation

The first phase of the war is of little practical interest. The exact sequence of who did what to whom is at best now a matter for international lawyers. The Ayatollah Khomeini attacked the Baath regime almost from the start, and Iran first announced that it was no longer committed to the Algiers Accord and claimed full control over the Shat al-Arab on 14 September 1979. Iraq made its claim in turn on 31 October 1979, and from that point on both sides constantly protested the other's provocations.[26] By April 1980, a low-level border war was clearly under way. Iran had stepped up its attacks on the Baath, and Iraq had laid claim to the border territory the shah had promised, but not delivered, under the Algiers Accord, and demanded the return of the Tumbs and Abu Musa to the Arab states. Khomeini ordered the Iranian armed forces on full alert in response to Iraqi "attacks" and called for the Iraqi military to stage a coup. Saddam Hussein replied by threatening war against any state that attacked the popular government of Iraq.[27] Between April and September, both sides exchanged artillery fire, attacks on border posts, support for the other's opposition, and assassination attempts. In mid-September, this escalated to several aerial fighter duels and extended artillery bombardments.[28] By 20 September, Iran had called up its reserves and Iraq had started its offensive.[29]

Phase Two: The Iraqi Invasion

The Iraqi invasion strategy and the reasons for its timing have already been discussed, as have the basic reasons for its failure. On 22–23 September Iraq launched a massive air strike on 10 Iranian air bases, including the early-warning stations at Dehloran and Naft e-Shah. Although these included heavy attacks on at least six of Iran's fighter bases, most of the bombs dropped either misfired or missed their targets, and little damage was done to Iran's sheltered fighters. By the second day of the war, Iran's F-5s and F-4s had practical command of the air.[30] Then, at approximately 3 A.M. on the 23rd, six Iraqi divisions crossed the Iranian border at the positions shown in Map 16.1. A mechanized division in the north quickly overwhelmed the Iranian garrison at Qasr-e-Shirin and gained control of the Kermanshah-Hamadan road, which is the main route between Tehran and Baghdad. The other five divisions invaded Khuzestan along two major axes. The first axis spread outward toward various Iranian positions in Khuzestan, Dezful, and Ahwaz. The second crossed the Shat al-Arab and attacked Khorramshahr and Dezful. The attacks were supported by heavy artillery, and scattered and largely unsupported armored units advanced quickly.[31]

By the 24th, the Iraqi Army seemed to be advancing toward victory and claimed to be laying siege to Khorramshahr, Dezful, and Ahwaz. The Iranian Air Force, however, had already begun to strike at targets deep in Iraq. It hit military installations near Baghdad, oil facilities at Mosul and Kirkuk, and petrochemical plants at al-Basrah and Zubair. By the 25th, both sides were heavily attacking the other's oil facilities. Iranian ships and aircraft attacked al-Fao for the first time, and Iraq launched an unsuccessful attack on the main Iranian oil-loading facilities at Kharg Island. The Iraqi ground offensive continued, but began to slow at Abadan and Ahwaz as the Iranian forces stiffened their resistance, reserves were brought up, and the Iranian Air Force flew up to 150 close support sorties per day. Iraq claimed to have captured Abadan and Khorramshahr but did not take them. It did cut the major rail and road lines from Ahwaz to Khorramshahr.[32]

From the 26th to the 28th, the Iraqi advance continued, but it was halted at the outskirts of Ahwaz and Dezful. The Iraqi attack on Abadan bogged down in bloody fighting for each barrier, and Iran and Iraq began an exchange of artillery fire that eventually led to the virtual devastation of the city. The air war on oil installations continued, with Iran increasingly doing more damage than Iraq. The main refinery at al-Basrah was heavily bombed, and the Iraqi pipeline through Turkey was cut for the first time. Iraq made its first cease-fire offer on the 28th.[33] From 29 September to 23 October, Iraq continued to attempt to take Dezful and Ahwaz, and became involved in steadily bloodier fighting in Khorramshahr. The Iranians moved their reserves into Khuzestan and largely offset Iraq's initial advantage in strength. Iraq then gradually dug its forces in around the Dezful and Ahwaz fronts, and by mid-October, the ground war had begun to take on a World War I character, with heavily entrenched positions, extensive use of terrain barriers, artillery bombardments, and slow advances. Meanwhile, the air war continued, with Iran striking more and more heavily at Iraq. Iran bombed Baghdad successfully in early October, and Iraq again dispersed many of its aircraft to protect them. The Iraqi nuclear plant at Osirak was bombed for the first time.[34]

In late October and early November, Iraq won its last major success. Its troops succeeded in putting a pontoon bridge across the river and entered Khorramshahr. Between 24 October and 10 November, they fought their way slowly through the city and finally were able to make a serious claim to have conquered both Khorramshahr and Abadan on 10 November. Iran continued to dominate the air, however, and began to make increasing use of helicopter gunships. It poured reserves into the area and proved able to hold the Iraqi forces to token gains in the rest of Khuzestan.[35]

Phase Three: Iran's Strategic Oil Victory

The war approached a stalemate in early November 1980. However, Iran was to strike several strategic blows. The first was an air attack on Kuwaiti border posts on 12 and 16 November, which did a great deal to discourage any too overt support of Iraq by the other Arab Gulf states.[36] The second was a combined commando, naval, and air raid on Iraq's oil-loading facilities in the Gulf on 29–30 November, which left both Mina al-Bakr and al-Fao inoperable. It cut Iraq's oil-export potential from about 3 MMBD to about 1 MMBD. At the same time, it demonstrated that no ship could approach the Iraqi Gulf ports safely, and it left Iraq dependent on its vulnerable pipelines routes through Syria and Turkey.[37]

Phase Four: The Stalemate

Between December 1980 and May 1981, both sides fought for position without achieving any major victories. Iraq opened another division-sized "front" in the north near Panjwin, largely to protect Kirkuk. Attempts to use it to support an uprising by the Iranian Kurds proved unsuccessful. In most areas, both sides continued to dig in. Iran flooded some parts of Khuzestan while Iraq built raised and surface roads and

MAP 16—5
KEY FIGHTING AREAS IN THE IRAN-IRAQ WAR: 1980-1981

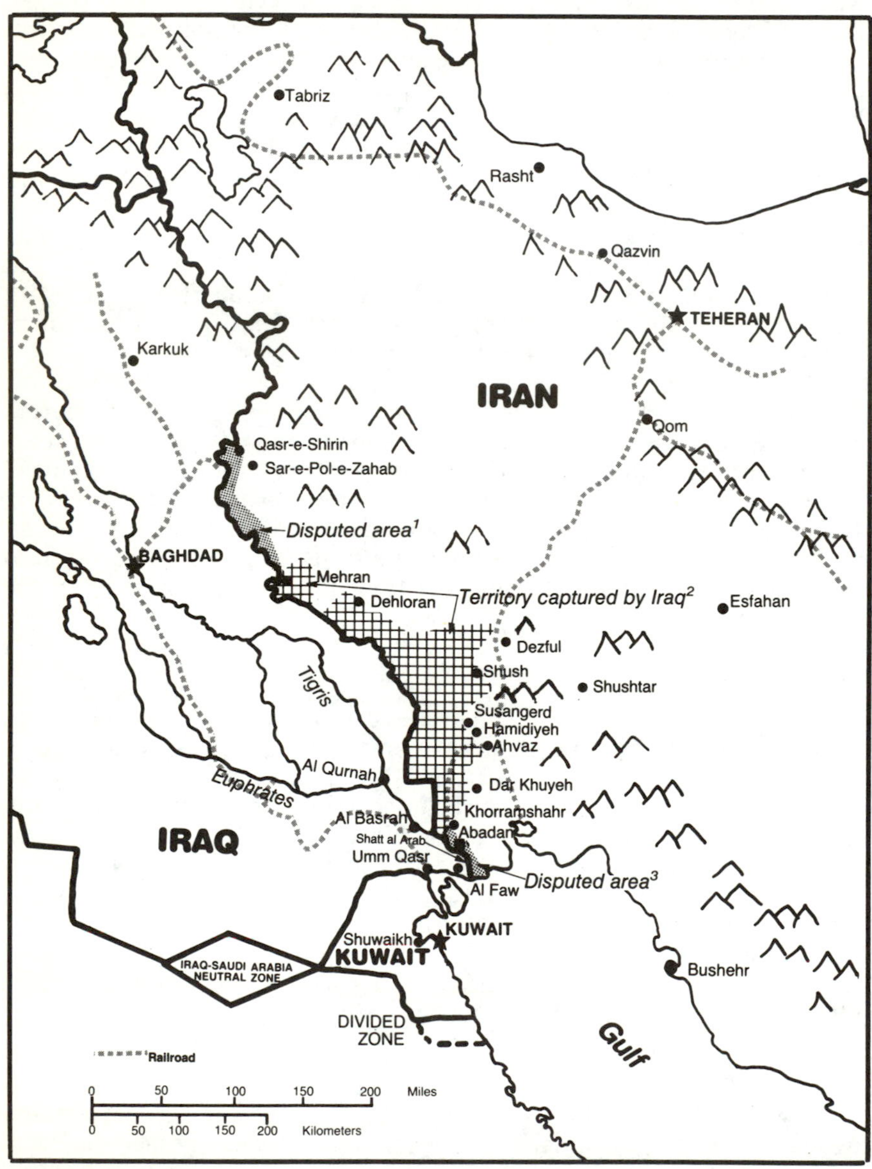

[1]*Area ceded by Iran to Iraq under 1975 Algiers Accord, but not turned over.*
[2]*Maximum line of advance.*
[3]*Claimed by Iraq, but ceded to Iran under Algiers Accord.*

Adapted from CIA maps by author.

heavy defensive positions. Iraq laid siege to Susangerd, but without significant results. On 11 December, Iraq began to talk officially for the first time of fighting a long war.[38] From mid-December on, Iraq's actions were largely defensive, and it began to mobilize for prolonged conflict. The air war gradually tapered off, although Iran successfully closed down facilities at Kirkuk for several weeks in December. Neither side seemed prepared to strike further at the other's major oil facilities or at its population centers, although artillery exchanges continued against the last Iranian positions in Khorramshahr and targets in al-Basrah.

Phase Five: Iran's Shift Toward Victory

The first major Iranian offensive of the war did little to indicate that this situation would change. By the end of 1980, Iran's President Bani Sadr was involved in a struggle for political survival with the Shi'ite clergy around Khomeini that finally forced him to flee the country in July 1981. He seems to have calculated that even a limited victory would allow him to retain power, and he launched an attack on Iraqi positions near Susangerd on 5 January 1981.

The Iranian Defeat at Susangerd. Bani Sadr's counteroffensive failed for many reasons. He committed the three under-strength regular armored regiments under his control to an assault without the support of the infantry provided by the Revolutionary Guards (Pasadran) loyal to Khomeini. He telegraphed his offensive to the extent that the Iraqis were well positioned and waiting for him, and he then attacked deep into the Iraqi line and penetrated almost as far as Hoveyzeh without combined arms support from the Guards and regular army. He ignored the fact that the terrain critically inhibited Iranian ability to conduct logistic resupply, and he failed to maneuver effectively when his armor entered the killing ground created by well-dug-in Iraqi tanks and infantry.[39] As a result, the Iraqis were able to surround the Iranian forces on three sides and to force the Iranians to abandon many of their armored vehicles because they could neither refuel nor resupply them. Several sources agree that, even though both sides fired at ranges under 1,000 meters and the firing was heavy and went on for some time, most of the losses occurred because of Iranian inability to maneuver and to resupply in the mud. Iranian armor was not so much defeated as stuck and abandoned. It is also clear, however, that Iraq showed little ability to exploit its victory and counterattack.[40]

Reports that Iraq lost 50 medium tanks, destroyed at least 40 Iranian tanks, and captured 100 more seem to be roughly correct. It also seems likely in retrospect that Bani Sadr caused the defeat by launching a poorly prepared attack, rather than that his attack was sabotaged. If he faced any problem from Khomeini, it seems to have been in the lack of support from the Revolutionary Guards, and even here, it seems as likely that Bani Sadr deliberately failed to use them properly as that they were withheld.

It is interesting to note that Iran was much more successful in May 1981, when it launched limited attacks along the Bustan-Susangerd front to secure the city of Susangerd. It launched a direct assault on the Iraqi forces in the Allah Akbar hills northwest of the city and in positions in front of it, and in three days of fighting it drove them back several key kilometers. This attack, however, was fully supported, and it demonstrated the new fighting power of Iranian infantry.[41]

The Iranian Victory at Abadan. Bani Sadr's January 1981 offensive proved to be the last battle Iran was to lose between early 1981 and its May 1982 attack. Following Bani Sadr's flight from Iran, the regular armed forces and Revolutionary Guards acted in comparative unity. This unity and competent command enabled Iran to retake Abadan during 26–29 September 1981. The full details of this battle are unclear, but Iran seems to have led Iraq to redeploy its forces from the Abadan front by launching a series of minor attacks on the front north of Susangerd, along the Karkeh River, and in various parts of the Khuzestan front.[42] Iran then attacked with a force roughly equivalent to two infantry divisions, plus armor and artillery, along the Bahamsheer River side of Abadan Island. From all reports, the Iranian attack was well organized and took Iraq by surprise. According to some reports, Iran made good use of night infantry attacks over a broad area to find weak spots and penetrate while pinning down the Iraqi forces in strongly held areas. Iran also seems to have been able to exploit its tactical successes and concentrate its forces quickly and responsively, while Iraq tended to freeze in position and await orders.

Both sides fought well in head-on confrontations, but the Iraqis seem to have been fatally slow in maneuvering and in adapting to the changing circumstances of battle. While the Iranian infantry showed amazing courage and a willingness to die in frontal assaults on Iraqi positions, the Iraqis held positions too long and were then outflanked as much by their own rigidity of command as by the initiative of their enemy.

The resulting Iranian victory seems to have cost Iraq the equivalent of one trained division, something like 600–1,500 killed and 1,500–3,000 captured, and the loss of hundreds of armored vehicles. It seems probable that Iran lost about 3,000 killed to achieve this victory, but it still was able to rout Iraq's 10th Armored Brigade when it tried to counterattack. It is possible that there is some truth to Iraq's claims that it made a strategic withdrawal across the Karun River to reduce casualties, but it is still true that the withdrawal allowed Iran to restore many of its critical lines of communication and destroyed much of the fighting capability of the Iraqi Army on the southern front.[43]

The War of Lies. Iran lost its top four commanders in a helicopter crash following the battle for Abadan, and in the months that followed, the war seemed to be largely a war of lies.[44] This was nothing new. Both sides had long exaggerated their victories and their opponent's losses. By January 1981, Iran had claimed that it had "bombed and destroyed" 500 Iraqi oil centers, military bases, airports, ports, and strategic and industrial targets. In fact, it might have done some damage—most of it slight—to as many as 50. During this same period, Iran's battle communiqués claimed to have destroyed something like 73% of the entire Iraqi Air Force, although a claim of 30% would have been exaggerated. A month later, Iran's claims added up to more than 100% of Iraq's aircraft. This was a definition of "air superiority" that even Curtis LeMay would have been proud of, but it failed to explain that a nonexistent Iraq Air Force flew over 150 sorties per day in late March. Iraq's battle communiqués countered by making absurdly precise estimates of Iranian losses, such as "8,413 killed, 588 warplanes, 1,098 tanks, 1,270 APCs, 115 multiple rocket launchers, 147 naval vessels, and 44 radar stations." The only thing that can be said about such Iraqi claims is that they indicated that Iraq was winning at the time when they were made, because Iraq claimed it had killed well over 100% of its opponent's air force almost four months before Iran claimed it had killed over 100% of the Iraqi Air Force. The true losses on both sides before Iran's March 1982 offensive probably approached 70,000 killed and 150,000–200,000 casualties. Each side had lost some 110–175 aircraft and over 700 tanks. The war had also created roughly 2 million new refugees.[45]

During the period between the Iranian victory at Abadan and Iran's spring offensive, these differing "victory" claims led to considerable confusion. From December to February, both sides issued a long series of conflicting bulletins over who controlled small towns and minor tactical objectives. These claims have made it virtually impossible to place much faith in the word of either side. Iran reported the recapture of towns that Iraq had not lost, and some Western papers accepted such Iranian claims at times when other papers had correspondents visiting the Iraqi forces in these same towns.

The fighting around Bustan and Qasr-e-Shirin in December and January led to particularly contradictory reports and made it impossible to validate what was then one of the most common interpretations of the war: that Iraq was unable to advance because of its unwillingness to incur casualties, but could hold most of its positions indefinitely. Iraq's losses during its initial attack on Khorramshahr, and its seeming unwillingness to incur casualties in later battles, were often cited as the reason why Iraq halted when it met serious Iranian resistance, why it bypassed or laid siege to other cities and key positions after the first few days of the war, and why its tactics were largely defensive after November 1980.[46] There is no doubt that Iraqi officials encouraged this interpretation. However, Iraq's tactics were much the same as those Iraq used in the war against the Kurds—although on a much grander scale—and it is far from clear that Iraq could have taken any more of its objectives if it had been willing to accept more casualties. In general, Iraq proved far less flexible and able to maneuver than Iran, less able to use air power, and less able to show initiative and exploit opportunities.

Iran's Operation "Undeniable Victory." Iran proved this during February and March 1982. It kept its newly won confidence and initiative in spite of the loss of its top commanders. It systematically built up its forces for a spring offensive near Dezful, and it repulsed repeated "spoiling attacks" by Iraq's Fourth Army, which were designed to disrupt the buildup of the Iranian attack. In fact, Iran inflicted serious losses on its Iraqi attackers during these spoiling attacks and forced them to dig in even further. Iran then pinned the Iraqi forces down. Where Iraq had rapidly rotated troops in and out of their forward positions early in the war, Iran forced Iraq to lock its most effective troops in place by hitting them with constant low-level attacks and skirmishes that exhausted their will and morale. Iran found that even minor infantry attacks could have this effect if they were pressed home consistently against a static enemy and on a broad front and that a combination of antiaircraft guns and man-portable SAMs like the SA-7 could drive off the Iraqi Air Force or make its attack sorties ineffective without having to commit its limited reserves of operational fighters.[47]

In the third week of March 1982 Iran launched its offensive in the Dezful-Shush area. It had built up a force of more than 100,000 soldiers, including some 30,000 Revolutionary Guards,[48] plus additional volunteers and logistic elements from a new popular force called the Army of 20 Million. This gave it the equivalent of four divisions, including an armored division redeployed from the Pakistani frontier.[49] The Iraqis had also built up their forces to three divisions, plus eight independent brigades, with the Iraqi 10th Armored Division in reserve.

Iraq struck first and launched a spoiling attack on Iran on 17 March, which produced significant casualties. However, the success of the attack misled Iraq into thinking it had a week to 10 days in which to reinforce its defenses. In reality, the Iraqi attack had had little impact on the organization of the Iranian offensive, and Iran was able to deploy one more division than the Iraqis had detected. Iran achieved considerable tactical surprise. On the night of 19 March the Iranians landed commando forces behind Iraqi lines. It waited until roughly 3:00 A.M. to launch its two-pronged armored attack from the north and the east, which led the Iraqis to assume they were dealing with a mere raid. The Iraqis also seem to have felt that Iran would not attack during its New Year's holiday, and they had not even manned their Soviet-made night sensor gear along the rest of the front. The Iranian armored attack also made excellent use of large numbers of small infantry units that were carefully trained to attack a given Iraqi position, and this tactic tied down Iraqi forces while misleading them regarding the extent to which Iran intended to use its armor. While some reports indicate that religious "commissars" had whipped the forces into a frenzy and that they carried papers guaranteeing them admission to paradise as "martyrs," Iranian forces were not employed suicidally and had excellent tactical command.[50]

The attack caught the Iraqis by surprise in two ways. First, they were not prepared for a late night attack; second, they were not prepared for an attack from the north or for the weight of another Iranian division. The Iranians were able to mass 45,000–50,000 men to Iraq's 25,000, although nothing like the 4:1 superiority Iraq claimed later. The Iranians also followed up effectively. Between 21 and 28 March, Iran launched waves of carefully staged infantry attacks that kept Iraqi forces pinned down in place. At the same time, Iran pushed two of its reorganized "armored divisions" forward in an enveloping movement around two Iraqi divisions that had dug in deeply on the front. In spite of press reports to the contrary, both sides fought heavily during the initial phases of the battle, but while the Iranians had trouble in pressing forward, they again were able to maneuver and exploit their opportunities, while the Iraqis tended to delay.

The Iranians were not totally successful. They failed to close their armored "pincers" on the Iraqi forces and reached only the frontier village of Dehloran, northeast of Dezful, rather than their overambitious objective of Al Amarah in Iraq. Iraq's forces were also able to withdraw with many of their units intact and to establish new defenses on the high ground west of the Deweirej River. However, Iran was able to outflank at least two Iraqi divisions. Iranian units also virtually destroyed the 10th Iraqi Armored Division when it attempted to check them, and made effective use of Sagger and Milan ATGMs. The resulting Iraqi losses included the 11th Special Mission Brigade, the 96th Infantry Brigade, the 60th Armored Brigade, and other independent elements.[51]

The Iranians conducted their offensive with only minimal air power. While Iraq flew over 150 sorties per day, including some with its new Mirage F-1s, the Iranians kept most of their 70–90 remaining operational fighters on the ground. The Iranians used some F-5s, but they relied on attack helicopters for most close air support and on curtain fire from their automatic weapons and antiaircraft guns, and on SA-7 fire to keep the Iraqi fighters from pressing home their attacks. This tactic enabled Iranian troops to absorb the rest of Iraq's badly delivered air strikes and occasional use of attack helicopters. News films of the fighting also show that the Iranians did a far better job of exploiting terrain and maneuvering in detail. The Iranians made excellent use of the hilly terrain in the area, both defensively and to find good terrain upon which to maneuver their armor. Far too often, the Iraqis either maneuvered too late and lost the terrain advantage, bogged down in the mud, or were enveloped in company- and battalion-sized elements and forced to surrender.

It is impossible to tell how much a loss of morale contributed to the willingness of Iraqi troops to surrender or abandon their armor, but it is clear that Iraq lost at least 320 tanks and armored vehicles and that the Iranians captured 350 more, including roughly 150 T-54 and T-55 tanks that had been abandoned in place.[52] Western correspondents on the scene also saw abandoned T-62s and some abandoned T-72s that could only have come from the elite troops that Iraq's President Saddam

Hussein used on his guard. Iran claimed that it had captured 165 artillery pieces, SA-6 missiles, and a key Iraqi-held radar site. Western press sources confirmed that Iraq had lost much of its artillery and was unable to conduct the orderly withdrawal of its rear-echelon equipment.[53]

The Iranians claimed that they had produced 25,000 Iraqi casualties, and some Western experts estimate that Iraq may well have suffered that many and lost at least 10,000 killed.[54] As many as 15,000 Iraqis seem to have been captured. However, the victory was not an easy one. Iranian casualties seem to have exceeded 10,000, with 3,500–4,000 killed and as many as 6,000 Iranians taken prisoner. The stress the fighting placed on Iraqi military capabilities is indicated by the fact that even before this battle, Iraq thrust foreign workers and children into the front. Some of these foreign workers included Egyptian peasants and farmers who had specifically been promised exemption from the fighting.

The exact areas where the fighting took place are difficult to locate because maps differ strikingly in their place names for the area. Iranian battle communiqués issued on 3 April claimed that their victories were being consolidated in the Ein Kosh (Duflak) region and Neshad west of Dezful and that Iran was pursuing the enemy at Saleh Abad, Sunar, Gilan-e-Gahreb, and Sar-el-Pol-e-Zahab. Iraqi and Western reports used other names. It is clear, however, that Iran pushed Iraq 24–28 miles nearer the border and threatened Iraqi positions along a 200-square-mile area just north of Bustan and west of Dezful. The Iranians also recaptured between 600 and 1,200 square miles of territory and moved within 5–10 miles of the Iraqi border.

Syria: The Impact of a Two-Front War. In early April, Syria transformed the conflict into a "two-front" war. Syria quietly accumulated 1.5 million barrels of Iraqi oil at the Syrian terminal of Baniyas, then seized the oil in mid-April. It simultaneously announced that it was ending the shipment of roughly 300,000 BPD of Iraqi oil through Syrian pipelines[55] and that it had signed a 10-year agreement with Iran to barter Syrian agricultural products and other exports for 8.7 million tons of Iranian crude oil annually (174,000 BPD).[56] Syria then closed its border with Iraq and announced that "Syria would stand beside the Iraqi people in their struggle to topple that [Saddam Hussein's] regime until they succeed."[57] Syria followed these political and economic hostilities by providing Iran with large numbers of SA-7 missiles, which it had obtained from Libya, and with roughly 90 more artillery pieces.[58] It repeatedly sent fighters over Iraq in an effort to divert the Iraqi Air Force.[59] Further, under the cover of strengthening its security forces in the area near the junction of the Turkish-Iraqi border, Syria helped Iranian and Kurdish agents blow up Iraq's last functioning oil pipeline through Turkey and to divert its flow into the Ceyhan River.[60] While the pipeline was flowing again within a week, even a temporary cut in Iraq's remaining oil exports cost Iraq $6 million a day and did nothing

MAP 16—6
THE GEOGRAPHY OF THE TWO-FRONT WAR

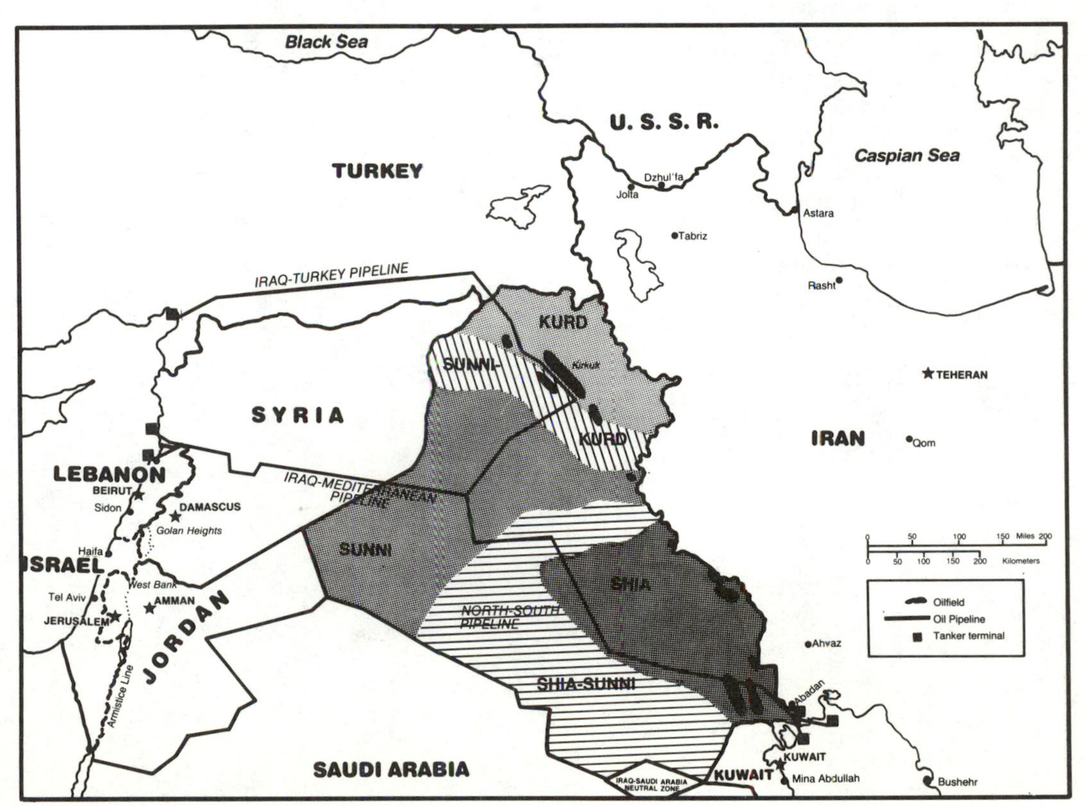

Adapted from CIA 626033 11-79

to help it pay for a war costing well over $1 billion a month or ease its economic burdens at a time when it was already $24 billion in debt to its neighbors in the southern Gulf.

The Syrian cutoff continued into 1983, in spite of repeated Saudi efforts to use its aid to Syria to persuade Assad to change his policies and resume the transit of Iraqi oil through Syria. Prince Abdullah made repeated visits to Syria, and at one point he shuttled back and forth between Damascus and Baghdad after Saddam Hussein flew to Riyadh to make a personal appeal for King Fahd's help. Not only did Syria refuse, but the foreign ministers of Syria, Iran, and Libya met in Damascus on 23 January 1983 and announced that the "Steadfastness and Confrontation Front" called for the overthrow of Saddam Hussein and opposed any move toward an Arab-Israeli peace. While Algeria, South Yemen, and the PLO were not present at the meeting, it was clear that Saudi threats to shut off aid to Syria had not succeeded in restoring Iraq's ability to export oil or in defusing the Front's threat to the Gulf.[61]

The May Offensive: Operation Jerusalem or Holy City. Iran gave Iraq no time to recover from its defeat in March. Iran redeployed three of the divisions it had used in its successful offensive near Dezful to the southern front. Then, on the night of 29-30 April, Iran launched a broad attack called Operation Jerusalem or Operation Holy City on the Iraqi positions in Khuzestan.[62] It attacked the Iraqi positions in three main thrusts. The first was to the north along the narrow access routes to the Iraqi-held town of Hoveyzeh about 12 miles southwest of Susangerd. The second was against the town of Jofeyr, the former Iranian fortress garrison of Hamid, and the only major rail and road route from Khorramshahr to Ahwaz and the Iraqi positions at Hoveyzeh. Finally, it launched a major attack across the Karun River just north of Hoseyniyeh, another key town on the main road and rail line, to recover the city of Khorramshahr.[63] The attack began with widespread night infantry attacks, supported by armor. These were followed by several major armored thrusts and attacks by limited numbers of fighters and more significant numbers of helicopters.[64] During its initial days, the attack seems to have recaptured something like 309 square miles of Iranian territory, although the Iranians had serious difficulty in their northern thrust against Hoveyzeh and in advancing through the well-entrenched Iraqi positions in front of Khorramshahr.

Iraq's performance was mixed. The regular Mohammed al-Qassem and Usama divisions around Hoveyzeh fought well. Iraq made better use of its defensive positions than it had around Dezful. It showed a new willingness to maneuver and to listen to the advice it received from Jordanian experts. Iraq also made good use of French advice and new deliveries of French Mirage F-1 fighters and made more effective use of its air power.[65] At the same time, the newly formed Iraqi volunteer units with three-number or "triple-digit" designations along the Hamid front tended to break or surrender without sufficient cause.[66]

By the second day of the fighting, each side claimed it had inflicted some 6,000 casualties on the other. Iran claimed sweeping advances; Iraq, that its Fourth Army had "completely crushed" the Iranian attack. Iraq seems to have been correct in claiming victory to the north, but Iran began to cut the highway that was Iraq's major line of communication south of Ahwaz, took Jofeyr, massively reinforced the positions across the Karun River near Hoseyniyeh it had won earlier, and breeched Iraq's defensive positions around Khorramshahr. Iran made unusually heavy use of its helicopters during this attack and seems to have captured some 2,500 Iraqi prisoners and inflicted over 5,000 casualties, at the cost of about 2,500 Iranian casualties at the Hamid front.

Iraq counterattacked on 3 and 4 May, making heavy use of its own helicopters and aircraft. It seems to have recovered some of the positions it had lost near Khorramshahr and to have launched two division-size counterattacks on the main Iranian thrust against Hoveyzeh. This thrust was constrained by terrain to a narrow line of advance, and the Iranians were repulsed with heavy losses. Iran responded by reinforcing its thrust south of Jofeyr, and its helicopters attacked the Iraqi town of Fakah (Fuka, Fuqa, Fukeh), about 200 miles south of Baghdad, in an effort to halt resupply of Iraq and to divert Iraqi forces. It also used helicopters to attack an Iraqi command post at the border town of Selamche.

By 7 May, at least 60,000 Iranian troops and 200 tanks were on the west bank of the Karun River around Taheri and Haloub.[67] U.S. intelligence experts estimated that each side had lost over 15,000 killed and that some 8,000 Iraqis had been taken prisoner.[68] Iran claimed a massive victory, although Iraqi sources claimed they were cutting off the Iranian bridgeheads, that 21,000 Iranians had been killed, and that 140 Iranian tanks had been destroyed.[69] Iraq flew up to 100 fighter sorties per day, while Iran flew nearly as many helicopter sorties.[70]

By 9 May, Iran had scored a major victory. It decisively cut the main road to Hoveyzeh, which is on a raised dike and is the key to defending the area. As a result the Iraqi forces in Hoveyzeh were cut off to the west by the Hawr el-Hawizah and Hawr el-Azim marshes and could no longer be supplied. Iraq's Usama and Mohammed al-Qassem forces had to abandon the front to Iran. Iran recaptured an additional 116-square-mile triangle north of Khorramshahr and approached positions on the Shat al-Arab southeast of Selamche and within 15 miles of Iraq's port of al-Basrah. By 12 May, Iran had nearly recaptured Khuzestan. It was on the Shat, was consolidating its position in Hamid and Hoveyzeh, and had gained an additional 366 square miles of its territory. It then recaptured the border town of Selamche, 15 miles north of Khorramshahr, and by 14-19 May, Iran threatened to cut off the Iraqi forces in a besieged Khorramshahr.[71]

From the Iraqi Defeat at Khorramshahr to the Iraqi Withdrawal. By the time the next round of fighting took place at Khorramshahr, the city was virtually undefendable, and the concentration of Iraqi

MAP 16—7
IRAN-IRAQ: IRAN RECOVERS KHUZESTAN

Adapted from the author's article on the Iran-Iraq War in the *Armed Forces Journal*, May, 1983, p. 38.

troops in the area threatened to allow Iran to cut off and destroy something like a quarter of the Iraqi army. While Iraq could provide a limited amount of resupply across the Shat, it had lost its main land routes, and the marshes surrounding the city made establishing new lines virtually impossible. Although Saddam Hussein talked of making Khorramshahr into Iraq's "Stalingrad," the battle was over virtually before it began. Iraq could not afford to lose 30,000–40,000 men in a city that was little more than rubble and that was a strategic liability rather than an asset. It also immediately became apparent that Iraq did not have the time to organize an effective defense. When the Iranians launched their first night attacks on 22-23 May, the Iraqi defenses quickly crumbled and the Iraqi commander was killed trying to reorganize the front. Within 36 hours, Iranian forces poured into the city and began rolling up an almost totally disorganized Iraqi defense.[72]

While Iraq desperately sought political support in stopping the battle from Saudi Arabia, the other Gulf states, Egypt, Jordan, and the West, Iran took something like 12,000–15,000 prisoners. Only Iraq's best regular forces withdrew in order, and they sustained heavy casualties. Iran's victory was so quick and sweeping that Iran changed the name of the city yet again to Kurramshahr (greenness and happiness).[73] The radical states in the Steadfastness Front, which were meeting in Algiers, celebrated Iran's victory by declaring on 24 May that Iran was a friend of the Arabs and that no Arab state should support Iraq.[74] In contrast, the foreign ministers of the Gulf Cooperation Council, which met in Riyadh shortly after the Iranian victory, had to back away from calls for support of Iraq and to concentrate on peace initiatives that might save the Baath regime.[75]

Phase Six: The New War of Attrition

During the next two months, Iraq variously claimed victory, offered to negotiate, and attempted to launch new bombing raids against Iranian cities and oil facilities to force Iran to show restraint. Iran methodically put pressure on every remaining Iraqi-held enclave in Iran. It also claimed it would not invade Iraq, but then stated it would not end the war until Saddam Hussein was punished as a war criminal, until the Iraqi people had a legitimate regime, and until it obtained reparations, which ranged at various times from new territory and the closing of the Shat to Iraq to payments of $50–150 billion.[76] Iraq was forced to seek more and more help from Egypt, while Saudi Arabia and the other Gulf states sought to persuade Syria that too strong an Iran would threaten it as well as the other Arab nations.[77]

A New Iranian Offensive. It was Iran, however, that had the military initiative, and it put continuing military pressure on Iraq throughout this period. Two days after Iraq acknowledged its defeat at Khorramshahr, Iran launched a new offensive on its central front near Sumar, only 80 miles northeast of Baghdad.[78] On 29 May Iran began to launch raids on Iraqi facilities across the Shat al-Arab.[79] The battle communiqués of both sides showed that Iran was able to inflict a constant series of minor defeats on Iraq while suffering only roughly the same casualties.

By this time, the Iraqi Army had suffered critical losses. In early March, it had had approximately 210,000 men, 2,300 tanks, 2,000 armored vehicles, and 335 combat aircraft. At the end of May, in spite of tens of thousands of replacements, it was down to 150,000 men, two of its four armored divisions had been reduced to brigade-size formations, and it had only about 100 flyable combat aircraft.[80] Several of its top generals had been killed or imprisoned, and every Iranian attack after early June put new pressure on an exhausted Iraqi army and air force.

Saddam Hussein attempted to hang on to his military positions in Iran in spite of these pressures. While the Iraqi position near Mehran has only limited value in defending Al Kut, Iraq also controlled a vital ridge on the central front that overlooked the river near Sar-el-Pol-e-Zahab and defended the main pass along the main route to Baghdad from Tehran. This position, and Iraqi control of the Iranian border town of Qasr-e-Shirin, was the last major barrier to an invasion by Iranian forces, and it was only 120 kilometers from Iraq's capital. Iraq's own border defenses on the same route near Khanaqin had nothing like the same defensive strength.[81]

Iran did not prove successful in breaking through Iraq's defenses, but it became clear by mid-June that Saddam Hussein had no chance of negotiating a peace as long as Iraq stayed in Iran, that there was a good chance the Iraqi Army would break if Iran launched an offensive after the month of Ramadan, and that Saudi Arabia could get Syria to end its pressure on Iraq only if Iraq withdrew. Khomeini rejected efforts to negotiate a cease-fire with Iraqi forces still in Iran, and Iraq's attempts to renew its strategic bombing did little more than further incite the Iranians and briefly halt Japanese oil shipments out of Kharg Island. In fact, Iran's oil revenues climbed sharply. Average Iranian oil exports rose from 500,000 BPD in December to 1,500,000 BPD in June.[82]

By the end of June, Hussein and the Baath had had enough. Hussein reorganized the Revolutionary Command Council and the top levels of the Baath party to leave nothing but the closest party loyalists, and on 20 June Baghdad announced that all Iraqi troops would leave Iranian soil.[83] On 30 June Iraq announced that it had completed its withdrawal and would maintain a unilateral cease-fire. All Hussein had to show for 21 months of occupation was defeat without peace, over 50,000 dead, nearly 50,000 Iraqi prisoners of war, a debt in excess of $40 billion, a far more vulnerable Shi'ite population than when the war began, disruption of the Iraqi economy and development effort, and the loss of over $100 billion in facilities and oil revenues.[84]

The Iranian Offensives of Summer 1982. By July 1982, the war had taken a different pattern. Iran seemed to have lost the ability to operate most of its fighters and helicopters and much of its armor. It no longer was able to keep its major combat equipment operating with the supplies available on the world market, and it had become heavily dependent on the light Soviet-made weaponry it could get through Libya, Syria, and North Korea. Its F-4Es presented a particular problem because they had extremely high maintenance requirements, and Iran's only supplier of key parts, Israel, no longer feared an Iraqi victory enough to provide significant support to Iran or risk further complications in its relations with the U.S. at a time when it was involved in a crisis in Lebanon.

At the same time, Iran faced problems within its armed forces. First, the Iranian high command seems to have divided from the ruling mullahs over the feasibility of invading Iraq without more logistic capabilities and supplies than Iran had available. The clerics won the debate, but this seems to have placed much of the planning of Iran's offensives under religious control and led the planners to place far too high a value on religious and revolutionary fervor. There may also have been some minor purges within the Iranian military, but in any case, the pattern of Iranian command and tactics changed. Large numbers of infantry and poorly prepared troops began to be committed in "human-wave" attacks without adequate tactical planning, heavy weapons and air support, and logistics backup.[85]

By early August 1982, Iran had launched three major drives into Iraq directed at cutting off al-Basrah. All had failed. The first major attack occurred on 13 July and drove 6–10 miles into Iraq. It led to at least one major Iraqi ambush of Iranian forces, and it was checked with heavy losses. Iran attacked again on the 21st and penetrated nearly 5 miles into Iraq, but it again lacked the tactical control, airpower, armor, and logistic support to sustain its penetration and was thrown back. It launched equally unsuccessful probing assaults during the rest of the week of 20 July and then launched a third major assault on 28 July. This attack accomplished nothing except to expend the lives of Iranian infantry, many of whom were poorly trained boys and teenagers rather than seasoned Revolutionary Guards.

Although any statistics are suspect, these offensives seem to have raised the total cost of the war to at least 80,000 killed, 200,000 wounded, and 45,000 captured. Some estimates went as high as 27,000 killed during these four offensive actions. The offensives gained Iran a narrow strip of Iraqi territory about 1–2 miles deep and 10 miles long, although the swamp area north of al-Basrah was strategically worthless. In strategic terms, the offensives demonstrated that Iran could not sustain an attack into Iraq without better leadership, equipment, and logistics than it then had available. At the tactical level, it showed that the Iraqi forces would fight with more determination for their own territory than for that of Iran and that there was no strong Shi'ite "fifth column" within the armed forces.[86]

Iran responded by stepping up its efforts to subvert the Shi'ites in Iraq and the Gulf and its attacks on Saudi Arabia. It also called for an Islamic oil embargo against the U.S. and increased its executions of various Marxist groups, Kurdish rebels, and members of the People's Mujahedin. At the same time, it showed increasing confusion regarding its war aims. The speaker of the Majlis, Hashemi Rafsanjani, insisted that Iran had "advanced as much as it planned." Moshen Rezai, a Revolutionary Guard commander, stated that Iran would be "forced to remove the Iraqi Baath party and put an end to its crimes." Ali Akbar Velayati, the foreign minister, stated that it was Iraq that must "annihilate" the Saddam Hussein regime.[87]

Iraq countered with still further consolidations of the Baath to ensure its support of Saddam Hussein, appeals to the southern Gulf states for more aid, appeals to the West and the USSR for more rapid arms deliveries, occasional charges that the U.S. and the USSR were prolonging the war, and a concerted effort to dig in and establish strong defensive positions. While Iraq continued to publicize atrocity stories about Iran's sending untrained boys into combat, it committed boys and teenagers of its own and desperately sought volunteers from other Arab states, including Sudan.

At the same time, Kuwait and Algeria made continuing—if unsuccessful—efforts to achieve peace. While Iran occasionally gave indications that it was interested in peace, it never clarified its position on whether it would accept Saddam Hussein's survival, and it fluctuated between demanding $150 billion in war reparations from Iraq and control of the Shat and hints that it would accept lesser amounts from the southern Gulf states.[88]

The Fall 1982 Iranian Offensives. The next Iranian offensive came on 30 September. Iranian forces launched an attack against Baghdad. They drove against Mandali, south of the main Iraqi defenses at the border town of Qasr-e-Shirin. This offensive involved between 50,000 and 100,000 troops and led to some of the bloodiest fighting of the war. While Iran lacked the armor and air power to punch through the Iraqi defenses, and repeated its rather careless use of human-wave tactics, both sides incurred significant casualties. The fighting also did not die down quickly. Iran launched another major attack on Mandali on 10 October, and according to one Western estimate, a single engagement cost Iran 4,000 killed, to only 300 Iraqis.[89]

By this time, both sides had been severely hurt. Iraq was exporting only 600–700,000 BPD and had to make an emergency appeal for $3.5 billion in additional funds from its southern Gulf neighbors. Although Iraq's losses were less severe than those of Iran, and the war was gradually turning its volunteers into more seasoned and professional troops, it was still suffering serious casualties and paying more than $1 billion a month in direct war costs. Iraq also was consuming much of the equipment it was getting from the USSR as soon as it was delivered. Iran had lost many of its seasoned troops and Revolutionary Guards, and many of its brigades had only two out of three maneuver battalions.

MAP 16—8
IRAN-IRAQ: IRAN'S OFFENSIVES OF 1982

A. THE MAIN THRUSTS

B. THE DRIVE ON BAGHDAD IN SEPTEMBER-OCTOBER

C. THE SCENE OF THE NOVEMBER OFFENSIVE

Adapted from the author's article on the Iran-Iraq War in the *Armed Forces Journal*, May, 1983, p. 40.

The losses among the Guards were particularly heavy because they lacked the professionalism to properly time their mass infantry assaults and they proved easier to ambush than the regular forces. Iran had virtually no operational fighters left, its one remaining armored division was short of spare parts, and it was forced to commit its airborne division as infantry because it lacked operable aircraft and helicopters.[90]

The war had clearly become one of attrition. Iraq had the advantage in terms of a defensive position and far superior equipment supply, but Iran had the advantage in terms of a rising oil income and greater political ability to sustain casualties. Iraq tried to counter this situation by first threatening, and then actually conducting, air attacks on tankers and facilities at Kharg Island and by launching air attacks and Scud missiles at cities in Iran. It launched a barrage of Scud missiles at Dezful in late October, killing 21 and wounding 107, and repeated air raids from October on. The result, however, was little more than harassment and irritation. The Iraqi attacks could not kill enough Iranians to have any serious military or political effect, and Iraq's MiG and Mirage fighters lacked the range, munitions, and pilot skill to inflict serious damage on the well-defended facilities at Kharg.[91]

Iran's Winter 1982 Offensives. Iran, in turn, launched a new offensive against Iraq on 2 November 1982. The offensive came through the foothills of the Zagros Mountains and struck near Fakah (Fuka) in Iraq. Its ultimate objective may have been the Iraqi provincial capital at Mishan, although it is unclear how Iran could have hoped to advance this far, given the lack of roads in the area. Iranian infantry, supported by M-60 and Chieftain tanks about 800 yards to the rear, attacked at night, to minimize the impact of Iraqi air power and artillery. The attack scored minor successes. Iran recaptured a small oil field at Bayat and came within artillery range of some of the key roads linking al-Basrah and Baghdad. Iran also secured the territory around the Iranian city of Dehloran and had some other minor successes. Although the Iranians had up to 4 regular and 12 Guard and volunteer divisions, three Guard brigades of about 10,000 men each seem to have led the attack and to have performed considerably better than the Guard units had at Mandali.

Iraq lost several hundred killed and several thousand prisoners, about 160–240 square miles of captured Iranian territory, and the small town of Tib in Iraq and the surrounding heights. Iraq also had to draw on its last reserves—by then reduced to two under-strength brigades in the Kirkuk-Mosul oil fields in the north and an army-sized formation south of Baghdad—to secure its defensive positions. Although Iraq was able to use its growing fighter and helicopter force without opposition from the Iranian Air Force, the Iranian units were able to down significant numbers of Iraqi planes using AA guns and SA-7 missiles. Thus Iraq was deprived of much of the advantage it should have gained from local air superiority. Nevertheless, Iraqi armor, artillery, fighters, and helicopters did halt the exploitation phase of the attack, contain Iran's limited tactical breakthroughs, and inflict serious casualties of their own.[92]

This offensive brought Iranian forces to new positions within shelling range of al-Basrah, but it did not achieve any major strategic effect except to weaken Kuwait's and the UAE's willingness to provide new funds and other support for Iraq. Although Iran may have briefly entered Mandali, it could not hold it, and its claims to have killed 5,000 Iraqis were totally false. Iraq kept most of its heavily fortified positions and retained an important edge in equipment. Iraq had about 3,000 operational tanks to 800–900 for Iran, 2,500 other armored fighting vehicles to 1,500 and 1,800 heavy artillery pieces to 900. Iraq was also able to operate over 300 first-line fighters to less than 50 F-4s and F-5s for Iran, and most of Iran's fighters had to be kept in reserve.[93]

The offensive thus ended in what was becoming a familiar pattern. More internal tension developed in both Iran and Iraq. Iraq made new appeals for aid and for help in achieving a peace. Iran issued new threats and demands for reparations and for Saddam Hussein's overthrow. At the same time, both sides faced another increase in their tactical problems. The Iranians suffered further attrition of the equipment they needed to sustain an attack and lost more experienced military personnel. The Iraqis remained locked in static defensive positions and tactics. They lacked the organization and leadership to use their reserves to launch counteroffensives—if indeed they had the strength and political will to do so. This, and their inability to use their air power effectively, meant they could not exploit their ability to halt an Iranian offensive to inflict decisive casualties or regain key territory.

Iraq did launch a new round of air raids against key oil facilities, strong points, and ships in the Gulf and made new claims to have inflicted damage on Kharg Island, tankers in the area, and Iranian ships. Yet Iraqi pilots still lacked the range, munitions, and training to achieve much lethality, particularly against a heavily defended target like Kharg Island, which had growing AA and SAM defenses and buried, sheltered, and redundant equipment. As had been the case with the Israeli Air Force in the October War, the Iraqis could not fly successful missions using regular ordnance against extremely dense SHORAD defenses. Not only did observers note that Iraqi pilots dumped their munitions offshore, rather than try to penetrate, but some sources indicate that Iraq brought in Egyptian pilots in an effort to improve the effectiveness of fighter missions.[94] Iraq also launched new air strikes on Iranian towns in the forward area and new Scud missile attacks on Dezful. While Iran reported 62 killed, 287 wounded, and 120 homes destroyed, it was taking advantage of the Iraqi attacks to launch a new wave of prowar propaganda. The Iraqi attack had little other effect.

Still more peace initiatives followed in late December 1982, with Kuwait and Algeria taking the lead. Rumors indicated that the southern

Gulf nations had increased their offer to Iran from $25 to $50 billion, but Iran continued to demand $150 billion. At the same time, Iraq continued its air attacks and Iran its border raids. Iran stepped up its shelling of Iraqi traffic transiting Kuwait. Iran made a "last demand" that Iraq accept its terms on 21 December; Iraq responded with a near-record 74-sortie attack against its oil facilities and positions on the 26th. While the year ended with Iraq still occupying some 9,560 square miles of Iranian soil, the positions were strategically of little value. At the same time, Iran could not drive into Iraq.

The First Offensives in 1983. During January 1983, both sides remained locked in the same position. Iraq remained on the defensive, using its tanks more as pillboxes than armor. Iran ground away at Iraq in light actions, making increasing use of Soviet-bloc equipment from North Korea, Syria, and Libya. Although Iran could no longer operate most of its aircraft and Cobra helicopters, it did rebuild its Revolutionary Guards to well over 200,000 men. Iraq had the advantage in equipment, but Iran had the advantage in expendable manpower.[95]

Iran launched another offensive on 7 February, called Operation Before Dawn. The attack involved 100,000–150,000 troops on each side and a front 20–40 miles wide. It came along an axis north of Dezful and west of Fakah toward Amarah in Iraq. It was timed to defeat Iran on the fifth anniversary of the resignation of the shah's last prime minister, Shapur Bakhtiar. The speaker of the Majlis, Hashemi Rafsanjani, described it as "the final military operation that will determine the final destiny of the region." The main force involved six Iranian divisions and hit about 80 miles north of the November 1982 offensive. Not only was it one of the largest offensives of the war, it was clearly intended to be decisive. The Iraqis captured battle plans showing that it had the objective of reaching Al Amarah and of cutting the main route from al-Basrah to Baghdad. Once again, Iran attacked at night to minimize the impact of Iraqi air power, artillery, and armor and used masses of poorly trained infantry backed by tanks several hundred yards in the rear.

Iran did recover some minor border posts, took the border villages of Sableh, Safariyeh, and Rushaidah, and regained roughly 120 miles of territory. Iran was unable, however, to achieve a major breakthrough, and it suffered heavy casualties. The Iraqis counterattacked in the morning, and while Iraqi armor moved very slowly in the center, Iraqi infantry outflanked the Iranians in a pincer movement and forced them back. The terrain Iran chose contributed to the problem. It may have achieved a degree of tactical surprise because it came in an unlikely area, but the area was also extraordinarily difficult to fight in. The Iranian forces had to attack three heavily fortified Iraqi lines of sand and earth among territory ranging from low hills to the edge of marshes between the Doveyrich River and the Tigris and Tib river marshes that form a near-semicircle around Al Amarah from the east. As a result,

MAP 16—9
IRAN-IRAQ: IRAN'S FIRST OFFENSIVE OF 1983

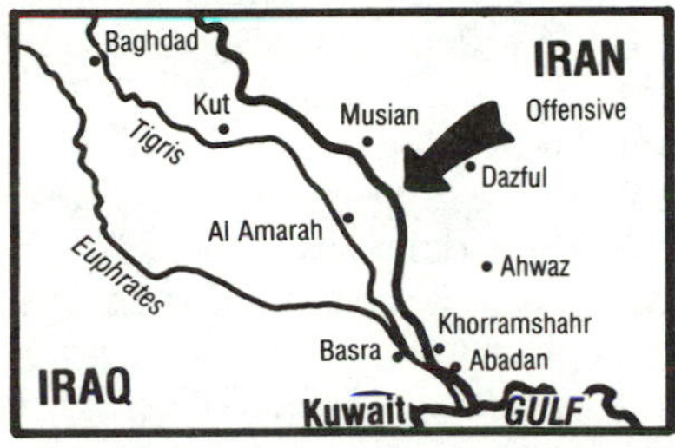

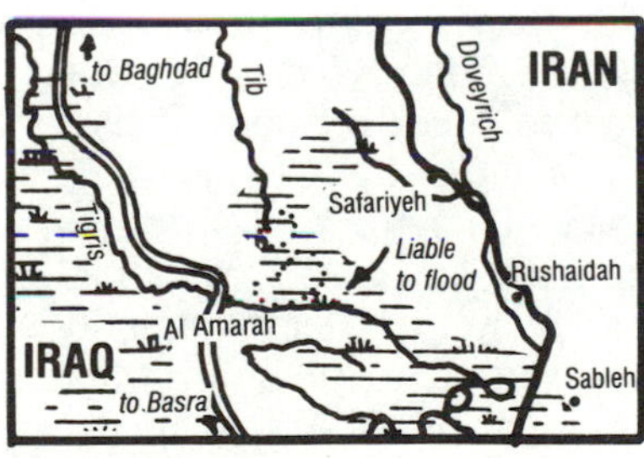

Adapted from the author's article on the Iran-Iraq War in the *Armed Forces Journal*, May, 1983, p. 43.

the Iranians had to attack across the wetlands or attack Iraqi positions on ridges and low hills across a relatively open plain.

Iraq again had local air supremacy and was able to fly over 200 sorties per day, although its fighters had limited effect. Iran had fewer than 60 fighters operational by its own count, and it kept them in reserve. Iraqi fighters thus enjoyed a virtual monopoly of the skies, which told when Iraq counterattacked on the morning after the Iranian attack and caught Iranian forces in the open. Iraq normally, however, could not acquire targets at the proper time or penetrate effectively against Iran's SHORAD. In contrast, Iraq's use of attack helicopters seems to have been timely and able to survive Iran's air defenses. According to British sources, the helicopters helped make up for Iraq's incompetence in using armored forces in defensive maneuvers, rather than positional warfare, and in using reserves to counterattack decisively.[96]

The end result was that Iran could not penetrate, and Iraq could not make its counterattacks decisive. For all its "final" character, the Iranian offensive seemed to signal that the war would continue until one side broke politically or economically rather than militarily. Further, while Iran had taken the offensive, it obviously had suffered heavy losses, and its infantry had shown signs of breaking under pressure. Iraqi claims of 15,258 killed were almost certainly exaggerated, but Western experts estimated that Iran had sustained the majority of the casualties, which amounted to about 7,000 killed and wounded, and that Iraq had taken some 5,000 prisoners.

In March 1983 both sides continued the pattern they had established in late 1982. Iran was attempting to build up for another offensive and was constantly testing Iraq's defenses. Iraq, in turn, sought to find some means that would put pressure on Iran and reduce the immense advantage Iran had gained through restoring its oil revenues. While the exact circumstances remain unclear, in February Iran seems to have suffered damage either from a tanker collision or from a storm to one of the offshore wells in its Nowruz field, which started to leak oil into the Gulf. On 2 March 1983, shortly after another demand by Hojatolislam Hasemi Rafsanjani that Saddam Hussein must go as the price for peace, Iraqi helicopters attacked other offshore wells in the Nowruz field. As later became apparent, some of these helicopters were specially equipped by French technicians to launch Exocet surface-to-surface missiles. The French later criticized the Iraqis for "wasting" two missiles to attack one well, but the attacks were at least partially successful.

The damaged wells started to pour anywhere from 1,500 to 10,000 barrels of oil a day into the Gulf. While this scarcely cut Iran's ability to export oil, it did create a major expansion of the oil conflict. In spite of attempt after attempt to mediate some truce that would allow the wells to be capped, neither side would compromise. Iran insisted on a partial settlement and Iraq upon a full one. The result, day by day, was to create an oil slick that gradually expanded to cover the entire western Gulf.

The potential importance of the oil slick was not apparent in most of March and April, however, and attention focused on charges that Iran had received Israeli help in reactivating the Phoenix missiles on its F-14s and that both Iran and Iraq were receiving large numbers of Chinese- and North Korean-made F-7 and F-6 jet fighters. Estimates issued at this time indicated that Iraq had lost a total of 79 Soviet-built fighters, including 35 MiG-19s and MiG-21s, several Tu-16 and Tu-22 bombers, and 6 Mirage F-1s. Iraq was said to be getting F-6s and F-7s (to replace these losses) that were transiting through Jordan and being assembled by Chinese technicians while Egyptians trained Iraqi crews. Iraq was also reported to have bought Egypt's remaining Soviet-made bombers and to have at least 30 F-6s. The remainder of its operational strength was estimated at 85 MiG-23s, 10 MiG-25 interceptors, 8 MiG-25 reconnaissance fighters, 150 MiG-21s, 40 MiG-19s (including some F-6s), 30 MiG-17s, 80 Su-20s, and 20 Su-7/Su-17s. In addition, Iraq was reported to have 13 Mi-24 Soviet attack helicopters, 10 Mi-8s, 15 French-made Gazelles, 6 Alouettes, and 12 Super Frelons and BO-105s.

The data on Iran were less precise but indicated that Iran was down to as few as 40 operational aircraft and that any North Korean deliveries of F-6 fighters were still highly limited. The net result was that Iraq had emerged with about 150 air defense and 150 ground attack fighters against an Iranian force of no more than 50—a six to one Iraqi superiority.

It was also clear that Iraq was slowly improving its performance in the air. While Iran found itself facing steadily improving Iraqi ground-based air defenses, and reduced its long-range strike and attack missions even further, the Iraqi Air Force was learning to use its remaining 38 Mirage F-1s in reasonably effective low-altitude attack missions. Iraq also improved its air-to-air performance with the F-1 when it shifted to a heavy emphasis on the Magic 530 semi-active radar-guided missile. While the 530 was not particularly effective, it did make up for the Iraqis' inability to push dogfight encounters to the point where they could use IR missiles successfully.

Nevertheless, Iran continued to have the advantage in terms of both oil and ground forces. Although the spill in the Gulf increased to 200,000 BPD, its main effect was to put pressure on the southern Gulf countries—particularly Bahrain, Qatar, and Saudi Arabia—which began to suffer serious losses in their fishing industry and had to shut down desalinization plants and other Gulf facilities. Iran continued to export at average levels of over 2.3 MMBD.

In mid-April, Iran launched another offensive called "Operation Dawn" near Fuka (Fakkeh), on the border of Iraq's Missan province, west of Dezful. Iran attacked three lines of entrenched Iraqi positions across an open plain, but the results were negligible. Iraq claimed to have killed 9,832 Iranians during the attack—it later became apparent that Iraq had lost up to 4,000 men in the fighting. It also was Iraq that called for an Islamic peace conference and that obviously was under the most political and financial pressure. It started new missile attacks on Dezful and increased its aircraft and helicopter attacks on tankers and oil facilities in the Gulf.

Iran, in turn, signed a new agreement with Syria in April that guaranteed the supply of 130,000 BPD at $25 per barrel ($5 below the

OPEC ceiling), 20,000 BPD for free for a year, and 10,000 BPD in a favorable swap for grain. This checkmated Saudi efforts to persuade Syria to reopen Iraq's oil pipeline through Syria. Iran also issued a book by its planning and budget organization that for the first time provided a detailed picture of the reparations it demanded and that set forth a bill for $90 billion.

May and June continued the war of attrition on both sides, while the southern Gulf states increased their efforts at mediation and at putting an end to the steadily growing oil slick in the Gulf. It seems fairly clear that Iraq was confronted with a virtual ultimatum that further attacks on offshore facilities would lead to massive cutbacks in its aid payments, and this eventually seems to have led to an informal cease fire which allowed Iran to cap at least some of its wells in September. Even so, French sources confirm that Iraq covertly carried out several additional missile attacks on Iranian wells.

There were few notable shifts in the fighting. The Red Cross did, however, announce that it estimated that Iran held some 45,000–50,000 Iraqi prisoners, to 6,800 Iranian prisoners in Iraq. This tended to confirm Iranian claims and contradict Iraqi claims regarding the recent course of the fighting. Iran also seemed to have the edge in its effort to simultaneously suppress its own Kurdish nationalists and exploit those of its opponent. By this point in the war, various Kurdish rebel groups had set up camps in a broad arc extending from Kermanshah in Iran north of Kirkuk in Iraq to Diyarbakir in Turkey. Each side backed the camps and movements on the other's territory while ruthlessly attempting to suppress any Kurdish dissident activity on its own soil. In late May, the situation in Iraq became so critical that Iraq gave Turkey permission to attack Kurdish rebel camps some 20 miles inside Iraqi territory. While Turkey originally claimed that it was conducting a joint operation and had used only 2,000 men, it later became clear that Turkey had acted alone, used forces of at least divisional size, and made extensive use of helicopter gunships and artillery. While Turkey directed its attacks at camps that had also been trying to create rebel movements among Turkey's 5.9 million Kurds (12% of Turkey's population), the fact remained that Iraq was so weak that Turkey had to suppress the Iranian-funded camps in Iraq.

The Super Etendards and Offensives in the North

The mediation efforts of Kuwait and the UAE occasionally seemed to make progress only to end in yet another impasse. Iraq, however, came under steadily greater financial pressure. It was getting only one-half to one-third its prior aid from the southern Gulf states and was forced to borrow money from Jordan, itself suffering from major cutbacks in Gulf aid payments and expatriate revenue. Iraq was forced to suspend payment to many European firms and to covertly appeal to France for more military aid. Iraq had by then been paying France roughly $2 billion a year for arms since 1980, and its civil and military debts had reached $5–7 billion, of which $1.7 billion was due in 1983 and could not be paid.

France had little choice but to cooperate. As a result, on 27 June 1983 France very publicly offered to lend Iraq five Super Etendard naval fighters with Exocet and announced that it had begun training of Iraqi crews in France. The Super Etendards provided a much better platform for attacking targets deep in the Gulf than Iraq's Super Frelon helicopters and F-1 fighters. They also offered a temporary substitute for the Mirage 2000s that France could not yet produce, although the French Navy had only 61 Super Etendard aircraft and could not easily spare the loan.

Iraq succeeded in using the French offer to put quiet pressure on its southern Gulf neighbors to buy Iran off by threatening further escalation of the war and blocking efforts to halt the still-growing oil slick in the Gulf. The main result was another conflict within OPEC at the July meeting of the oil ministers, at which Iran and Iraq attacked each other and then attempted to grab the vacant secretary-generalship of OPEC. The end result, fittingly enough, was a stalemate; OPEC remained without a head.

At the same time, the oil war in the Gulf became slightly hotter. Floating mines were reported off Ras Tanura, and the Defense Mapping Agency issued a warning that two ships—the *Annabella* and *Mokran*—might have been injured by mines and that another—the *Success*—might have been sunk. The warning was initially dismissed; it was taken more seriously when Qatar found a Soviet-made KB-1 20-kilogram mine drifting off its northeast coast.

Iraq then started a new diplomatic offensive. On 20 July Foreign Minister Tariq Aziz announced that Iraq would escalate attacks on oil facilities in Iran as part of an effort to weaken Iran's economy. He simultaneously announced that such attacks would continue to escalate indefinitely, that new executions of Shi'ite rebels had taken place, and that European and Japanese firms had agreed to accept deferred payment for their remaining activity in Iraq—an announcement at least one firm found to be something of a surprise. The foreign minister also used the opportunity to attack the U.S. for letting U.S. weapons "pour" into Iran. Iraq launched new air attacks on Iranian positions and missile attacks on Iranian cities; it simultaneously sought help from Japan—which was friendly to Iran—in ending the war.

None of this Iraqi activity prevented another Iranian offensive. The Iranians had steadily improved their absorption of the Soviet ground weapons they were getting from Syria, Libya, and North Korea during the preceding six months. They also proved able to recondition a considerable amount of the equipment the shah had procured from the U.S., using parts bought illegally in the U.S. and on the world market. Further, Colonel Shirazi, the acting chief of the Iranian ground forces, announced that Iran had again reorganized its army to bring its regular and revolutionary guard forces together.

Then, on 21 July Radio Tehran announced a new military offensive in northwest Iran, roughly 150 miles north of any previous major fighting and about 40 miles from the Turkish border. The Iranians again seem to have attacked at night and to have had Kurdish help. The extremely rough mountain terrain in the region offset the advantage of Iraq's armor and fixed positions, and Iran seems to have limited its offensive to objectives it could hold without exposing itself to counterattack or having to mass where Iraq could make effective use of its artillery or air superiority. Ironically, the Iraqi positions were near Zinu, a town near a road through the mountains from Rawandiz in Iraq to the Iranian border town of Piranshar, a key route Iraq used in supplying Kurds unfriendly to Iran.

The new Iranian offensive produced the usual war of lies over who had won, but this time it seemed to be Iran. Iraq lost about 3,800 men to Iran's 1,400. Iran captured a key Iraqi artillery position on the 7,800-foot "King Mountain" that dominated the area, drove 6–11 miles inside northern Iraq, captured a major Iraqi garrison point at Haj Omran, and at least opened the possibility of attacking toward Kirkuk along the Rowanduz Valley. The conflict also proved embarrassing to Iraq: It had to retract its victory claims on 4 August 1983, after Western correspondents toured much of the disputed territory with Iranian forces; and Iraqi air power had had little effect, although Iraqi fighters and helicopters seem to have flown over 200 sorties and to have had virtual air supremacy.

The new offensive resolved nothing. Iraq continued to hold its key positions, both sides continued to threaten a war of attrition and escalation, and the human and financial cost of the war continued to rise. There was no clear indication of whether the fighting would eventually force acceptance of a stalemate or lead to further escalation. There were, however, further indications of strain in Iraq. Saddam Hussein was forced to appeal to the women of Iraq to donate their jewelry to help finance the war (something no Iraqi woman seemed likely to do easily, given that such wealth usually constitutes a good portion of a family's liquid capital), and Iran threatened on 24 July to make the war Gulf-wide if Iraq attacked it with its Super Etendards. The U.S. immediately announced that it would keep the Gulf open to shipping, which produced an equally predictable Iranian rejection of the right of the U.S. to intervene.

The Last Half of 1983: Attrition or Escalation

The pressures that shaped the first half of 1983 continued during the second. Iraq continued to try to find means of forcing Iran to the conference table and of ensuring a steady flow of aid from the other Arab states in the Gulf. Iran continued to probe Iraq's northern border and to force it into a conflict of attrition. Iraq sought desperately to increase its oil revenues while Iran sought a rise in its OPEC quota from 2.4 MMBD to 3.2 MMBD.

As a result, the war threatened to escalate at several levels. Iraq made every possible effort to publicize the threat the Super Etendards posed to Iran's oil facilities. This resulted in a steadily escalating set of threats and counterthreats throughout October as the time for delivery approached. Iran attempted to block French delivery of the Super Etendards with Exocet by threatening to close the Gulf if Iran's oil exports were blocked, expanded its naval and maritime patrol aircraft activity near the Straits, and may have emplaced artillery on the Iranian islands nearest the Straits. The U.S. responded by declaring that it would keep the Gulf open; strengthening its naval and marine forces in the Indian Ocean, Japan attempted new peace initiatives; and the world's oil importers conducted a host of new studies to determine the damage Iraq could do and Iran's probable response.

By the time the 5 Super Etendards were delivered in early November, most analysts had concluded that they could threaten tanker traffic but not cripple Iranian oil export facilities and that Iran had little chance of mining the Straits of Hormuz or otherwise blocking Gulf oil traffic for an extended period of time. Nevertheless, even a limited threat to tankers raised the spectre of major increases in insurance, a halt in tanker movements in the Gulf, another rise in oil prices, and a confrontation between U.S.-Iranian naval and air forces. Given the fact that Iran could still operate most of its major ships and at least 40 fighter-bombers, and Iraq had at least 120 Mirage F-1 and MiG-23BM fighter-bombers it could use to attack Iran in addition to its Super Etendards, the risks remained serious.

Iraq also did more than posture. Throughout the last four months of 1983, it conducted occasional raids on ships in Iranian waters near Iraq. Several Iranian warships were sunk, and in early November one Greek tanker, the *Avra,* on its way to Bandar Khomeini, was seriously damaged and another, the *Antigoni,* was sunk. In late November, Iraq issued a formal warning to all merchant vessels to avoid the "war zone" at the northern end of the Gulf. Although Iraq had not made any major use of its Super Etendards by the end of December 1983—and may have launched all the Exocets it used against Iranian warships and commercial tankers from helicopters—Iraq's actions did seem to be successful in putting pressure on Iran.

During the second week of November, Iranian president Ali Khamenei stated Iran would not attack Iraq's remaining pipeline "out of consideration for Turkey." This may have been related to a new Iranian offensive, which will be discussed shortly, but Khamenei was also careful to down-play the risk of war with the U.S. Further, Hashemi Rafsanjani, the speaker of Iran's parliament, was careful to note that Iran would not have to react unless as much as half of its 2.4 MMBD in exports were blocked. Iran also capped about 100 offshore wells in its Nowruz and Ardeshir fields in December 1983. Significantly, Iran used concrete at the seabed, a process that will require redrilling once the threat ends. This did not affect Iran's ability to export at levels well above its OPEC quota, and Iran left some key wells flowing, but it represented a significant indication of Iran's concern regarding the Iraqi air threat.

At another level of escalation, Iran increased its pressure on the Southern Gulf states. This included even more virulent attacks on Saudi Arabia and new efforts to encourage Shi'ite insurgency and terrorist action. This may have included an attempt to blow up a meeting of the heads of the Gulf Cooperation Council states when they met at Doha in Qatar in early November. While Qatar was careful to label the plot's head as a "pro-Libyan prayer leader," it involved some thirty conspirators armed with rocket launchers and mortars, and may well have had Iranian backing.

There was no doubt that Iran expanded its support of Shi'ite and radical Islamic movements outside the Gulf, particularly in Lebanon. Groups with at least indirect Iranian support—as well as that of Syria—were responsible for a series of bloody car bombings of French, Israeli, and U.S. military facilities, and Iran made a concerted attempt to radicalize Lebanon's Shi'ites and supported Syria's efforts to strengthen its influence in Lebanon. Iran also seems to have been behind the bombing of the U.S. embassy and several other facilities in Kuwait on 12 December 1983. The group claiming credit for the bombing, the Islamic Jihad, was a Shi'ite group with at least ideological links to the Islamic Amal, the group headed by Hussein Musawi, which was generally given credit for bombings that killed 63 people in the U.S. Embassy in Beirut in April and a total of 298 American and French personnel in the peacekeeping force in Lebanon in October. While Iran denied a direct role in the bombings, Iranian President Ali Khamenei took the occasion of the Kuwaiti bombings to state that, "Iran would not allow the U.S. to enter the region, and let its allies live there, lord over others, and sell oil."

The ground fighting also involved some elements of escalation, although the war remained one of attrition. Iraq launched repeated Scud missile and air attacks on the Iranian towns near the border, and the missile attacks were clearly intended to kill civilians and put political pressure on the Iranian government. While Iranian charges that Iraq used gas seem false, the missile attacks did tend to escalate the fighting and Iran replied with artillery attacks on Iraqi towns and civilian targets.

Iran also launched another offensive in the north during the third week of October. The offensive took place on a 100-mile front and was directed at the Iraqi garrison towns of Penjwin and Garmak in Iraqi Kurdestan, about 90 miles from the Kirkuk oil fields and 30 miles from Sulaymanayah. Iran claimed it was trying to put its own border towns—Baneh and Marivan—out of Iraqi artillery range and striking at "counterrevolutionaries" supporting Iraq, who seem to have been Iranian Kurds. Iraq claimed the attacks were directed at its Kirkuk fields with the intent of isolating its Kurdish areas and launched new missile attacks on Iranian cities in the south—Dezful and Masjed Suleyman—also claiming to have mined the shipping routes to Bandar Khomeini.

While details of the fighting remain obscure, Iran does seem to have made excellent use of its infantry against relatively lightly held Iraqi positions and to have avoided the high casualties that had resulted from poorly coordinated use of "human wave" tactics during the earlier offensives in 1983. While the offensive did not involve major new casualties, it did continue into November and Iran launched several follow-up attacks in December. This brought the cost of the war to as many as 125,000 killed, with three to five times as many wounded and some 50,000 Iraqis and 8,000 Iranians taken prisoner. Iran also seems to have pushed 10–25 miles into Iraq and to have conquered 150–270 square miles of Iraqi territory, placing Iran within 75–85 miles of Iraq's pipeline to Turkey, which orginates at the city of Kirkuk. This raised growing doubts about Iranian claims that Iran would not cut Iraq's pipeline to Turkey, and seemed certain to lead Iraq to make new attempts at escalating its air and missile war against Iran's population centers and oil facilities should Iran resume its attacks in the spring.

At the end of 1983, the outcome of the war was impossible to predict, although the situation seemed to slightly favor Iran. Iraqi forces could lose, although this seemed as likely to occur because of internal pressure to overthrow Saddam Hussein as because of any Iranian military gains. In contrast, it seemed doubtful that Iran could lose. The prospects of any advance into Iran scarcely seemed attractive enough to lead Iraq into any further adventures in Khuzestan.[97] The one thing that did remain clear was that three years of fighting had not eliminated the threat the war would expand to threaten the other Gulf states and the West's oil supplies.

Tactics, Training, and Technology: The Lessons of the Fighting

Given the historical background, it is possible to understand the key lessons the war has so far taught regarding tactics, training, and technology. Admittedly, both the outcome and many of the details of the fighting remain unclear. There is, however, agreement in enough areas so that it can be said that "blind men" now see alike.

Armor and the Dominance of the Defensive

Iraq consistently failed to concentrate its armor in the initial stages of the war, and it consistently lost the advantages of time and space. It scattered its armored forces in its initial attack on the central front into elements the size of reinforced battalions and failed to concentrate them on advancing on Ahwaz, Dezful, or Susangerd.[98] Iraqi armored forces often halted in the midst of their initial tactical successes while they waited for orders. According to one source, Iraqi armored forces actually occupied Susangerd on 23 October 1980 and then withdrew in confusion. According to others, they entered and abandoned Susangerd twice and gave up critical positions near Dezful because they lacked clear orders and responsive command direction. According to all sources, the Iraqis failed to concentrate against Dezful and Ahwaz and occupy these towns or aggressively attack them while Iranian defenses were still weak. Iraq compounded this tactical mistake by sending armor to attack defended and built-up positions without infantry support. The inevitable result was that Iraq's superiority in armor and artillery would not be exploited, and Iraq sustained major losses every time its armor encountered infantry forces defending in built-up areas or using terrain barriers.

The tactics of the war have again validated the advantage of defensive positions against attacking forces that lack first-rate training and maneuver capability. Both sides have generally been able to halt superior enemy forces, and inflict greatly superior casualties, whenever they have been on the defensive. Position and terrain have also been critical, as has the ability to exploit prepared positions, although the Iranians have generally shown more skill than Iraq both in using such positions and in attacking them.

Neither side, however, has shown the ability to use its armor and reserve forces to counterattack or to deploy forces effectively across multiple fronts. Iran's major successes were in night infantry battles supported by tanks and in rough terrain or city fighting where it used tactics designed to counter its lack of armored maneuver capability. Although Iraq has improved its armored warfare performance since early 1982, it still seems unable to rapidly mass armor and launch counterattacks with the speed and weight necessary to inflict a major defeat on Iran's now largely infantry forces.

The Iranians have made good use of built-up areas, water barriers, and rough terrain since the first days of the war. They halted the Iraqis just outside Qasr-e-Shirin by using the rough terrain in the area. They delayed the Iraqi advance on Abadan by using water barriers and the built-up areas on Abadan Island, and they often halted the Iraqis elsewhere in the field by digging in their tanks and infantry at points where the terrain was favorable. Iran also used deliberate flooding to channel the Iraqis into a few routes of advance in low-lying areas in the south and to force them into a massive engineering effort simply to create their own defensive positions.

The Iraqis have proved almost as effective in using defensive positions against the Iranians. They have shown that they can rapidly construct dug-in positions and support them with hard-surfaced roads and shelter command posts and logistics, even when the terrain is not favorable. Both sides have shown that with the proper determination on the part of the defender, and lack of skill on the part of the attacker, "blitzkreig" becomes "sitzkreig." The Iraqi problem does not seem to have been one of exploiting defensive positions, but rather of the inability to reinforce and redeploy once such positions are penetrated or flanked. Iraq's newly raised double- and triple-digit units, with their largely political leadership, have tended to collapse under such pressures. Further, Iraq's overly rigid and slowly reacting command structure, and its relatively poor training in maneuver, have prevented it from using its reserves effectively and from reacting to changes on the battlefield.

Both sides have shown that they are still amateur armies in using their heavy weapons and have illustrated just how difficult it is to create a force that can maneuver effectively with modern armor. Virtually all the reports on the fighting have indicated that neither side can use its tanks and combined arms to maneuver quickly and innovatively by Western standards. In most circumstances this inability has led them into battles of attrition. Reliable reports from both sides indicate that Iraq and Iran are still not able to use their tank gunsights and fire controls with more than minimal effectiveness and that their tank forces go to battle by closing to 200–300 meters, or "boresight" range. This brings them well within range of the defender's dug-in tanks and infantry antitank weapons. Iran's superiority over Iraq does not imply that it can make effective use of its armor by Western standards.

Both sides have also tended to dig in to reduce the vulnerability of their tanks, rather than maneuver. The Iraqi tanks advancing on Abadan moved in grindingly slow phases in which tanks would provide cover while Japanese bulldozers and digging equipment carved out hull-down defilade emplacement positions. As news films of the advance show, during the initial fighting Iraqi armor advanced in this manner half a kilometer at a time, and then only after Iraqi artillery had pounded at possible Iranian positions.

Iraq and Iran have generally proved unable to properly coordinate tanks, infantry, and artillery, which has led them either to make serious military mistakes or to operate at the pace of an infantry advance or as if they were infantry occupying heavily fortified lines. According to one report, this problem resulted in a desperate Iraqi request to France early in the war to ship bulldozers for its tanks so they could dig in faster. In fact, Iraq's tanks have consistently dug in so well that they could not dig out and were outflanked and outmaneuvered by Iranian infantry.

The Iraqi "farms" of the Iranian tanks that Iraq captured during the first half of the war show that Iran abandoned tanks with no damage because of an inability to resupply them or minor repair problems, and reports from the Iranian side confirm that this has been true of the Iraqi tanks that Iran has captured in the fighting around Abadan and near Dezful. Abandoning armor intact is characteristic of poorly trained and commanded armies. Armor should not be kept dug in so long that it cannot maneuver or retreat, it should not be exposed where it cannot be refueled or supplied with ammunition, and it should not be left in positions where it becomes surrounded by enemy armor so that it is safer to leave the tank and run.

The fact that such tactical failures still occurred in late 1983, and the constant and growing problems both sides have had with maintenance and recovery, make speculation about the relative merits of given tanks or armored fighting vehicles meaningless. The problem is clearly one of training and command, and here the Iranians seem to have gotten better advice from the U.S. and UK than the Iraqis got from the USSR. At the same time, due credit should be given to the Iranians. The Iranian Army has been purged repeatedly and many of the officers from battalion commander up, who were the officers most closely associated with Iran's U.S. advisers, were forced to leave the armed forces or no longer have key positions. It is the younger officers, in their mid-thirties or younger, who now lead the Iranian forces. Some did have U.S. training, but most have been forged on the anvil of battle.[99] While Iran's armored tactics have scarcely matched those of its infantry, Iran's performance improved far more quickly than Iraq's until the mullahs took increased control in mid-1982. The Iraqis began to heed the advice they got from Jordan and France only in their May 1982 defense of Khuzestan.

There is one aspect of Iraq's use of armor, however, that may be of value to the West and the southern Gulf states. If Iraq has not maneuvered well on the battlefield, it has tended to maneuver well behind it. Iraq makes extensive use of tank transporters and lighter AFV transporters to quickly wheel its armor from one front or battlefield to another. These moves are conducted without the use of column formations, by what seem to be civilian drivers. They allow movement of 150 tanks or more, plus additional large numbers of AFVs on lighter transports, to occur faster and with less vulnerability to air attack than the formations common in NATO, and at speeds of up to 40 miles an hour.

Uncombined Arms

Most observers agree that both sides have shown a consistent inability to use combined arms effectively, although they have improved since the start of the war. Iraq sent tanks with minimal infantry support into built-up areas early in the war and promptly saw its armor destroyed by infantry. Iran evidently sent its tanks into combat against Iraq in largely unsupported and head-on maneuvers in its Susangerd offensive of 5 January 1981. Even in the Iranian offensives of 1983, both sides still used their artillery largely in area fire against a position occupied by the enemy, or to blast at dug-in enemy positions during the times when armor is advancing or digging in. Counterbattery fire has proved slow and mechanical. Only a few attacks, which involved long preparation, showed much attention to shifting and massing fire to support maneuver. The attention to target acquisition and probable effect of fire has been minimal. Tanks have been both sides' most effective short-range artillery.

It is impossible, incidentally, to draw any conclusions about the impact of mortars, antitank weapons and missiles, surface-to-surface missiles, and multiple rocket launchers on the war. They have been used too erratically, and by units whose training is unknown. It is true that antitank guided missiles have destroyed tanks and even helicopters, but no lessons to date can be drawn about the relative efficiency of given weapons or weapons combinations.

The Infantry: Courage as Usual

The infantry on both sides have usually proved to be dedicated and combat effective even when they have had minimal formal training. Although both sides have had desertions and some large-scale surrenders, their infantry have generally shown that they will fight with great courage even when they do not receive proper support from armor and combined arms. It was only after the formation of volunteer units, which were usually led by senior members of the Baath rather than by professional officers, that Iraqi infantry began to surrender or collapse without being defeated in detail. These units, which normally have double- and triple-digit designations, often had low-grade manpower with only one month of training and commanders appointed from the Baath. These units permitted many of the Iranian breakthroughs after early 1981 and were the source of many of Iran's prisoners, although many gradually hardened into competent units in 1982. Similarly, although there were increasing reports of Iranian units breaking or running away in early 1983, the Iranians showed great courage throughout 1983 even after it became apparent to virtually every soldier that Iran's tactics meant incurring major losses.

This courage has important implications for the West, since its forces encounter similar resistance in any built-up area or rough terrain, and both Iran and Iraq have shown that once their troops know the area, they have an ability to take advantage of position that makes up for formal training in tactics and weaponry. Any effort to commit U.S. troops without regard to the defensive fighting characteristics of local forces—many of which would be as likely to oppose U.S. troops as to regard them as liberators—could result in a military disaster.

The Importance of Independence and Initiative

Iraq has also had an important lesson from Iran in command and infantry tactics. At the start of the war, Iraq controlled its NCOs and junior officers so rigidly that they would not move without orders and waited rather than took the initiative. They were particularly unwilling to advance without orders or to maneuver around a position, once ordered to advance. This control cost Iraq many of its casualties in the first few weeks of fighting in Khorramshahr and Abadan. It became apparent to the Iraqis that initiative must begin at the NCO level and that even small, squad-size formations must have considerable independence in warfare in built-up areas. Iraq has since improved the freedom given to its small formations, junior officers, and NCOs. Unfortunately for Iraq, it did not succeed in giving its commanders enough freedom of action. Iraq also made the mistake of attempting to enhance its fighting capability by punishing or executing officers for comparatively small withdrawals or tactical failures, although it is difficult to see what this has ever accomplished in military history.

Training for Combat in Urban and Built-Up Areas

The Iran-Iraq War has illustrated the need for special training to fight in urban and built-up areas and for special tactics to avoid the problems raised by such areas. An analysis by Edgar O'Ballance indicates that Iraq initially attacked Khorramshahr by ferrying three armored regiments across the Shat al-Arab to the north of the city.[100] It then sent unsupported armored forces forward into an urban area where they were petrol-bombed and destroyed at short ranges. Iraq took the city only after virtually halting offensive operations for three weeks, while it gave special training to units from its special forces, paratroop units, and Presidential Guards. Even then, it took a total of 15 days and some 5,000 casualties to occupy a lightly defended city. When Iraq went on to attack Abadan Island, its forces were channeled into a few narrow approaches using the bridges it had captured and one additional pontoon bridge. The Iranians were able to fight a prolonged defense in detail using natural and man-made barriers and resupplying by boat and helicopter. In contrast, Iraq concentrated on trying to force the island into submission with mass artillery fire and conventional tactics. It failed to coordinate its naval and army operations and continued to concentrate on Abadan although its tactical and strategic importance was minor compared to that of key objectives like Ahwaz.

As the Saudis learned to their cost during the 1979 uprising at the Grand Mosque in Makkah, much of the most critical fighting in the Near East may be urban warfare of a highly unexpected kind. It is essential that southern Gulf and USCENTCOM forces train to fight in such warfare and that the U.S. avoid the kind of street fighting that would lock even the best-trained U.S. forces into fighting their way through a city step by step. Even if the U.S. had the time and force ratios to win in such combat, it would be politically unable to accept the resulting casualties.

The Use of Reserves

It is also possible to draw some important conclusions about the potential value of reserves, particularly in the defensive role. One of the key factors that enabled Iran to hold in the early days of the war was the use of reserves. Reserves allowed Iran to rapidly build up from a 6:1 local inferiority when the Iraqi attack began to no more than a 3:1 inferiority by mid-October. Reserves, or popular mobilization, to be more exact, have since allowed Iran to match the Iraqi buildup. The disarray in Iran's army that helped lead to the Iraqi attack unquestionably did exist, and Iranian forces in the forward area were seriously under strength. Even before the Iraqi attack, however, Iran was able to reinforce with large Revolutionary Guard forces that had a heavy stiffening of trained NCOs, technicians, junior officers, and enlisted men from the conscript intake to the Iranian Army. Many of the Guards had formerly had reserve assignments.

Although it was generally discounted at the time, Khomeini's call to move 125,000 men to the front by any possible means in mid-September 1980—after the first serious artillery duels and border incidents—reflected a realistic estimate of the number of volunteers available, and civil and military transport did move up to 100,000 men into the area by the time the full-scale Iraqi invasion started on 22 September. Iran seems to have been able to get as many as 200,000 men to the front by late November 1980, and it has built up its strength with such forces ever since. Although Iran deployed elements of only six to eight regular divisions during most of the fighting, it had something like five additional divisions' worth of manpower mobilized into Guard and other irregular elements. It is not surprising that such "untrained" Revolutionary Guards were often highly effective, particularly early in the war. Many were trained ex-soldiers, and in the early days of the fighting the sheer chaos of their organization forced them to act independently, get into situations in which they incurred high casualties, and improvise their supplies. Thus they had an advantage over Iraq's overcentralized forces, once they had time to learn.

In contrast, Iraq began the war using only 35,000 men of its popular militia. Although this total had risen to 400,000 men by February 1982, and Iraq was trying to mobilize a full-scale "People's Army" and a "task force" of 2.5 million, Iraq did not provide the kind of training and leadership necessary to make such forces effective, and it could not give them anything like Iran's patriotic and spiritual motivation. Iraq also desperately sought to recruit Jordanians, Egyptians, and other Arab volunteers, and not simply for purposes of political solidarity. The call by King Hussein of Jordan on 28 January 1982 for a volunteer Yarmouk brigade reflected quite serious Iraqi fears that Iran's ability to draw on members of its organized reserves, other ex-military and conscripts, and volunteers was proving decisive in allowing Iran to mass superior forces and suffer much heavier casualties.[101]

Iraq also initially seems to have concentrated so much on mass and morale that it failed to pay realistic attention to tactics and technical factors, which contributed to the tendency of its new volunteer units to collapse under pressure. Even as late as January 1982, interviews with senior Iraqis indicated that they did not focus on the true reasons for their reverses in the field or realize the shortcomings in their command and communications. They allowed themselves to believe in the myths of their own ideology and insisted that their commanders and intelligence officers be believers as well. In war, being able to hear bad news quickly and honestly is just as important as being able to hear good news.

Combat Engineering and Engineering Support

Both sides have proved relatively efficient in combat engineering and engineering support. Economic development in Iraq and Iran has created quite competent construction services, many locally operated, and these have played a major role in the war.

Iraq started building oil-mixed blacktop and hard-surfaced two-lane roads to the front on the second day of the war. It used such roads to support its positions before Dezful, Ahwaz, and Khorramshahr when the rainy season began and to successfully counter Iran's attempts at flooding. The roads proved particularly critical in allowing Iraqi forces to continue to operate near Ahwaz in spite of Iran's use of irrigation dams to flood part of the area. Iraq has been using its construction equipment to strengthen its lines of communication ever since. Construction equipment has been used to rapidly build defense positions and strengthen existing ones. Extensive use has been made of shelters, earth mounds, and excavation. Urban and built-up positions have been rapidly strengthened under fire using shovels and bulldozers. Artillery and air attack damages on roads and runways have been repaired within hours.

It is also interesting to note that Iraq's greatest tactical successes of the war occurred as a result of the ability of its combat engineers to rapidly cross water barriers for the first time in Iraq's military history. For example, the rapid construction of a 310-meter pontoon bridge on 10 October 1980 enabled Iraq's Saladin division to carry out an excellent night-crossing operation about 16 kilometers up the Karun (Qum) River from Khorramshahr. This operation resulted in the capture of the 50 M-60 tanks turned over to Jordan, several 175mm guns, large numbers of stocks, and many Iranian prisoners. It also enabled Iraq to threaten the Abadan-Ahwaz road and cut Iran's western pipeline net. Iraq's engineering was also good enough to support pontoon and barge operations across river barriers with tidal changes of 1.5 meters and considerable currents. This proved critical in assaulting Abadan Island on 24 October 1980, when Iraq was able to capture only one of the two existing bridges to the island.

Combat engineering and the extensive military use of civil construction equipment can be expected to be important features of any future war in the Gulf. It is obvious that both sides in the current war have learned to make combat engineering a critical aspect of their defensive tactics, and the rest of the region places so heavy an emphasis on its construction industry that it is likely to follow suit.

The Importance of Long-Range Artillery

Both sides have been successful in using long-range artillery in attacking cities, ports, and oil facilities. They have shown that such weapons can play a vital tactical role in the forces of developing nations. Iranian artillery, some firing from shelters built under the shah, proved critical in halting the Iraqi advance on Dezful and Ahwaz. It was Iraqi artillery, not airpower, that destroyed the refinery at Abadan, and artillery on both sides closed the Shat and provided critical support fire in the campaign to take Khorramshahr and in the fighting over Abadan Island.

At the same time, far too much of the fire on both sides has been little more than harassment. Both sides have fired far more ammunition than most targets have justified and worn out their artillery barrels prematurely.[102] It has once again become clear that military operations and day-to-day civilian life can go on even under intense bombardment once troops are used to the shock effect of artillery rounds. As was the case in wars as diverse as World War I and the Vietnam war, the shock effect of prolonged mass artillery fire existed only in the mind of the artillery propagandist or incompetent commanders. To be effective artillery must be "maneuvered" as much as armor, used as quickly and surgically as possible, and then switched to new targets. The disruptive effect of the 175mm and 130mm guns and Scud missiles firing sporadically into urban centers and rear areas has, however, had an importance out of any proportion to its lethality. Its impact on morale and economic activity has proved to be more important than the shock effect of prolonged barrages on troops, and both sides have clearly found every kilometer of range to be of great value in reaching such targets.

The Iraqis have complained about the Soviet failure to provide suitable fire control and communications equipment and the doctrine and computers to manage mass artillery fire. They have also found they lacked suitable communications gear and the doctrine and training to use forward controllers to call in artillery fire in support of armor while under maneuver. Officers in friendly Arab states are uncertain as to whether this is a fault of Soviet advice and equipment or of Iraqi planning, but they note that the USSR did not provide effective advice and support equipment to Egypt.

Special Forces and Mountain Units

The value of the Near East's equivalent of "special forces" showed up early in the war in the pipeline sabotage that cut Iraqi oil shipments through Turkey on 26 September 1980. It showed up again in a more spectacular series of incidents on 4–6 January 1982. On the 4th, saboteurs cut the Tripoli spur of Iraq's pipelines through Syria just 10 days after it opened. On the 6th, another attack cut Iraq's pipeline through Turkey some 68 kilometers from the border, cutting Iraq's oil shipments by 200,000 BPD and 750,000 BPD respectively.[103] These attacks temporarily reduced Iraqi oil exports from around 1 MMBD to 300,000 BPD, or less than a tenth of Iraq's prewar level of 3.7 MMBD. Still further incidents temporarily cut Iraq's oil exports through Lebanon just before Iran's March offensive and Iraq's pipeline through Turkey just before the start of Iran's May offensive.[104] Given Syrian and Lebanese Shi'ite hostility to Iraq, and the ability of Kurdish rebels to operate in Turkey, the seriousness of these attacks was far greater than the temporary halt in the oil flow might indicate. Iraq received a series of strategic warnings that its oil shipments might be cut at any time, which inevitably limited its willingness to use its air power against Iran.

It should be noted that Iraq's mountain divisions have shown the value of special training for mountain warfare in attacking Qasr-e-Shirin and Mehran in 1980 and that Iran's troops showed equal proficiency in their mountain offensive in the northwest in July 1983. Both sides have shown that mountain troops can conduct flanking movements with high speed in mountain terrain and in the face of hostile air superiority. These lessons again may be important for USCENTCOM, which seems to have had more desert training than training in mountain warfare, and which may now have to meet both Soviet forces trained in the mountains in Afghanistan and local Iranian or Iraqi forces with extensive training in mountain combat. Such mountain forces could make optimal use of airmobile and airborne units, but must be fully equipped and trained to fight under such conditions, rather than given a minor amount of dual capability.

Close Air Support and Helicopter Forces

Since the early days of the war, close air support has been conspicuous largely by its absence or its incompetence. Both sides, but particularly Iraq, have tended to use fighters only in key attacks, and usually in emergencies when the survival of their ground units was in question. The Iraqis have charged that many of their Soviet-made bombs and rockets are duds. Iraqi forces, however, had little meaningful training in the attack role—except in strafing and rocket attacks—before Iraq sought French and Jordanian help. Such foreign advice has since improved Iraq's air performance, but Iraq still displays little ability to coordinate air support when it could be most effective. Retired officers among the correspondents who have visited Iraqi forces have seen many missed opportunities and random air attacks.

The Iranians did better early in the war, although Iran did not face the problem of where and when to use close air support while Iraq was driving forward along every major line of advance. Iranian air support was effective in helping to halt the Iraqi advance on Dezful and Ahwaz on 28 September and may have been critical in helping to halt the Iraqi push on central Khuzestan on 1 October. Iran also seems to have had some almost accidental success in hitting Iraqi armor while it was massing on 3 October. Even so, Iran's success consisted largely of the shock effect of airpower on Iraqi formations that were not yet accustomed to using their antiaircraft guns and that placed too much reliance on missiles. Iranian fighters did not inflict significant damage on Iraqi forces, and their main impact was in hitting carelessly deployed ammunition and fuel. Iran also failed to successfully attack critical targets like bridges or other small fixed targets in flying its close air support missions.

Neither side pressed its air support missions home between Iraq's attack and the beginning of Iran's Operation Victory, but the Iranian offensives of 1982 forced Iraq to use its air power. Iraq flew up to 150 sorties per day in trying to check Iran's May 1982 offensive, and Iraq flew over 100 sorties per day in trying to check key Iranian offensives during 1983. Although Iraq has shown increasing ability to make effective use of its Mirage F-1s since January 1982, most of its attack sorties have not been highly effective. This is not simply a matter of the weaknesses in Iraq's air force. The Iraqi and Iranian armies quickly learned to use man-portable surface-to-air missiles, their automatic weapons, and AA guns to do a good job of discouraging the few attacks that occur when a major offensive is not under way. This ability, and their emphasis on dug-in positions, have sharply reduced their vulnerability to air power.

Again, there is a message for USCENTCOM and the southern Gulf states. As was the case in the October War and the recent fighting in Lebanon, the Iran-Iraq War has shown that the reconnaissance and air strike "cycle" must be structured to catch land forces while they are massing and moving, not once they have reached their combat positions. This means night air attacks, armed patrol, and very fast recce processing and reaction. Even under these conditions, Western air power must be prepared for mass gun and man-portable SAM fire. The problem is not likely to be an electronic warfare duel against sophisticated missiles like the SA-6, but mass fire of a kind that is much harder to suppress or avoid while flying attack misions on alert combat units.

Another problem with close air support in the Iran-Iraq War is that both sides have lacked competent forward air controllers, a C^3I net capable of bringing aircraft in at the right place, training for using air support in fluid battles on rough terrain, and the kind of reconnaissance and briefing capability necessary to prepare the pilot. The sortie limits imposed by serviceability and the unwillingness to incur casualties seem equally serious, as does the lack of realistic peacetime training in the role. Iraq still wasted many of its sorties in 1982 and 1983 because they came at the wrong time or were not properly directed.

Both sides have demonstrated their ability to use helicopters successfully as gunships, troop carriers, and emergency supply transports. There seems to be a general consensus that helicopters are survivable and able to play a critical role in making up for the lack of proper planning, maneuver, and support in emergencies. Iranian helicopters proved both survivable and of great tactical importance in limiting the

Iraqi advance around Mehran. They were critical to the Iranian supply of Abadan during the Iraqi siege, and Iran increasingly substituted helicopters for fighter close air support after the start of its March 1982 offensive. The Iraqis found helicopters critical in moving across water barriers and in small tactical troop movements around terrain barriers. So few helicopters have been operational, however, that they have not been proved in the offensive role in large numbers. If they had, it seems likely that they would often have been critical in bypassing the slow-moving and dug-in defenses on both sides. As has been the case in Afghanistan, it also has been possible to use helicopters to seek out and destroy targets that jet fighters cannot find and to operate in mountainous and built-up terrain where helicopters can locate and maneuver around light AA guns and man-portable missiles that fighters cannot spot and fly over.

This experience has been further validated by Britain's use of helicopters in the Falklands and Israel's use of helicopters in Lebanon. It indicates that properly structured USCENTCOM and southern Gulf forces could take advantage of the maneuver problems of the armies in the region through more extensive use of attack helicopters and heliborne forces.

Air Defense

Neither side has shown much proficiency in sophisticated air defense. The Iranians discovered early in the war that small, low-flying F-4 formations could strike virtually at will anywhere in Iraq. There are many reports, often by retired Western military personnel, that Iranian aircraft could easily defeat Iraqi SA-2 and SA-3 surface-to-air missiles by following the maneuvers the U.S. developed in Vietnam. As was the case in the October War, the SA-2 and SA-3 missiles proved important largely as deterrents to medium- and high-altitude strikes, and they seemed particularly vulnerable to such maneuvers at low altitudes because of their comparatively slow initial acceleration.[105] Iraq seems to have had more success with the SA-6, and deployed limited numbers into forward positions, but it evidently did not have enough SA-6s to provide more than occasional point coverage.[106]

While insufficient unclassified information is available on the precise variants of the SA-2, SA-3, SA-6, and Soviet support equipment available to Iraq, it is clear that Iran was able to fly under them and outmaneuver them without extensive use of sophisticated electronic countermeasures. There also is no doubt that the Iraqis—all public claims to the contrary—are deeply unhappy about the quality of the air defense radars and C^3I systems they bought from the USSR. The Iraqi investment in such Soviet systems has been immense. The Iraqis have about 70 batteries of surface-to-air missiles, although comparatively few SA-6s—which seem to be the only effective system they have. They also have bought large numbers of Soviet-built radars and associated C^3I systems. They have found, however, that Soviet training and doctrine are poor, that the operational reliability of their missiles and guidance equipment is low, and that the Soviet missiles were either designed for a far more sophisticated C^3I environment than the USSR made available to Iraq or designed to destroy targets flying at higher altitudes than the Iranian fighters had to operate in. While Iraqi readiness, education levels, and training are suspect, the fact remains that the Syrians had even worse luck against the Israelis in 1982, losing 19 SA-6 sites without hitting one Israeli fighter.[107] In any case, the result has been that the Iraqis have been forced to rely on earthmounds, other passive defenses such as barrage balloons, and AA guns to protect their cities, oil facilities, industries, and other rear installations.

The Iranians seem to have had serious trouble in operating or maintaining their Hawk, Rapier, and Tigercat surface-to-air missiles. Although the Hawk proved more effective than Soviet systems in the October War, there are no reports that Iran has been able to make effective use of its Western air defense systems.[108] Like the Iraqis, the Iranians have had to rely on their AA guns and the use of "curtain fire" from automatic weapons.

It is the SA-7 and AA gun that have emerged as the chief air defense weapons of the war. As was the case in the October War, once the hype over fighter cover and more advanced surface-to-air missiles died down, it became clear that SHORAD systems were the key to active air defense, even in rear areas. Few pilots press forward attacks on installations and facilities protected by large numbers of AA guns, particularly when radar-guided guns like the ZSU-23-4 are available. Any estimate of the overall lethality of such systems would be purely speculative, but both Western reporters and Arab military officers agree that both sides have learned the kind of curtain fire and automatic weapons fire techniques used in Vietnam and the October War and that these now standard air defense tactics, coupled with the defense of key positions by more advanced AA guns, are critical in protecting them from the effective delivery of conventional air ordnance.

There is a similar consensus that neither side has been particularly effective in air-to-air combat. Even though both sides had claimed to have destroyed more than 100% of their opponent's air force by the end of the first year of the war, most of the air-to-air combat seen by outside observers or on radars in Kuwait and Bahrain was inconclusive. Engagements that should have taken less than 2 minutes lasted as long as 20. In most cases, the more successful pursuer was then unable to keep his opponent from breaking off and escaping. This may reflect the fact that combat tended to "spiral down" to altitudes in which neither side was trained to fight and in which the IR missiles operated by both sides were relatively ineffective. The Iranians had the tactical edge and the fuel and endurance to "win" most such encounters during the first year of the war. They also seem to have had a distinct edge in training.

They did not prove able to bring most "victories" to a kill, however, and they have not engaged in extensive air combat since their numbers of operational fighters dropped sharply in early 1982.

As for the other aspects of air combat tactics, most reports agree that the flying done during the period between the first few days of the war and the time when Iran began to lose its air strength was in formations of twos and fours and that only Iran was able to consistently employ formation tactics in air-to-air combat. No attempt was made to use mass as a tactic for defending or countering the defense. Such saturation of contested airspace was one of the few Arab tactics that Israeli experts feared after the October War because of its ability to reduce the effectiveness of formations and to present firing opportunities to less capable pilots, although their successes in fighting Syria in June 1982 have shown that such tactics can be overcome when one side has the advantage of an AWACS like the E-2C.[109]

There is considerable speculation—even among those Arab officers most friendly to Iraq—that Iraq found its peacetime air combat training to be almost totally inadequate and that the Soviet emphasis on guided intercepts using air-to-air missiles had little practical operational value. One senior Arab military officer, who had been consulted on Iraq's problems, found that the Soviet training course given to Iraq's pilots had been too short, undemanding, and often further curtailed because of weather. His private reaction was that neither the training in the USSR nor the Soviet advice given regarding training in Iraq had served the Iraqis well and that Iraq had made things worse by cutting back further on its training effort to conserve aircraft during the transition to new aircraft types. Both he and several other Arab observers also indicated that Iraq had serious problems in keeping its avionics operational and may have had reliability and effectiveness problems with its Soviet air-to-air missiles. Iraq may have had particularly serious problems with the later models of MiG-21s until mid-1982. After this time Soviet support seems to have either improved or been significantly increased.

The Iranians had somewhat different problems. Only 10 of Iran's 77 F-14s seem to have been flyable when the war started, and none seem to have been able to fire more than AIM-9 missiles under close visual encounter conditions. The F-14 could be used as "mini-AWACS" only where it was flown in the rear behind Iranian air strikes or air intercepts and used to vector Iranian F-4s and F-5s against Iraqi fighters or to warn them of attempted Iraqi intercepts.[110] Interestingly enough, Israel used a more sophisticated version of this technique in achieving an 80:1 kill ratio over Syria in June 1982. It used its E-2C as an AWACS in the rear, and the radar of its F-15 to help vector fighters in forward combat and spot takeoffs from Syrian air bases. Iran also seems to have been unable to achieve radar missile kills with its F-5s and F-4s, and most sources agree that Iran had serious trouble in keeping its aircraft operational after late 1981. Even before this, the Iranian tendency to close to dogfight ranges to launch its infrared missiles raised questions about how many of its avionics were operational.

Several lessons emerge from this situation. First, the USSR has done a poor job of training and equipping developing nations with SAM and fighter defenses. The few air forces that have had any success with Soviet equipment—Egypt's and India's—have had this success largely because they rejected Soviet tactics and bought outside technical advice and support equipment. Others, like Iraq's and Syria's, have suffered serious losses. It is, of course, impossible to know just how much Soviet training and equipment differs in its "export" version, or how much worse it is than the French, Jordanian, and Egyptian advisory efforts Iraq has had since 1981, but it is clear that numbers can be largely discounted when a developing nation relies on Soviet equipment and advice.

Second, developing nations have almost as serious a problem in learning how to operate a cohesive air force as they do in learning how to operate and maintain individual aircraft. Sheer numbers of aircraft tell little about military behavior when nations lack the overall command and control structure, and tactical and strategic planning capability, to operate their aircraft as part of a coherent concept of operations. This argues that properly equipped and organized air forces in the southern Gulf states could have an effectiveness out of any proportion to their numbers.

Third, USCENTCOM air power is likely to have an importance out of proportion to its numbers precisely because it can operate as a force rather than as scattered small groups of aircraft. While the various combat conditions of the Middle East may not favor the U.S. soldier or marine because of the problems of terrain, the problems of fighting among at least partly hostile populations, and the difficulty of dealing with combat in built-up areas, they do favor U.S. air power. Like the advantages the U.S. might gain from concentrating on the kind of heliborne and assault helicopter forces that can overcome or bypass the previous problems, its superior training and technical capabilities should allow it to virtually brush aside most of the air forces in the region.

Fourth, southern Gulf forces will succeed or fail to the extent that their fighter and helicopter forces can avoid the trap of becoming showpieces and become highly trained combat forces. This is a demanding test, and one that even Saudi Arabia risks failing. Saudi air combat training, for example, is now far too easy and simulator oriented, and it lacks the kind of demanding low-altitude regime necessary for military effectiveness. These problems are exemplified in Saudi fighter attrition rates, which should be five to six times higher than they now are in air combat training; the aircraft are surviving in peace under conditions that will lead them to die in war. No other southern Gulf nation approaches Saudi Arabia's present level of proficiency, no nation has adequate attack mission training and reconnaissance capability, and no nation is creating effective attack helicopter forces—again illustrating the need for collective defense efforts and for the kind of centralized training and exercise facilities in Saudi Arabia that will allow the smaller Gulf states to become effective.

Fifth, the problems Iran and Iraq face in air battle management, target acquisition, and managing an efficient forward air control and rear area strike planning system should be a warning to both the southern Gulf states and USCENTCOM. There is a clear need throughout the southern Gulf for a system like a "mini-AWACS" that can extend the coverage of the Saudi E-3As and handle air battles over each Gulf state in a way that can combine radar and electronic support measures to both allow air defense and help guide attacking fighters and helicopters. There is an equal need for better reconnaissance and army air support aircraft to provide targeting data. Saudi Arabia is the only country buying such aircraft, and even it will lack the required targeting and C^3I aircraft until the late 1980s.

Interdiction and Strategic Bombing

As in the case of close air support, both sides have generally proved unable to use air power effectively in interdiction and other attack missions in support of their military forces behind the front lines. The Iraqis have largely failed to achieve any significant damage in flying interdiction missions since their initial attacks on exposed Iranian ammunition and fuel dumps in the early days of the war. Even then, Iraqi successes were not proportionate to the effort involved. This Iraqi failure initially resulted from the training and equipment problems in the Iraqi Air Force discussed earlier and later from the growing strength of Iranian SHORAD. It also resulted from the fact that the Iraqis have no way to acquire targets on a timely basis that cannot be seen by their ground forces, and it lacked the command structure to plan such attacks effectively. The Iranian Air Force was marginally better until most of its aircraft became inoperable, but numerous observers confirm that the Iraqi Army operated in the rear with almost total indifference to the risk of Iranian air attacks against anything other than large, fixed area targets even during the period when Iran dominated the skies. Iran had the same problems as Iraq. It has no way to acquire targets in the rear area or to exploit air strikes against tactical forces under conditions in which such bombing would have a significant effect.

Neither side showed much capability to hit medium-sized interdiction targets like bridges, or to attack even large daytime movements of armor unsupported by any air defense, during the initial two years of the war. Although Iraq did strikingly improve its sortie rate against attacking Iranian forces after mid-1982, it then could not penetrate their dense mix of AA guns and SA-7s with great effectiveness. This failure again confirms the general lesson that developing nations find it difficult, if not impossible, to efficiently execute attack missions unless directly supported by a Western air force, regardless of their performance on test ranges.

Strategic bombing is another story. Iraq's attempt to suppress the Iranian Air Force in the first two days of the war was an absolute disaster. Although it attacked 10 Iranian air fields and air facilities, it did virtually no damage. In fact, it did not even achieve enough shock value to impose more than the most minor delays in Iranian Air Force operations. While Iraq has since charged that the cause was defective Soviet-made bombs, the fact remains that Iran was able to hit at least two Iraqi air fields on the first day of combat, and with sufficient shock effect to force mass aircraft dispersals to Jordan and other Gulf countries that Iraq had not planned on when the war began. This, and Saddam Hussein's decision to withhold Iraq's bombers and MiG-23s from most of the fighting, left Iraq largely exposed to the Iranian Air Force. The result was that by the second day of the war, Iranian retaliation against Iraqi cities and oil facilities—evidently in response to Iraq's shelling of the refinery at Abadan—triggered the pattern of attacks on oil facilities that characterized the next month of the war. A few Arab experts, however, explain Iraq's forced dispersal of its aircraft as the result of the fact that it had comparatively few main operating bases, that most were fairly near Iran, and that while they were sheltered, most had large numbers of "soft" facilities. They feel it was the asymmetries in basing posture, rather than Iran's superior effectiveness, that forced Iraq to disperse.

Although Iraq did prove effective against targets like Iran's refineries and easily targetable unsheltered ammunition dumps—and forced fuel and ammunition rationing early in the war—the Iranians generally had the edge. This occurred in part because the key Iranian oil facilities in the Gulf were at Kharg Island, which was only barely within range of Iraq's fighter bombers and which Iraq proved unable to attack at its key points of vulnerability. Iraq proved barely able to hit such targets as oil storage tanks, but Iran was able to strike at smaller critical equipment targets. By the time Iraq organized such strikes more effectively in mid-1982, it confronted air defenses that denied it the ability to inflict major damage, and it lacked the targeting aids necessary to strike effectively at tankers moving in and out of the port.

The evidence is contradictory, but informed Western and Arab observers agree on the following points relating to Iran's superiority early in the war. First, Iranian proficiency and accuracy in delivering conventional attack ordnance like rockets and bombs were far greater than in the case of Iraq and owed a great deal to the fact that something like 100 U.S.-trained Iranian pilots were freed from jail in the first days of the war.[111] Second, Iranian missions were much better planned and indicated far better use of maps, and reconnaissance capabilities, and pilot briefings. Third, Iran did make effective use of Maverick on at least some occasions, including strikes on al-Bashrah. Fourth, the superior range and payload of most Iranian fighter-bombers proved absolutely critical against area targets. Iran's initial ability to deliver two to three times as many bombs or rockets per plane per sortie made up for much of the Iranian Air Force's lack of accuracy in using such munitions and had a telling effect on dispersed targets like refineries, tank farms, and petrochemical plants.

This Iranian success may hold an important lesson regarding the character of future wars because of the Iranian ability to strike at complexes like Ras Tanura (with its disastrously concentrated mix of oil and liquid gas facilities) or other central oil facilities in the Gulf. While none of the air strikes on either side indicated that they could attack small key targets like the sensitive equipment involved in refineries and oil extraction, Iran's potential ability to deliver a large number of individual rockets and bombs presents a serious problem. If Iran can get the parts to make and keep its remaining F-5s and F-4s operational, it will pose a significant threat to Western oil supplies and the independence of action of the southern Gulf countries.

At the same time, the actual damage done by such air strikes should not be exaggerated. Discussions with some of the Iraqi experts involved—confirmed by Arab, Western, and Japanese observers—indicate that air power had a much greater effect in forcing both nations to shut down operations than in doing actual physical damage. The psychological impact of burning oil tanks and petrochemicals plants tended to disguise the fact that most of the key equipment emerged intact and that the key military impact was to force a temporary shut-down of operations.

Iran must be given credit, however, for some relatively accurate and well-planned attacks on Iraqi power plants and for demonstrating considerable coordination in several attacks. This coordination was particularly striking in an attack it launched on Iraq's H-3 oil field complex and air base at al-Walid, where Saddam Hussein kept his Tu-22 and Il-28 bombers. This target is over 800 kilometers from the nearest Iranian air base at Reza'iyeh, indicating that Iran's F-4s had to refuel to carry out this attack.[112] Iran also showed considerable skill in planning its three air attacks on Kuwait. Its "accidental" bombings of Kuwait on 12 and 16 November 1980 hit at border areas that were beautifully chosen to discourage other Arab support of Iraq. Its follow-up raid on 7 June 1982 had the same effect, and its outright attack on Kuwaiti oil facilities on 2 October 1982 provided precisely the right signal that Iran still had the ability and will to threaten the rest of the Gulf. It is interesting to consider just what the Iranian Air Force would have accomplished if it had not been for political purges, and loss of its fuel supply at a critical phase in the war, and erratic spare parts supply.

It is also notable that both sides avoided strikes on each other's population centers during 1981–1982, concentrating on power plants, oil facilities, and other targets that would not encourage escalation to strikes against population centers. Neither side has yet made use of weapons like napalm or cluster bombs—although Iran has some 5,000 units of napalm in inventory and extensive stocks of cluster bombs.[113] While Iraq did fire some Scud missiles into Iranian cities in 1982 and carried out some minor harassment attacks on Iranian towns, it did not exploit its air advantage to strike at Iran's population and conducted only one major high-altitude strike with its Tu-22 bombers, which produced extensive damage to Iranian auto plants near Tehran. Iraq seems to have both feared the resulting impact on Iran's population in terms of new support for the war and realized that it lacked the tactical air strength for a major area bombing campaign.

It was only in 1983, when Iraq's financial and military positions became extremely serious, that Iraq expanded its air strikes to cover oil targets in the Gulf and began more serious missile strikes on Iranian cities. Even in December 1983, however, Iraq seemed to have trouble conducting effective long-range strikes, and to be more interested in political escalation than in military effectiveness. Iraq remained committed to the close air support role while it used the threat of its newly delivered Super Etendards to pressure Iran for concessions and its Arab neighbors for added funds.

Sea Power

Reporting on the naval battles between Iraq and Iran has been hopelessly confused by the tendency to call everything with weapons and an engine a major warship and by the exaggerated claims of both sides. It was clear during a visit to al-Basrah that at least some of the Iraqi ships sunk in the press had escaped that fate in real life. British and Omani military officials feel that the Iranian Navy remains largely intact, and Iran was certainly capable of destroyer and maritime patrol aircraft operations in the Strait of Hormuz in mid-1983. It is clear, however, that Iran's sea and air power have combined to give Iran the ability to deny Iraq's use of the Gulf to ship its oil and to receive imports through its ports. This is as meaningful a definition of naval victory as can occur between the two states, particularly as Iranian artillery now prevents the use of the Shat and Iraq's other ports. Iran won this victory early in the war. It launched successful air attacks on Iraq's main port of al-Basrah on the first day of the war. Its subsequent air attacks produced massive fires at the al-Basrah refinery and petrochemical plant on the 23rd of September, and its navy demonstrated on the 27th that it could attack Iraq's oil-loading facilities. Iran then cemented these victories on 29–30 November 1980, when its navy and commando forces were able to seize Iraq's two tanker loading points at Khor al-Amaja and Mina al-Bakr and to shell its facilities at al-Fao.

While Iraq claimed that it had sunk 76 Iranian ships by the time these engagements had ended (56% of the Iranian Navy), and Iran claimed 42 ships (66% of the Iraqi Navy), the actual naval losses seem unimportant. Western sources, for example, indicate that Iran lost only 3 significant ships and 3 fighters in the battles on the 29th–30th, while Iraq suffered maximum losses of 11 gunboats.[114] What is important is that Iraq emerged with nothing left but its pipelines to the West, that its ports were closed, that it was losing a billion dollars a month in foreign exchange holdings even before Syria halted Iraqi oil shipments through Syria, that 66 ships were trapped in the Shat, and that Iran could continue to supply Abadan Island by sea until it relieved the Iraqi siege in October 1981. In strategic terms, Iran used sea power to win a victory as important as or more important than any Iraqi victory on the ground.

There are no great insights about tactics, training, or technology to be gained from this situation. The main lessons are the vulnerability of the oil facilities in the Gulf and the value that special forces like commandos can play if they strike at truly critical targets. Gunfire and bombing alone might not have permanently damaged the terminals, but demolition teams did.

At the same time, there is no guarantee that these lessons will continue to be true in the future. One of the most striking aspects of Iraq's conduct during 1982 and 1983 was its inability to harass or attack tankers going to Iran by air or sea. Its inability to use its MiG-23s and Mirage F-1s is partly explainable by their lack of range and on-board avionics, coupled with appallingly bad SIGINT. Iraq could not identify land or naval targets with radar and lacks the range to loiter, identify, and destroy targets on Kharg from beyond the range of Iran's short-range air defenses.

Iraq's only successes seem to have arisen when it used French helicopters with Exocet or attacked targets in waters close to Iraqi territory. This, however, was enough to teach Iraq that its only practical form of sea power was air power. It made moderately effective use of French technical help in using the Exocet to attack offshore oil facilities and ships after March 1983, and its Super Etendards extend its range with Exocet significantly. The Super Etendard does lack the kind of radar that could effectively use Exocet to attack land targets in a dense, high-clutter radar environment like Kharg Island, and the ability to attack ships at port or offshore facilities without exceptionally high radar contrast. However, the Super Etendard is certain to be only the first of many similar attack systems to come. Maritime patrol aircraft and mine warfare aircraft are sure to follow with better sensors and range. The next generation of fighters will have better air-to-surface missiles, and avionics with much better targeting capability over the sea. There already is no reason that Iraq cannot remotely target tankers by SIGINT as they go into Kharg.

Such aircraft could be supplemented by small craft with ship-to-ship missiles and modern radars able to raid tankers in the Gulf and support seaborne commando operations against oil facilities or by attack helicopters. Maritime defense will become far more difficult in the 1980s, particularly as the southern Gulf states lack the vessels and expertise to use ships as a defensive screen. They again indicate the need for airborne platforms like the E-3A or mini-AWACS that can deal with the combined threat of ships, helicopters, and aircraft.

The Problem of Supply

The war provides a final set of lessons relating to supply, but not in the conventional sense of prewar stock levels or logistics. Both Iraq and Iran began the war with a history of being heavily dependent on foreign suppliers, from which they had been largely cut off for political reasons. The problem was particularly clear in Iran's case. The foreign and native technicians maintaining its sophisticated, and computer-assisted, logistic system had largely vanished and left Iran unable to find many of its holdings. It had some 20–30 million aircraft parts alone, and no way to find them.[115] The hostage crisis had cut it off from the U.S. and most Western suppliers, and the overall disruption of its forces and economy meant that it could not easily draw on stocks even if it knew where they were.

Iraq, however, was suffering from problems of its own. As only became apparent after its "cakewalk" into Iran turned into bloody and sustained fighting, Iraq lacked key spares and war reserves and had never gotten proper stock levels from the USSR. It is also clear from events that Iraq did not warn the USSR it was going to attack and knew that it would incur intense displeasure from the USSR when it did invade Iran. The most Iraq did to ensure resupply early in the war was to send Tariq Aziz, the deputy prime minister, to Moscow to explain the attack on the day the invasion began. Even this gesture was not particularly conciliatory, since he had severely criticized the Soviet role in the 1978 coup attempt and since it soon became apparent that Iraq had consulted with some of the conservative Gulf states much earlier.

Interestingly enough, Aziz responded to a question during an interview on his trip that asked if he was going to Moscow for resupply by asking if the reporter thought Iraq's leaders would be fools enough to begin a war and then have to turn around and beg for the supplies to fight it the next day. By 1 November, that answer must have been highly embarrassing. A combination of wartime losses, far greater consumption than had been estimated, and imbalance and inadequate stocks forced Iraq to start cutting back on its combat operations and use of artillery. It also may have forced Iraq to sharply curtail its air operations. By 11 November, Aziz was back in Moscow clearly "begging" for supplies. He went on to France, Czechoslovakia, and Bulgaria, and in each successive capital, more rumors arose that the USSR had put a leash on supplies and was trying to force Iraq to a cease-fire.[116] Iraq did have some success in getting Soviet-made arms, but only in the form of shipments of equipment already on order and relatively token shipments of tanks from Poland (possibly 100).

Iraq's major success was with France. France expedited delivery of the first four Mirage F-1s on 2 February 1981. It also agreed to sell 100 tanks, large amounts of 155mm self-propelled artillery, 40 transport helicopters, 20 light helicopters, and 50 light tanks and other AFVs. Further, it agreed to discuss sales of the Alphajet and Mirage 2000 and 4000. The only problem was one of time and training. France has not been able to deliver aircraft and other key weapons in the volume needed to meet Iraq's wartime needs, and Iraq did not have the time to train to operate new equipment. Further, although the chronology is uncertain, the Soviets initially retaliated by making further reductions in their shipments of military supplies.[117]

As a result, Iraq was forced to turn to Egypt—and to a Sadat it was then attacking for treason to the Arab cause—to get some of the key Soviet-bloc equipment, parts, and ammunition it needed. The largest single Egyptian shipment before Sadat's assassination provided over 4,000 tons of ammunition. Iraq has since obtained over $2 billion worth of arms from Egypt ($1.2 billion in 1982 alone), including large amounts of artillery, Tu-16 and Il-28 bombers, and AS-5 air-to-surface missiles. Such shipments were of crucial value because the only other Arab states with large surplus holdings of Soviet arms and equipment were Libya and Syria—both of which opposed Iraq and favored Iran[118]—and because the USSR refused to make major arms deliveries to Iraq until Khomeini decisively rebuffed Soviet attempts at friendship in early 1983. While the evidence involved is uncertain, Iraq was forced to "beg" for Soviet resupply of critical parts while seeking some $667 million more in supplies and equipment—including large amounts of artillery—from France. By the spring of 1982, it was obtaining substantial amounts of equipment from Egypt and Jordan, plus some arms from the southern Gulf states, and quietly buying something like $1 billion worth of arms and military equipment a month on the world arms market.

Iraq learned that it could not buy parts for its Soviet-made aircraft on the world market and that such aircraft can present major problems for a Third World country involved in sustained combat. Where Iran could often keep its fighters and other aircraft flying by buying parts or through "cannibalization," Iraq found that this does not work for Soviet aircraft. Such aircraft lack the "plug in–plug out" character of U.S. designs, and while they are rugged, major maintenance or overhaul is time-consuming and cumbersome. Even relatively minor combat damage or stress could knock out Soviet fighters, and the only solution in many cases was to obtain service or parts from the USSR, or an entire new aircraft.

The Iraqi miscalculation regarding resupply went further, however, than major shortfalls in ammunition, parts, and weapons. The U.S. refused Iran's early requests for resupply because of the hostage crisis, but Israel did not. In October 1980, in spite of protests to Begin by U.S. Ambassador Samuel Lewis, Israel started air shipments of critical arms to Iran via Cyprus. These shipments included 250 F-4 tires, critical M-60 and M-48 parts, and other key spares from French and Italian suppliers. While it is unclear that more than about 400 tons were involved, they involved the key equipment Iran needed to keep fighting and went on through at least July 1981.[119] Then, on 5 November 1980, President Carter signaled that the U.S. might resume shipments of arms if the hostages were released, and mention was made of shipping a $400 million backlog in orders and such weapons as the Harpoon and CBU 58 and CBU 71 cluster bombs. Although the Reagan administration decided against full resupply, one of the conditions of the hostage release was an easing of the constraints against shipping U.S. supplies to Iran.[120]

Although Israel eventually cut back on its assistance to Iran, the Iranians finally managed to trace many of the holdings in their computerized logistic systems, and Iraq's many other enemies rushed to provide supplies.[121] These enemies included Syria and Libya. Libya became a particularly important source of Soviet-made arms for Iran.

The U.S. never proved willing to provide significant arms, but the cutoff of Iraq's oil exports through the Gulf early in the war, and the survival of Iran's, allowed Iran to buy increasing amounts of U.S. arms illegally on the world or domestic market. The shift in revenues also led former friends of Iraq like North Korea to turn on Iraq and supply arms to Iran. Vietnam played both sides. It funneled captured U.S. arms to North Korea to sell to Iran while it professed friendship to Iraq. As much as $500 million worth of Soviet-built arms was channeled to Iran in this manner. And although Iran has been taken in some spectacular frauds, including a $58 million Syrian-Brazilian scam, it was initially able to find far more of its other requirements on the world market than Iraq.[122]

Perhaps worst of all from Iraq's viewpoint was the quiet Soviet tilt toward Iran. Although the evidence involved is uncertain, the USSR seems to have supported Syria and Iran in funneling funds and arms to the Iraqi and Kurdish opposition groups to Saddam Hussein's leadership beginning in early February 1981. It evidently provided indirect support to the National Democratic Front, and to the National Islamic Liberation Front, after meetings in Damascus in late February. It may have channeled similar aid to the Kurdish Democratic party and other opposition groups like the Iraqi Mujahideen and Dawa. It definitely supported the Iraqi Communist party in its calls to end the war and its attacks on the Baath, which began to be broadcast from the USSR in early March 1981.[123] Iraq found during 1981 that Iran had become a nation with many suitors, and one of the most ardent was the USSR. Not only did the mullahs around Khomeini become more tolerant toward the USSR—in spite of occasional slaps at the Tudeh—but Iran became steadily more dependent on Soviet aid. Iran and the USSR signed a new protocol for economic and technical cooperation on 15 February 1982, and the USSR clearly sought to become a major economic ally of the Khomeini government. It bought 16 million barrels of oil from Iran, and even though it was no longer getting gas shipments from Iran, the bilateral trade between the two countries rose to $1.2 billion in 1981, or twice the 1980 level. Trade volume was 30% higher than in 1978, when Soviet-Iranian trade reached its highest volume under the shah and at a time when Iran's principal export to the USSR was gas.[124]

This was an ominous spectre for Iraq, which had every reason to fear that the USSR might back a Shi'ite-dominated Syria and Iran rather than a relatively hostile Iraq, particularly one whose Sunni-controlled government might well fall to a Shi'ite revolution if the war continued to go against it. This fear took on a special meaning when Tariq Aziz went back to Moscow in early June 1982, this time to beg for Moscow's help in obtaining peace rather than for arms. Aziz's meeting with Deputy Prime Minister Ivan Arkhipov and Boris Ponomaryov, a candidate member of the Politburo, obtained nothing but a Soviet statement of neutrality—scarcely reassuring at a time when this amounted to tacit support of Iran.[125] Fortunately for Iraq, France provided the major arms sales discussed earlier, and Iran refused its suitor. From mid-1982 onward, the Khomeini regime began to systematically persecute members of the Tudeh and other pro-Soviet Marxists. This led the USSR to resume major fighter, armor, and artillery deliveries to Iraq, although several billion dollars in hard currency was a considerable additional incentive. The precedent can scarcely, however, have been a comfortable one. Iraq has no guarantee that the USSR might not back a more friendly regime in Iran, if one arises, and it must soon face the problem of whether it can rely on the USSR for the massive rearmament that must follow the war.[126]

The lesson here for both USCENTCOM and the southern Gulf states is twofold. First, there is a need to create an adequate mix of stocks that will ensure that southern Gulf forces can remain effective even if a major supplier should halt arms shipments or be unable to rapidly deliver spares or combat replacements. This issue is more complex than it seems. It is not U.S. supply, since the FMS program provides such stocks almost as a matter of course; it is the European supplier that can be a critical problem. Many lack the resources to maintain major production lines and high inventories, which makes balance stocking essential. Second, attacking the weaknesses in the supply system of threat powers may be far more effective than trying to attack the disperse-and-shelter logistics and supplies of industrialized states. There is a good chance that critical ammunition supplies, spares, and facilities will be left as high-payoff targets and that careful prewar planning could weaken a threat nation's ability to use its aircraft or heavy combat equipment.

Notes

1. This chapter draws on a wide range of sources and interviews, as well as the author's experience as an adviser to the Iranian Supreme Command Staff in 1972–1973. The author conducted extensive interviews in Iraq, Jordan, Egypt, Saudi Arabia, France, England, and the U.S., often with officials who cannot be cited.

2. The discussion of the war draws on Stephen R. Grummon, *The Iran-Iraq War*, Washington Paper no. 92, Center for Strategic and International Studies (New York: Praeger Publishers, 1982); Shirin Tahir-Kheli and Shaheen Ayubi, *The Iran-Iraq War: New Weapons, Old Conflicts* (New York: Praeger Publishers, 1983); a working paper entitled "A Strategic Analysis of the Gulf War" by William O. Staudenmaier of the Army War College, 9 December 1981; "The Persian Gulf on Fire," in *Middle East Military Survey* (Jerusalem: Born in Battle Press); the writings of Maj. Gen. F.W.E. Fursdon in the *Daily Telegraph* and *Jane's Military Annual, 1981*; Edgar O'Ballance, "The Iran-Iraq War," *Marine Corps Gazette*, February 1982; various editions of the *Economist*; Iranian and Iraqi official and propaganda publications such as Tariq Aziz's *Iraq-Iran Conflict* (London: Third World Center, 1981); the reporting of Thomas L. Friedman, R. W. Apple, and Drew Middleton of the *New York Times* and Jonathan C. Randal and George C. Wilson of the *Washington Post*; William F. Hickman, *Ravaged and Reborn: The Iranian Army, 1982*, Staff Paper (Washington, D.C.: Brookings Institution, 1982).

3. *Middle East Economic Digest (MEED)*, 19 February 1982; *8 Days*, 23 January 1982; *Wall Street Journal*, 24 February 1982; *Los Angeles Times*, 31 March 1982; *Arabia: The Islamic Review*, January 1982, pp. 43–44; *Washington Post*, 18 March 1982; *Middle East*, December 1981, pp. 12–13.

4. CIA, *World Factbook*, 1981, pp. 93–94; 1983, pp. 104–107.

5. Discussions with Iraqi officials, January 1982. See also the *Baghdad Observer*, 25 January 1982.

6. For typical reporting on these tensions, see the *Washington Post*, 10 July 1982.

7. *Wall Street Journal*, 2 October 1981; *Los Angeles Times*, 29 May 1982; CIA, *World Factbook*, 1981, p. 12; *Washington Post*, 2 February 1982.

8. Countless reports exist of these shifts. The Foreign Broadcast Information Service (FBIS) is the best source of shifts in Iranian rhetoric. The *Economist* provides good detail on the Iranian disruption of the pilgrimage in 1982 (18 September 1982, pp. 37–38). See the *Washington Post*, 26 January 1983; *New York Times*, 2 February 1983; *Economist*, 29 January 1983, pp. 57–60, 71, for typical background on the oil conflict.

9. For an interesting discussion of this problem see Enver M. Koury, "The Impact of the Geopolitical Situation of Iraq on the Gulf Cooperation Council," *Middle East Insight* 2, no. 5 (January-February 1983):28–36.

10. *Washington Post*, 9 November 1980. This conclusion is supported by Saddam Hussein's war aims speech of 28 September 1980; by conversations with Iraqi officials, those of the other Arab states, and various Western officials; and by a review of published and unpublished propaganda materials in Iraq in January 1982. For a contrary view see Aziz, *Iraq-Iran Conflict*. Grummon leaves Iraq's ultimate war aims somewhat ambiguous; see *Iran-Iraq War*, pp. 12–21. For additional background see Claudia Wright, "Implications of the Iran-Iraq War," *Foreign Affairs*, Winter 1980-1981.

11. Several Iraqi and Iranian counts of such incidents have been issued by their respective ministries of information. None go below 100 events.

12. The coup was attempted around 10 August.

13. CIA, *World Factbook*, 1981, pp. 92–93.

14. Most of these data are taken from Nicola Firzli, *The Iran-Iraq Conflict* (Paris: Editions du Monde Arab, 1981), especially pp. 37–55. While this work is somewhat propagandistic, it is useful for much of the history and data on Khuzestan. Also see Grummon, *Iran-Iraq War*, pp. 1–12; Michael M. J. Fisher's discussion of Iranian policy in the region in *Iran: From Religious Dispute to Revolution* (Cambridge, Mass.: Harvard University Press, 1980); various editions of the U.S. Army *Area Handbook for Iran*; and the four-volume series, *Security in the Persian Gulf* issued by the IISS (London: Gower, 1982), especially Vol. 2, pp. 13–15, and Vol. 3, pp. 41–48.

15. Firzli, *Iran-Iraq Conflict*, pp. 39–40.

16. *The Military Balance, 1981–82* (London: IISS, 1982).

17. These included estimates issued by the IISS, background briefings by British and U.S. intelligence officials, and a number of other expert sources well known to Iraq.

18. Based on discussions with British, Egyptian, Jordanian, and Saudi officers and officials.

19. This was routinely reported to Iraq by Arab officials and its own diplomatic personnel. Discussions in Iraq confirm that Iraqi officials were aware of such movements and Iranian capabilities.

20. William. O. Staudenmaier of the Army War College was among the first to point out the influence of the Kurdish conflict. Maj. Gen. Fursdon and other British experts have also raised this point. See Staudenmaier, "A Strategic Analysis of the Gulf War"; Tahir-Kheli and Ayubi, *Iran-Iraq War*, pp. 27–50.

21. A 1982 seminar on the war at the CSIS of Georgetown University revealed little consensus on the extent to which these purges influenced Iraqi capabilities. It seems likely from interviews in the Gulf, however, that they had a quite serious impact. See the *Washington Post*, 23 September 1980; Grummon, *Iran-Iraq War*, pp. 15–39.

22. See the discussions in Avi Plascov, *Security in the Persian Gulf: Modernisation, Political Development, and Stability* (Aldershot: Gower, 1982), pp. 14–55, 106–115; Grummon, *Iran-Iraq War*, pp. 1–15; Mohamed Hassaud Heikal, *Iran: The Untold Story* (New York: Pantheon, 1982), especially pp. 179–207.

23. Much of this analysis is again drawn from work done by William C. Staudenmaier and Maj. Gen. Fursdon.

24. Estimates of these figures differ. These numbers and many of the following figures are drawn from Staudenmaier, "A Strategic Analysis of the Gulf War." Other key sources include the writing of Maj. Gen. F.W.E. Fursdon in the *Daily Telegraph* and *Jane's Military Annual, 1981–82*; Grummon, *Iran-Iraq War*, pp. 15–32; and "The Persian Gulf on Fire."

25. See the bibliography for recent works on Gulf and Middle Eastern urbanization. This issue is discussed in Chapter 12. Avi Plascov provides a good summary discussion in *Modernization, Political Development, and Stability*, pp. 56–75, 115–134. Also see Allan G. Hill, "Population Migration and Development in the Gulf States," in Shahram Chubin, ed., *Security in the Persian Gulf: Domestic Political Factors* (London: IISS, 1981), pp. 58–82; J. S. Birks and C. A. Sinclair, *Arab Manpower, The Crisis of Development* (New York: St. Martin's Press, 1980); G. H. Blake and R. E. Lawless, *The Chaning Middle*

Eastern City (New York: Barnes and Noble, 1980); Ragaei El Mallakh, *Saudi Arabia: Rush to Development* (London: Croom Helm, 1982); and Hugh Roberts, *An Urban Profile of the Middle East* (London: Croom Helm, 1979).

26. See Robert Litwak, *Security in the Persian Gulf: Sources of Inter-State Conflict* (London: IISS, 1981); and Harvey Sicherman, "Iran and Iraq at War: The Search for Security," *Orbis* 24, no. 4 (Winter 1981):711–717, for a neutral history of the background to the dispute. For key dates, see the *New York Times*, 14 September 1979; *Washington Post*, 1 November 1979; 9 April 1980; and *New York Times*, 18 September 1980. According to some sources, Khomeini first formally called for a coup in Iraq in April 1980, and both sides began their military buildup. Iran informally denounced the Algiers Accord in October 1979, but did not legally renounce it until 17–18 September 1980.

27. *New York Times* and *Washington Post*, 9 April 1980.

28. *Washington Star*, 15 October 1980.

29. *New York Times*, 21 September 1980.

30. *The Middle East Military Survey, War Data*, no. 8, 1981, pp. 8–19.

31. Ibid., pp. 8–19; *New York Times*, 24 September 1980.

32. *Washington Post* and *New York Times*, 25 September 1980.

33. *New York Times*, *Washington Post*, *Washington Star*, 26, 27, and 28 September 1980; *Baltimore Sun* and *Washington Post*, 29 September 1980.

34. *Washington Post*, 4 October and 7 November 1980.

35. *Washington Post*, 4 October and 29 November 1980; *New York Times*, 29 November 1980.

36. *Washington Post*, 13 and 17 November 1980.

37. Ibid., 1 December 1980.

38. Ibid.

39. Staudenmaier, "Strategic Analysis of the Gulf War," p. 17; *Washington Post*, 5 January 1981; *New York Times*, 6 January 1981; Grummon, *Iran-Iraq War*, pp. 26–28.

40. O'Ballance, "Iran-Iraq War," p. 49.

41. Grummon, *Iran-Iraq War*, pp. 11–12.

42. O'Ballance, "Iran-Iraq War," p. 49.

43. *Washington Post* and *New York Times*, 23 September 1981; *Washington Post*, 3 October 1981.

44. *Washington Post*, 30 September 1981.

45. *Aviation Week*, 25 January 1982, p. 24; *Wall Street Journal*, 7 July 1981; discussions with U.S. officials in May 1982.

46. Part of the confusion arose because the front did move back and forth in a series of bloody small encounters. Both sides fought hard during this period, and although no major battle took place, there were substantial casualties on both sides. See the *Washington Post*, 1 February and 1 March 1981, and the *Christian Science Monitor*, 20 January 1982, for typical accounts.

47. *Washington Post*, 8 April 1982.

48. Ibid., 1 April 1982.

49. *New York Times*, 25 March 1982.

50. *Washington Post*, 3 and 8 April and 7 May 1982; *Economist*, 24 April 1982.

51. *Washington Post*, 3 April 1982; *Economist*, 24 April 1982.

52. *New York Times*, 31 March and 1 April 1982.

53. *Washington Post*, 31 March 1982.

54. *New York Times*, 1 April 1982; *Economist*, 24 April 1982.

55. *New York Times*, 15 April, 1982.
56. *Los Angeles Times*, 12 April 1982; *Christian Science Monitor*, 5 May 1982.
57. *New York Times*, 19 April 1982.
58. *Washington Post*, 7 May 1982.
59. *New York Times* and *Washington Post*, 14 April 1982.
60. *New York Times*, 28 April 1982.
61. *Economist*, 29 January 1983, pp. 30–31.
62. *Washington Post*, 9 May 1982.
63. *Washington Post* and *New York Times*, 10, 11, 12, and 13 May 1982; *Economist*, 8 and 15 May 1982.
64. *Washington Post*, 7 May 1982.
65. *New York Times*, 6 May 1982; *Washington Post*, 13 May 1982.
66. *Washington Post*, 9 May 1982.
67. *Washington Post*, 7 May 1982; *Wall Street Journal*, 6 May 1982.
68. Ibid.
69. *New York Times*, 6 May 1982.
70. *Washington Post*, 6, 7, and 13 May 1982; *New York Times*, 6 and 11 May 1982.
71. *Economist*, 15 May 1982.
72. *Washington Post*, *New York Times*, and *Wall Street Journal*, 22, 23, 24, 25, and 26 May 1982; *Los Angeles Times*, 29 May 1982.
73. *Wall Street Journal*, 25 May 1982; *New York Times*, 26 May 1982.
74. *Economist*, 29 May 1982.
75. *Washington Post*, 31 May 1982.
76. *Washington Post,* and *New York Times*, 27 May 1982; *Christian Science Monitor*, 27 May 1982.
77. *Economist*, 29 May 1982.
78. *New York Times* and *Washington Times*, 28 May 1982.
79. *Washington Post*, 30 May 1982.
80. *New York Times*, 29 May 1981.
81. *Economist*, 5 June 1982.
82. *Wall Street Journal* and *Chicago Tribune*, 3 June 1982; *New York Times*, 6 June 1982; *Los Angeles Times*, 29 May 1982.
83. *Washington Post* and *Baltimore Sun*, 21 June 1982.
84. *Los Angeles Times*, 29 May 1982; *Christian Science Monitor*, 1 July 1982; *MEED*, 2 July 1982.
85. *New York Times*, 14 July 1982, pp. 1, 14; 5 August 1982; Hickman, *Ravaged and Reborn.*
86. For typical reporting see the *New York Times*, 5 August 1982; and *Washington Post*, 8 August 1982. The reader should be aware that Iraqi and Iranian news releases and reports were generally worthless after May 1982. Virtually all the press information used from this point on draws on U.S. and British official background briefings and Gulf sources, primarily Kuwaiti, Jordanian, and Saudi. Israeli background briefings had a high misinformation content during the period because of the complex political problems resulting from its invasion of Lebanon.
87. *Middle East*, September 1982, pp. 6–7; *New York Times*, 25 August 1982; Reuters, 24 August 1982.
88. *New York Times*, 4 October 1982; *Economist*, 2 October 1982, pp. 38–39.

89. *New York Times*, 24 October 1982; *Economist*, 2 October 1982,, p. 38; 9 October 1982, p. 41; 16 October 1982, p. 62.

90. *New York Times*, 24 October 1982.

91. Ibid., 31 October 1982.

92. Ibid., 27 October, 4, 7, and 19 November 1982; *Washington Times* and *Washington Post*, 8, 17, and 19 November 1982.

93. *Washington Post*, 19 November 1982.

94. *New York Times*, 23 November and 10 December 1982; *Economist*, 11 December 1982.

95. *Washington Post*, 1 February 1983.

96. *Washington Post*, 8 and 10 February 1983; *New York Times*, 8 and 16 February 1983; *Christian Science Monitor*, 16 February 1983.

97. *New York Times*, 9 and 6 February, 3 March, 13, 14, 15, 17 and 24 April, 10 and 26 May, 28 June, 18, 20, 25–28 and 31 July 1983; *Christian Science Monitor*, 11, 20, and 26 July 1983; *Aviation Week*, 11 April 1983, pp. 11–14; 23 May 1983, p. 44; *U.S. News and World Report*, 18 April 1983, p. 9; *Wall Street Journal*, 25 April, 15 July, and 4 August 1983; *Washington Post*, 12 and 13 April, 8, 12, 13, 25, and 28 May, 20–26 and 28 July, and 1 August 1983; *Economist*, 9 February 1983, pp. 31–32; 4 June 1983, p. 51; 18 June 1983, pp. 53–54; United Press, 18 June 1983.

98. O'Ballance, "Iran-Iraq War," p. 45.

99. *Washington Post*, 8 April 1982.

100. O'Ballance, "Iran-Iraq War," pp. 45–46.

101. See the *Washington Post*, 31 January 1982; *Oman Daily Observer*, 1 February 1982; and *MEED*, 19 February 1982, p. 10.

102. *Strategy Week* 7, no. 20 (25–31 May 1981):1.

103. *New York Times*, 12 January 1982.

104. Ibid.

105. O'Ballance, "Iran-Iraq War," p. 48.

106. *Washington Post*, 3 April 1982.

107. *New York Times*, 11, 12, and 13 June 1982; *MEED*, 25 June 1982, pp. 14–15; *Economist*, 3 July 1982.

108. *New York Times*, 20 October 1982.

109. See the *New York Times* and *Washington Post* for 13, 15, and 16 June 1982.

110. *Aviation Week*, 25 January 1982, p. 24.

111. O'Ballance, "Iran-Iraq War," p. 48.

112. Staudenmaier, "Strategic Analysis of the Gulf War," p. 24.

113. *New York Times*, 20 October 1980; *Aviation Week*, 13 October 1980, pp. 24–25.

114. See Commander William L. Dowdy, "Naval Warfare in the Gulf, Iran Versus Iraq," *U.S. Naval Institute Proceedings* 107/6/940 (June 1981):114–117.

115. Staudenmaier, "Strategic Analysis of the Gulf War," p. 7; *New York Times*, 23 September 1980.

116. *New York Times*, 12 November 1980.

117. Ibid., 2 and 4 February 1981; *Washington Post*, 4 February and 3 March 1981.

118. *New York Times*, 1 April 1981. On 28 October 1981 Israeli Defense Minister Ariel Sharon accused the U.S. of selling arms to Iraq. The U.S. denied this claim the same day. Sharon's charges were made to counter leaks of Israeli sales to Iran, and Israeli officials confirm that Sharon knew they were false

when he made them. See *New York Times*, 29 October 1981; *Chicago Tribune*, 22 October 1982; and *Christian Science Monitor*, 16 February 1983.

119. See Phil Marfleet and Edward J. Mann, "Seeking Arms from the Devil," *Middle East*, June 1981, pp. 20–21, for one of many accounts of these events. Also *Sunday Times* (London), 26 July 1981; *Washington Post*, 27 July 1981; and Ariel Sharon's acknowledgment of such support as quoted in the *Washington Post*, 28 May 1982.

120. *New York Times*, 6 November 1980; 13 January 1981; *Baltimore Sun*, 22 January 1981. Bani Sadr on 21 January 1981 noted that shortages of U.S. arms and parts were hurting the Iranian war effort.

121. *New York Times*, 25 March and 25 May 1982; *Washington Post*, 8 April, 29 and 30 May 1982.

122. The U.S. did allow Hughes to sell 30 Model 500D and 30 Model 500C helicopters to Iraq for $25 million, as well as aircraft like 6 small executive jets. U.S. civilian equipment with even limited military applications formed a negligible proportion of the $745.9 million worth of exports the U.S. sold to Iraq in the first 10 months of 1982. *Washington Post*, 14 September 1982; *Wall Street Journal*, 15 December 1982.

123. *Washington Post*, 3 March 1981; *Chicago Tribune*, 27 May 1982; *New York Times*, 8 March 1982; *Middle East*, January 1982, pp. 20–23.

124. *Chicago Tribune*, 12 and 27 May 1982; *Christian Science Monitor*, 12 May 1982; *New York Times*, 8 March 1982; *Wall Street Journal*, 24 February 1982.

125. *Christian Science Monitor*, 17 June 1982.

126. *Washington Post* and *New York Times*, 14 November 1982.

17
Once the Fighting Pauses: The Trends in Iran and Iraq

The most important aspect of the Iran-Iraq War is what will happen once it is over. While no one can make any firm predictions, most of the alternatives are bad for both the Gulf and the West. Iran does not seem likely to drift into the Western camp or even become a moderate neutral. Iraq may well become a radical and hostile state.

Iran: From the "Sick Man of the Gulf" to the Colossus?

The extent to which Iran can emerge from revolution, civil war, and its conflict with Iraq to become the dominant power in the Gulf, and Iran's future political character and alignments, are the two most important uncertainties affecting Gulf security.[1] Although Iran has not yet demonstrated that it can invade Iraq any more successfully than Iraq invaded Iran, and Iran's air and naval strength are now limited, Iran has evolved a high level of capability as a "People's Army." The question is whether Iran will try to use this capability to become an expansionist power, and if so, whether it will rely on ideology and subversion as its main mechanism or try to rebuild the modern armor, air, and naval forces necessary to create a direct threat to the southern Gulf. Much will depend on how much of the shah's military legacy remains once the war is over and on Iran's internal stability. While the new Iranian armed forces are very different from those the shah created, they still are largely equipped with his arms purchases and are dependent on the support he obtained from the West in training and maintenance for their ability to operate high-technology weaponry. Similarly, although Iran's internal security problems are now radically different, they may eventually be as serious as those that brought down the shah.

The Iranian Army

The detailed history of the shah's immense arms purchases is traced in Table 17.1. There is no question that the shah built up the largest armed forces in the Gulf and that he left Khomeini a vast inheritance

TABLE 17.1 The Military Buildup in Iran, 1972-1983

	1973–73	1973–74	1974–75	1975–76	1976–77
Total population (millions)	30.5	30.8	32.2	33.18	33.8
Defense expenditures (billions)	0.915	2.01	3.225	10.405	9.5
GNP ($ billions)	15.09	22.5	35.6	56.8	n.a.
DE as % of GNP	6.06	9.38	9.06	18.49	12.0
Total military manpower	191,000	211,500	238,000	250,000	300,000
Reserves	–	315,000	300,000	300,000	300,000
Army					
Manpower	60,000	160,000	175,000	175,000	200,000
Reserves		300,000	300,000	300,000	300,000
Equipment					
Medium tanks	860	860	920	1,160	1,360
Major types	M60A1,47	M60A1,47	M60A1,47	M60A1,47	Chieftain M60A1,47
Other AFVs	1,200	2,000	2,000	2,000	2,000
Major types	BTR,M113	BTR,M113	BTR,M113	BTR,M113	BTR,M113
Artillery	105,155mm	105,155mm	664+	714	714
SP guns	–	–	–	175,203mm	175,203mm
ATWs	TOW	TOW	TOW	106mm,TOW	106mm,TOW
AA weapons	40,57,85mm	40,57,85mm	23,40,57mm	650	650
Missiles	SS11,12	Hawk,SS	Hawk,SS	Hawk,SS	Hawk,SS
Aircraft	104	104	119	171	308
Helicopters	84	82	58	110	247
Major types	AB-205/6A	AB-206A	AB-206A	AB-205A	Bell 214A
Navy					
Manpower	9,000	11,500	13,000	15,000	18,500
Total craft	51	41	41	56	61
Destroyers	1	3	3	3	3
Frigates	2	4	4	4	4
Patrol	28	14	14	29	29
Submarines	–	–	–	–	–
Minesweepers	6	6	6	6	5
Landing ships/craft	4	4	4	2	4
Other	10	10	10	12	16
Aircraft	24	16	34	35	47
ASW	–	–	–	–	6
Major types					S-65A
Transport	–	–	–	–	–
Major types					
Rescue/Search	–	–	–	–	6
Helicopters	24	16	34	35	35
Major types	AB-206A	AB-212	AB-206A	AB-206A	AB-206A

Source: The Military Balance (London: IISS, various years).

TABLE 17.1 (continued)

1977–78	1978–79	1979–80	1980–81	1981–82	1982–83
34.76	36.37	39.3	38.25	39.67	39.1
7.9	9.94	3.79	4.2	4.2	n.a.
75.1	76.1	81.7	n.a.	112.1	n.a.
10.9	13.06	4.6	n.a.	3.7	n.a.
342,000	413,000	415,000	240,000	195,000	235,000
300,000	300,000	300,000	400,000	400,000	440,000
220,000	285,000	285,000	150,000	150,000	150,000
300,000	300,000	300,000	400,000	400,000	400,000
1,620	1,620	1,735	1,735	1,410	1,770
Chieftain	Chieftain	Chieftain	Chieftain	Chieftain	Chieftain
M60A1,47	M60A1,47	M60A1,47	M60A1,47	M60A1,47	M60A1,47
2,250	1,075	1,075	1,075	6,407	680+
BTR,M113	BTR,M113	BTR,M113	BTR,M113	BTR,M113	BTR,M113
714	782	782	1,072+	1,065	1,265+
175,203mm	482	482	482	?	?
106mm,TOW	106mm,TOW	106mm,TOW	106mm,TOW	106mm,TOW	106mm,TOW
650	1,900	1,900	1,900	?	1,800+
Hawk,SS	Hawk,SS	Hawk,SS	Hawk,SS		Hawk
401	669	715	725	665	67
332	627	650	660	600	572
AH-1J	Bell 214A	Bell 214A	Bell 214A	Bell 214A	Bell 214A
22,000	28,000	30,000	20,000	10,000	10,000
56	48	50	52	54	
3	3	3	3	3	3
4	4	4	4	4	4
24	16	17	20	14	19
—	—	1	—	—	—
5	5	5	5	5	5
4	4	3	3	3	3
16	16	17	17	19	16
70	56	73	73	31	2
6	12	26	20	9	2
S-65A	SH-3D	SH-3D	SH-3D	SH-3D	D-3F
10	10	11	11	9	9
Shrike	Shrike	Shrike	Shrike	Shrike	Shrike
6	6	6	6	6	—
48	28	30	36	7	23
AB-206A	SH-3D	AB-206	AB-206	AB-212	SH-3D

of military equipment. Unfortunately, there is no way to know how much of this equipment has been lost in the war, or even how Iran's land forces are now organized. Further, even the best-informed sources also are uncertain as to how much of the army was purged before the war. This proportion may be critical in determining Iran's ability to build an army using advanced weapons and technology, since some estimates go as high as 50% of the army's prerevolutionary officers, NCOs, and technicians.

The IISS estimated in 1983 that Iran had armed forces of up to 2 million men and an army in excess of 150,000 men, with three armored "divisions," four infantry "divisions," an airborne "division," four SAM "battalions," and an army aviation command. It seems likely, however, that there are the equivalent of six to eight divisions' worth of additional formations—including forces from the Revolutionary Guards—and that Iran's land forces are now equal to at least 1 million men and probably to more than 1.5 million. While much of this manpower includes irregular forces, it is still probably true that the Iranian "regular" army now totals over 500,000 men and that at least 80% of its present manpower did not serve under the shah or saw only brief conscript service.

The present Iranian Army equipment pool is even harder to assess. Table 17.1 shows that when the shah fell, Iran's army had 875 Chieftain, 400 M-47/8, and 460 M-60Al medium tanks; 250 Scorpion light tanks; and well over 1,000 APCs and other AFVs. Iran had over 1,100 medium and heavy long-range artillery weapons, including more than 600 self-propelled tube and multiple rocket launcher weapons. It had vast numbers of TOW and Dragon ATGMs and extensive holdings of HAWK surface-to-air missiles, light SAMs, and AA guns, including 100 ZSU 23-4 self-propelled AA guns. It had the only major helicopter force in the region, with 205 AH-1J and 295 Bell 214A combat helicopters. It seems probable that at least 50–65% of these holdings may have been lost or rendered permanently inoperable by the war and revolution and that Iran may now be down to as few as 700 tanks, but the extent of such losses is highly dependent on Iranian repair capabilities and the availability of parts and replacements. The evidence available indicates that these capabilities are limited and that Iran's problems in repairing combat damage and keeping its U.S.- and British-made army equipment remain serious. While Iran has ample supplies for its infantry and evidently its artillery and has acquired some Soviet armor by reconditioning captured equipment and through transfers from Syria and North Korea, the ability of the Iranian Army to conduct armored deep offensive thrusts is now highly restricted.[2]

Even so, Iran will emerge from the war as a formidable force. The Iranian Army's ability to survive the revolution had four main causes: (1) revolutionary fervor coupled to intense nationalism and religious conviction, (2) the skills and innovativeness of its young officers and other ranks, (3) its vast prewar equipment stores, and (4) the massive training and education program conducted under the shah. While the Iranian Army's equipment pool is now vanishing, or at best being replaced with less capable or captured Soviet equipment, Iran's key resource—its combat-trained manpower—has grown sharply. In spite of its past purges, Iran now has a large army of comparatively well-trained junior officers and NCOs. They may lack the technical skills of the shah's officers, NCOs, and technicians, but they have proved to possess a good ability to lead and manage.

Further, the war and the continuing purges of the army by the Khomeini government seem to have brought the regular army together with the Revolutionary Guards and to have replaced much of the U.S.-trained officer corps with "revolutionary" and Islamic officers. While there are still recurrent reports of further purges, power struggles within the military, and conflicts between the Revolutionary Guards and pre-Khomeini professionals, the army now seems relatively united. The major purges designed to Islamicize the army during September 1979–September 1980, and the impact of Iran's first massive victory in March 1981, seem to have forged a force that can sustain its unity even in the face of repeated defeats.

It is also a force whose skills may be unfamiliar in the West, but which can have considerable effectiveness in the Gulf. The Iranian Army has gradually learned to use light Soviet-made equipment as a substitute for much of the heavy U.S. equipment it has lost during the fighting. It has learned to substitute infantry assault for the use it made of artillery, air support, helicopters, and armor in Operation Undeniable Victory. While such "human wave" tactics are often criticized in the West, it is unclear that they really inflict higher overall casualties than fighting the same battle with more advanced equipment, and they often have proved successful against Iraq's well-equipped forces, particularly in night attacks and on rough terrain.

Most important, Iran's new tactics have generally been relatively professional—given the limits enforced by Iran's steadily declining stores of modern equipment and the clerical pressures to launch offensives regardless of the immediate tactical situation—and its army presents a force that is difficult to attack with modern helicopters and air power precisely because of its emphasis on dispersed formations, limited logistics, night combat, infantry maneuver, and assault. Its revolutionary character gives it both defensive strength and the capability to support revolutionary conflict in the southern Gulf, even if it lacks the modern weapons and transport to launch any large-scale invasion. As long as its manpower is not subject to catastrophic losses or any further massive purges, Iran should be able to meet any threat from Iraq and to defeat any Gulf army where it is not required to face a highly capable air force or use large amounts of armor.

The Iranian Navy

Western observers gave the Iranian Navy under the Shah low effectiveness ratings. The Iranian Navy had severe manpower quality, maintenance, and logistic problems. Much of its more sophisticated sensors and weaponry were never properly operational, and its exercises revealed that it had severe problems in conducting even simple coordinated operations. While it could operate individual weapons systems and maritime patrol aircraft reasonably well, it lacked the ability to act as a cohesive force.

The navy suffered from constant changes in its high command under the shah, and this situation has grown worse since his fall. The navy has experienced major purges of its senior officers, including one exceptionally severe purge after the forced resignation of its head, Admiral Ahmed Madani, in July 1980. This resignation came about as a result of the conflict between Bani Sadr and the clergy, and it cut deeply into the navy's ranks.

According to some sources in the Gulf, the Iranian Navy now lacks the ability to fully operate the sensors and air defense weapons on its three guided-missile destroyers and on all but two or three of its six guided-missile frigates. However, its Harpoon surface-to-surface missiles are still reported to be operational. While many of Iran's naval assault, ASW, and mine-clearing helicopters are semi-operational (flyable without most sensors and equipment operating), Iran is still able to regularly fly two of its P-3F Orion maritime patrol aircraft. No reliable data are available on Iran's mining capabilities. While some loose mines have been found floating in the western Gulf, neither side seems likely to have significant mine warfare forces.

The problems in the Iranian Navy are relative. In spite of its operational problems, it did prove able to fight Iraqi vessels, to attack and destroy the Iraqi oil-loading facilities in the Gulf, and to help resupply Abadan and Khorramshahr. After the present war, it should be able to use a significant number of its missile-armed ships and patrol craft in strikes against tankers or offshore oil facilities. Iran retains a major naval base at Bandar Abbas and has major facilities at Bandar Khomeini and Bushihr. Its P-3Fs with Harpoon could still present a significant threat because they are fairly easy to keep flying and can locate and destroy vessels in the Gulf at long ranges and with little warning. Iran also is seeking to renew the order for West German light submarines placed by the shah and to obtain other naval equipment from the West.[3]

The Iranian Air Force

It was Iran's air force that led many Western experts to believe that the shah could dominate the entire Gulf region in the period before his fall. No other Gulf air force approached the offensive power shown in Table 17.1, and Iran had superior training, maintenance, logistic support, and munitions. If Iran was scarcely well organized enough to

MAP 17—1
IRAN

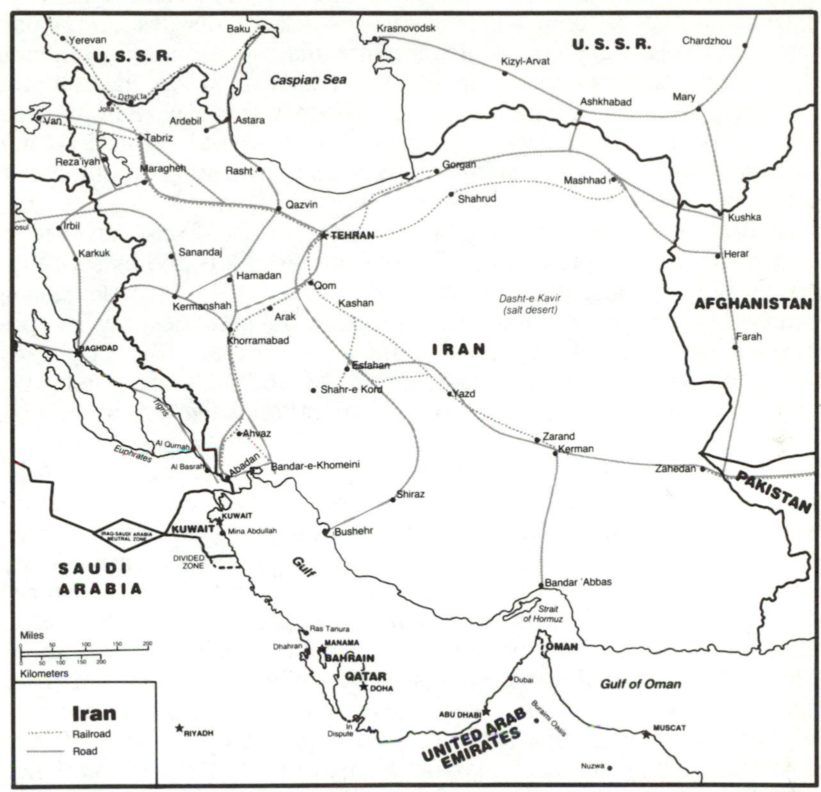

SOURCE: CIA 504190 (544499) 7-79

have a modern air force by Western standards, it still had the range and mass to pose a critical threat to any other Gulf state. For similar reasons, it is the future capability of Iran's air force that will determine Iran's ability to project its military power much beyond its borders, except as part of a revolution.

The air force was extensively purged before the war. Its high command suffered a particularly broad purge from September 1979 to the fall of 1980, and its officer corps and many of its NCOs were purged again following the failure of the U.S. hostage raid. (One intelligence expert estimates that something approaching half of the air force's pilots, and 15–20% of its officers, NCOs, and technicians, were imprisoned, dismissed, or relegated to minor roles.) There are also indications that the air force was purged again following the disclosure that it had assisted President Bani Sadr in his flight into exile in the summer of 1981 and that virtually all advanced pilot and technical training halted after 1981. It is also important to reiterate that the Iranian Air Force proved unable to act as a coherent air force in the Iran-Iraq War. It lacked tight battle management and failed to use its air-to-surface missiles and smart bombs effectively. Further, the air force has major equipment problems. Key avionics were removed from most of Iran's 76 F-14A fighters, and it has been virtually unable to use its Phoenix missiles. Before Israel started parts and tire deliveries, something like 40–65% of its F-4s and F-5s were inoperable and many of its sensor, warning, maintenance, and logistic systems were beginning to break down.

Iran dealt with this situation at the start of the Iran-Iraq War by freeing many of its imprisoned junior officers and pilots and by accepting aid from Israel.[4] These measures allowed it to fly 110–150 sorties during the early days of the war, and Iran sustained such sortie rates in spite of combat wear by cannibalizing many of its aircraft. By early 1981, however, its sortie rate had dropped sharply, and Western intelligence experts felt that it was down to 40–80 operational fighters at the end of 1983.

There are reports that Iran is getting several squadrons of North Korean MiG-19 and MiG-21 Fighters and up to 100 Chinese F-6 Fighters, but this can do little to improve Iran's air force. Such fighters have very poor attack and air combat capabilities by modern standards and are reliable only in terms of requiring limited routine maintenance. They are extremely difficult to repair or recondition after prolonged combat wear, and their lack of avionics necessitates high pilot proficiency.

The air force and army have a slightly different situation in terms of ground-based air defense. Iran started the war with 37 Improved Hawk surface-to-air missile batteries, and these were evidently effective against Iraq during the first year of the fighting, but as few as 3 may now be fully operational. The air force's Tigercat and Rapier units also seem to be largely nonoperational. Iran has, however, learned how to develop very dense and effective mixes of antiaircraft guns and shorter-range surface-to-air missiles like the SA-7 and SA-9. Like its infantry tactics, these allow for highly dispersed forces that are difficult to attack in detail, but that can be effective both in providing mobile support of ground forces and as static defenses.

The air force does seem to have learned how to cooperate with Iranian ground forces during the Iranian offensives of 1981, something it never learned under the shah. It seems to have conducted at least some joint operations with the navy before it curtailed operations because of lack of operational aircraft. It now seems to have the same "revolutionary Islamic" leadership as the army, and the purges of the air force do not seem to have led to the loss of more than half its technicians. While it has terminated virtually all its advanced and military school training, much of its infrastructure is also intact. Iran retains large modern air bases at Tabriz, Shahroki, Vahdati, Isfahan, Shiraz, Bushihr,

Mehrabad, Doshan Tappen, Meshad, Kerman, and Bandar Abbas. It seems able to service and fly those F-4 and F-5 aircraft for which it can get parts. It also has some 77 airfields with paved runways throughout the country; 14 have runways over 3,600 meters, 16 have 2,500–3,600-meter runways, and 68 have 1,200–2,500-meter paved and unpaved runways.[5]

It seems likely, therefore, that even if Iran does not make major new aircraft purchases, it should be able to gradually increase its number of operational aircraft after the war and be able to launch limited F-4 and F-5 strikes against targets in the Gulf. What will be in doubt is whether Iran will have the strength to press such attacks home, to win air superiority over any part of the southern Gulf supported by the Saudi Air Force, or to win the degree of air superiority over Iraq that it enjoyed in the first months of the war.

Iran's ability to make its ground-based air defense weaponry operational after the war is more uncertain. While it has been able to use ZSU-23-4s and SA-7s in the war, it has made little recent use of its advanced surface-to-air missiles like the Improved Hawk. This enabled Iraq to fly an increasing number of attack sorties deep into Iran in June 1982, after Iran's operational fighter strength had declined. While much of the Hawk equipment remains intact, Iran will be able to use it only if it can obtain a new source of Hawk missiles and major support from the U.S. or some other member of the NATO Hawk consortium.

The Problem of Resupply

These problems again illustrate how critical the issue of Iran's future source of parts and military equipment will be in determining the Gulf's future. Iran's smaller suppliers in the Iran-Iraq War—Greece, Israel, Italy, Libya, North Korea, Syria, and Vietnam—can meet only part of its needs if Iran seeks anything like the strength the shah built up before his fall. Iran has gotten significant supplies of U.S. parts and equipment, but not of the major items under tight U.S. export controls. It cannot maintain or recondition its fighters, helicopters, and armor without U.S. and British support. Although North Korea supplied about 40% of Iran's $2 billion worth of easily identifiable arms imports in 1982, most such arms were relatively light equipment.[6] This situation has not improved in 1983, although up to 150 North Korean tanks may have been delivered, and Iran seems to have spent $6.9–13.3 billion on defense.

Iran also will experience severe delivery problems with the West even if it can solve its political problems. Buying major amounts of new equipment will not be easy. Britain and France have now committed much of their production resources for the next few years, although they could deliver significant numbers of fighters in three to five years and several hundred medium tanks in two to three years. Even the U.S would be able to make the massive aircraft and tank deliveries Iran would require to replace its wartime losses only by diverting them from U.S. forces or allies who have already paid for such equipment.

This leaves Iran with three options. The first is to let its equipment stocks run down, to rely on a people's army for defense, and to confine any efforts to expand its influence to subversion or political warfare. The second is to reach some modus vivendi with Western suppliers—and they would have to include the U.S. or Britain for Iran to obtain the right weapons and technology. This course would enable Iran to rebuild its forces to a moderate level. However, it would also mean considerable Iranian dependence on the Western suppliers involved, since it would take several years to convert to European aircraft and to get suitable deliveries or to get suitable parts deliveries from the U.S. Iran could be cut off at any time during this supply process. The third is to seek immediate arms deliveries and large numbers of advisers from the Soviet bloc. The pressure to select one of the latter two choices will grow as more of Iran's equipment is lost in the war or becomes inoperable. Some Israeli sources indicate that Iran already is down to only 30% of its prerevolutionary fighter and tank strength, although the accuracy of such reports is unclear.

All the choices involving resupply are politically unpalatable, however, and it is important to note that any massive arms purchases from the West will require huge amounts of capital. Iran will face serious postwar financial problems if it has to pay for rebuilding its forces and its economy simultaneously. It also may well have to relocate most of its port and refinery facilities in Khuzestan as a strategic precaution, which will be almost as costly as any probable rearmament plan. Even though Iran has recovered a substantial part of its oil income and has been "winning" the Iran-Iraq War, it is far too soon to predict that Iran will become the military colossus of the Gulf that the shah once sought to build.

Iran's Internal Security

The future of Iran's internal security is essentially the future of the Iranian revolution, and this is a subject of almost complete disagreement among experts. There does seem to be a wide consensus that the clergy around Khomeini have succeeded in consolidating power in the short run, that they have largely suppressed the radical Marxists in the Mujahedin e-Khalq, purged the remaining "moderates" who supported figures like Bani Sadr and Ghotbzadeh, relegated the Tudeh party to a negligible role, removed rival major religious figures like Shariat Madari, and put down any immediate military challenge from Iran's Kurds, Azerbaijanis, and other minorities.

The traditional secular moderates were suppressed in the early months of the revolution and then purged from the Iranian government and Iranian industry, along with many technocrats. The Kurds and other ethnic minorities were systematically suppressed by force whenever they challenged the central government.[7] The armed forces were purged, and then Khomeini's secular supporters. The Mujahedin, which had helped Khomeini seize control of Iran, were hunted down and killed in a low-level civil war. President Bani Sadr was removed from office on 22–23 June 1981 and then forced to flee into exile in July, along with the head of the Mujahedin, Massoud Rajavi.[8] The communists in the Tudeh were purged from senior positions, and some were arrested as early as the winter of 1981.[9] Ex-Foreign Minister Ghotbzadeh was arrested along with 40 others in April 1982 for allegedly participating in a plot to kill Khomeini, and Khomeini's closest religious rival, the Ayatollah Shariat Madari, was implicated in the same plot. After some delay Ghotbzadeh was tried and finally was shot on 15 September.[10]

The Khomeini government officially reported 2,100 political executions and the sentencing of about 8,000 political criminals between 10 April and 20 October 1981.[11] The total number of executions reported between May 1981 and March 1982 was 4,000.[12] There is no way to reliably estimate the total cost of revolution in such terms, but a UN human rights report issued in late February 1983 estimated 4,000–20,000 executions, and a current total of 50,000 political prisoners. A European intelligence official estimates the death toll at over 40,000 from early 1980 to mid-1983, including various "criminals" who would not have been charged before the revolution and guerrillas like the Mujahedin. This same official estimates arrests at over 120,000, but admits such figures are extremely speculative. Amnesty International estimates a minimum of 4,658 actual executions after "trial" for the same period, including 2,500 after the departure of President Bani Sadr.[13] Some British experts indicate that deaths from trials have reached 15,000, plus 40,000 sentences approaching the status of "disappearance."

Most Western experts now discount the various Iranian opposition groups that are plotting to gain power. The Iranian government has reported that various exile groups like the Mujahedin e-Khalq have had 2,500 to 4,000 of their followers killed since early 1981, while Gulf intelligence officials estimate the true totals of such Marxist guerrillas to be 6,000–8,000 of executed plus 27,000 imprisoned.[14] Although many of the senior members of the Mujahedin have escaped arrest, their leader in Iran, Mussa Kheyyabani, was killed with 12 other leading members and Rajavi's wife on 8 February 1982, and between 15 and 20 other cadres were killed in March and April 1982. Claims that the Mujahedin still retain large paramilitary and terrorists forces do not seem valid, and most of its underground units of the kind that killed President Mohammed Ali Rajai, Prime Minister Mohammed Javad Bahonar, and the leader of Khomeini's Islamic Revolutionary party (IRP), the Ayatollah Mohammed Beheshti, on 28 July 1981 seem to have been hunted down and exterminated.[15]

Ex-Prime Minister Shapur Bakhtiar's National Movement of the Iranian Resistance, which Iraq supported during 1979–1981, has had almost no success, and Bani Sadr and the Mujahedin's leaders in exile seem to be faring little better. Iraqi efforts to support Iran's Kurds and Azerbaijanis with funds and arms have had limited success; major local battles continued in 1982 and 1983, but they have not threatened the government.[16] While both Iran and Iraq aid Kurdish groups opposed to the other state, both have been relatively successful in limiting Kurdish opposition. Iran recaptured the cities its Kurdish rebels had seized in 1981 and gradually opened up the main roads in its Kurdish areas in 1982, including the road between Piranshahr and Sar Dasht that Iran used in its July 1983 offensive against Iraq.

While the nationalist Kurdish National Democratic party and left-wing Komaleh movement have formed a coalition and still have some 5,000–10,000 part-time guerrillas in the hills, they remain more a spoiling force than any kind of serious political threat. The loose grouping of the various pro-shah military groups as part of the Azadegan (Born Free) movement has also had few tangible results beyond the hijacking of a few patrol boats. The Iranian Salvation Movement led by former army general Gholam Ali Oveissi and the monarchist movement led by the shah's sister Princess Ashraf and son Prince Reza Pahlavi, have done little more than talk.

Reports have surfaced that the two largest paramilitary groups—led by Rear Admiral Ahmed Madani (the former commander of the Iranian Navy and first defense minister under Khomeini) and General Bahram Aryana (the chief of staff of the army under the shah—have 6,000–8,000 men receiving paramilitary training in eastern Turkey, but these reports seem to have little substance. Neither they nor the Kurdish groups loosely associated with them now seem to have more than minimal military capability.[17]

This does not mean that civil fighting has stopped. Iran's political leaders were still surrounded by guards in late 1982 and were the objects of occasional assassination attempts in mid-1983. The speaker of Parliament, Hojatolislam Hashemi Rafsanjani, even took the precaution of traveling in an ambulance at one point in 1982, which started the grim joke that he had added a busload of mourners just in case.[18] The Ghotbzadeh plot also seems to have had military support in its plans to shell Khomeini's home in north Tehran.[19] Although Iran's security forces have been incredibly ruthless—far more so than the SAVAK at its worst—there is no question that Khomeini's consolidation of power has not meant internal peace. What it has meant is that no opposition group now seems to have the power to challenge the Khomeini movement as long as he remains alive or the clergy around him remains united. This, however, is now an area of acute controversy. Khomeini was at least 83 years old in 1983, and his health was increasingly uncertain.

There are also growing reports of divisions among his closest supporters.[20] According to most such reports, Khomeini's closest followers have become divided into two major political factions. The first faction is called the Maktabi, or "properly schooled," faction. It is reported to be headed by the deputy speaker of Parliament, the Hojatolislam Muhammad Musavi Khoeyni. This group evidently favors the selection of a single leader or Vellayat-e-Faghih (religious guide or guardian). Khomeini is said to prefer his former student, the Ayatollah Hussein Ali Montazeri, as his successor in this role. Khomeini also seems to support the movement in seeking land reforms, the nationalization of foreign trade, and other reforms designed to create an "Islamic" economy. Khomeini is the son of a peasant, and his speeches have long favored creating a largely rural and traditional society in which all share in the nation's wealth.[21]

While President Ali Khamenei is sometimes said to head a separate "imam's faction" that favors a more centralized economy, rule by three or four ayatollahs, and closer ties to the Soviet bloc, the main rival group is called the Hodjatieh. It has taken the stand that the twelfth imam will return to the earth and that no religious figure should be given improper power before his return. This group is reported to have been headed by Foreign Minister Velayati and Defense Minister Moussa Salimi. The Hodjatieh has had strong support from many of Iran's other religious leaders and the more traditional elements in Iranian society. It also has been supported by most of Iran's five other surviving grand ayatollahs (Maraj-e Taklid), who have had exceptional power because of their control of the Guardian Council, a body of religious law experts who must approve all reforms.[22]

There is no easy way to estimate the power of the two groups. However, the Maktabi may have the advantage. As many as 8 of the 12 members of the political committee of the IRP are said to be supporters of the Maktabi, and at least half of its 30-man Central Committee. Khomeini's son has publicly endorsed the Maktabi position, and the implication of the senior grand ayatollah, Shariat Madari, in Ghotbzadeh's April 1982 plot against Khomeini further weakened the Hodjatieh. Rafsanjani's alignment with the Hodjatieh is reported to have ended, as well as that of Foreign Minister Ali Akbar Velayati and Oil Minister Mohammed Gharazi. The Revolutionary Guards and the emerging military heroes of the war—like Col. Ali-Sayyad Shirazi, the young commander of the army—are reported to support the Maktabi.[23] Further, on 10 December 1982 the Maktabi won an election for an 83-man special assembly of experts to name a successor to Khomeini,[24] although the assembly did not meet until June, and the Hodjatieh does seem to have won some recent political battles to preserve traditional proper rights and prevent labor reform.

There is also no way to tell whether these splits will turn into any kind of open conflict or weaken the clergy. It is equally impossible to predict whether the victory of one faction would allow it to make broader alliances and further consolidate its rule or to dismiss the possibility that any major split in the clergy—particularly after Khomeini's death—would discredit its authority and bring Iran's emerging military leaders to power. A still unexplained uprising took place at Tehran's Lavizan military base on 27 March 1982, and Khomeini did call for the political purification of the armed forces on 18 April. There are also reports that a more serious coup attempt was made in June 1982 by a group called NIMA that was attempting to create a military government headed by a Col. Azar Dahkan. While the nature of this attempt is uncertain, it has evidently led to new purges within the military. Further, some senior Iranian officers, including the commander of the navy, were implicated in Iran's crackdown on the Tudeh party.[25]

Iran faces two other major problems. The first is its economy. The statistics now available on the Iranian economy are uncertain, but it is clear that the rise in Iran's oil revenue has not prevented widespread shortages of food and most consumer goods and that only the war has averted catastrophic unemployment. Iran also has had severe difficulties in raising funds and has repeatedly been forced to discount its oil.[26] Inflation exceeds 35%, and industrial production is down at least one-third since 1979. Imports exceeded $12 billion in 1981, while foreign reserves dropped from $14.5 billion in March 1980 to $1 billion in January 1982.

Oil production averaged about 2.4 million barrels in 1982 and 1983, with daily peaks as high as 3.2 million barrels, and Iran's continued willingness to undercut OPEC's price levels has produced $2 billion or more a month in income. Iran's foreign exchange reserves recovered to well over $7 billion in 1982. Iran is paying off its previous debts, and inflation has dropped from 60–70% to 18–25%. Iran is now able to afford its budget of roughly $1.5 billion a month and has reduced its foreign debt from $15 billion to $2 billion.[27] Nevertheless, the rationing started in reaction to the war has been followed by the creation of a large black market and extensive smuggling. At the same time, the agriculture, foreign trade, development, construction, and industrial sectors are still experiencing a serious decline. This helps explain why Iran pressed so hard for a rise in its quota from 2.4 to 3.2 MMBD at the OPEC Ministerial Meeting in November 1983. Iran did not get its demands, it is not exporting gas, and it is forced to import large quantities of spare parts and food. Coupled to the devastation of Khuzestan and some of Iran's largest oil facilities, these trends may create an economic crisis that could deeply divide Iran once the war is over.[28]

The second problem is the combined effect of the ethnic and class differences within Iran. Although Iran is 93% Shi'ite, with only 5% Sunni and 2% Zoroastrains, Jews, Christians, and Baha'is, it is only 63% Persian. The rest of the population is 3% Kurds, 13% Baluchis and other Iranian, 18% Turkic, 3% Arab, and 1% other. All of these groups have shown some signs of separatism, and elements of them have been involved in fighting with the central government.[29]

Iran also retains a powerful middle class. Although many of Iran's Western-educated middle class have left the country, most of the country's middle class is Iranian rather than Western educated. This class now supports Khomeini, although it has large numbers of technocrats and other secularly educated members who do not support many of Khomeini's religious reforms and who might be far more hostile to the Khomeini regime because of its economic failures if the nation were not at war. Even the most traditional members of the Iranian middle class, including the merchants of the bazaars, may cease to back the clergy, however, if it continues to cut deeply into their living standards, and the exiles are likely to pose a serious long-term problem.

Even Iran's lower classes are a potential source of unrest. In 1979 only 33% of the work force of roughly 12 million worked in agriculture. Roughly 21% worked in manufacturing, and 46% in services and government. Thus, about 67% worked at jobs dependent on Iran's modern economic sector, and it is far from clear how they will benefit from the economic policies of the Maktabi. The GNP declined by at least 25% per year during 1979–1981, and the average per capita income of $2,170 was cut by more than 50%. While the GNP rose to $66.5 billion in 1982, and per capita income rose to $1,621, much of this increase was consumed by the war. The Iranian budget totaled nearly $20 billion, and a good portion of Iran's $10.6 billion in imports went to support the fighting. Accordingly, the unity the war has brought could disappear if peace does not result in a major economic upturn.[30]

It is also important to note that Iran has budgeted $37 billion for the year beginning on 21 March 1983. This required $33 billion in oil and other income, which has proved optimistic given world oil prices, and Iran planned for $4 billion in additional special war funds. Iran faces a deficit of at least $4–8 billion in 1983, and it could be much worse. Iran has had to cut deeply into the $14 billion it plans for development and cut back even more on its civilian economy. This cutback, plus a steady stream of casualties, could have a serious political effect.[31]

Even so, it seems likely that Iran will remain under religious rule in the near term in spite of these pressures, but they obviously cut deeply into Iranian society. One cannot dismiss the possibility that Iran could return to civil war after Khomeini's death and that this could be followed by a military takeover or even by some coalition of the more radical clergy. There does not, however, seem to be much prospect of a takeover by the Tudeh, and the various underground Marxist factions like the Mujahedin. Nor does it seem likely that a new regime will lead to any sudden expansion of Soviet influence.

Reports surfaced late in 1981 that the Mujahedin's assassination of leading IRP officials like the Ayatollah Mohammed Beheshti had brought Turkic and pro-Moscow clerics to power, but such reports seem to have little merit. The officials generally named in such reports included

President Khamenei (who did receive training in revolutionary warfare in Libya), Deputy Speaker Khoeyni, Chief Justice Ayatollah Musavi Ardebili, Prosecutor General Hojatolislam Hussein Musavi Tabrizi, and former Foreign Minister Hossein Musavi (Khamenei). Virtually all these officials supported the continuing purges of the Tudeh and the removal of its officials from influence, the suppression of the Tudeh party newspaper, the removal of low-level party members from the civil service, and the expulsion of various Soviet officials. The conduct of Khomeini officials during 1982 and 1983 was far more that of radical Iranian nationalists than pro-Soviet agents. Virtually all also seem to have supported such initiatives as expanding Iran's trade with the West and building new pipelines through Turkey, and none seem to have taken any action preferential to the USSR.

It is also notable that in 1982 the USSR cancelled its usual February 11th editorials in praise of the "anniversary" of the Iranian revolution. Even low-level Soviet officials found problems in dealing with the various branches of the Iranian government, and TASS and *Pravda* correspondents lost their visas. By March 1983, Iran had arrested nearly 1,500 members of the Tudeh, and *Pravda* turned from printing Iranian accounts of the war to printing both Iranian and Iraqi accounts and wrote several long editorials attacking restrictions on Soviet and Iranian Communist party activity as "contrary to Iran's interests." This culminated on 4 May 1983, when Iran expelled 18 Soviet envoys and totally suppressed all Tudeh activity. By July, the USSR had joined the U.S. as a "satan," with few signs that the Tudeh commanded any political support or that any resistance was taking place to continuing arrests and executions.[32]

There are some intelligence officials who believe that Iran's internal tensions have not diminished, but rather are in a state of suspended animation, waiting for Khomeini's death. This seems possible, since no outsider can estimate the divisions within the clergy or the extent to which the Iranian middle class or other elements are quietly hostile to the regime. Nevertheless, the near-term prospect for Iran does seem to be a successor regime formed out of the leading clergy around Khomeini. Such a regime seems likely to continue to pursue its own ambitions and to be hostile to both the USSR and the U.S. There is little likelihood that it would face sufficient internal security problems to give up its ambitions to influence or control Shi'ite movements in the rest of the Arab world, to expand Iran's share of the world oil market, or to expand Iran's power and influence in the Gulf.

Iraq: The Problems of Avoiding Defeat

It is even more difficult to predict Iraq's future than that of Iran.[33] Few experts predicted that Iraq would suffer such rapid military reversals in 1981 and 1982, and the West is only beginning to consider what kind of regime might emerge if Saddam Hussein, the Takriti, or the Baath should lose power. It is equally difficult to predict what Iraq's future military capabilities will be, how its economy will develop, or how internal religious and ethnic pressures will affect its future.

One thing is clear: Even if Iraq survives the war without an Iranian invasion or the overthrow of Baath rule, its performance in the Iran-Iraq War will at least have reduced temporarily its influence and power in the Gulf. Its neighbors are all too aware that its defeat has been as much a self-inflicted wound as the result of Iranian military skill. Their present support of Iraq is more the result of their fear of the creation of a hostile regime and the loss of Arab control of Iraq and of a strategic counterweight to Iran than of any love of Iraq's current government. At best, Iraq faces a long period of trying to cope with Iran as a weakened and defensive power that must seek arms wherever it can find them and aid from the conservative Gulf states. More probably, it faces a period of considerable civil unrest, a change in regime, and the challenge of rebuilding its military capabilities in spite of the mistakes both of the Iran-Iraq War and in its previous military buildup.

The Structural Causes of Iraq's Military Failures: Politics, Purges, and Soviet Aid

It is important to note that many of the causes of Iraq's failures in the Iran-Iraq War go deeper than the strategic, tactical, and technical factors discussed earlier. They grow out of Iraq's political and military history and have become embedded in its military forces and government. Iraq is unique in the Arab world in that its military forces have been involved in over 40 conspiracies and 11 successful coups in the last half century. At the same time, they have been purged virtually on an annual basis, and by one count, they have fought 11 battles or wars against internal enemies.[34] The bloodiest of these battles was the campaign against the Kurds, which produced between 10,000 and 16,000 casualties.[35] Although Iraq fought in the 1973 war with Israel, and played a token role in previous Arab-Israeli conflicts, it did not fight serious battles except for one major encounter with the Israelis in 1973, in which it lost nearly 100 tanks in the course of a few hours. Iraq's only serious combat experience before the Iran-Iraq War was in fighting against its own citizens.

Once the Baath came to power in 1968, it spent as much time purging the military as it did trying to build up Iraq's forces to compete with the shah. The Baath's ruling Sunni elite could never forget that it was a military coup that had given the Baath power in 1968 and that even senior members of the Baath party might try to use the armed forces to overthrow the government. The Baath leadership had to execute one former army chief of staff shortly after coming to power. In 1970 it faced a coup attempt by General Abd-al-Ghani al-Rawi, and 40 army officers were publicly executed. Another minor coup attempt took place in July 1971. Nazim Kaazar, the Baath security chief, then made a serious coup attempt in 1973 that killed the defense minister, Hamad Shihab, and several other defense officials.

MAP 17—2
IRAQ

SOURCE: CIA 504065 3-79 (544444)

Western intelligence officials estimate that at least 100 officers were executed or imprisoned for plotting against the government every year from 1973 to 1978, when the KGB and Iraqi Communist party were found to have violated their agreement not to establish cells in the military. This discovery led to the execution of 21 officers for supporting the Iraqi Communist party during the period when Saddam Hussein replaced Field Marshal Hasan al-Bakr as head of state in 1978, and many more were arrested. At least 10 officers were quietly executed in 1979, and more were imprisoned.[36]

It is scarcely surprising, therefore, that in the years before the war, Saddam Hussein placed control of the Iraqi forces under such close allies as his half brother, Barzan Ibrahim, the chief of the al-Mukhabarat, or Internal Security Agency, and his cousin General Adnan Khayrallah Talfah, the minister of defense and chief of the army. Many of Iraq's senior national security officials were also Sunni, senior members of the Baath, and from the area around Takrit. These included the minister of the interior and security chief, Saadoun Shaker; General Al-Jabouri, chief of staff of the air force; Taha Jazrowi, head of the Popular Army; Mohammed Hanash, the chief of staff of the Popular Army; and General Saadoun Ghaidan, the minister of communications and transportation.[37] The administrative control of the armed forces was kept tightly under the Revolutionary Command Council. While Iraq did have a National Defense Council, defense planning in the Western sense was always subordinated to party authority. In fact, the Baath hierarchy was often a better indication than official position within the Iraqi government of who controlled the armed forces.

The details of Iraq's prewar military buildup are shown in Table 17.2, but they are somewhat misleading indicators of Iraq's military power. No other Arab state, not even the Yemens, spent as much time ensuring that no military officer or clique could threaten the regime, or was more willing to subordinate military professionalism to political loyalty. Iraq conducted its military buildup after British withdrawal from the Gulf with two contradictory goals. The first of these goals was political control of the armed forces, and it inevitably conflicted with the second goal of increasing military effectiveness. Virtually every promotion and assignment in the Iraqi armed forces after 1968 was influenced by the Baath's effort to ensure that the armed forces would remain loyal. Even after Iraq's offensive against Iran bogged down in 1981, Iraq consistently promoted Baath party officials, many of them without military expertise, to combat commands. At the same time, it ruthlessly punished any signs of political deviation at the front and any military "failure" by officers who were not members of the Baath.

Iraq also had a special internal security division for the armed forces, with parallel branches in each service, simply to ensure against a coup. The heads of these forces reported directly to the president, and a parallel security apparatus existed within the Baath party. It reported

TABLE 17.2 The Military Buildup in Iraq, 1972-1983

	1972-73	1973-74	1974-75	1975-76	1976-77
Total Population (millions)	9.75	10.14	10.74	11.09	11.49
Defense Expenditures ($ billions)	0.338	0.467	0.803	1.19	1.41
GNP ($ billions)	3.5	5.0	5.6	13.4	14.2
DE as % of GNP	9.65	9.4	14.33	8.88	9.6
Total military manpower	101,800	101,800	112,500	135,000	158,000
Reserves	250,000	268,000	250,000	268,000	304,800
Army					
Manpower	90,000	90,000	100,000	120,000	140,000
Reserves		250,000		250,000	250,000
Equipment					
Medium tanks	860	990	1,390	1,200	1,200
Major types	T-54,55,34	T-54,55,34	T-54,55,62	T-54,55,34	T-54,55,62
Other armored vehicles	300	1,300	1,300	1,300	1,600
Major types	AML,Ferret	BTR-152	BTR-152	BTR,BMP	BTR,BMP
Artillery	300	700	700	790	790
SP guns	—	—	—	90	90
ATWs	—	—	—	—	—
AA weapons	—	included	included	800	800
Missiles	—	—	FROG SSM	SA-7SAM	SA-7SAM
Navy					
Manpower	2,000	2,000	2,000	3,000	3,000
Total craft	20	30	26	29	28
Patrol	4	13	9	13	11
Sub-chasers	3	3	3	3	3
Torpedo craft	12	12	12	13	12
Minesweepers	—	2	2	2	2
Other (type)	—	—	—	—	—
Air Force					
Manpower	9,800	9,800	10,500	12,000	15,000
Total combat aircraft	189	224	278	247	299
Fighters	100	120	130	130	110
Major types	MiG-27,17	MiG-27,17	MiG-27,17	MiG-27,17	MiG-27,19
Fighter bombers	80	96	80	110	170
Major types	Su-7, Hunter	Su-7, Hunter	Su-7, Hunter	Su-7, MiG-23	Su-7B, Hunter
Medium-light bombers	9	8	8	7	19
Major types	Tu-16	Tu-16	Tu-16	Tu-16	Il-28,Tu-16
Transports	33	27	28	30	45
Major types	An-24,Il-74	An-24,Il-74	An-2,24	An-2,24	Il-14,An-24
Helicopters	46	69	101	101	134
Major types	Mi-4,Mi-8	Mi-4,Mi-8	Mi-4,Mi-8	Mi-4,Mi-8	Alouette III,Mi-4
Paramilitary (total)	16-17,000	17-18,000	18-19,000	18-19,000	54,800
National Guard	10,000	10,000	10,000	10,000	—
Security troops	3,800	4,800	4,800	4,800	4,800
Other	4-5,000	4-5,000	4-5,000	4-5,000	50,000[b]

[a] Some inaccuracy may occur due to war losses, and some Iranian equipment may have been taken into service.

[b] People's Army

TABLE 17.2 (continued)

1977–78	1978–79	1979–80	1980–81	1981–82	1982–83[a]
11.8	12.47	12.73	13.11	13.84	13.6
1.66	2.02	2.67	3.0	n.a.	n.a.
16.3	15.05	21.4	39.0	n.a.	n.a.
10.18	13.03	12.47	7.7	n.a.	n.a.
188,000	212,000	222,000	242,250	252,250	342,250
304,800	329,800	329,800	329,800	250,000	75,000
140,000	160,000	180,000	190,000	210,000	300,000
250,000	250,000	250,000	250,000	250,000	75,000
1,350	1,700	1,700	2,600	2,600	2,300
T-55,54,62	T-54,55,62	T-54,55,62	T-54,55,AMX	T-54,62,72	T-54,62,72
1,800	1,620	1,700	2,500	2,100	3,000
BTR,BMP	BTR,BMP	BTR,BMP	BTR,BMP	BTR,BMP	BTR,BMP
790	930	930	1,040	860	878+
90	130	130	240	?	?
Sagger,	Sagger,	Sagger,	Sagger,	Sagger,	Sagger,
SS-11	SS-11	SS-11	SS-11	SS-11	SS-11
800	1,200	1,200	1,200	1,200	1,200
27FROG	38FROG	38FROG	38FROG	19FROG	19FROG
3,000	4,000	4,000	4,250	4,250	4,250
31	35	49	48	50	?
14	14	31	29	28	?
3	3	—	—	—	—
12	10	40	10	10	?
2	5	5	5	8	?
—	3(LCT)	3(LCT)	4(LCT)	4(LCT)	3(LCT)
25,000	28,000	28,000	38,000	38,000	38,000
369	339	339	332	335	335
135	115	115	115	151	151
MiG-27,19	MiG-21	MiG-21	MiG-21	MiG-21	MiG-21
200	190	190	195	167	167
MiG-23,	MiG-23,	MiG-23,	MiG-23,	Su-20	Su-20
Su-7B	Su-7B	Su-7B	Su-7B	MiG-23	MiG-23
14	22	22	22	17	17
Il-28,Tu-16	Il-22,Il-28	Tu-22,Il-28	Tu-22,Il-28	Tu-22,Il-28	Tu-22,Il-28
47	45	45	56	68	58
Il-14,An-24	Il-14,An-2	Il-14,An-2	Il-24,26	Il-24,26	Il-24,26
135	227	237	276	366	397
Alouette	Alouette	Mi-8,Mi-24	Mi-8,24	Mi-8,24	Mi-8,24
III,Mi-4	III,Mi-4		Alouette	Alouette	Gazelle
54,800	79,800	79,800	79,800	254,800	11,800
—	—	—	—	—	—
4,800	4,800	4,800	4,800	4,800	4,800
50,000[b]	75,000[b]	75,000[b]	75,000[b]	250,000	7,000

Source: The Military Balance (London: IISS, various years).

on the loyalty of each military officer who was a member of the Baath. Since party membership was as important to a military career in Iraq as is Communist party membership in the Soviet Union, this acted as a powerful mechanism for checking on the behavior of each officer even if he did not come to the attention of the security forces. It also, however, ensured that for nearly 15 years, Iraq's officers were chosen on the basis of political dedication rather than military competence.

Iraq organized virtually its entire command structure and order of battle around the issue of military loyalty. The army units nearest the capital and Takrit were chosen on the basis of loyalty and were specially equipped to prevent coups. In addition, the Popular Army was originally set up as much to protect against the regular army as to provide a mobilization base, and additional commando units and armored infantry units were set up directly under the command of the Baath party. These forces reached 225,000 before the Iran-Iraq War began.[38] Even the air force was specially organized and deployed to prevent its use in a coup. All of Iraq's modern attack aircraft and bombers were directly under the command of Saddam Hussein, and their training was deliberately restricted to prevent a sudden diversion against the President's Palace. The Jordanian officers who came to Iraq as advisers after the war began found that the offensive training of Iraq's air force had been negligible by Jordanian standards. They also found that the officers of both the army and air force had had remarkably little access to Western and Israeli military works and only limited professional training for command, with a heavy emphasis on politics rather than war.

This background unquestionably helped shape Iraq's defeats in 1981 and 1982, but it is difficult to estimate its impact on the country's future. While the war has almost certainly done much to create a new class of Iraqi military professionals, it has cost as many of Iraq's career officers and NCOs their lives. Defeat also provides only a limited learning experience. Many of Iraq's regular forces have been taken prisoner since early 1982 and gained only limited combat experience. Many others have been forced into a period of continuous intense fighting that has given them no time to try to improve their use of military technology and tactics.

Further, it is impossible to dismiss the impact that the Baath's constant propaganda about Iranian numbers and its "suicidal" tactics will have in shaping the future thinking of Iraqi officers and NCOs. While virtually all Western reporting has assigned most of the blame for Iraq's defeat to its lack of military professionalism, senior Jordanian and Saudi officers confirm the fact that even Iraqi officers who do not support the present Baath regime tend to see the main cause of their defeat as being Iranian fanaticism and numbers, and the secondary cause as Soviet equipment and training. The politicization of the Iraqi armed forces, their lack of modern training, and their problems in using their modern weapons have gone virtually unmentioned. Nothing in Iraq's modern military history indicates that it will be able to see through its own lies and illusions, regardless of what government is in power.

The Iraqi Army

The dual character of the Baath's effort to expand Iraq's military forces and to make them a loyal arm of the Baath is clearly reflected in Iraq's army. Before the Iran-Iraq War, Iraq's forces were organized into three major corps areas. Five mountain infantry divisions held the north; the Republican Guards Brigade, two armored divisions, and the Baghdad Garrison held the center; and two mechanized divisions and three armored divisions (several reinforced brigades in the process of converting to division-size formations) held the south. Iran kept something like a third of its army in the north to ensure the loyalty of the Kurds—a step that seems prudent in view of the Kurdish contribution to the Iranian offensive of July 1983 discussed earlier. It kept its best armored and mechanized units near Baghdad to guarantee the regime's security against a coup. These included the Republican Guard mechanized division (sometimes reported as a brigade), a special infantry division, and an independent armored brigade. In addition, an armored division, a mechanized division, a special forces brigade, and a special infantry brigade were kept near Takrit. While the units near Baghdad and Takrit also covered the main Iranian invasion route to the capital, it was only after Khomeini's rise to power that Iraq began to commit its army units primarily to external, rather than internal, security.[39]

It is important to note, however, that Iraq suffered from two other major problems. The first was that it expanded its forces far too rapidly to make them effective; the second was that it failed to develop an effective general staff and borrowed Soviet methods for training and operations without making a rigorous effort to put them into practice. As Table 17.2 shows, the regular Iraqi Army expanded from 90,000 men in 1972 to 210,000 men in 1980. It also expanded from 6–7 to 12–13 divisions and from less than 900 to over 2,600 medium tanks. Iraq simultaneously built up the Popular Army and party armored infantry forces referred to earlier and a number of additional independent brigades, including a total of three special forces brigades. This was far too rapid an expansion for the Iraqi Army to make effective, even if it had not been subject to purges and politicization. Further, Iraq failed to develop an effective staff college system, to create suitable technical training schools, to adopt modern training technology, and to develop an effective C^3I system. It maintained a two-year conscript period with a manpower pool that was undereducated and often functionally illiterate. In short, Iraq conducted its arm race with Iran during the 1970s without the essential organization and resources to make its army work.

Iraq's problems did not stop there. Between 1970 and 1976, much of the Iraqi Army was locked up in a series of offensives against the Kurds and did little training in modern warfare. Since Iraqi tactics in fighting the Kurds relied heavily on "creeping" offensives using air power and artillery against an enemy that had only token supplies of modern weapons, Iraq learned little about armored warfare, modern infantry combat in other areas, or fighting in the very different mix of water barriers and built-up areas in the south.

Part of the blame for this inadequacy must fall on the USSR. From 1974 to 1978, the Iraqi Army received second-rate training from the USSR, a factor that led Iraq to begin its search for Western arms. Several Egyptian and Jordanian officers blame the Soviets for making only a half-hearted effort to assist Iraq, even in comparison with the often inadequate support given other Arab states. One senior Egyptian officer feels that the USSR deliberately restricted its support to Iraq once the Soviet Union and Iraq split over the Iraqi attacks on the Kurds. This same officer notes, however, that the Iraqis had many of the same problems with Soviet advisers in the late 1970s that he had had in the early 1970s:

> You only train in the field in small units, but you train as if you only could fight as a large mass. The book says wait until you assemble everything, fire everything, then advance. You don't really maneuver in any serious sense. Everything is combined arms mass and you win by being bigger.
>
> Equally importantly, you and your Soviet advisors know that you aren't really training well enough to make the concept work. It takes really excellent training to bring all these pieces together and make them work, and even better training to do it quickly enough to ever outflank or surprise. They know this isn't going to happen out here, but they aren't going to force the truth on anyone, particularly since this means confrontations with the officer of their host country.

After mid-1978, this situation became even worse. Iraq reacted to the attempted coup by the Iraqi Communist party by adding another layer to the problem. It kept most of its Soviet advisers, but it increasingly turned to the West for advice and equipment. Further, it attempted to convert to a higher level of technology without ever developing its own combat tactics and doctrine and while still relying on hybrid unit tables of organization and equipment that had little relation to Iraq's future needs.

The war caught Iraq midstream in this process. It had 50 T-72 and 100 AMX-30 tanks but had not conducted advanced firing training or simulated combat with either type. It had 200 Cascavels on order, but no real doctrine or experience in using its Soviet-made APCs and AFVs. It was just beginning to learn how to use attack helicopters and was taking delivery on 360 HOT antitank guided missiles from France. It had stocks of Milan ATGMs but had not trained its forces to use them effectively. Its infantry still had no training in urban warfare, no training in independent small unit action, and little training in the use of its new heavier infantry weapons. The army as a whole was layering its new Western technology over a Soviet system it had only half assimilated. Such structural problems will not be easy to overcome even with the experience the Iraqi Army has gained from three years of war.

It is also difficult to predict how the army's wartime buildup will be translated into future capabilities. The army had expanded to as many as 22 divisions by December 1983, but these averaged only about 8,000–10,000 men. While most were comparatively well equipped with Soviet armor, Iraq was having problems replacing its heavy losses of tanks and artillery, and even its newest T-72s lacked the fire-control equipment and laser range finders present on Soviet models. Iraq also had had to cancel virtually its entire advanced training program and continued to experience severe problems in middle-echelon leadership, compounded by the emphasis Saddam Hussein placed at the top on nationalism and political fervor, rather than military effectiveness. For all its battle experience and billions of dollars worth of new arms and military technology, the Iraqi Army seemed to be in the grip of many of the same political and organizational problems that had limited its effectiveness in the period before the war began.

The Iraqi Air Force

There were matching weaknesses in Iraq's other services. Table 17.2 reveals the same rapid expansion of the air force that took place in the army. With the air force, however, a far higher level of technology was involved, and Iraq's problems with politicization and inadequate training had an even greater impact. The effect of these problems has already been outlined in the discussion of Iraq's performance during the Iran-Iraq War, but it is important to note that from 1968 onward, Iraq tended to buy new aircraft and air defense technology while making only a limited effort to integrate them into an effective force.

Iraq did build modern air bases at Baghdad, Qayyarah west of Kirkuk, Mosul, Nasariya, al-Basrah, and at H-2 in the west near Rutba and the border with Syria. It gave these bases reasonably effective surface-to-air missile and antiaircraft gun defenses and developed a reasonably competent shelter program. It did not match this infrastructure, however, with suitable training facilities, simulators, or the other equipment necessary to forge a modern air force. It made little effort to test and evaluate what it bought. It had no real capability on its air staff to force its own doctrine and tactics on the basis of empirical trials and exercises. It made few practical attempts to test the effectiveness of its ground-based air defenses, its training in fighter combat, or its ability to carry out various types of offensive missions. Iraq borrowed technology and tactics from the Soviet Union and the West without validating what it borrowed and made little apparent effort to learn from previous wars. It did not develop an effective air operations staff, a targeting and reconnaissance capability, or an effective air defense command. It bought large numbers of SAMs, sensors, and AA guns without properly improving its training and welding these pieces into an effective system.

It expanded from a force of about 190 low-grade fighters at the time of the October War to 335 relatively advanced aircraft when the Iran-Iraq War began. Iraq also had an extensive network of civil and military airfields. It had 81 usable fields when the war began. Thirty-two had paved strips; one had a runway over 3,600 meters, 42 had 2,500–3,600-meter runways, and 12 had 1,200–2,500-meter runways. However, Iraq carried out this expansion without taking the time to fully train its forces in using the more advanced aircraft or setting up the C^3I systems necessary to employ them in battle. When the war began, Iraq had 73 MiG-23BM and 80 Su-20 aircraft on hand, but few units had completed conversion or had any advanced training. Iraq was also in the process of transition to yet another generation of fighters. It had ordered 150 more MiG-23/25/27s, and the MiG-25s were in the process of delivery. It also had ordered 60 Mirage F-1 fighters, Matra 530 and Exocet air-to-surface missiles, other advanced attack munitions, and Super 530 air-to-air missiles.

If Iraq had had several years to convert to these systems, it might have done much to compensate for the weaknesses of its earlier Soviet-supplied aircraft, SAMs, and munitions. However, Iraq was forced to rely on Soviet fighters and munitions with comparatively poor avionics, range, loiter time, payload, and lethality. It also was in a poor position to use its attack aircraft, Tu-22 medium bombers, and aging Il-28 light bombers. Not only did Iraq lack advanced avionics and offensive munitions, the president's personal control over these forces meant they had only limited training, and they had had no combat experience beyond set-piece attacks on Kurdish villages. According to some reports, the Soviet Union also began to restrict munitions and spare parts deliveries after the failure of the 1978 coup attempt, and Iraq had serious problems in maintaining its Su-7B, Su-7, MiG-21, and Su-20 fighters in fully operational condition. It also was not ready to conduct helicopter operations because it had only recently begun to take delivery of 100 French attack helicopters, 50 with antitank guided missiles.

The present Iraqi Air Force is a curious mixture indeed. Its front-line aircraft consist of 37 Mirage F-1 fighters, but 70% of its air force remains Soviet supplied. As has been noted earlier, it had 70–85 MiG-23 BMs, 22 MiG-25s (14 fighter and 8 recce), 70–100 MiG-21/F-7s, 40 MiG-19/F-6s, 30 MiG-17s, 80 Su-20s, and 20 Su-7/SU-17s in the fall of 1983. It also had 13–41 Mi-24 Hind attack helicopters, 30–150 Mi-8 assault helicopters, 15–50 Gazelles, 6–47 Alouettes, 11 Super Frelons, and some MMB BO-105s. This represented an extremely diverse force mix even within the range of Soviet types, and one that presented serious logistic and support problems. Iraq was virtually forced to permanently base its smaller holdings of given types of aircraft at given bases, regardless of their mission.

Iraq had 42 more Mirage F-1s on order in December 1983, in addition to the 5 Super Etendards it received in November. Although the Mirage F-1s are Iraq's most effective aircraft, and much of the blame may have to reside with Iraq, senior Arab officers indicate that the F-1s did not meet a single major reliability specification within 50%, had serious avionics problems, and required 3 to 10 times the scheduled maintenance per flying hour. These problems made it difficult to use the aircraft in sufficient numbers and to fly demanding missions, and they were compounded by problems with Iraq's Soviet aircraft. The USSR resumed major aircraft deliveries as the Khomeini government became steadily more hostile, and it is replacing some of Iraq's older aircraft with as many as 150 MiG-23s, MiG-25s, and MiG-27s. All three types, however, have comparatively limited avionics in at least the export versions provided to Iraq and require extremely high pilot proficiency. In at least some cases, Egyptian and Indian instructor pilots have had to fly combat missions because of a lack of suitable Iraqi crews.

Iraq also continues to have to rely on foreign advisers to help it with targeting and mission planning and to support the C^3I of its air operations. In spite of repeated training efforts, its pilots still regularly fail to follow instructions in flying air-to-air combat, fly too high in attack missions, and fail to obey instructions in releasing their munitions. Even the delivery of cluster bombs in the spring of 1983 did not ease Iraq's problems in using its ordnance. Further, Iraq has continued to expand a force structure it could not really man. It seems to have ordered 30–60 Chinese-built F-6 and F-7 fighters and bombers from Egypt. This is symbolic of the Iraqi obsession with numbers. The F-6s and F-7s simply lack the mission capability to make it worth Iraq's while to dilute its skilled manpower pool and C^3I structure to try to operate them.

Further, Iraq has ordered at least 40 more French helicopters and significant numbers of Soviet Mi-24 attack helicopters. It already has a shortage of skilled helicopter pilots—particularly the kind that can fly pop-up attack missions like those Iraq has learned from France. These will further dilute Iraq's over-strained pilot training and maintenance capabilities.

Iraq has had serious problems with its air defenses. As has been the case in all recent combat, its SA-2s have proved almost useless except as a means of forcing enemy fighters to fly low. Its SA-3s have also been relatively ineffective, and it has not made good use of its SA-6s. It does seem to have had better luck with its Franco-German Rolands, but the claims of the European manufacturer for this system rival Iraq's ability to exaggerate, and the truth of the matter is hard to ascertain. Like Iran, Iraq seems to have done far better with its antiaircraft guns and lighter surface-to-air missiles, although it lacks Iran's excuse of an inability to obtain resupply to explain the poor performance of its larger missile defenses. It would seem that Iraq, like Syria, has bought the

SA-2, SA-3, and SA-6 without getting the technical help, C^3I links, sensors, and siting assistance to really make them effective.

While the air force is learning from its conflict with Iran, its problems are structural and will continue once the war is over. The war has unquestionably taught Iraq many lessons, but it has also cost it many casualties, and it is unclear how many of its senior pilots will be around to help translate their lessons into future improvements in training and organization. While the Iraqi air staff has certainly benefited from French and Jordanian help and advice during the war, it is uncertain that it has improved enough to really learn from its mistakes, even if it is not purged again as part of Iraq's reaction to its current defeats. Further, the Air Force has had to suspend virtually all of its military school and advanced training programs since early 1982.

The Iraqi Navy

The Iraqi Navy was still essentially a river and coastal patrol force when the war began. It consisted mainly of Soviet guided-missile patrol boats, 12 of which were OSA I– and OSA II–class vessels, armed with obsolescent Styx ship-to-ship cruise missiles. It had negligible mine warfare and amphibious capability, and none of Iraq's three ports (al-Basrah, Umm Qasr, or al-Fao) could be described as a major naval base. Once again, Iraq was waiting for new weapons. Its navy was planning to acquire a meaningful military capability only after it had completed its $1.8 billion deal with Italy to exchange Iraqi oil for four 2,500-ton Lupo-class frigates, six 650-ton corvettes, and support vessels and equipment. This deal included modern sensors, radars, fire-control systems, guns, and missiles. It also included U.S. turbines for its frigates and a substantial amount of U.S.-licensed technology manufactured in Italy. The U.S. temporarily embargoed the turbines at the start of the war.

It is doubtful that the delivery of these ships would have made much difference, given Iraq's geographic disadvantages, its limited number of ports, and its vulnerability to Iranian aircraft. In fact, it is hard to see how Iraq can ever be effective as a naval power unless it can somehow achieve at least local air superiority over Iran or any other opponent or find contingency bases somewhere else in the Gulf. Iraq does, however, seem to recognize this. Tariq Aziz requested 5 Super Etendard naval attack aircraft with Exocet antiship missiles when he visited Paris in January 1983, and Iraq has actively sought Nimrods with AWACS and maritime surveillance capability and some form of air-to-ship missile from the British. Such systems would give it far more naval power in the Gulf without the limitations inherent in depending on such limited access to Gulf waters.

In fact, although Iraq's corvettes and frigates are now being completed in Italy, its surface navy can never be much more than a strategic practical joke as long as its access to the sea is within the range of

Iranian guns and Iraq has only 58 kilometers of coastline. It is doubtful that Iraq can safely transit its new Italian ships through the Gulf even in the face of a limited threat like the present capability of the Iranian Navy. This means that Iraq's future form of "sea power" almost has to be air power. While ships may look impressive, long-range naval attack and maritime patrol aircraft offer Iraq virtually its only practical way to exert military power in Gulf waters—a lesson that Iraq's helicopter attacks on Iran's offshore oil rigs and request for Super Etendards with Exocet indicate that Iraq may have learned.

Internal Security

It is almost impossible to discuss the internal security of Iraq at the present time. The forces unleashed by Iraq's defeat are too strong and too unpredictable to make any assessment based on past trends and on the opposition groups that existed before the war. Nevertheless, some factors do seem likely to have a bearing on Iraq's future stability and the conduct of any future government, whether Baathist or some replacement.

The impact of Iraq's defeat will inevitably be affected by the deep ethnic and religious divisions discussed in Chapter 11. Most experts feel that the regime was largely successful in pacifying the Kurds after 1975 and made major progress in improving their economic situation and dealing with their ethnic and political concerns until the Iran-Iraq War began. Iraq's Kurds also are largely Sunni and have little interest in seeing any Shi'ite religious regime replace Sunni rule or Iraq's present secular style of government—particularly one allied to a Khomeini regime that has been ruthless in suppressing Iran's Kurds. Nevertheless the Kurds are at least 18% of the population, and various Assyrian (0.7%), Turkoman (2.4%), and other (7.7%) minority elements seem likely to join them in pressing for greater autonomy and privileges.[40] The Kurds are, therefore, a somewhat unpredictable force. They might support the Baath or any other secular regime against an effort to give Shi'ite religious figures power, but they would probably support any new secular movement that offered them increased independence.

There are now three major Kurdish opposition groups, and they represent the best-organized paramilitary threat to the Baath government, although even this threat is weak. Western intelligence officials agree that these groups have received significant additional funds from Syria and Iran since 1979. The Kurdish Democratic party (KDP), or Pesh Merga, has been particularly well armed, has occupied some of the areas evacuated by the Iraqi troops sent to the front, and is reported to have as many as 5,000 men under arms. It is currently headed by Massoud and Idriss Barzani, the sons of the Mustafa Barzani who led the Kurds during the revolt that ended in 1975. The KDP is closely associated with Iran and has a base at Karaj, 30 miles from Tehran. The smaller groups include the Kurdish Socialist party (KSP), headed by Rasoul Memendeh, and the Kurdish Patriotic Union (KPU or PUK), headed by Jalal Talabani (which has close ties to the USSR and the Iraqi Communist party). These Kurdish groups have recently attempted to form a Kurdish front called the National Democratic and Patriotic Front (NDPF), and they have expanded their operations in Irbil, Kirkuk, and Sulaimaniya provinces and in the Badinau region. While feuding between them continues, the efforts at unity do seem to be having some effect, and violence between the KDP and PUK has been reduced.[41]

These groups may also have given Iran some support in its July–November 1983 offensives against Iraq, although such reports seem exaggerated. The Kurds had at most 3,000 low-grade guerrillas in the area, and while Barzani was allowed to occupy his father's old Pesh Merga headquarters at Haj Omran, it was Iran that did the fighting. The Barzani movement has long had Iranian funding and seems to have supported Iran, but the Iranian attack was launched partly to halt Iraqi aid to Iran's Kurds, and at least some Iraqi Kurdish leaders have long criticized Barzani's ties to Iran and any attempt to reach an accord with Iraq's radical Shi'ites.[41]

The rest of Iraq's diverse opposition movements seem to lack significant power. They have repeatedly tried to join with the Kurdish groups in a broad opposition front. One was set up in 1982, called the Iraqi Front of Revolutionary, Islamic, and National Forces (IFIRN), which included many of the disparate groups trying to overthrow the present Baath leadership. Efforts to create such a front had gone on since July 1981 and evidently were successful in February 1982. The front may also have created a Supreme Council in a meeting at Cyprus on 17 November 1982, although this is unclear. Any such unity presents difficult problems. The front must link such conflicting movements as the Kurds, rival elements of the Baath, Shi'ite fundamentalists, ex-military groups, and the Iraqi Communist party.[42]

These various opposition movements have previously been organized into smaller fronts, which tend to constantly shift membership or even name. These include the National Islamic Liberation Front (NILF), the National Democratic Front (NDF), and the Majlis Ulema. These three fronts seem likely to continue as independent political forces regardless of the establishment of the IFIRN. Each front represents major divisions in the opposition that severely weaken its ability to challenge the regime.[43]

The individual strength of each of these fronts is uncertain, but the NILF seems to be the strongest. It includes the KDP; the Shi'ite Muslim Iraqi Mujahedin (largely a religious movement), headed by Modhi Hakim and the strongest group outside Iraq; some pro-Syrian Iraqi Baathists; and dissident members of the military headed by General Hassan Mustafa Naqib. It has received substantial Syrian backing and seems to be a secular socialist movement that has radical elements but few ties to the USSR. Its party platform calls for parliamentary rule, national elections, a liberal economy with a substantial private sector, and full autonomy for the Kurds.

In contrast, the NDF includes the ICP, the KPU, and seven smaller parties, which evidently include the Iraqi Baath party (opposition) headed by Bakr Yassin. It also receives heavy Syrian support and may have more official backing from the Syrian Baath than does the NILF. Its platform is strongly anti-Western and covertly opposed to the conservative Gulf regimes; it calls for a radical socialist economy. Its strength is almost impossible to estimate because it is composed of groups with covert and cell-like organization, but it seems to be significantly weaker than the NILF.

The Majlis Ulema, or Mullahs' Council, is not a front in the normal sense. It is a group of religious leaders run by Mohdi Hakim's brother, Bakr, and is composed of Iraqi ayatollahs and clergy who are strongly influenced by Khomeini. It does not seem to have the official backing of Iran, however, which has given at least as much support to the KDU and NILF. Another religious movement, the Dawa, or Call, seems to have declined in strength since its leader, Ayatollah Bakr Sadr, was executed in April 1981, although it evidently still has volunteers fighting with Iran.[44]

If some recent reports are correct, all three fronts also now have some loose affiliation to a central IFIRN military command based in Iran with up to 10,000 men. This command is reported to be headed by General Hassan Naqib and calls itself the Iraqi Revolution. While Naqib is evidently affiliated with the NILF and the NDF, he has much broader credentials. He was part of the 1958 coup that overthrew the monarchy, was assistant chief of staff of the Iraqi Army, and served as ambassador to Spain and Sweden before going into exile after the attempted coup in 1978. No reliable details are available on the group's military strength, on whether it played any role in the fighting in 1983, or on the degree of unity this command represents, but the major elements of the IFIRN have a long history of feuding and occasional assassination.[45]

It seems doubtful that any of these groups will have more than a minimal chance of seizing power unless Iraq suffers additional serious defeats. With the exception of the KDP, all seem to lack substantial popular support even among a given ethnic or religious group. Most are typical of the small and divided opposition groups that arise in all Third World states. While Saddam Hussein and the Baath ruthlessly suppressed active opposition, there is a broad consensus that the Baath leadership did a comparatively good job of managing the nation's development after 1978 and that virtually all classes and groups in Iraq benefited greatly from the nation's increasing oil wealth. For most Iraqis, the period from 1973 to the first year of Iran-Iraq War represented a major increase in personal income, social services, and social privileges, and they had little incentive to support opposition movements that promised to do no better.

It is also important to note that Iraq's Shi'ites are less likely to form a united opposition than its Kurds. Deep splits exist within the various

Shi'ite opposition groups, which limits the potentially most important source of popular opposition to the present regime. Various intelligence officials note that recent studies of the Iraqi Shi'ites indicate that a substantial number have risen to the middle ranks of the Baath and that during the last 10 years, many Shi'ite towns and cities have benefited greatly from Iraq's new oil wealth.

Iraq seems to have paid considerable attention to the need to reduce any causes of Shi'ite unrest in structuring and implementing its development activities and to have done a great deal more to educate and secularize its ordinary citizens. Accordingly, although 55% of Iraq's total population is Shi'ite, it is far from clear that its Shi'ites would want to follow the path of Iran or would seek to overthrow the Baath, as distinguished from changing its leadership.[46]

Further, Iraq's various security services were comparatively efficient after the mid-1970s. There were few arbitrary arrests and little overt repression. The security services were not corrupt and, unlike in Iran, did not constantly interfere in the day-to-day lives of most of Iraq's citizens. Saddam Hussein was careful after the start of the war to minimize any security activity that affected the ordinary citizen, as distinguished from ruthless suppression of actual rivals and opposition groups, and to stress nationalism, the Arab cause, and economic incentives as his method of developing loyalty. The war actually eased the security situation in Iraq in the period before the country began to suffer major military reversals.

As a result, it is unlikely that if Hussein and the Takriti fall, it will be to any of the present opposition groups. Unless Iran can put one of these groups in power by force of arms, it seems probable that it will be some faction within the Baath, particularly the younger officials most affected by the war, or some man on horseback from within the military, that will take power. Even if Iran does put one of the present opposition groups in power, it seems likely that these "new men" will soon replace it. It is interesting to note in this regard that Saddam Hussein's June 1982 reorganization of the Revolutionary Command Council and the Baath party seems to have been designed to reduce the power of such new men and non-Takriti. The question is whether it is still possible to secure his authority against the internal forces of change.[47]

This shake-up purged those felt to be of uncertain loyalty to Saddam Hussein from the Regional Command on 27 June 1982. It then cut nine members from the Revolutionary Command Council (RCC) and eight members from the cabinet. Hussein became secretary general of the Regional Command, and the RCC was cut to 10 members personally loyal to him. Ten new ministers were created in what seems to have been both an adjustment to the civil demands of the war and an effort to broaden Saddam Hussein's contacts with the younger technocrats in the Baath.[48] The shake-up did not guarantee Hussein's security, however, and may have helped lead to a major assassination attempt. According to reports in the *Economist*, an armed force attacked Saddam Hussein at the small town of Ad Dujayal, 40 miles northeast of Baghdad, on 11 July 1982. These same reports indicate that up to 150 were killed and wounded in the fighting that followed and that 100 were arrested during the fighting in Ad Dujayal and at Balad, 5 miles to the north. The facts involved remain unclear, but car bombings and assassination attempts on Baath officials did take place in Baghdad in December 1982. Hussein was also forced to cancel his appearance at the nonaligned summit in New Delhi in March 1983 because of fears of assassination attempts. While he seems to have been far more afraid of Iran than of any Iraqi groups, it is still striking that he canceled in spite of sending an advance guard of nearly 150 commandos.[49]

These problems continued through the rest of 1983. Several bombing incidents took place in the fall of 1983, and in October Saddam Hussein removed three of his half-brothers from office: Barzan Ibrahim Al-Takriti, the head of the security services; Sabawi, a deputy head of security; and Watban, the governor of a province north of Baghdad. The cause was uncertain, and rumors flew about a family quarrel, Barzan's removal of two key loyalists without consulting Saddam, or perhaps a failure by these officials to uncover a plot for an internal military coup early enough. While Saddam replaced Barzan with a soldier, Hisham Sabah Pfakhri, who was regarded as a Saddam protegé, the fact remains that Pfakhri is the former commander of the 4th Army Group and that heading the security services is a new role for the army.

Hussein has also had to set up a corps of political guidance officers within the armed forces under Yasin Ramadan, the civilian head of the Popular Army, to act as the equivalent of the commisars. In addition, he seems to face a growing challenge over strategy from his chief of staff, General Abdel Jabar Shanshal, and his Defense Minister, Air Chief Marshal Adnan Khairrallah Talfah. Both seem to resent Sadam's personality cult and favor limited ground counteroffensives over showpiece attacks on Iranian towns or mass air attacks on Iranian oil facilities.

Finally, Saddam faced growing terrorist pressure from the Iraqi Mujahedin, the Islamic Action Organization, and the Islamic National Liberation Front, and even from small communist cells led by Aziz Muhamad. While these elements of the opposition fronts discussed earlier scarcely emerged as major threats, they did seem to be increasing their freedom of action and their ability to carry out bombings and assassination attempts. This reinforces the impression that Iraq's internal problems have begun to threaten Saddam's survival.

Other Factors Shaping Iraq's Future

Whatever Iraq's regime, it will have to cope with many of the same postwar problems as Iran. The reductions in Iraq's oil exports and the costs of the war forced it to borrow at least $15–25 billion between its attack on Iran and the end of 1981. By early 1982, the new costs of the fighting had reached as high as $2–4 billion per month. This caused more borrowing and probably raised Iraq's debt to around $25–30 billion by January 1982, while Iraq's foreign reserves dropped from $30 billion in September 1980 to $6–8 billion.[50]

Equally important, although Iraq kept its economy and development plans functioning until late 1981, they began to grind to a halt after the spring of 1982. This halt, plus the additional stress of trying to maintain the projects under wartime conditions, probably cost Iraq over $50 billion more, and there is no question that the war has done immense damage to its roads and other infrastructure. The cost of fixing this damage, creating new pipeline links through Saudi Arabia and Jordan, and paying for the war may well exceed $200 billion. Unless the conservative Arab states write off their loans and provide further funds, or a new Iraqi regime unilaterally refuses to repay, the Iraqi economy faces serious problems over the next two to three years.[51]

In the interim, Iraq will have increasing problems in paying for its war. While estimates differ sharply, Iraq earned only about $6 billion in oil income in 1982. The southern Gulf states may have paid only $9–15 billion of the $30 billion they pledged in 1982 and offered Iraq less than $6 billion of the $15 billion it requested for the first six months of 1983. Saudi Arabia and Kuwait seem to have quietly given Iraq 350,000 BPD of oil to market in late 1982, but Iraq was still forced to plan for a minimum of a $4 billion deficit for its budget year beginning in March 1983, and it projected only $6–10 billion in annual oil income. It was forced to borrow $500 million from commercial banks in November 1982 and to come to the U.S. for a $210 million wheat loan in December. In early 1983 it stopped payment on much of its aid to Jordan and to many large contractors, who it then asked to increase their self-financing by 30%. It stopped paying overruns on development projects and cut import licenses sharply. It also quietly warned France that it might be unable to make payments on the $7.15 billion it owed France or on $2.15 billion more in French guaranteed contracts.

By mid-1983, Saddam Hussein had been reduced to borrowing from Jordan and asking Iraqi women to donate all their gold jewelry to pay for the war. Many social services had been reduced, imports of consumer goods had been cut back sharply, and Iraq's education program had nearly been destroyed. Iraq was not paying some of its essential foreign labor, and its plans to expand its arable land by 25% by 1985 had been replaced by a minor loss of land under cultivation. New Zealand had temporarily suspended butter shipments for nonpayment, imports contracts had been cut in half, and Iraq had received only about half its scheduled payments on the more than $13 billion the southern Gulf states had pledged for 1983. Further, Iraq had been reduced to bartering future oil shipments in lieu of some $800 million in civil debts and $1,200 million in military payments it owed France.

Trade projections for 1983 indicate Iraq will have a deficit of $9–10 billion for 1982 and 1983, rather than the $4 billion projected in Iraq's budget. Iraq's foreign reserves have dropped from $35 billion in late 1980 to under $4 billion in spite of the fact the other Arab states increased their aid to $20 billion in reaction to the growing threat to Hussein's survival. Iraq had to increase its austerity program and cancel additional development projects throughout 1983, and its real economic activity has dropped by 5.7% versus 4.8% in 1982. These are all signs that Iraq faces a critical funding squeeze in a period when the southern Gulf states are also having problems with declining revenues.[52]

Even after the war is over, Iraq must try simultaneously to rebuild its economy and military strength and to recover a major share of the world oil market. Unlike Iran, Iraq cannot choose the solution of a popular army unless a new regime can establish secure and friendly relations with Syria and Iran. Iraq will be forced not only to buy the arms necessary to replace its wartime losses, but to buy the kind of military equipment and support that can make up for its numerical inferiority to Iran and correct the heritage of military incapability and incompetence left by Baath rule between 1968 and 1979. While Iraq has not suffered as much economic damage from the war as Iran, it probably faces an even steeper rearmament bill, and its ability to obtain a source of high-technology arms and support may be even more important. France would be a logical supplier, and Egypt might provide additional support, but the nature of Iraq's future economic alignments and of its effort to rebuild its military is now as unclear as its future government.

This same uncertainty affects the securing of Iran's oil supplies. Iraq has awarded a $70 million contract to Enka of Turkey to extend its pipeline from Kirkuk to the Turkish Mediterranean. The project will include five new pumping stations and raise the capacity of the six-year-old, 620-mile pipeline to 358 million barrels of crude a year versus the 255 million barrels it now can carry. This still, however, is a limited capacity. Jordan has agreed to jointly fund new pipeline links between H-3 in Iraq and Jordan's port of Aqaba. These links could be built fairly quickly since lines already exist from Saudi Arabia to Jordan's refinery at Amman, but they would probably have a maximum capacity of 600,000–700,000 BPD. Saudi Arabia has also formally given Iraq the right to build a 1.5-MMBD pipeline to a port on the Red Sea, and some reports have indicated that Saudi Arabia has agreed to finance its $2–3 billion construction cost. Most of these projects cannot be completed until the late 1980s, however, and then will furnish a maximum of 2.5 MMBD worth of capacity. This is far better than Iraq's current exports of 700,000 BPD, but much less than its pre-war exports of 3.2 MMBD, and the level Iraq needs to fund its current need for guns and butter.

Iran, Iraq, and the Problem of Nuclear Proliferation

There is another "wild card" that affects all these trends: the problem of nuclear proliferation.[53] This threat has diminished in the near term. The revolution in Iraq, the Iran-Iraq War, and Israel's successful attack on Osirak on 7 June 1981 have put an end to any near-term chance that Iran or Iraq could build nuclear weapons. Iran's nuclear effort disintegrated after the shah's fall, Israel's F-16s destroyed Iraq's Tammuz 1 reactor, and the new government of France has made it clear that it will not provide Iraq with weapons-grade fuel once it rebuilds its reactor.[54] Nevertheless, Israel and India already have a nuclear capability, Pakistan will probably acquire one at its facility at Kahuta no later than 1986, and it is impossible to dismiss the possibility that one of the northern Gulf powers may develop the capacity to produce nuclear weapons by the late 1980s.[55]

The potential seriousness of this threat is shown in Tables 17.3 to 17.5, which project various estimates of the rate of proliferation that could take place in the region. While such estimates have always overstated the probability of proliferation in the past, the fact remains that three regional powers—India, Israel, and Pakistan—will have nuclear weapons by the mid-1980s. The Gulf is also one of the few areas in the developing world where sufficient surplus funds exist to fund proliferation or the purchase of nuclear weapons from a third party at a level that could make such sales highly tempting.

It is hardly necessary to speculate on the role that nuclear proliferation might play in the Iranian-Iraqi arms race, and any form of nuclear proliferation presents special problems in the Gulf. As is discussed in more detail in Chapter 19, the Gulf states are exceptionally vulnerable to nuclear attack. One well-placed bomb on a capital could destroy the national identity and recovery capability of most of the smaller southern Gulf states, and only five to seven such strikes could probably destroy the national identity of Iraq, Iran, or Saudi Arabia. This makes the Gulf states vulnerable to both nuclear attack and nuclear blackmail.

Further, as Table 17.6 and Map 17.3 show, attacks on a small number of targets can shut off a substantial amount of the West's oil and threaten the economic viability of the West and the Gulf states without necessarily inflicting large casualties on Gulf populations. Map 17.3 shows, for example, that even a nuclear attack on Ras Tanura, which is comparatively close to Dhahran, Al Khobar, Dammam, and Jubail, could halt a major portion of the West's oil imports while inflicting only limited collateral damage. Many other key targets, such as Kharg Island, would involve even fewer collateral casualties.

Nuclear proliferation already affects Gulf security. Israel has seriously planned for nuclear war, including strikes that would deny the Arabs the use of the "oil weapons" by destroying key Arab facilities, since the October War. Israel's 26-Mwe reactor at Dimona has been operating

TABLE 17.3 The Move Toward a Regional Nuclear Weapons Capability: Shifts Toward the "Kit" Stage of Rapidly Assembling Nuclear Weapons

Technical Capability	1980	1985	1990
Build enrichment plant	India Israel	India Israel Pakistan	India Israel Pakistan Egypt
Build small plutonium production reactor (2-5 bombs/year)	India Israel Egypt? Iran? Iraq? Pakistan	India Israel Egypt Iran Iraq Libya? Pakistan Syria?	India Israel Egypt Iran Iraq Libya Pakistan Syria
Access to significant amounts of divertible material from civilian fuel cycle	?	India Israel Pakistan?	India Israel Pakistan Egypt Iran Iraq Kuwait Syria
Operation of nucleal power plants and start of nuclear infrastructure	India Israel Pakistan?	India Israel Pakistan Iraq?	India Israel Pakistan Iraq Egypt Iran Kuwait Syria

Source: Adapted from Lewis A. Dunn, "Persian Gulf Nuclearisation: Prospects and Implications," in Hossein Amirsadeghi, ed., *The Security of the Persian Gulf* (New York: St. Martin's Press, 1981), pp. 85-100.

without safeguards since 1974 and produces about 8 kilograms of fissile plutonium, or at least 1.6 bombs' worth, per year. Israel probably now has about 143 kilograms of weapons-grade plutonium stockpiled from the reactors, and since Israel diverted some 168 tons of natural uranium from the European Atomic Energy Community (EURATOM) in 1968, it could keep Dimona operating for almost 20 years even without the new supplies it has since obtained from South Africa.[56] Further, Israel

TABLE 17.4 Illustrative Estimate of Nuclear Weapons Production Capability Affecting Small Nuclear Forces in the Middle East and South Asia

	India	Israel	Pakistan	Iraq[a]
End of Year 1980				
Safeguarded	270	0	30	0–1
Unsafeguarded	50	27+	0	0
Total	320	27+	30	0–1
End of Year 1985				
Safeguarded	442	0	48	1–5
Unsafeguarded	85	35+	0+	0–3
Total	530[b]	35+	48+	1–8
End of Year 1990				
Safeguarded	614	0	66	1–5
Unsafeguarded	250	43+	0+	0–8
Total	860[b]	43+	66+	1–13

[a] Predates raid on Osirak
[b] Total rounded

Note: A "bomb equivalent" is either 5 kg of fissile plutonium or 15 kg of highly enriched uranium. Material is limited to what can be enriched in country. Centrifuge processes are assumed to be highly restricted or unavailable. Laser enrichment is assumed to be too sophisticated to affect the output of the nations listed before 1990, an assumption that may be unrealistic in the case of Israel and possibly of India and Pakistan. Weapons-grade material is assumed to require the same levels of enrichment as in Western weapons, and plutonium to have less than 7% U-240. This seems a dangerously conservative assumption.

For India, the MAPP 1 reactor is assumed to start at the end of 1981, MAPP 2 at the end of 1985, MAPP 1 at the end of 1987, MAPP-2 at the end of 1989, and R-5 at the end of 1984. All Tarapur plutonium is assumed to be safeguarded throughout the 1980s. If this is not the case, then an additional 200–300 bomb equivalents of plutonium would be unsafeguarded. The "+"s for Israel and Pakistan indicate that additional bomb equivalents may be available through unsafeguarded enrichment plants, but the quantities are unknown. The estimate predates the attack on Tammuz 1 (Osirak), which was assumed to start operation in 1982. The range of uncertainty reflected the lack of knowledge of fresh fuel kept at Tammuz 1 and whether the reactor would be blanketed with uranium (natural or depleted).

Source: Adapted from Wurtele, Jones, Rowen, and Agmon, "Nuclear Proliferation Prospects for the Middle East and South Asia," Pan Heuristics, 31-109-38-597, Marina Del Rey, Calif., June 1981, Table 3.4. The comments on laser and centrifuge enrichment, and enrichment standards, reflect technical notes in the SIPRI yearbooks, especially 1982, pp. 281–289.

probably diverted weapons-grade material from the U.S. and obtained over 100 pounds of highly enriched uranium from a firm called NUMEC, which was processing material for U.S. Navy reactors.[57] This led Robert Kennedy to warn as early as 1965 that Israel was stockpiling nuclear weapons and the CIA to publicly conclude in 1974 that "we believe that Israel has already produced nuclear weapons."[58]

Although President Zia of Pakistan had denied that Pakistan will build a bomb, Pakistan's development of nuclear weapons would add another member of this club and open up the possibility of an "Islamic bomb." While various reports that Pakistan has been massively funded

TABLE 17.5 Illustrative Estimate of Advanced Nuclear-Capable Delivery Systems Likely to Be Deployed in the Middle East and South Asia

Country and Date	Weapons System	Numbers	Range with 2,000-lb. Payload (km, radius for aircraft)
Algeria (306/132)			
1982	MiG-23BM	40	390–720[a]
	Su-20	12	600
	MiG-25A	18	1,100
1990	MiG-27I	50?	500–1,100[a]
	MiG-23I	50?	500–1,100[a]
	Su-24	50?	322–1,800[a]
	SS-21	?	120
	SS-22	?	350
	SS-23	?	1,000
Egypt (429/232)			
1982	Tu-16	14	4,800
	F-4E	35	750
	Mirage 5	40	600
	F-16A	10	900
	FROG 7	12	15
	Scud B	12	160–280
1990	F-16A/C	150+	900+
	Mirage 2000	50+	460–1,480[a]
	Saqr "X" SSM	?	600+
	E-2C	?	n.a.
India (635/227)			
1982	MiG 23BN/UM	10	390–720[a]
	Jaguar GR-1	16	720
	Su-7MkBM	45	175–320[a]
	Canberra B(I)-58	45	1,100
1990	Mirage 2000	150	460–1,480[a]
	Jaguar (Imp)	100	1,000+
	MiG-23BN/UM	72	390–720
	SS-23 SSM	?	1,000
Iran (217/130?)			
1982	P-3F Orion MPA	2	1,500
	F-4D/F	30–70	750
1990	?	?	?
Iraq (330/115)			
1982	MiG-23BM	75	390–720
	Su-20	80	600
	Mirage F-1	36	750
	Tu-22	9	3,100
	FROG	19	15
	Scud B	9	160–280
1990	MiG-23I	100	500–1,100[a]
	MiG-27	80+	390–720
	Mirage F-1	72	750
	Mirage 2000I	100+	460–1,480[a]
	SS-22	?	350
	SS-23	?	1,000
	Il-26/NIMROD (AWACS)	?	n.a.

[a] Radius for Lo-Lo-Lo to Hi-Lo-Hi missions. Note that range is more than twice radius and that many aircraft can be refueled. Nations with suitable technical capability are assumed to up-engine aircraft by 1990 or improve range with conformal tanks and munitions.

Note: The figures shown in parentheses beside each country name are, first, the total number of combat aircraft operational and, second, the portion dedicated to the attack mission.

TABLE 17.5 (continued)

Country and Date	Weapons System	Numbers	Range with 2,000-lb. Payload (km, radius for aircraft)
Israel (634/n.a.)			
1982	F-15A/B	40	2,000+
	F-4E	138	750
	F-16A	66	900
	E-2C (AWACS)	4	n.a.
	E-707 (ECM)	4	n.a.
	Lance SSM	12	8–120
	Jericho SSM	?	480–600
1990	F-15E/B-Mod	75–150	2,000+
	F-4E/P-110	100	900+
	Lavi	50	350–700[a]
	F-16C/B Mod/XL	150–250	1,200+
	Jericho II	?	?
	Lance SSM	12	8–120
Libya (555/218)			
1982	Tu-22	7	3,100
	Mirage F-1AD	14	750
	Su 20/22	100	600
	Mirage 5D/DE	45	600
	MiG-23BM/U	32	390–720[a]
	MiG-25U	5	1,100
	FROG 7	48	15
	Scud B	70	160–280
1990	MiG-23I	200	500–1,100
	Su-24	150	322–1,800
	MiG-25U	60	1,100
	Mirage F-1AD	44	600
	SS-22	?	350
	SS-23	?	1,100
	Candid (AWACS)	?	n.a.
Pakistan (219/62)			
1982	B-57 Canberra	14	1,100
	Mirage 5PA	34	600
1990	F-16B/C	150	1,200+
	E-2C/Nimrod (AWACS)	?	n.a.
	Chinese SSM	?	600+
Saudi Arabia (128/65)			
1982	n.a.	n.a.	n.a.
1990	F-15E	?	2,000+
	F-15A/B	60	2,000+
	E-3A (AWACS)	5	n.a.
Syria (450/205)			
1982	MiG-23BM	62	390–720[a]
	Su-20	40	600
	MiG-21 Bis	100?	400+
	FROG 7	24	15
	Scud B	70	160–280
1990	MiG-23I	150–250	500–1,100
	Su-24	150	322–1,800
	SS-22 SSM	?	350
	SS-23 SSM	?	1,100
	Candid (AWACS)	?	?

Source: Numbers for 1982 are taken from, *The Military Balance, 1982–83* (London: IISS, 1983). Only modern attack configured or potential long-range strike aircraft are included. Estimates for 1990 include types now on order or logical orders.

TABLE 17.6 Major Oil-Exporting Facilities in the Gulf, 1979

Country	Facility	Capacity (MMBD)	Actual 1979 Throughput (MMBD)
Saudi Arabia	Ras Tanura	6.0+	
	Abqaiq	7.2	5.8
	Juaymah	3.0	2.4
	Zuluf	1.85	0.7
	Yanbu	-2.2 (1981)	
Iran	Kharg Island	5.1-6.0[a]	
Iraq	Al-Fao (Mina al-Bakr and Khor al Amaja)	(4.3)[a]	(2.4)[a]
	Pipeline to Turkey	0.7	0.6
	Pipeline to Syria	1.4	0.3
	Kirkuk stabilizers	1-1.5 per plant[a]	
Kuwait	Mina al-Ahmade	2.4	
Qatar	Halul	0.4	
UAE	Jabal Dhanna		0.86
	Das Island		0.56
	Fateh		0.36

[a]Pre-Iran-Iraq War

Source: Adapted from Wurtele, Jones, Rowen, and Agmon, "Nuclear Proliferation Prospects for the Middle East and South Asia," 31-109-38-597, Pan Heuristics, Marina Del Rey, Calif., June 1981, p. 74.

by other Islamic states such as Libya are rejected by U.S. intelligence officials, and most feel that Pakistan will have to stockpile its entire weapons production for at least five years to meet the threat from India, it may well be willing to trade weapons for large amounts of aid or even to supply a major ally like Saudi Arabia. This might be particularly true if Pakistan did get major outside funding to expand its facilities once it demonstrated that it actually had an initial nuclear capability.[59]

It is also impossible to dismiss the prospect of another type of "Islamic" effort, involving such combinations as Libya, Syria, and Iran. Libya's previous effort to create domestic nuclear facilities was farcical, and the ability of any group of Islamic states to cooperate in such an effort is uncertain. However, Israel's acquisition of nuclear weapons, its attack on Osirak, the growing competition between the superpowers in the Near East, and the search for military equalizers or security after the Iran-Iraq War will all increase the incentive for nuclear proliferation. Iranian physicists are already working with Syrian experts and with Libyan funding, although the effort is now small.[60]

It is difficult to see how even the start of any such effort, particularly one involving Iran or Iraq, could now avoid creating a nuclear arms race throughout the Gulf. While Iraq might well see such weapons as an equalizer against Iran's popular army, Iran would be almost certain

MAP 17—3
BLAST EFFECTS OF A 70-KT GROUND BURST ON RAS TANURA
WEAPON RADIUS AGAINST A 2005 TARGET

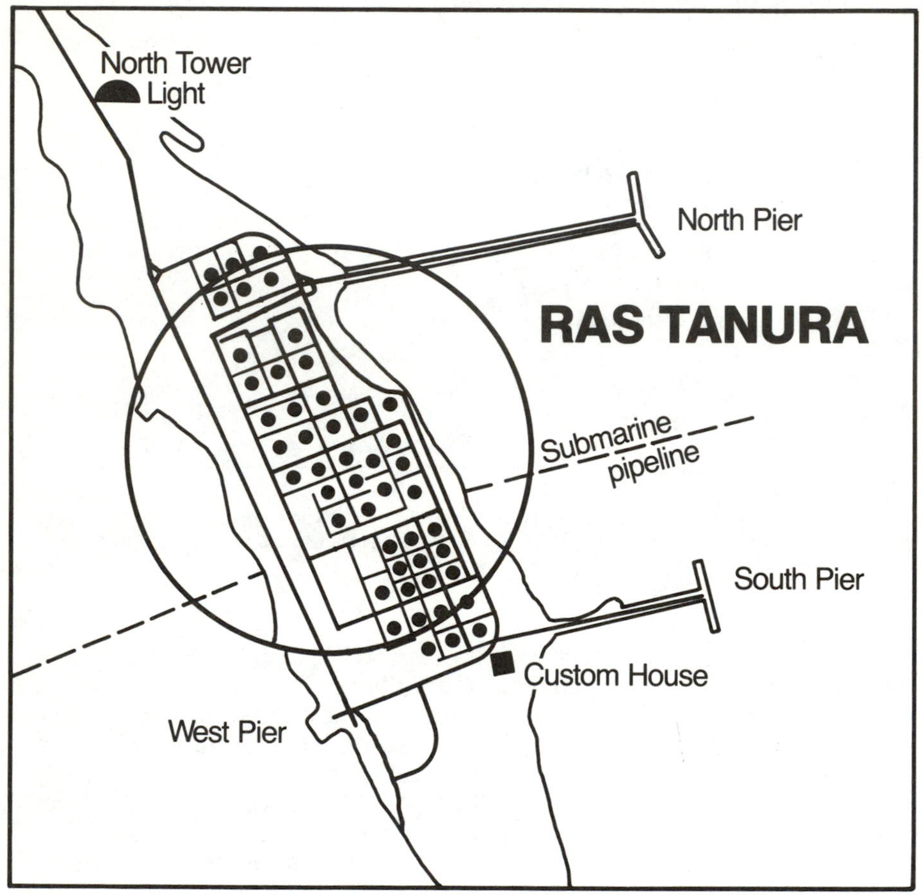

Adapted from Wurtle, Jones, Rowen, and Agmon, "Nuclear Proliferation Prospects," p. 7-6, and work by John Collins of the Congressional Research Service.

to seek its own nuclear weapons the moment it became aware that a serious Iraqi effort was under way. Saudi Arabia would probably then seek weapons from Pakistan, which would almost certainly lead to open Israeli deployment of a capability it has so far kept covert or to additional Israeli raids on any such nuclear facilities.

Fortunately, it seems doubtful that any proliferation can take place in a Gulf state before the mid-1980s. As a result, the West and the southern Gulf states can do much to plan contingency actions that would deter the use of such weapons, to improve the air defenses in the region, to discourage such proliferation diplomatically or through economic pressure, and to persuade the northern Gulf powers to find some other solution to their problems. These, in fact, must be major goals in dealing with the aftermath of the Iran-Iraq War and the future military buildup in the Gulf.

While it seems unlikely that any Gulf or regional power would use nuclear weapons except as an ultimate last resort, it is impossible to estimate the behavior of any future regime threatened with the kind of attacks that have characterized the Iran-Iraq War or to predict the pattern of nuclear escalation in future conflicts between the Arabs and Israel. It is also impossible to rule out the possibility that a Gulf nuclear power would use the threat of nuclear attack for political purposes or even use such weapons in comparatively low-level conflicts.

The Current Military and Political Probabilities

Speculations about the future of the Gulf are virtually always refuted by the ensuing events, and it should be clear from the previous discussion that this situation is not likely to change in trying to predict the results of the Iran-Iraq War. Nevertheless, it is equally impossible to avoid trying to summarize the current probabilities and their implications for the West and its allies in the Gulf. The major trends and probabilities that have emerged from Iran's victory at Khorramshahr may be summarized as follows:

- Iran will emerge from the war under a religious regime even if the morale of the troops at the front is crippled by continuing casualties. While there is increasing feuding among the clergy around Khomeini, and a division into traditional factions favoring the collective power of the clergy and a "Khomeini" faction favoring power for a single leader with some emphasis on land reform, the leftist militant and moderate factions have largely been suppressed. None of the various ethnic or dissident groups in Iran seem powerful enough to challenge the Persian religious leadership as long as it remains united.
- Iran's military forces will emerge from the war more a "People's Army" than a modern military power. Only about 50–100 of its fighters will be repairable and serviceable, many without full use of their avionics. Much of the advanced technology it has bought from the West, including many of its SAMs, ASMs, and sensors, will be nonoperational or have limited capability. It will take several years, and access to a major arms supplier, to change this situation, giving Saudi Arabia and the southern Gulf states a breathing space before any major direct Iranian military threat develops, although it will scarcely provide any protection against efforts at subversion.
- Iran's People's Army will pose a grave postwar (or interwar) threat to the southern Gulf states. Iran has developed massive cadres of highly

competent and experienced infantry and helicopter forces, which can conduct raids, train subversives, etc. This indirect threat to the southern Gulf will become extremely dangerous the moment the pressure of having to fight Iraq is removed. It is also unlikely that this threat can be avoided by southern Gulf aid or Iraqi reparations. If Iran accepts such aid, Iraq and the southern Gulf state will be under such pressure that they will have to continue paying even if Iran conducts extensive subversive activity. Any cease-fire or peace will, therefore, probably be followed by a growing security problem throughout the area.

• It is uncertain whether Iran will deeply invade Iraq or attempt to force Saddam Hussein's removal through political means. The Iranian Army has evidently advised that it lacks the resources for an invasion, but this may not determine the views of Iran's political leaders. If Iran does invade, Iraq may be able to hold defensively because Iran will lose much of its ability to exploit terrain and to use its infantry in the river plains, and it probably is only marginally superior to Iraq in armored maneuver. The outcome is still too close to call. Much will depend on Iranian ability to support continued offensives, on Iraqi ability to hold on in spite of a growing cash squeeze, on the casualty figures on both sides, on the political loyalty and will of the Iraqi forces, and on the extent to which the regular Iraqi Army and Air Force continue to learn from abroad.

• A negotiated peace cannot be ruled out, although Algeria virtually gave up its efforts to negotiate after the February 1983 offensive. Such a "peace," however, will come out of exhaustion, not commitment. Both states will remain enemies for years to come unless one forces the overthrow of the other's regime. "Peace" will mean political, economic, and revolutionary war and massive rearmament, not regional stability or even a lasting modus vivendi.

• It will take considerable luck for Saddam Hussein and/or the Takriti to survive even a military stalemate as the true nature of Iraq's losses, defeats, and economic situation become known. The extent to which this situation will precipitate the fall of the Baath party, as distinguished from changing its leadership, is uncertain. A shift to a Shi'ite religious regime seems unlikely and would probably lead to a civil war. It seems more likely that some form of secular regime will survive in spite of the threat from Iran, but that Saddam Hussein and the Takriti will be replaced.

• It seems unlikely that any new secular regime formed out of the various opposition fronts outside Iraq could long remain in power. The expatriate leaders and parties now openly opposing Saddam Hussein do not seem capable of leading the new Iraq that will emerge out of the pressures of the war. Even if they should temporarily gain power, it seems probable that any new secular regime will eventually be headed by the as yet unknown new military and political leaders who have emerged during the war.

• Most of Iraq's potential new leaders seem likely to preserve Iraq's current economic policy regardless of the language they use to describe it. However, a new regime will probably have to allow a higher degree of Kurdish autonomy or face renewed fighting. It will also have to compete with Iran and the southern Gulf states for oil sales, which may create new frictions between Iraq and its Arab neighbors.

• At a broader political level, Iran has already emerged as a major influence on the Shi'ites in Lebanon and throughout the Muslim world. Iran seems likely to continue to act as a powerful force in radicalizing Shi'ite movements and in supporting various insurgent and rebel groups. Much will depend on whether Iran works in concert with Syria and on the outcome of the present fighting in Lebanon, but Iran's influence seems likely to reach far beyond the Gulf.

• While some sort of Syrian-Iraqi-Iranian front may emerge out of the war, this seems unlikely to be more than an ephemeral political development. The historical, cultural, and political tensions among the three states are simply too great. Even the current coalition between Syria and Iran is inherently unstable, given Syria's secular regime and Iran's religious rule, although it is unclear that their present alliance against Iran will collapse. There is also a serious threat that Syria, Iran, South Yemen, Libya, Ethiopia, and the USSR will form some sort of loose coalition whose only true common interest will be to overthrow the conservative regimes of the southern Gulf and reduce Western influence in the region.

• Resupply will be a key indicator of the Gulf's military future. Iran may or may not choose to conduct a major high-technology arms buildup after the war. Some U.S. intelligence experts theorize that since Iran's present successes have come through a people's army, rather than high technology, and its ideology opposes high technology and Westernization, Iran will be satisfied to buy much more limited numbers of aircraft and tanks from a mix of Western and Eastern sources and avoid repeating the massive buildup that took place under the shah. Such a policy, however, would not allow Iran to compete with the advanced air defense forces and technology being deployed in the southern Gulf. It is also unclear how Iraq can avoid a massive arms buildup regardless of what regime is in power and how Iran can avoid competing. It seems far more probable that any "peace" will really be a pause for rearmament.

• If Iran does attempt to build up modern military forces, this may still push it into military dependence on the USSR, which is the only power aside from the U.S. capable of rapidly providing arms deliveries on the scale required. This dependence would threaten to eventually move Iran into the Soviet camp if the Iranian revolution should progress toward a counterreaction to religious rule.

• Iraq will also face a major resupply problem, and one thing is certain. If Iraq continues to depend on Soviet equipment and advice, it cannot rebuild its military strength in the near future. Its ability to learn from its mistakes, and to obtain the technical advice and support it needs, is dependent on access to European or U.S. arms. Since U.S. support is unlikely, Iraq may be forced to create some special relationship with France and to seek massive additional aid from its conservative neighbors. If it cannot create this relationship, it seems likely to be forced to turn to the USSR.

• Although there seems to be no urgent risk of nuclear proliferation in the Gulf following the war, the war will probably reinforce Iraq's interest in the bomb, and probably that of other Gulf states. Iran has already begun cooperation with Libya in a nuclear weapons effort. Coupled to the growing nuclear forces of Israel, and the nuclear developments in India and Pakistan, this interest seems likely to push the Gulf toward "nuclearization" in the late 1980s.

• Both Iran and Iraq face problems in repaying their war debts and restoring their economies and will have to compete sharply for oil sales. Both must pay for the acute economic damage suffered by each side. The direct costs of the war to Iraq have exceeded $2 billion per month since late 1981, and the indirect costs are probably in excess of $220 billion. Iran's direct costs may have exceeded $1.5 billion, and the indirect damage of the war, revolution, and civil war to its economy has probably exceeded $600 billion. Iran may be content with its new low-level economy and concentrate on revenue from oil exports rather than recovery simply because of the ideological preferences of its ruling clergy. However, it will still be forced into an "oil war" with the other Gulf states, and the competition for oil revenue may accelerate its attacks on Saudi Arabia and pressure on Kuwait.

• Iraq may be content to take aid from the southern Gulf states, but it too will have to compete for a share of the world's oil market and do everything possible to maximize its oil revenue. This need may force it into competition or conflict with the southern Gulf states regardless of what regime is in power and in spite of their aid and the construction of a pipeline through Saudi Arabia. An anti-Baathist regime, or even any successor regime to Saddam Hussein, might find it very tempting to renounce any debts to its wartime suppliers and join Iran in its "oil war." Both states will need money badly. It may not be possible for the southern Gulf states to buy peace, but they may be able to delay or diminish the threat to their security.

• In the long run, it also seems unlikely that any cease-fire or "peace" will be no more than the prelude to rearmament or revenge and that hatreds have been built up that will explode periodically into war even if one side does achieve "victory."

The ability of the West and the conservative Gulf states to deal with this situation will be determined largely by the extent to which they realize that the risks involved are not a passing phenomenon and that the best they can probably hope for is a pause in which to build up the collective defense capabilities of the southern Gulf states and to strengthen U.S. contingency capabilities to deal with any overt threat from Iran or Iraq. While Iran does not seem to be drifting into the Soviet camp, nothing about it indicates it will become pro-Western or an acceptable neighbor for the conservative Arab states in the Gulf region. Iraq now needs help from the conservative Gulf states, but there is little they can do but provide money and arms, and it is increasingly unclear that such aid will either preserve a friendly regime in the future or ever be repaid by the present regime's successor. There is little prospect that any serious links will be built up between Iraq and the U.S., or that the U.S. will provide the current Baath regime with the aid it needs to survive. It seems equally doubtful that Egypt can influence the situation.

The options open to the Gulf states and the West are, therefore, limited. They are not, however, in any sense bleak. Only the problem of subversion seems urgent, and this is a problem the conservative Gulf state seem fairly well equipped to handle. It will take Iran some years to become a major military threat, and this should be long enough for Saudi Arabia and the Gulf Cooperation Council to develop a combination of maritime and air capabilities that will deter any direct Iranian military action. It also should provide the time for the development of suitable U.S. contingency plans to help the southern Gulf states protect themselves against any threatening political upheavals in the northern Gulf states and even to deal with the possibility that some future Iranian or Iraqi regime might align itself with the Soviet Union.

Notes

1. Sources used in this section include John Keegan, *World Armies* (New York: Facts on File, 1979), pp. 325–336; Mark Hewish, Bill Sweetman, Barry C. Wheeler, and Bill Gunston, *Air Forces of the World* (New York: Simon & Schuster, 1979), pp. 158–167; Shirin Tahir-Kheli and Sheheen Ayubi, *The Iran-Iraq War: New Weapons, Old Conflicts* (New York: Praeger Publishers, 1983); various editions of *Jane's; The Military Balance* (London: IISS, various years); Otto von Pikva, *Armies of the Middle East* (New York: Mayflower, 1979), pp. 97–102; Mohamed Heikal, *Iran: The Untold Story* (New York: Pantheon, 1981); Alvin Z. Rubinstein, "The Soviet Union and Iran Under Khomeini," *International Affairs*, Autumn 1981, pp. 599–617; John Laffin, *The Dagger of Islam* (London: Sphere, 1979); Hossein Amirsadeghi, ed., *The Security of the Persian Gulf* (London: St. Martin's Press, 1981); Farhad Kazemi, *Poverty and Revolution in Iran* (New York: New York University Press, 1981); Michael M. J. Fischer, *Iran: From Religious Dispute to Revolution* (Cambridge, Mass.: Harvard University Press, 1980); "Iran: Two Years After," *MERIP Reports*, no. 98 (July-August 1981); "Khomeini and the Opposition," *MERIP Reports*, no. 104 (March-April 1982); William H. Forbis, *The Fall of the Peacock Throne* (New York: McGraw-Hill, 1981); Robert Litwak, ed., *Security in the Persian Gulf: Sources of Inter-State Conflict* (London: IISS, 1981); Avi Plascov, *Security in the Persian Gulf: Modernisation, Political Development and Stability* (Aldershot: Gower, 1982); Norriss S. Hetherington, "Industrialization and Revolution in Iran,"

Middle East Journal 36, no. 3 (Summer 1982):362–372; various books and articles by James Bill; Barry Rubin, *Paved with Good Intentions* (New York: Oxford University Press, 1980); Mohammad Reza Pahlavi, *The Shah's Story* (London: Michael Joseph, 1980); John D. Stempel, *Inside the Iranian Revolution* (Bloomington: Indiana University Press, 1981); Shaul Bakhash, *The Politics of Oil and Revolution in Iran*, Staff Paper (Washington, D.C.: Brookings Institution, 1982); William F. Hickman, *Ravaged and Reborn: The Iranian Army, 1982*, Staff Paper (Washington, D.C.: Brookings Institution, 1982); Fred Halliday, *Iran: Dictatorship and Development* (London: Pelican Books, 1979); P. Sciolino, "Iran's Durable Revolution," *Foreign Affairs*, Spring 1983, pp. 893–920; and a wide variety of media sources, including *Le Monde, Economist, 8 Days, Middle East*, and *Arabia: The Islamic World Review*.

2. *Chicago Tribune*, 27 May 1982. It seems likely that most transfers from Syria, Libya, and North Korea were confined to such comparatively easy items to transport as 130mm guns, ZSU-23-4 AA guns, and SA-7 missiles. Syria and Libya are reported, however, to have begun to airlift Soviet tank engines and parts in January 1982 to allow Iran to recondition the Soviet armor it captured from Iraq.

3. *New York Times*, 8 November 1982.

4. Ibid., 8 March 1982.

5. Ibid., 8 March 1982; 18 July 1983; *Washington Post*, 28, 29, and 30 May 1982; *Aviation Week*, April 1983.

6. *Christian Science Monitor*, 20 December 1982; *Time*, 25 July 1983, p. 26; *Chicago Tribune*, 23 June 1983; *New York Times*, 20 December 1982; 21 July 1983.

7. *Middle East*, August 1979, p. 16.

8. *New York Times*, 18 January 1982.

9. *Washington Post*, 16 February and 10 March 1982.

10. Ibid., 21 April 1982; *Economist*, 18 September 1982, p. 37.

11. *Christian Science Monitor*, 23 October 1982.

12. *Strategic Survey, 1981–82* (London: IISS, 1982), pp. 89–90.

13. *New York Times*, 21 November 1982; *Chicago Tribune*, 18 January 1983; *Economist*, 15 January 1983, pp. 35–36.

14. *Middle East*, December 1981, pp. 12–13; *Arabia: The Islamic World Review*, January 1982, p. 26; *Economist*, 13 February 1982, pp. 51–52; *New York Times*, 21 November 1982.

15. *Washington Post*, 9 February and 28 November 1982; 6 January 1983; Agence France Press, Tehran, 3 May 1982; *New York Times*, 18 January 1982; *Middle East*, February 1983, pp. 6–7; *Christian Science Monitor*, 27 July 1983.

16. *New York Times*, 30 June 1982; 10 January and 31 July 1983; *Middle East*, November 1982, pp. 18–20; February 1982, pp. 7–8; *Christian Science Monitor*, 27 July 1983; *Defense and Foreign Affairs*, May 1983, pp. 34–35; *Economist*, 21 May 1983, pp. 60–61.

17. *New York Times*, 7 March and 5 April 1982; *Middle East*, October 1982, p. 11; *Christian Science Monitor*, 12 October 1982.

18. *New York Times*, 21 April 1982.

19. Ibid., 28 June, 11 July, and 15 August 1982; *Baltimore Sun*, 15 August 1982; *Economist*, 18 September 1982, p. 37. The nature of the plot is uncertain, and Khomeini has used it, if it existed, to imprison or discredit many of his rivals. Iran also charged at one point that Prince Abdullah of Saudi Arabia

was implicated, although this charge seems to have been made largely for propaganda purposes.

20. See the *New York Times*, 19 February 1982; and *Washington Post*, 23 February 1982, for early reports; also *Christian Science Monitor*, 27 July 1983; and *Middle East*, February 1983, pp. 7–8.

21. *Christian Science Monitor*, 12 May and 1 July 1982; *Arabia: The Islamic World Review*, January 1982, p. 26; *New York Times*, 12 April 1982; *Middle East*, December 1982, pp. 12–13; February 1983, pp. 7–8.

22. Ibid.; *Jerusalem Post*, 11 June 1982, p. 7.

23. *Christian Science Monitor*, 12 May 1982.

24. *Washington Post*, 10 December 1982; *New York Times*, 11 December 1982; *Economist*, 18 December 1982.

25. *New York Times*, 19 April and 28 June 1982; *Christian Science Monitor*, 22 and 27 July 1983.

26. *Los Angeles Times*, 13 March 1982; *Chicago Tribune*, 12 May 1982; *8 Days*, 31 October 1981, pp. 54–55; *Washington Post*, 13 April 1982; *Economist*, 13 February 1982, pp. 51–52; *Wall Street Journal*, 1 August 1983.

27. *New York Times*, 15 December 1982; *Los Angeles Times*, 21 November 1982; *Wall Street Journal*, 7 and 8 July 1983; *Chicago Tribune*, 24 June 1983; *Washington Post*, 23 July 1983.

28. *Christian Science Monitor*, 28 April, 7 September, 8 and 15 November, 1982; *New York Times*, 23 February and 29 May 1982; *Arabia: The Islamic World Review*, January 1982, p. 43; *Wall Street Journal*, 9 November 1982.

29. CIA, *World Factbook*, 1981, pp. 92–93; 1983, pp. 104–105.

30. Ibid., 1981, p. 93; 1983, p. 104; *Chicago Tribune*, 12 May 1982.

31. *New York Times*, 20 January 1983.

32. See Alvin Z. Rubinstein, "The Soviet Union and Iran Under Khomeini"; and Muriel Atkin, "Tehran and Moscow," *New York Times*, 25 March 1982, for balanced discussion of Soviet influence in Iran. Reports of Soviet spy posts in Iran (*Time*, 8 March 1982, p. 32) have been denied by U.S. intelligence experts. For other recent background see Dusko Doder, "Soviets and Iran, Bolstering Strained Ties," *Washington Post*, 16 February 1982; and "Soviets Assess Tehran Ties," *Washington Post*, 10 March 1982; John F. Burns, "Soviet-Iranian Relations," *Washington Post*, 25 February 1982; Leslie H. Gelb, "East-West Rivalry for Influence in Iran," *New York Times*, 9 March 1982; Ralph Joseph, "Iran's New Clerics Tilt Closer to Moscow," *Christian Science Monitor*, 23 October 1981; R. W. Apple, "Soviet Influence in Iran Shows a Steep Decline," *New York Times*, 14 November 1982; *Middle East*, October 1982, p. 10; Shahram Chubin, "The Soviet Union and Iran," *Foreign Affairs*, Spring 1983, pp. 921–949; *Washington Post*, 2 and 5 May 1983; *Christian Science Monitor*, 28 March, 22 and 27 July 1983; *New York Times*, 12 May 1983; *Economist*, 14 May 1983, p. 55; *Los Angeles Times*, 23 June 1983.

33. Much of the material used in this section is taken from interviews in the Gulf, from interviews with intelligence and other officials in the U.S., UK, and France, and from various official and academic seminars and working papers in 1981 and 1982. Special recognition should be given to the contributions of Claudia Wright, Edmund Ghareeb, Phebe Marr, W. Seth Carus, and William Staudenmaier at these later sessions. Other sources include Keegan, *World Armies*, pp. 337–357; Hewish et al., *Air Forces of the World*, pp. 157–158; von Pikva, *Armies of the Middle East*, pp. 103–109; the sections on Iraq in Steve Weissman and Herbert Krosney, *The Islamic Bomb* (New York: Times Books,

1981); Richard F. Nyrop, *Area Handbook for Iraq*, Foreign Area Handbook Series (Washington, D.C.: American University, 1977); Amirsadeghi, *Security of the Persian Gulf*; the various books in the IISS *Security in the Persian Gulf* series cited earlier; and a wide range of news sources and publications.

34. W. Seth Carus, "Military Policy in Iraq," in Stephanie Neuman, ed., *Defense Planning in Less Industrialized States* (Lexington, Mass.: Lexington Books, 1983).

35. See Edmund Ghareeb, *The Kurdish Question in Iraq* (Syracuse, N.Y.: Syracuse University Press, 1981), pp. 172–175.

36. Keesing, *Contemporary Archives*, 6 October 1978.

37. This list is taken from a working paper by William O. Staudenmaier; Claudia Wright, "Iraq—New Power in the Middle East," *Foreign Affairs* 58, no. 2. (Winter 1979/80); Adeed I. Dawisha, "Iraq: The West's Opportunity," *Foreign Policy*, no. 4 (Winter 1980-1981):143–144.

38. Keegan, *World Armies*, pp. 337–351; Nyrop, *Iraq*, pp. 221–257.

39. See Keegan, *World Armies*. The unit count and deployment analysis are taken from Carus, "Military Policy in Iraq," and a working paper by William G. Staudenmaier, "A Strategic Analysis of the Iran-Iraq War," 9 December 1981.

40. CIA, *World Factbook*, 1981, pp. 93–94; 1983, pp. 104–106. Other sources indicate that the Kurds are well over 23% and that other non-Arab elements are much larger.

41. *Washington Post*, 6 and 29 July 1983; *Christian Science Monitor*, July 1983; *New York Times*, 24 July 1983; *Middle East*, October 1982, p. 11.

42. *New York Times*, 18 November 1982.

43. Edward Cody, "Kurds Join Other Rebels," *Washington Post*, 7 January 1982; *Washington Post*, 6 and 29 July, 2 August 1983; *Christian Science Monitor*, 14 July 1983; *New York Times*, 24 July 1983; *Middle East*, October 1982, p. 11; *Economist*, 29 January 1983, p. 30.

44. Johathan C. Randall, "Iraqi Opposition Groups Organize," *Washington Post*, 18 February 1982; Mordechai Abir, "A New Balance in the Gulf," *Jerusalem Post*, 11 June 1982, pp. 7–8; *Economist*, 19 June 1982, pp. 23–24; *Middle East*, October 1982, p. 11; *New York Times*, 18 November 1983; *Washington Post*, 2 August 1983.

45. *Washington Post*, 7 January 1982; *Economist*, 19 June 1982.

46. CIA, 630814 (U) 12-81. For typical recent on-the-scene reporting of Sunni-Shi'ite relations in Iraq see *Baltimore Sun*, 8 December 1982; *Washington Times*, 23 November 1982; and *New York Times*, 13 July 1982. Also see Hanna Batatu, "Iraq's Underground Shi'i Movements," *MERIP Reports*, no. 102 (January 1982):3–9, for a different view.

47. *Washington Post*, 28 June 1981; *Christian Science Monitor*, 30 June 1982; *MEED*, 2 July 1982, p. 11.

48. *MEED*, 2 July 1982, p. 10; *Middle East*, November 1982, pp. 18–19.

49. *Economist*, 4 December 1982; 29 January 1983, p. 30; *Washington Post*, 17 December 1982; *MEED*, 29 January 1983, p. 20; *Chicago Tribune*, 5 March 1983.

50. *Christian Science Monitor*, 14 May 1982; 20 and 31 January 1983; *Washington Post*, 17 May 1982; *MEED*, 19 February 1982, p. 10; Wall Street Journal, 16 December 1982; *New York Times*, 28 November 1982.

51. Ibid.; *Middle East*, December 1980, p. 25; December 1981, p. 60; *8 Days*, 24 October 1981, pp. 26–27, 35–36.

52. *MEED*, 28 January 1983, p. 19; 25 February 1983, p. 24; *Financial Times*, 11 May 1983; *Washington Post*, 17 December 1982; 16 March, 14 May, and 2 August 1983; *New York Times*, 7 and 24 July 1983; *Los Angeles Times*, 3 April 1983; *Wall Street Journal*, 16 December 1982; 5 July 1983; *Christian Science Monitor*, 20 and 31 January 1982; 3 August 1983; *Economist*, 5 and 12 February 1983.

53. This section summarizes the author's work in a section of a forthcoming book by Rodney Jones of the CSIS and draws on the results of several working papers and presentations at the seminars on proliferation that Jones and Samuel Wells of the Wilson Center held in 1982 and 1983. A wide range of other sources were consulted in writing this section. These include Roger F. Pajak, *Nuclear Proliferation in the Middle East*, Monograph 82-1 (Washington, D.C.: National Defense University Press, 1982); Rodney W. Jones, *Nuclear Proliferation: Islam, The Bomb, and South Asia*, Washington Paper No. 82, CSIS (Beverly Hills, Calif.: Sage Publications, 1981); Ernest W. Lefever, *Nuclear Arms in the Third World: U.S. Policy Dilemma*, (Washington, D.C.: Brookings Institution, 1979); Wurtele, Jones, Rowen, and Agmon, *Nuclear Proliferation Prospects for the Middle East and South Asia*, 31-109-38-5970 (Marina Del Rey, Calif.: Pan Heuristics, June 1981); Lewis A. Dunn, "Persian Gulf Nuclearisation," in Amirsadeghi, *Security of the Persian Gulf*, pp. 85-100; Paul Jabber, *A Nuclear Middle East: Infrastructure, Likely Military Postures, and Prospects for Strategic Stability* (Los Angeles: CACIS, University of California, 1977); Weissman and Krosney, *Islamic Bomb*; Robert E. Harkavy, *Spectre of a Middle East Holocaust: The Strategic and Diplomatic Implications of the Israeli Nuclear Weapons Program*, Monograph, Vol. 14, Book Four, University of Denver, 1977.

54. France announced on 12 January 1982 that it would provide only low-grade enriched fuel to Iraq. The 10% enrichment level is inadequate for nuclear weapons purposes, which require 20% enrichment. *Washington Post*, 13 January 1982.

55. Ibid., 8 December 1981, p. 17.

56. For a good, but pro-Israeli, summary of the evidence, see Weissman and Krosney, *Islamic Bomb*, pp. 105–128.

57. NUMEC was headed by Dr. Zalman Shapiro, a strong supporter of Israel, and was later fined $1.1 million for the loss of the material. The enriched uranium was processed as a gray powder or small pellets and was easy to transport. See *Middle East*, June 1980, for a worst-case analysis of this possibility, and Weissman and Krosney, *Islamic Bomb*, pp. 119–122, for a more balanced account.

58. *Prospects for the Further Proliferation of Nuclear Weapons* (Washington, D.C.: CIA, 4 September 1974), p. 1.

59. For a different view, which is largely Israeli, see Weissman and Krosney, *Islamic Bomb*, pp. 23–24, 28, 52, 59–61, 64, 88, 167, 172, 236–237, 313–314.

60. For a discussion of the Libyan effort, see ibid., pp. 23, 26, 52–60, 210–213.

18
The Military Threat from the Yemens, the Red Sea Nations, and Other Neighboring States

Developments in Iran and Iraq are the most immediate threat to Gulf stability, but other threats are developing in the Yemens, the Red Sea area, and Syria and Jordan. The developments in the Yemens are particularly important, but the growth of Soviet influence in Ethiopia, the instability in Sudan, the changing demographics of Jordan, and Syria's increasing role in Gulf politics may be equally important in the long run. South Yemen has approached the status of a Soviet client state, and North Yemen may follow. Developments in Ethiopia, Djibouti, Somalia, and Sudan could "radicalize" the southern coast of the Red Sea. Jordan is now stable, but Syria is not, and there is growing threat to the Gulf 's western flank.

The Problem of the Yemens: The Threat from the South

The key issue in determining the role the Yemens will play in the Gulf is the future political alignment of North Yemen. Unfortunately, there is no way to predict whether North Yemen will stay neutral, align itself with Saudi Arabia and the West, unite with South Yemen, or come under Soviet influence. It is typical of North Yemen's current political juggling act that President Saleh would visit Moscow to obtain more arms in October 1981,[1] hold yet another round of unity talks with South Yemen in November 1981, deploy more forces to guard the South Yemeni border, appeal to Saudi Arabia for emergency economic aid, and then break off the unification talks. Although Saleh now seems to be tilting toward Moscow for security assistance, he obtains arms from both the U.S. and the USSR and is seeking massive amounts of Saudi, other Arab, and Western economic aid. The game is still too uncertain to call.

MAP 18—1
THE YEMENS AND THE BAB EL MANDEB

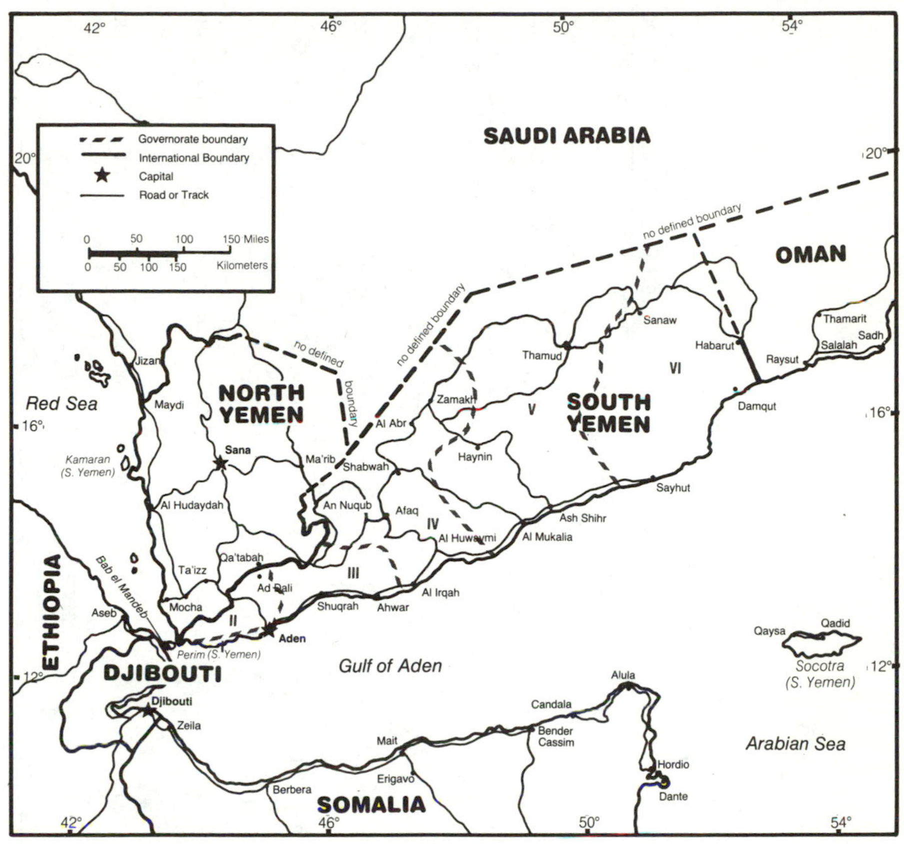

Adapted from CIA 501283 7-73

Military Trends in North Yemen

It is equally difficult to predict how soon North Yemen's growing military forces will acquire any real military effectiveness.[2] The recent trends in North Yemen's military buildup are shown in Table 18.1. These numbers are superficially impressive, but as was discussed in Chapter 13, North Yemen has never had the money and manpower resources to make its forces effective.

Any current count of North Yemen's military forces also has little meaning for the future. The ongoing deliveries of $1–1.5 billion in arms from the USSR (see Chapter 12) are producing massive increases in North Yemen's military equipment strength. The efforts of the growing

TABLE 18.1 The Military Buildup in the Yemen Arab Republic, 1973–1982

	1973–74	1974–75	1975–76	1976–77	1977–78	1978–79	1979–80	1980–81	1981–82	1982–83
Total population (millions)	7.0	6.4	6.5	6.9	7.0	7.3	7.5	5.3	5.4	7.2
Defense expenditures ($ millions)	13[a]	58	60	n.a.	79	n.a.	79	331	212	n.a.
GNP ($ millions)	460[a]	n.a.	n.a.	n.a.	1,200	1,500	3,800	4,490	n.a.	n.a.
DE as % of GNP[b]	n.a.	n.a.	n.a.	n.a.	6.6	n.a.	2.1	7.4	n.a.	n.a.
Total military manpower	20,900	26,900	32,000	39,000	39,850	38,000	36,600	32,100	32,100	32,050
Army										
Manpower	20,000	25,000	30,000	37,000	37,600	36,000	35,000	30,000	30,000	30,000
Equipment										
Medium tanks	30	30	30	30	30	220	232	864	704	714
Major types	T-34	T-34	T-34	T-34	T-34,54	T-34,54	T-34,54	T-34,54	T-54,M60	T-54,M60
Other AFVs	70	100	100	140	150	400	450	488	490	577
Major types	BTR-40	BTR-40	BTR-40	BTR-40	BTR-40	BTR-40	BTR-40	BTR-40	BTR,M-113	BTR,M-113
SP guns	50	50	50	50	50	50	50	50	50	50
Field guns/mortars	50	50	50	50	50	50	50	400	505	265+
AA weapons	100	n.a.	n.a.	37mm	37mm	37,57mm	37,57,mm	90 SP	96 SP	96+
ATWs	—	—	—	75mm RCL	Vigilant	20Vigilant	20Vigilant	20Vigilant	Vigilant,TOW	Vigilant,TOW
Missiles	—	—	—	—	—	—	—	—	—	SAMS
Navy										
Manpower	300	300	300	300	750	500	600	600	600	550
Total craft	7	5	5	5	8	8	10	10	11	13
Numbers/Types	5 patrol 2 landing	5 patrol	5 patrol	5 patrol	8 patrol	8 patrol	8 patrol 2 landing	8 patrol 2 landing	11 patrol	11 patrol 2 landing

TABLE 18.1 (continued)

	1973–74	1974–75	1975–76	1976–77	1977–78	1978–79	1979–80	1980–81	1981–892	1982–83
Air Force										
Manpower	600	1,600	1,700	1,500	1,500	1,500	1,000	1,500	1,500	1,500
Total Combat Aircraft	28	28	24[c]	28[c]	22	26	11	49	55	75
Fighters	12	12	12	12	8	12	3	49	55	75
Major types	MiG-17	MiG-17	MiG-17	MiG-17	MiG-17,21	MiG-17	MiG-17	Su-22	Su-22	MiG-21
Fighter-bombers	—	—	—	—	—	—	—	—	—	—
Major types										
Transports	1 sqn	1 sqn	n.a.	some	n.a.	6	14	11	11	11
Major types	C-47	C-47	C-47	C-47	C-47	C-47	An-26	C-47	An-26	An-26
Helicopters	1 sqn	1 sqn	—	n.a.	n.a.	3	3	15	27+	27+
Major types	Mi-4	Mi-4	—	Mi-4	Mi-4	AB-205	AB-205	AB-206	Mi-8	Mi-8
Other	16	16	22 trnrs	22 trnrs	22 trnrs	26 trnrs	26 trnrs	8 trnrs	8 trnrs	8 trnrs
Paramilitary Forces	20,000; tribal levies	20,000; tribal levies	20,000; tribal levies	20,000; tribal levies	20,000; tribal levies	20,000; tribal levies	20,000; tribal levies	20,000; tribal levies	20,000; tribal levies	20,000; tribal levies

[a]1970
[b]Calculated.
[c]Some aircraft believed to be in storage.
Source: The Military Balance (London: IISS, various years).

Soviet advisory team and the experience North Yemen's forces are gaining in fighting the National Front rebels should also produce significant increases in military effectiveness. At the same time, any improvement in actual military capability is likely to be slow and may be sufficient only to give the junta better control over North Yemen's tribes and the National Front. It is unclear that North Yemen's forces can achieve the level of professional military capability required to fight South Yemeni or Saudi forces. North Yemen's forces are now undertrained, under strength, and only about one-sixth literate. They are continuously drained of their skilled men, who leave for higher-paying jobs elsewhere in the Gulf.

North Yemen's Army. Some reports indicate that as many as 15,000 soldiers have deserted or left the army for jobs in Saudi Arabia during 1980–1982. The army has also experienced a high turnover in commanders for a variety of political reasons.[3] The North Yemeni army demonstrated poor unity and leadership during the fighting with South Yemen in 1979. The officers occasionally abandoned their men under fire, and the relationship between the staff in Sana and the units in the field was poorly organized and created serious morale problems. The army performed better in 1981, but it also faced less serious opposition from the National Front.

In late 1983, North Yemen's army was expanding into a force of six armored brigades (one a training brigade), one mechanized brigade, and nine infantry brigades (one a reserve unit). Twelve of these 16 brigades could be called active, although most were little more than reinforced battalions by U.S. standards. Eleven were Soviet advised, and one had both U.S. and Saudi advisers. The armor and mechanized units were relatively well equipped and have improved steadily relative to National Democratic Front forces since 1979, but they have serious manpower shortages and poor training, organization, and command. North Yemen also had a relatively effective parachute force, a guard force, and two commando units.

North Yemen had approximately 150 T-34, 500 T-54/T-55, and 64 M-60 medium tanks in inventory. It had 50 Saladin and Ferret armored cars, 12 M-106 mortar carriers, 90 M-113 APCs, 425 BTR 40/60/152 AFVs, and some Walid APCs. It had 5 independent artillery battalions, 250 76mm, 105mm, and 122mm multiple rocket launchers, and 200 82mm and 120mm mortars. It had two antiaircraft battalions armed with 72 M-163 Vulcan and 24 Soviet ZSU-23-4 antiaircraft guns. It had large numbers of SA-7s and Soviet-supplied antitank weapons, but only limited stocks of modern antitank guided weapons. Equipment maintenance was generally poor, with the exception of elite units, and overall proficiency was low.

The army's organization and staff procedures were heavily influenced by the Soviets at the top and had a more traditional character at lower echelons. Its commanders often acted more like feudal warlords than conventional army commanders. Training was weak except at the infantry level, and North Yemen's nominal "conscription" system continued to produce a low-quality manpower intake.

North Yemen's Air Force. Until major Soviet aid resumed in late 1979, North Yemen's air force was even less effective than its army. Maintenance problems were so acute that most planes were inoperative. As a result North Yemen's pilots received little flight time and experience with their machines. Recent deliveries and Soviet and U.S. training are correcting this situation, but the North Yemeni Air Force still lacks the ability to act as a coherent fighting forces.

In 1983 the Air Force was nominally organized into five fighter squadrons, based largely at Sana and Al Hudaydah. Two squadrons had a total of 40 recently supplied Soviet MiG-21s and another had 10 new F-5Es. These F-5Es are a result of the $390 million Saudi-U.S. arms deal funded in 1979, and lack the advanced avionics and munitions, such as the Maverick missiles, on their Saudi counterparts. North Yemen's other squadrons were equipped with 10 MiG-17Fs, which were barely flyable, and 15 Su-22s. Its transport and helicopter fleets were small and hampered by constant equipment and parts shortages. There was no modern air defense, except for a low-quality air defense regiment with 12 SA-2 launchers. Climatic conditions also caused serious problems in handling complex equipment, particularly at the main base at Al Hudaydah, and the lesser bases at Harib, Ta'iz, and Sa'dah.

It is unclear how this Air Force will cope with the arrival of additional MiG-21s and Su-22s. The Soviet advisory effort has been reasonably effective in making most of North Yemen's first-line fighters flyable and in improving basic training. Some units performed effectively against the National Front in 1981 and 1982, but the air force has little capacity to expand, and its overall capability seems likely to remain low through the mid-1980s.

North Yemen's Navy. The YAR's navy was barely able to carry out minimal coastal patrol and antismuggling missions in 1983, and it could not provide coastal defense. The 550-man force, based at Al Hudaydah, operated 2 Osa missile patrol boats with SS-N2b Styx missiles, 4 obsolescent, Soviet-supplied P-4 torpedo boats, 6 lightly armed patrol craft, and 2 light landing craft. Harbor facilities and equipment and spare parts holdings are limited, and the navy should experience little if any improvement in the foreseeable future.

Internal Security

North Yemen's internal security capabilities remained ineffectively clumsy, and oppressive in those areas under central government control. The National Democratic Front (NDF) remained active, with up to 5,000 guerrillas armed with Soviet weapons supplied by the PDRY, Libya, and Syria. Approximately 500 deserters from North Yemen's forces were included in this total. In contrast, North Yemen's 20,000-

man paramilitary tribal levies were as likely to oppose the government as to support it. Traditional tribal rule in the outlying areas also continued to be oppressive.[4] While some reforms are in progress, landowner and lender exploitation still divides the population into a "modern" faction, composed of the younger Yemenis who work as expatriates and in the "modern" service sector supported by expatriate remittances, and a traditional faction, composed of the declining traditional tribal rulers, merchants, and landowners.

North Yemen's main problems, however, lay in its economy. In addition to the problems discussed in Chapter 12, mismanagement of the nation's light manufacturing and service sector led to a serious recession in mid-1979 that still gripped the country in 1983. Remittances from foreign labor dropped from $1.5 billion in 1979 to $1.2 billion in 1980 and to $900 million in 1981, and they fell again in 1982.[5] North Yemen kept its currency overvalued and maintained a tariff and tax system that stifled internal development and led some 60–80% of North Yemen's major imports to be smuggled in from Saudi Arabia. As was discussed in Chapter 12, agricultural development remained limited, and smuggling crippled North Yemen's legal economy and deprived the government of key revenues. The smuggling issue also paralyzed the Saudi-Yemeni Cooperation Council and led to considerable tension between President Saleh and the Saudi minister of the interior, Prince Naif.[6]

The seriousness of North Yemen's problems was also indicated by the fact that its annual budget deficit exceeded $1 billion, and its overseas deficit grew to $662 million, or 25% of its GDP in July 1981. By September 1981, its foreign currency reserves had dropped to $883 million, a decline of 38% since July 1980. Even its 1982–1986 five-year plan projected annual deficits on current account of over $500 million through 1986. In 1980–1982, North Yemen's largest single export was biscuits, with a total annual value of about $3 million. Only income from expatriate workers and aid from Saudi Arabia and Kuwait kept North Yemen's economy and development plans from total collapse.

The development plans did have some success. The 1975–1980 plan provided vital infrastructure improvements and expanded its education program so that 37% of its youth attended school. However, the 1982–1986 plan had a projected cost of $6.5 billion and required at least $3 billion in grant aid. To make the plan work, North Yemen had to get 48% of the total cost in annual payments from Saudi Arabia, $150 million from other Arab states, $100 million from the West, and $200 million from sources ranging from COMECON to the World Bank.[7]

Such aid seems unlikely in view of the drop in Gulf oil revenues in 1982–1983, and it is unclear that it can keep Saleh's government alive even if it is forthcoming. As was discussed previously, the 1982–1986 plan concentrates on relatively grandiose projects and on making major changes in North Yemen's patterns of trade and agriculture. The Central

Plan Organization continues to overinvest in major projects and activities like the national airline, electric power plants, massive modern farming and irrigation projects, and inefficient state-run manufacturing and mining. The plan also requires imports to grow from $415 million (38% of GDP) in 1975–1976 to $2.1 billion (75% of GDP) in 1980–1981. The drop in oil income in 1982 has already reduced expatriate payments below the level called for in the plan, and North Yemen has little latitude for any drop in income. Living conditions remain so severe that the per capita was less than $800 in 1983, and the average life expectancy was only 42 years.[8]

Much will depend on how long President Saleh can sustain his complex juggling act and balance the conflicting interests of Moscow, Aden, and Riyadh. This, in turn, may depend on Moscow's calculations of the changes that South Yemen and the National Democratic Front will be able to seize the country and on the Saudi and U.S. response. North Yemen now owes the USSR over $700 million, and Moscow may prefer ties to Saleh to the uncertainties of civil war, but no one can guarantee that the PDRY will be held back by Soviet influence.[9]

In March 1982 the North Yemeni government arrested yet another group of "subversives" in Sana, and it was clear that the National Democratic (or Liberation) Front had started another offensive. Its leader, Sultan Ahmad Omar, claimed on 15 March that the NDF captured "hundreds" of prisoners and shot down two jet fighters. While these claims could not be substantiated, the NDF did attack government armored forces in Juban, early in March, and the fighting spread around Al-Bayda, Taiz, and Ibb. Saleh's troops seem to have repulsed these attacks and to have dealt the NDF a major setback, but Saleh's uncertainty regarding Soviet protection was indicated by the acceleration of his efforts to obtain British counterinsurgency aid in checking the NDF.

Major new arms shipments were discovered in November 1982,[10] and North Yemen's problems continued into 1983. North Yemen suffered an earthquake on 13 December 1982 that killed at least 1,500 people and caused $2.9 billion in damage. While North Yemen received extensive Saudi, Kuwaiti, and Japanese aid, the quake left 300,000 homeless. The quake came at a time when cuts in the number of jobs for foreigners in Saudi Arabia and the rest of the Gulf were reducing expatriate payments. Although Saudi Arabia evidently continued its economic aid to the central government, it is doubtful that this aid approached the $400 million level some sources reported, and Saudi Arabia seems to have given priority to payments to the Zaidi sheikhs in the north. These problems tended to reduce the government's financial ability to placate its opposition. They also accelerated the differences between the urban and younger Zaidi (who lost income) and the Zaidi sheikhs, and increased Shaafi tensions with the central government. While there had been no major new attacks on the government by mid-1983, the forces that had divided North Yemen since the coup against the imam again seemed to be on the upswing.

There is a good probability, therefore, that President Saleh's regime will be replaced by a more radical and pro-South Yemeni regime after 1985 or be forced into a firm alignment with the USSR and South Yemen. Such a regime could be more powerful than any previous government backed by Soviet aid. It might well complete the breakup of the tribal system, gain full independence from Saudi influence, and join with South Yemen, presenting a serious threat to both Saudia Arabia and Oman.

South Yemen: Arabia's "Heart of Darkness"

Although South Yemen's population of 2.1 million is about one-third of North Yemen's 5.7–7.2 million, South Yemen maintains a 26,000-man military force through a dual system of conscription and career service. South Yemen's radical government has also been more successful in centralizing state control. It has ruthlessly suppressed tribal loyalties and hostile political factions, and its forces do not face organized internal military opposition.

Military Forces

The PDRY's military buildup, shown in Table 18.2, has made South Yemen increasingly threatening to the conservative Gulf states and the West.[11] The PDRY's military forces have had combat experience in the NDF's 1979 campaign against North Yemen and in the Ethiopian campaigns against the Eritrean rebels. As many as 2,000 South Yemeni troops were deployed to Ethiopia in support of the government in 1978–1979. South Yemen has increasingly cooperated with other radical and Soviet-backed states. In August 1981 it signed a military alliance with Ethiopia and Libya. It has since exchanged observers at exercises and shared intelligence. It also has cooperated in backing radical causes and groups, including those as far away as Cuba and Nicaragua, although such cooperation seemed to decline slightly in 1982 and 1983.

South Yemen's forces, however, have significant problems. The effort to maintain centralized and highly politicized control of the armed forces has led to a long series of purges and defections. The selection of officers is often based on loyalty to the party rather than talent, and they often have limited leadership quality. Better Soviet-bloc training and increased numbers of Soviet-bloc advisers have, however, given South Yemen better military leadership than the YAR.

The South Yemeni Army. South Yemen's forces have absorbed an exceptionally large portion of South Yemen's total government expenditures and GNP. They have still been underfunded by Gulf standards, however, because the PDRY has remained one of the poorest nations in the region. The army is relatively well equipped and well trained, but it has suffered from purges, desertions, and a steady loss of draftage manpower due to emigration to Oman and Saudi Arabia.

TABLE 18.2 The Military Buildup in the People's Democratic Republic of Yemen, 1973–1982

	1973–74	1974–75	1975–76	1976–77	1977–78	1978–79	1979–80	1980–81	1981–82	1982–83
Total population (millions)	1.56	1.61	1.66	1.74	1.79	1.83	1.87	2.12	2.0	2.0
Defense expenditures ($ millions)	15.5[a]	41	n.a.	n.a.	43.7	56	124	124	n.a.	n.a.
GNP ($ millions)	140[b]	500[c]	n.a.	n.a.	224	500	997	997	n.a.	n.a.
DE as % of GNP[d]	—	n.a.	n.a.	n.a.	19.5	11.2	12.4	12.4	n.a.	n.a.
Total military manpower	9,500	14,000	18,000	21,300	21,300	20,900	20,800	23,800	24,300	26,000
Army										
Manpower	8,800	11,300	15,200	19,000	19,000	19,000	19,000	22,000	22,000	22,000
Equipment										
Medium tanks	50	50	50	200	200	260	260	375	375+	470+
Major types	T-34,54	T-34,54	T-34,54	T-34,54	T-34,54	T-34,54	T-34,54	T-34,54	T-54/62/34	T-54/62/34
Other AFVs	—	Saladins	Saladins	20	20	20	20	220	200	320
Major types				Saladins	Saladins	Saladins	Saladins	BTR-40	BTR, BMP	BTR, BMP
Field guns/mortars	some	105,122mm	25pdr,105mm	25pdr,105mm	25pdr,105mm	25pdr,105mm	25pdr,105mm	185	185	310
AA weapons	—	57,85mm	23mm,SP	23mm,SP	23mm,SP	ZSU-23-4	ZSU-23-4	140+	140+	140+
ATWs	—	—	122mm,RCL	122mm,RCL	122mm,RCL	122mm,RCL	122mm,RCL	122mm,RCL	122mm,RCL	?
Navy										
Manpower	200	200	300	300	300	600	500	500	1,000	1,000
Total craft	7	8	9	24	15	14	17	22	22	27
Number/types	2 subchsrs 2 minswprs 3 landing	2 subchsrs 3 minswprs 3 landing	2 subchsrs 2 MTB 3 minswprs 2 landing	2 subchsrs 2 MTB 3 minswprs 15 patrol 2 landing	2 subchsrs 2 MTB 3 minswprs 6 patrol 2 landing	7 patrol 2 MTB 3 minswprs 2 LCT	2 torpedo 9 patrol 3 minswprs 3 LCT	2 torpedo 11 patrol 1 minswpr 7 landing	4 torpedo 10 patrol 8 landing	6 FAC(M) 14 patrol 7 landing

TABLE 18.2 (continued)

	1973–74	1974–75	1975–76	1976–77	1977–78	1978–79	1979–80	1980–81	1981–92	1982–83
Air Force										
Manpower	500	2,500	2,500	2,000	2,000	1,300	1,300	1,300	1,300	3,000
Total combat aircraft	20	39[e]	27[e]	27[e]	33[e]	34[e]	109	111[e]	118	114
Fighters	15	12	12	12	12	12	50	40	36	36
Major Types	MiG-17	MiG-21	MiG-21	MiG-21	MiG-21	MiG-21F	MiG-21F	MiG-21F	MiG-21F	MiG-21F
Fighter-Bombers	12	27	15	15	15	15	47	59	74	70
Major types	Jet Prvst	MiG-17	MiG-17	MiG-17	MiG-17	MiG-17	MiG-17	MiG-17F	MiG-17F	SU-20/22
Bombers (light)	—	—	—	—	6	7	12	12	8	8
Major types					Il-28	Il-28	Il-28	Il-28	Il-28	Il-28
Transports	8	4	4	7	7	7	7	7	7	7
Major types	C-47	An-24	An-24	Il-14	Il-14	Il-14	Il-14	Il-14	Il-14	Il-14
Helicopters	6	8	8	8	8	8	8	14	14+	23+
Major types	Bell 47G	Mi-8	Mi-8	Mi-8	Mi-8	Mi-8	Mi-8	Mi-8,24	Mi-8,24	Mi-8,24
Other				3 trainers	3 trainers	3 trainers	3 trainers	3 trainers	3 trainers	3 trainers
Paramilitary forces	—	Popular Militia	Popular Militia	Popular Militia; 1,500 Public Security	Popular Militia; 1,500 Public Security	Popular Militia; 15,000 Public Security	Popular Militia; 15,000 Public Security	Popular Militia; 15,000 Public Security	Popular Militia; 15,000 Public Security	Popular Militia; 15,000 Public Security

[a]1971
[b]1970
[c]1972
[d]Calculated
[e]Some aircraft believed in storage
Source: The Military Balance (London: IISS, various years).

The 22,000-man army is organized into major service branches (armor, infantry, artillery, etc.), and its combat units are organized into 12 brigades: 1 armored, 1 mechanized, and 10 infantry. Each infantry brigade has a tank squadron of 12–18 T-34, T-55, or T-62 tanks. Three of these brigades are deployed near Oman, and nine near the border with North Yemen. Each has three combat battalions, an artillery battalion, and a small antiaircraft unit. The army also has a SAM regiment and a number of independent and supportive units that can be attached to parent units with relative ease.

The authorized manning of each brigade is about 1,500, with 300 men per battalion. Most, however, were at only 30–40% of authorized strength at the end of 1982, and even the best unit had only 1,200 men. About 60% of their manpower is conscripted, and conscription has created serious disciplinary problems.[12] It has also, however, improved the PDRY's manning levels over the last three to four years. Actual manning was only 300–500 men per brigade in 1978, versus 1,500 in 1983.

There are now three to five Soviet advisers per brigade, with one per combat battalion, one in the artillery regiment, and one in some of the tank squadrons. There are now about 1,000 Soviet military and civilians with the PDRY army, plus some East German and Cuban training companies and squadrons.[13] Training is conducted primarily at the unit level, and emphasis is placed more on small-unit training. The majority of technical and advanced officer training is done in the Soviet Union, and it involves extensive political indoctrination at all levels.

The army's organizational structure has reasonable flexibility, because battalions and other unit elements can be interchanged, and support units and the units of other combat arms can fit into the various brigade organizations, either organically or as attachments. The army has plans to expand from 22,000 to 40,000 men by 1985, but it is unlikely to achieve this goal.

Mobility is acceptable, despite the lack of good roads in the interior, and has been aided by the high rate of mechanization experienced in past years. South Yemen's inventory now includes 470 T-54/55 and T-62 medium tanks.[14] This tank inventory is smaller than that of North Yemen, but South Yemen is able to use its armor more effectively. South Yemen has a score of British Saladins and Ferrets and nearly 200 old 25-pounders and 105mm pack guns. Soviet equipment, however, is steadily replacing these last vestiges of the army's past ties to Britain. The army now has some BMP mechanized combat vehicles, 300 BTR-40 and BTR-152 APCs, 350 85mm, 100mm, and 130mm guns, 122mm BM-21 multiple rocket launchers, 120mm and 160mm heavy mortars, and FROG-7 rocket launchers. It also has a large number of towed and self-propelled AA guns, including the ZSU-23-4, and Soviet SA-2, SA-7, and SA-9 surface-to-air missiles. Its antitank capability is limited and includes a few antitank guns and older Soviet ATGMs.

The South Yemeni Air Force. The air force is the branch of South Yemen's forces that is most dependent on Soviet-bloc personnel, but it is reasonably effective. Some of its 113 combat aircraft are relatively old, but much of the force is modern, and the air force is relatively well trained and maintained. It seems capable of controlling indigenous airspace, providing tactical support for the ground forces and providing air transport.

Its combat elements are organized into a squadron of 10 Beagle light bombers and seven squadrons of fighter ground-attack planes. Two have a total of 30 MiG-17Fs, one has 12 MiG-21s, and another has 25 Sukhoi Su-20s and Su-22s. The PDRY would like to phase out its MiG-17s, and it is considering selling them to Nicaragua and replacing them with MiG-21s. The interceptor force has the remaining three squadrons and a total of 36 MiG-21Fs. A squadron of 15 MiG-23BMs is located near Aden, but it seems to be flown and maintained entirely by Soviets and dedicated to the defense of Aden, the capital city. Many of South Yemen's other combat and transport aircraft are evidently flown by Soviet and Cuban volunteers. Air transport capabilities include a squadron of four Il-14s and three An-24s. There is also a helicopter force of a few Mi-4s, 30 Mi-8s and 15 Mi-24 assault helicopters. There are a number of aircraft in storage, and one South Yemeni MiG-17 squadron. Up to 1,000 PDRY troops may still be in Ethiopia. The PDRY Air Force is now based mainly at Kormaksar and Beihan, but new bases are being built at Tahmud and Al Ghaydah.[15]

The South Yemeni Navy. The South Yemeni Navy has undergone considerable improvement in recent years, although it remains the least developed of the PDRY's armed forces. The navy lacks the ability to cover the vast sea area around Aden, but the 1,000-man force has one converted Soviet T-58 minesweeper, and six ex-Soviet Osa-class fast attack craft, four of which have Styx missiles. It also has a pair of SO-1 large patrol craft, two P-6 and two Mol fast torpedo boats, four fleet auxiliary craft, a pair of Zhuk-class patrol boats, a Pozharny-class harbor patrol craft, and a handful of support and landing vessels.

The navy's bases at Aden, Al Mukalla, and Socotra are slowly improving.[16] Officers and technicians are sent to naval schools in the Soviet Union, which provides spare parts and resupply. Soviet officers are present on most South Yemeni ships, and many of the harbor pilots in Aden are Russian. The Soviets also actively patrol South Yemeni waters with ships and aircraft and use facilities in the port of Aden, where further naval facility construction is under way.

Militia Forces and Internal Security

South Yemen has a 15,000-man People's Militia and internal security force to supplement the army, provide internal security, and act as a secret police. The militia formerly had PRC training, but the advisory effort is now led by cadres from East Germany. Trainees are usually tribesmen and local peasants, who serve in a military and also a civilian role and are responsible for the indoctrination of the populace. Many act as the directors of village administrations and cover such areas as defense, education, and economic and legal direction.

Although the PDRY is an effective police state, the Ali Nasr regime does have some internal security problems. It continues to regularly execute deserters, economic saboteurs, smugglers, and "gangs of subversion" and often accuses these of being CIA or Saudi agents. Ali Nasr has also had problems with his defense ministers. His ex-defense minister and first deputy prime minister, Col. Ali Antar, has been a particular problem. In spite of Ali Antar's ouster from power, he was shifted to managing local government, evidently because he had strong ties to South Yemen's Dahla tribes that kept him from being eliminated.[17]

The current defense minister, Brig. Gen. Salih Muslih Qassim, may also be a problem. Since 1981, he has steadily identified himself with the hard line of former President Ismail and is close to military supporters of Ali Antar. He was conspicuously out of the country when the head of the Soviet Navy, Admiral Sergei Gorshkov, visited South Yemen in April 1983. There also were increasing rumors that Qassim did not support Ali Nasr's suppression of the Voice of Oman Revolution, a PDRY-backed front broadcast from Aden, when South Yemen ratified its agreement with Oman on 6 November 1982, and that he opposed Ali Nasr's increasing economic cooperation with Kuwait and Saudi Arabia.

Nevertheless, the Ali Nasr government seems in control. It reduced the level of tension among the regular armed forces, the People's Militia, and the security forces in 1982. East German experts now seem to operate much of the internal security effort in Aden and the other urban areas, and they have reduced the use of violence, the erratic character of security operations, and the tendency to randomly purge members of the militia and armed forces. Further, regardless of any problems with Qassim, Ali Nasr seems to have had good talks with Admiral Gorshkov and continued to obtain aid from the USSR. Gorshkov's visit seems to have led to promises of more arms, and the minister of industry, Abd al-Qadir Ba Jammal, obtained promises of additional aid in industry and oil during a visit to Moscow in July 1983. As a result, it is likely that South Yemen will remain dependent upon the USSR in spite of its recent shift toward trade with the West. South Yemen needs Soviet military equipment and advisers, and it seems doubtful that South Yemen could make its economy viable, or even service its debts, if it had to compete on market terms. Further, Ali Nasr Muhammad seems strongly pro-Soviet and heavily dependent on his Soviet advisers.[18] These factors seem to ensure that South Yemen will remain a client state of the USSR, even if further purges take place within its leadership.

External Relations

This climate offers little prospect of regional stability and makes it difficult to predict how either North or South Yemen will align itself with other states. South Yemen has stuck to its agreements with Oman. It not only has kept its peace agreement, but restored full diplomatic relations in October. South Yemen also obtained Kuwaiti aid in exploring the oil potential of the Belhan region in the Shabwa governorate in June 1983 and exchanged ambassadors with Saudi Arabia in July for the first time since November 1977. It is impossible to know, however, whether this is a temporary expedient because of economic hardship or a serious long-term shift in policy.

As for North Yemen, the short-term trends also seem good. North Yemen has taken a steadily more anti-Iranian line as Saudi support of Iraq and Soviet problems with Iran have led the policies of North Yemen's principal sources of aid to coincide on the Iran-Iraq War. The Iranian daily, *Jomhuri-ye Eslami*, in its 29 March 1983 edition launched a major attack on North Yemen as having "sold out" to Saudi Arabia. In contrast, South Yemen has continued to back radical causes everywhere except in the Gulf, and it signed a letter of understanding with Iran in July 1983 to use its refinery in Aden to refine the oil Iran could not handle because of the destruction of its facilities in Abadan.

North Yemen's need for outside aid, and its fear of Iranian influence over its Zaidi Shi'ites, have led it to maintain close relations with Iraq and the conservative Gulf states. On the other hand, South Yemen continues to back Iran, and its recent friendly relations with its conservative neighbors may prove little more than a temporary expedient. If Saleh should fall or North Yemen should come under NDF or PDRY influence, North Yemen could suddenly tilt toward Iran and the support of radical movements in other Gulf countries.

Threats from the Red Sea and to the West

Most of the nations on the southern and western periphery of the Gulf states do not pose an immediate threat to the conservative Gulf states or the West's supply of oil imports. Sudan, Egypt, Jordan, and Djibouti are now pro-Western. Although they are scarcely stable, they do not seem likely to become radical or drift into the Soviet camp in the near future. Two states are, however, areas of potential concern: Ethiopia and Syria.

The Problem of Ethiopia

It is unlikely that Ethiopia will pose a short-term threat to Saudi Arabia. It has concentrated on its internal problems in recent years and sharply reduced its low-level border conflict with Sudan in June 1982. It does continue to back anti-Somali rebel groups, but it is possible Soviet use of Ethiopia as a staging area for the deployment of Soviet

MAP 18—2
THE RED SEA

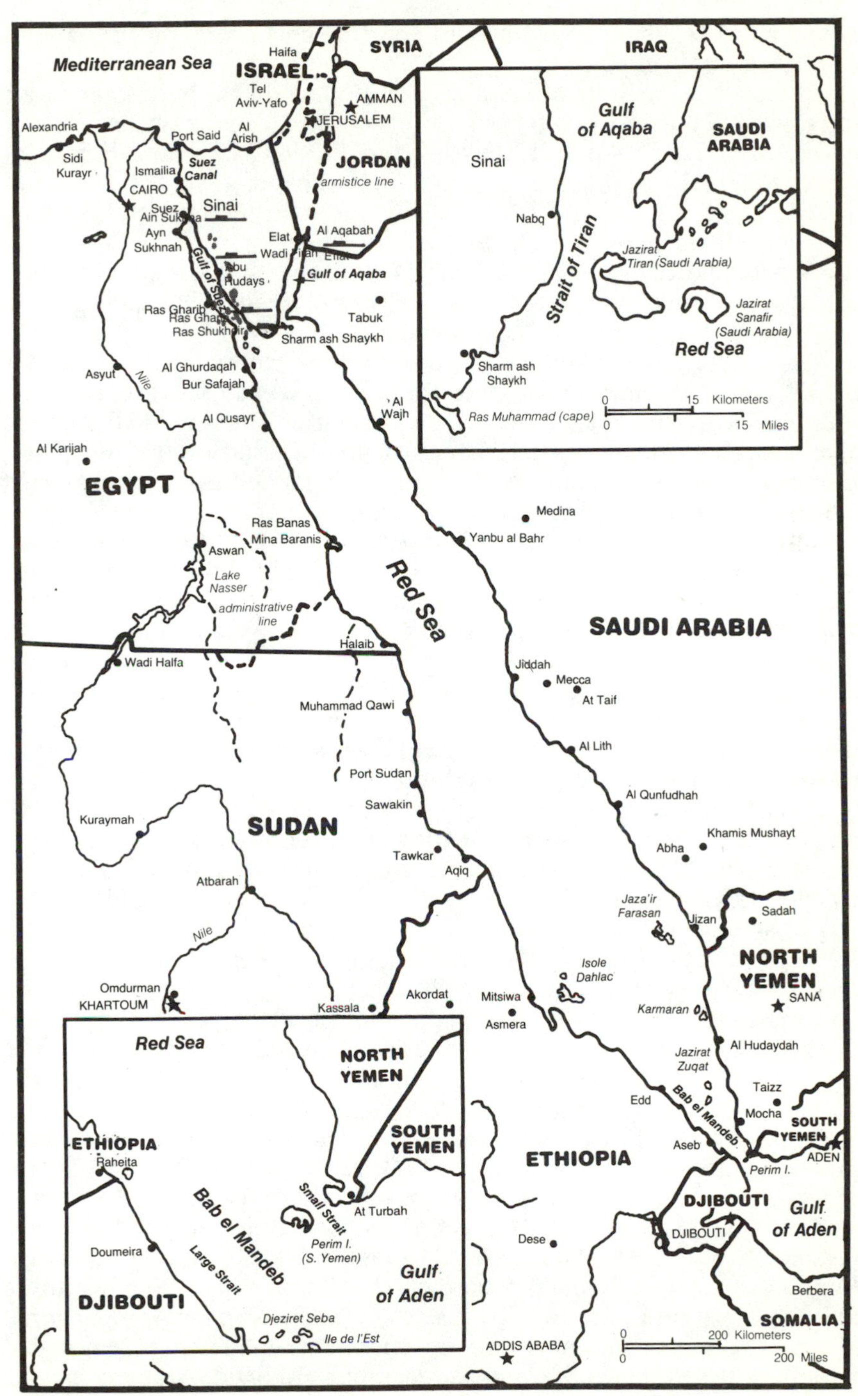

Adapted from Defense Mapping Service 504306 9-79 (541978)

or Cuban forces that seems likely to pose the greatest threat to the Gulf through the late 1980s.

Ethiopia's current air capabilities are modest. It has a 3,500-man air force with about 107 combat aircraft. These include an awkward mix of 10 MiG-17s, 65 MiG-21 shukois, and 20 MiG-23s. The Ethiopian Air Force (EAF) also has a limited COIN capability with T-28As and a few Saab T-17s. It has fairly extensive air transport resources, which include 14 An-12, 4 An-22, and 20 other medium- and long-range transports and 32 Mi-8 and 24 Mi-24 helicopters. Most of Ethiopia's remaining Western aircraft were put into storage in 1982–1983.

Many EAF aircraft now have "volunteer" pilots from Cuba, North Korea, and the Soviet bloc, and Ethiopian aircraft are critically dependent on 300 Soviet technicians for maintenance. Soviet advisers are, however, training large numbers of Ethiopian personnel, and the EAF may be able to deploy as many as 150 modern fighter aircraft by the late 1980s. Ethiopia is also expanding its helicopter lift capabilities and acquiring attack helicopters. Further, it is developing substantial air base facilities along the Red Sea coast. As a result, it may be able to challenge Saudi air capabilities in the Red Sea region by the mid-1980s or to support the PDRY. Soviet air units could deploy rapidly to Ethiopian bases.

Ethiopia may also develop a significant navy by Red Sea standards. While most of its U.S.-supplied ships are no longer operational, it now has nine large patrol boats, four OSA-II missile patrol boats with Styx, and more Soviet-bloc missile craft on order. It is improving its naval bases at Massawa and Assab, and these bases can now support a substantial Soviet naval presence.

It is difficult to make any prediction of how soon Ethiopia can free its land or air forces from the fighting with the Eritrean rebels, or the forces it now has to commit to checking the threat from Somalia. It is equally difficult to predict the extent to which Ethiopia would support Soviet action in the Red Sea or the Gulf. Ethiopia did not do well in its 1982 campaign—the "Red Star" campaign—against the Eritrean rebels, which was expected to be decisive. It used 90,000 of Ethiopia's 244,500 troops, backed by Cuban and Soviet advisers. They used half of the nation's 790 medium tanks and advanced on four fronts. The ELF, however, held its "capital" of Nakfa in Ethiopia's Sahel province; as many as 20,000 Ethiopian troops were killed while the ELF lost only 5,000; and the fighting continued at the end of 1983.[19] Ethiopia may have few forces free to threaten the Gulf as long as the 29-year-old war drags on and Saudi Arabia continues to fund the ELF. There are, however, some 11,000–16,500 Cuban troops, Soviet military and technical personnel, and 550–3,000 East Germans in the country.[20] Further, Ethiopia did attack Somalia's border in 1982, and its potential future military capabilities are so high that the West and Saudi Arabia cannot afford to ignore them. Saudi Arabia must plan for the contingency that Ethiopia's ties to the USSR and its resentment of Saudi Arabian backing of Somalia and the Eritrean rebels might lead it to put military pressure on Saudi Arabia's southern flank.

The Problem of Syria

Syria poses an equal threat to the Gulf. Its emergence as a dominant military power in the Levant is increasingly driving Jordan to seek Soviet arms or other sources of advanced weapons to compensate for the growth of Syria's forces. As was discussed in Chapter 17, Syria also poses a considerable threat to the key commercial lines of communication to the Gulf, to Iraq's oil pipelines and facilities, to Iraq, and to Saudi Arabia and the other states in the western Gulf. Its alignment with Iran and Libya, its developing ties to South Yemen, and its growing ties to the Soviet bloc raise the possibility that Syria might put pressure on the Gulf states to use their oil weapon, become a Soviet base, and/or forge an alliance with Iran. There is no doubt that its military capabilities (discussed in more depth in Chapter 20) are significant by Gulf standards.

Jordan

There are no current indications that Jordan is becoming hostile to Saudi Arabia. Quite to the contrary, Jordan has moved steadily closer to Saudi Arabia and the U.S. as it has searched for a peace with Israel and aid in countering Syria's growing military power. Jordan is, however, becoming more "Palestinian" in terms of demographics and politics. Jordan's total population is now about 3.16 million, with 2.34 million on the East Bank and 821,000 in the Israeli-occupied territories. Its East Bank population is growing at a rate of 3% by birth or marriage.[21] The days when Jordan's armed forces could be largely recruited among and officered by Bedouin are long over. Jordan increasingly recruits most of its military personnel from the Palestinian, or Palestinian-related, part of its population. By the mid-1980s, Jordan will have largely "Palestinian" forces, and it must recruit most of its civil service from these same sources.

These changes may mean little in the short run. Jordan's Palestinians have shown few recent signs of disaffection from the king, and Israel's recent invasion of Lebanon and Syrian pressure greatly weakened the PLO. Still, Jordan's political and strategic posture depends heavily on the life of one man. An assassination, a coup attempt, or death from natural causes could conceivably trigger events that would make Jordan a Palestinian state in political leadership as well as population. Although Crown Prince Hassan is popular and has proved highly competent, a coup might bring a much more radical regime to power, or one less sympathetic toward ties to Saudi Arabia and the U.S. Even King Hussein might be forced to turn away from the U.S. if President Reagan does not make progress in resolving the Arab-Israeli conflict. No strategic analysis of the Gulf can, therefore, ignore the fragility of Saudi Arabia's most important conservative buffer, and the fact that Jordan "looks two ways." The problem of Jordan's future is critical to both the Arab-Israeli conflict and the Gulf.

Sudan, Somalia, and Djibouti

The remaining Red Sea and Horn nations are not immediate military or political threats to Gulf or Western interests. All, however, are of growing strategic importance and present potential problems for the Gulf and the West. Sudan is undergoing a serious long-term economic crisis, and it has had significant problems with Libya. Somalia faces equally serious problems with its economy, must cope with a large refugee population, and faces a growing threat from a hostile Ethiopia and various rebel groups. Although Djibouti has held together surprisingly well since it became independent from France, it is a logical target for Ethiopian expansion and Soviet efforts to remove the French presence from the Red Sea area.

Sudan. Sudan's security problems acquired a high profile in early October 1981. Minor Libyan incursions into the country, which grew out of Libyan military intervention in the civil war in Chad, coincided with the assassination of President Sadat.[22] President Nimeiri of the Sudan capitalized on this situation to seek increased military and economic aid and to crack down on his internal opposition. Although the Libyan "threat" consisted of a few propeller-driven trainers that made minor air attacks on Chadian refugee camps, President Nimeiri claimed that Libya was preparing to invade Sudan and that Sudan faced an urgent air threat. Egypt supported these claims as part of its effort to get increased U.S. military aid. The U.S. responded by sending E-3A aircraft to Egypt and by promising Sudan increased military assistance, in an effort to check Qadaffi and demonstrate U.S. support of Egypt in the wake of Sadat's assassination.[23] The U.S also provided $100 million in additional military aid in FY1982, plus another $100 million in economic aid, and promised accelerated delivery of U.S. weapons. It made plans to provide $100 million in foreign military sales in FY1983 and FY1984, plus $75 million in MAP aid in FY1983 and $60 million in FY1984, of which $50 million was to be forgiven. This aid was to be used to buy more F-5 fighters, antiaircraft weapons, radars, patrol boats, and spares. Egypt and Saudi Arabia agreed to provide substantial additional military aid, and the U.S. agreed to train 490 Sudanese officers in Sudan and 120 in the U.S.[24]

Nimeiri had good political and economic motives for turning the border incident into a major Libyan invasion threat. Sudan had made little progress in development and had undergone a major increase in population. By October 1981, it was $3 billion in debt, and when the Libyan "crisis" began, it could not repay $250 million in overdue loans and faced major problems with the IMF. Sudan faced the prospect of an even bleaker future in the mid-1980s. Its balance-of-payments deficit was projected to exceed $1 billion a year, and some 85% of its foreign income already had to be used for fuel. Inflation was over 50% per year, unemployment was chronic, and much of its labor force had to emigrate to survive. Nimeiri was able to capitalize on the Libyan crisis to get $95–125 million annually in Economic Support Funding during FY1982–1984, $23–27 million annually in development aid, and $27–51 million in P.L. 480 food aid.[25]

Further, Nimeiri's political motives were those of one of the world's great political survivors. Nimeiri had experienced some 12 coup attempts since 1969, and he used the Libyan threat as a cover for nearly 10,000 arrests in October 1981. He also used the incident to whip up patriotic feeling, to bridge divisions between the "Arab" north and "African" south, and to push Egypt toward unification talks that were designed to help support his grasp on power.

Nimeiri used the same Libyan threat again in 1982 and 1983 in the face of worsening regional splits and growing tension between the Dinkas and the other tribes in the southern Sudan. He timed a February 1983 visit by his foreign minister, Mohamed Mirghani, to coincide with congressional problems with the Reagan administration's FY1984 aid request, and the foreign minister then proceeded to attack the Libyan buildup on the Sudan's border. This situation became somewhat embarrassing when the administration disclosed that it had diverted four AWACS from an exercise to cover the Libyan buildup at Egypt's request. Not only did the aircraft not find a threat, the announcement embarrassed Egypt at a time when it was trying to rebuild its ties to the Arab world.

At the same time, Nimeiri had a valid need for military aid. Sudan's military capabilities had declined steadily since Nimeiri had broken relations with the USSR in the early 1970s, and Sudan could no longer maintain its combat aircraft and armor. It had only 31 combat aircraft, with 4 F-5E/Fs, 8 MiG-21s, and 19 Chinese-made variants of the MiG-17 and MiG-19 (5 CH F-5s and 13 CH F-6s). Even this small air force was largely ineffective, however, because of a lack of spares and trained manpower. Sudan also could not operate much of its small tank inventory, which included 70 T-54s, 53 T-55s, 17 M-47s, 50 M-60A1s, and a diverse mix of other British, Chinese, French, and Soviet armored vehicles. Its navy had only 15 patrol craft and 3 landing craft; it was far too small to be effective.

There is, therefore, some justification for the aid the U.S. is providing. Sudan must have economic aid for a pro-Western regime to survive, and U.S. deliveries of 12 F-5 fighters, 50 additional M-60 tanks, TOW antitank weapons, and 120 M-113 APCs and aid in creating an air defense system involve a fairly modest effort. While the Libyan threat is minor, in spite of its large inventories of fighters and armor, Nimeiri's military forces have so declined that they probably could not provide internal security in the face of another outbreak of fighting between the northern and southern parts of Sudan or serious popular unrest.[26]

There is, unfortunately, no way to predict whether Nimeiri will survive even with the aid he has been promised. Sudan's problems are scarcely likely to be solved by any credible amount of foreign aid, and the country's political stability is uncertain and dependent on Nimeiri's personal survival. While the Libyan "crisis" may get Nimeiri or some pro-Western successor through the early 1980s, it is equally possible that the Sudan could split into a new civil war between the Arab north and tribal south, or that a new radical or anti-Western regime could take power at any time.[27]

Djibouti. Djibouti is the smallest member of the Arab League; it has an area of only 23,310 square kilometers and a population of only 316,000, plus roughly 30,000 refugees from Ethiopia. It has done surprisingly well since it obtained independence on 17 June 1977. Although its port has lost traffic to Jiddah—which has 45 modern quays and 20–25% lower level prices—Djibouti's role as one of Northwest Africa's key ports and the beginning of the 780-kilometer Djibouti–Addis Ababa railroad is growing. This economic growth has allowed the nation to survive in spite of a previous conflict between its dominant Afar and Issa tribes and the rerouting of much of Ethiopia's trade to the Soviet-modernized port at Assab.[28] Although there is continuing tension between the feuding ethnic elements, and most of the economy is still primitive, it has remained relatively stable and pro-Western.

Although Djibouti is a "nonaligned" nation, it continues to act as the home port for France's Indian Ocean Squadron, which normally includes about 12 combat vessels and a carrier. The agreement France and Djibouti signed on independence also allows France to station a squadron of aircraft and up to 4,000 troops. France normally maintains 12 fighters and the 5th Overseas Mixed Forces Regiment in the country. The French forces have AMX-13 tanks, a limited assault helicopter capability, and modern antitank weapons. An additional 12,000 Frenchmen are resident, and 60% of Djibouti's teachers are French. Djibouti has considerable strategic importance because it is only 150 miles from the growing Soviet base at Aden and because it acts as a strategic counterweight to the growing Soviet presence in Ethiopia.

Djibouti now receives extensive aid from both France and Saudi Arabia, and it seems likely to remain relatively stable and pro-Western as long as its Afar and Issa factions remain at peace. It also is now almost as important a U.S. port as a French one, and both navies now make an equal number of annual visits. Djibouti has, however, made a reasonably good effort to balance off East and West. It has made token arms purchases from the Soviet bloc, has reached an agreement with Ethiopia on joint ownership of the railroad and continued Ethiopian use of the port, and is seeking "neutral" Arab military aid. Its 2,400-man armed forces have only token military capability, and it has no combat air force. Its defense expenditures are about $3–4 million a year, or 3.5% of the central government budget.[29]

Somalia. Somalia's strategic importance to the Gulf is confined largely to its value as a potential staging point for U.S. or Soviet land and air forces and as a naval base. At present, Somalia is loosely aligned with the West and the conservative Gulf states, largely because of its dependence on outside aid and the increasing threat of internal subversion and outside guerrilla movements.

Saudi Arabia has provided Somalia with extensive financial support since 1978, and Kuwait has provided both grants and 100 reconditioned Centurion tanks.[30] The U.S. aid agreement with Somalia reached on 22 August 1980 provided for $45 million in military sales and credits in return for U.S. contingency bases at the airstrip and naval base at Berbera. The U.S. also provided an arms airlift to Somalia in July 1982 to help halt Ethiopian-backed rebels. It gave Somalia about $50 million annually in FMS loans during FY1982–1984, raised its MAP aid from $15 million to $40 million annually, increased Economic Support Funding from $20 to $35 million annually, and provided $36 to $42 million annually in development and P.L. 480 aid.[31] The U.S. is planning to spend up to $110 million to upgrade the 5,100-yard airstrip at Berbera and to build a longer loading dock at its port.[32] In return, the Somalis will get Vulcan M-167 20mm antiaircraft guns to defend the villages in the disputed Ogaden region, additional antiaircraft weapons, and military transportation, communications, and engineering equipment.

Western and Saudi aid seems likely to give Somalia marginal security for the early 1980s. It has long been clear, however, that Somalia is seeking a far larger amount of military and economic aid than can be obtained from the West and its Arab allies. It is equally clear that Mohammed Siad Barre's regime faces a steadily growing threat from Ethiopia and Ethiopian-backed rebels such as the Somali National Movement and the Somalia Democratic Salvation Front. The front took several northern Somali towns with Ethiopian aid in mid-1982, and renewed its attacks in 1983. Its spokesman, Mohamed Abshir, has already said Somalia "should be free of big power bases." These factors make it possible that Somalia may turn back toward the Soviet camp by the mid-1980s, and Siad Barre is now critically dependent on the military aid he is getting from the U.S., UK, PRC, Kuwait, Saudi Arabia, and Egypt to replace his Soviet armor and fighters.[33] Unless such aid is forthcoming, his regime seems unlikely to survive for even the next few years. His fall could threaten an increasingly unstable Kenya and significantly strengthen Soviet freedom of action in the Red Sea and Indian Ocean areas.

The Steadfastness and Confrontation Front

The individual threats to Western and Gulf interests discussed in previous sections may be compounded by the emergence of the Steadfastness and Confrontation Front. The front was originally formed in 1977, in reaction to Sadat's visit to Jerusalem, as a group of "hard-line" states that opposed compromise with Israel and that generally backed radical or Soviet positions in the Near East. It reemerged with new strength at a meeting of Libya, South Yemen, and Ethiopia in Aden in August 1981.[34] This meeting seems to have been designed to tighten the links between the pro-Soviet states in the Near East, and it led to the military alliance among South Yemen, Libya, and Ethiopia discussed earlier. It was followed in September 1981 by a meeting in Libya that included the heads of state of Algeria, Libya, South Yemen, Syria, and the Palestine Liberation Organization. Following the meeting a communique was issued over Tripoli and Damascus radio that declared the conferees had decided to

- call on the forthcoming Arab summit, scheduled for November in Rabat, Morocco, to take deterrent measures against all Arab states that continue to cooperate with Egypt
- declare the United States in a state of direct confrontation with the Arabs
- include the issue of U.S.-Arab relations on the agenda of the Arab summit and take a unified position on these relations
- regard the new U.S.-Israeli strategic "alliance" as direct U.S. participation in the occupation of Palestine (Israel) and other Arab territories and any form of U.S. military presence in the "Arab homeland" as "hostile to our nation to be fought and removed"
- call on the Arabs to use all their economic resources, including oil and dollar deposits in U.S. banks, to confront the new strategic alliance between Israel and the United States
- call on the Arabs to enter negotiations with the Soviet Union and achieve a qualitative upgrading in relations to restore the balance of power in the region[35]

While it is far too early to predict whether this "alliance" will create any serious military links among Libya, Syria, Ethiopia, South Yemen, and the PLO, it is scarcely a promising development. The front does seem to have produced increasing formal and informal cooperation among its members during 1981–1983 in supplying arms to Iran, in supplying and training various radical and terrorist groups, and in opposing such steps toward peace with Israel as the Fahd Plan.[36] It presents a serious risk that the conservative Gulf states and the West will have to deal with an increasingly united opposition.

The Impact on Gulf Security

Given the trends described in this chapter, the problem of stabilizing the Gulf goes far beyond improving collective security among the southern Gulf states. Stabilization requires the implementation of the following additional policies:

• The U.S. should continue to support Saudi Arabia's efforts to keep North Yemen in the conservative camp. The U.S. cannot play its own game in North Yemen; it lacks the area expertise to do so. It can, however, both provide the support Saudi Arabia needs and play the role of "honest broker," *when* this is useful. As long as the U.S. understands that North Yemen will not be an ally, and that the objective is to keep it from becoming a threat, it can tailor its effort accordingly.

- Like the Yemens, Ethiopia poses a major threat to the southern part of Saudi Arabia and Western lines of communication through the Red Sea. As with South Yemen, it is also impossible to predict the level of sophistication an air or naval attack might achieve because of the possible use of "volunteers" and the rapid deployment of new Soviet aircraft and/or ships. As a result, Saudi Arabia's economic development plans in the Hejaz, and the new pipeline to Yanbu and the Red Sea, will be continuously threatened through the 1980s. It is impossible to rule out the use of Ethiopia or South Yemen to launch attacks against any U.S. use of staging bases in Somalia, Oman, Diego Garcia, or Ras Banas in Egypt.
- The threat in the Red Sea creates a continuing Western interest in supporting Egypt's efforts to strengthen Sudan. While Sudan is not normally regarded as a Gulf power, it will acquire almost the same strategic importance as more oil shipments move out of the Red Sea. In spite of its instability, the West should try to block any effort to radicalize the Sudan.
- The West needs to do its best to keep Jordan in the conservative Arab camp and to support King Hussein and moderate elements in Jordanian society. Jordan is sometimes regarded as having limited strategic importance because it is treated only as a potential threat to Israel. Its role in regard to Saudi Arabia is far more significant and gives it great potential strategic importance in securing the West's oil supplies.
- The U.S. needs to pay more attention to Syria as a threat to the Gulf, as well as a problem in terms of the Arab-Israeli confrontation. This again emphasizes the necessity of finding a basis for an Arab-Israeli peace that would reduce Syria's need for Soviet military support.
- The U.S. should consider stepping up its aid to Somalia and encouraging Egypt to provide more training and advisory help. Siad Barre is now 63 years old, and he is firmly supported by only one tribe—the Marehan in the south. The U.S. and Arab states should encourage both a more balanced development plan to check the Ethiopian-backed rebels in the north and plans for some kind of orderly succession.

The threat to the Gulf and to the West's oil supply is both highly unpredictable and a "360 degree" threat. This has broad implications for both regional cooperation and Saudi ties to the U.S. The other conservative Gulf states cannot provide Saudi Arabia with support to cover the Red Sea or its western borders, and only Oman has an interest in checking the threat from South Yemen. As a result, Saudi Arabia must act alone in defending its southern borders. Saudi Arabia also must plan to deal with sudden increases in the forces of potential threat countries along these borders that cannot be predicted on the basis of the deployments and trends. These factors reinforce the need for a strategic partnership between Saudi Arabia and the United States and give Saudi Arabia an even stronger incentive to make provision for over-the-horizon reinforcements from the U.S. They also, however, make Egypt and Jordan more critical as potential allies and give them a major potential role in helping to stabilize both the Gulf and Red Sea. Thus any Arab-Israeli peace that could lead to broad military cooperation in the region and reduce the constraints on U.S. military assistance is of enormous strategic importance.

Notes

1. *Christian Science Monitor*, 28 and 29 October 1981.

2. The sources used for North Yemen include those listed in note 1 of Chapter 6 and Warren Richey, "North Yemen," three-part series in the *Christian Science Monitor*, 12 January 1983. In addition, for the army, see Richard F. Nyrop, *Area Handbook for the Yemens*, Foreign Area Handbook Series (Washington, D.C.: American University, 1977), pp. 226–239; John Keegan, *World Armies* (New York: Facts on File, 1979), pp. 801–808; *The Military Balance, 1981–82* (London: IISS, 1982), p. 49; for the air force, Nyrop, *The Yemens*, and *Military Balance, 1981–82*, as well as Mark Hewish, Bill Sweetman, Barry C. Wheeler, and Bill Gunston, *Air Forces of the World* (New York: Simon & Schuster, 1979), p. 164; for the navy, *Jane's*, Nyrop, *The Yemens*, and *Military Balance, 1981–82*.

3. Based on discussions in Oman, Saudi Arabia, and the UK.

4. Richey, "North Yemen."

5. World of Information, *Middle East Review, 1981*, p. 388.

6. *Middle East*, January 1982, pp. 14–15; September 1982, pp. 60–61; December 1982, p. 63; *MEED*, 7 May 1982, p. 2; 11 June 1982, p. 70; Associated Press International, wire service, 15 December 1982.

7. *Economist*, 15 May 1982, p. 87.

8. Ibid.; MEED working papers; World of Information, *Middle East Review, 1981*, pp. 385–390; *Christian Science Monitor*, 14 January 1983.

9. *MEED*, 19 March 1982, p. 55; interviews in Oman in January 1982; *Washington Post*, 21 April 1982; *Christian Science Monitor*, 12, 13, and 14 January 1983.

10. *8 Days*, 20 February 1982, p. 17; *Christian Science Monitor*, 13 January 1983.

11. Sources include those listed in note 1 of Chapter 12; Nyrop, *The Yemens*, pp. 144–159; Keegan, *World Armies*, pp. 809–815; and *Military Balance, 1982–83*, p. 50; Hewish et al., *Air Forces of the World*, p. 163; interviews in the region. See also Otto von Pikva's *Armies of the Middle East*, pp. 21–22, 142–143. Extensive use has been made of media sources, including *8 Days*, the *Middle East*, and *MERIP*.

12. Aside from desertions, many units cannot train in the field or deploy near their own tribal areas.

13. Omani sources.

14. Interviews in Oman, January 1982; *The Military Balance, 1982–83* (London: IISS, 1983), p. 64.

15. Views differ sharply over the status of these bases and plans to use the strip at Ataq and build a new base near Say'un.

16. Reports of 10 Soviet submarine pens at Socotra have not been verified. Only Soviet sensors seem to be present on Perim.

17. *Arabia: The Islamic World Review*, January 1982, p. 25; *Washington Post*, 23 April 1982. BBC ME/7392/A/1, 22 July 1983; *Defense and Foreign Affairs*, 4 April 1983, p. 1.

18. *Arabia: The Islamic World Review*, January 1982; *Washington Post*, 14 July 1982; BBC SU/7381/A4/1, 9 July 1983; ME/7392/A/1, 22 July 1983; *Oil and Gas Journal*, 20 June 1983, p. 76; Associated Press, 23 July 1983.

19. *Economist*, 30 January 1982, pp. 41, 59–60; and 26 June 1982, p. 41; 30 April 1983, p. 45; *New York Times*, 16 May 1982; 15 July 1982, p. 9; 25 July 1982, p. 1; *Wall Street Journal*, 23 August 1982, p. 19; *Middle East*, October 1982, p. 12; *8 Days*, 30 May 1981, pp. 22–23; 6 February 1982, pp. 30–31.

20. *New York Times*, 23 October and 21 December 1981; 25 July 1982. Such counts are very uncertain. Only about 9,000 Cubans are active as combat troops.

21. CIA, *World Factbook, 1981*, p. 103.

22. *Baltimore Sun*, 24 October 1981; *Washington Post*, 14, 17, and 24 October 1981; *New York Times*, 23 October 1981.

23. *New York Times*, 29 October 1981.

24. *Aviation Week*, 26 April 1983; *Economist*, 26 June and 23 October 1982; U.S. State Department, *Congressional Presentation: Security Assistance Programs, FY1984* (Washington, D.C.: April 1984), pp. 289–293.

25. See the *Middle East Annual Review*, 1982; *MERIP Reports*, no. 99 (September 1981):20–27; U.S. State Department, *Congressional Presentation: Security Assistance Programs, FY1984*; *Economist*, 28 May 1983, p. 50; *Los Angeles Times*, 23 April 1983.

26. The Libyan air attacks on Sudan were conducted by two obsolete Italian Macchi F-260 propeller-driven fighters, although Libyan MiG jets did fly over Sudan. Libya's forces consist of some 2,400 medium tanks and 450 combat aircraft, but only about 800 of the tanks have crews, and only 450 or less are combat employable. Similarly, only about 100 of Libya's jets are usable in combat. Libya had about 4,500 troops in Chad when the "crisis" began, but only 1,300 near Sudan. The Libyan armed forces lack the capability to support army units in extended operations away from their home bases or to deploy Libyan jet fighters remotely. Further, only 6,500 miles of Sudan's roads are paved, and Khartoum is 500 miles from the Libyan border and the roads are poor. A Libyan invasion through Chad would have had to move 600 miles by a poorly graded, single-track dirt road or desert tracks.

27. Sources include *8 Days*, *Middle East*, and various U.S. media, including the *New York Times*, 17 and 23 October 1981; *Washington Post*, 14 and 17 October 1981; 19 February 1983; *Baltimore Sun*, 24 October 1981; *Economist*, 23 October 1982; 28 May 1983, p. 50; *Wall Street Journal*, 18 February 1983; *Christian Science Monitor*, 1 March 1983; *Los Angeles Times*, 23 April 1983.

28. *8 Days*, 23 January 1982, p. 33.

29. Sources include various issues of *MEED*; the *Economist*; *8 Days*, 23 January 1982, p. 33; 20 February 1982, pp. 38–39; Keegan, *World Armies*, pp. 175–177; *The Military Balance, 1981–82* (London: IISS, 1982); World of In-

formation, *Middle East Review,* 1981, pp. 143–147; 1983, pp. 140–143; CIA, *World Factbook, 1983,* CR-83-11300, May 1983, p. 57.

30. *International Defense Review* 1 (1981):11.

31. *Aviation Week,* 26 April 1982, p. 22; *8 Days,* 30 May 1981, pp. 22–24; U.S. State Department *Congressional Presentation: Security Assistance Programs, FY1984,* pp. 285–287.

32. *Los Angeles Times,* 24 October 1981; *New York Times,* 21 September 1981; 15 and 26 July 1982; *Washington Post,* 27 July 1982; *Wall Street Journal,* 22 August 1982; *Economist,* 13 November 1982.

33. Sources again include various media, particularly Reuters, 23 October 1981; Keegan, *World Armies,* pp. 630–632; *Military Balance, 1981–82*; World of Information, *Middle East Review, 1981,* pp. 291–309; *Economist,* 19 February 1983, pp. 57–58; 30 April 1983, pp. 45–46; *New York Times,* 27 March 1983; *Washington Times,* 15 and 27 June 1983.

34. Geoffrey Godsell, *Christian Science Monitor,* 20 August 1981.

35. *Washington Post,* 20 and 23 September 1981.

36. *New York Times,* 21 September 1981; and 15 and 25 July 1982; *Los Angeles Times,* 24 October 1982; *Wall Street Journal,* 23 August 1982; *8 Days,* 30 May 1981.

19 U.S. and Soviet Power Projection Capabilities in the Gulf

Even the most successful collective security effort by the conservative Gulf states will not be sufficient to deter or defend against an all-out Iranian or Iraqi attack or against a major Soviet military move. Saudi Arabia and the other conservative Gulf states must ultimately depend on the West, and particularly on the United States, to guarantee their security. The question is what forces and capabilities the West and the U.S. can provide and what kind of relations can be created that will allow Western reinforcements to be effective.

Under President Carter, the U.S. sought to create formal military ties, direct military intervention capabilities, and a significant U.S. military and basing presence in the area. The Reagan administration has since focused more on the use of sea power and has gradually shown more sensitivity to the fact that it must work informally with its regional allies and cannot hope to obtain permanent bases in the region. This change in focus is critical to the success of Western policy. Friendly Gulf states must limit their cooperation to expediting U.S. capability to deploy over-the-horizon capabilities and to informal military relations. With the possible exception of Oman, no Gulf state can bear the political cost of having a U.S. base or permanently stationing U.S. combat forces on its soil. Such a U.S. presence would create unacceptable internal and regional security problems in terms of preserving national sovereignty, increasing friction with Iran and the USSR, preserving "nonaligned" status, dealing with the forces of Arab nationalism, and coping with the impact of giving such bases to Israel's chief ally.

Any strategic partnership between the U.S. and the conservative Gulf states must come to grips with this reality. At the same time, the question arises as to how real any difference between the U.S. position and that of the conservative Gulf states actually is. On the one hand, the U.S. search for direct power projection capabilities and permanent bases has had the character of a "paper chase." The U.S. has advanced plans to unilaterally protect the Gulf states, but it has lacked the forces to implement them. On the other hand, there has been an Arab tendency to "protest too much" about not needing the support of U.S. forces. Both sides have tended to bog down over the issue of granting formal basing rights when less formal arrangements can better serve their common interests. In fact, when U.S. capabilities are analyzed realistically, along with the needs and capabilities of the other conservative Gulf states, the differences between the two sides seem significantly less real and the value of their joint capabilities seem much greater.

The Fall of the Shah and the Invasion of Afghanistan

U.S. power projection capabilities in the Gulf have historically been limited to U.S. naval and air capabilities. Since 1946, the U.S. has been grossly inferior to the USSR in the land forces it could deploy and support in Iran and Iraq. U.S. strength has instead lain in a combination of strategic nuclear superiority, strong regional allies, and advanced naval and air capabilities. The gradual attrition of U.S. strategic nuclear superiority removed one of those underpinnings in the early 1970s, but the "two pillars" doctrine and the building up of Iran's military forces seemed to compensate. After a brief flurry of U.S. efforts to halt British withdrawal from east of Suez in the late 1960s, the U.S. came to rely more and more on the shah as a substitute for British power and U.S. projection capability.

The shah's fall on 16 January 1979 thus removed the remaining underpinning of a U.S. reliance on the forces of other powers. It exposed the absence of existing U.S. power projection capabilities in the Gulf and the decline in U.S. ability to create such capabilities from its other forces that followed the post-Vietnam deterioration of U.S. military strength. In effect, the U.S. found itself strategically isolated; its key regional military ally had now become a key potential threat. At best, the U.S. had little more to look forward to from Iran than a hostile regime and the prospect of prolonged civil war. At worst, it faced the constant possibility that a pro-Soviet faction would come to power in Iran or that some faction in Iran would request Soviet intervention.

The situation in the Gulf became even worse after the Soviet invasion of Afghanistan on 27 December 1979 (see Map 19.1). The invasion not only brought Soviet forces several hundred miles closer to the Gulf, it also triggered much broader increases in Soviet military capabilities in the region. Although the evidence involved is contradictory, the USSR has followed its invasion by steadily restructuring its basing, logistic, support, and readiness structure in such key military districts as the North Caucasus, Transcaucasus, Turkestan, and Central Asia. It has also acquired vast practical experience in operating and fighting in the region. The combination of the Soviet needs to support a prolonged war in Afghanistan, to react to the shah's fall, and to counter U.S. efforts to increase the U.S. strategic presence in the Gulf has led the USSR to steadily expand its presence in the areas surrounding the Gulf.

MAP 19—1
U.S.—SOVIET NAVAL FACILITIES IN THE GULF

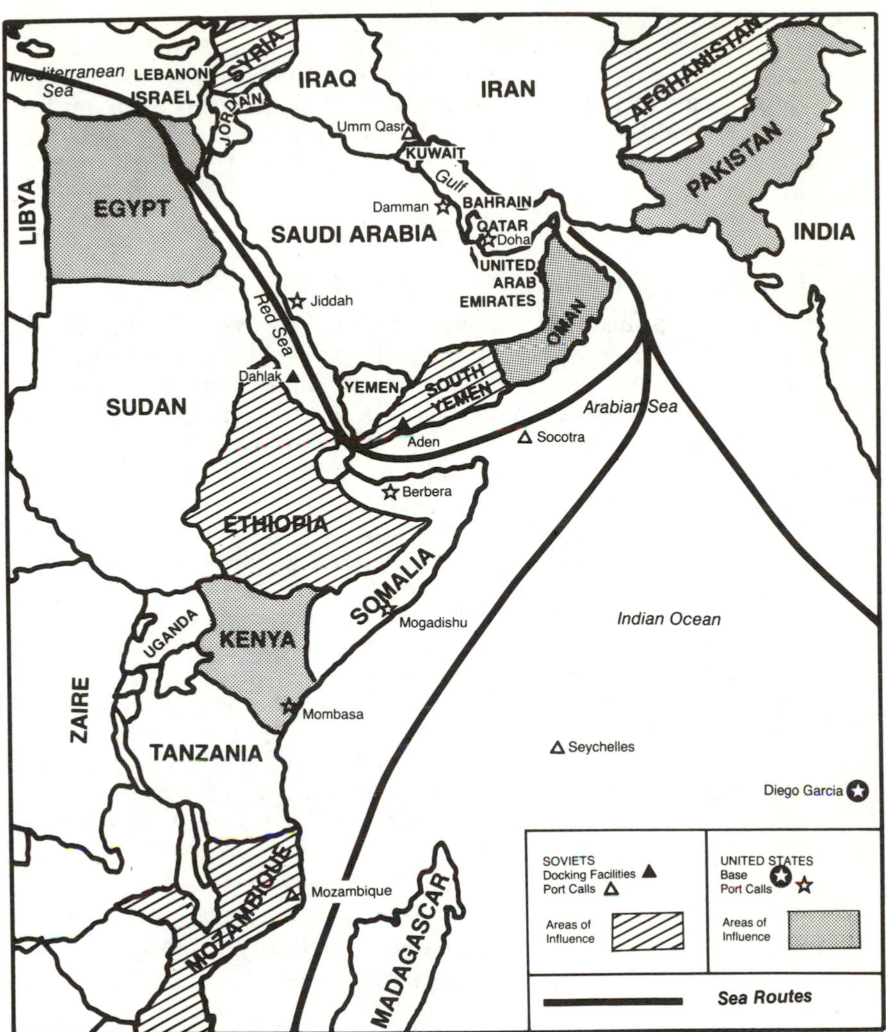

The Soviet Union now has an impressive pool of mechanized infantry and armored power to draw on. It has 1 tank, 21 motorized rifle, and 2 airborne divisions in the Transcaucasus, Turkestan, and North Caucasus military districts. There is considerable doubt as to the combat readiness of many of these divisions, which have previously been classified as Category 2 and 3, with most in Category 3. These categories are the lowest state of Soviet combat readiness.

While some U.S. analyses have indicated that the Soviet Union is strengthening its divisions in the Transcaucasus District so that up to one-third may be Category 1 (combat ready) and most of the remainder may be Category 2, this remains uncertain. It is equally unclear whether a Soviet "Southern Command" has been set up under Marshal Sokolov and actually commands all Soviet forces in the Turkestan, Transcaucasus, and North Caucasus military districts, or whether this is a unified command to handle all operations in Afghanistan. The former possibility would imply a more serious combined arms and land/air threat to Iran and the Gulf.[1]

U.S. Contingency Capabilities in the Gulf Region

The Carter administration reacted to the shah's fall and the Soviet invasion of Afghanistan by trying to build up new U.S. power projection capabilities that could offset the Soviet advantages in the region. It sought to create a Rapid Deployment Force that could deploy to the Gulf even faster than Soviet forces and confront any Soviet aggression with a U.S. presence in being. The administration emphasized strengthening U.S. capabilities to unilaterally intervene in the region, rather than seeking collective security, and meeting worst-case contingencies, rather than being able to deal with the most probable scenarios.[2] These policies triggered significant improvements in U.S. capabilities, but they called for larger forces than the U.S. had the resources to create. They also highlighted the discrepancies between U.S. and Soviet capabilities and raised serious doubts regarding the true U.S. objective in creating such forces on the part of many otherwise pro-Western or anti-Soviet Gulf nations. Even the most pro-Western countries in the region were frightened by the disclosure of a series of U.S. studies and contingency plans studying unilateral U.S. landings or assaults to protect the West's oil, and many came to question whether the U.S. was seeking to check the USSR or planning to seize key objectives and oil facilities.

U.S. Land Forces

Although the U.S. had many weaknesses in its ability to replace the shah with rapidly deployable U.S. forces, the most critical initial weakness was in land forces. U.S. land forces consisted of a total of 28 divisions, of which 19 (16 Army and 3 Marine Corps) were active and 9 (8 Army and 1 Marine Corps) were reserve units. These divisions, with an authorized strength of about 18,000 men each, were supplemented by nondivisional brigades and regiments (about 4,000 men each) and by separate maneuver, artillery, and aviation battalions. None of the reserve divisions could be made combat effective in time to reach the Gulf under most foreseeable contingencies, and 11 of the 19 active divisions required "round out" by battalion- or brigade-sized formations in order to reach full strength.

Further, none of these U.S. land forces were deployed near the Gulf, and virtually all had other commitments. The U.S. had two armored and two mechanized divisions, plus three additional independent regiments, committed to Europe. It had one brigade forward deployed in Europe out of a total of three additional active divisions based in the continental U.S. (CONUS). It had an active infantry division based in Korea, and it kept most of its remaining forces in CONUS at comparatively low readiness. The Marine Corps's three active divisions were located in Okinawa (with one brigade in Hawaii), at Camp Pendleton in California, and at Camp Lejeune in North Carolina. All three marine units had serious readiness and equipment limitations.

The Carter administration discovered that it was virtually impossible to quickly transform any part of this mix of land forces into an RDF that had any hope of successfully engaging Soviet forces in the northern Gulf. As a result, it launched a series of force improvement programs that gradually created the forces shown in Table 19.1. As was discussed in Chapter 7, however, every step in this process received heavy publicity, and the result was far more often to expose the weaknesses in the U.S. posture than to create an image of strength.

Even in 1983, after six years of effort—including significant changes in force structure and missions and the reorganization of the RDF into a U.S. Central Command tailored to fight in Southwest Asia, the Gulf, and the Horn of Africa, the U.S. still faces serious constraints. The forces assigned to USCENTCOM are shown in Table 19.1. They total only 4-2/3 division equivalents (3-1/3 Army and 1-1/3 Marine Corps), and many still require "round out" with additional battalions. Yet none are equipped with modern light armored vehicles or advanced attack helicopters. Most will not acquire all the artillery, TOW antitank weapons, and forward air defense weapons they need until the mid-1980s. The use of U.S. land forces is also constrained by the "earmarking" of virtually all army units in the U.S. force structure for Europe or Korea and by the need to rotate units back to the continental U.S. These problems would become especially serious if the United States should simultaneously become involved in crises with the USSR in the Gulf and some other areas.

In order to maintain combat effectiveness, 40% of all U.S. forces must now be rotated from overseas to CONUS assignments. Under situations in which the rest of the world remains quiet, four divisions (one airborne, one air assault, two mechanized infantry) would be available for the RDF. The use of airborne and air assault divisions would, however, leave the U.S. without any airborne capability for possible use in Europe or Korea. One of the divisions now committed to the RDF—the 24th Mechanized—was formerly under the jurisdiction of Pacific Command and might be unavailable if needed in Korea. It was the only theater reserve division available to the Pacific Command.[3] If simultaneous contingencies erupt, the United States might have as little

TABLE 19.1 Units Designated for USCENTCOM in Rapid Deployment Contingencies

Service	Units	Personnel
Army	82nd Airborne Division[a]	17,000
	101st Airborne Division (Air Assault)	18,000
	24th Mechanized Infantry Division	19,000
	6th Combat Brigade (Air Cavalry)	2,500
	Two Ranger Battalions	1,200
	Special Forces Units	Varies
	High Technology Infantry F Divisions	In formation
Marines	1 Marine Amphibious Force[b]	31,000
	7th Marine Amphibious Brigade	(12,000)
	1 MAGTF/NTPF	
	1–2 Marine Fighter Wings[c]	
Navy	3 Aircraft carrier battle groups (CVBGS)	Escorts and support vessels would vary depending on task
	1 Surface action group	
	5 Squadrons of maritime patrol aircraft	
	1 Amphibious Ready Group (ARG)	
	1 Naval Special Warfare Task Group	
	18 Near-term prepositioning ships (NTPS)	
	6 Enhanced NTPS	
Air Force	Strategic Projection Force including	
	2 B-52H bomber squadrons[d]	
	various other aircraft	
	7 Tactical Wings, including[e]	
	27th Tactical Fighter Squadron (F-15)	
	71st Tactical Fighter Squadron (F-15)	
	94th Tactical Fighter Squadron (F-15)	
	68th Tactical Fighter Squadron (F-4E)	
	70th Tactical Fighter Squadron (F-4E)	
	339th Tactical Fighter Squadron (F-4E)	
	353rd Tactical Fighter Squadron (A-10)	
	355th Tactical Fighter Squadron (A-10)	
	552nd Tactical Fighter Squadron (F-111)	
	563rd Tactical Fighter Squadron (F-4G)	
	2 reconnaissance squadrons	
	9 tactical airlift squadrons	
Total designated manpower	Combat Units	87,500
	Total Army	100,000
	Total Marine Corps	50,000
	Total Navy	42,000
	Total Air Force	30,000
	Total Force	220,000+

[a] Includes combat and combat support units.

[b] Includes aviation and logistic support elements of a marine air ground task force. A marine amphibious force normally consists of a reinforced marine division and a marine aircraft wing containing roughly twice as many tactical fighter aircraft as an air force fighter wing.

[c] Roughly equivalent to four USAF fighter wings.

[d] The Strategic Projection Force.

[e] First-line USAF fighters include more than 72 F-15s, 144 F-111s, 72 F-4s, and 85 A-10s.

Sources: DOD, *FY1984 Annual Report,* p. 195; James Wooten, "Rapid Deployment Forces," CRS Issue Brief IB80027, updated 23 March 1981, p. 4; USRDF *Fact Sheet,* HORDJTF Public Affairs Office, Miami, revised November 1981; OJCS, *Military Posture, FY1983,* p. 41; *Economist,* 11 December 1982, p. 63; DOD, "USCENTCOM," October 1982.

as one division available for use in Southwest Asia. The other units in CONUS might be required to rapidly reinforce other theaters. While other reserve forces could be committed to Southwest Asia in their place, this would deplete the "earmarked" reserves for other theaters. These are already considered a bare minimum, and any such shift would mean both deploying forces poorly trained and equipped to fight in the Gulf areas and greatly reducing combat effectiveness of any U.S. buildup in Europe or Korea.

The problems involved become clearer after an examination of the major combat units that would be the first to be deployed in a Gulf contingency. These units would probably be the 82nd Airborne Division, the 101st Air Assault Division, and the 7th Marine Amphibious Brigade (MAB), whose unit equipment is prepositioned on ships at Diego Garcia—about seven days' sail from the Gulf. These units could be followed up by two more marine brigades stationed at Okinawa if lift operations proceeded as planned.

Although the MABs are now increasing in mobility and firepower, they formerly had 12,000—16,000 marines and a total armored and mechanized capability of only 53 tanks and 1,200 vehicles of assorted types. This has been augmented by 36 artillery pieces, the majority of which are towed,[4] and a multipurpose air group, including UH-1 utility helicopters, CH-46 medium-lift helicopters, and CH-53 heavy-lift helicopters.[5] While the MABs will grow significantly in "punch," they will not have adequate numbers of TOW ATGMs, forward air defense weapons, or light armored vehicles before 1986. They will lack adequate numbers of modern attack and transport helicopters through the mid-1980s. The MAB can reach the Gulf in seven days using equipment prepositioned on ships at Diego Garcia.[6]

The 82nd Airborne is arranged in three infantry brigades, for a total of 16,000 paratroops. One brigade, the Division Ready Brigade, is on constant alert, with the reputed ability to move within 24 hours. The 82nd Airborne is the most combat-ready of all U.S. units; it undergoes yearly training evaluations that consist of drop and airmobile operations under live-fire conditions. The 82nd is improving in firepower and mobility; but it is still lightly armed and has little air defense and anti-armor capability. It can theoretically reach the Gulf in 5 days, but more than 14 days may be required in practice.

The 101st Air Assault Division, consisting of 17,900 troops, has heavier equipment than the 82nd. It has a steadily growing assault helicopter capability, and in early 1981 this included 48 AH-1S Cobras with TOW missiles and 90 UH-1H lift helicopters, which can carry 11 paratroopers. These helicopters are to be replaced in the mid-1980s with Apache AH-64 long-range, all-weather attack helicopters and Blackhawk UH-60 A armored utility helicopters.[7] Its assault helicopter force will also be enlarged and equipped with new ATGMs and target acquisition systems. The 101st does not have modern light armored fighting vehicles and heavy-lift helicopters. It is, however, being reorganized to improve its anti-armor, air defense, and forward fuel and ammunition support capabilities. It would currently take at least two weeks to reach the Gulf if the 82nd was deployed first, and it would probably have to move by sea and take 30–35 days.

The 82nd also has a complement of 54 improved Sheridan reconnaissance vehicles whose 152mm guns fire Shillelagh antitank missiles. It must be noted, however, that, in drop exercises, the Airborne has severely damaged a large number of Sheridans and that these weapons have proved unreliable and to have limited combat effectiveness. The army may have to phase out the Sheridans in favor of M-60s, which would not be air-dropable. It is, however, planning to procure light armored vehicles (LAVs) specifically designed for the USCENTCOM mission. Procurement of 969 (680 for the army and 289 for the marines) has been requested in the FY1982-1986 defense program.[8]

Both the 82nd and 101st divisions are relatively self-sustaining and have their own support command. They have both crew-operated and hand-held anti-armor weapons. Individual paratroopers are outfitted with M-47 Dragon and LAW antitank missiles. Crew-operated weapons consists of TOWs (tube-launched, optically tracked, wire-guided), which can be mounted on any carrier, including jeeps and helicopters. These anti-armor weapons would be successful only if they could be used from at least hastily prepared positions and in defense in depth in and around favorable terrain. They have limited lethality against Soviet T-72 tanks, although the Improved TOW is being procured and should be able to defeat Soviet T-72 tanks and their successors. An improved man-portable antitank rocket, like the Viper or an improved LAW, should be in service in the mid-1980s.

For antiaircraft defense, the 82nd and 101st divisions have improved Redeye shoulder-fired SAMs, crew-operated Stinger infrared missiles, and 46 Vulcan rapid-fire AAs. These weapons can provide a light, low-altitude air defense screen, and airborne units engaged in combat would be dependent on air defense support from either land-based or carrier aircraft. The numbers of such systems, and related training procedures, are now inadequate but they are improving.

The 24th Mechanized Division has a total of 216 battle tanks, APCs, and self-propelled guns. If the 24th was able to deploy in sufficient time, the USCENTCOM would have a total of 370 battle tanks,[9] which could leave it heavily outnumbered in terms of armored firepower even if it opposed only a few Soviet motorized rifle or tank divisions on terrain suited for armored operations. It would have no modern light armored vehicles and its manportable and other weapons would not be superior to those of Soviet or local forces. The U.S. would now have to choose whether to move the 101st or the 24th by sea. During the late 1980s, however, it will require enough added airlift capability to move both the 82nd and the 101st by air. It also is improving its sealift so that rapid deployment ships could carry even the 24th to the Gulf by sea in 12–17 days, beginning in 1985.

As is discussed later, even these units will have trouble moving according to schedule until the U.S. improves its airlift and sealift capabilities. They also will lack any real backup until the Marine Corps prepositions the equipment for two additional brigades on new maritime prepositioning ship task forces. The 7th MAB will complete this in late 1984 and acquire a significant roll-on/roll-off and self-sustaining capability. The other two MABs will acquire this capability in 1985 and 1986, but they will remain deployed at more remote locations.[10]

The remaining U.S. Army forces in CONUS will modernize more slowly. They now lack the equipment and training to be effective in RDF missions and in most contingencies. As a result, the 9th Infantry Division was converted to a High Technology Test Bed (HTTB) in June 1980. It is hoped that this will produce a strategically more deployable and mobile High Technology Light Division by FY1986 and allow conversion of the remaining divisions during the late 1980s. These units are already scheduled to acquire light armored vehicles, fast attack vehicles, and improved attack helicopter capability.[11] They will be trained and equipped for urban, anti-armor, and mountain and rough terrain warfare.

Difficulties with the Rapid Deployment Joint Task Force

USCENTCOM forces also still suffer from problems in combat readiness, but their readiness is now significantly better than at the time of the shah's fall. As of 1979, the 82nd Airborne was the only unit considered combat ready; it then suffered from shortages of necessary items such as radios, assault rifles, and transport vehicles. Both the 101 Air Assault and the 24th Mechanized were still rated C-4 in late 1980, which indicated that both units were not combat ready.[12] They have since been upgraded to C-1 and C-2, and the readiness of U.S. Marine Corps units is now comparatively high.

Support and logistic capabilities are also improving, but problems will remain until the late 1980s. Pentagon planners consider the minimum logistic support necessary for RDF operations to be support for 100,000 combat personnel. According to General Warner, former chief of the U.S. Readiness Command, deploying 100,000 troops would necessitate another 100,000 for support. The majority of these 100,000 support personnel would be deployed within the United States assisting the massive sealift and airlift operations that a Gulf contingency would involve.[13] The lack of air traffic controllers, traffic management personnel, maintenance personnel, and the like in the Gulf would require the U.S. to deploy a sizable logistical contingent into Southwest Asia along with its combat elements.

Any USCENTCOM operation would also have to contend with the hardships of mountain and desert warfare. U.S. forces have only limited training and equipment for the kind of mountain and rough terrain warfare characteristic of Iran and Iraq. In spite of a concentration on defending key passes or mountain barriers, U.S. forces lack the sensors, all-terrain vehicles, and firepower for such combat. The U.S. has recently increased its desert training and equipment and has run exercises and tests in Egypt and Oman. These tests indicate that new combat and service support units (ammunition, petroleum, oil, lubricants, water, medical, transportation, maintenance, and engineering) be created that are tailored to the particular difficulties associated with desert and mountain warfare. The army is now creating active units to provide such support for its airborne and air assault division, and will create dedicated or "dual hatted" support units in its reserve components to support follow-on deployments.[14]

The navy estimates that USCENTCOM's greatest special logistic requirement could be adequate water. USCENTCOM will have only moderate amounts of water desalinization equipment, and fresh water must be supplied by outside sources. Its tanker inventories are now sufficient to carry both fuel requirements and minimal water requirements (12 gallons per man per day.)[15]

As the failure of the U.S. raid to rescue the Iranian hostages illustrated, weather conditions in the desert are another source of concern. A desert sandstorm can immobilize units, and the intense midday heat (often exceeding 100° F) can have the same effect. Storms and winds of more than 10 knots can seriously hamper air drops or reinforcements. As a result, weather conditions in the Gulf region may have a severe effect on U.S. combat effectiveness and may limit activities to certain times of the day, such as airborne drops at night. In contrast, winter conditions in Iran and Iraq can involve freezing conditions in exposed mountain areas in the north and seas of mud in the south.

The training of USCENTCOM forces has improved sharply since 1981. They are now much better prepared for regional warfare, for independent operations, and for nonlinear situations. This preparation is correcting a serious lack of training for maneuver warfare and many small equipment deficiencies.[16] As a small illustration of this problem, the units that participated in the first Bright Star exercise in Egypt were outfitted in jungle fatigues and used vehicles with jungle camouflage, both highly visible in the desert. This problem was solved after the Bright Star exercises in November 1981, but each new series of exercises has revealed new problems and requirements. The desert is also only one of several special environments that exist in the Gulf. Much of the area consists of high mountain plateaus or rough terrain. The Iran-Iraq border area has complex water barriers. Gulf cities differ strikingly from those in Europe. USCENTCOM still lacks specialized training and equipment for urban and mountain warfare in the region, an adequate number of language specialists, and the ability to cope with a host of specialized problems such as the winters in Iran and Iraq, sand erosion on helicopter rotor-blade tips, sand clogging of engines and other equipment, weapons maintenance, and the inadequate range of many weapons, particularly the M-16 rifle.

The Command of USCENTCOM

The RDF initially had an awkward joint command structure that limited its ability to employ both land and air forces effectively. It was initially put under the jurisdiction of the Readiness Command (REDCOM), which was under an army general. REDCOM, rather than the RDF, had the authority from the RDF to decide which units would be assigned to the RDF. A marine general, P. X. Kelly, had complete operational command, but no authority to decide which units would be assigned to him. REDCOM has also assumed control over mission planning and military exercises for the RDF, which led to bitter disputes between the two commands.[17]

Interservice rivalry over the RDF's command carried over into the Joint Chiefs of Staff (JCS). The JCS was initially unable to form a workable theater command structure. Not only was responsibility for the RDF divided between RDF and REDCOM, but peacetime theater operations were divided between the European Command (EUCOM) and the Pacific Command (PACOM). EUCOM was under the army's authority, and PACOM under the Navy's. EUCOM is also attached to NATO, and if the command of the RDF remained attached to EUCOM, the U.S. would theoretically have had to consult with its European allies before taking action. The responsibilities of EUCOM and PACOM also were functionally divided between land- and sea-based operations. EUCOM was responsible for land-based operations and PACOM for sea-based. Southwest Asia was also geographically divided between them—the geographic demarcation line ran through the Strait of Hormuz.

Neither the JCS nor the then secretary of defense, Harold Brown, was able to achieve a consensus over how to change the situation before the Carter administration left office. Brown's successor, Secretary of Defense Casper Weinberger, has had more success. In April 1981 he managed to push a plan through the JCS that transformed the RDF into a separate command area for a Rapid Deployment Joint Task Force (RDJTF). This initiative created a separate command area for Southwest Asia on 1 October 1981. It removed the new RDF from the dual command of PACOM and EUCOM and placed it in the position of reporting directly to the National Command Authority through the JCS. Most important, it laid the groundwork for creating the first new geographic unified command in 35 years. The commander of the RDJTF became the commander-in-chief of USCENTCOM and all planning, exercises, and operations in Southwest Asia on 1 January 1983. The new command is based at MacDill Air Force Base in Florida, with a small 20-man forward headquarters on a U.S. Navy ship in the Gulf. It is rapidly expanding to include the full responsibility of a commander-in-chief, including security assistance programs. All the land and air units shown in Table 19.1 are now being trained and organized with support of a USCENTCOM task force as their primary mission, although the naval units necessary to move USCENTCOM forces remain under separate command.

U.S. Naval Capabilities

The "normal" deployment of the naval forces supporting USCENTCOM also raises serious problems. Of the three carriers theoretically assigned, one will be forward-deployed at the base at Diego Garcia, one will be held back, and the third will be drawn from the other fleets. The 7th fleet could also deploy a fourth carrier, if it was not needed in the Pacific, and an additional air wing could be removed from a carrier in dock for overhaul. If the U.S. had to fight both in Europe and Asia, however, it is possible that not a single aircraft carrier could be deployed to the Indian Ocean.[18] Only if no other contingency arose would three—or possibly four—carriers be available for RDF support, although the "swing" strategy now employed in the Pacific would probably give the Gulf–Indian Ocean area priority for the carriers of the 7th Fleet even if war broke out in East Asia.

To illustrate the problems involved, the navy maintains that it needs at least seven carriers in the Atlantic. Two of these might be forward-deployed in the Mediterranean. At least one more carrier is undergoing overhaul in stateside ports at all times. It was these constraints that forced the U.S. to borrow carriers from the Pacific Fleet to create the ad hoc TF-70 Task Force in the Indian Ocean in 1980, which reduced the ability of the U.S. Navy to meet its requirement to patrol the Pacific Ocean and deal with Asian contingencies. Although the Reagan administration's FY1984 defense plans call for an active force of 14 carriers, a Gulf task force will still have to borrow a carrier air wing to deal with most contingencies through the middle to late 1980s.[19]

The strain on U.S. carrier resources posed by Indian Ocean deployments is also likely to remain serious. In 1980 the aircraft carrier *Nimitz* had to be kept at sea in the Indian Ocean for over three months, and this long period at sea had a serious effect on crew morale and performance.[20] In 1981 the U.S. maintained two carrier battle groups in the Indian Ocean and four to five surface combatants in the Gulf. However, the carriers could not enter the Gulf. Navy planners consider the Gulf to be a "poor cockpit" for aircraft carriers because of the lack of maneuverability afforded by its relatively narrow channels. The carriers also faced the threat of Iranian Harpoon antiship missiles, and they would have so little warning of air attack that most of their fighters would be tied down in a defensive role. Thus U.S. carrier operations had to be conducted from the Gulf of Oman, which put naval aircraft far from the target areas of the Iran-Iraq War and the Saudi "core area."

While the deployment of the E-3A and radar picketships, and reductions in Iranian capability, have since decreased this threat, U.S. carriers will have to stand even further out in the Arabian Sea as more serious threats arise in the future, and the distances involved in flying to targets in the Western Gulf will then be similar to trying to operate against Gulf targets from Western Europe. Such distances would put a severe strain on both the F-18 and A-6 fighter-attack aircraft, which will be the principal long-range ground-attack aircraft on U.S. carriers, and will make use of the comparatively short-range A-V8B almost impossible. The A-6 has a maximum range of 1,100–2,700 miles, depending on ordnance, but it cannot use this range and preserve sufficient fuel to perform demanding attack sorties. Plus, it is slow maneuvering and vulnerable to short-range air defenses. Operating out of carriers in the Arabian Sea, the A-6 can cover only a small proportion of possible targets unless it can get airborne refueling. The F-18 and A-7 will face similar or more severe limitations.

As a result, carrier-based forces must draw on the tankers Saudi Arabia is buying from the U.S., U.S. tankers flying from Oman, or from some forward refueling base. They will also need local air control and warning to conserve fuel and fly optimal attack sortie profiles. The replacement of the A-6 with the F-18 in the mid-1980s will make this situation slightly worse because U.S. carriers will carry fewer and shorter-range attack aircraft.

U.S. naval forces in the Indian Ocean could be augmented by allied naval forces. During the beginning of the Iran-Iraq War, France, Great Britain, Australia, and New Zealand deployed a total of 19 naval vessels in the region, including one small aircraft carrier, as a warning to Iran not to close the Strait of Hormuz.[21] The French reinforced the 14 ships they kept in the Indian Ocean area with mine-countermeasure vessels in response to Iranian threats to mine the strait, although the Iranians lacked such mines and the currents in the area make any such effort dubious. The British also sent an ASW aircraft carrier task group with missile destroyer *Conventry* to the Gulf of Oman and then reinforced it with the frigate *Alacrity*. These ships were later relieved by the missile destroyer *Antrim* and the frigate *Naiad*. All the ships were part of a special Task Group that Britain had originally sent east of Suez in early 1980 after the shah's fall.

Britain further reinforced these forces in late 1980, after four Iranian destroyers attempted to enter Omani waters near the main shipping channels through the strait. It sent the missile destroyer *Birmingham* and the frigates *Apollo, Ardent*, and *Avenger* and kept them in the area through the spring of 1981. British forces were also reinforced in late 1980 by combat ships from Australia and New Zealand, and Britain was able to obtain basing support for its resupply ships and auxiliaries at Mombasa. Britain also announced in November 1983 that it was creating a "rapid strike" force of 1,200 paratroopers and a 700-man infantry battalion with armored cars, field guns, and helicopters. The entire force can be airlifted, and Britain is adding 6 Lockheed Tristar jets to its transport pool with a capability to lift 100 men up to 3,000 miles.

Thus the U.S. may be able to get significant allied support in an emergency that threatens Western oil supplies. Interestingly enough, the West Germans also sent four ships into the Indian Ocean in the summer of 1980. Accordingly, while NATO provides only limited coverage of any waters east of Suez, it cannot be ruled out of the balance of power in the area.[22] Both Britain and France later emphasized that if the strait had been closed, "action would have been taken." Although U.S. carrier battle groups would be the decisive element in any allied Indian Ocean fleet, allied naval forces could remove part of the burden on strained U.S. resources.

Naval equipment shortages could also pose problems, although some of these shortages are being corrected. Aircraft carriers normally carry 180 days worth of parts for aircraft maintenance. In 1980 the carriers in the Indian Ocean maintained only a 60-day supply. This resulted in a serious depletion of available carrier aircraft. Of 21 aircraft aboard the *Eisenhower* examined in a routine check in 1980, only 5 were mission capable.[23] U.S. aircraft carriers also suffered shortages of Phoenix and Sparrow air-to-air missiles, which preclude available aircraft from receiving the full amount of ordnance. While these shortages will be eliminated by the end of FY1987, if the FY1984 Reagan administration defense plan is funded, U.S. carriers will not be fully equipped until the mid-1980s to fly the very high numbers of attack sorties per day likely to be required against a Soviet attack in the Gulf.[24]

Further, U.S. carriers may experience serious difficulties in operating sufficient numbers of on-board special mission aircraft. These include early warning aircraft, photo reconnaissance, electronic and signal warfare aircraft, and airborne refueling aircraft. The total inventory of each of these special mission aircraft was less than 100 in 1981, and in many cases it was less than 10. These "cats and dogs" are vital to carrier operations. Serious shortages of any key type could seriously inhibit the viability of the U.S. carrier presence in the Indian Ocean.[25]

Finally, the U.S. Navy also has a shortage of fleet minesweepers, which would present problems if the Soviets or Iran should attempt to mine the passageways in and around the Gulf, although a mix of currents and geographic factors limit the ability to create mine barriers as distinguished from less effective mine "hazards."

U.S. Air Capabilities

At least for the foreseeable future, the U.S. Air Force will be limited more by base and support capabilities than by aircraft numbers or readiness. While the USAF would experience substantial problems in trying to deploy fighter aircraft if it were denied the use of allied bases and overflight rights, it now has at least seven wings of fighters available and could project as many squadrons to the Gulf as local air bases could support if the Gulf states chose to provide such facilities. The USAF could also tailor its forces to the threat with considerable flexibility, and the marines could deploy the equivalent of four additional USAF fighter wings. The U.S. could, in fact, commit up to 31 squadrons to the Gulf, in addition to those earmarked for NATO, committed for rotation, and so on. In the event of simultaneous contingencies, the U.S. could still afford to commit more than 26 squadrons to Southwest Asia.[26] This does not take into account aircraft grounded for maintenance. In the late 1970s, up to 40% of U.S. combat aircraft were grounded for maintenance,[27] but the USAF and Marine Corps will greatly enhance their readiness under the FY1981–1987 defense programs, have already sharply reduced such problems, and can further reduce such percentages in an emergency.

The U.S. Air Force does lack an attack fighter with the long range it needs for the Gulf and is losing its F-111s to attrition. It is, however, now evaluating options to acquire such aircraft and the Strategic Air Command has modified two B-52H squadrons to fly deep-penetrating missions in the region. It can now commit 28 B-52s and 7 associated reconnaissance and refueling aircraft, which can be based at Diego Garcia and the Darwin field in Australia.[28] This "strategic projection force" can now provide extensive contingency coverage of the Gulf and the capability to interdict rear-echelon Soviet forces at long distances. Other B-52s, F-15 fighters, and E-3A AWACS units are being trained and equipped to provide land-based defense of the carrier task forces in the Indian Ocean and to defeat the Soviet naval bomber and surface threat.[29]

In short, the key problem for U.S. air power will be forward basing. It is important to note in this regard that the "bare bones" kits designed to allow the USAF to deploy military basing capability by air have so far proved inadequate, particularly in supporting the F-4 and F-15. Accordingly, the USAF must draw on the base facilities, munitions, and AC&W capabilities of Saudi Arabia, or other friendly Gulf states, to fight any kind of intensive conflict in the Gulf.

Soviet Contingency Capabilities in the Gulf Region

The exact strength that the Soviet Union could commit to conflict in Southwest Asia is a matter of conjecture. A Soviet offensive in the Gulf region might include anything from an airborne assault in conjunction with indigenous forces to a full-scale invasion by several mechanized divisions in conjunction with commitment of Soviet naval forces. Table 19.2 illustrates Soviet military strength in the areas from which Soviet forces might most readily be drawn.

TABLE 19.2 Soviet Forces Available for a Gulf Contingency

Service	Units	Personnel (where applicable)
Army[a]	1 tank division [b]	11,000
	21–22 motorized rifle divisions	152,000
	2 airborne divisions	15,000
	3 artillery divisions	12,000
Naval Infantry	2 regiments[c]	5,000
Frontal Aviation[a]	2 tactical air armies[d]	6 fighter regiments 6 fighter bomber regiments
	34th TAA in Transcaucasus MD	300 MiG-21, -23, -27, YAK-27, SU-24, SU-25
	6th TAA in Turkestan MD	175 MiG-21, -23, -21R; Mi-8
Naval Aviation	Interdiction and antiship aircraft	Undetermined number of long- and medium-range bombers[e]
Navy	1 carrier battle group Guided missile cruiser battle groups Attack submarines (Pacific Fleet)	Size of Indian Ocean Task Force would depend on extent of conflict[f]

[a]Author's estimate. Does not include 1 airborne (105th), 7 motorized rifle divisions (54th, 66th, 201st, 360th, 346th, 5th, and 16th), and 5 air assault brigades, the 85,000–90,000 men in combat units, some 500–600 helicopters (200 Mi-24s), and several hundred Soviet fighters and bombers in Afghanistan.

[b]1 tank, 1 artillery, and 6 motorized rifle divisions in the North Caucasus MD; 11 MRD, 1 airborne, and 1 artillery division in the Transcaucasus MD; and 5 MRD and 1 artillery division in the Turkestan MD. In mid-1981, 5 were Category I, 5 were Category II, and 14 were Category III. About 50,000–150,000 reservists would be required.

[c]The Soviet Union has 2 naval infantry regiments in the Pacific Fleet, making up an operational division.

[d]The USSR could draw upon the resources of 3 tactical air armies with 600 aircraft and 18 regiments without drawing upon those in the military districts facing other fronts.

[e]Combat deployment of these aircraft is open to speculation. However, there are approximately 80 Backfire, B5s with AS-4 ASMs, 40 Blinders, and 270 Badgers available in the strike aircraft inventory of the naval air force. Probably no more than 100 bombers (from the Black Sea and Pacific fleets) are more immediately available.

[f]The Soviet Union might commit more of the Pacific Fleet plus reinforcement from the Black Sea Fleet. The size of a Soviet Indian Ocean contingent would depend on deployment necessary in other areas of conflict, if confrontation between the U.S. and USSR turned to other theaters. The Indian Ocean squadron has normally had about 20 ships, only 4–5 of which have been major combatants, but it has built up rapidly during the October War, Ethiopia-Somalia conflict, Iranian civil war, and other crises.

Sources: The Military Balance 1982–1983 (London: IISS, 1983), pp. 10–14; a telephone interview with John M. Collins, senior specialist for the Congressional Research Service; Thomas L. McNaugher, "The Soviet Military Threat to the Gulf," Brookings Working Paper, February 1982; Keith A. Dunn, "Constraints on the U.S.S.R. in Southwest Asia: A Military Analysis," *Orbis* 24 (Fall 1981):607–629.

Land Force Capabilities

The Soviet Union has approximately nine divisions and about 80,000–90,000 troops of the forces shown in Table 19.2 deployed near the Iranian border, plus approximately seven motorized rifle divisions, five air assault brigades, and one airborne division in Afghanistan, which might be temporarily withdrawn from counterinsurgency operations.[30] Only one of the nine Soviet divisions in the USSR near Iran is a tank division. This division is part of the North Caucasus Military District, and it is located at a somewhat greater distance from Iran than most motorized rifle divisions. However, this is relatively unimportant given the formidable armored "punch" of Soviet mechanized divisions. The Soviet Union's major problems are likely to lie in readiness and deployment rather than in a need for armor.

Most Soviet motorized rifle divisions now have three motorized rifle regiments and one tank regiment of three battalions. Each tank battalion has 36–40 tanks, giving the division an armored capability of some 216–266 tanks. Motorized rifle divisions in Europe that are up to full strength have an additional tank unit with about 50 tanks. Each motorized rifle regiment has a separate ATGW battery armed with Sagger or Swatter antitank missiles and a separate AA battery with four ZSU-23-4 AA guns or four SA-9 surface-to-air missiles. In addition to antitank and antiaircraft capabilities, the motorized rifle regiment contains about six 122mm howitzers and 112 APCs.

Divisional-strength Soviet mechanized infantry forces normally have a separate FROG or SS-21 battalion to attack rear-echelon forces and provide support in tactical nuclear warfare. They also have an artillery regiment with 18 100mm antitank guns and an additional 54 112mm howitzers. Their antiaircraft capability is augmented by a separate regiment of 24 57mm towed AA guns or a battalion of SA-6 or SA-8 SAMs. The combat-ready divisions have reconnaissance, engineer, and signals battalions and a chemical defense company.[31]

In contrast to a motorized rifle division's 266 tanks, a first-line Soviet tank division in Europe possesses a total of 335 tanks, but 40 of these belong to an attached motorized rifle regiment. The Soviet tank division is smaller than the motorized rifle division, with 11,000 men as opposed to 14,000.[32] In most Gulf contingencies, the additional armored capability of the Soviet tank division will add little to the motorized rifle division's offensive power. While a Soviet motorized rifle division has fewer tanks, it has more infantry support. Since large-scale armored battles seem unlikely, the more massive mechanized infantry forces in the motorized rifle divisions seem likely to provide a better capability to seize large areas and deal with probable mixes of indigenous and U.S. forces.

Soviet units are noted for their high tank-to-soldier and combat-to-support-personnel ("teeth-to-tail") ratios. Supply could be a serious problem as Soviet forces move southward, particularly if the advance involves heavy combat. The Soviets are beefing up their logistical capabilities, but their experience in Afghanistan indicates that they are still having problems and need one-half to one man in support for every man in a combat unit.[33]

The Soviet Union has seven divisions plus a training unit in reserve. At least two of these airborne divisions would be available for immediate action in Southwest Asia. One is the 104th, based at Korovabad in the Transcaucasus Military District, and the other is the 107th, stationed at Fargana in the Turkestan Military District. A third, the 97th Guards, is stationed at Alogorsk in the Trans-Baikal. These divisions grew from 7,000 to 8,500–12,000 men between 1975 and 1982; they have three brigades each.

Each airborne division has an inventory of 127 airliftable BMD combat vehicles and 30 ASU-57/85 airborne assault guns. In addition, airborne units have a contingent of 13 BRDM armored scout cars, some mounted with AT-4/AT-5 antitank missiles. Their artillery consists of 18 120mm heavy mortars, 18 D-30 122mm howitzers, and 18 M-1965 140mm multiple rocket launchers. Antitank capabilities are augmented by 18 73mm or 85mm antitank guns and 27 AT-3/AT-4 ATGW launchers. Antiaircraft weaponry includes 36 ZSU-23-4 self-propelled AA guns and SA-7 SAMs.[34] These divisions are being steadily augmented with battalion-sized elements of Mi-8, Mi-24A, and Mi-24D/E attack helicopters. One battalion in three of each motorized rifle regiment is being trained for helicopter operations. The USSR has also recently organized independent air assault brigades with 64 assault helicopters, a squadron of M-26 heavy-lift helicopters, and three air assault rifle battalions.[35]

The Soviet airborne division is essentially a portable mechanized division, which proved its tactical value during the Soviet invasion of Afghanistan. Elements of Soviet airborne forces airlifted into Afghanistan seized and held vital areas in and around Kabul.[36] These areas were held long enough for heavier motorized rifle divisions to cross the Afghanistan border and link up with airborne troops in place.

The key problem the Soviets face is the readiness of these units. While the airborne divisions are combat ready, the rest of the units are largely Category 3 units or worse, and Soviet manpower near Iran would have to grow from 170,000 men to 380,000 to fill out the Soviet force structure in the region. Fifteen of the 22–24 regular divisions in the USSR north of Iran had less than 25–30% of their wartime manning at the end of 1982. Five were Category 2 units with 30–75% of their manning, and five were Category 2 units at nearly full strength. Many had second- or third-rate equipment and were far short of the TOE strength of Category 1 units in Europe. While the USSR can unquestionably bring such units to their full manning levels rapidly by using reserve personnel, or by airlifting in regular troops, it is still far from clear how many of the Category 3 units can be made fully combat effective and how long this process would take. U.S. intelligence experts disagree over both these problems, over the extent to which the readiness of such divisions is being upgraded, and over the pace of the modernization of their combat equipment.

Amphibious Capabilities

The Soviet Union might also make use of its naval infantry, the Soviet "Marine Corps," in a permissive environment in which the U.S. did not oppose such operations. The Soviet Union has placed far less emphasis on amphibious operations than the United States, but it has shown increased interest in strengthening its amphibious forces. Although the naval infantry's total manpower has remained static, the USSR has augmented its amphibious lift capability and has outfitted it with a slightly more credible forced-entry capability. The naval infantry's inventory of light tanks increased about 60% from 1970 to 1979, and its inventory of APCs increased about 50%.[37]

The Soviet Union now maintains 2 naval regiments in the Pacific fleet, but the endurance of Soviet naval infantry is relatively limited. In spite of recent improvements, it still has a total of about 200 tanks, including obsolescent T-54/55 medium and PT-76 light tanks. Mechanization is limited to a total of about 750 APCs and AFVs, including BMPs and BTR-60P vehicles, and the Soviet naval infantry has no helicopters or tactical aircraft. This limited mix of heavy weapons is understandable in the light of Soviet amphibious tactics. In an amphibious assault, Soviet naval infantry is intended only to secure a beachhead, followed by heavier motorized rifle elements. Alternatively, it would conduct harassment or diversionary strikes along the flanks of heavier units.

Air Force Capabilities

The Soviet Union could commit two to three tactical air armies (TAAs) and 475–600 fighters to a Gulf conflict without drawing on tactical aircraft stationed in distant military districts (MD) or on its strategic air defense forces, the PVO Strany. Each Soviet TAA normally has three fighter and three attack regiments, giving it a total of 54 immediately available squadrons if the TAA is at full strength.[38] There are also an undetermined number of Soviet tactical aircraft in Afghanistan. Each squadron has between 10 and 15 aircraft, with an average of 12. Many key targets in Iraq and Iran would be in range of Soviet tactical aircraft operating out of bases in the Soviet Union and possibly Afghanistan, although targets in the southern Gulf would be beyond the range of most Soviet fighter types.

The new Su-24 strike fighter is greatly extending the range of Soviet TAAs, as is deployment of the MiG-23B and MiG-27. An A-10-like tank killer, the Su-25 or Frogfoot, is now entering service in Afghanistan, and an improved two-seat version of the MiG-25M is being deployed with pulse doppler look-down/shoot-down radars and AA-9 shoot-down missiles. The MiG-29 Fulcrum, an advanced variable-wing multirole fighter roughly equivalent to the F-18, will be deployed in the mid-1980s, and a new fighter called the Su-27 is in final development.[39] Although Soviet capabilities for air projection are increasing, and the USSR has built six new bases in southern Afghanistan, Soviet forces are still limited by the lack of well-placed airfields, the long ranges involved, and the mountainous terrain of the area, which impedes low-altitude strikes and radar coverage.[40]

The main threat Soviet air power poses to most of the Gulf now consists of long- and medium-range bombers. At least 16 Backfires are reported to be positioned in the Transcaucasus, and Bears can operate out of the USSR as well as Da Nang and Cam Ranh Bay in Vietnam. Such Soviet long-range aviation (LRA) and Soviet naval aviation (SNA) aircraft have an extensive combat radius. Badgers have a range of 2,605 NM, Blinders have a range of 1,215 NM, and Backfires have an unrefueled range of 4,350 NM.[41] The Backfires in Soviet naval forces now regularly practice AS-4 Kitchen missile strikes against U.S. carrier task forces in the Sea of Japan.

Such aircraft pose a threat to U.S. land-based forces in the Gulf region and could jeopardize the U.S. naval presence in the Indian Ocean and Arabian Sea. They are acquiring steadily better avionics and surface-to-air missiles, and a new Soviet bomber, a variable-wing type called the Blackjack A, is likely to be deployed in 1986.[42] Even today, intermediate-range bombers armed with antiship cruise missiles and operating in strike regiments with tankers and ECM aircraft might, with sufficient luck and air cover, be able to eliminate a U.S. carrier battle group.

Soviet Naval Capabilities

Estimates of the naval strength that the Soviet Union will be able to commit to a future conflict in the Gulf are affected by several major uncertainties.[43] The Soviet Pacific Fleet consists of 25 SSBNs, 95 other submarines, and 85 major surface combatants, including one 37,000-ton Kiev-class aircraft carrier (*Minsk*), and 104 submarines. It includes 215 minor combatants, 20 amphibious ships, 77 support ships, and 330 combat aircraft, including 120 bombers. Additional combatants and one full-sized 60,000-ton carrier are under development. The extent of Soviet deployment in the Indian Ocean now averages 3 submarines, 7 surface combatants, and 18 support ships. In a crisis, it would depend on Soviet reaction to the crisis and how widespread conflict with the U.S. became.

If conflict was limited to the Gulf region, the USSR could theoretically employ most of its Pacific Fleet and, if necessary, reinforce Indian Ocean naval forces with vessels from the Black Sea Fleet. If a conflict was global in scope, or threatened to escalate to such a level, Soviet resources for Gulf conflict would be limited. Soviet naval deployment would depend on how vital Soviet planners considered victory in the Gulf to be in a broader conflict and on their calculation of the U.S. reaction. If the Soviet Union did opt to commit sizable naval forces to the Indian

Ocean, a future Soviet Indian Ocean task force could consist of up to two Kiev-class carriers, possibly one Moskva-class carrier from the Black Sea Fleet, 1 Kirov nuclear-power guided weapons cruiser, a number of guided-missile cruisers, several guided-missile destroyers and frigates, and large numbers of submarines.[44]

Soviet Kiev-class carriers now have little tactical air power compared to U.S. carriers. They are 37,000-ton ships, as compared to 60,000 tons for a U.S. carrier. A Kiev-class carrier is designed primarily to launch SS-N-12 surface-to-surface missiles with 550 kilometer range, carry out ASW missions, and provide amphibious support. It has an aircraft inventory of 15 Yak-36 Forger V/STOL aircraft and 20 Ka-25 Hormone helicopters.[45] Moskva-class carriers are smaller, having only 18 Hormone ASW helicopters and no V/STOL aircraft aboard. This is scarcely sufficient air strength to survive against even one U.S. carrier task group. Adding arresting wires and catapults and Su-24 or Fencer variants to the aircraft complements on Soviet carriers could theoretically give Soviet carriers a strike ability by augmenting their existing V/STOL aircraft with multipurpose fighter/attack planes, but current Soviet carriers would still lack the space and arming capability to generate significant numbers of attack sorties. This situation will not change until the Soviet Union completes a large, 60,000-ton carrier similar to the U.S.S. *Forrestal*, with a projected complement of 85 aircraft, in the late 1980s, and even then the U.S. should retain a decisive edge in naval air power.

Soviet naval forces now stress guided-missile cruisers over sea-based air power. Even Kiev-class carriers are designed for a guided-missile role, with eight launchers for SS-N-12 antiship cruise missiles, and Hormone B helicopters for over-the-horizon targeting. Soviet guided-missile warships are designed to concentrate the maximum amount of firepower into the minimum amount of tonnage. The large Kirov has 20 SS-N-19 surface-to-surface missiles plus SS-N-14s. The Kresta- and Kara-class cruisers and Krivak III–class frigates all possess launchers for SS-N-14, SS-N-16, and possibly SS-N-12 antiship cruise missiles.[46] The new nuclear-powered Kirov-class guided-missile cruiser, which began sea trials in May 1980, symbolizes this aspect of Soviet sea power. It is introducing new generations of long-range air defense and antiship missiles. In July 1980 the USSR started sea trials of a new 8,000-ton Sovremennyy-class guided-missile destroyer, which also carries new antiship and antiair missiles, in July 1980, and of a new ship called Black-Com-1, which is an 11,000–13,000-ton command ship with long-range antiship capabilities, in early 1981.

Many Soviet attack submarines are also intended for a cruise missile role. The new Oscar class carries 24 antiship missiles with submerged launch capability. Some 42–70 Papa- and Charlie-class submarines are equipped to launch stand-off missiles; Charlie II–class submarines can launch eight missiles with 100-kilometer range from a submerged position, and more advanced attack and missile-carrying submarines are now being deployed. The missile on the Oscar class, for example, is estimated to have a range of over 450 kilometers.

Although the Soviet Union would lack air power, it could move a formidable armada of ships with antiship missiles into the Indian Ocean and Arabian Sea. In the event of naval confrontation with U.S. forces, the Soviet Union could deploy its surface combatants and attack submarines and emphasize stand-off weapons for single-shot kill probabilities far more advanced than the Exocets the Argentines used against the British in the Falklands. Although the number of cruise missiles aboard Soviet surface combatants is limited, and such ships can be tracked and destroyed by aircraft, the range of their missiles will exceed that of missiles like the Harpoon on U.S. ships and aircraft. The U.S. will gain the edge in missiles as well as aircraft as it deploys the Tomohawk cruise missile in 1984–1988, but the Soviet fleet may also increase its ship-destroying potential. Its ships can also target the air-launched antiship missiles carried aboard Soviet intermediate-range bombers.

Given the size, reach, staying power, and other characteristics of the Soviet Navy, it seems more likely that its role will be limited to that of a strategic sea interdiction force through the late 1980s. Further, most Soviet naval power in the Indian Ocean still operates out of Vladivostok. The tremendous distances involved, and the uncertainty of free passage through the Pacific sea lanes and choke points in war, are also likely to limit Soviet naval power in the region.

U.S. Strategic Reach

These measures of U.S. and Soviet force strength tell only part of the story regarding the relative capabilities of each side. The effectiveness of each side is also determined by the extent to which it has the "strategic reach" to deploy its forces rapidly and effectively and to sustain them once deployed. "Strategic reach" consists of 4 elements: (1) airlift, (2) sealift, (3) amphibious lift, and (4) prepositioning. A contingency distant from a nation's borders requires a proper mix of all four. Each element has tactical advantages that the others do not possess, and each element has disadvantages that can be compensated for only by use of the other three. In general, airlift has the advantage of speed, but the disadvantage of inefficient lift. Sealift has the advantage of adequate lift, but the disadvantage of much slower deployment. Amphibious lift has the advantage of providing self-contained and surprise assault, but the disadvantage of its dependence on naval and air superiority, its limitation to coastal areas, and its inadequate "follow on" capability. Prepositioning still requires theater mobility.

The U.S. is particularly dependent on having an appropriate mix of the four elements of strategic reach because of the enormous distances its forces must travel in a Gulf contingency. The USSR has an advantage in the northern Gulf because of its geographic proximity, and it can use lighter and shorter-range aircraft. U.S. "reach" also is heavily dependent on having a relatively "permissive" environment. Airlift, sealift, and the other aspects of U.S. strategic reach can be efficient only if the U.S. has the consent of the foreign governments involved to use intermediate staging bases and can deploy to the territory of one or more countries in the Gulf area. If the Afghanistan invasion is an indication of Soviet planning, the Soviets may prefer a "permissive environment" but are scarcely dependent on the full consent of a "host" nation.

U.S. Airlift Capabilities

Airlift is essential for the initial deployment of U.S. forces, given the time required to deploy adequate sealift. However, U.S. airlift capacity is limited. As a result, it would now take 30–35 days to transport a U.S. mechanized division from CONUS to the Gulf by sealift, but over 50 days of airlift.[47]

This difference between the ability to move mechanized forces by air and by sea will grow in the future as the U.S. procures fast cargo ships with roll-on/roll-off capability, shifts to ferriable or more easily transportable attack helicopters, and prepositions its armor. Even the largest air transports have serious problems in moving heavy armor. The C-5A is the only air transport in the U.S. inventory that can transport the 58-ton M-60A1 battle tanks in U.S. mechanized divisions, and a C-5A can carry only one M-60 per sortie. It would take the entire C-5A fleet to deliver 70 tanks, and—under operational conditions—it would take 400–450 C-5A sorties to deliver the tanks for one division. Carrying a full division without support would tie up all U.S. heavy lift for an extended period and leave no lift for other contingencies. It is also unclear that the C-5A could load the new M-1 Abrahms tank without sacrificing other cargo, and airlift for the new M-2 Bradley fighting vehicle would put an additional strain on U.S. lift resources. The air force now has 70 C-5As and 234 C-141s in its strategic airlift forces. Transporting an 18,500-man mechanized division requires more than 400 C-5A and 1,200 C-141 sorties.[48] USAF lift resources will be further strained by the fact that one-half of a mechanized division's equipment items can be transported only by a C-141 or C-5A.

It would be impossible to simultaneously transport major equipment for a mechanized division and the 82nd Airborne Division to the Gulf, since simultaneous airlift would require over 830 C-141s, and the total USAF inventory is less than one-third that amount. The smaller, but more numerous, C-130 transport planes have only a limited payload capacity to carry the 82nd's equipment and troops. While the 82nd can air-deploy a battalion in 48 hours, and ready two of its three brigades for air movement in 18 hours, U.S. air transport is now so limited that it is doubtful that the entire 82nd division can be deployed within its claimed five days even if no other units were being moved.

Transporting the heavier 101st Air Assault Division by airlift could take an additional month.[49] The statistics on total lift capacity for a Middle East or Gulf contingency are confusing because they vary from study to study, but it is clear that the U.S. now faces significant problems. Testimony before the House in July 1982 indicated that the present C-5A fleet could provide only 37% of the 39,880 tons needed for a Middle East contingency and 72% of the 24,740 tons needed for a limited contingency in the Gulf. The USAF announced later that it had only enough airlift capability to transport one and one-half light divisions and two fighter wings in 40 days (versus a mission requirement of 21 days) and that it had a 25-million-ton-mile deficiency in airlift capability. Forty percent of this deficiency was said to be in the outsize cargo capability that only a C-5 or C-17 could provide, and this did not take into account potentially serious problems in tanker and refueling capacity.[50]

Tactical resupply by air, as opposed to strategic deployment of airborne forces, would be easier. Tactical transports using the container delivery system can theoretically drop supplies accurately within a 400-meter area[51] and can drop vehicles using the low-altitude parachute extraction system with similar accuracy.[52]

The problems in U.S. airlift would be far worse if NATO were also threatened. "Nifty Nugget" and successor exercises suggest that the air force could not reinforce Europe effectively by airlift, let alone simultaneously support the Gulf and Southwest Asia. By 1986, airlift requirements for a NATO contingency will require 13,000 tons of material by the 10th day of conflict, 64,000 tons more by the 15th day, and 71,000 tons more by the 20th day. Ironically, the new consumption estimates made during 1981 and 1982 indicate that urgent load requirements for NATO are more than 129,250 tons, which exceeds current airlift availability by 80%. Even a "bare bones" supply of both NATO and the Gulf would require an immediate 43,870 tons, or 58% more lift than the U.S. could provide, versus a 28% deficiency for a Gulf contingency alone.[53]

Maintenance requirements and attrition would further limit U.S. strategic airlift capability. It can be assumed that transports would come under enemy fire, and downed aircraft could not be replaced, as none are presently being produced. The wings of the C-5A currently suffer from critical metal fatigue after 7,100 flight hours, and 12–20% of the total U.S. strategic transport force has been grounded at all times for maintenance. "Fixes" are now under way to the wings of all 77 C-5As in inventory to extend their life by 30,000 hours, or through the year 2000, but their success is still unproved. The ability of the C-5A to operate on primitive airfields, such as those that might have to be used in Southwest Asia and the Gulf, is also uncertain. Some of the C-5As tested on unprepared surfaces have experienced extensive damage, and C-5As with a payload of 550,000 pounds have taxied off the end of qualified runways during takeoff—even though the maximum payload of the C-5A is supposed to be 600,000 pounds. There are, however, 80 airfields in the region that can take the C-5A, 28 of which are in the southern Gulf and 20 of which are in Saudi Arabia.[54] The USAF has "stretched" its C-141s and added refueling to increase their payloads (at a cost of $3 million each). This permits them to carry 30% more payload and to eliminate at least one intermediate refueling stop on the way to the Gulf. The U.S. has also programmed funds during FY1983–1985 to buy the additional spares necessary to increase wartime utilization rates.[55]

Strategic air transport must rely on overflight and refueling rights, and the U.S. is heavily dependent on the use of Lajes Air Force Base in the Azores. While the U.S. has obtained new rights in Morocco, and is seeking such rights in the FRG, UK, Egypt, Tunisia, and Spain, it is still somewhat dependent on Portuguese permission to massively deploy to the Gulf by air. Such rights were denied to U.S. transport aircraft flying to Israel during the 1973 Arab-Israeli War. Other denials have occurred before and since, and it is possible that key overflight rights could be denied to U.S. transports flying to the Gulf and Southwest Asia.

In order to deal with this problem, and to augment existing U.S. airlift capability, the air force originally sought $10 billion to procure a new, larger transport aircraft called the C-17. This request was made in 1981 and met with major opposition. Even before the C-17's selection, the General Accounting Office accused the air force of requesting development funds without a clear idea of what requirements the C-X (the prior name for the C-17) should fulfill. Then, in a report on FY1981 defense appropriations, the GAO stated that the air force had emphasized a new transport without properly studying proposed C-5A modification options. The intended payload capabilities of the C-X required it to carry one to two M-1 battle tanks or the infantry/cavalry fighting vehicles, and the GAO charged that it could not carry this payload the required 2,000–2,400 miles without refueling.[56] These charges were exaggerated, since the USAF deliberately left its specifications loose to allow manufacturers to propose a wide range of options, including C-5 variants. Nevertheless, they helped block the program. Although the air force selected the McDonnell-Douglas variant of the C-X in August 1981, the Congress and the administration denied the program funding.

At the direction of the secretary of defense, the air forces dropped the C-17 and instead sought funding of 50 C-5Bs and 44 KC-10 tankers. Although the latter aircraft were not as capable in landing on short fields as the C-17s, they were chosen because they could be fielded in the mid-1980s rather than in 1988–1989, and because the OSD felt they effectively met the immediate airlift needs of the RDF.[57] This decision seems to be going ahead, along with further modifications to the C-5A to improve its short-range and rough field performance and improvements to existing U.S. tankers to increase their range and endurance. Further, development of the C-17 continues, now as a possible replacement for the C-130 and C-141. The first 15 C-5Bs are funded by the end of FY1985, and all 50 by the end of FY1988. The 50 C-5Bs and 44 KC-10s will provide 13 million ton-miles and will meet the immediate need for 10 million ton-miles of outsize cargo capacity. While the C-5Bs have escalated in cost from $9 to $11 billion and may be delayed, the force should still be ready by 1989.[58]

Civil Reserve Airlift

Some of these problems in U.S. airlift could be eased through utilization of the Civil Reserve Air Fleet (CRAF), which provides as much as 15% of total U.S. airlift potential. At present, there are 324 long-range commercial aircraft in the CRAF program. These include 90% of the long-range passenger and 100% of the long-range cargo aircraft in U.S. inventory; they are a mixture of DC-8s and DC-10s and Boeing 707 and 747 aircraft. About 215 of these are 747-equivalent passenger aircraft, and 109 are cargo aircraft. The Defense Department has requested that at least 70 of the 324 aircraft in the CRAF program be earmarked for Europe.[59]

Unfortunately, the smaller CRAF transport aircraft cannot carry the majority of the heavy equipment allocated to U.S. forces that would be involved in combat in the Gulf. They also are unsuited for rapid cargo handling at most Gulf airports and would require significant redesign for rapid cargo throughput. DOD hopes to enhance the ability of such CRAF aircraft to carry heavier payloads by modifying them to include side-loading cargo access, floor strengthening, and in-flight refueling. Civilian carriers have been hesitant to make these modifications, however, because of the costs involved and the greater fuel consumption of modified aircraft.

Transporting Fighters and Helicopters

Transporting tactical combat aircraft over intercontinental distances also poses serious strategic problems for the U.S. Tactical combat aircraft can be flown from the U.S. to the Gulf, but only if they are properly supported and they receive refueling from tanker aircraft at points along the entire route. This process absorbs a great deal of tanker capability and can exhaust the crews before they can reach the combat zone. Large numbers of tankers are critical to provide flexibility and recovery time for ferry missions.

In 1981 deploying the first 12 F-15s to Saudi Arabia required 36 KC-135 tankers to fly from Langley AFB in Virginia to the Gulf, although the number of tactical aircraft transported could have been doubled with the resources of just 4 more tankers. In a similar exercise, deploying adequate support facilities and equipment for 12 F-4Es sold to Egypt required the airlift of 378 personnel and 2,000 tons of equipment in 5

C-141 and 28 C-5 sorties.[60] Although the use of conformal wing tanks will ease F-15 refueling, air force and naval fighters will need a highly capable and flexible tanker force, and U.S. Army acquisition of the AH-64 attack helicopter, which has the ferry range to eliminate the need for constant refueling or transport by ship or air, will increase this requirement in the future. This is another major reason the U.S. is procuring 44 KC-10 tankers. Refueling tactical aircraft and helicopters, and the personnel and equipment needed to support them, would seriously strain SAC's present inventory of 615 aging KC-135 tankers. The purchase of 44 advanced KC-10 tankers, 24 of which will be deployed by FY1984, will both largely eliminate this tanker shortage and provide far greater flexibility in staging for the tankers. In addition to having greater range, the KC-10 can carry 350,000 pounds of fuel and extra cargo, which reduces the total number of tankers needed. These same factors explain why the U.S. will re-engine its KC-135As with current-technology CFM-56 engines, which will extend their life, reduce operation and maintenance needs, and significantly increase their range-payload. This program will be complete by 1988.[61]

Sealift and Prepositioning Capabilities

The alternative to relying on strategic air transport is to mix sealift and prepositioning, and it is an alternative that the Reagan administration has also emphasized. Historically, 90–95% of material bound for U.S. forces in Vietnam traveled by ship. The situation in Southwest Asia could, however, be different from that in Southeast Asia. Secure port facilities cannot be guaranteed, and the sea lanes to Southwest Asia could be subject to interdiction. Even fast sealift involves a major drawback in transport time. In the event of a crisis it would take at least 20 days to transport the initial units of a mechanized division to debarkation points in the Gulf, plus 5 days at each end for loading and unloading, and it would take 26–35 days by conventional ship. This period would be extended if scattered shipping had to be assembled.[62]

The Navy Military Sealift Command now owns outright 14 cargo and stores ships and 21 tankers and has another 23–26 cargo vessels and 10 tankers under charter.[63] It also acquired 8 SL-7 high-speed (29–33 knots) container ships in FY1981–1982, which it will convert to a roll-on/roll-off (RO/RO) configuration by 1984–1985.[64] The other ships required for a move to the Gulf would have to be provided by the National Defense Reserve Fleet (NDRF). The NDRF had a low funding priority before the shah's fall. Its capabilities have improved steadily, however, and the NDRF had a total of two RO/RO ships, one Seabee, and seven C-4/C-3 cargo ships available for use by the NDRF in early 1981. Two of the RO/ROs, the Seabee ships, and two of the C-4/C-3s were anchored at Diego Garcia as prepositioning ships.[65] Most of the 179 ships in the NDRF are mothballed in U.S. ports without crews and are 40 years old. Funds were requested in the FY1983 and

FY1984 budgets to create a Ready Reserve Force (RRF) of 29 dry cargo ships that could be ready in 5 to 10 days. This force will increase to 77 ships (61 cargo and 16 tankers) by FY1988 if current plans are funded.[66]

The U.S. also has an active and inactive commercial fleet of 289 cargo vessels and 555 tankers, with another 161 cargo ships and 9 tankers in reserve. Most of the vessels that carry U.S. cargoes are under foreign registry and are under the jurisdiction of the nation whose flag they fly.

The Military Sealift Command's controlled fleet of dry cargo ships has declined from 2,400 to 440 vessels since 1945. While 173 cargo vessels are available under contract or charter as part of the Sealift Readiness Program, only 104 are militarily useful. This fleet is becoming substantially less useful because of the shift from "break-bulk" ships that can carry outside cargo and off-load to ports without specialized container handling facilities. Only 8–25% of the equipment of typical U.S. combat units can be containerized, and the number of active dry carriers with optimal break-bulk capability dropped from 25 to 16 ships between 1982 and 1983.

The tanker situation is similar. In 1983 there were only 143 militarily useful tankers in the U.S. merchant fleet. Most operated in the U.S. coastal trade and were steadily being replaced with barges at a rate of 4–5 tankers per year. Such "handy size" tankers with a nominal 220,000-barrel capability to carry different POL products are now in such short supply that the U.S. would have to rely on foreign-flag carriers with foreign crews in a major conflict. This is almost inevitable in any case because the average U.S. merchant sailor is now 53 years old.[67]

Assembling even a fraction of these vessels would take time, and rapid assembly would require that mobilization plans proceed perfectly. Multiple contingencies could cause nightmares for the Military Sealift Command (MSC) as vessels in the MSC, NDRF, Merchant Marine, and under foreign registry were mobilized and assembled, although study is now under way of the use of standard container ship equipment that could rapidly modify and load any container vessel to meet U.S. military requirements.

The Military Sealift Command is currently capable of transporting only a part of the supplies required for sustained combat in the Gulf region using all these assets, even if no sealift resources are diverted to other theaters. Sealift vessels might also be vulnerable to interdiction if they were not provided with adequate protection, and the U.S. Navy lacks the strength to do this. The civilian crews of vessels chartered for sealift operations might also refuse to serve on unprotected vessels if the attrition rates were high enough. This situation will change, however, as the eight 33-knot SL-7 container ships are converted to RO/RO capability. The 24th Infantry Division could have all its equipment ready to load at Savannah, Ga., in as little as 72 hours and could load within 120. If the SL-7s are allowed through the Suez Canal and can keep up a steady 29 knots, they could reach the Gulf in as few as 12 days. Work on four SL-7s will be complete in 1983, and all eight are expected to be completed by early 1985.[68] Even if the canal cannot be adapted to allow such movements, or if the USSR or its proxies control traffic in the Red Sea, the SL-7s could go around Africa in 17 days.[69]

Even with such capability, sealift operations could result in the loss of substantial amounts of such equipment, plus other supplies and support, if U.S. shipping was subject to interdiction by Soviet bombers, ships, or attack submarines. The transit times for all other types of nonprepositioned vessels would also increase sharply if the U.S. was denied the use of the Suez Canal. Further, the use of such sealift assumes the availability of adequate and secure port facilities—i.e., a "permissive" environment. The USSR, or even Iran or South Yemen, might well try to cut off the U.S. supply lines and deny U.S. forces the use of port facilities in many contingencies.

U.S. Maritime, Prepositioning, and Amphibious Assault Options

Shore-based and maritime prepositioning provide further solutions to some of these lift problems. Both can greatly shorten the time necessary to deploy USCENTCOM units in combat strength and help compensate for the obvious deficiencies in U.S. airlift and sealift. Prepositioning equipment provides rapid mobility without sacrificing firepower, since the personnel for USCENTCOM units can be rapidly flown in by strategic airlift and "marry-up" with their prepositioned equipment. The presence of prepositioning can also be a significant deterrent.

U.S. land-based prepositioning options near the Gulf are restricted by several factors. First, there is the difficulty of predicting the exact area where such prepositioning would be required, given the large size of the Gulf. No matter what the requirement, it still will take time to load and move equipment from any contingency bases, and the equipment might then have to be off-loaded at comparatively primitive facilities. Third, the need to create special storage and loading facilities is almost as costly as providing prepositioned ships. Fourth, the conservative Gulf "host" countries face severe political difficulties in accepting large-scale prepositioning of U.S. equipment.

These factors have less impact on maritime prepositioning, however, and the U.S. already has made substantial progress in this area. The United States prepositioned 7 near-term prepositioning ships (NTPSs) at Diego Garcia in August 1980 and had raised this total to 17 by early 1983. Three ships contained the equipment needed for one marine air-ground task force (MAGTF), two had a 30-day stock of supplies, three had USAF and U.S. Army ammunition, four had 44 million gallons of fuel, one had 9 million gallons of drinking water, and two had mixed supplies.[70] The U.S. also planned to build up the total number of prepositioned ships for the marine amphibious brigades to 13. This would preposition equipment for three MABs, with the ships for the first brigade on station in 1984, the second in 1985, and the third in 1986.[71]

Much of this terminology is confusing; the following table shows the nature of U.S. prepositioning plans in the Gulf and gives a broad picture of the overall investment the U.S. is making in prepositioning US-CENTCOM forces (data represent brigade equivalents/number of ships).[72]

	FY1983	FY1984	FY1985	FY1986
Maritime prepositioning ships	0/0	1/4	2/8	3/13
Near-term prepositioned force	1/6	1/6	1/6	0/0
Depot ships	–/12	–/12	–/12	–/12
Total	1/18	2/22	3/26	3/25

The end result of the prepositioning program is that the U.S. will have the ability to rapidly deploy three marine brigades to even low-capability ports using Maritime prepositioning ships (MPSs), while keeping the supplies for early-arriving army and air units on the 12 depot ships. This will radically change the present balance of marine capabilities. The equipment for one additional marine amphibious force could now be deployed to the Gulf on its own amphibious sealift, but this would require virtually all of the amphibious resources of the U.S. Navy and take considerable time, because the required vessels are scattered or are mothballed. It would take at least two weeks to deploy one of the two MABs stationed at Okinawa to the Gulf by sea, although the transport time for a prepositioned unit would be a matter of days if its personnel were airlifted in. Assembling the necessary amphibious shipping would be time-consuming, and the U.S. might have to send marine contingents into a hostile area in a piecemeal fashion as ships became available.[73]

The ability of the maritime prepositioning ships (MPS) to rapidly off-load in low-capability ports will also ease the problem of vulnerability and the demands on U.S. amphibious lift.[74] The Reagan changes to the Carter prepositioning program do include providing air cover or a naval escort with antiship and antiaircraft capabilities, but the near-term prepositioned force (NTPF) has tacitly depended on a heavily defended, or unopposed, debarkation and off-loading. The MPS program greatly reduces the need for defense of the force during this phase. At the same time, it reduces the risk that Soviet aircraft or ships could sink enough vessels that the advantage of prepositioning would go down with them.

The ability to off-load directly from an MPS is important because the U.S. is only slowly modernizing its amphibious forces. Most of its present 63 amphibious vessels are obsolete, it has modern 20-knot lifts for only one brigade, and even many of the newer ships now scheduled to stay in service into the 1990s are inadequate. They lack the helicopter transports and cargo space to support effective marine operations. The U.S. does plan to procure 12 new landing ship docks (LSD-41s), and 3 have been authorized. It will also start work on the first of three modern 40,000-ton amphibious assault ships (LHD-1) with the ability to base AV-8Bs in FY1984. The USN will not replace eight low-capability helicopter-landing-platform ships until the mid-1990s, but it will fund a service-life extension for the LPHs and LPD-4s. It also plans to build a new landing-platform-dock ship, the LPDX, but this is still in the notional design stage. Production of modern air-cushioned landing craft (LCACs) will begin in FY1983, but only 6 will be in service by 1986. The program will then build 12 ships a year until a total of 54 are constructed.[75] Until these programs make substantial progress, however, the U.S. would have difficulty in mounting an amphibious assault that could overcome any effective opposition to an amphibious landing. The 40-knot LCACs are particularly important in this regard, as are the LHD-1s, because they will provide the quick reaction and deployment capability necessary to reduce the vulnerability of U.S. amphibious forces.

U.S. Basing and the Search for a Permissive Environment

All these factors help explain the search the U.S. has conducted for basing rights in the Gulf region. It is the logical result of a theater strategy that requires extensive staging facilities and a relatively permissive deployment environment whether or not the U.S. relies on a maritime strategy. Unfortunately, Britain's withdrawal from the Gulf and the shah's fall left the U.S. with military facilities only in Bahrain,[76] and Mahé Island in the Republic of Seychelles.[78] U.S. use of the facilities at Bahrain was severely restricted as a result of the October War, and while U.S.-Bahraini relations recovered, the U.S. was forced to keep a low profile. The facilities at Diego Garcia, while useful, are distant from the Gulf. And the facility at Mahé Island is vulnerable to shifts in Seychelles politics and has little value in a Gulf contingency. This forced the U.S. to adopt the strategy of seeking the staging bases shown in Map 19.2.

The U.S. has now reached agreements or arrangements that give it the contingency bases shown in Table 19.3. These give the U.S. a substantial number of staging areas and jump-off points from which to deploy its tactical air and sea power and from which it can initiate tactical airlift. They make a major improvement in U.S. capabilities. While Diego Garcia is 3,000 miles from Abadan, and almost as far from the Western Gulf as Dublin, Ireland, it is an ideal staging point for B-52 operations, prepositioned ships, and amphibious vessel assembly. U.S. combat aircraft flying from the new $170 million air base the U.S. is building at Masirah in Oman could cover most of the southern Gulf, and the airfield facilities at Masirah could prove indispensable for tactical

MAP 19–2
U.S. AND SOVIET POWER PROJECTION BASES IN THE MIDDLE EAST AND GULF

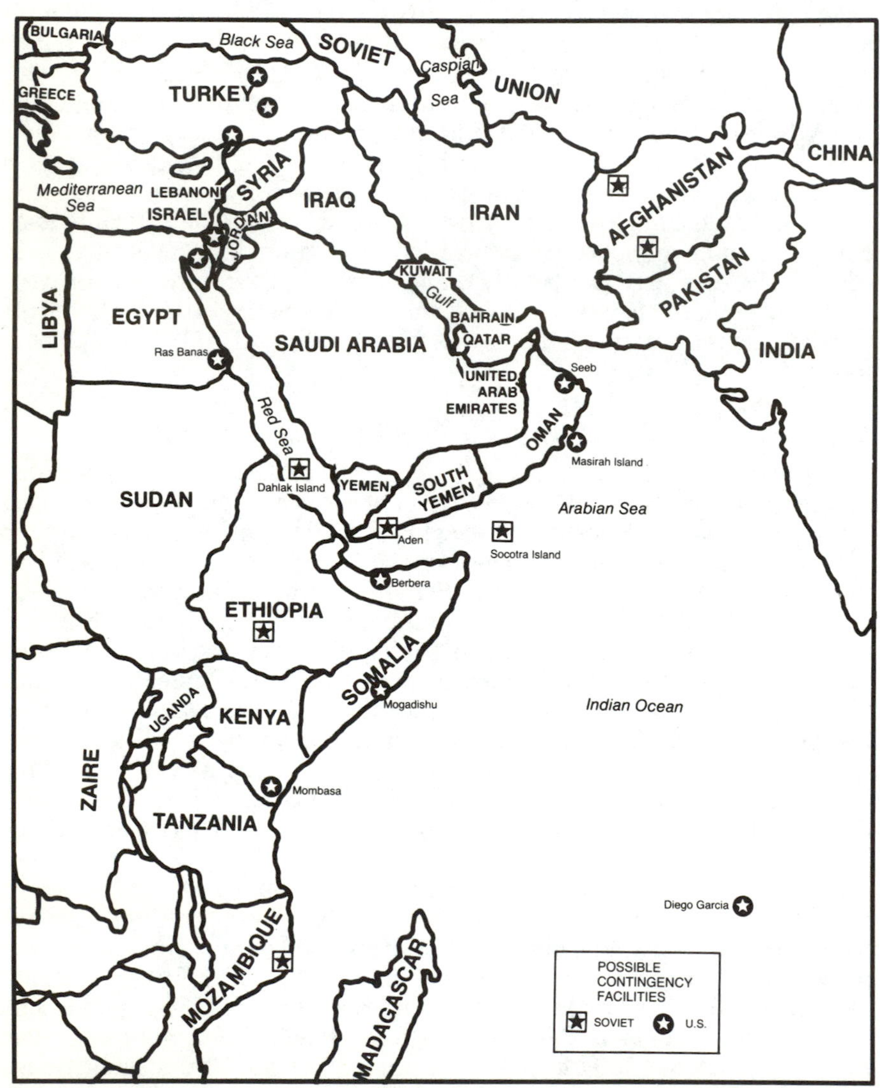

Adapted from *Newsweek*, 17 March, 1981, *New York Times*, 3 December, 1981, and Secretary of Defense, Annual Report, FY 1984, Washington, January, 1983.

TABLE 19.3 USCENTCOM Contingency Bases Affecting the Gulf

Country	Facility	Type
Portugal	Lajes[a]	air staging point
Oman	Seeb	airfield/port
	Thumrait	airfield
	Khasab/Goat Island	airfield/port
	Salalah	airfield
	Masirah[b]	airfield
Somalia[c]	Berbera	airfield/port
	Mogadishu	airfield/port
Kenya	Mombasa[d]	airfield/port
	Nairobi	airfield
	Nanyuki	airfield
Egypt	Ras Banas[e]	airfield/port
	Etzion	airfield
Great Britain	Diego Garcia[f]	airfield/port
Turkey[g]	Erzurum	airfield
	Batman	airfield
	Mus	airfield

[a] U.S. is improving base capability and fuel storage.

[b] U.S. is improving selected facilities for contingency use and is upgrading runways, taxiways, and aprons, as well as personnel and maintenance support facilities.

[c] U.S. improvements under negotiation.

[d] U.S. is upgrading airfield and dredging harbor.

[e] U.S. plans to upgrade airfield and port facilities and will build a cantonment. Funding not approved by Congress in FY1983.

[f] U.S. is increasing airfield capacity and building port facilities. A taxiway and strip exists for B-52 operations. 1,856 U.S. Navy and Marine personnel are now deployed.

[g] Bases in eastern Turkey. No formal contingency use agreement exists. Erzurum and Batman will be improved. Mus will be a new base.

Sources: Jeffrey Record, *The Rapid Deployment Force* (Cambridge, Mass.: Institute for Foreign Policy Analysis, 1981), p. 59; DOD, *FY1983 Annual Report,* pp. iii–108, and *FY1984 Annual Report,* pp. 202–204; *Economist,* 11 December 1982, pp. 62–65; *Aviation Week,* 16 August 1982, p. 15; *Time,* 25 October 1982, pp. 47–50; *U.S. News & World Report,* 29 November 1982, pp. 30–31; *Washington Post,* 7 November 1982, p. 1.

airlift operations. Other facilities at Seeb, and at Khasab on the Musandam Peninsula near the strait of Hormuz, are important for maritime patrol aircraft and sea control missions. The bases in Somalia at Berbera and Mogadishu could be useful in keeping the Red Sea open, and in keeping naval forces in the Arabia Sea supplied, although these will be "bare bones" bases. Ras Banas in Egypt is located across from Saudi Arabia's new port at Yanbu on the Red Sea.

Unfortunately, the political situation in the Gulf region prevents the U.S. from reaching formal agreements to obtain access to forward bases in the Gulf. As was discussed in Chapters 10, 11, and 13, the conservative and moderate regimes in the Gulf cannot grant such facilities in peacetime without raising massive internal security problems and risking ostracism from the Arab world. Any hint of a permanent U.S. military presence could spark vigorous protest from key elements of the population and from Iraq and other neighboring states. Even the host nations on the periphery of the Gulf that have agreed to U.S. basing rights have done so on the condition that they retain full sovereignty over the bases—i.e., can deny facilities to the United States at any time—and that no formal security arrangements exist between the U.S. and the host nation. The upgrading of such facilities must also be done solely at U.S. expense, although the improved facilities then belong completely to the host nation.

These conditions have proved particularly difficult in Egypt because the U.S. Congress has been unwilling to accept informal assurances from the Mubarak government that the U.S. would be allowed to use Ras Banas and transit nuclear-powered warships through the Suez Canal. The Mubarak government is unable to take the same high profile in making formal commitments to the U.S. that helped lead to President Sadat's assassination, and this has presented the usual problems in U.S.-Arab relations because of U.S. insistence on formal commitments that are no more binding in practice than informal commitments. Further, the Office of the Secretary of Defense mishandled its relations with both Egypt and the Congress. Under Secretary of Defense Harold Brown, it refused Egypt's offer to allow nuclear-powered warships to transit the Suez Canal and to resolve the issue simply by setting a precedent rather than reaching a formal agreement. In the spring of 1983, senior officials under Secretary of Defense Caspar Weinberger failed to properly explain the Ras Banas issue to Congress and turned U.S.-Egyptian differences over the formal language regarding U.S. use of Ras Banas into a "crisis" that led the Congress to delay funding of improvements of the base.

Another difficulty arises from the tensions between potential host nations. Egypt and Israel are the most obvious example, but friction between Kenya and Somalia, or Oman and its neighbors, could be another source of problems. Somalia has made sporadic claims to the Northern Frontier District of Kenya. During the Ogaden crisis, Kenya allowed war material to be shipped through Mombasa into Ethiopia, and there were reports that Kenyan troops participated in the conflict with Ethiopian and Cuban contingents.

The need for U.S. payment of economic and military aid in return for basing rights also presents problems. Somalia originally requested $2 billion in aid in return for the use of Berbera, but the final figure has come down to $20 million annually in military aid (although the majority of equipment to be transferred is "nonlethal") and $5 million in economic aid. Kenya will receive a $50 million aid package, although it originally requested far more, and Egypt has requested arms sales in the billions in return for U.S. basing facilities. The gap between the original host nation request and the actual U.S. aid is often severe enough so that a given host country may not be inspired to make good on the agreement if any political problems arise or if allowing U.S. use of such bases presents serious risks.

The cost of upgrading bases in the Gulf region must be added to the cost of the aid necessary to obtain them. All the basing facilities shown in Table 19.3 require expensive improvements. The U.S. appropriated $224 million in FY1980–1983 to improve facilities in Oman, as well as to provide prestocking for air units and the marines and a regional headquarters at Masirah. Ras Banas is currently mined and subject to flooding. Improvements will initially cost $91 million, and completion will cost another $400 million. Improving the facilities in Somalia will cost over $54 million.[79] The port of Mombasa will need $26 million worth of improvements, and the total cost of improving facilities in Kenya will be over $58 million. Improving Lajes is budgeted at $67 million.[80] Yet the investment in acquiring these bases will be absolutely useless if the United States is denied use of the facilities for political reasons.

Turkey has been a consistent ally of the U.S. for more than a quarter century. The air bases the U.S. is improving and building at Erzurum, Mus, and Batman in eastern Turkey are not formally designated as USCENTCOM contingency bases, but if Turkey should make them available, they would put U.S. aircraft only 550 miles from Tehran and 700 miles from Abadan. These distances contrast with 1,000 miles to the western Gulf from Ras Banas in Egypt and 3,000 miles from Diego Garcia. The difference could be of critical importance. Even if the U.S. could operate out of Oman, Iran is 900 miles wide (roughly the distance from London to Warsaw), and it is 1,200 miles from Tabriz to Chah Bahar (the distance from Inverness to Zagreb). Turkey also, however, has NATO's longest border with the USSR. It and the U.S. must act with extreme caution to avoid escalation that might drag Turkey into a major war with the USSR. In many contingencies, the role of the bases in Turkey may have to be limited to that of a deterrent, and in most contingencies, their use will have to be limited or will pose grave risks.

The only fully secure U.S. base in the region is on the British atoll of Diego Garcia, which the United States obtained from Great Britain in spite of considerable congressional objection. While Diego Garcia is roughly 2,500 miles from the Gulf, it has both port and air base facilities. It can now accommodate B-52s, C-141s, C-130s, and C-5As, as well as four permanent air combat squadrons. Its facilities required extensive further improvement, however, to support the air and sea traffic that would result in a combat situation. Its airstrip now lacks apron taxiway and maintenance facilities to support B-52 operations in the area for any length of time. The cost of upgrading Diego Garcia is now budgeted at $435 million for FY1980–1983.

The Reagan administration is also planning to diversify operational support and provide much better support facilities in intermediate arenas. It is seeking new tanker facilities with a 40-million-gallon capacity in the Azores and will greatly expand the refueling and service facilities now available in Morocco.

The Overall Rate of U.S. Force Improvements

It is obvious from these data that U.S. capabilities will be in transition through the late 1980s, with different enhancements arriving at different times. These enhancements involve a wide mix of tactical, technical, political, and financial uncertainties that make it difficult, if not impossible, to predict U.S. capabilities at any given time. Nevertheless, the U.S. is making impressive progress, albeit at an impressive cost. This cost is shown in the following table.[81] It symbolizes the extent of the U.S. commitment to defending the Gulf and making up for the military weakness it had at the time of the shah's fall. It is also important to note just how much the U.S. has been able to achieve through informal cooperation with friendly states, through a renewed emphasis on sea power, and by shifting from the Carter focus on forces in being and unilateral intervention to the Reagan focus on over-the-horizon reinforcement and cooperation.

	FY1984	FY1985	FY1986	FY1987	FY1988	FY1984-1988
Southwest Asia specific	622	805	893	1,204	852	4,376
Other	1,618	1,479	1,580	1,717	2,783	9,177
Total	2,240	2,284	2,473	2,921	3,635	13,533

Soviet Strategic Reach

Soviet strategic reach also has its strengths and weaknesses. Soviet airlift is growing, but its capability is still restricted. Soviet airlift is still limited and highly vulnerable, and Soviet amphibious capabilities are just beginning to take on serious proportions. Accordingly, the USSR faces serious problems in operating in the Gulf the moment that its forces cannot move along the land routes contiguous to the USSR.

Soviet Airlift Capabilities[82]

In early 1983 the USSR had a total of 55 An-22 (comparable to the C-5A) and 150 Il-76 (comparable to the C-141) aircraft in its strategic transport inventory, and an additional 31 An-22 and 2 I1-76 aircraft in Aeroflot inventory. The An-22 and the Il-76 have maximum payloads of 80 tons and 40 tons respectively or can transport 175 and 140 people. Both these aircraft types can fly from the USSR to off-loading areas in the Gulf with maximum payload. The An-22 has a range of 4,200 kilometers, and the Il-76 has a range of 5,300 kilometers.[83] It would take 25 An-22s or 50 Il-76s to airlift two lightly equipped airborne divisions to an air base in Iran, Iraq, or Afghanistan.

Another strategic transport, the An-40, is still in final development, but it will be the world's largest operational transport when it is deployed. The An-40 is estimated to have the ability to carry 120 tons for a range of 5,000 kilometers. This exceeds the capabilities of the C-5A, which can carry only 100 tons for the same distance. The An-40 should also be able to out-perform the C-5A in terms of shorter take-off and landing distances.

The bulk of Soviet airlift capabilities are still built around tactical rather than strategic transport, but they could provide significant airlift because of the Soviet Union's proximity to the region. The most common Soviet tactical transport is the An-12 (comparable to the C-130), with 400 in military transport aviation and 350 more available. The An-12 has a maximum payload of 20 tons or 91 people and a range of 1,400 kilometers.

The Soviet Military Transport Command (VTA) has 8 Il-62s, 20 Il-18s and 20 Tu-134s. The Il-62 has a payload capacity of 26 tons for a distance of 6,680 kilometers, and the ranges of Soviet tactical transports like the Il-18 and Tu-134 are over 1,600 kilometers. If these aircraft were involved in a simultaneous lift, they could transport about 13,900 tons.[84] Although the Soviet Union would not commit all its An-12s to an airlift operation in the Gulf, the VTA's airlift potential remains formidable and helps compensate for the relative payload limitations of Soviet strategic transport aircraft. The VTA's total of over 600 tactical transports also has the advantage over strategic transport that the USSR could dispatch more aircraft in a simultaneous lift and achieve a greater element of surprise, and the new An-72 STOL transport will soon provide a capability to eliminate air drops for an airborne assault wave.

While most Soviet lift assets and exercises are concentrated in the western USSR and Europe, the USSR tested its airlift potential in massive airlift operations in the Gulf region in a 1978 exercise. Observers noticed a very heavy amount of Soviet air traffic to Ethiopia during this exercise, with Soviet transports flying from bases near the Black Sea landing every 15 minutes. Roughly 225 transports flew over Yugoslavia to Ethiopia, while other transports took off from bases in Tashkent, flew over Afghan airspace, and landed in South Yemen.[85] It has been suspected that the Soviet Union has been prepositioning equipment in South Yemen in order to supply airborne troops or even provide the equipment for a motorized rifle division. Reports of a Soviet 40,000-man, multinational airborne exercise in South Yemen, however, have been refuted by U.S. intelligence experts.

In summary, existing Soviet military transport resources enable the Soviet Union to airlift 2 fully equipped airborne divisions, or about

14,000 troops, to a country in the northern Gulf in a matter of days. Some observers of the 1978 exercise feel that a fully mobilized and departure-ready unit could be lifted in as little as 10 hours. Alternatively, the USSR could airlift the personnel of two motorized rifle divisions (24,000 troops) to "marry up" with prepositioned equipment, or transport almost fully equipped elements of one motorized rifle division.[86] Such airlift capabilities might enable the USSR to seize key targets with complete surprise, although the staying power of the units would be limited.

Soviet airlift potential can be further increased by drawing on the resources of Aeroflot. Aeroflot aircraft carried Soviet troops for the 1968 invasion of Czechoslovakia, and applicable Aeroflot aircraft can add 1,100 medium- and long-range transports to Soviet airlift capacity. These include 31 An-22, 132 An-12, and 2 Il-76 transports. If Aeroflot was mobilized, the USSR could airlift elements of a third airborne division simultaneously or increase the overall cargo payload of the VTA by about 40%. Adding just the resources of Aeroflot's An-12s to the VTA's An-12s would increase the total potential payload of this tactical transport type by 34%.[87] The total passenger-carrying potential of Aeroflot aircraft could transport 120,000 troops if time allowed these aircraft to be assembled.

Aeroflot is well suited for such a military role. In peacetime its administration falls under the jurisdiction of a Soviet air marshal, and the majority of Aeroflot's 400,000–500,000 employees are in the military reserves or have had military experience. Around 20,000–25,000 of Aeroflot's pilots would be available for military transport duty if the situation warranted. If the Soviet Union planned massive airlift operations against the Gulf and/or Europe, it could combine the resources of the VTA and Aeroflot in a relatively short time. The pool of available aircraft would then be flexible enough for simultaneous lift of fully equipped assault forces and elements of heavier "follow-on" forces. If the transport exercises to South Yemen and Ethiopia are an indication, the USSR could transport two airborne divisions.

Soviet transport aircraft are also designed for relatively short "hops" in austere environments. They lack the in-flight refueling capability of U.S. transports, but they are designed to operate on unprepared surfaces and require shorter take-offs and landings. The An-26 and An-24 aircraft are equipped for rocket-assist take-offs, and most of the newer aircraft have tire pressure regulators for improved operations on loose, sandy soil. On-board cargo-handling facilities give Soviet transports added flexibility (Il-76 and An-22 aircraft have on-board winches for loading heavy vehicles), and they are also designed for a minimum of maintenance. The Il-76 has tools and spare parts on board and a mechanic is a member of the flight crew; these arrangements can keep the Il-76 in operation for up to 90 days without major maintenance.[88]

Soviet Sealift Capability

Soviet sealift to the Gulf is limited by choke points that constrain Soviet access to major oceans. The maritime staging area out of Murmansk and Archangel confronts the Greenland-Iceland-UK gap. Ships passing out of the Baltic Sea must pass between Denmark and Sweden. Soviet maritime traffic out of the Black Sea must navigate the Dardanelles. Any ships bound for the Pacific or Indian Ocean must travel either through the Strait of La Perouse or the Strait of Tsushima, and the seasonal Soviet "lift" moving through the Caspian consists largely of ferries that offer little advantage over the use of land routes. Soviet maritime traffic must also normally move well within range of land-based aircraft, and Soviet sealift bound for the Gulf region is vulnerable not only to Western airpower, but also to Western antishipping operations.

The Soviet Navy depends heavily on light support vessels. It had 214 principal auxiliary ships in early 1983. Some 28 were fleet replenishment oilers, 28 were support tankers, 19 were submarine tenders, 32 were repair ships, and 107 were support, supply, and cargo ships that had some sealift capability. The key to Soviet sealift, however, is the Soviet merchant fleet. The Soviet merchant fleet has 2,300 vessels, and roughly 1,725 could be adapted for sealift. About 350 vessels of this total are tankers, and 1,375 are cargo vessels. Many of these cargo vessels are well suited for sealift operations. The USSR has emphasized the building of RO/RO ships over container ships, which are less suited for transporting military equipment. It now has 40 RO/RO vessels with large ramps suited for heavy military lift. Soviet merchant tankers are often utilized for direct fleet support and could be diverted almost immediately from civilian tasks. The exact number of Soviet cargo vessels that could be transferred to sealift operations remains classified; but the Soviet Union could mobilize sealift resources from its Pacific merchant fleet, which would be compatible with military lift operations and could be dispatched quickly.[89]

Soviet maritime traffic in the Pacific has been reduced considerably since the invasion of Afghanistan. Prior to the invasion, the USSR was operating about 10 cargo lines to Pacific ports; this number has recently fallen off to about 3. Nevertheless, the USSR maintains sizable merchant traffic to areas in Southeast Asia, particularly Vietnam. The resources available for Soviet sealift could be enhanced by the amount of this traffic, which forms the bulk of Soviet maritime potential in the Pacific. Turnaround times would be smaller, and the USSR could commandeer all available merchant vessels if required.

Soviet Amphibious Lift Capabilities

The same geographic factors that constrain Soviet sealift also limit Soviet amphibious lift. Amphibious operations would be further strained by the relatively small number of Soviet amphibious vessels. The USSR has only one amphibious transport dock (LPD) and 25 landing ship tanks (LSTs), for a total of 26 vessels. The Soviets, however, have steadily expanded their amphibious capability. Up until 1975, the USSR had only 15 LSTs as its entire amphibious lift potential.

The *Ivan Rogov*—which is the sole LPD in the Soviet amphibious force—is a 13,000-ton ship capable of landing 550 naval infantrymen along with their equipment. It also has facilities for operating high-speed air-cushion landing craft and for 6 Hormone helicopters. It is about three times the size of any previous Soviet amphibious ship. It deployed to the Indian Ocean in April 1980. The next largest amphibious vessel—the Alligator class—is capable of landing 375 troops and 26 tanks. The USSR also has 60 LSMs, largely Polnocny-class vessels.[90] If all 14 Alligator-class vessels were mobilized, as well as the 25 smaller Ropucha-class LSTs and the *Ivan Rogov*, the USSR could land the majority of its naval infantry forces in the Gulf. This, however, would mean the commitment of the entire Soviet amphibious capability, the scope of which is small to begin with. The USSR would have to commit an entire arm of its "reach" potential in a highly vulnerable manner to support a deployment that would be of dubious military value in most contingencies.

Potential Soviet Bases

Soviet Pacific forces and Soviet maritime traffic affecting the Gulf and Indian Ocean have historically been linked to Vladivostok. The USSR has, however, steadily expanded its alliances and potential basing facilities to decrease its dependence on Vladivostok and to increase its power projection capability in the Indian Ocean and the Pacific. As Map 19.2 shows, the Soviet Union has acquired several strategically located allies around the Indian Ocean and the Gulf region that could threaten Western sea lines to communication and U.S. naval forces.

Utilizing its alliance with Vietnam, the USSR has acquired use of the former U.S. facilities at Da Nang and Cam Ranh Bay. These will allow the USSR to increase its deployments into the Indian Ocean and make a Soviet naval presence more difficult to suppress than if it were based at Vladivostok. The USSR has brought a submarine tender into Cam Ranh Bay, and Echo- and Charlie-class submarines have been sighted operating out of Soviet facilities in Vietnam. Such deployments could signify a substantial increase in the future Soviet attack submarine threat to U.S. naval LOCs, since such submarines could disperse into open water with far less reliable warning than if they were deployed from Vladivostok. Soviet intermediate-range bombers have been flying out of bases in Vietnam. If they were deployed in sufficient number, they could pose a serious threat to the U.S. naval presence in, and access to, the Indian Ocean. The USSR could move a substantial number of its surface combatants out of Vladivostok before the U.S. had the opportunity to close off the choke points.

The Soviet Union has established "bases," or obtained facilities, at Dahlack, Massawa, and Assab in Ethiopia. These are well situated to control the Red Sea and traffic through the Suez Canal. The USSR has docking facilities across from Ethiopia at Aden near the entrance to the Red Sea, plus control of the former RAF base at Khormasters. It also has facilities at Socotra. While rumors of up to 10 submarine pens may be untrue, the USSR regularly flies Il-38 maritime reconnaissance aircraft from Aden. The Soviet Union thus has potential contingency bases on both sides of the entrance to the Red Sea and could support a substantial naval presence in Southern Arabian waters. Soviet naval aviation or tactical aviation may be able to use these same bases to seek control of the Red Sea even without the use of sea power.

The USSR has been seeking a more permanent presence of its own in the Seychelles, whose facilities include a deepwater port and several airfields. Although facilities in the Seychelles would need substantial upgrading (only one of the airfields is paved), a Soviet presence there would counterbalance the U.S. presence at Mombasa in Kenya and would provide an effective staging area for Soviet naval aircraft and ships. In addition, the USSR has shown interest in leasing Gan in the Maldives, which does have a surfaced runway and is within striking distance of the crucial U.S. facilities at Diego Garcia.[91] These efforts have reportedly failed, due mainly to Indian intervention.[92]

These changes in Soviet basing will become steadily more important as Soviet naval and air forces expand. Soviet forces operating out of Cam Ranh Bay could also restrict U.S. access to the Indian Ocean through the Pacific. If the USSR can develop major bases in Ethiopia and South Yemen—and facilities in the Seychelles and Maldives—it may be able to close the Indian Ocean to U.S. sealift and naval forces or to inflict serious losses. This, however, would require at least a decade of further effort, a major improvement in both Soviet ship and aircraft strength and capability, and a U.S. failure to complete its present plans to expand its air and naval capabilities in the region.

Lessons of the Invasion of Afghanistan

Both the U.S. and the USSR face serious difficulties in operating in Southwest Asia. Both sides also lack practical experience in such warfare. USCENTCOM forces have conducted intensive exercises, but these are only exercises, and the failure of the U.S. hostage raid in Tehran has demonstrated how uncertain such exercises can be.

The Soviet invasion of Afghanistan[93] is, however, providing a limited test of Soviet strategic "reach," and of Soviet ability to deploy its forces directly along the major northern land routes into Southwest Asia. It is also providing a test of Soviet airlift and armored mobility, has given Soviet troops extensive experience in mountain and rough terrain warfare, and has furnished the first serious tactical test of Soviet attack helicopters, particularly the impressive Mi-24. In addition, the seizure of the air bases in Afghanistan has placed Soviet tactical aircraft several hundred miles closer to some targets in the Gulf region and given it six new air bases in southern Afghanistan, although few of these targets are of significant strategic value.[94] Soviet intermediate-range bombers operating out of Afghanistan have achieved somewhat broader coverage of the Indian Ocean and the Gulf and might help the USSR capitalize on the antiship capabilities of its naval aviation forces.

It is unclear, however, that the Soviet invasion provides a clear model of Soviet ability to take on more sophisticated forces. When the USSR intervened in Afghanistan in December 1979, it already had over 16,000 troops in the country and had built up cadres of advisers and supporters necessary to paralyze the nation's security forces, governmental apparatus, and communications. The USSR also left nothing to chance in military terms. It applied a tremendous force to secure itself against an army with negligible capability for modern warfare and that lacked political leadership and will. This is illustrated by the sequence of Soviet operations at the start of the invasion.

While accounts differ, elements of the 105th Paratroop Division seem to have been deployed near Kabul airport on the night of 24 December, while elements of the 103rd and 104th Paratroop divisions deployed near Bagram Air Base to the north. On the night of the 27th, all communications were cut, and the paratroops seized complete control of the air bases and critical facilities in Kabul. During the first two days of the invasion, between 100 and 180 Soviet Il-76, An-22, and An-12 transports flew 5,000 additional Soviet paratroops into Afghanistan, and within four days some 10,000 were deployed in the country.[95] At the same time as the major paratroop actions began, the 360th and 201st Soviet MRDs advanced from the Central Asian Military District. Both divisions crossed the border at Termez and then advanced as rapidly as possible on Kabul by the two main routes available (Marzar-Baghlan and Kunduz-Baghlan). They quickly captured small border airfields at Kunduz and Mazar-Sharif, and Soviet attack helicopters were immediately deployed to provide additional air support. The 375th and 66th MRDs crossed the border simultaneously from Turkestan at Kushka and seized air bases at Herat and Shindand.

Overall operations were coordinated by the Soviet first deputy defense minister, Marshal Sergei Sikolov, from the Soviet General Headquarters at Moscow, using satellite links to the 105th Paratroop Division at Kabul and the 40th Army headquarters at Termez, with relay links to each of the major combat elements involved. By early January, over 50,000 Soviet troops were in control of most of the country, and the 40th Army headquarters was relocated to Bagram Air Base. The 16th and 54th MRDs were sent in as reinforcements in mid-January, and the 33rd MRD was sent to control the Salang Tunnel area, the Khyber Pass, and the Kandahar–Khojak Pass route into Pakistan. A fighter-bomber unit was deployed at Herat, and MiG-21 and Mi-24 squadrons were deployed at Shindand and Kandahar to cover the south.[96]

It is important to note that this Soviet sledge hammer failed to crack the Afghan walnut. By mid-1981, the USSR had built up to about five motorized rifle divisions and one airborne division, plus about six fighter squadrons, four Mi-24 squadrons, 2 An-12 transport squadrons, and some Tu-95 bombers. The fighting then forced the USSR to reduce the tank inventories of its divisions in favor of BMP fighting vehicles and Mi-24 attack helicopters, because it found that tanks were relatively ineffectual in suppressing the Afghan guerrillas and led to casualties of 500 or more per week.[97] The USSR also had to bring in 170 combat aircraft and 150 helicopters to "support" the Afghan Air Force in counterinsurgency operations by the fall of 1981.

During 1982, the Soviets were again forced to massively reinforce their air strength and start harsh reprisals against population centers in their efforts to suppress the Afghan "*mujahidin*" (popular guerrillas). Although the USSR launched major offensives against Kandahar in the south and Parvan, north of Kabul, in the winter of 1981–1982, and massive offensives against the *mujahidin* strongholds in the Panjsher Valley (60 miles north of Kabul) and Paghman (a mountain area 12 miles from Kabul) in the spring, summer, and fall of 1982, it had little success. The rebels remained strong, and the Afghan Army cooperated with the *mujahidin* more often than it attacked. Soviet efforts to use General Abdul Qadar to end the feuds between the Khalqis and Parchamis in the army had no success. Even in mid-1983, the army remained at around 30,000 men. It also had had roughly 20,000 desertions and 8,000 casualties, more than enough to offset draconian Soviet efforts at forced conscription during 1981–1983.

This situation was particularly striking because the USSR had suffered 2,500–5,000 killed and 5,000–10,000 seriously wounded by mid-1982, in spite of its buildup. It had seven divisions (tentatively the 105th Airborne and 5th, 16th, 54th, 66th, 201st, and 346th Motorized Rifle Divisions) in the country, plus up to five air assault brigades. It was operating 500–650 helicopters (200 of which were modified Mi-24s), it was using toxic agents, it was making heavy use of T-72s and M-1973 self-propelled 152mm howitzers, it was using its latest SU-25s and MiG-27s—and still it could not move safely, even in armored convoys.

This situation forced the USSR into further reinforcement in late 1982. By early 1983, it had raised its forces from 85,000 men at the end of 1981 to at least 105,000 men, had 3,000 to 5,000 more "advisers" in country, had 30,000 more men in "rear guard" duty just over the border, and was training at least 2,000 Afghan military annually in the USSR. Yet it still could not even secure Kabul. The city's entire power supply was knocked out temporarily on 8 February 1982; and the Soviets could not move enough fuel into the capital to heat it for the winter. Similar attacks continued through the end of 1983. Further, although the USSR steadily increased its efforts to control key towns and population centers, at least one-third of Afghanistan's 280 district capitals remained outside Soviet control, and the fighting threatened to go on indefinitely.[98]

Soviet forces are, however, acquiring practical experience that could be of great value in any future intervention in Iran. They have tested every weapon, from the smallest to the largest. Soviet troops in Afghanistan have been outfitted with the new AK-74 assault rifle, which is the lighter-weight version of the AKM. They also are equipped with new self-propelled artillery and FROG and SCUD surface-to-surface missiles, although the latter weapons have no possible utility in counterinsurgency operations. Thus they have been able to test the use of artillery and possibly potential tactical nuclear weapons in a combat situation. The Soviet units in Afghanistan also conducted "exercises" in biological and chemical warfare early in the invasion, and the Reagan administration has since accused Soviet troops of utilizing chemical warfare to kill at least 3,000 Afghans and Afghan guerrillas.[99]

The Soviets' most extensive lesson, however, has been in learning how to conduct effective air support strikes with its fighters, to fight the Mi-8 and the Mi-24 attack helicopter and to conduct rapid tactical movements through mountain areas. It has now modified the Mi-24 to fly in the cold and at high altitudes and has changed its weapons mix to suit mountain warfare. The USSR is reported to have deployed well over 200 modified Mi-24s to Afghanistan, and these play a vital role in suppressing guerrillas, particularly in a counterambush role.

Such Soviet experience with modern warfare, under conditions similar to those that would occur in any attack or intervention in northern Iran or Iraq and using similar lines of communication, may ultimately be the greatest value the USSR gets from its invasion. At the same time, it may also be a massive deterrent to intervention in any situation in which the USSR is not certain of a friendly people as well as a sympathetic regime.[100] The invasion has been costly. In addition to at least 15,000–30,000 Soviet casualties and 5,000 killed, Soviet-occupied Afghanistan lacks friends, a stable regime, and an effective army.[101] Rebel operations continue, with a total force of up to 100,000 men and active forces of 10,000–20,000, and the resistance was still able to operate parallel governments in major cities like Kandahar and Herat at the end of 1983.[102]

The only tangible benefits the USSR obtained for expenditures in excess of $2 billion a month were slightly enhanced supplies of Afghan natural gas at preferential prices; 19 air bases, including greatly strengthened facilities at Kandahar, Kailagai, and Bagram; and new bases in Shindand, near Kandahar, and Jalalabad in the south and southwest. The USSR was also able to annex the Wahan Corridor, the only part of Afghanistan bordering China, bring Tadjik settlers to displace the Afghans in the area, and to build six new airfields in the desolate and large uninhabited northeastern provinces of Badakhshan. This strengthened the Soviet position relative to the PRC and Pakistan.[103]

The strategic value of invading Afghanistan may otherwise be limited. Even if the intensified Soviet pacification effort in Afghanistan does not drag on indefinitely, "victory" seems likely to leave Afghanistan a highly troublesome client state. A thrust through Afghanistan would be of marginal advantage to any Soviet movement against Iran or the Gulf. The USSR would find it far more difficult to move troops through the northwestern land routes in Afghanistan centered around Herat than to move through Tedzhen and Ashkhabad in the USSR. Movement through Afghanistan would also expose Soviet forces to guerrilla attacks and might double or triple the movement time to reach any key objectives in northeastern Iran. Unless the USSR moved against Pakistan or Baluchistan, which seems likely to end in a worse strategic morass than invading Afghanistan, it would also draw only limited benefit from trying to deploy through Afghanistan to reach the Gulf. There is only one suitable road net connecting southwestern Afghanistan with Iran, which is centered on the Zaranj-Zabol axis. The capacity of these routes is low, distances are long, and Iran east of Kerman is strategically unimportant. Moving west from Kerman would force the USSR to deploy over one of the worst road systems in Iran, through many natural defensive barriers, and across a mix of desert and salt plateaus that is one of the most unpleasant areas in the world for military operations.[104]

The Impact of Afghanistan on a U.S.-Soviet Conflict in the Eastern Gulf and Gulf of Oman

The new roads, bridges, and ports that the USSR is building in Afghanistan will change this situation marginally. The permanent road and rail bridges over the Oxus, new paved roads, expanded ports at Hairatan and Sher Khan, and twin oil and diesel pipelines from Termez through Mazar-e Sharif and Oålaqai to Kabul will allow more rapid passage to Iran or Pakistan. At the same time, the Soviet Union seems likely to continue to face serious problems in securing its movements and rear areas. As a result, it is the Soviet air bases at Farah, Herat, Serdeh Band, and Kandahar that may be the most serious Soviet advantage. These already base MiG-27s and MiG-25Rs. Such bases will bring Soviet air operations only about 300 NM closer to targets in Iran, and most Afghan air bases are further from the key Soviet objectives in Iran than the Soviet bases along the Iran-USSR border, like that at Ashkhabad. The Afghan air bases might, however, have more value to the USSR in striking at other targets in the Gulf.

Soviet tactical air power could use such bases to strike at virtually all key targets in the southeastern Gulf. Soviet antiship aircraft, such as the Backfire, could also partially compensate for the relative inferiority of Soviet surface combatants. It is also conceivable that Soviet transports could use bases in Afghanistan as a staging area or help compensate for the lack of adequate Soviet overland access to the Gulf region by supporting a surprise airborne assault. Such an airborne assault could seize strategic areas and hold out for heavier units to make the slow passage into the region.

A Comparison of U.S. and Soviet Military Capabilities in Southwest Asia

Differing U.S. and Soviet capabilities do not lend themselves to any simple net assessment. It is virtually impossible to predict the contingency in which the "building blocks" of military capability on each side would be employed, or the political conditions that would limit their actions. While it is easy to make worst-case comparisons for the West, such as a U.S.-Soviet war for the control of northern Iran, the previous chapters have shown that Gulf conflicts rarely arise in the form of theoretically logical geopolitical wars. Many of the key factors that will shape the outcome of any fighting between U.S. and Soviet forces are in considerable transition. Both sides are steadily improving their ability to project forces into the region, as well as the readiness and capability of the forces they can project. More significant, both sides are experimenting with different equipment, tactics, and training. Given the experience of recent years, it is unlikely that most of these new concepts will be fully implemented or even reach a high degree of stability until the mid-1980s. Nevertheless, some trends do emerge in the U.S.-Soviet balance.

The Land Force Balance

The USSR has an obvious advantage in the land forces it could deploy in the northern Gulf. This advantage is shown in the comparison in Table 19.4 and it is clear that the Soviet forces now in the area outnumber the total forces the U.S. can rapidly deploy by at least two to one. This Soviet lead would be far greater if the U.S. did not have ample warning, did not deploy its forces into the area before a conflict began, and did not have time enough to improve its airlift and sealift. In many contingencies, the Soviet superiority in the northern Gulf could be well in excess of six to one. Further, the USSR has far more armor and attack helicopter capability in any contingency that allows it to move into Iran.

Several problems arise, however, in making such comparisons. The first is the role of indigenous forces, which will be discussed shortly. The second is the nature of the intervention or conflict: Much depends on whether a given side must make a forced entry into the area or whether it is welcomed in. The third is the readiness of each side's forces. The Soviet units near the region are largely reserve forces, and opinion differs sharply on how rapidly they can be made combat effective. Some experts, for example, feel Category 3 divisions can be made ready in as little as seven days; others think it might take over three weeks. A fourth problem arises out of the kind of fighting that would be required. The problems in desert warfare have been discussed earlier, but much of the area is mountainous, and most of the population and key objectives are in built-up or urban areas. Thus, the units on both sides must be ready to fight three kinds of relatively unconventional

TABLE 19.4 Comparison of U.S. and Soviet Forces Available for a Gulf Contingency

	United States		USSR	
Service	Units	Personnel	Units	Personnel
Army	82nd Airborne	16,200	1 tank division	9,500
	101st Air Assault	17,000	22 motorized rifle	152,000
	24th Mechanized	12,300	1 airborne	7,000
	48th Mechanized Brigade	3,600	3 artillery	12,000
	Ranger Battalions (2)	1,200		
	1 air cavalry brigade special forces units	2,500		
Amphibious	1 amphibious ready group 1 Marine amphibious force (Div, 1 air wing) 1 Marine amphibious brigade	47,400	2 naval infantry regiments	4,800
Total		100,200		185,300
Air Force	Combat aircraft		Combat aircraft	3 tactical air armies (about 1,350 aircraft), *plus* the tactical combat aircraft of the naval air forces, probably no more than 90 aircraft and 75 helicopters immediately available.
	Interdiction aircraft	35 B-52Hs (2 squadrons)	Interdiction aircraft	Undetermined numbers of intermediates and long-range bombers
	F-15s 72 (1 wing) F-111a 144 (1 group) F-4Es 72 (1 wing) A-10s 85 (1 wing) Total 373			
Navy	3 Aircraft Carrier Task Forces	Escorts and support would vary depending on task	1 carrier battle group; Guided missile cruiser Battle groups Attack submarines	Size of Indian Ocean Task Force would depend on extent of conflict
	ASW aircraft	5 squadrons		
	Prepositioned support ships	17		

Sources: James Wooten, "Rapid Deployment Forces," CRS Issue Brief IB80027, updated 23 March 1981; ***The Military Balance, 1982–83*** (London: IISS, 1983).

warfare in a highly political environment and under conditions that can range from a unilateral intervention in an uprising or civil war to conflict with another superpower. Worse, both sides must be prepared for escalation to nuclear or chemical warfare.

While little unclassified data is available on the details of the recent training activities of each side, it is doubtful that either U.S. or Soviet land forces have yet decided how to deal with all these possibilities. Soviet capabilities for desert warfare are an area of major uncertainty to U.S. intelligence experts, and probably to Soviet commanders as well. While the USSR has extensive advisory experience with countries that fight desert warfare, its exercise experience seems relatively limited except for one large-scale, 100,000-man land and naval infantry exercise in the Baltic and Belorussian military districts called Zapad-81. This involved 80 ships from all four Soviet fleets, 27 landing craft, and extensive air support. While it seems to have been directed at the FRG and Denmark, it may have been designed for global power projection purposes. The U.S. has conducted extensive exercises over the last few years, but these have exposed many problems, and the U.S. Army and Marine Corps are only beginning to reequip, retrain, and reevaluate tactics and doctrine.[105]

The Soviets have now acquired extensive experience in mountain warfare, and the U.S. has some relevant experience from its long involvement in South Korea and Vietnam. However, several key uncertainties arise. Mountain warfare tends to favor the defender and/or the best-trained and most experienced force. The ability to conduct offensive maneuvers in mountain areas requires exceptional training and leadership against well-equipped defenders, and without it, moutain warfare can become highly static even in attacks against sharply inferior defending forces. At the same time, the helicopter is rapidly changing the rules for such conflicts. The Soviets have already proved this with their use of the Mi-24 in Afghanistan, although the Mi-24 lacks the maneuver capability needed for some aspects of such conflicts and cannot operate with full effectiveness at high altitudes and high temperatures. The U.S. is also reequipping and retraining its USCENTCOM forces to use helicopters in desert, mountain, and urban warfare and to use combinations of light armor, helicopters, and infantry. This effort is, however, still in its experimental stages, and the U.S. Army will need a new divisional organization, new attack and tactical lift helicopters, and improved antitank missiles, AFVs, and short-range air defense weapons to implement its current concepts. The U.S. will be in serious trouble if it has to fight before it can deploy its AH-64 attack helicopter and light armored vehicle and its new division structure.

As the Iran-Iraq War has shown, urban warfare can be the most difficult fighting of all. The U.S. does have a number of special units trained to intervene in urban fighting and to help put down uprisings or civil conflicts. These units are, however, comparatively small and unproved. Similarly, the Soviet Army, the KGB, and East Germany all have specially trained urban intervention forces, although little is known about their size and actual readiness. Even less clear is what would happen in a major war that involved fighting in a capital or other large city. This could involve brigade- or division-sized forces, and the relative performance of U.S and Soviet forces is almost impossible to predict.

As a final major complication, all of these types of fighting might be transformed into prolonged guerrilla warfare of the kind that has occurred in Afghanistan. Such warfare could tie down large numbers of U.S. and Soviet forces in fighting local and highly political military actions and could seriously threaten their already extended and vulnerable supply routes and lines of communications. It would also place an extremely heavy burden on the C³I capabilities of the forces on each side, and both are only now beginning to acquire dedicated command and communications facilities suitable for fighting in the Gulf region. Finally, it would require large numbers of specially trained and equipped forces, which seem to be lacking on both sides.[106]

It is impossible under such conditions to predict the true force ratio or importance of numbers and mass on each side. Both armies are, after all, largely peacetime armies. While they have fought limited military actions since World War II, neither force has tested itself against an equally well-trained and -equipped force in the quarter century since that war. It is easy to advance arguments about the probable result of fighting between them; it is far more realistic to say that the results will be highly unpredictable and may be determined as much by unquantifiable factors as by force numbers.

The Importance of Air Power

The U.S. would, however, have a potential advantage in the number and quality of the combat aircraft it could deploy from U.S. carriers and friendly bases. If Saudi Arabia, other southern Gulf states, Turkey, or Iran made suitable bases, AC&W capability, and refueling available, the U.S. should be able to win superiority over both any Soviet tactical aircraft and bomber forces developed in Afghanistan and the southern USSR, except in northern and central Iran. While the three tactical air armies in the area would nominally give the USSR a total deployable force of 350–600 combat aircraft,[107] and reinforcements could be brought in from other military districts, it is still unlikely that the USSR could actually base and support enough aircraft to win air superiority south of the Elbruz Mountains.

Much would be determined by the further effectiveness of the Soviet naval forces and the long-range fighters and bombers based in Afghanistan and the USSR, and by their ability to threaten friendly air bases and U.S. sea-based operations. The U.S. would need good forward air bases and depend heavily on naval superiority to win an air conflict in the Gulf, particularly given the emphasis the Reagan administration is placing on carrier operations and maritime mobility. Successful attacks on such bases or interdiction of U.S. carriers by Soviet long-range aviation, naval aviation, and/or submarines could spell disaster in supporting USN and USMC fighters and U.S. sealift and amphibious operations. The rate at which the USSR deploys its new long-range attack fighters, Backfire, with improved antiship cruise missiles, and Blackjack A, into the region will be a particularly good indicator of whether it can shift the air balance.[108]

Relative Naval Capabilities

Improved Soviet air-based antiship capabilities and submarine-launched missiles would also be necessary to compensate for the present inferiority of Soviet naval forces. Although Soviet surface combatants are geared for an antiship role, they probably cannot now survive engagement with U.S. carrier task forces, and they have limited at-sea support and staying power even with support by the Soviet Merchant Marine. Soviet surface combatants also carry a limited number of antiship missiles because of the Soviet emphasis on single-shot kills, and once these missiles are exhausted, the surface combatants must return to their basing facilities for replenishment. The Soviet reliance on stand-off missiles rather than saturation fire results in the complete vulnerability of Soviet naval vessels once these missiles are exhausted, and U.S. carrier-based aircraft should be able to locate and destroy these vessels before they are within range to launch antiship missiles. Once again, the issue is one of the relative pace of the force improvements on each side.

Amphibious and Lift Capabilities

The Soviets do have significant advantages in some aspects of strategic reach, which are shown in Table 19.5. While the force numbers are not particularly unfavorable to the U.S., the USSR has a distinct advantage over the U.S. because of its proximity to the Gulf. It is 7,000 air miles from the U.S. East Coast to the Gulf and 12,000 miles around the Horn. It is more than 12,000 miles from the U.S. West Coast to the Gulf. In contrast, it is 800 miles from Kivrobad to the headwaters of the Gulf, and 2,000 miles from Kivrobad to Aden. Although the U.S. has more strategic airlift, the USSR can substitute its tactical airlift while the U.S. cannot. As a result, the Soviet Union can now use airlift to deploy and maintain more of its available ground forces in the northern Gulf.

This advantage in airlift is unlikely to change before the late 1980s, but the Reagan administration's use of sealift, amphibious lift, and prepositioning should compensate, except in the northern Gulf. Such U.S. success in increasing and using its sealift and prepositioning will, however, be dependent upon sufficient time to deploy U.S. naval superiority and access to adequate basing facilities. In contrast, Soviet use of sealift will hinge on the degree of U.S. naval superiority in the

TABLE 19.5 Comparison of U.S. and Soviet Lift Capability

	U.S.			USSR	
	Number		Type	Number	Type
Military Airlift					
Strategic					
Active	70		C-5A	55	AN-22
	234		C-141	150	Il-76
Total Strategic	304			205	
Tactical					
Active	218		C-130	400	AN-12[a]
Reserve	19		C-7/C-123	40	AN-24/26
	294		C-130	20	Il-14
				20	Il-18
				8	Il-62
				20	TU-134
Total Tactical	531			508	
Utility/Cargo Helicopters[b]					
Active	333	(Army)	CH-47/CH-54	1,800	?
	153	(Marine)	CH-46/CH-53		
	(4,349)	(Both)	UH-1/UH-60[c]		
Reserve	169	(Marine)	CH-46		
	18	(Marine)	CH-53		
Total	673			1,800	
Civil Air Reserve Fleets[d] (total)	324		long-range	1,300	medium- and long-range
Tankers	128		KC-135	70	(Navy) Tu-16 Badger
	12		KC-10	35	(LRAF) Mya-4 Bison
				10	(LRAF) Tu-16 Badger
	140[e]			115	
Military Sealift					
Active[f]					
Cargo SL-7	88		misc.	107	misc.
Tanker Other	37		misc.	56	misc.
Total	45			163	
Reserve					
Ready Reserve	29		misc.	–	–
NDRF	167		misc.	–	–
Total	196				
Sealift Total[g]	241			163	
Amphibious Lift[h]					
Amphibious vessels					
Amphibious command ship (LCC)	2		Blue Ridge	0	n.a.
Amphib. cargo ship (LKA)	6		Charleston	0	n.a.
Amphib. tnspt (LPA/LPD)	14		Austin, Raleigh	1	Ivan, Rogov
Landing ship dock (LSD)	13		Anchorage, Thomaston	4	MP-4
Landing ship tank (LST)	18		Newport	28	Alligator, Rupucha
Helicopter carriers (LPH, LHA)	12		Taruwu, Iwo-Jima	0	n.a.
Total	65			33	

[a] Aircraft numbers and types for Soviet tactical airlift capability taken from *The Military Balance, 1982–83.* Estimate for total may be inaccurate due to conflicting counts of smaller aircraft.

[b] U.S. utility/cargo helicopter estimate includes U.S. Marine Corps.

[c] UH-1/UH-60 helicopters are not normally shown as mobility assets, but they could have significant tactical value. Not counted in totals.

[d] Aircraft numbers and types for U.S. and Soviet civil reserve fleets taken from *The Military Balance, 1982–83.* Estimate for U.S. Civil Reserve Air Fleet (CRAF) includes 109 cargo/convertible and 215 passenger aircraft. The Soviets include about 200 Cubs and Candids, and 1,000 medium- and long-range passenger transports.

[e] 107 U.S. KC-135s are assigned to NORAD.

[f] Estimate for active U.S. sealift vessels include those 24 owned outright by the Military Sealift Command, those under charter, and those under foreign registry; it does not include 2,300 ships of Soviet merchant fleet.

[g] Merchant carriers dominate this aspect of sealift but do not lend themselves to simple counts. See the previous discussion in the text.

[h] Amphibious lift for the Soviet Union does not include the estimated 56 Hovercraft vessels and 35 LCUs.

Sources: DOD, *Annual Report,* FY1983 and FY1984; OJCS, *Military Posture,* FY1984; John M. Collins, *U.S.-Soviet Military Balance, 1960–1980* (New York: McGraw-Hill, 1980), pp. 528–537; *The Military Balance, 1982–83* (London: IISS, 1983).

Gulf. Although Soviet sealift is increasing, it cannot be used without local sea and air superiority, and the USSR seems likely to be forced to rely on land and air transport.

The Importance of Geography and Communications

Given the mix of capabilities on either side, neither emerges as clearly superior in a conventional conflict, and the outcome of such a U.S.-Soviet conflict would be likely to depend on such factors as (1) the precise location and timing of the conflict; (2) the availability to the U.S. of forward air bases in Saudi Arabia, or in some other Gulf nation, and Turkey; and (3) the fight for the control of critical passes through Azerbaijan, the Elbruz Mountains shielding Tehran, Isfahan, and Shiraz, the mountains in Kudistan shielding the northern Mesopotamian river plain; and the Zagros Mountains, shielding the oil-rich Iranian territory in Khuzestan. Once the conflict moved into an area where Soviet land movement could be blocked—such as the Elbruz or Zagros mountains—the U.S. would have the advantage on the sea, while the USSR would have the advantage on land. The balance would then tend to depend on which belligerent controlled the air and on the relative effectiveness and innovativeness of its ground troops and air units.

There is no way to predict the extent to which current U.S. plans to restructure its ground forces to use antitank weapons and attack helicopters to hold mountain areas will succeed against Soviet efforts to use airborne forces, helicopters, and mechanized infantry to secure them or outflank defenses. A wide range of tactical alternatives exist, and both armies are experimenting with new approaches and training methods. It seems likely, however, that the outcome will be decided not by mass but rather by tactics and speed of reaction.

U.S. and Soviet Military Capabilities in a Collective Security Context

It seems unlikely, however, that any superpower confrontation in the Gulf will be limited to U.S. or Soviet forces or be fought as if the military forces in the region were neutral or merely provided bases and facilities. In fact, it is far more likely that future U.S. or Soviet military action in the Gulf will be limited or indirect in nature and that such action will be aimed at political rather than purely military objectives and be conducted in cooperation with allies in the region. Seen from this perspective, U.S. conventional options and capabilities in most of the Gulf are greater than the previous comparison would indicate.

The Impact of Regional Forces on the U.S.-Soviet Balance

Table 19.6 shows the current balance of forces in the Gulf in terms of their alliance with the West or Soviet bloc. While such alliances have

TABLE 19.6 Comparison of Gulf Forces Related to the West and the USSR, 1982-1983

	Manpower	Medium Tanks	Other AFVs	Artillery	Combat Aircraft	Helicopters	Paramilitary Forces	Reserves
Soviet-equipped/oriented								
Ethiopia	250,500[a]	640	600+	700+	173	47	169,000	20,000
South Yemen	26,000	470+	320+	310+	114[b]	23+	15,000	–
Total	276,500	1,110+	920+	1,010+	287	70+	184,000	20,000
Western-equipped/oriented								
Kuwait	12,400[c]	240	407	90+	49	32	18,000	–
Oman	15,000[c]	18	36+	85+	37	30	3,300	–
Qatar	5,000	24	201	14	9	14	some	–
Saudi Arabia	52,200	450	1,390+	18	174[d]	38	31,500+	–
UAE	48,500	118	486+	70+	52	44	some	–
Total	133,100	850	2,520+	277+	321	128	52,800+	–
Uncertain								
Iran[e]	235,000	1,110	680+	1,265+	90	648	35,000	400,000
Iraq	342,250	2,300	3,100	828+	335	397	31,800	75,000
North Yemen	32,050	714	577	365	75[f]	27	20,000	–
Total[e]	609,300	4,124	4,357+	2,458+	500	1,072	86,800	475,000
Potentially pro-Western								
Egypt	452,000	1,250	3,330	2,124	429[g]	178	139,000	335,000
Potentially pro-Soviet								
Cuba	127,000	660	400+	150+	189	112	165,000	190,000

[a] Incorporating 150,000 People's Militia; some 18,000 Cubans and 1,150 Warsaw Pact technicians are engaged in Ethiopia, operating aircraft and heavy equipment; some South Yemeni troops may also serve there.
[b] Some believed in storage; some flown by Soviet and Cuban crews.
[c] Excluding expatriate personnel.
[d] Includes 46 BAC-167 COIN/trainers.
[e] Real figures believed much less; serviceability of much equipment is low; aircraft figures operation only.
[f] Some aircraft in storage.
[g] Spares for Soviet equipment are short; active holdings being reduced to one-third of listed total; replacement by Western hardware under way.

Source: The Military Balance, 1981-82 (London: IISS, 1982). These figures are general order of battle figures before the Iran-Iraq conflict and do not represent the limited capabilities of the peripheral or related states to introduce forces into the area.

often proved tenuous, the previous chapters have discussed a number of ways the U.S. can build up the security of Saudi Arabia and the conservative Gulf states and improve U.S. relations with Iraq without jeopardizing U.S. relations with Israel. At least in the near term, the alignment of regional forces shown in Table 19.6 favors the U.S. in any contingency other than one in which Iran invited the USSR to deploy its forces on Iranian territory or some conflict in which Iraq either sought direct Soviet support or otherwise welcomed a Soviet presence.

Iran is, of course, the major "wild card" in the region and is likely to remain so for the next decade. It is impossible to rule out the possibility that a pro-Soviet regime will come to power in Iran or that Iran will either invite Soviet military intervention to ensure its "sovereignty" or simply gradually fall into Soviet hands. At the same time, the control of Iran is losing some of its strategic importance. The Iran-Iraq War, Iranian revolution, and Iranian civil war have severely cut Iran's near-term oil- and gas-production capabilities and quite probably its ultimate recovery potential. Iran's economy is still weak, and the West has learned to live without a heavy dependence on Iranian gas and oil. Iran's politics may make any firm Soviet presence untenable for years to come. Accordingly, a Western "defense" of Iran could be limited to de facto partition at the Zagros or Elbruz mountains. It might even be limited to ensuring that Iran's navy, air force, and southern military facilities do not become Soviet bases and that the Iranian-held islands in the Gulf are transferred to friendlier hands. While the West can scarcely "write off" a former friend with more than 35 million people, it also cannot prevent it from writing itself off.[109]

As for the rest of the Gulf, the USSR seems unlikely to use direct military intervention to achieve changes in the alignments shown in Table 19.6. What seems far more probable is that it will try to shift such alignments to make various Gulf regimes more dependent on the USSR and to create regimes more hostile to the conservative Gulf states and Western interests. The problem is not likely to be Soviet invasions, but rather Soviet-backed radical regimes like South Yemen that present a constant military threat to the West's allies in the region, that support limited or indirect aggression, and that back revolutionary movements in the conservative Gulf countries. At worst, such states could act as Soviet proxies with the kind of Soviet, East German, Cuban, and North Korean "volunteers" that have provided a military stiffening to other Soviet-backed efforts.

The Importance of Air Power

This kind of limited conflict would deprive the USSR of its superiority in deploying armored and mechanized forces in the northern Gulf and would further constrain the size of the air forces the USSR could deploy. Unlike in an all-out Soviet military attack on the Gulf, the USSR would have to limit its military support to a level more appropriate to the

TABLE 19.7 National Strength of U.S. Navy and Marine Corps Air Wings

	Aircraft Type	Function	Squadrons	Aircraft
Carrier Air Wing	F-4, F-14 (TARPS)	Fighter (reconnaissance)	2	24
	A-7, F/A-18	Light attack	2	24
	A-6, KA-6D	Medium attack, tanker	1	14
	S-3A	ASW (fixed wing)	1	10
	SH-SH	ASW (rotary wing)	1	6
	EA-6B	Electronic warfare	1	4
	E-2C	Airborne early warning	1	4
Total			9	86
Marine Corps Air Wing	F-4, F-18	Fighter	4	48
	A-4, A-18, AV-8A	Light attack	2–3	38–57
	A-6	Medium attack	1–2	10–20
	KC-130	Tanker/transport	1	12
	EA-6B	Electronic warfare	1	4
	RF-4	Reconnaissance	1	7
	OV-10	Observation	1	12
	AH-1	Attack helicopters	1	24
	CH-53, CH-46	Transport/utility helicopters	6–7	131
	UH-1	Helicopters	9	120
Total			27–30	403–435

Source: DOD, *FY1984 Annual Report,* p. 163.

Somali-Ethiopian conflict, or to the Dhofar and Yemeni civil wars described in Chapter 12. It could not send in regular troops except in small numbers, and it would have difficulty using its Cuban proxies to do more than provide training and occasional leadership cadres.

It might well be possible to limit the U.S. response to such Soviet-backed efforts to providing the threatened Gulf states with support in equipment and military advice. The U.S. may also be able to deter most such Soviet attempts by backing the efforts of the conservative Gulf states to develop collective security capabilities and their ability to reinforce each other in dealing with internal security threats. However, friendly Gulf states would still need U.S. military forces or reinforcements to deal with major revolutionary or guerrilla attacks that were backed by their neighbors, to deal with major border incursions, or to counter outright invasions by neighboring Soviet-backed states.

Even so, the U.S. may be able to use limited amounts of air power to check any such a threat to a Gulf ally. As Table 19.1 has shown, the U.S. has a tremendous potential over-the-horizon capability to provide air reinforcements to a Gulf state. Although the U.S. is limited in its ability to provide land reinforcements to the northern Gulf, it has immense reserves of tactical air power it can draw upon without affecting its forces in Europe. Table 19.7 shows that even a single U.S. carrier or marine air wing could tilt the balance in favor of a pro-Western

Gulf state in many local contingencies. In fact, in some ways, U.S. tactical airpower capabilities operating from friendly bases or carriers under limited war conditions could reverse the usual imbalance in land forces.

The USSR is also unlikely to be able to project enough Soviet tactical air power from Yemen, Ethiopia, Iran or Iraq to threaten U.S. control of the air over the southern Gulf and Red Sea for some years to come. This means the U.S. can offer the conservative Gulf states the air reinforcements they will need to deal with many, if not most, Soviet-backed military contingencies. Such U.S. air reinforcements are "non-threatening" in that they cannot be used to intervene in internal affairs or seize Gulf oil facilities, but they would almost certainly be capable of allowing a Gulf nation to win local or total air superiority. They could strike at rebel bases with impunity and strike at the local ground forces used in a border war or invasion. In short, they provide the basis for a natural strategic partnership between the U.S. and the southern Gulf states.

The Importance of the AWACS Package

As has been discussed earlier, such a partnership in tactical forces will be facilitated by the U.S. success in selling the AWACS package to Saudi Arabia. U.S. deployment of the E-3A to Saudi Arabia has confirmed that the E-3A can play a vital role in a Gulf conflict in economizing the use of U.S. tactical aircraft resources, in winning air superiority, and in ensuring the ability to operate with the friendly Gulf air forces. The USAF E-3As are now planned to remain in Saudi Arabia until its E-3As go on station. According to U.S. Navy and Air Force sources, the Saudi E-3A force will be able to handle an entire U.S. carrier or Marine Corps air wing, up to two air wings of USAF fighters, and Saudi air defense forces when it is deployed. The Saudi E-3As would be equally effective in coordinating USAF and Saudi F-15 operations, USAF F-16 reinforcements, and joint attack missions. Further, additional USAF AWACS could be deployed to Saudi Arabia to defend a second front.[110]

The KC-3 tankers Saudi Arabia is buying will also allow U.S. carrier aircraft to extend their range and endurance, to minimize the risks inherent in deploying carriers into the Gulf or near Gulf waters, and to support both the deployment of U.S. fighters from CONUS or other U.S. bases abroad and their operations from Saudi bases against distant tactical targets in the Gulf. So, for that matter, will most Saudi munitions and spare parts reserves and the technical manpower used to support Saudi fighters as part of the Peace Hawk and Peace Sun programs. As a result, many of the time and mobility force constraints inherent in trying to move air units into a new area of operations would be removed.

Air Power and Land Lines of Communication

The importance of U.S. air power capabilities is also enhanced by the geography of the region. Map 19.2 has already shown how the over-the-horizon staging bases the U.S. is acquiring will give it the capability to rapidly move air power into bases in friendly host countries. Once this is done, the terrain tends to favor the U.S. and its allies in operating in a defensive role. Even in the areas in the western and southern Gulf that are comparatively flat, land force movement is restricted largely to a few roads or fixed lines of communication. Most Gulf forces would find it difficult to sustain large-scale, off-road or desert operations, and such operations rarely offer the concealment from aircraft typical of operations in Europe or other more sheltered areas. These conditions make hostile land forces uniquely vulnerable to a combination of U.S. and allied tactical airpower, particularly given the uncertain training, lack of discipline, and uncertain air defense capabilities of the forces that would have to be used in such an attack.

The rest of the region has more difficult terrain, which tends to channel offensive land movements even further. This is true of the Yemens, Oman, most of northern Iran and Iraq, the Asir, and much of western Saudi Arabia. While such terrain factors will limit U.S. and Soviet land movements alike, they also increase the impact that strong U.S. tactical air forces operating out of friendly bases could have on a Soviet-backed invasion. Any major Soviet intervention in Iran or Iraq, for example, would force the USSR to rely on land lines of communication through the Zagros and Elburz mountains, which have peaks of 12,000–19,000 feet. Since the USSR does not have a common border with Iraq, it would be forced to move to Iraq by air or through Iran. Any land movements would require use of the limited road routes through the mountains in Azerbaijan and Kurdestan. Quite aside from the fact that this might expose Soviet movements to U.S. and NATO land and air operations from eastern Turkey, it would also mean reliance on an almost endless series of vulnerable cutouts, small tunnels, and bridges and an extreme climate in summer and winter. There are no broad river basins through the mountains, just narrow gorges. Recent U.S. targeting studies have shown that these areas are at least moderately vulnerable to interdiction and harrassment by U.S. air power and that with limited deployments of ground troops and attack helicopters, they could be held for some time against superior forces.[111]

These same factors would limit Soviet operations against Iran if Iranian forces chose to fight in their own defense. While it is virtually impossible to defend the northern Iranian plain along the southern edge of the Caspian, and cities like Mashad, Tabriz, Ardebil, and Rasht are probably undefendable, the Elbruz Mountains form a natural defense barrier around Tehran. Even if this barrier is penetrated, the lines of communication south of Tehran offer a mixture of rough terrain and dried-out salt seas that virtually force any invasion to rely on movement by roads. The Iranian "plateau" is also generally 2,000–4,000 feet above sea level and is crossed by lines of hills 6,000–7,000 feet high. If this terrain is crossed, the Zagros Mountains become another defensive barrier where it is far easier for the U.S. to achieve air superiority. It would also take several weeks for Soviet forces to deploy to the Iranian oil fields or the strait of Hormuz in any strength, and they would be exposed to air and helicopter attack most of the way.

Further, in any extensive offensive, the Soviet Union could make use of only one major rail link, the Trans-Caucasus railroad, which runs from Tehran through Julfa to Tabriz and then to Baku in the USSR. This railroad is a slow, twisting route with many vulnerable points and requires a change of guage at Julfa.[112] Roads are limited in the west to one low-capacity route from Yerevan to Jolfi to Tabriz and one from Baku to Rasht to Qazviv. In the east, the Soviets would be limited to a low-capacity route linking Mashad to the Soviet Mary-to-Ashkhabad railspur and the route in Afghanistan from Shindand to the Iranian border. The terrain through which these roads pass consists of high mountains and narrow twisting gorges. The Soviet Union could also use the Volga River, which empties out into the Caspian Sea, and Soviet forces could conceivably make use of the extensive barge traffic on the Volga to link up with Iranian ports on the Caspian. This route, however, is seasonal and slow moving at best. Further, many of these rail and road links are congested even in peacetime, and all the major Soviet supply routes, as well as any Soviet land force movements along them, are highly vulnerable to air attack.

The Soviet Union would be particularly vulnerable if the U.S. could operate from air bases in Turkey, which would bring U.S. air power far closer to the key targets in any Soviet advance south from the Transcaucasus Military District. Operating from Turkey would present obvious complications. It would involve Turkey in a Gulf conflict and might cause the USSR to attack Turkey's weak air defenses or to try to involve Syria as a counterbalance. However, the use of Turkish bases would allow the U.S. to generate high sortie rates against critical road and rail routes and help make air interdiction more effective. The U.S. has already made limited initiatives to secure the use of such bases. It reached an agreement in December 1981 to create a high-level joint defense consultation group, to plan jointly for the improvement of air bases in eastern Turkey and their use by the RDF, and to upgrade the base at Incirlik.[113] As was noted earlier, this resulted in an agreement in the fall of 1982 to expand two bases in eastern Turkey into major operating bases, create a new base at Mus, and improve seven others.

Implications for U.S. Land Force Capabilities

Such an emphasis on U.S. air power does not mean that the U.S. and its regional allies will not need U.S. land forces. The U.S. must be prepared to use ground troops to help halt or delay any Soviet incursion. It does not necessarily, however, have to destroy Soviet forces in detail. It may be enough to interdict Soviet forces by defending key passes or lines of communication while attacking key junctures of supply and command and communication. This means that the U.S. will not need to equal Soviet land power in any "force matching" sense. It should be enough in most contingencies to provide the kind of advisory and support team that could help friendly Gulf armies overcome their lack of experience, management and combat skills, and support problems. In many contingencies, the USCENTCOM forces might have only to provide COIN, attack helicopter, anti-armor, and reconnaissance units to complement local forces. Special urban warfare and point defense teams might be equally useful, particularly if it was clear that they would be deployed in limited strength and in ways that clearly protected a Gulf host rather than threatened it. At higher levels of conflict, even the limited forces now available to USCENTCOM also might be sufficient to hold key strong points in cooperation with host country forces, provided that the U.S. won air superiority and could operate from friendly bases. The future balance will, of course, depend on how rapidly both the U.S. and USSR improve the readiness and strength of the forces they can deploy.

What the United States cannot do is act as a latter-day Xenophon and operate alone in a Gulf state. It cannot hope to check the USSR unless it is supported by key Gulf states. It cannot hope to rescue and sustain an unpopular regime, or to secure objectives like the oil fields, in the face of popular opposition. Even if the U.S. could successfully deploy its land forces in such contingencies and could avoid a direct conflict with the USSR, the U.S. would ultimately still face the problem of how to withdraw. It seems likely that such a withdrawal could generally be accomplished only at the cost of creating a more threatening postwithdrawal situation than existed before U.S. intervention.

If the U.S. chooses to exploit its opportunities, it has strengths in the Gulf that are not apparent in a direct comparison of U.S. and Soviet forces, or in any analysis of U.S. capabilities that is based on U.S. forces operating in isolation or seizing a base, beach, or bridgehead. U.S. strengths complement those of its allies in precisely the areas where U.S. forces seem most likely to serve both U.S. interests and those of friendly Gulf states. If the U.S. is to be successful, however, it must fully reject the emphasis the Carter administration placed on using the Rapid Deployment Force as a unilateral intervention force and consider how it can best develop USCENTCOM's abilities to operate with friendly Gulf nations. It also is not enough to refocus U.S. plans on a maritime strategy, as has been done by the Reagan administration. The U.S. must accept the fact that its primary role is to provide quick and effective over-the-horizon reinforcements, particularly in the form of tactical air power. It must improve its ability to deal with sensitive political scenarios without appearing to threaten its Gulf allies or make itself the natural political scapegoat for every hostile or radical political movement in the region.

The Nuclear Dimension

Finally, the U.S. and its regional allies must also plan for the contingency that a Gulf war may lead to nuclear exchange between the superpowers.[114] The U.S. has already run war games in which the U.S. compensated for its weaknesses in land forces by initiating the use of tactical nuclear weapons and in which both sides responded by the large-scale employment of tactical weapons. In one such case, the total yield of the weapons employed on both sides totaled 26 megatons. While such exercises employ nuclear weapons far more readily than the U.S. or USSR would in reality, it is still true that the strategic value of the Gulf is so great that both the Reagan and Carter administrations have signaled the USSR that the U.S. would use nuclear weapons rather than suffer a decisive loss of Gulf oil.[115]

Any such nuclear escalation would present a wide range of new difficulties, not the least of which is the asymmetric vulnerability of the U.S. and USSR. The Soviet Union could virtually destroy the Gulf's near-term oil-export capability by launching nuclear attacks at only three targets in Saudi Arabia: Abqaiq, Ras Tanura, and Juaymah. Their destruction could reduce Saudi oil production by up to 6 MMBD for up to several years. The USSR could similarly halt most of Iran's oil-export capability with several low-yield strikes at Kharg Island, and a similarly limited number of strikes could destroy the export capability of Kuwait, the UAE, and/or Iraq. This leaves the U.S. with the alternative of having to deter by the threat of countervalue strikes against the USSR, and the credibility of such retaliation is uncertain. This, however, may be a more drastic scenario than the USSR would need to follow. If it were to conduct even one demonstrative strike near a Gulf target, it is uncertain that any Gulf state would continue to support the U.S. or allow the U.S. to conduct military operations from its soil. The southern Gulf nations have such small and concentrated populations that they are uniquely vulnerable. Even Saudi Arabia could lose most of its national identity with something like five nuclear strikes, and the other conservative Gulf states could not survive one. A nuclear attack on Baghdad might at least force a new government on Iraq, and a nuclear strike on Tehran could have a similar effect. Soviet nuclear strikes on Tehran, Mashad, Qom, Isfahan, and Shiraz might well destroy Iran's Persian identity.

While the probable world reaction to such Soviet strikes, and particularly that of the Arab world to nuclear strikes on an Arab nation, might help deter Soviet action, the problem remains that no nuclear war in the Gulf can necessarily be confined to the battlefield or even military targets. Further, it is uncertain that southern Gulf states will accept even the risk of such Soviet attacks to help defend a northern Gulf state. The unique dependence of the conservative Gulf states on the Saudi air base at Dhahran also means that even a single Soviet strike at a military target might destroy the collective security structure of Gulf air power and the willingness of the conservative Gulf states to cooperate with the West.

Unfortunately, the only answer to such Soviet threats or actions seems to be a U.S. ability to launch limited strikes against the USSR. While the risks of such strikes are serious, the U.S. has no choice but to plan for them and to use such forces as its SLBMS and SLCMs to assure the USSR that the U.S. will retaliate against any Soviet strike on critical countervalue targets in the Gulf by inflicting equal damage on the Soviet Union. Even with such steps it will be difficult to persuade the Gulf states to accept the risk of nuclear escalation. Such persuasion will require a great deal of prior consultation and planning. While most Gulf states may now be sufficiently unsophisticated to have failed to think out the full consequences of a major superpower confrontation in the Gulf, they are unlikely to remain so in view of the number of widely publicized U.S. studies of nuclear options.

Notes

1. *Washington Star*, 16 April 1980, p. 1; *New York Times*, 3 July 1982, p. 2; 14 November 1982, p. 21. Conversations with intelligence experts indicate that some evidence does exist to support this conclusion, but that no firm consensus exists. See also Thomas L. McNaugher, "The Soviet Military Threat to the Gulf: The Operational Dimension," Brookings Institution working paper, 1982, pp. 4–7.

2. This was worsened in the spring of 1980 by mistaken intelligence estimates that forecast an immediate Soviet invasion of Iran. These forecasts concentrated U.S. planning on defense of Iran.

3. John M. Collins, *U.S.-Soviet Military Balance, 1960–1980* (New York: McGraw-Hill, 1980), p. 215.

4. Jeffrey Record, *The Rapid Deployment Force* (Cambridge, Mass.: Institute for Foreign Policy Analysis, 1981), p. 49.

5. Congressional Budget Office, "The Marine Corps in the 1980s," p. 14.

6. DOD, *FY 1984 Annual Report*, pp. 128–129; *Armed Forces Journal*, July 1982, pp. 50–56; Congressional Budget Office, *Rapid Deployment Forces: Policy and Budgetary Implications* (Washington, D.C.: CBO, February 1983), pp. 45–49.

7. 315 AH-64s were requested in the FY1982–1986 defense program, with 16,911 remote-designated laser-guided Hallfire missiles and 354 UH-60s. Funding of the extremely advanced and expensive AH-64 was uncertain. DOD, *FY 1984 Annual Report*, pp. 128–129.

8. Ibid., pp. 125–127.

9. *New York Times*, 10 December 1980, p. 24.

10. DOD, *FY 1984 Annual Report*, p. 201.

11. Ibid., pp. 123–125; Maj. Gen. Jack Galvin, "The Heavy/Light Concept," *Armed Forces Journal*, July 1982, pp. 66–88.

12. *Daily Oklahoman*, 31 August 1980, p. 1.

13. *Washington Star*, 9 April 1981, p. 1.

14. DOD, *FY 1984 Annual Report*, pp. 199, 214, 215.

15. Bright Star II saw the first use of the new reverse-osmosis-process water-purification units. Apparently, the problem is now one of water distribution rather than of production. See "Bright Star in the Desert," *Army*, February 1982, p. 40.

16. See *U.S. News and World Report*, "Adding Up the Results of 'Bright Star,'" 30 November 1981, pp. 33–34; Frank Greve, "A Desert War Might Leave U.S. Forces High and Dry," *Philadelphia Inquirer*, 15 November 1981, p. 1.

17. *New York Times*, 10 December 1980, p. 24.

18. John M. Collins and Clyde R. Mark, *Petroleum Imports from the Persian Gulf: Use of U.S. Armed Forces to Ensure Supplies*, CRS Issue Brief IB79046 (Washington, D.C.: Library of Congress, Congressional Research Service, 1982), p. 6.

19. DOD, *FY 1984 Annual Report*, p. 142.

20. *New York Times*, 15 April 1981, p. 7.

21. The French Indian Ocean Squadron normally comprises an oiler, four guided-missile escorts of the Commandant Rivière class, a maintenance support ship, and six patrol craft, reinforced by a naval task force of ASW destroyers, AA frigates, conventional attack submarines, amphibious warfare ships with naval infantry, and an occasional aircraft carrier, as well as an on-call mine-sweeping task force of three ships. Also, the French operate SAR missions and a squadron of Mirage III C interceptors at Djibouti. The main base is at Réunion. The British Royal Navy maintains a permanent presence of a command helicopter cruiser, five frigates, one nuclear-powered attack submarine, four escorts, two oilers, and three replenishment ships, with the last afloat maintenance ship soon to be decommissioned. Both Britain and France have heavy commitments to NATO, however, and both governments have issued defense plans that may cut these forces. Australia, on the other hand, has made a significant contribution to the naval balance in the Indian Ocean recently, with deployment of an ASW aircraft carrier task group and increased allied operations out of Perth. Lastly, the German Bundesmarine has also seen deployment of a small group of destroyers and a support ship. See Diego Ruiz Palmer, "Western Naval Power in the Indian Ocean," *F.Y.E.O.*, no. 37 (3 March 1982).

22. The NATO ministers agreed to collective contingency planning for the defense of the Gulf at the spring 1982 ministerial meeting. This, however, was more a recognition that U.S. forces earmarked to NATO had a de facto commitment to the Gulf than a change in NATO roles and missions.

23. *Washington Post* and *Washington Star*, 4 October 1980.

24. DOD, *FY 1984 Annual Report*, p. 142.

25. "Indian Ocean Unpreparedness," *Defense Electronics*, June 1980, p. 98.

26. Collins and Mark, "Petroleum Imports from the Persian Gulf," p. 6; DOD, *FY 1983, Annual Report*, p. III-103.

27. Stephen P. Glick and Stuart L. Koehl, "The Rapid Deployment Farce," *American Spectator*, January 1981, p. 19.

28. DOD, *FY 1984 Annual Report*, p. 195; Lt. Col. William R. Ligget, "Long Range Combat Aircraft and Rapid Deployment Forces," *Air University Review* 33 (July-August 1982):74–81.

29. DOD, *FY 1983 Annual Report*, pp. 145–146; *Aviation Week*, 30 August 1982, p. 9; *Washington Post*, 7 October 1982, p. 21.

30. *The Military Balance, 1981–82* (London: IISS, 1982), pp. 10–11.

31. For a full account of Soviet armored and mechanized power, see John Keegan, *World Armies* (New York: Facts on File, 1979), pp. 739–740; Keith A. Dunn, "Constraints on the U.S.S.R. in Southwest Asia: A Military Analysis," *Orbis*, 25, no. 3 (Fall 1981):609–629: McNaugher, "Soviet Military Threat to the Gulf"; Dennis M. Gormley, "The Direction and Pace of Soviet Force Projection Capabilities," *Survival* 24, no. 6 (November-December 1982):266–276.

32. Figures for Soviet divisions in Europe per *The Military Balance, 1982–83* (London: IISS, 1983), p. vii. In the author's opinion most Soviet divisions in this region have about 200 tanks for an MRD and 270 for a tank division and only 75% of the manpower figures shown. Most intelligence experts do not agree.

33. See David C. Isby, "Afghanistan 1982: The War Continues," *International Defense Review* 11 (1982):1523–1528.

34. U.S. Army Threats Office, "Organization and Equipment of the Soviet Army"; *The Mid-East Military Survey—2, War Data*, no. 9, 1981, pp. 84, 94. The latter source estimates the four reserve divisions and an increase in manning to 12,000 men.

35. Isby, "Afghanistan 1982," p. 1526; *Weapons and Tactics of the Soviet Army* (London: Jane's, 1981). Also see Viktor Suvorov, *Inside the Soviet Army* (London: Hamish Hamilton, 1982).

36. Israeli sources indicate that Soviet exercises have air-dropped 8,000 men and 160 armored vehicles at ranges over 1,000 miles in less than 22 minutes.

37. See the sources in note 20; John Collins, *U.S.-Soviet Military Balance*, Appendix 4, Table 38; and Gormley, "Direction and Pace of Soviet Force Projection Capabilities."

38. Some Israeli sources quote figures of 2,500–3,500 aircraft, but it is difficult to see how these could be deployed or supported. See "The Mid-East Military Survey," *War Data*, no. 9, 1981, pp. 81–90.

39. See *International Defense Review* 12 (1981):1609–1612; 8 (1982); 9 (1982); *Jane's Defence Review* 3, no. 6 (1982):559.

40. *Jane's Fighting Ships 1980–81*, pp. 207–212; *Aviation Week*, 7 June 1982, pp. 54–56; *New York Times*, 14 November 1982.

41. *Jane's Fighting Ships 1980–81*, pp. 486–487; *Military Balance, 1982–83*, p. 16.

42. *Washington Post*, 9 November 1982, p. 16.

43. The assessment of Soviet naval capabilities in this section is more critical of Soviet forces and trends than many sources on the subject. For contrasting or additional views, see Paul J. Murphy, *Naval Power in Soviet Policy*, Studies in Communist Affairs (Washington, D.C.: Government Printing Office, 1978); Mordechai Abir, "Persian Gulf Oil in the Middle East and International Conflicts," *Jerusalem Papers on Peace Problems*, no. 20, Hebrew University of Jerusalem, 1976; W.A.C. Adies, *Oil, Politics, Seapower, and the Indian Ocean Vortex*, National Strategy Information Center (New York: Crane, Russak & Co., 1975); Alvin J. Cottrell, *Sea Power and Strategy in the Indian Ocean*, CSIS (Beverly Hills, Calif.: Sage Publications, 1981); Normal Polmar, *Soviet Naval Developments*, 2nd ed. (Annapolis, Md.: Nautical and Aviation Publishing, 1981); the various forewords to *Jane's*; Gormley, "Direction and Peace of Soviet Force Projection

Capabilities"; James H. Hasen, "Zapad 81," *Defense and Foreign Affairs*, December 1982, pp. 26–27.

44. Telephone interview with John M. Collins on 10 July 1981; *Military Balance, 1982–83*, pp. 14–16.

45. *Jane's Fighting Ships 1980–81*, pp. 486–487; DOD, *FY 1973 Annual Report*, Annex A, pp. 39–48; *Military Balance, 1982–83*, p. 15.

46. *Jane's Fighting Ships 1980–81*, pp. 408–503; and *Military Balance, 1982–83*, p. 15.

47. Record, *Rapid Deployment Force*, p. 21; USCENTCOM background briefing paper, November 1982, p. 6.

48. "Nation's Ability to Transport by Air and Sea Eroded," *Sunday Oklahoman*, 19 October 1980, p. 1; *Atlanta Journal*, 22 August 1982, p. 22.

49. *Economist*, 11 December 1982, pp. 62–64; USCENTCOM background briefing paper, November 1982, p. 6; *Atlanta Constitution*, 22 August 1982, p. 22; *Armed Forces Journal*, July 1982, p. 54.

50. *Armed Forces Journal*, July 1982, p. 54; *Aviation Week*, 26 July 1982, p. 21.

51. "The Airborne/Air Force Team—Spearhead of Rapid Deployment," *Air Force Magazine*, 3 April 1980; Col. Alan L. Gropman, "The Compelling Requirement for Combat Airlift," *Air University Review* 33 (July-August 1982):2–15, 58–67, 72–81.

52. Ibid.

53. "U.S. Looks to Civil Aircraft," *Aviation Week and Space Technology*, 31 March 1980, p. 48.

54. "USAF Asked Why Not Updated C-5 Instead of New CX," *Armed Forces Journal*, April 1980, p. 17; DOD, *FY 1982 Annual Report*, pp. 200–201; DOD, *FY 1984 Annual Report*, p. 212; "CX Cargo Plane Takes a Direct Hit," *Washington Post*, 22 October 1980, p. 8.

55. DOD, *FY 1984 Annual Report*, pp. 211–213.

56. "Modernizing the Means of Mobility," *Air Force Magazine*, June 1979; DOD *Annual Report FY 1982*, p. 203.

57. *F.Y.E.O.*, no. 39 (31 March 1982).

58. *Armed Forces Journal*, March 1979, p. 12; July 1982, p. 54; Caspar W. Weinberger, *Annual Report to the Congress, FY 1983*, p. III-92; *New York Times*, 6 August 1982, p. 6; 5 October 1982, p. 10; 26 October 1982, p. 13; *Newsweek*, 23 August 1982, pp. 50–51; Fred Kaplan, "The Flying Lazarus," *Washington Monthly*, February 1983, pp. 48–52, 53–56.

59. DOD, *FY 1984 Annual Report*, p. 210; *Armed Forces Journal*, July 1982, p. 56; Paul D. Tuck, "A Uniform National Air Cargo System," *Air University Review* 33, no. 5, pp. 7–12.

60. *Aviation Week*, 7 July 1980, p. 16.

61. "Air Force Will Ungrade Aerial Refueling Capabilities," *Aviation Week and Space Technology*, 11 August 1980, pp. 57–60; DOD, *FY 1983 Annual Report*, pp. III-93–94; Office of the Joint Chiefs of Staff (OJCS), *Military Posture, FY 1983* (Washington, D.C.: DOD, February 1982), pp. 55, 94–98; DOD, *FY 1984 Annual Report*, pp. 200, 224–225, 334.

62. Record, *Rapid Deployment Force*, p. 21.

63. DOD, *FY 1984 Annual Report*, pp. 212–215.

64. Ibid., pp. 200–335; Deborah M. Kyle, "Sea Lift," *Armed Forces Journal*, July 1982, pp. 57–58.

65. James Wooten, "Rapid Deployment Forces," CRS Issue Brief IBP0027, p. 6; DOD, *FY 1983 Annual Report*, pp. III-97, III-106; USCENTCOM background briefing paper, November 1982, p. 6.

66. DOD, *FY 1983 Annual Report*, p. III-99; OJCS, *Military Posture, FY 1983*, p. 98; DOD, *FY 1984 Annual Report*, p. 214.

67. OJCS, *Military Posture, FY 1984*, pp. 32–33.

68. See Carl O. Schuster, "SL-7 Conversion Program," *F.Y.E.O.*, no. 35 (3 February 1982); *Economist*, 11 December 1982, p. 62.

69. *Armed Forces Journal*, July 1982, p. 60; *Journal of Commerce*, 15 June 1983.

70. "The Marine Corps in the 1980's," Congressional Budget Office Budget Issue Paper for FY1981, p. 52; OJCS, *Military Posture, FY 1983*, p. 98; *Economist*, 11 December 1982, p. 63.

71. Record, *Rapid Deployment Force*, p. 19; discussions with various DOD officials in November and December 1981; OJCS, *Military Posture, FY 1983*, p. 98; DOD, *FY 1982 Annual Report*, pp. III-98–99; DOD, *FY 1984 Annual Report*, pp. 216–217.

72. Adapted from DOD, *FY 1984 Annual Report*, p. 198. Note that only MPS ships have an RO/RO capability or can use ports with only limited equipment. Does not include two 200-bed hospital ships to be deployed in 1986 or programs to provide modular off-loading for container vessels and tankers, new army watercraft, and mobile piers or "elevated causeways" that can be installed within 72 hours.

73. DOD, *FY 1983 Annual Report*, pp. III-47–110; OJCS, *Military Posture, FY 1983*, pp. 98–100.

74. Record, *Rapid Deployment Force*, p. 49.

75. DOD, *FY 1983 Annual Report*, pp. III-27–28; DOD, *FY 1984 Annual Report*, pp. 153–154; OJCS, *Military Posture*, FY 1983, p. 90; FY 1984, p. 47.

76. The U.S. military presence in the Gulf was modest until 1979. A small naval force, the Middle East Force (MIDEASTFOR), consisting generally of a flagship and two destroyers, has been assigned to the Gulf since 1949. These U.S. naval vessels enjoyed access to port and support facilities at Jufair in Bahrain under informal agreements with the United Kingdom. The command flagship was homeported at Jufair. With the end of the British treaty a new agreement between the United States and the government of Bahrain (GSB) was implemented by an exchange of diplomatic notes on 28 June 1977. The agreement resulted from negotiations conducted over a year between the two governments and accommodated the GSB's desire to cease formal "homeporting" of the Middle East Force in Bahrain. The agreement terminated this homeporting but provided for a 65-man DOD administrative support unit to be stationed in a 10-acre compound in Bahrain to carry out "administrative functions," including support of ship and aircraft visits, which had exactly the same effect. Further, the GSB agreed to extend the status of forces protection accorded under the 1971 agreement to DOD personnel who "reside in or visit Bahrain for purposes related to functions of the DOD Administrative Support Unit." Report of the Senate Foreign Relations Committee (SFRC), "United States Foreign Policy Objectives and Overseas Military Installations," 96th Congress, 1st Session, CP-808/35-9950, April 1979, p. 112; *Time*, 25 October 1982, pp. 47–50; *U.S. News and World Report*, 29 November 1982, pp. 30–31.

77. Diego Garcia is an atoll located about 1,000 NM south of the tip of India in the very center of the Indian Ocean. It is in the Chagos Archipelago,

which is the only remaining part of the original British Indian Ocean Territory. In an action that later aroused considerable criticism, the British Government during the mid-1960s bought up the existing plantation leaseholds and relocated about 1,000 residents of the archipelago to Mauritius. The island has a large natural harbor protected on three sides by coral formations. In 1979 the base included a highly classified intelligence and communications facility. It had a 12,000-foot runway capable of handling four-engine transports, a protected harbor capable of containing an aircraft carrier and support ships (i.e., a carrier task group), and fuel storage capacity for 380,000 barrels of aviation fuel and 320,000 barrels of fuel oil, enough to supply a carrier task group for about 30 days. The harbor contained both an anchorage and 550 feet of berthing for loading and unloading fuel. The facility was seldom used by navy ships before 1974 as it was not convenient to normal sailing patterns. The fuel stored at Diego Garcia was primarily for contingency use. SFRC, "United States Foreign Policy Objectives," p. 96.

78. Mahé Island, lying about 1,200 NM east of the African coast at about the latitude of Zanzibar Island, Tanzania, is the largest island in the Seychelles group. Formerly a British colony, the islands became the independent Republic of Seychelles in June 1976. The country has a total population of 50,000, the bulk of which is concentrated on Mahé. The economy is dominated by plantation crops and tourism. More than half of the country's export income derives from the sale of copra to India. The U.S. maintains a satellite tracking system on Mahé staffed with USAF and NASA personnel. The station also functions as a communications link between Diego Garcia and other U.S. bases. The United States holds a 10-year lease on the station site for which it pays an annual rent of $1 million. Ibid., p. 94.

79. "Rapid Deployment Scrutinized," *Aviation Week and Space Technology*, 14 March 1980, p. 4; *Aviation Week*, 27 June 1983, p. 13; *Washington Post*, 21 May 1983; *Washington Times*, 25 May 1983; *New York Times*, 24 June 1983.

80. *New York Times*, 12 March 1981, p. 6; DOD, *FY 1984 Annual Report*, p. 203; Congressional Budget Office, *Rapid Deployment Forces: Policy and Budgetary Implications* (Washington, D.C.: CBO, February 1983), pp. 45–49; *Defense Week*, 7 February 1983, p. 2.

81. DOD, *FY 1984 Annual Report*, p. 198.

82. "Aeroflot," *Armed Forces Journal*, May 1981, p. 42; *Military Balance, 1982–83*, pp. 16–17.

83. DOD, *FY 1983 Annual Report*, Annex, p. 35.

84. "Soviets Exercise Their Airlift Capability," *Air Force Magazine*, March 1978, p. 27.

85. "Aeroflot," p. 40.

86. Ibid., p. 57; DOD, *FY 1983 Annual Report*, Annex A, pp. 36–37; *New York Times*, 20 May 1983.

87. "The Soviet Transport Air Force," *International Defense Review*, June 1979, p. 948; *Military Balance, 1982–83*, p. 17.

88. Ibid., *Los Angeles Times*, 16 May 1983.

89. Telephone interview with the Office of Maritime Affairs, Department of State; *Military Balance, 1982–83*, p. 16.

90. DOD, *FY 1983 Annual Report*, Annex A. p. 49.

91. The potential strategic value of the Seychelles has been appreciated for some time. In 1965 the British joined the lightly populated Seychelles island

groups of Aldabra, Desroches, and Farquhar, the Crown Colony of Mauritius, and the Chagos Archipelago (including Diego Garcia) into a new crown colony called the British Indian Ocean Territory. This action was taken in conjunction with the general reduction of Britain's military position east of Suez and with the objective of providing locations for joint UK-U.S. bases. Part of the plan was for an air-staging facility on Aldabra, an atoll that also contained a good protected anchorage. The Aldabra plan, however, fell victim to environmental objections—the coral atoll possesses some unique plant and animal species—and to UK defense budget cuts. The anchorages available at Desroches and Farquhar also were not developed. Britain transferred the Seychelles Islands from the British Indian Ocean Territory back to the Republic of Seychelles upon independence in 1976.

92. "DOD Says U.S. Does Not Want to Compete with U.S.S.R. for Key Indian Ocean Base," *Armed Forces Journal*, July 1980, p. 29; *U.S. Policy Objectives and Overseas Military Installations*, CFR (Washington, D.C.: Government Printing Office, 1979); DOD, *FY 1982 Annual Report*, Annex A, pp. 83–87; OJCS, *Military Posture, FY 1983*, pp. 6–8.

93. Many sources are used in this section. See Jiri Valenta "From Prague to Kabul: The Soviet Style of Invasion," *International Security*, Fall 1980, pp. 114–141; *The Middle East Military Survey*, *War Data*, no. 8, 1981, pp. 2–8; and McNaugher, "Soviet Military Threat to the Gulf," pp. 8–10; David T. Griffiths, "Afghan Problems Stall Soviets," *Aviation Week*, 21 April 1980, pp. 18–19; Leo Heiman, "Soviet Invasion Weaknesses," *Military Review*, August 1969, pp. 38–45; Nancy Peabody and Richard S. Newell, *The Struggle for Afghanistan* (Ithaca, N.Y.: Cornell University Press, 1981); Anthony Arnold, *Afghanistan*: *The Soviet Invasion in Perspective* (Stanford, Calif.: Hoover Institution Press, 1981); David C. Isby, *Jane's Military Review, 1982–83*, and "Afghanistan 1982: The War Continues," *International Defense Review* 11 (1982):1523–1528; U.S. Department of State, "Afghanistan: Three Years of Occupation," Special Report no. 106, December 1982; Yacov Vertzberger, "Afghanistan in China's Policy," *Problems of Communism*, May-June 1982, pp. 1–23; Alvin Z. Rubinstein, "Afghanistan: Embraced by the Bear," *Orbis* 26, no. 1 (Spring 1982):135–153; and Beverley Male, *Revolutionary Afghanistan* (London: Croom Helm, 1982).

94. *New York Times*, 3 July 1982, p. 2; 14 November 1982, p. 21; *Sunday Telegraph*, 8 August 1982, p. 11; *Christiain Science Monitor*, 5 April 1983; *Washington Post*, 6 May 1983.

95. For an interesting comparison of these moves with those in Czechoslovakia, see Donald E. Fink, "Afghan Invasion Likened to 1968 Action," *Aviation Week*, 14 July 1980, pp. 20–23; and map in *Aviation Week*, 14 January 1980, p. 13.

96. The State Department estimated Soviet forces as totaling approximately 75,000–80,000 men during this period. See INR, U.S. State Department, "Afghanistan: Two Years of Occupation," prereleased edition, 26 December 1981.

97. Avigdor Haselkorn, "Analysis of Soviet Military Casualties in Afghanistan: Knowns and Unknowns," Analytical Assessments, AAC-WN-8011, April 1980; *Baltimore Sun*, 27 August 1980, p. 4.

98. *Christian Science Monitor*, 30 March, 3 May, and 7 July 1983; *Washington Times*, 18 July 1983; *Washington Post*, 9 February, 6 April, 11 and 26 May, 22 June 1983; *Economist*, 11 June 1983, p. 66; *Long Island Newsday*, 11 March 1983; *New York Times*, 23 December 1982, p. 7; 25 December 1982, p. 1; 10 March and 1, 4, and 18 May 1983.

99. Chemical weapons may have been used as early as six months before the invasion on Mujahidin guerillas. Attacks are reported by Il-28 bombers based in Shindand beginning on November 1979, and the U.S. has reports of 47 attacks between mid-1979 and 1981, with 24 confirmed by chemical evidence. Aircraft, mines, and Mi-24 and Mi-8 helicopters may have been used. *New York Times*, 9 and 23 March 1982; 21 May 1983; "Chemical Warfare in Southeast Asia and Afghanistan," Special State Department Report to Congress, 22 March 1982; Isby, "Afghanistan 1982," p. 1527; State Department Special Report no. 106, p. 5; *Defense and Foreign Affairs*, June 1983, pp. 30–31.

100. *Baltimore Sun*, 5 January 1982; *Economist*, 27 February 1982, pp. 54–55; *New York Times*, 8 March 1982; *Washington Post*, 13 February and 13 April 1982.

101. INR, "Afghanistan: Two Years of Occupation"; *New York Times*, 27 December 1981, p. 3; 1 May 1983; *Baltimore Sun*, 5 January 1982, p. 4.

102. *Baltimore Sun*, 30 September, 3 October, and 20 December 1981; *Los Angeles Times*, 4 December 1981; *Christian Science Monitor*, 11 September 1981; 16 March 1982; 30 March and 7 July 1983; *Washington Post*, 28 September and 27 December 1981; 3 March 1982; 6 April 1983; *New York Times*, 20 December 1981; 12 January 1982; 1 May 1983; *Economist*, 11 June 1983, p. 66.

103. Isby, "Afghanistan 1982," p. 1528; *New York Times*, 3 July 1982; *Business Week*, 4 April 1983, p. 52. Reports differ sharply over the number and location of the new bases. Herat, Mazar e-Sharif, and Badakhsan are often cited.

104. For a view assigning a much higher value to Afghanistan, see Thomas T. Hammond, "Afghanistan and the Persian Gulf," *Survey: A Journal of East and West Studies* 26, no. 2 (115) (Spring 1982):83–101.

105. U.S. exercises tend to be highly praised or highly attacked, depending on the source. The key recent exercises are Bright Star (which is held annually: one year in the U.S. and the next in Southwest Asia) and Jade Tiger 83, which was held in Oman, Sudan, and Somalia in late 1982. These are supported by annual exercises like Gallant Knight, Gallant Eagle, Bold Eagle, and Bold Star. In general, the U.S. seems to be making acceptable progress in these exercises, but it is important to stress that Jade Tiger 83 was far too small to really test USCENTCOM capabilities even in the air defense and air interdiction roles. Its amphibious landing phase had only token value, although it did allow some joint training with the sultan of Oman's forces. Its most valuable aspect was to test B-52 operations and the use of E-3As and F-15s against Soviet bombers.

There is a serious need to test U.S. readiness and force improvements in cooperation with Gulf forces, particularly as U.S. forces build up to their full projected capability in FY1986–1988. This cannot, however, be done on the high-profile, mass-exercise basis the U.S. has attempted in the past. A new approach is needed to combine command post (CPX) and small field training exercises (FTX) that will allow the U.S. to cooperate "invisibly" with local forces and jointly simulate large-scale operations.

106. See Isby, "Afghanistan 1982," for the deficiencies in Soviet forces in Afghanistan, which seem to be remarkably severe given the length of the fighting. See Richard Halloran, "Army's Special Forces Try to Rebuild," *New York Times*, 21 August 1982, pp. 8–9, for a good summary of U.S. problems. The U.S. effort is now heavily oriented toward Central America and Africa.

107. *Aviation Week*, 14 January 1980, p. 13; McNaugher, "Soviet Military Threat to the Gulf," p. 13; Dunn, "Constraints on the U.S.S.R.," pp. 614–616.

108. The Blackjack A was undergoing flight testing at the Ramenskoye flight test center in late November 1981. It is a variable-geometry bomber slightly larger than the B-1B with an estimated unrefueled range of 7,300 NM and dash speeds of Mach 2.3. Improved Soviet air-to-ship missiles for Backfire are in final development. *Aviation Week*, 14 December 1981.

109. The U.S. might pursue a "value denial" strategy as a means of reducing the risks inherent in any defense of Iran. Such a strategy would require that the U.S.

- take every possible step to encourage Iraq and Saudi Arabia to build additional pipeline capacity through Turkey and Janbu, and to connect the other Gulf states;
- encourage rapid exploration and development of the oil and gas fields in Oman. While these are small now, there are recent indications of major new discoveries that might be exploited to increase oil-load capacity outside the Gulf;
- encourage its European and Asian allies to shift even further away from dependence on Iranian oil. This should be fairly simple, given the fact that Iran's production dropped from 5.2 MMBD before the shah's fall to 1.66 MMBD before the Iran-Iraq War began, and it now averages only about 2.5 MMBD. For similar reasons, the West should also be extremely careful about any economic investment in or credits to Iran;
- prepare contingency plans to deny the USSR access to military facilities near the Gulf. If necessary, the U.S. should be prepared to use B-52 strikes against Iranian air and naval bases to permanently interdict their use;
- prepare to fight the war it is best equipped to fight and draw an invisible line somewhere north of Kerman and Dezful below which it simply will not allow the USSR to build or occupy the air and naval facilities necessary to exploit any occupation of Iran;
- make this policy tacitly clear to both the USSR and the Iranian government and be prepared to enforce it with consummate ruthlessness;
- quietly encourage articles and studies that would examine how the U.S. might aid Iraq in seizing Khuzestan. In effect, the U.S. should make it clear to any Iranian government that U.S. neutrality in the Iran-Iraq War will cease immediately if Iran brings in a major Soviet advisory presence or invites in Soviet troops;
- use the same unofficial and unattributable means to make it clear that the U.S. would support the Arab Gulf states in regaining control of the Abu Musa and Tumb islands that Iran seized following Britain's withdrawal from the Gulf and that the U.S. would either seize the Qu'oin Islands in the mouth of the Gulf of Hormuz or encourage Oman to do so;
- make it clear that the U.S. would aid the Arab states to gain control of all Gulf oil fields in open water and that it would occupy the strategic islands of Kharg, Lavan, Kish, Forur, and Sim and take effective control of Iran's southern coast;
- make it clear to Iran and the USSR that the U.S. would never allow Iran's oil and gas facilities to fall intact under Soviet control and that it would show the same ruthlessness in destroying such facilities as it would Iran's southern military bases.

110. These figures are taken from Pentagon sources as of September 1981.

111. For a detailed discussion of the Soviet problems in moving through Iran see Joshua M. Epstein, "Soviet Vulnerabilities in Iran and the RDF Deterrent," *International Security*, Fall 1981, pp. 126–158; McNaugher, "Soviet Military Threat to the Gulf," pp. 21–29; Dunn, "Constraints on the U.S.S.R.," pp. 617–619; and Heiman, "Soviet Invasion Weaknesses." Stephen L. Canby has also completed several excellent working papers on this issue.

112. Even the railroad from Iran's Caspian coast directly to Tehran goes through 69 tunnels of 12 miles total length and takes 41 miles of turns to go a straight-line distance of 22 miles. McNaugher, "Soviet Military Threat to the Gulf," p. 27.

113. *New York Times*, 5 and 6 December 1981; *Baltimore Sun*, 6 December 1981. See also Epstein, "Soviet Vulnerabilities in Iran," pp. 126–180; and Michael C. Dunn, "Exposed Flank," *Defense and Foreign Affairs*, April 1983, pp. 15–17.

114. Little has been written on nuclear war in the Gulf; this subject is discussed in more detail in the next chapter. For an interesting discussion of Soviet behavior in this area see Francis Fukuyama, "Nuclear Shadowboxing: Soviet Intervention in the Middle East," *Orbis* 25, no. 3, (Fall 1981):579–605.

115. Based on informal discussions with DOD officials.

20
U.S.-Soviet Competition in Gulf Arms Transfers

The U.S.-Soviet competition in arms transfers is as important to the strategic stability of the Gulf as their competition in power projection capabilities. This competition has long been a major factor in shaping the dynamics of the military buildup in the region and the current military capabilities of each Gulf nation. There is little doubt that it will continue to accelerate during the 1980s and that the capability of each superpower to meet the demands of the Gulf nations will be a powerful factor in determining their relative influence.[1]

Tables 20.1–20.4 provide a broad overview of how U.S. and Soviet arms transfers have affected the flow of arms of the Gulf nations and their neighbors. Table 20.1 shows the annual arms flow to each country in current dollars; Table 20.2 shows these same data in constant dollars. Tables 20.3 and 20.4 show the trend in terms of weapons numbers and the dollar value of the arms supplied by major exporters, which provides a rough indication of Western and Soviet-bloc "influence" over each importing nation. The subtotals in Tables 20.1, 20.2, and 20.3 show the arms flows into major areas of political confrontation and provide a rough measure of how arms flows may affect future conflicts and confrontations in these areas.

Arms Flows to the Gulf

As might be expected, Tables 20.1 and 20.2 reflect the massive buildup in arms imports described in earlier chapters, and the steady increase in Western and Soviet-bloc competition to use arms sales to obtain influence. Even in constant dollar terms, the rate of increase is astronomical. In 1970 the Gulf states spent only $392 million in constant 1977 dollars. By 1978, they were spending over $5 billion in constant dollars, or thirteen times more in real terms. While the fall of the shah led to some reductions in 1980, there are preliminary indications that the Iran-Iraq War increased regional arms purchases to over $12 billion (in 1977 dollars) in 1981 and that the Gulf states have spent even more

TABLE 20.1 Annual Trends in Arms Imports by the Near East and Gulf (current $ millions)

	1971	1972	1973	1974	1975	1976	1977	1978	1979	1980	1976–80
Gulf States											
Bahrain	n.a.	n.a.	0	0	0	0	0	0	20	20	40
Iran	320	525	525	1,000	1,200	2,000	2,500	1,900	1,600	220	8,300
Iraq	40	140	625	625	675	1,000	1,500	2,600	2,100	1,600	8,800
Kuwait	5	5	0	0	50	80	310	300	60	50	800
Oman	10	5	10	10	40	10	50	270	10	100	430
Qatar	n.a.	0	0	0	10	0	40	20	20	90	170
Saudi Arabia	20	100	80	340	250	440	875	1,100	925	1,400	4,700
UAE	n.a.	10	10	50	30	100	130	40	150	160	575
South Yemen	5	20	40	40	40	40	120	140	250	240	775
North Yemen	0	10	5	10	20	20	30	90	450	490	1,100
Total	400	815	1,295	2,075	2,315	3,790	5,555	6,460	5,585	4,370	24,690
Arab-Israeli Confrontation States											
Egypt	350	550	850	230	350	150	250	380	625	500	1,900
Jordan	50	30	40	70	70	140	120	170	100	525	1,000
Lebanon	5	20	20	10	10	10	0	20	20	40	100
Syria	110	280	1,300	825	380	625	650	900	2,000	2,400	6,600
Subtotal	515	880	2,210	1,135	810	925	1,020	1,470	2,745	3,465	9,600
Israel	260	300	230	950	725	975	1,100	925	525	825	4,300
Total	775	1,180	2,440	2,085	1,535	1,900	2,120	2,395	3,270	4,290	13,900

TABLE 20.1 (continued)

	1971	1972	1973	1974	1975	1976	1977	1978	1979	1980	1976–80
Related Northern Tier											
Turkey	260	150	50	150	220	320	140	220	170	250	1,100
Afghanistan	20	20	80	80	40	40	110	90	200	10	460
Total	280	170	130	230	260	370	250	310	370	260	1,560
Indian Ocean											
Bangladesh	n.a.	32	62	28	12	12	23	5	0	27	70
India	240	270	190	190	170	490	725	290	525	725	2,800
Pakistan	50	110	130	100	100	190	220	170	190	280	1,000
Nepal	0	0	0	10	5	0	0	0	0	0	0
Sri Lanka	10	10	10	0	0	10	0	0	10	5	20
Total	300	422	392	328	287	702	968	465	725	1,037	3,890
The Horn of Africa											
Ethiopia	10	10	10	10	30	50	440	1,100	210	480	2,300
Sudan	5	20	10	30	0	50	190	120	100	100	575
Somalia	0	20	40	90	70	100	80	240	130	190	750
Total	15	50	60	130	100	200	710	1,460	440	770	3,625
Related States											
Cyprus	0	0	0	0	0	0	0	0	10	0	10
Greece	270	110	40	100	260	525	430	310	380	250	1,900
Turkey	260	150	50	150	220	320	140	220	170	250	1,100
Libya	100	160	180	330	550	1,000	1,200	2,000	2,300	2,100	8,600
Total	630	420	270	580	1,030	1,845	1,770	2,530	2,860	2,600	11,610

Source: ACDA, *World Military Expenditures and Arms Transfers, 1971–80,* Tables II and III.

TABLE 20.2 Annual Trends in Arms Imports by the Near East and the Gulf (1979 constant $ millions)

	1971	1972	1973	1974	1975	1976	1977	1978	1979	1980	Total
Gulf											
Bahrain	n.a.	n.a.	0	0	0	0	0	4	20	18	42
Iran	547	862	815	1,419	1,555	2,465	2,901	2,063	1,600	199	14,432
Iraq	68	229	971	887	874	1,232	1,744	1,738	2,100	1,450	11,293
Kuwait	8	8	0	0	64	98	360	325	60	45	968
Oman	17	8	15	14	51	12	58	293	10	90	568
Qatar	n.a.	0	0	0	12	0	46	21	20	81	180
Saudi Arabia	34	164	124	482	323	542	1,017	1,194	925	1,269	6,074
UAE	n.a.	16	15	70	38	123	151	43	150	145	751
South Yemen	8	32	62	56	51	49	139	152	250	217	1,016
North Yemen	0	16	7	14	25	24	34	97	450	444	1,111
Total	682	1,335	2,009	2,942	2,993	4,545	6,456	5,926	5,585	3,958	36,435
Arab-Israeli Confrontation States											
Egypt	598	903	1,320	326	453	184	290	412	625	453	5,564
Jordan	85	49	62	99	90	172	139	184	700	475	2,055
Lebanon	8	32	31	14	12	12	0	27	20	36	192
Syria	188	459	2,020	1,171	492	770	755	977	2,000	2,175	11,007
Subtotal	879	1,443	3,433	1,610	1,047	1,138	1,184	1,594	3,345	3,139	18,818
Israel	444	492	357	1,348	939	1,202	1,279	1,004	525	747	8,337
Total	1,323	1,935	3,790	2,958	1,986	2,340	2,463	2,598	3,870	3,886	27,155

TABLE 20.2 (continued)

	1971	1972	1973	1974	1975	1976	1977	1978	1979	1980	Total
Related Northern Tier											
Turkey	444	246	77	212	285	394	162	238	170	226	2,454
Afghanistan	34	32	124	113	51	61	127	97	200	9	848
Total	478	278	201	325	336	455	289	335	370	235	3,302
Indian Ocean											
Bangladesh	n.a.	32	62	28	12	12	34	5	0	27	212
India	410	344	295	269	220	604	843	315	525	657	4,482
Pakistan	85	180	202	141	129	234	255	184	190	253	1,853
Nepal	0	0	0	14	6	0	0	0	0	0	20
Sri Lanka	17	16	15	0	0	12	0	0	10	4	74
Total	512	572	574	452	367	862	1,132	504	725	941	6,641
The Horn of Africa											
Ethiopia	17	16	15	14	38	61	511	1,194	210	435	2,511
Sudan	8	32	15	42	0	61	220	130	100	90	698
Somalia	0	32	62	127	90	123	93	260	130	172	1,089
Total	25	80	92	183	128	245	824	1,584	440	697	4,298
Related States											
Cyprus	0	0	0	0	0	0	0	0	10	0	10
Greece	461	180	62	141	336	647	500	336	380	226	3,269
Turkey	444	246	77	212	285	394	162	238	170	226	2,454
Libya	171	262	279	468	712	1,232	1,395	2,172	2,300	1,903	10,894
Total	1,076	688	418	821	1,333	2,273	2,057	2,746	2,860	2,355	16,627

Source: ACDA, *World Military Expenditures and Arms Transfers, 1971–80,* Table II.

TABLE 20.3 Arms Import Flows by Source, the Near East and Gulf (cumulative in 1976–1980 current $ millions)

	Total	USSR	U.S.	France	UK	FRG	Czech.	Italy	Poland	Switz.	Yugo-slavia	Others
Gulf												
Bahrain	40	–	5	20	–	–	–	5	–	–	–	20
Iran	8,300	625	6,200	200	250	380	–	300	–	100	–	250
Iraq	7,800	5,000	–	950	90	160	90	130	30	10	695	625
Kuwait	800	50	390	130	220	–	–	–	–	–	–	10
Oman	430	–	10	–	400	–	–	–	–	–	–	10
Qatar	170	–	5	70	90	–	–	–	–	–	–	10
Saudi Arabia	4,700	–	2,000	700	975	350	–	150	–	130	–	380
UAE	575	–	20	450	60	40	–	10	–	–	–	10
South Yemen	775	725	–	–	–	–	–	–	–	–	–	10
North Yemen	1,100	625	170	80	–	10	–	5	100	–	–	100
Total	24,693	7,075	8,800	2,400	2,085	940	90	600	130	240	675	1,415
Arab-Israeli Confrontation States												
Egypt	1,900	20	430	600	180	370	10	60	–	–	–	230
Jordan	1,060	–	725	–	280	5	–	–	–	–	–	50
Lebanon	85	–	40	10	20	5	–	–	–	–	–	10
Syria	6,620	5,400	–	290	100	100	440	–	10	–	–	280
Subtotal	9,665	5,420	1,195	900	580	480	450	60	10	–	–	570
Israel	4,390	–	4,300	–	60	–	–	30	–	–	–	–
Total	14,055	5,420	5,495	900	640	480	450	90	10	–	–	570

TABLE 20.3 (continued)

	Total	USSR	U.S.	France	UK	FRG	Czech.	Italy	Poland	Switz.	Yugo-slavia	Others
Related Northern Tier												
Turkey	1,100	–	600	–	–	240	–	210	–	–	–	40
Afghanistan	460	450	–	–	–	–	10	–	–	–	–	–
Total	1,560	450	600	–	–	240	10	210	–	–	–	40
Indian Ocean												
Bangladesh	70	20	–	–	10	–	–	–	–	–	–	30
India	2,800	2,300	50	50	160	10	70	40	30	–	10	30
Pakistan	1,100	20	220	390	20	50	–	10	–	–	–	350
Nepal	–	–	–	–	–	–	–	–	–	–	–	–
Sri Lanka	20	10	–	5	10	–	–	–	–	–	–	5
Total	3,990	2,350	270	445	200	60	70	50	30	–	10	415
The Horn of Africa												
Ethiopia	2,225	1,900	80	10	–	5	40	30	10	–	10	140
Sudan	515	10	140	5	–	360	–	–	–	–	–	–
Somalia	560	150	–	40	10	10	–	340	–	–	–	10
Total	3,300	2,060	220	55	10	375	40	370	10	–	10	150
Related States												
Cyprus	10	–	–	–	–	–	–	–	–	–	5	5
Greece	1,900	–	1,200	270	20	260	–	50	–	–	–	100
Turkey	1,090	–	600	–	–	240	–	210	–	–	–	40
Libya	8,125	5,500	–	410	50	460	280	575	–	–	–	850
Total	11,125	5,500	1,800	680	70	960	280	835	–	–	5	995

Sources: ACDA, *World Military Expenditures and Arms Transfers, 1971–80,* Tables III and IV.

TABLE 20.4 Patterns in Weapons Transfers to the Near East and South Asia (number of weapons and regional share)

Weapon (% of Third World supply for decade)		Suppliers						
		USSR	Other European Communist	U.S.	Major West European	Minor West European	Other	Total
Tanks and SP guns (69.8%)	1972–76	4,640 (40.5%)	2,360 (20.5%)	2,525 (22.0%)	1,125 (9.8%)	— —	810 (7.0%)	11,450
	1977–81	5,205 (48.2%)	1,960 (18.1%)					
Light armor (71.3%)	1972–76	4,285 (43.0%)	765 (7.6%)	3,280 (32.9%)	1,230 (12.3%)	— —	395 (3.9%)	9,955
	1977–81	6,500 (38.1%)	80 (0.4%)	7,210 (42.3%)	2,280 (13.4%)	30 (0.1%)	920 (5.4%)	17,020
Artillery (over 100mm) (49.0%)	1972–76	4,455 (34.5%)	2,070 (16.0%)	775 (6.0%)	845 (6.5%)	1,485 (11.5%)	3,265 (25.3%)	12,895
	1977–81	5,115 (36.8%)	1,580 (11.3%)	1,015 (7.3%)	935 (6.7%)	2,120 (15.2%)	3,115 (22.4%)	13,880
Major surface warships (29.8%)	1972–76	13 (40.6%)	4 (12.5%)	2 (6.2%)	13 (40.6%)	— —	— —	32
	1977–81	19 (42.2%)	8 (17.7%)	7 (15.5%)	11 (24.4%)	— —	— —	45
Minor surface warships (30.4%)	1972–76	28 (15.6%)	2 (1.1%)	23 (12.8%)	96 (53.6%)	2 (1.1%)	28 (15.6%)	179
	1977–81	10 (7.7%)	5 (3.8%)	10 (7.7%)	56 (43.4%)	25 (19.3%)	23 (17.8%)	129
Guided-missile patrol boats (56.6%)	1972–76	28 (100.0%)	— —	— —	— —	— —	— —	28
	1977–81	33 (57.8%)	— —	— —	20 (35.0%)	— —	4 (7.0%)	57

TABLE 20.4 (continued)

Weapon (% of Third World supply for decade)		Suppliers						
		USSR	Other European Communist	U.S.	Major West European	Minor West European	Other	Total
Submarines (23.6%)	1972–76	7 (87.5%)	— —	— —	1 (12.5%)	— —	— —	8
	1977–81	3 (33.3%)	— —	1 (11.1%)	4 (44.4%)	1 (11.1%)	— —	9
Supersonic combat aircraft (69.5%)	1972–76	1,250 (59.8%)	35 (1.6%)	470 (22.4%)	200 (9.5%)	— —	135 (6.4%)	2,090
	1977–81	1,635 (64.8%)	— —	430 (17.0%)	240 (9.5%)	— —	215 (8.5%)	2,520
Subsonic combat aircraft (40.5%)	1972–76	210 (35.2%)	40 (6.7%)	290 (48.7%)	20 (3.3%)	— —	35 (5.8%)	595
	1977–81	150 (61.2%)	25 (10.2%)	35 (14.2%)	30 (12.2%)	— —	5 (2.0%)	245
Helicopters (47.4%)	1972–76	280 (20.8%)	— —	285 (21.1%)	760 (56.5%)	— —	20 (1.4%)	1,345
	1977–81	620 (49.4%)	55 (4.3%)	15 (1.1%)	540 (43.0%)	10 (0.7%)	15 (1.1%)	1,255
Other military (28.2%)	1972–76	20 (3.3%)	100 (16.6%)	210 (35.0%)	155 (25.8%)	80 (13.3%)	35 (5.8%)	600
	1977–81	100 (9.7%)	195 (18.9%)	285 (27.6%)	200 (19.4%)	125 (12.1%)	125 (12.1%)	1,030
Surface-to-air missiles (84.4%)	1972–76	10,595 (80.1%)	150 (1.1%)	1,695 (12.8%)	780 (5.9%)	— —	— —	13,220
	1977–81	9,495 (56.0%)	150 (0.8%)	5,595 (32.9%)	1,390 (8.1%)	130 (0.7%)	200 (1.1%)	16,960

Countries in the Near East and South Asia are Afghanistan, Algeria, Bahrain, Bangladesh, Egypt, India, Iran, Iraq, Israel, Jordan, Kuwait, Lebanon, Libya, Morocco, Nepal, Oman, Pakistan, Qatar, Saudi Arabia, Sri Lanka, Syria, Tunisia, United Arab Emirates, North Yemen, and South Yemen.

Source: Adapted from U.S. State Department, *Conventional Arms Transfers in the Third World,* Special Report no. 102, August 1982, p. 14.

in 1982 and 1983. This would mean a thirtyfold increase in real terms in about 10 years. To put these figures in perspective, the total GNP of all the Middle Eastern and Gulf states did not even double in real terms during 1977–1980, in spite of massive transfers of oil wealth to some states. The annual arms imports of these same nations have increased six times in real terms, and did so in spite of the massive buildups that had previously occurred as a result of the Arab-Israeli conflict, the Dhofar rebellion, the Yemeni wars, and tensions between the Gulf powers.

The Case of Iran

Ironically, this steady increase in arms sales to the Gulf region has not been matched by an increase in either Soviet or U.S. influence. This is clearly illustrated by the case of Iran. Iran was the leading arms importer in the region and the developing world until 1979. It obtained most of its imports from the United States and, in spite of occasional efforts to diversify its sources of arms for political purposes, Iran made commitments during FY1978 that would have further increased the U.S. share of its total arms imports. The U.S. also had a major military assistance presence in Iran, kept most of Iran's more sophisticated military equipment operational, and conducted an extensive military training effort for Iranians in the U.S. None of this prevented the total collapse of both the shah and the major U.S. strategic shield in the Gulf.

The Failure of the U.S. Military Assistance Effort. The lack of U.S. success in using military exports to influence Iran must, however, be kept in careful perspective. As is now a matter of public record, this U.S. effort had grave defects that were not typical of most U.S. military assistance efforts overseas. The Nixon administration reacted to the shah's growing egocentricity, and token efforts to diversify his sources of arms, by giving him a "blank check" to buy virtually any U.S. arms he wanted. The Nixon administration assigned to Iran a military assistance chief who was chosen because he would not challenge this policy, and it cut off the ties between the shah and the U.S. military advisers who had served in Iran in the past. It suppressed warnings from the U.S. Embassy staff and military attachés in Tehran regarding the problems the shah's purchases were creating and removed U.S. officials who questioned the wisdom of U.S. policy.

The Nixon administration further reinforced U.S. willingness to meet the shah's demands for arms in reacting to the 1973 oil embargo and the following rises in oil prices. While Presidents Ford and Carter did clean up some of the recurring corruption in the U.S. military assistance effort and put some important checks on the actions of U.S. defense contractors, both administrations largely sustained the Nixon administration's blank check approach to the shah and actively discouraged efforts to offer independent advice that challenged the shah's ambitions and preconceptions.[2]

While the Iranian military forces had reasonable effectiveness in the comparatively primitive tribal guerrilla conflict that took place during the Dhofar rebellion in Oman, they had only a limited ability to maintain modern combat equipment after the expulsion of the U.S. advisory effort. Ironically, Iran's best combat troops in the Iran-Iraq War were not the U.S.-trained and -organized forces. The U.S.-trained air force did have a major impact, but it was the Revolutionary Guards that carried out the bulk of Iranian fighting with the Kurds, Baluchis, and Iraqis. In short, massive U.S. military sales and assistance to Iran did more to destabilize Iran than to stabilize it, and the U.S. failure to provide honest and objective military advice both hastened the shah's fall and increased the hostility to the United States of his successors.

The Soviet Economic Assistance Effort. The Soviet effort to wean the shah away from the U.S. by arms sales and transfers in the late 1960s did equally little to strengthen the Soviet position.[3] However, CIA studies indicate that the USSR did benefit from its limited economic aid and trade relations with Iran.[4] The Soviet experience in Iran before the shah's fall thus makes an interesting contrast to the U.S. efforts to obtain influence through arms sales. In contrast to the Soviet-bloc dealings with most other Gulf and Middle Eastern countries, the Soviet connection with Iran focused on economic, not military, aid. Iran, as the developing world's largest arms buyer, placed less than 5% of its orders in communist countries after early 1967 and never hosted more than 100 communist military advisers. However, the Soviets were able to establish a low-key economic relationship with Iran that survived even the shah's fall.

Moscow's first development aid to Iran, in 1963, provided assistance for a dam on the Aras, Iran's boundary river with the USSR. Over the following 16 years, the USSR gradually extended $1.1 billion of aid, and Eastern Europe, $685 million. The Soviets built Iran's first steel plant, a project turned down by Western commercial interests. This plant became one of Iran's largest industrial enterprises, employing 10,000 Iranian workers and accounting for 70% of Iran's steel capacity. Soviet aid also helped to improve Iran's port facilities and transport links with the USSR, provide grain storage facilities, contribute to the development of Iranian fisheries, increase Iran's electric power and irrigation facilities, and make possible the annual export of 13 billion cubic meters of natural gas, which Iran had previously flared. Iran's $200 million in annual earnings from these gas exports was more than enough to service Tehran's military and economic debt to the USSR and marks one of the few cases in which Soviet aid resulted in a "profit" to the recipient country.

In further contrast to most Soviet aid efforts, the Soviet program in Iran was kept relatively apolitical throughout the 1960s. As a result, relations were sufficiently friendly that the quadrupling of world oil prices in 1973–1974 resulted in a major upsurge in Soviet-bloc commercial relations with Iran. A joint commission was established for long-term planning, and a 15-year economic cooperation agreement was signed to promote a $3 billion development effort on both sides of the Soviet-Iranian border under commercial and credit arrangements. The next year, Iran awarded more than a billion dollars' worth of commercial contracts to the USSR for power plants, a heavy-machinery complex at Kerman, and other projects. East European trade with Iran moved up to nearly a billion dollars annually, and more than one-third of Iran's nonoil and nongas exports went to Soviet-bloc countries.

This Soviet success was limited. Although Iran was the largest Third World market for Soviet goods in 1978, trade with the USSR never amounted to more than 5% of Iran's total trade. Soviet-Iranian aid relationships were also affected by the shah's fall. His departure led to the cancellation of the 1,500-kilometer IGAT-II pipeline to the Soviet border, which was to have delivered 17 billion cubic meters of gas annually from fields in southern Iran.

Even so, Soviet-Iranian relations allowed the USSR to ride out the revolution better than the U.S. Iran's first postrevolutionary oil sales were to the USSR. Roughly 2,000 of the 4,000 Soviet economic and military technicians who left in 1978 were back in place by late 1979, and work had resumed on most projects begun before the revolution.[5] Soviet technicians also played a significant role in aiding Iran during the initial phases of the Iraqi attack. They helped deal with the inevitable bottlenecks in Iran's northern rail system resulting from the shift of imports from Iran's Gulf ports to rail links to Turkey and the USSR and provided locomotives and extra rolling stock. Soviet technicians returned to project sites threatened by Iraq the moment Iranian troops managed to secure them from Iraqi attack. They played a critical role in completing the steel plant at Isfahan, expanding its power plant, and electrifying the Tabriz-Julfa railroad.

Although the Soviet Union did not provide any economic aid to Iran in terms of transfers of cash or goods during 1980–1982, it did increase the total number of Soviet-bloc economic technicians to 2,450 and provided 3,500 Cubans. This aid, plus Iran's dependence on transshipments of goods from the USSR, almost certainly helped prevent the Khomeini regime's suppression of the Tudeh party as it began to crack down on all Marxist movements in 1981 and shifted to imprisonment and execution in 1982. It did not prevent the eventual suppression of the Tudeh during mid-1982 to May 1983 or the steady worsening of relations with the USSR. It is notable, however, that there is a direct correlation between the hardening of Iran's relations with the Soviet Union and its military and economic recovery. Iran acted only after its oil exports to the West had recovered and after it had obtained an alternative source of technicians from nations like Japan. This indicates that aid and trade were the major factors tying the USSR and Iran together during the first two years of the revolution.

Iran's trade with the USSR recovered rapidly from the revolution. While exports dropped from a 1979 high of $350 million in 1978, $210 million in 1979, and $116 million in 1980, they rose to $630 million in 1981. East European exports rose from a high of $550 million in 1978 to $1,118 million in 1980 and $878 million in 1981. The Soviet bloc provided 6% of Iran's imports in 1978 and 14% in 1981. Trade levels reached $1 billion in both 1981 and 1982, even though Iran was no longer exporting gas to the USSR. Although much of this increase in trade occurred because of the Iran-Iraq War, it occurred at a time when the OECD share of trade with Iran dropped from 80% in 1978 to slightly over 60% in 1981.

Iran signed an "accelerated economic and technical cooperation agreement" with the USSR on 15 February 1982 and agreed to new projects for gas exports, power plants, and dams. The Iran-Iraq War expanded use of trade routes through the USSR, raised transits to a record 3.4 million tons per year, and led to new rail, sea, and truck accords expanding Soviet access to Iran. This civilian trade compared with about $220 million worth of Soviet arms sales to Iran between the shah's fall and the end of 1981. In contrast, the West had sold about $350 million, and North Korea well over $600 million.

Yet, for all this success, the USSR then seemed to end in the same political box as the United States. Once Iran began to recover its oil revenues in 1982, it steadily shifted its imports to the West. Although no reliable figures are yet available, it is clear that this trend continued in 1983. Preliminary data indicate that the total value of U.S.-Iranian trade bottomed out in 1981 at $364 million, then rose to $706.7 million in 1982 and to $234 million in the first five months of 1983. Iran also began to hold covert meetings with its old U.S. prime contractors, including firms once denounced by the government like the Fluor Corporation and William Brothers Engineering. Iran also tacitly consented to a third-party purchase of oil for the U.S. strategic petroleum reserve, knowing that the U.S. Department of Defense was the true end buyer. While this was scarcely a return to the $6.6 billion in U.S.-Iranian trade reported in 1979, it indicated that the Khomeini government preferred the "satan" with the most money and the most goods.

Iranian activity in Europe also indicates that Iran is shifting its markets back toward the West, and this tilt seems to have accelerated since Iran expelled 18 Soviet officials in May 1983. Iran has also made at least some reductions in the limited number of Soviet military and economic technicians in Iran and seems to have systematically eliminated those who might have had political influence or who showed any signs of intelligence or political activity.[6]

A Comparison of the U.S. and Soviet Experiences in Iran. The ironies of this situation are obvious. By violating its own practice in giving military and economic aid, and by "moralizing" the oversupply of arms to an unstable national leader, the U.S. contributed to the alienation of a key ally. This is especially ironic because a more pragmatic reliance on the normal methods of allocating and administering U.S. military assistance might have had just the opposite effect.

As was shown in Chapter 17, the Soviet Union was initially successful in maintaining its economic ties to Iran, and its presence in that country, in spite of the takeover by an otherwise ideological hostile regime, until Khomeini formally suppressed the Tudeh party and began to expel Soviet technicians in May 1983.[7] As a further irony, this Soviet success was at least partly the result of the fact that the USSR reversed its normal practices in giving military and economic aid and followed procedures that were far more characteristic of those the U.S. followed in dealing with Third World states. Economic aid may still enable the USSR to maintain a limited opening to Iran that could prove critical in the post-Khomeini era.

Iran thus provides a classic case study of the fact that the style or method by which U.S. and Soviet aid and arms transfers are made is often more important than its scale or the ideology of the seller/donor. It also demonstrates the risks of moralizing the U.S. aid process and the importance of examining the method of U.S. and Soviet arms transfers by country in estimating their impact.

The Case of Iraq

Iraq provides an equally discouraging picture of a superpower's ability to transform arms transfers into influence. The Soviet Union agreed to provide massive arms transfers to Iraq from 1958 onward. These transfers totaled $4.5 billion in deliveries between early 1975 and 1980. They did not, however, involve major changes in the usual pattern of Soviet military assistance, and they proved as unsuccessful in giving the USSR influence over Iraq as did U.S. military assistance in giving the U.S. influence over Iran.[8]

The data in Tables 20.1–20.3 describe Iraq's massive arms buildup. This buildup accelerated even further during the late 1970s, and ACDA data indicate that the USSR sold Iraq $3.6 billion worth of military exports during its peak sales period of 1974–1978, out of worldwide sales of $27.2 billion. Table 20.5 shows how these sales fit into the broader context of Soviet worldwide arms transfers and indicates that the USSR has trained over 4,400 Iraqi military personnel in the USSR and another 800 in Eastern Europe; it had as many as 1,000 Soviet-bloc military technicians in Iraq when the Iran-Iraq War began.[9] A total of 550 Soviet-bloc military and 13,000 civilian advisers and technicians were still in Iraq in early 1983.[10]

The sheer volume of these Soviet arms sales and the Soviet military assistance effort was so impressive during the late 1970s that it led some Western analysts to treat Iraq as a Soviet satellite and to credit Iraq with substantial military capability. The CIA, for example, reported in October 1980 that "Soviet military aid to Iraq has outrun economic

TABLE 20.5 Trends in Soviet-Bloc Arms Sales and Military Aid by Target Country

	Arms Exports[a] (current $ millions)		Soviet and Cuban Military Technicians[b] 1977		1979		1981		LDC Military Personnel Trained in Communist Countries[b]		
	1967–76	1976–80	Soviet and Eastern Europe	Cuban	Soviet and Eastern Europe	Cuban	Soviet and Eastern Europe	Cuban	1956–77	1977–79	1979–81
World Total	22,053	38,600	10,250	21,850	15,865	34,315	18,205	39,175	46,975	4,955	5,865
Africa	2,501	11,300	5,715	21,340	6,825	33,060	9,900	36,960	13,175	3,005	2,150
N. Africa	1,315	7,300	1,600	15	2,835	15	4,600	50	3,525	610	395
Algeria	315	1,800	615	15	1,015	15	2,000	n.a.	2,250	—	—
Libya	1,005	5,500	1,000	—	1,820	?	2,600	?	1,275	320	395
Sub-Saharan Africa	290	2,830	4,115	21,325	3,990	33,045	5,300	36,910	7,880	4,165	1,755
Angola	190	550	500	19,000	1,400	19,000	1,600	23,000	—	60	120
Equatorial Guinea	5	10	50	250	40	200	?	?	200	—	—
Ethiopia	—	1,900	500	100	1,250	13,000	1,900	12,000	—	1,790	305
Guinea	50	50	125	200	85	50	50	10	900	45	60
Guinea-Bissau	5	30	50	150	60	50	50	50	100	—	—
Mali	25	110	175	—	180	—	205	—	350	20	125
Mozambique	15	180	200	50	525	275	550	1,000	—	430	100
Somalia	181	150	?	?	?	?	?	?	2,550	—	45
Tanzania	30	320	?	?	?	?	?	?	1,425	555	235
Other	685	700	2,515	1,575	450	530	945	850	2,355	545	765
Latin America	520	2,000	100	10	110	255	225	1,715	625	155	270
Cuba	355	1,100	?	n.a.	?	n.a.	8–10,000	n.a.	?	?	?
Nicaragua	—	—	?	?	?	?	125	1,700	?	?	?
Peru	165	900	100	—	?	—	100	—	625	155	270
Other	—	—	—	10	?	?	—	15	—	—	—

TABLE 20.5 (continued)

	Arms Exports[a] (current $ millions)		Soviet and Cuban Military Technicians[b]						LDC Military Personnel Trained in Communist Countries[b]		
			1977		1979		1981				
	1967-76	1976-80	Soviet and Eastern Europe	Cuban	Soviet and Eastern Europe	Cuban	Soviet and Eastern Europe	Cuban	1956-77	1977-79	1979-81
East Asia	3,204	2,800	—	—	—	—	—	—	9,300	?	—
Indonesia	5	—	—	—	—	—	—	—	9,275	—	—
Kampuchea	5	10	—	—	—	—	—	—	25	?	—
Vietnam	2,481	1,900	?	—	—	—	?	—	?	?	?
Other	713	890	—	—	—	—	—	—	—		—
South Asia	1,535	2,800	555	—	4,180	—	2,155	—	6,775	?	1,570
Afghanistan	100	450	350	—	4,000	—	2,000	—	4,025	?	1,570
Bangladesh	35	20	50	—	30	—	—	—	450	—	—
India	1,365	2,300	150	—	150	—	150	—	2,250	—	—
Pakistan	25	20	—	—	40	—	—	—	50	—	—
Sri Lanka	10	10	—	—	—	—	—	—	?	—	—
Other	—	—	5	—	—	—	5	—	—	—	—
Middle East	6,982	12,500	3,880	500	4,780	1,000	5,925	500	17,100	1,775	1,875
Egypt	2,365	20	—	—	—	—	—	—	6,250	—	5
Iran	611	625	—	—	—	—	—	—	325	—	80
Iraq	1,795	5,000	1,150	150	1,065	?	550	—	4,075	325	10
Jordan	—	—	—	—	—	—	—	—	?	—	—
Kuwait	0	50	?	—	?	—	?	—	?	?	?
Syria	2,015	5,400	2,175	—	2,480	—	3,300	—	4,350	1,105	60
N. Yemen	35	625	100	—	130	—	700	—	1,175	185	700
S. Yemen	151	775	350	350	1,100	1,000	1,100	500	875	220	20
Other	10	55	105	—	5	?	275	—	50	—	1,000

[a] Includes USSR, East Germany, Czechoslovakia, and Poland.

Sources: Arms export data from ACDA, ***World Military Expenditures and Arms Transfers,*** various editions; other data from U.S. Department of State, "Soviet and East European Aid to The Third World, 1981," and various editions of CIA, "Communist Aid Activities in Non-Communist Less Developed Countries."

aid nearly 15 to 1 and has made Baghdad the U.S.S.R.'s largest arms buyer. The Communist military supply program has transformed the Iraqi military from a counterinsurgency force after the July 1958 *coup* into a large, well-equipped military establishment capable of sizable modern military operations."[11]

The Soviet Failure of Iraq. While the CIA was undoubtedly correct about the size of the Soviet military assistance effort in Iraq, this assessment ignored the weaknesses in Iraq's forces discussed in Chapter 13, and the Iran-Iraq War showed that Iraq was far from "capable of sizable modern military operations." Similarly, major qualifications need to be made about the success of Soviet military assistance efforts in influencing Iraqi policy, either domestically or in support of Soviet foreign policy.[12] In fact, the entire history of modern Soviet-Iraqi relations is essentially one of Iraq's playing off the USSR for its own interests. Although the Soviet Union has been the principal supplier of arms to Iraq since the first Iraqi-Soviet arms transfer agreement was signed in November 1958, the USSR has seen various Iraqi governments steadily purge the Iraqi Communist party, often in the form of mass executions, and allow the ICP to participate in Iraq's politics only as a ploy. The USSR also has tried several times to embargo arms to Iraq only to see Iraq ride out the arms embargo or turn to the West and pursue its own foreign policy objectives.

The Baath coup that overthrew Abd al-Karim Qassim in February 1963 was followed by the execution of about 2,500–3,000 members of the ICP, and the resulting Soviet arms embargo did little to catalyze the following coup in November by General Abd al-Salam Arif. As a result, the USSR resumed arms exports in June 1964, with little to show in terms of direct influence. It was limited to the "spoiler" role of supporting a strongly anti-Western state in the process of nationalizing its oil industry. The period between 1964 and 1967 also saw only *pro forma* Iraqi tolerance of the ICP and support of Soviet foreign policy interests. While the 1967 Arab-Israeli War catalyzed a brief Soviet-Iraqi rapprochement, and the USSR encouraged the deployment of Iraqi forces to Jordan and Syria, this period also marked the start of a growing Iraqi conflict with the Kurds. In the years that followed, Iraq often departed from the Soviet line on the Middle East and violently rejected ICP efforts to reach an accommodation with the Kurds. Accordingly, although some 7 to 10 Iraqi-Soviet arms transfer agreements were reached between 1968 and 1971, these did not bind Iraq to the USSR, and this period saw the gradual emergence of strong and independent Iraqi nationalists with no practical interest in Soviet ideology or the Soviet form of socialism. Iraq also continued to harass the ICP throughout this period and to oppose the USSR in such key policy decisions as refusing to provide Iraqi support to the Palestinians during their conflict with Jordan.

The Iraqis did tilt back toward the USSR during 1972–1975, but only to achieve Iraqi goals that generally failed to serve Soviet interests and that ultimately increased Iraq's independence. The Iraqi-Soviet friendship treaty of 9 April 1972 resulted primarily from the Iraqi need for Soviet help in fully nationalizing the Iraq oil fields. This nationalization, however, ultimately gave Iraq the revenues and influence it needed to buy arms on the world market. Similarly, when Iraq signed a massive arms agreement with the USSR in September 1972, it did so to pacify its army while the Baath systematically purged it of pro-Soviet elements. It then suppressed the Kurds, who were being supported by the USSR, and it used its arms to checkmate the shah's arms buildup after his May 1971 "blank check" meeting with President Nixon. In fact, Iraq bought enough Soviet arms to obtain considerable long-term independence from Soviet resupply. It also pressured the USSR into delivering advanced arms such as the MiG-23, Su-7, and Blinder medium bombers in 1973. It then refused an urgent Soviet request to supply Syria with 500 tanks during the October War and instead sent Iraqi troops in a fashion that maximized Iraqi prestige while doing little to help Syria.

Iraqi independence continued even though the USSR delivered more than $1.7 billion worth of arms between 1971 and 1975, or more than twice the total value of arms the Soviets had previously delivered since the fall of the monarchy. The USSR got in return virtually nothing but occasional Iraqi political support of its foreign policy initiatives. In contrast, Iraq got arms to use against the Kurds, Iranians, and Israelis. It also built up its military strength enough to help persuade the shah to negotiate the Algiers Accord of 15 March 1975 and to end his support of the Kurdish rebels on terms largely acceptable to Iraq. This, in turn, allowed Saddam Hussein to reassert his control over the Iraqi government and to use Iraq's new oil wealth to assert the country's independence. The impact of this shift on the USSR was quick and brutal. Iraq altered its trade patterns so that the Soviet Union dropped from Iraq's largest trading partner in 1973 to fourth in 1975, accounting for less than 10% of Iraqi imports. Iraq promptly re-engaged in its long-standing feud with Syria at a particularly inopportune moment for the USSR and provided de facto aid to Egypt in the form of covert shipments of Soviet arms and parts. The Iraqi leadership again suppressed the ICP. By the time the USSR attempted another arms embargo in July 1975, Iraq had enough arms to sustain the end of the Kurdish war without Soviet resupply. Even so, Iraq immediately reacted to the embargo by shifting to France as a major source of arms. In fact, by late 1975, Iraq had concluded arms sales agreements with France equal in value to any previous set of agreements with the USSR.

The Syrian intervention in Lebanon—which was another case of a Soviet arms buyer's acting against Soviet guidance—led to still another brief rapprochement between Iraq and the USSR in 1976, but this again benefited the Iraqis to the exclusion of the USSR. The Iraqis ended up with T-62 tanks, more MiG-23s, the SA-6, Scud, and massive artillery shipments. The USSR ended up with nothing other than a secret agreement that allowed it to transmit airlift through Iraqi air bases and whose validity depended on Iraqi interests and policy on a given day. In fact, Iraq began to quietly tilt toward a rapprochement with the conservative Gulf states in 1976 and again systematically suppressed the ICP.

This step may have led the USSR to try to use its remaining supporters in the army and the ICP to try to launch a coup d'etat in late 1977 and early 1978. However, the result of the coup attempt was the execution of 21 communist leaders, a brief Iraqi rapprochement with Syria, and the ruthless suppression of the ICP and any Iraqi officers, officials, and students suspected of being successfully indoctrinated by the USSR. Saddam Hussein also reacted by seeking even larger French arms supplies, made major arms purchases from Italy, and started quiet arms dealing with the Germans and Swiss. By May 1979, Iraq was making more arms purchase commitments to the West than to the USSR, and some reports indicate that Iraq made over $2.3 billion worth of new commitments to the West during the first six months of 1979.

Near-Term Prospects. Since 1978, Iraqi-Soviet military relations have been exceedingly uneasy. Both nations still find value in their military and economic relationship, particularly now that Soviet-Iranian relations have become increasingly hostile, but Iraq's need for the USSR has declined as it broadened its military trade with France and Italy. Iraq reacted sharply to the Soviet invasion of Afghanistan—perhaps seeing a model of what might happen in Iraq—and further limited the role of the Soviet military in working with Iraqi forces. While the USSR still provided $5.0 billion of the $7.8 billion in arms that Iraq imported between 1975 and 1979, the balance of new orders for all military goods and services has changed, and Iraq is ordering the majority of these goods and services from Western Europe.[13]

Although Iraq's development plans have been upset by the Iran-Iraq War, its economic ties have clearly shifted to the West. Iraq originally planned to spend some $22.5 billion on development in 1981 and purchase over $3 billion from the European Community and nearly $2 billion from Japan. Its projected imports from the U.S. were to exceed $725 million, while its projected purchases from the entire Soviet bloc were only about $700 million. France emerged as a particularly strong trading partner, and France's trade and investment agency had mid-1981 trade guarantees for French exports equal to $4.5 billion. In fact, French exports to Iraq rose from about $300 million in 1978 to over $1 billion in 1981. France also became Iraq's major arms supplier in terms of new orders once the Iran-Iraq War began. It was to France that Iraq turned after the war began, placing some $660 million in "rush" arms orders. Iraq and France also discussed a possible deal that would sell Iraq 60–100 Mirage 2000 fighters, a new national air defense radar and AC&W system, guided missiles, and missile patrol boats for

Iraqi oil, although at one point Iraq also tried to buy 100 Panavia Tornados. According to some reports, the initial wave of French arms sales reached well over $3 billion by early 1981, with $1.6 billion more in the final negotiating stages.

As was discussed in Chapter 18, French sales in 1982 and 1983 grew at a rate of several billion dollars a year, and France had virtually become financially committed to the survival of Saddam Hussein's regime. While no firm figures are available, Iraq seems to have bought as much as $3–5 billion worth of equipment from France, increasingly on credit or deferred payment terms.[14]

Iraq has turned to the USSR to resupply the massive amounts of equipment it lost in the Iran-Iraq War. This scarcely seems likely, however, to lead to close Iraqi-Soviet military relations if the Baath regime survives, and most potential successor regimes seem unlikely to do anything more than play the USSR off against the West, or rely on the USSR for weapons and technology, unless they have no choice. It was France, not the USSR, that rushed advisers to Iraq as an assurance that France still supported Iraq and that delivered Mirage F-1 fighters in spite of its declared neutrality.[15] In contrast, the grudging Soviet deliveries of armor through Poland in 1981 did nothing to offset Iraq's belief that Soviet arms and training were a primary cause of its failure to win a rapid victory. Indeed, the Iraqi tendency to blame Soviet equipment and training for its military performance in the October War turned into open contempt for Soviet equipment and tactics since Iraq's defeat by Iran and Syria's defeat by Israel.

The situation has changed to only a limited degree since the USSR resumed deliveries of major weapons and fighters in 1982. It was all too clear to the Iraqis that such Soviet deliveries were largely a reaction to the USSR's growing problems with Iran, that the USSR was providing Iraq with far slower deliveries than those to Syria, and that Iraq was being charged far higher prices than Syria and India. Although Iraq had to pay several billion dollars in hard currency for Soviet arms between 1981 and 1982, deliveries were limited in volume, and they did not convince the Iraqi military that they were getting equipment equivalent to that available from the West.[16] Rightly or wrongly, the Iraqi military blame Soviet equipment and advice for many of their problems and make no secret of the fact that they are accepting Soviet support and equipment in many areas only because no other source is readily available. A new regime might, of course, bring new officers to power, but these views seem to be broadly held within the senior ranks of the present Iraqi military.

Iraq as a Case Study in the Problems in the Soviet Military Assistance Effort. Iraq also serves as an interesting case study of some of the other problems in the Soviet military assistance effort. One of these problems is the broad degree of antagonism that has built up between the Iraqi military and the 600-man Soviet military advisory team in Iraq, which reflects a general problem the USSR has had in dealing with developing societies because of the racial and ethnic orientation of the Soviet military toward White Russia. The Soviet military remains an extremely ethnocentric force whose "worldwide revolutionary consciousness" is offset in the real world by the belief that Arab and African peoples are racially and culturally inferior.

The Soviet military has had little of the softening exposure of U.S. military contacts with other nations, and the problems the Soviet military have with the country's Asian minorities scarcely produce the same kind of day-to-day lessons in race relations that the U.S. forces have had to learn in dealing with a growing black minority in every military service. As a result, Iraqi military personnel who have trained in the USSR or who have had day-to-day contact with the Soviet military often have become all too aware of Soviet contempt for the Arab in general and for the Arab soldier in particular. This friction has been reinforced by the defeat of Soviet-trained and -equipped Arab forces in the last three Arab-Israeli wars, although the Soviets have gone to immense lengths since 1971 to create a cadre of professional military assistance personnel who do not show such attitudes and prejudices.

The USSR has also had problems with the 4,500 Iraqi military personnel it has trained in Soviet-bloc countries since 1955. Many Iraqi military personnel also complain that the Soviets have failed to provide their Arab clients with adequate offensive training in armored warfare; they refer to the "Frunze Academy Syndrome." This had led at least some senior Iraqis to believe that the USSR deliberately attempts to keep the Arabs weak in war-fighting capability and to limit them to a defensive role. Since the Syrian and Egyptian officer corps have similar beliefs, there may be some truth in this Iraqi attitude.[17]

Although covert Soviet efforts to politicize the Iraqi armed forces and government were more sophisticated between 1975 and 1978, they were still obvious enough so that many Iraqi military got the impression that they were being drilled in an alien ideology with little relation to their own culture and the needs of the Arab world. This seems characteristic of the way most Soviet-trained military in developing nations react to Soviet attempts at political indoctrination and subversion.

There seems ample reason, therefore, to question whether the USSR's arms transfers to Iraq will enable it to draw any substantial long-term benefits from any given outcome of the Iran-Iraq War or the probable internal political developments in Iraq. The more likely result would seem to be to replace one group of military nationalists with another. The 13,000 Soviet-bloc economic technicians in the country, 8,000 of whom are Poles working under hard-currency contracts, seem even less important as a political lever. Even if Iraq's future leadership does not come from Takrit, it seems unlikely to come from Moscow.

The Case of Saudi Arabia

U.S. relations with Saudi Arabia have already been discussed at length. They have generally been a more successful model of military assistance than U.S. relations with Iran or Soviet relations with Iraq, for several reasons. First, the Saudi government has been much more broadly based than that of Iran and has never suffered either from the problems of one-man rule or from any illusions that Saudi Arabia, with its limited population, could become a major military power. Second, U.S. goals and objectives in Saudi Arabia have always been more constrained than in Iran. The U.S. has sought to preserve Saudi security and friendship—not to make it into a proxy power in the Gulf—and Saudi Arabia has relied on a combination of U.S. and other foreign advisers. Third, the Saudis have not attempted the impossible. Their effort to build up Saudi forces has been slow and methodical and has paid more attention to the realities of the required pool of trained manpower and infrastructure and to the problems of dependence upon foreign advisory groups and training than that of nations like Iran. The Saudis have understood the risk that their military may become politicized and alienated by contact with U.S. advisers and training centers. And finally, both nations clearly need each other, without needing a patron-client relationship, and have largely recognized this fact.

Accordingly, although, as Tables 20.1, 20.2, and 20.4 show, roughly the same growth occurred in U.S. military exports to Saudi Arabia during 1969–1979 that occurred in the case of Iran, the U.S. military assistance effort to Saudi Arabia has so far proved more successful in meeting both countries' objectives. This seems likely to continue in spite of the recent growth in Saudi purchases shown in the data in Table 20.6, which provides more current data on U.S. arms transfers. Although these data are not directly comparable with the ACDA data in Tables 20.1, 20.2, and 20.4, they provide an important perspective on recent U.S. efforts.

It is important to reiterate, however, that the majority of U.S. military sales have not been weapons sales. State Department working data—current as of October 1981—showed that the U.S. had signed $34.2 billion worth of arms agreements with Saudi Arabia during 1950–1980 and delivered about $12 billion. About 18.2 billion of the total was construction, with $6.2 billion delivered through 1980. Some $7 billion was in "other services," largely program management and support.[18] The U.S. thus contracted for $6.3 billion but delivered only about $2.7 billion worth of major U.S. military systems to Saudi Arabia between 1950 and 1980. Total U.S. FMS agreements with Saudi Arabia in FY1980 and FY1981 did, however, include a higher proportion of arms, and the State Department estimates for such transfers are higher than the DSAA data shown in Table 20.6. The State Department reports $4.5 billion in FY1980 and $2.15 billion in FY1981.

These figures reflect the U.S. inability to sell Saudi Arabia the arms it needs to make use of its vast investment in military infrastructure

TABLE 20.6 U.S. Military Sales Deliveries to the Gulf, FY1976–FY1984 (current $ millions)[a]

	Actual Deliveries							FY1976–1982		Planned New Sales and Agreements		
	FY1976	FY1977	FY1978	FY1979	FY1980	FY1981	FY1982	Deliveries	Sales	FY1982	FY1983	FY1984
Bahrain												
FMS	b	b	b	b	2	1	3	6	12+	6	5	5
Military Aid	—	—	—	—	—	—	—	—	—	—	—	—
Commercial Exports	b	b	b	b	b	2	1	3+	3+	1	1	2
Total	b	b	b	b	2	3	4	9+	15+	7	6	7
Iran												
FMS	1,554	2,525	1,931	2,409	—	—	—	8,479	3,973	—	—	—
Military Aid	—	—	—	—	—	—	—	—	—	—	—	—
Commercial Exports	108	138	133	110	7	—	—	496	496	—	—	—
Total	1,662	2,663	2,064	2,519	7	—	—	8,975	4,469	—	—	—
Kuwait												
FMS	16	157	188	71	78	65	85	660	564	—	—	—
Military Aid	—	—	—	—	—	—	—	—	—	—	—	—
Commercial Exports	6	b	2	3	b	1	5	18+	18+	—	—	—
Total	22	157	190	74	78	66	90	678+	582+	—	—	—
Oman												
FMS	b	b	b	b	8	17	32	57+	97+	24	40	40
Military Aid	—	—	—	—	—	—	—	—	—	0.1	0.1	0.1
Commercial Exports	1	1	1	1	b	1	1.5	6.5+	6.5+	1.5	3	3
Total	1+	1+	1	1+	8	18	33.5	63.5+	103.5	25.6	43.1	43.1
Saudi Arabia												
FMS	461	1,066	1,129	941	1,152	1,363	1,785	7,897	20,818	7,419	5,700	8,120
Military Aid	—	—	—	—	—	—	—	—	—	—	—	—
Commercial Exports	93	44	166	44	29	72	50	498	498	50	50	400
Total	560	1,110	1,292	985	1,181	1,435	1,835	8,395	21,316	7,469	5,750	8,520

TABLE 20.6 (continued)

	Actual Deliveries							FY1976-1982		Planned New Sales and Agreements		
	FY1976	FY1977	FY1978	FY1979	FY1980	FY1981	FY1982	Deliveries	Sales	FY1982	FY1983	FY1984
UAE												
FMS	b	b	2	b	b	2	3	7+	23+	0.1	30	200
Military Aid	—	—	—	—	—	—	—	—	—	—	—	—
Commercial Exports	3	1	3	2	5	4	2	19+	19+	2	5	10
Total	3	1	5	2+	5+	6	5	26+	42+	2.1	35	210
North Yemen												
FMS	b	22	27	70	72	49	39	207+	337	17.6	20	20
Military Aid[c]	b	b	b	1	1	1	—	3+	3+	1.2	1.2	1.5
Commercial Exports	b	b	b	b	b	b	b	b	b	0.1	1	2
Total	b	22+	27+	71+	73+	50+	39+	210+	340+	18.9	22.2	23.5
Total												
FMS	2,031	3,770	3,277+	3,491+	1,312+	1,480+	1,947	17,253+	25,824+	7,446.7	5,795	8,385
Military Aid	b	b	b	1	1	1	—	4+	4+	1.3	1.3	1.6
Commercial Exports	211	183	305+	162+	41+	80+	60+	1,043+	1,043+	54.6	60	417
Total	2,242	3,953	3,582+	3,654+	1,354+	1,561+	2,007	18,300+	26,871	7,502.6	5,856.3	8,803.6

[a] Qatar is not included because it averaged only $200,000 annually in FMS. Licensed commercial arms exports, however, are planned to rise to $2 million annually in FY1982 and FY1983 and to $4 million annually in FY1984.

[b] Less than $0.5 million.

[c] International Military Education and Training only.

Source: Based on DSAA working data as of September 1982 and State Department programs as of April 1983. FY1982–1984 data are subject to significant change due to congressional action.

(see Chapters 7 and 10). It also has encouraged the Saudis to buy from France, Britain, and Germany. The ACDA estimates that during 1971–1980, Saudi Arabia acquired $3.6 billion worth of arms, munitions, and direct spares. The U.S. provided $1.8 billion worth (50%), France sold $290 million worth (8%), Britain $900 million (25%), Italy $130 million (4%), and other countries $470 million (13%).[19]

This situation remains a major long-term threat to Saudi-U.S. relations and will not be resolved by the Reagan military sales program shown in Table 20.6 even if it is fully funded by Congress. The totals for FY1982–1984 in Table 20.6 seem high, but they disguise the fact that the administration has had to tell the Saudis it cannot sell them their full requirement for major armor, more F-15s, bomb racks for the F-15s, new fighters, or other equipment that might cause political problems with Israel and its supporters in an election period. Further, Saudi Arabia is still expanding its investment in a military infrastructure that the U.S. is effectively refusing to arm. In FY1982, $1.8 billion out of $7.4 billion in new FMS agreements will still be construction. The figure will be $700 million out of $5.7 billion in FY1983 and $1.7 billion out of $8.1 billion in FY1984. The U.S. inability to fully support Saudi force modernization is not fading with time, and it poses an increasing embarrassment for both countries in a period in which Saudi Arabia faces significant budget constraints and must pay the costs of buying from an unnecessarily wide range of suppliers.

The Case of Oman

The trends in the arms transfer data for Oman in Tables 20.1 and 20.2 are shaped by both the cost of defeating the Dhofar rebellion and the current threats posed by Iran and South Yemen. Table 20.3 shows that Britain has historically been Oman's chief source of arms and military assistance, with only limited supplies coming from the U.S., Italy, and a variety of other countries. Table 20.6 shows, however, that Oman has recently shifted its arms purchases to depend heavily on U.S. assistance and imports. This change is largely the result of the fact that Sultan Qabus is reacting to the growing threat from Iran and South Yemen by seeking an alignment with the United States. As was discussed in Chapters 17 and 18, the sultan has sought to trade Omani staging bases for U.S. forces for U.S. security assistance guarantees and increased supplies of U.S. military equipment. Unlike the other conservative Gulf rulers, Qabus can make such arrangements because he does not have large minorities of foreign labor, has little to fear in terms of further worsening his relations with the radical Gulf states, and cannot make dissenting radical elements in Oman any more hostile than they already are. Oman has little to lose in terms of internal security and much to gain in terms of external security from ties to the U.S.

As a result, Oman will provide a major U.S. staging facility at Masirah. The growth in U.S. aid stemming from this agreement is not yet fully reflected in the currently declassified data shown in Table 20.6, but the U.S. will provide at least $40 million more in FMS credits in FY1983 and has proposed $40 million more for FY1984, plus $3 million annually in commercial exports. It is discussing means to provide $200–250 million in forgiven loans, grant aid, or offsets under the joint economic cooperation agreement signed in 1981. The U.S. will provide $15 million annually in Economic Support Funding during FY1982 to FY1984 plus $563,000 in P.L. 480 aid over the same period.[20]

As was discussed in Chapter 18, the U.S. has already spent $224 million to upgrade contingency facilities in Oman, and this total may eventually reach $1.5 billion. It already flies two P-2C Orion maritime patrol aircraft out of Seeb airport and bases a command destroyer and four frigates in the area. Under the agreement, it will lengthen the airstrip at Masirah to be a main C-5 and C-141 base, improve its port facilities, add predeployment storage facilities, and set up a major aircraft repair and maintenance facility with 100 permanently based U.S. technicians. It will extend the air base at Thamarit to help defend against South Yemen and that at Khasab to help defend the Strait of Hormuz, and it will help create a new naval facility north of Muscat at Wudham. The U.S. is also developing an air defense system to cover Oman. While all these actions will help secure U.S. power projection capabilities, they will also help Oman deter Iran and South Yemen.[21]

Oman is thus a good example of a country where a limited U.S. commitment can achieve major strategic advantages. The air facilities in Oman are approximately 2,000 miles closer to the Gulf than the base the U.S. currently leases in Diego Garcia, and although the air base at Seeb has the disadvantage that the U.S. must operate with high visibility near the international airport in the capital city of Muscat, the base on the island of Masirah has the advantage of having a very low profile on an underpopulated island with negligible local water supplies and population. The airfield is now too small for staging major B-52 strikes, but it can take virtually all other U.S. aircraft. By 1984, it will be improved to allow landing of the B-52 and C-5B and provide prepositioned stocks for U.S. air operations in the Gulf. Masirah allows Oman to offer the U.S. contingency bases with a minimal U.S. presence on its soil and with the assurance that little friction need take place with the local population. Such arrangements will also leave the U.S. well positioned to help Oman deter another round of fighting in the Dhofar and to use Oman as a potential staging base for support of the Gulf area. The arms transfers and tacit security guarantees it will provide for the use of Omani facilities will pay off directly for both the U.S. and Oman by helping Oman to deal with its internal security problems and deterring direct or indirect aggression from South Yemen.

Such a combination of U.S. arms transfers to Oman and the provision of power projection facilities does, however, present two interrelated problems. The first is that it may renew the tensions that arose over the "Muscat Mafia," the foreign advisers surrounding Sultan Qabus in the late 1970s, and channel any new hostility against the U.S. The second is that Oman's provision of staging points to the U.S. may divide Oman from the other conservative Gulf states. Kuwait and the UAE are particularly vulnerable to external and internal security pressures that may force them to criticize Qabus's links to the U.S. and even to avoid any collective security links with Oman.

There are no easy answers to these problems, and much will depend on the extent to which the U.S. can keep its advisory effort small and well disciplined and help develop an improved partnership between Oman and Saudi Arabia. There are obvious potential advantages to all three nations in such an arrangement.[22] Further, although Saudi Arabia and the other conservative Gulf states have sometimes made ritual criticisms of Oman for providing the U.S. with such facilities, they recognize the benefit from these bases. U.S. facilities in Oman are also far less provocative than such bases directly near the Gulf's oil facilities, because they can be useful to the U.S. only if a Gulf nation actively seeks U.S. help. As U.S. over-the-horizon reinforcements contribute to the defense of the conservative Gulf states, and as long as the U.S. avoids giving its presence in Oman too high a profile, Gulf criticism of Oman can probably be contained within limits that will allow Oman to fully participate in any collective security arrangements in the Gulf.

The Case of the Yemens

The events discussed in Chapters 12 and 17 have given the USSR bases with immense potential strategic value in South Yemen. They also have created a pattern of Soviet military assistance to South Yemen different from that the USSR gives to other Near Eastern countries. South Yemen's radical regime has been heavily dependent on Soviet-bloc economic assistance for its survival since its independence from Britain, and it is now dependent on Soviet military aid to help maintain internal control over a divided and often chaotic state. In spite of Saudi and Iraqi attempts to reverse the situation, the Soviet Union has come to almost totally dominate arms exports and military assistance to South Yemen and has received basing rights and substantial political and paramilitary support in return.

CIA data show that the size of the Soviet military assistance team in South Yemen reached 1,100 in 1979, plus an additional 1,000 Cubans. The USSR also deployed some 1,300 civilian technicians, who virtually ran key parts of the South Yemeni economy.[23] As is shown in Table 20.5, the USSR provided South Yemen with $775 million in arms exports during 1976–1980.[24] About $200 million of this total was provided in 1980, and it may since have increased by more than a third. For this expenditure, plus $330 million in economic aid between 1954 and 1981, the USSR has obtained access to the best naval facility in the Arabian Peninsula and air bases capable of receiving a massive Soviet air and airborne buildup. It has also been able to establish a civilian-military advisory team that totaled more than 2,000 Russians, 500 Cubans, and 325 East Germans in early 1983.[25]

The Soviet Union has also been heavily involved in South Yemen's internal politics. As was described in Chapters 12 and 17, the USSR steadily built up a client faction in the ruling party and then deliberately backed its head, Abd al-Fattah Ismail, in his overthrow of the more moderate, and pro-Iraqi, Rubai Ali in June 1978. Although reports differ, the USSR seems to have used its military advisers, plus those of Cuba and East Germany, to directly help Ismail in overthrowing Rubai Ali in much the same way the USSR later used its advisers in Afghanistan. It was equally deeply involved in the events that then led to the deposition of Abd al-Fattah Ismail and brought Ali Nasr Muhammed to power and in the complex politics that made Ismail's former security chief, Mushin al-Shargabi (the "Beria of South Yemen") ambassador to Bulgaria. While the details are unclear, Moscow seems to have backed Ali Nasr in taking a more moderate position relative to his Gulf neighbors in 1981 and 1982, but allowed Ismail and Mushin to develop something approaching an opposition movement. Ali Nasr reacted by recalling Mushin in mid-1982 and throwing him into the "death camp" at Fatah and by exiling his chief of staff, Ahmad Salim Ubaid, to London. He could not, however, break with the USSR or suppress all of Ismail's supporters. It was clear that Moscow was still able to ride two horses at once in South Yemen in early 1983 and was backing Ali Nasr publicly while preserving Ismail as a hard-line alternative.[26]

This is an interesting example of the shift in the Soviet advisory effort to maintain a parallel structure of political subversion in the nations in which it operates military assistance efforts. Although it is impossible to document the extent of such operations, the end result is that the USSR may now be able to use South Yemen as its proxy in Arabia (at least to the extent that South Yemen's ambitions and Soviet policy do not violently conflict). It can pressure Saudi Arabia by threatening to increase its military aid to South Yemen or to support it in a future border conflict, and can threaten the U.S. by increasing its military and naval presence.

The situation in North Yemen is different, but the trend also seems to favor the USSR. As described in Chapters 12 and 17, the USSR has been able to use its military assistance effort in North Yemen to checkmate U.S. and Saudi efforts to bring North Yemen into the conservative and/or pro-Western sphere of influence. Its success, however, is as much the result of the weaknesses in the U.S. and Saudi aid efforts and of vicissitudes of Yemeni politics as of Soviet efforts. Although the U.S. began to replace the USSR as North Yemen's principal source of arms in 1976, with Saudi Arabia funding most of the key arms transfers, U.S. arms deliveries proved grindingly slow. The U.S. lacked the equipment stocks and production base to meet even minimal North Yemeni needs, and the "bilateral" U.S. aid effort with Saudi Arabia broke down because of Saudi efforts to keep the North Yemeni government firmly under Saudi control.

As was described in Chapter 12, the U.S. and Saudi Arabia offered North Yemen expedited arms deliveries after its border clash with South Yemen in March 1979. This offer, however, did little more than demonstrate the limits to U.S. aid. The Soviets responded by helping to oust Ismail, installing a more "moderate" government in South Yemen, and offering North Yemen faster arms deliveries on far more advantageous terms than the U.S. The USSR delivered $625 million worth of arms to North Yemen during 1976–1980, and Poland $100 million, versus about $170 million for the U.S.[27] The Soviet Union delivered $415 million worth of this total in 1980 and also reacted to the threat of increased U.S. aid by delivering three times as many combat aircraft and four times as many tanks in 1980 as the U.S. could offer. It continued such deliveries in 1981 and increased its military advisory presence to over 700 men, plus 175 economic technicians, whereas the Saudis and the U.S. had only a token presence.[28] By 1983, the U.S. was delivering only $23 million worth of arms and military aid annually while the Soviet Union was delivering annual increments of a $1.5 billion arms agreement. North Yemen thus serves as a warning of the advantages the USSR enjoys over the U.S. in using arms transfers because of its vastly larger weapons stocks and production rates.

The Other Conservative Gulf Nations

The future impact of U.S. and Soviet arms sales on the other conservative Gulf states is now highly uncertain. Kuwait has been the only conservative Gulf state to buy Soviet equipment and to make any serious effort to balance U.S. and Soviet military influence. It bought $50 million worth of Soviet arms and $390 million worth of U.S. arms during 1971–1980, out of a total of $800 million, and has increasingly opted for British and French arms.[29] Bahrain, Qatar, and the UAE have previously chosen to rely principally on European equipment and advisers. Although the smaller Gulf states have spent over $2 billion on arms since 1971, they have not aligned themselves with either the U.S. or the USSR in buying their equipment.[30]

As was described in Chapters 11 and 15, however, the smaller conservative Gulf states cannot hope to develop effective military forces if they do not cooperate in the future. If they are to create effective naval and air defenses they must link their defenses with Saudi Arabia and improve the standardization and integration of at least their military electronics. Such arrangements will become even more important when the smaller Gulf states have to react to the military buildup of the larger Gulf states that seems certain to follow the Iran-Iraq War. They will be forced to make still further purchases of advanced military equipment, none of which will be effective without collective security arrangements.

The issue is now whether they will actually buy the equipment they need and whether they can transform their individual arms purchases into the ability to achieve collective security. It now seems unlikely that any will turn to the USSR, although some additional Kuwaiti purchases seem certain. Their most likely course of action is to rely on Europe for most deliveries, given the problem of U.S. ties to Israel and their need to maintain existing European equipment, but to buy enough U.S. or compatible British equipment to integrate their air defense forces and sensor and C^3I systems. Fortunately, they may be able to develop sufficient cooperative defense capabilities by emphasizing interdependence and interoperability as a substitute for standardization.[31]

It is still too early to predict, however, whether the conservative Gulf states can properly rationalize their military procurement efforts, find ways of drawing on Western technical expertise to achieve interoperability, and build an effective collective security effort. A successful effort to create full interoperability with potential U.S. over-the-horizon reinforcements seems even more uncertain. The links to the Saudi AWACS and air defense system discussed in Chapters 9, 10, and 15 will allow the smaller Gulf air forces to integrate their fighter operations over the Gulf, but it seems unlikely that the UAE, Kuwait, Bahrain, or Qatar will make any arrangements that would help support U.S. fighter operations from their bases. While interoperability with U.S. air units would involve comparatively limited purchases of selected items of U.S. equipment, and possibly only the provision of key equipment and munitions for rapid deployment from Saudi Arabia and U.S. staging points in the Gulf, it is doubtful whether any of the smaller conservative Gulf nations will take such steps.

Future Trends in U.S. and Soviet Military Assistance in the Gulf Area

In summary, neither the United States nor the Soviet Union has yet acquired an advantage through its arms transfers to the Gulf area. Barring some crisis as a result of the Iran-Iraq War, the effect of Soviet aid to Iraq will probably continue to be the creation of a strongly nationalist and independent Arab state whose oil wealth will make its Baathist radicalism more and more theoretical and transform it into a buffer protecting the conservative oil-producing states. The U.S. is likely to achieve even less from its past aid and arms sales to Iran. The fall of the shah may still—with luck—forge an equally independent and nationalist state, but it is increasingly hard to rule out a possible Iranian shift toward military dependence on the Soviet Union. This could occur as Iran seeks military resupply as a result of the Iran-Iraq War or as the result of the ongoing civil war between Iran's political factions.

The U.S. has a broad advantage in the fact that most of the southern Gulf states are now conservative and will seek military aid from Europe or East Asia, if not the United States. At the same time, the Arab-

Israeli conflict and its domestic political impact on the U.S. ability to sell arms to the conservative Gulf states and improve its relations with Iraq favor the USSR. Much also depends on the ultimate outcome of the Iran-Iraq War, and the trends now seem more favorable to the Soviet Union than to the U.S.

The Soviet Union has achieved an advantage over the U.S. in the southeastern Red Sea area because of the basing capability and proxy forces it has gained through its presence in South Yemen and its growing presence in North Yemen. As a result, the future of U.S.-Soviet military competition in the Gulf area is extremely volatile, even if the U.S. is fully successful in creating a matching set of contingency bases in Oman. Finally, the USSR also may be able to achieve many of its objectives in the region simply by using its arms sales to play a "spoiler" role. If it can capitalize on the post–Iran-Iraq War rearmament effort, or on a future coup d'etat in any Gulf state, to tie additional Gulf states to the Soviet military assistance effort, the USSR will have significant additional leverage over all the other Gulf states. In the long run, therefore, U.S. ability to counter the USSR is likely to be highly dependent on U.S. success in establishing a more stable pattern of military assistance efforts to Saudi Arabia and the other Gulf states or in encouraging Europe in a joint effort to achieve the same ends.

The Impact of U.S. and Soviet Arms Exports on the Arab-Israeli Confrontation States

The impact of U.S. and Soviet arms transfers on the Gulf cannot be divorced from the impact of these transfers on the other states in the region. The broad flows of arms shown in Tables 20.1–20.4 show trends in neighboring states that will have a powerful effect on the stability of the Gulf. This is particularly true of the sales to the Arab-Israeli confrontation states.

Current data on U.S. military sales to these states is shown in Table 20.7. Unfortunately, current data are not available on Soviet exports because recent CIA reports do not provide a country-by-country breakdown of Soviet military exports to the region. CIA figures do show, however, that the USSR massively increased its arms shipments to the entire Middle East in the early 1980s, after a sharp decline in 1978 and 1979.[32] The data in Tables 20.1, 20.2, 20.4, and 20.5 do, however, reflect several trends that seem likely to affect U.S.-Soviet competition in the 1980s: the end of Soviet military supply to Egypt (which continued for two years after the October War and long after the expulsion of Soviet advisers from Egypt), the increase in Iraqi independence discussed earlier, the reassertion of Soviet military influence on Syria, and the continued buildup and military dominance of Israel.

TABLE 20.7 U.S. Military Sales and Aid Deliveries to the Arab-Israeli Confrontation States, FY1976–FY1984 (in millions of current dollars)

	Actual Deliveries							FY1976–1983		Planned New Agreements and Sales		
	FY1976	FY1977	FY1978	FY1979	FY1980	FY1981	FY1982	Deliveries	New Agreements	FY1982	FY1983	FY1984
Israel												
FMS	821	869	825	339	581	1,042	972	5,449	5,006	656	1,900	800
Military Aid	—	—	—	—	—	—	—	—	—	—	—	—
Commercial Exports	190	222	123	174	272	267	150	1,398	1,398	150	150	300
Total	1,011	1,091	948	513	853	1,309	1,122	6,897	6,404	806	2,050	1,100
Arabs												
FMS	78+	111+	166	280	394	329	1,212+	2,570	6,953	2,273.2	920	1,330
Military Aid	65+	7	63	42	49	66	20	312	312+	5.4	4.4	6
Commercial Exports	2+	5+	19+	8+	62+	47+	67	210+	210+	66.5	81.5	121.5
	145+	123+	248+	330	505+	442+	1,299+	3,092+	7,475+	2,345.1	1,005.9	1,457.5
Egypt												
FMS	[a]	10	51	192	203	203	1,052+	1,711	5,369	2,122.7	560	1,000
Military Aid	—	—	—	—	—	—	—	—	—	2.4	2	2
Commercial Exports	1	1	7	1	7	4	15	36	36	15	30	70
Total	1+	11	58	193	210	207	1,067+	1,747	5,405	2,140.1	592	1,072
Jordan												
FMS	73	101	106	80	175	113	123	771	1,442	141	300	300
Military Aid	65	7	63	42	49	66	20	312	312	2	1.4	2
Commercial Exports	[a]	4	9	4	54	42	50	163+	163+	50	50	50
Total	138	112	178	126	278	221	193	1,246+	1,917	193	351.4	352
Lebanon												
FMS	5	[a]	9	8	16	13	37	88+	142	9.5	60	30
Military Aid	[a]	—	—	—	—	—	—	[a]	[a]	1	1	2
Commercial Exports	1	[a]	2	3	1	1	2	10+	10+	1.5	1.5	1.5
Total	6+	[a]	11	11	17	14	39	98+	142+	12.0	62.5	33.5
Syria												
FMS	—	[a]	—	—	—	—	—	—	—	—	—	—
Military Aid	—	—	—	—	—	—	—	—	—	—	—	—
Commercial Exports	[a]	[a]	1	[a]	[a]	—	—	1+	1+	—	—	—
Total	[a]	[a]	1	[a]	[a]	—	—	1+	1+	—	—	—

[a] Less than $0.5 million.

Sources: DSAA working data as of September 1982; State Department programs as of April 1983. FY1982–1984 data are subject to significant change due to congressional action. Israeli totals are likely to average $2 billion annually after such action. Note that data on FMS financing, often confused with agreements, are shown in Chapter 20.

The Case of Syria

Syria has recently been far more dependent on the USSR than has Iraq, and Soviet-Syrian relations have lacked the continuing tension that has been created by Iraqi treatment of the Kurds and the ICP.[33] Syria has also had more regional goals and interests in common with the USSR than has Iraq. There are, however, some striking similarities in the Soviet aid effort to the two countries. There has been tension between Syria and the Soviet Union over such issues as the Syrian intervention in Lebanon, the Soviet handling of the October War cease-fire negotiations with the U.S., relations with the PLO, the quality of Soviet arms, and the reliability of Soviet support. Syria has often taken a harder line toward the PLO, at least internally, than Moscow has desired.

Problems in the History of Soviet Arms Transfers to Syria. There has also been considerable friction between the Syrian military and their Soviet advisers, and the Syrian forces have had as much reason to question the quality of Soviet military assistance as have the Iraqi. This friction has been slower to emerge in Syria than in Iraq and Egypt. Major Soviet military deliveries to Syria began only in 1971 and 1972, when the USSR sought to build up a combination of strong Syrian forces and contingency bases in Syria's airfields and ports. This policy minimized Syrian and Soviet military contact during the formative period in the Soviet military assistance effort, when its racial and ideological problems were most apparent.

Syria did, however, experience problems with Soviet military equipment and assistance during the October War. The Syrians had brutal practical evidence of their inability to compete with Israeli armor and fighters. They had further problems with the inadequacy of key aspects of Soviet training—particularly in urban warfare and the management of artillery fire—during the initial phases of their intervention in Lebanon. As a result, the Syrians sought to diversify their military training and equipment purchases from 1974 onward, to buy key Western fire-control equipment and C^3I software, and to reduce their dependence on Soviet military equipment. This effort showed some signs of success during 1976–1979, when Syria's search for military independence was encouraged by the Saudis, and both Iraq and Syria started to buy systems like the HOT and Milan antitank guided missiles and 35 Gazelle helicopters equipped with AS-11 or HOT from France.[34]

The vicissitudes of Arab politics, however, then left Syria isolated from Jordan, Iraq, and Egypt and facing a major internal security threat. Syria also never found a stable external source of arms funding that would allow it to phase down its dependence on Soviet equipment, replace preferential Soviet credit terms, and receive European equipment with any security and consistency. Further, the Soviets improved the quality of the equipment they were willing to sell and of their advisers, as they faced the potential loss of their final center of influence. As a result, Syria reasserted its military ties to the USSR in 1979–1981 and greatly increased the Soviet military presence in the country. Syria signed a Friendship and Cooperation treaty in November 1980 that implied Soviet protection if Syria should be invaded, and it signed a new major arms agreement in January 1982.[35] The Syrian government particularly expanded the Soviet role in assisting Syrian internal security forces and the various "black operations" groups under the command of President Assad's brother.

The USSR had 2,480 military technicians in the country in 1979 and increased the number of Syrian military personnel trained in the USSR (the CIA reports that a total of 4,250 were trained during 1955–1979). The number of Soviet-bloc military technicians was twice that in Iraq and was second only to the number in Afghanistan. In addition, the USSR provided large numbers of economic technicians, at least some of whom provided covert internal security assistance.[36] These numbers also increased during 1980–1981. A total of 3,300 Soviet military and 4,100 civilian "technicians," plus 210 Germans and 5 Cubans, were present in mid-1981. The number of Syrian military personnel training in the Soviet bloc also increased to over 600 per year.[37]

Syria also has begun to receive considerable amounts of modern Soviet aircraft and armor, such as the new T-72 tank and 122mm and 152mm self-propelled guns. It acquired large numbers of BMP-1s and BTR-60s to replace its BTR 40/50s and BTR-152s, and of new MiG-23, MiG-27, Su-20, and MiG-25 fighters. These deliveries of modern Soviet aircraft and of SA-9 and upgraded SA-6 surface-to-air missiles led to several Syrian attempts to reassert its air strength against Israel during 1981. These attempts, however, resulted in Israel's first air-to-air kill of a MiG-25, and Syria still had not won an air-to-air encounter with Israel when the fighting started in Lebanon in 1982.

Soviet-bloc arms transfers to Syria reached nearly $2 billion a year in 1981 and over $3 billion in 1982 and $2.5 billion in 1983 because of Soviet transfers to compensate for the losses inflicted by Israel. These transfers, however, have done little to match the improvements in Israel's capabilities.[38] As was the case in Iraq, massive deliveries of modern Soviet arms have produced only limited increases in military effectiveness. This was largely the fault of Syria, but it was also the result of the USSR's inability to provide effective equipment, training, and advice in the period before the June 1982 fighting. Syria was unable to get effective Soviet support in offensive and large-unit training. It was unable to get the USSR to provide adequate air combat and air attack training or support in teaching it how to effectively operate and integrate its new air and surface-to-air missile equipment. Although some aspects of Syrian training were disrupted because of its military involvement in Lebanon, and because of its military posturing against Jordan and Iraq, many Syrian officers feel that the USSR has deliberately failed to improve Syria's training base because it wants a dependent state that cannot challenge Israel rather than a regional ally that will acquire the strength to act on its own. Discussions with Western intelligence officers also indicate that although the USSR provided massive deliveries of radars, it failed to provide the truly advanced electronic warfare equipment, military software, C^3I systems, and advanced air munitions Syria needed to use its modern Soviet combat equipment effectively. Although Syria got export versions of some of the latest Soviet fighters, these export versions lack the avionics, radars, and modern air-to-air missiles to survive combat with the IAF.

Soviet "Parallel Operations" in Syria. The expansion of Soviet arms deliveries was also accompanied by expanding Soviet support of Assad's internal security efforts. Soviet personnel were involved in the suppression of anti-Assad coups within the Syrian military in 1982 and in the bloody suppression of various dissidents that Syria groups under the label of the "Muslim Brotherhood," including the fighting to suppress them in Aleppo, Homs, and Hammah. The Alawite-led armed forces generally remained loyal after an attempted coup by air force and naval officers in the spring of 1982, which was followed by an uprising in Hammah that led the government to decimate the city; but the attempts of Syria's small Alawite elite to maintain its security has led to a growing alienation of Sunni Syrian officers and officials, to a resentment of the often clumsy process of arrests and security review, and to the increased isolation of Assad, his brother, and his clan.[39]

This Soviet role in Syrian internal security has not endeared the Soviet Union to either the bulk of the military or Syria's Sunni majority, and it is clear that the USSR has not solved the broader attitudinal problems of the Soviet military training teams in Syria or the USSR. Arabs who deal extensively with the Syrian military indicate that they continue to complain about the covert racial contempt some Soviet advisers show for the Syrians and about their contempt for the Baath ideology of the Syrian government, no matter how "fraternal" that government may be. Further, a few Soviet officers have evidently been outspoken about the corruption that permeated the Syrian forces as they exploit their occupation of Lebanon to compensate for low pay and Syria's lower standard of living.

The Future of Soviet-Syrian Military Cooperation. The future of Soviet-Syrian cooperation is difficult to predict. While Israel's invasion of Lebanon initially acted to divide the two countries, it has since brought them together. Iran did send volunteers, but it became clear that Syria had few Arab supporters. As a result, Syria turned to the USSR and sought a strengthened security treaty that was to all intents and purposes a request for Soviet military guarantees.[40] Israel's destruction of up to 19 Syrian SA-6 missile batteries, 80 MiG-21 and MiG-23 fighters, and large quantities of tanks and other armor in the first week of the fighting also forced Syria immediately to seek Soviet resupply.[41]

The Soviet response was initially mixed. The USSR conspicuously refused to expand its friendship and cooperation treaty with Syria beyond the defense of Syrian territory. The Soviet Union paid lip service to the PLO during the fighting in Lebanon in 1982, but ignored its calls for military support, even when these were backed by Syria. In fact, Soviet support of the Arab cause was so lukewarm that Qadaffi called in the Soviet-bloc ambassadors to Libya for a 5-minute tongue-lashing on 27 June, and Salah Khalaf, the second ranking official in the PLO, publicly criticized the USSR for its limited support.[42] The USSR also did not offer Syria any new arms or technologies during the fighting, although it became clear that many of Syria's military problems were caused by the inability of its Soviet-made MiG-23 and MiG-25 fighters and SA-6s to compete with Western and Israeli weapons. The fact that the deputy commander of the Soviet air defense forces had to be rushed to Syria to determine how Israel could have been so effective in defeating the SA-6 was scarcely an advertisement for Soviet arms or tactics.[43]

This Soviet response to the Israeli invasion created a considerable Syrian backlash against the USSR for being a "fair weather" friend and pushed Syria to demand the most advanced weapons and technology in Soviet forces. This seems to have been the reason why the USSR then agreed to fully replace Syrian losses in the fighting in Lebanon, provided SA-5 missiles to Syria in early 1983, provided deliveries of more advanced MiG-25s and MiG-23s and air-to-air missiles, and gave Syria advanced SS-21 surface-to-surface missiles.[44] The poor performance of Soviet equipment and the USSR's conspicuous failure to aid Syria during the fighting over Lebanon confronted the USSR with a serious risk that it could lose its main card in the region. As a result, it increased its presence to 5,000–7,000 Soviet military and 4,100 economic technicians. It also provided all Soviet crews for two SA-5 batteries with 12 launchers each. Although the SA-5 missiles dated back to the 1960s, they had a 150–190-mile range and had never before been deployed to a Third World nation. Further, the USSR provided most of the cadre of the 500–1,000-man crew each battery required and began deployment of a fully integrated air defense system, including the required electronics, advanced fighters, and overlapping layers of SA-6, SA-8, SA-9, and SA-11 missiles.[45] In addition, it provided Soviet personnel to help operate the improved air defense system and gave Syria aid in developing counter-measures to Israel's air defense suppression capabilities.

This sets an ominous precedent for the Gulf. It implies that whatever nation turns to the USSR in the future can count on a far more sophisticated level of Soviet advice and technology, which could be particularly important in terms of shaping the future threat from Iran and Iraq if either turns to the USSR after the war. If such a system were combined with the new Soviet Candid-2 AWACS, it would also do much to offset the advantages Saudi Arabia can gain through the

E-3A and its F-15s and would require far tighter cooperation among the southern Gulf nations. They would, in fact, probably be forced to buy significant numbers of "mini-AWACS" with ELINT capabilities to counter the ability of such a Soviet-supplied system to provide air cover and radar ducting penetration.[46] It is also unclear that the USSR has much other choice. The fighting in Lebanon, the Iran-Iraq War, and the Falklands have raised the Third World's consciousness of the advantages of Western technology and of the weaknesses in at least the export versions of Soviet systems to the point where the USSR virtually must do something.

Even so, the USSR may not be able to preserve its present influence in the country. Arms transfers will not keep the USSR from being identified with Assad and the Alawites, and Syria may well face division or civil war if Assad is assassinated or dies. It is unclear that any new Syrian leadership will pursue the present conflict in Lebanon or struggle with Israel, and Syria faces a steadily building economic crisis and competing demands for resources. It also has always been apparent that Assad treats with the USSR out of necessity, not out of love. He has repeatedly tried to break away from the Soviet orbit. He went so far during 1980 and 1981 as to open "unity" talks with Libya in an effort to get an independent source of funding and equipment. Syria also continues to seek expanded Saudi aid and may have made offers in 1981 to reduce its dependence on the USSR if the Gulf oil-producing states would provide suitable military aid and economic assistance. While the USSR may have "bought" itself an ally, it has scarcely acquired a friend.

The Case of Egypt

The situation in Egypt has also changed radically over the last few years, and scarcely in favor of the USSR. By 1983, only a few hundred Soviet economic technicians and a small volume of trade remained from a relationship that had brought Egypt $2.7 billion worth of Soviet economic aid and $4 billion of Soviet-bloc military equipment.[47]

The Failure of the Soviet Military Assistance Effort in Egypt. The result of one of the most massive Soviet military assistance efforts in the postwar era[48] was Sadat's expulsion of Soviet military technicians in 1972, Egypt's unilateral abrogation of the Soviet-Egyptian Friendship Treaty in 1976, Cairo's cotton embargo in 1977, a massive dispute over repayment of Egypt's military debt, and Sadat's expulsion of 400 Soviet economic technicians and canceling of all outstanding contracts shortly before his death. The legacy to Egypt was a $3–4 billion debt, vast stores of unusable military equipment, and the collapse of a Soviet-backed economic development program in midstream.[49]

The *volte-face* in Egypt's relations with the USSR had many causes, but it was at least partly the result of endemic problems in the Soviet military assistance effort to the more advanced developing nations. First, there is no doubt that the Soviets in Egypt, and those who trained Egyptians in the USSR, often showed nearly open contempt for the Egyptian forces. While the Soviet aid efforts to Iraq and Syria have since made an effort to reduce this problem, racism was blatant during the period of close Soviet military relations with Egypt and was made worse by the professional contempt that many Soviet advisers displayed for the Egyptian officer corps. Somewhat similar problems have occurred in U.S. military aid efforts to nations like Vietnam, Saudi Arabia, and Iran, but they have been far less serious and far more episodic in character. The Soviets have had much more serious problems with the ethnocentricity of their advisers than the U.S., and Egypt was only the worst and most obvious example of this in the Near East.

The USSR had equally serious problems in establishing a clear policy toward technology transfer. While it did provide advanced SAMs and advanced radars, it conspicuously omitted providing all of the equipment necessary to "net" such equipment into an effective air defense system and modern electronic warfare equipment, and it either failed to or could not provide the training necessary for the Egyptian forces to take advantage of the transfers. The Soviets also proved unwilling to provide their most advanced fighter munitions and avionics and provided minimal and often irrelevant air combat training.[50] Whether the USSR did this because it felt the Egyptians could not absorb the equipment, because it feared Israeli seizure of key technology vital to Soviet defense, or because it sought to keep Egypt dependent on the USSR is uncertain. But the net effect was to deny Egypt much of the potential benefit of its fighter and air defense purchases.

Finally, Soviet training of the Egyptian army remained essentially defensive and had a small-unit character. The USSR failed to help the Egyptians develop the ability to operate their armor offensively except in the most limited staff-college-textbook sense of the term, and Egyptian military historians generally seem correct in giving Egypt credit for virtually every detail of the planning and training for the Egyptian offensive in 1973.[51] It is unclear whether this represented a fundamental weakness in the Soviet aid effort or a Soviet calculation that Egypt was not ready to absorb such assistance, or whether it again was a deliberate Soviet effort to limit Egyptian capabilities and maintain Egyptian dependence on the USSR. The net effect, however, was that the Soviets not only did not provide the army training Egypt needed, but conspicuously failed to do so in terms of Egyptian perceptions.

Putting aside the complex politics behind the Soviet expulsion from Egypt, the Iraqi, Syrian, and Egyptian experience with the USSR raises a common set of doubts about Soviet ability to use arms exports and assistance to exert sustained influence over recipient states.[52] In spite of the advantages the USSR enjoys in providing arms exports because of its ability to provide large and rapid deliveries, advantageous credit terms, and freedom from the political and moral constraints of the

West, it has severe difficulties in conducting military assistance efforts that involve extensive work in the host country or the training of Third World forces in the USSR.

U.S. Military Assistance to Egypt. At the same time, there is no question that the Egyptian shift to relying on U.S. military assistance in 1976 has exposed different problems in the U.S. aid effort. After some abortive attempts to obtain its arms imports from Britain and France, Egypt sought broad U.S. assistance in replacing the USSR as its principal source of arms, a trend that is reflected in Table 20.7. As a result, U.S. FMS and MAP agreements with Egypt rose from zero during FY1970–1975 to $161 million in FY1978, $447 million in FY1979, and $2.388 billion in FY1980.[53] This trend established the U.S. as Egypt's principal arms supplier. It has made the Egyptian Air Force heavily dependent on U.S. technical assistance for its first-line aircraft, although Egypt has decided to procure the French Mirage 2000. It also meant that Egyptian military strength became linked to U.S. support and supply for a 5- to 10-year cycle of conversion and rearmament using Western arms. This dependence, as well as Egypt's overall weakness, has been further increased by the reductions in Arab military assistance following the Camp David accords, by reductions in Saudi credits to buy European arms, by cancellation of plans to set up an "Arab" arms industry in Egypt, and by massive Soviet arms transfers to Libya, which have strengthened Sadat's principal opponent.

The U.S. agreed to provide Egypt with $3.6 billion in military aid between FY1979 and FY1981 as part of the Camp David accords and $900 million in further aid in FY1982. The Reagan administration increased these FMS credits to $2.1 billion in FY1982 and requested $425–450 million in forgiven loans and $850–900 million in guaranteed financing for FY1983 and FY1984. It is considering providing $1.2 billion in all grant aid each year during FY1985–1986. The U.S. has already allocated $2.95 billion for FMS contracts through FY1982, and Egypt has signed contracts for $4 billion under the cash-flow financing permitted for FMS. This is roughly 21% of the total U.S. security budget request.[54]

By the end of 1982, U.S. sales included 35 F-4E and 80 F-16 A/B fighters, 12 batteries of Improved Hawk surface-to-air missiles, 439 M-60 tanks, 1,214 M-113 APCs, 100 M-106A2 and M-125A2 armored mortar carriers, 200 TOW missile launchers, 1,500 regular TOW missiles, 2,500 Improved TOW missiles, 52 M-901 TOW armored fighting vehicles, 129 tank recovery vehicles, 18 C-130 transport aircraft, and many other items of combat equipment. The sales included modern air combat training, armored warfare training, and aid in building up the Egyptian base on the Red Sea at Ras Banas and other Egyptian bases and C^3I capabilities. Further, Egypt was talking to the U.S. about buying 40 more F-16s with AMRAAM air-to-air missiles (with an ultimate force goal of 120–140 F-16 aircraft), F-5G fighters, 4 E-2C Hawkeyes, 20 more

C-130s, 400–600 M-60A3s (with 128 under letter of offer), 500 more M-113s, up to 12 more batteries of Improved Hawks, 24 Cobra gunships with TOW, 200 more TOW launchers, and 2,500 Improved TOW missiles, plus a large quantity of other weapons, missiles, and military electronics.

Such U.S. aid led President Sadat to go so far as to talk about joining NATO before his assassination. The U.S. cannot, however, provide the equipment numbers required to allow Egypt to build back to its military strength of the early 1970s, and it may have trouble sustaining the domestic political consensus necessary to provide the required arms deliveries and credits. The potential problems involved are illustrated by the fact that the U.S. has identified $8 billion worth of additional requirements over the next eight years while Egypt has identified $27–32 billion and is seeking $1.7 billion in annual U.S. aid rather than the $900 million to $1.4 billion the U.S. has promised.[55] These differences may be unimportant as long as President Mubarak is willing to abandon Egypt's past efforts to achieve a military solution with Israel, and Mubarak has proved his commitment to peace in his moderate response to Israel's invasion of Lebanon. Still, any major shift in Egyptian policy that led it to arm against Israel would virtually force Egypt to seek arms elsewhere.

Egypt can produce $240 million worth of its own arms annually, obtain another $60 million worth through local vendors, and $100 million worth from the Arab Organisation for Industrialization. It is seeking to purchase arms from France, including Matra Crotale missiles and 12–24 Gazelle helicopters with ATGM (in addition to the 40 in inventory), and has already purchased up to 80 Mirage 2000 fighters and 30 Alphajet trainers.[56] It may buy the Skyguard air defense system from Italy, with 35mm radar-controlled guns, and Selina Aspide missile.[57] Egypt is also improving its efforts to maintain and recondition its Soviet-built MiG-21s.[58]

In spite of this massive shift to the West, Egyptian military dependence on the U.S. is still a weak lever for exerting U.S. influence. Internal political pressures have already led to President Sadat's assassination. The U.S. military assistance program to Egypt is also vulnerable to any radical action by Israel or shift in Egypt's commitment to the Camp David accords.

Further, the U.S. aid effort has run into serious internal and external problems. The U.S. still has not established a smooth military contracting and sales relationship with Egypt. In early 1983, General Dynamics Corporation was maintaining all the F-16s in Egypt out of contract because Egypt could not agree on terms to provide U.S. technical support. The 35 F-4Es the USAF transferred to Egypt were in wretched condition, and the Egyptian Air Force proved unable to maintain them, as the GAO had warned before the sale, and had to sell them to Turkey.[59] Similar problems had arisen in training Egyptians to operate and fly U.S. helicopters and transport aircraft and to operate and maintain U.S.

Army equipment. Further, a serious scandal arose over the role Egypt's ex–defense minister and current foreign minister, Kamal Hassan Ali, played in giving a company called EATSCO rights to ship U.S. military equipment to Egypt. EATSCO took some $30 million in fees for $21 million worth of shipping. While the evidence is unclear, Ali may have received substantial funds through Hussein K. Saleh, a former associate and intelligence officer, who founded EATSCO in 1979.[60]

Egypt also encountered problems in using U.S. economic assistance. Although the U.S. budgeted $7.6 billion between 1975 and 1983, or roughly $1 billion per year by 1982, about $400 million annually of this total was allocated to projects the U.S. had to approve. Unlike the $250 million annually that went to Food for Peace and the $350 million that went to commodity imports, this approval process bogged down in the Egyptian and U.S. civil services. This built up a backlog of $2.7 billion by early 1983, affecting 13% of the 66 major and 2,000 minor projects that the Agency for International Development (AID) was asked to fund.[61] While AID attempted to work this out and rationalize the program, both the U.S. and Egypt were still encountering serious administrative difficulties in mid-1983.[62]

There is no question, however, that Egyptian officers prefer ties to the U.S. and France to ties to the USSR and that many of them have a deep and abiding dislike of the Soviet officers with whom they worked. This distaste for the Soviet bloc has been reinforced by the low-level conflict between Egypt and Libya since 1976 and by the Chad and Sudan crisis of 1981, which involved Soviet-bloc as well as Libyan personnel. Accordingly, the Egyptians are not likely to turn back to the USSR lightly. They will do so only if the U.S. fails to respond with reasonable increases in its military aid or seriously miscalculates its influence, or if Egyptian-Israeli relations degenerate to a major crisis. In fact, even if Mubarak should fall or reverse his course, it seems likely that a successor regime would seek to get European arms with the support of the Arab oil states rather than resume ties to the USSR, unless it became committed to conflict with Israel.[63]

The Case of Jordan

Jordan provides a more graphic illustration of the problems the U.S. faces in dealing with the Arab world because of close U.S. political and military ties to Israel. As Jordan has become steadily more modern, urbanized, and "Palestinian," the limited amount of military and economic assistance that U.S. domestic politics have allowed the U.S. to provide to Jordan has had less and less impact. King Hussein has steadily increased his dependence on the Arab world for economic grants and military aid, and during 1978–1979 he began a tilt toward Iraq.[64] This led him into the position of being Iraq's strongest Arab supporter in the Iran-Iraq War and helped provoke a serious political conflict with Syria during December 1980, which culminated in a major military buildup at the Jordanian-Syrian border.[65]

King Hussein's motives in tilting toward Iraq have been military, economic, and political. Iraq's new oil wealth allowed it to act as a major supplier of economic and military assistance to Jordan until the war crippled Iraq's economy in late 1982. Unlike the U.S., Iraq could offer direct aid rather than credits and was significantly easier for Jordan to deal with—and more willing to provide actual cash—than Saudi Arabia. King Hussein's alliance with Iraq also allowed him to identify his regime more closely with the mix of Palestinian and Arab factions that now make up most of Jordan's population. In contrast, Hussein's former ties with Syria had many disadvantages: Syria lacked oil wealth and had growing internal political and economic problems; and ties to Syria increased the possibility of confrontation with Israel and offered far less control over the elements of the Palestinian movement that Hussein has found most threatening to his regime.

King Hussein used the aid he obtained to reduce his dependence on U.S. arms sales. Jordan purchased the 275 British made Shir-I tanks that the shah had on order at the time of his fall. It took delivery of 36 French Mirage F-1 fighters it purchased from France at a cost of $75 million, plus advanced French air-to-air and air-to-surface missiles. While Jordan sought the U.S.-made F-20A and F-16, it also discussed buying up to 72 Mirage F-1s and making its entire next generation of first-line combat aircraft French.

After the U.S. refused to sell Jordan mobile air defense systems to supplement the 14 fixed Hawk batteries the U.S. had sold it in 1974, Jordan turned to the USSR.[66] This shift took place, however, only after the Israeli raid on the Osirak reactor overflew Jordan, after Israeli reconnaissance flights continued to cover Jordan and Tabuk in Saudi Arabia, and after Israel continued to treat the East Bank of the Jordan River as Israeli airspace. In the process, Jordan found that its Hawk missiles and radar system were vulnerable to Israeli ECM and ineffective against Israeli fighters.[67] It was this development that finally catalyzed Jordan into procuring Soviet SA-8 surface-to-air missiles after nearly a decade of threatening to buy arms from the USSR. Jordan obtained $225 million in aid from Iraq, and in November 1981 Jordan purchased 10 SA-8 mobile surface-to-air missile launchers and 16 ZSU-14/4 radar-guide AA guns from the Soviet Union.

These arms purchases have led to some Jordanians' receiving Soviet training and have made Jordan a Soviet arms client for the first time. However, they have scarcely been fatal to Jordanian-U.S. relations or to U.S. interests in preserving Jordan's ties to the Gulf. They have led King Hussein to align himself with Iraq in ways that have so far contributed to creating Saudi-Iraqi-Jordanian relations that are helping to secure the Gulf's western flank. Further, Jordan is increasing its air defense ties to Saudi Arabia and is still making extensive military purchases from the U.S. Talks between King Hussein and President

Reagan in November 1981 averted any immediate risk of a serious split, and Secretary Weinberger has since sought to increase U.S. arms sales to Jordan.[68] Jordan received $54.9 million worth of guaranteed FMS loans in FY1982, and the Reagan administration has proposed $75 million worth in FY1983 and $115 million worth in FY1984.[69]

Equally important, the administration reached a confidential agreement with Jordan that it would provide $220 million in secret aid to allow Jordan to buy air lift, amphibious armored vehicles, bridgelayers, TOW missiles, short-range air defense weapons like Stinger, and improved land mobility for two Jordanian "brigades" totalling about 8,000 men to act as a rapid reinforcement force for the Gulf. It also initiated discussions of an aid package of roughly $700 million, to include F-16C aircraft and improved Hawk missiles, if Jordan could find a way to more actively support the Reagan peace plan. While Israel leaked the details of this plan to the U.S. press in an effort to block it in the fall of 1983, that tactic is more likely to delay such U.S. aid than to block it. If the U.S. Congress funds the Reagan program and Saudi Arabia proves willing to fund Jordan's arms purchases from Europe, Jordan is unlikely to drift away from the West or the moderate Arab states.[70] Jordan has backed President Reagan's peace initiatives, and its new independence has not reduced its friendship for the U.S. Jordan's relations with Iraq have reduced King Hussein's dependence on Syria and Jordan is now as threatened by Syria as Israel.

As was discussed in Chapter 19, there also seems to be only a limited prospect that any successor regime—which would probably have to depend heavily on the backing of the Jordanian military—would move toward the USSR. There is no question that Jordanian officers are loyal to the king and generally regard Soviet equipment as sharply inferior to what is available in the West. They also distrust the nature of current Soviet operations in Syria and have heard many Iraqi and Egyptian complaints about the nature of the Soviet aid effort. Even if Jordan should expand its purchases of Soviet equipment, the Jordanian officer corps could almost certainly absorb such equipment without an extensive Soviet advisory effort. Accordingly, while a more radical Jordan might pose a significant political threat to the Gulf and the West, such a development seems unlikely.

Although the Middle East is far too volatile for any firm predictions, Jordan's diversification of its military equipment purchases may thus ultimately serve both Arab and U.S. interests. This illustrates a broad advantage the U.S. has in its competition with the Soviet Union: The U.S. does not need direct influence as long as a nation is strongly independent. It has no need to inflict its ideology on other nations, and it does not need to tie its military assistance to a single revolutionary ethic.

The Case of Israel

Israel is one of the largest single buyers of U.S. military equipment. Israel has received $3 billion in U.S. military aid as part of the Sinai accords and is steadily increasing its U.S. arms imports.[71] It received $4.3 billion worth of U.S. arms during 1977–1980, or 2.2 times the U.S. arms sold to Saudi Arabia.[72] Israeli FMS purchases averaged close to $1 billion a year during FY1975–1982.

Even these figures disguise the true nature of Israel's recent relationship with the U.S. Israel got $500 million in payment waivers for U.S. military goods in FY1980 and FY1981 and $550 million in FY1982. It got $500 million more in guaranteed FMS loans in FY1980, $900 million in FY1981, and $850 million in FY1982. In addition, Israel bought $271.8 million in commercial arms in FY1980, $267.3 million in FY1981, and about $750 million in FY1982. This was well over its FY1975–1979 average.[73] Israel will receive 2.2 billion in military and related economic support for FY1982 and $2.6 billion in FY1983. It is programmed to receive $2.485 billion in FY1984 and similar amounts in FY1985–1989.

The economic part of this aid has been all grant aid, and Israel has generally received 50% forgiveness on FMS sales, as well as concessionary interest rates of 3–5% versus a normal rate of 14%.[74] Senator Alan Cranston proposed still further increases in U.S. grants in early 1982, however, and the Congress approved these over the objection of the Reagan administration in late 1982. They gave Israel $475 million more than the administration had intended, raised Israel's share of total U.S. worldwide military assistance to 27%, and set a precedent amounting to near-forgiveness of all future loans and sales.

The Congress again raised the administration's aid request in April and July 1983,[75] and during the visit of Prime Minister Shamir in November 1983, the Reagan administration agreed to convert all its military aid to Israel to grant aid beginning in FY1985. Coupled to agreements to fund development of the Lavi fighter, this will raise U.S. FMS grants to $1.4–1.7 billion in FY1985, plus another $1.2 billion in economic support funding.

In spite of such U.S. aid and sales, however, several factors limit the influence the U.S. can exert over Israel:

- Short-term cutbacks in U.S. military aid are likely to have little immediate effect. The Israeli armed forces are having problems in absorbing the U.S. military equipment they have already received. As a result, the IDF may already have bitten off more U.S. equipment than it can chew and seems unlikely to suffer from any temporary dip in the flow of arms in the early 1980s.
- Second, Israel has the choice of either striking while it is strong or waiting out a temporary break in U.S. arms supplies. The aftermath of its invasion of Lebanon has shown that U.S. pressure is unlikely to be consistent or even particularly deep. As long as Israel does not face

a threat from Egypt or Jordan, and the assessment of the balance in Chapters 13 and 21 indicates it does not, Israel can either pursue its own military objectives or largely ignore all but the most serious political and military pressure from the U.S.

• Third, the IDF has had enough munitions and spare parts since mid-1975 to avoid dependence upon the U.S. for immediate military resupply after another major round of fighting with the Arabs. For the first time in its military history, Israel can fight against its probable opponents and still remain independent of resupply for at least a year or two. In this sense, the IDF's tendency to grossly overbuy during the middle and late 1970s has acted to Israel's advantage.

• Fourth, Israel is emerging as a major arms exporter on its own. It sold $1.3 billion in arms between April 1980 and April 1981, or roughly 40% more than it did the previous year. It is able to produce its own ships, fighter aircraft, tanks, and missiles, and many of these systems, like the Merkava (Chariot) tank, may have an important world market. Israel also has a new generation of ship-to-ship missiles in development, can recondition and upgrade armor and artillery for export, and seems likely to use a non-U.S. engine for its Lavi (Lion) fighter if the U.S. does not grant it the export licenses it initially denied it for the Kfir. This should give Israel increasing independence in the future and make any cutoff in U.S. sales more likely to stimulate Israeli arms production rather than shift Israeli policy.

• Fifth, and most important, the U.S. lacks the domestic political consensus to allow it to act. In the absence of a clear Arab commitment to peace and recognition of Israel within its 1967 boundaries, U.S. administrations have lacked the ability to sustain any pressure on Israel in the face of the Congress's concern with domestic politics.

The U.S. can certainly influence Israel, but it proved to have tenuous leverage over Israel during Israel's invasion of Lebanon in 1982 and withdrawal from the Chouf in 1983, has had little practical impact in restraining Israel when Israel feels it must act out of military necessity. The political aftermath of the invasion of Lebanon has also done little to convince Israel it cannot ride out any U.S. threats of sanctions, arms cutoffs, and other U.S. measures. Israel seems likely to see its FMS purchases put on full grant aid in FY1985, in spite of the hostile U.S. reaction to its attacks on Beirut during the 1982 fighting, and the beginning of the 1984 presidential campaign has shown that Israel's domestic political influence in the U.S. remained as strong as ever.

Israel also has sufficient military supplies and superiority that it can ignore short-term pressure from the U.S. In spite of the massive Soviet buildup of Syria in 1983, Israel can still afford to attack any likely Arab opponent and wait until it can rebuild its political ties to the U.S. While the growing Soviet presence in Syria may deter Israeli action because of its fear of Soviet involvement, it is not clear that sudden U.S. pressure in a crisis could have the same effect. Israel could attack

Syria in the almost certain knowledge that the U.S. would not abandon it in the face of any Soviet reaction. Further, any dramatic U.S. efforts to use arms transfers to force Israel's hand over a major security issue might either lead it to act preemptively by attacking Syria or annexing the West Bank, or end in leading Israel to shift to a strategy of declared reliance on nuclear weapons.

Broad Trends in U.S.-Soviet Competition

As was the case in the Gulf, an analysis of U.S. and Soviet military assistance and arms exports to the Arab-Israeli confrontation states indicates that it is far harder for both superpowers to use arms transfers to exert direct influence over third nations than it might seem. It is also again unclear that the USSR can successfully exploit its theoretical advantages from being able to rapidly supply equipment, provide larger equipment deliveries and military assistance teams, and pursue a consistent policy line without the limits enforced by U.S. domestic politics. If anything, the long-term problems in Soviet military assistance to Syria seem likely to more than offset any short-term advantages from its ties to its one remaining ally in the region.

South Asia and Afghanistan

U.S.-Soviet competition in arms exports and military assistance in South Asia has followed a different pattern from that in the Gulf and Middle East. Until 1981, the USSR gave South Asia a far greater priority than did the U.S. It successfully sought to extend its influence in the area, to counter U.S. and PRC influence, and to improve its influence and capabilities in the Indian Ocean area. The USSR first began its penetration into South Asia when it provided military aid to Afghanistan in 1954, and it has provided a broad mix of military assistance and economic aid to several key nations in the region since the early 1960s. In contrast, the U.S. did not offer Afghanistan significant military aid at any time after 1952, and it proved indecisive as to whether it should play an even-handed role in the Indian-Pakistan conflict or back Pakistan until it finally reached an agreement to renew military assistance to Pakistan in late 1981.

The trends in U.S.-Soviet competition in the region are again shown in Tables 20.3–20.6. More recent CIA data on Soviet military relations with South Asia show that all Soviet military agreements in the region totaled $5.4 billion in 1956–1979 and peaked at $1.3 billion after the Bangladesh war in 1975. These agreements dropped to a low of $270 million in 1976, although they rose back to $400 million before the invasion of Afghanistan. Soviet arms transfers to India alone reached $3.5 billion during 1977–1980, while the U.S. sold India only $80 million worth of arms and Pakistan only $300 million.[76] The USSR also concentrated much of its declining economic aid in the region. In 1980 it gave India $800 million and Afghanistan $395 million in economic aid out of a worldwide total of $2.1 billion. It gave the region $100 million in 1981 out of a worldwide total of $445 million. The number of economic technicians in South Asian countries reached 5,945 in 1979 and 6,895 in 1982, but this reflected a growing Soviet-bloc trend toward selling technical services rather than providing aid.[77]

Table 20.8 provides a picture of recent trends in the U.S. military sales and aid effort to South Asia and shows that the U.S. effort lacked thrust and impact in the late 1970s. This reflected a U.S. decision to limit rearmament to Pakistan after its war with India and to try to use a cutoff of U.S. aid to block Pakistan's effort to develop nuclear weapons. It also reflected a U.S. effort to rebuild its military relations with India after Indira Gandhi's defeat.

New U.S. FMS sales and MAP aid agreements with Pakistan dropped from a high of $146 million in FY1977 to only $22.2 million in FY1979, before the Soviet invasion of Afghanistan. Even in FY1981, they totaled only $78.4 million. Although U.S. FMS agreements reached $146 million in FY1982, and total U.S. military sales and economic support reached $151 million, this aid was still worth far less in real terms than U.S. aid in FY1977. U.S. FMS sales to India rose from negligible levels in the early 1970s to $7.0 million in FY1979, but they remained unimportant relative to Soviet sales. As Table 20.8 shows, U.S. arms transfers during 1976–1980 were worth $50 million compared to $2.3 billion in Soviet transfers out of worldwide transfers of $2.8 billion. U.S. sales to Bangladesh, Nepal, and Sri Lanka were negligible, and no government-to-government sales and only token military aid were provided to Afghanistan. The Reagan administration's reassertion of U.S. ties to Pakistan, which increased U.S. aid to Pakistan to $450.6 million, represented the first major U.S. military assistance initiative in the Indian Ocean area since FY1977.

The Case of Afghanistan

Afghanistan is again important as a demonstration of Soviet actions and capabilities in the region.[78] It provides a case study of how a massive Soviet military and economic aid program can give the USSR de facto control of the government of a developing state and in the techniques that the Soviet Union may apply in other nations as part of its increasing efforts to tailor its aid program to key recipients so that it can sponsor a coup d'etat if its client starts to shift away from dependence on Soviet aid.[79]

It is important to understand, however, that the Soviet aid effort had nearly 30 years in which to take control of the Afghan government and that the USSR was aided in this process by the primitive nature of the recipient state and its proximity to the USSR. Further, much of the Soviet penetration into Afghanistan came largely as a result of U.S. inaction. Although the Soviets had trained the Afghan army and air

TABLE 20.8 U.S. Arms Transfer Sales and Aid to South Asia, FY1974–FY1984 (current $ millions)

	Actual Deliveries										Planned Agreements and Sales		
	FY1974	FY1975	FY1976	FY1977	FY1978	FY1979	FY1980	FY1981	FY1982	FY1976–82	FY1982	FY1983	FY1984
Afghanistan													
FMS	—	—	—	—	—	—	—	—	—	—	—	—	—
Commercial sales	—	—	a	a	a	a	a	—	—	a	—	—	—
MAP	—	—	—	—	—	—	—	—	—	—	—	—	—
Training and education	a	a	a	a	a	a	—	—	—	—	—	—	—
Total	a	a	a	a	a	a	a	—	—	a	—	—	—
India													
FMS	a	2	3	1	1	1	6	1	1	14	0.8	0.5	0.5
Commercial sales	1	a	6	9	9	10	3	5	5	47	5	5	40
MAP	a	a	1	a	a	a	a	a	a	a	—	—	—
Training and education	a	a	a	a	a	a	a	a	a	a	0.1	0.1	0.2
Total	1+	2+	10+	10+	10+	11+	9+	6+	6+	61	5.7	5.6	40.7
Pakistan													
FMS	12	13	15	39	45	59	53	78	146	435	1,524.3	150	300
Commercial sales	2	2	1	5	9	4	5	11	5	39	5	5	30
MAP	—	—	—	—	—	—	—	—	—	—	—	—	—
Training and education	a	a	a	a	1	a	a	—	1	2+	0.6	0.7	0.8
Total	14+	15+	16+	44+	55	63+	58	89	152	476+	1,529.9	155.7	330.8
Bangladesh													
FMS	—	—	—	—	—	—	—	—	—	—	—	—	—
Commercial sales	a	a	a	1	a	a	1	a	1	3+	1	1	1
MAP	—	—	—	—	—	—	—	—	—	—	—	—	—
Training and sales	—	—	—	a	a	a	a	a	a	a	0.2	0.2	0.2
Total	a	a	a	1+	a	a	1+	a	1+	3+	1.2	1.2	1.2
Sri Lanka													
FMS	—	—	—	a	—	a	—	—	—	—	—	—	—
Commercial sales	a	—	a	a	a	a	a	—	—	—	—	—	—
MAP	a	—	—	—	—	—	—	—	—	—	—	—	—
Training and education	—	—	—	a	a	a	a	a	a	a	0.1	0.1	0.15
	a	—	a	a	a	a	a	a	a	a	0.1	0.1	0.15
Nepal													
FMS	—	—	—	—	—	—	a	—	—	—	—	—	—
Commercial sales	—	a	a	—	a	a	a	—	—	a	—	—	—
MAP	—	—	—	—	—	—	—	—	—	—	—	—	—
Training and education	a	a	a	a	a	a	a	a	a	a	0.1	0.1	0.1
Total	a	a	a	a	a	a	a	a	a	a	0.1	0.1	0.1

[a] Less than $0.5 million.

Sources: DSAA working data as of September 1982; State Department FY1984 program data as of April 1983. Data for FY1982–1984 are subject to major change due to congressional action.

force in the 1920s, they were largely replaced by European and Turkish advisers in the 1930s. Unfortunately, when the United Kingdom pulled back from India, the U.S. decided to avoid becoming involved in military assistance to Afghanistan and repeatedly refused Afghan requests for military assistance during 1953–1955. The Soviets were quick to exploit this situation and agreed to provide $25 million worth of arms in August 1956, including T-34 tanks, MiG-17 aircraft, and I1-28 bombers. This required a heavy Soviet military presence in the country, because of the primitive nature of the Afghan forces, and extensive technical training of the Afghan army in the USSR. The Soviets quickly found that they could further exploit the situation by manipulating fuel and spare parts supplies, and they systematically expanded their advisory presence down to the platoon level. Soviet advisers were even managing most of the minor military fuel depots and military storage operations in Afghanistan by the early 1960s.

At the same time, the Soviets used their indoctrination of the Afghan military to build up support to displace Turkey as the adviser to the Afghan police and internal security apparatus, a process they largely completed by 1963. The king failed to maintain more than minimal control over this process, and the Soviets enjoyed virtual carte blanche in political indoctrination. During 1956–1970, the Soviets trained some 7,000 Afghan officers; the U.S. trained only 600. They steadily expanded their influence by shipping arms during 1963–1980, and each step in Afghan military modernization expanded Soviet presence and control.

The Soviets also coupled their military aid effort to Soviet economic aid. By the time the Soviets invaded in December 1979, the USSR had become Afghanistan's largest source of economic and military assistance, an important influence on cultural and educational programs, and its principal trading partner. The Soviet upgrading of Afghan military forces that began in 1956 was coupled to Soviet credits for Kabul's first five-year economic development plan. This mix of Soviet and military aid was provided on more advantageous terms than for any other less developed country (LDC); it came to total $2.5 billion before the invasion. This gave the Kremlin a dominant role in Afghan economic and military development. Soviet aid provided about one-half of Kabul's import requirements for Afghan economic projects, and although Afghan gas exports to the USSR briefly created a favorable balance of trade in the mid-1970s, the first Marxist takeover quickly reversed this. A combination of economic development and a need for food and petroleum imports created a $100 million deficit after 1978 and made Afghanistan even more dependent on both Soviet technical aid and economic assistance.

When Mohammed Daoud Khan deposed King Zahir Shah in July 1973, both Daoud and the other officers involved in the coup had been trained by the Soviets, and it is interesting to note that Daoud and many of the other officers involved had run leftist political indoctrination seminars since the late 1960s. The Daoud coup led to a period of close

Soviet-Afghan military ties, but the Soviets seem to have overplayed their hand. In 1976 they were removed from an advisory role at the company level and restricted to battalion training and above. Daoud also seems to have planned to use his new gas wealth to distance himself at least slightly from the USSR. This almost certainly contributed to the next coup in April 1978, in which Daoud was killed. It was led by Nur Mahammad Taraki, one of the Soviet-trained officers who had been a principal force in the 1973 coup.

The new coup was accompanied by yet another set of Soviet arms transfers—including T-62 tanks and modern fighters—and another increase in the number of Soviet advisers. By 1979, the Soviet presence had built up to about 4,000 military technicians and advisers, and the USSR was providing over 97% of Afghanistan's arms imports, which totaled $460 million during 1976–1980. Thus the Soviet advisers had virtual control over the Afghan military and security forces. This situation contrasted sharply with only 150 Soviet military technicians in India, 40 in Pakistan, and 30 in Bangladesh. Training of regional military personnel in the USSR reflected a similar emphasis during 1955–1979. The Soviets trained about 3,700 from Afghanistan, 2,200 from India, 430 from Pakistan, 450 from Bangladesh, and 10 from Sri Lanka.[80] The Soviet bloc also built up the number of "economic technicians" it deployed in Afghanistan to 3,700 by 1979, and they came to dominate police operations and to control key facilities like telecommunications and the Afghan airfields. It is interesting to note that this buildup paralleled the buildup that supported the Soviet-backed coup in South Yemen in April 1978. It also parallels the Soviet buildup in Syria, which may be an indicator of a potential Soviet interest in controlling Syria in the future.

Soviet control expanded after the April 1978 coup because of Taraki's massive purge of the Afghan officer corps, and only about 1,000 of an original total of 8,000 officers were still on duty at the time of the invasion. The Soviets also used the coup as an opportunity to force out the small number of West German advisers that Daoud had brought into his police force. Throughout this period, the Soviets also built up the infrastructure necessary to control Afghanistan. In the late 1950s and early 1960s they constructed the two major land roads later used by their invading forces, built or improved most of Afghanistan's international airports, built its air bases, and set up such key supporting systems as the files used by the internal security forces and the related communications and reporting software.

By 1979, the Soviets already were able to use their arms transfers and assistance to exert a significant degree of control and influence over Afghanistan and to use their increasing emphasis on internal security aid to great advantage in overthrowing the Afghan government. This Soviet control was not as apparent as it might have been in more developed nations because Afghanistan remained a relatively primitive society that required only a small cadre of modern services. Thus a high degree of Soviet control was possible with comparatively limited manpower, and the extent of Soviet technical support was not visible on a day-to-day basis. Even in 1982, in the midst of a major war with the Afghan rebels and with well over 100,000 combat troops in country, the USSR still had only 2,000 military personnel serving as advisers and 3,750 economic technicians, plus 100 additional Cubans, in the country. These figures are incredibly low when compared to the support the U.S. had to provide South Vietnam.

The USSR was also able to so exploit the Afghan economy that it provided virtually no economic aid in comparison with the U.S. effort in Vietnam. Roughly $400 million of the $800 million in aid the USSR provided through 1982 was financed through Afghan transfers of gas and increases in the Afghan debt, and the USSR was able to cut aid from $395 million in 1980 to $25 million in 1981. The Soviet Union was able to help pay for its invasion by controlling Afghan trade. It signed a five-year (1981–1985) trade agreement with the government designed to triple trade over the 500-million-ruble level of 1980. It reshaped Afghan transportation and maintenance facility plans and investment to support military supply and movement. It obtained agreement to provide 150,000 tons in wheat as a "grant" and signed a 300,000-ton agreement that gave the USSR a virtual monopoly over the sale of petroleum products.

The USSR also continued work on development projects of value to the Soviet Union in spite of the fighting. These included oil and gas development, the half-billion-dollar Ainak copper complex, agricultural development and processing projects, and a $200 million power transmission project. The Soviets even conducted third-party aid deals that helped benefit the Soviet economy. Most of the $170 million in East European aid provided after the Soviet invasion went to agriculture and aid projects that may eventually make Afghanistan a productive part of the Soviet bloc. This includes Czech aid in refurbishing the U.S.-built Helmand Valley irrigation project, Bulgaria's agricultural development and processing projects, and East Germany's communications and power projects.

While it may be argued that the Soviets have so far failed in achieving their major objective of securing a client state, and they certainly failed to achieve control without having to launch an invasion, the Soviet "failure" seems to be an unavoidable result of Afghan politics rather than of any defects in the Soviet aid effort. The Soviet effort was, in fact, managed well enough to obtain de facto control over the economy, the armed services, and the apparatus of the state. It gave the USSR influence and control over virtually every organized modern element in Afghani society.

The Case of India

The Soviet Union has also achieved some success from its arms sales and aid to India. It has again been able to use a combination of military and economic aid to achieve at least some of its major policy goals. Soviet military equipment deliveries have largely displaced India's partial reliance on Western arms, except for aircraft. They have provided the backbone of Indian military capabilities since 1971 and constituted about 80% of Indian arms imports during 1971–1980 and $2.3 billion worth of the $2.8 billion worth of arms India bought between 1976 and 1980. At the same time, the USSR used $3.0 billion in economic aid between 1955 and 1980, $800 million of which was granted in 1980, to try to influence India's economic development projects and to expand trade relations.

Soviet aid to India effectively deprived the West of most of its ability to control the Bangladesh war and the following India-Pakistan conflict. While the resulting division of Pakistan and Pakistan's decisive military defeat by India were not the direct result of Soviet policy, they did eliminate Pakistan as the one power in the region whose ties to the U.S. and PRC represented a significant threat to Soviet interests, and they helped open up the Indian Ocean to Soviet influence.

The election of Morarji Desai as Indian prime minister in March 1977 did offer a brief opportunity for the U.S. to try to reassert its ties to India. This was a primary reason why President Carter was initially willing to allow India to buy 38 tons of nuclear fuel for the Tarapur reactor and why Britain offered to sell India Jaguar attack fighters and trainers on particularly advantageous terms. The resulting $1.8 billion British sale to India,[81] coupled with other French sales and a U.S. offer of $400 million in credits, might even have gradually shifted India back to dependence on the West if Indira Gandhi's opposition had stayed in power.[82]

Gandhi swept back to power in January 1980, however, and the Soviets immediately took initiatives to restore their military ties to India. They provided $1.6 billion worth of arms in May 1980 on the extremely advantageous terms of 2.5% interest over 17 years and at prices that Western intelligence experts felt provided the equivalent of $4–5 billion worth of Western military equipment. They provided immediate delivery of a token number of MiG-23s, agreed to coproduction of advanced models of the MiG-21, and made clear their intention to sell India virtually any Soviet military equipment it requested.

While Prime Minister Gandhi sustained India's purchase of the Jaguar and coproduction of 45 Jaguar fighters, and finally decided to buy 150 Mirage 2000s as well, she launched a formal investigation into the Jaguar sale.[83] She also increased Indian purchases of Soviet equipment, including 63 MiG-23BM, 13 MiG-23UMs, Mi-24 attack helicopters, 2 Nanuchka corvettes, 6 Polnocny LCTs, 130 T-72 tanks, and BMP-1 armored fighting vehicles,[84] and reactivated the Indian nuclear weapons program, which Desai had phased down. Her tilt toward the USSR went so far as to include Indian support of the Soviet invasion of Afghanistan and cooperation with the KGB in exchanging intelligence on the PRC. It also helped allow the USSR to increase its pressure on Pakistan to limit aid to the Afghan rebels, to exploit the threat of "hot pursuit" across the border with Pakistan, and to threaten to provide aid to dissident elements in Pakistan like the Baluchis. Soviet aid to India has also allowed it to count on a form of Indian "neutrality" in the Indian Ocean area, which often seems considerably less "neutral" toward the U.S. in opposing U.S. naval movements and the creation of U.S. contingency bases.

At the same time, Soviet arms sales to India have not provided any significant increase in Soviet influence over Indian society or the Indian armed forces. Although India tilted back toward the USSR following Gandhi's election, it still purchased 40 Mirage 200 fighters from France in April 1982, with an option to coproduce 110 more. The $1 billion sale did include 9.2% financing, but it was far less attractive than the Soviet offer and terms, which involved coproducing the MiG-23 -25, and/or -27. The Indian military insisted on Western arms to meet the "threat" posed by the U.S. F-16 sale to Pakistan. They also insisted on an advanced Western doppler radar with look-down/shoot-down capability, on advanced attack avionics, and on French air-to-air missiles, area munitions, and laser guided bombs.[85] In mid-1983, India was not only heavily dependent on Western technology for its air force, it was acquiring West German submarines, 8 Sea Harrier fighters for its World War II–vintage carrier, the Vikrant. It was close to concluding a $900 million purchase of U.S. artillery and was using Western technology in its new Vijayanta main battle tank.[86]

India has also been extremely careful to limit Soviet influence over its military and, indeed, has had only limited need of such Soviet help. There were only 150 Soviet military technicians in India in 1979, versus 205 in a nation like Mali or 700 in North Yemen.[87] The USSR also provided training for only 2,200 Indian military personnel during 1955–1979 and trained only 85 more between 1979 and early 1982. This is a token effort, given the size of Indian military imports—only about 60% of the number of Iraqi military personnel trained in the USSR during the same period.

The Case of Pakistan

The case of U.S. aid to Pakistan is more complex. Pakistan's awkward strategic position, and its economic and military inferiority to India, have long placed it in the position of having to seek more military aid and equipment than any Western ally would be willing to provide. At the same time, Pakistan has had to seek such aid without sufficient funds to buy even the limited amount of equipment available to it on the world market. As a result, Pakistan has often had to accept military and economic aid on virtually any terms it could get. This need for aid preserved Pakistan's willingness to claim at least *pro forma* status as a U.S. ally even in the face of considerable U.S. indecisiveness, as U.S. support has swung back and forth during the Bangladesh crisis, the search for closer U.S. relations with India, the nonproliferation crisis, and periods of U.S. dissatisfaction with various Pakistani governments.

The one consistent result of these pendular shifts in U.S. policy has been the continuing erosion of Pakistani military capability. U.S. military sales and assistance provided Pakistan with virtually all of its modern arms through 1969, and FMS and MAP deliveries totaled $727 million during FY1955–1969. The U.S. cut arms sales to Pakistan after the Bangladesh war, however. FMS agreements dropped from $80.8 million in FY1970 to $20 million in FY1971 and $300,000 in FY1972, and they remained at $10–37 million annually in FY1973–FY1975. The U.S. did fund much of Pakistan's limited rearmament after its defeat in its war with India over Bangladesh. The U.S. provided $34.3 million worth of FMS in FY1975, $93.4 million in FY1976, and $139.4 million in FY1977. As Table 20.8 shows, however, deliveries were slow and the flow of new agreements was halted again in FY1978, when the Carter administration attempted to cut all arms sales, to halt Pakistan's nuclear weapons effort, and to tilt toward India. New U.S. military sales agreements dropped to only $43.6 million in FY1978, $21.4 million in FY1979, and $29.1 million in FY1980.

These swings in U.S. policy left Pakistan dependent on the PRC and France at a time when India was making major increases in its forces. They also left Pakistan acutely vulnerable to Soviet pressure after the Afghan invasion, and the four-year "gap" in U.S. military deliveries to Pakistan means it will now take at least five years to restore Pakistani military forces to a level at which they can act as more than a token deterrent to Soviet action. This, in turn, creates the specter of an impossible contingency requirement for USCENTCOM forces if the USSR should attack Pakistan to hit at the Afghan rebels or exploit internal divisions in the country.

Ironically, when the U.S. first attempted to rebuild its ties to Pakistan after the fall of the shah in 1979, the gulf between Pakistani military demands and U.S. military assistance capabilities had become almost unbridgeable. President Zia responded to a U.S. offer of $400 million in credits by calling it "peanuts," and the U.S.-Pakistan aid talks collapsed. While the Reagan administration finally reached an agreement with Pakistan in 1981 on a multibillion-dollar aid package, the agreement was not effective until FY1982. Pakistan got only $59.9 million in new FMS agreements in FY1981, although it received $1,524.3 million in FY1982, $150 million in FY1983, and $300 million in FY1984. Under the financing program it also had to borrow only as it received deliveries, so actual FMS loan guarantee financing began with $275 million in FY1983 and $300 million in FY1984.[88] Thus Pakistan remained without major U.S. resupply for at least two years following the Soviet invasion of Afghanistan and the shah's fall.

Fortunately for the U.S., China and Saudi Arabia played a significant role in supplementing U.S. military assistance during the period the U.S. cut its aid. CIA reports indicate that the Chinese, viewing Pakistan much as the Soviets had once viewed Eygpt, made Pakistan their largest recipient of economic and military aid. The PRC gave Pakistan more than 15% of its economic commitments to the LDCs and nearly 60% of its military commitments. This PRC aid provided about half a billion dollars' worth of military equipment between 1961 and 1982. Further, China gave Pakistan rapid arms deliveries during those periods of crisis when the U.S. and UK withdrew their support for political reasons. The PRC has thus made an important contribution to the maintaining of Pakistan's military establishment, and it replaced the U.S. after 1969 in providing the backbone of Pakistan's air and ground force inventories.[89]

The PRC also provided Pakistan with the core of a modern arms industry. This has helped to reduce the acute problems the Pakistan Air Force (PAF) had in using Chinese jet fighters, which require major overhauls after only 100 hours of operation and which at one point kept something like 20% of the PAF fighter inventory nonoperational while it was shipped to China, overhauled, and returned. More important, it allowed Pakistan to advance to the point at which it could assemble and recondition Mirage III and V fighters, which were becoming available on the world market, and consider coproducing the Northrop F-5G.

Table 20.9 shows, however, that despite PRC military equipment, Saudi financial aid, and French technical support, Pakistan was still hopelessly vulnerable to either Soviet or Indian military action. China's own growing military inferiority relative to the USSR, and the growing relative backwardness of virtually all its military equipment, made the PRC an ineffective competitor with the Soviet Union for any recipient that had to have modern major combat equipment.

As was noted earlier, the U.S. now recognizes this problem, and the Reagan administration has signed an aid agreement to give Pakistan a more stable pattern of U.S. military assistance and a $3.2 billion military and economic aid package. Even so, Pakistan's first deliveries under the FY1982 and FY1983 aid packages will consist of only 100 M-48 A5 tanks, 75 M-113 APCs, 24 M-901 TOW vehicles, 1,000 TOW missiles, 10 AH-1S attack helicopters, 75 M-198 towed 155mm howitzers, 100 M-109A2 self-propelled artillery weapons, and 40 F-16 attack fighters. While U.S. aid is planned to climb from $275 million in FY1983 to $525 million in FY1984, this still will not allow Pakistan to make up for the years in which the U.S. provided virtually nothing.[90]

In contrast, India already has 1,028 T-54/T-55/T-72 tanks, 1,100 Vijayanta main battle tanks, over 850 major artillery weapons, 13 MiG-23 BN/UMs, 48 Su-7s, and 300 MiG-21F/PF/MF/Ns. While Pakistan

TABLE 20.9 Comparative Defense Aid and Buildup in Pakistan and India

	India	Pakistan
1981 defense budget ($ billions)	$5.26	$1.89
Arms transfers 1977–1980 (current $ billions)[a]	5.6	1.15
France		0.5
PRC		0.15
FRG		0.2
USSR	3.5	
U.S.	0.1	0.3+
Other free world	2.0	
Total military manpower	1,104,000	478,600
Medium tanks[b]	2,050	1,285
Modern tanks on hand	78 T-72s 1,100 Vijayanta	250 M-47/8s
Modern tanks on order	130 T-72s	100 M-48Ss[c]
Total combat aircraft	635	219
Modern combat aircraft on hand	48 Su-7BM/KU 300 MiG-21s[d] 16 Jaguars 10 MiG-23s[e]	17 Mirage III EPs 34 Mirage IV PA/DPs
Modern combat aircraft on order	150 Mirage 2000s 75 MiG-23s[f] (85 Jaguars)[g] ? MiG-21Ns 8 MiG-25s 62 MiG-23 BMs 13 MiG-23 UM and MiG-21 bis 40 Ajeets	40 F-16s 35 Mirage V PA/DPs 18 Mirage IIIs
Nuclear weapons	Up to 6–12 high-yield fission assemblies transportable in the B-I-58 and possibly MiG-23?	2–3 years before device could be ready?[h]

[a]Source is State Department.

[b]The M-47/8 is not modern, but it is Pakistan[s best tank. It is uncertain that standard guns and rounds in Pakistan can defeat frontal armor on India's T-72. Some M-48s are A5s (with 105mm) that could penetrate, provided with Israeli kinetic rounds.

[c]The U.S. arms package for Pakistan is heavily defensive and oriented to mountain warfare against the USSR. It includes 100 M-48A5s, 75 APCs, 24 TOW vehicles, and 1,000 TOW missiles.

[d]Many are advanced MiG-21Ns.

[e]One more squadron is forming.

[f]More may be on order. The USSR has offered to provide larger numbers of MiG-23s, and possible MiG-27s, to India.

[g]Mirage 2000 purchase will evidently replace most Jaguar purchases.

[h]Author's estimate.

Source: The Military Balance, 1982–83 (London: IISS, 1983).

has an additional 35 Mirage 5 DA/PAs and 18 Mirage IIIs on order, India has bought 150 far more advanced Mirage 2000s, 75 more MiG-23s, and unknown numbers of MiG-21-Ns.[91]

Pakistan may, however, be aided by its expanding ties with Saudi Arabia and the other Gulf nations. Although Saudi military aid to any nation outside the Gulf has traditionally been limited, there are strong indications that Saudi Arabia has arranged for the contingency deployment of Pakistani forces in Saudi Arabia in return for Saudi funding of a major rearmament package for Pakistan.[92] If so, Saudi assistance will both serve U.S. strategic interests in Pakistan and help support the Saudi military buildup. It will also reduce the impact of the Arab-Israeli issue on strengthening Saudi defense capabilities and help lower the "profile" of the U.S. in Saudi Arabia. The emergence of such collective security arrangements between Saudi Arabia and Pakistan would help to protect the U.S. against the consequences of some of the structural weaknesses in its military assistance effort.

The Other South Asian Nations

U.S. and Soviet arms exports and military assistance to Bangladesh, Nepal, and Sri Lanka have had little recent importance. U.S. and Soviet relations with Bangladesh are dominated by that country's internal political and economic problems. While they receive military aid from several sources, both Bangladesh and Nepal are also effectively under India's military control. Sri Lanka has been lucky enough to enjoy virtual immunity from external military pressure, and whatever its other mistakes, it has had the good sense to use that immunity to avoid purchasing arms it does not need.

A Summary of the U.S.-Soviet Military Assistance Competition in South Asia

The USSR has recently been more successful in exploiting military assistance ties to South Asia than has the United States, and its success has helped to expand Soviet influence near the Gulf and in the Indian Ocean area.[93] The USSR has built relatively solid ties with India, and its military assistance effort in Afghanistan has probably been as successful as Afghan politics permitted. In contrast, U.S. inconsistency in Pakistan has left Pakistan too weak to defend itself.

There is, however, nothing inevitable about this trend. U.S. relations with Pakistan are now being rebuilt and the USSR may have gotten about as much as it can out of its relations with India. The Soviet success in Afghanistan must also be transformed into either the creation of a true satellite state or absorption of a primitive and largely hostile culture. Accordingly, future U.S.-Soviet competition in South Asia may be less favorable to the USSR. There are also indications that India is becoming concerned about the scale of the Soviet buildup in the region. India significantly improved its relations with Pakistan in 1982, and its armed forces remain independent and highly nationalistic. Further, it seems unlikely that India would support the USSR if it occupied Iran or took significant political advantage of Pakistan's and Iran's present weakness.

It also seems worth noting that the Soviet military assistance effort in South Asia has paid off largely because of years of consistent Soviet behavior in pursuing a reasonable strategy in both India and Afghanistan. In contrast, the U.S. effort has failed because the U.S. has not been consistent in its behavior, had no overall strategy, and lacked a well-defined picture of its interests in the region. The Reagan administration seems to have reversed this situation.

The Overall Impact of U.S.-Soviet Competition

The trends in arms sales and military assistance are sufficiently contradictory that it is impossible to say that they clearly favor either the U.S. or the USSR. The current trends in the Gulf and neighboring regions reveal a jockeying for position between the U.S. and USSR whose outcome is impossible to predict. Similar uncertainties affect the position of both states in the Horn and East Africa and in dealing with Greece and Turkey. A major miscalculation by either superpower might well drive a critical ally or potential ally into alliance with the other superpower. The Soviet Union, for example, has shown a considerable genius for alienating those Arab states it has done most to furnish with military equipment and advice. At the same time, critical states like Iran remain uncommitted, and the U.S. faces a constant uncertainty in its dealings with the Arab states because of its commitment to Israel.

The Major Factors Shaping the Impact of U.S. and Soviet Arms Sales to the Gulf in the 1980s

It is possible, however, to identify some critical issues and risks that will affect the success of any strategic partnership among the U.S., the Gulf states, and its other allies in the area.

• First, U.S. ability to use military assistance effectively throughout the entire region from Egypt to Bangladesh hinges on the ability of the U.S. to create a long-term relationship with Saudi Arabia, and at least indirectly with the other conservative Gulf states. The fall of the shah has tied the success of U.S. security assistance policy in the Near East to the success of U.S. military relations with Saudi Arabia. Without such success, U.S. arms sales to Israel, Egypt, Pakistan, and the smaller conservative Gulf states cannot offer a high credibility of securing U.S. interests. With such success, U.S. assistance to the other countries in the region tends to act as a buffer to stabilize the Gulf and check Soviet influence.

• Second, much will depend on the next round of the arms race in the Gulf and the outcome of the "logic of arms" discussed in Chapters 13 and 16. It is hard to see how Iran and Iraq can avoid a massive effort to expand their arms following the Iran-Iraq War or how the other Gulf states can avoid reacting to the end of the war by attempting to increase their strength and deterrent capabilities. At the same time, the Lebanese, Syrian, and Osirak crises of 1981 have triggered a massive arms race between the Arab states and Israel that seems likely to further stimulate the arms race in the Gulf. The same is true of the Soviet intervention in Afghanistan, the renewal of U.S. military assistance to Pakistan, and India's increases in its arms purchases from the USSR.

• Third, the USSR will have a significant advantage in its superior arms production capacity, which is shown in Table 20.10. While European arms production helps to offset this Soviet advantage, the fact remains that the Soviet bloc is the only arms manufacturer capable of massive deliveries of new, advanced equipment on short notice. This advantage is now offset by the West's lead in technology and the fact that the Reagan administration is in the process of increasing U.S. arms production. Nevertheless, a key Gulf nation like Iran might find itself forced to turn to the USSR if it suffered further major equipment losses as a result of the Iran-Iraq War.

• Fourth, the "style" or character of future U.S. and Soviet assistance will be also of critical importance. The problems the U.S. has encountered in its past dealings with Saudi Arabia and Iran have been matched or exceeded by the awkward character of Soviet aid to Iraq, Syria, and Egypt. There is no doubt that both superpowers have tended to weaken or alienate their allies through poorly organized military assistance efforts, and the USSR has compounded this problem by a past inability to deal with other nations on an equal basis. It is, however, now trying to minimize the racial and ethnic problems in its military advisory effort and to improve its organization and training.

These issues and uncertainties are particularly important because so much depends on U.S. military relations with Saudi Arabia, whether Iraq continues to pursue an independent course in the Gulf and diversify its sources or arms, and Iran's future procurement policies. A major shift in any of these areas could suddenly hand the Soviet Union a massive strategic advantage in the Gulf and several important options for countering. It seems likely that the future stability of the Gulf and Western influence in the region will depend as much on the extent to which the U.S. and its allies manage their arms sales assistance as on any other factor affecting the region.

Recommendations for Policy Action

As for the course of action the West should pursue, there is nothing particularly subtle about what should be done.

TABLE 20.10 Comparative U.S. and Soviet Production of Major Military Equipment

	U.S. versus USSR					
	Average Annual Production, 1972–1976[a]			Average Annual Production, 1978–1982[b]		
	USSR	U.S.	USSR : U.S.	USSR	U.S.	USSR : U.S.
Tanks	2,770	469	5.9 : 1	2,250	650	3.5 : 1
Other combat vehicles	4,990	1,556	3.2 : 1	4,800	850	5.6 : 1
Artillery	1,310	162	8 : 1	2,450	170	14.4 : 1
Combat aircraft	1,090	573	1.9 : 1	700	400	1.8 : 1
Military helicopters	666	733	0.9 : 1	400	150	2.7 : 1
ATGMs	27,000	27,351	1 : 1	—	—	—
Major surface ships	—	—	—	8	10	.8 : 1
Attack submarines	—	—	—	9	3	3 : 1

	NATO versus Warsaw Pact[c]					
	Average Annual Production, 1978–1982			Production, 1982		
	Warsaw Pact	NATO	Warsaw Pact : NATO	Warsaw Pact	NATO	Warsaw Pact : NATO
Tanks	2,650	1,050	2.5 : 1	2,500	1,200	2.1 : 1
Other armored vehicles[d]	5,500	1,800	3.1 : 1	4,500	1,300	3.5 : 1
Artillery (over 100mm)	2,800	400	7 : 1	3,750	300	12.5 : 1
Tactical combat aircraft[e]	850	600	1.4 : 1	700	650	1.1 : 1
Military helicopters	400	300	1.3 : 1	500	200	2.5 : 1
SAMs (not man-portable)[f]	28,000	8,500	3.3 : 1	28,000	7,200	3.9 : 1
Major naval surface combatants (over 1,000 tons)	10	22	0.5 : 1	10	27	0.4 : 1
Attack submarines	9	8	1.1 : 1	6	7	0.9 : 1

[a] Adapted from DOD, *FY1978 Annual Report,* p. 114; *U.S. News and World Report,* 11 February 1980; and *New York Times,* January 1980.
[b] Source: FY1984, "DOD Program for RD&A," p. II-11.
[c] Includes France.
[d] Includes light tanks, infantry combat vehicles, armored personnel carriers, reconnaissance vehicles, and fire-support and air-defense vehicles.
[e] Includes tactical fighter, attack, reconnaissance, electronic warfare, and all combat-capable tactical training aircraft.
[f] USSR and WP figures include SAMs for other countries.

• First, the U.S. must preserve a balance in its arms sales to Israel and its Arab friends. No single factor could so thoroughly shift the trends in the Gulf and neighboring states against the West than the conviction on the part of the conservative and moderate Gulf states that they could not count on the supply of key U.S. military technologies and equipment to deal with the arms buildup in the region.

• Second, the West must avoid a situation in which any Gulf nation is trapped into turning to the Soviet Union as its only source of supply. The sheer diversity of the West as a source of arms is partial insurance that a Gulf state can always obtain part of its arms supplies from the West, but Iran in particular may be unable to find a Western supplier, particularly with the amount of equipment it will need.

• Third, the U.S. should increase its production base and build up a pool of U.S. military equipment to allow rapid emergency sales and deliveries. It may also be necessary, however, for the West to work out a contingency plan through which Iran can buy arms from Britain or Germany. Iraq's dependence on France, and the recent tensions between the U.S. and Iran, might otherwise preclude Iran from turning to the West for military supplies.

• Fourth, the U.S. needs to give its military assistance and arms sales efforts in the region the personnel and high profile they deserve. No single area of U.S. official relations with the Gulf merits more careful management and better U.S. personnel. It is particularly important that the U.S. do everything possible to minimize friction between U.S. advisers and Gulf military personnel and to convince the Gulf states they are getting advisers who will be quickly responsive to their needs and can reach the higher policy levels in Washington. It is equally important that the U.S. exert very tight management over the quality of its training efforts and contract personnel. The attitudinal problem will be as important in this regard as the substantive one. Gulf military personnel must feel they are being treated as equals and not patronized.

• Fifth, the same priority exists for improving the quality of the long-term planning of military assistance to the other Gulf states that exists for improving U.S. military assistance to Saudi Arabia. While the U.S. may never be able to develop equally close military relations with the other Gulf states, it can accomplish a great deal by offering the air defense and maritime surveillance systems and support programs that will help them achieve collective security. It may even be able to persuade them to enhance their contingency capability to support over-the-horizon U.S. reinforcements.

• Sixth, as part of this effort, the U.S. needs to act in the role of an honest adviser. Simply selling the Gulf states anything they want is not a solution to effectively organizing the U.S. arms sales and military assistance effort, nor is attempting to recycle petrodollars. The Gulf states must feel confident that the U.S. is pursuing an effort to enhance their security and not simply to profiteer. This will also be of crucial importance in dealing with the new class of highly trained native officers and defense officials that is building up in most conservative Gulf states. These technicians are far better able to determine the effectiveness and honesty of Western advice and arms sales than their predecessors, and they have historically been a major source of coups d'etat and internal instability whenever they have felt their own defense system was corrupt or being exploited from the outside.

• Seventh, the U.S. needs to consistently strengthen Turkey as well as Pakistan and to provide both nations with predictable and adequate amounts of aid. It does not need to endorse the Turkish presence in Cyprus, but it does need to reject the more extreme efforts of the Greek-American lobby, such as demands that seventy cents of aid be provided to Greece for every dollar of aid to Turkey. The Reagan administration has recognized this need in its recent aid plans and has rejected the 7 : 10 ratio since FY1981. The FY1984 Reagan program for Turkey called for $343 million in FMS loan guarantees in FY1982, $355 million in FY1983, and $525 million in FY1984. It sized its financing program for Greece at a constant $280 million annually over this period, which would have shifted the aid ratio from 0.8 : 1 to 0.5 : 1. More important, it allowed Turkey to make $526 million in new FMS agreements in FY1982, $420 million in FY1983, and $900 million in FY1984—a major step toward rebuilding Turkey's force posture. The issue is whether the Congress will allow this trend to be sustained long enough to be effective.[94]

The U.S. needs to keep in perspective its efforts to prevent Pakistan from developing nuclear weapons, as well as its need to consider India. Once again, the U.S. is doing this in its FY1984 aid program, and the issue is whether this aid will be sustained. Turkey and Pakistan are critically important strategic allies. Greece is less important, and its status as an ally far more uncertain. India may be a friend, but it is extremely unlikely to become a strategic asset. Selfish as it may be, the U.S. must both reward its friends and back its allies.

Finally, the U.S. must carefully distinguish between the broad effort to improve regional security and its efforts to improve the basing for USCENTCOM forces. This distinction has often been forgotten in the years since the shah's fall, but it is a crucial one. The threat of an overt Soviet attack on the Gulf is still relatively limited except in the case of Iran. In most Gulf states the problem will be to help the states help themselves and improve their own security. This goal not only should have priority over improving the effectiveness of the RDF in most cases, it may often mean deliberately avoiding options to strengthen U.S. power projection capabilities in order to reduce the threat of internal or regional instability.

Notes

1. Numerous sources are available on the impact of U.S. and Soviet aid. This section draws on ACDA, SIPRI, and CIA publications and computer printouts. Among the books consulted are Bruce E. Arlinghaus, *Arms for Africa* (Lexington, Mass.: Lexington Books, 1983); E. J. Feuchtwanger and Peter Nailor, *The Soviet Union and the Third World* (London: Macmillan, 1981); Ammon Sella, *Soviet Political and Military Conduct in the Middle East* (London: Macmillan, 1981); Yaacov Roi, *The Limits to Power, Soviet Policy in the Middle East* (London: Croom Helm, 1979); U.S. Department of State, *Conventional Arms Transfers in the Third World,* Special Report no. 102, Washington, D.C., August, 1982; U.S. Department of State, *Soviet and East European Aid to the Third World, 1981,* Special Report 9345, February 1983; Soviet Ministry of Defense, *Whence the Threat to Peace,* 2nd ed., (Moscow: Military Publishing House, 1982); U.S. Department of Defense, *Soviet Military Power* (Washington, D.C.: Government Printing Office, November 1981); Milton Leltenberg and Gabriel Sheffer, eds., *Great Power Intervention in the Middle East* (New York: Pergamon Press, 1979); Lawrence L. Whetten, *The Canal War: Four Power Conflict in the Middle East* (Cambridge, Mass: M.I.T. Press, 1974); Stephanie G. Neuman and Robert E. Harkavy, *Arms Transfers in the Modern World* (New York: Praeger Publishers, 1980); Stephen S. Kaplan, *Diplomacy of Power* (Washington, D.C.: Brookings Institution, 1981); Stephen S. Kaplan and Barry M. Blechman, *Force Without War: U.S. Armed Forces as a Political Instrument* (Washington, D.C.: Brookings Institution, 1978); Andrew J. Pierre, *The Global Politics of Arms Sales* (Princeton, N.J.: Princeton University Press, 1982); John D. Glassman, *Arms for the Arabs* (Baltimore: Johns Hopkins University Press, 1975); Barry Rubin, *Paved with Good Intentions,* (New York; Oxford University Press, 1980); James H. Noyes, *The Clouded Lens,* 2nd ed. (Stanford, Calif.: Hoover Institution, 1982); Hossein Amirsadeghi, ed., *The Security of the Persian Gulf* (New York: St. Martin's Press, 1981); Shahram Chubin, *Security in the Persian Gulf: The Role of Outside Powers* (London: IISS, 1981); Alvin Z. Rubinstein, *Soviet Policy Towards Turkey, Iran, and Afghanistan: The Dynamics of Influence* (New York: Praeger Publishers, 1982); U.S. State Department, *Congressional Presentation: Security Assistance Program, FY1984* (Washington, D.C., 1983); U.S. State Department, *International Security and Development Cooperation Program,* Special Report no. 108 (Washington, D.C., 4 April 1983); U.S. State Department, *Conventional Arms Transfers in the Third World, 1972–81,* Special Report no. 102 (Washington, D.C., August 1982); U.S. State Department, *Soviet and East European Aid to the Third World, 1981* (Washington, D.C., February 1983); Anthony H. Cordesman, "The Soviet Arms Trade Patterns for the 1980's," *Armed Forces Journal,* June 1983, pp. 96–105; August 1983, pp. 34–45. Saudi and Arab League sources estimate that new Gulf arms sales agreements made between 1980 and 1983 may exceed $40 billion.

2. The author served as a U.S. adviser to the Iranian Supreme Command Staff during many of these events. Written sources are listed in the bibliography. The best single source on the U.S. advisory role is Rubin, *Paved with Good Intentions,* but several interesting essays are presented in Amirsadeghi, *Security of the Persian Gulf.* Mohamed Heikal also provides an interesting, if unreliable, perspective in *Iran: The Untold Story* (New York: Pantheon, 1982).

3. The Soviet policy described here differs sharply from its mixture of threats and intervention in earlier periods. See Richard A. Stewart, "Soviet Military

Intervention in Iran, 1920–46," *Parameters, Journal of the U.S. Army War College* 11, no. 4(1981):24–33.

4. CIA, "Communist Aid Activities in Non-Communist Less Developed Countries, 1979 and 1954–79," ER-80-10318U, October 1980.

5. Ibid.

6. *Chicago Tribune,* 24 June 1983; *Wall Street Journal,* 8 July 1983; *Washington Post,* 16 February, 10 and 12 March 1982; *New York Times,* 25 February, 8 and 9 March 1982; *Christian Science Monitor,* 23 October 1981; Alvin Z. Rubinstein, "The Soviet Union and Iran Under Khomeini," *International Affairs,* Autumn 1981, pp. 599–617.

7. See R. W. Apple, "Soviet Influence in Iran Shows a Sharp Decline," *New York Times,* 14 November 1982, for typical reporting on the growing friction between the Soviet Union and the Tudeh party and the Khomeini regime. Iran formally suppressed the Tudeh and began major expulsions of Soviet technicians in early May 1983. *Washington Post,* 4 May 1983.

8. ACDA, *World Military Expenditures, 1971–80,* p. 119.

9. CIA, ER 80-1031 (U), p. 29.

10. DOD, *FY 1983 Annual Report,* Annex A, p. 84; U.S. State Department, *Soviet and East European Aid to the Third World,* 1981, pp. 8, 14, 15. Israeli Ministry of Defense estimates indicate that no significant change occurred through early 1983.

11. CIA, ER 80-1031 (U), p. 29.

12. The following discussion draws extensively upon work done by Francis Fukuyama of the RAND Corporation in such papers as "The Soviet Union and Iraq Since 1968," RAND N-1524-F, July 1980, and on the various writings and working papers of Phebe Marr, Christine Helms, and Shahram Chubin.

13. ACDA, *World Military Expenditures and Arms Transfers, 1971–1980,* p. 119.

14. See *8 Days,* 14 February 1981, pp. 2–3; 24 October 1981, pp. 24–26, 36–38; *Middle East,* June 1979, p. 20; and *War Data,* no. 8.

15. France secretly delivered the first four *Mirage* F-1 fighters to Iraq via Cyprus in February 1981. Fifty-six more F-1s are in delivery. *8 Days,* February 1981, p. 2.

16. *Washington Post,* 14 November 1982; *Aviation Week,* 12 July 1982, p. 15; *Christian Science Monitor,* 20 and 31 January 1983; Stephen R. Grummon, *The Iran-Iraq War,* Washington Paper 93, CSIS (New York: Praeger Publishers, 1982), pp. 63–71.

17. These comments are based on the author's visits to Iraq and on the views of French, Jordanian, and Saudi visitors and advisers to the Iraqi forces during 1981 and 1982.

18. Unclassified working paper, Department of State, 28 October 1981.

19. ACDA, *World Military Expenditures, 1971–1980,* pp. 62, 104, 129.

20. *Aviation Week,* 26 April 1982, pp. 22–23; *U.S. News and World Report,* 4 March 1982; *Washington Post,* 7 April 1982; U.S. State Department, *Presentation to Congress: Security Assistance Programs, FY 1984,* p. 137.

21. *Norfolk Virginian Pilot,* 7 March 1982; *U.S. News and World Report,* 8 March 1982; *Washington Post,* 7 April 1982; DOD, *FY 1984 Annual Report,* p. 203.

22. The U.S. was not in this role in late 1981. Squabbles between U.S. military advisers and career State Department officials in the U.S. Embassy in Oman were a subject of local gossip.

23. CIA, *World Factbook, 1983,* CR 83-11300, pp. 104–107. Note that such data are controversial. The full range of statistics involved are discussed in Chapter 12.

24. ACDA, *World Military Expenditures, 1971–1980,* p. 119.

25. DOD, *FY 1983 Annual Report,* Annex E, p. 84; DOD, *Soviet Military Power, 1983,* p. 95; State Department publication 9345, pp. 14–19. Egyptian sources estimated 1,500 Soviets and 3,000 Cubans in December 1981. *Aviation Week,* 14 December 1981, p. 48.

26. Patrick Sale, "Soviet Influence Slipping in Aden," *Jerusalem Star,* 2 September 1982, p. 8.

27. These numbers are slightly misleading, and the reader should rely on the data in Chapter 12. Unclassified data are not available on recent arms transfers, and the 1970–1979 totals exaggerated the U.S. and Saudi role. Out of total transfers of $625 million, $80 million were French, and $110 million were "other," largely Saudi. ACDA, *World Military Expenditures, 1970–1979,* p. 129.

28. DOD, *FY 1983 Annual Report,* Annex E, p. 84; U.S. State Department, *Soviet and East European Aid,* pp. 14–21.

29. ACDA, *World Military Expenditures, 1971–1980,* p. 119.

30. None bought significant Soviet arms during 1970–1980. Bahrain bought less than $5 million worth of U.S. arms out of total purchases of $40 million. Qatar bought $5 million in U.S. arms out of a total of $170 million, and the UAE bought $20 million out of $575 million. Only Bahrain had committed itself to extensive U.S. purchases by the spring of 1983. More recent purchases in the U.S. are shown in Table 20.6. Ibid., p. 119.

31. The UAE seems to have accepted British proposals for an integrated air defense system. Bahrain is studying a $180 million proposal to provide F-20A fighters by 1986, along with technical support and training. This would create a de facto contingency base at Bahrain's main airport, which has a 13,000-foot runway. *Washington Post,* 23 September 1982.

32. CIA ER-80-1031 (U), p. 29.

33. The bulk of this analysis is based on the author's interviews with Syrian and other Arab military personnel.

34. *War Data,* no. 8, p. 26.

35. *8 Days,* 23 January 1982, p. 4; *Washington Post,* 15 January 1982; *New York Times,* 19 January 1982.

36. Several were eventually assassinated for this reason by the Muslim Brotherhood.

37. DOD, *FY 1983 Annual Report,* p. 84; *Aviation Week,* Annex E, 14 December 1981, p. 49; State Department publication 9345, pp. 14–21.

38. CIA working estimate. Recent ACDA data show that Syria received $6.6 billion worth of arms during 1971–1980, with $5.4 billion coming from the USSR, $290 million from France, $100 million from West Germany, $100 million from the UK, and $730 million from other sources. ACDA, *World Military Expenditures, 1971–1980,* p. 129. See also *Near East Report,* 8 January 1982, p. 7; *New York Times,* 19 January 1982, p. 3.

39. *Washington Post,* 3 May 1982; Stanley F. Reed III, "Dateline Syria: Fin de Regime," *Foreign Policy,* no. 39 (Summer 1980):176–189; *Baltimore Sun,* 30 May 1982; Yosef Bodansky, "In the Wake of Lebanon," Jewish Institute for National Security Affairs, September 1982, p. 1; Nikolaos Van Dam, *The Struggle for Power in Syria* (London: Croom Helm, 1981); *New York Times,* 6 and 21

February, 8 and 24 March, 29 May, 7 November 1982; *Washington Times,* 24 November 1982; *Economist,* 6 February 1982, pp. 55–56; 27 February 1982, pp. 51–52; 15 May 1982, p. 60; *Christian Science Monitor,* 16 February and 19 May 1982.

40. The extent to which Syria sought Soviet help and a strengthened security treaty is still unclear, although it is certain that Syria did appeal to Moscow for help and tried to use the threat of such a treaty to get the USSR to put pressure on the U.S. *Christian Science Monitor,* 11 June 1982.

41. *Newsweek,* 21 June 1982, p. 24; *Time,* 21 June 1982, p. 20; *Washington Post,* 17 June 1982; *Christian Science Monitor,* 16 June 1982.

42. The Soviets were conspicuously silent about providing anything more than moral support. While they did eventually issue a threatening statement two weeks after the Israeli invasion, this referred only to the "interests of the USSR" and made no direct threat of military intervention. It also was issued at a time when the major fighting seemed to be over. *New York Times,* 15 June 1982; *Washington Post,* 16 June 1982; *Wall Street Journal,* 28 June 1982.

43. Col. Gen. Yevgeny S. Urasov arrived on 13 June, the night after the day Israel destroyed most of the 19 SA-6 sites in Lebanon and in Syria near the Lebanese border and shot down 29 Syrian MiGs without a single loss. Israel conducted a heavy disinformation campaign as to how it suppressed the Syrian SA-6 units, but it seems to have used modified Ryan Firebee drones to obtain the data it needed to program the ECM pods on its fighters to jam the semi-active radar homing on the missiles and to reduce the effectiveness of their guidance radars. At the same time, Israel used its standard recce capabilities and E-2Cs to exactly locate the missile sites. On the day of the attack it sent in a force that eventually amounted to some 90 aircraft and flew a mix of attack sorties, with some fighters equipped with Shrike anti-radiation missiles (ARM) and some with a combination of Mavericks, laser-guided bombs, and regular bombs and rockets. The Israeli-modified Shrikes were used against any Syrian radars that became active while the regular ordnance was used to destroy the SA-6 sites. F-16s seem to have performed the major attack missions, in which timing was critical and which required high accuracy because the SA-6 can also be fired optically and because of the presence of AA guns and SA-7s in the area. The F-15s provided forward radar warning and air defense cover, and the E-2C, advanced electronic warfare analysis. *Washington Post,* 14 and 24 June 1982; *New York Times,* 12 June 1982; *Time,* 21 June 1982.

44. Virtually all losses were replaced by October 1982. *New York Times,* 24 October and 12 December 1982; *Washington Times,* 25 October 1982; *Washington Post,* 3 December 1982.

45. *Wall Street Journal,* 18 January and 22 June 1983; *Washington Post,* 5–18 January, 8 February, 29 May, and 22 June 1983; *Boston Globe,* 18 January 1983; *New York Times,* 18 and 20 January, 2 March, and 17, 25, and 29 April 1983; *Baltimore Sun,* 25 January 1983; *Economist,* 23 April 1983, p. 54; 4 June 1983, pp. 49–50; 11 June 1983, p. 51.

46. The thermal currents over the Gulf extend or contract normal radar coverage by 10 to more than 100 miles at given altitudes and locations. An attacker can predict the gaps in ground radar or E-3A coverage and fly through them undetected. An "AWACS on AWACS" duel offsets most of the advantages of a single AWACS. The only countermeasure is large numbers of small AWACS flying unpredictable flight paths with sufficient electronic support measures to detect enemy AWACS and fighters.

47. CIA ER-80-1031 (U), p. 29; State Department publication 9345, pp. 7, 19.

48. For varying views on the U.S. and Soviet advisory roles in the region, and the Soviet role in Egypt, see the essays on U.S. problems in Neuman and Harkavy, *Arms Transfers in the Modern World,* and in Leltenberg and Sheffer, *Great Power Intervention in the Middle East.* Several Egyptian sources, including Shazly and Anwar Sadat, have written on Soviet-Egyptian military relations, but more balanced accounts are available in Alvin Z. Rubinstein, *Red Star over the Nile* (Princeton, N.J.: Princeton University Press, 1977); Whetten, *The Canal War;* and in the case studies by Paul Jabber, Roman Kolkowicz, and Alvin Z. Rubinstein in Kaplan, *Diplomacy of Power.*

49. All major military equipment maintenance was done in Soviet military compounds, which Egyptians were normally not allowed to enter. When the USSR withdrew, it took its skills, equipment, and many key spares with it.

50. In addition to the sources in note 35, See Yaacov Bar Simon Tov, *The Israeli-Egyptian War of Attrition, 1969–1970* (New York: Columbia University Press, 1980); Glassman, *Arms for the Arabs;* the various writings of Sadat and Heikal; Hassan el Badri, Taha el Magdoub, and Mohammed Dia el Dia Zohdy, *The Ramadan War, 1973* (New York: Hippocrene, 1974; Lt. Gen. Saad El Shazly, *The Crossing of the Suez* (San Francisco: American Mideast Research, 1980).

51. For a detailed account see al-Shazly, *Crossing of the Suez.*

52. For another view see Roger F. Pajak, "Soviet Arms Transfers as an Instrument of Influence," *Survival,* July-August 1981, pp. 165–173; and Pierre, *The Global Politics of Arms Sales,* pp. 73–80, 136–210.

53. OJCS, *Military Posture, FY 1984,* p. 52; *New York Times,* 5 February 1983, p. 3; DOD, DSAA, *Foreign Military Sales, Foreign Military Construction, and Military Assistance Facts,* September 1982.

54. See *Aviation Week,* 14 December 1981; 12 and 26 April, 29 November 1982; U.S. State Department, *Presentation to Congress: Security Assistance Programs, FY 1984,* pp. 111–114. The U.S. also provides $750 million per year under the economic stabilization fund. Under the Camp David accords, one-third must be repaid over 40 years, with 10 years' grace in which 2% interest is paid, with 3% thereafter. Two-thirds of the fund is in the form of grants. Others FMS loans have the normal Treasury interest rate. The U.S. also provides about $275 million a year worth of food under P.L. 480; this amounted to 1.5 million tons of grain and flour in 1980.

55. Ibid.

56. France is negotiating this sale on the basis of 4% loans. Egypt has also negotiated for the Northrop F-20A. See *Washington Post,* 4 January and 6 October 1982, p. 1; *8 Days,* 23 January 1982, p. 16; *Aviation Week,* 18 January 1982, pp. 16–17; *Baltimore Sun,* 6 October 1982; *Wall Street Journal,* 14 October 1982.

57. Egypt is also negotiating coproduction of Lynx multirole helicopters and has bought 5 Vosper Ramadan FPG with Otomat SSM and Sapphire radars. It has 15 British SRN-6 Hovercraft on order and 3 on hand, plus 6 Sea King helicopters. It also has Beeswing and Swingfire ATGMs.

58. Although Egypt has had mixed success in keeping its Soviet equipment operational, it still plans to keep much of it in operation over the next five years. Its 1983 inventory of Soviet equipment includes more than 100 MiG-21s; more than 80 MiG-17s; more than 50 MiG-15s; about 35 Su-7s

(half operational); 15 Su-20s (most inoperable); 60 MiG-17s (most operable); 16 Tu-16 bombers (most operable), with AS-5 Kelt missiles; roughly 200 SA-2 launchers plus 1,000 missiles; the same number of SA-3s; more than 50 SA-6 launchers and 500 missiles; about 1,000 SA-7 launchers and 3,500 missiles; 100 ZSU-23-3 radar-guided AA guns; and more than 500 twin 23mm AA guns. Efforts to recondition these aircraft and upgrade their avionics have generally been a failure. The same has been true of up-engining and reconditioning Egypt's 850 T-54/55 and 750 T-62 medium tanks. Egypt is now considering producing a modified form of the BMP combat vehicle. It now has 200 BMPs; 80 PT-76s; 2,500 OT 62/64 and BTR 40/50/60/15Zs; some 1,300 Soviet towed guns; 250 Su-200 and ISU-152 SP guns; 300 Soviet multiple rocket launchers, 30 FROG-4/7s; and 24 Scud Bs. *War Data,* no. 9, pp. 40–53; *Aviation Week,* 14 December 1981; *Military Balance, 1982–83.*

59. *Baltimore Sun,* 20 February 1982; *Christian Science Monitor,* 20 January 1982; *Washington Post,* 6 January 1983, p. 18. Even new F-4Es require 30 hours of maintenance time for every hour of flight time. Egypt averaged only 2 operational F-4Es out of 35 at any given time.

60. *Washington Post,* 10 and 13 October 1982; *Baltimore News American,* 7 October 1982.

61. *Wall Street Journal,* 28 January 1983; *Christian Science Monitor,* 28 January and 3 February 1983.

62. *Washington Post,* 7 November 1982; 27 January 1983; *Christian Science Monitor,* 28 January 1983.

63. It is rather disturbing, however, that the U.S. Embassy staff in Eygpt has grown to 500, and become the second largest in the world, after the U.S. Embassy in London, and that only 15 of these 500 are fluent Arabic speakers. In 1967 the U.S. Embassy staff was 7, and in 1970 it was only 15. There are now 12 attachés and 255 personnel in the office of military cooperation. There is no clear indication that these numbers are justified or that they have been selected and trained with sufficient care. See Anne Crittenden, "Huge American Presence in Egypt," *New York Times,* 19 October 1981, for more details.

64. Syria concentrated several divisions at the same area where it had deployed forces in September 1980. Jordan responded by deploying its armor, and at the height of the crisis some 50,000 men and 1,000 tanks were deployed. The crisis was avoided by Saudi mediation.

65. It is worth noting, however, that 85% of Jordan's $600 million in arms imports during 1970–1979 still came from the U.S.

66. The Hawks cost $450 million. The unsheltered systems are very vulnerable since Israel can hit their fixed and well-known locations with great precision and virtually no warning.

67. Saudi and Jordanian officials separately confirm that the Israeli fighters overflew Jordan and not western Saudi Arabia and that the Hawk both proved vulnerable to Israeli EW and failed to fire.

68. *Washington Post,* 6 November 1981. The U.S. was still negotiating follow-on arms sales in May 1982.

69. *Aviation Week,* 26 April 1982; *New York Times,* 5 February 1982, p. 3; U.S. State Department, *Presentation to Congress: Security Assistance Programs, FY 1984,* pp. 121–123; Congressional Quarterly, *CQ Weekly Report* 41, no. 23 (18 June 1983):1227–1233.

70. *War Data,* 9., pp. 29–39; *Aviation Week,* 25 April 1983, p. 23.

71. Israel also receives economic aid from the U.S. economic stabilization fund, on roughly the same terms as Eygpt, as a result of the Camp David accords.

72. ACDA, *World Arms Transfers, 1971–1980,* p. 119.

73. DOD, DSAA, *Foreign Military Sales, Foreign Military Construction, and Military Assistance Facts,* September 1982.

74. *Aviation Week,* 14 December 1982, pp. 44–45; *Chicago Sun Times,* 2 March 1982. FY1983 military aid will be $500 million in waivers and $900 million in guaranteed loans. *Aviation Week,* 26 April 1982.

75. *Washington Post,* 28 September and 14 December 1982; OJCS, *U.S. Military Posture, FY 1974,* pp. 51–53. For an interesting discussion of these issues see Thomas R. Wheelock, "Arms for Israel: The Limits of Leverage," *International Security* 3, no. 2(Fall 1978):123–137; State Department, *Presentation to Congress: Security Assistance Programs, FY 1984,* pp. 117–120; *CQ Weekly Report* 41, no. 23(18 June 1983):1227–1233.

76. State Department working paper, 28 October 1981.

77. CIA ER-80-1031 (U); State Department publication 9345.

78. This discussion is based on the sources listed in the Afghanistan case study in Chapter 17, plus Patrick J. Garrity, "The Soviet Military Stake in Afghanistan," *RUSI Journal,* September 1980; and Alvin Z. Rubinstein, "The Last Years of Peaceful Coexistence: Soviet-Afghan Relations 1963–1978," *Middle East Journal* 36, no. 2 (Spring 1982):165–283.

79. *Chicago Sun Times,* 26 February 1982.

80. CIA ER-80-1031 (U).

81. The $1.8 billion deal sold 40 Jaguars outright, provided for assembly of 45 more at Bangalore, and then provided for full production of additional aircraft in India.

82. The British sale constituted over 80% of the $2.08 billion the West sold India during 1977–1980. In contrast, the USSR sold India $3.5 billion worth of arms. U.S. State Department working paper, 28 October 1981.

83. *Washington Post,* 23 October 1981, p. 11; *Christian Science Monitor,* 26 October 1981, p. 16; *Financial Times,* 24 May 1982, p. I.

84. *Military Balance, 1982–83,* pp. 85–86.

85. *Aviation Week,* 26 April 1982; *Financial Times,* 24 May 1982.

86. *Washington Post,* 31 July 1982, p. 17; *New York Times,* 30 July 1982, p. 2. The U.S. sales package potentially included 200 self-propelled and 200 towed 155mm weapons at a cost of $200 million, including ammunition and spares. The $1 billion figure is the total life-cycle cost of the weapons. If the sale goes through, it will be a major change. Since 1950, India has received a total of $79 million in FMS sales, $144 million in commercial arms exports, and $90 million in MAP aid from the U.S.

87. There were 1,550 Soviet economic and military technicians in India in mid-1981. DOD, *FY 1983 Annual Report,* Annex E, p. 84.

88. This is largely to buy 34 F-16 fighters. The first 6 are being paid for in cash. The military assistance package is planned to total $1.7 billion. Economic Support Funding is planned to be $100 million in FY1982, $200 million in FY1983, and $225 million in FY1984. P.L. 480 (food) aid will be $103 million in FY1982, $68 million in FY1983, and $57 million in FY1984. *Aviation Week,* 26 April 1982; *Chicago Sun Times,* 26 February 1982; *New York Times,* 30 November 1982, p. 1; U.S. State Department, *Congressional Presentation: Security Assistance Programs, FY1984,* p. 139.

89. CIA ER-70-1031 (U).

90. *New York Times,* 5 February 1983, p. 3.

91. Anthony H. Cordesman, "U.S. Arms Sales to Pakistan: This Time Can We Begin with a Few Facts," *Armed Forces Journal,* December 1981, pp. 26–27; *Washington Post,* 3 December 1982; *Military Balance, 1982–83,* pp. 91–92; *Aviation Week,* 6 December 1982, p. 19.

92. See Shirin Tahir-Kheli and William O. Staudenmaier, "The Saudi-Pakistani Military Relationship: Implications for U.S. Policy," *Orbis,* Spring 1982, pp. 155–171.

93. See Shahram Chubin, "Gains for Soviet Policy in the Middle East," *International Security,* Spring 1982, pp. 122–173, for a broader treatment of these trends.

94. *New York Times,* 5 February 1983, p. 3; *Washington Post,* 6 May 1983.

21
Achieving a Strategic Partnership in the Gulf: The Problem of Peace

If there is a "bottom line" to the preceding chapters, it is that the West and the conservative Gulf states can draw great mutual benefits from an informal strategic partnership.[1] The strengths and weaknesses of the United States complement those of friendly Gulf states. The right combination of U.S. military assistance and over-the-horizon reinforcements can provide the conservative Gulf countries with the added security guarantees they need and can do so without threatening their internal security. In turn, the Gulf states can turn their own forces into a reasonably effective deterrent to deal with lesser threats and to protect their internal security. This partnership will reduce the need to station U.S. or other Western forces in the Gulf area, help secure the free world's oil supplies, and reduce the strains on U.S. power projection capabilities.

The problem with this "bottom line" is twofold: First, the U.S. and its potential partners in the Gulf must come to realize just how much they have to gain from such a partnership and act to make it a reality. Second, the U.S. must walk a delicate tightrope in expanding its military relations with the Gulf states in ways that allow it to preserve its alliance with Israel. No amount of historical argumentation or strategic analysis will alter the fact that the U.S. is now the ultimate guarantor of Israel's security and will not retreat from that position. The moral and political imperatives that tie the U.S. to Israel do allow considerable flexibility in U.S.-Israeli relations and allow the U.S. to press Israel to accept a just peace. They *do not* allow for fundamental changes in the United States's status as Israel's principal supplier of armaments, military and economic aid, and guarantees against Soviet pressure. As a result, a close U.S. military partnership with the Gulf states will affect the trends in the Arab-Israeli military balance, and both Israel and its U.S. supporters fear that the expansion of U.S. strategic ties to Saudi Arabia may weaken U.S. support of Israel. The extent to which such pressures have hurt Saudi-U.S. military relations in the past has already been discussed, and there is no doubt that they are now a major obstacle to expanding U.S. strategic ties to its natural allies in the Gulf and the rest of the Arab world.

The Gulf Reaction to U.S. Ties to Israel

The U.S. relationship with Israel now threatens any Gulf state that allies itself to the United States. No Arab state can afford to ignore the extent to which its youth, military, and politically conscious citizens see the Arab-Israeli conflict as the key test of Arab nationalism, independence, and success in foreign and military relations. The occasional attempts to deny this are as futile as those that demand a major reduction in U.S. ties to Israel. Both positions are at best wishful thinking and are more commonly an invitation to folly.

Every Arab now living has grown up in an environment in which the Arab-Israeli conflict has been a central focus of his political education and of the actions of his political leaders. This is particularly true of the large population of Arab students and youths, which is becoming the demographic majority of every Arab state. The Arab defeat in June 1967, the relative resurgence of Arab military capability in October 1973, and Israel's invasion of Lebanon in June 1982 are the key events in modern history for most young Arabs. The shifts in the military balance, and events in Lebanon, the Golan, the West Bank, and the Sinai dominate their daily news. The Palestinian movement, regardless of its recent defeat and its problems and divisions, is a central focus of the Arab media. The Palestinian issue has become the Arab equivalent of the American morality play.

Equally important, a complex web of interactions has been established between Palestinian and Gulf political leaders. A similar web exists linking Palestinian expatriates working in the Gulf, Jordanian and other advisers from the Arab confrontation states, and the native population of the Gulf. This web reinforces the importance of the Palestinian movement. So has the evolution of the Arab intelligentsia. Virtually every cultural and political movement that now seeks power in the Arab world must pay at least lip-service to the Palestinian cause. While Arabs often disagree on means, political alliances, and the need to use force, all agree on the need to solve the Palestinian issue.

The Gulf militaries are part of this broad political consciousness within the Arab world. They are subject to the same political conditioning, plus the special pressures of having to structure their forces and military training in response to six Arab-Israeli conflicts and the trends in the Arab-Israeli military buildup. While this has led many officers, NCOs, and senior technicians in the Gulf countries to develop great respect for Israeli military skills, it has also made the view the resolution of the Arab-Israeli conflict as a military imperative that transcends nationalism and national boundaries. The younger the Arab officer or NCO, the more urgent this goal seems.

The practical result is that no Arab state can divorce itself from political support of the Palestinian cause, regardless of its failures or internal divisions, or avoid challenging U.S. support of Israel, until a peace settlement takes place. At the same time, there is no doubt that most of the political leaders of the Arab world, no matter what they may say publicly, fear their Arab neighbors at least as much as they fear Israel. They also fear the effect of the Arab-Israeli arms race on their societies, the consequences of the daily conflict between the Palestinians and Israel, and the disaster inherent in any future war with Israel. It is all too obvious to most Arab leaders, and certainly to those of the conservative Gulf states, that the Arab-Israeli conflict has become a constant source of internal conflict and tension and a potential source of radicalism. They fully realize the risks inherent in having to maintain a distance from the U.S.—the risk that their military relations with the U.S. may suddenly be severed and the risk that they may find themselves forced to use the "oil weapon" in ways that disrupt their political, economic, and/or military development.

The Gulf leaders are conscious that the delicate web of political and economic relationships with the other Arab and Third World states, upon which they depend for their security as much as on their military forces, can suddenly become hopelessly tangled or distorted by the impact of a new outbreak of tension or conflict in the Arab-Israeli struggle. They have faced a constant series of threats of this kind. These currently include the internal political instability in Egypt, the problem of dealing with constant flare-ups in the Israeli conflict with Syria, the transformation of Lebanon into an Arab-Israeli "killing ground," the growing Israeli pressure to make Jordan a "Palestinian state" and Jordan's uncertain role on the West Bank, the explosive divisions within the PLO, the risk that Iraq may be dragged into a growing confrontation with Syria, the various adventures of Libya, and the uncertain future of the Palestinian movement. Any of these specters could suddenly shatter the stability provided by months of quiet diplomatic and economic effort to secure a Gulf state's position.

The Strategic Problem for the U.S. and the Conservative Gulf States

The ideal solution to these problems would be an Arab-Israeli peace that resulted in a stable Arab recognition of Israel as a state, Israel's recognition of Palestinian self-determination, and return of the Golan Heights to Syria. The prospects for such a peace may have been slightly enhanced by President Reagan's peace proposal of September 1982 and the Arab summit at Fez that followed. But such a peace now seems as far away as it did in 1967 and 1973. Israel seems committed to retention of the Golan and West Bank, Syria is actively pursuing its own ambitions in the region, and the Palestinian movement is now deeply divided and unwilling to negotiate a peace. Finding a form of Palestinian "self-determination" that is mutually acceptable to Israel, Jordan, Syria, and the Palestinians may well prove to be impossible. Israel's annexation of the Golan on 14 December 1981, Prime Minister Begin's attempts on 3 May 1982 to persuade the Knesset never to return the West Bank, and Israel's invasion of Lebanon have offset the positive impact of Israel's return of the Sinai on 26 April 1982. While Jordan and Lebanon have made significant progress in showing their willingness to reach a mutually acceptable peace, Syria and the PLO have proved as rigid as Israel's Likud governments.[2]

In the near term, therefore, the Arab-Israeli conflict will continue to limit any U.S. strategic ties to the Gulf states. The U.S. seeks to create an indirect partnership while trying to deal equitably with both sides in the Arab-Israeli conflict. In practice, this means that U.S. ties with the Gulf states will hinge on

- U.S. ability to provide Saudi Arabia and potentially the other southern Gulf states with the military equipment they need
- The degree of "balance" or "equity" in U.S. military relations with Israel and friendly Arab states
- The extent to which the U.S. provides convincing evidence that it is actively seeking to implement President Reagan's September 1982 peace proposal and to build on the Camp David accords to achieve an equitable peace between the Arab states and Israel
- U.S. policy in dealing with the aftermath of Israel's invasion of Lebanon
- U.S. willingness to accept the Palestinian cause as "just" to the extent of supporting some form of self-determination for the occupied territories

The regional security situation in the Gulf states is so precarious that the leaders of most conservative Gulf states will expand their strategic ties with the U.S. as long as the U.S. accepts tacit rather than formal arrangements, provides military aid and equipment, and makes an obvious and honest effort to settle the Arab-Israeli dispute. While the Gulf leaders urgently desire a rapid peace settlement among the Palestinians, the Arab confrontation states, and Israel, most accept slow progress as a substitute for an unachievable immediate peace.

At the same time, the U.S. position in the Gulf will hinge on its military relations with Saudi Arabia, particularly on U.S. ability to give Saudi Arabia the military equipment and assistance it needs in spite of pressure by Israel and special-interest groups supporting it in the U.S. Even the best relations with Oman cannot substitute for close ties to Saudi Arabia, and no collective security effort can work without Saudi leadership. The AWACS debate has not established U.S. credibility in this role. The Reagan administration has not yet convinced the Congress, the American public as a whole, or most American Jews and Israelis that Saudi-U.S. military relations can expand without presenting an unacceptable threat to Israel. The success of U.S. policy in the Gulf thus depends on convincing the Congress and the American public that Saudi Arabia lacks the ability to threaten Israel and that U.S. arms sales to the Gulf will not seriously affect the other changes taking place in the Arab-Israeli military balance.

Current Saudi Military Capabilities Against Israel

The task of demonstrating that a U.S. strategic partnership with the conservative Gulf States is compatible with U.S. ties to Israel should not be impossible if an administration pursues it with suitable depth and consistency. The previous chapters have shown that Saudi Arabia lacks the military strength and manpower to engage Israel unilaterally and that the other conservative Gulf states will lack any offensive capability against Israel until well into the 1990s. Saudi Arabia can at most provide the same symbolic forces in support of the Arab cause that it has provided in past Arab-Israeli wars. Saudi troops have never had a significant engagement with Israeli forces.[3] Saudi Arabia did not contribute any significant forces in 1948 or 1956. It supplied about 4,500 men, 10 tanks, and 40 aircraft to assist in the defense of Jordan in 1967, out of a total Arab strength of over 250,000 men, 2,000 tanks, and 950 aircraft. Saudi forces, however, arrived only after the lightning pace of the Six-Day War had already ensured a decisive Israeli victory. Saudi Arabia contributed 1,500 men, about one tank squad, and some replacement aircraft in the 1973 war, but in a defensive role in support of Jordan and Syria that resulted in only minor combat.[4] Saudi Arabia's contribution to the Arab forces arrayed against Israel has otherwise been limited to stationing troops in Jordan and the Golan during periods of peace.

Saudi Arabia's forces are far better developed today than they were in 1973, but they still lag far behind the current capabilities of Israeli forces.[5] Saudi Arabia's diverse mix of armor leads to major problems in operational readiness and serviceability, and Saudi Arabia lacks the ability to provide logistical, service, and combat support to project a significant part of its forces. The rest of the Saudi Army is in a process of acute transition to new equipment and is unprepared to move against Israel in any strength.[6]

The RSAF is excellent is excellent by Gulf standards, and it is better prepared to conduct operations against Israel than the Saudi Army, but it will scarcely pose a major threat to Israeli forces. It is just beginning transition to the 45 F-15 fighters and 15 F-15 trainers it has on order, and its active first-line air defense fighters are still dependent on fewer than 17 short-range, aging British Lightnings. These Lightnings have proved extremely difficult to keep serviceable and are now dependent on support by contract personnel from the British Aircraft Corporation. They lack the avionics and maneuver capability to be effective in low-altitude combat with modern fighters, and the oldest are beginning to show signs of structural failure, such as cracking fuselages.

Saudi Arabia's "offensive" air capabilities consist of 65 F-5E fighters, which have the avionics to use Maverick air-to-surface missiles. These F-5E *Tigers* are limited in range and avionics capability and cannot compete effectively with the Israeli Air Force, although they are well configured to match current Gulf air forces and are generally superior in clear-weather attack mission capability to most of the Soviet aircraft operated by potentially hostile nations. Saudi Arabia also has 16 F-5Bs and 24 F-5Fs in operational conversion units, and 35 BAC-167 trainer-COIN aircraft, but these could have little value in an Arab-Israeli conflict.

Equally important, Saudi Arabia's ability to operate against Israel is severely limited by its basing structure. As Map 21.1 shows, Saudi Arabia currently has only three airstrips in the vicinity of Israel, and only the strip at Tabuk is on a fully equipped military air base. Similarly, the only major Saudi army base near Israel is at Tabuk, and the token Saudi army facilities at Sakaka, Kar, Turki, Badana, and Rafha cannot support offensive armored operations. Even when Saudi Arabia completes its military city at Hafr al-Batin, this complex will be more than 350 NM from the Israeli border and will be unsuited to support offensive ground or air operations against Israel.

Thus Saudi Arabia is effectively limited to acting in support of Jordan, although it might be able to provide limited air support to Egypt. The Saudi Army is not equipped with the tank transporters, mobile support equipment, and support forces it needs to operate at long distances from its main western support bases at Tabuk and Hafr al-Batin. While it could operate in a reserve or static defense role in an area like the Golan, it could not support and sustain intensive armored combat. The Saudi Army's breakdown rate, lack of recovery and repair capability, and lack of supply and support capability would quickly cause even brigade-level forces to collapse. Even if Saudi forces operated out of Jordan and were supplied by the closest Saudi base at Tabuk, it is 200 kilometers from Tabuk to Eilat and 450 kilometers to Jerusalem by air and roughly 350 kilometers and 600 kilometers by road. This is a long "tail" for a force so dependent on central support bases and foreign personnel. The facilities at Tabuk also can support only two Saudi brigades—assuming additional major service and combat support by Jordan—and only one brigade without Jordanian support.[7]

In terms of air operations, Tabuk can currently support a maximum of three Saudi squadrons, and its capacity will expand only to four squadrons when base improvement plans are completed in 1985. It is currently defended by three Hawk missile batteries, but it lacks shelter facilities. It will have four Improved Hawk batteries and the same

MAP 21—1
SAUDI ARABIAN MILITARY BASES IN THE VICINITY OF ISRAEL

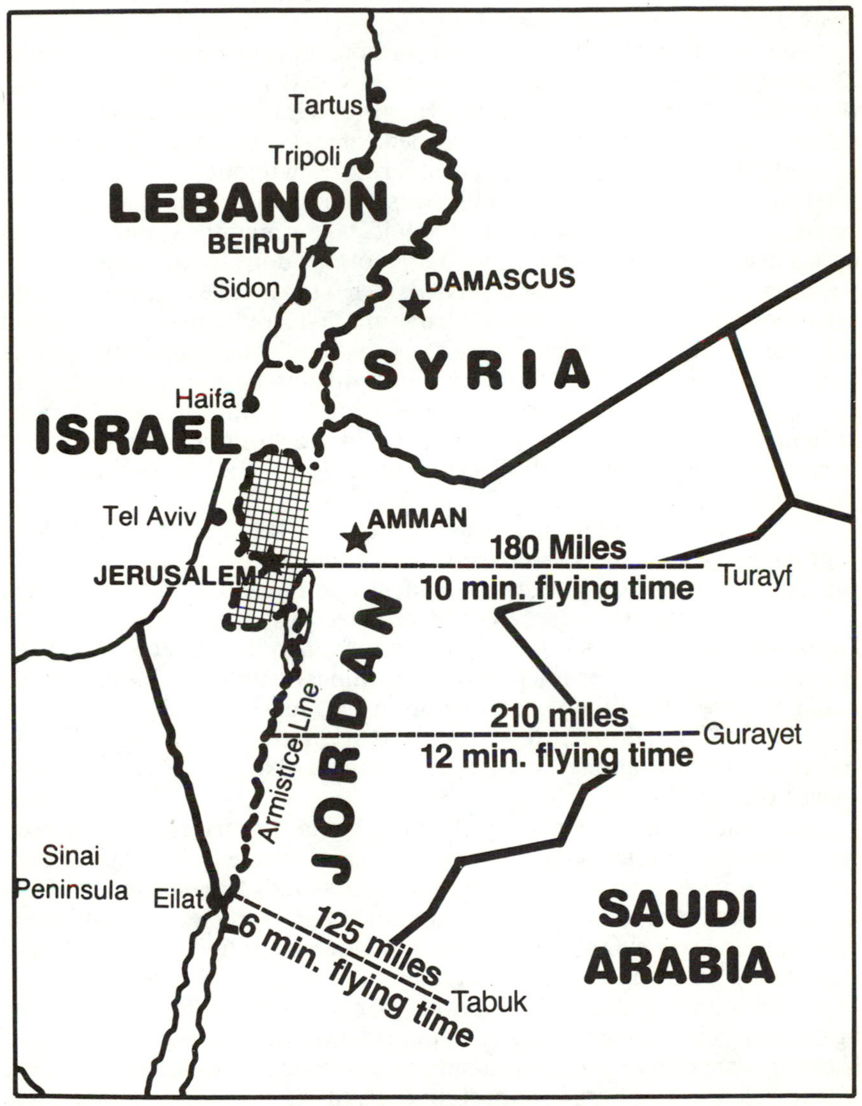

Adapted from AIPAC, "F-15s to Saudi Arabia—A Threat to Peace," Jan., 1978, p. 10.

shelters as the Saudi base at Dhahran by the mid-1980s, but it will still be limited to 60–75 combat aircraft. The strips at Turayf and Gurayat are suitable for dispersal and recovery, but they lack all the facilities to act as main operating bases and will not acquire such capabilities in the foreseeable future. Aside from Hafr al-Batin, the nearest alternative main air base will be at Taif, nearly 1,000 kilometers away.

Saudi Arabia's ability to conduct air combat will be severely limited by other factors. Saudi Arabia informally stated in 1978 that it did not plan to deploy its F-15s at either Tabuk or Hafr al-Batin. In practice, this means that it cannot move its dedicated F-15 support equipment, or use U.S. contract personnel at either base, without U.S. permission. Even assuming that Saudi Arabia was willing to accept the risk of a cutoff of U.S. technical support, it would take a month to move critical equipment to Tabuk, and this could not be done without providing warning and risking a pre-emptive Israeli strike. These factors would limit any Saudi "surprise attack" using the F-15 refueling at Tabuk and the limited numbers of forward sorties that could be backed by service at a rear base like Taif. This situation will not be materially affected by supplying KC-3 tankers or F-15 conformal fuel tanks to Saudi Arabia, although it might enable Saudi Arabia to provide a limited fighter screen over eastern Syria or northeastern Jordan when Hafr al-Batin is fully operational.

Under current conditions, Saudi Arabia will be limited to the 17–25 Lightning fighters that it will keep operational at Tabuk to compensate for its inability to operate the F-15 and to no more than 40 operational F-5Es and/or BAC-167s. If the U.S. does agree to support F-15 operations from Hafr al-Batin or Tabuk in the future, Saudi Arabia will still be dependent on U.S. technicians and technical support. Saudi Arabia could not sustain air defense operations against Israel by more than 45–60 aircraft for even a few days, and it would have acute difficulty in sustaining operational availability of more than 45 aircraft for any longer period.[8]

The Saudi ability to launch effective offensive strikes will be even more limited. While Tabuk will be sheltered by the mid-1980s, it will remain vulnerable to suppressive raids that would deprive Saudi Arabia of its one major operating base in the area. Although some Saudi pilots have logged over 1,000 hours, and have demonstrated excellent flight proficiency in flying against top-grade U.S. "aggressor" squadrons, the Saudi Air Force is also not ready to fly air combat or offensive missions against Israel. It would lack the endurance, basing, air control and warning capability, and command structure to avoid extremely high loss-to-kill ratios.[9] Perhaps most important of all, Saudi Arabia will lack the aircraft strength and pilot numbers to accept such losses without crippling its air capabilities and its ability to defend its oil fields for years to come. The fact that Saudi Arabia is moving toward a considerable self-defense capability against air threats in the Gulf area does not indicate that it now has a significant capability against Israel or that it could afford to send more than token forces against Israel without the risk of catastrophic losses.

The Saudi Air Defense Enhancement Package and Saudi Capabilities Against Israel in the Middle to Late 1980s

The Air Defense Enhancement Package will affect Saudi Arabia's future capability to threaten Israel, but long debate over the sale of the package has indicated that the U.S. can provide it with safety. Saudi acquisition of the AWACS, and the other air defense equipment necessary to create an effective Saudi air defense system, will change Saudi capabilities largely by increasing the attrition the Israeli Air Force would have to suffer to win air superiority. The sale of the equipment (see Table 9.2) will do little to enhance Saudi offensive operations against Israel, although it may have a significant effect on deterring Israeli strategic strikes on or through Saudi Arabia.

Lack of Offensive Capability

The continuing debate over the AWACS issue is more political than real. The E-3A will not be delivered until the mid-1980s, and it will then require U.S. support for the life of the aircraft. The E-3A has a systems mean time between failure of 27.4 hours and will need U.S. support at maximum intervals of three days to stay operational. There are also sound technical and operational reasons why the E-3A will not be a threat to Israel.

The capabilities and noncapabilities of the E-3A are summarized in Table 21.1, which shows that, although the E-3A is of major value to Gulf air defense, it has far less value in air operations against Israel. It has none of the signals intelligence capability provided on the Nimrod or Israeli-operated EC-2 Hawkeye. Saudi Arabia could not acquire such a capability covertly, and the U.S. personnel operating the E-3A would be provided with at least a year of warning during the period in which Saudi Arabia learned how to operate it. The Saudi version of AWACS will also lack the advanced Have Quick and Seek Talk jam-resistant, frequency-agile voice links and the JTIDS digital data links necessary to prevent the Israeli use of electronic countermeasures. The APY-2 radar of the AWACS will have no value in detecting movements by land force equipment. As a result, the AWACS cannot be used to assist in attack missions or in analyzing army operations.[10]

The confusion that emerged during the debate over the AWACS sale over the inability of AWACS to cover ground targets stemmed from the difference between the collection capability of the radar on the E-3A and its ability to process and analyze the resulting signal. The APY-2 radar will collect all movements by any object capable of radar reflection

TABLE 21.1 Mission Capabilities and Noncapabilities of the Saudi-Configured E-3A

Capability	No Capability
Detect and track all aircraft, even at low altitudes • 175 NM for MiG-21–sized targets • 240 NM for SU-24–sized targets above horizon line • 360 NM for Backfire above horizon line	See any moving object on the ground • Cannot see all ground-force equipment such as tanks, troops Cover most helicopter movements • Can occasionally pick up large rotors
Detect aircraft above the horizon beyond 208 NM for range only with radar	Cover any moving object not within prolonged line of sight • Virtually all Israel immune without survival point
Detect ships and low-speed aircraft over water • 35–208-NM range • Must be metal and of given size • Depends on sea conditions	Predict fighter movements or actions Acquire "Tactics Program" for Arab-Israeli War Deliver munitions Take photos or provide radar mapping
Analyze and manage Gulf- and Yemen-scale war using Saudi ground stations and aircraft with secure IFF	Collect SIGINT or ELINT Analyze air war in any region that lacks software
Link Saudi F-15, Hawk, ships • Take advantage of superior F-15 low-altitude coverage	Analyze enemy attack missions or training in detail Perform jamming
Link to USN and USAF systems	Track and sense surface-to-air missile launchers and AA guns
Identify "friendlies" with IFF transponders	Act as a command post for large-scale war
	Identify "friendlies" without secure IFF
	Monitor Israeli airspace without Israeli knowledge
	Shift E-3A or F-15 bases without U.S. support or knowledge

within its line of sight when it is operated in the high-PRF pulse-Doppler mode. In doing so, however, it collects a large volume of "clutter" signals from land objects that cannot be processed and interpreted by the IBM CC-2 computer and radar correlator on the aircraft. This limitation forces the electronics and computer on the E-3A to reject all radar data reflected by land objects moving at less than 80 NM an hour and to treat as "ground clutter" most objects moving at less than 100 NM per hour at altitudes of less than 200 feet. For obvious reasons, no army operates, or has in design, land weapons that operate at these speeds and altitudes. In fact, the E-3A is extremely erratic in tracking low-altitude helicopter movements, although it can occasionally track the motion of large rotor blades.

The Saudi version of the AWACS also has the capability to use its radar to receive signals from medium-sized or large metal ships at sea moving at speeds above 10–15 knots by using the radar's low-PRF, compressed-pulse mode. This coverage is dependent on the sea state, and it has no value over land since it produces a chaotic mixture of information and false signals, or "noise." The "interleave" mode of the AWACS allows near-simultaneous air and maritime coverage, but no land coverage. No upgrade or refit of the E-3A can give it land coverage.

Inability to Use the AWACs in Air Combat over Israel

The Saudi E-3As will face massive survivability problems if Saudi Arabia attempts to use them to support air combat over Israel and most of Jordan and Syria. Unlike the relatively flat terrain of the Gulf, the terrain of Israel, the Sinai, Jordan, Syria, and Lebanon is filled with ridges and mountains. These terrain barriers severely "shadow block," or limit, the line-of-sight coverage of the E-3A at low altitudes. Thus a Saudi E-3A would have to fly over Jordan or Syria to provide reasonable low-altitude coverage of Israel. Since Israel's E-2Cs can passively detect the operation of the E-3A at ranges of up to 400 NM, the Saudi AWACS could not hope to achieve surprise and would be a "sitting duck" well within the kill range of Israeli F-15s. USAF studies have shown that even if the E-3As operate north of Tabuk in the "notch" in the Saudi-Jordanian border area close to Israel (shown in Map 21.2), their low-altitude coverage of Israel would be severely reduced by terrain-shielding. It would offer little benefit over land-based radars in Jordan and Syria.

What is "sauce for the Gulf" proves to be "blood for the Gaza." To cover the low-altitude areas near Israel's air bases and fighter flight corridors, an AWACS must move into a position where it cannot defend itself.[11] This means the Saudis could do little more than lose an aircraft worth hundreds of millions of dollars, deprive themselves of the minimal number of AWACS they need to cover the Gulf, and sacrifice the future U.S. support necessary to make the Saudi Air Force work as well as an investment of over $20 billion in the overall air defense system.

Since Israel will operate an air force of roughly 600 combat airplanes from a territory with about 3% of the airspace of Saudi Arabia, most Israeli sorties could not be determined as attacks on the AWACS until they were within minutes of reaching it and were virtually assured of a kill. Further, Israel would have the electronic warfare capabilities to jam the AWACS flying in such fixed predictable orbits, to jam or read its communications, and to enter its IFF system as "Saudi aircraft." These capabilities could expose the Saudi E-3As to instant attack.[12]

The Value of AWACS to Saudi Arabia in Defending Against Israeli Strategic Strikes

The E-3A and Air Defense Enhancement Package could offer Saudi Arabia significant benefits if the U.S. agreed to support F-15 operations at Tabuk and if the E-3As operated in defense of Saudi airspace. If the

MAP 21—2
AWACS "INFINITE SMOOTH PLAIN" COVERAGE OF ISRAEL FROM SAUDI ARABIA

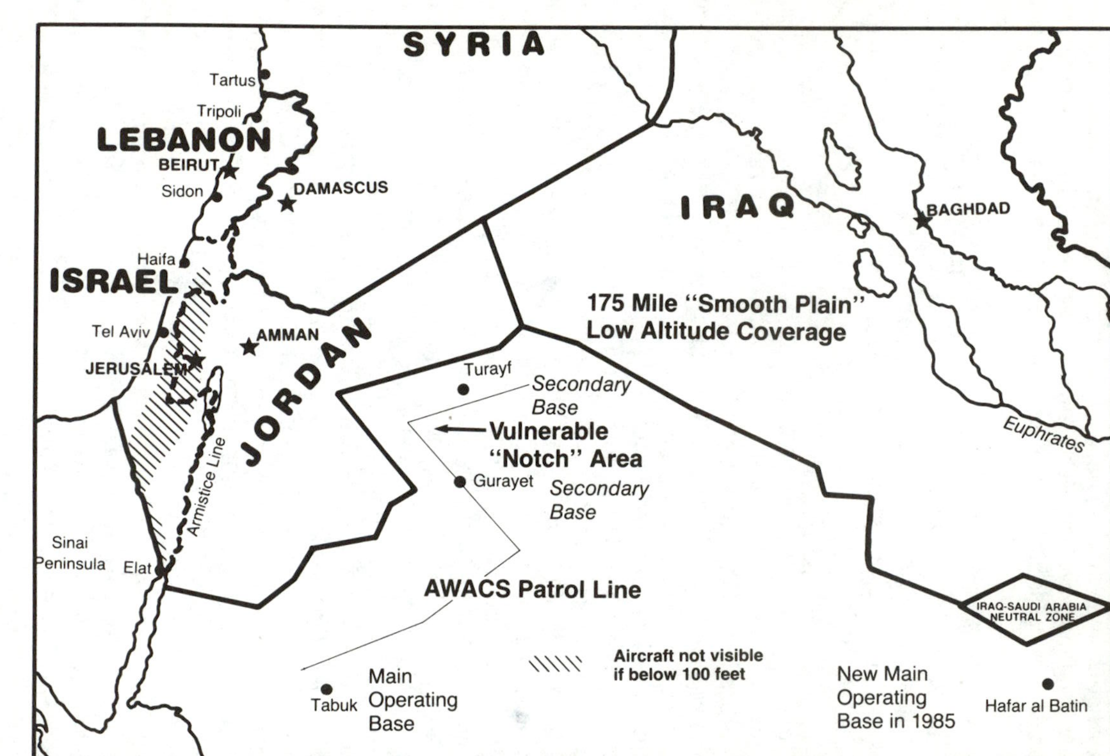

Adapted from U.S. Air Force briefing chart. Only two Israeli air bases would be in the shaded region. The E-3A could not detect air operations over Israel's other air bases below 700-1,500 feet.

E-3As flew in a patrol area centered on an axis north from Tabuk and about 150 NM within the Saudi border, it could provide both low-altitude coverage and survivability. The AIM-9Ls would add an increase in dogfight capability, and the KC-3 tankers and conformal fuel tanks will give the F-15 the endurance and range to maintain a significant air screen. The package would thus allow Saudi Arabia to deploy its fighters effectively in defending its border area, reduce the need for combat air patrol, and provide warning and vectoring for air-to-air combat. Assuming the survival of AWACS, and limited Saudi success in electronic countermeasures to prevent local jamming and Hawk suppression, Saudi Arabia might shift the exchange ratios to air-to-air combat in defense of Saudi airspace from about 6–9:1 in Israel's favor to 3–6:1[13,14]—a significant increase in the effectiveness of Saudi air defenses.

Even in a such defensive role, the E-3A will be vulnerable to Israeli saturation and preemptive Israeli attack, as well as to many of the tactics discussed in Chapter 9. Further, any substantial F-15 and F-5E losses will mean a critical loss of first-line RSAF pilots. Saudi Arabia would also risk the loss of U.S. technical support and of its future ability to operate the bulk of its air force equipment unless it was fighting purely in self-defense.

In sum, the Air Defense Enhancement Package will act to deter Israel as well as Saudi Arabia. The combination of the Saudi F-15, F-5E, AIM-9L, and Hawk will almost certainly be formidable enough to discourage any Israeli attack on Saudi Arabia. Israel would also experience major problems in conducting selective strategic air strikes against Saudi ports, cities, or oil facilities of the type the IDF planners have discussed since 1973 and executed against Iraq in the Osirak raid of 1981.[15]

Limited Value of AWACS to Saudi Ground Forces

The Air Defense Enhancement Package can also do little to strengthen a Saudi Army attack on Israel. Saudi acquisition of AWACS, the AIM-9L, the KC-135, and the FAST fuel kits will allow the Saudi Air Force to fly far better air cover over Saudi Army forces in the Gulf and to "net," or link, the Saudi fighters with the Saudi Hawk and Shahine missiles operated by the army. It will not, however, give the Saudi Army much aid in large-scale offensive operations against Israel. The AWACS cannot survive if it operates near Israel, and Saudi Hawk missiles will not have suitable mobility to provide forward area defense.

The Impact of Saudi Purchases of More Advanced Fighters and Armor

The Air Defense Enhancement Package will be only one key step in expanding U.S. strategic ties to Saudi Arabia. The U.S. will almost certainly have to furnish additional arms and equipment to Saudi Arabia to meet the threat in the Gulf and help it integrate the equipment it buys from Europe into its force structure. Saudi Arabia needs more F-15s and will have to replace or supplement its F-5E aircraft by the middle to late 1980s. The F-20A or F-16C would be a logical replacement. The RSAF will need to give its F-15 dual capability in the attack role and to acquire a modern multirole fighter like the Strike Eagle by the end of the 1980s. The National Guard will need to obtain more advanced equipment to strengthen its internal security and local defense capabilities,[16] and the Saudi Army will need additional equipment to overcome the imbalances and obsolescence in its force structure. U.S. ability to provide such equipment will be a key to strengthening U.S. ties to the Gulf.

Purchase of More Army Equipment

In spite of the M-1 tank fiasco discussed in Chapter 10, the U.S. should be able to make these sales without creating a meaningful increase in the threat to Israel. As has been discussed earlier, the Saudi Army is now forming two armored brigades. One, with French armor, will soon be largely up to strength, and another, with U.S. armor, is still forming. It is finishing formation of two mechanized brigades and will eventually convert at least two of its remaining infantry brigades to mechanized status. It is seeking to form two combat-capable paratroop battalions, a Royal Guard battalion, and three artillery battalions by the mid-1980s and would like to create a small air mobile or assault helicopter force.[17] Although manpower estimates differ, the Saudi Army is now somewhat over 30,000 men and is seeking to build up to a force structure of about 45,000–50,000.

It is doubtful that Saudi Arabia can reach these force goals by 1985, and it will definitely still suffer from the equipment problems discussed in Chapters 6 and 10 and be short of trained officers, NCOs, enlisted men, and technicians. While unclassified sources differ, present plans for the future force mix of the Saudi Army appear to be approximately the levels shown in Table 21.2. Major increases in these figures will still leave the Saudi Army under strength in coping with the threats it faces from Iran and the Yemens, and they offer Saudi Arabia little hope of engaging Israel without destroying irreplaceable cadres of trained manpower. The numbers of Table 21.3 also exceed the limit of what Saudi Arabia can credibly operate through the mid-1980s, even with large-scale foreign logistic and maintenance support. They represent Saudi purchases that are intended more to guard against the loss of a major foreign supplier than to meet projected unit requirements.

Follow-on Saudi army equipment modernization is also unlikely to pose any serious threat to Israel. Saudi Arabia would benefit from rationalizing its wide mix of equipment types and replacing its current AMX-30 tanks with types better able to deal with the T-72, T-80, and

TABLE 21.2 Major Saudi Arabian Army Equipment Plans

Category and Type	On Hand	On Order	Total
Medium tanks			
AMX-40	.0	?	?
AMX-30	300	0	300
M-60A1	150	(150)[a]	150
Other armor			
AMX-10P MICV	250	60	310
AML-60/90 armored car	200	0	200
Ferret scout car		0	?[b]
Fox scout car	100	0	100
M-113 APC	600	?	600
Panhard M-J APC	1,000	?	?
Engesa armored cars	0	?	?[b]
Antitank weapons			
TOW ATGM[c]	50	200[d]	250
Dragon ATGM[e]	4,000	0	4,000
Artillery			
105mm pack howitzer		?	?
105mm SP howitzer	56	?	?
135mm SP howitzer		?	?
M-198 towed 155mm howitzer	18	0	18
FH-70 155mm howitzer	0	72	72
Antiaircraft			
Improved Hawk[f]	6	16	28?
Shahine (Crotale)	48	?	48
Redeye[g]	400	?	400
Vulcan 20mm SP	?	?	?
M-42 40mm SP	?	?	?
AMX-30 SA 30mm	46	40	86
35mm	86	0	86
Helicopters	n.a.	10–90	10–90

[a] M-60 A3 conversion kits.
[b] SIPRI estimates up to 647.
[c] Includes 1,000 missiles on hand: more than 1,000 Improved TOWs are on order.
[d] VCC-1 TOW AFVs.
[e] 172–344 trackers.
[f] Total of 580 Hawk missiles. 16 Batteries.
[g] On 20 vehicles.

Sources: The Military Balance, 1982–83 (London: IISS, 1983); John Keegan, *World Armies* (New York: Facts on File, 1979), p. 618; SIPRI computer printouts; *War Data* no. 8 (Jerusalem: Eshel-Dramit, Ltd.).

successor tanks that potential threat nations are likely to deploy in the late 1980s and early 1990s. However, Saudi conversion to a new tank like the AMX-40, Leopard II, or Abrahms M-1 is unlikely to be completed before the late 1980s and would not produce major changes in Saudi armored capability relative to Israel until well after the mid-1980s.[18]

Purchases of More Combat Aircraft

The impact of Saudi Air Force purchases is more difficult to analyze. It is interesting to consider the effect of an incremental purchase of 100 F-20As, F-16Cs, Tornados, or Mirage 2000s[19] as an example of the largest and most sophisticated aircraft purchase Saudi Arabia could absorb by 1990. Such fighters cannot be delivered before 1985–1988, and it would normally take a Western air force between three and five years to fully accomplish such a conversion, assuming a suitable pool of pilots, ground crew, and support and suitable training facilities. As a rough guess, it would take the Saudi Air Force at least six to eight years to fully absorb 100 more advanced fighters, although it could make squadron-sized units effective more quickly.

Thus Saudi Arabia can complete conversion to large numbers of new fighters only in the late 1980s or early 1990s. While it might then acquire a significantly increased air defense capability against medium-scale Israeli attacks, and a limited offensive capability to operate over southern Israeli air space, this seems unlikely to remain a key issue. An Arab-Israeli peace settlement may take time, but if it takes forever, the U.S. will have far more serious problems to worry about than aircraft sales.

Giving Saudi Arabia the multiple ejection racks (MER) necessary to use its F-15 in the attack mission would improve Saudi Air Force offensive attack capability more quickly. Once again, however, this seems likely to pose a minimal "real-world" threat to Israel. Saudi Arabia now could not carry out such a conversion before 1985–1986, and then it could not afford the large F-15 losses that would result, even if it could get U.S. support in forward basing. While the F-15 has a considerable range-payload in attack missions, the Saudi F-15s would lack the avionics to use sophisticated offensive munitions effectively and would be forced into vulnerable attack profiles in the target area. This factor would further enhance Israel's advantage in dog-fighting capability and its ability to use its longer-range AIM-7E and AIM-7F air-to-air missiles.

The Saudi F-15 C/Ds are well suited for attack missions in the less sophisticated environment Saudi Arabia faces on its other borders, but they are considerably less lethal in attack missions against armored forces than even the F-16 A/B.[20] They will lack the mix of computer capability, sensors, and avionics to penetrate Israel's far more capable air defenses. The F-15 C/Ds do not approach the attack mission capabilities of the F-16C, F-16E, or F-15E, which will have far superior tactical situation displays, advanced terrain-following capability and synthetic aperture radars (SAR) to provide long-range target imaging and all-weather strike capability, forward-looking infrared, and LANTIRN capability to provide long-range infrared target identification.[21]

Similar problems will affect the Saudi F-5E IIs. As was mentioned in Chapter 10, these planes are excellent short-range fighters with good dogfight and moderate attack capabilities, but they lack the avionics and data display to allow effective netting with the digital system on the AWACS. They require the pilot to fly relatively vulnerable attack profiles in order to use Maverick or other advanced air-to-ground munitions of a kind unsuited for combat with Israel. While modifications like ring-laser gyros will help keep the F-5Es effective against Gulf or Red Sea air forces, the F-5Es lack the radar, data display sophistication, combination of thrust-to-weight ratio and wing-loading and air-to-air missile range to engage Israeli pilots. Northrop and USAF studies indicate that any attempt to upgrade the F-5E to counter these problems would not be cost effective: it could cost almost the same as buying a new fighter aircraft. The F-5Es cannot be replaced before the late 1980s, however, and any such conversion would directly compete for manpower resources with any Saudi effort to expand its forces.

The Impact of the AWACS Sale to Saudi Arabia on Arab Military Capabilities in the Middle to Late 1980s

The U.S. can meet Saudi Arabia's military needs and those of any of the smaller Gulf states without making significant increases in Saudi capabilities against Israel through the late 1980s. The validity of a Saudi military threat is, however, only part of the problem. U.S. arms sales to Saudi Arabia might also affect the image of military superiority that is Israel's chief deterrent, improve the effectiveness of the forces of other Arab nations through equipment transfers or data sharing, or alter the outcome of a full-scale Arab attack on Israel. The seriousness of such issues depends on (1) how much Arab capabilities have improved relative to those of Israel, (2) how the use of AWACS could change these capabilities, (3) how credible the resulting Arab threat to Israel would be, and (4) how Arab capabilities might change by the late 1980s.

The Present Arab Threat to Israel

Even in a region as politically volatile as the Near East, the Arab threat to Israel has been minimized by Israel's invasion of Lebanon and is likely to be further reduced by a number of other political factors.[22] These include (1) the broad pattern of inter-Arab rivalries; (2) moderate-radical splits within the Arab world; (3) the Egyptian commitment to peace with Israel; (4) Egyptian dependence on the U.S. for the conversion of its armed forces from Soviet to U.S. equipment at a significantly lower ultimate force strength, (5) Jordanian tensions with Syria; (6) the destruction of Palestinian forces in Lebanon; (7) serious internal political unrest in Syria; (8) Syria's continuing involvement in Lebanon; (9) Iraq's conflict with Iran; and (10) Iraq's continuing feud with Syria. Even if these political problems did not exist or seem likely to continue through the mid-1980s, the fighting in Lebanon has shown that the Arab-Israeli balance has shifted in Israel's favor.

The Force Numbers. The key trends in the force numbers on each side are shown in Table 21.3. Taking into account qualitative differences, these numbers indicate that the growth of Israel's forces has roughly matched that of Arab forces. Given these numbers, no combination of Jordan and Syria, or Syria alone, can seriously threaten Israel. Even if a post-Mubarak regime should reverse Egypt's commitment, it would still take until the late 1980s for Arab forces to train and reequip to operate effectively. Such a reversal now seems unlikely in view of Egypt's long-term dependence on the U.S. to reequip its forces, Egypt's conduct during Israel's invasion of Lebanon, President Mubarak's continuing reassertion of Egyptian support for the Camp David accords, and Egypt's quiet reaction to Israel's earlier annexation of the Golan. No combination of Arab forces without Egypt presents a serious threat to Israel, and the forces the Arabs could actually field would be far smaller than the totals shown in Table 21.3. For example, even when Iraq eventually reaches a peace settlement with Iran, it will still be able to support only about two to three divisions in full-scale combat against Israel and a maximum of 100 of its first-line combat aircraft.

The force ratios in Table 21.3 are also misleading in their inability to communicate the qualitative changes that have taken place in the forces on both sides. Israel showed during its June 1982 invasion of Lebanon that it has done a far better job of learning from the October War than its Arab neighbors. It has made major improvements in its warning and surveillance systems and in its intelligence organization. Israel has corrected many of the defects in its reserve system. It now has a far more effective call-up system, does a much better job of locating and preparing reserve equipment, provides much more realistic training, and calls up entire reserve units rather than battalion-size elements. It has also vastly improved the training and armament of its territorial defense forces.

The Limits of Using AWACS in a Combined Arab Attack

The trends outlined in the previous section indicate that Israel is now far stronger than in 1973. But it is the problems most Arab states have in managing an air war that caused most of the debate over AWACS and that seem likely to shape any future debates over U.S. arms sales to Saudi Arabia. Many of the opponents of the sale saw the E-3A as

TABLE 21.3 Illustrative Arab-Israeli Force Ratios: Credible Versus Incredible Threats

Israel versus	Medium Tanks			Combat Aircraft		
	Israel	Arabs	Israel : Arabs	Israel	Arabs	Israel : Arabs
Jordan						
1973	2,000	420	1:0.2	340	52	1:0.2
1978	3,175	500	1:0.2	620	76	1:0.1
1983	3,600	616	1:0.2	769	94	1:0.1
Syria						
1973	2,000	1,170	1:0.6	340	326	1:1
1978	3,175	2,500	1:0.8	620	392	1:0.6
1983	3,600	3,990	1:1.1	769	534	1:0.7
Jordan and Syria						
1973	2,000	1,590	1:1	340	342	1:1
1978	3,175	3,000	1:0.9	620	470	1:0.8
1983	3,600	4,606	1:1.6	769	628	1:0.7
Jordan, Syria, and Egypt						
1973	2,000	3,980	1:2	340	910	1:2.7
1978	3,175	4,600	1:1.4	620	945	1:1.5
1983	3,600	6,706	1:1.9	769	1,057	1:1.4
Jordan, Syria, and Iraq						
1973	2,000	2,820	1:1.4	340	560	1:1.6
1978	3,175	4,800	1:1.5	620	797	1:1.3
1983	3,600	6,906	1:1.9	769	874	1:1.2
Jordan, Syria, Iraq, and Egypt						
1973	2,000	5,780	1:2.9	340	1,128	1:3.3
1978	3,175	6,400	1:2.0	620	1,272	1:2.1
1983	3,600	8,959	1:2.5	769	1,408	1:1.8
Jordan, Syria, Iraq, and Saudi Arabia						
1973	2,000	2,905	1:1.5	340	630	1:1.9
1978	3,175	5,125	1:1.6	620	934	1:1.5
1983	3,600	7,356	1:2.0	764	1,086	1:1.4
Jordan, Syria, Iraq, Egypt, and Saudi Arabia						
1973	2,000	5,805	1:2.9	340	1,198	1:3.5
1978	3,175	6,725	1:2.1	620	1,409	1:2.3
1983	3,600	9,456	1:2.7	769	1,515	1:2.0

Source: The Military Balance (London: IISS, various years). The data for 1983 are conservative in that they reflect end 1982–early 1983 strengths as estimated by the IISS and not the higher 1983 figures estimated by the author that are used elsewhere. See Table 13.13 and 13.17–13.19 for the author's estimate of the impact of recent arms acquisitions and transfers. These shifts generally improve Israel's position relative to that of the Arabs and Syria's position relative to that of the other Arab states.

an "instant" solution to the problems the Arab states faced in making their air forces effective. These opponents failed to realize that any attempt to use the AWACS in such a role would encounter a wide range of problems, in addition to those Saudi Arabia would face in supporting its own forces:

- It would require a massive joint training effort and close cooperation over a period of years.
- The only permanent E-3A basing and service facilities would be at al-Kharj, and the E-3A requires semiannual depot maintenance in the U.S.
- The AWACS could not provide coverage of Israel from points of survivability.
- Israel's E-2Cs could detect the Saudi E-3A at 400 NM. The Israeli F-15 could enter the Saudis' E-3A "net" as "friendlies" or jam it.
- The E-3A will require daily U.S. technical and programming support through the life of the aircraft.
- The E-3A requires special software programming for such a role that could come only from the U.S.
- The E-3A has no IFF compatibility with most Arab aircraft and could not function efficiently against Israel without it.
- The Saudi E-3A lacks an adequate independent data-management capability. It is configured to operate through C^3 ties to Saudi ground stations. It has no IFF security in operating with other Arab air forces.
- No field-portable downlink equipment would be provided from the U.S.
- The Saudi E-3A will not have secure UHF/HF/VHF communications links. It will have no compatibility with Soviet-built aircraft in key communications links since they use a different spectrum of the VHF band.
- Effective use of the E-3A requires standardization in training, intercept procedures, attacks, armament, and on-board aircraft sensors.
- The E-3A is unsuited to coordinate attack missions in the mid-1980s. The MiG 23-27s, Su-24s, and Mirage F-1s in Arab hands could not benefit from the use of the aircraft.
- Saudis cannot base their F-15s forward without U.S. support and could not provide minimal sustained screen.
- The five Saudi sector coordinating centers are fixed and not oriented toward combat with Israel. Most other Arab ground radars are unsuited to link with the E-3A. Aside from Jordan and Egypt, Arab C^3I, radar, and air defense ground environment (ADGE) terminals cannot operate with the E-3A.
- Jordanian TPS-63 radars will provide nearly equal low-altitude coverage over most of Israel almost five years before the Saudi E-3As become operational.

- Syria is the one remaining Arab power seriously competing in an arms race with Israel, but it is Soviet equipped, organized around a Soviet C^3I air control and warning system, and lacks any C^3I equipment, IFF, and training compatible with the E-3A.

Using AWACS to Provide Low-Altitude Coverage of Israel

Even if these problems are ignored, the E-3A sale can offer the Arabs only limited advantages against Israel. The E-3A's main purpose in an Arab-Israeli war would be to provide warning of low-flying Israeli aircraft once they became airborne. It could provide such warning only to the extent that such aircraft were not shielded by any ridge or mountain and their mission could be clearly identified even in an environment where several hundred aircraft would be in near-continuous operation.

This might deprive Israel of the ability to fly ultra-low-altitude missions below existing Arab land-based radars. The E-3A radar can provide such low-altitude coverage with higher jam and ground-clutter resistance than any competing aircraft. It is, however, vulnerable to a noise-jamming defense of the Israeli border, and the Arab states already have considerable low-altitude radar coverage of Israel. They can also acquire other airborne platforms by the late 1980s with a similar capability. These include the British AEW Nimrod, possible variants of the E-130, the E-2C already operated by Israel, the Soviet Tu-126, and a developmental Soviet variation of a Candid 2 AWACS that is now in test deployment.[23] In fact, it seems possible that variations of the MiG-23 or MiG-25 may be available by the early 1980s that could give Syria and Iraq a low-altitude surveillance capability to cover border areas with considerably greater survivability.

Even then, such an incremental warning and tracking capability would have only limited operational value in Israel's small airspace. The average combat air support or interdiction mission flown from Israel—now that the Sinai has been returned to Egypt—involves only 6–7 minutes of flight time to the target area once an Israeli fighter reached the 200-foot altitude an AWACS can cover. Even if Israel had to mass its aircraft for a combination of fighter cover and strike roles, the AWACS could not predict intentions until the Israeli fighters actually moved against a target and would not be able to give more than a few minutes of warning.

Similarly, the Saudi E-3A or any other AWACS would have little ability to deprive Israel of the advantage of "surprise," given the special combat conditions in the region: (1) Israel constantly engages in large-scale exercises, and an AWACS could not distinguish these from an attack;[24] (2) AWACS could predict only the initial vector of an attack once it developed and not the ultimate destination, although it could track the attack's development; and (3) it would take all the Saudi AWACS to provide continuous coverage of Israel for even a few days, and Israel would be able to passively detect whether the AWACS was operating and attack the moment it stood down. Given Israeli skill with surprise, one can even speculate on the extent to which the Israelis might exploit AWACS and the false sense of security it might give the Arab states.

Capability for Battle Management in an Arab-Israeli Air War

The E-3A could also be used to provide the Arab side with precise range and elevation data on large numbers of Israeli aircraft and Arab aircraft, to quickly analyze their vector and maintain real-time tracking, and to home Arab fighters and advanced surface-to-air missiles like the Hawk in attacking Israeli aircraft. Given the high density of combat, the extremely short flight profiles common in an Arab-Israeli conflict, Israel ECM and low-altitude flight capabilities, and the availability of terrain masking from ridges and mountains in the forward area, these AWACS capabilities could be used effectively only if the Arab fighter receiving information from AWACS was capable of accepting an automated data link with AWACS and of providing information the pilot would need in the form of an advanced "heads up" tactical situation display.[25] Not only will most Arab fighters lack the equipment to receive such data from the Saudi E-3A, they will lack the secure digital data links to provide them with the speed and information density required. Most Arab fighters will also lack until the late 1980s on-board radars with the "look-down" capability to fight low-flying Israeli aircraft.[26]

Most hostile Arab fighters are also likely to lack air-to-air missiles equivalent to the AIM-9L/AIM-9M, AIM-7E/AIM-7F, and their successors. They will lack the avionics for a competitive intercept with Israeli pilots and aircraft. Arab-operated Hawk or SAM batteries also generally will not have the advanced automated data-processing capability to benefit from an AWACS, given the short flight distances in an Arab-Israeli conflict and vulnerability to Israeli countermeasures. Further, the U.S. controls the software necessary for the AWACS to recognize or count such systems as friendly, and no other nation has a credible hope of providing such software support.

If Israel used its typically high fighter sortie densities, the AWACS would be forced to control the defending Arab fighters directly to ensure suitable reaction times. The Saudi E-3A can theoretically handle a maximum of 6 simultaneous and 12 near-simultaneous intercepts, but in practice it can usually only handle one per controller. Even if Israeli fighters did not enter the E-3A's IFF "net" as friendlies, they could still saturate its defensive direct intercept control capabilities.

In short, the E-3A is not designed to manage melee warfare in complex terrain and in airspace of less than 16,000 square kilometers. (Israel has an airspace of about 21,000 square kilometers using its 1967 boundaries.[27]) It could locate and identify aircraft, but it would be hopelessly unable to deal with the problem of intentions and short reaction times.[28] Further, the Arabs would risk being "blinded," or having their immense investment in training and configuring to use the AWACS severely degraded, by the almost inevitable loss of the AWACS aircraft if it flew close enough to cover the low-altitude airspace over Israel or by Israeli communications jamming.[29]

The Impact of Saudi-Jordanian Cooperation

If the sale of the Air Defense Enhancement Package presents any realistic risk to Israel, it lies in the use of a combination of Saudi and Jordanian aircraft, and Saudi and Jordanian Hawk units, to create a more effective defensive air screen over eastern Jordan.[30] Such a Saudi-Jordanian air defense screen would be effective, however, only in a limited war in which the Israeli Air Force had a limited incentive to press the attack and was not willing to penetrate deeply into Saudi Arabia and attack its air bases. Its success would also depend upon tactical concepts that have not been operationally proved, on Jordan's acquiring mobile Hawk missiles it cannot make operable until the late 1980s, on Israeli inability to develop effective ECM against vulnerable AWACS communications links and the same Improved Hawk that is operated by Israel, and on optimal Saudi-Jordanian use of terrain factors.

Such Saudi-Jordanian cooperation would also require relatively deep Israeli penetration into Jordan to be effective. Under any other conditions, the fighters or missiles flying in the forward area of Jordan—which includes all its cities, major economic facilities, ports, and probable land combat areas—would have to fire or engage immediately, since the reaction times would be so tight that they could not wait for AWACS data links to characterize the attack. Given current Hawk radar capabilities, and the search/track radar capabilities of the fighters Jordan is likely to have in the mid-1980s, AWACS would provide only limited additional data, and reliance on the E-3A to control a forward air defense mission might actually reduce the Arab ability to force Israeli attack aircraft to abort their strike mission and the Arab kill-to-loss ratio.

Finally, Israel's June 1982 air combat with Syria indicates that any attempt to mass Arab attack aircraft, and then alter mission profiles using AWACS, might well expose the Arab attack aircraft to far more Israeli kills than flying without inputs from the E-3A. The Israeli E-707s, E-2Cs and F-15s could almost certainly use their radars and C^3I gear to react far more quickly than such an uncoordinated, multinational Arab force. The same story might well apply to air-to-air combat for the same reason that AWACS cannot be used effectively in the forward air defense of Jordan.

The Arabs could almost certainly achieve better results by first trying to exhaust Israeli reaction capabilities through threatening fighter sorties and false alarms, firing long-range surface-to-air missiles like the SA-5 to disrupt Israel's E-2C and F-15 radar aircraft, massing their air defense

TABLE 21.4 The Human Cost of the Four Arab-Israeli Wars

	Killed		Wounded		Total	
	Arabs	Israelis	Arabs	Israelis	Arabs	Israelis
1948 War	15,000	6,000	25,000	15,000	40,000	21,000
1956 War[a]	1,000	189	4,000	899	5,000	1,000
1967 War	4,296	983	6,121	4,517	10,417	5,500
1973 War	8,528	2,838	19,549	8,800	28,077	11,638
1982 War[b]	12,000	500+	25,000	2,500	37,000	3,000+
Total	40,824	10,510+	79,670	31,716	120,494	42,226

[a]Totals do not include captured or missing or European and Egyptian losses resulting from the Anglo-French invasion of 1956.
[b]Estimated by the author. Includes civilian casualties on the Arab side.
Source: Adapted from Trevor N. Dupuy, *Elusive Victory: The Arab-Israeli Wars, 1947–1974* (New York: Harper & Row, 1978), pp. 124, 212, 333, 610.

fighters to force Israel to engage, and then simultaneously launching their attack fighters in preplanned missions while using their air defense fighters to engage Israeli aircraft on a target-of-opportunity basis. Even so, Israel's recent tactics in using its E-2C "AWACS," RPVs, E-707 ELINT and jamming aircraft, and its F-15s as "mini-AWACS" to guide Israeli fighters from the rear, should give Israel a decisive edge through the late 1980s.

Israel's Perceptions of the Trend in the Arab-Israeli Balance

Saudi military modernization does not present even a serious "worst case" threat to Israel in the 1980s. This conclusion, however, is based on Western perceptions of Arab capabilities, *not* on Israeli perceptions of the importance of the overall threat from Arab forces in the mid-1980s, of the Saudi threat, and of AWACS.

Israeli Inability to Accept Casualties

Israeli defense planners differ fundamentally from Western experts in their perception of the near-term Arab threat. They have different attitudes regarding the deterrence of combat losses of major equipment or life and about the giving up of any territory. As a result, Israel reacts sharply to even limited changes in Arab capabilities that might increase Israeli losses or casualties.

Americans have little real idea of how limited Israel's casualties have been in most of its four major wars with the Arabs. While statistics vary, Trevor Dupuy's estimates, shown in Table 21.4, provide an illustration of Israel's incredible success in avoiding the intensity of losses that Western analysts would predict for a similar level of armored and air combat in Europe. To put Table 21.4 in perspective, U.S. war games that model manpower losses would predict casualty rates from 7 to 20 times greater than Israeli losses in the October War. No one can fault Israeli planners for seeking to preserve this situation, particularly because they have suffered serious losses in the fighting in Lebanon, and even limited losses are a significant percentage of Israel's population of less than 3.2 million Jews.[31] Nevertheless, these attitudes drive them to seek the unattainable. Israel has recently pursued steadily more dangerous and uncertain long-run strategic options to avoid short-term losses and risks. It also has found it impossible to accept more than the most limited increases in U.S. military ties to the Arab states.

The Israeli Economic and Social Crisis

Israeli perceptions of the Arab threat are also inevitably shaped by the almost devastating social, economic, and manpower costs of maintaining Israel's military forces.[32] Israel is spending something like 60% of its government budget and one-third of its GNP on defense and defense-related debt repayment. Its total military import payments exceeeded $2.2 billion in 1980 and 1981, and they exceeded $2.5 billion in 1982. Its debt service payments on previous arms purchases reached $750 million a year in 1983, in spite of U.S. grants and nearly 50% U.S. forgiveness of loans, and will exceed $1.1 billion annually by the early 1990s. Israel's total foreign debt reached $45 billion in June 1983, and its total annual debt repayments will soon exceed $5 billion. Israel already must pay to the U.S. over $1 billion in annual debt repayments, which now exceed U.S. foreign aid to Israel. Israel's defense budget is now averaging about $8 billion, close to the limit Israel's economy can bear. The invasion of Lebanon has cost Israel at least $3 billion and will drive its future defense spending even higher.[33]

The resulting pressures on the Israeli economy helped produce 133% inflation in 1980 and 105% inflation in 1981. Although before its invasion of Lebanon Israel had projected less than 90% inflation for 1982, inflation actually reached 135%, and it averaged 160% in the first half of 1983.[34] These pressures are a major reason why Israel's real economic growth has dropped below 2.5% and why its trade deficit grew from $1.7 billion in 1977 to $2.7 billion in 1980, exceeded $4 billion in 1982, and increased 35% in the early part of 1983. Israel has gotten $25 billion in aid from the U.S. between 1948 and 1982 and now gets roughly 14% of its GNP from U.S. aid. The pressures are forcing Israel to expand its foreign debt to $45 billion, or more than a year's GNP, even though it already gets 12.8% of its GNP from U.S. aid, and into massive additional private borrowing. They inhibit the modernization, restructuring, and expansion of Israel's rapidly aging economic infrastructure.

When the Israeli cabinet met on the 1982 budget before Israel's June invasion of Lebanon, it was forced to make serious cuts in social services to avoid a rate of inflation that Israel's finance minister, Yoram Aridor, warned would otherwise exceed 200%. As a result, roughly two-thirds of the resulting "austerity" budget of $26.4 billion was committed to defense and to servicing a defense-dominated national debt. Immediately after the invasion, Israel had to impose a 25% increase in the 12% value added tax, a 2% tax on stock market transactions, and a new fees for travel aborad. These increases, however, covered only $1 billion of the cost of the war. Israel estimated in early 1983 that its direct and indirect costs were at least $5 billion.[35]

By August of 1983 Israel was forced into another massive devaluation and budget cuts of nearly $1 billion, including $400 million in defense. By the end of 1983, inflation exceeded 140%, the foreign debt was over $27 billion, and Israel's trade deficit was over $3.5 billion annually. GNP growth was below 2%, and Israel's banks had finally given up trying to index their shares to compensate for inflation.

Israel faces even worse problems in the future in spite of U.S. economic aid averaging over $1.2 billion annually, and direct and indirect U.S. subsidies to Israel's defense of $1.4–1.9 billion a year, which are now equivalent to 38–50% of its defense budget. As Table 21.5 shows, Israel received over $12 billion in U.S. military aid between FY1976 and FY1982, of which more than $5.5 billion was in the form of payment waivers or the equivalent of direct grants. U.S. military aid to compensate Israel for withdrawal from the Sinai involved a special $3.7 billion aid package, of which $900 million was in grants. In FY1982 (1 October 1981–30 September 1982), Israel received $2.6 billion from the U.S. and requested $2.475 billion for FY1983. It is receiving $1.7 billion in military assistance in FY1983, of which $750 million was in grants.[36] It received $1.7 billion again in FY1984, of which $850 million was in grants, and it will receive at least $1.4 billion, all in grants, in FY1985.

Yet Israel will face growing strain, even if the U.S. eventually buys $300 million worth of Israeli-made military equipment annually as part of the new strategic ties between the U.S. and Israel agreed to in September 1981 and November 1983.[37]

This level of U.S. assistance to Israel will be enough to fuel attacks on the U.S. throughout the Arab world and to offset many of the political benefits of U.S. military aid to Egypt and Pakistan.[38] It will not, however, be enough to meet Israel's military goals. Israel set its annual aid requirement at $3.45 billion in FY1981 and only trimmed it back to $2.9 billion in FY1982. It has since presented plans to the U.S. calling for $17–25 billion in military aid over the next 10 years.[39] On the basis of these aid requests, Israel would need about $4–5 billion worth of annual aid in 1982 dollars for at least the next five years to sustain both its present level of military capabilities and a viable domestic economy, and it would still have to export about $1 billion worth of arms annually. As a result, even if the U.S. is willing to continue paying something like 25–33% of Israel's defense bill, this level of U.S. aid will still not be enough.[40]

TABLE 21.5 U.S. Military Sales and Assistance to Key Middle Eastern States, FY1976–FY1984 (current $ millions)

	FY1976	FY1877	FY1978	FY1979	FY1980	FY1981	FY1982[a]	FY1976–82	FY1950–82	FY1983[b]	FY1984[b]
Israel											
FMS agreements	966	496	1,385	829	542	132	656	5,006	9,772	1,900	800
FMS construction	–	–	–	3	–	–	–	3	3	–	–
Commercial sales	190	222	123	174	272	267	150	1,398	1,639	150	300
MAP aid	–	–	–	–	–	–	–	–	–	–	–
IME aid	–	–	–	–	–	–	–	–	–	3	3
Total	1,156	718	1,508	1,006	814	399	806	6,407	11,414	2,053	1,103
FMS payment waived	350	500	500	500	500	500	1,400	4,250	5,500	750	550
FMS direct loans	–	–	–	–	–	–	–	–	1,667	–	–
FMS loan guarantees	350	500	500	2,700[c]	500	900	850	6,840	7,737	950	1,150
Egypt											
FMS agreements	66	1	162	427	2,286	324	2,102	5,368	5,369	560	1,000
FMS construction	–	–	–	–	–	–	20	20	20	–	–
Commercial sales	1	1	7	1	7	4	15	36	36	30	75
MAP aid	–	–	–	–	–	–	–	–	–	–	–
IME aid	–	–	*	*	*	1	–	2	2	2	3.9
Total	67	2	169	428	2,293	329	2,137	5,426	5,427	592	1,078.9
FMS payment waived	–	–	–	–	–	–	200	–	200	425	450
FMS direct loans	–	–	–	–	–	550	–	550	550	–	–
FMS loan guarantees	–	–	–	1,500[c]	–	–	700	2,200	2,750	900	850
Jordan											
FMS agreements	354	95	68	74	342	368	141	1,442	1,773	300	300
FMS construction	*	4	9	4	54	42	50	163	163	–	–
Commercial sales	*	4	9	4	54	42	–	113	113	50	50
MAP aid	52	52	55	42	28	1	*	230	493	–	–
IME aid	1	1	1	2	1	1	2	9	13	1.2	1.2
Total	407	156	142	126	479	454	193	1,957	2,555	351.2	351.2
FMS payment waived	–	–	–		–	–	–	–	–	–	–
FMS direct loans	–	–	–		–	42	–	42	56	–	–
FMS loan guarantees	83	75	71	67	50	–	60	406	484	75	115
Lebanon											
FMS agreements	*	–	28	23	31	55	9	146	166	60	30
FMS construction	–	–	–	–	–	–	–	–	–	–	–
Commercial sales	1	*	2	3	1	1	2	10	14	1.5	1.5
MAP aid	–	–	–	–	–	–	–	–	14	–	–
IME aid	*	*	*	1	*	*	2	6	13	0.7	0.7
Total	1	–	31	27	33	57	13	162	207	62.2	32.2
FMS payment waived	–	–	–	–	–	–	–	–	–	–	–
FMS direct loans	–	–	–	–	–	20	–	20	29	–	–
FMS loan guarantees	–	25	–	43	22	–	10	100	120	15	15

TABLE 21.5 (continued)

	FY1976	FY1977	FY1978	FY1979	FY1980	FY1981	FY1982[a]	FY1976–82	FY1950–82	FY1983[b]	FY1984[b]
Iran											
FMS agreements	1,667	1,912	359	36	—	—	—	3,974	12,557	—	—
FMS construction	—	—	—	—	—	—	—	—	1	—	—
Commercial sales	108	138	133	110	7	—	—	496	671	—	—
MAP aid	—	—	—	—	—	—	—	—	767	—	—
IME aid	—	—	—	—	—	—	—	—	67	—	—
Total	1,775	2,050	492	146	7	—	—	4,470	14,063	—	—
FMS payment waived	—	—	—	—	—	—	—	—	—	—	—
FMS direct loans	—	—	—	—	—	—	—	—	176	—	—
FMS loan guarantees	—	—	—	—	—	—	—	—	327	—	—
Saudi Arabia											
FMS agreements	1,996	1,309	2,707	4,929	3,023	1,280	5,574	20,818	23,297	5,000	6,420
FMS construction	5,454	648	667	1,021	1,552	877	1,846	12,065	18,938	700	1,700
Commercial sales	93	44	166	44	29	72	50	498	566	50	400
MAP aid	—	—	—	—	—	—	—	—	24	—	—
IME aid				—	—	— *	—	—	12	—	—
Total	7,543	2,001	3,540	5,994	4,604	2,229	7,470	33,381	42,837	5,750	8,520
FMS payment waived	—	—	—	—	—	—	—	—	—	—	—
FMS direct loans	—	—	—	—	—	—	—	—	65	—	—
FMS loan guarantees	—	—	—	—	—	—	—	—	189	—	—

* Less than $500,000.

[a]Economic Support Funding (ESF) for FY1982 is $806 million in grants for Israel; $10 million in loans and $5 million in grants for Jordan; $771 million in grants for Egypt; $6 million in grants for Lebanon; and $11.08 million in Mideast regional grants.

[b]Preliminary figures only. ESF for both FY1983 and FY1984 is $785 million for Israel, $525 million in grants; $20 million for Jordan; and $750 million for Egypt, $500 million in grants. Lebanon will get $145.5 million in ESF in FY1983. The FY1984 total is unclear. Israel has requested $1.97 billion in military aid for FY1984, with $835 million in grants (*Philadelphia Inquirer*, 26 October 1982, p. 1; *Midwest Observer*, 15 February 1983, p. 3; *Washington Report on Middle East Affairs*, 21 February 1983, p. 5).

[c]Includes $1.5 billion for Egypt and $2.2 billion for Israel in FY1979 authorized by P.L. 96-35 and appropriated by P.L. 96-38.

Sources: DSAA, *Foreign Military Sales, Foreign Military Construction Sales, and Military Assistance Facts*, 1982; U.S. State Department, *International Security and Development Cooperation Program*, Special Report no. 108, 4 April 1983. Does not show expected impact of congressional action, which will raise FY1984 total for Israel to around $2.2 billion. "FMS agreements" includes equipment and support agreements; "FMS construction" includes construction agreements. "Commercial exports" include purchases licensed under the Arms Export Control Act. "MAP" is military assistance program, including excess defense articles program. "IME" is international military education and training. Total may not add due to rounding. Definitions differ from those of similar data used earlier.

Israel's defense effort also involves a massive social cost. It has meant disrupting Israel's educational system and lowering the quality of its secondary school and university system at a time when the increase in the proportion of less well-educated Middle Eastern Jews to 55% of the total Jewish population of Israel is causing serious problems in terms of labor and military skills. The defense effort is channeling Israel's industry and exports into military construction.

Israel's embattled society and economy have produced critical cutbacks in immigration from outside Israel, and the number of Soviet Jews emigrating but not settling in Israel has risen from 4.3% in 1973 to 85% in 1981.[41] The *New York Times* has reported that there are now 350,000 Israelis in the U.S. and that as much as 15% of Israel's Jewish population has left Israel at least temporarily.[42] Even Israel's Ministry of Labor and Social Welfare, which does not count most expatriates as permanent departures, says 510,528 Israelis left Israel between 1969 and 1979, versus 384,000 immigrants. Only the recent world recession slowed this outflow in 1982.[43] At the same time, Israel faces the social strain of making a large percentage of its draft-age males perform internal security missions or become involved in the complex brutality of the Lebanese civil war.[44]

The expansion of the IDF to a mobilized force structure roughly equivalent to that of France or Germany, but drawing from a total population of less than 3.5 million, created massive manpower problems even before the invasion of Lebanon.[45] To quote a leading Israeli defense expert, this search for manpower has not only forced Israel to go to the "bottom of the barrel" for manpower, but "to dig deeply into the wood."[46] Israel has had to sharply relax both the physical and educational standards in its combat personnel and is now accepting service and logistic personnel it would previously not have allowed to enter the armed forces or to serve in their current occupations.

Israel has been able to make its force structure work in spite of these problems only because of the immense experience of key serving and reserve Israeli military personnel and their ability to compensate for the weaknesses of new conscripts and recruits. Even with the new battle-trained forces it has acquired from its June 1982 fighting, this cadre of experienced personnel will slowly disappear in the mid-1980s, and the relative quality of the Israeli intake will decline steadily through the late 1980s. Ignoring emigration, Israel faces three unavoidable reasons for this decline: (1) the increase in demand for technical skills imposed by the steady increase in the sophistication of Israeli equipment and tactics; (2) the demographic shift in Israel to more Oriental Jews with poorer education and skill levels; and (3) the steady disruption of the Israeli educational system forced by the extension of the Israeli call-up and conscription procedures, which particularly affects the quality of personnel available for training as officers and technicians.

These social, economic, and military costs are so high that they raise serious questions as to whether Israel can maintain its capability to win a war with the Arabs without suffering a strategic defeat in having to endure the economic and social strains of its current state of "peace." They have thrust Israel into a continuing crisis that will be accelerated by its 1981 election budget and the June 1982 fighting in Lebanon.

Israeli Exaggeration of the Current Arab Threat

Israel has a legitimate need for military superiority over any combination of the military forces of the most likely Arab confrontation states. The reality of Israeli military superiority is the only way in which it can deter hostile military action or the escalation of a conflict or crisis once it begins. It is the only way Israel can avoid being forced into a peacetime or quasi-wartime struggle of attrition in which the Arab states simply deploy to Israel's borders, keep making threatening moves, or otherwise force Israel into a constant state of mobilization that would destroy or fatally weaken its economy without large-scale conflict taking place.

This fact, does not, however, justify Israel's tendency to treat the Arab states as one hostile mass for military planning purposes, which so exaggerates the threat as to make U.S. cooperation with any Arab state impossible:

- It ignores the almost total isolation of the PLO and Syria during the June 1982 fighting and the fact that the Arabs have never attained such unity in any of their previous wars.
- It ignores the fact that Saudi Arabia cannot commit all its forces to an attack on Israel and Iraq; its rhetoric has been extremely cautious in committing its forces to battle with Israel.
- It ignores Jordan's current commitment to peace, its traditional restraint, the fact that Jordan and Syria were at war in 1970, that Jordan largely stayed out of the 1973 war, that Jordan and Syria came close to war in 1980 and 1981,[47] and that Jordan did nothing during the fighting in 1982.
- It ignores Jordan's serious equipment weaknesses.
- It ignores the divisions among various Palestinian groups and the conflicts inherent in their dispersal and changing alignments with Syria, Jordan, and the PLO.
- It ignores the almost overwhelming evidence that most Arab forces have bought advanced military technology without really being able to absorb it.
- It ignores Iraq's poor performance in the Iran-Iraq War.
- It ignores Syria's long involvement in Lebanon in kinds of fighting that have precluded effective training of Syrian forces and that have scarcely provided combat experience of the kind valuable in fighting Israel.
- It ignores Syria's long and growing tension with Iraq and with many Palestinian factions.

- It ignores Syria's continuing poor performance in air-to-air combat and inability to effectively operate the new C³I and other advanced military technology it has received from the USSR since 1982.
- It ignores Egypt's patent commitment to peace with Israel, its slow conversion to U.S. military equipment over the next half decade, and plans to make major cuts in its force structure.

While the pace of Israel's first invasion of Lebanon in the Litani Operation of March 1978 may not have fulfilled Israeli expectations of instant victory, it was an effective use of combined arms and air power that no realistic combination of Arab confrontation states will soon be able to match. Israel's second invasion in June 1982 has shown that Israel has an even more decisive superiority. The continuing Israeli air victories over Syria, the inability of Syrian surface-to-air missiles to hit Israeli fighters, and the successes of Israel's strike at the Osirak reactor should also show Israelis that they are likely to retain their past edge over the Arabs in spite of the USSR's delivery of the SA-5 and other new arms to Syria.

The Threat Against Israel After 1985

Nevertheless, Israeli security in the late 1980s may not equal that of the mid-1980s. While U.S. arms sales to the Gulf states will have a negligible impact on the Arab-Israeli balance, Israel could face a steadily increasing threat from Syria and the other "hardline" Arab states. Israel does seem to be approaching the absolute limit of its manpower resources, and its manpower may decline in educational quality even if more Israelis do not emigrate. Israel's Matmon Bet (Treasure B) plan of 1974 was almost certainly overambitious in calling for an IDF of 17 divisions, 5,000 tanks, and 750 combat aircraft by 1986.

The Matmon C plan of 1979 set a goal of 10 armored divisions for the containment of sudden ground attacks on all fronts and theaters of Israel, plus 3 divisions as a strategic reserve. It also called for 15 infantry brigades, including 2–3 assigned to airborne missions, 10 of which were to have an organic tank battalion. Each armored division was to contain 3,330 tanks, 600 APCs, 72 155mm SP guns, and 36 long-range antitank launchers on APCs. The basic force goal, which is still of interest in spite of increases under Sharon and Arens, was 4,500 tanks (4,000 of which were to be capable of engaging T-72/T-80/Chieftains), 9,000 APCs of M-113 quality or better, 1,000 155mm SP artillery weapons of M-109 quality or better, 200 or more M-107 modern guns, and 600 armored fighting vehicles with TOW or more modern antitank guided weapons. In addition, Matmon C called for 80–100 attack helicopters, 200 advanced air superiority fighters, 250 dual-capable high-performance fighters, 250 high-performance attack fighters, 6 Mohawks, 6 KC-135s, 60 heavy-lift helicopters, 24 modern short-range surface-to-air missile batteries, and 24 Improved Hawk or Patriot batteries. The navy goal was 30 missile patrol boats equipped with 100 Harpoon missiles. Neither this plan nor later variants provide any indication that Israel could achieve higher force levels in the late 1980s.[48]

In contrast, Arab states like Egypt, Syria, Jordan, and Iraq can eventually increase the mass or strength of their armed forces as well as their quality. They will be able to bring far more mass against Israel with steadily less warning as their forces improve in aircraft range, mobility, and basing.

The Impact of New Military Technology on the Arab-Israeli Balance

It is also hard to disregard the fact that many of Israel's advantages over the Arab states have stemmed from the dependence of the key Arab confrontation states on Soviet military technology that was inferior to Western technology in many critical ways and that exacerbated the training and organizational weaknesses in Egyptian and Syrian forces. These technological weaknesses have included

- Lack of modern air defense avionics, modern aircraft cannon, and related air-intercept computers. The Arabs had to depend on the unreliable and ineffective Soviet AA-2 Atoll, a copy of the U.S. AIM-9A. The AA-2 Atoll air-to-air missile and the Soviet AA-8 have recently proved no more effective in Arab hands, which has crippled Arab air-to-air combat capability in most wars.
- A lack of effective command and control for the massive Arab ground-based air defenses, and the need to use large numbers of incompatible, vulnerable, and jam-prone land radars. These weaknesses made the massive Arab investment in land-based air defenses largely ineffective.
- A lack of attack aircraft with effective avionics for low-altitude penetration and accurate munitions delivery and a lack of modern attack munitions, which made Arab offensive air strikes largely ineffective.
- Reliance on Soviet antitank guided missiles requiring incredible degrees of operator proficiency, which could not engage at ranges of less than 200–500 meters, and which were highly vulnerable to suppressive fire because of the need for total concentration on the part of the operator. This made Arab ATGMs effective only in well-entrenched, set-piece defense and armor ambush actions.
- Reliance on Soviet T-54, T-55, and T-62 tanks whose low profile was achieved at the cost of being unable to fire effectively in the defilade mode common in desert "ambush" warfare, and whose simple stadiametric range finders and awkward loading and firing sequence made them grossly inferior to Israel's tanks, especially at long ranges. These problems led to an almost incredible Israeli advantage in tank-to-tank kill ratios.

- A lack of self-propelled artillery and modern artillery fire-control systems, which obfuscated the impact of Arab superiority in artillery numbers.
- Reliance on World War II–level SIGINT and electronic warfare equipment, which left the Arabs vulnerable to Israeli countermeasures and deprived their own massive SIGINT and electronic warfare effort of much of its value.

The data in Table 21.6 are only a rough indication of how radically this situation will change in the late 1980s, especially if peace is not achieved, as the Arab states react to the Israel-Syria-Lebanon crisis, the Israeli attack on Osirak, the annexation of the Golan and Jerusalem, the de jure annexation of the West Bank, and the lessons of the Iran-Iraq War. They do, however, provide a grim promise that by the late 1980s, Israel must either find some way to make further massive increases in its defense effort or lose the kind of technical edge over the Arabs it has maintained in the past.

The Israeli Fear of Close Saudi-U.S. Relations

Its military concerns help explain why Israel seeks to block further U.S. arms sales to Saudi Arabia, but they probably are not the major reason for such Israeli efforts. Israeli planners almost certainly fear the political leverage Saudi Arabia could acquire from establishing stable military relations with the United States far more than the almost nonexistent military threat that Saudi Arabia would pose to Israel. Unlike Egypt and Jordan, which have little economic or oil power, Saudi Arabia is of vital strategic value to the U.S. It is natural that Israel's leaders are concerned that Saudi Arabia's oil and growing economic power could give it a degree of influence over the United States that might threaten U.S. willingness to support Israel in a crisis and that closer relations with Saudi Arabia may eventually lead the U.S. to broaden its contacts with other Arab powers and the Palestinians.

What is less natural is that these concerns should blind Israel's leaders to the advantages of U.S. ties to the conservative and moderate Arab states. In the long run, any limited increase in the military threat to Israel that would result from U.S. arms sales to Saudi Arabia, or from the expansion of U.S. strategic ties to the conservative Gulf states, will be more than offset by the extent to which such ties would align Saudi Arabia and its neighbors with the West, make them dependent on continued U.S. military assistance, and encourage their continued moderation in taking positions on the Arab-Israeli conflict.

Peace as the Best Defense

All of the points discussed earlier argue that an Arab-Israeli peace is as important to Israel as to the U.S. and the Gulf states. They also

TABLE 21.6 Recent or Planned Weapons Purchases Affecting the Arab-Israeli Balance

	Army Systems		Air Force Systems	
	Nos.	Model and Type	Nos.	Model and Type
Israel	125	M-60 tanks	20	F-15
	100	Merkava tanks	75	F-16A
	800	M-113 APCs	8	F-16B
	200	M-109 AB1 155mm SP howitzer	200	Improved Hawk SAMs
			30	H-500 attack helicopters
	60+	175mm SP guns	36	AH-1S attack helicopters
	?	Lance SSM	600	Maverick ASM[a]
	?	TOW ATGM	600	AIM-9L AAM[a]
	7000	Dragon ATGM	470	AIM-7F AAM[a]
			200	Shrike AAM[a]
			?	New fighter
			?	Cluster bombs
Egypt	189	M-60 A3 tanks	20	Mirage 2000
	750	M-113 APCs	45	Alphajet
	52	M-901 TOW SP	16	Mirage 5E2
	2000	Swingfire ATGM	70–80	F-16 A/B
	100	Vulcan AA	20	Gazelle with HOT
	4	Crotale SAM	6	C-130H transport
	200	TOW launchers	600	Maverick ASM[a]
	1500	TOW missiles	70	AIM-7E AAM[a]
	2500	Improved TOW missiles	100	AIM-9E AAM[a]
			100	AIM-9P AAM[a]
	100	M-106A2 and M-152A2 mortar carriers	?	CSA-1 SAM
			12	Hawk batteries[a]
			4	AS-61 helicopters
	100	Kuerassier SP ATK guns		
Syria	?	T-72 tanks[b]	?	MiG-25
	?	BMP-1 AFV	38	MiG-27
	?	BTR-60	?	MiG-23
	?	122mm SP howitzer	26	Su-22
	?	152mm SP howitzer	50	Mi-8 attack helicopters
	?	FROG SSM	18	AB-212 attack helicopters
	?	SCUD SSM	50	SA-342K attack helicopters
	?	HOT ATGM	21	Super Frelon
	1200	AT-3 ATGM[a]	?	R-530 AAM
	1000	Milan ATGM[a]	?	AA-6 AAM
	?	Spigot ATGM[a]	24?	SA-5
	?	SA-6 SAM	200	SA-6 SAM[a]
	?	SA-8 SAM	200	SA-8 SAM[a]
	?	Gazelle helicopter	300	SA-9 SAM[a]
			?	ASM
			?	SA-11
Jordan	248	Khalid tanks	36	F-16C,
	40	M-60A3 tanks[c]	36	F-20A
	78	M-113 APCs	20	Mirage F-1
	?	Stinger SAM	24	AH-1Q helicopter with TOW
			280	AIM-9J AAM
			?	R-530 AAM
			?	Matra ASM
			16	ZSU-23/4 SA-8
Lebanon[d]	7	M-48 tanks[e]	6	Gazelle helicopters
	228	M-113 APCs	6	F-5 E/F
	18	155mm guns		
	200	Milan ATGM		
	100	TOW ATGM		

TABLE 21.6 (continued)

	Army Systems		Air Force Systems	
	Nos.	Model and Type	Nos.	Model and Type
Iraq	150	T-72 tanks[a]	75	MiG-23 BM
	600+	T-62 tanks	?	Mirage 2000
	100+	AMX-30 tanks	150?	MiG-23/25/27
	100	Cascavel, Jararaca	24?	Mirage F-1C
			?	CH-6
			?	CH-7
			?	Super Etendard
			10	Gazelle, Lynxhelis
			?	M-24, AB-212
			?	AS-61TS helicopters
		AFVs	?	Super 530 AAM
	80	Urutu, EE 11 APCs	90	SA-6 SAM
	?	SP-74, SP-73 SP	?	SA-8/9 SAM
		Howitzer	?	Crotale SAM
	?	Sucuri SP antitank	?	Roland II SAM
	?	SCUD B SSM	?	Exocet SAM
			144	R-550 ASM
Saudi	150	M-60A3 kits	4	F-5E
Arabia	200	VCC-1 TOW AFV	5	AWACS
	60	AMX-10P APCs	31	F-15
	72	FH-70 155mm howitzer	40	C-272-200
	?	Enjesa ar. cars.	?	F-15 Fast kits
	?	Shahine SAM bty	15	TF-15
			10	RF-5E
			6	KC-135 tankers
			916	Maverick ASM
			600	AIM-9L AAM[a]
			850	AIM-9J AAM[a]
			600	AIM-9P AAM[a]
			20-90	Helicopters
			1	F-SF Trainer
			1	747 Transport
Libya	100	Leopard (Lion)	140	MiG-23
		IOF-40 tanks	50	MiG-25
	300	T-72 tanks	40	Mirage F-1
	?	Fiat 6616 AFV	160	SF-260 Warrior
	100	Urutu APCs	?	Super 530 AAM[a]
	30	SCUD-B/C SSM	300	SA-2/3/6[a]
	?	SA-9 SAM	?	SA-9 SAM[a]
	?	SA-8	12	G-222 transport
	?	SA-11	10	Twin Otter transport
	200	Palmaria 155mm	70	SF-260 trainers
		SP howitzer	?	Gazelle helicopters
			?	A-109 helicopters

[a]On delivery.
[b]May be converted to use Western sights and range finders.
[c]Includes captured Iranian tanks provided by Iraq.
[d]Lebanon is to receive aid from the U.S. in small arms and other hardware to equip three infantry brigades. See *Washington Post,* 23 October 1982.
[e]Ex-Jordanian.

Sources: Primary sources include the *Military Balance, 1981-1982* (London: IISS, 1982), SIPRI, *Aviation Week, Armed Forces Journal,* and *International Defense Review.* See Tables 13.18 and 13.20 for more details.

argue that Israel should give peace a higher priority than annexation and should show more tolerance and objectivity toward U.S. relations with Saudi Arabia and the other conservative Gulf states during the time it takes to negotiate a peace. The alternative, after all, is to force Saudi Arabia and the conservative Gulf states, as well as Egypt and Jordan, into a steadily more exposed position that will force them to back the more radical and hostile states in the Arab world.

In pursuing short-term political and military advantages, Israel may deprive the U.S. of the option of seeking to encourage Iraq's recent movement away from the Soviet bloc, preclude the kind of U.S. relations with the Palestinians that will encourage a peace settlement, and end Arab willingness to seek peace on terms that would give Israel security within its 1967 boundaries.

There is little prospect, however, that Israel's perceptions of the Arab threat and the risks inherent in U.S. ties to the Arab world can be moderated to reassure Israel as long as the U.S. does not take additional steps. Without such steps, Israel is almost certain to oppose future arms sales and encourage its U.S. supporters to do so. As a result, the U.S. must take the following steps to help meet its major policy goals in the Near East:

The U.S. must structure its military assistance to the Gulf states to take into consideration both Gulf interests and tensions with Israel. The AWACS package was the fifth major military modernization effort that the U.S. encouraged Saudi Arabia to undertake without adequate long-term planning and at least the third that took place without the kind of dialogue and preparation that would have minimized Israeli concerns.

There is a clear need for more forthright U.S. efforts to communicate to Israel the rationale for given U.S. arms sales to the Gulf states. It is not fair to blame Israel, or the various U.S. political groups that support Israel, for all of Israel's overreaction to the AWACS package or its resistance to any long-term expansion of U.S. ties to the conservative Gulf states. The U.S. has made far too little effort to develop a process of tacit communication among its major allies in the near East or to encourage their understanding of the degree to which a modus vivendi among them can serve a common interest and create a true "strategic consensus." The U.S. has failed to stress the advantages to Israel of U.S. military relations with Saudi Arabia and the other friendly Gulf states that encourage the moderation of the Gulf states, that can meet their military needs without threatening Israel, and that are based on stable, long-term plans and common understandings that greatly reduce the risk of creating the kind of unified Arab threat that Israel most fears. Improved long-term planning is as important to achieving strategic stability as it is to reducing the problems in military modernization in the Gulf and tensions between the Gulf and the United States.

The U.S. must restructure its military and economic assistance to Israel to give it security after a peace settlement. The U.S. cannot hope to achieve strategic stability in the Gulf or Middle East by restricting arms to Saudi Arabia, the other friendly Gulf states, Jordan, and Egypt in an effort to reduce the "worst case" threat to Israel. The end result will be to destroy the U.S. position in the region and possibly to create a unified Arab opposition to the U.S. and Israel that could ultimately make such "worst case" Arab threats a reality, increasing the probability of renewed Soviet politico-strategic intervention. Such restrictions would also have little effect on the Arab military buildup other than making friendly Arab states buy from other nations (like the USSR). Yet the U.S. cannot hope to expand its military relations with the Arab states without finding some method of reducing Israeli concerns and developing domestic U.S. political support for such an effort.

The near-term alternative is for the U.S. to sustain its support of Camp David and the Reagan peace proposals, even though it may take years to bring them to a successful conclusion, and to compensate Israel for expanding U.S. military relations with Saudi Arabia and the Arab world in ways that can serve Israeli and Arab interests alike. The new "strategic relationship" that President Reagan offered Prime Minister Begin in September 1981 and renewed in his November 1983 discussions with Prime Minister Shamir is not a valid mechanism for doing this.[49] Such a strategic relationship is militarily purposeless and hopelessly unstable without an Arab-Israeli peace, and any U.S. use of Israel as a base for USCENTCOM forces would do the West far more harm than good. The end result of any U.S. use of Israel to deal with a contingency in any Arab state would be to destroy the legitimacy of all Arab regimes friendly to the U.S. and to kill any U.S. hope of strategic partnership with the Gulf states. Similarly, such a relationship does not provide a convincing U.S. security guarantee to Israel by joint naval and air force exercises or prestocking equipment in Israel.[50] The net effect of such policies will be to isolate the U.S., weaken moderate Arab states, and increase the threat to Israel.

Although it may be some time before the opportunity arises, the U.S. should focus on trading economic and military assistance to Israel for Israel's support of peace and not for "surrogate" forces. Specifically, the U.S. must (1) guarantee Israel that it will provide at least the current level of economic assistance on a long-term basis, (2) increase its military assistance enough to reduce Israeli fear of any buildup in the Arab threat and replace the current mix of loans and grants with an all-grant program, (3) establish a long-term defense planning effort with Israel tailored to dealing with the kind of Arab threat that may arise in the late 1980s, and (4) develop long-term U.S. security guarantees that will help assure Israel that any reduction in Israeli capabilities to defend itself in an all-out Arab-Israeli conflict will be made up by U.S. assistance or forces.

These steps are essential to ensure security and to create a climate in which Israel can ultimately accept the increases in the threat to its security that will result from even the most favorable peace settlement. They are essential to avoid future situations in which Israel strikes preemptively at Arab states friendly to the U.S. or increases its reliance on nuclear weapons. Further, they are essential to avoid a separation of U.S. and Israeli strategic interests because of Israel's different perception of its need to use military options.

The U.S. does *not* have the option of "blackmailing" Israel into peace—and its Arab friends must be persuaded of this. The U.S. can set reasonable conditions for its aid and put pressure on Israel for restraint and limited concessions, but any effort to use aid as a means of force would be no more tolerable to Israelis than it would be to Americans. Such U.S. efforts would instead exacerbate all the negative trends in Israeli politics and strategy, increase the risk of another Arab-Israeli war and of further incidents like the Israeli invasion of Lebanon, and erode the credibility of the military and economic incentives the U.S. could offer for progress in offering self-determination for the West Bank.[51]

Above all, such actions would cast the credibility of U.S. guarantees of Israel's security into further doubt at precisely the time when some degree of Israeli belief in that guarantee is the only hope of achieving a peace between the Arabs and Israel based on a solution that offers the Palestinians dignity and hope. Although it is no fault of the Arabs, it is a grim fact that the collective Western guilt for the Holocaust and centuries of anti-Semitism erodes the credibility of such guarantees enough without further U.S. action. Such a U.S. policy position will inevitably limit U.S. freedom of action in the short run and risk temporarily alienating many Arabs friendly to the U.S., but it is the best approach in the long run to serving the interests of Arab and Israeli alike.

The U.S. must act to halt further Israeli attacks and escalation. In the interim, the price for U.S. aid, and a more meaningful form of the "alliance" President Reagan offered Prime Minister Begin in September 1981,[52] should be a firm quid pro quo with Israel that halts Israel's use of U.S. arms in "defensive attacks" on Arab targets outside Israeli territory.

The U.S. must put tighter controls on the arms it sells Israel and must limit the escalation of future military incidents and the drift toward another Arab-Israeli war. It cannot continue to accept actions like Begin's annexation of the Golan in December 1981 or Israel's invasion of Lebanon. The U.S. must establish firm rules and penalties for the use of U.S. military equipment that both sides understand, that will be applied consistently over time, and that are not tied to an immediate crisis or U.S. effort to force Israel into a specific course of action in such a crisis. Such new controls will inevitably involve compromise on the part of both Israel and the United States, but more effective controls on the Israeli use of U.S. military equipment do not have to be punitive or prejudicial to Israel's security, *if* they are agreed on in the context of U.S. compensation. Such a bargain will also make it far easier for the U.S. to provide the military equipment Saudi Arabia and other Arab allies of the U.S. will need in the future, since Israel will have a much clearer picture of the long-term impact that U.S. aid to both Israel and the Arabs will have on the Middle East balance. It should also establish a better climate for peace negotiations.

The U.S. must accept that there can be no "strategic consensus" without resolving the Palestinian issue. Finally, the U.S. has to accept that it must oppose Israel at least to the point at which the U.S. continues to support a peace settlement acceptable to the Palestinians living on the West Bank and in Gaza. As former Presidents Carter and Ford stated in their joint press conference following President Sadat's funeral, the U.S. must encourage Israel to deal with Jordan and the PLO and to reach a settlement with the Palestinians.[53] The virtual destruction of the PLO's armed forces during Israel's invasion of Lebanon and the PLO's struggle with Syria have helped make this easier and more urgent.

As President Reagan has already proposed, a settlement does not have to mean immediate agreement to an ultimate peace treaty or transferring the West Bank to the present leadership of the PLO. It does not have to mean a rigid adherence to Israel's 1967 boundaries. It might well mean preserving an Israeli military presence in the occupied territories for some years and granting recognition of an eventual Palestinian right to self-determination without recognizing any current group of Palestinian leaders as formal heads of state or attempting to resolve all the complex issues of the relations between such a new state and Jordan, the PLO, Syria, and Lebanon.

It may even be enough to trade Israel's formal recognition of the Palestinian right to self-determination, and to obtain some form of actual or near sovereignty within a set time period, for broad Arab recognition of Israel's right to exist, limited territorial adjustments, and the need for special security measures on the West Bank to limit the risk to Israel. As long as the settlement corrects the critical gaps in the Camp David accords and creates a negotiating climate that puts an end to Israeli efforts to absorb the occupied territories, it should be enough to allow a tacit modus vivendi to develop between Israel and Saudi Arabia, end the isolation of Egypt from the rest of the Arab world, and ease the current tension between the U.S. and Jordan.

Without progress in these areas, U.S. relations with Saudi Arabia, the other friendly Gulf states, Egypt, and Jordan will constantly be threatened by the political dangers posed by the U.S. commitment to Israel and by growing political hostility in the Gulf and Arab world. These risks will grow regardless of how well the U.S. conducts its military assistance efforts. The stability of the Egyptian-Israeli peace treaty will be constantly threatened, particularly now that the Sinai has been returned to Egypt, and U.S. ability to strengthen Eygpt politically and economically will almost inevitably be affected by Israeli efforts to limit U.S. aid. Similar problems will arise in dealing with Jordan and in maintaining any unity in Lebanon.

The settlement of the Arab-Israel peace issue is the key step. It is as vital to all sides today as at any time in history. It is the only step that can allow the U.S. to minimize the risks of upheaval in the Gulf and of the loss of the West's oil supplies. It is the only alternative to a constant escalation of the military buildup in the Near East and to tensions that are virtually certain to cause the loss of critical U.S. security interests in the Gulf and force yet another Arab-Israeli conflict. Painful and time-consuming as they may be, U.S. efforts to negotiate a valid peace settlement are the only step that can avoid another major war between Israel and Syria and Israel's steady drift toward an annexation of occupied territories.

Such annexation will eventually prove as dangerous to Israel as to U.S. and moderate Arab regimes. As former Israeli Foreign Minister Abba Eban has put it, Israel has only two alternatives to peace in trying to annex an Arab population whose birthrate will inevitably force new deportations or make it a majority within an expanded Israel. The first is to try to fully integrate the Arabs into Israel and become another Lebanon. The second is to keep the Arabs an oppressed minority and become another South Africa. Both are, in the long run, disastrous.

In contrast, if Israel eventually can reach a peace settlement, Israel's relations with the U.S. will eventually be transformed from a moral obligation to a strategic asset worth far more than the cost of any increases in U.S. aid. It will enable Israel to deal with the conservative and friendly Arab states. It will create the hope, eventually, of bringing true strategic stability to the Gulf and Near East and of freeing billions of dollars annually for use in civil development.

Notes

1. This chapter draws heavily on John Keegan, *World Armies* (New York: Facts on File, 1979); *Military Balance* and *Strategic Survey* (London: IISS, various years); the *War Data* and *Born in Battle* series; Trevor N. Dupuy, *Elusive Victory, The Arab-Israeli Wars, 1947–1974* (New York: Harper & Row, 1978); various writings by Geoffrey Kemp; numerous U.S., British, Israeli, and Arab media sources; and interviews during 1980, 1981, 1982, and 1983.

2. *New York Times,* 15 December 1981; 26 and 28 April, 4 and 29 May, 11 and 13 August 1982; *Washington Post,* 25 April, 10 May, 12 September, 10 October, 10 December 1982; *Christian Science Monitor,* 4 May 1982; *Baltimore Sun,* 4 and 30 May, 13 August 1982; *Los Angeles Times,* 4 May 1982.

3. See Dupuy's authoritative *Elusive Victory.*

4. Figures taken from Otto von Pikva, *Armies of the Middle East* (New York: Mayflower, 1979), pp. 23, 32. It should be noted that in testimony before the Senate Foreign Relations Committee on 21 September 1976, Professor Alan Dowty of the Department of Government and International Studies of the University of Notre Dame claimed that 12 Saudis were captured by Israel in

the October War, although it is unclear whether they were in a rear area combat or support role.

5. Current strengths are based on *Military Balance, 1981–82;* Keegan, *World Armies,* pp. 607–622; and *War Data,* nos. 8 and 9.

6. See Chapters 7–9 for full details.

7. This problem would be worsened by the fact that Saudi Arabia's only combat-capable armored brigade is French equipped, as are all major Saudi units operating out of Tabuk. Jordan could not support French equipment effectively, and Saudi Arabia will not have combat-ready, brigade-strength, U.S.-equipped units at Hafr al-Batin until the late 1980s.

8. Assumes performance equivalent to peak USAF performance standards. Saudi Arabia currently does not train below 10,000 feet in Saudi Arabia or practice jamming or any other form of electronic warfare.

9. The Arabs suffered 14 : 1 air-to-air loss ratios in 1973. Dupuy, *Elusive Victory,* p. 609.

10. These details are taken from White House briefings of 23 April 1981; DOD background papers of 24 April 1981; and various DOD background papers of August and September 1981. More details are available in Royal United Services Institute/Brassey, *International Weapons Developments* (London, 1980), pp. 161–163; various editions of *Jane's All the World's Aircraft;* Jane's *Defense Review* 2, no. 2 (1981):133–139.

11. This would be just as true of the Nimrod as of the E-3A. While rumors have surfaced that Saudi Arabia might also buy 3–5 Nimrods, these lack the range of the E-3A and would be even more vulnerable. *Christian Science Monitor,* 6 May 1982.

12. The IDF could read E-3A UHF transmissions with only commercial encryption up to 200 kilometers on a line-of-sight basis. The predictable orbit made the E-3A vulnerable to low-powered noise jammers, as well as dedicated logic jammers, and the Israelis could adapt their IFF to show up on the E-3A's radar as Saudi fighters.

13. Any such ratios are highly approximate, but these ratios seem logical given the shifts in training and technology that would occur with AWACS and in view of the comparison of the exchange ratios in Dupuy's study of the October War and in combat environments like Vietnam.

14. This again assumes some solution to operating the F-15 out of Tabuk. It is unclear how effective any temporary arrangement would be, however, and Saudi performance without such a solution would be much worse than these estimates indicate.

15. For example, see Israel Tal, "Israel's Defense Doctrine: Background and Dynamics," *Military Review,* no. 58 (March 1978):23–37; Benny Morris, "New Strategic Thinking in Israel," *Armed Forces Journal,* September 1980, pp. 82–91; Hirsh Goodman, "Strategic Crossroads," *Jerusalem Post,* 5–11 April 1981; Douglas J. Murray and Paul R. Viotti, *The Defense Policies of Nations* (Baltimore: Johns Hopkins University Press, 1982), pp. 371–402.

16. The National Guard is now armed only with 150 V-150 Commando APCs and Vulcan AA guns. It has 20,000–35,000 men, depending on the estimates, many serving part time. See Chapter 11.

17. The Saudi Army was discussing plans to buy up to 90 helicopters by 1985–1986, before major cuts occurred in its oil revenues. In late 1981 seven companies—Bell, MBB, Sikorsky, Boeing, Vertol, Hughes, Aerospatiale, and Westland—were asked to make proposals for an initial force of 15 observation

and 12 utility helicopters to be deployed at three bases in Saudi Arabia. The types being considered were the UH-60, Bell 214, OH-58, CH-47, Hughes 500 MD, Gazelle, Super Puma, Dauphine 2, BO-105, and Lynx. Some options involved links to the existing Northrop or Lockheed support effort. The National Guard also was studying an initial purchase of 12 helicopters for frontier patrol, troop transport, and liaison. The Bell CH-47, Super Puma, and Commando 3 were under consideration. The status of these discussions is now uncertain. *International Defense Review* 2 (1982):136.

18. Saudi Arabia will also not have any main tank equivalent to the Israeli Merkava, the 278 Khalid on order by Jordan, or the Soviet-built T-80s likely to then be in the Syrian and Iraqi inventories. The capability of the Saudi AMX-30 to defeat the main armor on the Isralei Markava main battle tanks at long ranges is uncertain.

19. Britain was actively seeking FRG permission to offer the Tornado to Saudi Arabia in late 1981. Rumors that the Saudis have financed the development of the Mirage 2000 by Dassault as a "private venture" seem to be correct.

20. The Saudi F-15 will not have the U.S. program support package (PSP) to use its radar to optimal advantage in the attack role. Its APG-63 radar lacks the signal processor for high-resolution radar ground mapping or raid assessment. The Saudi F-15 can detect only city-sized targets or land-water contrast. It has no MTI capability, and the U.S. "threat" tape is not releasable to foreign nationals. It also lacks Mark IV IFF. These features are unimportant in a Gulf defense role but critical in a conflict with Israel.

21. Many of the technical issues involved are discussed in the "Combat Aircraft," *International Defense Review,* special edition, 1976, pp. 51–74. The technical description of the Strike Eagle is taken from a 1981 McDonnell-Douglas press release. Also see "The U.S. Export Fighters," *International Defense Review* 1 (1981):83–87. The analysis in this section has been confirmed with USAF and McDonnell-Douglas sources.

22. The numbers and analysis used in this section are taken from a variety of sources. These include *The Military Balance, 1982–83* (London: IISS, 1983); SIPRI special computer printouts on arms transfers to the Near East; von Pikva, *Armies of the Middle East;* Keegan, *World Armies;* various articles in the *Armed Forces Journal* and *International Defense Review;* the "National Security" section of the Joint Economic Committee, *Political Economy of the Middle East, 1973–78,* (Washington, D.C., 21 April 1980); articles by various Israeli authors, including Yoram Peri, "Israel's Defense in the 1980s," *Defense Attache,* August 1980, pp. 35–43, and the Israeli-published *Born in Battle* series (Jerusalem: Eshel-Dramit); and interviews with various Western and local experts.

23. The Nimrod may be significantly less vulnerable to jamming.

24. Israel used this technique, plus ECM, to deceive Jordanian and Iraqi radars during the IAF's attack on the Osirak reactor. *New York Times,* 10 June 1981, p. 27.

25. It cannot be stressed too firmly, however, that this analysis applies only to the Arab use of the Saudi-configured E-3A against Israel, and not to Israel's use of the E-2C, E-3A, or even the radar on the F-15 in defense of Israel. In contrast to the Arabs, Israel "looks out" of a small airspace into large surrounding airspace that it cannot cover with ground-based radars. It would thus benefit significantly from the E-3A's low-altitude coverage of its territory, its vast improvement in medium-to-high altitude coverage and low-altitude coverage in selected areas not subject to terrain masking, and its ability to send secure,

digitally processed data to Israel's homogeneous, well-equipped, and tightly disciplined fighter force. Although an Israeli AWACS would still be vulnerable, it would give Israel enough additional air defense battle-management capability to deal with any credible Arab "saturation" attacks and would effectively "extend" Israel's airspace by providing sensor coverage of many Arab air movements far beyond Israel's border and of a number of key Syrian, Egyptian, and Jordanian main air bases. Unlike the Arabs, Israel is strong enough to operate the E-3A only part time, rather than in the continuous surveillance mode, and thus reduce its vulnerability and predictability. While the AWACS may be too expensive for the IAF, it is a potentially important tool in providing Israel with the technical compensation it would need to give up the Sinai airspace and sensor coverage it has had in the West Bank and Golan.

26. The MiG-25 variant with look-down/shoot-down capability is optimized against bombers and is not really suited for high-intensity fighter combat with Israel.

27. Israel's "occupied" air space shrank from 60,000 square kilometers to about 21,000, including the Golan and West Bank, after full return of the Sinai in April 1982. CIA, *National Basic Intelligence Fact Book* (Washington, D.C.: Government Printing Office, July 1979), pp. 96–97.

28. According to various DOD background briefings, the AWACS would also require a reprogramming of its software to do even an inefficient job of battle management under these conditions. Since sale of the AWACS does not provide access to its software programming, which is perhaps the most complex single aspect of its technology, it is unclear where Saudi Arabia could get such support. This again raises the prospect of risking a $20 billion investment to provide a marginal increment to Arab military capabilities.

29. As was discussed earlier and shown on Map 21.2, such a mission requires AWACS to operate the radar in the pulse Doppler and elevation scan mode. In this mode, AWACS has a maximum range of about 208 NM flying at 29,000 feet and a usual operating range of only 175 statute miles. It would still be subject at this altitude to slant masking by a number of terrain features in the area. Saudi Arabia could fly such missions from Saudi airspace near bases at Turayf, Gurayat, and Tabuk. It would probably, however, have to move much closer to Israel and operate from over Jordan or Syria to provide optimal coverage in this role, which would make it far more vulnerable than in flying in Gulf defense modes. See Kenneth Munson, "Boeing's E-3A *Sentry,*" *Jane's Defense Review* 2 (1981):129–133; *Aviation Week,* 24 March 1980, pp. 40–42; 30 March 1981, pp. 61–63; *Air Force,* June 1979.

30. This would require creating such a Saudi-Jordanian capability without U.S. or Israeli detection by covertly buying AWACS data terminals and down links for Jordan's 14 Improved Hawk batteries, massively restructuring Jordan's C^3 system and AC&W center, and training Jordanian pilots and SAM crews in Saudi Arabia. It must be regarded as extremely unlikely.

31. CIA, *World Factbook, 1981,* p. 96.

32. Current statistics are taken from numerous sources, including the *Washington Post,* 2 January and 18 August 1980; 11 May and 14 July 1983; *Baltimore Sun,* 12 September 1979, p. 2; 16 October 1982; 17 and 26 June 1983; *Washington Star,* 19 June 1980, p. 6; *Aviation Week,* 25 August 1980, p. 11; *Wall Street Journal,* 15 July 1980, p. 1; 26 June 1981; 14 June, 14 and 16 July 1982; 7 April, 26 May, 13 July 1983; *New York Times,* 26 June 1981; 14 July and 8 August 1982; 1, 10, and 26 May, 15 June, 5 and 10 July 1983; *Christian Science Monitor,* 9 August and 8 December 1982; 5 July 1983.

33. *Washington Post,* 13 August 1982; *Los Angeles Times,* 13 August 1982; 13 and 26 May, 5 and 12 July 1983; *Newsweek,* 1 November 1982, pp. 46–48; GAO, *U.S. Assistance to the State of Israel,* ID-83-51 (Washington, D.C.: GAO, 24 June 1983), pp. 24–40, 76–81.

34. *Wall Street Journal,* 16 April 1982; *Baltimore Sun,* 16 October 1982; *Christian Science Monitor,* 8 December 1982.

35. *New York Times,* 22 February 1982; 26 May and 5 July 1983; *Wall Street Journal,* 14 June 1982; *Washington Post,* 13 August 1982; 26 May 1983.

36. Total aid to Egypt and Israel was originally requested in the amount of $4.8 billion, with $2.5 billion for Israel and $2.3 billion for Egypt. Israel would receive $500 million in forgiven FMS loans and $900 million in FMS loan guarantees. On 30 November 1982 the Congress provided $125 million in additional economic aid and shifted $350 million in military aid from loans to grants. Jordan would receive $75 million in loan guarantees. This was out of a worldwide total of $1.73 billion in FMS loans and $3.92 billion in loan guarantees. *New York Times,* 28 March 1982; 26 May 1983; *Aviation Week,* 26 April 1982, pp. 22–23; *Chicago Sun Times,* 2 March 1982; *Christian Science Monitor,* 14 December 1982; *Washington Post,* 11 May 1983.

37. *Baltimore Sun* and *Christian Science Monitor,* 11 September 1981; *Washington Post,* 11 September and 19 December 1981; *New York Times,* 12 September and 31 December 1981; 28 March 1982; 15 June and 10 July 1983; *Washington Times,* 27 May 1982; 15 June 1983; GAO, *U.S. Assistance to the State of Israel,* pp. 37–40, 42–58.

38. Before President Sadat's death, the U.S. had agreed to spend $100 million to upgrade the Egyptian base at Ras Banas over a three-year period—a program that is now the subject of considerable U.S. and Egyptian debate over how it should be funded and over U.S. rights once the project is completed. It also had agreed to provide about $1 billion (in FY1980 dollars) in military sales every year through FY1987. President Carter had extended $2.05 billion in FMS credits for purchases that included 35 F-4s, 12 Improved Hawk batteries, 1,300 APCs, 311 M-60 tanks, and 40 F-16 jets. Secretary Haig indicated U.S. aid would be further increased the day after President Sadat's funeral, and this was done in the U.S. aid request for FY1982. *Baltimore Sun,* 8 Septmeber 1981, p. 4; *Washington Post,* 12 September 1981, p. 1; *Aviation Week,* 26 April 1982.

39. See Anthony H. Cordesman, *Jordan and the Middle East Balance* (Washington, D.C.: Middle East Institute, February 1983); *Congressional Record,* 7 April 1981, p. H1359; and *Washington Post,* 2 January and 18 August 1980, for background on these estimates.

40. Israel received not only $2.206 billion in FY1982 from the U.S. government, but also $285 million in gifts whose tax-free status is subsidized by the U.S. taxpayer.

41. David Shipler, "Soviet Jews," *New York Times,* 13 September 1981; *Washington Post,* 17 June 1982.

42. Drora Kass and Seymour Lipset, "America's New Wave of Jewish Immigrants," *New York Times Magazine,* 13 September 1981, p. 44.

43. Shipler, "Soviet Jews"; Jewish Agency, press release, December 1982.

44. Lally Weymouth, "Begin vs. Peres, What It Means to America," *Parade Magazine,* 14 June 1981, p. 48.

45. In January 1981 the total population of Israel was 3,814,000, excluding East Jerusalem and the occupied territories, with a 2.3% growth rate—predom-

inantly composed of Oriental Jewish and Arab births. The population was 85% Jewish and 15% non-Jewish—largely Arab. The religious composition was 85% Jewish, 11% Muslim, and 4% Christian and other. The labor force was 1,252,000, with 24% in industry, 30% in public services, 7% in construction, 7% in finance and business, 7% in personal services, and 6% in agriculture. Literacy was 88% among Jews and 48% among Arabs. CIA, *World Factbook, 1981,* p. 96.

46. Peri, "Israel's Defense in the 1980's," p. 42.

47. Iraq deployed only two divisions in 1972 and allowed only limited forces to fight under its own control. There is still considerable debate as to whether Syria "set up" Iraqi and Jordanian forces so they would take heavy casualties and escalate their involvement. Officers in the armies and air forces of both nations have mentioned their suspicions in this regard.

48. Peri, "Israel's Defense in the 1980's," p. 42.

49. *New York Times,* 19, 21, 22 December 1981; *Washington Post,* 19, 22, 31 December 1981; *Baltimore Sun,* 19 December 1981.

50. *New York Times, Christian Science Monitor, Washington Post,* and *Baltimore Sun,* 11 September 1981. Interestingly enough, IDF spokesmen later claimed that U.S. forces with equipment dispositions in Israel could reach Dhahran overland in 3 days and Kuwait in 36 hours vesus 20 days from the U.S. and 17 days from Ras Banas. They neglected to explain how the U.S. would pass through Jordan or Syria, or move unopposed at maximum road speed from Israel across states with which Israel was at war. *New York Times,* 9 October 1981.

51. See the *Christian Science Monitor,* 9 August 1982; *Economist,* 13 February 1982; *Baltimore Sun,* 26 February and 11 March 1982; *Los Angeles Times,* 26 February 1982; *New York Times,* 14 April 1982; *Washington Post,* 13 August 1982, for only a few of many indications that this is likely.

52. A "senior U.S. defense official" made this point in a press conference timed to coincide with the Reagan-Begin meeting. *New York Times,* 12 September 1981, p. 3. For the agreements text see the *New York Times,* 19 December 1981.

53. *New York Times* and *Washington Post,* 12 December 1981.

Abbreviations

AA: antiaircraft
AACO: Arab Air Carriers Organisation
AAM: air-to-air missile
ACDA: Arms Control and Disarmament Agency
ACM: air combat maneuver
AC&W: air control and warning
ADC: army air defense control
ADDF: Abu Dhabi Defense Force
ADIZ: Air Defense Intercept Zone
AEI: Associated Electronics Industry
AEW&C: airborne early warning and control
AFB: air force base
AFV: armored fighting vehicle
AID: Agency for International Development
AISC: Arab Iron and Steel Company
ALBA: Aluminium Bahrain
ANM: Arab Nationalist Movements
APC: armored personnel carrier
APPU: Arabian Peninsula People's Union
ARAMCO: Arabian-American Oil Company
ARIG: Arab Reinsurance Group
ARM: antiradiation missile
ASM: air-to-surface missile
ASW: antisubmarine warfare
ATC: air traffic control
ATGM: antitank guided missile
ATGW: antitank guided weapon
AWACS: airborne warning and air control system

BAC: British Aircraft Corporation
BANOCO: Bahrain National Oil Company
BCF: billion cubic feet
BCFD: billion cubic feet per day
bd: brigade
BDM: Braddock, Dunn, and McDonald
bn: battalion
BPD: barrels per day
bty: battery

C^2: command and control
C^3: command, control, and communications
C^3I: command, control, communications, and intelligence
CAP: combat air patrol
CASOC: California Arabia Standard Oil Company
CENTO: Central Treaty Organization
CGE: central government expenditures
CIA: Central Intelligence Agency
CIEC: Conference on International Economic Cooperation
COMECON: Council of Mutual Economic Assistance
COMINT: communications intelligence
CONUS: continental United States
CRAF: Civil Air Reserve Fleet

DB: decibel
DIA: Defense Intelligence Agency
DLF: Dhofar Liberation Front
DOD: Department of Defense
DOE: Department of Energy
DSAA: Defense Security Assistance Agency
dwt: deadweight ton

EAA: Engineering Assistance Agreement
EAF: Ethiopian Air Force
ECCM: electronic counter-countermeasures
ECM: electronic countermeasures
EEC: European Economic Community
ELF: Eritrean Liberation Front
EIA: Energy Information Administration
ELINT: electronic intelligence
ESM: electronic support measures
EURATOM: European Atomic Energy Community
EW: electronic warfare

FAC: fleet auxiliary craft
FEBA: forward edge of the battle area
FGA: fighter ground attack
FLOSY: Front for the Liberation of South Yemen
FMS: foreign military sales
FRG: Federal Republic of Germany

GAO: General Accounting Office
GARMCO: Gulf Aluminium Rolling Mill Company
GCC: Gulf Cooperation Council
GCI: ground-controlled intercept
GDP: gross domestic product
GIB: Gulf International Bank
GNA: Gulf News Agency
GNP: gross national product
GOC: General Operating Center
GOSP: gas-oil separator
GPDC: Gulf pipeline Development Council

HTTB: high-technology test bed
HUD: heads-up display
HUMINT: human intelligence

IAF: Israeli Air Force
ICBM: intercontinental ballistic missile
ICP: Iraqi Communist party
IDA: International Development Authority
IDF: Israeli Defense Force
IEA: International Energy Agency
IFF: identification friend or foe
IFIRN: Iraqi Front of Revolutionary, Islamic, and National Forces
IFV: infantry fighting vehicle
IISS: International Institute for Strategic Studies
IMF: International Monetary Fund
IR: infrared
IRBM: intermediate-range ballistic missile
IRP: Islamic Revolutionary party

JCEC: Joint Commission on Economic Cooperation
JCS: Joint Chiefs of Staff
JTIDS: Joint Tactical Information Distribution System

KAF: Kuwaiti Air Force
KDP: Kurdish Democratic party
KPU: Kurdish Patriotic Union
KSP: Kurdish Socialist party

LAV: light armored vehicle
LCAC: air-cushioned landing craft
LCM: landing craft medium
LCT: landing craft tank
LCU: landing craft utility
LDC: less developed country
LGB: laser-guided bomb
LOA: letter of agreement
LOC: line of communication
LPC: light patrol craft
LPD: amphibious transport dock

LPG: liquid propane gas
LRA: long-range aviation
LSL: light logistic support ship
LSM: landing ship medium
LST: landing ship tank

MAB: marine amphibious brigade
MAP: Military Assistance Program
MAGTF: marine air-ground task force
MBD: thousand barrels per day
MBT: main battle tank
MCC: Military Command Council
MCFD: million cubic feet per day
MD: military district
MEED: *Middle East Economic Digest*
MER: multiple ejection rack
MMB: million barrels
MMBD: million barrels per day
MOD: Ministry of Defense
MODA: Ministry of Defense and Aviation
MOFF: Muscat and Oman Field Force
MPS: maritime prepositioning ship
MRBM: medium-range ballistic missile
MSC: Military Sealift Command
MTI: moving target indicator

NATO: North Atlantic Treaty Organization
NCO: noncommissioned officer
NDF: National Democratic Front
NDFLOAG: National Democratic Front for the Liberation of the Occupied Arab Gulf
NDPF: National Democratic and Patriotic Front
NDRF: National Defense Reserve Fleet
NGL: natural gas liquids
NILF: National Islamic Liberation Front
NLF: National Liberation Front
NM: nautical mile
NORAD: North American Air Defense
NSC: National Security Council
NTPF: near-term prepositioned force
NTPS: near-term prepositioned ship

OAPEC: Organization of Arab Petroleum Exporting Countries
OBU: overseas banking unit
OECD: Organisation of Economic Co-operation and Development
OJCS: Office of the Joint Chiefs of Staff
OPEC: Organization of Petroleum Exporting Countries
OSS: Office of Strategic Services

PAF: Pakistani Air Force
PC: patrol craft
PCG: patrol chaser (missile) craft
PCM: patrol craft medium
PDFLOAG: People's Democratic Front for the Liberation of the Occupied Arab Gulf
PDRY: People's Democratic Republic of Yemen
PDS: passive defense system
PFLO: Popular Front for the Liberation of Oman
PFLOAG: Popular Front for the Liberation of the Occupied Arab Gulf
PGG: light guided missile patrol craft
PGM: patrol craft (guided missile) medium
PGM: precision-guided missile
PIC: Petrochemical Industries Corporation
PLO: Palestine Liberation Organization
POL: petroleum, oil, and lubricants
PRC: People's Republic of China
PSP: program support package
PUK: Kurdish Patriotic Union

QRA: quick reaction alert

RAF: Royal Air Force
RAMIS: reporting, analysis, and management information system
RCC: Revolutionary Command Council
RCL: recoilless rifle
R&D: research and development
RDF: Rapid Deployment Force
RDJTF: Rapid Deployment Joint Task Force
REDCOM: Readiness Command
reg: regiment
RFP: request for proposal
RO/RO: roll-on/roll-off
RRF: Ready Reserve Force
RSAF: Royal Saudi Air Force

SAC: Strategic Air Command
SABIC: Saudi Arabian Basic Industries Corporation
SAF: Sultan's Armed Forces
SAM: surface-to-air missile
SAMA: Saudi Arabian Monetary Agency
SAMP: Saudi Arabian Mobility Program
SAR: synthetic aperture radar
SAS: Special Air Services
SAVAK: Iranian Secret Police
SCC: sector coordinating center
SDECE: Service de la Documentation Extèrieure et du Contre-Espionage
SDR: special drawing right
SFRC: Senate Foreign Relations Committee
SHORAD: short-range air defense
SIGINT: signal intelligence
SIPRI: Stockholm International Peace Research Institute
SLBM: submarine-launched ballistic missile
SNA: Soviet naval aviation
SNEP: Saudi Naval Expansion Program
SOAF: Sultan of Oman's Air Force
SOC: sectoral operating center
SOCAL: Standard Oil of California
SOLF: Sultan of Oman's Land Forces
SP: self-propelled
SPM: single-point moorings
SPR: strategic petroleum reserve
sqn: squadron
SSBN: nuclear ballistic missile submarine
SSM: surface-to-surface missile

TAA: tactical air army
TAFT: Technical Advisory Field Team
TOE: table of organization and equipment

UAE: United Arab Emirates
UAEAF: United Arab Emirates Air Force
UAR: United Arab Republic
UAS: United Arab States
UASC: United Arab Shipping Company
UDF: Federal Union Defense Force
UN: United Nations
UNRWA: United Nations Relief and Works Agency
USAF: United States Air Force
USCENTCOM: U.S. Central Command
USCINCEUR: U.S. Commander-in-Chief, Europe
USMTM: U.S. Military Training Missions
USN: United States Navy

VLCC: very large crude carrier
VTA: Military Transport Command

YAR: Yemen Arab Republic
YSP: Yemeni Socialist party

Bibliography

Abdullah, Muhammad Morsy. *The United Arab Emirates, A Modern History.* New York: Barnes and Noble, 1978.

Abed, George. "Arab Oil-Exporters in the World Economy." *American-Arab Affairs*, no. 3 (Winter 1982-1983):26–40.

Abellera, James W., and Rolf Clark. "Forces of Habit: Budgeting for Tomorrow's Fleets." *Foreign Policy and Defense Review* (AEI) 3, no. 2-3 (1981).

Abolfathi, Faird, Keyon, Gary, et al. *The OPEC Market to 1985*. Lexington, Mass.: Lexington Books, 1977.

Aburdene, Odeh. "Falling Oil Prices and the World Economy." *American-Arab Affairs*, no. 4 (Spring 1983):46–52.

Adan, Abraham. *On the Banks of Suez*. San Francisco: Presidio, 1980.

Adie, W.A.C. *Oil, Politics and Seapower, The Indian Ocean Vortex*. National Strategy Information Center, Inc. New York: Crane, Russak & Co., 1975.

Aerospace Daily.

Akehurst, John. *We Won a War: The Campaign in Oman, 1965–1975*. London: Michael Russel, 1982.

Alama, Muhammad. *Arabia Unified: A Portrait of Ibn Saud*. London: Hutchinson Benham, 1980.

Alessa, Shaiman Y. *The Manpower Problem in Kuwait*. London: Keegan Paul, 1982.

Alexander, Yonah, and Allan Nanes, eds. *The United States and Iran: A Documentary History*. Frederick, Md.: University Press of America, 1980.

al-Farsy, Foud. *Saudi Arabia: A Case Study in Development*. London: Stacey International, 1978.

Allan, J. A. *Libya: The Experience of Oil*. Boulder, Colo.: Westview Press, 1981.

Allon, Yigal. *The Making of Israel's Army*. New York: Bantam Books, 1971.

Almana, Mohammed. *Arabia Unified: A Portrait of Ibn Saud*. London: Hutchison Benham, 1980.

Amirsadeghi, Hossein, ed. *The Security of the Persian Gulf*. New York: St. Martin's Press, 1981.

Amos, John W. *Arab-Israel Military/Political Relations*. New York: Pergamon, 1979.

Anthony, John Duke. *Arab States of the Lower Gulf*. Washington, D.C.: Middle East Institute, 1975.

ARAMCO, *ARAMCO Handbook*, various years.

ARCO Series of Illustrated Guides. New York: Salamander Books, ARCO, 1982: *Weapons of the Modern Soviet Ground Forces; The Modern U.S. Air Force;*

The Modern Soviet Air Force; Military Helicopters; The Israeli Air Force; The Modern Soviet Navy; and *The Modern U.S. Navy.*

Arlinghaus, Bruce. *Arms for Africa.* Lexington, Mass.: Lexington Books, 1983.

Armed Forces Journal International.

Arnold, Anthony. *Afghanistan: The Soviet Invasion in Perspective.* Stanford, Calif.: Hoover Institution, 1981.

Auer, Peter, ed. *Energy and the Developing Nations.* New York: Pergamon, 1981.

Aviation Week and Space Technology.

Aviation Week. *Egypt's Shift to the West.* New York: McGraw-Hill, 1982.

Ayoob, Mohammed, ed. *The Middle East in World Politics.* London: Croom Helm, 1981.

Aziz, Tareq. *Iraq-Iran Conflict.* London: Third World Center, 1981.

Badri, Maj. Gen. Hassan el, Magdoub, Maj. Gen. Taha el, and Zhody, Maj. Gen. Mohammed Dia el Dia. *The Ramadam War, 1973.* New York: Hippocrene, 1974.

Bakhash, Shaul. "The Politics of Oil and Revolution in Iran." Staff paper. Washington, D.C.: Brookings Institution, 1982.

Ball, Desmond. *Can Nuclear War Be Controlled?* Adelphi Paper no. 169. London: International Institute for Strategic Studies, 1981.

Ball, George W. "The Coming Crisis in Israeli-American Relations." *Foreign Affairs,* Winter 1979–1980, pp. 231–256.

Baltimore Sun.

Banks, Ferdinand. *The Political Economy of Oil.* Lexington, Mass.: Lexington Books, 1980.

Bar Simon Tov, Yaacov. *The Israeli-Egyptian War of Attrition, 1969–1970.* New York: Columbia University Press, 1980.

Baram, Amazia. "Saddam Hussein—A Political Profile." *Jerusalem Quarterly,* no. 17 (Fall 1980):115–144.

Barker, A. J. *Arab-Israeli Wars.* New York: Hippocrene, 1980.

Bass, Gail, and Bonnie Jean Cordes. *Actions Against Non-Nuclear Energy Facilities: September 1981–September 1982.* Santa Monica, Calif.: Rand Corporation, April 1983.

Baylis, John, and Segal, Gerald, eds. *Soviet Strategy.* Totowa, N.J.: Allanheld, Osmun & Co., 1981.

Be'eri, Eliezer. *Army Officers in Arab Politics and Society.* New York: Praeger Publishers, 1970.

Behbehani, Hashim S. H. *China's Foreign Policy in the Arab World.* London: Keegan Paul, 1981.

Beling, Willard A., ed. *King Faisal and the Modernisation of Saudi Arabia.* Boulder, Colo.: Westview Press, 1980.

Bell, J. Bowyer. *The Horn of Africa.* Strategy Paper no. 21, National Strategy Information Center. New York: Crane, Russak & Co., 1973.

Ben Horin, Yoav, and Barry Posen. *Israel's Strategic Doctrine.* Santa Monica, Calif.: Rand Corporation, September 1981.

Ben Porat, Yeshayahu, et al. *Kippur.* Tel Aviv: Special Edition, 1973.

Benton, Graham M., and George H. Wittman. *Saudi Arabia and OPEC: An Operational Analysis.* Information Series no. 138. Fairfax, Va.: National Institute for Public Policy, March 1983.

Bertram, Christoph, ed. *Third World Conflict and International Security.* London: Macmillan, 1982.

Betts, Richard K. *Surprise Attack.* Washington, D.C.: Brookings Institution, 1982.

________. *Cruise Missiles.* Washington, D.C.: Brookings Institution, 1981.

Bidwell, Shelford. *Brassey's Artillery of the World.* London: Brassey, 1981.

Bill, James A. "Iran and the Crisis of '78." *Foreign Affairs,* Winter 1978–79, pp. 323–342.

Bin Talal, El Hassan. "Jordan's Quest for Peace." *Foreign Affairs,* Spring 1982, pp. 803–813.

Birks, J. S., and Sinclair, C. A. *Arab Manpower, The Crisis of Development.* New York: St. Martin's Press, 1980.

Bishara, Ghassan. "The Political Repercussions of the Israeli Raid on the Iraqi Nuclear Reactor." *Journal of Palestine Studies,* Spring 1982, pp. 58–76.

Blake, G. H., and Lawless, R. E. *The Changing Middle Eastern City.* New York: Barnes and Noble, 1980.

Boutros-Ghali. "The Foreign Policy of Egypt in the Post-Sadat Era." *Foreign Affairs,* Spring 1982, pp. 769–873.

Braibarti, Ralph, and Abdul-Salam, Al-Farsy. "Saudi Arabia: A Developmental Perspective." *Journal of South Asian and Middle Eastern Studies,* Fall 1977, p. 1.

Brassey's Defense Yearbook (later *RUSI and Brassey's Defense Yearbook*). London, various years.

Brodman, John R., and Hamilton, Richard E. *A Comparison of Energy Projections to 1985.* International Energy Agency Monograph Series. Paris: OECD, January 1979.

Campbell, John C. "The Middle East: House of Containment Built on Shifting Sands." *Foreign Affairs,* 1981, pp. 593–628.

Caradon, Lord (Sir Hugh Foot). *The Future of Jerusalem.* National Defense University Series No. 80-1. Washington, D.C., 1980.

Carlsen, Robin Woodsworth. *The Imam and His Islamic Revolution.* New York: Snow Man Press, 1982.

Carroll, Jane. *Kuwait, 1980.* London: MEED, 1980.

Carswell, Robert. "Economic Sanctions and Iran." *Foreign Affairs,* Winter 1981–82, pp. 247–265.

Carus, W. Seth. "The Military Balance of Power in the Middle East." *Current History,* January 1978.

Carver, Michael. *War Since 1945.* London: Weidenfeld and Nicolson, 1980.

Casadio, Gian Paolo. *The Economic Challenge of the Arabs.* London: Saxon House, 1977.

Chalian, Gerard. *Guerrilla Strategies.* Berkeley: University of California Press, 1982.

Chambers, Everett A. "Airlift: Finding the Plane to Fit the Mission." *Armed Forces Journal,* November 1982, pp. 40–47.

Chibwe. *Arab Dollars for Africa.* London: Croom Helm, 1976.

Choucri, Nazli. *International Politics of Energy Interdependence.* Lexington, Mass.: Lexington Books, 1976.

Christian Science Monitor (Boston).

Chubin, Shahram. "Gains for Soviet Policy in the Middle East." *International Security,* Spring 1982, pp. 122–173.

Chubin, Shahram. *Security in the Persian Gulf: The Role of Outside Powers.* London: International Institute for Strategic Studies, 1981.

———. "The Soviet Union and Iran." *Foreign Affairs*, Spring 1983, pp. 921–949.

Chubin, Shahram, ed. *Security in the Persian Gulf: Domestic Political Factors.* London: International Institute for Strategic Studies, 1980.

Cittadino, John, and McLeskey, Frank. "C³1 for the RDJTF." *Signal*, September 1981.

Clark, Ian. *Limited Nuclear War.* Princeton, N.J.: Princeton University Press, 1982.

Clark, Wilson, and Page, Jake. *Energy, Vulnerability, and War.* New York: W. W. Norton, 1981.

Clarke, John I., and Bowen-Jones, Howard. *Change and Development in the Middle East.* New York: Methuen, 1981.

Clemens, Walter C. *The U.S.S.R. and Global Interdependence.* Washington, D.C.: American Enterprise Institute, 1978.

Clements, F. A. *Oman, The Reborn Land.* New York: Longman, 1980.

Cleron, Jean Paul. *Saudi Arabia 2000.* London: Croom Helm, 1978.

Cline, Ray S. *World Power Assessment: A Calculus of Strategic Drift.* Boulder, Colo.: Westview Press, 1975.

Collins, John M. *U.S.-Soviet Military Balance, 1960–1980.* New York: McGraw-Hill, 1980.

Collins, John M., and Cordesman, Anthony M. *Imbalance of Power.* San Rafael, Calif.: Presidio Press, 1978.

Collins, John M. and Mark, Clyde R. *Petroleum Imports from the Persian Gulf: Use of U.S. Armed Force to Ensure Supplies.* Issue Brief IB 79046. Washington, D.C.: Library of Congress, Congressional Research Service, 1979.

Collins, Joseph. "Afghanistan: The Empire Strikes Out." *Parameters, Journal of the U.S. Army War College* 12, no. 1 (1982).

Collins, Michael. "Riyadh: The Saudi Balance." *Washington Quarterly*, Winter 1981.

Cooley, John K. *Libyan Sandstorm.* New York: Holt, Rinehart and Winston, 1982.

Congressional Budget Office. *Cost of Modernizing and Expanding the Navy's Carrier-Based Air Forces.* Washington, D.C.: Congressional Budget Office, May 1982.

———. *Rapid Deployment Forces: Policy and Budgetary Implications.* Washington, D.C.: CBO Press, February 1983.

Congressional Research Service, Library of Congress. *Oil Fields as Military Objectives.* No. S6-S520. Washington, D.C.: Government Printing Office, 1975.

———. *Project Interdependence: U.S. and World Energy Outlook Through 1990.* No. 95-31. Washington, D.C.: Government Printing Office, 1977.

———. *Soviet Policy and the United States Response in the Third World.* Washington, D.C.: Government Printing Office, 1981.

Corcoran, Kevin R. *Saudi Arabia: The Keys to Business Success.* London: McGraw-Hill, 1981.

Cordesman, Anthony H. "After AWACS: Establishing Western Security Throughout Southwest Asia." *Armed Forces Journal*, December 1981, pp. 64–68.

———. *American Strategic Forces and Extended Deterrence.* Adelphi Paper no. 175. London: International Institute for Strategic Studies, 1982.

———. "The Falklands Crisis: Emerging Lessons for Power Projection and Force Planning." *Armed Forces Journal*, September 1982, pp. 29–46.

———. *Jordan and the Middle East Balance*. Washington, D.C.: Middle East Institute, 1978.

———. "Lessons of the Iran-Iraq War." *Armed Forces Journal*, April-June 1982, pp. 32–47, 68–85.

———. "Saudi Arabia, AWACS and America's Search for Strategic Stability." International Security Studies Program, Working Paper no. 26A. Washington, D.C.: Wilson Center, 1981.

Cottrell, Alvin J. *The Persian Gulf States*. Baltimore: Johns Hopkins University Press, 1980.

Cottrell, Alvin J., and Hanks, Robert J. "The Strait of Hormuz: Strategic Chokepoint." In *Sea Power and Strategy in the Indian Ocean*. Beverly Hills, Calif.: Sage Publications, 1981.

Crane, Robert D. *Planning the Future of Saudi Arabia: A Model for Achieving National Priorities*. New York: Praeger Publishers, 1978.

Croan, Melvin. "A New *Afrika Korps*?" *Washington Quarterly*, no. 3 (Winter 1980):21–37.

Cummings, J. H., Askari, H., and Skinner, M. "Military Expenditures and Manpower Requirements in the Arabian Peninsula." *Arab Studies Quarterly* 2 (1980).

Curtis, Richard H. *A Changing Image: American Perceptions of the Arab-Israeli Dispute*. Washington, D.C.: American Educational Trust, 1982.

Daniels, John. *Abu Dhabi: A Portrait*. London: Longman, 1974.

David, Steven. "Realignment in the Horn: The Soviet Advantage." *International Security*, no. 4 (Fall 1979):69–90.

Davis, Jacquelyn K., and Pfaltzgraff, Robert L. *Power Projection and the Long Range Combat Aircraft*. Cambridge, Mass.: Institute for Foreign Policy Analysis, June 1981.

Dawisha, Adeed I. *Saudi Arabia's Search for Security*. Adelphi Paper no. 158. London: International Institute for Strategic Studies, Winter 1979-1980.

———. "Iraq: The West's Opportunity." *Foreign Policy*, no. 41 (Winter 1980-81):134–154.

Dawisha, Karen. *Soviet Foreign Policy Towards Egypt*. New York: St. Martin's Press, 1979.

Day, Bonner, ed. "Conserving Energy and Combat Readiness." *Air Force Magazine*, October 1969, p. 67.

Dayan, Moshe. *Breakthrough*. New York: Alfred A. Knopf, 1981.

De Gaury, Gerald. *Faisal: King of Saudi Arabia*. New York: Frederick A. Praeger, 1966.

Digby, James. "Alternatives to Nuclear Weapons." *Wall Street Journal*, October 13, 1982, p. 30.

Doran, Charles F. "Leading Indicators of the June War: A Micro-Analysis of the Conflict Cycle." *International Journal of Middle East Studies*, no. 11 (February 1980):23–58.

Dougherty, James E. *The Horn of Africa: A Map of Political-Strategic Conflict*. Cambridge, Mass.: Institute for Foreign Policy Analysis, 1982.

Dunn, Keith A. "Constraints on the U.S.S.R. in Southwest Asia: A Military Analysis." *Orbis* 25, no. 3 (Fall 1981):607–629.

Dunn, Lewis A., and Kahn, Herman. *Trends in Nuclear Proliferation, 1975–1995* (HI-2479/2-RR). Croton-on-Hudson, N.Y.: Hudson Institute, 1977.

Dupuy, Trevor N. *Elusive Victory: The Arab-Israeli Wars, 1947–1974*. New York: Harper & Row, 1978.

———. *Numbers, Predictions and War.* New York: Bobbs-Merrill, 1979.
Durby, Phillip. *British Defense Policy East of Suez, 1947–68.* London, 1973.
Economist.
8 Days, Middle East Business (London: Falconwood Publications).
Eilts, Herman F. "Security Considerations in the Persian Gulf." *International Security* 5, no. 2, pp. 79–113.
Elazar, David. *The Camp David Framework for Peace.* American Enterprise Institute no. 236. Washington, D.C., 1979.
El-Edroos, Brigadier S. A. *The Hashemite Arab Army, 1908–1979.* Amman, Publishing Committee, 1980.
Epstein, Joshua M. "Soviet Vulnerabilities in Iran and the RDF Deterrent." *International Security* 6, no. 2 (Fall 1981):126–180.
Eshel, David. *Born in Battle.*" Series nos. 1, 3, 12, and 16. Tel Aviv: Eshel-Dramit, 1978 and 1980.
———. *The Israeli Air Force.* Mid-East Wars Series. Tel Aviv: Eshel-Dramit, 1978.
———. *War Data.* Series nos. 1, 2, 5, and 8. Tel Aviv: Eshel-Dramit, 1979 and 1981.
Eshel, Lt. Col. D. *The Israeli Air Force.* Tel Aviv: Eshel-Dramit, 1980.
Eshel, Lt. Col. D. *Peace for Galilee.* Special edition of the Born in Battle Series. Tel Aviv: Eshel-Dramit, 1982.
Europa. *The Middle East and North Africa, 1981–82.* London: Europa, 1981.
Evans-Smith, William. *Iran: A Country Study.* Foreign Area Handbook Series. Washington, D.C.: American University, 1978.
Eveland, Wilbur Crane. *Ropes of Sand: America's Failure in the Middle East.* New York: W. W. Norton, 1980.
Evron, Yair. *An American-Israeli Defense Treaty,* no. 14. Tel Aviv: Center for Strategic Studies, Tel Aviv University, December 1981.
Feldman, Shai. "A Nuclear Middle East." *Survival* 23, no. 3 (May-June 1981):107–116.
———. "Israel's Security." *Foreign Affairs,* Spring 1981, pp. 756–780.
———. *Israeli Nuclear Deterrence, A Strategy for the 1980s.* New York: Columbia University Press, 1982.
Feuchtwanger, E. J., and Nailor, Peter. *The Soviet Union and The Third World.* London: Macmillan, 1981.
Fiennes, Sir Ranulph. *Where Soldiers Fear to Tread.* London: Hodder & Stoughton, 1975.
Financial Times (London and Frankfurt).
Fischer, Michael M. J. *Iran: From Religious Dispute to Revolution.* Cambridge, Mass.: Harvard University Press, 1980.
Fisher, W. B. *The Middle East: A Physical, Social and Regional Geography.* New York: E. P. Dutton & Co., 1963.
For Your Eyes Only (F.Y.E.O.), 1981–2 World Armed Forces Strength Assessment. New York: Simulations Publications, 1982.
Forbis, William H. *The Fall of the Peacock Throne.* New York: McGraw-Hill, 1981.
Freedman, Robert O., ed. *World Politics and the Arab-Israeli Conflict.* London: Pergamon, 1979.
Fukuyama, Frances. *The Soviet Union and Iraq Since 1968.* Santa Monica, Calif.: RAND, N-1524, AF. 1980.

Furlong, R.D.M. "Israel Lashes Out." *International Defense Review* (Geneva) 15, no. 8 (1982):1001–1003.

Gail, Bridget, "The West's Jugular Vein: Arab Oil." *Armed Forces Journal International*, 1978, p. 18.

Gazit, Shlomo. "Risk, Glory and the Rescue Operation." *International Security*, Summer 1981, pp. 111–135.

Ghadar, Fariborz. *The Evolution of OPEC Strategy*. Lexington, Mass.: Lexington Books, 1977.

Ghassan, Salameh. *The Kurdish Question in Iraq*. Syracuse, N.Y.: Syracuse University Press, 1981.

———. "Saudi Arabia: Development and Dependence." *Jerusalem Quarterly*, no. 16 (Summer 1980):137–144.

Ghareeb, Edmund. *The Kurdish Question in Iraq*. Syracuse, N.Y.: Syracuse University Press, 1981.

Glassman, John D. *Arms for the Arabs*. Baltimore: Johns Hopkins University Press, 1975.

Grace, Col. J. J., U.S.M.C. (Ret.) "Land the Landing Force Where It Will Do the Most Good: A New Look at an Old Mission." *Proceedings of the Naval Institute/Naval Review*, 1981, pp. 114–131.

Grayson, Leslie E. *National Oil Companies*. New York: John Wiley, 1981.

Greene, Joseph N., et al. *The Path to Peace, Arab-Israeli Peace and the United States*. Mount Kisco, N.Y.: Seven Springs Center, 1981.

Griffith, William E. *The Middle East 1982: Politics, Revolutionary Islam, and American Policy*. Cambridge, Mass.: M.I.T. Press, 1982.

———. "The Revival of Islamic Fundamentalism: The Case of Iran." *International Security* 5, no. 4 (Spring 1981):49–73.

Grimaldi, Fulvio. "Whose War in the Yemens?" *Middle East*, April 1979, pp. 56–57.

Gross Stein, Janice. " 'Intelligence' and 'Stupidity' Reconsidered: Estimation and Decision in Israel, 1973." *Journal of Strategic Studies*, no. 3, (September 1980):147–177.

Grummon, Stephen R. *The Iran-Iraq War*. Washington Paper 92, Center for Strategic and International Studies. New York: Praeger Publishers, 1982.

Gulf Cooperation Council. *Cooperation Council for the Arab States of the Gulf, Information Handbook*. Riyadh: Bahr Al-Olum Press, 1982.

Gulf States (London: Middle East Newsletters, various years.

Haddad, George M. *Revolutions and Rule in the Middle East*. 3 vols. New York: Robert Speller and Sons, 1965.

Haley, P. Edward, and Snider, Lewis W., ed. *Lebanon in Crisis*. Syracuse, N.Y.: Syracuse University Press, 1979.

Halliday, Fred. *Arabia Without Sultans*. London: Pelican, 1975.

———. "Yemen's Unfinished Revolution: Socialism in the South." *MERIP Reports*, no. 81, Spring 1981, pp. 3–20.

Hammond, Thomas T. "Afghanistan and the Persian Gulf." *Survey: A Journal of East-West Relations* 26, no. 2(115) (Spring 1982):83–101.

Handel, Michael I. *Israel's Political Military Doctrine*. Cambridge, Mass.: Harvard University Press, 1973.

Hanrahan, Brian, and Fox, Robert. *I Counted Them All Out and I Counted Them All Back, The Battle for the Falklands*. London: BBC, 1982.

Hardt, John P. "Soviet Energy: Production and Exports." Issue Brief no. 1B75059, Library of Congress, Congressional Research Service. Washington, D.C., 1979.

Hargraves, D., and Fromson, S. *World Index of Strategic Minerals.* New York: Facts on File, 1983.

Harkabi, Yehoshafat. "Reflections on National Defence Policy." *Jerusalem Quareterly*, no. 18 (Winter 1981):121–140.

Hart, Jane Smiley. "Basic Chronology for a History of the Yemens." *Middle East Journal* 17 (Winter-Spring 1963):144–153.

Hawley, Donald. *The Trucial States.* London: George Allen & Unwin, 1970.

———. *Oman and Its Renaissance.* London: Stacey International, 1980.

Hedley, Don. *World Energy: The Facts and the Future.* London: Euromonitor, 1981.

Heikal, Mohamed. *Iran: The Untold Story.* New York: Pantheon, 1982 (also published as *The Return of the Ayatollah.* London: Andre Deutsch, 1981).

———. *The Road to Ramadan.* New York: Quadrangle, 1975.

Heikal, Mohamed Hassaud. *The Sphinx and the Commissars: The Rise and Fall of Soviet Influence in the Middle East.* New York: Harper & Row, 1978.

Heller, Mark. "Begin's False Autonomy." *Foreign Policy*, no. 37 (Winter 1979–80):111.

———. *A Palestinian State: The Implications for Israel.* Cambridge, Mass.: Harvard University Press, 1983.

Helms, Christian Moss. *The Cohesion of Saudi Arabia.* Baltimore: Johns Hopkins University Press, 1981.

Henze, Paul B. "Arming the Horn." Working Paper no. 43. Washington, D.C.: International Studies Program, Wilson Center, 28 July 1983.

Herzog, Chaim. *The Arab-Israeli Wars.* New York: Random House, 1982.

———. *The Arab-Israeli Wars: War and Peace in the Middle East.* London: Arms and Armour Press, 1982.

Hetherton, Norris, S. "Industrialization and Revolution in Iran: Forced Progress or Unmet Expectation." *Middle East Journal* 36, no. 3 (Summer 1982):362–373.

Hewish, Mark, Sweetman, Bill, Wheeler, Barry C., and Gunston, Bill. *Air Forces of the World.* New York: Simon & Schuster, 1979.

Hickman, William F. *Ravaged and Reborn: The Iranian Army, 1982.* Staff paper. Washington, D.C.: Brookings Institution, 1982.

Holden, David, and Johns, Richard. *The House of Saud.* London: Sidgwick and Jackson, 1981.

Holland, Max. "The Militarization of the Middle East." Philadelphia: American Friends Service Committee, 1983.

Holshek, C. J. "East Asia and the Western Pacific: The Military and Strategic Balance." East Asia Studies Program Special Report. Washington, D.C.: Woodrow Wilson Center, 1982 and 1983.

Hopwood, Derek, ed. *The Arabian Peninsula: Society and Politics.* London: George Allen & Unwin, 1972.

Hottinger, Arnold. "Arab Communism at Low Ebb." *Problems of Communism*, July-August 1981, pp. 17–32.

Hourani, Albert. *The Emergence of the Modern Middle East.* Berkeley: University of California Press, 1981.

Howard, Harry N. *Turkey, the Straits and NATO Policy.* Baltimore: Johns Hopkins University Press, 1974.

Hurewitz, J. C. *Middle East Politics: The Military Dimension.* New York: Praeger Publishers, 1969.

Hyman, Anthony. *Afghanistan Under Soviet Domination, 1964–81.* London: Macmillan, 1982.

Ibrahim, Saad Eddin. *The New Arab Social Order: A Study of the Social Impact of Oil Wealth.* Boulder, Colo.: Westview Press, 1982.

International Defense Review (Switzerland), 1976–1982.

International Defense Review, Special Series.

International Energy Statistical Review (Washington, D.C.: National Foreign Energy Assessment Center), 1978–1982.

International Institute for Strategic Studies. *The Middle East and the International System.* Parts I and II. Adelphi Papers no. 114 and 115. London, 1975.

———. *Survival* (London, various years).

———. *Strategic Survey* (London, various years).

———. *The Military Balance* (London, various years).

Iraq, Minister of Culture. *Revolution et développement en Iraq.* Baghdad: Ministre de la Planification, 1980.

Iraq, Ministry of Culture and Information. *Revolution and Development in Iraq.* Baghdad, 1980.

Isaac, Rael Jean. *Israel Divided, Ideological Politics in the Jewish State.* Baltimore: Johns Hopkins University Press, 1976.

Isby, David C. "Afghanistan: The Unending Struggle." In *Military Annual* (London: Jane's, 1982), pp. 28–45.

———. "Afghanistan 1982: The War Continues." *International Defense Review* 11 (1982):1523–1528.

———. *Weapons and Tactics of the Soviet Army.* New York: Janes, 1981.

Israel, Tareq Y. *The Iran-Iraq Conflict.* Toronto: Canadian Institute of International Affairs, 1981.

Jackson, Robert. *The Israeli Air Force Story.* London: Tandem, 1970.

Jane's. *All the World's Aircraft.* London, various years.

———. *Armour and Artillery.* London, various years.

———. *Aviation Annual.* London, various years.

———. *Combat Support Equipment.* London, various years.

———. *Defense Review.* London, various years.

———. *Fighting Ships.* London, various years.

———. *Infantry Weapons.* London, various years.

———. *Military Annual.* London, various years.

———. *Military Communications.* London, various years.

———. *Naval Annual.* London, various years.

———. *Weapons Systems.* London, various years.

Jenkins, Brian Michael, et al. "Nuclear Terrorism and Its Consequences." *Society* 17, no. 5 (July-August 1980):5–25.

Johany, Ali D. *The Myth of the OPEC Cartel: The Role of Saudi Arabia.* New York: John Wiley, 1982.

Johnson, Major Maxwell Orwe, U.S.M.C. "U.S. Strategic Operations in the Persian Gulf." *Proceedings of the Naval Institute*, February 1981.

Jones, Rodney W. *Nuclear Proliferation: Islam, the Bomb and South Asia*, Washington Paper no. 82, Center for Strategic and International Studies. Beverly Hills, Calif.: Sage Publications, 1981.

Joyner, Christopher C., and Shah, Shahqat Ali. "The Reagan Policy of 'Strategic Consensus' in the Middle East." *Strategic Review*, Fall 1981, pp. 15–24.

Jureidini, Paul, and McLaurin, R. D. *Beyond Camp David.* Syracuse, NY.: Syracuse University Press, 1981.

Kanovsky, Eliyahu. "Saudi Arabia in the Red." *Jerusalem Quarterly*, no. 16 (Summer 1980):137–144.

Kazemi, Farhad. *Poverty and Revolution in Iran.* New York: New York University Press, 1980.

Keegan, John. *World Armies.* New York: Facts on File, 1979.

Kelly, J. B. *Arabia, the Gulf and the West: A Critical View of the Arabs and Their Oil Policy.* New York: Basic Books, 1980.

_______. "Great Game or Grand Illusion?" *Survey,* Spring 1980, pp. 109–188.

Kemp, Geoffrey, and Vlahas, Michael. "The Military Balance in the Middle East in 1978." Working paper prepared for congressional testimony.

Khadduri, Majid. *Arab Contemporaries.* Baltimore: Johns Hopkins University Press, 1973.

Khalifa, Ali Mohammed. *The United Arab Emirates: Unity in Fragmentation.* Boulder, Colo.: Westview Press, 1979.

Klass, Philip J. "Israeli Aviation." *Aviation Week and Space Technology,* 10, 17, and 24 April, 1 May 1978.

Kohler, Foy D., Coure, Leon, and Harvey, Moses L. *The Soviet Union and the October 1973 Middle East War.* CAIS. Coral Gables, Fla.: University of Miami Press, 1974.

Korb, Edward L., ed. *The World's Missile Systems.* 7th ed. Pamona, Calif.: General Dynamics, Pamona Division, 1982.

Kramer, Martin. "The Ideals of an Islamic Order." *Washington Quarterly,* no. 3 (Winter 1980):3–13.

Krapels, Edward, N., ed. "International Oil Supplies and Stockpiling." In proceedings of a conference held in Hamburg, 17 and 18 September 1981. London: Economist Intelligence Unit, 1982.

_______. "Oil and Security," Adelphi Paper no. 136. London: International Institute for Strategic Studies, 1977.

_______. *Oil Crisis Management.* Baltimore: Johns Hopkins University Press, 1980.

Kuwait. *Annual Statistical Abstract.* Kuwait City: Ministry of Planning, Central Statistical office, various editions.

Kuwaiti News Service. *The Gulf Cooperation Council,* Digest no. 9, KUNA, Kuwait, Ninth Issue, 3rd ed. Kuwait: Kuwaiti Universal News Agency, December 1982.

Lacey, Robert. *The Kingdom.* London: Hutchinson & Co., 1981.

Laffin, John. *Fight for the Falklands.* London: St. Martin's Press, 1982.

Laffin, John L. *The Dagger of Islam.* London: Sphere, 1979.

Laqueur, Walter. *The Struggle for the Middle East.* London: Routledge and Keegan Paul, 1969.

Le Monde (Paris).

Lee, Air-Chief Marshal Sir David. *Flight from the Middle East.* London: Her Majesty's Stationery Office, 1980.

Lefever, Ernest W. *Nuclear Arms in the Third World: U.S. Policy Dilemma.* Washington, D.C.: Brookings Institution, 1979.

Leites, Nathan. *Soviet Style in War.* New York: Crane, Russak & Co., 1982.

Leltenberg, Milton, and Sheffer, Gabriel, eds. *Great Power Intervention in the Middle East.* New York: Pergamon Press, 1979.

Lenczowski, George. *The Middle East in World Affairs,* 4th ed. Ithaca, N.Y.: Cornell University Press, 1980.

_______. *Middle East Oil in a Revolutionary Age.* Washington, D.C.: American Enterprise Institute for Public Policy Research. 1976.

———. *Soviet Advances in the Middle East.* Washington, D.C.: American Enterprise Institute for Public Policy Research, 1971.

Lewis, William J. *The Warsaw Pact: Arms, Doctrine, and Strategy.* New York: McGraw-Hill, 1982.

Library of Congress. "The Persian Gulf: Are We Committed?" Washington, D.C., 1981.

Liebov, Robert J. "Energy, Economics and Security in Alliance Perspective." *International Security,* Spring 1980, pp. 139–163.

Litwak, Robert, ed. *Security in the Persian Gulf: Sources of Inter-State Conflict.* London: International Institute for Strategic Studies, 1981.

Long, David E. *The Persian Gulf: An Introduction to Its Peoples, Politics, and Economics.* Rev. ed. Boulder, Colo.: Westview Press, 1978.

———. "Saudi Oil Policy." *Wilson Quarterly,* 1979.

———. "U.S.-Saudi Relations: A Foundation of Mutual Need." *American-Arab Affairs,* no. 4 (Spring 1983):12–22.

Long, David E., and Reich, Bernard, eds. *The Government and Politics of the Middle East and North Africa.* Boulder, Colo.: Westview Press, 1980.

Looney, Robert E. *Saudi Arabia's Development Potential.* Lexington, Mass.: Lexington Books, 1982.

Lottam, Emanuel. "Arab Aid to Less Developed Countries." *Middle East Review,* 1979-1980, pp. 30–39.

Lubin, Peter. "Gulf Follies." *Middle East Review,* Spring 1980, pp. 9–22.

Luckner, Helen A. *A House Built on Sand: A Political Economy of Saudi Arabia.* London: Ithaca Press, 1978.

Luttwak, Edward, and Horowitz, Dan. *The Israeli Army.* New York: Harper & Row, 1983.

MacDonald, Charles G. "Iran's Strategic Interests and the Law of the Sea." *Middle East Journal,* Summer 1980, pp. 302–323.

MacDonald, Charles G., "The U.S. and Gulf Conflict Scenarios." *Middle East Insight* 3, no. 1 (May-July 1983):23–27.

MacGwire, Michael, and McDonnell, John, eds. *Soviet Naval Influence.* New York: Praeger Publishers, 1977.

McNaugher, Thomas L. "Rapid Deployment and Basing in Southwest Asia." In *Strategic Survey* (London: International Institute for Strategic Studies, April 1983), pp. 133–137.

———. "The Soviet Military Threat to the Gulf: The Operational Dimension." Working paper. Washington, D.C.: Brookings Institution, 1982.

Madelin, Henri. *Oil and Politics.* London: Saxon House, 1975.

Male, Beverly. *Revolutionary Afghanistan.* London: Croom Helm, 1982.

Mallakh, Ragaei El. *OPEC: Twenty Years and Beyond.* Boulder, Colo.: Westview Press, 1982.

———. *Saudi Arabia: Rush to Development.* London: Croom Helm, 1982.

———. *Qatar: Development of an oil Economy.* London: Croom Helm, 1979.

Mallakh, Ragaei El, and Mallakh, Dorothea H. El. *Saudi Arabia: Energy, Development Planning, and Industrialization.* Lexington, Mass.: Lexington Books, 1982.

Malone, Joseph J. *The Arab Lands of Western Asia.* Englewood Cliffs, N.J.: Prentice-Hall, 1973.

Mansfield, Peter. *The Middle East.* New York: Oxford University Press, 1980.

Mansur, Abdul Kasim (pseud.). "The American Threat to Saudi Arabia." *Armed Forces Journal International,* September 1980, pp. 47–60.

Margiotta, Franklin D., ed. *Evolving Strategic Realities, Implications for U.S. Policymakers*. Washington, D.C.: National Defense University Press, 1980.

Mark, Clyde R. *Egyptian-Israeli Peace Treaty*. Issue Brief no. 1B 79076. Washington, D.C.: Library of Congress, Congressional Research Service, 1979.

_______. *Palestine and the Palestinians*. Issue Brief no. 1B 76048. Washington, D.C.: Library of Congress, Congressional Research Service, 1979.

Mendelsohn, Everett, et al. *A Compassionate Peace*, a report prepared for the American Friends Service Committee. New York: Hill and Wang, 1982.

Meyer, Lawrence. *Israel Now: Portrait of a Troubled Land*. New York: Delacorte, 1982.

Middle East (London).

Middle East Economic Digest (London).

_______. *Oman: A Practical Guide*. London, 1982.

_______. *Saudi Arabia: A Practical Guide*. London, 1981.

_______. *UAE: A Practical Guide*. London, 1982.

Middle East Economic Digest Special Report Series. *Bahrain*. London, September 1981 and September 1982.

_______. *France and the Middle East*. May 1982.

_______. *Oman*. November 1982.

_______. *Qatar*. August 1981 and August 1982.

_______. *UAE: Tenth Anniversary*. November 1981.

_______. *UK and the Gulf*. December 1981.

Middle East Insight.

Middle East Journal (Washington, D.C.: Middle East Institute).

Miller, Aaron David. *Search for Security: Saudi Arabian Oil and American Foreign Policy, 1939–1949*. Chapel Hill: University of North Carolina Press, 1980.

Miller, Lt. Col. D.M.O., Kenney, Col. William V., Jordan, John, and Richardson, Douglas. *The Balance of Military Power*. New York: St. Martin's Press, 1981.

Moore, Capt. John E. *The Soviet Navy Today*. London: MacDonald and James, 1975.

Morton, Theodore H. "Iranian Defense Expenditures and the Social Crisis." *International Security* 3, no. 3 (Winter 1978-79):178–192.

Morris, Benny. "New Strategic Thinking in Israel." *Armed Forces Journal*, September 1980, pp. 82–91.

Mostyn, Trevor. *Saudi Arabia*. London: MEED, 1981.

_______. *UAE*. London: MEED, 1982.

Mottahedeh, Roy Parviz. "Iran's Foreign Devils." *Foreign Policy*, no. 38 (Spring 1980):19–34.

Murphy, Paul J. *Naval Power in Soviet Policy*. 2 vols. Washington, D.C.: United States Air Force, 1978.

Murray, Douglas J., and Viotti, Paul R. *The Defense Policies of Nations*. Baltimore: Johns Hopkins University Press, 1982.

Nakhleh, Emile A. *The West Bank and Gaza*. American Enterprise Institute No. 232. Washington, D.C., 1979.

National Foreign Assessment Center. *International Energy Statistical Review*. Washington, D.C.: Photoduplication Service, Library of Congress, 1978–1981.

_______. *The World Oil Market in the Years Ahead*. ER79-10327U. Washington, D.C., August 1979.

"Nearby Observer." "The Afghan-Soviet War: Stalemate or Solution?" *Middle East Journal*, Spring 1982, pp. 151–164.

Neff, Donald. *Warriors at Suez.* New York: Linden, 1981.

Neuman, Stephanie, and Harkavy, Robert E. *Arms Transfers in the Modern World.* New York: Praeger Publishers, 1980.

New York Times.

Newell, Nancy Peabody, and Newell, Richard S. *The Struggle for Afghanistan.* Ithaca, N.Y.: Cornell University Press, 1981.

Newson, David D. "America Engulfed." *Foreign Policy,* no. 43 (Summer 1981):17–32.

Niblock, Tim, ed. *State, Society, and the Economy in Saudi Arabia.* London: Croom Helm, 1982.

———. *Social and Economic Development in Arab Gulf States.* London: Croom Helm, 1980.

Noyes, James H. *The Clouded Lens.* Stanford, Calif.: Hoover Institution, 1982.

Nyrop, Richard F. *Area Handbook for Iraq.* Foreign Area Handbook Series. Washington, D.C.: American University, 1971.

———. *Area Handbook for the Persian Gulf States.* Foreign Area Handbook Series. Washington, D.C.: American University, 1977.

———. *Area Handbook for Saudi Arabia.* Foreign Area Handbook Series. Washington, D.C.: American University, 1977.

———. *Area Handbook for the Yemens.* Foreign Area Handbook Series. Washington, D.C.: American University, 1977.

O'Ballance, Edgar. *The War in the Yemens.* Hamden, Conn.: Anchor Books, 1971.

———. "The Iran-Iraq War." *Marine Corps Gazette,* February 1982, pp. 44–49.

Ochsenwald, William. "Saudi Arabia and the Islamic Revival." *International Journal of Middle East Studies* 13, no. 3 (August 1981):271–286.

Odell, Peter R., and Rosing, Kenneth E. *The Future of Oil: A Simulation Study.* London: Nichols, 1980.

Ofer, Guri. "Israel's Economy: Diagnosis and Cure." *Jerusalem Quarterly,* no. 20 (Summer 1981):5–161.

Office of Technology Assessment. *The Effects of Nuclear War.* Washington, D.C.: Government Printing Office, 1979.

Oman and Its Renaissance. London: Stacey International, 1980.

Oman: A Practical Guide. London: MEED, 1982.

Oman, Sultanate of. *Oman '80.* Muscat: Ministry of Information and Youth Affairs, 1981.

———. *Oman in Ten Years.* Muscat: Ministry of Information, 1980.

———. *Second Five Year Plan, 1981–85.* Muscat Development Coucil, 1981.

Osborne, Christine. *The Gulf States and Oman.* London: Croom Helm, 1977.

Osgood, Robert. *Limited War Revisited.* Boulder, Colo.: Westview Press, 1979.

O'Sullivan, Edmund. *Bahrain.* London: MEED, 1981.

Otaiba-Al, Mana Saeed. *OPEC and the Petroleum Industry.* London: Croom Helm, 1975.

———. *Petroleum and the Economy of the United Arab Emirates.* London: Croom Helm, 1977.

Pahlavi, Mohammed Reza. *The Shah's Story.* London: Michael Joseph, 1980.

Pajak, Roger F. *Nuclear Proliferation in the Middle East.* National Defense University, Monograph 82-1. Washington, D.C., 1982.

Peres, Shimon. "A Strategy for Peace in the Middle East." *Foreign Affairs,* Spring 1980, pp. 887–901.

________. *David's Sling*. London: Willmer Brothers Ltd., 1970.

Peres, Shimon (sponsor). *Military Aspects of the Arab-Israeli Conflict*. Tel Aviv: UPP, 1975.

Peretz, Don. "A Different Place." *Wilson Quarterly* 2 (1983):62–81.

Peri, Yoram. *Between Battles and Ballots: Israeli Military in Politics*. New York: Cambridge University Press, 1983.

________. "Israel's Defence in the 1980's," *Defense Attache*, August 1980, pp. 35–43.

Perlmutter, Amos. "A Palestinian Entity?" *International Security*, Spring 1981, pp. 103–116.

________. *Politics and the Military in Israel, 1967–1977*. London: Cass, 1978.

________. *Egypt: The Praetorian State*. New Brunswick, N.J.: Transaction, 1974.

Perlmutter, Amos, Handel, Michael, and Joseph, Uri Bar. *Two Minutes over Baghdad*. London: Corgi, 1982.

Perry, Charles. *The West, Japan, and Cape Route Imports: The Oil and Non Fuel Mineral Trades*. Cambridge, Mass.: Institute for Foreign Policy Analysis, 1982.

Peterson, J. E. *Oman in the Twentieth Century: Political Foundations of an Emerging State*. London: Croom Helm, 1978.

________. *Yemen: The Search for a Modern State*. Baltimore: Johns Hopkins University Press, 1982.

Philadelphia Inquirer.

Pierre, Andrew J. "Beyond the 'Plane Package': Arms and Politics in the Middle East." *International Security* 3, no. 1 (Summer 1978):148–161.

________. *The Global Politics of Arms Sales*. Princeton, N.J.: Princeton University Press, 1982.

Pincus, Joseph. "Syria: A Captive Economy." *Middle East Review*, Fall 1979, pp. 49–57.

Plascov, Avi. "A Palestinian State? Examining the Alternatives." Adelphi Papers no. 163. London: International Institute for Strategic Studies, 1981.

________. *Security in the Persian Gulf: Modernisation, Political Development and Stability*. Aldershot: Gower, 1982.

"Population Revolution: Running to a Standstill." *Middle East*, July 1979, pp. 57–60.

Poullada, Leon B. "Afghanistan and the United States, The Crucial Years." *Middle East Journal*, Spring 1981, pp. 178–190.

Pradas, Col. Alfred B. *Trilateral Military Aid in the Middle East: The Yemen Program*. Washington, D.C.: National Defense University, 1979.

Price, D. L. *Oman: Insurgency and Development*. Conflict Studies No. 53. London, 1975.

Qatar. *Year Book 1978–79*. Ministry of Information, 1978.

Quandt, William B. *Saudi Arabia in the 1980s: Foreign Policy, Security and Oil*. Washington, D.C.: Brookings Institution, 1981.

________. *Saudi Arabia's Oil Policy: A Staff Paper*. Washington, D.C.: Brookings Institution, 1982.

Ramberg, Bennet. *Destruction of Nuclear Energy Facilities in War: The Problems and the Implications*. Lexington, Mass.: Lexington Books, 1980.

Ravi, Yehoshua. "Arab-Israeli Balance." *Jerusalem Quarterly*, no. 18 (Winter 1981):121–144.

Record, Jeffrey. *NATO's Theater Nuclear Force Modernization Program*. Cambridge, Mass.: Institute for Foreign Policy Analysis, 1981.

———. *The Rapid Deployment Force.* Cambridge, Mass.: Institute for Foreign Policy Analysis, 1981.

Reed, Stanley F. "Dateline: Cairo: Shaken Pillar." *Foreign Policy*, Winter 1981-82, pp. 175–185.

Richardson, Douglas. *Naval Armament.* New York: Jane's, 1981.

Roberts, Hugh. *An Urban Profile of the Middle East.* London: Croom Helm, 1979.

Robinson, Clarence A., Jr. "Cairo Turns to West for Weapons." *Aviation Week and Space Technology*, no. 14 (December 1981):39–45.

Roi, Yaacov. *The Limits to Power, Soviet Policy in the Middle East.* London: Croom Helm, 1979.

Rosen, Steven J. *Military Geography and the Military Balance in the Arab-Israeli Conflict.* Jerusalem: Hebrew University, 1977.

Rosen, Steven. "What the Next Arab-Israeli War Might Look Like." *International Security* 2, no. 4 (Spring 1978):149–173.

Ross, Dennis. "Considering Soviet Threats to the Persian Gulf." *International Security* 6, no. 2 (Fall 1981).

Rouleau, Eric. "Khomeini's Iran." *Foreign Affairs*, Fall 1980, pp. 1–20.

———. "The War and the Struggle for the State," *MERIP Reports*, no. 98 (July-August 1981):3–8.

Royal United Services Institute/Brassey. *International Weapons Development.* 4th ed. London: Brassey's, 1981.

Rubin, Barry. *The Arab States and the Palestinian Conflict.* Syracuse, N.Y.: Syracuse University Press, 1981.

———. *Paved with Good Intentions.* New York: Oxford University Press, 1980.

Rubinstein, Alvin Z. *Soviet Policy Towards Turkey, Iran, and Afghanistan: The Dynamics of Influence.* New York: Praeger Publishers, 1982.

———. "Afghanistan: Embraced By the Bear." *Orbis* 26, no. 1 (Spring 1982):135–153.

———. "The Last Years of Peaceful Co-Existence: Soviet-Afghan Relations 1963–1978." *Middle East Journal*, 36, no. 2 (Spring 1982):165–183.

———. *Red Star over the Nile.* Princeton, N.J.: Princeton University Press, 1977.

RUSI/Brassey, *International Weapons Developments*, 4th ed. London: Brassey's 1981.

Russi, Pierre. *Iraq, the Land of the New River.* Paris: Les Editions, J.A., 1980.

Ruszkiewicz, Lt. Col. John J. "A Case Study in the Yemen Arab Republic." *Armed Forces Journal*, September 1980, pp. 62–72.

Sabah-Al, Y.S.F. *The Oil Economy of Kuwait.* Boston: Keegan Paul, 1980.

Sabini, John. *Armies in the Sand: The Struggle for Mecca and Medina.* New York: W. W. Norton, 1981.

Sadik, Muhammad, and Snavely, William P. *Bahrain, Qatar and the U.A.E.* Lexington, Mass.: Lexington Books, 1972.

Safran, Nadav. *From War to War.* New York: Pegasus, 1969.

———. *Israel: The Embattled Ally.* Cambridge, Mass.: Harvard University Press, 1978.

Sagan, Scott D. "Lessons of the Yom Kippur Alert." *Foreign Policy*, no. 36 (Fall 1979):160–178.

Saikal, Amin. *The Rise and Fall of the Shah.* Princeton, N.J.: Princeton University Press, 1980.

Sampson, Anthony. *The Arms Bazaar*. New York: Viking Press, 1977.

Sciolino, P. "Iran's Durable Revolution." *Foreign Affairs*, Spring 1983, pp. 893–920.

Scott, Harriet Fast, and Scott, William F., eds. *The Soviet Art of War: Doctrine, Strategy and Tactics*. Boulder, Colo.: Westview Press, 1982.

Sella, Ammon. *Soviet Political and Military Conduct in the Middle East*. London: Macmillan, 1981.

Shamir, Yitzhak. "Israel's Role in a Changing Middle East." *Foreign Affairs*, Spring 1982, pp. 789–802.

Shazly, Lt. Gen. Saad El. *The Crossing of Suez*. San Francisco: American Mideast Research, 1980.

Sherbini-El, A. A., ed. *Food Security Issues in the Arab Near East*. New York: Pergamon Press, 1979.

Shirrelf, David. "Five Year Plan Goes Back to the Drawing Board." *MEED*, 30 May 1980.

Sid-Ahmed, Mohamed. "Shifting Sands of Peace in the Middle East." *International Security* 5, no. 1 (Summer 1980):53–79.

Siekiewicz, Stan. "National Security and Nuclear Proliferation." *Comparative Strategy* 3, no. 1, pp. 25–43.

Simpkins, Brigadier Richard E. *Antitank—An Air Mechanized Response to Armored Threats in the 1990s*. London: Brassey's, 1982.

________. *Mechanized Infantry*. London: Brassey's 1980.

________. *Tank Warfare: An Analysis of Soviet and NATO Tank Philosophy*. London: Brassey's, 1979.

Sisco, Joseph J. "Middle East: Progress or Lost Opportunity." *Foreign Affairs*, Spring 1983, pp. 611–640.

Stauffer, Thomas R. *U.S. Aid to Israel: The Vital Link*. Middle East Problem Paper no. 24, Washington, D.C.: Middle East Institute, 1983.

Stempel, John D. *Inside the Iranian Revolution*. Bloomington: Indiana University Press, 1981.

Stewart, Richard A. "Soviet Military Intervention in Iran, 1920–46." *Parameters, Journal of the U.S. Army War College* 11, no. 4 (1981):24–34.

Stobaugh, Robert, and Yergin, Daniel, eds. *Energy Future*. New York: Random House, 1979.

Stockholm International Peace Research Institute. *Tactical Nuclear Weapons: European Perspectives*. New York: Crane, Russak & Co., 1978.

________. *World Armaments and Disarmament*: *SIPRI Yearbook*, various years (computer printout for 1982). London: Taylor E. Francis, Ltd.

Stoff, Michael B. *Oil, War, and American Security: The Search for a National Policy on Foreign Oil, 1941–47*. New Haven, Conn.: Yale University Press, 1980.

Stookey, Robert W. *South Yemen: A Marxist Republic in Arabia*. Boulder, Colo.: Westview Press, 1982.

________. *Yemen: The Politics of the Yemen Arab Republic*. Boulder, Colo.: Westview Press, 1978.

Sullivan, William H. "Iran: The Road Not Taken." *Foreign Policy*, no. 40 (Fall 1980):175–187.

________. *Mission to Iran*. London: W. W. Norton, 1981.

Sunday Times Insight Team. *War in the Falklands, The Full Story*. New York: Harper & Row, 1982.

Szuprowicz, Bohdan O. *How to Avoid Strategic Materials Shortages.* New York: John Wiley, 1981.

Tahir-Kheli, Shirin, and Shaheen Ayubi. *The Iran-Iraq War: New Weapons, Old Conflicts.* New York: Praeger Publishers, 1983.

Tahir-Kheli, Shirin, and Staudenmaier, William O. "The Saudi-Pakistani Military Relationship: Implications for U.S. Policy." *Orbis,* Spring 1982, pp. 155–171.

Tal, Israel. "Israel's Security in the Eighties." *Jerusalem Quarterly,* no. 17 (Fall 1980):13–18.

Thompson, Sir Robert, ed. *War in Peace.* New York: Harmony Books, 1982.

Thompson, W. Scott. "The Persian Gulf and the Correlation of Forces." *International Security,* Summer 1982, pp. 157–180.

Till, Geoffrey, ed. *Maritime Strategy in the Nuclear Age.* London: Macmillan, 1982.

Tillman, Seth P. *The United States in the Middle East: Interests and Obstacles.* Bloomington: Indiana University Press, 1982.

Timerman, Jacobo. *The Longest War.* New York: Alfred A. Knopf, 1982.

"Too Hot to Handle (Iran-Iraq War)." *Middle East,* November 1980, pp. 10–16.

Tow, William T., and Feeney, William R., eds. *U.S. Foreign Policy and Asian-Pacific Security: A Transregional Approach.* Boulder, Colo.: Westview Press, 1982.

Tucker, Robert W. "Lebanon: The Case for the War." *Commentary* 74, no. 4 (October 1982):19–30.

Turner, Louis, and Bedore, James M. *Middle East Industrialization: A Study of Saudi and Iranian Downstream Investments.* London: Saxon House, 1979.

United Arab Emirates, Ministry of Information and Culture. *A Record of Achievement, 1979–1981.* Abu Dhabi, 1981.

U.S. Arms Control and Disarmament Agency. *World Military Expenditures and Arms Transfers, 1966–1975 and 1969–1978.* Washington, D.C., 1980.

U.S. Army Armor Center, Threat Branch. *Organization and Equipment of the Soviet Army,* ST 30-40. Fort Knox, Ky., 1981.

U.S. Budget Office. *Costs of Expanding and Modernizing the Navy's Carrier-Based Air Forces.* Washington, D.C., 1982.

U.S. Central Intelligence Agency. *Economic and Energy Indicators.* DOI, GI EEI. Washington, D.C.: Government Printing Office, various years.

———. *Handbook of Economic Statistics.* CIA ER 76-10481, September 1976.

———. *The International Energy Situation: Outlook to 1985.* No. 041-015-00084-5. Washington, D.C.: Government Printing Office, 1977.

———. *International Energy Statistical Review.* NFAC, GI-IESR. Washington, D.C.: Government Printing Office, various years.

———. *The World Factbook—1981.* NFAC, GS WF 81-001. Washington, D.C.: Government Printing Office, 1981.

U.S. Comptroller General. *U.S. Assistance to the State of Israel.* GAO/ID-83-51. Washington, D.C.: General Accounting Office, 24 June 1983.

U.S. Congress, House of Representatives, Committee on Foreign Affairs. *Saudi Arabia and the United States: The New Context in an Evolving 'Special Relationship.'* No. 81-494 0. Washington, D.C.: Government Printing Office, 1981.

———. *U.S. Interests in, and Policies Toward, the Persian Gulf, 1980.* No. 68-184 0. Washington, D.C.: Congressional Printing Office, 1980.

———. *U.S. Security Interests in the Persian Gulf.* No. 73-354-0. Washington, D.C.: Government Printing Office, 1981.

U.S. Congress, Joint Economic Committee. *The Political Economy of the Middle East, 1973–78*. No. 51-623 0. Washington, D.C.: Government Printing Office, 1980.

U.S. Congress, Senate, Committee on Energy and Natural Resources. *Geopolitics of Oil*. No. 96-119. Washington, D.C.: Government Printing Office, 1980.

U.S. Department of Energy, Energy Information Administration. *Monthly Energy Review*. Washington, D.C.: Government Printing Office, 1978–1981.

________. *1980 International Energy Annual*. DoE/EIA-0219 (80). Washington, D.C.: Government Printing Office, 1981.

________. *1980 Annual Report to Congress*. Vols. I, II, and III. DoE, EIA-0173 (80). Washington, D.C.: Government Printing Office, 1981.

U.S. Department of Energy, International Affairs. *International Energy Indicators*. DoE/IA-0010. Washington, D.C.: Government Printing Office, various years.

U.S. Department of State, Bureau of Public Affairs. *Afghanistan: Three Years of Occupation*, Special Report no. 106. Washington, D.C., December 1982.

U.S. Defense Security Assistance Agency. *Foreign Military Sales, Foreign Military Construction Sales and Military Assistance Facts as of September 1982*. Washington, D.C.: Government Printing Office, 1983.

U.S. News and World Report.

Van Cleave, William R., and Cohen, Sam T. *Tactical Nuclear Weapons*. New York: Crane, Russak & Co., 1978.

Van Creveld, Martin. *Military Lessons of the Yom Kippur War: Historical Perspectives* Washington Paper no. 24. Beverly Hills, Calif.: Sage Publications, 1975.

Van Dam, Nikolaos. *The Struggle for Power in Syria*. London: Croom Helm, 1981.

________. *The Struggle for Power in Syria: Regionalism and Tribalism in Politics*. New York: St. Martin's Press, 1979.

Van Hollen, Christopher. "Don't Engulf the Gulf." *Foreign Affairs*, Summer 1981, pp. 1064–1078.

Vatikiotis, P. J. *Politics and the Military in Jordan, A Study of the Arab Legion 1921–1957*. New York: Praeger Publishers, 1967.

Vernon, Graham D., ed. *Soviet Perceptions of War and Peace*. Washington, D.C.: National Defense University Press, 1981.

Vertzberger, Yaacov. "Afghanistan in China's Policy." *Problems of Communism*, May-June 1982, pp. 1–23.

von Pikva, Otto. *Armies of the Middle East*. New York: Mayflower Books, 1979.

Walinsky, Louis J. *The Implications of Israel-Arab Peace for World Jewry*. New York: Waldon Press, 1981.

Wall Street Journal.

Waltz, Kenneth H. "A Strategy for the Rapid Deployment Force." *International Security* 5, no. 4 (Spring 1981):49–73.

________. "The Spread of Nuclear Weapons, More May Be Better." Adelphi Paper no. 171, London: International Institute for Strategic Studies, 1981.

War Data. Special editions of the "Born in Battle' series. Jerusalem: Eshel-Dramit.

Ward, J.W.D., and Turner, G. N. *Military Data Processing and Microcomputers*. London: Brassey's, 1982.

Washington Post.

Washington Star.

Weeks, Col. John, ed. *Jane's 1981–82 Military Annual.* London: Jane's Publications, 1982.
Weinbaum, Marvin G. *Food Development, and Politics in the Middle East.* Boulder, Colo.: Westview Press, 1982.
Weinberger, Caspar W. *Soviet Military Power.* Department of Defense. Washington, D.C.: Government Printing Office, 1981.
Weissman, Steve, and Herbert Krosney. *The Islamic Bomb.* New York: Times Books, 1981.
Weizman, Ezer. *On Eagle's Wings.* New York: Macmillan, 1976.
———. *The Battle of Peace.* New York: Bantam Books, 1981.
Wells, Donald A. *Saudi Arabian Development Strategy.* Washington, D.C.: American Enterprise Institute, 1976.
Weltman, John J. "Nuclear Devolution and World Order." *World Politics* 32, no. 2 (January 1980):69–193.
Wenner, Manfred W. *Modern Yemen, 1918–1966.* Baltimore: Johns Hopkins University Press, 1967.
Wheelock, Thomas R. "Arms for Israel: The Limits of Leverage." *International Security* 3, no. 2 (Fall 1978):123–137.
Whelan, John, ed. *Saudi Arabia.* London: MEED, 1981.
Whetten, Lawrence L. *The Canal War: Four Power Conflict in the Middle East.* Cambridge, Mass.: Massachusetts Institute of Technology, 1974.
Whittier, Charles H. *Islam in Iran: The Shi'ite Faith, Its History and Teaching.* Washington, D.C.: Congressional Research Service, 11 September 1979.
Williams, Louis, ed. *Military Aspects of the Arab-Israeli Conflict.* Tel Aviv: University Publishing Projects, 1975.
Wittam, George H. "Political and Military Background to France's Intervention Capability." National Institute for Public Policy, McLean, Va., June 1982.
Witton, Peter. *UAE—10th Anniversary.* London: MEED, 1981.
World of Information. *Middle East Review, 1981.* London, 1981.
World Industry Information Service. *Energy Decade: A Statistical and Graphic Chronicle.* San Diego, Calif., 1982.
Wright, Claudia. "The Iran-Iraq War." *Foreign Affairs,* Winter 1980-81, pp. 275–304.
———. "Iraq—New Power in the Middle East." *Foreign Affairs,* Winter 1979–1980, pp. 267–277.
Wright, John. *Libya: A Modern History.* London: Croom Helm, 1982.
Wurtele, Jones, Rowen, and Agmon, *Nuclear Proliferation Prospects for the Middle East and South Asia.* 31-109-38-597. Marina Del Rey, Calif: Pan Heuristics, June 1981.
Yariv, Aharon. "Strategic Depth." *Jerusalem Quarterly,* no. 17 (Fall 1980):3–12.
Yariv, Aharon, and Gabriel Ben-Dor. "The War is Lebanon," Memorandum no. 8. Tel Aviv: Center for Strategic Studies, 1983.
Zahlan, Rosemarie Said. *The Creation of Qatar.* London: Croom Helm, 1979.
Zamir, Dani. "Generals in Politics." *Jerusalem Quarterly,* no. 20 (Summer 1981):17–35.
Zeev, H., et al. *The Gaza Strip.* Jerusalem: Carta, 1974.
Zelniker, Shimshon. *The Superpowers and the Horn of Africa.* Center for Strategic Studies, Tel Aviv University, Paper No. 18, September 1982.
Zonis, Marvin. *The Political Elite of Iran.* Princeton, N.J.: Princeton University Press, 1971.

Index

About the Book and Author

The Gulf and the Search for Strategic Stability: Saudi Arabia, the Military Balance in the Gulf, and Trends in the Arab-Israeli Military Balance

Anthony H. Cordesman

This book provides the most extensive military and strategic analysis yet made of the Gulf and the Arabian Peninsula, assessing the regional military balance, the internal security and stability of each Gulf nation, the evolution of each nation's forces from 1969 into 1983, and the impact of defense spending and Western and Soviet-bloc arms sales in the region. Comprehensive statistics are provided on arms transfers to each country since 1969 and on the forces each nation is capable of deploying in the Gulf.

Mr. Cordesman focuses initially on the strategic importance of the Gulf in view of the shifts in world oil demand and oil prices. Looking in depth at the major forces affecting U.S. security policy in the Gulf and the conflicting objectives of the U.S. and the Soviet Union, he examines the relative importance of each Gulf nation to Western interests, then concentrates on Saudi Arabia as the potential keystone for building a strategic partnership between the Gulf and the West, as well as regional cooperation. He traces the history of Saudi military relations with the West, the build-up of Saudi forces, and the factors now influencing Saudi Arabia's internal security. Detailed tables provide data on the development of Saudi forces from 1950 to 1983, the relationship between the Saudi military build-up and that of its neighbors, and the impact of the Western advisory efforts on Saudi Arabia.

Turning again to the other Gulf nations, Mr. Cordesman covers the historical forces shaping the development of their political alignments and military capabilities and looks at the overall military balance in the Gulf. The current military and internal security situation in each Gulf nation is analyzed, and each nation is assessed in terms of social and economic stability, political and ethnic tensions, and future willingness to cooperate with the West. Tables on each nation's military development accompany an analysis of recent and current conflicts such as those in Oman, in the Yemens, and between Iran and Iraq.

Anthony H. Cordesman has had many years of experience in the Office of the Secretary of Defense, the State Department, and the Department of Energy in analyzing the military balance and strategic situation in the Gulf region and Near East. He has served as a U.S. government official in Iran and has made extensive visits to the region, most recently as a Woodrow Wilson Fellow and as international policy editor of the *Armed Forces Journal.*